MULTINATIONAL ENTERPRISES
AND THE
GLOBAL ECONOMY

International Business Series

Consulting Editors

Professor Neil Hood, Strathclyde Business School and Scottish
   Development Agency, UK
Professor Bob Hawkins, Rensselaer Polytechnic Institute, USA

Editorial Board

Dr Michael Z. Brooke, Brooke Associates (Manchester) Ltd,
   UK
Professor John Dunning, University of Reading, UK
Professor David Eitemann, UCLA, USA
Professor Hiroyuki Itami, Hitotsubashi University, Tokyo
Dr K.C. Kwan, National University of Singapore
Professor K.C. Mun, Chinese University of Hong Kong
Professor S.G. Redding, University of Hong Kong
Professor Stephen Young, Strathclyde Business School, UK

Other Titles in the Series

International Marketing and Export Management   *G. Albaum,*
  J. Strandskov, E. Duerr and L. Dowd

MULTINATIONAL ENTERPRISES AND THE GLOBAL ECONOMY

John H. Dunning

State of New Jersey Professor of International Business, Rutgers University
and Emeritus Professor of International Business, University of Reading

Addison-Wesley Publishing Company

Wokingham, England · Reading, Massachusetts · Menlo Park, California · New York
Don Mills, Ontario · Amsterdam · Bonn · Sydney · Singapore
Tokyo · Madrid · San Juan · Milan · Paris · Mexico City · Seoul · Taipei

In appreciation of my colleagues and students – past and present

Cover designed by Pencil Box Ltd, Marlow, Buckinghamshire
and printed by The Riverside Printing Co. (Reading) Ltd.
Typeset by Columns Design and Production Services Ltd, Reading.
Printed and bound in Great Britain by William Clowes Ltd, Beccles, Suffolk.

First Printing 1992.   Reprinted 1993 and 1994.

British Library Cataloguing in Publication Data
A catalogue record for this book is available from the British Library.

Library of Congress Cataloging in Publication Data
Dunning, John H.
    Multinational enterprises and the global economy / John H.
Dunning.
        p.   cm.
    Includes bibliographical references and index.
    ISBN 0–201–17530–4
    1. International business enterprises.   2. International economic
relations.   I. Title.
HD2755.5.D868   1992
338.8′8—dc20   92–41390
                                                              CIP

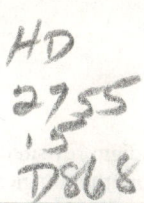

CONTENTS

v

ACKNOWLEDGEMENTS

It gives me great pleasure to recognize the help of many people and institutions in the preparation of this book. First, I would like to thank ICI for generously financing a four year Research Professorship at the University of Reading, during the tenure of which this book was written. I am grateful to the (UK) Economic and Social Research Council for awarding me a personal research grant for the first nine months of 1988.

Second, I would like to acknowledge the very considerable help and encouragement I have received from the Transnational Corporations and Management Division, Department of Economic and Social Development (formerly the United Nations Centre on Transnational Corporations [UNCTC]) of the UN; and, in particular, from Karl Sauvant, Chief of the Research and Policy Analysis Branch, and his colleagues. I am happy to recognize that Chapter 6 draws extensively on the Centre's study *The Determinants of Foreign Direct Investment*, published early in 1992; while the latter part of Chapter 17 contains some of the material in their paper *Economic Integration and Transnational Corporations Europe 1992, North America and Developing Countries*, first published in 1990. Persa Economou and Paz Tolentino have also been generous with their time in providing me with some of the latest statistical material, set out in Chapter 2.

Third, I owe a debt to two of my other publishers. The first is Routledge of London and New York (who acquired Unwin Hyman in 1991). Chapter 12 of this book uses some of the material first published as Chapter 9 in *Multinational Enterprises, Technology and Competitiveness* in 1988; while parts of Chapter 5 and 22 draw upon material first contained in *Explaining International Production*, also published in 1988. The second publisher is Taylor and Francis of New York who in 1989 contained an earlier and abbreviated version of Chapter 4 in a volume entitled *International Trade, Existing Problems and Prospective Solutions* (edited by K. Fatemi).

Fourth, although appearing under my name, in many respects this volume is very much a compendium of the work and views of many colleagues, who, over many years, have helped fashion my own thoughts and ideas. I have done my best to acknowledge their writings. If I have failed to refer to some important books or papers, I hope the authors will accept my apologies!

In the preparation of this book, I have been greatly helped by the research assistance provided by two of my Ph.D. students at Rutgers University. Sumit Kundu has given generously and cheerfully of his time to help me compile the extensive bibliography at the end of this book. Rajneesh Narula had the no less painstaking, and perhaps even more frustrating, task of helping me gather statistical data for various parts of the book, and particularly Chapter 2. He too managed to keep a smile on his face – for most of the time at any rate!

The typing of the several drafts of this book has been a challenging task, and I have been extremely fortunate in having the services of two highly skilled and dedicated secretaries – Melanie Waller of the University of Reading and Phyllis Miller of the Graduate School of Management at Rutgers University. I warmly thank both of them, not only for their sterling work, sometimes undertaken under great pressure, but for their patience and understanding of my many idiosyncrasies and constant drafting changes. I also thank Diane Bott of the University of Reading and Senta Butzel of Rutgers University, who made a valuable secretarial contribution at an earlier stage of the book.

Last, but not least, I wish to acknowledge the warm and enthusiastic support of my wife, Christine. Not only has she shared in some of the typing and editing of this work, but over its long gestation period, and particularly in the past year, she has had to put up with an unusually withdrawn and pre-occupied husband. I cannot promise her this will be my last book; only that I do not intend writing anything of quite this length again!

John H. Dunning
Rutgers and Reading Universities, June 1992

Acronyms and Initials

A&M	Acquisitions and Mergers	GATT	General Agreement on Tariffs and Trade
ANDEAN	Andean Sub-Regional Integration Agreement	GDP	Gross Domestic Product
ANZCERTA	Australia–New Zealand Closed Economic Relations Trade Agreement	GNP	Gross National Product
		GPA	General Purpose Alliance
APA	Advanced Pricing Agreement	HDI	Human Development Index
ASEAN	Association of South East Asian Nations	HRD	Human Resource Development
		IBRD	International Bank for Reconstruction and Development
CACM	Central American Common Market	ICC	International Chamber of Commerce
CARICOM	Caribbean Community	IDB	Inter-American Development Bank
CFIUS	Committee on Foreign Investment in the United States	ICFTU	International Confederation of Free Trade Unions
CUP	Comparable Uncontrolled Price	IFC	International Finance Corporation
C–USFTA	Canadian–US Free Trade Agreement	IIO	International Investment Organization
DVA	Domestic Value Added	ILO	International Labour Organization
EC	European Community	IMF	International Monetary Fund
ECIP	European Community Investment Partners	IRS	Internal Revenue Service
		ISTEC	International Superconductivity Technology Center
ECOWAS	Economic Community of West African States	LAFTA	Latin American Free Trade Area
EFTA	European Free Trade Area	LAIA	Latin American Integration Association
ESCAP	Economic and Social Commission for Asia and the Pacific	MIGA	Multilateral Investment Guarantee Agency
ESP	Environment/Systems/Policy	MITI	Ministry of International Trade and Industry
ESPRIT	European Strategic Project on Information Technology		
EUREKA	European Research Coordinating Agency	MNE	Multinational Enterprise
		NAFTA	North American Free Trade Area
FAO	Food and Agricultural Organization	NATO	North Atlantic Treaty Organization
FDI	Foreign Direct Investment	NCMS	National Center for Manufacturing Sciences
GAIC	General Agreement on International Corporations	NIC	Newly Industrializing Country
		NVA	National Value Added
GAII	General Agreement on International Investment	OECD	Organization for Economic

	Cooperation and Development	TRIPS	Trade Related Intellectual Property Rights
OLI	Ownership/Location/Internalization		
OPEC	Organization of Petroleum Exporting Countries	UN	United Nations
		UNCTAD	United Nations Centre for Trade and Development
PTA	Southern and East African Preferential Trade Area	UNCTC	United Nations Centre on Transnational Corporations
R&D	Research and Development		
RBP	Restrictive Business Practices	UNDP	United Nations Development Program
RCA	Revealed Comparative Advantage		
RV	Retained Value	UNESCO	United Nations Educational, Scientific and Cultural Organization
SBA	Strategic Business Alliance		
SEMATECH	Semi-conductor Manufacturing Technology	UNIDO	United Nations Industrial Development Organization
TPM	Transfer Price Manipulation	WHO	World Health Organization
TRIMS	Trade Related Investment Measures		

INTRODUCTION

This volume is intended to accomplish two main objectives. First it aims to present a fairly detailed, but broadly based, survey of the history and present day role of multinational enterprises (MNEs) in the global economy. In doing so, it draws upon a wealth of statistical, institutional and analytical material which has been compiled by academic scholars, business practitioners and data supplying agencies over the past half century or more, but particularly since 1960. The coverage of the volume is intended to be comprehensive. Indeed, it is my hope that it will serve as a reference book for all those interested in the determinants and consequences of foreign direct investment (FDI) and MNE activity. While inevitably there will be some lacunae both in subject matter and the sources drawn upon, I have attempted to present the reader with a 'state of the art' description and appraisal of the mainstream writings on the ways in which MNEs interact with the global economy which they have so much helped to shape since the Second World War.

Second, the monograph seeks to couch its descriptive and analytical contents within a uniform and consistent conceptual framework. The framework chosen is that which I have developed in my writings since 1976, *viz* the eclectic (or OLI) paradigm of international production. The paradigm avers that an explanation of both the determinants and the impact of MNE activity can be viewed in terms of the juxtaposition between the competitive (or ownership [O] specific) advantages of firms and the competitive (or location [L] specific) advantages of countries and, in the light of these advantages, of the organizational modes by which both firms and countries (or, more specifically, governments of countries) seek to acquire and organize their re-

sources and capabilities. The methods of organizing value-added activities studied in the volume are essentially three – *viz* markets, hierarchies and some form of inter-firm collaboration. While most of the literature on MNEs concentrates on their preference for internalizing cross-border intermediate product markets (the I-specific component of the eclectic paradigm), *de facto* most MNEs are also actively engaged in a variety of cross-border collaborative arrangements, which do not necessarily involve an equity ownership on their part.

It is the precise configuration of the ownership, location and internalization (OLI) advantages (and disadvantages) facing firms, and their strategic reaction to them, that will determine, *at any given moment of time*, the nature, level, and structure of MNE activity. And it is the impact of this activity which, when coupled with the macro-strategy of governments in organizing the location-bound resources and capabilities within their jurisdiction, that, *over a period of time*, will determine the consequences of international production for national and global economic welfare.

The volume is divided into four main parts. These deal with the causes, organization and effects of MNE activity, and the consequential response of national governments and supra-national authorities to both inward and outward direct investment. In particular, we shall analyse the ways in which the interface between the competitive advantages of firms and those of countries determine the *kinds* and forms of foreign production undertaken and *in which sectors and countries* it is concentrated. We shall discuss the consequences of different types of FDI for the welfare of different kinds of Nation States, as well as for the same Nation States over time. Finally, we shall analyse the efficacy of particular macro- and micro-organizational policies which governments may pursue in their efforts to maximize the benefits of MNE activity in terms of the balance between the O-specific advantages and opportunity costs of the investing companies, and the L-specific advantages and opportunity costs of the countries seeking to attract such investments.

The structure of this volume proceeds in the following way. First, in Chapter 2 we present the most recent information available on the current role of MNEs in the world economy. In this chapter we draw substantially on the data compiled by the Division of Transnational Corporations and Management of the Department of Economic and Social Development of the UN.[1] Chapters 3 and 4 concern themselves with the motives for and determinants of MNE activity. Chapter 3 identifies four main reasons for engaging in FDI and suggests that each of these needs to be explained in very different ways. Chapter 4 sets out the theoretical underpinning for much of the rest of the monograph. Chapters 5 and 6 then seek to use the eclectic paradigm to explain the emergence, growth and contemporary industrial and geographical structure of MNE activity. Both chapters draw extensively on the work of other scholars, but present their findings within a common analytical framework.

The second part of the book, from Chapters 7 to 9, views the MNE as an organizational entity and seeks to review some of the explanations provided by organizational theorists and business analysts of the way in which decisions are taken on the internationalization of value-added activities and on the form of its governance. As in other parts of the monograph, we seek, wherever possible, to take a dynamic or developmental view of the interface between the competitive advantages of firms (and, within firms, of different operating units) and that of countries. These chapters pay especial attention to the changing character of MNE activity over the past half century or so, and the implications of this for organizational structures, the locus of decision taking and the form of inter-firm relationships.

Part 3 of the book, which comprises Chapters 10 to 19, deals with some of the more important consequences of MNE activities for the global economy and for the countries in which its home or foreign operations are based. Here we hypothesize

that, depending on the OLI configuration facing firms, the competitive advantages of countries – including the strategies and policies pursued by governments – and the type of foreign production undertaken, the consequences of any given amount of MNE activity will differ. While separate chapters will deal with specific impact areas, the reader is invited to consider these as part of an economic and social system. At the end of the day, it is the impact of MNEs on this system and on the economic and political objectives of Nation States, which is our main concern.

Again, whether dealing with the consequences of MNEs for the technological capacity of home or host countries, or for industrial productivity, or for the upgrading of human resources, or for market structure, or for competition, or for the structure and organization of cross-border trade, or for regional integration, or for the environment and national cultures, we try, rather than to give general answers, to set an analytical framework within which it is possible to examine the impact of specific types of MNE activity in specific circumstances.

Generalizing on the appropriate national economic policies to pursue in the light of the presence of MNEs is no less difficult than generalizing about their impact. So much depends on the assumptions made about the distinctiveness of MNE activity and what would have occurred in its absence. In fact, we prefer to avoid generalizations about what governments should or should not do in particular circumstances and, instead, concentrate on identifying the kinds of actions that need to be taken by governments if MNEs are to make the fullest possible contribution to national economic and other objectives. In doing so we consider both unilateral and multi-lateral policies towards MNE activity.

The kind of schema used in this book for analysing the role of MNEs in the contemporary global economy is illustrated in Exhibit 0.1. The triadic relationship between the ownership-specific advantages of firms, the location-specific advantages of countries and the way in which firms and governments (on behalf of countries) organize the use of resources and capabilities within their domain is presented in the top three boxes. The resulting interaction gives rise to a series of intra-firm and external transactional relationships, the outcome of which will affect the welfare of both MNEs and

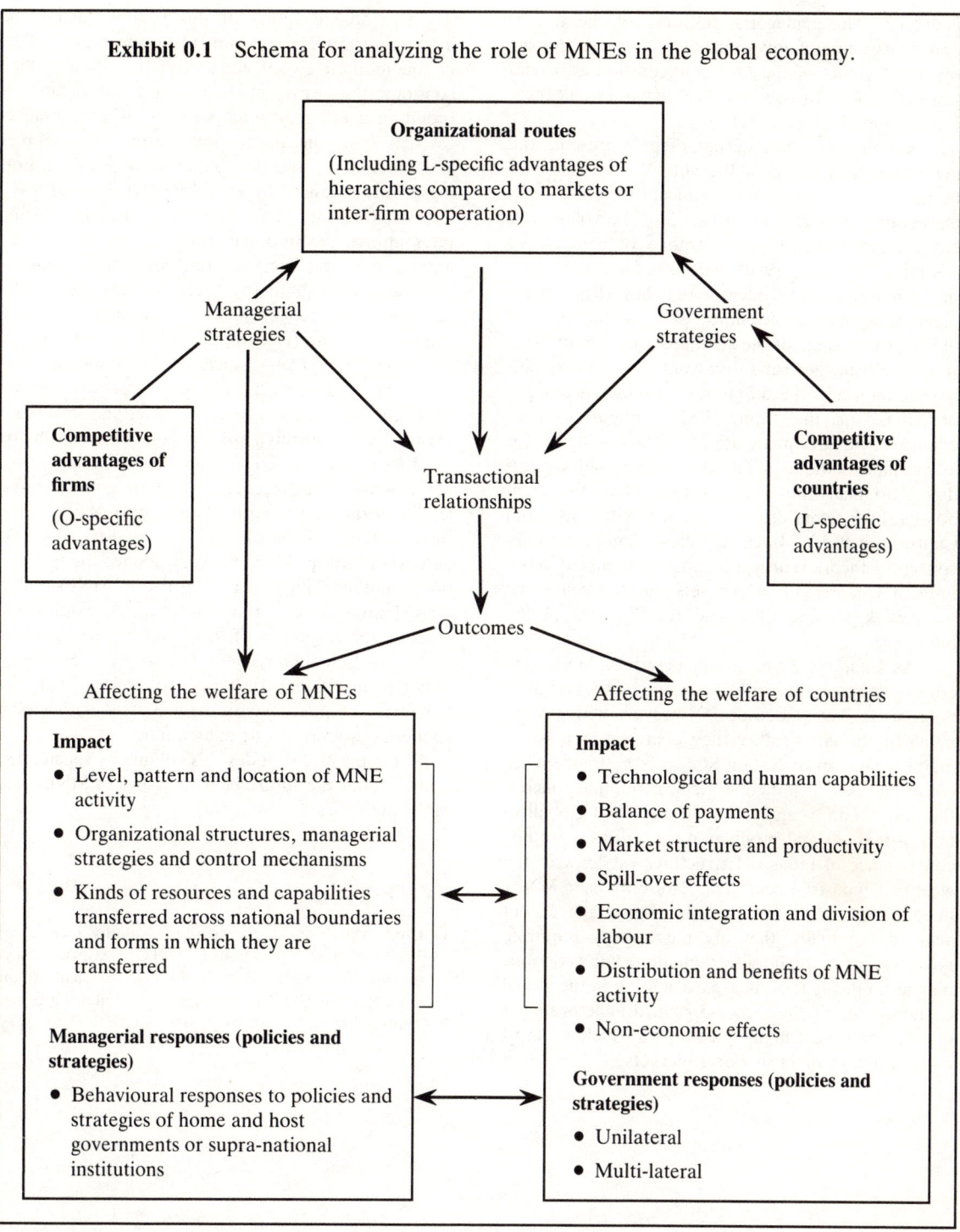

Exhibit 0.1   Schema for analyzing the role of MNEs in the global economy.

Organizational routes

(Including L-specific advantages of hierarchies compared to markets or inter-firm cooperation)

Managerial strategies

Government strategies

Competitive advantages of firms

(O-specific advantages)

Transactional relationships

Competitive advantages of countries

(L-specific advantages)

Outcomes

Affecting the welfare of MNEs

Affecting the welfare of countries

Impact

- Level, pattern and location of MNE activity
- Organizational structures, managerial strategies and control mechanisms
- Kinds of resources and capabilities transferred across national boundaries and forms in which they are transferred

Managerial responses (policies and strategies)

- Behavioural responses to policies and strategies of home and host governments or supra-national institutions

Impact

- Technological and human capabilities
- Balance of payments
- Market structure and productivity
- Spill-over effects
- Economic integration and division of labour
- Distribution and benefits of MNE activity
- Non-economic effects

Government responses (policies and strategies)

- Unilateral
- Multi-lateral

countries. The managerial response of the former and the reaction of governments will, in turn, impact on the structure of the OLI configuration at a later time. Chapter 10 sets out the dynamics of these interactions in more detail.

Although the eclectic paradigm represents the main analytical thrust in the volume, we have not hesitated to draw upon other concepts, theories, and paradigms. For example, in Part 3 of the volume we have found both Porter's 'diamond of competitive advantage' (Porter, 1990) and Koopman and Montias' Environmental System and Policy (ESP) paradigm (Koopman and Montias, 1971) as helpful ways of identifying some of the attributes of a country's L-specific advantages (and disadvantages). In examining the impact of the different O-specific advantages of MNEs on the future ESP configurations of countries, we have made use of the technological (or as we shall choose to call it) asset-accumulation paradigm, originally put forward to explain the technological trajectory of countries by Pavitt (1987) and Cantwell (1989c). Each of these complementary concepts, theories or paradigms is discussed more fully in Chapter 10, which sets out the schematic framework for the third and fourth parts of the book.

As Chapters 2 and 5 will describe, MNEs are critical actors on the world economic stage, and have been so for many decades. However, whereas for much of the last century they operated in a world mainly made up of Nation States, largely independent of each other in their strategic economic policies, the past twenty years have seen a gradual globalization of markets and production, as well as a gradual convergence of industrial structures, at least in the wealthier industrial countries.[2] Not only have MNEs been partly responsible for this convergence, but also, in the 1990s, they are increasingly requiring governments to reappraise their domestic economic policies in the light of their participation in the global economy and of the macro-organizational strategies pursued by governments of countries which are most competitive to them in world markets.

The final chapters of this volume review the interaction between governments, markets and MNEs in the modern global economy. In particular they consider the ways in which this interaction is requiring a more systemic strategy by governments towards both the macro-organization of resources and capabilities, and the role of MNEs in contributing to this organization in a socially beneficial way.

In particular, Chapter 21 argues that the existing international institutional regimes for setting the ground rules for cross-border, commercial transactions are inadequate to meet the demands of the modern global economy. This is because they were framed at a time (*viz.* the late 1940s) when trade in goods was the main vehicle of international commerce, and when such trade was largely conducted between independent parties. Neither condition exists today. Foreign production undertaken by MNEs – either via FDI or some kind of collaborative agreement – has replaced trade in goods as the leading form of international commerce. At the same time, a large volume of trade is now driven by FDI and occurs within MNE networks. Since the international market failures that give rise to MNE-related activity are different from that of arm's-length trade – as are the responses of firms and national governments to these failures – it follows that the supranational machinery designed to ensure that the behaviour of governments is consistent with global economic welfare needs overhauling.

Chapter 22 concludes this volume by speculating a little about the future characteristics of MNEs and MNE activity.

NOTE

1 Until March 1992 the United Nations Centre on Transnational Corporations (UNCTC). Because most of this book was written prior to this date, we shall use the nomenclature UNCTC throughout the following pages.
2 Throughout this volume, Germany refers to West Germany prior to 1991.

PART 1
FACTS, THEORY AND HISTORY

This first part of the book consists of six chapters. Chapter 1 introduces the reader to the distinctive nature of MNEs and goes on to describe some of the data used by scholars in their search to understand better the causes and consequences of MNE activity. Chapter 2 then surveys the extent and pattern of foreign direct investment (FDI) and MNE activity in the modern global economy. While most of the available data relates to the stock and flow of international direct investment, Chapter 2 also presents some information on the sales and employment of MNEs and their foreign affiliates, as well as on the significance of their activities to both home and host economies. The chapter concludes by setting out some recent data on the role of foreign-based firms in the newly emerging market economies of Central and Eastern Europe.

Chapters 3 and 4 present the theoretical core of the volume. Chapter 3 identifies the motives for several kinds of MNE activity. The distinctions set out in this chapter are important ones, and are used throughout the rest of the book. Chapter 4 then surveys the various explanations of the growth of MNEs and MNE activity that have been put forward by economists and business analysts over the past 30 years. After a review of a group of theories to explain particular kinds of FDI or different aspects of MNE activity, attention is given to three more general theories or paradigms. These include the author's own eclectic paradigm of international production, which is the central analytical concept used throughout the volume. The chapter concludes by considering some of the lacunae in current theoretical thinking, and suggests some of the likely courses such thinking might take in the 1990s.

The final two chapters of Part 1 examine some of the facts relating to the evolution of international business activity, its contemporary form, and its industrial and geographical scope. But they do so in the light of the partial and general theoretical explanations put forward in Chapter 4. Chapter 5 traces the changing nature and value of the competitive advantages of firms and countries over the past century or more and the way in which this has led to the growth of value-added activities of firms outside their national boundaries. Chapter 6 then goes on to summarize some of the very considerable amount of empirical research on the determinants of FDI and MNE activity. *Inter alia* this chapter reveals that most explanations offered by scholars tend to relate to specific kinds and aspects of foreign production and are more complementary than competitive to each other. Some, for example, concentrate on the 'where' of MNE activity; others on the 'what kind' of activity or on the contribution of MNEs or their affiliates to the output, capital stock or employment of the countries in which they produce. Using the eclectic paradigm, the chapter attempts to identify the consensus of scholars as to the particular ownership, locational and internalization variables which are most likely to be important determinants of which kind of MNE activity. As the chapter will show, the answer is critically dependent on the context in which these variables are evaluated, and particularly the countries which are home or host to MNEs or their affiliates, the industries in which they operate and the characteristics of particular MNEs, including the strategic behaviour of their management.

CHAPTER 1

THE ACTIVITIES OF MULTINATIONAL ENTERPRISES: SOME INTRODUCTORY REMARKS

1.1 THE NATURE OF A MULTINATIONAL ENTERPRISE

1.1.1 A working definition

A multinational or transnational enterprise is an enterprise that engages in foreign direct investment (FDI) and owns or controls value-adding activities in more than one country.[1] This is the threshold definition of a multinational enterprise (MNE), and one that is widely accepted in academic and business circles, by data collecting agencies such as the Organization for Economic Cooperation and Development (OECD), the United Nations Centre on Transnational Corporations (UNCTC) and by most national governments. At the same time, some scholars and practitioners have found it desirable to distinguish between the universe of enterprises undertaking foreign production and those that have substantial overseas commitments and/or pursue an integrated managerial strategy towards their foreign and domestic operations. In particular, business analysts like to distinguish between MNEs that govern a group of largely independent multi-domestic foreign subsidiaries, each of which produces goods and services mainly for the local market, and those that treat their affiliates as part and parcel of a regionally or globally coordinated network of production and marketing activities.

The literature has identified several criteria for assessing the degree of an enterprise's multi- or transnationality.[2] These include:

(1) the number and size of foreign subsidiaries or associate companies it owns or controls,

(2) the number of countries in which it engages in value-adding activities such as mines, plantations, factories, selling outlets, banks, offices and hotels,

(3) the proportion of its global assets, revenue, income or employment accounted for by its foreign affiliates,

(4) the degree to which its management or stock ownership is internationalized,

(5) the extent to which its higher value activities, for example, research and development (R&D), are internationalized; this measure is intended to capture the *quality* or *depth* of foreign production,

(6) the extent and pattern of the systemic advantages arising from its governance of, and influence over, a network of economic activities located in different countries.

While each of these criteria helps delineate different types of FDI and international production, there is no escaping the fact that the choice of the point at which an enterprise is deemed to become a multinational – not to mention a global corporation – is bound to be arbitrary. Moreover, the multi- or transnationality of an enterprise is best considered as a multi-dimensional, rather than a unidimensional concept (Raghunathan and Chandran, 1991).

A rather different kind of dissatisfaction of confining the scope of a MNE to the foreign value-added activities it *owns* is that many such companies also engage in a variety of cross-border non-equity cooperative ventures, for example licensing agreements, turnkey operations and strategic alliances, which may give them some degree of control or influence over the foreign production associated with these ventures. At the same time, MNEs are also increasingly participants in international networks of economic activity involving, for example, suppliers and industrial customers, in which the transactional relationships between the members of the network, though less formally specified, are frequently, by custom or tradition, no less binding. Section 1.1.3 of this chapter takes up this point in more detail.

1.1.2   The distinctive features of a MNE

The MNE is one of several institutions that engage in international business, the characteristics of which are set out in Exhibit 1.1. In particular, it has two near relations. The first is the international trading firm, like which it exchanges goods and services across national boundaries, but unlike which it transacts these internally before or after adding value to them from the assets it owns or controls in a foreign country. Second, like a domestic multi-activity or diversified firm, it engages in multiple economic activities,[3] but unlike this type of firm it undertakes at least some of these in a country, or

countries, other than the one in which it is incorporated.

An MNE has, therefore, two distinctive features. First, it organizes and coordinates multiple value-adding activities across national boundaries and, second, it internalizes the cross-border markets for the intermediate products arising from these activities. No other institution engages in *both* cross-border production and transactions.

An MNE may be privately or publicly (i.e. state) owned and managed. It may originate from a market or a socialist country. It may be motivated by private or social objectives. It may be a large diversified global corporation owning or managing a network or coalition of activities in many countries or a small, single-product firm that operates only one foreign marketing venture. Its assets may be owned and controlled by citizens or institutions of a single country, such as Virgin Atlantic, Mars, Tatung; nationally controlled but internationally managed and owned, such as Ford, Rhone Poulenc, Sony, Samsung; or internationally owned and controlled, such as Agfa-Gevaert, SAS, Royal Dutch Shell. In practice, most MNEs are nationally controlled but internationally owned, although the extent and form of their cross-border equity and non-equity participa-

---

Exhibit 1.1   Types of international business

(1)   International business occurs whenever an individual, corporation or public institution located in one country engages in a commercial transaction with an individual, corporation or public institution in another country.

(2)   Most international business transactions occur between corporations and other corporations or individuals. Usually, they take the form of *assets*, *goods* or *services* exported or imported for a money price. Exceptions include *counter-trade*, that is, the exchange of goods for services for other goods and/or services.

(3)   (a)   Trade may be conducted between independent buyers and sellers at arm's length prices, or between different parts of the same organization at an internally set (i.e. transfer) price.

 (b)   Trade in financial assets is called international or foreign investment. Such trade, and trade in non-financial assets (e.g. knowledge and organizational systems), may be portfolio or indirect where it is between independent economic entities, or direct where it is undertaken within the same economic entity.

 (c)   Trade in products may consist of *final* goods or services (television sets, a life insurance policy, etc) or of *intermediate* goods or services, which are used by the purchasers to create additional value.

Exhibit 1.2

Foreign direct investment

(1) The investment is made *outside* the home country of the investing company, but *inside* the investing company. Control over the use of the resources transferred remains with the *investor*.

(2) It consists of a 'package' of assets and intermediate products, such as capital, technology, management skills, access to markets and entrepreneurship.

Foreign indirect (i.e., portfolio or contractual) transfer of resources

(1) Specific assets and intermediate products (e.g. capital, debt or equity, technology) are separately transferred between two independent economic agents through the modality of the market. Control over the resources is relinquished by the seller to the buyer.

(2) Only these resources are transferred.

---

tion varies a great deal between industries and firms, and even within the same firm over time.

1.1.3   Forms of foreign involvement by MNEs

Traditionally, the territorial expansion of a firm's production outside its national boundaries has been achieved by the act of a foreign direct investment. FDI is different from foreign portfolio (or indirect) investment in two important respects (see Exhibit 1.2). First, the former involves the transfer of a package of assets or intermediate products, which includes money capital, management and organizational expertise, technology, entrepreneurship and access to markets across national boundaries; the latter involves only the transfer of money capital.[4]

Second, unlike arm's length trade in assets and intermediate products, FDI does not involve any change in *ownership*; in other words, the *control* of decision taking over the use of the transferred resources remains in the hands of the investing entity. Put another way, while the indirect exchange of assets and intermediate products is organized by the market, the direct exchange is administered by, and within, investing hierarchies.

De jure, the boundaries of a uninational or multinational enterprise are determined by its ownership. In cases of shared ownership with another firm

or firms, provided it has a majority equity stake, it has a legal right to control all the activities of the joint venture; where it has a minority interest, it has, at best, a shared right. Yet most countries treat a foreign investment as direct whenever a single investing company is perceived able to exert a significant control or influence over decision taking in a foreign company. Indeed, FDI is defined in the IMF *Balance of Payments Manual* (5th edition) as 'investment that involves a long-term relationship reflecting a lasting interest of a resident entity in one economy (direct investor) in an entity resident in an economy other than that of the investor. The direct investor's purpose is to exert a significant degree of influence on the management of the enterprise resident in the other economy' (1993). There is, however, no international consensus on the minimum equity stake deemed necessary for such an effective voice, but for the majority of countries it varies between 10% and 25% of the total equity stake of an enterprise.[5] Neither are the accounting systems used to compile direct investment data always comparable between countries.[6]

Once one moves from control to *influence* as a criterion for delineating the boundaries of a firm, one opens up a Pandora's box. There are as many instances of MNEs exerting very little *de facto* influence over the day-to-day decision taking of their 100% owned affiliates as there are of such enterprises with only a minority foreign shareholding exercising a substantial influence. And if influence or voice is the criterion, why confine attention to a minority equity investment? What of firms that engage in a Keiretsu network of inter-firm cooperation? What of the strong power relationships between Germany, banks and industrial corporations? As later chapters in this volume will illustrate, companies that enter into subcontractual agreements with firms in other countries may sometimes build into these agreements the right for them to exercise substantial financial or operational control over the subcontractors. Some scholars have referred to these agreements as quasi-internalization; quasi-, in this instance, suggesting a partial, specified and time-limited control, unlike that stemming from an equity interest which is assumed to be total and without time limit.

The problem does not, however, end there. Even more difficult to handle are the cooperative alliances now being forged by firms to undertake specific functions. If Tata (an Indian corporation) agrees with TLF (a French corporation) for the latter to market its leather products in Europe, to whom are the sales credited? If Philips of Eindhoven and Siemens of Western Germany (that is, the part of Germany previously known as West Germany) agree to share the cost and the fruits of research and development in microchips, how are these allocated in their respective income statements?

It is but one step further to incorporating the influence of a MNE on its suppliers, customers and competitors. If an automobile assembly firm subcontracts its production of shock absorbers to an independent component supplier and is the sole customer of that supplier, then in a very real sense, the latter might be thought to be controlled by the former. Similarly, if an aluminium fabricating firm is totally dependent on a single bauxite producer for its raw materials, then it might be said to be controlled by that firm. Finally, in a variety of ways, a dominant MNE in a particular sector might be able to influence the strategy, performance and behaviour of its smaller competitors.

For these and more practical reasons (see Section 1.2.2) the approach in this volume is to define a MNE as an enterprise that engages in FDI and organizes the production of goods or services in more than one country. In practice, many MNEs own or control a plurality of economic activities. In

1990, for example, Philips of Eindhoven operated 346 manufacturing plants in 46 countries. It was also a partner in several hundred cross-border strategic alliances, a leading participant in more than 60 regional or international research-based consortia, and its foreign subcontractors were numbered in thousands. It is also understandable that since foreign production is highly concentrated among the world's largest firms,[7] scholars often focus their attention on MNEs of a certain size or with a minimum geographical spread of activities,[8] or on those that pursue particular strategies towards their domestic and foreign operation.[9] At the same time, there is a growing consensus that minority joint ventures, cooperative alliances and networking relationships should be considered as part and parcel of a MNE's sphere of influence and control.

1.2 MEASURING THE EXTENT AND PATTERN OF MULTINATIONAL ACTIVITY IN THE GLOBAL ECONOMY

1.2.1 Types of data available

In attempting to assess the extent and pattern of the activities of MNEs in the global economy, the analyst may appear to have several sources of data open to him. In practice, however, his choice is seriously constrained by the quality and comparability of the information regularly published. Exhibit 1.3 illustrates the kind of data that is available. Naturally, which statistics are sought and used will depend on the purpose for which they are being collected and the level of analysis being made. The informational requirements of organizational scholars is likely to be different from that of marketing scholars or economists, while those of the MNEs themselves are not likely to be the same as that of governments or labour unions. The data most appropriate for assessing the role of affiliates in host countries or sectors will be different from that needed to evaluate the impact of MNEs on the structure of the world economy. Assessing the impact of FDI on the quantity and quality of the world's labour force will clearly require employment data. For evaluating their effects on the balance of

Exhibit 1.3

Data availability on MNE activity

	Sources	*Orientation of data*
MACRO		
	International agencies (UNCTC, World Bank)	Global/industrial/geographical
	Regional agencies (EC, NAFTA, ASEAN)	Regional/country
	Countries (US, Japan, India)	Industrial/geographical
	Trade associations (Electronics, Pharmaceuticals, Hotels)	Sectoral Global Regional National
	Firms (IBM, Sony, Fiat, Siam Darby)	Company; number, location, size, ownership of MNEs and their affiliates
MICRO		

Kind of data available

Input	Labour (employment) Capital assets (stock) Employee compensation Investment
Output	Gross output Sales (value of end product) Value added (net output)
Other	Employee compensation Number, ownership and age of affiliates Income earned

payments, statistics on trade and investment flows, profits and dividends may be more relevant, while data on research and development (R&D) expenditure and intra-firm technology payments may be a useful starting point for assessing the contribution of MNEs to innovatory capacity. At a more micro-level more detailed operational and financial data may be needed for an evaluation of particular foreign investment projects.

However, as an indicator of the overall or sectoral economic significance of MNE activity, the best measure is the value added created by such firms outside their national boundaries, and more particularly that part of the value added accruing to the investing or recipient countries. Throughout this volume, as far as possible we shall be using this measure to analyse the interaction between the domestic and foreign production of MNEs and the economic welfare of the Nation States in which they operate. In practice, statistical data on MNEs and their activities, though markedly better than they were even a decade ago, are fragmentary, variable in quantity and rarely comparable between countries, industries and firms, or over time. This is well illustrated by reference to three major reference sources *viz* the *World Investment Directory* compiled by the UNCTC (UN 1992b, 1993),[10] *The World Directory of Multinational Enterprises* edited by John Stopford (1982, 1992) and the annual *World Investment Surveys* published by the UNCTC. In addition, there are several national, international and industrial business directories, such as *Who Owns Whom?*, that identify the more important MNEs, together with their foreign affiliates classified by country of operation.

These publications confirm that there are two primary and several secondary sources of data on MNEs and their activities. The primary sources are the enterprises themselves (or their affiliates) and the governments of the home and host countries in which they operate.[11] Secondary sources include most international or regional economic agencies, including the UNCTC, The World Bank, IMF, ILO, OECD, and EUROSTAT,[12] industrial and commercial trade associations, and academic scholars.

Country data reveals that while some governments, for example, those of the US, Canada, Germany, Australia and Singapore, compile a fairly comprehensive range of statistics on inward and outward MNE activity, most countries limit their data gathering to the foreign direct investment stake (usually compiled irregularly on a survey or sample basis)[13] and direct investment flows (obtained largely from balance of payments statistics). Recipient countries, in which the affiliates of foreign MNEs play an important role, usually publish more data as part of the normal collection of information on the activities of all firms producing within their boundaries. Such data includes the sales, employment, exports and imports, wages and profits of foreign affiliates. Again, problems of coverage and classification make it difficult to make meaningful cross-country comparisons, but the UNCTC directory does give a reasonable indication of the geographical and sectoral orientation of inward and outward direct investment and the relative significance of such investment to home and host countries. Chapter 2 will present some of this data.

1.2.2   Sources of data

An examination of the various available sources of data reveals that comprehensive and comparable statistics are only available for three indices of multinational activity, *viz* the outward and inward foreign capital stake, the income earned on that capital stake and new investment flows.[14] However, even the latter data is not always comparable as it does not always include information on reinvested profits.[15] Some sectoral data on these variables and on the number of the affiliates of MNEs is also published by the major investing and recipient countries.[16] However, information on other input and output measures, such as employment, R&D expenditure, imports and exports is better obtained from directories reproducing data supplied by the leading MNEs or their affiliates. Data in these directories varies in coverage and scope but, at the end of the day, it is only as good as the statistics provided by the enterprises and the ability of the compilers of the directories to interpret them. Exhibit 1.4 illustrates the type of information that it is possible to extract from the published statistics of one country and one firm. Of course, there is a vast amount of other quantitative and qualitative data on the scope and pattern of the activities of MNEs, much of which is contained in the hundreds of monographs and reports, and thousands of papers and articles, written on this subject over the past 30 or more years.

Statistical data on the non-equity involvement of, or collaborative alliances between, MNEs is even more difficult to obtain. Only a few countries (notably the US, UK and West Germany) publish details on the receipts and payments made for cross-border sales of technology and management, administrative and marketing services, or on the number of international non-equity agreements concluded. Most data so far published on acquisitions and mergers (A&Ms) and on strategic alliances has been compiled by banks, accountancy firms, business consultancies and academic scholars from information supplied by individual enterprises or derived from trade and financial directories, magazines and newspaper reports.[17] However, some governments (e.g. the UK and US) and the European Commission now publish data on Acquisitions and Mergers

Exhibit 1.4   Illustrations of data provided by a country (US) and a MNE (ICI) of its foreign value-adding activities

	Foreign activities of all US multinationals End 1990 or in 1990 ($ million)	Foreign activities of ICI End 1990 or in 1990 (£ million)
1. (a) Value of foreign direct capital stake	421 494	3 573
(b) As a % of global[1] capital stake	na	56.1
2. (a) Capital expenditure (1990)[2]	57 962	na
(b) As a % of global capital expenditure	na	na
3. (a) Value of sales accounted for by foreign affiliates of non-bank MNEs (1988)	1 194 816	6 780[4]
(b) As a % of global sales	29.7	52.5
4. (a) Number employed in foreign affiliates (000s) (1988)	64 038	78.4
(b) As a % of global employment	26.3	59.3
5. (a) Employee compensation of (4) (1988)	151 098	na
(b) As a % of global employee compensation	20.4	na
6. (a) Income earned abroad[3]	54 444	734
(b) As a % of global income	na	71.3
7. (a) Geographical distribution of foreign direct capital stake (% of total foreign assets):		
● The Americas	34.3	39.5
● Europe	48.4	34.0
● Asia and the Pacific	15.2	22.1
● Other	2.1	4.4

1   Global is defined as domestic plus foreign activities of US MNEs or ICI.
2   By majority owned affiliates.
3   Before tax and depreciation.
4   After deduction of intra-area transactions.

(A&Ms) involving foreign firms. Some industrial trade associations also collect information about the foreign activities of their member firms. Much useful data on the international operations of MNEs in the auto, pharmaceutical, consumer electronics, petroleum, banking and insurance firms is obtainable from such sources.

1.2.3   Deficiencies in the quality of statistical data

Quite apart from differences in the coverage of data published by national governments – for example, data on the foreign capital stake varies from an estimated 85 to 95% coverage of all firms in the case of the US, West Germany and the UK, to a much lower proportion in many developing countries –

there are several reasons for exercising considerable caution in the interpretation of published statistics. Six of these deserve special mention; several are common to evaluating the economic activity of all firms, but some are specific to MNEs.

The first relates to the value of the capital stake. In most cases, this is represented by the book value of assets of MNEs or their affiliates, which are likely to be a considerable underestimate of their current market value. For example, according to US Department of Commerce data, at the end of 1988 the stock of foreign direct investment of the US was some $327 billion and that of foreign direct investment in the US was $329 billion. However, when these assets were recalculated by Eisner and Pieper (1990) at replacement value, the respective figures were $747 million and $389 billion.[18] *Inter alia*, this data suggested that the stock of foreign direct investment in the US was of much more recent origin than that of outward direct investment.[19]

Secondly, countries differ in the way in which they deal with currency translation adjustments.[20] Take, for example, statistics on FDI compiled by the US and Mexican Governments. While US parent companies have to submit details of the foreign exchange gains and losses of their Mexican affiliates to the US authorities, these same affiliates do not have to convert their assets from pesos to dollars when reporting their changes in investment to the Mexican Government.

Thirdly, countries vary in their accounting conventions, particularly the way in which they depreciate assets and value trade investments (OECD, 1991b).[21] Moreover, some countries present data based on FDI intentions, others on investments actually authorized and undertaken.[22] Fourthly, countries organize the collection of data relating to MNE activity in different ways and (rather irritating to the academic researcher) at different times. Moreover, the quality and accuracy of the data are likely to vary according to confidentiality safeguards surrounding the collection process, and whether or not the data is provided voluntarily or compulsorily. Fifthly, because of the cross-border transfer pricing practices of MNEs, intra-firm sales, costs and profits actually recorded may under- or overestimate their arm's length values. Finally, several countries do not regularly collect data on the stock of FDI. Instead they estimate such data by aggregating past invest-

ment flows. However, sometimes these flows include reinvested profits and in other cases they do not. Moreover, such data can easily be distorted by flight capital (especially in the case of some developing countries, for example, Zimbabwe in the 1970s and the Philippines in the 1980s) and, in a given year, by sizeable A&Ms, intra-company loans and/or repayments and divestments.

It is not surprising that, in the light of the above and other problems associated with the collection and recording of FDI and similar data, it is sometimes difficult to reconcile statistics on the same MNE-related variable provided by home and host countries.[23] For example, according to US data, the Japanese foreign direct investment stake in the US in 1989 was $53.3 billion while according to Japanese data it was $71.8 billion.[24] Asymmetries in investment flow data are even greater (Fujita, 1990). According to EUROSTAT (1991) – and taking two random examples – German sources recorded a direct investment outflow to Italy in 1988 of 512 billion ECU, while Italian sources recorded an inflow of investment from Germany of 335 billion ECU. In the same year the Netherlands recorded an outflow of direct investment to France of 195 million ECU, but the French authorities recorded an inflow of investment from the Netherlands of 857 million ECU. There is little that the analyst can easily do about these problems – not, at least, in making macro-economic comparisons – except frequently to remind himself that all estimates are only as good as the data on which they are based, and that in many cases, because they are not adequately defined or carefully analysed, they may be subject to misleading and injudicious interpretations.

1.2.4   Identifying the nationality of MNEs

Most MNEs can be readily identified as originating from a single country. Everyone, for example, identifies ICI as a British firm, Ford as a US firm, NEC as a Japanese firm, Volvo as a Swedish firm, Siemens as a German firm and Samsung as a Korean firm. Yet each of these MNEs has its shares quoted on a number of stock exchanges throughout the world and the membership of their Board of Directors is multinational, while an increasing proportion of their value-added activity is undertaken outside their home countries. Even more difficult is to identify the true nationality of ownership of a MNE that is, itself, fully or partly owned by foreign interests. As global or regional integration increases, it is likely that these 'spin-off' or secondary MNE activities are likely to increase.

The globalization of many enterprises is reducing the significance of the nationality of ownership as a feature influencing the contribution of such firms to national economic welfare. Less and less is the prosperity of such MNEs tied to their home nation's economic success or failure. Of the 300 largest industrial enterprises in the world in 1987, 102 or 34% produced more than 40% of their output from their foreign subsidiaries[25] (UNCTC, 1988). MNEs, such as Nestlé, BAT Industries, Seagrams, Norsk Hydro, Alcan Aluminium, Solvay and CIE each recorded a foreign production ratio of 80% or more. Moreover, on average, and for most MNEs – particularly non-US MNEs – this ratio has risen markedly since the early 1960s.

From the perspective of a host country, it is quite possible that a foreign-owned subsidiary could be contributing more to the upgrading of workforce skills, R&D and productivity than an indigenous company. In 1989, more than one-third of Taiwan's trade surplus with the US came from US corporations making or buying products there, then selling or using them in the US (Reich, 1990). The same corporate sourcing practices account for a substantial share of the US trade imbalance with Singapore, South Korea and Mexico, while the net export contribution of Japanese motor vehicle affiliates in the UK is considerably superior to that of other UK-based manufacturers. Between 1986 and 1990, American corporations increased their overseas R&D spending by five times more than in the US, while an increasing proportion of indigenous R&D expenditure in the US is being accounted for by foreign-owned firms.

In some industrial sectors dominated by global producers, it is becoming increasingly difficult to distinguish between the nationality of the ownership of value-added activities in any meaningful way. Some implications of this fact are discussed in some detail in Parts 3 and 4 of this volume.

NOTES

1 In this volume, we shall use the terms 'transnational' and 'multinational' interchangeably. The former terminology was adopted by the United Nations Centre on Transnational Corporations (UNCTC) in 1974, at the request of some Latin American countries who wished to distinguish between companies domiciled in one country of Latin America, which might invest in another, from those originating from outside the region. The latter is the preferred nomenclature of the developed countries, the business community and most academic scholars, and is the one we shall most frequently use in this study. Over time, the terminological differences have become increasingly obscure, and today most scholars, businessmen, labour leaders and politicians use the terms 'multinational' and 'transnational' as meaning the same thing. However, even among academia, the term 'transnational' is being increasingly used to mean a 'MNE that practises a fully integrated and multi-dimensional organizational strategy'. See, for example, Bartlett and Ghoshal (1989). The terms 'enterprise', 'firm', 'corporation' and 'company' also tend to be used synonymously, although we recognize that each has a particular legal connotation. The term 'global' corporation has a more specific meaning, referring to an enterprise that engages in value-added activities in each of the major regions of the world and which pursues an integrated strategy towards these activities. For further details, see Part 2 of this volume.

2 For a recent summary of this literature, see Raghunathan and Chandran (1991). Broadly speaking, scholars have tried either to quantify the value of an enterprise's foreign production (or some proxy for it), or to identify the extent to which its management attitudes, organizational procedures, operational strategies and performance calculations are internationally rather than domestically orientated. Examples of the former approach, which, *inter alia*, are now employing scaling techniques and entropy methods of measurement, are contained in Rolfe (1969), UNCTC (1973), Stopford *et al.* (1980), Stopford (1982), Yang *et al.* (1985), Michel and Shaked (1986), and Kim (1989); and of the latter, Behrman (1969), Aharoni (1971), Vernon and Wells (1981), Kogut (1983), Cheng and Ramaswamy (1989), and Bartlett and Ghoshal (1989). For an attempt to operationalize and evaluate the significance of various attributes of internationalization see Sullivan (1992b).

3 A single economic activity is defined as an activity that adds value by converting an input or combination of inputs into a single identifiable output. The end product of such an activity may be an intermediate or final goods or service. Final goods and services are

defined as those that are used for consumption only. Intermediate goods and services are defined as those used for further value-added activity. These may include finished goods or services that still require additional production (e.g. marketing and distribution) before they are sold to the final consumer.

4   Similarly, the separate transfer of the other assets or intermediate products that make up FDI, for example, technology, managerial capability and marketing rights, may be perceived as a form of portfolio resource transfer.

5   Countries treating an investment by foreigners within its boundaries (inward investment) or investment by its own individuals or companies outside its boundaries as direct, rather than portfolio, whenever the ownership of ordinary shares or voting power is 10% or more, include the US, Canada and Australia. By contrast, the normal cut-off percentage for Germany and France is 20%, and for New Zealand 25%. The OECD (1991b) has recommended to its member countries that 10% be the minimum equity stake deemed to classify an investment as 'direct'. For further details see Dunning and Cantwell (1987), UN (1992b, 1993) and EURO-STAT (1991).

6   For example, some countries adopt fully consolidated accounting systems, while others cover only investment in directly-owned enterprises. The US follows a third system by which FDI is defined as investment in every foreign enterprise in which 10% or more of the voting stock is directly or indirectly attributable to the direct investor (OECD, 1991b).

7   For further details see Chapter 2.

8   In his pioneering study of the extent and pattern of the foreign activities of multinational enterprise in the 1960s, Raymond Vernon took as his criterion an enterprise that owned manufacturing affiliates in at least six countries.

9   Jack Behrman, in particular, has always been particularly careful to distinguish between discrete and largely self-contained acts of foreign direct investment by firms and the pursuance of an integrated and coordinated strategy towards a firm's global operations. He prefers to limit the expression 'multinational' enterprise to these latter groups of enterprises. See, for example, Behrman (1969).

10   This study is an extension of an earlier statistical survey co-edited by Dunning and Cantwell (1987).

11   Thus, for example, the US now undertakes quiquennial benchmark surveys on US direct investment abroad, while the UK collects data on the foreign assets of UK companies and assets of foreign-owned companies in the UK every three years. The different attitude of countries towards publishing data on the activity of multinational firms partly reflects differences in their capability to collect such data, partly the importance they attach to it, and partly their attitudes towards publishing the data. Thus, several developing countries obtain quite a lot of data on inward direct investment but choose not to release it. Other countries, including some developed countries (e.g. Switzerland) do not conduct official enquiries on the activities of either domestic or foreign-based multinationals, and the information we can glean about their activities comes only from private enquiries.

12   See, for example, a report by EUROSTAT (1991) for the European Commission on Direct Investment of the European Community 1984–1988.

13   Who, in turn, often collect the data directly from the MNEs or their affiliates.

14   It should be noted that data such as this is necessary but not sufficient to make such an assessment. The actual employment of MNEs or their affiliates must be set against the employment that would have been generated in their absence. The methodology of assessing the *impact* as opposed to the *extent* and *pattern* of multinational activity is discussed further in several chapters in Part 3 of this volume.

15   Normally investment by one country's firms in another country comprises net capital flows plus reinvestment profits plus changes in intra-company accounts. However, according to the IMF, several countries do not include reinvested profits in the investment data they provide to the IMF *Balance of Payments Year Book* (various editions).

16   As set out, for example, in Dunning and Cantwell (1987) and UN (1992b, 1993).

17   Examples include data banks on strategic alliances constructed by scholars at the London Business School INSEAD, and at FOR (an Italian institution, see Chapter 9), and those on A&Ms compiled by scholars at the Stern School of Business (New York University) and by several management and/or financial consultants – e.g. KPMG (see its regular quarterly publication *Deal Watch*) and Securities Data Corporation (both of whom are US firms). The investment advisory corporation Translink International also publishes regular reviews of European mergers and acquisitions.

18   To calculate the replacement values of net assets, the authors used investment goods price indices or, where these were not available, the gross domestic product implicit price deflator, sometimes supplemented by consumer price indices. They also made estimates of the market value of the inward and outward investment stakes based on stock price indices. These gave broadly similar results to replacement values.

19   Partly, this was because Japanese data is based on an approval or notification basis; they also exclude reinvested profits; and are based upon the fiscal year

ending 31 March not 31 December as in the case of US data. Other estimates made by US scholars reveal an even greater discrepancy between the book and replacement values of US capital stake data. However, data on the sales of US foreign affiliates and foreign affiliates in the US tells a rather different story. In 1989, for example, the former amounted to $1015 billion and the latter to $1041 billion. For a critical appraisal of the US direct investment data system, see Stekler and Stevens (1991). For a more general analysis on the problems of estimating a nation's international investment position, see Cantwell (1992) and Miranti and Gray (1992). For a revision of income earned on US foreign direct investments to take account of currency translation adjustments, see *Survey of Current Business* (August 1990).

20 The US has recently revised the way in which it treats capital gains and losses associated with currency translation adjustment for US direct investment abroad. These are now excluded from direct investment, income and capital outflows, and, instead, are classified as valuation adjustments to the direct investment position. For further details, see *Survey of Current Business* (August 1990, p. 57).

21 For a good analysis of differences in accounting and other conventions between countries, see Clegg (1987).

22 For example, between 1 January 1988 and 1 July 1990, the EC reported that some 4905 joint ventures involving non-East European partners had been registered in Eastern Europe. However, by the end of 1991, it is improbable that more than 15% of these were operational.

23 In its examination of asymmetries in intra-EC investment flows, EUROSTAT (1991) identified four main reasons. These are (i) those caused by differences in the definition of an investor and of a direct investment enterprise, (ii) those resulting from differences in the way of identifying the link between the investor and the direct investment enterprise, (iii) those produced by differences in the definition of a direct investment flow, and (iv) those resulting from differences in recording the same flow.

24 Quite apart from the fact that the US data for 31 December 1989 (as published by the *Survey of Current Business*) and the Japanese for 31 March 1990 (as published by the Ministry of Finance), the Japanese data on direct investment includes investments made through third countries while the US data does not. For further details of differences between the Japanese and US data on Trans-Pacific investments, see Fujita (1990).

25 Further details are presented in Chapter 2 of this volume.

CHAPTER 2

THE EXTENT AND PATTERN OF FOREIGN ACTIVITIES BY MNEs

2.1 INTRODUCTION

The purpose of this chapter is to present a broad overview of the extent and pattern of the global activities of MNEs in the late 1980s and of the main changes that have taken place in these activities over the previous two decades. Chapter 5 will trace some of the more important historical landmarks in the transnationalization of economic activity over a longer time period.

the present chapter makes use of two main sets of data. The first is that published by national governments or government agencies on the activities of their own MNEs and those of foreign firms which operate subsidiaries or associated companies within their boundaries. In the main, these statistics are collected in the course of official and mandatory inquiries, and are obtained from either the universe, or a very large sample, of corporations. Some of this data is also collated and reproduced by regional or international agencies, such as The European Commission, ASEAN, International Monetary Fund (IMF), OECD and UNCTC. Perhaps the single most comprehensive source is a five-volume *World Investment Directory* (1992b, 1993) published by the UNCTC.[1]

The second set of data is that which, directly or indirectly is provided by the MNEs themselves, mostly in the form of company accounts or accompanying statements. In some cases, the provision of information is statutory. For example, US corporation law requires US MNEs to disclose certain information about their foreign assets, employment, sales and profits. In others it is voluntary. However, most of the latter data is only likely to be made available to governments, shareholders, trade associations or *bona fide* researchers by the larger MNEs in selected industrial and service sectors.

2.2 A GENERAL OVERVIEW

2.2.1 The position in the late 1980s

In 1990, the total value of the foreign direct capital stake of MNEs from all countries was estimated at $1,644 billion, an amount equivalent to about 8% of the combined gross domestic products of industrial market economies and developing countries. Later estimates by the UNCTC (UN 1992a) put the figure in 1991 at nearer $1,900 billion. The total capital controlled and employed by such companies outside their national boundaries in that year was considerably higher – probably in the order of $2,100 billion – while the combined domestic and foreign net assets of such enterprises, as recorded in their balance sheets, was nearer to $5,500 billion.[2]

Estimates of the sales and value added[3] generated by this capital stake,[4] and calculated by the UNCTC (1992a), suggest that MNEs accounted for between 25% and 30% of the gross domestic product of the world's market economies in the mid 1980s. They were also responsible for around three-quarters of the world's commodity trade,[5] and four-fifths of the trade in technology and managerial skills[6] of these economies. This data excludes the assets, output or trade arising from non-equity contractual agreements or strategic alliances in which MNEs are involved, although these also are known to be substantial.[7] The data also excludes the activities of foreign firms in the Central and East European economies and in the People's Republic of China, as well as outward direct investment by state-owned transnational activities by non-market economies.[8] Though these estimates are approximate and should be treated with a great deal of caution, they do give some idea of the dimensions and significance of MNEs in the global economy. Later sections in this chapter will pay more attention to the industrial and geographical composition of MNE activity and to the contribution of individual and particular groups of enterprises.

Our best estimate of the number of separately owned MNEs in 1988 is between 17 500–20 000. This estimate excludes the foreign subsidiaries of MNEs which themselves undertake FDI, and as far as possible only embraces MNEs that are actively engaging in foreign-based value-adding activities. The number of new MNEs is currently increasing at a rapid rate, particularly from Third World countries. However, the largest 300 MNEs are thought to account for 70% of the total foreign direct investment stake.[9] This data is drawn from the official statistics of some 65 countries, which, between them, currently account for 95% of all MNE related activity. Table 2.1(a) sets out some other facts about the extent of MNE activity in the late 1980s.

2.2.2   Trends since 1960

The only reasonably comprehensive and reliable time-series data on the activities of MNEs is that on their foreign direct investment stake and annual investment flows. Some information is also available on the foreign and global production of the world's largest industrial companies since 1962. To gain some idea of the changing role of MNEs in the global economy, this data may be related to a variety of macro-economic variables and, in particular, to gross domestic product and world trade.

Table 2.1(b) sets out some relevant details. *Inter alia* it reveals that in the early 1980s the value of the two indices of multinational activity identified has consistently outstripped that of both the world gross domestic product and world exports. The table also suggests that the rate of growth of such activity was fastest since the 1960s, although the latter part of the 1980s also showed a marked acceleration in the pace of new investment by MNEs.

It should be observed that this and other data on MNE activity is derived from different sources. Data

on investment flows, for example, is derived mainly from balance of payment statistics. Unfortunately, these are not always directly comparable between countries, as sometimes reinvested profits are included and in other cases they are not.[10] However, the data suggests that until 1981 there was a steady increase in the money value of outward direct investment flows from the major investing countries, but that in the following four years these dropped sharply, primarily because of the economic recession, the growing debt crisis and a realignment of the major currencies. By 1986, however, capital exports had recovered to a new peak, while between 1987 and 1989 they were more than four times that of the first half of the 1980s. The fact that with a few exceptions the value of the foreign production of MNEs continued to rise throughout the period, suggests that such production has been financed increasingly from local partners, banks or from the local or international capital market.[11]

The following paragraphs will show that the international data on MNEs is strongly influenced by those of US origin which, in the late 1980s, were still accounting for about two-fifths of all new FDI. Most of the fall in the new investment by MNEs in the early 1980s was explained by a dramatic decline in the profitability of US affiliates in Europe and the repatriation of capital invested by American corporations in the Netherlands Antilles and other tax havens. By contrast, the second half of the 1980s saw a marked recovery of the profitability of US outward direct investment. However, the largest upsurge in foreign production originated from Japanese MNEs, while the opening up of new markets in Eastern Europe, North America, India and East Asia encouraged foreign firms from all countries to pay more attention to these regions or countries.

2.3   THE LEADING OUTWARD INVESTORS

2.3.1   The facts

In 1988, ten developed countries identified in Table 2.2 accounted for 97.2% of the total stock of outward direct investment. The leading four – the US, the UK, Japan and West Germany – accounted for 65.6%. Eight years previously, of some 98 000

Table 2.1   The significance of multinational enterprises in the world economy.

(a) In 1988

1. Number of enterprises with foreign affiliates[1]	17 500 to 20 000
2. Number of foreign affiliates[2]	120 to 125 000
3. Global assets of MNEs	$9–10 trillion
4. Total assets of foreign affiliates	$3.0 trillion
5. The foreign direct capital stake	$1.1 trillion
6. Value of worldwide sales	$13.5 trillion
7. Value of sales of foreign affiliates	$4–4.5 trillion
8. Worldwide employment	50 to 55 million
9. Employment in foreign affiliates	14 to 15 million

(b) Since 1960

	Growth of foreign direct capital (at book value stake)	Foreign direct investment flows[3]	Gross domestic world product	World trade (at current prices)
1960–67 (1960 = 100)	165.7	164.6[4]	142.9	168.8
1967–73 (1967 = 100)	188.3	223.2	180.7	270.3
1973–80 (1973 = 100)	253.9	204.1	209.4	357.3
1980–85 (1980 = 100)	129.3	142.2	131.2	97.8
1985–88 (1985 = 100)	155.6	200.7	141.6	146.9

1   Excluding the foreign subsidiaries of MNEs which may themselves engage in FDI.
2   Some adjustment has been made by the author to allow for the fact that not all approved or registered investments are operational.
3   Represents the growth of investment flows of last two years of the period over that of the first two years of the period (e.g. for 1960–67) investment flows of 1966 and 1967 of investment flows of 1960, 1961, the latter being taken as 100.
4   1962–66.

Source: (a) Estimates of author based on data published in IMF *Balance of Payments Year Book* and *Direction of Trade Statistics* (various editions), UN (1992b, 1993) and various national surveys, notably *US Department of Commerce* (1991). Where data is incomplete, it is grossed up on the basis of the industrial or geographical information that is available.
(b) Data originally published by IMF and UNCTC (as above) and *UN Statistical Year Book* (various editions).

foreign affiliates of MNEs identified by the United Nations Centre on Transnational Corporations (UNCTC) in 1983, those based in these same countries also accounted for 97.2%, while the four leading foreign direct investors at that time – the US, the UK, West Germany and The Netherlands – were responsible for 70.2% (UNCTC, 1983b).

Though the US continues to be by far the largest outward direct investor, its share of the world direct capital stake over the past three decades has steadily fallen from 47.1% in 1960 to 40.0% in 1986 and 30.5% in 1988. In 1982, the US accounted for 44.1% of the 483 largest industrial companies in the world compared with 60.5% of the 500 largest industrial companies in 1962 (Dunning and Pearce, 1985). Trends in outward investment flows are even more revealing. Table 2.3 shows the continuing relative decline of the US as a major new foreign direct

Table 2.2 Outward stock of foreign direct investment by major home countries and regions (billions of US dollars).

Countries/regions	1967			1973			1980			1988		
	Value	% of total	% of GDP	Value	% of total	% of GDP	Value	% of total	% of GDP	Value	% of total	% of GDP
Developed market economies	109.3	97.3	4.8	205.0	97.1	5.1	535.7	97.2	6.2	1108.8	97.2	8.0
United States	56.6	50.4	7.1	101.3	48.0	7.7	220.3	40.0	8.2	345.4	30.5	7.1
United Kingdom	15.8	14.1	14.5	15.8	7.5	9.1	81.4	14.8	15.2	183.6	16.2	26.1
Japan	1.5	1.3	0.9	10.3	4.9	2.5	36.5	6.6	3.4	110.8	9.8	3.9
Germany (FRG)	3.0	2.7	1.6	11.9	5.6	3.4	43.1	7.8	5.3	103.4	9.1	8.6
Switzerland	2.5	2.2	10.0	7.1	3.4	16.2	38.5	7.0	37.9	44.1	3.9	23.9
Netherlands	11.0	9.8	33.1	15.8	7.5	25.8	41.9	7.6	24.7	77.5	6.8	34.0
Canada	3.7	3.3	5.3	7.8	3.7	6.1	21.6	3.9	8.2	50.7	4.4	11.6
France	6.0	5.3	7.0	8.8	4.2	3.8	3.8	3.8	3.2	56.2	5.0	5.9
Italy	2.1	1.9	2.8	3.2	1.5	2.4	7.0	1.3	1.8	39.9	3.5	4.8
Sweden	1.7	1.5	5.7	3.0	1.4	6.1	7.2	1.3	5.8	26.2	2.3	16.4
Other[1]	5.4	4.8	0.8	20.0	9.5	1.7	17.4	3.2	1.9	64.0	5.6	4.7
Developing countries	3.0	2.7	0.6	6.1	2.9	0.6	15.3	2.8	0.7	31.7	2.8	1.1
Total[2]	112.3	100.0	4.0	211.1	100.0	4.2	551.0	100.0	4.9	1140.5	100.0	6.7

1 Australia, Austria, Belgium, Denmark, Finland, Greece, Ireland, New Zealand, Norway, Portugal, South Africa and Spain.
2 Including a small amount of outward FDI by centrally planned economies, especially in 1980 and 1988.

Source: United Nations Centre on Transnational Corporations, based on J. H. Dunning and J. Cantwell, *The IRM Directory of Statistics of International Investment and Production* (New York, Macmillan, 1987) and official national and international data. *World Development Report* (various editions).

investor and a sharp increase in the relative significance of Japan and the marginal increase of that of major EC countries. In the period 1980–4, for example, the US accounted for 28.1% of the worldwide investment flows and Japan for only 8.9%. By 1989 and 1990, these percentages had been almost reversed, with Japan accounting for 30.8% of all new investment and the US for 19.5%. Over these same years, the three leading European capital exporters increased their share of investment flows from 33.5% to 49.7% of all new investment.

To a large extent, the relative decline in the US's position as an international direct investor was inevitable. It primarily reflects the reinstatement of the Continental European countries as leading outward investors and the emergence of Japan as a major global player. In 1988, the four main European investors (the UK, Western Germany, the Netherlands and France) and Japan accounted for 46.9% of the accumulated stock of foreign direct investment compared with only 26.3% in 1960. More particularly, between 1980 and 1988, the net increase in the foreign capital stake of the UK, Western Germany and Japan rose by $237 billion – nearly twice that of the US of $125 billion.

Two other features of the data set out in Table 2.2 are the sharp increase in the Canadian outward direct investment stake since 1980[12] and – after doubling their share between 1960 and 1975 – the unchanged contribution of third world MNEs in the following decade.[13] The latter data, however, disguises the substantial increase in new foreign direct investment by some Asian industrializing countries, such as South Korea, Taiwan, the People's Republic

Table 2.3 Outflows of foreign direct investment from five major home countries.

Home country	1985	1986	1987	1988	1989	1990	1980–84	1985–90
	(Billions of dollars)						(Percentages)	
France	2.2	5.4	9.2	14.5	19.4	34.8	6.0	10.0
Germany	5.0	10.1	9.2	11.2	13.5	22.5	7.4	8.3
Japan[1]	6.4	14.5	19.5	34.2	44.2	48.1	8.9	19.5
United Kingdom	11.1	16.5	31.1	37.0	32.0	21.5	19.4	17.4
United States[2]	8.9	13.8	28.0	13.3	26.5	29.0	28.1	13.9
Total	**33.7**	**60.2**	**97.1**	**110.2**	**135.6**	**155.9**	**69.8**	**69.2**
Developed countries	52.1	84.7	132.6	155.4	187.1	216.7	98.4	96.7
Developing countries	1.2	1.7	2.4	5.9	8.9	8.1	1.6	3.3
All countries	**53.3**	**86.5**	**135.0**	**161.3**	**196.1**	**224.8**	**100.0**	**100.0**

1 Data for Japan do not include reinvested earnings.
2 Excluding outflows to the finance (except banking), insurance and real estate sectors of the Netherlands Antilles. Also excludes currency translation adjustments.

Source: International Monetary Fund, Balance of Payments tapes; UNCTC *World Investment Reports* 1991 and 1992.

of China, Singapore and Hong Kong. The number of foreign affiliates or approved foreign investments of MNEs from these first three countries rose from 988 to 1626 between 1986 and 1988. Some smaller developed countries, *viz* New Zealand, Norway, Israel and Portugal, have also stepped up their foreign investments over the past decade (Akoorie and Enderwick, 1991; Almor-Ellemers and Hirsch, 1992; Simoes, 1992; UN, 1992a).

In general, over the past 25 years, there has been a gradual convergence between the share of outward direct capital stake of the leading industrial countries and their share of the exports of manufactured goods and services. In 1960, for example, the ratio between the US's share of the world stock of FDI and that of her export of goods and services was 2.74%. The corresponding ratios for the UK, France, Germany and Japan were 2.01, 0.99, 0.12 and 0.20. By 1988, the ratios were 1.92, 2.54, 0.79, 1.05 and 1.57.

2.3.2 The significance of outward direct investment to home countries

Table 2.2 also shows that, relative to the gross domestic product of the leading developed market economies, the significance of the outward capital stake increased between 1960 and 1988 in all countries except the Netherlands, Switzerland and France. The table also suggests that the comparative importance of the foreign activities of their own MNEs varies markedly between Nation States, with the smaller European economies, for example, Switzerland and the Netherlands, recording the highest significance ratios and some of the larger industrial economies, such as the US, Japan, France and Italy, the lowest. The United Kingdom is an exception. In 1988, her outward stock of FDI was more than one-quarter the value of her GDP.

The figures presented in Table 2.2 are not adjusted for changes in the value of the US dollar in foreign exchange markets. In some cases, such changes can markedly affect the significance ratio (UNCTC, 1989). For example, between 1980 and 1985 the $/£ exchange rate depreciated from 2.39 to 1.45, that is, by 38%. This resulted in a fall in the dollar value of the UK gross domestic product, but

Table 2.4 Outward direct investment and direct investment stake of selected developing countries.

	Investment flows (annual averages, US $m)			Capital stake 1989	
	1975–80	1981–85	1986–89	US $m	As % of GNP
Asia and Pacific					
Hong Kong	na	2058.1[1]	2879.0[2]	13 978.7[3]	30.2
Papua New Guinea	1.4[4]	1.2	−0.3[2]	na	na
People's Republic of China	na	30.0	386.5	465.2[3]	0.2
Philippines	25.0	34.8	1.7[2]	39.5[5]	0.1
Republic of Korea	17.0	66.9	214.3[2]	1 119.2[5]	0.7
Taiwan	10.0	52.4	2960.0	3 969.4[5]	1.1
Thailand	2.2[6]	1.0	60.0	258.4	0.4
Singapore	85.3	57.6	122.5	1 523.5[5]	5.9
Latin America					
Argentina	−48.3[8]	−45.0[9]	na	144.0[7]	0.5
Brazil	195.9	197.3	221.8	1 750.8	0.5
Chile	15.8[8]	10.8	9.25	151.8[10]	0.9
Columbia	16.8	32.9	27.4[2]	370.6[5]	1.0

1	1984–85	5	1988	9	1981–83
2	1986–88	6	1978–80	10	1984
3	1987	7	1981	na	not available
4	1976–80	8	1977–80		

Source: UN (1992a), *IMF Balance of Payments Year Book* (various editions); *World Development Report* (1989, 1990, 1991); Dunning and Cantwell (1987).

not that of the foreign capital stock (the initial value of which is expressed in non-UK currencies). As a consequence, the UK significance ratio rose more than it would otherwise have done. By contrast, in the case of countries whose currency appreciated *vis à vis* the dollar in the first half of the 1980s (e.g. Germany and Japan), the rise in the significance ratio underestimates the growing importance of their foreign direct investments. Even so, the figures set out in Table 2.2 paint an unmistakable picture. For Japan, at least, all the signs are that the foreign activities of their own MNEs are likely to play an even more important role in the future. Outward direct investment is also beginning to be of some consequence for the economies of several developing nations – particularly the newly industrializing countries such as Hong Kong, Singapore, South Korea and Taiwan and the oil rich countries of the Middle East. Table 2.4 sets out some details.

2.4 THE LEADING INWARD INVESTORS

2.4.1 The facts

The structure of the accumulated stock of inward direct investment is less concentrated than that of the outward capital stake. Even so, 15 countries accounted for 70.4% of the world's total in 1988, and the leading three of these – the United States, Canada and the United Kingdom – for 45.6%. In contrast to the relatively minor share of outward direct investment accounted for by developing countries, these same nations received some 21.3% of inward direct investment. However, four countries – Brazil (ranked 5th), Mexico (ranked 12th), Indonesia (ranked 14th) and Singapore (ranked 15th) – accounted for 35.7% of all the foreign capital stake in developing countries. Of the 130 developing countries that were members of the United Nations in 1990, 115 shared less than one-tenth of the total stock of inward investment.

This data and changes in the geographical distribution of the inward investment stock are set out in Table 2.5. Because of differences in coverage, definitions, reporting systems and the recording of errors and omissions, together with the fact that the data is based on that supplied by host countries rather than home countries (as in the case of Table 2.2), the estimates of the aggregate stock of inward and outward investment are not directly comparable with each other.

Table 2.5 also gives details of the significance of the inward capital stake relative to gross domestic product of developed and developing countries and how this has changed over the past two or more decades. Perhaps the most obvious conclusion to be

drawn from the data is that while, as a group, developing countries have attracted a smaller share of MNE activity, such activity has become a more significant component in their domestic economies. In any event, the share of the new investment going to developing countries is part of a longer term phenomenon,[14] which now appears to have been partially arrested, mainly as a result of the rapid growth of foreign manufacturing and service investment in South East Asia.

No less significant, however, have been the very marked changes in the distribution of MNE activity among developed and developing countries. Within developed countries, for example, there has been a shift of interest of foreign investors away from some traditional resource-rich countries such as Canada and Australia to the leading industrial nations, and especially the US and continental Europe. Japan is

Table 2.5   Inward stock of foreign direct investment by major host countries and regions 1967–88 (billions of US dollars).

Countries/regions	1967			1973			1980			1988		
	Value	% of total	% of GDP	Value	% of total	% of GDP	Value	% of total	% of GDP	Value	% of total	% of GDP
Developed market economies	73.2	69.4	3.2	153.7	73.9	3.8	403.4	78.5	4.7	959.5	78.7	6.9
Western Europe	31.4	29.8	4.2	73.8	35.5	5.6	186.9	36.4	4.2	444.5	36.5	8.4
UK	7.9	7.5	7.2	24.1	11.6	13.9	63.0	12.3	12.0	119.6	9.8	17.0
Germany	3.6	3.4	1.9	13.1	6.3	3.8	47.9	9.3	5.8	83.5	6.8	6.9
Switzerland	2.1	2.0	8.4	4.3	2.1	9.8	14.3	2.8	14.1	23.2	1.9	12.6
United States	9.9	9.4	1.2	20.6	9.9	1.6	83.0	16.2	3.2	328.9	27.0	6.8
Other[1]	31.9	30.2	4.2	59.3	28.5	4.2	133.5	26.0	8.7	175.7	14.4	4.8
Japan	0.6	0.6	0.3	1.6	0.8	0.4	3.3	0.6	0.3	10.4	0.9	0.4
Developing countries	32.3	30.6	6.4	54.7	26.3	5.4	110.3	21.5	5.4	259.8	21.3	9.0
Africa	5.6	5.3	9.0	10.2	4.9	8.7	13.1	2.6	4.1	30.9	2.5	9.7
Asia	8.3	7.9	3.9	15.3	7.4	3.6	34.9	6.8	5.0	114.0	9.3	8.9
Latin America and the Caribbean	18.5	17.5	15.8	28.9	13.9	12.3	62.3	12.1	8.4	114.9	9.4	14.2
Other[2]	na	na	na	0.3	0.1	0.1	na	na	na	na	na	na
Total	105.5	100.0	3.8	208.1	100.0	4.1	513.7	na	4.8	1219.3	na	7.2

1   Other developed economies: Australia, Canada, Japan, New Zealand, South Africa, Africa – Sub-Saharan Africa, Algeria, Egypt, Tunisia and Morocco.
2   Other developing countries: Fiji, Papua New Guinea, Saudi Arabia, Turkey, Yugoslavia, Kuwait and UAE.

na   not available

Source: As for Table 2.2.

the main exception; in 1985 it still accounted for less than 1% of the inward stock of foreign direct investment. Partly this restructuring of FDI has reflected the growing significance of the secondary and tertiary sectors in most economies, and partly a realignment of exchange rates, which itself reflects changes in the attractiveness of countries to foreign investors. The US is by far and away the leading inward direct investor (having replaced Canada in this role in 1979), and in 1988 accounted for no less than 27.0% of all inward investment (34.2% of that of developed countries) – more than that attracted either to all of Europe or to the developing countries.

Within developing countries, the share of Asian countries (outside the Indian subcontinent) of the capital stake of foreign multinationals rose from 14.8% in 1960 to 39.6% in 1988. Most of the growth has been concentrated in the newly industrializing economies of South Korea, Taiwan, Hong Kong and Singapore. However, since the mid 1980s, the second generation of the manufacturing 'tigers' of the Far East, *viz* Malaysia, Thailand and the Philippines, have noticeably increased their share of new inward investment, especially from Japan. By contrast, the share of the foreign capital stake attracted to Africa and the Middle East fell from 25.6% in 1960 to 16.2% in 1988, and that of India and Sri Lanka from 2.0% to 0.3%. Latin America and the Caribbean have maintained a steady share of inward investment directed by MNEs to developing countries of around 50%.

These geographical patterns also reflect a shift of interest of foreign firms away from resource-based to manufacturing activities, with newly industrializing nations in Latin America and East Asia recording growth rates in manufacturing industry of well in excess of 10% per annum for most of the past 25 years.

In general, it may be said that flows of foreign direct investment since 1960 have been increasingly concentrated among the industrial and richer industrializing market economies, with the latter recording the most pronounced increases in share in the 1980s. Indeed, no less than 88% of all the foreign direct investment stake in 1985 was concentrated in the twenty wealthiest industrial market economies and upper middle income developing countries (as identified in the World Bank *World Development*

Report), compared to 75% in 1960. In the same year, these two groups of countries had only a quarter of the world's population. From the perspective of MNEs taken as a whole, then, most of the world is currently of little interest to them. This perspective may change dramatically in the 21st century should four of the world's most highly populated countries, *viz* the People's Republic of China, India, the USSR and Japan (which between them, in 1985, attracted less than 2% of the total foreign capital stake), open their doors more widely to foreign enterprises.[15]

2.4.2   The significance of inward direct investment for host countries

It would be incorrect to infer from the previous paragraphs that the economic impact of foreign-owned MNEs on the least developed countries is unimportant. Far from it; as Tables 2.5 and 2.6 demonstrate, some of the poorest economies are among the most dependent on inward direct investment.

In at least 19 countries – of which ten were in Africa – with a gross national product per capita of less than $2,300 per head in 1988, the foreign direct investment stock as a per cent of gross national product was 10% or more. By contrast, in only two upper-middle income developing countries and seven industrial market economies did the accumulated capital stake reach this percentage. While the economies of these developing countries are largely natural resource based, in South East Asia industrialization and an increasing foreign presence have gone hand in hand. Thus, in the five leading industrializing countries in South East Asia, *viz* South Korea, Singapore, Hong Kong, Taiwan and Malaysia, the inward foreign direct capital stake grew on average by 4.2 times between 1980 and 1988 compared with an increase of their gross national product (GNP) of 2.2 times. For Asia as a whole, the share of the foreign direct investment stake rose from 3.6% in 1973 to 9.3% in 1988.

By contrast, until the mid 1980s the growth of inward direct investment in most parts of Western Europe lagged behind that of the growth in gross national product. The opportunities and challenges offered by the completion of the EC's internal

Table 2.6   Estimated economic significance of inward direct capital stock to selected countries (1988).

| | Total | Inward investment stock as % of gross domestic product number of countries | | | |
		Under 5%	5%–9.9%	10%–19.9%	Over 20%
Industrial market economies	18	5	6	2	5
Developing economies					
Upper-middle income economies[1]	9	5	2	0	2
Lower-middle income economies	22	6	6	5	5
Low income economies	7	4	3	0	0
All countries	56	20	17	7	12

1   Includes high income oil exporting economies.

Source: *World Investment Report* (UN, 1992a) and *The IRM Directory of Statistics of International Investment and Production*; *World Development Report 1991*.

market in 1993 has prompted a resurgence of interest by foreign multinationals in this area. Between 1986 and 1988, for example, the EC accounted for 32.5% of new investment by the US, Canada, Japan and five EC countries (Denmark, France, Germany, the Netherlands and the United Kingdom) compared with 24.7% in the previous three years and 24.3% between 1980 and 1982. Nevertheless, it has been the United States that has recorded the most substantial increase in the economic significance of inward investment in recent years, with the annual rate of growth of the stock inward investment being two-and-a-half times greater than the increase in the gross national product. Table 2.5 reveals that between 1973 and 1988 the share of the inward investment stake to the US gross domestic product rose from 1.6% to 6.8%.

2.4.3   The geographical pattern of foreign activity by MNEs

In principle, it should be possible to supplement the data just described by data on the distribution of the production of the affiliates of MNEs – at least by broad geographical region. In practice, this is more easily said than done, mainly because only a relatively small number of MNEs publish the regional breakdown of their value-added activities,

and where they do they do not always define regions in the same way.

Data on the output of foreign affiliates in individual countries is rarely published, although some information is available on their geographical distribution. The data bank prepared by scholars at the Harvard Business School in the late 1960s and early 1970[16] was a pioneering attempt to compile such information on the affiliates of US, European and Japanese MNEs. However, this data does not go beyond 1971. In the early 1980s, the UNCTC produced some data on the geographical distribution of some 98 000 foreign affiliates of the leading MNEs from 18 developed countries in 1980 (UNCTC, 1983b). Some relevant statistics are presented in Table 2.7. In aggregate, they reveal a similar picture to that of the foreign direct investment stake (see Table 2.6). They also display some differences in the geographical distribution of foreign affiliates according to their country of ownership. Thus, while MNEs from the richer Western European countries and Canada own a larger number of foreign affiliates in developed countries, those from the US, Australia, Japan, the poorer European countries and the three developing countries own a larger proportion of their affiliates in developing countries. There are also marked differences in the pattern of affiliate activity *within* developed and developing countries. While, for example, US MNEs have a more pronounced

Table 2.7 Distribution among regions of foreign affiliates of multinational enterprises from selected home countries 1980 (percentage).

Home countries	Host countries										
	Developed market economies				Developing countries						
	North America	Europe	Other[1]	Sub-total	Latin America	Africa	West Asia	South and East Asia	Europe	Sub-total	Total
Developed market economies											
Australia	8.7	19.8	27.9	56.5	1.7	0.7	0.7	40.5	–	43.5	100.0
Austria	6.2	72.2	2.8	81.2	9.8	1.2	3.5	3.5	0.8	18.8	100.0
Belgium	5.2	74.4	2.2	81.8	6.1	9.7	0.6	1.5	0.2	18.2	100.0
Canada	34.9	39.7	8.1	82.7	12.6	1.3	0.4	2.8	0.2	17.3	100.0
Denmark	7.3	73.3	4.9	85.5	4.9	3.5	1.0	4.9	0.2	14.5	100.0
Finland	11.4	80.5	1.2	93.1	3.2	1.6	1.2	0.8	–	6.9	100.0
France	8.2	58.0	3.3	69.5	7.7	18.7	1.1	2.9	0.1	30.5	100.0
Germany (FDR)	9.0	68.2	5.2	82.4	9.2	3.0	0.8	4.4	0.2	17.6	100.0
Italy	7.4	63.0	3.5	73.9	15.0	6.7	1.1	2.6	0.7	26.1	100.0
Japan	17.1	19.5	5.2	41.8	13.4	2.2	0.8	41.7	–	58.2	100.0
Luxembourg	1.4	88.8	0.6	90.8	7.9	0.7	–	0.7	–	9.2	100.0
Netherlands	6.3	70.9	5.0	82.2	6.7	5.0	1.1	5.3	0.3	17.8	100.0
New Zealand	4.2	10.8	61.7	76.7	0.9	0.4	0.2	21.5	0.2	23.3	100.0
Norway	8.8	74.6	2.8	86.2	3.6	3.0	1.9	5.3	–	13.8	100.0
Portugal	–	57.2	–	57.2	21.4	–	–	–	–	42.8	100.0
Spain	2.4	62.1	1.0	65.5	27.7	4.8	–	2.1	–	34.5	100.0
Sweden	9.4	73.1	4.5	87.0	7.1	1.3	0.5	4.0	0.1	13.0	100.0
Switzerland	8.1	72.7	5.6	86.5	6.9	1.7	0.8	4.0	0.1	13.5	100.0
United Kingdom	14.1	15.2	26.5	75.8	4.7	7.7	0.9	10.4	0.5	24.2	100.0
United States	12.9	42.6	9.7	65.3	21.4	2.3	2.3	0.9	0.1	34.7	100.0
Average (developed market economies)	9.2	56.9	9.1	76.1	9.6	4.9	0.9	8.4	0.2	23.9	100.0
Developing countries											
Hong Kong	–	16.3	24.9	44.8	4.3	19.5	0.3	31.0	0.1	55.2	100.0
Malaysia	–	29.1	10.9	40.0	2.3	2.3	–	55.4	–	60.0	100.0
Singapore	1.9	8.7	6.2	16.8	1.2	0.5	–	81.5	–	83.2	100.0

1 Australia, Japan and New Zealand

Source: UNCTC (1983b).

presence in Latin America, foreign direct investors from the Far East and Pacific tend to favour Asian locations, whereas those from the UK and France prefer Southern Europe and the African continent.

Later sections in this chapter and Chapter 4 will further discuss these and other characteristics of the geographical structure of international production.[17] Further data is also contained in the UNCTC's *World Investment Directory* referred to earlier.

2.5 THE BALANCE BETWEEN INWARD AND OUTWARD DIRECT INVESTMENT

Combining the data presented in the previous two sections, two outstanding conclusions emerge. First, the foreign activities of domestic MNEs and those of the affiliates of foreign multinationals are becoming an increasingly important component of the national output of both industrialized and industrializing market economies. In 1967, the value of the combined inward and outward direct investment stock of the US was only 8.3% of its gross domestic product; by 1973 it had risen to 9.3% and by 1988 it was 13.9%. The corresponding percentages for the UK, Germany, Japan and Switzerland were 21.7%, 3.3%, 1.2% and 18.4% for 1967, 23.0%, 7.2%, 2.9% and 26.0% for 1973, and 43.1%, 15.5%, 43% and 36.5% for 1988.

Second, there appears to be a growing symmetry between outward and inward foreign capital stake in the case of most countries. Table 2.8 presents some salient details. Particularly worthy of note is the quite dramatic change in the ratio of the outward to inward stake of the United States – from 5.72 in 1967 to 0.95 in 1988. (By 1990, this ratio had risen marginally to 1.04.) The growth of outward direct investment has also lagged behind that of inward direct investment in the UK and Sweden. By contrast, Canada, Germany, Italy, Australia and some developing countries have improved their relative international direct investment positions, and Germany and Italy are now net outward investors. Contrary to these movements towards a more balanced international investment position, is the widening of the net credit or debit status of some other developed nations, notably Japan and, to a lesser extent, Switzerland and France.

Table 2.8   Ratio of outward to inward direct capital stake (1960–88).

Market economies	1960	1967	1975	1985	1988
Developed countries					
North America					
US	4.61	5.72	4.48	1.36	0.95[6]
Canada	0.19	0.10	0.28	0.60	0.65[5]
Western Europe					
France	na	na	1.16	1.06	1.35
Italy	na	na	0.36	0.86	1.02
Netherlands	na	na	2.14	1.98	1.60
Sweden	na	4.55	3.28	2.47[4]	3.40
Switzerland	na	1.19	5.50	1.95	1.96[6]
UK	2.16[1]	2.00	1.58[2]	1.73	1.59[5]
Germany (FDR)	0.56	0.83	1.04[3]	1.67	1.24
Asia and the Pacific					
Japan	3.68	2.50	10.60	13.70	14.57
Australia	0.11	na	0.13	0.23	0.46
Developing countries					
Latin America					
Brazil	na	na	na	0.08	0.06
Chile	na	na	na	0.07	na
Columbia	na	na	0.04	0.13	na
Asia and the Pacific					
Singapore	na	na	na	0.11	0.09
South Korea	0.0	0.0	0.10	0.26	0.28
Taiwan	na	na	na	0.04	0.14

1 1962	3 1976	5 1987
2 1974	4 1984	6 1989
na not available.		

Source: As per Table 2.2 and Dunning (1985).

To some extent these changes reflect a repositioning of the changing international competitiveness of countries, as suggested by the realignment of exchange rates which has taken place over the past 20 years.[18] It is no coincidence that the industrial countries that have most improved their net international investment positions since 1960 (i.e. Japan and Germany) are those whose currencies have appreciated the most. At the same time the US, whose currency has depreciated the most, has had the greatest deterioration in its outward/inward capital stake. The fluctuating position of the UK as a net capital exporter also accords well with a currency which bought $2.4 US in the early 1970s, dropped to $1.1 in 1979 and had recovered to $1.86 by December 1991. However, government policy and other changes in the macro-economic climate and the structure of production and trade, which are less readily reflected in exchange rate changes, are no less important reasons. Thus, in spite of a fall in the value of the Canadian dollar relative to the US dollar for most of the 1980s, Canadian direct investment has increased sharply in the US – especially in the non-tradeable service sectors. Also the rapid increase in the foreign value-added activities of Swedish MNEs has mirrored the higher (or expected higher) profitability of these activities relative to their domestic equivalents, and continuing doubts over the competitiveness of the Swedish economy, particularly in labour-intensive sectors.[19] The growth of intra-industry strategic alliances has also contributed towards the cross-hauling of trade and production by MNEs.

As far as developing countries are concerned, the emergence of their own MNEs has coincided with the generation of new competitive advantages (Lall, 1983) which are best exploited through foreign production. To start with, these advantages were usually based on the national resources of the home country. Examples included Indian shrimp canners, Argentine meat packing firms, Malaysian rubber companies, Brazilian and Nigerian coffee processing firms, Taiwanese pulp and paper producers, Thai timber firms and so on. Latterly, some Third World MNEs, especially from Brazil, Singapore and India, have developed quite a sophisticated range of products and services, and are actively participating in such sectors as consumer electronics, aircraft and hotels (World Bank, 1989). A number of Asian and Mexican MNEs have also acquired quite substantial companies in sectors like cement, glass, chicken and fish canning.[20] There are also several state-owned MNEs from developing countries in the oil and steel industries (Wells, 1983; Lall, 1983; Khan, 1987).

2.6   THE SECTORAL COMPOSITION OF OUTWARD AND INWARD INVESTMENT

2.6.1   The main orders of economic activity

Just as there is some geographical concentration of the countries supplying and receiving FDI, so there is a marked preference as to the industrial sectors in which MNEs choose to produce. While the pattern of this concentration differs according to the home country of the investing firms as well as to the countries in which their affiliates are located, some general conclusions may be drawn both from the data on the stock of FDI published by countries and from those of the foreign assets, employment and production reported directly by the leading MNEs.

Table 2.9 sets out the broad sectoral distribution of the outward FDI stake of seven of the largest capital-exporting countries in 1975 and 1988. The table shows that, taking an unweighted average, in the latter year 35.6% of multinational investment was directed to the manufacturing sector, about 47.4% to services and 17.0% to the primary product sector. The corresponding percentages for 1975 were 42.1%, 33.4% and 24.5%. The table also reveals that there are some marked differences in the sectoral distribution of the capital stake, as between home countries. These differences largely reflect the stage of internationalization and the structure of resource endowments and capabilities of home countries (cf Japan with West Germany). Other data reveals that recipient countries also vary in their propensity to attract different kinds of FDI (Dunning and Cantwell, 1987; UN, 1992b, 1993). Nations rich in natural resources but with small populations (e.g. Canada, Australia, the oil rich Middle Eastern and several African countries) tend to attract a higher percentage of inward investment in the primary sector. On the other hand, industrial or industrializing economies (e.g. West Germany, Japan, Singapore and Mexico) attract an above average share of inward investment in the secondary sector. France, Switzerland, Hong Kong, the US and Fiji are among the countries that record the highest share of tertiary investments.

Generally speaking, the significance of inbound MNE activity in the service sector rises as income

Table 2.9 Changes in the sectoral composition of the stock of outward foreign direct investment of major investing countries (1975–88).

Country	Period	Sectors			Total
		Primary	Secondary (% share)	Tertiary	
Canada					
Composition	1975	21.1	50.5	28.4	100.0
	1987	13.1	43.3	43.4	100.0
Growth rate[1]	1975–87	12.2	26.0	28.3	26.3
France[2]					
Composition	1975	22.1	38.2	39.7	100.0
	1988	15.0	36.6	48.3	100.0
Growth rate[1]	1975–87	12.1	15.1	16.6	16.4
Germany (FDR)					
Composition	1976	4.5	48.3	47.2	100.0
	1988	2.8	43.4	53.7	100.0
Growth rate	1976–88	7.6	10.7	12.9	11.5
Japan					
Composition	1975	28.1	32.4	39.5	100.0
	1989	6.7	26.0	67.0	100.0
Growth rate[1]	1975–89	10.0	19.9	26.5	21.8
Netherlands					
Composition	1975	46.8	38.6	14.6	100.0
	1988	36.4	24.7	38.8	100.0
Growth rate[1]	1975–88	5.9	4.2	16.5	7.9
United Kingdom[3]					
Composition	1981	—	—	35.6	100.0
	1987	26.9	34.4	38.6	100.0
Growth rate[1]	1981–87	—	—	12.3	11.3
United States[4]					
Composition	1975	26.4	45.0	28.6	100.0
	1989	16.7	40.9	42.3	100.0
Growth rate[1]	1975–89	4.7	7.4	11.4	8.2

1 Compound general growth rate.
2 Based on cumulative flows of direct investment from 1972.
3 Data for primary and secondary sectors is not available separately for 1981. The combined growth rate of the two sectors for the 1981–87 period was 10.3%.
4 The vertically integrated petroleum industry is included in the primary sector in 1975. In 1989, only the extractive portion of the industry is included in the primary sector, with processing included in the secondary sector and marketing and distribution in the tertiary sector.

Source: UNCTC estimates, based on UNCTC, 1991a.

Table 2.10 Changes in share of foreign direct investment stake accounted for by services in selected host countries during the 1980s.

Developed countries			Developing countries		
Europe			**Latin America**		
France	1980	61.6	Argentina	1981	25.0
	1989	66.7		1986	23.0
Germany	1980	40.2	Brazil	1976	21.1
	1989	60.5		1988	25.5
Italy	1980	31.1	Columbia	1980	18.2
	1989	50.6		1986	11.3
Netherlands	1980	39.5	Ecuador	1981	50.0
	1989	46.2		1986	46.2
Norway	1980	59.0	Peru	1980	22.2
	1988	58.2		1986	28.6
Portugal	1980	47.5	Venezuela	1981	33.9
	1989	64.0		1986	27.1
United Kingdom	1981	28.1			
	1987	34.7			
North America			**Asia**		
Canada	1980	25.0	India	1980	38.6
	1989	34.2		1988	19.0
United States	1980	41.0	Indonesia	1980	10.7
	1986	48.3		1989	10.3
			Korea	1980	32.3
				1988	37.7
			Malaysia	1980	38.7
Asia and Pacific				1987	24.3
Australia	1980	46.0	Pakistan	1980	38.5
	1988	51.1		1988	49.8
Japan	1980	22.2	Philippines	1980	30.3
	1989	34.8		1989	21.8
			Singapore	1980	45.2
				1989	57.4
			Thailand	1980	54.7
				1989	48.0
			Africa		
			Morocco	1980	53.3
				1988	57.2
			Nigeria	1980	36.4
				1988	36.8

Source: Derived from UNCTC (1988), UN (1992b, 1993).

levels increase. In the mid 1980s, this sector accounted for around 45% of the inward investment stock in developed countries and about 30% of the stock in developing countries (UNCTC, 1988). No less worthy of note is the fact that in more than two-thirds of the countries for which data was available, the share of new FDI received by the service sector rose sharply in the 1980s (UNCTC, 1988; UN, 1992a). This data is further confirmed by that set out in Table 2.10, which details the changes in the share of new investment directed to the services sector by some developed and developing economies. The only countries that recorded a decreased share are those for which FDI in manufacturing industry markedly increased in the 1980s.

The changing composition of international production so far outlined in this chapter reflect part of a longer term trend, the features of which will be explored in more detail in Chapter 5. Suffice it to mention, here, that in the case of most industrialized developed countries, FDI was initially directed to the extraction of minerals and the harvesting of raw materials and foodstuffs for consumption or further processing in the investing countries. Of the leading outward investors of the 19th century, Germany was the only nation that had few foreign interests in the primary sector. It is no coincidence that it was not a major colonizing power. Of the foreign activities of US, British, French and Dutch MNEs in developing countries, the great majority of these – probably four-fifths – was directed to the primary sector.

After the Second World War, this all changed. In the first place, foreign-owned production became more oriented towards the industrialized countries to supply markets which, for one reason or another, could not be serviced, or serviced as cheaply, by exports. In the second place, nationalization and expropriation programmes of several host developing nations in the 1960s and 1970s drastically reduced the role of many MNEs, particularly in the natural resource sectors. Thirdly, the growth of export-processing manufacturing investment since the early 1970s and, more recently, a rapid expansion in trade and pre-industrialization in both developed and developing economies has diminished the relative significance of FDI in the primary sector in almost all host countries.

2.6.2   The composition of FDI within broad orders of activity

Comprehensive and comparable data on the industrial distribution of value-added activities by MNEs, or their affiliates, within the sectors identified in previous paragraphs is even more difficult to obtain. Except in the case of a very few countries, data is not available beyond the three-digit level of (US) standard industrial classification (SIC). Table 2.11 sets out some details on the sectoral composition of the outward direct investment stock of MNEs from selected countries. Table 2.12 presents similar data for the activities of foreign affiliates in some leading host countries.

The data in these tables leads to a number of broad conclusions. First, within the primary sector, investment by multinational petroleum companies accounts for about three-quarters of the outward investment stock of both the developed and developing countries, although relative to all MNE activities, those of the oil companies are more concentrated in the latter countries. For example, in 1988 Brazil, Chile, India, Mexico, Korea and Taiwan all owned petroleum companies which were among the largest 500 non-US industrial firms in the world (Fortune, 1990). While investment by petroleum MNEs dominates the foreign-owned primary sector of most host countries some, such as Spain, Ecuador, Indonesia, Morocco, Liberia, Thailand, Botswana, Namibia and the Cameroons, attract substantial investments in agricultural cash crops like rubber, tobacco, sugar, palm oil, cocoa, pineapples and bananas. Still others, including Canada, Papua New Guinea, Chile, Malaysia, the Congo, Gabon, Zambia and Zimbabwe, are important suppliers of hard minerals like bauxite, copper, zinc and tin. There is also some foreign direct investment in the fishing industry in several African and Asian countries.

Second, in the manufacturing sector there are two main groups of industries favoured by MNEs. First are the capital intensive processing industries, which are often based on foodstuffs, minerals and raw materials supplied by other, or the same, foreign investors in the primary sector. They produce both intermediate products and high income, differentiated consumer goods. Table 2.11 suggests that the most important of these are coal and petroleum-based products, chemicals, food, drink and tobacco, metal processing, textiles and clothing, paper and allied products, stone clay and glass and rubber products. Such sectors accounted for about three-fifths of the foreign manufacturing activities of MNEs and about one-third of the total investment stake in the late 1980s. These same sectors account for a fluctuating share of the inward investment stake in host countries. In the US, Sweden and some developing countries that are rich in non-mineral primary products, it was more than 75%, whereas in most industries in the newly industrializing nations of South East Asia it ranged from 40% to 60%.

The second group of industries favoured by MNEs are the technology and/or human capital intensive sectors, and those which can benefit from the economies of large scale production. These are largely the fabricating industries, such as mechanical engineering, electrical and electronic equipment, computers and motor vehicles. In the late 1980s these sectors accounted for about one-third of all outward manufacturing investment, with the ratios varying between over 50% in the case of Germany, Sweden and the Netherlands to 20% in the UK. The attraction of the fabricating industries to foreign direct investors varies considerably between host countries. It is markedly above average in the case of the Netherlands, Argentina, Hong Kong and the UK, and markedly below average in the Philippines, Thailand, Malaysia and the US. Within both groups of industries FDI tends to be concentrated in:

(1)   the most technologically advanced and capital intensive sectors,

(2)   those supplying products with an above average income elasticity of demand and a high degree of product differentiation, and

(3)   those where there are substantial economies of scale or scope to be gained from plant specialization, but a geographical diversification of activities.

In the service sector which, as we have seen, is attracting an increasing share of MNE activity, the overwhelming amount of FDI is concentrated in trade and financial services. As Table 2.13 shows, in the great majority of countries for which data is available, the share of both the outward and inward investment stock in these activities (which include wholesale and retail trade, banking, insurance and finance) exceeds 60%, although MNEs are taking an increasing interest in other services, including tourism, telematics, engineering and business consultancy and professional services, as well as construction and real estate investment. However, with one or two exceptions (e.g. Thailand, Taiwan and Singapore, as depicted in Table 2.13), these activities still do not figure significantly in their overall investment portfolios.

Table 2.13 also suggests that there are some differences in the composition of activities of MNE affiliates in the service sectors of host countries. These differences largely reflect the role of services in economic development and the attitude of host governments towards foreign participation in sensitive sectors. Although in all countries, trade and finance related services account for the bulk of inward direct investment, in the faster growing developing countries, the share of investment directed to infrastructural services like construction, transport, telecommunications and hotel accommodation is above average, while the developed economies seem to attract a larger share of inward investment in securities and diversified financial services (Daniel, 1991). There are also significant inter-country differences in the role of particular services. Compare, for example, the overwhelming importance of tourism in Spain, the Caribbean, Fiji and Tanzania, with those of trade and financial activities in the UK, Hong Kong and Singapore. Producer services are largely concentrated in the major cities of the Triad countries.

2.7   THE ECONOMIC SIGNIFICANCE OF DIFFERENT TYPES OF INDUSTRIAL ACTIVITY BY MNEs

2.7.1   Some home country data

From time to time some countries publish data on the relative significance of the foreign activities of their own MNEs in particular sectors. A selection of this data is set out in Table 2.14. It suggests that for the leading investing economies, the outward MNE significance ratio (defined as the ratio of the foreign output, assets or employment of MNEs to the indigenous output, assets or employment of their home countries) varies considerably both between

Table 2.11 Industrial distribution of outward direct capital stock for selected countries in the late 1980s (percentages).

	Developed countries								
	Australia (1989)	Canada (1989)	France[1] (1989)	Germany (1989)	Italy (1989)	Japan[2] (1989)	Norway (1988)	UK (1987)	US (1989)
Primary	19.2	6.4	13.4	2.7	8.2	6.7	11.6	27.0	16.7
Agriculture	0.3	neg	0.2	0.4	0.3	0.7	neg	1.0	0.1
Mining and quarrying	18.9	6.5	neg	0.5	neg	6.0	neg	nsa	1.3
Oil	neg	neg	13.2	1.8	7.9	neg	11.6	26.0	15.3
Secondary	18.2	51.6	39.9	41.7	33.6	26.0	33.5	34.3	41.0
Food and drink products	nsa	6.1	7.7	0.6	2.2	1.3	0.6	6.8	4.9
Chemicals and allied products	0.9	7.2	6.7	15.6	8.8	3.4	21.9	9.4	9.5
Metals	3.7	16.1	9.2	2.3	2.3	3.5	3.4	0.7	2.2
Mechanical engineering	1.7	nsa	1.5	4.0	6.3	2.6	4.3	1.6	7.1
Electrical and electronic goods	nsa	nsa	5.4	6.9	nsa	5.8	neg	3.8	3.1
Motor vehicles	0.1	nsa	2.5	6.1	2.6	3.5	neg	1.1	5.9
Textiles, clothing and leather goods	nsa	nsa	0.8	1.0	1.1	1.3	0.3	nsa	0.5
Paper products	7.7	11.7	1.1	0.9	nsa	1.1	2.2	2.9	2.3
Rubber products	nsa	nsa	0.5	1.3	nsa	nsa	nsa	nsa	1.7
Coal and petroleum products	nsa	7.0	nsa	0.1	nsa	nsa	nsa	nsa	3.5
Other manufacturing	4.1	3.5	4.5	2.9	11.3	3.5	0.8	nsa	2.8
Tertiary	62.5	42.0	46.7	55.6	58.2	67.0	54.9	38.6	42.3
Construction	2.0	nsa	1.8	0.4	nsa	0.8	neg	1.8	0.3
Transport and communications	3.5	2.1	1.3	0.9	0.8	6.0	10.5	2.1	0.8
Trade and distribution	5.3	4.8	5.2	19.6	7.2	9.9	1.6	9.0	11.7
Real estate	nsa	nsa	4.4	9.7	nsa	13.7	nsa	nsa	0.7
Finance and insurance	47.6	27.6	26.1	17.9	44.7	22.6	40.8	13.4	26.5
Other services	4.1	7.5	7.9	7.1	5.5	14.0	2.0	12.3	2.3
Total	100.0	100.0	100.0	100.0	100.0	100.0	100.0	100.0	100.0
Value national currencies (billion)	A$ 33.4	$C 79.9	FF 433.1	DM 206.6	L 63 407	$ 253.9	K 18.1	£ 86.7	$ 380.0

Table 2.11   continued.

	Developing countries					
	China[3] (1988)	Columbia (1988)	India (1988)	Korea[4] (1989)	Taiwan[5] (1988)	Thailand (1989)
Primary	26.0	3.7	3.1	42.3	1.1	0.3
Agriculture	10.2	3.0	3.1	9.1	1.1	0.2
Mining and quarrying	8.4	0.6	neg	33.3	neg	0.1
Oil	nsa	nsa	neg	neg	neg	neg
Secondary	45.0	17.8	81.7	32.8	65.6	17.4
Food and drink products	1.1	15.4	3.8	4.5	2.9	13.1
Chemicals and allied products	1.2	nsa	21.2	2.3	13.5	0.2
Metals	12.1	0.1	13.0	11.3	1.8	0.3
Mechanical engineering	0.2	0.5	6.4	0.4	0.5	neg
Electrical and electronic goods	4.4	nsa	1.3	2.2	30.1	0.1
Motor vehicles	neg	nsa	nsa	1.4	nsa	nsa
Textiles, clothing and leather goods	4.6	0.1	15.5	6.8	3.9	neg
Paper products	0.6	0.7	11.5	nsa	4.4	3.6
Rubber products	0.4	0.9	1.2	nsa	4.5	neg
Coal and petroleum products	0.2	nsa	1.9	nsa	nsa	neg
Other manufacturing	20.2	0.1	5.9	3.9	4.0	0.1
Tertiary	29.0	77.8	15.3	24.9	33.2	82.3
Construction	2.7	0.2	1.2	3.4	1.2	0.1
Transport and communications	3.7	nsa	nsa	0.3	neg	3.5
Trade and distribution	5.6	3.4	1.9	9.4	5.8	2.0
Real estate	1.5	2.0	2.7	2.8	3.7	neg
Finance and insurance	nsa	67.5	nsa	nsa	nsa	77.1
Other services	15.5	4.7	9.5	9.0	16.7	−3.2
Total	100.0	100.0	100.0	100.0	100.0	100.0
	Yuan	$	R	Won	NT$	B
Value national currencies (billion)	1.7	0.37	1.2	765.6	19.8	6.6

1 Cumulative direct investment flows since 1972.
2 Cumulative direct investment flows since 1951.
3 Cumulative direct investment flows since 1979.
4 Cumulative direct investment flows since 1962.
5 Cumulative direct investment flows since 1959.

nsa   not separately available.
neg   negligible.

Source: Various national authorities and UN (1992b, 1993).

Table 2.12 Industrial distribution of inward direct capital stock for selected countries in the late 1980s.

	Developed countries								
	Australia (1983)	Canada (1987)	France[1] (1987)	Germany (1988)	Italy (1987)	Portugal (1983)	Japan[2] (1989)	UK (1987)	US (1989)
Primary	25.2	23.9	1.5	0.7	3.5	4.5	neg	29.1	11.0
Agriculture	1.6	neg	0.2	0.1	0.1	1.8	neg	0.2	0.5
Mining and quarrying	} 23.5	4.4	0.3	0.2	neg	} 2.7	neg	neg	1.8
Oil		19.5	1.0	0.5	3.4		neg	28.9	8.8
Secondary	27.8	43.1	37.1	46.7	50.1	52.9	65.2	36.2	40.0
Food and drink products	4.1	8.1	8.0	3.7	3.3	4.8	1.8	5.7	6.0
Chemicals and allied products	4.8	6.7	8.0	9.2	11.6	13.0	17.4	7.8	11.5
Metals	5.3	18.9	7.4	3.5	0.9	2.9	3.2	2.0	4.6
Mechanical engineering	} 6.0	nsa	3.1	7.1	} 19.2	} 19.1	} 34.3	4.6	2.6
Electrical and electronic goods		nsa	1.6	6.3				6.0	4.1
Motor vehicles	3.9	nsa	0.9	4.3	7.7			4.2	1.0
Textiles, clothing and leather goods	0.9	0.8	1.8	0.6	1.8	3.5	0.3	0.3	0.4
Paper products	0.8	6.2	1.7	1.2	nsa	6.9	neg	2.4	0.6
Rubber products	nsa	neg	0.7	2.4	nsa	nsa	0.5	nsa	1.5
Coal and petroleum products	nsa	nsa	nsa	nsa	nsa	nsa	4.4	nsa	nsa
Other manufacturing	1.0	2.4	3.9	8.4	5.6	2.7	3.3	3.2	7.7
Tertiary	46.9	33.0	61.5	52.6	46.4	42.6	34.8	34.7	49.0
Construction	1.3	nsa	0.1	0.2	nsa	0.8	0.5	0.3	1.0
Transport and communications	1.0	nsa	2.0	1.0	0.7	1.3	1.6	0.3	1.0
Trade and distribution	23.9	7.7	15.5	16.3	7.4	27.6	14.1	9.8	17.8
Real estate	} 18.8	nsa	19.0	22.7	nsa	} 11.7	3.7	neg	8.9
Finance and insurance		20.1	13.9	9.1	30.5		5.1	18.0	13.4
Other services	1.9	5.2	10.9	3.3	7.8	13.3	9.8	6.3	6.9
Total	100.0	100.0	100.0	100.0	100.0	100.0	100.0	100.0	100.0
	A$	$C	FF	DM	L	ES	$	£	$
Value national currencies (billion)	18.1	101.5	234.9	148.7	36 660	38.5	15.7	54.6	400.8

Table 2.12   continued.

	Developing countries								
	Argentina (1986)	Brazil (1988)	Columbia (1988)	India (1989)	Korea (1988)	Singapore (1989)	Taiwan (1988)	Thailand³ (1989)	Turkey⁴ (1990)
Primary	14.6	3.4	48.2	6.1	0.9	neg		9.1	3.1
Agriculture	2.0	1.0	0.6	2.9	0.7	neg	nsa	1.3	2.1
Mining and quarrying	11.6	2.5	47.7	0.6	0.2	neg		0.8	1.0
Oil		neg		2.6	neg	neg		7.0	neg
Secondary	62.4	71.0	40.4	89.1	61.5	42.4	88.3	42.8	52.2
Food and drink products	7.5	6.0	6.4	3.5	4.0	1.4	1.8	3.6	5.5
Chemicals and allied products	12.2	15.1	nsa	28.5	16.9	6.0	17.9	5.7	9.5
Metals	4.4	6.6	2.6	10.6	2.9	2.5	4.1	4.5	3.7
Mechanical engineering	3.9	8.6	0.5	8.8	5.3	2.5	10.9	2.1	0.5
Electrical and electronic goods	3.6	8.6	5.5	11.6	18.9	14.0	28.0	14.9	7.9
Motor vehicles	13.2	8.8	neg	9.2	9.9	nsa	0.3		11.7
Textiles, clothing and leather goods	2.5	1.8	2.6	1.4	0.5	8.3	4.1	2.5	3.0
Paper products	0.6	1.9	5.3	0.1	0.7	0.8	2.3	nsa	2.8
Rubber products	1.8	2.7	nsa	3.5	nsa	0.6	4.5	nsa	2.6
Coal and petroleum products	nsa	nsa	nsa	nsa	nsa	10.6	nsa	1.3	nsa
Other manufacturing	12.7	9.2	18.3	10.7	1.5	3.5	10.2	6.6	5.0
Tertiary	23.0	25.5	11.3	4.8	37.6	57.5³	11.7	48.0	44.7
Construction	1.6	nsa	neg	0.5	1.0	1.55	0.1	11.6	0.3
Transport and communications	0.6	0.2	nsa	0.1	0.6	15.9	4.7	2.6	0.9
Trade and distribution	4.5	3.9	5.1	1.5	0.7	13.9	0.3	16.6	7.6
Real estate	0.3	0.5	0.4	nsa	nsa	6.7	nsa	4.2	nsa
Finance and insurance	12.2	5.3	5.3	0.3	7.8	25.0	nsa	6.6	16.0
Other services	3.8	15.6	0.8	2.4	27.5	4.7	nsa	6.4	16.9
Total	100.0	100.0	100.0	100.0	100.0	100.0	100.0	100.0	100.0
Value national currencies (billion)	$ 6.6	$ 32.0	$ 3.0	R 14.1	Won 2706.6	S$ 50.7	NT$ 191.1	Baht 142.2	TL 3 867 500

1   Cumulative direct investment flows since 1972.
2   Cumulative direct investment flows since 1951.
3   Cumulative direct investment flows since 1970.
4   Cumulative direct investment flows since 1954.

nsa   not separately available.
neg   negligible.

Source: As for Table 2.11.

Table 2.13 Composition of the services sector in outward and inward direct investment stock (National currency in billions; latest available year).

A. Outward investment

Developed countries	Year	Value of stock	Construction	Distributive trade	Transport and storage	Communication	Finance and insurance	Real estate	Other
Canada (Canadian dollar)	1987	28.7	nsa	12.6	4.9	nsa	64.7	nsa	17.9[1]
France (French franc)	1988	153.5	3.8	12.4	3.4[2]	0.2	55.0	8.6	16.7
Germany (FDR) (Deutschmark)	1988	98.9	0.9	38.2	1.5		31.8	17.4	10.2
Italy (Italian lira)	1987	20.3	nsa	14.2	0.7		82.5	nsa	2.6
Japan (US dollar)	1988	120.9	2.0	16.6	10.2		34.6	17.5	19.9
Netherlands (Guilder)	1988	57.5	0.8	22.6	3.1		35.7	nsa	37.8
Spain (Peseta)	1983	135.3	7.5	21.3	2.7		65.3	nsa	3.2
UK (Pound sterling)	1987	33.5	4.7	23.3	5.4	nsa	34.8	nsa	31.8
US (US dollar)	1989	160.8	0.6	27.7	1.1	0.7	62.7[3]	1.7	5.5

B. Inward investment

	Year	Value of stock	Construction	Distributive trade	Transport and storage	Communication	Finance and insurance	Real estate	Other
Austria	1988	37.4	nsa	42.2	11.3		29.8	nsa	16.6
Belgium/Luxembourg (Belgian franc)	1987	632.6							
Canada (Canadian dollar)	1987	33.5	nsa	23.2	nsa	nsa	60.8		16.0[1]
France (French franc)	1988	144.4	0.2	25.2	3.3[2]	nsa	22.6	31.0	17.7
Germany (FDR) (Deutschmark)	1988	78.2	0.5	31.0	1.8		17.2	43.1	6.4
Italy (Italian lira)	1987	170.1	nsa	15.8	1.5		56.7	nsa	16.9
Japan (US dollar)	1988	3.8	1.9	44.3	2.1	2.8	10.4	3.9	34.5
Netherlands (Guilder)	1988	42.9	2.8	37.1	3.6		15.5	nsa	41.1
Spain (Peseta)	1983	237.0	4.6	56.2	4.0		30.9	nsa	4.3
UK (Pound sterling)	1987	18.9	0.8	28.3	1.0	nsa	51.9	nsa	18.0
US (US dollar)	1989	196.4	19.7	36.3	2.0	0.3	27.4[3]	18.3	13.8

C. Inward investment (continued)

	Year	Value of stock	Construction	Distributive trade	Transport and storage	Communication	Finance and insurance	Real estate	Other
Argentina (US dollar)	1986	1491.4	7.4	1.9	neg	2.3	53.2	1.1	16.3
Indonesia (US dollar)	1987	0.8[4]	17.1	17.4	2.1	4.9	nsa[4]	nsa	58.5
Korea (Won)	1988	1017.0	2.7	1.8	1.5	nsa	20.6	nsa	73.3
Malaysia (Ringih)	1987	5.3	8.9	30.1	nsa	nsa	58.7	nsa	2.3
Singapore (Singapore dollar)	1981	8.5	2.6	27.8	6.7	nsa	43.4	11.6	8.1
Taiwan (New Taiwanese dollar)	1988	16.5	1.0	3.0	40.3[2]	nsa	nsa	nsa	55.8
Thailand (Bhat)	1988	45.1	27.9	37.0	7.0[5]	nsa	13.2	4.6	10.4

1 Includes utilities.
2 Transport and storage represents transport only.
3 Includes holding companies.
4 Banking and insurance are excluded.
5 Consists of transport and travel.

nsa not separately available.
neg negligible.

Table 2.14 Share of domestic output of MNEs from leading source countries accounted for by foreign affiliates.

	France (1977)	Germany (1982)	Italy (1987)	Japan (1979)	Sweden[1] (1978)	UK[2] (1981)	US (1987)
Primary							
Agriculture	na	na	na	46.7	na	34.4	60.2
Mining and quarrying	28.3	5.4	na	61.2	44.0	29.5	120.6
Petroleum	21.2	nsa	49.1	na	na	30.3	592.2
Secondary							
Food and drink products	na	4.8	59.6	21.7	26.0	23.4	35.9
Chemical and allied products	12.1	54.4	20.8	4.6	35.0	34.4	47.4
Metals	10.6	10.2	24.0	9.8	29.0	23.7	29.1
Mechanical engineering	1.7	13.6	30.0	1.7	40.0	8.7	67.2
Electrical and electronic goods	4.1	24.3	25.6	4.8	44.0	10.2	39.3
Motor vehicles	12.5	25.4	15.1	3.1	na	6.1	56.8
Textiles, clothing and leather goods	3.6	8.7	5.7	5.3	30.0	16.1	16.6
Paper products	14.2	8.1	3.2	41.9	23.0	21.9	19.0
Rubber products	nsa	9.5	164.0	nsa	na	nsa	59.0
Coal and petroleum products	nsa	2.0	0.8	nsa	na	nsa	40.1
Tertiary							
Construction	3.7					10.5	36.2
Transport and communications	nsa					18.8	11.0
Trade and distribution	0.3	na	na	na	na	22.8	56.7
Real estate	nsa					nsa	nsa
Finance and insurance	nsa					nsa	12.8
Other services	nsa			32.4		nsa	72.2
Total	na	na	26.1	na	na	na	39.2

1 Share of domestic employment.
2 Share of domestic assets.
na not available.
nsa not separately available.

Source: Derived from a wide variety of national sources, Dunning and Cantwell (1987) and UN (1992b, 1993).

sectors and countries. Generally speaking, the ratio is highest in chemicals, electrical engineering, motor vehicles and petroleum, and lowest in most of the service sectors. There are major differences between countries according, for example, to the structure of their resource endowments and capabilities, their stage of development and their experience in international production. For example, the outward significance ratio for Belgium, West Germany and the UK is highest in chemicals. In the Netherlands and Sweden it is highest in electrical engineering, in the US in motor vehicles and in Japan in primary products and food and drink. Relative to other investing countries, the UK and Japan have a higher

percentage of their foreign value-added activities in medium to low research intensive industries, while the US, Germany and Sweden appear to have a comparative investing advantage in the high to medium research intensive sectors (Clegg, 1987).

Data on the foreign production of the world's leading industrial companies supports these conclusions. This is set out in Table 2.15 which shows that the contribution of the sales of foreign affiliates to the global sales of MNEs is above average in four sectors:

(1) those industries supplying products which, in part or in whole, cannot be economically

produced in the home country; examples are natural resource intensive products such as oil, forestry, tobacco and rubber products;

(2)   research-intensive sectors, such as computers, electronic equipment and pharmaceuticals; the main exception is aerospace – a strategically sensitive industry in which governments usually disallow majority FDI;

(3)   mass production fabricating sectors, such as motor vehicles and consumer electronics;

(4)   processing industries that are capital intensive and produce differentiated products with a high income elasticity and demand.

Table 2.15 also reveals there are substantial differences in the foreign sales ratios of particular countries. For all industries, the ratios are highest for the smaller industrialized European countries, notably Switzerland, Sweden and the Netherlands, and above average for the UK whose outbound investments date back to the last century and beyond. They are lowest for countries with the least experience in foreign investments, *viz* Japan and other (mostly developing) countries. Differences in the ratios for particular industries reflect the comparative innovatory and natural resource advantages of countries. However, as the comparable macro-economic data suggests, there are a number of genuinely international industries that consistently record higher than average foreign production ratios.

Other data shows that the foreign sales ratios of the leading industrial companies rose between 1972 and 1982, fell back in the following three years, since when they have risen again. This data is, however, strongly influenced by the behaviour of US MNEs, which in 1982 accounted for about one-half of the sales of all MNEs. As we have seen earlier in this chapter, the share of US foreign direct investment fell sharply in the 1980s. This, together with a marked improvement in the domestic sales of US firms, explains the fall in the foreign sales ratio of US MNEs from 28.5% in 1982 to 25.7% in 1985. Towards the end of the 1980s, however, the growth of foreign production accelerated again, particularly via acquisitions and takeovers in Western Europe. According to the US Department of Commerce (1990), the sales of foreign affiliates of non-bank US MNEs rose by 32.3% between 1985 and 1988,

compared with a corresponding increase in their domestic sales of 9.3%. European firms have also stepped up their investments both elsewhere in Europe and in the US. Overall, however, the fastest rates of growth of overseas production have been recorded by Japanese companies, especially in the transport and electrical machinery sectors (Hyun and Whitmore, 1989).

There are few published statistics on the degree of transnationality of firms in the primary and tertiary sectors. Macro-economic data shows that, in relation to the domestic production of services, Japanese and UK firms are among the most internationalized and German, US and French firms the least internationalized. Sectoral data suggests that Japan is among the most internationalized countries in wholesale trade and banking; the US in finance, advertising, retailing, accounting, business consultancy and fast food chains; the UK in trade, banking, publishing, insurance and law, and hotels; Germany in reinsurance, airlines and railways; Switzerland in airlines and reinsurance; France in tourism and construction; Korea in trade and construction; Hong Kong in airlines and hotels; and Greece in shipping. Further data on the degree of transnationalization of US MNEs in service activities reveals that in 1984, 20% or more worldwide sales of MNEs in the advertising, engineering services, motion pictures, construction and wholesale trade sectors were accounted for by their foreign affiliates. By contrast, the foreign sales ratio of MNEs in the transportation, telecommunications, public utilities, hotels, rental equipment and health services sectors ranged between 3.1% and 7.6% (UNCTC, 1988). It is also worth observing that each of these ratios is below that recorded by US MNEs in the manufacturing and petroleum sectors. At the same time, the internationalization of most service sectors is increasing at a faster rate than in most manufacturing sectors.

2.7.2   Some host country data

Next, we consider the contribution of foreign-owned affiliates to the output of the host countries. Here, there is a great deal of data, most of which is derived from regular or specially commissioned surveys by government departments or agencies (usually depart-

Table 2.15 Average foreign production ratios[1] of 509 of the world's largest industrial enterprises by industry, area and major country in 1982 (all figures are expressed in percentages).

	USA	Europe	Germany	France	UK	Sweden	Switzerland	Japan	Canada	Other countries	Total
Aerospace	9.4	3.5	–	nsa	nsa	–	–	–	–	–	8.4
Office equipment (including computers)	33.6	nsa	–	–	nsa	–	–	nsa	–	–	33.3
Electronics and electrical appliances	24.9	38.5	24.3	nsa	34.4	nsa	nsa	19.7	nsa	nsa	25.7
Measurement, scientific and photographic equipment	26.8	nsa	–	–	–	–	–	–	–	–	25.5
Industrial and agricultural chemicals	24.2	40.4	39.1	31.8	39.9	nsa	nsa	2.9	nsa	nsa	29.7
Pharmaceuticals and consumer chemicals	27.4	28.8	22.3	28.1	29.6	nsa	–	2.8	–	–	26.2
Total high research intensity	26.2	35.7	29.9	21.7	34.6	49.7	68.8	7.5	nsa	19.1	27.2
Industrial and farm equipment	24.5	33.0	3.3	–	38.9	46.5	nsa	11.4	nsa	nsa	27.3
Shipbuilding, railroad and transportation equipment	nsa	nsa	–	–	–	nsa	–	nsa	–	–	4.7
Rubber	34.8	51.6	nsa	–	nsa	–	–	5.4	–	nsa	31.9
Building materials	24.7	48.2	–	nsa	44.2	–	nsa	6.9	nsa	34.6	36.5
Metal manufacturing and products	18.0	22.0	10.4	13.4	40.6	22.9	–	3.1	18.5	9.2	15.2
Total medium research intensity	22.0	29.9	9.1	32.0	42.7	39.3	64.7	4.6	37.3	21.1	21.2
Textiles, apparel and leather goods	11.8	46.5	nsa	–	49.0	–	–	9.3	–	–	17.8
Paper and wood products	15.1	26.0	–	–	26.9	nsa	–	0.4	20.8	20.8	17.6
Publishing and printing	5.3	36.2	nsa	–	nsa	nsa	–	nsa	nsa	nsa	23.4
Food	25.1	57.6	–	27.0	33.8	–	nsa	4.8	nsa	nsa	36.1
Drink	24.2	22.4	–	–	22.4	–	–	–	60.6	60.6	26.2
Tobacco	22.4	66.8	–	–	66.8	–	–	–	nsa	nsa	44.3
Total low research intensity	21.3	50.5	36.2	27.0	41.3	44.9	nsa	6.6	38.4	35.4	31.4
Petroleum	44.9	39.1	nsa	nsa	nsa	nsa	–	1.1	0.3	0.0	38.4
Other manufacturing	17.5	5.3	nsa	–	nsa	–	nsa	–	nsa	nsa	13.8
Total	31.6	37.1	23.0	30.9	41.2	44.3	77.5	5.5	32.0	14.1	29.9

nsa   Results not given for reasons of confidentiality and disclosure. The information is, however, included in the appropriate aggregates.

1   Sales of overseas affiliates and associate companies (excluding goods imported from parent for resale) as a percentage of worldwide sales of group.

–   No enterprises in this category.

Source: Sales data *Fortune* 22 May and 22 August 1983. Ratios obtained from survey by Dunning and Pearce (1985) and sources listed therein.

Table 2.16　Share of (gross) output in selected host countries accounted for by foreign affiliates.

	Developed countries											
	Australia (1983)	Belgium (1975)	Canada[1] (1986)	France (1982)	Germany[2] (1982)	Italy[2] (1985)	Japan (1986)	Netherlands[2] (1987)	Portugal (1978)	Spain[2] (1977)	UK (1988)	US[2] (1987)
Primary												
Agriculture	na	3.1	nsa	na	0.5	nsa	nsa	na	1.2	17.0	na	1.0
Mining and quarrying	33.6	nsa	40.5	na	10.1	2.2	nsa	30.0	31.0	48.0	na	8.4
Petroleum	na	77.7	nsa	51.4	25.0	1.7	nsa	na	31.0	14.0	na	na
Secondary	21.6	44.0	49.0	25.3[2]	15.8	na	2.2	14.0	19.6	46.6	20.7	7.3
Food and drink products	25.6	22.5	29.4	nsa	17.7	12.8	0.5	18.0	15.8	52.0	14.6	8.8
Chemical and allied products	65.7	55.6	75.8	40.0	21.8	62.4	3.4	nsa	31.0	77.0	33.0	23.5
Metals	30.7	16.1	17.5	15.0	30.4	5.6	0.2	8.0	22.6	28.0	8.5	6.7
Mechanical engineering	32.9	57.7	50.2	nsa	16.3	12.6	2.2	nsa	14.1	45.0	22.7	5.8
Electrical and electronic goods	43.3	87.3	60.6	34.0	18.8	44.4	3.0	23.0	67.3	82.0	21.2	9.3
Motor vehicles	61.9	54.7	87.2	14.9	18.9	9.2	0.4	nsa	51.3	99.0	69.2	6.5
Textiles, clothing and leather goods	22.3	11.3	50.0[5]	7.2	4.8	1.9	0.1	9.0	9.3	na	4.2	3.2
Paper products	15.6	30.4	25.9	24.1	7.6	4.0	0.3	19.0	25.4	na	32.2	5.5
Rubber products	41.1	59.8	88.2	24.8	24.4	16.6	nsa	nsa	46.2	63.0	22.2	6.5
Coal and petroleum products	59.0	nsa	66.7	nsa	61.0	nsa	29.0	nsa	26.0	12.0	nsa	39.5
Tertiary	na	na	na	na	na	na	na	4.0	na	na	na	na
Construction			5.7		1.8		nsa	2.0	9.8	22.0		0.8
Transport and communication			na		6.3		nsa	1.0	4.4	39.0		2.6
Trade and distribution	na	na	24.6[6]	na	3.5	na	0.6	3.0	12.5	33.0	na	3.6
Real estate			na		nsa		nsa	nsa	nsa	nsa		2.3
Finance and insurance			na		6.3		nsa	8.0	8.1	93.0		4.4
Other services					2.6		0.3	13.0	2.1	nsa		1.2
Total	na	na	33.0	na	na	11.8	na	na	na	46.6	na	na

Table 2.16   continued.

	Developing countries						
	Brazil (1987)	Hong Kong (1987)	Mexico² (1985)	Morocco (1987)	Singapore¹ (1975)	Taiwan (1981)	Thailand (1986)
Primary							74.8
Agriculture	22.8		3.8				6.5
Mining and quarrying	2.7	na	0.1	na	neg	na	93.6
Petroleum	34.0		6.5				21.5
Secondary	34.2	17.3	20.2	14.0⁷	62.9⁸	16.7²	43.2
Food and drink products	17.7	28.9	6.5	9.9	67.3	6.8	22.0
Chemical and allied products	38.9⁴	50.8	44.7	10.1	97.2	28.8	72.0
Metals	34.1	12.9	10.6	3.5	96.7	4.4	60.8
Mechanical engineering	46.4	8.2	32.1	20.8		24.5	80.3
Electrical and electronic goods	50.9	48.2	45.6	27.7	88.7	48.6	89.4
Motor vehicles	80.6	nsa	96.4	25.5		nsa	59.8
Textiles, clothing and leather goods	11.7	6.3	nsa	14.1	98.0⁴	nsa	nsa
Paper products	19.4	12.4	nsa	22.4	45.4	6.5	nsa
Rubber products	44.7	8.8	nsa	12.1	70.5	7.9	30.5
Coal and petroleum products	nsa	nsa	nsa	22.0	100.0	nsa	77.7
Tertiary	8.3		na		18.1⁸		30.3
Construction	5.1		nsa				30.4
Transport and communication	2.0		nsa		10.1		52.4
Trade and distribution	11.2	na	2.3	na	25.5	na	37.6
Real estate	9.2		nsa		17.9⁸		4.8
Finance and insurance	8.5		nsa		14.5		10.8
Other services	9.6		3.2				37.5
Total	17.1	na	10.9	na	na	na	39.3

na   not available.
nsa   not separately available.
1   Share of assets.
2   Share of employment.
3   Food only.
4   Chemicals only.
5   Textiles only.

6   Wholesale trade only.
7   Share of assets in 1982.
8   Excluding construction.
9   Including business services.

Source: Derived from a wide variety of national sources, Dunning and Cantwell (1987) and UN (1992b, 1993).

ments of industry or employment), or by *ad hoc* field studies undertaken by trade associations, research institutions and academic scholars. A selection of this data is reproduced in Table 2.16 to give the reader a feel for the fact that the significance of foreign affiliates varies considerably both between sectors and between countries. Further details are contained in the UNCTC's *World Investment Directory* (UN, 1992b, 1993).

The data suggests that the role of foreign affiliates is generally most pronounced in those sectors in which the foreign significance ratio of outward MNE activity is the highest, *viz* chemicals, motor vehicles and electrical engineering. At the same time, there are some countries that differ in the competitive advantages they can offer foreign-based MNEs (Porter, 1990). The US, for example, has a high propensity as an outward investor in automobiles, but foreign firms account for a relatively unimportant (but growing share) of domestic production. In contrast, the significance to the British economy of inward investment in automobiles is much greater than that of the activities of its own MNEs in that sector. As one would expect, the inward significance ratios in the technology intensive sectors and in those producing high income consumer goods tends to be higher in developed countries than in developing countries, whereas those in the labour intensive sectors tend to be more pronounced in developing countries. The significance ratios of foreign affiliates in sectors characterized by oligopolistic competition and the economies of scale tend to be higher in the smaller industrialized economies than in the larger ones. Countries that are rich in natural resources tend to be less dependent on inward investment in the processing of these resources than those that are deficient in them.

We will explore some of the reasons for country-specific differences in the patterns of MNE activity in more detail in Chapter 4. Suffice, for the moment, to record that there is some evidence to suggest that the structure of inward and outward investment will be most divergent at the early stages of industrialization but is likely to converge as economic development proceeds. Moreover, technological developments in the past decade have encouraged an international division of labour and the specialization of trade and foreign production within industrial sectors, and this

has led to more intra-industry FDI.[21]

Indeed, it is now possible to identify genuine global industries. These are those dominated by groups of large corporations of different nationalities each of which produces and sells its products in most of the major markets of the world. The number and nationality of such firms varies between industries. However, as more countries become industrialized, the membership of the global club is likely to increase. The oil industry is a global industry *par excellence*. Not only do the major oil companies have a presence in most countries of the world, but also tend to integrate their cross-border activities vertically and horizontally, and adopt a global strategy towards them. In the past decade there have been many new MNE entrants in the automobile and consumer electronics industries, with companies from Korea, Malaysia, India and Czechoslovakia joining those from developed countries in penetrating world markets. MNEs and their affiliates account for a substantial and increasing proportion of the output of the rubber tyre, pharmaceutical, tobacco, soft drinks, fast food, financial consultancy and luxury hotel sectors in both developed and developing countries. MNE activity in these sectors is also characterized by a high degree of intra-firm trade. This point is taken up further in Chapter 15.[22]

2.7.3 Some country-specific differences in the pattern of MNE activity

Previous tables in this chapter have revealed that there are considerable differences in the propensity of firms to engage in foreign production and of countries to be outward or inward direct investors. In 1987, Japan, with a gross domestic product (GDP) three times that of the UK, had a combined inward and outward direct investment stake per capita of only one-third of that of the UK. Sweden and Switzerland are currently substantial net outward investors; Norway and Australia, with about the same living standards, are both substantial net inward investors. Mexico, Hong Kong, Malaysia and South Korea are examples of developing countries that are fully integrated into the international economy and are highly attractive to MNE investors. By contrast, until very recently, India, The People's

Republic of China and several Latin American and African countries pursued a development strategy that allowed foreign companies only a limited role. The industrial composition of inward direct investment is totally different in Taiwan and Brazil from that in New Guinea and Jamaica. The geographical structure of Austrian and Swiss outbound MNE activity is strongly oriented to the rest of Europe, while that of Canada and Mexico is primarily directed to the US. The Eastern bloc countries engage in only a limited amount of FDI (McMillan, 1987, 1991), and have only recently opened their borders to inward investment.

Moreover, over time the international direct investment position of a country may dramatically change. In 1975, US MNEs had a foreign direct investment stake 4.5 times as high as that of foreign MNEs in the US. By 1985 this multiple had fallen to 1.4, and by 1989 to 0.99%. In the 1960s Canada was the world's leading inward direct investor, but for much of the 1980s, the outward investment of Canadian multinationals was considerably greater than that of inward investment. West Germany, too, has dramatically changed its position from being a substantial net debtor on the direct investment account to being a substantial net creditor in the space of a decade. In 1975 the foreign assets owned by Korean companies abroad were only 10% of those owned by foreign companies in Korea, but by 1988 this had risen to 28%.

Earlier tables in this chapter have also shown that the industrial composition of MNE activity varies between countries. Partly this reflects the geographical origin or destination of FDI and, related to this, the characteristics of the home and host countries. Table 2.17 illustrates some differences between the geographical distribution of some of the major outward direct investors, and Table 2.18 some differences in the geographical pattern of inward investment of a group of developed and developing countries.

We now turn to make a few observations about the data set out in the tables and also that derived from other sources (e.g. UN, 1992a). A more detailed explanation of this data is presented in Chapters 3 and 4.

2.8   THE GEOGRAPHY OF MNE ACTIVITY

2.8.1   Outward direct investment

Although there are broad similarities in the geographical distribution of MNE activity by the leading investing countries, there is also some evidence of differences in the pattern of clustering (UN, 1992b, 1993). Such clustering is of two kinds. The first reflects the fact that, *ceteris paribus*, in their initial venturing outside their national boundaries firms tend to prefer to invest in neighbouring territories or in those with which they have the closest economic, political, language and cultural ties. In 1987, for example, 75.7% of Canadian investment was elsewhere on the American continent, while 50.3% of Indian investment was elsewhere in Asia. Spanish and Italian MNEs have a higher propensity to invest in Latin America than do other European MNEs, while there is some concentration of UK, French, Dutch and Indonesian FDI in their ex-African and Asian colonies. Scandinavian countries are more prone to invest in each other's territories than are other European or US MNEs. The great majority of Latin American and Asian foreign direct investments are made elsewhere in the region.[21] US MNEs have a much stronger propensity to invest in Mexico and Brazil than do their European or Japanese counterparts.[23]

The second kind of cluster is that which is more associated with established MNEs operating in global industries; they may perceive that it is in their economic or strategic interests to own or control production facilities in each of the main markets of the world. The clustering of manufacturing and service MNE activity in the Triad of the US, the EC and Japan has increased noticeably in the past decade, and the great majority of acquisitions and mergers (A&Ms) since 1980 have been between firms within the main Triad. In 1989, some 60.8% of the combined outward and inward direct investment stake of the US was in, or by, the EC and Japan, compared with 45.3% in 1980. The corresponding percentages for Japan in the US and the EC were 58.0% and 37.5%, and for EC countries in the US and Japan 71.6% and 66.7%. There is also some suggestion that MNEs from some developing countries (particularly from newly industrializing coun-

Table 2.17 Geographical distribution of the outward capital stake of selected countries 1980 and 1988 (percentage figures).

Host country	Year	World total (billion)	Developed countries					Developing countries				Eastern Europe
			Western Europe	Japan	US	Others	Total	Latin America	Asia	Other	Total	
Developed countries												
Australia	1980	1.9	14.1	0.0	15.3	14.7	44.0	0.0	8.2	47.8	56.0	0.0
Australian dollars	1988	28.2	41.0	0.0	15.9	15.4	72.3	0.0	1.4	26.2	27.7	0.0
Canada	1980	27.0	18.1	0.4	62.2	3.4	84.2	11.4	3.9	0.5	15.8	0.0
Canadian dollars	1987	66.1	16.2	0.4	65.1	2.06	83.8	10.5	5.4	0.2	16.2	0.0
France	1982	100.4	44.1	0.7	34.3	−1.3	77.8	8.5	0.7	68.6	77.8	0.5
French francs	1989	317.9	51.7	0.4	32.3	1.6	86.0	3.4	0.9	81.7	86.0	0.3
Germany (FDR)	1980	84.5	48.9	1.2	21.6	5.7	77.4	12.3	2.0	8.2	22.5	0.1
Deutschmarks	1988	184.1	49.0	2.2	27.0	5.4	83.7	8.7	2.3	5.2	16.3	0.1
Italy	1980	6 486.0	58.3	0.0	8.6	0.0	66.9	0.0	0.0	33.1	33.1	0.0
Italian lira	1987	37 285.0	61.6	0.4	11.4	1.1	74.4	13.6	0.0	12.0	25.6	0.0
Japan	1980	36.5	11.7	0.0	24.3	8.8	44.8	16.9	26.9	10.8	54.6	0.5
US dollars	1989	253.9	17.6	0.0	41.1	7.0	65.7	14.5	15.9	3.7	34.2	0.1
Netherlands	1980	89.7	52.6	0.0	18.8	10.0	81.4	11.3	4.4	2.8	18.6	0.0
Guilders	1988	148.0	45.6	1.1	33.9	6.8	87.4	7.8	3.9	0.9	12.6	0.0
UK	1981	28.5	23.1	0.7	27.9	26.5	78.1	6.0	8.3	7.5	21.9	0.0
Pounds sterling	1987	86.7	31.0	1.1	35.3	16.4	83.8	7.7	5.7	2.6	16.1	0.1
US	1980	220.1	43.8	2.8	0.0	25.5	72.1	19.7	3.9	4.3	27.9	0.0
US dollars	1989	380.0	46.4	5.1	0.0	22.2	73.7	17.9	5.4	2.9	26.3	0.0
Switzerland	1986	55.7	50.8	0.0	0.0	1.5	81.3	11.2	5.2	2.3	18.7	0.0
Swiss francs	1989	78.7	51.8	0.0	0.0	1.5	78.8	13.8	5.3	2.0	21.1	0.0
Developing countries												
Brazil	1980	0.6	11.0	0.8	62.2	0.0	74.0	24.7	0.0	1.2	26.0	0.0
US dollars	1988	1.7	11.04	0.6	48.7	0.0	60.4	37.0	0.9	1.7	39.6	0.0
China	1984	0.3	6.7	1.9	148.3	0.8	57.8	4.5	26.2	11.6	42.3	0.0
Yuan	1987	1.7	6.5	1.2	13.8	45.3	66.7	3.5	21.9	7.8	33.1	0.0
India	1985	1.2	1.01	0.0	0.4	0.1	1.4	0.0	57.0	41.6	98.5	0.0
Indian rupees	1988	1.1	6.09	0.0	1.4	0.3	7.7	0.1	50.3	41.4	91.8	0.5
Korea	1980	93.6	7.4	7.4	20.5	1.2	31.8	4.8	28.8	34.6	68.2	0.0
Won	1988	765.6	3.7	2.7	35.6	13.6	55.5	2.3	22.7	19.5	44.5	0.0
Taiwan	1980	3.7	nsa	nsa	43.4	13.1	56.5	nsa	33.4	10.1	43.5	0.0
New Taiwanese	1988	19.8	nsa	nsa	60.5	10.8	71.3	nsa	24.4	4.3	28.8	0.0

Source: Derived from UN (1992b, 1993).

Table 2.18 Geographical distribution of the inward direct capital stake of selected countries 1980 and 1988 (percentage figures).

Host country	Year	World total (billion)	Developed countries					Developing countries				Eastern Europe
			Western Europe	Japan	US	Others	Total	Latin America	Asia	Other	Total	
Developed countries												
Australia	1980	11.1	42.8	6.3	40.2	3.3	92.5	2.7	2.6	1.9	7.2	0.2
Australian dollars	1988	60.9	51.4	9.7	32.2	0.0	93.3	0.0	2.3	4.4	6.7	0.0
Canada	1980	61.7	17.9	1.0	78.9	0.1	97.9	1.7	0.2	0.2	2.1	0.0
Canadian dollars	1987	101.5	21.5	2.5	71.1	0.4	95.5	1.6	2.6	0.2	4.5	0.0
France	1982	93.3	75.0	1.7	13.1	0.4	90.1	1.1	0.0	8.3	9.4	0.4
French francs	1989	234.9	70.8	3.0	13.5	1.9	91.2	0.6	0.2	7.7	8.5	0.5
Germany (FDR)	1980	93.3	38.1	2.5	31.6	0.6	72.9	1.1	0.3	2.3	3.7	0.4
Deutschmarks	1988	148.7	39.9	5.4	23.9	0.9	70.1	0.9	0.4	1.5	2.8	0.5
Italy	1980	827.4	81.2	0.0	18.5	0.0	99.7	0.0	0.0	0.3	0.3	0.0
Italian lira	1987	3666.0	76.0	0.7	14.9	0.5	92.2	1.8	0.0	6.1	7.9	0.0
Japan	1980	3.0	23.3	na	54.1	2.6	94.3	0.6	3.1	2.1	5.7	0.0
US dollars	1989	15.7	23.2	na	50.5	1.2	86.8	0.0	2.9	10.3	13.2	0.0
Netherlands	1980	40.8	43.1	1.5	34.4	4.9	83.8	14.9	0.4	0.8	16.2	0.0
Guilders	1988	92.7	52.2	3.3	25.4	4.3	85.2	13.1	1.6	0.1	14.8	0.0
UK	1981	17.0	26.7	1.9	56.4	10.1	95.1	1.2	3.1	0.6	4.9	0.0
Pounds sterling	1987	54.6	35.9	3.5	45.8	9.7	95.0	2.9	1.6	0.6	5.0	0.0
US	1980	83.0	65.8	5.7	0.0	15.6	87.0	11.7	0.3	1.0	13.0	0.1
US dollars	1989	400.8	65.3	17.4	0.0	9.6	92.3	5.1	0.9	1.6	7.7	0.0
Developing countries												
Argentina	1980	5.4	52.4	0.6	38.6	3.5	95.2	4.4	0.1	0.3	4.8	0.0
US dollars	1986	6.8	47.5	0.9	41.5	5.2	95.1	4.3	0.1	0.6	4.9	0.0
Brazil	1980	17.5	47.3	9.9	28.6	4.3	90.0	7.1	0.3	2.6	10.0	0.0
US dollars	1988	32.0	47.9	9.5	29.3	4.8	91.5	5.5	0.4	2.6	8.5	0.0
China	1984	16.0	14.6	5.8	16.9	4.5	41.8	1.5	56.3	0.5	58.2	0.0
Yuan	1987	58.1	9.5	7.2	15.8	2.5	35.0	0.5	63.9	0.6	65.0	0.0
India	1985	9.7	69.5	0.4	22.6	3.0	95.5	nsa	nsa	4.5	4.5	0.0
Indian rupees	1988	9.3	70.3	0.5	21.1	3.7	95.5	nsa	nsa	4.5	4.5	0.0
South Korea	1980	752.3	9.6	60.5	19.6	0.1	90.0	5.4	2.1	0.7	8.2	0.0
Won	1988	2706.5	12.8	52.0	27.7	0.2	92.8	1.5	3.9	0.4	5.8	0.0
Taiwan	1980	98.0	9.7	18.6	35.0	0.0	63.2	0.0	26.0	10.4	26.8	0.0
New Taiwanese	1988	3020.2	13.4	26.9	32.1	6.0	72.3	0.0	17.1	10.6	27.7	0.0

Source: As for Table 2.17.

tries) are investing in Western Europe and the US both to service the local market and to acquire assets which (they perceive) will strengthen their own competitive positions. In 1988, no less than 60.5% of Taiwanese direct investment stake was in the US. Similarly the Korean direct investment stake in developed market economies has increased from 31.8% in 1980 to 55.5% in 1988.

As firms become more global in their production and marketing strategies, the structure of their domestic and foreign investments tends both to complement, and converge with, each other. Naturally, since home countries differ in their competitive strengths and weaknesses (Porter, 1990), MNE activity, like those of trade, will reflect these strengths and weaknesses. Canada, Australia, New Zealand and Norway, for example, are resource rich nations and make few investments in resource-based activity in developing countries. On the other hand, their inbound investments tend to originate from advanced industrial nations and are concentrated in high value processing or fabricating industries. Japan, Belgium, Switzerland and Singapore are examples of countries that predominantly invest abroad to exploit their industrial competitiveness or to acquire resources not available domestically. Inward investment tends to be from countries that can offer advanced technologies, managerial skills or access to foreign markets.

A great deal has been made by some writers of the differences between the geographical distribution of FDI between the major industrial countries, and particularly between Japan and the US (Kojima, 1990). However, it is becoming increasingly acknowledged that many of these differences, originally thought to reflect differences in the goals or perspectives of MNEs or that of their home governments, reflect the position of particular countries in their investment development cycle,[24] as well as their geographical and psychic positioning in relation to that of their neighbours.

2.8.2   Inward direct investment

Many of the characteristics of the geographical pattern of the outward direct capital stake are mirrored in that of the inward direct capital stake. However, first we would make two additional observations on the data set out in Table 2.18.

First, while the great majority of direct investment received by developed countries originates from other developed countries, some developing countries, particularly the least advanced countries in Africa, Latin America and Asia, draw a larger proportion of their investment from other (and particularly neighbouring) developing countries.

Second, the dependency of host countries on particular home countries as a source of inward investment varies considerably both between developed countries (compare, for example, the Netherlands with the UK, and Canada with Australia) and between developing countries (compare, for example, Zimbabwe with Gabon, Bangladesh with Indonesia, and Brazil with Colombia). Partly these differences in the geography of inward investment reflect differences in its industrial structure, and partly the comparative needs and capabilities of investing countries to undertake such investment. It also partly reflects differences in the relative locational costs and benefits of home and host countries (compare, for example, the costs of shipping goods from Japan and the US to Brazil, or the differential production costs between German and Hong Kong investors in Thailand). Finally, it reflects the relative incentives of firms of different nationalities to own their value-added facilities in a particular foreign country, rather than license or subcontract a local producer to undertake the work.[25] As might be expected, with the growing participation of Japanese firms in international production, the origin of inward investment has become more pluralistic in character, particularly in the manufacturing and service sectors.

2.9   THE STRUCTURE OF THE WORLD'S LEADING MNEs

So much for the industrial and geographical composition of MNE activity. We now turn to consider some other features of the world's leading MNEs.

Earlier we indicated that between 17 500 and 20 000 companies engage in value-added activities outside their national boundaries. However, by far the greater part of these activities is undertaken by a comparatively small number of global enterprises which operate a network of subsidiaries and associated companies throughout the world. It is, perhaps,

Table 2.19 Largest firm concentration ratios[1] by main industrial and service sectors (1962–90).

Industrial sectors	1962	1977	1982	1990
Food	38.8	34.9	35.1	31.5
Drink[2]	50.0	52.8	53.2	54.4
Tobacco[2]	58.2	59.8	68.9	61.4
Textiles, apparel and leather goods	29.0	26.7	24.8	na
Paper and wood products[3]	29.5	28.6	26.3	29.9
Industrial and agricultural chemicals	32.7	26.4	27.7	33.8
Pharmaceuticals and consumer chemicals	48.6	32.8	31.8	30.9
Petroleum	47.7	38.8	35.9	38.1
Rubber[4]	52.3	56.0	56.1	54.3
Building materials[5]	44.6	52.6	50.1	51.1
Metal manufacturing and products[6]	31.7	27.3	31.4	28.7
Electronics and electrical appliances	41.8	35.4	28.8	30.1
Shipbuilding, railroad and transportation equipment[7]	74.0	58.8	67.2	na
Motor vehicles	66.7	50.5	41.3	38.6
Aerospace[8]	42.7	39.4	37.3	42.1
Office equipment (including computers)[4]	65.4	68.3	67.7	67.0
Industrial and farm equipment	34.7	29.6	24.0	34.0

1 Except where otherwise specified, the sales of the three largest firms in the world as a percentage of the sales of the 20 largest firms in the world.
2 Sales of the three largest firms in the world as a percentage of the nine largest firms in the world.
3 Sales of the three largest firms in the world as a percentage of the 19 largest firms in the world.
4 Sales of the three largest firms in the world as a percentage of the eight largest firms in the world.

5 Sales of the three largest firms in the world as a percentage of the ten largest firms in the world.
6 Sales of the three largest firms in the world as a percentage of the 18 largest firms in the world.
7 Sales of the three largest firms in the world as a percentage of the seven largest firms in the world.
8 Sales of the three largest firms in the world as a percentage of the 15 largest firms in the world.

Service sectors	1962	1976	1983	1988
Banking[9]	na	na	na	36.3
Finance and securities	na	51.6[4]	20.6	29.4
Insurance	na	24.1	25.7[6]	29.3[9]
Reinsurance	na	65.4[1]	64.1[6]	63.0[7]
Wholesale trading	na	na	49.4	35.9
Retail trading	na	38.4	40.6	31.2
Accounting[3]	na	na	33.0	47.6[11]
Advertising	na	30.1[4]	26.3	22.5
Market research	na	na	na	50.4[8]
Construction	na	na	42.2	24.4
Publishing	na	38.2[2]	29.9	20.4
Hotels	na	50.4[5]	49.3	37.1

1 Sales of the three largest firms in the world as a percentage of the 15 largest firms in the world.
2 Sales of the three largest firms in the world as a percentage of the 12 largest firms in the world.
3 Sales of the three largest firms in the world as a percentage of the 15 largest firms in the world.

4 1975.
5 1977.
6 1980.

7 1985.
8 1987.
9 1986.

10 1990.
11 1989.

Source: *Fortune: Annual Surveys of Largest 500 US and 500 Non-US Industrial Companies*, UNCTC (1991a) and UNCTC data bank on billion $ companies.

these enterprises that conform most readily to the popular image of an MNE. Data on the 500 largest US and 500 largest non-US industrial corporations published in the mid 1980s (Dunning and Pearce, 1985) suggest that the largest 50 of these companies account for about 35% of total foreign production, the largest 100 for about 50%, the top 250 for 65% and the top 500 for 75%. Comprehensive data on service MNEs is less readily available, but what there is suggests that a comparatively small number of firms account for the bulk MNE activity in such sectors as insurance, banking, accounting, advertising, construction, hotels and airlines (UNCTC, 1988).

Table 2.19 shows that within particular sectors the degree of concentration among the world's largest enterprises – most of which are also MNEs – varies a good deal. The measure of concentration used is the global sales of the three largest industrial enterprises in a particular sector as a proportion of those of the largest twenty industrial enterprises identified by *Fortune* magazine in that sector,[26] and, either that of sales or the number of affiliates of the three largest service enterprises as a proportion of those of the leading 20 enterprises in their sector (UNCTC, 1988). The table reveals that with around an (unweighted) average concentration ratio of 39.4% at the end of the 1980s, the tobacco, office equipment, rubber products, reinsurance, general trading and market research sectors recorded the highest ratios, while industrial and agricultural chemicals, industrial and farm equipment, textiles, apparel and leather goods, law, construction and publishing recorded the lowest. Over the previous decade, the concentration ratios fell in most of the sectors listed, but rose in the tobacco, rubber, office equipment, accounting, advertising and market research sectors.

Data compiled by the European Commission in the mid 1970s (European Commission, 1976) revealed that although in 1971 there were 55 enterprises that owned more than 20 foreign affiliates and 215 that owned more than ten affiliates, 85% of the 9500 firms that engaged in FDI owned one or two affiliates. More recently, a study by the UNCTC (1990b) of some 735 small and medium size MNEs from developed countries,[27] showed that on average such MNEs owned 3.2 foreign affiliates. Although it might be reasonable to expect the latter proportion

to fall as existing foreign investors increase their degree of multinationality, there are always new companies starting up foreign ventures, while some never expand beyond a certain point. Currently, the fastest rate of growth is being recorded by MNEs from Japan and the developing countries, as well as by small and medium size firms in the newer industrial sectors (e.g. biotechnology) and the more information-intensive service sectors (e.g. computer advisory services[28]). The smaller multinationals tend to make their investments in neighbouring countries or those with which the parent company or country already has strong political, trading or cultural ties. There is also some suggestion that the relative significance of these companies tends to be greater in smaller developed and less prosperous developing countries (UNCTC, 1990b). The bulk of FDI from developing countries, for example, is in other developing countries, although that directed to North America and Europe by some Third World MNEs has increased significantly since the 1970s.[29]

Tables 2.20 and 2.21 set out some vital statistics for a selection of the largest MNEs. These lists are derived from data compiled by the UNCTC on the largest MNEs in both industrial and service sectors. They are intended to illustrate the geographical and industrial origin of MNEs and the extent of their multinationalization. Later data published by *Fortune* magazine reveals that in 1990, twenty-two of the forty largest industrial enterprises with foreign direct investment were classified to the petroleum or motor vehicles sectors, six to the electrical engineering sector and five to the chemical sector. Many of these companies were, however, widely diversified outside the sectors to which they are classified (Pearce, 1989).[30] Data on some of the largest service enterprises is ranked by their employment because of the difficulty in making meaningful comparisons of assets between such sectors as banking and retailing, or hotels and advertising. Table 2.21 shows that with a few exceptions (e.g. wholesale trading and banking), the foreign investment stake by service companies is both absolutely and proportionately of less significance than that of their industrial counterparts (UNCTC, 1988).

Earlier data set out in Table 2.15 revealed that in 1982 the foreign production ratios of the world's largest industrial companies varied considerably both across industries and countries. Since that date, the

Table 2.20 Vital statistics of a selection of the world's largest industrial companies in 1989 ranked by net sales (all currency figures in millions of US dollars).

Company	Home country	Primary industry	Sales		Assets		Employment
			Global	% foreign	Global	% foreign	Global
General Motors	USA	Automotive	123 212	26.9	173 297	24.1	775 000
Ford Motor	USA	Automotive	96 146	33.3	160 893	19.0	366 600
Exxon	USA	Petroleum	86 656	82.1	83 219	55.8	104 000
Toyota	Japan	Automotive	67 659	na	62 053[1]	na	96 849
International Business Machines	USA	Electronics	62 710	59.0	77 734	48.6	383 220
British Petroleum Company	UK	Petroleum	57 222	73.5	61 033	na	119 850
KOH Nederlands Petroleum Naatscha	Netherlands	Petroleum	56 857	53.0	61 216[2]	56.1	134 000
General Electric Company	USA	Electrical	53 884	13.8	128 344	8.8	292 000
Hitachi	Japan	Electronics	52 093	23.4	57 445	na	290 811
Daimler-Benz	Germany	Automotive	51 099	61.3	46 161	na	368 226
Mobil	USA	Petroleum	50 220	74.7	39 080	51.1	67 900
Fiat	Italy	Automotive	46 297	45.9	56 862	23.5	286 294
Matsushita Electric Industrial	Japan	Electronics	44 181	43.7	57 785[3]	na	198 299
Volkswagen	Germany	Automotive	43 714	63.8	38 038	na	257 561
Nissan Motor Company	Japan	Automotive	41 548	na	42 284[3]	na	na
Siemens	Germany	Electrical	40 888	48.1	51 702[4]	na	365 000
Shell Transport & Trading	UK	Petroleum	40 283	50.4	43 530	58.4	135 000
Philip Morris Companies	USA	Food	39 011	28.8	38 528	14.8	157 000
Nestlé	Switzerland	Food	37 675	98.1	27 767	na	196 940
Du Pont (E.I.) de Nemours	USA	Chemicals	35 534	39.8	34 715	29.5	145 787
Chrysler	USA	Automotive	34 922	26.3	51 038	11.0	121 947
Renault	France	Automotive	34 278	43.3	23 984	34.6	174 573
NV Philips	Netherlands	Electronics	33 941	93.4	33 835	na	304 800
Veba	Germany	Diversified	32 915	29.3	27 703	na	94 514
Texaco	USA	Petroleum	32 416	42.3	25 636	20.3	37 067
Basf	Germany	Chemicals	31 851	68.1	23 496	na	136 990
Toshiba	Japan	Electronics	31 294	31.6	38 134[3]	na	142 000
Hoechst	Germany	Chemicals	30 701	77.2	23 040	13.8	169 295
Peugeot	France	Automotive	30 050	53.5	21 032	23.8	159 100
Chevron	USA	Petroleum	29 253	23.7	33 884	22.6	54 826
Bayer	Germany	Chemicals	28 963	41.2	24 171	na	170 200
Unilever	Netherlands	Food/Detergents	25 761	32.8	15 163	na	142 000
Imperial Chemical Industries	UK	Chemicals	25 427	77.9	21 759	37.1	133 800
NEC	Japan	Electronics	25 349	25.9	27 114[3]	na	114 599
Brown, Boveri & Co.	Switzerland	Electrical	25 038	na	29 364	na	na
Asea	Sweden	Machinery	24 103	na	27 464	na	184 424
Procter & Gamble	USA	Chemicals	24 081	39.9	18 487[1]	35.3	89 000
Amoco	USA	Petroleum	23 966	28.5	30 430	32.7	53 653
British Telecommunications	UK	Utilities	23 774	na	36 963[3]	na	245 665
Thyssen Ag Vorm August Thyssen-Hue	Germany	Metals	22 909	48.5	15 426[4]	na	133 824
Nippon Steel	Japan	Metal products	21 880	na	30 918[3]	na	55 863
Total-Cie Francaise Des Petroles	France	Petroleum	21 197	71.0	17 370	na	35 889
Sony	Japan	Electronics	21 196	69.8	32 164[3]	na	95 600
Robert Bosch	Germany	Automotive	20 460	26.5	15 317	na	174 742
Boeing	USA	Aerospace	20 276	na	13 278	na	159 200
Occidental Petroleum	USA	Petroleum	20 068	6.4	20 741	10.1	53 500

NB. Foreign sales, assets and employment represent those accounted for by foreign affiliates.

1 30th June 1990.
2 31st December 1988.
3 31st March 1990.
4 30th September 1989.

Source: Various but especially data provided by UNCTC.

Table 2.21 Vital statistics of a selection of the world's largest service companies in 1989 ranked by employment (all currency figures in millions of US dollars).

Company	Home country	Primary industry	Sales Global	Sales % foreign	Assets Global	Assets % foreign	Employment Global
Sears, Roebuck & Co.	USA	Retail trading	53 794	7.7	86 972[2]	3.7	500 000
K. Mart Corporation	USA	Retail trading	29 533	3.7	13 145[4]	na	365 000
McDonalds	USA	Food services	66 340	33.4	10 667	33.1	169 000
ITT	USA	Telecommunications	20 054	28.6	45 503[2]	18.2	119 000
American Express	USA	Financial services	25 047	19.4	130 855[2]	21.6	107 542
RWE Aktiengesellschaft	Germany	Utilities	25 943	19.7	32 744[5]	na	97 596
National Westminster Bank	UK	Banking	28 336	40.3	224 303[2]	46.1	96 000
Trust House Forte	UK	Hotels and motels	4 023	22.1	7 135[7]	na	92 900
Citicorp	USA	Banking	37 970	13.2	230 643[2]	37.8	92 000
Bougyues	France	Construction	10 468	17.1	11 402	na	64 373
Klynveld Peat Marwick Goerdler	USA	Accounting firm	3 900	42.0	na	na	63 700
British Airways	UK	Air transportation	9 112	77.7	7 518	na	50 204
Holiday Corporation	USA	Hotels and motels	1 597	na	2 139	na	43 600
Thomson	Canada	Newspapers	5 003	73.3	6 954	50.7	41 600
Fluor	USA	Construction	7 446	13.0	2 476	11.1	17 876
Saatchi & Saatchi	UK	Advertising	7 428	17.5	1 860	na	16 614
Interpublic Group of Companies	USA	Advertising	1 368	56.2	2 584	43.8	14 700
Sanwa Bank	Japan	Banking	28 999	na	448 625[1]	na	13 604
Mitsui & Co.	Japan	Wholesale trading	123 387	29.8	46 570	20.8	10 772
Mitsubishi Corp.	Japan	Wholesale trading	115 139	21.9	70 012	18.4	8 005
Salomon Inc.	USA	Financial services	6 146	25.8	74 747[2]	16.3	8 000

NB. Foreign sales, assets and employment represent those accounted for by foreign affiliates.
1   31st March 1989.
2   31st December 1989.
3   31st March 1988.

4   31st January 1989.
5   30th June 1990.
6   3rd February 1989.
7   31st December 1990.
Source: UNCTC *World Services Directory* (1991).

degree of multinationalization of the world's leading firms has continued to increase, particularly those of Japanese origin in the car and electronics sectors.[31]

The degree of multinationalization among service producers is generally less than that of industrial firms. According to the US Department of Commerce (1986), in 1984 the ratio of the foreign to global sales of US MNEs in the service sector was 16.6% (compared with that in manufacturing of 27.3% and in petroleum of 41.7%). Among the most transnationalized service sectors were wholesale trading (24.8%), engineering consultants (23.9%)

and advertising (20.3%). Among the least transnationalized were health services (3.1%), transportation, communications and utilities (6.5%) and hotels (7.6%) (UNCTC, 1988).

Broadly speaking, this company-specific data tells a similar story to the macro-data presented earlier. Time-series data also suggests that the fastest growing larger MNEs (measured in terms of total sales) are those that have the highest degree of internationalization, or those that are expanding their foreign operations the most (Dunning and Pearce, 1985).

Table 2.22 Examples of state-owned multinationals.

	State-owned MNEs		
Enterprise	Sectors of activity	Home country	Degree of internationalization[1]
Aerospatiale	Aerospace	France	78.2
Agip (ENI)	Petroleum products	Italy	na
Assi	Paper products	Sweden	79.9
Alcatel Alsthom	Electronics	France	na
CEA Industries	Nuclear power	France	na
DSM	Chemicals, fertilizers, plastics	Netherlands	14.1
Elf-Aquitaine	Petroleum, chemicals	France	29.0
Embraer	Aircraft	Brazil	na
INI	Motor vehicles	Spain	na
Keppel Shipyard	Shipbuilding	Singapore	na
Norsk Hydro	Petroleum, chemicals	Norway	94.6
IRI	Metals	Italy	na
Petrobras	Petroleum	Brazil	na
Renault	Motor vehicles	France	51.3
Rhone-Poulenc	Chemicals	France	54.7
Salzgitter	Iron and steel products	Germany	79.2
Thomson	Electrical and electronic products	France	61.2
Voest Alpine	Metals	Austria	35.7
YPF	Petroleum products	Argentina	na
Kemira Oy	Chemicals	Finland	50.0
Neste Oy	Petroleum, chemicals	Finland	70.1
	State-owned MNEs in the process of multinationalization		
British Coal	Mining	UK	1.5
Bharat Heavy Elect	Electrical engineering	India	na
Pemex	Petroleum products	Mexico	na
Matra	Aerospace	France	na
Siderbras	Iron and steel products	Brazil	na
Japan Tobacco	Tobacco products	Japan	na
Valmet	Industrial and farm equipment	Finland	na
Petrleos de Venezu	Petroleum products	Venezuela	na
Bull	Computer company	France	na
Enso-Gutzeit	Wood products	Finland	na
Sino-chem	Chemical products	China	na[2]

1 Defined as proportion of world-wide assets or output accounted for by foreign affiliates.
2 But is known to have 66 foreign subsidiaries employing 5000 people (*Transnationals*, 1992).

Source: *Fortune* magazine (various issues), *Worldscope*; annual reports of corporations.

2.10 STATE-OWNED MULTINATIONAL ENTERPRISES

There are two kinds of state-owned MNEs. First, there are those from the non-socialist countries which are wholly or partially owned by the governments or government agencies of their home countries. Until the mid 1980s, these companies were a spreading phenomenon. In 1965, 19 of the world's top 200 industrial enterprises outside the United

States were state-owned companies. By 1975 the same group were found to include 29 state-owned enterprises, nine of which were multinational. Ten years later, the number of state-owned enterprises had risen to 38, including 18 with foreign direct investments. Since 1985, the renascence of faith in the market economy has led to the privatization of several publicly-owned corporations, particularly in Europe. Examples include British Steel and British Leyland in the UK, Thomson and St Gobain in France, and ENI in Italy.

There were three main reasons for the growth of state-owned MNEs in the 20 years prior to 1985. The first was a spate of nationalization of private firms, particularly by the French and UK governments in the 1970s. The second was that the sectors in which governments had a stake were among the fastest growing sectors: examples included aerospace, oil products and motor vehicles. Thirdly, the past 20 years has witnessed the emergence of MNEs from Third World countries in which, generally speaking, the state tends to play a more dominant role (Anastassopoulos *et al.*, 1987). Examples include Keppel Shipyards (Singapore), Kuwait Petroleum Corporation (Kuwait), Embraer (Brazil), Bharat Heavy Electricals (India) and YPF (Argentina).

Table 2.23 Distribution of former Comecon investments by host country by number of investments (1991).

Host country	Investing country							Total
	Bulgaria	Czechoslovakia	Hungary	Poland	Romania	USSR	Yugoslavia	
Developed countries								
Western Europe	58	76	134	97	23	132	201	721
Austria	8	5	36	12	1	8	30	100
Belgium	3	3	2	7	0	12	4	31
Denmark	1	0	1	1	0	3	2	8
Finland	0	1	1	1	0	10	2	15
France	4	6	6	9	4	14	21	64
Germany	12	24	38	26	4	25	61	190
Greece	6	0	4	1	2	2	5	20
Italy	7	12	9	2	5	11	17	63
Luxembourg	0	0	1	1	0	1	0	3
Netherlands	2	4	3	5	0	6	12	32
Norway	2	1	1	1	0	5	1	11
Portugal	0	0	1	0	0	1	0	2
Spain	2	3	5	4	1	5	1	21
Sweden	2	4	2	6	0	7	6	27
Switzerland	4	2	9	5	2	7	11	40
UK	5	11	15	16	4	15	28	94
North America	5	9	13	19	5	20	40	111
Canada	2	5	3	3	2	12	8	35
US	3	4	10	16	3	8	32	76
Other	4	3	4	6	0	8	6	31
Australia	2	3	2	3	0	6	2	18
Japan	2	0	2	2	0	2	4	12
New Zealand	0	0	0	1	0	0	0	1
Total	67	88	151	122	28	160	247	863
Developing countries	29	41	46	82	52	60	74	386
All countries	96	129	197	204	80	220	321	1249

Source: *East-West Business Directory 1991/92*; East-West Project Database.

Table 2.24 Estimated value of authorized capital invested in the West by former Comecon countries by principal activity, 1991 (in thousands of current US dollars).

Principal activity	Bulgaria		Czechoslovakia		Hungary		Poland		Romania		USSR		Total	
Primary														
Minerals	499	0.92%	0	0.00%	0	0.00%	0	0.00%	0	0.00%	0	0.00%	499	0.04%
Secondary														
Manufacturing	16 281	29.95%	2 822	2.86%	12 304	9.15%	616	0.42%	0	0.00%	8 005	1.14%	40 028	3.26%
Tertiary														
Commercial	21 357	39.29%	73 737	74.62%	23 233	17.28%	52 650	36.03%	7 714	8.28%	116 635	16.67%	295 326	24.08%
Financial[3]	12 372	22.76%	13 120	13.28%	74 526	55.42%	73 906	50.58%	85 300	91.51%	518 535	74.13%	777 759	63.41%
Transportation	2 423	4.46%	120	0.12%	1 742	1.30%	2 224	1.52%	202	0.22%	36 571	5.23%	43 282	3.53%
Other services	1 399	2.57%	516	0.52%	4 419	3.29%	1 813	1.24%	0	0.00%	10 198	1.46%	18 345	1.50%
Not classified[1]	32	0.06%	8 504	8.61%	18 263	13.58%	14 916[2]	10.21%	0	0.00%	9 526[2]	1.36%	51 241	4.18%
Total	54 363	100.00%	98 819	100.00%	134 487	100.00%	146 125	100.00%	93 216	100.00%	699 470	100.00%	1 226 480	100.00%

1 Not classified elsewhere because of diversified activity of enterprise.
2 Diversified includes investment in fisheries.
3 Excludes Western branches of Eastern headquartered banks.

Source: *East–West Business Directory 1991/92.*

Table 2.22 identifies some of the leading state-owned MNEs from non-socialist countries in 1989. As in the case of the privately-owned MNEs, the petroleum industry is well represented, but there are others, for example, shipbuilding, iron and steel, coal mining and aircraft, that do not figure substantially in the activities of private investors precisely because they are the most likely sectors to be publicly owned. Excepting the oil industry, however, the degree of multinationalization of state-owned corporations is generally quite small.

The second kind of state-owned MNEs are those from (erstwhile) socialist countries. These, too, have become an important form of cross-border FDI and industrial cooperation in recent years. In 1991, the number of MNEs originating from Central and Eastern Europe was estimated at 300 (UN, 1992a), while China recorded some 553 outward direct investors. In December 1990, the estimated value of authorized capital invested in foreign enterprises by the former Comecon countries was over $1 billion. By the end of 1989, as Table 2.22 shows, state enterprises from these countries had established some 827 branches, subsidiaries and affiliates in the member countries of the OECD – a figure that can be compared with our estimate of 120–125 000 foreign affiliates of MNEs from developed

or developing market economies. The estimated authorized equity capital invested by these companies in that year was $1.1 billion, of which those from the former Soviet Union accounted for 65.3%, Polish companies for 9.0%, Czech companies for 7.7%, Hungarian companies for 6.6% and Romanian companies for 5.0% (*East-West Business Directory*, 1990/1; *Economou*, 1990).

Other data published by the East–West Business Directory 1991/2 reproduced as Table 2.23 shows that at the end of 1990, MNEs from Central and Eastern Europe countries had also set up 386 foreign affiliates in developing countries. Of these, Africa accounted for 153, Asia for 66, Latin America for 80 and the Middle East for 79.

An analysis of the sectoral distribution of equity ventures from socialist countries, as set out in Table 2.24. Other data suggests a different industrial distribution for developed and developing market economies. According to information provided by the East–West Center at Carleton University, in the developed market economies 96% of these ventures were in the service sectors, especially in import-export trade and related marketing functions. Trading firms are, in fact, the single largest group of affiliates in developed market economies. Their principle task is to establish a foreign marketing infrastructure to promote the export of goods and services produced in socialist countries. However, in terms of the value of the investment, the financial services sector accounted for by far the largest share of Comecon investment – well over two-thirds in developed countries. In developing countries, primary and manufacturing activities are relatively more important and accounted for 27% of the total number of foreign affiliates from Central and Eastern Europe in 1990.

Just over one-half of investment by Comecon countries currently takes the form of majority-owned joint ventures. However, the equity split between Comecon and foreign partners varies considerably. In 1983, Czechoslovakia recorded the highest proportion (34.4%) of 100% owned foreign affiliates while 90.0% of Romanian and 59.3% of Hungarian investments were 50–50 or minority-owned ventures. However, the proportion of 100% owned affiliates in developed countries was only one-third of that in developed countries (7.3% and 22.8% in 1983).

A special institutional factor may also play a role in explaining the trade-supporting character of most of the equity ventures originating in socialist countries. In all these countries, specially established foreign trade organizations have typically been the only firms permitted to engage in foreign trade and, hence, in the overwhelming bulk of foreign value-adding activities (UNCTC, 1988).

NOTES

1   The first compendium of statistics on international investment and production was compiled by the present author and John Cantwell for the Geneva-based Institute of Research in Multinationals (IRM), and published in 1987. With the demise of the IRM, the UNCTC took over the responsibilities for the production of a much more ambitious directory under the guidance of John Cantwell and the present author.

2   Estimated from data contained in John Stopford (ed.) *The World Directory of Multinational Enterprises* (1982, 1992), McMillan (1987, 1991), and the *UNCTC Billion Dollar Directory of MNEs* (see, for example, UNCTC, 1988) and updated to 1988.

3   Gross output equals the value of output produced; net output, or value added, equals gross output less purchases from other firms. Net output is the value of the firm's contribution to economic activity and is

available for distribution to the factors of production responsible for that output and to governments (e.g. through direct taxes).

4   This estimate is derived from (and cross-checked with) a variety of sources, including that contained in the *World Directory of Multinational Enterprises*, *The IRM Directory of International Investment and Production Statistics* (edited by John H. Dunning and John Cantwell, 1987), the 1982 and 1989 Benchmark Surveys *US Direct Investment Abroad* and data on the value added of foreign affiliates of MNEs compiled by several leading host countries.

5   Derived from the above data and that contained in J. H. Dunning and R. D. Pearce *The World's Largest Industrial Enterprises*, Gower Press (1985).

6   Derived from data on cross-border royalties and fees between non-affiliated companies published by the US, German and UK governments. See also Dunning and Cantwell (1987), Table A11.

7   For example, if one assumes that royalties and fees represented 10% of value added of the companies paying them, and adds this figure to the value added generated by multinational enterprise, the 25% to 30% of gross domestic product would rise to 30% to 35%.

8   For the most part, until the late 1980s the former group of activities was limited to some joint venture activity by Western European and US MNEs in Yugoslavia, Hungary and Poland (for further details, see McMillan, 1987).

9   As set out by Dunning and Cantwell (1987).

10   For most major investing countries, direct investment flows represent new capital outflows plus reinvested profits plus (or minus) changes in intra-country balances. However, for some countries data is only published on net capital flows. The figures then underestimate the total amount of FDI in any one year. It should be noted that all data is converted into US $ and thus may reflect changing values of the dollar as well as any real factors. This is particularly important in the case of major outward investors, such as the UK, whose value currency in $ terms has fluctuated between 2.43 in 1979 and 1.09 in 1983, and then to 1.96 in early 1991.

11   It should be observed that foreign production is the total value of output of foreign affiliates, irrespective of how this production is financed. Thus the total output of a 30% owned foreign affiliate is treated in the same way as that of a 100% owned affiliate, or that of a majority-owned affiliate which has financed its capital outlays mostly with international loans. Foreign production is hence more a measure of the extent of control exercised by multinational enterprises than of the financial ownership of such enterprises.

12   Table 2.4 also shows the increasing share of Canada in the outward investment flows since 1981.

13 These latter figures are the most suspect of all. Other estimates (based on those contained in a chapter by J. H. Dunning in an edited volume by K. Khan on *Multinationals of the South*, Francis Pinter, 1987), suggested that the total foreign capital stake of less developed countries in 1985 is more likely to have been between $20 and $25 billion, excluding investment in tax haven countries, and $33 to $39 billion including tax havens.

14 In 1958, for example, developing countries were host to 65.7% of the estimated cumulative stock of foreign direct investment. For further details, see Chapter 3.

15 Speculating just for a moment, if these countries, which accounted for two-fifths of the world population, attracted an inward capital stake *per capita* equal to, say, Thailand – a middle income developing country – this would increase the total stock of foreign investment by 35%.

16 The results of which are contained in two volumes by J. W. Vaupel and J. P. Curhan: *The Making of a Multinational Enterprise*, Cambridge, Mass: Harvard University Press, 1969, and *The World's Largest Multinational Enterprises*, Cambridge, Mass: Harvard University Press, 1974.

17 Table A7 in this volume sets out the geographical distribution of the outward capital stake of the leading investment countries. Like Table 2.7 in this chapter, it reveals some interesting differences on the preferences of US, European and the Far Eastern and Pacific MNEs.

18 The relationship between changes in the net outward investment positions of countries and changes in relative exchange rate is a complex one. Most certainly, because they affect the comparative profitability of investment in different countries, some kinds of investment respond to (i.e. lag) changes in exchange rates. However, others lead or reinforce movements in exchange rates, such as capital exports generated by a low expectation of the future economic opportunities in the home countries. It is also important to distinguish between fluctuations in the short or medium term competitiveness of countries, such as the UK and US, and the long term consequences of industrialization and income growth, as in the case of Japan and the newly industrializing countries.

19 This situation changed in 1991 and the first half of 1992 as a result of a change in economic policy introduced by the new Swedish Government and the announcement that Sweden had applied for membership of the EC.

20 Examples include the purchase in 1988, by the Indonesian MNE Mantrust, of 'Chicken of the Sea' in the US for $260 million, and in 1989, that by the Thai company Unicord of 'Bumble Bee', the third largest canning firm in the US. For further details see Haude (1991).

21 For further details see Dunning (1988a).

22 See also Porter (1990), Prahalad and Doz (1987) and Bartlett and Ghoshal (1989).

23 On the basis of investment data from the leading source countries it is estimated that about 40% of FDI stock in Africa is in the resource based sector.

24 A concept further discussed in Chapter 4. See also Chapter 5 of Dunning (1988a).

25 This kind of reasoning is further explored in Chapter 4.

26 As regularly published each year, usually in the April and August editions of *Fortune*.

27 Defined as firms that employ less than 500 people in manufacturing, less than 100 in wholesale trade, and less than 50 in retail trade and other sources.

28 Some statistical testing by Cantwell and Randaccio (1990) confirmed that, on average, over the period 1972 to 1982 for large firms with smaller amounts of foreign production in the former year grew faster than those with larger amounts and that the catching-up process took place mainly with rather than between industries.

29 For example, according to the UNCTC (1990), the share of the Korean foreign investment accounted for by the US and Europe increased from 14% in 1974 to 41% in 1988, and that of Taiwan from 43% in 1980 to 60% in 1988. For many years now, the bulk of outward Latin American investment has been concentrated in developed countries, but most of this originated from the tax haven countries of the Bahamas, Cayman Islands, Netherlands Antilles and Panama, which accounted for 78% of all outward investment stock by Latin American countries in 1988 (UNCTC, 1990b, p. 14). Recent data suggest that developed countries now account for 75% of Chinese outward direct investment (*Transnationals*, 1992).

30 Since modern technologies are breaking down traditional industrial boundaries, it is becoming increasingly difficult to classify the giant multinationals like Unilever, Philips, Matsushita, ITT and General Electric to a single sector.

31 In terms of worldwide employment, for example, 10 of 14 of the largest banks and two of the largest insurance companies employed 50 000 people or more in 1986. American Express employed 78 747, Merrill Lynch (securities) 45 100, Sears Roebuck (retailing) 485 000, Arthur Anderson (accounting) 36 117, Bechtel (construction) 30 000, and British Airways (air transport) 39 498 (UNCTC, 1988).

CHAPTER 3

THE MOTIVES FOR FOREIGN PRODUCTION

3.1 INTRODUCTION

The following two chapters consider the motivations for, and the determinants of, the foreign value-added activities by MNEs. The present chapter describes some of the reasons prompting firms to undertake FDI, and distinguishes between four main types of production financed by such investment. Chapter 4 describes and evaluates some of the theories and paradigms that have been put forward over the past 30 years to explain the existence and growth of MNEs, and of their foreign activities.

3.2 WHY DO FIRMS WISH TO ENGAGE IN FOREIGN PRODUCTION?

Chapter 2 has shown that the great majority of MNE activity is undertaken by private business enterprises from market economies. This suggests that, like their domestic counterparts, MNEs are motivated primarily by what they perceive to be in the interests of their stakeholders, rather than that of the wider community of which they are part. These stakeholders include employees, managers and shareholders,[1] all of whom must be recompensed for their contributions to the production process by an amount at least equal to the opportunity cost of the resources and capabilities they provide (i.e. the highest return they could earn for their resources and capabilities if they were deployed differently). Most of the literature in the tradition of neo-classical economics asserts that any residual of income earned by a firm over and above the opportunity cost of the stakeholders will accrue to the owners of the business in the form of profits, and that it is the maximization of these

profits (net of tax and depreciation) in relation to the capital invested, which is the driving force of the modern business enterprise. This may be expressed in the equation:
Maximize:

$$\Pi = \frac{TR - TC}{K} \qquad 3.1$$

where Π is the rate of return, TR is the total sales revenue, TC is the total cost of production and K is the owner's capital invested.

A modification of the above formula, which takes account of the fact that the value of a firm's earnings will vary according to when they are earned, is set out below. Assuming that over a three-year period a firm will aim to maximize its total income, including that which is derived from reinvesting the profits earned in the first two years,[2] the appropriate formula then becomes:
Maximize:

$$\Sigma\Pi_{1\rightarrow3} = \Pi_1 (1 + r)^2 + \Pi_2 (1 + r) + \Pi_3 \qquad 3.2$$

where r is the maximum income a firm can earn through reinvesting profits earned in years 1 and 2.

Each of these two formulae assume that the value of the owner's investment stake does not change independently of the profits earned. However, once one allows for this possibility (perhaps as a result of an appreciation or depreciation of property values, or changes in future earning capacity of the firm), it may be more appropriate to think of the goal of the owners of a firm as maximizing the value of their equity stake over a given period of time. Equation 3.2 would then need to be modified as follows:

Maximize:

$$\Sigma \Pi_{1 \to 3} + \Sigma \Delta K_{1 \to 3} \qquad\qquad 3.3$$

where $\Sigma \Delta K_{1 \to 3} = \Delta K (1 + r)^2 + \Delta K_3 (1 + r)$
$+ \Delta K_3$

Alternatively, it is possible to conceive of the firm as a collection of assets, the value of which its owners wish to increase as much as possible over a given period of time. The formula to achieve the objectives of the wealth maximizing firms, as set out in most micro-economic textbooks, assuming a three-year time period, is as follows:
Maximize:

$$NPV_{(t=3)} = \frac{Y_1}{(1 + r)^2} + \frac{Y_2}{(1 + r)} + Y_3 \qquad 3.4$$

where NPV is the net present value of the expected income of a firm at time t^3, Y is the net expected income of the firm in time 1, 2 and 3, and r is the opportunity cost of K invested to earn that income.

The fact that an enterprise produces outside its national boundaries is not generally thought to affect the objectives of the owners of equity capital except, perhaps, in the case of publicly-owned or state-controlled companies.[3] However, as with any multi-activity or multi-plant company, it may open up the possibility of a conflict of interests not only between the various groups of stakeholders, but also between the same group of stakeholders (e.g. shareholders, management and labour) in one country and that in another. As Chapter 8 will suggest, the interests of the management and employees of an affiliate of an MNE will not necessarily coincide with those of the parent company. Conflicts may arise not only about the distribution of surplus profits, but also on decisions about the capital structure of the affiliate, the sharing of risks and responsibilities, the pricing of intra-firm transactions, the sourcing of inputs, the kind of markets served, the timing of income flows and the amount of production undertaken by the affiliate.

Post neo-classical theories of the firm assert that where output is supplied in other than perfectly competitive market conditions, the owners of enterprises need not necessarily be constrained to maximizing the rate of return on their capital. Wherever

the equity[4] stakeholders can earn above the opportunity cost of their capital, they have the freedom to pursue other objectives. These range from maximizing the sales of the company or increasing its market share, to driving competitors out of business, undertaking risky investments which otherwise would not have been made and advancing the welfare of the other stakeholders. Alternatively, behaviourists (e.g. Simon, 1959; Cyert and March, 1963) argue that because of the difficulty of identifying the appropriate conditions for profit maximization and to avoid attracting new competition or unwelcome government attention, firms will be content to earn 'satisfactory' rather than 'maximum' profits.

Each of the above theories suggests that, if they should so desire, the owners of a firm may trade off part or all of surplus profits against other goals. At the same time, depending on their bargaining power, the other stakeholders (e.g. the employees) might be able to appropriate part of these profits for themselves (Dunning and Stilwell, 1978).

The introduction of risk and uncertainty into factor or product markets adds a further complication in evaluating the motivation of firms. Is a capital project with a 75% chance of a 15% return being earned and a 25% of 12% being earned likely to interest a firm more or less than an investment with a 100% chance of a return of 13.5%? Economists can give no hard and fast answers without knowing the preference functions of the owners of the firm. In the above example, much will depend on the decision taker's perceived attitude to risk taking. Such an attitude is likely to vary between owners, making it difficult to give it an objective value, except in so far as it may be associated with certain (measurable) attributes of decision takers. Moreover, when it is impossible to calculate the risk, then one's judgement of the nature of that risk may itself vary.

Later chapters will describe the various ways in which MNEs can and do evaluate risk and uncertainty, and how they may react to environment volatility. We shall see that much depends on the kinds of risk and uncertainty under consideration. While an increase in some risks, such as the possibility of nationalization of a firm's foreign assets, is likely to reduce FDI, an increase in others, for example, the unreliability of foreign-owned suppliers or the inefficiency of independent foreign sales agents, may increase it.

It is further worth observing that most economic and behavioural explanations of international (or foreign)[5] production do not explicitly specify the motivation of firms engaging in that production, but only the variables likely to determine their behaviour. Moreover, most explanations are concerned with explaining what firms *actually* do rather than what they *should* do. In other words, rather than hypothesizing that a fall in real wages in Thailand will increase FDI in Thailand because it will increase profits, most theories of FDI first attempt to establish whether labour costs *are* an important factor in influencing profits, and hence investment, and if they are, what is the nature of the relationship. A few analysts[6] have used a composite variable, for example, some measure of profitability, growth of sales or market share, to explain the industrial or geographical distribution of FDI, but most have chosen to identify the variables that may be expected to influence these objectives.[7]

In this volume we shall assume that the principal objective of private enterprises in undertaking foreign production is to advance their long-term profitability. However, it is important to note that this profitability is made up of two components. First, there is the profitability of the foreign affiliate itself. Second, the effect that foreign production has on the profitability of the rest of the investing organization. This latter effect might be positive, where, for example, FDI leads to an increase in, or lowering of the costs of, domestic production. Alternatively, it might be negative where, for example, it replaces the production of another foreign affiliate. Equation 3.1 may then be reinterpreted as:
Maximize:

$$\Pi_{fp} = \frac{(TR_f + \Delta T_r) - (TC_f + \Delta TC_r)}{K_f + \Delta K_r} \qquad 3.5$$

where fp are the profits as a result of MNE activity, f indicates the foreign affiliate and r is the other producing units of MNE.

Equations 3.2 to 3.5 may be similarly reinterpreted. Thus maximizing the NPV of the MNE by engaging in FDI makes it necessary to consider both the effect of FDI on the NPV of the foreign affiliate and that on the rest of the MNE's operations.

In practice, MNEs operate in an environment in which both intermediate and final product markets are imperfect, and where the outcome of business decisions is uncertain. This being so, it is even more difficult to generalize about the strategic behaviour of such firms than about that of their domestic equivalents. Partly this is because of the greater range of options open to MNEs; partly to the differences in perception of decision makers in the MNEs towards these options; and partly because of differences in attitudes towards risk taking. Thus, some firms may place a higher value on the risk spreading opportunities of FDI than others; while MNEs that compete in oligopolistic markets may gauge the value of their foreign activities as much by their anticipated repercussions on their competitors' market position as on any profits that the affiliate may earn. This suggests that some firms may produce outside their national boundaries as part of a coherent and coordinated global competitive strategy, rather than to earn profits on a specific FDI. This is, however, more likely to be the case with experienced and globally integrated MNEs rather than with smaller firms undertaking their first foreign investment.

With these introductory points in mind, we now turn to examine the main kinds of foreign production that firms undertake.

3.3   THE MAIN TYPES OF FOREIGN PRODUCTION

Broadly speaking, we might identify four types of MNE activity. Borrowing and extending from an earlier taxonomy used by Jack Behrman (1972) they are:

(1)   resource seekers
(2)   market seekers
(3)   efficiency seekers
(4)   strategic asset or capability seekers.

The characteristics of each are set out in the following paragraphs. It is, however, worth noting that in the early 1990s many of the larger MNEs are pursuing pluralistic objectives, and most engage in FDI that combines the characteristics of each of the above categories. Moreover, each type of MNE activity may be *aggressive* in the sense that the investing company is seeking to take pro-active action to advance its strategic objectives, or *defensive* in the sense that its behaviour is in reaction to actions taken (or perceived likely) by its competitors or by foreign governments which require it to protect its market position.

The motives for foreign production may also change as, for example, when a firm becomes an established and experienced foreign investor. Initially, most enterprises invest outside their home countries to acquire natural resources or gain (or retain) access to markets. As they increase their degree of multinationality, however, they may use their overseas activities as a means by which they can improve their global market position by raising their efficiency or acquiring new sources of competitive advantage.

3.3.1 The resource seekers

These enterprises are prompted to invest abroad to acquire particular and specific resources at a lower real cost than could be obtained in their home country (if, indeed, they are obtainable at all). The motivation for the FDI is to make the investing enterprise more profitable and competitive in the markets it serves (or intends to serve) than it would otherwise be. Most, or all, of the output of the affiliates of resource seekers is exported, and mainly, although not exclusively, to developed industrialized countries.

There are three main types of resource seekers. First, there are those seeking physical resources of one kind or another. They include primary producers and manufacturing enterprises, from both developed and developing countries, who are driven to engage in FDI by the motives of cost minimization and security of supply sources. The resources they seek include most minerals, raw materials and agricultural products, but especially those whose production requires the kind of complementary capabilities and markets that MNEs are especially well equipped to provide. Chapter 2 has suggested that these include minerals, such as oil, zinc, copper, tin and bauxite; and agricultural products, such as rubber, tobacco, sugar, bananas, pineapples, palm oil, coffee and tea. Some FDI in service activities is also intended to exploit location-bound resources. Examples include tourism, car rentals, oil drilling, construction, medical and educational services. One feature of this first

kind of resource intensive MNE activity is that it usually involves significant capital expenditure. Moreover, once the investment has been made, it is relatively location-bound.

The second group of resource seeking MNEs comprise those seeking plentiful supplies of cheap and well motivated unskilled or semi-skilled labour. This kind of FDI is usually undertaken by manufacturing and service MNEs from countries with high real labour costs, which set up or acquire subsidiaries in countries with lower real labour costs, to supply labour intensive intermediate or final products for export. Most of this type of MNE activity is in the more advanced industrializing developing countries such as Mexico, Taiwan and Malaysia. However, within Europe and North Africa there is also some labour seeking investment in Spain, Portugal and Morocco. Frequently, in order to attract such production, host countries have set up free trade or export processing zones. Home countries have sometimes allowed their own MNEs tariff concessions on products imported from their foreign subsidiaries. The economic implications of this kind of MNE activity are explored in some detail in Chapters 13 and 17.

The third type of resource seeking FDI is prompted by the need of firms to acquire technological capability, management or marketing expertise and organizational skills. Examples include collaborative alliances concluded by Korean, Taiwanese and Indian companies with EC or US firms in high technology sectors; executive search subsidiaries set up by US firms in the UK; and R&D listening posts established by UK chemical companies in Japan. Each of these value-added activities parallels the investment made, for example, by Belgian MNEs in Africa or Japanese MNEs in Australia and SE Asia in the natural resources in which their home countries are deficient.

As Chapter 5 will show, much of the FDI by European, US and Japanese firms in the 19th century was prompted by the need to secure an economic and reliable source of minerals, primary products for the (then) investing industrializing nations of Europe and North America. Indeed, up to the eve of the Second World War, about three-fifths of the accumulated foreign direct capital stake was of this kind. By the mid 1980s, resource based investment had declined to about one-third of worldwide

MNE activity, and about 45% of that in developing countries. The rising importance of other kinds of investment coupled with the voluntary or involuntary indigenization of many primary sectors (e.g. oil, rubber, tin, copper etc) previously dominated by MNEs, was responsible for this. More recently, the declining role of unskilled or semi-skilled labour in the value-added process of several manufacturing activities has reduced the incentives for MNEs to seek out cheap supplies of labour. On the other hand, FDI to gain access to technology, information and specialized management skills is more important than it used to be. Not only are Third World MNEs investing in the industrial nations to gain access to knowledge, there is increasing evidence of foreign investors in industrialized countries diversifying their R&D activities, at least within the Third World.

3.3.2   The market seekers

These are enterprises that invest in a particular country or region to supply goods or services to markets in these or in adjacent countries. In most cases, part or all of these markets will have been serviced previously by exports from the investing company which, either because of tariff or other cost-raising barriers imposed by host countries or because the size of the markets now justifies local production, are no longer best supplied by this route. Sometimes, however, an enterprise may seek to replace its exports to a foreign market by investing in a third country and exporting to that market from there.[8] One scholar (Nicholas, 1986) found that no less than 94% of the UK MNEs with foreign manufacturing investments in 1939, first supplied the countries in which they then produced by exports.

Market-seeking investment may be undertaken to sustain or protect existing markets or to exploit or promote new markets. Apart from market size and the prospects for market growth, there are four main reasons which might prompt firms to engage in either sorts of market-seeking investment. The first is that their main suppliers or customers have set up foreign producing facilities and that to retain their business they need to follow them overseas. One recent example of this kind of FDI is that by some 300 Japanese auto-component suppliers which have set up manufacturing subsidiaries in the US, or con-cluded joint ventures with US firms, to supply US plants of the leading Japanese auto assemblers. In the services sector, cross-border acquisitions and mergers (A&Ms) among accounting, auditing, law and advertising firms in the 1980s were considerably stimulated by the need to offer their globally-oriented clients a presence in the leading markets of the world (Dunning, 1990).

The second reason for market oriented FDI is that quite frequently products need to be adapted to local tastes or needs, and to indigenous resources and capabilities. In addition, without familiarizing themselves with local language, business customs, legal requirements and marketing procedures, foreign producers might find themselves at a disadvantage *vis a vis* local firms in selling consumer goods like washing machines, stereo equipment and a wide variety of food and drink products, as well as those supplying intermediate products such as construction machinery, petrochemicals and forestry products, financial and professional services.

The third reason for serving a local market from an adjacent facility is that the production and transaction costs of so doing are less than supplying it from a distance. Obviously, this decision will be highly industry- and country-specific. The production of goods that are relatively costly to transport and can be produced economically in small quantities is more likely to be located near the main centres of consumption than are those that cost relatively little to transport and yield substantial economies of scale in their production. Firms from countries that are geographically removed from important markets are more likely to engage in market-seeking FDI than those that adjoin to those markets (compare French or Dutch investment with US investment in West Germany). In some cases, government regulations, import controls or strategic trade policy may prompt firms to relocate their production facilities. For example, the Canadian telecommunications MNE, Northern Telecom, moved many of its production facilities to the US in the late 1980s so that it could win Japanese contracts. At the time, Japan favoured the US as a source of telecommunication equipment because of the politically sensitive US–Japan trade gap.

The fourth and increasingly important reason for market-seeking investment is that an MNE may consider it necessary, as part of its global production and marketing strategy, to have a physical presence in the leading markets served by its competitors. Thus most of the larger MNEs in sectors dominated by international oligopolists (e.g. oil, rubber tyres, pharmaceuticals, semiconductors and advertising) not only operate production units in each of the Triad areas, but also are increasingly engaging in R&D.[9] Such strategic market-seeking investment might be undertaken for defensive or aggressive reasons. Much of the 'follow my leader' or 'band-wagon' type of investments (which are analysed more fully in the following chapter (see p. 72)) are of the former kind. Aggressive investments are those designed to advance the global interests of a firm by investing in an expanding market. The response of MNEs to the completion of Europe's internal market (EC, 1992) and to the opening up of Eastern Europe to FDI is essentially of this kind, although the belief that EC 1992 might be restrictive in its policies towards imports from non-EC countries has also led to some defensive strategic investment by non-EC MNEs.

However, undoubtedly the single most important reason for market-seeking investment remains the action of host governments encouraging such investment. The traditional instrument chosen by governments has been to impose tariffs or other import controls. History suggests that the majority of first time manufacturing and service investment were undertaken to circumvent such trade barriers. Governments have also attempted to attract inward investment by offering a gamut of investment incentives ranging from tax concessions to subsidized labour and capital costs and favourable import quotas. We shall discuss these measures in more detail in Chapter 20.

Unlike those engaging in other kinds of FDI, market-seeking MNEs tend to treat their foreign affiliates as self-contained production units rather than as part of an integrated network of cross-border activities. In consequence, they tend to be the most responsive to local needs and requirements.[10] The affiliates of market seeking firms will normally produce similar products to those supplied by their parent companies, though usually a truncated range. Usually, too, the output will be sold in the country in which it is produced, although there may be some exports to adjacent markets. In regionally integrated markets like the EC, however, production in one or a few countries might service all the countries in the region. At the end of the 1980s, market-seeking MNEs probably accounted for about 45% of global direct investment and about 30% in developing countries.

3.3.3 The efficiency seekers

The motivation of efficiency seeking FDI is to rationalize the structure of established resource based or market-seeking investment in such a way that the investing company can gain from the common governance of geographically dispersed activities. Such benefits are essentially those of the economies of scale and scope and of risk diversification. They stem from cross-border product or process specialization, the learning experiences that result from producing in different cultures and the opportunities for arbitraging cost and price differentials across the exchanges. The intention of the efficiency seeking MNE is to take advantage of different factor endowments, cultures, institutional arrangements, economic systems and policies, and market structures (country-specific ESP configurations) by concentrating production in a limited number of locations to supply multiple markets.

Usually, the efficiency seekers will be experienced, large and diversified MNEs producing fairly standardized products and engaging in internationally accepted production processes. In the past, such FDI has usually occurred once resource based or market-seeking investments have become sufficiently numerous and important to warrant some degree of rationalization. Increasingly, however, investment by new entrants, such as by the Japanese in the EC, are being undertaken on a product-by-product basis as part of a carefully integrated regional or global marketing strategy.

In order for efficiency seeking (or rationalized) foreign production to take place, cross-border markets must be both well developed and open. This is why it flourishes in regionally integrated markets. In practice, the efficiency seeker is likely to be a global corporation competing on the basis of the products it offers for sale and its ability to diversify its assets and capabilities by exploiting the benefits of producing in several countries.

Efficiency seeking FDI is of two main kinds.

The first is that designed to take advantage of differences in the availability and cost of traditional factor endowments in different countries. This explains much of the division of labour within MNEs producing in both developed and developing countries, with capital, technology and information intensive value-added activities being concentrated in the former, and labour and natural resource intensive activities in the latter. The second kind of efficiency seeking investment is that which takes place in countries with broadly similar economic structures and income levels and is designed to take advantage of the economies of scale and scope, and of differences in consumer tastes and supply capabilities. Here, traditional factor endowments play a less important role in influencing FDI, while 'created' competences and capabilities, the availability and quality of supporting industries, the characteristics of the local competition, the nature of consumer demand and the macro- and micro-policies of governments play a more important role.[11]

3.3.4   The strategic asset seekers

The fourth group of MNEs comprise those which engage in FDI, usually by acquiring the assets of foreign corporations, to promote their long-term strategic objectives – especially that of sustaining or advancing their international competitiveness. The investing firms involved include both established MNEs pursuing an integrated global or regional strategy and first time foreign direct investors seeking to buy competitive strength in an unfamiliar market. The motive for strategic asset seeking investment is less to exploit specific cost or marketing advantages over their competitors (although these may sometimes be important) than to add to the acquiring firm's existing portfolio of assets, others which they perceive will either sustain or strengthen their own overall competitive position *or* weaken that of their competitors. Increasingly, too, strategic and rationalized FDI are going hand in hand as firms restructure their assets to meet their objectives.[12] An example was Grand Metropolitan's sale of Inter Continental Hotels to a Japanese conglomerate in December 1988 for $3.3 billion, and its purchase in the same year of Pillsbury Mills, a large US food producing company and fast food

chain for $5.8 billion.

Like the efficiency seeking MNE, the strategic asset acquirer aims to capitalize on the benefits of the common ownership of diversified activities and capabilities, or of similar activities and capabilities in diverse economic and potential environments. Chapter 4 will analyse the nature of these benefits in more detail. They all arise from the imperfections of the product markets in which MNEs operate and the opportunities open to these companies to exploit, or indeed add to, these imperfections. In some cases, the strategic asset seeker is a conglomerate primarily concerned with the management of financial assets denominated in different currencies. Companies like Hanson Trust, for example, are primarily institutional portfolio investors even if they own a majority of equity shares in the companies they invest. At the same time such MNEs may, and often do, inject their own organizational systems and management styles into the companies they acquire, even if they do not involve themselves in the day-to-day management functions. However, in the case of the great majority of strategic investments (including those of some quite small MNEs) the expectancy is that the acquisition or joint venture will bring some benefits to the rest of the organization of which it is part. This it might do, for example, by opening up new markets, creating R&D synergies or production economies, buying market power, lowering transaction costs, spreading administrative overheads, advancing strategic flexibility and enabling risks to be better spread.[13]

While some specialist multinational conglomerates tend to be service rather than goods producing companies, and often their foreign investments are free standing, most foreign A&Ms are currently undertaken by MNEs that fall into one of the other three categories just described. Strategic and economic good sense usually go hand in hand. However, on certain occasions and for certain purposes, strategic considerations may be the dominant motive for FDI. One company may acquire or engage in a collaborative alliance with another to thwart a competitor from so doing. Another might merge with one of its foreign rivals to strengthen their joint capabilities *vis à vis* a more powerful rival. A third might acquire a group of suppliers to corner the market for a particular raw material. A fourth might seek to gain access over distribution outlets to better promote its own brand of products. A fifth might buy out a firm producing a complementary range of goods or services so it can offer its customers a more diversified range of products. A sixth might join forces with a local firm in the belief that it is in a better position to secure contracts from the host government, which are denied to its exporting competitors. All these are examples of strategic FDI to protect or advance the investing firm's long-term competitive position.

There are no statistical data on the significance of efficiency seeking or strategic asset acquiring FDI[14] by MNEs, particularly as they cannot easily be separated from the other two kinds of value-adding activity. What does seem certain, however, is that these investments are accounting for an increasing share of the global activity by MNEs, particularly within the major markets of the world, and that they are concentrated in the technology and capital intensive manufacturing, and information intensive service sectors.

3.3.5   Other motives for MNE activity

There are other reasons for MNE activity which do not easily fit into the four categories just described. We shall classify these into three groups *viz* (i) escape investments, (ii) support investments and (iii) passive investments. Let us consider each of these in turn.

(i)   *Escape investments*   Some FDI is made to escape restrictive legislation or macro-organizational policies by home governments. We are not here concerned with 'flight' capital which may be associated with political unrest or dire economic circumstances, for example, as occurred in Argentina, Zimbabwe, South Africa and the Philippines in the 1980s. Examples of the kind of 'escape' investments we have in mind include outbound MNE activity by Indian companies to circumvent restrictions on the share of domestic production they might attain; that by Israeli firms in the EC to by-pass the Arab boycott on products exported from Israel (Almor-Ellemers and Hirsch, 1991); that by Swedish, US or Nigerian firms because opportunities for investments in some sectors are limited by their home governments; that by Japanese banks in Europe which

engage in a wider range of services for their customers (notably investment banking) than they are allowed to undertake in Japan (Hawawini and Schill, 1992); and that by BASF, a German company, who confronted with the legal and political challenges from the local 'green' movement, shifted its cancer and immune system research from Germany to the US (*Business Week*, 1990).

Escape investments, such as those just described, are obviously most likely to originate from countries whose governments pursue strongly interventionist macro-organizational policies; and they tend to be concentrated in those sectors – especially service sectors – which are most regulated. With the renaissance of pro-market economic strategies and the liberalization of many markets in recent years, one might anticipate rather less 'escape' MNE activity to occur in the 1990s. The one exception might be where firms are 'pushed' to relocate their value activities as a result of trade barriers imposed on home country exports.

(ii)   *Support investments*   The purpose of these investments is to support the activities of the rest of the enterprise of which they are part. Such affiliates are rarely self-contained profit centres. Their activities incur costs but the major benefits accrue to the rest of the MNE.

Foremost among support investment are trade-related investments of MNEs, which are essentially designed to promote and facilitate the exports of goods and services from the investing (or other) companies, and/or to assist in the purchasing of foreign produced goods and services from the investing (or other) companies. As Chapter 2 indicated, specialist trade-related investments are the single most important service investment by US, Japanese and UK MNEs,[15] and their share of total FDI has increased considerably over the past two decades.

The kinds of value-added activity undertaken by MNE trading affiliates include not only wholesale and retail distribution and marketing, but also a whole range of import facilitating which they undertaken on behalf of the investing company. The Japanese Soga Sosha and the Korean Chaebol companies are trading MNEs *par excellence*. There are many others. Examples are the leading clothing wholesale and retail outlets in Europe and the US such as Sears Roebuck, K. Mart and C&A which purchase substantial quantities of clothing and foot-wear from Asian suppliers, and delegate the sub-contracting arrangements (including the monitoring of quality control) to their buying subsidiaries in Hong Kong, Singapore, Thailand etc. Similarly, the sale of sophisticated intermediate products and those which need regular after-sales maintenance and servicing may need the presence of trained personnel and of warehousing facilities for spare parts. Often trade-related subsidiaries also provide other market-ing and public relation services for their parent companies. Finally, as Chapter 7 will show, such activities are frequently the first step to the setting up of market seeking or resource seeking production facilities.

There are other kinds of support services which might be provided by the foreign affiliates of MNEs. These are usually undertaken by regional or branch offices. Regional offices act as an intermediate centre of control and administration between the head office and the foreign operating units. Various studies[16] have shown that the functions performed by these offices vary a great deal. Typically they involve both the coordination of the activities of the operating units and the provision of financial and marketing information for the parent company. They may also undertake such services as manpower recruitment, the search for additional investment opportunities for the parent company, site selection, public relations and liaison with host governments and/or regional authorities.

Branch offices which are independent of trade and operating units are less common. However, the idea of setting up a listening and monitoring arm of the parent company has gained credence in recent years, particularly, for example, in the case of US firms contemplating investments in the EC, and of Japanese finance-based MNEs seeking a presence in the City of London.

(iii) *Passive investments*   Chapter 1 indicated that a foreign investment is treated as direct if the investing entity has a financial equity interest in a foreign company sufficient to give it some control or influence over the latter's decision taking. *De facto*, data collecting agencies assume this to be somewhere between 10% and 25%. We have also suggested that direct investment is differently motivated than is portfolio investment. The latter kind of investment is an expression of faith in the existing organization and management of the company, and is undertaken to earn profits or to gain capital appreciation. By contrast, direct investment is designed to inject new resources and management skills into the company or to acquire new assets to increase its own profits. Portfolio investment is presumed to involve *passive* management whereas direct investment is presumed to involve *active* management.

In practice, most direct investments vary in the degree of active management pursued by their owners, ranging from 'complete' to 'non-existent'. Those which veer to the passive end of the spectrum are of two kinds. The first are those of large institutional conglomerates that specialize in the buying and selling of companies. Examples are T. Boone Pickens (US) and Lonrho (UK). However, although the investments are motivated by income potential or capital gain, some direct managerial input is usually involved. Rarely is an acquired company left to its own devices. Some investments are undertaken to improve technological, marketing, financial or organizational capabilities; others may involve asset stripping. Most real estate involvement (in land, hotels etc) is based on some expectation of future land and property values. The greater the fixed capital stake of an investment, the more important it is to take account of possible move-ments in future exchange rates (Aliber, 1970).

Nevertheless, it is true that the motivation of such investment may be primarily financial, and the 'foreign-ness' impact on the use of the assets acquired may be very limited. A good deal of Arab FDI in the 1970s, for example, in London hotels, was of this kind. More recently, the dramatic increase in the acquisition of prestigious real estate in the US by Japanese MNEs has smacked of 'passive' rather than 'active' investment.[17]

The second kind of passive investment is that made by small firms and individual investors in real estate. Often this is simply to foster the foreign ownership of holiday or second homes. However, sometimes it is undertaken purely in anticipation of an appreciation in land and property prices. Here, the mainstream theories of FDI described in the next chapter are left wanting. This is because, although classified as direct, these purchases have more the attributes of portfolio investment.

There is some suggestion that the passive element in the foreign operations by MNEs may be increasing. Certainly, this is more likely to be a feature of cross-border A&Ms than of greenfield investments; as shown in Chapter 2, the former have escalated in the past decade. Moreover, the rate at which firms have changed ownership, particularly in real estate related activities has increased dramatically. The problem of identifying the passive or portfolio component of a direct investment is not unique to FDI. Indeed, one school of thought has viewed the growth of the firm as being motivated by the pursuance of profitable and wealth appreciation activities.[18] While most firms would be reluctant to accept this perception, and prefer to follow an 'every cobbler sticks to his last' philosophy, most undertake some kind of 'trade' investments. Although there isn't much the academic scholar can do about separating the portfolio component of any direct investment, he should be aware of its relevance. At least for some kinds of investment (e.g. in real estate), he should try and incorporate the kind of variables that influence such investment into his explanatory models.

3.4   THE POLITICAL ECONOMY OF OUTWARD FDI

The previous sections have dealt with some of the economic and strategic motives for foreign direct investment. However, in so far as the governments of the investing countries are also interested in the outcome of the activities of MNEs, then, by influencing the conduct of such firms or their affiliates, they may affect the amount and pattern of FDI. Chapter 5 will, indeed, show that throughout history much MNE activity has either been undertaken directly by Nation States or with their support and encouragement. Such encouragement has only been forthcoming if the investment was perceived to advance the long-term economic and political goals of the home country.

Most early British investments in North America and 19th century investments by European colonial powers in the developing countries were of this kind (Svedberg, 1982). History is replete with examples of private MNEs being used as instruments of the economic policy of metropolitan governments. Indeed, until the outbreak of the First World War the UK and French colonies were sometimes forbidden to accept inward investment from other than the mother country, who at the same time might give incentives to its own firms. Even in the second half of the 20th century there have been several cases of uneasy alliances being concluded between MNEs and their home governments (UNCTC, 1983b, 1988), while in the early 1990s there is increasing evidence of home governments supporting FDI by their own MNEs, especially in Eastern Europe and some developing countries, in the belief that it serves their own political or strategic objectives. These issues will be explored in more detail in Chapters 5 and 19.[19]

Chapter 2 observed that there are several important state-owned MNEs. Though the great majority of these are from countries that would not normally wish to use FDI as a political instrument, in the case of those from the erstwhile communist countries this is one of their explicit goals. The question of the tactics pursued by state-owned MNEs and the extent to which home governments may affect the behaviour of private MNEs operating outside their home territories is an altogether different matter which is taken up in more detail in later chapters.

3.5   CONCLUSIONS

The above paragraphs have demonstrated that the types of foreign value-added activities undertaken by MNEs may be very differently motivated. Because of this, it is difficult to perceive an all-embracing theory of the determinants of these activities in the sense of encompassing, within a single explanatory equation, a set of variables that can fully explain each at the same time. The most the economist or business analyst can reasonably do is to formulate paradigms to provide an analytical framework for explaining the various kinds of MNE activity or theories designed to explain particular kinds of FDI.

The consensus of scholarly research and business case histories over the past 30 years support this contention. Thus, the factors that explain Rio Tinto's investment in copper mines in New Guinea or Geest's investment in a banana plantation in the

Windward Islands are totally different from those that explain Coca-Cola's investment in a bottling plant in Arusha, Tanzania, Bata's investment in a shoe factory in Belgium, the purchase of the Rockefeller Center in New York by the Mitsubishi Estate Corporation of Japan, or an investment by the Indonesian company Summa in the first foreign owned bank in Vietnam. Likewise, each of these investments is motivated by a different set of considerations than those driving IBM's, Royal Dutch Shell's or ABB's strategies towards the globalization of their R&D facilities, or AT&T's attempts to build up an international network of communication facilities, or Club Mediterranee's policy to own or franchise hotels in each of the world's major tourist regions.

However, it is one thing to argue that different explanatory variables are required to explain different kinds of foreign production, but quite another to assert that it is not possible to formulate a general paradigm or, as Kuhn (1960) puts it, 'a disciplinary matrix which seeks to set out a common analytical approach' to explaining all kinds of MNE activity. A reading of the literature suggests that there is some division of opinion as to the nature of the distinction between a theory and a paradigm. As we see it, a theory is a set of propositions about the nature and form of the behavioural relationships between a set of phenomena, the validity of which can be empirically tested. In some cases there may be alternative theories to explain the same phenomena; these may be called competing theories. In others, different phenomena may (and usually do) require different explanations, in which case the theories would be non-competing. Most partial theories of the MNE or FDI fall into one or other of these categories.

A paradigm, on the other hand, seeks to present a general framework for analysing the relationship between phenomena from which it is possible to formulate a variety of competing or non-competing theories. Perceived in this way, a theory is a derivative of a paradigm, but one paradigm may be able to accommodate several theories.

The following chapter takes up these points in more detail with respect to some of the theories and paradigms that have been put forward to explain the determinants of the existence and growth of MNEs and of their global value-added activities.

NOTES

1   In a sense, the government is also a stakeholder in that it receives taxation from any profits earned.

2   Π, of course, represents the difference between TR and TC. Clearly, to maximize Π over a three-year time period a firm will attempt to earn as much of the (total) revenue in the early part of the period and postpone the incurring of its (total) costs to the latter part of the period.

3   Thus a publicly-owned company in a mixed economy, such as the National Coal Board in the UK, may be required to adhere to certain social accounting conventions and/or goals in its home country, but abroad may seek to maximize the return on the invested capital. By contrast, in a centrally planned economy, state-owned MNEs may be expected to represent the state from which they originate in their overseas activities, and this takes on a quasi-ambassadorial or political role.

4   Under perfect competition, it is assumed that in conditions of equilibrium, all factors of production, including entrepreneurial capital, earn only the opportunity cost of their services.

5   We use these words interchangeably, although some writers use 'international' to embrace both the foreign and domestic activities of firms. We accept, however, that to undertake foreign production there must be a linkage between domestic and foreign operations through the internal trade of intermediate products. We further accept that, in globally integrated MNEs, the prosperity of domestic and foreign operations is closely intertwined.

6   See particularly the work of those scholars who have attempted to explain the geographical distribution of the US foreign direct stake in Europe as, for example, reviewed by Yannopoulos (1990) and UN (1992a).

7   To be more explicit, theories of the firm are concerned with identifying the optimum levels of investment, output or price. To determine these levels, some assumptions must be made about the motivation of firms. Such assumptions are not necessary to explain foreign production or changes in foreign production.

8   For example, to overcome import quotas levied by EC countries on Japanese produced goods some Japanese firms have set up or acquired manufacturing facilities in South East Asia (e.g. Singapore and Malaysia) and exported to the EC from there.

9   See Chapter 11 for more details.

10 See Chapter 8 for more details.

11 In Michael Porter's terminology, the three other facets of the diamond of competitive advantage. See especially Porter (1990), Dunning (1992a) and Rugman (1991).

12 For example, in the years 1988 and 1989, US firms reported that they had increased their foreign equity by $26 billion, mostly by the acquisition of existing companies. In these same years, however, they repatriated $37 billion of assets mainly through the sale of foreign affiliates. New investment and disinvestment normally go hand in hand.

13 For a recent review of the reasons for cross-border acquisitions see Hong-Jen Chiu (1992).

14 Some years ago, Kopits (1979) attempted to give a breakdown between the first three groups of investment, and came to the conclusion that the proportion of the direct foreign investment stake owned by US multinational companies, which can be classified as conglomerate investment, rose from 14.1% in 1962 to 23.3% in 1968.

15 Excluding those undertaken in primary, secondary or tertiary MNEs.

16 See, for example, those by Daniels (1986, 1987), Grosse (1982), Dunning and Norman (1979, 1983, 1987) and Van den Bulcke (1984).

17 The value of the capital stake of such investment has risen to $34.7 billion by March 1990.

18 As described, for example, by Edith Penrose (1958) and Lloyd Amey (1964).

19 See also Dunning (1993b).

CHAPTER 4
THE DETERMINANTS OF MNE ACTIVITY

4.1 INTRODUCTION

This chapter seeks to review some of the leading economic and behavioural explanations of the existence and growth of MNEs and of the foreign value-added activities they own or control. Chapter 1 identified MNEs as multi-activity firms that engage in foreign direct investment. At the same time, it acknowledged that many MNEs also participate in a variety of cross-border non-equity alliances and/or clusters of value-adding activities over which they may exert considerable influence. Chapter 1 further suggested that MNEs have two near relatives. First, like international trading companies, they undertake cross-border transactions outside their home countries, but unlike them, they own and control foreign production facilities. Second, like multi-plant domestic firms, MNEs operate two or more production units and internalize the transactions between these units. Unlike them, however, at least one of these production units is located in a foreign country and the markets internalized are transnational rather than domestic.

The theory of the determinants of MNE activity must then seek to explain both the *location* of value-adding activities, and the *ownership* and *organization* of these activities. As such, it needs to draw upon and integrate two strands of economic thought. The first is the theory of international resource allocation based upon the spatial distribution of factor endowments and capabilities. This theory chiefly addresses itself to the *location* of production. The second is the theory of economic organization, which is essentially concerned with the *ownership* of that production and the ways in which the transactions relating to it (including those which may impinge on its location) are managed and organized.

In traditional (classical or neo-classical) models of trade, which were the dominant paradigms in international economics until the 1950s, only the first issue, *viz* the 'where' of production, was addressed. Questions relating to the ownership and organization of economic activity were ignored. This was because the market for the cross-border exchange of goods and services was assumed to be a costless mechanism. Resources were assumed to be immobile across national boundaries but mobile within national boundaries. Firms were assumed to engage in only a single activity. Entrepreneurs were assumed to be profit maximizers. Managerial strategy was assumed to be confined to identifying the optimum level of output and minimizing the costs of supplying that output.

However, once one allows for imperfections in goods or factor markets, the possibility of alternative patterns of ownership of firms and/or organizing transactions arises. For example, in place of one firm selling its product through the market to another firm which then adds value to it, the same firm may coordinate both sets of activity and, in so doing, replace the market as a mechanism for allocating resources between the two firms, or for any transactions in which they were both previously involved. Foreign production occurs when at least one of these activities spans national boundaries. The factors influencing the modality of organizing cross-border activities are therefore at the heart of the theory of the MNE; indeed, some scholars go as far as to assert that it is the only real question of interest.

Taking a different starting point, one might equally ask why, given the ownership of firms and the way in which they organize production and transactions, they should choose to locate at least some of their value-added activities in a foreign country. In this case, the spatial distribution of factor endowments may be as relevant as it is in explaining some kinds of trade. Put another way, the introduction of market imperfections and multiple activities not only opens up the possibility of foreign production, but also requires a reappraisal of traditional trade theory. Indeed, some types of international transactions, such as intra-industry trade, can only be explained by drawing upon the theory of industrial organization.

From the above paragraphs, it should be evident that any attempt to theorize about the extent and pattern of MNE activity crucially rests on the type of question one wishes to answer. It is primarily 'Why do firms own foreign production facilities?'; or 'Why do firms locate their activities in one country rather than another?'; or 'What specific attributes demarcate MNEs from uninational enterprises?'; or 'Why does the participation of foreign, relative to indigenous, firms differ between countries and sectors?'; or 'Under what conditions will firms finance their foreign activities in the currencies of their home country rather than in those of another (i.e. engage in foreign direct investment)?' Even a cursory review of the literature on international production[1] suggests that frequently researchers address themselves to related, but very different questions.

Similarly, scholars differ in their choice of the unit of analysis. At the one end of the spectrum are the political economists who view the internationalization of firms as an inevitable outcome of the capitalist system, and as a means of increasing the monopoly power of the investing firms and/or countries (Baran and Sweezy, 1966; Cowling and Sugden, 1987). At the other end, business analysts and organizational theorists have sought to identify the main factors that determine the foreign investment decision process of firms (Aharoni, 1966). In between these two extremes, it is possible to identify three main theoretical streams of thought. The first emanate from a group of scholars who have taken a macro-economic perspective to MNE activity and have concerned themselves with why *countries* engage in FDI. These economists, such as Kojima (1973, 1978, 1982, 1990), usually take neo-classical type trade models as their starting point and then extend them to explain the extent and pattern of foreign production. Not surprisingly, they tend to focus on location-specific variables and why firms of particular nationalities have different propensities to engage in trade and foreign production. Others, more interested in the behaviour of the individual business enterprise, draw upon the theory of the domestic firm (which seeks to answer very different questions than that of international trade) to explain the existence and growth of the MNE *qua* MNE. This school of thought, of which Buckley (1990, 1991), Casson (1987, 1992), Buckley and Casson (1976, 1985), Hennart (1982, 1986a, 1989, 1991), Rugman (1982, 1986a) and Teece (1981a, 1985) are leading exponents, looks upon the MNE as an organizational hierarchy which internalizes the market for cross-border intermediate products. The school derives its methodology and approach both from the founder of modern transaction cost economics – Ronald Coase (1937, 1960) – and from organizational theorists such as Herbert Simon (1947, 1955), Alchian and Demsetz (1972) and Oliver Williamson (1975, 1985, 1986).

A third group of analysts, more closely allied in background to the second than the first, address the question of why firms of one nationality are better able to penetrate foreign markets than indigenous firms located in those markets, and why they wish to control value-added activities outside their national boundaries. Stephen Hymer (1960, 1968) was the progenitor of this type of explanation of foreign production which, he argued, could not occur without the investing firms possessing some kind of monopolistic advantage over and above that possessed by indigenous competitors. In his explanation, he drew not so much on the theory of the firm as on the theory of industrial organization, which had been developed a few years earlier by Bain (1956) to explain the pattern and ownership of US domestic industry.

In reviewing the literature on the determinants of MNE activity, it is important to distinguish between these three approaches, because what may be an exogenous variable in one may be endogenous in another. It follows that there is no all-embracing explanation of international production, only a correct answer to particular questions, each of which may add to our understanding about the cross-border organization of economic activity.

Finally, as previous chapters have demonstrated, the nature of FDI undertaken by MNEs is extremely varied. Because of this, both the motives for and the determinants of international production will differ. The parameters influencing a UK pulp and paper company to invest in a new forestry project in Botswana are unlikely to be the same as those influencing the purchase of a French food processing company by a US MNE. Similarly, those determining the pattern of rationalized production in the EC by a large and geographically diversified US motor vehicle MNE will be quite different from an investment by a Korean construction management company in Saudi Arabia, or a US pharmaceutical company establishing R&D facilities in Japan.

In summary, we would argue that it is not possible to formulate a single operationally testable theory that can explain all forms of foreign-owned production any more than it is possible to construct a generalized theory to explain all forms of trade or the behaviour of all kinds of firms. It is fully accepted in the literature that inter-industry trade needs different explanations than intra-industry trade, and that any theory of the firm critically depends on the assumed motivation of enterprises. At the same time, as the previous chapter has indicated, we believe that it is possible to formulate a general paradigm of MNE activity, which sets out a conceptual framework and seeks to identify clusters of variables relevant to an explanation of all kinds of foreign-owned output. Within this framework, we believe that most of the partial micro- and macro-theories of international production can be accommodated. Also, while the relevance and significance of the variables identified by each theory will differ, they should be more properly viewed as complementary, rather than substitutable, explanations for the cross-border activity of firms.

The rest of this chapter proceeds in the following way. Section 4.2 identifies and briefly reviews a selection of the leading theories of international production which were put forward by economists between 1960 and the mid 1970s. These theories were primarily focused on explaining the initial decision of firms to engage in FDI. In the last 15 years or so, attention has been switched to explaining the sequential investment of firms and to formulating more general explanations of MNE activity and the emergence of the global corporation.[2] Section 4.3 will pay special attention to the eclectic paradigm of international production, which

is, perhaps, the most ambitious attempt to integrate each of the main theoretical strands described earlier. This paradigm will then be compared and contrasted with two of the more influential contemporary economic theories of the MNE or MNE activity, *viz* the internalization theory and the macroeconomic theory of foreign direct investment propounded by Kiyoshi Kojima. Section 4.4 concludes the chapter by examining some contributions of organizational and management scholars to the debate, as well as some possible directions which theorizing about the MNE and MNE activity might take in the 1990s.

4.2   THEORIES OF THE MNE AND MNE ACTIVITY: 1960–76

4.2.1   Prior to the 1960s

Prior to the 1960s there was no established theory of the MNE or of FDI.[3] Attempts to explain the activities of firms outside their national boundaries represented an amalgam of:

(1) a fairly well formalized theory of (portfolio) capital movements (Iversen, 1935);

(2) a number of empirical and largely country-specific studies on the factors influencing the location of foreign direct investment (Southard, 1931; Southard *et al.*, 1936; Barlow, 1953; Dunning, 1958);

(3) a recognition by some economists, notably Williams (1929), that the internationalization of some industries required a modification to neoclassical theories of trade;

(4) an appreciation that the common ownership of the cross-border activities of firms could not only be considered as a substitute for the international cartels and combines (Plummer, 1934), but could be explained, in part at least, by the perceived gains of vertical or horizontal integration (Penrose, 1956, 1958; Bye, 1958).

Bye's contribution, which was (and still is) generally neglected by economists was particularly perceptive. It was he who coined the expression 'the multi-territorial firm' and used the case of the international oil industry to demonstrate that 'real and financial size enables firms to cross varying thresholds of growth either by extension or integration, and so assure them of a certain bargaining position' (Bye, 1958, p. 161).

The 1960s saw two influential and path breaking contributions to the theory of the MNE and MNE activity. Each was put forward quite independently of the other, and approached its subject matter from a very different perspective. The following paragraphs briefly describe the main features of the two approaches.

4.2.2   The contribution of Stephen Hymer

The first contribution was that of Stephen Hymer (1960, 1968) who, in a PhD thesis, expressed his dissatisfaction with the theory of indirect (or portfolio) capital transfers to explain the foreign value-added activities of firms. In particular, he identified three reasons for his dissatisfaction. The first was that once risk and uncertainty, volatile exchange rates and the cost of acquiring information and making transactions were incorporated into classical portfolio theory, many of its predictions, for example, with respect to the cross-border movements of money capital in response to interest rate changes, became invalidated. This was because such market imperfections altered the behavioural parameters affecting the conduct and performance of firms and, in particular, their strategy in servicing foreign markets.

Secondly, Hymer asserted that FDI involved the transfer of a package of resources (technology, management skills, entrepreneurship, etc), and not just finance capital which portfolio theorists such as Iversen (1935) had sought to explain. Firms were motivated to produce abroad by the expectation of earning an economic rent on the totality of their resources, including the way in which they were organized. The third and perhaps most fundamental characteristic of FDI was that it involved no change in the ownership of resources or rights transferred, whereas indirect investment, which was transacted through the market, did necessitate a change in ownership. In consequence, the organizational modality of both the transaction of the resources (e.g. intermediate products) and the value-added activities linked by these transactions was different.

In this connection, it is perhaps worth observing that Hymer was only interested in FDI in so far as this was the means by which firms were able to control the use of property rights transferred to their foreign subsidiaries.

In his thesis, Hymer broached many other issues which were subsequently taken up more rigorously by other scholars. For example, Aliber (1970, 1971) developed a formal model of FDI based on the failure of international financial and currency markets to perform efficiently, while Hymer's identification of the international firm as a firm that 'internalizes or supersedes the market' provided a useful prologue to the theory of internalization as a means for transferring knowledge, business techniques and skilled personnel (Hymer, 1960, pp. 48 and 60). However, Hymer's work is best known for its application of an industrial organizational approach to the theory of foreign production. His argument ran as follows. For firms to own and control foreign value-adding facilities they must possess some kind of innovatory, cost, financial or marketing advantages – specific to their ownership – which is sufficient to outweigh the disadvantages they faced in competing with indigenous firms in the country of production.[4] These advantages, which he assumed to be exclusive to the firm owning them (hence the expression 'ownership' advantages), imply the existence of some kind of structural market failure.

In seeking an explanation of these imperfections, Hymer turned to Joe Bain's classic treatise on the barriers to competition in domestic markets (1956). In extending this analysis to explain the cross-border activity of firms, he argued that such firms had to possess some kind of proprietary or monopolistic advantage. However, in so far as some ownership advantages may arise from the ability of firms to improve the allocation of resources or organize transactions more efficiently than markets, the word 'monopolistic' is an inappropriate one, even though the advantage(s) may, but not necessarily will, allow the owning firm to enjoy a temporary economic rent. Hymer then went on to examine the kind of ownership advantages that firms contemplating FDI might possess or acquire, as well as the kind of industrial sectors and market structures in which foreign production was likely to be concentrated.[5]

Elsewhere in his thesis, Hymer examined other

issues germane to MNE activity. In particular, like
Bye, he was interested in the territorial expansion of
firms as a means of exploiting or fostering their
monopoly power. And, although his writings show a
clear awareness of the failure of markets to perform
efficiently, he always seemed to compare the welfare
implications of resource allocation by international
hierarchies with those of Pareto optimality offered
by perfect markets. In consequence, Hymer overlooked the fact that increased profits from the
superior efficiency of foreign firms is not necessarily
a social loss if the prices of the final products are not
higher than they would otherwise be (Teece, 1985).
The emphasis placed by Hymer on the organization
of economic activity by MNEs as a means of
advancing monopoly power, rather than of reducing
costs, improving product quality or fostering innovations, also led him to consider the alternatives
between FDI and other forms of international
involvement in normative terms, rather than by a
reasoned analysis of the costs and benefits of these
options.

In a later paper, first published in French,
Hymer (1968) took a rather different approach to
explaining international production. Here, he sought
– in his own words 'to consider things from the firm's
point of view . . . and the reasons for it to become
multinational as well as the obstacles it may
encounter on the way'. In developing his analysis,
Hymer drew very heavily on the ideas of Coase
(1937), whose work he did not acknowledge in his
thesis. Hymer applied the analysis of Coase to
suggest reasons why firms might wish to engage in
cross-border vertical integration. Although he did
not fully develop his argument, Hymer did appear to
acknowledge that MNEs might help to improve
international resource allocation by circumventing
market failure. To this extent at least, his 1968
contribution is a natural point of departure for the
more rigorous work of the internalization economists
in the following decade.[6]

4.2.3   The product cycle

If Hymer used industrial and organizational economics to explain MNE activity, Raymond Vernon

and his colleagues at Harvard were the first to
acknowledge the relevance of some of the newer
trade theories put forward in the 1950s and 1960s[7] to
help explain this phenomenon. In a classic article
published in 1966, Vernon used a micro-economic
concept – the product cycle – to help explain a
macro-economic phenomenon, *viz* the foreign activities of US MNEs in the post-war period. His starting
point was that in addition to immobile natural
endowments and human resources, the propensity of
countries to engage in trade also depended on their
capability to upgrade these assets or to create new
ones, notably technological capacity. He also hypothesized that the efficiency of firms in organizing
these human and physical assets was, in part at least,
country-specific in origin.

Drawing upon some earlier work by Posner
(1961), Vernon argued that the competitive or
ownership advantages of US firms – particularly their
capacity to innovate new products and processes –
was determined by the structure and pattern of US
factor endowments and markets. However, it was
quite possible that any initial competitive advantage
enjoyed by innovating enterprises might be eroded
or eliminated by the superior competence of firms in
other countries to produce the products based on
them. Without explicitly bringing market imperfections into his analysis, Vernon then switched his unit
of analysis to the firm and particularly the location of
its production. Initially, the product (or more
correctly, the value-added activities based on the
firm's proprietary assets) was produced for the home
market in the home country near to both its
innovatory activities and markets. At a later stage of
the product cycle, because of a favourable combination of innovating and production advantages offered
by the US, it was exported to other countries most
similar to the home country in demand patterns and
supply capabilities.

Gradually, as the product becomes standardized
or mature, the competitive advantages of producing
firms changes from those to do with the uniqueness
of product *per se*, to their ability to minimize the
costs of value-adding activities and/or their marketing expertise. The pressure to ensure cost efficiency
mounts as imitators start making inroads into the
market. At the same time, as demand becomes more
price elastic, as labour becomes a more important
ingredient of costs and as foreign markets expand,

the attractions of siting value-added activities in a foreign, rather than in a domestic, location increase. This might be hastened by the imposition of trade barriers or in anticipation of competitors setting up in these markets. Eventually, Vernon argued, if conditions in the host country are right, the subsidiary could replace exports from the parent company or even export back to it.

This approach to explaining foreign production was essentially an extension of the neo-classical theory of the spatial distribution of factor endowments to embrace intermediate products, together with an acknowledgement that strategic factors, arising from an oligopolistic market structure in which MNEs were observed to compete, influenced the response of firms to these endowments. It did not, however, address organizational issues. Since the competitive advantages of firms were assumed to be country-specific, little attention was paid to the kinds of advantages that arose specifically from the internalization of cross-border markets. In a later contribution, however, Vernon (1983) did explicitly identify the reduction of organizational risk as a motive for, and determinant of, FDI.

The product cycle model was introduced in the 1960s to explain market seeking production by firms of a particular nationality or ownership. It did not explain, nor purport to explain, resource based, efficiency seeking or strategic asset acquiring FDI. Like Hymer, Vernon offered a theory which was partial in that it addressed itself to only some of the issues surrounding MNE activity. On the other hand, the product cycle was the first dynamic interpretation of the determinants of, and relationship between, international trade and foreign production. It also introduced some novel hypotheses regarding demand stimuli, technology leads and lags, and information and communication costs, which have subsequently proved useful tools in the study of foreign production and exchange.

4.2.4 Follow up developments

Since the early 1970s there have been various attempts by economists to refine and test the theories of Hymer and Vernon. Of the former, the work of industrial economists like Caves (1971, 1974a, 1974b),

Horst (1972a, 1972b), Johnson (1970), Magee (1977a, 1977b), and a second generation of researchers such as Swedenborg (1979), Pugel (1981), Calvet (1980), Owen (1982), Lall (1979b, 1980), Lall and Siddharthan (1982) and Kumar (1990), is particularly worthy of note. Essentially, this group of scholars have sought to identify the kind of ownership advantages possessed by MNEs. Why is it (as we showed in Chapter 2) that FDI tends to be concentrated in certain primary, manufacturing and service sectors? Why does the share of the domestic output of a particular country accounted for by foreign-owned affiliates vary so much between economic activities?

Most of the above studies, and others which are discussed in some detail in Chapter 6, concentrated on trying to identify and assess the significance of specific intangible assets, such as technological capacity, labour skills, product differentiation, marketing skills and organizational capabilities, which afford a firm of one nationality an ownership advantage over that of another. Not surprisingly they found that the relevant variables varied between industry, country and sometimes between firms as well. Thus, whereas the privileged possession of, or access to, information technology and human capital explained much of US direct investment in producer goods and intermediate service industries, product differentiation and quality, as proxied by advertising intensity, was revealed as the dominant ownership advantage of US MNEs in consumer goods industries. A favoured access to markets or to large amounts of investment capital explained much of early UK investment in the mining and agri-business industries (Hennart, 1986b); just as it was later to attract a flood of Japanese investment into the European banking and finance sector in the 1980s. Advantages specific to European and Japanese owned MNEs were perceived to differ from each other and from those of their US counterparts – mainly because the economic and social characteristics of their countries of origin were different (Franko, 1976). The advantages that best explained the structure of US outward investment of the 1960s and 1970s failed to explain the pattern of inward investment in the US in the 1970s and 1980s (Lall and Siddharthan, 1982).

Stephen Magee (1977a, 1977b), in a more detailed examination of technology as a valued intangible asset, took rather a different line. He was primarily interested in why the incentive of firms to internalize the market for technology varied over time. He coined the concept of the industry technology cycle, which built upon the Vernon hypothesis that the competitive advantages of firms was likely to change over the life of the product. He argued that firms were unlikely to sell their rights to new and idiosyncratic technology for two reasons. First the fear that as a result of information inadequacy, the buying firm was unlikely to pay the selling firm a price that would yield at least as much economic rent as it could earn by using the technology itself. Second, the fear that the licensee might use the technology to the disadvantage of the licensor, and even become a competitor to it. As the technology matured, however, and lost some of its uniqueness, the need to internalize its use evaporated and the firm would consider switching its modality of transfer from FDI to licensing.

Around the same time, another group of scholars began to focus more specifically on the variables influencing the decision of firms to license their property rights as an alternative to FDI (Telesio, 1979; Contractor, 1981). However, although these scholars began to identify, more carefully, the circumstances in which firms might wish to control the use of the technological assets they possessed, they did not really grapple with the more fundamental issue of the organization of transactional relationships as part of a general paradigm of market failure. This task was left to another group of economists (see Section 4.3 of this chapter).

Other researchers – mainly from a business school tradition, and often from Harvard itself – built on the Vernon approach. A monograph summarizing some empirical research on the product cycle appeared in 1972 (Wells, 1972). Work on UK, Continental European and Japanese MNEs closely paralleled that on US MNEs (Franko, 1976; Stopford, 1976; Tsurumi, 1976; Yoshino, 1976). Perhaps of greater significance for the development of the theory of foreign production at this time were the findings of a group of Vernon's students, notably Knickerbocker (1973), Graham (1975) and Flowers (1976), that it was not just locational variables that determined the spatial distribution of the economic activity of firms but their strategic response to these variables and to the anticipated behaviour of their competitors. In a perfectly competitive market situation, strategic behaviour (like the firm itself) is a black box. This is simply because the firm has no freedom of action if it is to earn at least the opportunity cost on its investments. Its maximum and minimum profit positions are one and the same thing. However, once markets become imperfect as a result of structural distortions, uncertainty, externalities or economies of scale, then strategy begins to play an active role in affecting business conduct.

Nowhere is this more clearly seen than in an oligopolistic market situation where economists, for more than a century, have acknowledged that output and price equilibrium depends on the assumptions made by one firm about how its own behaviour will affect that of its competitors, and how, in turn, this latter behaviour will impinge upon its own position. Knickerbocker (1973) argued that, as risk minimizers, oligopolists, wishing to avoid destructive competition, would normally follow each other into new (e.g. foreign) markets, to safeguard their own commercial interests. An analysis of the timing of FDI by US MNEs in manufacturing industry prior to 1971 seemed to support this proposition (Knickerbocker, 1973), while since the mid 1970s there has been a good deal of bunching of Japanese MNE activity in the US and European auto and consumer electronics industries. In another study, Flowers (1976) showed that the Knickerbocker proposition also held for Canadian and European investment in the US as well as for US investment in Europe, whereas Graham (1975) viewed European investment in the US as a reaction by European firms to the incursion of their own territories by US MNEs. In particular, Graham hypothesized that an MNE which found its home territory invaded by a foreign MNE would retaliate by penetrating the invader's home turf. A frequently quoted example of the so-called 'exchange of threats' hypothesis is the entrance by Royal Dutch Shell in the US in the 1900s in response to Standard Oil's entry into Far Eastern markets which were previously dominated by Shell. Others include the cross-border activities of leading MNEs in the rubber tyre, automobile, colour television, advertising, banking and hotel sectors.[8]

Mention at this point should also be made of the pioneering work of Yair Aharoni in his attempt to trace and evaluate the decision-making process of firms contemplating FDI. His was primarily a micro-organizational study of the factors influencing: first, whether or not a firm is likely to contemplate making a foreign investment; second, the kind of feasibility study it undertakes to evaluate the costs and benefits of such investments; third, the decision to commit resources to a foreign investment; fourth, the terms negotiated with reviewing bodies in host countries; and fifth, the implications of the foreign commitment for the global organizational structure and strategy of the firm. Based on data provided by some 38 US MNEs that had undertaken foreign investments in the 1950s and 1960s, Aharoni identified both the kind of enterprise most likely to become an MNE and some unique properties of FDI. These include the relatively high information, search, negotiating and learning costs, and the associated risks.[9] *Inter alia*, Aharoni suggested these properties may explain why proportionately fewer small firms undertake foreign than domestic investment, and why licensing is sometimes a preferred modality of international involvement.

In retrospect, the work of these scholars and Vernon himself (1974), who acknowledged that the nature of a firm's foreign investment strategy would depend on its position in the product cycle, was not only pathbreaking in that it emphasized the behavioural interaction between firms, but also because it pinpointed a particular type of market failure, which was later formalized and incorporated into the organizational theories of the late 1970s.

To summarize, by the mid 1970s the two streams of explaining MNE activity pioneered by Hymer and Vernon were beginning to converge, although their focuses of interest remained very different. The industrial organization approach, which was concerned with identifying the main ownership-specific advantages of MNEs, was beginning to recognize that the way in which assets were created, acquired and organized was an advantage in its own right. By the mid 1970s, the trade/location approach had also begun to acknowledge the role of market imperfections, not only in affecting the ownership of firms, but also of the way in which firms chose to organize their cross-border activities. But, whereas Hymer viewed FDI as an aggressive strategy by firms to advance their monopoly power, Vernon and his colleagues perceived it more as a defensive strategy by firms to protect their existing market positions.

4.2.5 Other theoretical contributions: a selected view

To complete this short historical review, we briefly consider two other approaches to explaining MNE activity which, though outside the mainstream of thinking, when reinterpreted in terms of contemporary theorizing, offered (and still offer) valuable insights into both the location and ownership of international economic activity. Both approaches were developed by financial or macro-economists.

(i) *The risk diversification hypothesis* The risk diversification hypothesis was first put forward by Agmon and Lessard (1977), Lessard (1976, 1982) and Rugman (1975, 1979, 1980). Building on some earlier work by Grubel (1968) and Levy and Sarnat (1970), these scholars argued that the MNE offered individual or institutional equity investors a superior vehicle for geographically diversifying their investment portfolios than did the international equity market. This partly reflected the failure of the equity market to evaluate efficiently the risks or the benefits of risk diversification, and partly the fact that, compared with their domestic counterparts, MNEs possessed certain non-financial advantages that enabled them to manage the risks associated with international diversified portfolios more effectively. Empirical research (Agmon and Lessard, 1977) seems to support the idea that investors do recognize the benefits of diversification provided by MNEs. Rugman (1979) also found that the variance of US corporate earnings in the 1960s was inversely related to the ratio of their foreign to domestic operations, while Michel and Shaked (1986) have demonstrated that the MNEs are less likely to become insolvent than are domestic corporations. However, there remains some doubt as to the extent to which the gains of international diversification are reflected in the cost of equity to, or the share prices of, the investing firms.

Rugman and Lessard have further argued that, given that firms deemed it worthwhile to engage in FDI, the location of that investment would be a function of both the firm's perception of the uncertainties involved and the geographical distribution of its existing assets. In the absence of country specific hazards (foreign exchange risk, political and environmental instability, etc) firms would simply equate the returns earned on their assets in different countries at the margin, even if this meant concentrating these assets in only one country. However, as the uncertainty attached to the returns varied with the amount and concentration of assets, this would affect the geographical distribution of their foreign investments. In a later contribution, Rugman (1980) acknowledged that the risk diversification hypothesis is best considered as a special case of a more general theory of international market failure based upon the desire and ability of MNEs to minimize cross-border production and transaction costs.

(ii) *Macro-financial and exchange rate theories: The Aliber model* Robert Aliber (1970) took as his starting point the failure of financial markets identified by Hymer in his PhD thesis. However, unlike Hymer, Aliber was not concerned with why firms produce abroad but why they finance their foreign assets in their domestic currencies. He explained this in terms of the ability of firms from countries with strong currencies to borrow or raise capital in domestic or foreign markets more cheaply than can those from countries with weak currencies, which, in turn, enabled them to capitalize their expected income streams at different rates of interest. Aliber further argued that structural imperfections in the foreign exchange market allow firms to make foreign exchange gains through the purchase or sales of assets in an undervalued or overvalued currency.

Aliber's theory does not attempt to deal with many of the questions tackled by other scholars and should not therefore be judged by the same criteria. But neither does it have strong claim to be a general theory of FDI. It is difficult to see how it explains the industrial structure of foreign production or the cross-hauling of direct investment between weak and strong currency areas. It does, however, present some interesting ideas about the timing of FDI, particularly that of foreign takeovers, and of fluctuations around a long-term trend. It also offers some reasons as to why countries might shift their international investment status over time.

In many respects, Aliber's theory is better regarded as an extension of portfolio capital theory to incorporate market failure rather than as a theory of FDI *per se*. Indeed, his whole thesis rests on the presence and characteristics of imperfections in the capital and/or exchange markets. He asserts that such market failure tends to confer advantages on firms whose assets are denominated in certain currencies rather than others, and as a result affects the location of where they invest these assets. It is, however, unclear why firms should wish to control these assets. Hence, so is the distinction between the motives for direct rather than portfolio investment.[10] Finally, in practice it is the difference in the non-financial assets owned by enterprises that enables them to exploit imperfections in the financial exchange markets. To this extent, Aliber's theory is best regarded as one that is complementary to other explanations of FDI.

To the best of our knowledge, Aliber has never subjected his theory to rigorous empirical testing. However, an examination of the pattern of British direct investment in the US in the 1980s during which time there were substantial fluctuations in US and UK interest rates and the $/£ exchange rate reveals that there is only limited support for his thesis – at least as the predominant explanation for such investment.[11]

(iii) *Macro-financial and exchange rate theories: Exchange rate models* The role of exchange rates in influencing the location of MNE activity is acknowledged by many economists and business analysts. And yet it is only comparatively recently that the relationship has been systematically explored using macro-economic data. Frost and Stein (1989) present a model in which currency movements affect the geography of MNEs by altering relative wealth across countries, and demonstrate a significant negative correlation between the value of the US dollar and the propensity of foreign firms to invest in the US. However, other writers, like Cushman (1985) and Culem (1988) have argued that, rather than reflecting relative wealth, exchange rate movements mirror changes in relative real labour costs, and it is these that determine FDI. In a test of these alternative propositions, Klein and Rosengren (1990a) have demonstrated that the correlation between the exchange rate and US inbound direct investment during the 1980s supports the former rather than the latter hypothesis. In a subsequent paper, Klein and Rosengren (1990b) show that relative wealth is also an important determinant of outward US investment, especially when Japan (where there are significant barriers to acquisitions and mergers by foreign firms) is excluded as a host country.

4.3   GENERAL EXPLANATIONS OF MNE ACTIVITY

4.3.1   Introduction

By the mid 1970s it was becoming clear that none of the theories so far put forward to explain the foreign activities of MNEs could claim to be a general theory or paradigm, and that most were not seeking to explain the same phenomena. Of all the explanations, Hymer's original thesis and his 1968 article offered the most promise as a general paradigm, although those parts of it to which later researchers paid the most attention were primarily concerned with identifying the reasons why some firms, and not others, engaged in foreign production, rather than why cross-border value-added activities were organized in one way rather than in another.

In the mid 1970s three attempts were made to offer more holistic explanations of the foreign activities of firms, each of which has attracted widespread attention in the literature. Each uses a different unit of analysis; two are quite similar in approach, but the third is very different. These are, respectively, the internalization theory of the MNE, the eclectic paradigm of international production and the macro-economic theory of foreign direct investment.

4.3.2   Internalization theory

Internalization theory is essentially directed to explaining why the cross-border transactions of intermediate products are organized by hierarchies rather than determined by market forces. It was first put forward in the mid 1970s by a group of Swedish, Canadian, British and US economists working largely independently of each other.[12] Its basic hypothesis is that multinational hierarchies represent an alternative mechanism for arranging value-added activities across national boundaries to that of the market, and that firms are likely to engage in FDI whenever they perceive that the net benefits of their joint ownership of domestic and foreign activities, and the transactions arising from them, are likely to exceed those offered by external trading relationships. The core prediction of internalization theory is that, given a particular distribution of factor endowments, MNE activity will be positively related to the costs of organizing cross-border markets in intermediate products.

Internalization theory is primarily concerned with identifying the situations in which the markets for intermediate products are likely to be internalized, and hence those in which firms own and control value-adding activities outside their natural boundaries. Like earlier attempts to explain the growth of domestic firms (Penrose, 1958), it seeks to explain the international horizontal and vertical integration of value-added activities in terms of the relative costs and benefits of this form or organization relative to market transactions. Certain types of transactions between certain types of buyers and sellers incur higher costs than others. Hierarchical organizational costs are also likely to be industry, country and firm specific.

Internalization theory may be considered a general theory in so far as it is able to predict the situations in which firms choose to internalize foreign markets. In many respects, however, as one of its protagonists (Buckley, 1990) has recently suggested, it is better described as a paradigm than a theory, in as much as the kinds of market failure that determine one form of foreign added value activity may be quite different from that of another. For example, in some consumer goods or service industries, the inability of the market to ensure a seller of an intermediate product sufficient control over the quality of the final product which may bear the seller's name may be a reason for replacing that market by forward integration. By contrast, backward integration may be motivated by a perceived need to reduce the risk of interrupted suppliers or price hikes, while the common governance of multiple activities in dispersed locations may be prompted by the desire to gain economies external to the activities in question but internal to the firm owning them.

We shall discuss the concept of market failure in more detail in the following section of the chapter, which sets out a paradigm which, while accepting the logic of internalization theory, argues that it is not, in itself, sufficient to explain the level and structure of the production of a country's own firms outside their national boundaries, or of the production of foreign-owned firms in its midst. To a certain extent, this criticism is accepted by some of the internalization theorists. Both Buckley (1987) and Casson (1987) have acknowledged the need to integrate location-specific variables with internalization variables (which one admits are not independent of each other) to present a holistic theory of the MNE activity. The role of ownership specific variables set out by Hymer is rather more contentious. In the static model of internalization, these variables, which are the outcome of structural market imperfections and exist prior to the foreign investment being made, are taken to be exogenous. Others which are the result of a firm engaging in foreign production may be said to be the outcome of the act of internalization. However, viewing the growth of the firm as a dynamic process, the legitimacy of this assumption is questionable. For a firm's current core competences, for example, its innovatory ability, systemic organizational skills, marketing strategy, executive development or raising and managing capital, are the outcome of past decisions which, at the time they were taken, were endogenous to the firm. Here, once again, strategic considerations enter the picture (Buckley, 1991). We shall give more attention to this point in the final section of this chapter.

4.3.3   The eclectic paradigm

Introduction

The eclectic paradigm seeks to offer a general framework for determining the extent and pattern of both foreign-owned production undertaken by a country's own enterprises and also that of domestic production owned by foreign enterprises. Unlike internalization theory, it is not a theory of the MNE *per se*, but rather of the activities of enterprises engaging in cross-border value-adding activities. Neither is it a theory of foreign direct investment, in the Aliber sense of the word, as it is concerned with the foreign-owned output of firms rather than the way that output is financed. At the same time, it accepts that the propensity of firms to own foreign

income generating assets may be influenced by financial and/or exchange rate variables. Finally, the eclectic paradigm chiefly addresses itself to positive rather than normative issues. It prescribes a conceptual framework for explaining 'what is' rather than 'what should be' the level and structure of foreign value activities of enterprises.

The theory of MNE activity stands at the intersection between a macro-economic theory of international trade and a micro-economic theory of the firm. It is an exercise in macro resource allocation and organizational economics. The eclectic paradigm starts with the acceptance of much of traditional trade theory in explaining the spatial distribution of some kinds of output (which might be termed Heckscher-Ohlin-Samuelson (H-O-S) output). However, it argues that to explain the ownership of that output and the spatial distribution of other kinds of output which require the use of resources that are not equally accessible to all firms, two kinds of market imperfection must be present. The first is that of structural market failure which discriminates between firms (or owners of corporate assets) in their ability to gain and sustain control over property rights or to govern multiple and geographically dispersed value-added activities. The second is that of the failure of intermediate product markets to transact goods and services at a lower net cost than those which a hierarchy might have to incur.

Such variables as the structure of markets, transaction costs and the managerial strategy of firms then become important determinants of international economic activity. The firm is no longer a black box – neither are markets the sole arbiters of transactions. Both the distribution of factor endowments and the modality of economic organization are relevant to explaining the structure of trade and production. Moreover, firms differ in organizational systems, innovatory abilities and in their appraisal of and attitude to commercial risks and, indeed, in their strategic response to these (and other) variables. This framework is no less applicable to explaining certain kinds of trade where the advantages of the trading firms are not *country* but *firm* specific.

The economics of the paradigm

Economic involvement by one country's enterprises

in those of another may be for the purpose of supplying foreign or domestic markets, or both. Production for a particular foreign market may be wholly or partly located in the home country, in the foreign market, in a third country, or in a combination of the three. Similarly, production for the home market may be serviced from a domestic or a foreign location.

The capability and willingness of one country's enterprises to supply either a foreign or a domestic market from a foreign location depends on their possessing or being able to acquire certain assets not available, or not available at such favourable terms, to another country's enterprises. Such assets we have already referred to as ownership-specific (hereafter O) advantages because they are assumed to be unique to firms of a particular nationality of ownership. The word 'assets' is used in the Fisherian sense (Johnson, 1968) to mean resources capable of generating a future income stream. They include not only tangible assets, such as natural endowments, manpower and capital, but intangible assets or capabilities such as technology and information, managerial, marketing and entrepreneurial skills, organizational systems and access to intermediate or final goods markets. Such assets might be specific to a particular location (hereafter referred to as location-specific (L) assets) in their origin and use, but available to all firms. These include not only Ricardian type endowments, but also the cultural, legal, political and institutional environment in which they are deployed, market structure and government legislation and policies (Dunning, 1991a). Alternatively, the assets may be owned by (i.e. be proprietary to) particular enterprises of the home country, but capable of being used with other resources and capabilities in the home country or elsewhere. Such assets may take the form of a legally protected property right or a commercial monopoly. They may arise from the size, diversity or technical characteristics of firms, and the economies of joint production, sourcing and marketing. They may embrace resource availability, financial strength, entrepreneurial vision and managerial competence.

For some kinds of trade, it is sufficient for the exporting country to have only an L advantage over the importing country. That is to say, it is not necessary for the exporting firms to possess any O-specific assets over their indigenous competitors in the importing country. Much of the trade between developed and developing countries (which is of the Ricardian or H-O-S type) is of this kind. Other trade, such as that which mainly takes place among developed industrialized countries, involves innovatory or Schumpeterian type products, and is based more on the O advantages of the exporting firms. However, this presupposes that it is better to use these advantages in combination with L-bound assets in the exporting rather than in the importing (or in a third) country. Where, however, these latter assets favour the importing (or a third) country, foreign-owned production will replace trade.

To summarize, an act of MNE activity combines the export of intermediate products, requiring inputs in which the home country is relatively well endowed, with the use of resources in which the host country is relatively well endowed. But if this were all there were to it, we would not need a separate theory of international production: an extension of international trade theory to incorporate trade in intermediate products, allowing for the mobility of at least some resources, would be sufficient. On the other hand, attempts to explain patterns and levels of MNE activity without taking account of the distribution of location-bound endowments and capabilities are like throwing the baby out with the bathwater!

We have argued that the failure of the factor endowment approach to explain international production completely or, in some cases, even partially, arises simply because it predicates the existence of perfect markets both for final and intermediate goods. In neo-classical trade theory, this leads to all sorts of restrictive assumptions, such as atomistic competition, equality of production functions, the absence of risk and uncertainty and, implicitly at least, that technology is a free and instantaneously transferable good between firms and countries. Since the 1950s, economists have grappled to incorporate market imperfections into trade theory but, in the main, their attention has been directed to the final rather than the intermediate goods markets. Partly because of this, little attention has been paid to the organization of production and transactions across, or indeed within, national boundaries. Exceptions include the work of Batra and Ramachandran (1980), Ethier (1986), Gray (1992), Helpman and Krugman (1985), Horstman and Markusen (1986) and Markusen (1984). In situations where firms have some locational choice in the production of intermediate products, this is assumed to influence the export versus licensing decision on a foreign firm, rather than the export versus foreign production decision.

We have suggested that the lack of interest by traditional trade economists with ownership or governance questions arises because they have tended to assume – again implicitly rather than explicitly – that firms engage in only a single value-added activity. The effect on trade patterns of the vertical integration or horizontal diversification of firms or their reaction to uncertain markets or government intervention is rarely discussed in the literature.[13] Since the option of internalizing domestic markets for intermediate products within a country has not generally interested trade economists, it is hardly surprising that they have been relatively unconcerned with issues of international production.[14] Yet the unique characteristics of the MNE is that it is both multi-activity and engages in the internal transfer of intermediate products across national boundaries. Indeed it is the difference between domestic and international market failure that distinguishes multinational from uninational multi-activity firms. It is the inability of the market to organize a satisfactory deal between potential contractors and contractees of intermediate products that explains why one or the other should choose the hierarchial rather than the market route for exploiting differences in L-specific assets between countries. It is the presence of structural and cognitive market failure that causes firms to pursue different strategies towards the exploitation of O and L assets.

Several types of market failure are identified in the literature by such scholars as Anderson and Gatignon (1986), Buckley and Casson (1976, 1985), Casson (1979, 1982a, 1985, 1987) and Teece (1981a, 1985). In their assessment of the contribution of Hymer's thesis to the theory of MNE, Dunning and Rugman (1985) distinguished between *structural* and *transactional* market failure. The former, which Hymer tended to emphasize, gives rise to monopoly rents as a result of the presence of entry barriers which the constituent firms may seek to erect or increase by a variety of means, including the acquisition of competitors (which is itself a form of internalization).

However, a no less important, but very different, type of market imperfection (later acknowledged by Hymer (1968)) reflects the inability of the *qua* market to organize transactions in an optimal way. There are three reasons for this. The first is that buyers and sellers do not enter the market with complete (or symmetrical) information or perfect certainty about the consequences of the transactions they are undertaking. Such cognitive deficiencies give rise to bounded rationality, opportunism, adverse selection, moral hazard and information impactness which are the innate characteristics of some markets (Williamson, 1985; Teece, 1981, 1985). This kind of market failure is particularly likely to be associated with cross-border transactions. The MNE, if nothing else, engages in foreign production to protect itself against the opportunities of foreign buyers and sellers as well as to counteract (and in some cases exploit) political and environmental volatility (Kogut, 1985b). Such risks are particularly noteworthy in capital intensive primary product and high technology industries that typically incur high development costs; where there is a danger of disruption of supplies; where there is a likelihood of property rights being dissipated or abused by foreign licensees; and where a threat of the pre-emption of markets or sources of supplies by rival oligopolists will encourage a follow-my-leader strategy by firms (Vernon, 1983).

The second reason for transactional market failure is that the market cannot take account of the benefits and costs that arise as a result of a particular transaction, but which are external to that transaction. Where products are normally supplied jointly with others, or are derived from a common input or set of inputs, this may provide a good reason for different stages of the value-added chain, or the same stage of different value-added chains, to be coordinated under the same governance. Cross-border transactions may give rise to additional advantages of common ownership such as those which exploit the imperfections of international capital and exchange markets and different national fiscal policies.

The third cause of transactional market failure arises wherever the demand for a particular product, while infinitely elastic, is insufficiently large to enable the producing firms fully to capture the economies of size, scope and geographical diversification. In other words, there is an inevitable tradeoff between the overall costs of a set of value-added activities and the opportunities they offer for synergistic economies (Galbraith and Kay, 1986). Such economies may be in direct production, in the sourcing, marketing, innovatory and financial activities of firms or, indeed, in their strategies towards risk reduction and the behaviour of competitors.

It is these and other market deficiencies which may cause enterprises, be they uninational or multinational, to diversify their value-adding activities and in so doing realign the ownership and organization of these activities. They do so partly to maximize the net benefits of lower production or transaction costs arising from common governance and partly to ensure that they gain the maximum economic rent (discounted for risk) from the O advantages they possess. We shall refer to such perceived advantages of hierarchical control as internalization (I) advantages. Again, the only difference between the actions of multinational and uninational producers in this respect is the added dimension of market failure when a particular transaction or diversification of economic activity is undertaken across the exchanges. Moreover, market failure may vary according to the characteristics of the parties engaging in the transactions. Here, too, country-specific factors may enter the equation. Returning to our parallel between firms engaged in international trade and international production, it is quite possible that while both may engage in exactly the same value-added activities, the former will do so within a single country and export their final product, whereas the latter will locate at least part of their production outside their national boundaries.

The distinctive characteristic of the MNE activity is, then, that it marries the trans-border dimension of value-added activities of firms with the common governance of those activities. While the former draws upon the economics of the spatial distribution of immobile resources and the theory of market structures to explain the location of production independently of its ownership, the theory of market failure helps to explain the organization and ownership of production independently of its location. The precise character and pattern of the resulting international production will depend on the configuration of the O assets of firms and the L assets of countries, as well as on the extent to which firms perceive that

they (rather than markets) possess net I advantages in organizing these O and L assets. Given these variables, it will also depend upon the strategic options open to firms and how they evaluate the consequences of these options.

The main tenets of the paradigm

The principal hypothesis on which the eclectic paradigm of international production is based is that the level and structure of a firm's foreign value-adding activities will depend on four conditions being satisfied. These are:

(1) The extent to which it possesses sustainable ownership-specific (O) advantages *vis-à-vis* firms of other nationalities in the particular markets it serves or is contemplating serving. These O advantages largely take the form of the privileged possession of intangible assets as well as those which arise as a result of the common governance of cross-border value-added activities. These advantages and the use made of them (see 2 and 3 below) are assumed to increase the wealth creating capacity of a firm, and hence the value of its assets.[15]

(2) Assuming condition (1) is satisfied, the extent to which the enterprise perceives it to be in its best interest to add value to its O advantages rather than to sell them, or their right of use, to foreign firms. These advantages are called market internalization (I) advantages. They may reflect either the greater organizational efficiency of hierarchies or their ability to exercise monopoly power over the assets under their governance.

(3) Assuming conditions (1) and (2) are satisfied, the extent to which the global interests of the enterprise are served by creating, or utilizing, its O advantages in a foreign location. The distribution of these resources and capabilities is assumed to be uneven and, hence, depending on their distribution, will confer an L advantage on the countries possessing them over those who do not.

(4) Given the configuration of the ownership, location and internalization (OLI) advantages facing a particular firm, the extent to which a

firm believes that foreign production is consistent with its long-term management strategy.

The generalized predictions of the eclectic paradigm are straightforward. At any given moment of time, the more a country's enterprises – relative to those of another – possess O advantages, the greater the incentive they have to internalize rather than externalize their use, the more they find it in their interest to exploit them from a foreign location, then the more they are likely to engage in outbound production. By the same token, a country is likely to attract investment by foreign MNEs when the reverse conditions apply. Similarly, the paradigm can be expressed in a dynamic form. Changes in the outward or inward direct investment position of a particular country can be explained in terms of changes in the O advantages of its enterprises relative to those of other nations, changes in its L assets relative to those of other countries, changes in the extent to which firms perceive that these assets (and any others it may acquire) are best organized internally rather than by the market, and changes in the strategy of firms which may affect their reaction to any given OLI configuration.

Table 4.1 identifies some of the more important OLI advantages. Some of these can best explain the initial act of FDI. Others, and particularly those which are to do with the common governance of geographically dispersed activities, are more helpful in explaining sequential acts of foreign production (Kogut, 1983). Industrial organization theory mainly explains the nature of the O advantages that arise from the possession of particular intangible assets. Elsewhere (Dunning, 1988a) we have called these asset advantages (Oa). They are to be distinguished from those that arise from the ability of a firm to coordinate multiple and geographically dispersed value-added activities and to capture the gains of risk diversification. These we refer to as transaction cost minimizing advantages (Ot). The theory of property rights and the internalization paradigm explain why firms engage in foreign activity to exploit or acquire these advantages. Theories of location and trade explain the factors determining the siting of production. Theories of oligopoly and business strategy explain the likely reaction of firms to particular OLI configurations.

The eclectic paradigm suggests that all forms of foreign production by all countries can be explained by reference to the above conditions. It makes no *a priori* predictions about which countries, industries or enterprises are most likely to engage in foreign direct investment, but it does hypothesize that at least some of the advantages identified in Table 4.1 will not be evenly spread across countries, industries and enterprises. It also accepts that such advantages are not static and that a firm's strategic response to any particular OLI configuration may affect the nature and pattern of its O and I advantages in a later period of time (Dunning, 1991b).

Although the three strands in the explanation of international production interact with each other, conceptually there is something to be said for considering them separately. Certainly the location and mode of foreign involvement are two quite independent decisions which a firm has to take, even though the final decision on where to locate its production will itself depend on the network and characteristics of its O advantages and the extent to which it perceives that that location might help it to internalize intermediate product markets better than another. It may also depend on the extent to which, as a result of any bargaining power it may have *vis-à-vis* a foreign government, it may be able to raise its O advantages or the advantages of the country in which it is contemplating an investment (Grosse and Behrman, 1992).[16] Take also the distinction between O and I advantages. O advantages may be internally generated (e.g. through product diversification or innovations) or acquired from other enterprises. If acquired, for example, by way of a purchase (be it domestic or foreign) of another enterprise, the presumption is that this will add to the acquiring firm's O advantages *vis à vis* those of its competitors. Elsewhere (Dunning, 1988a) we have argued that it is useful to distinguish between the *capacity* to organize value-added activities in a particular way and the *willingness* to opt for one mode of organization rather than another.

We have suggested that the eclectic paradigm offers the basis for a general explanation of international production. We illustrate this point by reference to Table 4.2 which relates the main types of foreign activities by MNEs, set out in Chapter 3, to the presence or absence of the OLI advantages making for such activities. Such a matrix can be used as a starting point for an examination of both the

Table 4.1   The eclectic paradigm of international production.[1]

1.   *Ownership-specific advantages* of an enterprise of one nationality (or affiliates of same) over those of another.

(a)   Property rights and/or intangible asset advantages (Oa); the resource (asset) structure of the firm. Product innovations, production management, organizational and marketing systems, innovatory capacity, organization of work, non-codifiable knowledge: 'bank' of human capital experience; marketing, finance, know-how, etc. Ability to reduce costs of intra and/or inter-firm transactions.

(b)   Advantages of common governance, that is, of organizing Oa with complementary assets (Ot).

   (i)   Those that branch plants of established enterprises may enjoy over *de novo* firms. Those resulting mainly from size, product diversity and learning experiences of enterprise (e.g. economies of scope and specialization). Exclusive or favoured access to inputs (e.g. labour, natural resources, finance, information). Ability to obtain inputs on favoured terms (e.g. as a result of size or monopsonistic influence). Ability of parent company to conclude productive and cooperative inter-firm relationships, for example, as between Japanese auto assemblers and their suppliers. Exclusive or favoured access to product markets. Access to resources of parent company at marginal cost. Synergistic economies (not only in production, but in purchasing, marketing, finance, etc, arrangements).

   (ii)   Which specifically arise because of multinationality. Multinationality enhances operational flexibility by offering wider opportunities for arbitraging, production shifting and global sourcing of inputs. More favoured access to and/or better knowledge about international markets (e.g. for information, finance, labour, etc). Ability to take advantage of geographic differences in factor endowments, government intervention, markets, etc. Ability to diversify or reduce risks (e.g. in different currency areas and creation of options and/or political and cultural scenarios). Ability to learn from societal differences in organizational and managerial processes and systems. Balancing economies of integration need to respond to differences in country-specific resources and consumer demands.

2.   *Internalization incentive advantages* (i.e. to circumvent or exploit market failure).
   To avoid search and negotiating costs.
   To avoid costs of moral hazard and adverse selection, and to protect reputation of internalizing firm.
   To avoid cost of broken contracts and ensuing litigation.
   Buyer uncertainty (about nature and value of inputs, for example, technology, being sold).
   When market does not permit price discrimination.
   Need of seller to protect quality of intermediate or final products.
   To capture economies of interdependent activities (see (b) above).
   To compensate for absence of future markets.
   To avoid or exploit government intervention (quotas, tariffs, price controls, tax differences, etc).
   To control supplies and conditions of sale of inputs (including technology).
   To control market outlets (including those which might be used by competitors).
   To be able to engage in practices, such as cross-subsidization, predatory pricing, leads and lags, transfer pricing as a competitive (or anti-competitive) strategy.

3.   *Location-specific variables* (these may favour home or host countries).
   Spatial distribution of natural and created resource endowments and markets.
   Input prices, quality and productivity (e.g. labour, energy, materials, components, semifinished goods).
   International transport and communication costs.
   Investment incentives and disincentives (including performance requirements, etc).
   Artificial barriers (e.g. import controls) to trade in goods and services.
   Societal and infrastructure provisions (commercial, legal, educational, transport and communication).
   Cross-country ideological, language, cultural, business, political differences.
   Economies of centralization of R&D production and marketing.
   Economic system and strategies of government: the institutional framework for resource allocation.

1   These variables are culled from a variety of sources, but see especially Dunning (1981b, 1988b) and Ghoshal (1987).

Table 4.2 Types of international production: some determining factors.

Types of international production	(O) Ownership advantages (The 'why' of MNE activity)	(L) Location advantages (The 'where' of production)	(I) Internalization advantages (the 'how' of involvement)	Strategic(s) goals of MNEs	Illustration of types of activity that favour MNEs
Natural resource seeking	Capital, technology, access to markets; complementary assets; size and negotiating strengths.	Possession of natural resources and related transport and communications infrastructure; tax and other incentives.	To ensure stability of supplies at right price; control markets.	To gain privileged access to resources vis-à-vis competitors.	(a) Oil, copper, bauxite, bananas, pineapples, cocoa, hotels. (b) Export processing, labour intensive products or processes.
Market seeking	Capital, technology, information, management and organizational skills; surplus R&D and other capacity; economies of scale; ability to generate brand loyalty.	Material and labour costs; market size and characteristics; government policy (e.g. with respect to regulations and to import controls, investment incentives, etc).	Wish to reduce transaction or information costs, buyer ignorance, or uncertainty, etc; to protect property rights.	To protect existing markets, counteract behaviour of competitors; to preclude rivals or potential rivals from gaining new markets.	Computers, pharmaceuticals, motor vehicles, cigarettes, processed foods, airline services.
Efficiency seeking (a) of products (b) of processes	As above, but also access to markets; economies of scope, geographical diversification, and international sourcing of inputs.	(a) Economies of product specialization and concentration. (b) Low labour costs; incentives to local production by host governments.	(a) As for second category plus gains from economies of common governance. (b) The economies of vertical integration and horizontal diversification.	As part of regional or global product rationalization and/or to gain advantages of process specialization.	(a) Motor vehicles, electrical appliances, business services, some R&D. (b) Consumer electronics, textiles and clothing, cameras, pharmaceuticals.

Strategic asset seeking	Any of first three that offer opportunities for synergy with existing assets.	Any of first three that offer technology, markets and other assets in which firm is deficient.	Economies of common governance; improved competitive or strategic advantage; to reduce or spread risks.	To strengthen global innovatory or production competitiveness; to gain new product lines or markets.	Industries that record a high ratio of fixed to overhead costs and which offer substantial economies of scale or synergy.
Trade and distribution (import and export merchanting)	Market access; products to distribute.	Source of inputs and local markets; need to be near customers; after-sales servicing, etc.	Need to protect quality of inputs; need to ensure sales outlets and to avoid under-performance or misrepresentation by foreign agents.	Either as entry to new markets or as part of regional or global marketing strategy.	A variety of goods, particularly those requiring contact with subcontractors and final consumers.
Support services	Experience of clients in home countries.	Availability of markets, particularly those of 'lead' clients.	Various (see above categories).	As part of regional or global product or geographical diversification.	(a) Accounting, advertising, banking, producer goods. (b) Where spatial linkages are essential (e.g. airlines and shipping).

Table 4.3 Some illustrations of how OLI characteristics may vary according to country-, industry-, and firm-specific circumstances.

OLI variables	Country or region	Structural variables — Industry or activity	Firm
Ownership	Factor endowments (e.g. resources and skilled labour) and market size and character. Government policy towards innovation, protection of proprietary rights, competition, education and training, and industrial structure. Government attitudes towards internalization of business and cross-border alliances. The organizational culture and wealth-creating ethos of a country. The nature of corporate governance and inter-firm rivalry and/or cooperation.	Degree of product or process technological intensity; nature of innovations; extent of product differentiation; production economies (e.g. if there are economies of scale); transaction economies (e.g. if there are economies of scope); importance of favoured access to inputs and/or markets.	The structure of the asset (resource) base, size, extent of production, process or market diversification; extent to which enterprise is innovative, marketing oriented or values security and/or stability (e.g. with respect to sources of inputs, markets); extent to which there are economies of joint production and entrepreneurial vision; attitudes to risk taking and the strategy of asset accumulation and usage.
Internalization	Government intervention and extent to which policies encourage MNEs to internalize transactions (e.g. transfer pricing); government policy towards mergers; differences in market structures between countries with respect to transaction costs, enforcement of contracts, buyer uncertainty etc; adequacy of technological, educational and communications infrastructure in host countries; and their ability to absorb contractual resource transfers.	Extent to which vertical or horizontal integration is possible/desirable (e.g. need to control sourcing of inputs or markets); extent to which internalizing advantages can be captured in contractual agreement (cf. early and later stages of product cycle); use made of ownership advantages (cf IBM with Unilever type operation); extent to which local firms have complementary advantages to those of foreign firms; extent to which opportunities for output specialization and international division of labour exist.	Organizational and control procedures of the enterprise; attitudes to growth and diversification (e.g. the boundaries of a firm's activities); attitudes towards subcontracting and contractual ventures such as licensing, franchising, technical assistance agreements; extent of which control procedures can be built into contractual agreements.
Location	Physical and psychic distance between countries; government intervention (e.g. tariffs, quotas, taxes, assistance to foreign investors or to own MNEs). An example is the Japanese government's financial aid to Japanese firms investing in South East Asian labour-intensive industries.	Origin and distribution of immobile resources; transport costs of intermediate and final goods product; industry-specific tariff and non-tariff barriers; nature of competition between firms in industry; can functions of activities of industry be split? Significance of 'sensitive' locational variables, e.g. tax incentives, energy and communication costs.	Management strategy towards foreign involvement; age and experience of foreign involvement (position of enterprise in product cycle, etc); psychic distance variables (culture, language, legal and commercial framework); attitudes towards centralization of functions such as R&D and market allocation; geographical structure of asset portfolio and attitudes to risk diversification.

industrial and geographical composition of FDI.

In seeking to test the kind of hypotheses implied in Table 4.2, in Chapter 6 we shall find it useful to distinguish between three contextual or structural variables that will influence the OLI configuration affecting any MNE activity, *viz* those which are specific to particular countries (or regions), to particular types of activities (or industries) and particular firms. In other words, the propensity of enterprises of a particular nationality to engage in FDI will vary according to the economic *et al.* specific characteristics of their home country and the country(ies) in which they propose to invest, the range and types of products (including intermediate products) they intend to produce, and their underlying management and organizational strategies. Some of these characteristics are set out in Table 4.3.

Combining the data in Tables 4.1 and 4.3, we have the core of the eclectic paradigm which, we believe, offers a rich conceptual framework for explaining not only the level, form and growth of MNE activity, but the way in which such activity is organized. Furthermore, as Parts 3 and 4 of this volume will seek to show, the paradigm offers a robust tool for analysing the role of FDI as an engine of growth and development; for predicting the economic consequences of MNE activity for the Nation States in which it operates; and for evaluating the extent to which the policies of home and host governments are likely both to affect and be affected by that activity.

The eclectic paradigm and other explanations of MNE activity

What, then, is the unique value of the eclectic paradigm? The paradigm avers that, given the distribution of specific assets, enterprises that have the most pronounced O advantages and perceive they can best exploit these by combining them with others in a foreign territory are likely to be the most successful international or global players. Enterprises will engage in the type of internationalization most suited to the factor combinations, market situations and government intervention with which they are faced. For example, our analysis would suggest not only that R&D intensive industries would tend to be more globally managed and controlled than others, but also that the incentive for internalization of

foreign-based raw material markets is likely to be greater for enterprises from economies that have few indigenous natural resources than for those that are self-sufficient; that the most efficient MNEs will exploit the most profitable foreign markets; and that the participation of foreign affiliates is likely to be greatest in those sectors of host countries where there are substantial economies of enterprise size. These conclusions are consistent with Horst's conclusion (1972a) that most of the explanatory variables of FDI may be captured in the size of an enterprise. Indeed, one would normally expect a firm's size and its propensity to internalize intermediate product markets to be closely correlated, and for MNEs to be better equipped to spread risks than national multi-product firms.

What does the eclectic paradigm predict that the other theories of international production do not? Taking the theories as a group, probably very little, except in so far as the independent variables set out in these theories fail to capture the advantages of internalization. Indeed, it could be argued that the paradigm is less an alternative theory of international production than one which pinpoints the essential and common characteristics of each of the mainstream explanations. At the same time, there are some important differences of emphasis. The eclectic paradigm, for example, argues that it is not only the possession of technology *per se* that gives an enterprise selling goods embodying the technology to foreign markets (irrespective of where they are produced) an edge over its competitors, but also the gains that follow from internalizing the use made of the technology. It is not the orthodox type of monopoly advantages that give the enterprise an edge over its rivals – actual or potential – but the gains that may accrue from internalizing the use of these advantages, for example, by transfer price manipulation and control over market access. It is not surplus entrepreneurial resources *per se* that lead to FDI, but the ability of enterprises to combine these resources with others to take advantage of the economies of scale and scope. It is not just the avoidance or reduction of political or exchange risks that influences the location of MNE activity, but the wider benefits that arise from operating in diverse environments.

In other words, without the incentive to internalize the markets for intangible assets and without the economies of scale and scope offered by the common governance of activities, FDI in technology-based industries would normally give way to cross-border licensing agreements and/or the outright sale of knowledge on a contractual basis. Without the incentive to lower the transaction costs of cross-border markets, there would be much less reason to engage in vertical or horizontal integration, and again trade would take place between independent firms. This, it could be argued, is the distinctiveness of the eclectic paradigm.

At the same time, the main difference between the determinants of intra-national and international production lies in the unique economic, political and cultural characteristics of separate sovereign states. Any theory of MNE activity must then seek to identify and evaluate OLI advantages, which specifically arise from foreign production; and how the strategic response of firms to these advantages might differ because they are operating within and between different environments. For example, why do US auto subsidiaries in some countries buy out a higher proportion of their components than in others? What are the particular common governance advantages which arise by producing in different currency areas? What is the role of government regulation in affecting the choice between foreign and domestic investment?

Finally, we would observe that various components of the eclectic paradigm are similar (though rarely identical) to those used by scholars interested in explaining the globalization of markets and production. To give just one example, at this point, the O advantages of the paradigm embrace the competitive advantages of firms as identified by Michael Porter in his various studies (Porter, 1981, 1985, 1986). However, we prefer our nomenclature as a firm may possess intangible assets which are better described as monopolistic rather than competitive. An exclusive access to a critical raw material is one such example. Similarly, Porter's 'diamond' of competitive advantages (Porter, 1990) offers a useful framework for analysing the interaction between some of the main advantages of countries, while his analysis of the factors influencing the extent to which an enterprise coordinates its value activities across national boundaries (i.e. the way it utilizes its I advantages) draws heavily on the work of internalization scholars.

In the course of this volume, we shall not hesitate to make use of the work of Porter and several other scholars from various disciplines as and when it helps to illuminate our understanding of the transnationalization of economic activity and its impact on the competitiveness of Nation States. Chapter 10, in particular, will set forth a general model of the interaction between FDI, asset accumulation and economic development, which is eclectic both in its approach and its sources of inspiration!

4.3.4 Some dynamics of MNE activity

Recent contributions to the literature on the determinants of MNE activity have increasingly distinguished between the initial act of foreign direct investment and sequential investment. In a chapter in a book edited by Kindleberger and Audretsch (1983), Bruce Kogut persuasively argued that although the possession of superior intangible assets may give rise to the initial act of foreign production, once established abroad the advantages of multinationality *per se*, that is, those gained from the spreading of environmental risks and the common governance of diversified activities in dispersed locations, become more significant. In a later paper, Kogut also related the international strategy of MNEs to the source of these sequential advantages[17] and to their learning experiences in coordinating domestic and foreign production (Kogut, 1987). On similar lines, Bartlett and Ghoshal (1988, 1990) have asserted that MNEs operating in a variety of environments are exposed to multiple stimuli which enable them to develop competencies and learning opportunities not open to domestic firms.

At the same time, as Chapters 2 and 3 have shown, an increasing proportion of intra-Triad investment by both established and first time MNEs is undertaken to acquire assets that will sustain, or add to, their own O advantages. Though this hypothesis has not been subject to any formal testing, there is sufficient casual evidence to suggest that, as markets become internalized, large MNEs are increasingly viewing the geographical portfolio of their assets and the formation of cross-border alliances as an integral part of their global marketing strategies.

Progress on advancing understanding about the

dynamics of foreign production has been less satisfactory. The literature identifies three main strands. The first is an extension of the product cycle model which examined the process of the internationalization of production. Most of this kind of research has so far been directed to explaining either how the location of value-added activity arising from the Oa advantages of firms or the modes of exploiting these advantages might vary over time. The general proposition is that as a firm becomes more international, it will first replace exports of low value activities by foreign production. This may later be followed by the foreign production of high value activities (Vernon, 1966, 1974). An alternative view is that as a firm moves through its technology cycle – from the innovatory to the mature stage – there is less reason to suppose it will need or wish to internalize the markets for that technology. Hence foreign-owned production might expect to be replaced by licensing (Magee, 1977). More recently, economists and business analysts have paid more attention to the nature of the O advantages (as described above) of MNEs and the location of the different kinds of activities that create these advantages. For example, the increasing dispersion of R&D laboratories by MNEs, especially in industrial countries, is now being put down to their need to establish an innovatory presence in the main technology producing centres of the world, *viz* Western Europe, the United States and Japan.[18]

The second strand looks at a firm's strategy as a dynamic force that bridges its internationalization posture of a firm at different periods of time. The argument runs as follows. At any given moment of time, a firm is faced with a configuration of OLI variables and strategic objectives to which it will respond by engaging in a variety of actions relating to technology creation, market positioning, the formation of corporate alliances, organizational structure, political lobbying, intra-firm pricing, etc. These actions, together with changes in the value of the exogenous variables it faces, will influence its overall competitive position and hence its OLI configuration at a future date. An explanation of the strategy of MNEs then becomes central to an understanding of the dynamics of international production. Not only will the kind of firm-specific characteristics set out in Table 4.3 be important, but so also will how the firm perceives that its competitors will react to any

change in its own internationalization strategy. Here economic and behavioural theories of the firm interact with each other.[19]

Third, and linked to the other two strands, have been attempts by economic theorists and political economists to model the extent to which the internationalization of production is linked to the ability of firms to accumulate, integrate and control O advantages across national boundaries. There are a number of variants of this approach. We shall consider just two. The first is the so-called technological accumulation approach (Cantwell, 1989, 1990) which draws upon some ideas of Rosenberg (1976, 1982) and suggests that the innovation of firm-specific technology is a cumulative process. The creation of new technology and new technological systems is best understood as a series of time-related adjustments and refinements. Each firm, because of the differences in its OLI configuration and its strategic response to these variables, will develop a unique and differentiated technological trajectory or path, each step of which needs to be learned and coordinated with that which preceded it. The more complex, path dependent and widely dispersed the technology is, the more the learning process needs to be internalized. However, although technological competence is often a firm-specific asset, its creation and sustenance is often dependent on the innovating capabilities and market characteristics of the countries in which the firm locates its production. It is also likely to vary according to the extent of a firm's multinationalization and its strategy towards the cross-border organization of its R&D activities (Cantwell, 1991;[20] Dunning, 1992d). The path of international production, then, requires an appreciation of the interaction between the technological assets of firms and the specific endowments of countries over time, as well as at a given moment of time.

It is possible to extend this approach to incorporate other O-specific advantages. The sequential analysis of Kogut (1983) also touches upon this. It is worth observing that while there is nothing automatic about a firm increasing the internationalization of its production, recent technological developments and the lowering of cross-border transport and communication costs have probably raised rather than reduced the incentive of firms to conclude collusive agreements to protect or advance their market power. This is in line with the earlier contention of Hymer that the MNE is an instrument of monopoly capitalism. However, the empirical evidence on this question is mixed. While the data shows that large multinationals are continuing to account for the bulk of foreign production and that cross-border non-equity alliances are growing, there appears to be no letting up in the competition for markets between MNEs. Indeed, as a result of the emergence of new foreign investors (especially those of medium size and of Japanese origin) and of the dispersal of production facilities, the evidence suggests that MNEs are at least as responsive to changes in the environment in which they operate as they are shapers of that environment.

4.3.5   The investment development path

Finally, we turn to consider an application of the OLI paradigm to explain the changing level and pattern of MNE activity into and out of a country as it proceeds along its development path. In doing so, we shall make use of the concept of the investment development cycle or path (Dunning, 1981, 1986, 1988a). The basic hypothesis of the concept is that, as a country develops, the configuration of the OLI advantages facing foreign-owned firms that might invest in that country and of its own firms that might invest overseas, changes, and that it is possible to identify the conditions making for the change as well as its effect on the trajectory of development. The concept also suggests ways in which the interaction between foreign and domestic firms might itself influence the country's investment path, but only recently has this aspect been incorporated into the literature (Tolentino, 1992).

The investment development path identifies several stages of development a country may pass through.[21] The first stage is one of pre-industrialization in which a country is presumed to attract no inward, or engage in any outward, investment, in the first case because it has insufficient L (or ESP) attractions, and in the second because its own firms possess inadequate O advantages. Moving to its next stage of development, then, depending on how successfully it has managed to upgrade its resources and capabilities and enlarge its markets, the OLI configuration facing its own foreign investors will change so as to first attract inward investment in resource-based sectors, in the traditional and labour-intensive manufacturing sectors, in trade and distribution, and transport and communications, construction, and perhaps some tourism.

Depending very much on the extent to which the country is able to create a satisfactory legal system, commercial infrastructure and business culture, and to provide both domestic and foreign firms with the transport and communication facilities and human resources they need; and depending on government policy towards inward direct investment (cf Japan, which largely disallowed such investment in the 1960s, with Germany, which adopted an open-door policy towards it), its L attractions will increase. Also, because foreign firms are likely to have more experience in manufacturing the goods and services now likely to be demanded, inward investment will grow. Gradually it and any investment by indigenous firms will affect both supply and demand conditions for the products supplied by foreign firms and their desire to internalize their markets for the competitive advantages. To begin with, L and O advantages are likely to complement each other. Then, as supply capabilities improve they give rise to agglomerative or cluster-type economies and increases in labour productivity. The introduction of new machinery and production methods is likely to lead to lower real labour costs and scale economies. The latter are also made possible by growing markets.

The improvement in the L specific advantages of a country may also help indigenous firms to develop their own O advantages. The growth of Japanese outward investment and, more recently, that of several developing countries is entirely consistent with a reconfiguration of the OLI advantages of indigenous firms brought about by the development process. Once again, the values of both exogenous and endogenous variables will change and affect each of these components. In these initial stages of development, the role of government is especially important (Porter, 1990). In an unpublished paper, Ozawa (1989) shows the absolutely critical role of the Japanese government in influencing the ability of Japanese firms to generate competitive advantages relative to their competitors and to locate their value-added activities outside Japan. It has also affected the strategy of the Japanese companies themselves. Studies of other East Asian economies point to a similarly important role of governments (Wade, 1989).

As countries move along their development paths, the OLI configuration facing outward and inward investors continues to change. Some foreign (and domestic) firms, which earlier found the country attractive to invest in because of its low labour costs or plentiful natural resources are no longer tempted to do so. At the same time, new L advantages arise based upon larger markets and the ability of a country to accumulate created assets such as human capital and innovatory capacity. This, in turn, makes it possible for domestic firms to develop their own O advantages and begin exporting capital.

Eventually, as and when countries reach some degree of economic maturity, the OLI configuration facing their own firms may be such that their propensity to engage in outward direct investment exceeds that of foreign-based firms to engage in inward investment. Again, whether or not this actually happens rests on the strategy of firms and governments to generate the resources and capabilities necessary to attract domestic and foreign investors. The literature is replete with examples of the kind of variables likely to influence the way in which the OLI configuration changes over time and the determinants of the value of these variables. Predictions for individual countries are difficult because they involve predicting the behaviour of governments. Different countries at the same stage of their development paths seem to display different propensities for different reasons. Thus, in the early 1990s both Sweden and Japan are significant net outward investors. However, whereas the foreign venturing by Japanese firms represents a positive restructuring to make way for the upgrading of their domestic industries, in the Swedish case it is more symptomatic of the falling competitiveness of the domestic economy.

We have dwelt at some length on the investment development path because it does introduce a dynamic element into the theory of international production. The configuration of OLI variables affecting (say) Japanese firms in the world economy in 1988 is a function of the OLI configuration facing them in (say) 1968 as well as of changes in the endogenous and exogenous variables which have affected their behaviour in the intervening period.

Of these, there is strong evidence that the way in which these two sets of variables interact is, itself, an important factor determining the movement towards a new OLI configuration. We also believe that the concept outlined is very relevant in explaining the growth of outward investment from Third World countries, especially from Korea, India, Singapore, Hong Kong and Taiwan.

4.3.6   A macro-economic approach to understanding MNE activity

Both the internalization and eclectic paradigms of international production are essentially micro-economic or behavioural explanations in the sense that they attempt to identify and evaluate the variables that determine the foreign activities of particular firms or groups of firms. Using the same data to explain the determinants of a country's propensity to engage in foreign production is legitimate only in so far as the actions of individual producers do not affect the value of the variables that they – the producers – take to be endogenous. After this point, the scholar not only has to move from a partial to general equilibrium perspective, but the type of questions he seeks to answer. Thus, rather than trying to explain why firms choose to undertake a particular value-added activity in a particular country, the macro economist is more interested in explaining *which* activities of firms are best undertaken in particular countries. In the former case, a comparison is made between the *absolute* costs and benefits of producing in different locations. In the latter, the distribution of value-added activity both within a country and between countries can only be explained in terms of *comparative* costs and benefits.

With this important distinction between micro- and macro-explanations of foreign production in mind, let us now consider Kiyoshi Kojima's macro-economic theory of FDI. This theory is essentially an extension of the neo-classical theory of factor endowments to explain trade in intermediate products, notably technology and management skills. But Kojima is as much interested in normative as in positive issues. A major part of his thesis, set out in Kojima (1973, 1978, 1982, 1990) and in Kojima and Ozawa (1984), is that whereas Japanese direct investment is primarily trade oriented and responds to the dictates of the principle of comparative advantage, US direct investment is mainly conducted within an oligopolistic market structure, is anti-trade oriented and operates to the long-term disadvantage of both the donor and recipient countries.

Kojima essentially believes that FDI should act as an efficient conduit for trading intermediate products, but that the timing and direction of such investment should be determined by market forces rather than by hierarchical control. His prescription is that outbound direct investment should be undertaken by firms that produce intermediate products that require resources and capabilities in which the home country has a comparative advantage, but that generate value-added activities that require resources and capabilities in which that country is comparatively disadvantaged. By contrast, inbound direct investment should import intermediate products that require resources and capabilities in which the recipient country is disadvantaged, but the use of which requires resources and capabilities in which it has a comparative advantage. To this extent, the Kojima thesis is quite consistent with any macroeconomic inferences that might be drawn from the eclectic paradigm – at least in respect of some kinds of FDI.

The point at which Kojima's theory ceases to be satisfactory as a general explanation of MNE activity is precisely that at which neo-classical theories fail to explain much of modern trade. That is because they countenance neither the possibility of market failure nor the fact that firms are both producing and transacting economic agents. This means that they cannot explain the kind of trade flows (including trade in intermediate products) that are based less on the distribution of factor endowments and more on the need to exploit the economies of scale, product differentiation and other manifestations of market failure. Neither can they explain trade in intermediate products based upon the advantages of common governance, which itself reflects the inability of the market mechanism to ensure the first-best international allocation of economic activity in situations in which the costs and benefits of transactions extend beyond those who are parties to the exchange; where there is uncertainty of the outcome of such exchanges; and where there is an asymmetry of knowledge between buyers and sellers.

To the extent that Kojima uses trade models to explain patterns of foreign direct investment, he follows in the Vernon tradition. To the extent that he regards MNEs as creators or sustainers of market imperfections whose impact on resource allocation must be less beneficial than that predicated by perfect competition, the geneology of this thought can be traced back to Hymer. The result is that whereas he formulates a useful analysis of the cross-border transactions in intermediate products and correctly identifies some activities of MNEs as being the result of structural market distortions, he pays little attention to the impact of transaction costs on international resource allocation, and hence fails to appreciate that, in conditions of market failure, multinational hierarchies may improve rather than worsen such an allocation. The means by which this is accomplished, which include geographical diversification, exploitation of the economies of joint supply, better commercial intelligence and the avoidance of costs of enforcing property rights, have been well spelled out by Gray (1982).

A very recent contribution by Kojima (1992) has acknowledged that MNEs may sometimes need to internalize intermediate product markets to promote their economic efficiency. However, rather than seeking to identify and evaluate the significance of the particular forms of market failure likely to determine different kinds of FDI, Kojima chooses to analyse the circumstances in which firms will use internal or external markets to optimize their transactions of intermediate products. He finds that the key determinant of the sourcing strategy of firms lies in the relative strength of the internal and external economies facing the firms, which, in turn, reflect the technical characteristics of their production functions.[22]

4.4   FUTURE CHALLENGES FOR THE THEORY OF MNEs AND MNE ACTIVITY

4.4.1   Issues resolved and unresolved by contemporary theory

In this chapter we have described the evolution of the theory of international production over the past three decades. As of the early 1990s, we have a galaxy of partial theories that purport to explain particular aspects of foreign production, particular kinds of foreign production or the behaviour of particular types of MNEs. Most of these have been tested – usually by the use of multiple regression techniques or, in the case of less quantifiable variables, by factor, cluster or multidiscriminant analysis. As Chapter 6 will demonstrate, most have sought to identify either the particular OLI variables likely to affect the geographical or industrial distribution of foreign production or the strategic response of MNEs to these variables. Few have attempted to evaluate the extent to which foreign-owned affiliates actually do record higher profits than their indigenous competitors, or whether they earn higher rates of return than could have been earned had the same activity been undertaken in the home country, although in the 1960s and early 1970s there were attempts to do so from the viewpoint of the efficiency of resource allocation. Stevens (1974) and Caves (1982) offer good summaries of the relevant empirical studies.

In the past decade, the focus of attention has been directed to more general – and even interdisciplinary – explanations of international production, of which the eclectic paradigm is probably the most ambitious. Clearly, it is easy to criticize such paradigms. Indeed their very strengths – the encompassing of a large set of disparate variables – makes any systematic testing very difficult. However, it is worth repeating that the idea of the eclectic paradigm is to produce an analytical framework within which particular explanations of the determinants of MNE activity can be evaluated. To this extent, the debate between the view of those who argue that market failure is a necessary and sufficient condition to explain the existence of MNEs and those who assert that the eclectic paradigm offers a useful framework for analysing the extent and patterns of MNE activity, is more meaningful than that between both schools of thought and those who argue for and against generalist explanations.

At the same time, there remain many unresolved issues in international business that require attention. We believe that some contemporary events, including the rapid growth of service MNEs, the emergence of Third World MNEs and the opening up of East Europe and the People's Republic of China to FDI, require only minor modifications to either the internalization or eclectic paradigms.

Similarly, together with a theory of strategic behaviour, both can satisfactorily explain the reasons why firms prefer to conclude joint ventures rather than engage in 100% owned foreign production. They can even explain the determinants of the locus of control within firms. However, there are other trends in international business that might require a more fundamental appraisal of existing modes of thought. We shall identify just three of these.[23] Part 2 of this volume will take up some of the issues raised in more detail.[24]

4.4.2 Cooperative alliances

The blurring of the boundaries of firms brought about by the growth of inter-firm collaborative agreements opens up new challenges to the researchers. At one time, the distinction between markets and hierarchies as modes or organizing transactions seemed fairly clear. Nowadays, an increasing proportion of transactions seem to involve cooperation or affiliation between firms. According to Richardson (1972), cooperation is more likely to appeal to two (or more) firms than a market or a hierarchical relationship when each engages in complementary but dissimilar activities. Coordination of economic activity by cooperation is preferred to that by hierarchies as it involves lower transaction costs for organizing dissimilar activities, whereas it is preferred to the market because coordination requires matching the plans of separate enterprises rather than matching aggregate supply to aggregate demand (which is the main task of markets).

The delineation of the role of the market, hierarchies and cooperation among hierarchies in terms of the matching of activities to capabilities rather than in terms of products and processes, is only now beginning to receive the attention of economists and business analysts (Contractor and Lorange, 1988). Yet this approach might well be the clue to incorporating networks of inter-firm alliances into the received theory of the MNE. Using Richardson's terminology, if technological advances encourage MNEs to specialize in similar activities across national boundaries, but that engaging in these activities requires their particular O advantages to be combined with a different, but complementary, set of intangible assets, then inter-firm cooperation

may be the preferred organizational form to maximize the value added from the inputs required for
these activities.

4.4.3   Network analysis

Whereas most of the analysis of cooperative alliances
has centred on the relationship between pairs of
firms, that is, bilateral transactional relationships, it
is clear that contemporary MNEs are adopting a
more pluralistic approach to their overseas activities.
At the same time, the transactional relationships
they forge with other firms, for example, their
suppliers and customers, are not independent of each
other. Hence, it becomes appropriate to consider the
behaviour of groups or networks of value-added
activities in which MNEs participate, rather than the
MNEs themselves. Moreover, the form and structure
of these networks may well affect the modality of the
relationships forged between the firms in the network.

The network approach to theorizing about the
foreign activities of MNEs owes its origin to a group
of Swedish and Japanese scholars. The basic proposition of these scholars is that in order to survive,
organizations require resources that can be obtained
only by interacting with other organizations that own
or control these resources. A network relationship
implies that there is some overlap in the transactions
of firms within the network. For example, Firm A
trades with Firm B, which trades with Firm C, which
trades with Firm A. There is a conscious division of
work among firms in the network, which means that
the supply capabilities of firms are interdependent.
However, the activities are coordinated neither
by the market nor by a central hierarchical plan, but
by the establishment of a set of relationships
between the members of the network. These networks are assumed to be stable and changing, while
the established bonds may vary from the formal to
the informal; and the transactions may be based on a
written contract or a verbal agreement.

The network approach, which has been used to
explain the process of the internationalization of
production by Imai (1985) and Johanson and Mattson (1987a, 1987b), has been contrasted with the
internalization model discussed earlier. At the same
time, most of the research conducted on networks

has concerned itself with bilateral relationships (or
links in the network) rather than with multi-lateral
relationships (or the network itself). To this extent,
the literature on strategic alliances and networks
overlaps. But one of the interesting features of at
least some of the MNEs of the early 1990s is that
their choice of network partners may well be
influenced by the relationship between these partners
and other firms, which may themselves have a
separate relationship – be it one of competition or
collaboration – with the first firm. The idea of a
galaxy or groupings of firms, each of which is to
some extent reliant on the other for its economic
prosperity, implies that the composition of the galaxy
is not independent of the role played by the
constituents of other competing galaxies. According
to this view, each firm performs a dual function: as a
cooperator in the group(s) of which it is a member,
and as a competitor in the supply of end products
and the demand for factor inputs. To this extent,
network analysis would seem to have a lot more to
offer than it has so far been able to demonstrate, but
it needs to be integrated with work now being done
by industrial organizational economists and especially that on the theory of oligopoly and contestable
markets.

Finally, mention should be made of the work of
Bartlett and Ghoshal (1990) who argue that the
MNE itself is best regarded as a controller of a
network of interrelated activities. These interactions
may both be internal (within the MNEs) or external
(between the MNEs and other organizations). Bartlett
and Ghoshal assert that the extent and form of these
link-ups will rest on the resource and capability
configuration of the MNEs, which in turn will
depend on the types of activities and the countries in
which they are engaged. They further suggest that
the allocation of decision taking within MNEs will
depend upon the related positions of the headquarters and subsidiaries in the total network of
activity. Chapters 8 and 9 discuss these issues in
more detail.

4.4.4   The role of strategic
management

The developments just described suggest the forging
of new kinds of cross-border relationships between

and within firms. They have been brought about both by changes in the OLI configuration facing firms, as a result of *inter alia* technological and organizational changes over the past two decades or more, and the strategic response of firms to these changes. The third challenge to the received theory of foreign production derives from the fact that the behavioural options to firms as to both the kind of value-added activities in which they engage and the organization of such activities, have themselves widened. This, we suggest, is because of the inadequacy of both pure markets and pure hierarchies to offer an optimal solution as to the way in which resources and capabilities should be organized.

On the one hand, we see the majority of industrial activity being dominated by large firms, diversified in their product and geographical structure, but competing as national or international oligopolists within their main product markets. On the other, because of the growing interdependence among economic functions, rapid technological change and the speedier rate of obsolescence, and the growing importance of the economies of scope, we observe that in an increasing number of instances neither pure markets nor pure hierarchies can ensure that resources and capabilities are allocated in a way that is acceptable to the participants. Moreover, as we have already seen, not only does the extent and form of market failure impinge on the OLI configuration facing firms, but it also affects the strategic response of firms to that configuration. In turn, such a response may affect the values of, and relationships between, the OLI variables at a later time.

The widening strategic options open to firms require a reappraisal of the received theory of MNE activity in a number of ways. Basically, however, the challenge to scholars is to switch their mode of thinking away from explaining individual cross-border transactions or acts of foreign production to explaining a system of transactions or acts of foreign production. Most research on the comparative efficiency of markets and hierarchies has tended to focus on the transaction of particular goods or services, or on particular decisions related to these transactions. However, because of the growing interdependency among trade in intermediate and final products and of the ways in which the production of products is organized among firms, the approach to understanding organization or foreign

production needs to be much more pluralistic than it has been in the past. No one model of the MNE is likely to be adequate. Whatever the organizational form any one activity may take, in its strategy towards its foreign value-added activities the MNE is likely to use an amalgam of organizational forms – varying from markets, through collaborative agreements, to hierarchies. These will differ according to activities, market structure, age and experience of firms and the countries involved.

Any future modelling of MNE activity must also pay more attention to strategic-related variables. Strategic management is concerned with the ways in which managers plan and act to achieve their objectives in conditions of market failure (Dunning, 1993b). It embraces not only decisions as to how resources are acquired, created and utilized, and the way in which markets are identified and serviced, but on how transactions relating to these decisions are organized. Like the choice of what and how to produce and sell, the various strategic strands of the governance of cross-border activity must be integrated. It is then the totality of this strategy rather than its individual component parts that is likely to determine the competitive success of MNE hierarchies.

The full incorporation of strategic-related variables into a general theory or paradigm of MNEs or MNE activity has yet to be accomplished.[25] Conceptually this should not be difficult to do. At any given moment of time, the level and pattern of the foreign value-added activities by any group of firms represent a point on a set of trajectories towards (or, in some cases, away from) the internationalization of production. The trajectory itself is set by the continuous and iterative interaction between the OLI configuration facing firms at particular periods of time and their strategic response to these configurations, which, in turn, will influence the OLI configuration at a later time. Strategic choice then becomes a 'dynamized add-on' variable[26] which, together with changes in other variables affecting the OLI configuration, explains the changing propensity of firms to engage in MNE activity.

Strategic management is essentially concerned with the ways in which managers act to achieve their long-term objectives in conditions of market failure. It embraces decisions about how resources are acquired, created, and utilized, the way in which markets are identified and served, and how transactions relating to these decisions are organized. It is concerned with the ways in which firms with different mixtures of physical human and financial assets deploy these strengths between countries with very different cultures, institutional structures and economic systems. Like the choice of 'what', 'how' and 'where' to produce, these various strategic strands must be integrated, and it is the extent to which an MNE is successful in this task that is increasingly determining its ability to sustain or advance its competitive position in global markets.[27]

There are other areas in which our knowledge about the determinants of MNE activity leaves much to be desired. One is in the dynamics of international production. Here, as an earlier section shows, scholars have yet to tackle the interaction between entrepreneurship, innovation and the management of human resources – the main engines of business growth – and the way in which the output of these assets affects both the OLI variables identified earlier and the strategy of firms towards their international operations. Tremendous changes have taken place in the extent and pattern of MNE activity over the past fifty years. Clearly these events would not have occurred to the same extent without changes in technological development, in the organization of firms, in population, in social and cultural values, and in the role of governments. Whereas, at a given moment of time, it may be correct to analyse the response of firms to these variables, over time, both at a micro- and macro-level, this is unjustifiable. This is now being recognized as scholars (e.g. Casson, 1987, 1990; Cantwell, 1989; Pavitt, 1987) are giving more attention to issues of innovation and entrepreneurship as they impinge upon the internationalization of business. We believe that, if and when, a new breakthrough in our understanding of foreign production occurs, it will probably be in this direction.

Finally, we believe that economists interested in explaining trade-related activity need to widen their sights to incorporate FDI and international production. Nowhere is this more clearly seen than in the current round of trade negotiations (the Uruguay round) about the nature of services. In these negotiations, at least one of the major industrial countries (the United States) is claiming that the

definition of trade ought to include foreign direct investment as trade in some services is impossible without a physical presence. Whatever one might think of the logic of this argument, there can be no dispute that the modalities of servicing foreign markets, both with goods and services, are becoming increasingly interdependent.

NOTES

1 For example, as set out by Agarwal (1980), Cantwell (1991), Calvet (1981) and Dunning (1991b).
2 Also referred to as sequential investment (Kogut, 1983).
3 Although various economists from the time of the Mercantilists onwards had something to say about the subject. Their views are set out in Cantwell *et al.* (1986) and Dunning (1988b, Chapter 3).
4 These include language barriers, lack of knowledge about the local economy, business customs, laws, suppliers and industrial relations, and the possibility of discrimination against foreign firms, of expropriation and of exchange risks.
5 See also some earlier empirical studies by Southard (1931), Barlow (1953) and Dunning (1958).
6 For a recent assessment of Hymer's contribution to the theory of the MNE, see Horaguchi and Toyne (1990).
7 As summarized by Hufbauer (1970) and Stern (1975).
8 For further details of some of these studies, see Chapter 6.
9 All characteristics of cross-border market failure later identified by the internalization economists (see Section 4.3).
10 In distinguishing between the goals of the portfolio capitalist and the direct investor, Kindleberger (1969) gives the capitalization formula as $C + I/r$, where C is the value of the capital asset, I is the income stream it produces and r is the return on investment. 'The theory asserts that direct investment occurs when the foreign firm can earn a higher I than the local firm whereas ordinary capital movements reflect a lower r' (Kindleberger, 1969, p. 24).
11 For example, although the Aliber thesis helps to explain the sharp upward movement of the acquisitions of US companies by UK firms in the late 1970s when the US dollar was undervalued in relation to the pound, it does not explain a similar sharp upward movement in the mid 1980s when the dollar was probably overvalued in relation to the pound.
12 Notably Lundgren (1977) and Swedenborg (1979) of Sweden, McManus (1972) of Canada, Buckley and Casson (1976, 1985) of the UK and Hennart (1982) of the US.

13 The exception being the work of strategic trade economists. For a useful recent appraisal of this literature, see Stegemann (1989).

14 Exceptions include the work of scholars such as Horstman and Markusen (1986) and Helpman and Krugman (1985).

15 I am indebted to Mr M. Itaki, one-time visiting research scholar at the University of Reading, for reminding me that the value of an ownership advantage must be expressed in terms of the capitalization of the income stream generated by such an advantage, which accrues to the owners of that advantage. The greater that income stream (net of payments made to other factor inputs that helped create that advantage or add value to it), the greater the advantage. I also accept that the ability of the owners of the firm to extract the maximum value added from the various factor inputs it utilizes, and the way in which it coordinates these factors, will determine the size of its ownership advantage. For a detailed criticism of the eclectic paradigm, see Itaki (1991).

16 For example, as a condition for entry into a country, an MNE may insist on a host government granting it protection from competitive imports. Alternatively, it may 'bargain up' the tax concessions offered or 'bargain down' the performance requirements imposed by the host government.

17 For example, in their exploitation of economies of scale, MNEs are in a better position than their uninational counterparts to practise a balanced strategy of national product segmentation and international aggregation of demand, whereas their ability to update and monitor cross-border information and to acquire their inputs from the cheapest source, helps them further build on their learning advantages, and those that arise from the geographical dispersion of plants.

18 This point is further taken up in Chapters 11 and 12.

19 For an attempt to embrace dynamic and organizational factors in extending internalization theory, see an interesting paper by Hill and Kim (1988). For a more general analysis of the dynamics of international production, see Dunning (1993b).

20 In his contribution, John Cantwell argues the case for a technological competence theory of international production. In doing so, he first identifies the specific characteristics of technological innovation, within a dynamic setting. Second he analyses some of the firm- and country-specific characteristics of technological competence. Third, he discusses its likely locational implications. And fourth, he considers some of the aspects of the theory for the competitiveness of countries and national innovatory capacities. This last point is discussed further in Chapters 11 and 12 of this volume.

21 The reader should observe that these stages are not quite the same as those identified in Chapter 10.

22 At the same time, Kojima claims that Western economists and business analysts tend to stress those internalizing advantages which are market distorting rather than market facilitating. For a riposte to this assertion, see Buckley (1991). Kojima also criticizes the eclectic paradigm for failing to find the determinants of the choice between the internalizing and externalizing cross-border transactions. However, the eclectic paradigm has never sought to do this. Its main purpose is to identify and evaluate the kind of variables likely to affect the choice between internalizing and externalizing transactions.

23 Other issues that need the attention of scholars are identified by Casson (1991) and Buckley (1990).

24 See also the 'Introduction' to Dunning (1992a).

25 For a first attempt to do so, see Dunning (1991b, 1992b).

26 Compare with Caves (1980) who argues that the concept of strategic groups and mobility barriers 'do not add up to a tight formal model' but serve as a dynamized add-on to the traditional structure-product-performance paradigm.

27 There is a growing literature on the resource-based model of the firm which argues that a firm's sustainable competitive or O advantages arise from its ability to strategically deploy its own unique mix of rent-yielding resources (or assets) that are valuable, rare, partially substitutable and imperfectly imitable. An explanation of the origin and use of these resources by firms of different national origins and outside their natural boundaries poses additional challenges for the research scholar, as he is required to link the managerial strategy of the firm to the location-specific attributes (as identified by Porter (1990)) of the countries in which they have (or are contemplating) value-added activities. The resource-based theory of the firm is further discussed by such writers as Wernerfelt (1984), Bartlett and Ghoshal (1989), Barney (1991), Collis (1991), Conner (1991), Kogut (1992), Prahalad and Hamel (1990) and Tallman (1991).

CHAPTER 5

THE EMERGENCE AND MATURING OF INTERNATIONAL PRODUCTION: AN HISTORICAL EXCURSION

5.1 INTRODUCTION

Since the dawn of modern civilization, individuals, social groups, institutions and governments have always sought to advance their economic prosperity by three sets of spatial activity. The first is by the emigration or immigration of people, and particularly of professional, managerial and skilled workers. The second is by trade in assets, goods and services. And the third is by the acquisition or colonization of new territory. To promote these various activities, it is not long before there is a need for some kind of foreign-owned production. In the case of migration, new settlers may not only bring their savings capital and knowledge with them. Often their translocation is fostered by, or leads to, institutional investment. In trade, the foreign involvement might take the form of buying or selling agencies, reception, warehousing and storage facilities. At the very least, colonization requires some resources and capabilities to establish trading outposts or bridgeheads until the settlement becomes self-sufficient. Frequently these basic activities need supportive services, such as banking, insurance and ship maintenance, and before long a rudimentary network of international commercial activities has been established.

Clearly, there are certain prerequisites for any international value-adding activity to occur. These include the perception or knowledge that *foreign*[1] territories of some economic value exist. The history of FDI is largely the story about the increasing ease of, and motivation for, wealth-producing entities to engage in production and transactions outside their national boundaries. In the following pages we shall describe these developments within the context of the eclectic paradigm set out in the previous chapter. In particular, we shall see that the early cross-border activities of firms were largely dependent, first, on their perceived need and ability (or that of their home countries) to acquire resources or markets beyond their national boundaries; second, on the facilities available for transporting goods, people and information across geographical space, and particularly across water; and third, on the relative costs and benefits of the alternative modalities of undertaking trans-border transactions of intermediate products.

The following sections summarize the main features of international production from the Middle Ages onward, although earlier examples of embryonic MNEs can, most surely, be found in the colonizing activities of the Phoenicians and the Romans and, before that, in the more ancient civilizations of the Near and Middle East, China and South America. However, this sort of history, which almost certainly would provide us with some fascinating glimpses of how our forefathers dealt with many of the economic issues with which this book is concerned, still remains to be written.

5.2 COLONIZING AND MERCHANT CAPITALISM

Prior to the industrial revolution, most value-adding activities initiated by economic entities – be they the state, private corporations, families or individuals – outside their national boundaries were prompted by three factors. The first was the desire to foster trade and financial activities consistent with the needs of the state or that of individual producers or consumers. The second was to acquire new territories and new forms of wealth. The third was to discover new avenues for the use of domestic savings.

For much of the period from the 13th to the 18th century, the state was directly or indirectly involved in most kinds of overseas ventures. Most transactions were hierarchical or personalized. Neither capital nor intermediate product markets, as we know them today, existed. Such overseas investment as there was, was usually intended to advance the political or strategic goals of the governments of the home countries. It was undertaken primarily by chartered land companies, merchants and wealthy family groups.

Three characteristics of this period are particularly worth noting. First, up to the 19th century at least, it was generally quicker and cheaper to conduct commerce across water than by land. Because of this, the development of export-oriented industries proceeded faster than that of their domestic counterparts (Williams, 1929). To give just one example, the modern factory, based as it is on the contracting out system, originated in the medieval towns of the Low Countries and Italy, which manufactured goods primarily for export. The second characteristic is that since a lot of trade was between metropolitan countries and their colonies, little or no distinction was made between internal and cross-border transactions; each was organically related to the other. The third characteristic of the period was that migration and investment were handmaidens of each other. Indeed, expatriate investment was one of the most important forms of international commercial activity in the Middle Ages (Cunningham, 1902).

Douglass North (1981, 1985) traces some of the earliest international business ventures to the Commenda, which dominated caravan and maritime trade in Medieval Europe. The Commenda was an arrangement by which a principal investor, or group of investors, entrusted their capital (or merchandise) to an agent, or manager, who then traded with it and returned to the investor his principal and an agreed share of profits. Much of this commerce involved the transfer of resources across national boundaries. It was conducted by parties who were personally known to, and trusted by, each other, and who came from similar cultures. This, according to North (1985, p. 561), minimized the need for the formal rules and compliance procedures which characterize impersonal exchanges.

In addition to the Commenda, in the early Middle Ages there were numerous trading firms, based in different parts of Europe, which set up offices and representatives in many of the important cities of the continent. These companies were the ancestors of the 16th and 17th century merchant capitalists, and the modern Japanese and Korean trading companies. They were normally partnerships formed for a short period of time, at the end of which the profits would be distributed and the partnerships dissolved. However, there were two important exceptions. The first was the Hanseatic League, a cross-border trading company owned and operated by a group of Hanseatic merchants based at Lubeck in Germany. The League was, *par excellence*, a 14th century organizer and promoter of Western European and Levantine commerce. Its particular O-specific advantage was its ability to coordinate and diffuse the use of capital, entrepreneurship and goods throughout Europe. Among its many achievements, it helped to develop various branches of agriculture in Poland, sheep-rearing in England, iron production in Sweden and general industry in Belgium (Williams, 1929).

The second example of an early trading MNE was that of the Merchant Adventurers, a powerful consortium of UK wool and cloth companies which was set up to promote marketing outlets for its members' goods in the Low Countries. Some of these early merchant adventurers also developed banking services *inter alia* to provide loans and credit for their customers.

Later in the 14th century, the centre of gravity of international commerce switched to Italy. Capitalizing on its geographical position between the Western and Eastern hemispheres, this was the time when the hegemony of the Italian banking and trading houses was at its peak. Banking dynasties such as Bardi, Acciauoli and Peruzzi operated branch offices in London, Bruges and Paris. According to one estimate (Hawrylyshyn, 1971), by the end of the 14th century there were 150 Italian banking firms which were truly multinational in their operations. Among the best known of these was the Medici, which dominated the business and political life of Florence. The company had at least eight trading and banking houses scattered throughout Europe (Heaton, 1973). Some of these early ventures also engaged in foreign mining activities. Genoese merchants poured money into Polish salt mines. The Fugger family, which in 1525 was reputed to be the wealthiest company in Europe, invested in silver and mercury mines in Spain and Latin America, and chain stores in most of the larger cities of Europe.

The 16th and 17th centuries saw new developments in international business. Gradually, as transborder communications improved and the boundaries of commerce widened to embrace new cultures, relations between the trading partners became less personal and began to be based more on formal documentation. Throughout this period, FDI continued to be of two kinds. First and foremost it was intended to support the trading activities of the home countries. This, indeed, was the era of the first major colonizing ventures of Western European companies. Unlike their medieval predecessors, however, most of the companies in this era were directly set up or supported by the state and enjoyed its patronage only as long as they advanced its economic and political objectives. Among the best known trading firms of this period were the British East Indian Company (chartered in 1602), the Dutch East India Company (chartered in 1600), which became deeply involved in India and the Far East, the Muscovy Company (chartered in 1553), formed to pioneer the North East Passage, the Royal African Company (chartered in 1672), and the Hudson's Bay Company, which was one of the first companies to set up a major wholesale trading operation in North America.[2]

Like the Hanseatic League, some of these trading hierarchies also helped to foster foreign value-added activities and, in many respects, may claim to be the progenitors of the modern MNE.[3] The domination by the Hudson's Bay Company of the production and trading of Canadian furs is one such example. Another is the Dutch East India Company which established a plant in Bengal in 1641 to refine saltpetre and a print works for textiles for ten years. By 1717, the company was reported to be employing over 4000 silk spinners in Kaimbazar (Prakash, 1985). In other cases, the initiative was taken by individual entrepreneurs. In 1632, for example, two Dutch merchants – Andrei Vinius and Peter Marselis – established water-powered ironworks, 150 kilometres south of Moscow (McKay, 1970). Both capital and technology were exported from Holland. This venture was followed by others,[4] and by the end of the 19th century almost three-fifths of all large industrial plants in Russia were reputed to be owned by foreign enterprises (McKay, 1974).

The second kind of FDI in this period was to promote colonization and land development. In the early 17th century, most attention was focused on America, and several companies, for example, the Virginia Company, Massachusetts Bay Company and the Providence Company, helped to settle the Eastern seaboard of America. Most of these companies originated from England, which, at that time, offered appropriate incentives to emerging international entrepreneurs. Like the trading companies, these colonizing ventures soon branched out into other activities. For example, the Massachusetts Bay Company helped to cultivate a New England economy based on fishing, boat-building and simple manufacturing industries, while in Virginia, British capitalists initiated a plantation economy based primarily on cotton and tobacco. In both cases, expatriate capital, migrant workers, absentee investors and some direct investment played a critical role. As well documented by Coram (1967) and Wilkins (1989), many of these pre-revolutionary industries were started with European (mainly British) money and technology, machinery and skills. Other chartered companies also helped to colonize other parts of the world, notably in Africa.

Apart from the Middle Eastern trading ventures of the early medieval period, most international business ventures in the pre-industrial era originated from the major cities of the Low Countries and England. In addition, two Swiss families – the Jenny and the Blumers – were active in banking and trading ventures in Italy in the 18th century (Wavre, 1988). During the latter part of the period, American colonial merchants also began to set up branch outposts in England and the West Indies (Lewis, 1938).

5.3 THE EARLY 19TH CENTURY: THE FORERUNNERS OF THE MODERN MNE

5.3.1 Introduction

The industrial revolution dramatically changed both the ability and the incentive of firms and countries to engage in trade and colonizing activities. The 19th century also led to a massive cross-border movement of people, especially from Europe to North America. Capital, technology, management and entrepreneurship all followed to support and sustain these activities. At the same time, firms were prompted to invest abroad for new reasons, in particular to acquire minerals and raw materials for their domestic industries and foodstuffs for their population and/or to protect or widen their indigenous markets. While the first kind of investment was generally trade creating, rather than trade substituting (except where prior to the investment, the resources were being imported from independent foreign suppliers), the second often reduced trade in as much as the markets were previously serviced by exports. However, both market- and resource-seeking foreign investors aimed to produce goods and services that would advance domestic economic welfare and the colonizing policies of metropolitan governments.

The industrial revolution affected both the nature and organization of the value-added activities of firms. It introduced the factory system and helped to fashion the business enterprise as we know it today. It also dramatically influenced the way corporations were managed, the techniques of production and the range of value-added activities that could be efficiently undertaken by a single hierarchy. It created the demand for new sources of energy and industrial materials. By helping to raise living standards, it also increased the demand for the kinds of food and other products that the temperate industrial countries could not produce, or produce economically. It led to new and more efficient forms of transport, and drastically reduced inter- and intra-firm communication costs. It necessitated changes to the legal and financial status of companies and altered the character of exchange relationships. Personal transactions based upon trust and mutual forbearance were replaced by impersonal transactions backed up by legally binding contracts and elaborate monitoring

devices (North, 1981; Jones, 1987).

The growth of industrial capitalism also led to more specialization and division of labour both between and within business enterprises. This, in turn, fostered the roundaboutness of production and a reorganization of transactional mechanisms wherever the production or exchange of one product yielded costs and benefits to the production or exchange of other products. Embryonic hierarchies began to emerge, although these did not reach maturity until the third quarter of the 19th century (Chandler, 1980).

Finally, the industrial revolution greatly enhanced the role of technological capacity, money capital and human competences in the production process. Unlike natural resources, however, these assets had to be created. Once created, they often became the proprietary rights of the owners (i.e. they were ownership specific). They were also potentially mobile across space, opening up the possibility that firms might utilize the human and physical assets they generated or acquired in one country to produce goods and services in another.

Taken together, these events heralded a watershed in the history of international business. The age of merchant capitalism which had dominated international commerce for the previous two centuries was now replaced by an era of industrial capitalism (Cantwell, 1989b). Although the MNE, as we know it today, did not emerge until later in the 19th century, firms from Europe and North America began to invest in foreign plantations, mines, factories, banking, sales and distribution facilities in large numbers. We can identify three main kinds of foreign direct investment in the first half of the 19th century. The following paragraphs describe the main characteristics of each.

5.3.2 The individual entrepreneurs

The era prior to the emergence of managerial capitalism and limited liability was dominated by small firms, often owned and operated by a single entrepreneur or family group. Some of these entrepreneurs were internationally oriented from the start. Among those of US origin identified by Mira Wilkins (1970, p. 17) were: William Wheelwright, who established several businesses in Latin America in the second quarter of the 19th century; Henry Meiggs, who was instrumental in developing a network of transport and communications facilities in Chile; Hiram Walker, who erected a distillery in Windsor, Ontario in the 1850s; and Joseph Dyer, who set up a factory in Manchester, England to manufacture American-designed machinery around 1820.

At the same time, attracted both by market prospects and generous incentives offered by state legislatures (Wilkins, 1988), European businessmen were migrating to the US. Like their American counterparts, the European entrepreneurs usually invested only small amounts of capital but considerable amounts of technological expertise and management experience. Since most, and in particular the UK, governments saw the US as a potential industrial competitor, they did their best to discourage this transatlantic export of capital and technology. These efforts were generally unsuccessful, and up to the American Civil War at least, there was a steady migration of skilled workers, innovators and managers across the Atlantic. Entrepreneurs such as Andrew and William Macallum in carpet manufacturing, John Ryle in silk, Thomas Lewis in iron, Peter Ballantine in brewing and the Wright brothers in the umbrella business played a vital role in the development of American manufacturing industry.[5]

English-speaking entrepreneurs such as Charles Baird, a Scottish iron maker, also played a major part in the industrialization of Russia, particularly in the textile, machinery and railroad equipment industries (McKay, 1974). Among the ventures pursued by British entrepreneurs in Europe in the early 1800s – not all of which were successful – were engineering factories by William Cockerill in Belgium (in 1807) and by Aaron Manby near Paris in 1819 and a brewery operation by the Scottish distiller John Stein in St Petersburg around 1802 (Corley, 1992).

In as much as many of the early 19th century entrepreneurs migrated with their capital, the subsequent investment which they made cannot be considered 'foreign' or 'direct' in the sense that it is defined today. At the same time, as a kind of free-standing investment and in so far as both its motives and its contribution to the economic development of the host country were concerned it had many of the

features of FDI. Thus it may be legitimately viewed as one of the precursors of the modern MNE.

5.3.3   The finance capitalists

If the entrepreneurs brought only a small amount of money capital to foreign ventures, the finance capitalists brought little else. It was unusual for them to be involved in the management or organization of the businesses they funded. Indeed, for most of the 19th century the cross-border trade in financial assets was largely independent of that of technology and entrepreneurship. One exception appears to be the close relationships between French capital exports and entrepreneurship. Rondo Cameron (1961), for example, identified several sizeable French FDIs in Europe and Africa in the first half of the 19th century, which were accompanied by French management and technology.

Britain first began exporting capital on a major scale after the Napoleonic Wars to finance the reconstruction in Europe, followed by an investment boom in Latin America during the 1820s (Rippy, 1959). Much of this capital had been accumulated by UK industrialists and represented the first fruits of the industrial revolution. The British government initially supported such foreign investment, but after about 1840, apart from investment directed to the British colonies, it generally adopted a non-interventionist stance (Stopford, 1974, p. 308). By far the greater part of these capital exports prior to 1850 were portfolio rather than direct, although in a few cases they were substantial enough to give the investor a voice in the management of the foreign company. For the most part, it was Europe (rather than the US, which at that time was a major importer of capital) that supplied the finance, with British mercantile and investment banks playing a leading facilitating role.

Overseas companies financed by European capital were of three kinds. The first were those which raised money – mainly on the London market – from portfolio investors, but then organized its deployment abroad. Often, these were free-standing investments in the sense that, apart from maintaining a small head office in the home country, all the value-added activity was undertaken elsewhere. Mira Wilkins (1988a) suggests that between 1870 and 1914 there were literally thousands of British free-standing companies involved in a diverse range of activities including copper mining in Russia, cattle in the United States, railroads in Brazil, mortgage companies in Australia and meat packing in Argentina.

At the same time, at least some of the foreign activities were closely managed by the parent organization. The main O advantages of this group of foreign investors were their access to the UK capital market and their organizational skills in managing foreign investments. Some of the free-standing investments – particularly in the petroleum industry – were the forerunners of today's giant MNEs.

The second type of overseas companies were those set up by local entrepreneurs and managers, but which needed external capital. The main categories of enterprises registered overseas were UK railway, public utility and mining companies, and some Continental European owned railway companies. It has been estimated that there were 2640 of the former companies registered in 1914; most had only a small head office in London (Houston and Dunning, 1976). They invested their resources mainly in foreign mining and plantation investments. Such firms as Rio Tinto, Consolidated Gold Fields and deBeers were among the most active of these MNEs.

A third group of overseas investors were the British-based investment groups, which mainly comprised entrepreneurial or family concerns whose names and reputations were used to float a variety of foreign mining, manufacturing and tertiary enterprises. In some respects, these groups fall in between the first two categories of finance capitalists, and certainly many of them would be identified as free-standing investments by Wilkins (1988a). However, they deserve especial mention in that they were the natural descendants of the giant trading conglomerates of the 17th and 18th centuries. Essentially, their task was to facilitate all kinds of UK trade and commerce; frequently, in pursuance of this goal, they engaged in FDI. Typical of such investment groups were Matheson and Co., Jardine Skinner, Finlay and Co., Wallace Bros, Harrison and Crosfield and E. D. Sassoon and Co., which, between them, owned cotton and jute mills, coffee and tea estates, rubber plantations, shipyards, sugar refineries, copper, diamond and gold mines in India, China and the Far East (Chapman, 1985).[6] While the foreign activities of some of these mercantile groups were organized from their head offices in the UK, many, like expatriate firms, were often managed by local managing agents. This system was particularly prevalent in India,[7] from whence it spread to Iran and Malaysia (Davenport-Hines and Jones, 1989; Tomlinson, 1989).

Nevertheless, most of the investment outside the UK by British firms, at the time, took the form of portfolio capital. During the first half of the 19th century finance capital poured into Europe and the US to help construct public utilities, canals and railroads. As late as 1850, these activities accounted for more than one-half of UK capital exports. Other capital was directed to the 'white' Dominions and to Latin America, but only rarely did the sizeable investments involve any managerial influence or control.

5.3.4   The embryonic MNEs

The third kind of foreign investment consisted of that directed to the territorial expansion of a firm's domestic value-added operations. Such investment included that undertaken by the embryonic manufacturing MNEs. Sometimes they first exported to the country in which they made their investments; in other cases they did not. In a few cases, a company began life in one country, began investing in another and then, over time, became an MNE from the foreign base. Geoffrey Jones (1986) refers to these companies as migrating MNEs. In every instance, however, the investing company perceived itself to have a particular competitive or O-specific advantage over its domestic competitors or those producing in the host countries. Often this advantage was embodied in the products offered for sale or in production processes. However, in the case of resource-based investment, access to foreign markets was no less important. In some cases, high spatial transaction costs provided the initial impetus to produce abroad; in others, foreign investment followed exports as the local market began to expand.

In the main, this kind of investment was within the (then) developed world and was intended to produce goods and services for the local market. One exception, identified by Corley (1992), was a coconut-crushing plant set up in Ceylon (now Sri Lanka) by Prices Patent Candle Company of London to provide oil for candles made in the UK. Certainly manufacturing investment accounted for the bulk of the early activities of US MNEs (Lewis, 1938). As early as 1804, two Americans built a paper mill in Quebec; over the next half century, several US-owned companies set up branch factories in Canada. By the mid 1850s, American technology had already overtaken European technology in a wide range of metal-using industries and in those utilizing mass production techniques (e.g. machine tools, agricultural equipment, firearms and sewing machines).

Greatly encouraged by the response to their exhibits at the Crystal Palace exhibition in London in 1851, US firms tried to capitalize on their advantages by stepping up their sales to the UK. Frequently, however, they found it uneconomic to export from their American plants. The firms then had two options. One was to conclude licensing arrangements with British producers. This was the modality chosen by Cyrus McCormick, who in 1851 licensed the British firms Burgess and Key to make agricultural reaping machines. The other was to set up a foreign manufacturing affiliate. This was the route of entry preferred by Samuel Colt, who established the first US-owned factory in the UK in 1852 (Wilkins, 1970). The UK branch was designed to produce revolvers that were exact copies of those produced in its US factory.

The main O-specific advantage of the Colt Company was its ability to design and mass produce interchangeable parts for firearms. However, it was the fear that he might lose the European market to his competitors, unless he produced in their territories, that was the main locational stimulus to Colt to engage in FDI. The UK was chosen as a production site mainly because of the size of the local market and for language reasons. Three years later another US firm – J. Ford & Co. – set up a vulcanized rubber plant in Scotland. The factory was American financed, designed, equipped and managed. As it happened, neither venture was profitable and both were sold out to British interests within a decade of their establishment (Dunning, 1958; Jones, 1988).

European firms also set up subsidiaries in the US in the first half of the 19th century. One example was the Dupont Company, founded in 1801 by French capital and management. However, it was the tariffs imposed in the second half of the 19th century which prompted the first major wave of inward direct investment into US manufacturing industry. There was also some intra-European MNE activity, but it is difficult to pinpoint how important it was. The Englishman William Cockerill established a branch factory to produce textile machinery in Prussia in 1815. According to White (quoted in Wilkins, 1977a), much British capital entered France after the Napoleonic Wars to establish textile factories and (later) to construct railroads. Jenks (1938) observed that by 1840 about 20 textile plants and iron foundries had been built and were being operated by Englishmen in various parts of France. There were also sizeable Swiss direct investments in the Italian textile industry throughout the 19th century. Clough (1964) reports the case of a Zurich-owned company – J. Egg – employing 1300 workers in a cotton mill in Italy in 1834.

The first half of the 19th century also saw the continued growth of foreign-owned trading and sales ventures, and the establishment of the first foreign banking and insurance affiliates. American mercantile banks opened branch offices in London and Paris, while the first US merchants to promote the American–West Indian Sugar Trade were set up in Cuba in 1838 (Lewis, 1938). The European banking houses of Baring, Rothschilds and Lazard were extremely active in financing infrastructure projects in Continental Europe and the US, while in Asia, the Oriental Bank Corporation, founded in 1845, was for several decades the most important British bank in the East (Davenport–Hines and Jones, 1989). The first foreign insurance affiliate – the Phoenix Assurance Company – was set up in the US (by UK interests) in 1804. Several European land companies also established affiliates in the US to purchase and farm large tracts of agricultural land (Lewis, 1938).

The emergence of industrial capitalism, then, generated a variety of activities financed or managed by foreign investors. Add to these the expansion of existing trading investments and some early French and British plantation investments in Africa, and we have quite an impressive package of international business activities. The growing O-specific advantages of enterprises – particularly in processing industries, insurance, banking and shipping – a gradual reduction of inter-country locational barriers, and the need to gain access to both foreign input and output markets, led many firms not only to look beyond their national borders for intermediate or final products, but also to control the production and marketing of these products. Nevertheless, by the mid 1850s, the development of international production as we know it today was still in its infancy.

5.4 FROM 1870 ONWARDS: THE MODERN MNE EMERGES

5.4.1 New technological and organizational advances

It is difficult to put a precise date on the second watershed in the history of FDI and MNE activity. This is because a series of interrelated events occurred between the mid 1830s and mid 1870s, which, between them, had far-reaching implications on the nature, organization and location of production. In terms of the OLI paradigm, the second half of the 19th century witnessed organizational and technical innovations that not only better enabled firms to create or acquire proprietary rights and to produce at a much larger scale of output, but also provided them with opportunities to become multi-product and multinational producers. In particular, dramatic advances in domestic and international transport, communications and storage techniques created new market opportunities and led firms to reappraise their locational strategies. These developments, together with the emergence of a professionally trained cadre of managers and administrators, led both to a widening and deepening of value-added chains and to a growth in the transactional sector of the industrial economy.

In contrast to the technical and organizational advances of the previous fifty years, those of the mid and late 19th century most affected the fabricating industries, notably the engineering and metal-using sectors, rather more than the processing industries. Partly because of this, as well as the different resource, production and transactional needs of the two sectors, the organizational leadership of the new industries shifted from owner-managed and family firms to joint stock companies. These newer industries were characterized by a higher ratio of non-operative

to operative workers as well as by the substantially larger number of separate economic activities (and, hence, transactions) required to produce a given end product.

Compared to most European countries, the US was better suited both to create and to take advantage of these events. Indeed, the institutional mechanisms and organizational structures which had evolved to meet the needs of the first phase of the industrial revolution proved inappropriate and, in some cases, acted as a handicap in the second. As an emerging industrial nation, the US was well equipped to meet and fully exploit the challenges and needs of the last quarter of the 19th century, while the innovations, themselves, were both influenced by, and more suited to, its own natural resources, organizational capabilities and markets (Wright, 1990).

The last half-century before the First World War introduced a wave of technological advances which in many ways were more profound and far reaching than their predecessors. They were stimulated and supported by the creation of new transport and communications networks, which helped increase both the demand for and the supply of goods and services. Electricity and the internal combustion engine, the inter-changeability of parts and the introduction of new continuous processing machinery were the main technological lynchpins of the second industrial revolution.[8] They combined to make possible economies of scale in production and economies of scope in marketing. At the same time, the new and more capital-intensive production techniques required a reliable and sustained supply of intermediate products, an uninterrupted flow of work on the factory floor and assured and stable markets and distribution networks if they were to be profitably exploited.

Such technological changes fundamentally affected the production frontiers of firms, their capacity for, and strategies of, growth, and the market environment in which they operated. They made possible new kinds of O-specific advantages, which both added to the ability of enterprises to exploit foreign markets and affected their organizational cultures. For, compared to those that preceded them, these advantages created many more barriers to the entry of firms not possessing them as well as to their transfer to other countries. These included the growing cost-effectiveness of large plants, the economies of process, product or market coordination, and the protection offered by the international patent system. They encouraged further technological and organizational changes, which eventually led to a greater concentration of industrial output and to the transformation of some location-bound advantages of countries into the proprietary rights of enterprises.

The innovations of the later 19th century were different in another sense. Although the earlier discoveries in metallurgy, power generation and transport were interrelated and mutually reinforcing, such interdependence rarely extended across national boundaries. The implications of the later advances were truly transcontinental. By drastically reducing transport costs and improving the preservative qualities of primary products, the railroad, the iron-steamship and the innovation of new refrigeration and temperature controlling techniques opened up new sources of food and raw materials from distant countries. *Inter alia* these developments led to an increase in the size of the foreign trade sector.

Two other features about the newer technologies are worth mentioning. First, they demanded a higher and more consistent quality of inputs (e.g. technology, management, skilled labour) than their predecessors. At the same time, the materials they used were geographically more dispersed. Often the possession of these inputs generated advantages to firms which were not only exclusive (at least for a period of time) to the firms possessing them, but were transferable across national boundaries via FDI or by contractual agreement. Second, they tended to be more complex than their predecessors in that their output required a larger number of divisible production processes, both lateral – in the case of fabricating industries – and vertical – in the case of continuous processing industries. Yet to be fully effective these separate processes frequently needed to be coordinated within the same firm. Hence, economies of scale and specialization went hand in hand with economies of joint production. This integration extended beyond the production process to the purchasing of inputs and the marketing of outputs. Indeed, some writers, notably Chandler (1977), have asserted that access to and control over distribution networks was fundamental to the successful commercial exploitation of the new technologies.

As a result of these developments, many firms grew into multinational, multi-regional and multi-activity units. According to Chandler (1980), the modern industrial enterprise did not grow primarily by producing something new or by a different way; it grew by

> 'adding new units of production and distribution, by adding sales and purchasing offices, by adding facilities for producing raw and semi-finished materials, by obtaining shipping lines, railroad cars, pipelines and other transportation units and even by building research laboratories' (Chandler, 1980, p. 397).

Putting the Chandlerian thesis in another way, the competitive advantages of firms were becoming less based on the natural resources of the countries in which they produced and more on their capabilities and willingness to innovate new products and methods of production, and to coordinate these with a series of complementary assets and related value-adding activities. In the pursuance of creating and sustaining these advantages, firms increasingly took on organizational functions previously undertaken by the market. In the generation of O-specific assets and the internalization of the market for these advantages, the first and second conditions for the existence of the modern MNE, as set out in Chapter 4, were fulfilled. At the same time, events were occurring which favoured the location of at least some of these activities outside the home country of the innovating firms.

Chapter 3 distinguished two main reasons why firms initially choose to engage in FDI. The first is to obtain and control the production and marketing of intermediate products which are inputs to other value-adding activities of the investing firms; such investment was referred to as *resource-seeking investment*. The second is to acquire control over the production of goods and services embodying intermediate products which are also produced by the investing firms; such investment was called *market-seeking investment*. Data on the industrial distribution of both the European and US foreign direct capital stake in 1914 suggests that in the preceding half-century or so the amount of the two kinds of investment was about even. Most resource-based investment was going to the developing countries and most market-seeking investment was being attracted to Europe and North America. Of an estimated $2.6 billion of US FDI in 1914, $1.4 billion (54.6%) was in petroleum, mining or agricultural activities; the balance was in manufacturing, railroads, utilities and sales and marketing organizations (Lewis, 1938). Of the 3373 UK enterprises that operated wholly or very largely overseas and were quoted on the London Stock Exchange in the same year, 1802 (53.4%) were engaged in primary production and the balance in manufacturing or service activities (Houston and Dunning, 1976).

In his study of Continental European MNEs, Franko (1976) identified 167 manufacturing subsidiaries that had been set up by 85 large European MNEs before 1914. In addition, these firms owned 48 mining, petroleum or plantation operations. No separate data of investments in other primary product sectors is available. In an analysis of Swedish direct investments before 1927, Lundström (1986) found that most were made by manufacturing companies seeking foreign customers. Outbound German MNE activity also tended to be market seeking, with the US chemical and electrical engineering sectors attracting the largest share of capital exports (Hertner, 1986; Wilkins, 1988b).

French business interests abroad date back to the mid-19th century when St Gobain established a branch plant in Germany. By 1914, French MNEs were operating in a wide range of sectors, either to exploit natural resources or to seek new markets. Swiss MNEs, which were already active in several consumer good sectors and in hotels, were particularly renowned for their quality control techniques (Himmel, 1922). The Société Générale de Belgique was one of the largest diversified Belgian international investors of the late 19th century. At the other end of the scale, Wilkins (1990a, p. 27), referring to some work of Van der Wee and Goosens (1990), reported that 'individual Belgian entrepreneurs had many direct investments abroad'.

The main thrust of Japanese MNE activity in the late 19th and early 20th centuries was to promote her industrial exports and ensure that her domestic factories had adequate supplies of raw materials. Hence the importance attached to building up an efficient network of trading companies. Outside trade, most Japanese investment was directed to neighbouring territories, particularly to China, which, according to the Bank of Japan (quoted in Wilkins, 1986), accounted for 77.5% of Japan's foreign business investments at the turn of the century.

China, in fact, had already attracted a good deal of Western investment in such sectors as ship repair and maintenance, silk processing, soy bean manufacturing and railroads. This was noticeably speeded up as a result of the Shimonoseki Treaty in 1895 which permitted, for the first time, foreigners to manufacture in Chinese treaty ports. However, according to Wilkins (1986), some 36% of the 136 foreign-owned cotton plants set up between 185 and 1913 were Japanese owned. The Chinese match industry was exclusively in Japanese hands and there waer substantial Japanese direct investments in the coal, iron and shipping sectors. Wilkins (1986) also observes tha tthe main O-spoecific advantages of Japanese firms (*vis à vis* Chinese companies) at the time lay in their substantially greater industrial experience, their entrepreneurial initiative, their strong motivation to tap foreign markets, and the fact that they frequently had good financial support from their own banks. The following paragraphs explore the reasons for these two kinds of foreign production in more detail.

5.4.2 Market-seeking investments

Although the structure of market-seeking MNE activity differed according to its country of origin, each was prompted by the desire or necessity to exploit perceived competitive advantages through the establishment of foreign value-adding facilities. These O-specific advantages varied according to the extent of a firm's industrial or geographical diversification, the nature of its production and managerial capabilities and the market structure of the investing country.

In an analysis of 119 UK manufacturing firms that undertook FDIs in the 1870–1939 period, Nicholas (1982) found that one-half set up factories abroad to exploit a perceived technological advantage. A later study by Archer (1986), based on information provided by 187 UK MNEs, suggested that the possession of brand names and trademarks, and the ability to supply high quality, differentiated goods and services, was ranked next to superior technology and managerial competence as the principal O advantage. This finding is consistent with the fact that the greater part of the market-seeking investment by UK foreign investors before the First World War was in the processing and consumer goods sectors, and that UK affiliates abroad were producing goods at the later stage in the product cycle (Vernon, 1966).

By contrast, US direct investment abroad was primarily directed to the newer capital-intensive mass production and fabricating sectors. To quote from Mira Wilkins (1970, p. 66):

> 'The US triumph abroad was one of ingenuity, new products, new methods of manufacturing and new sales and advertising techniques. Americans who made overseas commitments had something distinctive to offer foreign customers. They sought not only to cater for, but to create foreign demand. From sewing machines to drugs to oil to insurance, aggressive and imaginative marketing gave Americans an advantage. Americans went abroad when they discovered their advantage.'

The competitive advantages of Continental European firms seemed to be strongest in the chemical and electrical engineering sectors. In his study of some of the largest Continental MNEs, Franko (1976, p. 77) concluded that product and process innovations tended to be biased towards material savings and 'working class and luxury products'. Notable exceptions were Nestlé's mother's milk substitute and a series of electrical innovations by Siemens and AEG of Germany and Philips of Eindhoven. Taking a host-country perspective, Brown (1979) concluded that superior production techniques by European MNEs, relative to indigenous firms, helped to develop and modernize the ship repair and maintenance and silk industries in China. In his analysis of MNE activity in Japan between 1899 and 1931, Mason (1987) argued that although the amount of foreign capital invested was small, the impact was 'very great indeed'. *Inter alia* it provided advanced production methods and valuable knowledge about Western management methods and financial control systems,[9] and training and skill development for Japanese workers.

In spite of the differences in the organizational structures of US and European MNEs in the late 19th century,[10] the early US and European MNE firms had two features in common. The first was that they were managed by dynamic entrepreneurs who were willing to take the risk of venturing into unfamiliar territories. In his examination of British manufacturing MNEs prior to 1914, Stopford (1974, p. 318) observed that they were all led by men who shared a global vision. Examples included William Lever (of Lever Brothers), Thomas Johnston (of Nobel Explosives) and A. Dewhurst (of English Sewing Cotton). Sometimes the business leaders were themselves foreigners. For example, Henry Welcome and Silas Burroughs (of the British firm Burroughs and Welcome) were US citizens.[11] Continental Europe also produced its entrepreneurs, such as Henri Deterding (of Royal Dutch Shell) and Lars Ericsson (of Ericsson). In the US, too, men such as Alexander Graham Bell, Thomas Edison, George Westinghouse, George Eastman and Isaac Singer all played an active role in the internationalization of their businesses.

The second common feature of both European and US market-seeking investments was that they were strongly concentrated in sectors characterized by oligopolistic competition. This was also a time when companies were beginning to use foreign production as a strategic tool. The two decades before the First World War saw the emergence of a group of industries, for example, pharmaceuticals, tyres, electrical equipment, oil and motor vehicles, in which the leading firms vied with each other to establish some kind of presence in the larger and more promising foreign markets.

While the possession of some kind of competitive advantage was a necessary prerequisite for market-seeking FDI, the impetus to engage in foreign production was entirely based on the perceived net economic benefits of such production *vis-à-vis* exports from a home-based factory. Here the evidence is very clear. In particular, four specific factors appeared to have been of paramount importance in influencing MNE activity.

The first was the imposition, by host governments, of a variety of import barriers on foreign made goods and services. Between 1860 and 1904, the US, Canadian and most European governments sharply increased their tariffs on a wide range of imported manufactured products. Before the Civil War, for example, three-quarters of the trade of J. & P. Coats had been with the United States. A 50% tariff imposed in 1864 forced the company, and other cotton thread producers, to relocate their manu-facturing activity in the US. That this was success-fully accomplished is shown by the fact that by the outbreak of World War I, British-owned subsidiaries accounted for four-fifths of the cotton thread pro-duced in the US (Wilkins, 1989).

Up to 1890, the United States bought 70% of the tinplate produced in South Wales. Then an *ad valorem* tariff of 90% was imposed as a result of which some 60 Welsh mills were closed down (Berthoff, 1953). In an effort to recapture the market, there was a steady migration of capital, technology and labour across the Atlantic. Earlier tariffs imposed by the US government had had a similar effect. In 1867 W. and S. Butcher of Sheffield, maker of crucible steel and tools opened a steelworks in Philadelphia (Corley, 1992). In 1864 two British chemists began to produce aniline oil and magenta in a New York factory (Wilkins, 1989). However, perhaps the largest exodus of capital and people occurred in the British silk industry. It is estimated that some 16 000 people migrated from Macclesfield in England between 1870 and 1893. Several United Kingdom companies moved the whole or part of their plants to the United States. Sometimes they crated their machinery and moved lock, stock and barrel with their employees (Mason, 1920). They fared rather better than the tinplate manufacturers; in particular, they captured most of the US market in velvet and satins.

From their examination of business histories, both Archer (1986) and Jones (1986) concluded that tariffs were the single most important trigger leading to foreign investment by market-seeking British MNEs before 1914.[12] Increased import duties also led German dyestuff, pharmaceutical and electrical manufacturers to set up production facilities in France and Russia (Hertner, 1986); Swiss textile firms to manufacture in Italy (Wavre, 1988);[13] Dutch soap and food processing firms to relocate some of their activities in Belgium and Germany (Franko, 1976); and the American Tobacco Company to enter into the UK market in 1901 (Dunning, 1958). Likewise, much of the early US manufacturing investment in Canada was laid at the door of the Canadian Tariff Act of 1879 (Marshall *et al.*, 1936). There are also instances of US firms investing in the UK in order to gain favoured access to Common-wealth markets.[14]

Along with tariffs and import controls, foreign governments often used other means to attract inward direct investment. The Russian government, for example, limited its purchases of many industrial products to domestically located firms (Kirchner, 1981). Patent legislation and, in particular, the insistence by some governments that foreign-owned patents should be locally exploited, prompted such companies as Dunlop to set up rubber tyre factories in France and Germany (Jones, 1984); Siemens to invest in France to supply electric lighting equip-ment; Bell Telephones to manufacture telephone equipment in Canada; Badische and Hoechst to produce dyestuffs in England (Jones, 1988); and several US firms to establish production facilities in the UK (Lewis, 1937; Wilkins, 1970; Jones, 1988). On the other hand, the absence of any legal obligation to use patents granted by the US ad-ministration meant that German dye makers could supply most of the US market by exports or by becoming US companies (Hertner, 1986).

There are also several instances of governments offering a variety of tax and other incentives to foreign investors. A reading of business histories suggests that such incentives influenced Lever to invest in South Africa, American steel companies to set up plants in Canada, and Vickers (the armaments firm) to manufacture in several European countries. Many US states also offered generous fiscal induce-ments to tempt foreign firms into their, rather than other, regions. Contemporaneously, there are other cases of host governments deliberately discouraging inward investment, for example, in Mexican and Canadian railroads (Wilkins, 1970, p. 170).

The second locational factor prompting overseas investment may be labelled competitive strategy. Earlier, we suggested that most firms that engaged in foreign production in the late 19th century operated in oligopolistic industries. While this was not, itself, a sufficient motivation for foreign investment, it was most certainly a contributory factor and an important determinant of its timing. Perhaps the best known example of oligopolistic strategy influencing foreign production was Royal Dutch Shell's investment in the US. Other examples include the establishment of Dunlop's factory in Japan in 1899 as a pre-emptive move against US tyre companies; the setting up of Swiss and German synthetic dyestuff firms in Russia and France to 'match the international moves of rivals to maintain a certain share of the whole European market for their product' (Franko, 1976); the establishment of Japanese textile companies in China, which was a direct response to the opening up of Shanghai and other ports to Western manufacturers (Wilkins, 1986); and the widespread practice of subsidiary matching by Dutch margarine firms in Continental Europe (Franko, 1976, p. 95).

The third impetus for 19th century firms to produce abroad was to reduce freight and production costs. Much of US direct manufacturing investment in Europe and European investment in Commonwealth countries in the late 19th century was geared to this end. Clearly, such an impetus was most pronounced where the goods supplied were bulky, fragile or perishable commodities, and where labour, raw materials and energy costs were substantially lower in the foreign than in the home country. Industries such as cement, chocolates, brewing, flour, milking, and iron and steel manufacturing fell into this category. Examples ranged from Anglo Swiss Condensed Milk's venture in Norway to produce condensed milk and Tobler's investment in Italy to supply chocolate, to Westinghouse's manufacture of brakes in Paris. Political, cultural and economic ties also help to explain the preference of UK companies for production sites in the White Dominions and the Indian subcontinent; Belgian and French investment in parts of Africa; and US investment in South America. The ability to raise finance in the City of London was also a factor in influencing the locational choice of US companies setting up subsidiaries in Europe (Jones, 1988).

Fourth, firms engaged in FDI to be near the market and to cater to the specific and special needs of local customers. This was the reason given by the Western Electric Company and the International Bell Telephone Company for their decision to manufacture telephone equipment in Belgium in 1882 (Wilkins, 1970, p. 51). This became more important as markets grew, and was especially noticeable where differences in factor endowments and consumer tastes required adaptation of the products supplied by, or the production methods used by, foreign firms. Frequently – particularly in service sectors such as banking and restaurants – foreign firms were set up to meet the needs of previously established foreign subsidiaries and/or of migrants.[15] The use of the inch system in the UK

apparently influenced the decision of SKF, the Swedish ball- and roller-bearing company to start manufacture in the UK in 1910 (Lundström, 1986). The British firm John Lysaght set up a factory in Australia in 1884 to produce wire netting to curb the spread of rabbits (Blainey, 1984).

In some cases, for example, American consumer goods manufacturers, the foreign invaders sought to create and fashion demand (Wilkins, 1970, p. 66). In others, such as Nestlé baby food, the attraction of large, high income markets made local manufacturing a viable proposition. By the turn of the century, Mercedes had formed a joint venture with the US piano producer Steinway to produce luxury vehicles in the US, while Daimler and Benz had begun production of their handcrafted luxury cars in Britain in 1893 and in the US some years later. Market-seeking investment to serve consumers in developing countries sometimes required even greater adaptation as a result of differences in tastes and needs, or of local supply capabilities. A good example is the (UK) Gramophone Company's investment in India, which was prompted by the perception that Indian consumers wanted records of indigenous, rather than of American, music (Stopford, 1974).

So much for the L-specific variables influencing market-seeking investment in the late 19th century. The final motive for such MNE activity reflected the preference for firms to internalize the markets for their competitive advantages. Why, for example, did not the innovators of the 19th century license the right to use the fruits of their innovations to foreign firms? Why did so many manufacturing investors prefer to own their sales and distributing facilities rather than use local agents?

Contemporary business historians suggest that there were two main reasons why firms preferred to engage in FDI. The first, which has been particularly well enunciated by Chandler (1980), is that just as the growth of the domestic corporation led to the 'creation of multi-unit enterprises, administered through managerial enterprises', so did the extension of these firms outside their national boundaries produce a similar result. Moreover, in each case the reason was the same, *viz* to reduce the transaction costs of the invisible hand of the market by vertical or horizontal integration. At the same time, distance and producing in an unfamiliar political, economic and cultural environment added to the costs and uncertainties of transportation, inventory control, worker motivation, supplier reliability and the protection of quality. Such market failures as these provided an additional reason for FDI.

The second reason is closely allied to the first, but rests less on the advantages of common governance than on the need to minimize the transaction costs of selling the output of a particular asset. Here the main rationale was to protect property rights and the interests of the investing firm. For example, Nicholas (1983) has suggested that the failure of independent sales agents to act (or be perceived to act) in the best interests of the exporting company was a powerful reason for early British investment in overseas sales and marketing activities.[16] The argument can be readily extended to explain Singer's preference for owning and managing its own retail and servicing outlets. Singer was one of the first firms to master a functional administrative structure which would characterize a later generation of MNEs (Davies, 1969). By 1914 it was reported that Singer had 1000 distribution centres scattered over Tsarist Russia (Kirchner, 1981). In the company's own words, independent agents 'did not pay sufficient attention to the product, did not know how to service it, failed to demonstrate it effectively and did not seek new customers aggressively'. Other well-known US manufacturers, such as the agricultural implement producers, chose to use franchise dealers (Chandler, 1980, p. 399). Further up the value-added chain, although some US companies had licensed their property rights to the foreign manufacturers, most perceived that FDI would better protect these rights from misuse or dissipation. Moreover, in some instances the production processes and equipment were so new that there was insufficient local know-how (or know-why!) for their successful implementation.

While both kinds of market failure just described influenced all kinds of market-seeking investments, those undertaken by the processing industries (e.g. chemicals, food, drink and tobacco) tended to rest more on the second, while those by the fabricating sectors (e.g. metal using and engineering) tended to be of the first. This is partly because managerial hierarchies were more pronounced in the latter sectors, which also recorded a higher ratio of transactions to value added. It also explains why the

advantages of common governance were most visible in large and diversified firms. An analysis of the industrial composition of pre-1914 foreign activities by US MNEs reveals that there was a clear bias towards sectors that possessed assets and capabilities best organized by managerial hierarchies. By contrast, European FDI was more likely to be undertaken by firms whose competitiveness rested on their favoured possession of specific intangible assets (Chandler, 1980; Franko, 1976).

An examination of the leading US market-seeking foreign affiliates established before 1914 reveals that about three-fifths were concentrated in the fabricating industries and the rest in processing industries (Wilkins, 1974). The respective proportions for UK firms were one-third and two-thirds, and for Continental European firms one-quarter and three-quarters (Vaupel and Curhan, 1970). Interestingly, the pattern of Swedish manufacturing investment more closely resembled that of the US than that of the rest of Europe (Lundström, 1986). Of some 27 US firms identified by Jones (1988) as having set up manufacturing subsidiaries in the UK before 1914, all but seven were in fabricating industries, whereas 15 of the 23 affiliates of Continental European investors were in the processing sectors. All of the Swedish manufacturing affiliates in the UK were in fabricating sectors. However, by US standards most of these investments were small and their parent companies were usually much less vertically integrated than their American counterparts.

The conclusion of the above paragraphs is that it is difficult to generalize about either the characteristics or the determinants of market-seeking MNE activity before 1914. The Chandlerian view of the growth of large firms in terms of the advantages offered by vertical or horizontal integration (i.e. the Ot advantages identified in Chapter 4) is certainly pertinent in explaining some kinds of FDI – particularly that of the larger and more diversified US firms. However, it is less convincing in accounting for the kind of foreign production that rests on the investing firm owning a specific intangible asset (i.e. the Oa advantages identified in Chapter 4) which, because of imperfections in the market for that asset, or its rights, the firm perceives that it can best utilize itself from a foreign location.

5.4.3   Resource-seeking investments

As the industrialization of the Western world proceeded, there was an increasing need for additional or new sources of materials to those available locally. At the same time, the innovations of the late 19th century tended to require different kinds of minerals and materials (e.g. oil, bauxite and rubber) than those required previously. In addition, as incomes rose consumers from temperate climates were increasingly demanding tropically produced food and drink products.

Since most of the resources involved were specific to particular locations, the factors explaining the 'where' of FDI are easily identified. In cases where investors had some choice, shipping costs, political and cultural ties and the quality of the infrastructure (e.g. roads, docks and public utilities) were among the key L-specific determinants. Many of the German investments in French iron ore mines prior to the First World War were designed to strengthen the position of the German iron and steel makers *vis à vis* their French competitors (Franko, 1976). For both economic and political reasons, British, French, Belgian and Dutch manufacturers preferred to source their raw materials from their colonial territories. American firms favoured Canada, Mexico and Chile for minerals and Mexico and the Caribbean for raw materials and agricultural products (Lewis, 1938), while Japanese firms owned valuable iron ore deposits and coal mines in China. On several occasions, particularly in colonial territories, MNEs themselves built roads, railroads, docks and warehouse facilities, and supplied the necessary housing and educational facilities for their workers.

Earlier in this chapter we suggested that much of world trade prior to the industrial revolution was organized by chartered trading or land companies. On occasions, these companies also invested in the local production and processing of the imported products they acquired. Generally speaking, however, this was not encouraged by the metropolitan powers. Industrialization vastly increased the demand for most raw materials, minerals and foodstuffs. At the same time, improved farming and mining techniques, a reduction in sea and land transport costs, and new storage techniques made this a practical possibility. Between 1800 and 1875, UK imports of primary products rose twenty fold in real terms. While the majority of these products were supplied by indigenous producers, an increasing proportion – though we have no record of how much – was provided by MNE affiliates.[17] The interesting question is 'why'?

The answer, suggested by the previous chapter, lies in the lower transactional costs of organizing the transnational purchase of primary products within the same firm rather than through the market. This, in itself, presupposes that the investing firm perceives it has sufficient O-specific advantages to produce and/or market these products, or expects to gain such advantages by FDI. The previous chapter also identified the nature of these advantages and the conditions under which MNEs preferred to exploit them via FDI rather than by licensing or other non-equity arrangements.

The late 19th century brought about a number of important economic changes which fundamentally changed the nature and organization of trade in intermediate products. The first was the increasingly technological and capital intensity of the production of primary products. This was, perhaps, most clearly seen in the petroleum and non-metallic mining sectors. However, the years preceding the First World War were also the heyday of the large plantation economy for many foodstuffs and raw materials. The second was the increasing importance attached to quality consistency and delivery reliability of some products by both industrial and domestic consumers: examples are petroleum, copper, bauxite and several agricultural products (e.g. pineapples, bananas and coffee). Each of these events clearly favoured the large producers and those best able to coordinate their production and marketing functions. These assets and organizational skills were, in the main, only available in the high income purchasing countries.

The third economic development was the growth of large and standardized markets. Since these markets were largely in developed countries, it was only natural that enterprises from these countries had privileged access to them and the knowledge of how best to supply them. These three factors, and the bargaining power which they afforded the investing firms, explain why they frequently dominated the production and trade of foreign-based natural resources.

The question, however, remains. Why should a firm wish to own intermediate products? Why not license the right to use the assets that it possessed? Internalization theory suggests several strategic and economic reasons why a firm might wish to engage in cross-border backward vertical integration. The first is to gain control over the supply of essential resources in order to protect or strengthen its market position. In the late 19th century firms aggressively sought control of the supply of primary products both to close the markets to their competitors and as a defence against competitors pursuing such a strategy.

The second, and no less powerful, motive for backward integration is to forestall a foreign supplier from using his options (e.g. vary output, raise prices, vary quality, alter delivery dates, etc) to the buyer's disadvantage. This certainly was an important reason cited, for example, by British firms investing in the US and Argentinean cattle-raising industry, as well as US MNEs involved in hard mineral ventures in Chile and Bolivia (Lewis, 1938; Coram, 1967). The third reason is to ensure that the quality and efficiency of the intermediate products supplied meet the purchaser's requirements and standards. This suggests that the purchaser has superior knowledge which he perceives that, without ownership, cannot or will not be implemented by the supplier. Sometimes this might be because the supplier perceives that the capital investment required is not economically justifiable. Alternatively it might be because the supplier does not have the managerial or organizational skills to implement and monitor the use of advantages. Much US and European FDI in agribusiness ventures in developing countries was undertaken for this reason (Wilkins, 1988b).

In their respective analyses of US, British and Continental European MNEs investing in resource-based sectors, Wilkins, Stopford and Franko each tell a similar story. Wilkins observes that by far the largest number of foreign investments by US MNEs prior to 1914 were in sales or manufacturing activities, while only a few companies had supply-oriented investments in more than one country. She attributes this situation to the fact that, for most of the 19th century, the US was self-sufficient in most minerals, raw materials and foodstuffs. Indeed, right up to the outbreak of the First World War, the US was a substantial exporter of crude petroleum.

Nonetheless, she names nine US companies which had extraction or agricultural holdings in more than one country in 1914 (Wilkins, 1970, p. 216). In addition, she and other scholars (e.g. Lewis, 1938; Stopford, 1974) have also identified several manufacturing companies engaged in backward vertical integration in the late 19th or early 20th century. These included the leading rubber tyre producers (e.g. Dunlop and Firestone) which owned plantations in Malaysia and Liberia, respectively; Singer, which owned iron mines and timberlands in Russia; the meat processing companies (e.g. Armour and Swift) which owned cattle ranches in Argentina and Uruguay; American Tobacco, which owned tobacco plantations in Cuba and Turkey; Diamond Match, which owned forests in Canada; Amalgamated Copper, which owned copper mines in Mexico; and Dupont, which owned potash mines in Chile.

Most US mineral and oil producers initially made their investments abroad to sell their domestic output rather than engage in primary production. Again, tariffs were a major contributory factor. The hard mineral companies led the way. These included the Oxford Nickel & Copper Company, set up in 1878 to exploit nickel deposits in Canada; the Batopilas Mining Company (a consortium of five silver companies), to mine silver in Mexico; and the American Smelting and Refining Company, which was to become one of the foremost miners and smelters of lead and silver in Mexico. In Chile, American capital – drawn by a highly stable domestic environment and generous investment incentives – dominated the initial development of the copper industry, with the Braden Copper Company and the Guggenheim family each playing a major entrepreneurial role (O'Brien, 1989). In Canada, US interests were primarily directed to the asbestos and precious metals industries, while in the Caribbean, inward investors were attracted to the opportunities offered by asphalt and iron ore.

The oil companies first entered the FDI arena as market seekers. It was not until the first decade of the 20th century that US MNEs began producing crude oil, primarily in Mexico, Canada, Peru and Rumania. Of these companies, none pursued a more aggressive international strategy than Standard Oil. By 1900 this company was already an established MNE, and by 1907 it had acquired control of 55 foreign enterprises. As the world demand for oil rose rapidly, Standard Oil searched for new markets. It tried to obtain a stake in the Far East – notably in Burma and the Dutch East Indies – but was thwarted in so doing by the British and Dutch governments. Apart from small investments in Canadian, Romanian and Mexican fields, it engaged in no further oil exploration prior to its dissolution in 1911. However, between 1911 and 1914 several other US companies increased their investment in Mexican oil fields (Lewis, 1938).

In the raw material and agricultural sectors, US capitalists invested heavily in Canadian forests – in 1909 it was estimated that 90% of the available timber in British Columbia was controlled by US citizens or enterprises – Mexican rubber plantations and cattle raising. Most US interest in the late 19th century, however, was directed to the Caribbean. Many of today's giant agribusiness MNEs had their origins in these years. Wilkins (1970, p. 151) tells of how US trader turned investor Captain Lorenso Dow Baker started the banana trade in 1870, and Andrew Preston marketed the fruit in the US. The two merged their interests in 1885, and the new firm, Boston Trust Company (later acquired by the United Fruit Co.), soon decided that 'in order to secure a reliable source of fruit' (Wilkins, 1970, p. 151) it should grow as well as purchase and market bananas. To this end, the firm bought plantations in Jamaica and Santo Domingo.

Elsewhere in the Caribbean, defaults on loans made to Cuban sugar growers by US merchants resulted in companies like Atkins and Company acquiring sugar plantations in the 1880s. By 1885 it was reported that there were 200 US engineers and machinists engaged in Cuban sugar estates (Jenks, 1928). Exempt from US import duty and employing the latest production techniques, sugar production proved highly profitable for American investors, and by 1909 US affiliates were producing 40% of Cuban sugar (Lewis, 1938).

The story of United Fruit's foreign operations is well known.[18] It is one of the most fascinating in the early history of MNE activity. When the company was formed in 1889, it owned or leased 322 000 acres of land in the West Indies. The land was not only allocated to the production of bananas, but also to that of oranges, coconuts, rubber and sugar. Initially the United Fruit Company bought 65% of its bananas on the open market and through contracts.

However, it soon decided to purchase additional land with a view to producing four-fifths of the fruit it marketed. According to Wilkins (1979, p. 158), this policy was prompted by the need to improve quality consistency and the failure of local growers to respect contracts.

In addition, United Fruit began to acquire its own transportation and distributing facilities to protect itself against delivery uncertainties. It owned railroads in several banana producing countries, and steamship companies to transport its products to the US. It was one of the first resource-based companies to realize and exploit the benefits of the common governance of cross-border production, purchasing, transport and marketing activities. It installed sewage, drainage and water systems, built roads, established company towns and invested in hospitals.[19] By 1899 United Fruit controlled 90% of the banana imports of the US. By 1915 it was one of the largest MNEs in the world and owned assets of nearly $90 million (Read, 1983).

The involvement of US direct investment in the agricultural sector of the Caribbean is also an excellent example of the early interaction between home government and business interests. This, again, is a well documented story[20] which culminates in the action of President Taft sending gunboats and marines into the Caribbean to protect US-owned property and the commercial interests of American affiliates. There are many other less dramatic examples of the US authorities influencing the amount, kind and course of FDI in the early years of the 20th century,[21] while host governments were not slow to offer tempting concessions to foreign companies to promote indigenous resource development.

In South America, US investments in agribusiness were differently focused. There was some investment in rubber plantations in Peru, Bolivia and Brazil, as well as some cattle ranching in Paraguay. American meat packers, however, did not integrate backwards into cattle lands. Instead they expanded horizontally when they were faced with growing competition to their own exports from Argentine meat packers. By 1914, most US meat packing plants had investments in Brazil, Paraguay, Uruguay and Argentina. Their primary motive was to protect their existing markets; the evidence suggests they were prepared to pay a substantial price to do so.

Resource-seeking investments by British manufacturing firms were also prompted by the need to counteract market failure. For example, by owning and controlling their own sources of oil and rubber, companies such as Shell and Dunlop could better offer their customers secure and stable supplies, while lessening their own dependence on unfriendly market forces. As processing activities became more capital intensive, so the cost of supply irregularities mounted. Some firms, too, integrated backwards to gain information on mining or cultivating techniques (Jones, 1986). Rather than rely on bilateral contractual agreements, UK manufacturers increasingly preferred to own and control their primary sources of production.

Examples of cross-border vertical integration prompted by this concern included Cadbury's investments in cocoa plantations in the Gold Coast and Trinidad; those of Crosfield (later Unilever) in vegetable oil plantations in Dutch West Africa; those of Fitch Lovell in cattle raising and meat packing plants in the US; those of Imperial Tobacco of tobacco leaf in Nyasaland; and those of Turner Brothers (later Turner & Newall) in asbestos mines in Rhodesia and South Africa (Stopford, 1974; Houston and Dunning, 1976). British and Russian tea merchants were also active in promoting a higher and more uniform quality of leaf tea produced in China.

No less important than security of supply was the need by industrial customers to obtain primary products at a reasonable price. William Lever, for example, was greatly suspicious of the combines and rings among foreign raw material producers, and was convinced they worked to the disadvantage of the purchasing manufacturers. As a result, in the early 1900s Lever began to acquire vegetable oil plantations in the Solomon Islands, Belgian Congo and Nigeria.

Unlike their US counterparts, however, most British companies investing in foreign natural resources did not engage in similar operations in the UK. However, the London market was instrumental in financing most of the overseas mining and commodity ventures, and many free-standing companies were floated there. These included MNEs such as Rio Tinto Zinc, Gopeng Tin Mining, Consolidated Gold Fields of South Africa and Borax Consolidated Ltd, whose O-specific advantages were based partly on the expertise and experience in

mining *et al.* built up over the years, partly on their favoured access to the international (and particularly the UK) capital market[22] and partly on their privileged access to final product markets. These assets enabled them to offer host countries a superior package of assets to those of their competitors.

The late 19th century also witnessed a variety of more speculative UK foreign investments directed to the mineral sector. Between 1851 and 1913, at least 174 British mining companies owned or controlled copper-pyrites, iron, lead and silver mines in Spain. Together with French and German interests, they dominated the Spanish minerals sector (Harvey and Taylor, 1987).[23] Another study (Wilkins, 1989) has identified 659 companies which were registered in Britain between 1880 and 1904 to promote mining ventures in the US alone. By 1889 it was estimated that foreign (mainly UK) owned companies accounted for more than 25% of the copper mining output of the US. There was also some activity by UK MNEs in the iron and steel industry in the American South, prompted by high tariffs and the perception that, unless they produced in the US, they would lose the market to indigenous firms. Individual entrepreneurs, or groups of entrepreneurs, initially played a crucial role, but these later gave way to syndicates like the Southern States Coal, Iron and Land Company, which helped found the industrial town of South Pittsburgh in Tennessee in 1877 (American Iron and Steel Association, 1887). In the main, these investments were unsuccessful, primarily, it seems, because of the incompetence (and sometimes dishonesty) of local management, an inadequate appreciation of local mining conditions and unanticipated organizational problems (Coram, 1967).

In general, there was little attempt by British – or indeed by European – investors to exploit the benefits of vertical integration. Wilkins (1989) puts this down to the fact that, while US companies invested abroad to acquire intermediate products for their domestic factories, European MNEs primarily invested in the US to sell to the local market.[24]

British interests were also active in promoting agricultural activities in the US. Foremost among these was cattle raising. Here, British investors were attracted by the very high profits being earned by indigenous cattle firms in the 1860s and 1870s. Much of the capital originated from Scotland and was channelled through mortgage and investment brokers whose managers were well experienced in financing the animal husbandry business in their home country. Between 1879 and 1889, there were some 41 acquisitions by British companies of cattle ranches in the American West; over £10 million was invested (Wilkins, 1989). Large acreages of cattle ranches in Texas, Wyoming, Colorado and New Mexico were owned by British companies (Lewis, 1938).

Not only capital, but also expertise was transferred across the Atlantic. Cattle breeds improved as imported British pedigree animals bettered the US stock. Scottish husbandry and breeding techniques were transferred to America, and there was also some migration of cattlemen from Scotland. At the same time, the cattle raising companies did not integrate forwards into meat packing, although, as we have already seen, several UK meat packers set up branches in the US in the 1880s.

However, dwarfing all other resource-based foreign investments were those of the British and Anglo-Dutch oil companies. By the turn of the century, Royal Dutch Shell already owned oil wells in the Dutch East Indies (now Indonesia).[25] From there, it acquired new fields in Russia and Rumania. By 1914 Shell controlled almost 20% of the total Russian oil production (Davenport-Hines and Jones, 1988). The discovery of oil in the Middle East did not occur until 1908. Royal Dutch Shell's purchase of oil fields in California and Oklahoma in the early 1900s was in direct retaliation to Standard Oil's incursion into the Far East. However, it was also made to gain access to the world's largest market for oil. As John Stopford puts it (Stopford, 1974, p. 332), Royal Dutch Shell 'though only 40% British-owned was a classic example of British capital at work to exploit natural resources on a worldwide scale'.

Continental European investments in the primary activities were mainly concentrated in the extractive sector. One of the first (but unsuccessful) ventures was that of a Dutch sugar refining company in a maple sugar subsidiary in upstate New York in 1792 (Wilkins, 1989). Franko (1976) tells of how several large European manufacturing enterprises integrated backwards into coal, bauxite, iron ore, nickel, copper, zinc and oil. A substantial proportion of these investments were located elsewhere in Europe; only a few appear to have been directed to colonial or other developing territories. It would

seem that Continental European governments were anxious not to be unduly dependent on foreign supplies which might be cut off by English sea power or the closure of the Suez Canal (Franko, 1976, p. 52).[26]

Apart from the Dutch, there was little interest by Continental European firms in foreign oil exploration. By World War I, the Belgian MNE, Union Miniere, was beginning to extract copper and other non-ferrous ores from the Congo; its later role in that country has been compared to that of the United Fruit Company in the Caribbean.

There were few Continental European equivalents to the free-standing investments of British companies in minerals, raw materials and agricultural products. French and German companies seemed to prefer either to invest in UK enterprises which, themselves, engaged in free-standing investments, or to own and manage their own foreign affiliates. French companies, for example, mined silver in the US, copper in Spain and the US, and phosphate in the US and North Africa. The Germans were among the world's largest traders in zinc and lead. Drawing upon their long experience and technical expertise, they integrated backwards into US and Latin American smelting and refining operations.

Some large US mining companies were also started by German expatriates. There was a substantial German involvement in US potash mines, while in the early 1900s a US subsidiary of the German precious metals firm DEGUSSA supplied most of the cyanide required by US industry. There was also some European direct investment in Russian coal mining which, according to one economic historian (McKay, 1974), was accompanied by new techniques in the washing, sorting and coking of coal, as well as in the ventilation, electrification and centralization of pits.

On a different continent, the first major foreign investment by an Australian company occurred in 1882 when the Colonial Sugar Refining Company (CSR) began investing in the Fijian Sugar Industry (Bureau of Industry Economics, 1984). This was a defensive horizontal investment intended to prevent the Fijian Sugar Industry becoming a competitive threat to the Queensland industry. Australian MNEs were also among the first and most successful iron, tin and gold mining investors in Malaya (now Malaysia). Such investment dates back to the 1880s. According to Birch (1976), by 1930 Australian companies accounted for a sizeable stake of the foreign mining sector in both Malaya and Siam (now Thailand).

Finally, there was some supply-oriented foreign investment which originated from retailers. One example was the investments by the Englishman, Thomas Lipton, in US meat packing plants in the period 1880–1902. Others were directly involved in the wholesale and retail meat trade, but again, these investments were mostly short-lived.

5.4.4   Other investments

Finally, brief mention should be made of MNE activity that does not easily fit into the 'market' or 'resource' seeking categories. Foremost among these were FDIs in railroads, shipping and public utilities. However, although sometimes there was active foreign organizational and managerial participation, for example, by Japanese companies in Chinese shipping (Wilkins, 1986), most of these investments were of the free-standing kind rather than extensions of established domestic enterprises. There was more direct foreign control over railroad investments in developing countries, notably in India and Argentina, than in the US where there was adequate local manpower and technological capacity. The main problem of absentee foreign investors in this sector (as indeed in others) was to know who to trust and how (and to whom) to delegate responsibility.

By 1914, 60% of UK foreign portfolio and direct investment was in railroads (Houston and Dunning, 1976, p. 44); of all inward investment in the US, about one-third was in the sector (Lewis, 1938). However, there were few genuine multinational railroad companies. Similarly, most foreign participation in public utilities took the form of portfolio rather than direct investment, although in some developing countries, European and US MNEs dominated the gas and electric power supply sectors.

The late 19th century was also an active period for syndicated foreign investment. Substantial amounts of British capital poured into the US to acquire granaries, grain elevators, flour mills and breweries. In the period 1888–91, for example, 24 English syndicates acquired 80 breweries and two malt houses. Their reported investments amounted to $90 million (Coram, 1967). However, because of injudicious entrepreneurship and bad management, most of these ventures lost money and few remained in British ownership at the beginning of the First World War.

In the half-century before 1914, there was also some foreign production in a variety of service sectors. Multinational banks, such as Barclays (UK), Deutsche Bank (Germany), Société Générale (Belgium) and Banque de l'Indochine (France), established a network of offices in many parts of the world (Jones, 1992). By 1913, the 28 UK registered banks had already established 1286 foreign branches and agencies (Jones, 1990), more than double the number of branches set up by German and French banks (Aliber, 1984). Jones (1990) identifies the (then) O-specific advantages of UK banks as their ability to raise finance on the world's largest capital market at a lower cost than their competitors; the presence of related or supplier industries in the City of London, their organizational capabilities; their ingenuity in offering multiple services and differentiating their products; and their focused strategy on following their customers abroad.

By contrast, US banks lacked these capabilities. In addition, they were subject to statutory restrictions on branching. In consequence, as Wilkins (1990) observes, there were not many American banks with foreign operations before 1914 (p. 222). Wilkins (1986, 1990b) records that the Yokohama Specie Bank – the predecessor of the Bank of Tokyo – had set up an agency in New York City in 1880 while it was operating a branch in Bombay in 1894. According to another source (Tanaki, 1990) the same bank had established at least 21 overseas banking units (Taniaki, 1990). Chinese banks, which were later to become particularly prominent in South East Asia, had already set up affiliates in Malaya and the Straits Settlements (now part of the Federation of Malaya) by 1912 (Brown, 1990).

European shipping, cable and wireless companies were active in the US – the Marconi Company was the leading enterprise in the field of radio communication (Wilkins, 1989). Swiss hoteliers owned or managed hotels in Italy, France and North Africa (Himmel, 1922), while there were substantial Belgian investments in foreign tramways (Van der Wee and Goosens, 1990). There was a sizeable foreign direct investment stake in insurance, though mainly of US and UK origin. Best's Insurance Report for

1914 recalls that the First Bulgarian Insurance Company of Roustchouk, Bulgaria, operated offices in seven European countries and the US. Accounting, consultant engineering and construction firms from Europe and the US were represented in several developing and developed countries.

By the turn of the century, Japanese trading companies were accounting for one-half of the total exports of Japan (Yonekawa, 1985), while Japanese MNEs owned or controlled an important part of trans-Pacific shipping operations. By 1881 fourteen Japanese trading companies had branches in New York City; the purpose of which was both to promote Japanese exports, notably of silk, and to procure materials and machinery for domestic manufacturers. In 1914, one Japanese Trading Company, Mitsui, was reported as handling more than 30% of US raw cotton exports to Japan (Sugiyama, 1988, quoted by Wilkins, 1990). British, German and French companies were also actively involved in import/export merchanting, particularly in primary products.

5.4.5   The position prior to 1914: a resumé

Studies published in the past two decades suggest that earlier scholars considerably underestimated the role of FDI as a vehicle for the international transfer of intangible assets in the 40 years prior to the First World War (Dunning, 1983). By assembling widely disparate estimates of both the inward and the outward direct capital stake of countries, it would appear that by 1914 at least $14.5 billion had been invested in enterprises or branch plants in which either a single or a group of non-resident individuals or firms owned or controlled a majority (or a substantial minority) of the equity interest, or which were owned or controlled by first-generation expatriates who had migrated earlier. This amount represented about 35% of the estimated total long-term international debt at the time.

There is also little doubt that from the viewpoint of some home and host countries, MNE activity, both as a channel for the transfer of resources and capabilities between countries and as a means of controlling the use of these and complementary local assets, played a scarcely less important role than it

had since the mid 1950s, and a far greater one than it did in the inter-war period. Moreover, the territorial compass of FDI was probably wider than it had been for most of the last half century. Both Eastern Europe and China, for example, were attractive outlets to foreign businessmen in the years preceding the First World War. According to one estimate (McKay, 1974), between 1880 and 1913 roughly 50% of all capital invested in industrial corporations doing business in Russia was of foreign origin, while many of the coastal industries and trade of Eastern China was controlled by Japanese firms. It is also worth recalling that there were few governmental controls on either inward or outward investment flows in the late 19th and early 20th centuries, or on the scope or behaviour of the activities of MNEs or their subsidiaries.

While for the first three-quarters of the 19th century, direct capital exports[27] mainly comprised expatriate investment or finance raised in the home country by corporations or individual entrepreneurs, the subsequent 40 years saw the infancy and adolescence of the type of FDI that predominates today, *viz* that owned and controlled by firms already producing in their home countries. This latter thrust began around the middle of the 19th century and accelerated after 1875. By 1914 the MNE had become firmly established as a major vehicle of international economic involvement.

As revealed in Table 5.1, the UK was by far the largest foreign capital stakeholder in 1914. However, even at that time US investments were more directed to the growth sectors in foreign countries, and a much larger proportion represented the activities of affiliates of MNEs rather than of absentee equity owners.[28] Such country-specific differences reflected differences in resource endowments and capabilities, institutional mechanisms and trading propensities of the investing countries. Thus, while Europe had accumulated a pool of entrepreneurial and managerial expertise and was already a major portfolio capital exporter, the US, with none of this background, was building a strong comparative advantage in corporate technology and management skills, which were often best exploited within the enterprise generating them.

Table 5.2 also shows that about three-fifths of the foreign direct capital stake in 1914 was directed to today's developing countries. However, taking a definition of such countries, at the time, to include

Table 5.1 Estimated stock of accumulated foreign direct investment by country of origin 1914–60.

	1914		1938		1960	
	$m	%	$m	%	$bn	%
Developed countries	14 402	100.0	26 350	100.0	62.9	99.0
North America						
USA	2 652	18.6	7 300	27.7	31.9	48.3
Canada	150	1.0	700	2.7	2.5	3.8
Western Europe						
UK	6 500	44.6	10 500	39.8	10.8	16.3
Germany	1 500	10.3	350	1.3	0.8	1.2
France	1 750	12.0	2 500	9.5	4.1	6.2
Belgium					1.3	2.0
Italy					1.1	1.7
Netherlands	1 250	9.6	3 500	13.3	7.0	10.6
Sweden					0.4	0.6
Switzerland					2.3	3.5
Other developed countries						
Russia	300	2.1	450	1.7	neg	neg
Japan	300	2.1	750	2.8	0.5	0.8
Australia					0.2	0.3
New Zealand	180	1.2	300	1.1	na	na
South Africa					na	na
Other	neg	neg	neg	neg	2.5	3.8
Developing countries	neg	neg	neg	neg	0.7	1.1
Total	14 582	100.0	26 350	100.0	66.1	100.0

na   not available.
neg   negligible.

Source: As for Table 5.2.

all areas outside Western Europe and the US, the figure would rise to more than four-fifths. The distribution among recipient nations was quite diffused, with the combined Russian and Chinese share exceeding that of Western Europe and only slightly less than that of North America. The importance of non-resident capital and expertise in the development of both economies is often underestimated.

About 55% of the global FDI stake in 1914 was directed to the primary product sector, 20% to railroads, 15% to manufacturing activities, 10% to trade, distribution, public utilities and banking. Manufacturing investments, which were largely of a market-seeking variety, were mainly concentrated in Europe, the US, the UK Dominions and Russia. Apart from iron ore, coal and bauxite, almost all mineral investments were located in the British Commonwealth or in other developing countries.

Of especial significance in this era were raw material and agricultural investments. This was the heyday of the large plantations (rubber, tea, coffee and cocoa); of cattle raising and meat processing; and of the emergence of the vertically integrated MNEs in tropical fruits, sugar and tobacco. Indeed, apart, perhaps, from some transnational railroad activity in Europe and Latin America, it was in the agricultural sector that the international hierarchical organization first flourished. It was especially prominent in economies whose prosperity was highly dependent on a single cash crop, the production, distribution and marketing of which was controlled by a few foreign companies.

Table 5.2   Estimates stock of accumulated foreign direct investment by recipient country or area 1914–60.

	1914		*1938*		*1960*	
	$m	*%*	*$m*	*%*	*$bn*	*%*
Developed countries	5 235	37.2	8 346	34.3	36.7	67.3
North America						
USA	1 450	10.3	1 800	7.4	7.6	13.9
Canada	800	5.7	2 296	9.4	12.9	23.7
Europe						
Western Europe:	1 100	7.8	1 800	7.4	12.5	22.9
of which UK	(200)	(1.4)	(700)	(2.9)	(5.0)	(9.2)
Other Europe	1 400	9.9	400	1.6	neg	neg
of which Russia	(1 000)	(7.1)	—	—	—	—
Australasia and South Africa	450	3.2	1 950	8.0	3.6	6.6
Japan	35	0.2	100	0.4	0.1	0.2
Developing countries	8 850	62.8	15 969	65.7	17.6	32.3
Latin America	4 600	32.7	7 481	30.8	8.5	15.6
Africa	900	6.4	1 799	7.4	3.0	5.5
Asia	2 950	20.9	6 068	25.0	4.1	7.5
of which China	(1 100)	(7.8)	(1 400)	(5.8)	(neg)	(neg)
India and Ceylon	(450)	(3.2)	(1 359)	(5.6)	(1.1)	(2.0)
Southern Europe					0.5	0.9
Middle East	400	2.8	621	2.6	1.5	2.8
International and unallocated	neg	neg	na	na	na	na
Total	14 085	100.0	24 315	100.0	54.5	100.0

Sources of Tables 5.1 and 5.2: The data contained in these tables has been derived from a large number of sources but the main ones have been as follows:

1914   Allen and Donnithorne (China and Japan, 1954); Bagchi (India, 1972); Callis (South East Asia, 1942); Frankel, S. H. (Africa, 1938); Hou (China, 1965); Houston and Dunning (UK, 1976); Lewis (various, 1938, 1945); McKay (Russia, 1970); Pamuk (Ottomon Empire, 1981); Paterson (Canada, 1976); Rippy (Latin America, 1959); Svedberg (various, 1978); Wilkins (various, 1988).

1938   Allen and Donnithorne (China and Japan, 1954); Bagchi (India, 1972); Callis (South East Asia, 1942); Conan (Sterling Area, 1960); Hou (China, 1965);

Lewis (various, 1938, 1945); Svedberg (various data collected by him, 1978); Teichova (East Europe, 1974); United Nations (1949).

1960   Various government publications are cited in United Nations (UNCTC, 1981) and especially those of the United States (Department of Commerce); United Kingdom (Department of Trade); and Canada (Dominion Bureau of Statistics). See also Conan (Sterling Area, 1960) and Kidron (India, 1965).

1971   OECD (various dates); United Nations (UNCTC, 1978, 1981) and various government publications as cited therein.

1983   US Department of Commerce (1986); Dunning and Cantwell (1987).

By 1914, FDI was increasingly taking the form of branch plant activity by MNEs. Both resource-based and market-seeking investments were becoming strongly motivated by the desire to exploit the gains of vertical or horizontal integration of production as well as the desire to minimize the uncertainties of intermediate product markets. Increasingly, too, such cross-border activities were being conducted by international oligopolies. While dynamic entrepreneurship continued to be a key O-specific advantage, strategic considerations began to play a more important role in affecting foreign investment decisions.

5.5   THE MATURING OF FOREIGN PRODUCTION: 1918–39

5.5.1   Introduction

The First World War and the years that followed saw several changes in the level, form and structure of international production. The war itself caused several European belligerents to sell some of their investments, while consequential political upheaval and boundary changes further reduced intra-continental European corporate activity and eliminated it altogether from Russia. Of the major investing countries, only the US emerged unscathed by these events. However, along with other countries, it suffered from the collapse of international capital markets in the late 1920s and early 1930s. Nevertheless, because American MNE activity was largely directed to sectors supplying products with an above average income-elasticity of demand, the US share of the world direct capital stake rose from 18.5% in 1914 to 27.7% in 1938.

Overall, as Table 5.1 shows, the international capital stake rose quite substantially in the inter-war years. Although there were some sizeable West European investments in Central Europe (Teichova, 1974), the amount invested in Russia fell dramatically, particularly after 1930. The Americas continued to attract more than two-thirds of the US direct investment stake. While the role of intra-European and US participation in Europe fell in the 1920s, it partially recovered in the 1930s, as did European investments in the US. There was also some retrenchment of European economic involvement in Latin America – particularly in the railroad sector. This was partly compensated by a modest increase in UK direct investment in Commonwealth countries in an attempt to recapture export markets lost during the war.[29] Prior to the Sino-Japanese War, there was also a sharp rise of Western and Japanese business activity in China.

The case of Germany as an outward direct investor in the inter-war years is particularly interesting. Having lost most of her foreign assets in or after the First World War, German MNEs displayed a certain reluctance to invest abroad. Moreover, a shortage of financial resources and foreign exchange constrained their options. Instead, German enterprises turned to international cartels and contracts as a means of assuring the supplies of critical raw materials and protecting market shares in the leading industrial countries (Schroter, 1988).

One of the most popular areas for German direct investments in the inter-war years was Scandinavia. Sometimes, such involvement took the form of FDI (e.g. in Norwegian iron ore mines, nitrogen production, etc.), sometimes by cartel (e.g. that formed by ASEA, AEG and Siemens in the field of electrical power and by Dupont and I.G. Farben in chemicals), and sometimes by long-term contract. Examples of such contracts are those between the German iron and steel producers and the Swedish firm Granges for iron ore, and between I.G. Farben and the Danish dairy cooperative Valio for a chemical process designed to conserve livestock fodder (Schroter, 1988).

There was also quite a lot of new MNE activity in the developing world in the inter-war years. This included investments by US firms in new oil fields in the Mexican Gulf, the Dutch East Indies (now Indonesia) and the Middle East; in copper and iron ore in Africa; in bauxite in Dutch and British Guyana (now Surinam and Guyana); in nitrate in Chile; in precious metals in South Africa; and, perhaps most noteworthy of all, in nonferrous metals in South America. Indeed, in 1929 two experts on mining observed that 'the bulk of productive mineral resources of South America are owned by American interests' (quoted by Wilkins, 1974, p. 106). Outside the mineral sector, the growing industrial demand for rubber led both US and European tyre manufacturers to increase their capital stake in Liberia, Malaya and the Dutch East Indies. At the same time, rising real incomes in industrial countries prompted a further flurry of activity by MNEs in sugar, tropical fruit and tobacco. There was also a sizeable expansion of public utility investments in Latin America by US firms. Both US and UK MNEs extended their foreign sales and marketing ventures into production in these years.

Yet though the number of new subsidiaries set up by MNEs continued to rise throughout the period, it was only in the 1930s that the value of the foreign direct capital stake exceeded its pre-war figure. Investments by Continental European firms were directed mainly to other parts of Europe and the US, while those of US MNEs were strongly oriented to South America, Canada and the larger European countries. The first four foreign manufacturing affiliates of the largest Japanese corporations existing in 1970 were set up between 1920 and 1938 (Vaupel and Curhan, 1974). During this period, many of the major Japanese cotton spinners established local production bases in China, mainly to defend their market shares (Kuwahara, 1989), while some of the general trading firms (e.g. Mitsui and Mitsubishi) were active in setting up import/export merchanting agencies on the West Coast of the US (Kawabe, 1989).

In general, the climate for transnational commerce was considerably less favourable than in the years prior to 1914. Increasing tariffs and other import controls inhibited trade based on the specialization of country-specific resources and capabilities and efficiency-seeking foreign production. The resulting international economic environment encouraged import substituting investment and the formation of cross-border cartels to protect the participants against destructive competition. On the other hand, new technologies and organizational advances helped to push out the industrial and territorial boundaries of firms and to encourage product and process diversification. The demand for raw materials and foodstuffs from developed countries outstripped their supply from these countries. Sometimes this resulted in more FDI, for example, by European firms in their colonies and US firms in Latin America and the Caribbean. In other cases, it led to the replacement of imported materials by synthetic substitutes which the home country could produce.

The net result of these developments was to increase defensive market-seeking manufacturing investments and to slow down the growth of aggressive and efficiency-seeking manufacturing investment. Resource-based MNE activity continued to expand, especially from Continental European countries, but at a reduced pace as man-made materials (e.g. rayon, plastics, synthetic rubber) began to replace their natural competitors.

Another feature of the inter-war years was the decline of syndicate and free-standing FDI, and an increase in all kinds of MNE activity. The growth of foreign production increasingly took the form of vertical integration or horizontal diversification. This was a period in which both the average size and number of internal transactions of firms increased sharply. Cross-border acquisitions and mergers rose relative to greenfield investments. Asset acquiring FDI (see Chapter 3) increased as firms sought to protect or strengthen their market positions and/or reduce their production or transaction costs. At the same time, the strategy of domestic oligopolists widened to embrace international markets.

For much of the inter-war year period, international cartels flourished. Trade restrictions also forced MNEs to replicate the same value-added activities in several countries, with the result that sustainable levels of production were rarely attained. Governments both tolerated the suppression of domestic competition and encouraged international market-sharing schemes. The net result was that either markets were assigned to firms of particular nationalities or, as Franko puts it, 'oligopolistic matching of the markets gave way to entry en famille in manufacturing subsidiaries jointly owned by international rivals' (Franko, 1976, p. 95).

The propensity of firms to engage in one form of international economic involvement rather than another again varied by sector, country and enterprise. There were, for example, few cooperative agreements in the fast-growing motor vehicle industry, where the technological and marketing advantages of US MNEs were particularly strong. Each firm produced a limited range of products. Substantial economies of scale enabled US producers to acquire and apply a knowledge of production and management techniques which were not available to motor manufacturers elsewhere in the world. Also, the earlier experience gained by American firms in machine tool technology and the Taylor system of organizing production was to prove an invaluable O-specific advantage (Foreman-Peck, 1982). By contrast, in the electrical equipment industry and some branches of the chemical and heavy engineering industries, where cartels were rife, these conditions were largely absent.

Moreover, contractual technological exchanges were favoured by the recuperating large companies of Western Europe – particularly those of German origin – as a way of penetrating the American market without a substantial capital investment. This also explains why joint ventures were more common among European firms investing in the US than vice versa. During this time, there was also an easing of some kinds of vertical direct investments as new international commodity markets were set up. On the other hand, in those primary sectors characterized by large indivisible costs where high barriers to entry kept the number of firms small and the need to protect against fluctuations in output was especially important (e.g. oil, tropical fruit, rubber and several nonferrous metals), MNEs tightened their hierarchical control.

5.5.2   Market-seeking investments

The pattern of country-specific O advantages of established US and European manufacturing MNEs prior to 1914 continued throughout the inter-war years. For example, because of the structure of their supply capabilities and the size and nature of their domestic markets, US firms continued to gain strength in many fabricating industries. Indeed, by 1939 they probably accounted for two-thirds of the world's foreign direct capital stake in the engineering and motor vehicles sectors. Added to the new product and process innovations in these fields were important developments in managerial, organizational and working practices. Enlarged domestic markets also enabled US firms better to exploit the economies of vertical and horizontal integration which had prompted the growth of many domestic corporations prior to World War I.

With a few exceptions (e.g. the match, steel, tobacco and insurance industries, which lost some of their earlier competitive advantages),[30] US MNEs maintained a vigorous growth in the 1920s. Most of this growth was directed to Canada and Western European countries which, between them, accounted

for 72% of all US outbound manufacturing investment between 1919 and 1929. Between 1925 and 1929 alone, 303 new American factories were set up in Europe and Canada – 31% of all those operating in 1929 (Lewis, 1938, p. 599). Most of these were intended to produce goods in which US-owned firms had a competitive advantage, *viz* the newer metal-using and technology-intensive processing industries, and the high income, product differentiated, consumer goods sectors.[31] Their impact was viewed with some disquiet by the Europeans – particularly in the UK and Germany – so much so that the Americans were forced to disguise their origins or enter into joint ventures with host country partners (Wilkins, 1974). Anxiety was also voiced in other parts of the world, such as Latin America and Australia. By contrast, in Japan, inward investment was generally welcome, although frequently it was undertaken jointly with one or other of the leading Japanese companies or Zaibatsu. Mason (1987) documents a number of cases of knowledge transfers by European and US MNEs in the 1920s, including those by Western Electric (US), Dunlop Rubber (UK) and Siemens (Germany).[32]

As American corporations expanded into more foreign countries, the character of their O-specific advantages changed from those based on the possession of particular intangible assets to the way in which these and other assets were organized and coordinated across national boundaries. Increasingly, as MNEs added to their foreign assets (i.e. engaged in sequential investments) and established a presence in more countries, the role of their affiliates changed from being simply appendages of the parent firms to becoming part of a systemic network of cross-border value-added activities. While the advent of the global enterprise was not yet nigh, the movement towards the globalization of products and markets certainly began in the 1920s, and was primarily of US origin.

British and European MNEs continued to develop new O-specific advantages in the processing industries. In Europe, where the ratio of material costs to labour costs was so much higher than in the US and there was a greater reluctance to rely on foreign-sourced raw materials (e.g. rubber, fertilizers, dyestuffs),[33] every encouragement was given to the development of synthetic substitutes and the more efficient use of existing materials. More specific reasons, such as the introduction of state-supported health insurance and retirement schemes in Germany, conditioned other innovations. In his analysis of European MNEs, Franko (1976) suggests that while in the US most innovations were directed to a large middle-income market and were of a labour-saving kind, in Europe the markets served were at the luxury or lower end, labour was relatively cheap and many materials were either expensive or had to be imported. Within Europe, conditions differed. For example, French institutional structures and vocational training opportunities were generally less conducive to innovation than their German counterparts. Nevertheless, the French helped to pioneer the synthetic rayon and aluminium industries.

The European MNEs further developed their competitive advantages in two types of activities. The first was in the processing sectors, and particularly the chemical industry. Between 1920 and 1939 the growth of US patents granted to European chemical firms completely outstripped those granted to North American firms (Cantwell, 1992b). By 1940, the Germans were producing 90% of the world's output of synthetic dyestuffs. The second was in niche markets in the fabricating industries. The Germans again led the way in supplying luxury motor cars and high quality electrical products, or, as Franko (1976, p. 25) puts it, 'in the supply of unique goods or goods produced with a unique process'.

The two most noticeable characteristics about UK market-seeking MNEs in the inter-war years were the growth in their number and their preference for Commonwealth locations. In a survey of 448 pre-1939 UK manufacturing MNEs, Nicholas (1982) found that 52% of those set up post-1914 were located in such areas compared with 34% prior to 1914. Partly, this preference reflected the fact that the leading British enterprises of the time were very oriented towards Commonwealth territories, partly because they frequently followed the lead of US or German MNEs, and partly because they generally regarded such territories as easier to penetrate than the tougher industrialized markets (Stopford, 1974).

In the case of British chocolate manufacturers, the war so damaged their exports to the Canadian and Australian markets that they found the only way to regain those markets was by FDI (Jones, 1984). For a very different reason, George Kent, the UK instrument producer, set up a Canadian subsidiary to attack 'on their own ground US companies selling water meters and instruments in Europe' (Archer, 1986, p. 299). However, the company chose Canada rather than the US because American firms were less active in the former country. There was some investment by UK firms in the US and Europe in the inter-war years,[34] although by the late 1930s, the political climate in Germany had reduced the flow of new MNE activity to a trickle. Again, most of the newcomers were in the processing and relatively mature and low technology sectors.[35] Indeed, the record suggests that UK MNEs in these sectors generally improved their global competitive performance in the inter-war years (Houston and Dunning, 1976).

In the technologically advanced and vertically integrated fabricating sectors, however, the UK lagged behind. This has been put down to the lack of incentive offered to UK firms to modernize or rationalize its activities, deficiencies in the British educational system and the slowness of UK firms to adapt to the kind of managerial and organizational structures most suited to these sectors (Chandler, 1980).

As in the period before the First World War, the leading UK MNEs continued to be managed by their owners. While this sometimes resulted in strong entrepreneurial leadership (e.g. Robert Barlow of Metal Box, Eric Bowater of Bowater and Harry Jephcott of Glaxo[36]), family-owned companies were generally less willing to engage in any form of expansion that might require a dilution of ownership or control.[37] In addition, MNEs like ICI, Courtaulds, Pilkington and Metal Box limited their foreign production because of cross-border licensing or cartel agreements. In some cases, cartels expressly disallowed FDI by their members. In 1933, for example, British manufacturers of wire nails reached an agreement with their Continental counterparts which prohibited the latter from erecting nail factories in Britain (Jones, 1988). In other instances, UK firms were permitted to produce in Commonwealth countries, but not in the US. Examples include arrangements concluded between ICI and Dupont, and Metal Box and Continental Can.

If the character of the O-specific advantages of market seeking MNEs in the inter-war years was broadly similar to those of the previous period – except that those germane to cross-border 'learning cost externalities' (Kogut, 1983) were beginning to be of some significance – the factors influencing the location of the value-adding activities arising from these advantages changed dramatically. Protectionism in the form of tariffs and other import restrictions escalated. Empirical studies at the time (Southard, 1931; Marshall *et al.*, 1936; the Royal Institute of International Affairs, 1937) concluded that most market-oriented FDI in developed countries was defensively motivated. In Canada, Marshall, Southard and Taylor found that tariffs were 'of overwhelming importance in the branch plant movement' (p. 201). By contrast, the same writers estimated that only between 15% and 20% of Canadian–American branch factories owed their existence 'in any measurable extent to transportation savings', while the factory costs of US companies in Canada were 'in most cases definitely higher than those in the parent company' (p. 207).

In Europe, Southard (1931) concluded that US firms were prompted to establish branch plants mainly by their need to customize goods (particularly consumer goods) to local supply capabilities and demand idiosyncrasies, to save on transatlantic transport costs (especially for bulky, perishable or fragile articles) and by the prevalence of non-tariff barriers (e.g. discriminatory government procurement policies and 'buy home produced goods' sales pitches). Nationalist pressures by the Australian, Indian, Italian and Irish governments were identified by Nicholas (1982) as a powerful inducement for raw UK manufacturing investment in those countries, while Egypt's tariff reform of 1930 directly led to three major UK textile firms setting up factories in that country (Tignor, 1987). Some US firms also sought to forestall the entry of European firms into US markets through the acquisition of European companies.

During these years, too, as markets became less secure and more compartmentalized, firms sought locations that were politically, culturally and sociologically similar to their own. This explains the preference of UK investment for Commonwealth countries and US investment for Canada, Latin America and parts of Asia. By contrast, the political situation in Europe was volatile, while local firms were buttressed by cartels and government protectionist policies.

Finally, as previous paragraphs have pointed out, although the transaction costs of cross-border hierarchical activities fell in the inter-war years, the benefits perceived to arise from alternative organizational forms were greater. Recession, monetary instability (which led to distorted price relationships) and a relaxed attitude towards collaborative agreements promoted a climate in which territorial and market sharing agreements flourished. The result was that a major impetus for forward integration was removed. Moreover, because of segmented markets, MNEs with subsidiaries in several countries did not find it beneficial to engage in inter-plant product specialization. Intra-firm trade remained small. The result of all these forces was that, although the internalization of domestic (and particularly US) markets continued to increase, those across national boundaries were mainly confined to selling activities.[38]

The role of some investing governments was no less important. After 1929, for example, the export of capital from the UK was restricted by exchange control. At the same time, British policy looked more favourably on foreign manufacturing than it did in pre-1914 days. In part, this change of attitude was influenced by the expansion of intra-industry oligopolistic competition and the recognition that in some instances home and foreign investment might be complementary, rather than substitutable, to each other.

There is little substantive evidence on the reasons why firms internalized their cross-border intermediate product markets in the inter-war years. Stopford and Turner (1985) assert that UK companies generally eschewed the licensing option because of a lack of enforceable patent legislation or difficulties in monitoring the licensees' performance. However, a review of company histories and archive material reveals other reasons why UK firms opted for FDI rather than a cooperative non-equity arrangement. These include the difficulty of finding suitable subcontractors or licensees; the failure to agree on acceptable contractual terms and conditions; and the concern lest a licensee might become a future competitor of the licensor (Archer, 1986).

5.5.3   Resource-based investments

Supply-based FDI in mining and agribusiness recorded a mixed performance in the inter-war period, and was largely dominated by American and British interests. Perhaps the most dramatic increase occurred in foreign-owned oil production. We have seen that before 1914 US MNE activity was mainly designed to seek markets for US oil. By the 1920s and 1930s, however, American companies were investing large sums of money in the exploration and production of crude oil in Latin America, Russia, the Middle East and the Dutch East Indies. By 1928, Venezuela had become the second largest supplier of oil to the UK (Wilkins, 1970). When the US placed a tariff on Venezuelan oil imports in 1932, American petroleum affiliates in Venezuela began exporting to Europe. Similarly, US-owned oil production in Russia was sold mainly to European markets. At the same time, as American oil companies opened up new sources of production, built new pipelines and refineries, increased their tanker fleets and widened their distribution networks, the two main European oil companies – BP and Shell – also diversified their production interests, and by 1939 had invested in most of the territories of their US competitors.

Except in some of the newer metals, FDI in mining rose only slightly during the inter-war years. As in the oil sector, US and British MNEs made most of the running, although the Belgian-owned firm Union Miniere de Haut Katanga was a leading nonferrous ore producing company in Katanga, while there were substantial German and French interests in bauxite in Southern and Eastern Europe (Franko, 1976). Frequently, these ventures were partly or wholly state owned.[39] However, as mentioned earlier, the inter-war years saw the establishment of several American and European energy and mineral cartels, particularly in coke, tin and copper. There was also some mineral investment in European colonies, while investments in rubber plantations in Malaysia and Liberia, and in forestry products in various parts of Africa and Asia, grew rapidly.

Generally speaking there was little secondary processing activity by MNEs in the developing countries in this period, and few attempts by host governments to disinternalize foreign investments in natural resources. But in the late 1930s, new commodity and futures markets (e.g. in rubber, tea and coffee) began to emerge, which were eventually to erode many of the advantages of vertical integration. In 1968, Reddaway, Potter and Taylor (1968) observed that by the late 1950s few UK firms directly owned foreign assets in the raw materials sectors which they had dominated half a century earlier. One other feature about supply-oriented investments in this period was that an increasing proportion of their output was supplied to industrialized countries other than the investing country. There was also some increase in cross-border intra-firm trade.

5.5.4   Other investments

The limited amount of FDI in services in the inter-war years reflected the deceleration of MNE activity in other sectors. However, there were exceptions to this rule: for example, Japanese trading companies were active both in Europe and the US. In Europe, Mason (1992) observes that such companies not only expanded their range of traded products, but assumed increasingly important roles as sources of market intelligence for home-based firms. Japanese insurance companies, such as Mitsubishi Marine and Tokio Marine, also set up or expanded their British operations in the inter-war period.

In the US, in the 1930s, the branches and agencies of the Yokohama Specie Bank were financing more than half of Japan's imports from the US and were a major participant in financing Japan's exports to the US (Wilkins, 1990). By that time, all the major trading companies had branches in the United States, each of whom played a critical role in fostering trans-Pacific commercial transactions, technology transfers and assisting in the start-up of US joint ventures in Japan. The trading companies were further supported by a network of Japanese-owned shipping and insurance companies. Indeed, Wilkins goes as far as to argue that the inter-war Japanese direct investments in the US 'provided the basic infrastructure for Japanese commerce' (ibid, p. 598).

By contrast to the growth of Japanese trading companies and banks, those of UK origin recorded a lower rate of growth in the inter-war years. This was partly due to a loss of trade by the UK manufacturers to their foreign (especially Indian and Japanese) competitors following the First World War. But UK banks also lost some of their original O advantages in foreign markets with the advent of local banks, the creation of central banks, the growth of banking regulations, the relative decline of the City of London as the world's leading financial centre, and the inability or unwillingness of UK banks to adapt their organizational structures to respond to changing environmental circumstances (Jones, 1992).

5.5.5 The inter-war years: conclusions

In spite of a less hospitable international economic and political climate, MNE activity continued to grow in the inter-war years, particularly in the 1920s. The most significant features of the period were:

(1) the maturing of US direct investment and, in particular, the emergence of the diversified and integrated MNE;

(2) the growth of defensive market seeking investments, particularly in Europe;

(3) the entry by foreign investors into new resource-based activities, particularly oil, nonferrous metals and phosphates;

(4) the substitution of foreign production by international cartels in several sectors which had previously attracted a great deal of FDI; and

(5) the role played by the Japanese trading companies in Japanese–American commerce and Japanese economic development.

These features together with the organizational and communication advances of the period led to a further pushing back of the territorial borders of firms and the opening up of new markets. At the same time, the developing world continued to attract the bulk of resource-based investment and the developed world most of the market-seeking investment. There were glimpses of rationalized or efficiency-seeking FDI as foreign affiliates began to specialize in some of their product and process activities and to engage in cross-border intra-firm trade. There were also the beginnings of strategic asset acquiring activity as MNE oligopolies moved towards more global production and marketing.

5.6 THE EARLY POST-WAR PERIOD: 1945–60

5.6.1 Some facts

If the inter-war years witnessed a maturation, but deceleration, in the growth of international business,

the years since the end of the Second World War have seen almost uninterrupted expansion of all kinds of trade and investment. The period, which has seen the emergence and maturity of global capitalism (Cantwell, 1989b), may be conveniently divided into two phases. The first – up to around 1960 – was one in which the US dominated new MNE activity. Of the increase in both the world direct capital stake since 1939 and in the number of manufacturing subsidiaries of 174 of the world's leading MNEs identified by Vaupel and Curhan in their 1974 study, the US accounted for about two-thirds. The second period, spanning the following three decades, has witnessed the increasingly important role first of Continental European, then Japanese and finally some Third World countries as international direct investors. This period has also seen the opening up of new territories, especially Eastern Europe, to foreign-owned production, the liberalization of many cross-border markets, advances in regional economic integration, and the emergence of truly global MNEs.

The effect of the Second World War was similar to that of its predecessor in that each of the main European belligerents was forced to divest many of its foreign direct assets. However, unlike the 1914–18 war, the second generated a series of major technological advances, while its aftermath produced an international economic and political climate particularly favourable to cross-border business activities. Also, it was not too long before the UK and the leading Continental European nations, apart from West Germany, began to rebuild their foreign investments. By 1960, for example, the foreign direct assets of French and Dutch companies had more than matched their pre-war levels.

As a percentage of both world output and trade, the global FDI stake rose modestly between 1938 and 1960. During this period there was a continuation of the pre-war trend for MNEs to favour developed countries for new venture activity. In 1938 something like two-thirds of the foreign assets owned by corporations were located in developing countries; by 1960 the proportion had fallen to 40%. Partly this reflected another major structural change, namely the increased interest shown by international firms in market-seeking activities, which were aimed at circumventing trade barriers of one kind or another. In 1960 about 35% of US- and British-owned foreign assets were within the manufacturing sector, compared with about 25% in 1938 and 15% in 1914. By contrast, interest in agricultural and public utility activities declined markedly, while – taken as a whole – mining investments recorded about average rates of growth. Yet some of these latter investments, notably those made by UK and US MNEs in nonferrous metals (copper in Chile and Peru, bauxite in the Caribbean, etc) and oil in the Persian Gulf, grew rapidly.

Although this period saw the start of enforced divestment or nationalization programmes by some host countries and the setting up of new international producers' cartels, it was not until the 1960s that the growing economic power of some developing countries was fully revealed.[40] Apart from state-owned oil companies, European MNEs were not very active in the primary sector; the major capital exporters in the 1950s, *viz* the Netherlands, France and Switzerland, preferred to invest in manufacturing, trade and service activities (including finance and insurance). As in the inter-war years, UK MNEs directed their attention mainly towards Commonwealth countries. Indeed, such countries increased their share of the total capital stake from around one-half in the 1930s to over 70% in 1960. During the early post-war period, first South Africa, and then Australia and Canada attracted the bulk of the new UK direct investment. By contrast, the focus of interest of US MNEs was strongly directed to Canada and Western Europe.

Two other points might be made about this era of international business expansion. First, the relative significance of new foreign subsidiaries, surveyed by Vaupel and Curhan (1974), which were established by greenfield ventures (as compared with acquisition, merger or reorganization) fell from 55% in 1946–52 to 48% in 1959–61; the corresponding figures for the pre-1914 period and 1919–39 were 67% and 58%, respectively. Second, in the case of both US and non-US based MNEs, the proportion of affiliates in which they had a 95% or more equity stake fell from 60% in 1946–52 to 54% in 1959–61.[41]

Both market-seeking and resource-based MNE activity rose sharply in the immediate post-war period. As before the war, the former was directed mainly to developed countries, particularly Western Europe and Canada, and the latter largely to developing countries as well as to Canada and Australia. There was a less noticeable increase in rationalized investment and hardly any MNE activity aimed at acquiring new competitive advantages. However, the first half of the post-war period did herald a number of important changes in the organization and location of FDI. These are described in the following paragraphs.

5.6.2 Changes in the organization of international business

Several events in the first decade and a half after 1945 combined to affect the organizational form of international business. First, as Chapter 2 has already described, the US dominated the supply of new capital, innovations and entrepreneurship for much of the period. Second, these were years when a great deal of idiosyncratic and non-codifiable technology and managerial expertise was produced, for which the international market was extremely imperfect. Third, anti-trust legislation, particularly in the US, made both domestic and international mergers or combines much more difficult to conclude than in pre-war days. Fourth, the advent of jet travel and the computer initiated a new era of transport and communication facilities which reduced hierarchical transaction costs. Fifth, while for the first decade after the war international markets of almost all kinds were in disarray, the underlying economic environment for FDI and trade, created at Bretton Woods and Havana, was both more congenial and stable than that which faced policy makers in the inter-war years. Add to these factors the types of sectors in which world output was expanding the fastest, the countries which were most eager to entice foreign entrepreneurship, technology and capital, and the relative unattractiveness of alternative routes of resource transfer, and it is not surprising that international production rose so markedly in these years.

This period also saw a continuation of the pre-war trend to a more integrated product and market structure on the part of established MNEs. At the same time, a reading of the many country studies of FDI published in the late 1950s and 1960s[42] suggests that rationalized production, as we know it in the early 1990s, was still the exception rather than the rule within the manufacturing sector. Certainly, intra-firm manufacturing imports and exports by MNEs were a small fraction of their current level and, for the most part, these firms engaged in little cross-border product or process specialization. Indeed, the early field studies of Dunning (1958), Stonehill (1965), Safarian (1966) and Brash (1966) all suggested that, in the main, US manufacturing subsidiaries were truncated replicas of their parent organizations and, after a learning period, tended to conduct their affairs with minimal parental interference.

This leads us to a general observation. While the setting up of a foreign affiliate may be likened to that of establishing a new branch plant of the parent company in the home country, it has also some of the characteristics of a *de novo* firm. This being so, a purely Chandlerian explanation (e.g. Chandler, 1962) of the growth of a large enterprise within a country may not be wholly applicable to the initial decision to undertake foreign production. This is not only because the majority of MNEs are small or medium size firms, but because a foreign investment decision, unlike its domestic counterpart, is often initially prompted by the need to protect an *existing* market, that is, to relocate rather than to expand production. If, then, we include all kinds of barriers to trade associated with traversing space between two countries, quite a lot of manufacturing and service investment over the past hundred years – but especially in the inter-war and early post-war period – originated in this way. For example, some 75% of the UK and US MNEs operating in the mid 1970s first set up outside their home countries in the post-1945 period (Vaupel and Curhan, 1974). The proportion was probably nearer 85% in the case of German firms and 95% in the case of Japanese firms.

Both in the capital-intensive resource-based and technology-intensive manufacturing sectors, there is some evidence of the bunching of new activities by rival MNE oligopolists in this period (Knicker-bocker, 1973). We have already argued that this behaviour is a form of risk-minimizing strategy which, in a wider context, helps to explain much of the imperative among MNEs to integrate their global activities. At the same time, capital investment entails its own uncertainties which, as and when these outweigh the risk-reducing aspects of internalization, may lead firms to prefer a cooperative or contractual route to exploiting foreign markets.

5.6.3 Changes in locational determinants

In the period 1945–60, the overriding and unique variable that influenced the locational choice of value-added activity by international firms was the world shortage of US dollars. In particular, this frequently obliged US firms to produce overseas to sell their products. There were also push factors at work, such as the growing differential in labour costs between the US and other industrialized countries and a revival of American anti-trust policy which checked growth by acquisition and merger (A&M) in the domestic market. Anxious to be the leaders in exploiting their new technological and marketing advantages in foreign markets, US oligopolists in the motor vehicle, pharmaceutical, electrical goods, computer, industrial instrument and other industries were quick to establish branch plants in Europe, Canada, Australia and in some wealthier Latin American countries. Again, investing firms initially perceived these ventures less as an expansion of their domestic activities and more as a replacement for part of them.

Much early post-war European direct investment was also of this kind and there was a certain pattern to it. First, a sales and service facility was set up to promote exports, then came local production using imported materials and components, followed by production with a higher local value-added content. This process was frequently observed in the 1960s in both UK and US manufacturing investments. Again, rising markets, often protected by import controls, were the main inducements, together with the fear of losing existing or potential markets to competitors. The abandonment of international cartel arrangements led several UK firms to set up production facilities in the US, while others saw such investment as the best way to obtain access to American technology.

The rapid growth in industrial output following the end of the Second World War led to an unprecedented demand for raw materials to sustain that output, so increasingly the main industrial countries were forced to seek new sources of supply. For reasons exactly parallel to those prompting backward vertical integration in the 19th century, large firms purchasing primary products for processing and fabrication sought to internalize their sources of supply. Thus the surge outwards to supply-oriented investment was in direct proportion to the growth in manufacturing output and domestic incomes in the industrialized north. At the same time, there was growing concern among the producing nations about the increasing presence of foreign firms in their key natural resource sectors. This was not just a matter of the ability of such firms to extract monopoly rents. No less important was their perceived governance of the way in which local resources were used, their rates of exploitation, and to whom, on what terms, and by what means they were sold. There was also disquiet about some of the ways some MNEs earned (or were perceived to earn) their economic rent, for example by manipulating cross-border transfer prices. Many of these costs of FDI were attributed to the internalizing of transactions between MNEs and their affiliates.

The story about the reactions of recipient countries to these events is well known; we shall consider these in some detail in Part 4 of this volume. Suffice it to say at this point that by the mid 1960s several host governments were encouraging or enforcing divestments by MNEs in many resource-based sectors, while attempting to change the terms in which others – particularly new investors – could be involved. Public fiat replaced firm fiat, while as a result of the increasing competition among MNEs and the growth of indigenous firms, the markets for many intermediate products became less imperfect.

The consequence of these events was that there was a decline in the relative importance of supply-based foreign investments in the 1960s and 1970s, except in some resource-rich developed countries, such as Canada, Australia and the UK (for North Sea Oil), and in countries in the Far East whose governments were of a similar political persuasion to those of the main investors. It was for example in this latter region that Japanese investors made their first major thrust in the 1960s. Three decades later, they have a much larger stake in resource-based activities than either their US or European counterparts. These investments are closely controlled, either directly or indirectly, by Japanese industrial or trading companies.

5.7   TOWARDS THE GLOBALIZATION OF PRODUCTION: 1960–90

5.7.1   Introduction

Chapter 2 has already described the most recent trends in the growth and pattern of FDI and MNE activity. In particular, it emphasized the growing number of countries generating outward direct investment and the convergence in the net outward direct investment position of the leading industrial nations since the mid 1970s. Over the past 25 years, international production has increasingly come to resemble international trade in the sense that countries now view the activities of their own MNEs, and those of the affiliates of foreign MNEs in their midst, as a way of benefiting from the international division of labour and the globalization of markets. Opportunities for such specialization and growth could not have occurred except within a relatively free trading and investment environment.

Although the activities of home- and foreign-based MNEs have assumed a greater significance in the most industrialized market and developing economies,[43] perhaps the most significant features of international business activity since 1960 have been threefold. First, the predominant form of MNE involvement has shifted from market-seeking and resource-seeking to rationalized and, more recently, strategic asset-acquiring investment. At the same time, the first two kinds of investment have been increasingly viewed from a global perspective and as part of a geocentric or transnational organizational strategy by MNEs.[44] *Inter alia* this is shown by the very considerable growth in all forms of *intra-firm* trade – both between foreign affiliates and parent companies, and between affiliates within developed countries – especially in such integrated regions as the EC and North America.

Second, the organizational forms of international business have become more pluralistic. In particular, all forms of non-equity cooperative ventures have mushroomed. In the early 1990s, international business scholars are as much concerned with explaining the growth of cross-border strategic alliances and networks of suppliers and customers as part of the global compound of MNE activity as they are with FDI *per se*.

Third, in the past two decades many MNEs have

evolved new attitudes and strategies towards their international activities. Divestment and new investments now go hand in hand. Expansion in one sector or territory is often accompanied by contraction in another. Organizational forms and decision-taking structures are constantly being revised to meet new environmental or technological challenges. As fast as new cross-border alliances are formed, old ones break up. Increasingly the MNE is coming to resemble a controller of a system of interlocking value-added activities, the composition and organization of which is constantly adjusting both to exogenously determined events and the priorities and strategies of the MNEs themselves.

Later chapters in this volume will concern themselves in more detail with these events, while a final chapter will speculate a little about the future course of MNE activity. To place them in historical perspective, however, they represent a continuum in the evolvement of international business, the nature and form of which has been fashioned both by technological developments, the influence of governments on the structure of resources and capabilities within their jurisdiction, and the level and form of international commerce. Certainly, one of the most distinctive features of the world economy of the early 1990s is the ease with which the kinds of assets and intermediate products that determine a nation's prosperity and growth are able to move across national boundaries. As a vehicle for housing and controlling the organization and location of these resources and competences, MNEs remain in a class of their own.

The following paragraphs consider some of the more important organizational and locational changes as they have affected MNEs over the past 30 years.

5.7.2   Changes in organizational form

The past 30 years have seen considerable changes in the organization and management of cross-border value-added activities, the net results of which have not only been to decrease the role of MNE hierarchies in some sectors and in some countries and to increase it in others, but also to alter the shape and form of such hierarchies. Supporting the former tendency has been an improvement in the efficiency of intermediate product markets. Reinforc-

ing this has been the voluntary divestment by MNEs and the enforced use of the market route by some host governments in many primary industries and in some key secondary and tertiary sectors. So, international production, initially designed to exploit a unique intangible asset, the value of which is usually time limited, has tended to fall except in countries where user capacity is still inadequate. By contrast, MNEs continue to flourish in innovating sectors in which technology is idiosyncratic, complex and not easily codified, as well as in sectors where the governance over a geographically dispersed set of assets and capabilities brings its own particular benefits.

However, both these phenomena are part of the same story and fit in well with the ideas contained in the product or industry technology cycles. Where MNEs are conceived primarily as transferors of competitive advantages and as tutors in the use of these and related assets, their presence in any particular country is likely to be a transient one, unless they can upgrade these advantages or create new ones. Hence, as was said earlier, one would expect the outward direct investment of a country to be positively related to the quality and rate of growth of its indigenous entrepreneurship and innovatory capabilities, both absolutely and compared with that of its competitors.

However, quite apart from the ebb and flow of these kinds of international production, the most marked organizational developments of the past 20 years have been the emergence of the truly global enterprise and the mushrooming of all forms of cooperative alliances. This is the natural extension of what Mira Wilkins has referred to as the third phase in MNE development (Wilkins, 1974). Here the motive for foreign production is not so much to gain the economic rent that marketable advantages can earn, as to capture the economies of integration and diversification arising from such production. This multi-divisional form of FDI may result in rationalized production between a group of foreign affiliates, or between their affiliates and their parent companies.

Such rationalization tends to be of two kinds. The first is a reorganization of a group of largely import-substituting activities in a number of countries which were initially designed to meet domestic needs. If and when the markets are large enough and/or become integrated, then the MNE may find it economic to pursue a different strategy based upon the economies of product or process specialization and intra-group trading. Secondly, corporate integration may take the form of export platform manufacturing investment or downstream processing of primary products, where the division of labour tends to be between different stages of the value-added chain and is based on international cost and marketing differences.

The expansion of these and similar forms of FDI has been made possible both by a reduction of trade barriers between countries and by continued improvements in transnational organizational competences. However, in some cases (particularly within the EC) what, in fact, has happened is that an MNE has transferred an organizational system to each group of its affiliates located in a particular region. It is less the potential gains from internalized transactions between parent and affiliates that has led to new foreign production, and more those that might result from common governance of the value-added activities of the affiliates. In this case, systemic advantages experienced in the multi-divisional form in the parent company may be usefully replicated at a regional level. Examples are the benefits of centralized purchasing, the use of sophisticated accounting systems, the reduction of environmental risks and the ability to move top personnel between subsidiaries.

Once again, one observes differences in the modes of international economic involvement by MNEs from different home countries and according to the countries in which they invest. Very often these reflect industry- or firm-specific characteristics. Reference has already been made to the interdependent behaviour of MNE oligopolists. In the late 1960s and early 1970s, this was noticeable in the timing of US direct investment in the European semiconductor and drug industries. Likewise, in the 1990s Japanese-owned motor vehicle and electronic MNEs are actively seeking new production outlets in both Europe and the US. Davidson and McFetridge (1985) have suggested that international transfers of technology are more likely to be internalized if the transferor already operates an affiliate in the recipient country and if previous transfers have been internalized. Certainly, the preference of US manufacturing MNEs (relative to those of other nationali-

ties) for the full ownership of their affiliates in the 1970s was at least partly because of their greater degree of international product and process integration. In the current decade, however, both European and Japanese MNEs are increasingly adopting systemic strategies towards their global or regional value-added activities.

Although, since around the mid 1960s, the US's share of world direct investment has been steadily falling, it is the established US MNEs that have most pursued a Chandlerian strategy towards international production. At the same time, the newly emerging MNEs, which were accounting for an increasing share of international production by the end of the 1970s, did not seem so prone to integrate their foreign and domestic operations. At a macro level, however, there is reason to suppose that Japanese foreign and domestic investments are more interrelated than, for example, their US counterparts. Finally, with innovations in trans-border information flows, some of the obstacles to hierarchical growth are being further eroded.

Previous paragraphs have suggested that changes in the advantages of alternative modalities for organizing the use and location of the competitive advantages of firms have played a significant role in affecting the level and patterns of international production over the post-war period. In particular, the internalization model explains why, in sectors where the market for transacting either inputs or outputs (including intermediate outputs) has improved, the contribution of MNEs has fallen. But in other sectors, where the O-specific advantages of firms have become more idiosyncratic or related to the coordination of interrelated activities, it has become even more important. We have also argued that while Chandlerian-type theories may not be very helpful in explaining the *initial* foreign investment decision by firms, the growth of established subsidiaries of MNEs – particularly those located in large integrated markets – is increasingly following the pattern of their domestic counterparts. Indeed, it might be hypothesized that the generally faster rate of growth of international production, *vis-à-vis* domestic production, may be attributed to the anticipated gains that stem specifically from the common governance of foreign value-added activities.

These gains may arise through a more efficient

organization of trans-border production within MNEs as well as between MNEs and other firms with which they have dealings. Chapters 8 and 9 will examine these issues in some depth. Suffice it to mention at this point that the past decade and a half has witnessed a profound metamorphosis in the cross-border bonding between firms. The 1980s, in particular, saw a prolific growth in all forms of alliances, especially within the Triad. The difference between these coalitions and those that preceded them lies essentially in the way in which they are organized and assimilated into the global strategy of the participating firms. As we observed in Chapter 4, the MNE is now an orchestrator of a set of geographically dispersed, but interrelated, assets and capabilities. Some of these, which represent its core competencies, it will wish to own, while others (which may be no less critical to its success) it will jointly supply or purchase from independent suppliers.

5.7.3   Recent locational changes

We now consider some of the characteristics of changing the location of MNE activity over the past two and one-half decades. Partly as a result of the enlargement of markets – occasioned *inter alia* by rising living standards and regional economic integration – and partly as a consequence of changes in the production and marketing strategies of MNEs, the factors influencing the geographical distribution of FDI have dramatically changed. It now rests less on the kind of determinants of discrete market-oriented or resource-based investments, and more on those relevant to the spatial optimization of an interrelated set of value-added activities. In this respect, there are considerable similarities between the inter-regional and inter-country specialization of production. There are also parallels with the explanation of the location of similar activities across national boundaries but under separate ownership, which give rise to intra-industry trade.

The best illustration of this latter form of FDI is that undertaken by US MNEs in the EC since around 1960. To capture the economies of scale and centralization of production while taking advantage of a free trade area, MNE affiliates, which were previously truncated replicas of their parent companies, have found it worthwhile to concentrate the

production of particular products in one or more European plants, the output of which is supplied to the entire EC. The choice of location of these plants and the effect of rationalization on the totality and distribution of the capital stake is partly determined by the disposition of existing capacity, partly by the relevant production and transaction costs, and partly by country-specific variables (e.g. the availability of skilled labour and materials, transport and communication costs, consumer tastes, government regulations and so on). The result has been a geographical distribution of production which is as much based on the comparative resource endowments of a country as on the absolute advantages offered by particular locations.

In this respect, companies may behave as countries. The allocation of the activities like Philips of Eindhoven, Honeywell, Ford and International Harvester in the EC is based on this type of strategy. It helps to create substantial economies of integration and can usually only be successfully achieved through the internalization of resource transfers. This, in turn, is only viable as long as there are no restrictions on trade in goods and services, and policies towards international direct investments are reasonably well harmonized.

In Europe, North America and, to a lesser extent, Latin America, the kind of trade associated with this type of efficiency-seeking investment is not predominantly based on differences in the distribution of factor endowments in the classical or neo-classical sense. However, in other parts of the world, another type of rationalized investment – the export platform type – is of this kind. In the late 1970s, the most rapidly growing activity of manufacturing MNEs in East Asia, Mexico and some parts of Southern Europe was to take advantage of cheap, plentiful and well motivated labour to produce products or processes that required such a resource. The main locational impetus giving rise to such activity was the growth of manufacturing capacity in a number of newly industrializing countries (NICs) and the generally liberal attitude of these countries to export-oriented FDI. However, in the 1980s, as a result of *inter alia* the rising cost of labour in some NICs and advances in computer aided design and manufacturing technologies, several MNEs in industries such as electronics, textiles and clothing have found it profitable to relocate some of their activities back to their home countries.[45]

It is worth observing that much of the first and some of the second kind of rationalized production reflects a form of *growth* of foreign participation rather than an *initial* means of entry. Essentially, such production represents 'specialization within diversification'; the resulting benefits are entirely those of the economies of scale and scope. Some of these economies may be specific to geographical diversification, such as those which give rise to intra-firm trade. These strongly suggest that the common ownership of spatially separated production units *does* influence the way in which resources are allocated.

To conclude this section, we would make two other observations. The first is on the changing origin and destination of MNE activity. Chapter 2 has already set out some of the salient facts. However, from an historical perspective, perhaps the most interesting aspect of this phenomenon has been the growing number of countries that have become significant outward direct investors, while at the same time the established capital exporters have become hosts to an increasing volume of trans-national activity (with the noticeable exception of Japan). This phenomenon is entirely consistent with the predictions of the investment development path and, as far as East Asian countries are concerned, the flying geese paradigm[46] analysed in Chapter 4. It suggests that over time as the relative ESP configuration of Nation States changes, so does the strategic response of firms that invest or might consider investing in these countries. In turn, for reasons which later chapters will elaborate upon, the response of these firms leads to a realignment of the world's investing and invested-in nations. To repeat just one example highlighted in Chapter 2: in 1965 the ratio of the US's direct capital stake in the EC to that of the EC's capital stake in the US was 3.19; by 1990 this had fallen to 0.75.

The second point relates to the gradual liberalization of the attitudes of many governments towards both outward and inward direct investment in the past decade. At the same time, as a result of the learning process of governments, policies with respect to entry, performance and exit conditions of foreign firms have become more enlightened (see Chapter 20). Partly too, while the world recession has made countries more aware of the potential gains of inward direct investment, it has also caused MNEs to cut back on some of their foreign operations to protect their domestic interests. This has been particularly noticeable in the case of US MNEs and, in part at least, is a reflection of the weakness of the dollar.

By contrast, the expansion of European and Japanese direct investment in the US illustrates the increasing benefits of investing in, rather than exporting to, the US. Again, this shift in the pattern of international production is primarily of location substitution although, as Chapter 2 has suggested, part of it is most certainly intended to protect or advance the global strategy of the investing companies. To make things more complicated, part of the investment classified as FDI in official statistics may in fact be portfolio investment as no *de facto* supervision is exercised over the capital exported. A great deal of Middle Eastern direct investment in Europe and the US falls into this category.

5.8   CONCLUSIONS

The growth of international production in modern history essentially reflects the way in which changes in the structure and organization of the world's resources and capabilities impinge on the cross-border production and transaction strategies of companies. While historically the role of the MNE has been both a pro-active and re-active one – and is certainly a very pro-active one today – the discovery of new territories, increases in population, advances in the stock of knowledge of production and organizational techniques, and the response of governments to these changes have been the prime movers.

Enterprises have responded to these developments by realigning the extent, form and geography of their value-added activities. From engaging in the production of simple and single products, they have increased their range and depth of value-adding activities as tasks and production processes have become more specialized. Furthermore, as the factory system has substantially replaced the 'putting out' system and firms have integrated their production and marketing functions, new forms of organization have heralded changes in the transactional relationships between economic agents.

Central to these developments has been the growth of MNE hierarchies. Throughout history, hierarchies, either singly or jointly, have gradually replaced markets as a modality for transacting intermediate products. In many ways the growth of international production is a microcosm of changing commercial relationships, as they evolved from the personal trading of individuals in the early civilizations, through the impersonal trading of the Mercantilist era, and the industrial (muscle replacing) revolution of the 19th century, to the computer (intellectual replacing) revolution of the 1980s.

In describing the history of MNE activity, we have made use of the eclectic paradigm set out in Chapter 4. More particularly, we have pinpointed a number of watersheds in the emergence and maturing of FDI, and have shown both how it has affected and been affected by changes in the O-specific advantages of firms, the L advantages of countries, and the strategic response of firms to these variables, particularly as it affected the organization of their global markets and production. We have seen that each watershed was triggered by a major technological or organizational advance, or by the actions of Nation States, or groups of Nation States, which have affected the motivation and capability of firms to manage geographically diversified assets as well as their attitudes towards the uncertainties associated with cross-border market failure.

Sometimes the trigger has been innovations which have reduced the cost of making transactions over distance and facilitated new forms of organization and management. Sometimes the advances have come in the guise of new production technologies or the introduction of new products, which have had implications for the sourcing of foreign materials or the securing of distribution channels of firms. Sometimes the initiative has come from governments through advances in military technology to defend themselves against aggressive neighbours or through import controls to protect themselves against economic warfare. Sometimes the impetus has been an expanding market brought about by colonization, population increase or rising incomes.

In all these cases, the initiatives have had widespread consequences on the revenue and costs of both domestic and foreign production. They have affected the innovation of new products and methods; the organization of value-added activities between

and within firms; the organization of transactions both between firms and markets and within firms as well as the location of these activities; and the interaction between the state and producing and transacting economic agents.

The history of MNE activity is, then, the story of a series of political and social events that have affected the ownership, organization and location of international production. The powerful role of the MNE in the contemporary global economy reflects its capabilities and willingness to organize, for good or bad, cross-border production and transactions more effectively than any alternative institutional mechanism. This chapter has sought to demonstrate that the eclectic paradigm takes us a long way in understanding the history of the changing significance of MNE activity. And, as later chapters in this volume will seek to show, it is also helpful for our understanding of the consequences of such activity on those most affected by it.

NOTES

1   By foreign, we mean outside the *physical* confines of a particular country. Using this definition, colonies and overseas possessions are treated as foreign territories.

2   All these companies, save the Hudson's Bay Company which is still in existence, had been disbanded or wound up by the mid-19th century.

3   Carlos and Nicholas (1988) argue that the basic *raison d'être* of the early trading companies was to economize on a high number of cross-border transactions. This they did by replacing owner-managers of single product firms with a team of salaried managers organized into MNE hierarchies. By internalizing market imperfections across time and space, they helped reduce transaction costs and exploit the economies of governance of separate, but related, activities.

4   According to Joseph Fuhrmann, as quoted in McKay (1974, p. 339), between 1637 and 1662 Dutch entrepreneurs built 10 iron factories in Russia, while Russian nobles built three and the state one.

5   Further details of early cross-border entrepreneurial ventures are given by Wilkins (1988b), Coram (1967), Clarke (1916) and Lewis (1938).

6   Other examples of UK investment groups with interests in Latin America, Russia and South Africa are given in Chapman (1982).

7   Tomlinson (1989) notes that managing agency houses

run by British expatriate businessmen were involved in 'almost all sections of the organized economy of the Indian continent' (p. 96) by the late 19th century, and that by 1914 foreign firms exercised a dominant influence over much of the non-traditional marketing processes (p. 97).

8 By the 1880s, continuous processing machinery and plant had been developed for the production of such products as cigarettes, matches, breakfast cereals, flour, soap and a wide variety of canned goods (Chandler and Daems, 1974). See also Wilson (no date). However, a paper by James (1983) suggested that in the US over the period 1850–90, technological advances alone did not explain firm size. See also Wilkins (1976, 1977a, 1977b, 1989).

9 For more details, see particularly the History of the Western Electric and NEC (Nippon Electric Company, 1984).

10 In particular, the failure of UK companies to adopt hierarchical organization systems, to update their management practices or to encourage the recruitment of university trained engineers and business graduates, led to their inability to participate fully in the newer and internationally oriented sectors, such as electrical engineering, standardized machinery and vertically integrated branded packaged products (Chandler, 1980).

11 Archer (1986, 1990) also gives examples of UK companies with unimpressive records of internationalization, which he puts at the door of poor entrepreneurship. These included Rio Tinto Zinc (prior to 1900), Burmah Oil (prior to 1904) and Bryant and May (prior to 1901).

12 In general, investors regarded the geographical diversification of their factories with some unease. The view of Western Electric (quoted by Wilkins, 1970, p. 51) is fairly typical: 'This multiplication of factories is an evil imposed by the necessity of working for Governments which refuse to buy outside their own countries'.

13 By 1900, Warre (1988) reports that there were 46 Swiss-owned cotton manufacturers producing in Italy.

14 One such example was Jököping and Vulcan's decision to establish a match factory in the UK in 1910 to export to Australia where matches of UK origin paid only 50% of the standard import duty.

15 Wilkins (1989, p. 337) cites an example of a Japanese soy sauce manufacturer – Kikkoman – setting up a manufacturing plant in Colorado in 1892 to produce soy sauce for Japanese immigrants.

16 In a study of British MNE investment before 1939, Nicholas (1982) found that 88% of the firms entered into an agency agreement prior to making an investment in a sales branch abroad, and that few British market-seeking MNEs began overseas production without first establishing sales subsidiaries. In another article (Nicholas, 1983, pp. 684–5), the author concluded that the propensity of UK firms to set up foreign sales units was greater:

'the larger were the number of sales, the more complex the product, the greater the idiosyncratic investment in spearhead capital and brand name by the principal, and the greater the appropriable rents from opportunism by agents'.

17 There are no details of intra-firm trade in this period. However, from company records we do know that in several industries (cocoa, rubber, tropical fruit, oil, etc), most of the leading producers were affiliates of MNEs from developed countries.

18 A good summary is contained in Wilkins (1970) and Read (1983). For a detailed analysis of the history of the American banana trade see Wilson (1947).

19 This was not an untypical practice among MNEs investing in poor agricultural areas. Lever did the same in the Belgian Congo in the early 1900s.

20 As described, for example, in Wilkins (1970, pp. 168–9).

21 See, for example, Bemis (1943) and Munro (1934).

22 This appeared to be particularly important in the tin industry. Indeed Hennart (1986) claims that the inability of the Malayan tin companies to obtain the necessary finance for capital development (e.g. in dredging techniques) explains the dominance of Western enterprise in that sector.

23 In their article, Harvey and Taylor provide some fascinating glimpses of the costs and benefits of resource-based investment to the host country. In particular, they quote (pp. 187–8) the opinion of one Spanish mining engineer, expressed in 1891, that while foreign investors had provided the Spanish mineral sector with 'capital, spirit of enterprise and business ability' the Spanish mineral industries had failed to promote 'the permanent good of the country' merely creating 'a fugitive and ephemeral prosperity'. A more virulent attack on British investors was contained in a Spanish pamphlet issued in Huelva in 1913, which stated that 'the English burgess has entered this province, and with the cunning of a Carthaginian, the ambition of an American, and the arrogance of the British, threatens to rend it, gouging its flesh, sucking its blood, into slavery'.

24 Indeed, Wilkins gives examples of UK iron and steel manufacturing firms investing or participating in the formation of free-standing US iron mining companies not to access raw materials but to market their UK manufactured products.

25 Oil was discovered in the Dutch East Indies in 1880. A decade later, the forerunner of Royal Dutch Shell was

set up in the Netherlands to work these properties. It built a refinery in Sumatra in the Far East. In 1895–86, the English firm M. Samuel & Company, which became Shell Transport and Trading Co Ltd in 1897, was producing oil in Dutch Borneo. In 1894 the Swedish Nobel family invested in Russian oil.

26 Franko (p. 52) reports that 49% (68% if Shell's operations are excluded) of the extractive operations of all continental firms were located in the continent before 1946. Commercial oil was discovered in Tutusville, US, in 1859 and by 1871 US-refined products were exported, mainly to Europe. In the mid 1880s US oil products met competition in Europe from Russian oil.

27 The definition of FDI – in so far as nineteenth century investment is concerned – is still a matter of dispute among economists. But current thinking, as articulated especially by Svedberg (1978, 1981), Stone (1977) and the authors of industry and country studies, suggests that quite a large part of investment originally classified as portfolio by the statisticians of the day was, in fact, managed or controlled by non-residents, while contemporary estimates of direct investment often exclude reinvested profits.

28 Using data derived from business histories and company archives, Nicholas (1982) has set out details on the industrial structure of 119 UK MNEs which made a FDI between 1870 and 1930, and has compared this with that of a sample of pre-1914 US MNEs and of the largest 50 UK firms in 1919 and 1930. His findings about the structure of large UK and US firms at that time closely correspond to those of earlier writers, such as Chandler (1977). However, his study also reveals a considerable similarity between the sectors that dominated the UK corporate economy and those that dominated UK direct investment.

29 Particularly in textiles and branded consumer goods in which the UK had a previous comparative trading advantage.

30 Wilkins (1970) quotes the case of the Diamond Match Company which once had a world leadership in match-making technology. By the 1920s it had lost much of its technological supremacy to the Swedish Match Company.

31 US foreign subsidiaries were also the first to introduce new methods of instrumentation. Jones (1988) quotes the case of H. J. Heinz installing automatic controls in their London factory in 1929 before British food canners had introduced any form of control.

32 As a general observation, business historians are increasingly providing the international business scholar with illustrations and case studies of the O advantages possessed by the early MNEs, and how these have impinged upon the economies of the Nation States in

which they operate. For a review of some of the more important contributions in this area, see two recently edited volumes by Wilkins (1991) and Jones (1992).

33 In particular, the recurrent fear of naval blockades constituted a powerful incentive to countries to reduce their dependence on some imported raw materials (Franko, 1976, p. 39). In other cases, for example, oil, by keeping the price high foreign cartels encouraged the users to seek substitutes (in this case electricity).

34 Nicholas (1989) records that 11% of post-1914 UK MNEs were set up in the US (compared with 13% pre-1914). The corresponding percentages for Europe were 43% and 27%. He also reports two-thirds of all UK post-1918 investment in Germany occurred between 1918 and 1933.

35 Of 55 UK industrial companies with producing subsidiaries in at least four foreign countries in 1938, no less than 40 were in the processing industries, with only 15 in the engineering and metal product sectors.

36 In writing on Sir Harry Jephcott, Davenport-Hines (1986, p. 140) writes:

> 'His strategic perception of Glaxo Laboratories business dominated its decisions and performance in Britain and abroad from 1935 until the mid-1960s. Its major product diversifications, into vitamin foods in 1924 and antibiotics twenty years later were also substantially at his initiative'.

37 Archer (1986) gives several examples of mergers or amalgamations between UK MNEs where there was little organizational rationalization and, in consequence, many economies of common governance, including (in the case of ICI) those of research and development, were not realized. See also Stopford (1974) and Hannah (1976).

38 Nicholas (1982) and Archer (1986) give examples. They include Thomas Fenner, maker of leather belts for machinery, who established a branch selling outlet in India in 1929 after reporting that Indian sales agents were unsatisfactory, and Brunner Mond's preference for owning its overseas selling companies because it did not trust independent agents to look after its interests properly. Glaxo, on the other hand, internalized its finished good markets in the belief that its success depended on 'precise and systematic marketing by carefully selected men bound by exact instructions and contracts' (Archer, 1986, p. 246).

39 For example, Union Miniere du Haut Katanga was partly owned by the Belgian government; Compagnie Française des Pétroles was partly owned by the French government; while Vereinigte Aluminum Werke (VAW) was owned by the German government.

40 For example, of 1369 instances of nationalization recorded by the United Nations (UNCTC, 1978)

between 1960 and 1976, 67% was recorded in the final six years. Of some 19 producers associations existing in 1976, only one (OPEC) existed in 1960.

41   The corresponding figures for pre-1914 and 1919–39 were 62% and 63%, respectively. Throughout these years, the propensity of US MNEs to operate wholly owned subsidiaries was greater than that of non-US MNEs.

42   Some of which are identified and described in Chapter 6.

43   See Chapter 2. To give just one figure as a proportion of world GNP, the combined inward and outward capital stake rose from 7.8% in 1967 to 13.9% in 1988.

44   For an elaboration of the meaning of a geocentric and transnational organizational strategy, see Chapter 7.

45   This point is further taken up in Chapter 15.

46   Both of which were analysed in Chapter 4.

TESTING THE THEORY OF THE DETERMINANTS OF MNE ACTIVITY

6.1 INTRODUCTION

6.1.1 Types of empirical research

This chapter reviews some of the more recent attempts by economists and business analysts to evaluate empirically some of the theories of MNE and MNE-related activity described in Chapter 4. Broadly speaking we can identify three main strands of research. The first is the original field study, which is usually conducted on an *ad hoc* basis by way of questionnaires and direct interviews with a selected group of firms. The second is an analysis and interpretation of secondary statistical and other data. For the most part, this data is collected and published by government departments, international agencies, regional authorities and trade associations (see Chapter 1). The third is by information obtained directly or indirectly from individual MNEs. Such information may range from that contained in chairmen's reports, company statements and articles in trade journals and the financial press, to business histories and detailed case studies. This kind of empirical research tends to be favoured by business analysts and economic historians.

While some empirical studies have attempted to test one particular theory or paradigm of MNE activity, most have sought to identify and evaluate the most significant variables associated with such activity.[1] The studies have involved a variety of investigative and statistical techniques, although the great majority of those most rigorously pursued have employed multiple regression, variance, factor and discriminant analysis, by which specific hypotheses are expressed as functional relationships and are systematically tested.

Empirical research has also varied according to the particular aspect of MNE activity that is being explained. Most early studies, for example, were concerned with the determinants of the 'where' of international production, particularly that of US direct investment in Europe and Canada (Southard, 1931; Southard *et al.*, 1933). Scholars were interested in identifying and evaluating the main variables influencing the location of value-added activities. This type of research has continued to attract the attention of scholars interested in four groups of choices which MNEs, or potential MNEs, have to take. These are:

(1) whether to export or engage in foreign production, and, if the latter, in which country to locate their value-added activi-ties;

(2) on the determinants of the sourcing of raw materials and intermediate products;

(3) where to locate export platform or offshore investment;

(4) where to site value-added activities within a regionally integrated area, for example, the EC and LATFA.

Location economists have also sometimes sought to assess the importance of specific locational variables, such as material and labour costs, investment incentives, transport costs and taxation, on MNE activity.

A second group of scholars has been more interested in explaining the sectoral composition of international production. Essentially they have sought to answer two questions. First, why do MNEs and/or their foreign affiliates tend to concentrate in some industrial sectors rather than others? Second, why is the sectoral distribution of MNE-related activity different from that of uninational firms? Essentially, these scholars have tried to identify and evaluate the significance of the O-specific advantages of MNEs and/or their affiliates *vis à vis* those of uninational firms *in a given location*. These have been the most extensive of the empirical studies, and we shall analyse some of their findings later in the chapter.

A third group of studies has focused on testing the theory of the MNE *per se*. Such studies have also been of two main kinds. First, there are those that seek to explain why firms engage in FDI rather than in some other modality of exporting the right to use the O advantages they possess. Most of these studies have concentrated on the variables influencing the investment versus the licensing decision, but occasionally, and especially as related to the question of market entry strategy, attempts have been made to identify and evaluate the variables affecting multiple forms of entry. Second, there are those that have attempted to measure the costs and benefits of the internalization of intermediate product markets by MNEs.

6.1.2   The burgeoning of empirical research since the 1960s

We would make one other introductory point. This concerns the way in which empirical research on the determinants of MNE activity has evolved over the past 30 years. As we have already suggested, the first rudimentary efforts to evaluate the determinants of international production took place in the 1930s, 1950s and early 1960s. These were based mainly on original field studies undertaken to pinpoint and, in some cases, qualitatively assess the significance of, the main situational variables influencing FDI and the preference of the investing firms for one foreign location rather than another. Some examples of this work are given in the next section of this chapter. In the late 1960s and 1970s, these studies were supplemented by econometric work, which used both time series and cross-sectional data to explain the growth and regional distribution of US direct investment in Western Europe. There were also some attempts to apply risk diversification analysis to explain the geographical allocation of MNE investment (e.g. Rugman, 1979). At the same time, a

number of scholars began to undertake a series of bi-country studies, which sought to explain the sectoral distribution of US investment in a series of host countries according to the O-specific advantages possessed by such firms.

However, perhaps the most significant leap forward in our knowledge and understanding on the emerging role of MNEs in the world economy in the late 1960s and early 1970s came from the Multinational Enterprise Project of the Harvard Business School under the direction of Raymond Vernon. Not only did this provide two major statistical source books on the origin and growth of the largest US and non-US manufacturing corporations (*viz* Vaupel and Curhan, 1969, 1974), but also field research unearthed valuable new data that enabled a series of hypotheses, propounded by the Harvard scholars, to be tested. Three examples should suffice. First, the product cycle hypothesis, outlined in Chapter 4, was put to the test by Hufbauer (1966), Hirsch (1967), Gruber, Mehta and Vernon (1967), Keesing (1967) and several writers in Wells (1972) in a series of industry and country case studies. Vernon himself, in summarizing some of the results of the Harvard research (Vernon, 1972), identified several historical instances that supported the concept. Second, Knickerbocker (1973) and Graham (1975) used the statistical material assembled by Vaupel and Curhan to test a number of hypotheses about the timing of FDI by MNEs that operated within an oligopolistic market structure. Third, in a detailed examination of the ways in which a group of 38 US MNEs decided to invest overseas (Aharoni, 1966), Yair Aharoni, another of Vernon's students, was able to make sense of his findings in terms of the product cycle sequence.

Since the mid 1970s, the area of empirical work has been extended in four ways. First, as an increasing number of home and host countries have begun to publish data on MNE-related activity, more studies – particularly those involving non-US MNEs – have sought to identify and evaluate the main OLI variables influencing the pattern of these activities. There have been literally hundreds of attempts to assess why firms from country X invest in country Y rather than country Z, and why firms from country X prefer to invest in country Y rather than to export goods to country Y, or to license firms in country Y to produce these goods. Increasingly, cross-sectional studies have become *multi* country rather than *bi* country in character.

Second, scholars have become increasingly interested in explaining the *growth* of MNE activity, rather than the reasons for the *initial* investment. So far there have been few quantitative research projects on this subject, but a good deal of case study material is now beginning to emerge from the field work of such business analysts as Prahalad and Doz (1987), Bartlett and Ghoshal (1989) and Kogut (1985, 1987).[2] There has also been a mushrooming of historical studies on the growth of MNE activity, both of particular firms and of countries and industries. Some of the more path-breaking of these studies are described in Wilkins (1991) and Jones (1992).

Third, scholars have begun to ask a wide variety of new questions about the determinants of MNE activity. Examples are 'How does the significance of MNE involvement change with economic development? Does the emergence of Third World MNEs require modification to the theory of FDI? Does the choice of entry modes differ between MNEs engaged in service and goods producing activities? What determines whether entry by joint venture occurs through the takeover or the greenfield route? What is the significance of changes in government economic policy on the location and form of inward investment? Does one need a new theory of MNE activity to explain the growth of cross-border alliances among firms?'

Fourth, the statistical methodology used to identify and evaluate the independent variables affecting investment has become more sophisticated. Not only have multiple regression measures been improved by the use of cluster and logit analysis, but increasingly factor, discriminant and correspondence techniques have been used to embrace some of the less easily quantifiable variables.

The consequence of all these developments is that there is now a fairly substantial body of knowledge on the empirical determinants of FDI and MNE activity. The rest of this chapter describes some of the more important findings of this research.[3] First, we shall review the conclusions of a selection of field studies and the company data available on the motivation and determinants of MNE activity. Second, we shall summarize the results of the econometric investigations that have sought to test

various theories of international production and MNE involvement. We shall consider both cross-sectional and time-series studies, and explanations of both outward and inward direct investment. A final section of the chapter will argue that, in spite of a plethora of research, our knowledge about the determinants of MNE activity is still very incomplete, particularly when it comes to explaining the organization of international collaborative ventures and strategic alliances.

6.2   FIELD SURVEYS AND RELATED STUDIES

6.2.1   Introduction

Field studies based on questionnaires and/or interviews with MNEs and on historical evidence have played a useful role in advancing our understanding of the determinants of FDI. Earlier studies of this type, some of which are summarized in Table 6.1, made an important contribution by detailing some of the key influences identified by business respondents at the time, which later become incorporated into more formal econometric models. Another value of these studies has been their ability to identify and evaluate less quantitative explanatory variables.

The limitations of field analyses are well recognized and have been described elsewhere (Dunning, 1973). Most obviously, the information obtained by investigators represents the subjective judgement of the respondents to questionnaires or of the interviewees. More often than not, past surveys have failed to distinguish between the motives for and determinants of MNE activity. Rarely do they state the assumptions underlying the answers given or make any attempt to normalize for the differences in the characteristics of firms (size, age, international experience, regional distribution, etc). Furthermore, most surveys report on the *ex post* determinants of *particular* FDI decisions, while the primary interest of policy makers is directed to the factors perceived as *generally* most relevant by firms *ex ante*. Indeed, it is quite possible that the factors that firms believe to be most important to their decision making are not those that are *de facto* the most influential. Data obtained by scholars from the records of companies, or that provided directly or indirectly by MNEs, also

Table 6.1 Summary of determinants of foreign direct investment (suggested by early field studies); number of times factors mentioned.

	Foreign investment in general					Investment in specific countries			
Name of researcher	Robinson[1]	Behrman	Basi[2]	Kolde	Forsyth(a)[3]	Brash	Deane	Forsyth(b)[3]	Andrews[4]
Date of publication	1961	1962	1966	1968	1972	1966	1970	1972	1972
Number of firms in sample	205	72	214	104	105	100	139	105	80
Marketing factors									
Size of market	262	—	141	—	—	—	21	—	—
Market growth		19	158	7	82	89		14	28
To maintain share of market or match a rival's investment	130	—	126	12	35	—	30	6	—
To advance exports of parent company	—	1	—	—	2	—	—	1	—
Need to maintain close contact with customers	—	7	—	—	5	—	15	9	—
Dissatisfaction with existing market arrangements	—	3	—	25		—	—	—	—
Export base for neighbouring markets	104	3	—	—	—	30		—	39
	496	33	425	44	124	119	66	30	57
Barriers to trade									
Barriers to trade	130		—	21	28	78	76	—	11
Preference of local customers for local products	—	14	—	—	1	24	—	—	—
	130	14	—	21	29	102	76	—	11
Cost factors									
To be near source of supply	—	—	—	—	3	—	14	2	—
Availability of labour	209	—	—*	—	—	—	—	53	—
Availability of raw materials	—	12	114	—	—	—	7	—	—
Availability of capital/ technology	—	—	78	—	—	—	—	11	—
Lower labour costs	79	—	103	—	—	—	—	18	
Lower other production costs	—	7	—	20	—	11	—	—	40
Lower transport costs	—	—	—	—	—	22	—	18	
Financial (et al.) inducements by governments	50	—	—	—	1	13	—	52	45
General cost levels more favourable (less inflation)	—	—	134	—	—	—	14	—	—
	338	19	429	20	4	46	35	154	85

Table 6.1 continued.

Name of researcher	Foreign investment in general					Investment in specific countries			
	Robinson[1]	Behrman	Basi[2]	Kolde	Forsyth(a)[3]	Brash	Deane	Forsyth(b)[3]	Andrews[4]
Date of publication	1961	1962	1966	1968	1972	1966	1970	1972	1972
Number of firms in sample	205	72	214	104	105	100	139	105	80
Investment climate									
General attitude to foreign investment	—[5]	—	145	6	—	—	10	—	—
Political stability	115	—	159	—	—	—	—	—	—
Limitation on ownership	20	—	—	—	—	—	—	—	—
Currency exchange regulations	105[6]	—	—	—	—	—	—	—	—
Stability of foreign exchange	—	—	151	—	—	—	—	—	—
Tax structure	—	—	131	4	—	—	—	—	—
Familiarity with a country	—	—	100	—	—	—	—	—	—
	240	—	686	10	—	—	10	—	—
General									
Expected higher profits	182	20	144	—	—	—	—	—	—
Other[7]	252	14	112	5	14	37	39	43	50[8]
	434	34	256	5	14	37	39	43	50
Total	1638	97	1796	100	171	304	226	227	203

* Included in lower labour costs.
1 Number of times factors are ranked 1 to 3 in a 6-point scale.
2 Listed as 'crucially' or 'fairly important' in Basi's 3-point scale.
3 Forsyth (a) refers to reasons given by firms on decision to invest outside the US.
4 Andrews' survey was concerned with identifying reasons for investing in Ireland.
5 Dealt with in a separate part of the survey and regarded as crucially important.
6 Classified as financial stability.
7 Including 192 mentions for availability of infrastructure, power and banking facilities.
8 Including forty mentions 'to take advantage of Ireland's entry into the Common Market should that occur'.

Source: Dunning (1973).

provides grist for the researcher's mill. While a lot of the information – particularly that obtained from trade and financial publications – needs to be treated with some caution, a great deal of historical and contemporary evidence has now been assembled, which provides a useful starting point for testing some of the general and specific hypotheses set out in Chapter 4.

Most of the field studies of the past two decades are similar in kind to those of the 1960s and early 1970s in that they seek to identify and, in some cases, quantitatively evaluate (e.g. by use of Delphi and other ranking procedures) the main variables affecting the decision to undertake FDI. Usually, the data for these studies is provided by the executives of MNEs, either by personal interview or completion of a questionnaire. However, company histories and related secondary material also offer quite a rich source of material on the *raison d'être* for MNE activity. Most of the studies tend to be home or host country specific and to focus on the reasons why MNEs prefer to service foreign markets from one location rather than another. Most also direct their attention to market- and efficiency-seeking MNE activity rather than to resource-seeking or strategic asset acquiring activity.

It would be tedious, and somewhat repetitive, to describe these surveys in any detail. Although the evaluating techniques vary among researchers, time and time again scholars have identified the same variables as affecting MNE activity and assessed them similarly. Where differences do occur, they reflect primarily the kind of FDI undertaken; the countries, industries or firms being considered; or the particular aspect of MNE activity being analysed.

We shall attempt to present the sense of the findings of a selection of some recent surveys in Sections 6.2.2 and 6.2.5.[4] In doing so, as far as possible we have tried to relate these findings to some of the mainstream theories even though, in most cases, the investigators have not attempted to do so. Two exceptions include an historical examination of the factors influencing the decision of 187 companies to invest overseas in the 19th and 20th centuries (Dunning and Archer, 1987), and our own study of Japanese participation in the UK manufacturing industry (Dunning, 1986). Both these studies attempted to identify and evaluate both the motives for foreign investment and the kind of OLI variables which the managers of firms perceived to be the most relevant in explaining their foreign operations. The following paragraphs briefly summarize the findings of recent field studies.

6.2.2   The motives for FDI

Chapter 3 has already described the main motives for FDI. As these have been derived mainly from historical and contemporary company data and field studies, little needs to be added. Such surveys reveal a mixture of *defensive* and *aggressive* motives for the *initial* act of foreign production. However, in the case of market-seeking investment at least, the overwhelming consensus of research scholars is that the possible loss of an existing market is the paramount driving force. An exception is the case of Japanese MNE activity in European manufacturing industry where the most common motive stated by some 270 investing firms was 'as one of the steps for the globalized business strategies of the company' (JETRO, 1990). For sequential investments, however, it is the anticipated growth of markets that is usually the principal motive. However, in the case of FDI in oligopolistic sectors, the protection of a global competitive position continues to be an important consideration.

In the case of resource-based and rationalized investment, local markets are a less important locational pull than the availability of indigenous resources and capabilities, and the avoidance of cross-border transportation and other transfer costs. In the case of strategic asset seeking investment, the main motive is to sustain or advance a firm's competitive position. The evidence suggests that the acquisition of technology and markets and the gathering of information have been particularly important motives for foreign firms investing in the US (Graham, 1974; Ajami and Ricks, 1981) and for Japanese firms investing in Europe (Hyun and Whitmore, 1989).[5]

6.2.3   The basis for FDI: O-specific advantages

Previous chapters have suggested that the ability of a firm to engage in FDI (and, for that matter, other forms of international economic activity) is usually based upon some competitive advantage of the investing company. In producer goods industries, this advantage is usually to do with the nature of the products supplied and the firm's ability to produce at lower cost or take advantage of the economies of large scale production. In consumer goods sectors, the possession of branded products and trademarks together with the ability to offer a reliable product customized to the needs of the local market are the main O advantages usually identified.[6]

However, it is clear that the significance of these O advantages varies between MNEs, and is both industry and country specific. Thus, comparing the O advantages of US firms investing in the UK in the 1950s with Japanese firms investing in the 1980s, the present author found that those of the former mainly comprised their ability to innovate particular goods and services, their managerial and marketing skills in producing and marketing these goods, and their capacity to exploit large and fairly homogeneous markets; the O advantages of the Japanese firms primarily consisted of their competence to produce differentiated, fault-free products at competitive prices (Dunning, 1988b). Other studies (Stopford, 1974; Dunning and Archer, 1986) show that throughout history UK MNEs have generally enjoyed a comparative O advantage in mature, relatively low technology sectors and in consumer goods industries, whereas their German equivalents have recorded noteworthy performances in most of the high technology sectors. New Zealand firms, on the other hand, appear to compete more successfully in sectors in which price, product design or quality are at a premium (Akoorie and Enderwick, 1991). The most important O advantage of Korean MNEs was identified by Kumar and Kim (1984) as 'their ability to start overseas manufacturing projects at costs lower than those cited by their competitors' (p. 49). According to the authors, Korean firms have been able to accomplish this by 'careful planning, lower costs of expatriate staff, minimum spending on infrastructure and by supplying necessary inputs at low prices' (p. 49). Chen (1983) and Schive and Hsueh (1985) found that Hong Kong and Taiwanese MNEs were able to compete against First World MNEs, particularly in other developing countries, because of their greater familiarity with the host countries' environment and their more appropriate management styles. On the other hand, a World Bank study (1989) has suggested that Third World MNEs have increasingly penetrated US and European markets to gain access to technology and market information. Parry (1982) identified the ability of Australian firms to adapt foreign technology to meet the needs of smaller markets as a decisive competitive advantage, while Rugman (1987) argued that Canadian firms in mature and resource-based sectors which invest in the US, excel at marketing their products, building up a network of foreign distributors and establishing close long-term contractual relationships with their customers and suppliers.

However, these and other field studies have also found that underpinning these O advantages are systemic organizational and institutional capabilities. Research suggests that these are likely to be less industry specific and more culture or firm specific in nature. The holistic approach of Japanese companies, their ability to reduce market failure by Kievetsu-type relationships and their particular approach to human resource management underlies their particular O advantages, while those of European and US MNEs have been found to possess different kinds of competences (Dunning, 1990; JETRO, 1990).

The types of O advantages enjoyed by foreign direct investors is also seen to vary according to the degree of multinationality of companies. This, in its turn, is likely to be a function of the age and experience of MNEs. The sequential theory of MNE activity expounded by Kogut (1983) and later extended by Bartlett and Ghoshal (1989) suggests that the way firms organize their assets may be as important an advantage as the assets themselves. This appears to be borne out by field studies. In his study of growth of UK MNEs (Archer, 1986), the advantages identified by established investors in the 1970s and 1980s were quite different from those 50 or 100 years earlier, and could be traced increasingly to their ability to exploit the economies of common governance and the reduction of transaction costs arising from geographical diversification.

6.2.4 The L variables: the decision to engage in, or expand foreign production

Market-seeking investments

The significance of the variables influencing the 'where' to produce vary with the type of FDI and the stage of development of both the investing and recipient countries. The one exception is the political stability of the recipient country. Almost invariably this is a necessary, though not a sufficient, condition for MNE activity. For *market-seeking* investments, the size and growth of host markets, the competition for these markets, the relative costs of producing goods in different countries, the lack of opportunities for expansion in the home country, the extent to which product adaptation and customization is required, the cross-border transfer costs (i.e. transport costs and tariff barriers) and the need to diversify risks, are all frequently mentioned in the surveys identified on page 140. Host government import controls, which, at one time, were a decisive factor in influencing the decision to produce abroad, are probably less important today. Exceptions include the restrictions imposed by some European governments on the import of Japanese motor vehicles and some electronic goods. Of some 8790 Japanese firms surveyed in 1987, only 10% considered host government policies were a critical influence on their decision to produce abroad (Hyun and Whitmore, 1989). Similarly, the anticipation of lower production costs in a foreign location does not figure as an important variable in most surveys.[7]

In their choice of manufacturing outlets in Europe in the late 1980s, Japanese firms ranked the 'environment for physical distribution' as the most important situational variable (JETRO, 1990). Historical studies also reveal a host of country-, industry- and firm-specific factors influencing the siting of foreign production units (Archer, 1986; Franko, 1976; Wilkins, 1974, 1980) which make it difficult for scholars to generalize on the significance of particular variables. Moreover, the locational determinants have changed over time. Restrictions on trade in the 1990s are less important than in the 1930s; labour and material costs make up a lower component of total costs than once they did, while the availability of skilled manpower and good communications facilities are more relevant. In their study of the strategic variables influencing the locational decisions of 23 leading UK manufacturing companies, Shepherd *et al.* (1985) identified 'the need to be close to the market which is being supplied' as the most important. Currency appreciations in Japan, Taiwan and Korea, together with import restrictions imposed by European and US governments, have a major 'push' factor making for FDI from those countries. Survey evidence has further confirmed that the locational determinants of MNE activity are likely to be activity specific. Dunning and Norman (1987), for example, in a study of the siting of the offices of some 120 MNEs in the mid 1980s, found that, while proximity to clients and familiarity of language were identified as the most important reasons influencing the choice of a European location by management and business consultants, other variables (e.g. availability of specialist and related services, quality of local professional or technical staff, availability of the right premises and the quality of telecommunication services) were ranked higher by computer software companies, engineering consultants and wholesale trading and financial concerns.

Resource-based investments

These are, to a certain extent, self-evident. Since firms invest to acquire resources and capabilities,

then it is not surprising (and this is confirmed by surveys) that firms will invest where the resources are available at the lowest real cost. However, the role of complementary assets necessary to extract raw materials and minerals, farm the land, and market the final output, may be no less relevant. Again, numerous field studies have identified the transportation infrastructure (road, rail, harbour and airport facilities), power and water supplies and sewerage systems, together with the appropriate institutional and legal framework for conducting business as important variables. Certainly, the processing of materials is strongly influenced by the availability of the appropriate labour skills and the presence of related industries (Porter, 1990).

Efficiency-seeking investments

In Chapter 4 we distinguished between two types of rationalized investment. The first was that designed to take advantage of the differential costs of natural factor endowments. The second was that intended to exploit the economies of specialization and scale. As regards the first, most surveys on the factors influencing the location of offshore production have established that production costs (and especially real labour costs) are an important determinant. Similarly, tax and other fiscal inducements offered by governments, which exert only a modest influence on market-oriented and resource-based investment, appear to be a more important determinant of efficiency-seeking investment.[8]

For the second type of efficiency-seeking investment, which is usually more capital or technology intensive, unskilled or semi-skilled labour and raw materials are likely to be less significant, and that of skilled labour, transport and communication costs more significant. Here the evidence suggests that while fiscal incentives may exert some influence, far more important is the role of government in creating the appropriate economic and cultural environment for inward investment, and in ensuring that the essential manpower and infrastructural services are available. Survey evidence suggests that the location of both kinds of efficiency-seeking investment are determined by supply rather than demand conditions.

6.2.5 When to invest and when to license: the internalization (I) decision

Only a few field studies and surveys specifically address the question of why firms engage in FDI rather than license foreign firms to use their proprietary assets. Yet there is a great deal of casual empiricism to support a number of propositions that firms invest overseas to lower cross-border transaction costs. Let us give just three examples:

(1) Many US and UK companies setting up resource-based investments in the 19th century as well as their Japanese equivalents in the post-1945 era have indicated that they did so to protect themselves against supply disruptions and price hikes. On occasions it was also done to prevent competitors from gaining access to critical primary products (Archer, 1986; Wilkins, 1974; Ozawa, 1989). Similarly, Nicholas (1982) and Stopford and Turner (1985) have shown that forward integration into cross-border sales and distribution ventures has been prompted by the perceived need to gain control of selling outlets, to ensure that the product exported is efficiently marketed and a proper standard of after-sales servicing is maintained. By contrast, the desire of Japanese companies to monitor closely the quality and price of imported materials and intermediate products was one of the main reasons prompting the internationalization of Japanese trading companies. Their main O advantage lay in their access to and knowledge of the Japanese market but they soon gained a trading, financial and shipping expertise of their own through their control over a diversified but linked group of service activities (Wilkins, 1990b).

(2) There is considerable historical evidence to suggest that foreign production has been preferred to licensing either because of the lack of a suitable licensee or because it was feared that a licensee might become a competitor. Archer (1986) cites the examples of UK companies, such as Delta, Bridon, BICC and Hawker Siddeley, setting up factories in the Commonwealth in the 1950s rather than engaging in licensing for these reasons.

(3) Finally, the literature contains several instances of the significance of the economies of common governance arising from FDI. Mostly, this is reported as a need to maintain control over the types of products produced, export markets served and the sourcing of intermediate products. It is largely revealed in the preference for the full ownership of foreign affiliates, particularly by the globally integrated MNEs. We shall deal with this issue in more detail in Chapter 7. For the moment, we observe that the rationalization of US direct investment in the EC in the 1960s and 1970s, and the reasons given by Japanese firms for wishing to control their European affiliates in the 1980s, accord well with the theoretical propositions put forward by scholars such as Anderson and Gatignon (1986), Hennart (1986) and Buckley and Casson (1985).

There have been very few original field studies aimed at testing the internalization theory of MNE. We might identify three such studies. The first is an investigation by the present author who, in 1983, interviewed 24 Japanese manufacturing affiliates about their reasons for investing in the UK (Dunning, 1986). The respondents were asked to rate a number of reasons for preferring equity investment (FDI) to a licensing arrangement (using the term 'licence' to embrace all forms of non-equity participation). The most important factor reported for not licensing (and therefore in favour of FDI) was the 'difficulty of guaranteeing quality control' in such arrangements, which may be linked to the realization that it would not be possible 'to ensure Japanese work style/management philosophy' in the licensees' operations. Also rated of considerable importance were factors relating to the difficulty of achieving an adequate licensing agreement, including the: 'difficulty of locating an appropriate licensee'; 'inability to negotiate a satisfactory price for the ownership-advantage'; and 'difficulty of enforcing patent or trademark rights'. The other key internalization variable pinpointed in the survey was the expected synergistic benefit of MNE operations which, it was felt, a licensing agreement could not fully capture. The three factors identified under this heading ('unable to capture full economies of scope and organizational synergy via licensing'; 'need to maintain full product, process or market flexibility'; and 'need to control distribution outlets') were all thought to be important by the respondents. A later study by the present author reveals that the ability of firms to internalize some markets is partly country specific. Thus Japanese MNEs in Europe have a stronger revealed I advantage in transaction-intensive sectors, both within and between firms, than their US counterparts (Dunning, 1993a).

The second glimpse into the way in which cross-border market failure might influence MNE activity is given by Buckley and Mathew (1979) who, in a study of the motives of 52 UK companies that had invested in Australia for the first time between 1959 and 1972, identified the desire to replace local marketing and distribution agents who had failed to look after their interests satisfactorily, as the most important single reason for engaging in FDI.

The third attempt to identify some of the reasons why firms might opt to engage in FDI rather than conclude a non-equity agreement with a foreign firm was made by Dunning and Norman (1987) in their survey of the location of MNE offices identified earlier. They found that the three main reasons given – in order of significance – were the need to capture the benefits of integrating their activities in the UK with the rest of their foreign operations, the difficulty in controlling the product quality of the licensee and the fear of under-performance by the licensee.

6.2.6   Behavioural factors influencing foreign production

Finally, survey data has shed some light on the strategy of firms towards their foreign operations. A substantial amount of industry, country and firm case study material has been assembled in support of Vernon's product cycle thesis (see especially Hufbauer, 1966; Hirsch, 1967; and Wells, 1972). However, in more recent years, for reasons set out in Chapter 4, empirical work has produced rather more mixed results (Mullar-Sebastian, 1983). Much casual evidence has also been accumulated to support Knickerbocker's 'follow my leader' and Graham's 'exchange of threats' hypotheses. Wilkins (1974) and Archer (1986), for example, give examples of several investments made by Courtaulds and Dunlops in Europe in the inter-war years. More recently, in the

1970s and 1980s such a rationale for new or sequential investment appears in the chairmen's reports of such UK companies as BP, ICI, Redland and Unilever; while an examination of the dates of entry of Japanese firms into European manufacturing reveals a 3–5 year bunching in such sectors as colour television sets, video recorders, cars, photocopiers and rubber tyres (JETRO, 1991).

Increasingly, however, it is the need to protect or advance global competitiveness that has led firms to seek out and acquire foreign-based intangible assets, particularly in the major countries of the Triad. An analysis of the rationale for A&Ms in the 1980s, contained in the annual statements of many MNEs, reveals that this is frequently the case. Sometimes this is achieved by buying into markets for particular products (e.g. the investment by Sony in Columbia records in 1989); sometimes by better enabling the economies of scale or scope to be reaped; and sometimes by gaining entry into a new market in an industry with surplus capacity (e.g. Sunitomo's investment in Dunlop). Taiwanese and Korean firms have been particularly active in concluding technology-sharing joint ventures and acquiring companies for their brand names or industry reputation in the US (World Bank, 1989). In addition, as we shall see in Chapter 8, firms have concluded cross-border strategic alliances to achieve these and other objectives.

6.2.7   Conclusions of field studies

Over the years a considerable amount of evidence has been amassed from field studies on the reasons for foreign-owned value-added activities. One of the more recent studies, which separates the main influences on FDI decisions according to whether the investment is being made in developed or developing countries, is set out in Table 6.2. While it is difficult to generalize about this and other data reviewed in the previous sections, there are some clear indications that the eclectic paradigm does provide a useful framework for identifying the main determinants of MNE activity. At the same time, any attempt to evaluate the determinants of particular types of FDI, or those from particular countries, industries and firms, may need to draw upon more specific theories.

The evidence from field studies indicates that

Table 6.2 Some main influences on FDI decisions by 52 leading firms.[1]

	Reasons for FDI in			
	Developed countries		Developing countries	
	per cent of respondents mentioning a factor in their 'top three'			
	1970	1983	1970	1983
A Market seeking				
A1 Access to host country's domestic market	89	67	82	87
A2 Access to markets in host country's region	41	37	29	34
A3 Avoidance of existing or anticipated tariff barriers	24	16	51	43
A4 Avoidance of existing or anticipated non-tariff trade barriers	13	18	29	28
A5 Inducements offered by host country	11	12	16	13
A6 Need for local market presence	6	5	3	0
A7 Development of local market	3	3	3	0
B Resource seeking				
B1 Access to raw materials	13	10	13	11
B2 Comparative labour cost advantages	4	6	11	13
B3 Comparative material cost advantages	4	6	2	4
C Rationalized (efficiency) seeking				
C1 Integration with company's existing investment	26	37	4	17
C2 Changes in industry's structure	20	22	11	9
D Strategic asset seeking				
D1 Acquisition opportunities	3	3	0	0
E General				
E1 Slower growth of home market	17	18	11	11
E2 Integration with other companies' investment	4	8	4	4
E3 Shifts of political and social stability of host country	2	8	9	8
E4 Tax advantages	6	4	7	0
E5 Distribution of risk	0	5	0	3
E6 Exchange rate movements on siting (not financing) investment	0	2	0	0

1 Companies were asked to rank the six most important influences on new foreign direct investment in industrial countries and in less developed countries, in both 1970 and 1983, by writing the number '1' for the most important factor, '2' for the second most important factor, and so on.

Source: Adapted from *Group of 30*, 1984.

many of the partial theories outlined in Chapter 4 do have some empirical support, but that none can claim to be a general explanation of the MNE or MNE activity. This is well borne out by the wide variety of motives identified by developing country MNEs in their foreign investment strategies (World Bank, 1989). Even in the case of some general theories, such as the internalization paradigm, the relevant variables reflecting the extent and form of market failure differ according to the type of investment and the stage of economic development of the investing and recipient countries.

6.3   STATISTICAL STUDIES

6.3.1   The nature of the studies

Most of the more recent scholarly research seeking to evaluate different theories of MNE activity has used existing published data, and has sought, by the use of a variety of econometric techniques, to identify the more significant explanatory variables, most of which are drawn from field studies and company-specific information.

These studies mostly fall into two broad categories. The first attempt to explain the geographical and industrial structure of MNE activity, or the modality of such activity at a particular point in time or, in some cases, between two or more points in time. These are cross-sectional or latitudinal studies. The second examine the temporal changes of MNE activity in a particular country or industry, or sometimes between countries and industries. These are time series or longitudinal studies. Sometimes, the two types of studies are combined, as in the case of pooled cross-sectional studies.

Both types of research have been used to suggest reasons for different kinds or aspects of MNE activity, as set out in the previous paragraphs. Some have sought to explain the structure of outward investment of particular countries or industries, but the majority have been concerned with the composition of inward investment. Most studies have been bi-country, although more recently, some multi-country studies have been undertaken (see, for example, Clegg, 1987).

With a few exceptions (to be described later), the econometric studies have not sought to evaluate the merits of alternative theories of MNE and MNE activity. Moreover, most have been *inductive* rather than *deductive*. They have tended either to test the predictions of a particular theoretical model, or to identify *which* of the OLI variables (e.g. as set out in Table 4.1) are the most (statistically) significant determinants of MNE activity. We shall present the results of a selection of these studies by first considering the cross-sectional studies then the time-series studies.

6.3.2   Cross-sectional studies: outward MNE activity

Introduction

Studies of the determinants of MNE using home-country data are of two types. First, there are those that attempt to explain either the total foreign production of a country's firms, or (more usually) its significance relative to the global or domestic production of such firms. The main questions addressed by these studies are: 'To what extent, and in what way, does the industrial composition of the foreign value-added activities of firms differ from that of its domestic equivalent?', and 'What explains the industrial distribution of outward direct investment by a particular country's MNEs?'

The second group of studies directs its attention to the ways in which foreign markets are serviced and/or the ways in which inputs used by domestic companies are sourced. Here the issues addressed primarily relate to the location of economic activity. Such questions as 'Why do Japanese firms produce in the EC rather than export to it?' and 'Why do Swedish companies source their intermediate products from Asian subsidiaries rather than produce them in their Swedish factories?', are the types of questions that this group of studies has sought to answer.

The composition and relative significance of outward MNE activity: the evaluation of O-specific advantages

These studies tend to analyse either the whole of the foreign value-added activities of firms or industries, or that of specific host countries or areas. Investigations that have attempted to compare the structure of such activities by several source countries include those of Clegg (1987), who made a comparative analysis of US, UK, Swedish, German and Japanese investments, and Pearce (1989) who analysed a multi-country sample of the world's largest enterprises.

The main purpose of these studies is to identify and evaluate the kinds of competitive or O-specific advantages possessed by firms that engage in foreign production. However, as Lall (1980a) astutely observes, it is not the absolute level of O advantages that will determine the ability of one country's firms to penetrate a particular market, but the relative strength of these advantages *vis à vis* those of firms of another country – and, in particular, those of the country in which the investment is made. It is also worth recalling that although these advantages may be necessary to explain the foreign activities of MNEs, they are not, in themselves, sufficient to explain such activities.

With these precautionary remarks in mind, we now consider the main findings of scholars who have attempted to identify the importance of the individual O variables identified earlier.

(i)   *O asset (Oa) advantages: proprietary and human capital*   The field research already described has suggested that many firms perceive their innovatory capabilities to give them an important competitive advantage over their foreign competitors.

Econometric studies of the determinants of US FDI (see, for example, Pugel, 1978, 1981; Grubaugh, 1987; Owen, 1984; Lall, 1980a; Wolf, 1977; Bergsten *et al.*, 1978) confirm that technological intensity is a positively and statistically significant explanatory variable of the industrial composition of such investment. The statistical significance rises sharply when resource-intensive products are eliminated from the sectors considered. In a study of 16 manufacturing industries in the early 1970s, Dunning and Buckley (1977) offer some support for the hypothesis that the strength of US FDI in the UK, compared to UK FDI in the US, is positively related to the relative strength of R&D activity in the investing countries. The appropriate regression equation was expressed in both linear and log linear form. In his study of the world's largest industrial enter-

prises in 1982, Pearce (1989) also found the R&D intensity of US firms to be significantly and positively correlated with their propensity to engage in foreign production. He further concluded that research intensity was a significant influence on the FDI of Continental European firms, but not on that of UK firms. This result is consistent with the fact that a higher proportion of UK outbound investment tends to be in resource-intensive sectors. For Japanese firms, Pearce's results suggested that their propensity to engage in overseas production was positively correlated to the *average* research intensity of industries, but that *within* industries there seemed to be some tendency for the less R&D-intensive firms to record a higher overseas production ratio.[9]

More recent work by Kogut and Chang (1991) on Japanese investment in the US confirms these results. They also suggest that as well as exploiting existing technological advantages, Japanese firms are currently investing in the US (particularly via the modality of joint ventures) to acquire access to US technology.[10] The explosive growth of Japanese banks in London in the 1980s can be explained by their desire to diversify their banking services into securitization – a course of action not open to them in Japan – and thus compete more efficiently in global markets. In competing with Western banks, their main O advantages were (i) their access to Japanese clients, (ii) their ability to obtain capital (from Japan) at low interest rates and (iii) their exceptional low operating costs/asset ratio (0.6% cf. 2.5% in the case of Western banks for 1988/90) (Hawawini and Schill, 1992).

In a five-nation study which used pooled cross-sectional sets of data for the years 1965, 1970 and 1975, Clegg (1987) found that R&D expenditure was the most positively significant determinant of outward FDI for US, Swedish and West German MNEs. However, in the case of Japanese MNEs the statistical relationship was both negative and significant, while for the UK it was similarly signed but insignificant. Swedenborg (1979) also discovered R&D intensity to be a positively significant determinant of the structure of all overseas production by Swedish firms in 1974, but not of that in particular countries. Using an output measure of technological capability (*viz* registered patents), Cantwell (1987) showed that there was a positive and significant relationship between the comparative patenting advantages of German and Japanese firms in a selection of 12 manufacturing sectors and their share of the total foreign production in these sectors.[11]

Turning now to the skill content of employment as an O-specific advantage, Lall (1980a) found that the average wage per employee (as a measure of the general level of human competence in an industry) tended to be positively and significantly related to the foreign production of US firms. Swedenborg obtained similar results for Swedish firms. In his study of West German MNE activity in developing countries, Juhl (1979) also established that it was positively related to a measure of human capital intensity. This countered the author's expectation that MNEs would be more inclined to invest in the less skilled sectors in these countries. One possible reason for these findings is that the firms that are most innovative and skill intensive in Germany are also those most prone to engage in an international division of labour, which includes their participation in the more labour-intensive activities *within* a sector in developing countries.

In other cross-industry studies of US FDI, Pugel (1978, 1981) concluded that the share of managers in total employment was positively correlated with the propensity of firms to engage in foreign production. In his five-country study, Clegg (1987) took non-operative wages and salaries as a measure of the skill intensity of managerial manpower as a possible O advantage. Perhaps surprisingly, this relationship proved to be insignificant for the US and Swedish firms, but was significantly positive for UK, Japanese and German firms.

(ii) *Financial asset advantages* Another frequently hypothesized Oa of MNEs, or potential MNEs, is their ability to raise capital at preferential rates. An interesting analysis of early European direct participation in Malaysian tin mining (Hennart, 1986a, 1986b) suggests that the critical advantage of the investing companies lay in their privileged access to capital. There are several reasons for this. First, MNEs are usually larger and more efficient than their uni-national competitors, and are therefore likely to have greater bargaining power with financial institutions. Second, and this is a direct result of their multinationality, they may have superior knowledge of, and access to, foreign sources of capital. These advantages may, in Pugel's words 'be trans-

ferred to a subsidiary either through the direct flows of funds from the parent, or indirectly in the subsidiary's efforts, backed explicitly or implicitly by the parent, to acquire external funds' (Pugel, 1981, p. 233). Thus, it might be hypothesized that the greater the capital intensity of a sector, the more significant the role of FDI is likely to be.

Pugel (1978) formulated a capital requirements variable, measured as the financial capital necessary to enable a firm to operate at its minimum efficient scale of production. This was found to be an insignificant determinant of FDI, which Pugel suggested may have reflected 'the failure to control for the separate influence of scale economies, which would tend to favour centralization of output rather than FDI' (1981, p. 233). When this was done (Pugel, 1981), the variable was found to be significantly and positively related to FDI in a cross-sectional industry study of US FDI. However, in a related study Lall (1980) discovered no significant relationship between a measure of capital intensity (total net fixed assets in each industry divided by total employees) and the propensity of US firms to undertake FDI. Further, Grubaugh (1987), using a sample of 300 US firms, found no significant relationship between a measure of labour intensity (used as the inverse of capital intensity) and the likelihood of the firm becoming an MNE.

In his five-country study Clegg (1987) detected important inter-country differences when using the variable 'net tangible fixed assets at book values per employee' as a measure of capital intensity. For US and UK FDIs, this variable was positively signed and significant; for Japan it was negatively signed and significant; while it was insignificant for Sweden (negative sign) and for Germany (positive sign). Clegg observes (1987, p. 102) that the US and the UK

> 'have notably large and well-established MNEs, for whom the cost of capital is lower than for firms from more recent foreign investing nations, because of their own internal funding and their size, commanding lower interest charges. As such, they will be relatively advantaged in capital-intensive industries'.

By contrast, Japanese firms involved in FDI over the period were 'typically small firms in standardized-product and labour-intensive industries . . . (which)

are in no way exploiting a general capital advantage'
(Clegg, 1987, pp. 107–8).

(iii) *Product composition and differentiation*
Following Caves (1971), a number of researchers
have hypothesized that the ability of firms to
differentiate their products – particularly high
income consumer goods and services[12] – may be a
key O advantage leading to foreign production.
Moreover, the efficient exploitation of these types of
expertise in major markets may require adaptation
of the products being sold to local supply capabilities
and demand idiosyncrasies; this may further stimulate the implementation of local producing facilities.

The commonly used proxy for this type of
intangible O advantage is advertising expenditure as
a proportion of sales. While, as Pugel (1978, 1981)
observes, advertising does not capture such key
attributes of product differentiation as the ability and
willingness of MNEs to customize their products or
provide special services, it does quite accurately
reflect the extent of product branding and marketing
expenditure. Other econometric studies by Caves
(1974a, 1974b), Grubaugh (1987), Owen (1982),
Bergsten *et al.* (1978), Lall (1980) and Kumar (1990)
all confirm a positive and significant relationship
between advertising intensity and outward US FDI.
In consumer goods industries, it is often shown to be
the most significant variable. In addition, Owen
utilized an alternative marketing proxy (ratio of sales
expenditure to industry sales) which was again found
to be positively related to FDI.

(iv) *O transaction (Ot) advantages: Economies of
plant size* Researchers have derived different predictions as to the effect of the size of a firm's plant
engaged in foreign production. Pugel (1981, p. 223),
for example, argues that

> 'the importance of scale economies in production
> favours centralization of production in order to
> exploit fully these economies. The importance of
> scale economies then should be negatively related
> to the extent of FDI across industries'.

In his analysis of the foreign activities of US firms in
the 1970s, Pugel found 'the share of the total US
market accounted for by a factory of minimum efficient
scale' was significantly and negatively related to the
propensity to undertake FDI. From a similar stand-

point, Lall (1980, p. 110) offers a different hypothesis. To quote his words:

> 'new facilities are set up in the US and the
> benefits of scale are reaped there; there is thus an
> initial non-transferability, which ends when the
> domestic facilities reach a certain size and foreign
> markets grow large enough to permit the transfer
> of capital for economic operation abroad. We
> expect to find, therefore, that scale economies
> promote outward investment'.

Using value added per establishment in each industry
as a measure of scale economies, both Lall and
Owen concluded that this variable was positively
related to the propensity of US manufacturing firms
to invest abroad.

In her study of Swedish MNEs, Swedenborg
(1979, p. 88) tested the hypothesis that 'scale
economies affect the firm's choice between foreign
and domestic production primarily by discouraging it
from setting up foreign production outlets before
such economies have been full exploited at home',
and derived limited support for the implied negative
relationship. On the other hand, Dunning and
Buckley (1976) discovered that, although the ratio
between the foreign production of US and UK
foreign firms was positively related to a plant
economies of scale variable, the relationship was not
a significant one (as it was, for example, in
explaining the ratio between US and UK exports).

(v) *Economies of firm size* From Horst (1972a)
onwards, many scholars have suggested that the
propensity of firms to undertake foreign production
is likely to be positively related to their size,
although it is accepted that size itself might represent
a composite variable for other variables affecting this
propensity. For example, large size may be associated
with a concentrated or oligopolistic market structure,
both of which tend to encourage FDI. In addition,
the larger a firm, the more likely it is to be involved
with overseas markets which, given other conditions,
will typically include some foreign production.

Horst (1972a) confirmed that size, more than
any other variable, explained the propensity of US
firms to invest in Canada in the 1960s. Bergsten *et al.*
(1978, p. 243) produced results that indicated that
for US firms 'size is critical *within* an industry but not
between industries. Within any given industry, the

large firms clearly tend to be the foreign investors, but, in some sectors, average firm size is large but (FDI is) small'. Studies by Owen (1982), Pearce (1989) and Li and Guisinger (1992) – the latter for service MNEs – have also demonstrated a positive relationship between the size of US firms and FDI, while Grubaugh (1987) found that size was positively related to the likelihood of a US firm being an MNE. In his analysis of German manufacturing FDI, Juhl (1979) concluded that firm size was a positive and significant determinant. However, in a broader based investigation of the world's largest industrial enterprises, Pearce (1989) ascertained that there was no statistically significant relationship between size and the degree of multinationality of firms, once allowance was made for differences in industrial structure.

A rather different approach to the relationship between size and FDI was taken by Kimura (1989). Using a pooled set of firm level data on the foreign activities of leading Japanese semiconductor firms between 1978 and 1982, the author concluded that although a firm's domestic size was a powerful influence on the amount of its FDI, this variable was highly correlated with a group of strategic related advantages, viz technological innovation, product diversification and vertical integration. He also concluded that as a result, firm size might best be regarded as a surrogate for these advantages. This finding is consistent with that of Blomström and Lipsey (1991) who, in an investigation of the propensity of US firms to invest abroad, using data from the 1982 Benchmark Survey (US Department of Commerce, 1985), found that once a firm has overcome the entry barriers into foreign production, size has no effect on the proportion of its resources devoted to foreign activity. At the same time Kimura's research also suggests that firm size exerts its own influence on FDI independently of that of strategic advantage.

(vi) *Oligopolistic interaction* We have suggested that a casual inspection of the timing of the initial FDI by firms in oligopolistic industries lends some support to the 'follow my leader' hypothesis put forward by Knickerbocker (1973) to explain the foreign activities of US MNEs, and (Flowers, 1976) to explain the activities of European and Canadian affiliates in the USA. In their empirical work, these scholars used the concept of an entry concentration index, which was designed to measure the extent to which the setting up of foreign affiliates by leading MNEs in a particular market was 'bunched' over a period of time. In doing so, they found such an index was positively related to the concentration of output in the home country up to moderately high levels of concentration, before decreasing in the most concentrated industries. They also discovered that as soon as one leading firm in an industry initiated foreign production, its main rivals quickly followed, fearing that unless they did so the pioneering enterprise might gain favoured access to foreign customers or new supply capabilities. Finally, it was found that in very concentrated industries, some form of tacit agreement to avoid excessive proliferation of foreign production was likely to operate.

These early studies have been supported by later empirical research on 'imitation' investment in the US tyre and textile industries (Yu and Ito, 1986); on Japanese investment in the European and US motor vehicle and consumer electronics sectors (Micossi and Viesti, 1991); on the FDI behaviour of the top 20 US advertising agencies (Terpstra and Yu, 1988); and on the globalization of 168 of the largest service firms in more service sectors over the period 1976–86 (Li and Guisinger, 1992).

In a related, but somewhat different approach, Graham (1975) has argued that post-war European direct investment in the US was a direct and defensive response by European MNEs to the incursion of their own markets by US firms. Graham discovered that this response was strongly correlated with a number of variables associated with FDI, including the extent of industrial concentration in the home countries of the MNEs. He concluded that such investment represented both an 'exchange of threats' motive associated with oligopolistic competition in standardized products and an 'exposure of innovatory' stimuli motive associated with new products.

(vii) *Natural resource availability* As already indicated, the kind of O advantages relevant to explaining outward direct investment is likely to vary according to the motives for the investment. In the case of resource-based MNE activity, the firms are assumed to venture abroad to acquire resources necessary for their domestic production. In their studies, Owen (1982) and Pugel (1978) found dummy variables of such natural resource dependence to be positively and significantly related to US FDI. On the other hand, in his investigation of West German FDI, Juhl (1979) found an often significant negative relationship between German industry's dependence on imported raw materials and its investment in developing countries. This he attributed to a preference of the governments of these countries for the local ownership of primary products, and that of German MNEs for undertaking the secondary processing of these products in the home country. Swedenborg (1979) formulated a natural resource dummy variable based on the two industries (paper and pulp, iron and steel) in which Sweden had a strong comparative advantage, and found that the relationship between this variable and outbound MNE activity was both positive and significant. Other evidence of a positive link between a home country's possession of natural resources and the pattern of its FDI is supplied by Rugman (1987) for Canada and the Bureau of Industry Economics (1984) for Australia.

(ix) *Other factors*   Other factors that have received more sporadic treatment in empirical tests of outward FDI may be briefly mentioned. Juhl (1979) tested for a correspondence between the level of effective protection received by a West German industry and its propensity to engage in FDI in developing countries. He suggested that where an industry's relative competitiveness against imports from developing countries declines, two of its options are to relocate production to these countries and to seek protection from the imports. It may, then, be hypothesized that the more successful a country is in securing protection, the less the need for foreign production. However, in contrast to the negative relationship hypothesized, Juhl's tests showed a persistently positive and weakly significant relationship between an industry's effective protection and its FDI in developing countries. The offered explanation is that although the level of effective protection may provide a good indicator of the industry's state of vulnerability, firms do not see it as an adequately reliable support for domestic production and therefore resort to the FDI alternative.

Swedenborg (1979) found a persistently positive and significant association between the length of time a Swedish foreign subsidiary had been operating and its relative share of its parent company's global output. In their study of the internationalization of the US advertising industry Terpstra and Yu (1988) confirmed that the extent of a firm's foreign operating experience was a powerful O-specific advantage. Other studies of several service sectors[13] suggest that the experience of firms in meeting the needs of their business clients in domestic markets gives them an important competitive edge when they follow them abroad. Pugel (1981) failed to find support for a hypothesized negative correlation between US FDI and a measure of transport costs. Pearce (1989) established a positive connection between the extent to which an industry is subject to 'penetration' by the diversified operations of firms from other industries and the FDI by firms from that industry. Where such penetration is high, firms in the industry feel the need to respond in some way to their perceived vulnerability; one such response is to strengthen their commitment in overseas markets.

Several studies have emphasized that some of the O-specific advantages of MNEs are likely to reflect their countries of origin. One example is that of Kumar and Kim (1984) who ascertained that Korean-based MNEs perceived their main O advantage to be their ability to initiate and operate overseas products at relatively low costs and the commitment of their expatriate staff. Their study also revealed the role played by the Korean government in assisting at least some of its firms to become MNEs.

One influence of outbound MNE activity that has received scant attention in the literature is the role of the home country's economic and political conditions. Yet some recent research by Tallman (1988) indicates that such variables as the level of home country development are positively related to FDI in the US. His research also shows that the less stable the political regime in the home country (in this case only Western industrialized countries were considered) the greater the propensity for its firms to invest in the US. In his various writings, Lall (e.g. 1985) has frequently stressed that, far from their intention, the macro-economic and organizational policies of the Indian government have forced its own firms to invest abroad to maintain their competitiveness in world markets.

Finally, in a macro-oriented analysis of US direct investment in six industrial countries, Klein and Rosengren (1991), using ordinary least squares (OLS) regression analysis, estimated that over the period 1979–88, one of the key determinants of such investment was relative wealth, as measured by the dollar value of the US stock market divided by the dollar value of the stock market of the host economy. By contrast, they found relative labour costs to be a relatively insignificant variable.

Methods of servicing markets; locational variables

We now turn to consider the second kind of scholarly research on outward MNE activity. This research has been concerned with the determinants of the location of the production by MNEs. Are, for example, foreign markets serviced by exports or local production? Are domestic markets supplied by foreign affiliates or by domestic production facilities? To what extent are exports or imports substitutes or complementary to FDI?

For the most part, the literature does not consider the ways in which the O characteristics of firms might affect the ways in which they service their markets. Two exceptions are the works of Buckley and Pearce (1979) and Kravis and Lipsey (1982). The first pair of authors, in a regression analysis of 156 of the world's largest industrial enterprises, concluded that size was the most important single variable determining their propensity to service an overseas market by foreign production rather than exports. They further argued that while standard location theory was useful in explaining most of the sourcing choices of firms, it needed to be modified in the light of the internalization of cross-border markets. In addition, they considered that these modifications were likely to be most pronounced in the case of R&D intensive and larger firms.

Kravis and Lipsey take a rather different approach. They argue that the locational strategies of MNEs (and, in this case, US MNEs) are likely to be influenced by the technical and behavioural characteristics of their parent companies. To quote their words

> 'The choices made by parent companies among different locations for their affiliates follow an "opposites attract" tendency. Within given

industries, low-wage, low-capital-intensity parents tend to place affiliates in high-wage, high-capital-intensity countries, and vice versa for high-wage, high-capital-intensity parents' (Kravis and Lipsey, p. 222).

At the same time, most scholars acknowledge that the mode by which foreign markets are serviced will also be determined by the structure of the L advantages of countries and the response of firms to them (and, in some cases, their ability to affect them) (Rugman and Verbeke, 1989). Thus the dependent variable of most market servicing tests – depending on whether outward or inward FDI is being examined – takes the form of either exports (imports) or foreign production divided by exports (imports) plus foreign production, that is, one or other component of the foreign market divided by the total foreign market. Occasionally, too, a distinction is made between inter- and intra-firms exports (Sleuwagen, 1985). We shall discuss each of these servicing ratios in turn.

(A)   Servicing foreign markets

The following are some of the L-specific variables that scholars have hypothesized as influencing the propensity of firms to service foreign markets by foreign production rather than exports (hereafter referred to as the foreign production servicing ratio (FPSR)).

(i)   *Relative innovatory capabilities of home and host countries*   As well as being a factor influencing the O advantages of firms, the presence or absence of innovatory capability in a capital exporting or importing country may affect its ability to attract value-added activities by both foreign and domestically owned MNEs.

In his analysis of the way US firms serviced their foreign markets in 14 manufacturing industries and 20 host countries in the late 1970s, Hollander (1984) included several innovatory related variables. The US share of the expenditure of some of the leading industrial nations on R&D in a particular sector was revealed to be significantly and positively correlated with the propensity of US firms to service their foreign markets in that sector by local production rather than by exports. By contrast, the R&D intensity of an industry (i.e. R&D expenditure per dollar of sales in the US) was significantly, but negatively, related to FDI. Using similar data,[14] Sleuwagen (1985) confirmed these results. However, whereas he found a particularly close positive correlation between the R&D intensity of US firms and their *internal* exports of intermediate goods, he also discovered that non-intra-company exports by US parent companies displayed a much lower R&D content.

In another cross-country, cross-industry analysis of US FDI based on 1972 data, the present author (Dunning, 1980) did not find a host country based 'skilled employment ratio' to be significantly related to the choice between exporting and foreign production (despite it being a positively signed influence on both components). In a firm-level analysis of the servicing of global markets by 458 of the world's leading industrial enterprises in 1972, Pearce (1990a) established that the predominant (and often significant) relationship between measures of R&D intensity and FDI was a negative one. The most notable exceptions were two low-technology industries, *viz* food and metals.

(ii) *Market characteristics* It has been argued by some economists (Horst, 1974) that in the early stages of the internationalization process, foreign production and exports are complementary ways of exploiting a foreign market, but that, after the market has reached a certain size, the two become substitutable for each other. If this is the case, it should be reflected in the relationship between host country market size and the servicing ratio. In their study of UK firms, Papanastassiou and Pearce (1990) ascertained that foreign production was persistently and positively related to the GNP of foreign markets, but only significantly so for two of eight industries (transport equipment and chemicals). They also established that GNP per capita was usually positively correlated to the servicing ratio, but only significantly so for one industry (chemicals). In a multi-country study, Dunning (1980) did not find a 'relative market size' variable to be significantly associated with the ratio between the foreign production and exports of US MNEs, despite it being a significant determinant of both components of the ratio. However, the same investigation did unearth some evidence of a positive relationship between the FPSR and the market growth of host countries relative to that of the US. Cross-industry support for this basic hypothesis was also provided by Horst's (1972a) analysis of the servicing of Canadian markets, where the ratio between US exports and US exports plus the local production of US firms in Canada was significantly and negatively related to the ratio of Canadian market size to US domestic production for each industry. By contrast, Buckley and Dunning's (1976) analysis of US sourcing in the UK revealed that neither 'relative market size' nor 'relative market growth' was an important variable influencing the way in which the markets were serviced.

Not all firms, of course, have a choice in their modality of servicing markets. Many service-based firms, for example, need to have a physical presence in a market to sell their products. Such research on the importance of market size in influencing FDI in these sectors is mixed. Terpstra and Yu (1988), for example, verified that FDI by the 20 largest US advertising agencies was positively and significantly related to size of markets, but Nigh *et al.* (1986) could discern no such association in the case of US banking firms.

(iii) *Barriers to trade* As a situational factor, tariffs might be expected to influence servicing ratios by encouraging the substitution of overseas production for exports. Hollander's (1984) tests of the servicing of foreign markets by US firms across both industries and host countries found this variable to be positively and statistically significant. In a cross-industry analysis of US sourcing in Canada, Horst (1972b) established that tariffs were significantly negatively related to the share of exports in US firms' total supply, but Orr (1975) found this association disappeared when 3-digit rather than 2-digit data was used. Buckley and Dunning (1976) demonstrated the effective tariff rate was positively, but generally insignificantly, related to the participation of US firms in UK industry while Kumar (1990) found the same for foreign firms in India. More generally it would appear that tariffs are a less important determinant of FDI than once they were, although intra-regional trade barriers remain an important obstacle to rationalized or efficiency-seeking MNE activity.

Non-tariff barriers have also been a powerful inducement to FDI, especially in countries that impose strict technical and quality control standards and whose governments discriminate against foreign imports in their procurement policies. At the same time – particularly in some service sectors like banking – protected markets may act as barriers to entry to FDI. In a careful study of US FDI in the banking sector, Sagari (1990) revealed that the regulatory framework of host countries was a statistically significant factor influencing the siting of their activities.

(iv) *Psychic distance* The concept of psychic distance as an impediment to trade and/or FDI was first developed by Beckerman (1956) to explain intra-European trade patterns. It was subsequently taken up by Vahlne and Weidersheim-Paul (1973), Hornell *et al.* (1973) and Nordström (1991) to explain the geographical distribution of the foreign subsidiaries of Swedish firms. Psychic distance has been defined by Vahlne and Nordström (1992, p. 3) as 'the factors preventing or disturbing firms learning about and understanding of a foreign environment'. Essentially, it represents a transaction cost of doing business between countries, although psychic distance costs may also be expected to vary between any two countries according to the nature of the economic activity.

The empirical studies of Vahlne and Weidersheim-Paul (1973), Hornell *et al.* (1973), Johanson and Vahlne (1977) and Nordström (1991) show that there is a positive and significant correlation between the actual or perceived psychic proximity between Sweden and other countries and the geographical distribution of Swedish manufacturing and sales subsidiaries. In particular, the association is shown to be most pronounced in the early stages of the firm's internationalization process. The kind of explanatory variables used by the Swedish scholars included differences in the levels of economic development, education, culture and languages, while the Hornell study focused on the perceptions of Swedish managers. The rankings of the two sets of data were similar to each other and to Hofstede's ranking of the cultural similarities of countries, which was based on a composite of four dimensions – *viz* power distance, uncertainty avoidance, individualism and masculinity – (Hofstede, 1980).

In both the Swedish studies, which covered almost all Swedish firms with manufacturing or sales

operations abroad, psychic proximity/distance was found to be positively and significantly correlated with the number of foreign affiliates, each of which was weighted according to whether the establishment is the first, second, third, etc in the country. In the fifteen countries about which data could be obtained, Vahlne and Nordström (1992) obtained a positive rank correlation of 0.89 between the two variables.

It is one thing, of course, to identify a relationship between psychic proximity and the location of FDI, and quite another to explain its significance in relation to other L-specific variables, or, indeed, to identify the role of psychic distance in determining the modality of foreign participation by MNEs. Unfortunately, there have been few attempts to do this, although in a multiple regression analysis combining psychic distance with GDP, growth of GDP and population Nordström (1991) found the first variable only moderately significant as an explanatory factor. In a more recent study, Vahlne and Nordström (1992) have shown that, in spite of the trend towards globalization and the convergence of consumer tastes, there is little evidence that the foreign establishment pattern of foreign firms has changed.

(v) *Real wage costs* A locational variable that has received surprisingly little support in explaining the mode of servicing foreign markets is that of relative wage costs. For example, Papanastassiou and Pearce (1990) discovered that a measure of host country real wages was a generally weak and inconsistently signed influence on the foreign servicing ratio of UK firms. In their study of the location of production for exports by the affiliates of US MNEs, Kravis and Lipsey (1982) found the labour cost component of four variables considered *viz* labour cost, real GDP, GDP^2 and the 'openness' of host countries, to be the least important coefficient. Though negative (as predicted) in 15 or 20 industries, it failed to reach a 5% significance level in any case. Likewise, Dunning (1980) ascertained that relative wage rates were always correctly signed as a determinant of a sourcing ratio for US firms, but rarely significantly so. In a cross-industry study of US sourcing in the UK, Buckley and Dunning (1976) also discovered that relative (UK compared with US) wage rates were an insignificant determinant. More generally it would appear that real wage costs are more likely to influence the mode of servicing developing than developed country markets. At the same time, changes in the relative real wage costs of Japanese and US workers have been an important determinant of the growth of Japanese FDI in the US (Frost and Stein, 1989). Yamawaki (1991) has revealed a statistically significant negative correlation between real labour costs and the geographical distribution of Japanese investment in Europe.

(vi) *Transport costs*   Another L-specific factor that field studies have identified as influencing the choice between exports and foreign production is transport costs. In fact, Hollander (1984) identified 'average cost of shipping per dollar of value of US imports in an industry' as being an insignificant determinant of the US FDI, a result supported by Buckley and Dunning (1976) in their analysis of the servicing of UK markets. By contrast, Papanastassiou and Pearce (1990) found a host country's distance from the UK to be a persistently positive (significantly for several industries) determinant of the propensity of UK firms to serve foreign markets through foreign production rather than exports.

(B) Sourcing domestic markets from foreign production

Chapter 3 has indicated that an important motive for FDI is to supply intermediate products to the investing company or country. Resource-seeking subsidiaries usually play narrow and carefully defined roles within an MNE's globally integrated network, the most significant of which is to combine the O advantages of the investing company with the particular resource endowments of foreign countries to undertake upstream value-added activities at the lowest real cost. These operations have sometimes been fostered by the governments of both home and host countries. For example, computation of the tariff charged on imported goods made by US subsidiaries in certain countries on a value-added rather than on a gross value basis has meant that the costs of shipping foreign-produced goods are less likely to cancel out any costs saved by foreign production. Similarly, the establishment of export processing zones together with the provision of infrastructure and tax concessions offered by host country governments have served to assist the

growth of export-oriented foreign affiliates. We now consider some of the variables influencing the propensity of MNEs to service their domestic markets with products from these affiliates.

(i) *Innovatory capability*   Lee (1986) has argued that the more R&D intensive an industry is, the less likely it is that MNE manufacturing subsidiaries located in developing countries will source their parent companies with a wide range of intermediate products. However, where significant labour-intensive stages exist within the value-added chain, offshore processing might be economically viable in developing countries, even in technologically advanced sectors. This leads Lee to predict that a positive relationship should exist between R&D intensity and the relative significance of imports, subject only to value-added tariff provisions (e.g. under the US Tariff Schedule 806.00 and 807.30) originating from US subsidiaries in developing countries. This was confirmed in statistical tests in which the R&D variable was strongly and persistently positively related to the sourcing of US imports from US affiliates in developing countries, but not to those imported from other developed countries.

In the analysis of Kirkpatrick and Yamin (1981), and in line with the reasoning set out in Chapter 4, R&D intensity is treated primarily as a determinant of the extent to which cross-border intermediate product markets are internalized. Kirkpatrick and Yamin also agree that if high R&D implies continuous innovation and the predominance of 'new' products in an industry's output, then exporting by foreign affiliates to their parent companies may be relatively unimportant, that is, R&D intensity may be negatively related to the need to seek particular foreign L-specific advantages for cost reducing reasons. In fact, the persistence of significant positive signs for R&D intensity in Kirkpatrick and Yamin's results confirms the prevalence of internalization-related influences.

(ii) *Product composition and differentiation*   Though the foreign sourcing of intermediate products by MNEs is clearly motivated by the need to reduce real costs, both Kirkpatrick and Yamin (1981) and Lee (1986) provide cogent evidence that advertising and marketing may sometimes be significant factors. In particular, they suggest that if advertising intensity reflects the propensity of firms to engage in product differentiation as a competitive strategy, then the cost savings of offshore production may be a less consequential locational variable. If this is so, then advertising intensity may be expected to be negatively related to the propensity of a firm to engage in foreign production. However, it is precisely because such foreign production is aimed at its home country's market that it may be positively related to advertising intensity. Moreover, advertising intensity may be positively related to quality-based competition, which favours internalized sources of supply.

In line with the indeterminate hypothesizing, neither Kirkpatrick and Yamin (1981) nor Lee (1986) discovered measures of advertising intensity to be consistently associated with MNE activity. In their empirical work, more direct tests of the role of marketing barriers proved quite successful. Thus Lee found 'the degree of forward integration of manufacturers into distribution' (i.e. the proportion of industry shipments in the US made to distributors owned by the manufacturing company) to be consistently and often significantly positively related to the foreign sourcing ratio. This was as hypothesized, since industries experienced in this type of linkage were able to use offshore production very effectively. Similarly, market service variables ('the frequency of pre-sale and after-sale services' for Lee and 'expenditure on after-sales service as a percentage of sales' for Kirkpatrick and Yamin) were always positively signed and usually significant.

(iii) *Scale economies* Lee (1986) observes that if an industry is characterized by substantial economies of scale, then new entrants, especially from developing countries, may find it difficult to develop that industry as an independent exporting sector. However, if it is possible to separate stages on the value-added chain, and if these stages are not themselves affected by economies of scale, then their relocation to overseas sites may be viable. In the absence of an adequate measure of the 'separability' of manufacturing processes within an industry, Lee uses a proxy of the minimum efficient scale of the industry, since a larger scale of production may mean more work processes to divide. This implies both more potential for offshore production by US MNEs and higher barriers to entry to foreign exporters into the

US market. The positive sign then predicted between minimum efficient scale and Lee's dependent variable was found (usually significantly) for both developed and developing economies. By contrast, arguing directly from the characteristics of final products (i.e. omitting the process separability possibilities noted by Lee), Clark et al. (1989) discovered a significant negative relationship between minimum efficient scale and the likelihood of offshore production in an industry.

(iv) *Differential resource costs* Field studies have confirmed that much of resource-based MNE activity is to take advantage of the lower costs of primary production in foreign countries. There have been few econometric tests of this hypothesis – perhaps it is regarded as self-evident! However, more attention has been given to cross-border differences in labour and capital costs as variables influencing the sourcing of products from foreign affiliates. Thus Moxon (1975) and Clark et al. (1989) found that a measure of labour intensity (*viz.* employee compensation related to value added) to be positively and usually significantly related to the presence of offshore production in developing countries. Clark et al. (1989) also discovered that their proxy for capital intensity (gross book value of depreciable assets divided by total employment) to be significantly and negatively related to their dependent variable, while Kirkpatrick and Yamin (1981) also found their surrogate for capital intensity (value added per production worker) to be persistently, and usually significantly, negative.

(v) *Transport costs* The growth of intra-firm trade is, of course, the natural complement of the increasing international division of labour practised by MNEs. It is a corollary of this that the same factors that constrain trade are likely to lessen the use of such subsidiaries. Therefore, trade-related factors might be expected to play a role in influencing the location of efficiency-seeking FDI.

It is obviously important that transport costs do not outweigh any cost savings gained by offshore production. In the electronics industry, the significantly negative relationship found by Moxon (1975) between a value-to-weight index and the propensity of firms to import from their offshore affiliates suggests the pertinence of such factors.

Similarly Clark *et al.* (1989) demonstrated that the '*ad valorem* international transport change' was significantly negatively related to the propensity of firms to engage in offshore assembling operations. By contrast, Lee (1986) found 'freight and insurance costs relative to the value of imports' to be insignificantly related to the dependent variable, that is, they did not affect the proportion of offshore production imports in total US imports.

(vi) *Import restrictions* If tariff levels imposed by the capital exporting country are relevant to the decisions of MNEs to supply their domestic markets from foreign sources, the most likely relationship would be a negative one. One reason for this is that high tariffs protect domestic producers and reduce their need to seek enhanced competitiveness through the cost savings of foreign production. Moxon (1975) found a negative association between offshore production and *ad valorem* tariffs, but this never approached statistical significance. However, Clark *et al.* (1989) discovered a positive relationship (marginally significant at 10%) between tariff levels and the likelihood of MNEs investing in offshore plants. The authors offer no explanations for a positive sign. It is, for example, unlikely that firms using offshore assembly provisions would see the tariff rate as indicating a margin of benefit from the value-added provisions.

(vii) *Import competition* Another hypothesis to explain the growth of foreign production to supply the investing country is that it frequently represents a defensive response to the import penetration of that country's markets. Both Moxon (1975) and Clark *et al.* (1989) found the use of offshore production to be significantly positively related to measures of import penetration, providing comprehensive support for this influence.

(viii) *Other influences* It has been frequently argued that since offshore production is labour intensive, it may be perceived as exporting jobs and might be more difficult to implement in highly unionized industries. Lee (1986) uses a variable 'percentage unionization of production workers in each industry' and predicts that this will be negatively related to the propensity to source intermediate products from foreign affiliates. However,

since most imports might be perceived as employment displacing, this prediction depends on offshore production imports being especially provocative to unions. This is plausible, since offshore production is a most visible form of FDI and provides a distinct target for union pressure. Lee's tests confirm his hypothesis but the relationship is never a significant one.

Another determinant of the foreign sourcing of intermediate or final products is a measure of sales growth. Moxon (1975) hypothesized

> '*that products experiencing rapid sales growth in the US would be more likely to be made offshore, other things being equal, since the establishment of an offshore facility would then not be likely to require the added costs of closing certain US facilities*'.

In his empirical testing, Moxon found the relationship was positively signed but statistically insignificant.

6.3.3   Cross-sectional studies: inward MNE activity

Introduction

There have been a prolific number of empirical studies of the determinants of MNE activity using host country data. These studies have generally been conducted across industries or countries. The former usually take, as their dependent variable, the share of the production in a particular sector in a host country accounted for by foreign-controlled firms. One advantage of this kind of study is that it is possible to consider both O and L variables influencing foreign production and to get some idea of the relative importance of each.

Most cross-country studies have been bilateral, with the US being the main investing country. However, there have been at least three attempts to use this approach in a multi-country context. The first of these was that of Clegg (1987) which analysed inbound direct investment in the US, UK, West Germany, Sweden and Japan using host country data for all variables. The second was that of Dunning (1980) which used US investment in 14 industries and seven countries to derive a particularly broadly based data set. The third was that of Levy (1983) which compared and contrasted the determinants of US investment in 11 sectors in five countries. Nevertheless, in each of these cases, the attempt to broaden the geographical scope was forced to limit the number of industries and independent variables covered. One of the main advantages of single-country studies is that by narrowing the geographical scope it is possible to widen the coverage of sectoral and independent variables.

A particularly interesting study in this vein was that of Lall and Siddharthan (1982) for FDI in the US, since it is US's *outward* investment that dominates most other studies. Two results of the Lall and Siddharthan study are that R&D and advertising, which, we have seen, are both powerful explanations of outbound FDI, are insignificant explanations of foreign investment in the US. Lall and Siddharthan argue that this supports the proposition that the O advantages of MNEs must be seen in *relative* terms and that, in the main, and at the time the study was undertaken,[15] US FDI was concentrated in the innovatory and high income branded goods sectors. By contrast, MNE activity in the US was either directed to exploiting niche domestic markets, particularly in the processing industries, or to acquiring the assets and capabilities necessary to sustain or advance the global competitive portion of the investing firms. It is the latter type of FDI – particularly by European MNEs – that has accounted for the predominant share of foreign acquisitions and takeovers over the past decade (Tolchin and Tolchin, 1988; Graham and Krugman, 1989; Walter, 1991).

The cross-country approach to inward investment serves mainly to focus on L-specific advantages which are not amenable to treatment within the cross-industry type studies. In some cases, the approach is to analyse the host-country distribution of the *outward* investment of particular countries, while others use the total inward investment of countries.

O-specific advantages

Most researchers have tended to concentrate on identifying specific proprietary rights that offer the foreign affiliates of MNEs a competitive edge over their indigenous competitors. These O-specific assets have elsewhere (Chapter 4) been referred to as Oa

advantages. Occasionally, those benefits that arise from the efficient coordination of these assets across related activities and in different countries – the so-called Ot advantages – are also considered, but usually under some umbrella variable, e.g. the economies of scale or scope. In the following paragraphs Oa advantages are considered in (i)–(iv) and Ot advantages in (v)–(vii).

(i) *Proprietary knowledge* The proposition to be tested here is that there is likely to be a positive relationship between the share of a local industry accounted for by foreign-owned affiliates and the R&D intensity of that industry. An econometric appraisal of the industrial composition of FDI (mostly US FDI) in Canada (Caves, 1974a; Caves *et al.*, 1979; Saunders, 1982; Owen, 1982; Gupta, 1983) provides strong statistical support for this hypothesis. Similarly, Caves (1974a) found R&D to be significantly related to total FDI in the UK, while Buckley and Dunning (1976), using a UK measure of R&D intensity, established it to be a significant determinant of US FDI in the UK. In his cross-sectional analysis of the determinants of US direct investment in Mexico, Korea, South Africa, India and Brazil, Levy (1983) verified that US-owned firms were significantly more likely to participate in technology-intensive sectors of industry than were their local counterparts. As earlier observed, Lall and Siddharthan (1982) did not find R&D intensity to be a significant determinant of FDI in the USA. However, there is some evidence that foreign MNEs engage in strategic asset acquiring investment in R&D-intensive sectors (Kim and Lyn, 1987; Kogut, 1991). Clegg (1987) found R&D intensity to be positively and significantly associated with all non-resident investment in the UK, Japan and Germany, but insignificantly negatively related to that in the USA and significantly negatively related to that in Sweden. This data supports the idea that this kind of O advantage of MNEs is likely to be country specific. This conclusion is supported by a comparison between the structure of Japanese and US direct investment in the UK (Dunning, 1988a, 1993a).

In a study covering 49 (3-digit) manufacturing industries in India (using data averaged over 1978 to 1981), Kumar (1990) ascertained a significantly negative relationship between the share of an industry's output accounted for by foreign-controlled companies and the percentage share of R&D expenditure in industry sales in India. By contrast, Kumar recorded a significantly positive connection between inward direct investment and 'total royalty, technical and other professional fees paid abroad as a percentage of net industry sales'. This investigation broadly corroborated the findings of an earlier study conducted by Lall and Mohammad (1983) of FDI in 28 manufacturing industries in the large private sector of Indian industry, except that these authors could establish no significant correspondence between the foreign share of activity and locally measured R&D intensity. Both groups of researchers explain the apparent contradiction in their results by the negative correlation that exists between the pattern of Indian R&D expenditure and that of developed countries, and the fact that the level of technology imports is probably a better indicator of an industry's technological capabilities than its stated R&D expenditures.

In their cross-country study of UK outward direct investment, Papanastassiou and Pearce (1990) used the proportion of scientists and engineers in total employment as an indicator of the host country's technological capability. Here the content of the hypothesizing is somewhat different than that used in the cross-industry studies. The cross-industry studies, for example, take the general technological capability of the host country as a given parameter and predict that the highest levels of FDI will be in the more technology-intensive industries. By contrast, in the cross-country studies it is hypothesized that as the ratio of scientists and engineers to the total employment in a country rises from very low levels, inbound foreign investors can more capably exploit their own technological O advantages. However, at higher levels a rise in this ratio may reflect the improved ability of a country to generate its own competitive advantages, thus making FDI penetration less easy. At the same time, as Chapter 2 has already observed, there is a tendency among the more globally oriented MNEs to seek a presence in each of the leading industrial nations.

The Papanastassiou and Pearce study showed that, for a group of resource-based low-technology industries (notably food, drink, tobacco and paper), the relationship between the ratio of scientists and engineers employed and inward FDI is essentially positive. The authors go on to suggest that where

technology is non-proprietary it is likely to take the form of an L advantage, which stimulates foreign firms to utilize other L-specific endowments such as mineral or agricultural resources. In most other industries, however, a negative relationship is more strongly indicated. The implication is that in such industries a high proportion of scientists and engineers is likely to generate proprietary advantages to local enterprises, which may deter investment by foreign MNEs.

(ii) *Knowledge capital* Along with, but distinct from, technological capability as an Oa of MNEs, is their ability to create, acquire and organize human skills and competence. In cross-industry studies in Canada, Caves *et al.* (1979), using Canadian data, found that inward direct investment was positively and significantly related to the 'professional and technical employees in the total labour force' while Saunders (1982) discovered a similar relationship between FDI and a US measure of the percentage of managerial personnel in total employment. Earlier Caves (1974a) had demonstrated that three measures of human capital (*viz* non-production workers as a percentage of total employees, payroll per employee in the Canadian industry, and wages per production worker in the Canadian industry) were insignificantly correlated with (the industrial composition of) FDI when other variables were included in the equations. However, in a multi-variable study of US FDI in the UK, Buckley and Dunning (1976) concluded that the 'proportion of non-operatives to all workers' was a cardinal O-specific advantage and significantly correlated with FDI.

Again, however, it would appear that the relevance of this particular advantage is partly host country (or perhaps, more accurately, home–host country) specific as neither of the two indices of human capital tested by Lall and Siddharthan (1982) (*viz* average employee remuneration in each US industry and the ratio of non-production to all employees in US industry), as possible determinants of FDI in US, were found to be significant.[16] Similarly, in his five-country analysis Clegg (1987) discovered that 'wages and salaries per non-operative' was only positively and significantly related to inward investment in one country, *viz* Sweden. By contrast 'wages and salaries per operative' was significantly negatively related for Sweden and also for the US, and insignificantly related for the other three countries. Finally 'non-operatives as a proportion of total employment', serving as a proxy for the scientific, engineering and managerial know-how, was significantly and positively associated with inbound investment in the US, Japan and Sweden; positively but not significantly signed for Germany; and negatively signed for the UK. Similarly, Dunning (1980), in a cross-industry cross-country study, found a skilled employment ratio (the ratio of salaried employees to production employees for all firms in the host countries) to be the single most important determinant of inward US FDI, although in this instance he did not use an R&D expenditure variable in his analysis.

Finally, in their studies of FDI in India, both Lall and Mohammad (1983) and Kumar (1990) demonstrated that the share of high-earnings employees in the total wage and salary bill to be a positively significant determinant. In addition, Kumar recorded an alternative skill measure, viz 'the share of non-production workers in the total workforce' to be positively significant, though Lall and Mohammad found 'average wages for all employees (US data)' to be negatively significant (at a 10% level).

(iii) *Financial asset advantages* If the hypothesis that MNEs – partly because of their size and partly because of their multinationality *per se* – are in a favoured position to raise capital, this should result in their being especially well represented in sectors in which capital availability is important. In their tests of FDI in Canada, Caves (1974a) and Gupta (1983) used a surrogate for capital requirements in the form of 'the minimum efficient scale of plant multiplied by the asset–sales ratio'. While Gupta established this ratio to be persistently positively significant, Caves found it to be both insignificant and often wrongly signed. Clegg (1987) discovered 'net tangible fixed assets at book values per employee' to be positively related to inward direct investment for each of the five developed countries studied, but only significantly so for the US. In his study of FDI in India, Kumar (1990) found 'total capital employed per firm' to be insignificant as an independent variable, while Lall and Mohammad (1983) demonstrated that two measures of capital intensity were significantly negatively related to FDI in India. According to the authors, the latter result is possibly explained by 'the

peculiarities of the Indian licensing system which have led to massive capital-intensive facilities being set up, usually in excess of demand, by large powerful Indian business houses'. Using OLS estimates in a logistic model, Levy (1983) concluded that the *disadvantage* of local firms in their access to finance capital was a statistically significant factor in explaining the participation of foreign firms in India, Brazil, Korea, Mexico and South Africa.[17] However, Kumar (1990) unearthed no evidence to suggest that Indian firms were hampered in their access to sources of capital, while Kim and Lyn (1987) observed that foreign investors in the US tended to favour sectors not requiring large capital outlays.

(iv) *Product differentiation and marketing advantages* Studies of MNE activity in Canada by Caves (1974a), Caves et al. (1979), Saunders (1982), Owen (1982) and Gupta (1983), all lend support to the proposition that advertising intensity (i.e. advertising expenditure as a percentage of sales, using either US or Canadian data) is a positive and significant determinant of the structure of inward investment, especially in consumer goods industries. The hypothesis is also upheld for the UK by the investigations of Caves (1974a) and Buckley and Dunning (1976). However, in the case of MNE activity in the US, Lall and Siddharthan found that foreign firms did not tend to concentrate in advertising intensive sectors, possibly because US firms tend to be more competitive in these sectors. This finding was supported by Kogut and Chang (1991) in their analysis of Japanese FDI in new US plants and joint ventures, but not for acquisitions. The authors offer the view (which is consistent with the strategic asset-seeking hypothesis) that acquisitions are often used to acquire trademarks and access to channels of distribution. For very different reasons, Lall and Mohammad (1983) obtained similar results for FDI in India. In this case, they argued that 'at the low and relatively unsophisticated consumption levels of the Indian economy, large domestic firms are able to compete fully in marketing their products with foreign ones'. In a later study, and using a more extended database, Kumar (1990) found that in most of the multi-regression equations he tested – again in respect of FDI in Indian industry – the advertising intensity had a positive sign and the level of significance was 5% to 10%.

(v) *Plant economies of scale* In the case of cross-industry inward direct investment studies, there are two conflicting hypotheses about the effect of economies of scale. The first suggests that they represent a barrier to market contestability, which MNEs are generally better able to overcome than other potential entrants. However, quite often these MNE advantages are incorporated in other explanatory variables. This is especially true in the case of capital requirements, which is often advocated as a scale-based barrier to entry and which MNEs are particularly adept at circumventing. By contrast, the higher the manufacturing economies of scale in an industry, the fewer foreign plants an MNE is likely to operate, and therefore, *ceteris paribus*, the less likely any given host country is to attract one of them.

For Canada, both Saunders (1982) and Gupta (1983) found a variety of proxies for the minimum efficient scale of plant to be insignificantly related to inbound investment in the previous decade. Earlier, Caves (1974a) had revealed this variable to be often significantly positive in some sectors. Buckley and Dunning (1976) found 'minimum efficient scale' to be insignificant as a determinant of FDI in the UK. Owen (1982) discovered plant economies of scale (whether measured from US or Canadian data) to be a significant positive determinant of FDI in Canada. By contrast, Lall and Siddharthan (1982) concluded that such economies of scale were significantly negatively related to FDI in the USA and went as far as to say that 'in the special case of US production, foreign MNEs would be at a disadvantage in industries where scale was significant'.

(vi) *Economies of common governance: size of firms* As noted earlier, the validity of absolute firm size as an independent variable may be compromised by its being related to other explanatory variables included in any multi-regression equation. Thus, in obtaining a significant positive relationship between 'percentage of shipments in US market accounted for by firms with sales of $100 million or more' and the production of foreign affiliates in Canada, Caves (1974a) reserved judgement on the independent nature of the influence of size. In any case, Saunders (1982) found the same relationship to be insignificant. Owen (1982) demonstrated that the structure of inward investment in Canada was positively related to the degree of capital intensity, whether this was measured in US industries or for *all* firms in Canadian industries. However, when only Canadian-controlled firms were used to measure firm size, a negative relationship emerged. This would suggest that the size of a host country's own firms may be an important deterrent to FDI, independently of the size of the investing country's firms. Alternatively, reversing the causation, Owen argued that 'large Canadian domestic firms may be present in sectors where large firms have advantages, yet other motivations for foreign firms entering the Canadian market are absent'.

In their study of FDI in India in the 1970s, Lall and Mohammad (1983) found it to be significantly and positively related to two measures of firm size: fixed assets per firm (Indian data) and value added per establishment (US data). The authors suggested that this could be explained by 'the inherited importance of foreign investors in scale-intensive sectors' or the possibility that 'the government has consciously permitted foreign entry or expansion in activities requiring high minimum investments'. In his analysis of the penetration by US firms in several industrial sectors in Korea, South Africa, Mexico, Brazil and India, Levy (1983) ascertained that a size variable (using a similar measure to that of Caves (1974a, noted above)) was a positive and often a statistically significant determinant in each of the five countries except Korea.

(vii) *Economies of common governance: multiplant operations* To what extent does the fact that MNEs tend to operate in multi-plant industries confer certain O-specific advantages on their affiliates? Three of the studies of FDI in Canada (Caves, 1974a; Caves *et al.*, 1979; Saunders, 1982) included a variable measuring the extent to which an industry is populated by multi-plant firms. All of them found the variable to be a positive and significant determinant of FDI. The implication is that where a domestic industry is characterized by multi-plant firms, it is likely that this feature will be extended to cross-border operations. In Caves' (1974a) analysis of FDI in the UK, the multi-plant variable was again positive, but not often significant. Lall and Siddharthan (1982) found the same variable to be a significant positive determinant of FDI in the US, and suggested that foreign MNEs are particularly adept at penetrating US industries where multi-plant operations are prominent. Here, in fact, the causal line of argument may be reversed, in as much as MNEs that have developed expertise in cross-border intra-firm coordination and communication may find this a valuable asset in producing in the large and dispersed US market.

L-specific advantages

(i) *Relative wage costs*   Among the L-specific variables that might influence the structure of MNE activity in particular host countries, relative labour costs are among those most frequently cited. The hypothesis that foreign-owned affiliates will tend to be concentrated in sectors where relative wage costs most favour the recipient rather than the investing country has been extensively investigated by scholars. The results, however, are inconclusive. Gupta (1983) and Owen (1982), for example, reported there was no significant relationship between 'relative US and Canadian employee compensation' and the structure of US direct investment in Canada. By contrast, using 'employee compensation per unit of output' as an index of labour costs, Caves *et al.* (1979) and Saunders (1982) found the relationship to be correctly signed and positive. In their study of US FDI in the UK, Buckley and Dunning (1976) concluded that US firms tended to invest in sectors where the relative wage costs most favoured the UK, but the relationship was an insignificant one. Dunning (1980) also found the same variable to be correctly signed but insignificant in his study of US FDI in 14 industries in seven countries. Among OECD countries, there appears little evidence that real labour costs are a significant locational determinant (Culem, 1988; Veuglers, 1991), but that in the technologically more advanced sectors inward investment is positively associated with the skill level of employees (VEV, 1984).

Against her expectations, Swedenborg (1979) showed that the average wage of workers in the foreign manufacturing subsidiaries of Swedish firms, relative to that paid by their parent companies, was found to be persistently and significantly positively related to FDI in the 1970s. However, in the light of the importance of skilled labour to Swedish FDI Swedenborg concluded that high wages paid to foreign workers reflected their skill intensity, which

acted as an L attraction to Swedish MNEs. By contrast, in a related study of UK MNE activity by Papanastassiou and Pearce (1990), the authors could discern no significant relationship between real wage costs and the location of that activity.

The statistical evidence about the significance of wage costs for attracting FDI to developing countries is also mixed. Agodo (1978), in an investigation of the investments of 33 US companies with African countries, found that the lower cost of African labour did not have a significant stimulatory effect on FDI in Africa. This, perhaps, is not surprising in the light of overwhelming significance attached to other explanatory variables, notably, political stability. However, in a wide ranging cross-country study of 54 developing countries, Schneider and Frey (1985) found wage costs to be a significant influence on the geographical distribution of MNE activity.

Perhaps more than most explanatory variables, relative labour costs or relative labour costs per unit of output demonstrate how difficult it is to generalize about the determinants of foreign production. Clearly, the significance of this variable is likely to vary according to the proportion of labour to total costs of production as well as to the average differences in employee compensation across both industries and countries. It will also be influenced by the number and significance of the other explanatory variables contained in any regression equation. Compare, for example, the importance of political stability in countries like Nigeria and Burma with that in Sweden and New Zealand. The significance of low real wages is likely to vary between industries and according to a country's stage of development. In some advanced countries, for example, high labour costs may reflect the presence of a cadre of well trained and motivated labour which, in high technology sectors in particular, may act as an incentive to inward investment. In their search to reduce the production costs of relatively easy to produce goods (e.g. some textiles, clothing and leather goods), low real wages may, and do, act as a critical inducement to foreign investors.

(ii) *Barriers to trade*   The hypothesis that, other things being equal – especially in market-seeking investment – inbound investment will be positively related to levels of effective protection imposed by host countries has mixed support from econometric research. It is not generally upheld by the cross-industry studies of FDI in Canada (Caves, 1974a; Caves *et al.*, 1979; Owen, 1982; Saunders, 1982; Gupta, 1983). However, Saunders (1982) suggests that an explanation of these results could be that the tariff rates in existence at the time of the investigations were different from those prevailing when much of the rapid growth of foreign investment in Canada occurred, i.e. in the 1960s. In other words, tariffs may have been high in sectors that initially attracted non-resident participation, but were then lowered once the investment had occurred. By contrast, Lall and Siddharthan (1982) found effective protection to be a persistently significant determinant of the industrial composition of foreign-owned activity in the US. Kumar (1990) demonstrated that effective protection just missed significance (at a 10% level) as a determinant of FDI in India, while Agodo (1978) concluded that protection did not have a significant effect on the participation of US companies in Africa.

In the case of efficiency seeking and some asset acquiring FDI, import restrictions are likely to have a negative effect on inbound investment. Several studies of FDI in Western Europe, following the establishment of the EC, reveal a marked increase in those types of MNE activity designed to exploit the advantages of the international (or a regional) division of labour. The hypothesized negative relationship between government-imposed restrictions on trade and FDI is explored further in Section 6.4.2 and in Chapters 14 and 17. In a global economy increasingly characterized by both intra-industry and intra-firm trade, it is the absence, rather than the presence, of these restrictions which is more likely to stimulate the further internationalization of MNE activity.

(iii) *Market size and characteristics* We have already suggested that the size and characteristics of domestic and adjacent markets is one of the most powerful L-specific variables influencing the industrial and geographical composition of market-seeking investment by MNEs. Using Gross National Product (GNP) or Gross Domestic Product (GDP) as a measure of market size, several researchers have demonstrated this variable to be positively and significantly associated with inward direct investment. Examples are the geographical composition of

the activities of the largest UK industrial firms by Papanastassiou and Pearce (1990); that of Swedish FDI by Swedenborg (1979); that of US FDI by Green and Cunningham (1975) and by Dunning (1980); and that of FDI into some 54 developing countries by Schneider and Frey (1985). Likewise, Kobrin's (1976) factor analysis of FDI found that the combination of the size of a country's GDP and its population was a positive and significant determinant of US manufacturing investment in all countries and in developing countries separately. Market size has long since been one of the main attractions of the US market for inward investors (Ajami and Ricks, 1981; Kim and Lyn, 1987).

In addition to the significance of the size of a country's GNP, Papanastassiou and Pearce (1990) showed that GNP per capita was persistently and positively related to the host country's distribution of UK manufacturing FDI; this relationship was significant for five of eight industries tested separately, and for all manufacturing industry. By contrast, Swedenborg (1979) found GNP to be negatively, and sometimes significantly, related to inward direct investment, although the author accepted that this relationship might have been compromised by a multi-collinear relationship between this variable and relative wage rates in the equation.

In their comprehensive analysis of the geographical pattern of FDI in developing countries, Root and Ahmed (1979) concluded that the *rate of growth* of GDP was a more significant discriminating factor than the *size* of the GDP. This conclusion may well reflect the fact that current levels of national income in many developing countries are so low that they attract little, if any, inward investment, whereas those countries in which living standards are improving the most are those which are likely to offer the best prospects for inbound MNE activity. However, Agodo (1978) found the opposite results for US investments in Africa, with GDP being a significant and GDP growth an insignificant, determinant. Kobrin's (1976) factor analysis of US manufacturing FDI concluded that a factor incorporating growth of GNP and growth of GNP per capita was both positively and significantly related to the formation of new MNE activity. This conclusion was supported by Culem (1988) in his examination of the location of FDI within the industrialized countries.

Other market characteristics influencing FDI

have been identified by scholars. Davidson (1980), for example, in a wide ranging study of the foreign investment projects of 190 large MNEs from their inception to 1975, concluded that the similarity in the market characteristics between the home and host country was a critical variable influencing their choice of location. US firms, in particular, favoured nations with which they already had established trading or investing associations. Davidson also found that as firms became more internationalized, the uncertainty previously attached to producing in near and similar cultures began to disappear, and in the more globally integrated companies had all but disappeared.

(iv)   *Other locational factors*   There is a good deal of fragmentary statistical evidence about the influence of other L advantages on inbound MNE activity which generally supports the predictions of theory and field investigations. Considering cross-border transport costs first, Caves *et al*. (1979) and Saunders (1982) both found a measure of this variable was negatively related to the industrial distribution of inward investment in Canada. In explaining this result, Saunders suggested that the positive relationship expected in the case of horizontal investment may be explained by the multi-plant variable included in both studies, while cross-border transport costs may deter vertical FDI. However, in a cross-country study of UK MNE activity, Papanastassiou and Pearce (1990) discovered that the location of this resource-seeking investment was positively related to distance from the UK (which might be regarded as a proxy for transport costs). In the same study, a dummy variable for EC countries was positively signed and significant for several industries, while a dummy for Commonwealth countries was positive and significant for most sectors.

A measure of the export propensity of Canadian-based firms in the 1970s was discovered by Caves *et al*. (1979) and Saunders (1982) to be positively related to inward FDI. Possible reasons why FDI (especially from the US) was attracted to Canada at that time include the need to gain access to Commonwealth preference schemes and/or to Canadian sources of raw materials. Kumar (1990) discovered a dummy variable for consumer good industries to be positively related to inbound investment in India and concluded that 'the selective policy towards foreign

collaborations which the Government of India has followed throughout the post-Independence period seems to have discouraged them in consumer goods sectors where local skills have been available' (1987, p. 339). In a very different policy background, Owen (1982) did not find a dummy for consumer goods industries to be significantly related to the presence of foreign firms in Canada.

As suggested by field studies, the significance of the availability and costs of natural resources influencing the choice of the modality of foreign involvement is strongly country specific. Owen (1982), for example, found a dummy for natural resource intensity to be a positive and significant determinant of FDI in Canada, though Buckley and Dunning (1976) found a similar dummy to be insignificant (and negatively signed) for the UK. Kumar (1990) tested a variable (*viz* the ratio of imports to total industry output in 1960/61) which proxied the potential for import-substitution FDI in India. As hypothesized, this variable was discovered to be positively and significantly related to such investment. In his explanation of the geographical composition of US manufacturing FDI, Kobrin (1976) demonstrated that a recipient country's share of US exports – which he used as a surrogate for its prior involvement with or knowledge about the investing country – to be of major significance.

In his investigation of US direct investments in Africa, Agodo (1978) recorded that the presence of development planning by local governments was positively and significantly related to FDI. In his own words (1978, p. 104) 'it is not development planning *per se* that attracts the foreign investor; rather it is the organized economic environment that it creates and the positive economic climate that frequently is associated with it'. The same study also identified the presence of primary infrastructure to be a positively significant determinant of FDI. Root and Ahmed (1978, 1979) confirmed that the quality of a country's transport and communications infrastructure was a significantly positive influence on manufacturing FDI in developing countries. Although field studies and the work of Porter (1990) suggest that infrastructure might be no less important a factor attracting inward investment to advanced countries, it does not appear to have been considered in any econometric studies. Using a technique known as communality analysis,[18] cultural relatedness, as captured in a language variable, was shown to be the most important factor influencing the intra-OECD distribution of the foreign affiliates of MNEs in 1980 (Veuglers, 1991), followed by the size of the neighbouring markets and the neighbouring relationship. This same study also suggested that a complementarity relationship existed between exports and foreign production, which the authors partly attribute to the specialization of value-added activity both by and within MNEs.

Finally, some studies on the location of MNE activity have attempted to identify the most important *deterrents* to such activity. Schneider and Frey (1985), for example, discovered that both balance of payments deficits and the rate of domestic inflation were negatively and significantly related to inbound FDI. Both of these variables were presumably seen by foreign firms as symptoms of economic and political vulnerability in the host countries, which are generally unwelcome by foreign investors both for themselves and the policies and measures they may force host governments to take. There is also some suggestion that the location of FDI is negatively associated with the stringency of environmental standards and pollution control regulations (Leonard, 1984; Kumar, 1991).

It will be observed that many of the studies described in this section date back to the 1970s or early 1980s and were primarily concerned with explaining new (or relatively recent) FDI in market-seeking or resource-seeking activities. In the last decade, the great majority of MNE activity has taken the form of sequential efficiency seeking, or strategic asset-seeking investment. The emphasis of L-specific explanations of these latter types of foreign production is very different from those mainly described in this chapter. Local supply capabilities, the absence of trading barriers and the efficiency of government macro-economic policies and organization strategies are likely to be more important pulls to inward investment. Taking a broader perspective, country-specific differences in environmental rules and regulations (e.g. with respect to pollution, health and safety standards) have increasingly entered into the cost calculations of MNEs. Finally, the role played by regional authorities (e.g. state governments in the US and the European Commission) as a factor influencing the location of MNE activity, both as between and within regions, is becoming increasingly important. Using a conditional logit model to evaluate the determinant of the spatial distribution of FDI in the US, Coughlin *et al.* (1991) found that while state taxes and wage levels were deterrents to such investment, per capita income, the density (or clustering) of manufacturing activity, the extensiveness and quality of the transportation network (including airport facilities) and state promotional expenditures were all positively, often statistically significant, inducements to foreign firms.[19]

6.3.4 The mode of exploiting O advantages: the internalization (I) dimension

Much of the empirical work on the mode by which firms exploit their O advantages in foreign countries has been limited to an evaluation of the determinants of the licensing *versus* FDI decisions. Here the work of Contractor (1981, 1984a, 1984b, 1991), Contractor and Lorange (1988), Davidson and McFetridge (1984, 1985), Kogut and Singh (1988) and Kumar (1990) is especially worthy of note. In his 1984 contribution, Contractor, after identifying the various reasons why a firm should wish to internalize the use of its proprietary assets, considers some host country specific factors that have influenced the propensity of US firms to transfer through technology. By way of OLS linear regression analysis and using data on the transactions of US firms with 30 foreign countries in 1977–80, Contractor finds that the ratio of income from unaffiliated licensees to US direct investment or investment income increases with the indigenous technological capability of a country. He also obtains some support for the proposition that the proportion of licensing increases, *ceteris paribus*, with government scrutiny regulation and decreases as more concessions are offered or direct investors.

Interestingly, this relationship is only partially upheld in a study by the present author (Dunning, 1988a) which considered the propensity of UK firms to engage in licensing agreements rather than FDI. In a cross-sectional analysis embracing 40 countries, Dunning found that the relationship between GNP and the ratios between the royalties and fees received from unrelated foreign firms and that received from affiliated firms was U or J shaped, with both low and high GNPs per head being significantly associated (at a 5% level) with below average propensities to engage in licensing agreements. However, when incorporated in a multi-regression equation which included the structure of economic activity in the host country and the openness of an economy to international trade as other explanatory variables, this apparent paradox is explained. High GNPs per capita are associated with shifts in the value of these other variables which, in some cases, counteract the proposition of Contractor (1984) that transaction costs for marketing intermediate products fall as GNP per head increases, and hence FDI becomes relatively more significant.

In a more recent paper, Contractor (1991) offers further insight into the role of governments in affecting the organization of cross-border production. In particular, he examines the impact of the liberalization of foreign investment regulations on the level of equity participation held by US foreign investors between 1977 and 1982. Using multi-regression analysis, he shows that in developing countries the reduction in government-imposed mandates (e.g. limits on the share of foreign ownership, local content requirements, etc) is the most significant factor explaining the fall in the proportion of joint ventures to wholly owned affiliates. This result accords well with some earlier work by Kobrin (1986). For industrialized countries, however, such restrictions were of little relevance. Instead, such factors as the need for local partner skills and/or the need to share large capital risks were found to be much more important in the choice of joint ventures. This result also adds credence to some earlier research by Beamish (1985) and is entirely consistent with the reasons stated by many firms for concluding international strategic alliances.

The Davidson and McFetridge (1985) study is an interesting one in that it attempts to view the mode of transferring technology (an O-specific advantage) as a function of the nature of the activity of the firm as well as that of economic, social and cultural attributes of home and host countries. The authors used a logit statistical model examining some 1226 intra-firm and market transactions undertaken by 32 US MNEs between 1945 and 1978. They found that technology was *least* likely to be internally transferred:

(1)   for newer technologies,

(2)   for technologies with fewer previous transfers,

(3)   for technologies in the same 3-digit SIC class as the transferor's principal line of business,

(4)   the more R&D intensive is the transferor's industry,

(5)   if the transferor had an affiliate in the receiving country prior to the transfer,

(6)   for transferors with the largest number of previous technology transfers.

Further examination of these variables suggests that the presence of each is likely to be associated with one or other of the attributes of market failure identified in Chapter 4, and, hence, are candidates suitable for hierarchical control. At the same time, the authors found that public policy variables were among the most significant country-specific variables influencing the choice between FDI and licensing.

The work of Kogut and Singh (1988) addresses the question as to the relevance of cultural distance between the investing and recipient countries and the desire to avoid uncertainty on the part of firms, on the modality of involvement by the latter. As firms are likely to perceive both as variables likely to raise the costs of operating a wholly owned foreign subsidiary, it might be hypothesized that the greater their value the more likely that a firm will exploit its O-specific advantages via the market or by a joint venture. In fact, in their analysis of entries by foreign firms into the US between 1981 and 1983, Kogut and Singh found that this proposition was strongly supported and that both variables were significant at a 5% level with positive coefficients.[20]

The final, and in some ways the most satisfactory, approach to evaluating the unique characteristics of FDI *vis à vis* their modes of organizing O-specific advantages across national boundaries is to compare and contrast structural differences between the two forms. This is what Kumar (1990) sought to do in his study of the interaction between FDI and foreign licensing in Indian manufacturing in 1977. Undertaking a cross-sectional regression analysis of some 49 branches of industry, Kumar found that FDI was the dominant mode of operation in those sectors which, in his wods, were 'characterized by a high level of product differentiation or are intensive in the use of idiosyncratic knowledge' (p. 47). By contrast, the incidence of licensing arrangements was more in evidence in those sectors which were 'intensive in the use of knowledge embodied in capital goods'. Somewhat surprisingly, Kumar discovered that the R&D intensity of local industry was inversely related to the intensity of FDI, but positively related to licensing. Kumar explains this finding by the fact that indigenous R&D in India is usually of an adaptive nature, and that the tendency to adapt decreases as the complexity of technology increases. Finally, Kumar established that the FDI policy of the Indian government was also an important factor in explaining why, in most consumer goods sectors or in those requiring skills that were adequately available in India, MNE activity played a very limited role.

A very different approach to identifying the determinants of the mode of international business activity is to be found in the bargaining literature. We shall take this point up further in Chapters 9 and 20. Suffice for the moment to observe that, *ceteris paribus*, host countries which are in a strong bargaining position *vis à vis* incoming investors are better able to insist on a particular ownership structure of an MNE affiliate than those who are in a weak bargaining position. The relative bargaining strength of the two parties will merely depend on their respective opportunity costs which, in turn, is likely to rest on what benefits each can offer the other (Lecraw and Morrison, 1991). Moreover, the *outcome* of the bargaining process *de facto* affects the balance between the O advantages of firms and the L advantages of countries[21] (Grosse and Behrman, 1992).

We would, however, make one final point. The rationale for international joint ventures is currently undergoing a profound change. Balanced against the desire to control the use of existing proprietary assets is the need to share the financial risks associated with the creation and exploitation of these assets. Counteracting the wish to appropriate the full economic rent on a particular O advantage is the increasing incentive to cooperate with other firms to acquire complementary or synergistic assets. These are the sorts of reasons behind the recent explosive growth of all kinds of cross-border coalitions. As Chapter 9 will show, these new collaborative ventures are being primarily undertaken between firms located in advanced countries and in sectors in which the 100% equity is the normal mode of foreign involvement. Inter-firm cooperation sits a little uneasily alongside

the hierarchical and market modes of organizing value-added activities. Such empirical research as has been undertaken as to why firms prefer to engage in non-equity alliances rather than FDI is set out in Chapter 9. What does seem clear is that the rationale for such ventures and their structural characteristics are sufficiently different from that of the traditional form of inter-firm association to warrant especial attention from scholars.

As observed at the beginning of this chapter, our review of the literature of the testing of the theory of MNEs or MNE activity cannot hope to encompass the findings of a large number of country, industry and firm case studies. However, as there have been relatively few attempts specifically to test the propositions of the internalization paradigm – although admittedly a great deal of that relating to the very nature of the MNE offers some valuable insights – we shall make brief reference to just one important industrial case study, *viz* that of the offshore oil production industry by Hallwood (1990).

In this study, the author examines the main organizational arrangements found in the oil-gathering industry and the reasons why these were chosen. In particular, he argues – and argues very persuasively – that the fact that oil companies purchase, or hire on a contract basis, over 90% of the purchases of the oil-gathering industry can be explained by use of the transaction cost paradigm. At the same time, the study is especially valuable as it examines the alternative forms of arrangements for the production and exchange of oil-gathering products, including those of quasi-integration and the invited tender bid auction. The main conclusion of the author is that there are several alternative institutional arrangements open to oil firms to appropriate the rents and protect the value of their idiosyncratic assets apart from FDI and that these arrangements warrant further attention by international business scholars.

Before considering some time-series studies, brief mention should be made of an attempt by two scholars – Agarwal and Ramaswami (1992) – not only to evaluate the significance of particular O, L or I variables, but also the interaction between these variables in determining the form of foreign economic involvement by firms. Taking, as their case study, the mode by which 97 US leasing firms penetrated those of their foreign markets, and by a combination of factor and multinomial logistic regression analysis, the authors were able to test (on the basis of the perceptions of Chief Executive officers from sample companies) a series of hypotheses about the possible interface between the entry modes and the O characteristics of firms and the L characteristics of countries. The results generally lent support to the propositions examined; and added a further dimension to our knowledge (albeit in respect of just one industry) of the kinds of OLI configuration most likely to lead to FDI, as compared with exporting, a contractual arrangement, or, indeed, no foreign involvement at all. To give just three examples; first, small firms with limited foreign experience were found to prefer entry into markets that were perceived to have a high potential through a joint venture; second, those leasing firms which claimed to have a particular O advantage in supplying differentiated products showed a strong preference for servicing foreign markets through FDI rather than exporting; and third, the preference for the export mode was found to be relatively low with a high potential for markets, which, the authors suggest, indicates that high return/high risk investment modes are the preferred entry modes in such markets (Agarwal and Ramaswami, 1992, pp. 20–21).

6.3.5   Time-series studies

Introduction

We now turn to consider some attempts by economists and business scholars to identify the most important variables affecting MNEs in particular countries or groups of countries over time. As a group, these longitudinal studies have proved illuminating in two ways. First, they have confirmed the key importance of market size among the determinants of market-seeking FDI. Second, they have helped us better to measure the effects on FDI of critical changes in the ESP configurations of countries. A good example of this latter kind of study is the considerable attention given by scholars to the impact of inward investment in Western Europe following the formation and subsequent enlargement of the EC. Section 6.4.2 will consider these studies separately. An excellent review of the more impor-

tant of these studies is contained in Yannopoulos (1990) and UN (1992c).

US FDI in the EC

Explanations of the growth and pattern of US FDI in the EC have mainly focused on the size and rate of growth of the internal market, the effects of the formation and expansion of the Community and the consequences of the US (voluntary or mandatory) capital controls programme of 1965 to 1972.

(i)   *Market size*   It may be hypothesized that once a market attains a size that permits local production to become cost-effective, *ceteris paribus*, at and after that point, the level of FDI in that market is likely to be closely related to its size. As an explanation of the growth of US FDI in the EC, this hypothesis has been consistently verified. In their studies, Bandera and White (1968), Scaperlanda and Mauer (1969, 1973), Schmitz and Bieri (1972), Lunn (1980) and Scaperlanda and Balough (1983) have all shown market size to be a salient explanatory variable.

(ii)   *Rate of growth of market*   In tests in which both the level of GNP and growth of GNP are included as explanatory variables, the specific effect of the rate of market growth on US FDI in the EC has been enigmatic and inconsistent. For example, Scaperlanda and Mauer (1969) tested three EC growth variables and found each to be insignificantly associated with inbound US investment, and often wrongly signed. Schmitz and Bieri (1972) discovered that the EC's share of total US FDI was negatively (and sometimes significantly) related to the EC's rate of growth for the period 1952 to 1958, but positively for 1959 to 1966.

(iii)   *Import barriers*   Though the theory of international production does not provide unequivocal predictions about the effect of economic integration of inward direct investment, most analysts in the 1960s (e.g. Krause, 1966) believed that the formation of the EC would have a stimulatory effect. This was for two reasons. The first was that the imposition of a common external tariff would lead to more import substitution FDI in the EC by non-EC MNEs. The second was that the removal of intra-EC trade barriers would better enable foreign (as well as domestic) firms to engage in regional cross-border product and plant specialization.[22]

In the time-series analyses of the effects of the EC on inward investment, two approaches may be distinguished. The first is simply to test for any differences in the share of inward investment which may be attributed to the Community's existence. This may be done either by running separate regressions for two different periods or by incorporating intercept-shift and/or slope-shift dummy variables in an equation covering both before and after periods. The second approach is to test the relationship between US FDI and a variable that proxies the implementation and evolution of tariff changes resulting from the formation of the EC.

Notwithstanding problems of data consistency and econometric testing, most of the early studies of the first approach supported the proposition that the EC did, in fact, lead to the member states attracting a larger share of inward investment. At the same time, scholars agreed it was exceedingly difficult to separate the EC effect from the other reasons for the growing prosperity of EC countries.

In their pioneering attempt to proxy the implementation of tariff changes resulting from the formation of the EC, Scaperlanda and Mauer (1969) used the ratio of US exports to the EC divided by intra-EC exports. However, as other analysts, such as Goldberg (1972) and Lunn (1980), have pointed out, this measure may capture not only the trade *diversion* and trade *creation* effects of the EC, but also other influences. In addition, the direction of causation is difficult to establish. Suppose, for example, that as a result of an increase of autonomous FDI by US firms in the EC, US exports to the Community fall and intra-EC exports increase. This would suggest a negative association between the tariff proxy and inward FDI. In fact, in their tests (which spanned the period 1952 to 1966), Scaperlanda and Mauer (1969) established that not only was this proxy never significant, but it was often wrongly signed. Goldberg's (1972) revision of it provided 'inconclusive results'.

Lunn (1980) employed US exports to the EC divided by US exports to the world minus the same ratio from the previous year, as an explanatory variable, which he believed to be superior to that of Scaperlanda and Mauer. This he found to be persistently and significantly negatively related to

inward direct investment as hypothesized. Earlier, Schmitz and Bieri (1972, p. 268), using a similar variable, concluded that 'after the EEC was formed, US direct investment in that region significantly increased while the growth in US exports to the EEC significantly decreased'.

An important refinement of these tests of tariff discrimination occurred with Scaperlanda and Balough's (1983) formulation of a variable that directly measured the progressive dismantling of tariffs on intra-EC trade. This was found, as predicted, to be persistently and positively related to US FDI in the EC. In line with the comment (Scaperlanda and Balough, 1983, p. 389) that the measure 'might be made more sophisticated by introducing modifications in the EEC's common external tariffs both as a result of the Community's evolution and General Agreement of Tariffs and Trade (GATT) negotiations', it is worth observing that this result probably owes more to the internal trade *creation* of lowering barriers to intra-EC trade than to the trade *diversion* of increasing the difference between the common external tariff and internal tariff levels.

In an intriguing refocusing of the analysis of the consequences of the accession of the UK to the EC in 1972, Blair (1987) tested the determinants of the UK share of US FDI in the UK and in the original six members of the EC. He established that, normalizing for the rate of GNP growth in the UK and the EC, the formation of the EC in 1958 without the membership of the UK did divert US FDI from the UK to the European Continent. However, following its announcement that it would be joining the Community, the UK gained an increased share of new US investment, particularly between 1972 and 1976. A later analysis of US MNE activity in Spain and Portugal before and after their succession to the EC in the mid 1980s points to a similar conclusion (UNCTC, 1991a).

(iv)   *The US capital control programme*   Several of the studies of US FDI in the EC have incorporated dummy variables to test for the effectiveness of the capital controls programme implemented by the US between 1965 and 1974.[23] Using data for 1952 to 1969, Scaperlanda and Mauer (1973) found a capital control dummy to be significantly negative in a test of all US FDI in the EC, but only insignificantly negative for manufacturing investment. Scaperlanda and Balough (1983) replicate these results for 1953 to 1972, but find that when the time series is adjusted to 1957 to 1977, the capital control dummy becomes insignificantly positive for both total and manufacturing investment. Scaperlanda and Balough also discovered the control dummy to be positively related to US manufacturing firms' EC plant and equipment expenditures, insignificantly so for 1957 to 1972 but significantly so for 1957 to 1977.

Scaperlanda and Balough (1983) interpret the results of that survey as suggesting that US FDI to the EC did not recover after the ending of the programme as might have been predicted. They comment (1983, p. 386) that

> 'since from a theoretical perspective the controls were a second best policy solution to offset disequilibrium fixed exchange rates, the empirical finding here implies that a variable is needed to explain the effects of the floating exchange rates of the post-1972 period since with their introduction the "controls" became market determined rather than administratively determined'.

Lunn (1983) points out, however, that the ramifications of changes in the international economy after 1973 extended well beyond the breakdown of fixed exchange rates and suggests that any attribution of change of behaviour in the model to this factor alone may be misleading.

In a more recent evaluation of the capital controls programe Scaperlanda (1992) concluded that, although overall it resulted in an increase in the indebtedness of US MNEs to foreigners of around $10.5 billion, within a relatively short period of time the interest payment on that debt would reverse any initial programme-related balance of payments gains. However, the author also considered that the programme had a salutary effect in that it counteracted the distorting consequences of a fixed exchange rate, which inflated the cost of making an FDI.

Time-series studies involving other countries

There have been several other attempts by economists to pinpoint the more significant variables influenc-

ing changes in foreign-based MNE activity over time. Usually these studies do not seek to test a particular theory of the MNE or MNE activity and few distinguish between different kinds of FDI. Instead, most confine themselves to pinpointing a number of likely explanatory variables and then trying to trace the extent to which changes in these affect inward and outward direct investment. We shall briefly consider just a selection of these studies.

The first is that by Petrochilas (1984, 1989) who analysed time-series data to explain inward investment in Greece for the period 1955 to 1978, using mainly L-specific variables. As with US direct investment in the EC, Petrochilas found that market size (GDP lagged by one year) was a positive and almost invariably significant explanatory variable. By contrast, measures of market growth were never significant and the former was wrongly (i.e. negatively) signed. Tariff protection was found to be a significantly positive influence on inward investment. The Greek discount rate, lagged by one year, was found to be negatively, and often significantly, related to FDI. The author interprets this as demonstrating the relevance of a source of complementary local capital as an L-specific advantage to foreign MNEs. By contrast, US long-term bond yields (measuring the opportunity cost of capital to a major group of potential investors) was never a significant variable, though it was negatively signed as hypothesized.

Using broadly similar techniques to those of Petrochilas, Torrisi (1985) investigated the determinants of inward FDI in Colombia for the years 1958 to 1980. Once again, market size proved to be a significant positive determinant, while the growth rate was positively signed but never significant. Torrisi also included a trade balance variable (i.e. total exports minus total imports of Colombia, lagged by one year). For all inward investment, this variable was found to be consistently and significantly negative; for US FDI alone, the relationship was also negative but never approached significance. Finally, Torrisi considered a dummy variable to take account of the creation of the Andean Common Market. In doing so, he assigned a value of 'zero' for 1958 to 1969 (prior to the conclusion of the Andean Pact) and 'one' for 1969 to 1980. This dummy was found to be persistently negatively signed though insignificant. The likely interpretation of this result is that while the market growth effects of regional integration might have encouraged FDI, some of the other consequences of the Andean Pact (especially the phased divestment elements of Decision 24) repelled it.

Third, we consider a study of FDI in the US between 1970 and 1986 undertaken by Hultman and McGee (1988). In line with previous research, the authors found GNP to be a statistically significant determinant of inward investment both in all industries and in four separate sectors. The value of the US dollar was also found to be significantly positively related to FDI in the US in all cases. As far as the relationship between FDI and exchange rates is concerned, this result may reflect the prevalence of 'speculative' over 'real' influences. Thus the hypothesis that provides Hultman and McGee (1988, p. 1061) with a possible positive result is 'that anticipations are important in the investment decision; thus, an appreciating (depreciating) dollar leads to anticipated gains (losses) such that foreign investment increases (decreases)'. By contrast, a negative sign could have emerged because 'if the dollar appreciates (depreciates), investment in the US costs more (less)'.

In a related analysis on the determinants of European direct investment in the US between 1961 and 1987, Kennett (1989) found that the effective US exchange rate of the dollar against other currencies was negatively associated with inward investment – although the association was only statistically significant at a 10% level. He also discovered that US equity prices on the stock market were negatively correlated with inward investment in the 1960s and 1970s but not in the 1980s. Other research by Frost and Stein (1989) and Klein and Rosengren (1990a), referred to in Chapter 4, established that the correlation between the exchange rate and US inward FDI from seven industrial countries during the 1980s was more appropriately attributable to the interaction between this variable and relative wealth than to changes in relative wages. Klein and Rosengren also demonstrated that the major changes in the tax legislation of the US in the 1980s, including a substantial cut in corporate taxes, had little effect on inward direct investment.

Finally, we shall make brief reference to Riedel's (1975) study of export-oriented FDI in Taiwan between 1955 and 1971. This research used multiple regression analysis to test the importance of changes in (relative) unit labour costs between Taiwan and three investing countries, and also of two important changes in the host government's strategy. Riedel took as his dependent variable a three-year moving average of inward investment approvals in Taiwan from Hong Kong, Japan and the US. In each case, this variable was found to be negatively and significantly related to changes in real wages, that is, as relative wages rose in Taiwan, FDI decreased.

The first of the policy changes constituted a change in the development strategy of the Taiwanese government from an import-substitution to an export-led orientation. This included the liberalization of trade policy and the implementation of direct incentives to FDI, mainly in the form of tax concessions. In the statistical tests, this policy change was covered by a dummy variable taking the value 'zero' up to 1960 and 'one' thereafter. The second change comprised the establishment, in 1966, of Export-Processing Zones (EPZs), which exempted investors from virtually all trade restrictions and helped to provide an adequate infrastructure at reasonable cost. This was also covered by a dummy variable taking the value 'zero' up to 1966 and 'one' thereafter.

The multiple regression tests carried out by Riedel revealed that both policy changes had significant positive effects on FDI in Taiwan from Hong Kong and Japan. In the case of the 1960 policy change, this result confirms a visible upturn in FDI, but in the 1966 case, the dummy (for these two countries) turned out to be significant despite the absence of any substantial visible shift in the trend of FDI at that time. By contrast, Riedel found that US FDI was not significantly affected by either of the policy changes. Riedel observes that in the light of the magnitude of wage differences between the US and Taiwan, which at the time were considerably larger than those between Taiwan and Hong Kong and Japan, it is not surprising that the marginal pecuniary incentives provided by tax concessions and EPZs had little effect.

To what extent, then, do the statistical tests on time-series data add to our understanding of the determinants of the FDI of firms and MNE activity? The answer must surely be that while the need to both pinpoint and evaluate some of the significant variables – mostly L specific, it might be added – which, over time, have certainly been associated with more or less MNE activity, they rarely seek to test these against the specific attributes that distinguish MNEs from other firms. Also the results of the tests seem to be critically dependent on the number and kind of other explanatory variables included in the equations. Moreover, few time-series studies have either distinguished between different kinds of MNE activity or normalized their results for industry-, country- or firm-specific characteristics. None has attempted to compare and contrast alternative hypotheses for the phenomena they are seeking to explain.

6.3.6   The testing of theory: a developmental perspective

There have been no substantive attempts to test the dynamics of FDI theory[24] and only very exploratory efforts to explain the changing international direct investment position of countries at different stages of their development. One of the latter has been that of the present author who sought to examine the determinants of the gross and net outward direct investment position at different stages of their development. Two separate statistical exercises were conducted. Both used cross-sectional data of countries at varying income (GNP) levels as a surrogate for longitudinal data of a country at particular stages of its development.

The first study was based on data of the accumulated inward and outward investment flows for 61 countries between 1967 and 1975. The theoretical underpinning for the research was described in Chapter 4. The hypothesis was that as a country developed, its propensity to be an outward and inward direct investor changed in a systematic way because the configuration of the OLI advantages facing its own firms and inward foreign investors itself changed.

An examination of the data revealed that most very low income countries attracted little or no inward investment and undertook no outward investment. Middle income developing countries attracted considerable amounts of inward investment, but engaged in only a modest amount of outward

investment, while industrialized upper income developing countries attracted large amounts of inward investment and were becoming quite important capital exporters. The data also demonstrated that the more developed countries were both substantial importers and exporters of direct investment capital, but only a few of the richest industrialized nations were *net* outward investors. At the same time, as Chapter 2 has revealed, the international position of the leading industrial nations has fluctuated over the last two decades. Therefore, it would seem that *relative competitiveness* of a country's firms and its L-specific assets, rather than the *absolute* income level of GNP, is the main determinant of this position. Later data also suggests that as they seek to penetrate global markets, developing country MNEs are engaging in more strategic asset acquiring investment than once they were (World Bank, 1989; UN, 1992b).

Since it was hypothesized that a wide variety of variables other than GNP per head were likely to affect the international investment position of a nation, the 67 countries were clustered into three main groups using a technique known as correspondence analysis.[25] The first group of countries broadly comprised those with some outward investment; the second comprised those which had considerable inward investment but little or no outward investment. The third group was made up of 20 very poor developing countries which attracted only a small amount of inward investment. This analysis of clustering also identified distinct sets of O, L and I variables within each cluster. We then used these variables to calculate a series of stepwise multiple regression equations to help identify the determinants of both outward and inward direct investment. The results obtained may be summarized as follows:[26]

(1)   Although outward investment was positively associated with the stock of human capital and research and development expenditure, only significant relationships were recorded for countries whose most educated and trained workers accounted for 10% or more of the population and whose R&D expenditure as a percentage of gross national output was normally 1.6 or above.

(2)   There was some suggestion that outward invest-

ment per capita is greater in industrialized than in resource-rich countries, but apart from this, in the lower income countries (Groups 2 and 3), the possession of natural resources was positively associated with outward investment.

(3) There was a generally positive association between average earnings and outward direct investment, but a generally negative association between the growth in industrial output and such flows, at least for Group 1, *viz* the most developed, countries. For most of the other locational variables, the association was in the reverse direction to that predicted, but we believe this primarily reflects their 'pull' on inward investment rather than their 'push' to outward investment.

(4) There is some reason to suppose that above-average outward investment is associated with the degree of cross-border market failure, but the relationship is not a significant one.

(5) There is no clear association between population size and the propensity to engage in outward investment. Looking at individual data, of the 12 countries with an average outward investment of more than $10 per capita, five had populations of more than 50 million and five of less than 22 million.

(6) The relevant L advantages determining inward investment vary according to the stage of development of the recipient country. In Groups 2 and 3 the availability of natural resources and the degree of urbanization were the most significant 'pull' variables, whereas in Group 1, one of the O-specific variables, *viz* stock of human capital, was positively, but not significantly, related to inward investment.

The second statistical exercise (set out in Dunning, 1986c, 1987, 1988a) examined the extent of outward direct investment of a group of 25 developing countries in 1982. It was hypothesized that this would be determined by five independent variables, *viz* GNP per head, a proxy for human capital, the percentage of labour employed in non-agricultural activities, the propensity of the country to engage in international trade and an urbanization index. Using stepwise log linear OLS regression equations, it was found that GNP per head was consistently the most

significant explanation of outward investment. In a bivariate regression alone it had an explanatory power (R^2) of 0.75. Of the other variables, the ones that were the *least* correlated with each other, *viz* trade intensity and a measure of economic structure, were also positively and significantly correlated to outbound investment, although their highest levels of significance, *viz* at a 1% level, were recorded when the independent variable to the equations was expressed in non-log form.

As we have indicated, cross-sectional studies of the kind described are an imperfect substitute for longitudinal analyses, but as yet the data has been inadequate to permit satisfactory statistical analysis. A brave attempt to do so for one country – the Philippines – has been undertaken by Tolentino (1992). In any event, to explain properly the dynamic interaction between the O-specific advantages of firms and the L advantages of countries as both affect the latter's international investment position, a more dynamic model of MNE is required. This is yet to be developed, but Chapter 10 does suggest a framework by which this might be done.

6.4   A DISCUSSION OF SOME PARTICULAR VARIABLES AFFECTING FDI

6.4.1   Introduction

In addition to the studies so far identified, which have essentially tried to test the propositions about the likely determinants of different kinds of MNEs, scholars have also paid some attention to evaluating the significance of specific variables on the propensity to engage in or expand foreign production. We shall conclude this chapter by examining two of these which have attracted special interest. These are, first, specific actions taken by governments to affect the flow of inward investment, and second, the role of political risk.

6.4.2   Government incentives and the regulatory environment

The survey evidence reviewed earlier in this chapter suggests that tax and other fiscal incentives offered by host governments are rarely of critical importance in determining whether or not particular foreign investment projects are undertaken. However, the field research also testifies to the fact that, after this decision is taken and providing there is some latitude in the siting of an MNE activity, such incentives may become relevant. This is particularly the case for export-oriented investments that do not require substantial amounts of location-bound resources. Moreover, it is the consensus of most analysts that while the 'carrot' of tax holidays and investment allowances are rarely decisive influences on the decision of MNEs to invest in particular countries, they are often considered as welcome 'rewards' for such investment. Both these points suggest that incentive strategies of host governments may frequently involve unnecessary, expensive and inefficient competitive bidding among themselves.[27] For their part, MNEs would be unwise to consider such inducements as either permanent or of lasting significance. The rationale and effectiveness of government incentives is further discussed in Chapter 20. Here, some evidence from studies aimed directly at evaluating the role of such measures in influencing the extent and location of MNE activity is evaluated.

The companies surveyed in the analysis of Reuber *et al.* (1973) of foreign investment projects in developing countries were 'asked to identify which of these incentives was deemed so important that its absence would have caused abandonment of the project or major changes in it'. In respect of export-oriented projects, 48% of respondents named 'financial incentives' (tax holidays, duty remissions, accelerated depreciation), 22% 'protection of markets' and 26% 'other incentives' (probably access to infrastructure and various risk-reducing guarantee schemes) with 4% indicating that 'incentives are of no importance'. Of the projects designed to provide goods for sale in the local market, 'protection of the market' was notably more relevant (56% of responses) with 'other incentives' (15%) and 'financial incentives' (9%) relatively unimportant and 20% of projects considering 'incentives of no importance'. In interpreting these results, it should be observed that Reuber addressed his attention to the location of particular investment projects rather than any broader decision of companies to engage in FDI. In this context, the prevalence of 'financial incentives'

among the more 'footloose' export-oriented projects is as would be expected.

In their analysis of the determinants of MNE activity in 41 developing countries, Root and Ahmed (1978) classified these countries as 'unattractive', 'moderately attractive' or 'highly attractive', according to the annual per capita inflow of non-extractive FDI over the period 1966 to 1970. Forty-four variables were then chosen as potentially significant discriminators of the three groups of countries. Among the six policy-related discriminators were three relating to tax levels. Of these, corporate taxes proved to be an effective discriminator at the 5% level (there were six effective discriminators at this level, of which this was the only policy factor). However, tax incentive legislation – measured in terms of its perceived complexity and the liberality of tax concessions – was not an effective discriminator.

Agodo (1978) analysed a sample of 33 US firms which owned 46 manufacturing investments in 20 African countries. Tax concessions were found to be insignificant explanatory variables in both simple and multiple regression equations. Phillips (1969) analysed 52 companies operating in Nigeria under 'pioneer company' provisions and, therefore, receiving tax incentives. Only 17 of the 52 identified these tax incentives as being the critical influence on the decisions of these companies to set up. Indeed, this variable was ranked eighth of the twelve considered. Furthermore, 25 of 37 respondents said they would probably (22) or definitely (3) have gone ahead with the investment without the incentives.

In a cross-country multi-variate study, Lim (1983) tested the relationship between the 'generosity of fiscal incentives' and FDI inflows in 27 developing countries between 1965 and 1973. The other variables included in the regression equation were a measure of natural resource strength, the level of economic development and GDP growth. In the tests, the fiscal incentives variable was discovered to be significantly negatively correlated with FDI. In offering an explanation for this unexpected result, the author suggested that 'fiscal hypergenerosity was seen by potential foreign investors as a danger signal (a disincentive) and not as a lure (an incentive)', that is, it reflects the country's pessimistic view of its own L advantages. A related version of this hypothesis that does not involve direct causation is the 'illusory compensating effect'. Here, the host country's pessimistic view of its L advantages leads it to offer high incentives. However, these are ignored by foreign investors who continue to react to poor L advantages, which results in a negative relationship between FDI and investment incentives.

Field studies have also suggested that foreign investors may react unfavourably to performance requirements inflicted on them by host governments, or indeed to regulatory and other devices which they perceive to reduce the opportunities for profitable investment. As we have already suggested, a recent study by Contractor (1991), drawing on data published by the US Department of Commerce on the changing attitudes of governments towards inbound direct investment over the period 1977 to 1982, confirms this proposition. Contractor found a positive and significant relationship between the extent to which governments had liberalized policies towards foreign investors and the FDI flows over the period.

Finally, extensive analyses by the UNCTC (1988, 1989) have suggested that for many years now the regulatory environment has been an important determinant of the level and pattern of FDI in service-based sectors. Indeed, it has been argued that the proclivity of rules and regulations governing the establishment and operation of foreign-owned service companies, in both developed and developing countries, is the main explanation for the lower degree of the internationalization of production in the service sector relative to that in the goods sector (see Chapter 2). By the same token, the liberalization of many service markets and the current movements toward regional integration are causing MNEs to reappraise the locational strategies of their service-based activities.

However, up to now there has been little quantitative research on the impact of government regulation on the location of FDI in services. The one exception is a recent study by Li and Guisinger (1992). Using a measure intended to reflect the openness of developed host countries (or regions) to the establishment of new foreign service affiliates, the authors demonstrate that the variable had a positive and statistically significant impact on the investment behaviour of 168 of the world's largest service firms over two time periods: 1976–80 and 1980–86. Like Contractor (1991), they show that the liberalization of national restrictions on inward investment during the early 1980s has had a significant impact on the foreign involvement of service-based MNEs.

6.4.3 Political instability and risk

Chapter 4 has suggested that depending on its characteristics, the presence of uncertainty may either induce or inhibit MNE activity. When the uncertainty arises from cross-border market failure, then firms may respond by undertaking or increasing their ownership of foreign assets. Where, however, it is perceived adversely to affect the economic viability of a firm's present or future value-added activity, it is likely to lead to a reduction of FDI. Political volatility normally falls into this second category of risk.

Early field studies of the influences on FDI (e.g. Basi, 1964) all suggested that political risk ranked very high among the variables taken into consideration by MNEs in determining the location of their overseas operations. However, later statistical studies which have embraced political environment indicators have yielded more ambiguous results. Bennett and Green (1972), for example, found political stability in 46 host countries to be insignificantly related to inward investment from the US; this was the case for both developed and developing country subsamples. However, since the dependent variable was the US foreign capital stake in 1965 and the political stability measure embraced events over the previous 8 or 16 years, the practical implications of the findings are questionable. A similar study by Green and Cunningham (1975), which incorporated fewer (25) countries but a larger number of explanatory independent variables, confirmed that political stability was again insignificant.

More comprehensive studies of the importance of the political risk variable have been carried out by Kobrin (1976, 1978) and Root and Ahmed (1979). Using a dependent variable comprising the number of new manufacturing subsidiaries established in eleven developed countries and 48 developing countries between 1964 and 1967 by 187 leading US manufacturing MNEs (Vaupel and Curhan, 1974), Kobrin (1976) applied factor analysis to 33 political, social and economic variables. This factor analysis produced six 'clusters' of variables of which three (labelled by Kobrin as 'rebellion', 'government instability' and 'subversion') were politically oriented. In a range of multiple regression tests, none of the 'clusters' emerged as statistically significant determinants of US manufacturing FDI. In a later reworking of the data for the 48 developing countries, Kobrin (1978) identified three types of 'political violence'. Of these only 'conspiracy' (e.g. assassinations, coups, revolutions, general strikes) was significantly negatively related to FDI. This result also held strongest where it was most likely to result in a response inimical to the interests of the foreign investors (i.e. at 'relatively high levels of socio-economic development and a relatively efficient bureaucracy').

A related statistical technique, *viz* discriminant analysis, was applied by Root and Ahmed (1979) to a sample of 58 developing countries, which were classified as 'unattractive', 'moderately attractive' or 'highly attractive' for FDI according to their annual average per capita inflow of non-extractive FDI between 1960 and 1970. Of 38 economic, social and political variables, only six emerged as significant discriminators (at 5%) between the groups. Of these, only 'the number of regular (constitutional) changes in government leadership' between 1957 and 1967 was a significant political variable. Though both 'number of armed attacks by internal groups' (1956 to 1967) and the 'role of government in the economy' were significant (negatively and positively, respectively) at 10%, the 'degree of nationalism' was insignificant at that level. These results were broadly supportive of those of Agodo (1978) who, in an analysis of 33 US firms which had 46 manufacturing investments in 20 African countries, found that political stability had a positive and significant effect on the locational choice of MNEs. They have most recently been confirmed by a 54-country study undertaken by Akhter and Lusch (1991) based on World Bank data for each year from 1975 to 1980.[28]

In his analysis of the determinants of annual average inflows of FDI in 25 developing countries, Levis (1979) considered the significance of two perceptions of political stability over two periods – 1962–4 and 1965–7. The first, and most common, view is that which equates political stability with the 'absence of domestic civil conflict and violent behaviour'. The measure used is that of Feierabend and Feierabend (1976) who defined political instability as

'the degree of the amount of aggression directed by individuals or groups within the political system against other groups within the political system against other groups or against the complex of office holders and individual groups associated with them' (quoted in Levis, 1979).

Levis uses stepwise regression equations to show that this variable was the third most important of the seven tested, and was significant as a determinant of FDI for the period 1962 to 1964. However, it was seventh and insignificant for the lagged period 1956–67. The second indicator of political instability is based on the perceived authority of the host country's government or, in Levis's words, 'the extent to which the political system and its outputs are accepted as right and proper by the population' (Levis, 1979, p. 62). The indicator used for this was ranked sixth and insignificant for the unlagged period, but fifth and significant in the lagged period.

In another analysis of the determinants of FDI in 54 countries in the late 1970s, Schneider and Frey (1985) ascertained that political instability was persistently and significantly negatively related to FDI in regressions (either with GNP per capita as the sole 'control' variable or with a wider selection of independent variables). Though 'government ideology' was never significantly related to FDI, the proportion of a country's foreign aid coming from Western sources was found to be a significantly positive determinant and that from East European sources significantly negative, while the amount of multi-lateral aid was also significantly positive.

An analysis by Nigh (1985) broadens the studies already described in two ways. First, by pooling time-series data on US manufacturing FDI in 24 countries for 21 years (1954 to 1975), the possibility of systematic investigation of lags is opened up. Second, four separate dimensions of political events are distinguished by taking account of both conflictive and cooperative events, both as within host countries (intra-nation events) and between countries (inter-nation events). Explicitly

(1) conflictive inter-nation events are unfriendly acts directed by the host country at the US,

(2) cooperative inter-nation events are friendly acts directed by the host country at the US,

(3) conflictive intra-nation events are associated

with a worsening political environment in a host country,

(4) cooperative intra-nation events are associated with an improved political environment in a host country.

For developing countries, Nigh (1985) found that both conflictive and cooperative inter-nation events and conflictive intra-nation events were significant deterrents to inbound FDI at a one per cent level when the latter variable is lagged by one year. When unlagged data was used, both types of inter-nation event were insignificant, but both types of intra-nation event were significant. For developed countries, both types of inter-nation political events were significant (signs as predicted), at a one per cent level, whether lagged or unlagged data was used.

In another analysis, Nigh (1986) applied the same methodology to eight Latin American countries for a similar period. Here, both types of inter-nation political events were shown significantly to affect inward investment, after a one-year lag, while both types of intra-nation events were found to be a significant influence when unlagged, but insignificant when lagged. Thus Nigh's results suggest, first, that the differentiation between inter-nation and intra-nation political events adds an extra dimension of subtlety to the analysis. Second, they demonstrate that part of this subtlety is reflected in differences between developed and developing host countries (with only inter-nation events being of any significance to firms contemplating investments in the former). Third, they indicate that the response of foreign investors to intra-nation events seems to be speedier than that to inter-nation events.

Finally, mention might be made of a study by Osenghale (1992), who undertook a statistical investigation into the reactions of US MNEs to adverse changes in host government policies towards inward FDI, inter-nation conflict, political instability and market size in eight Latin American countries for the years 1948–1983.[29] Using a longitudinal multiple regression analysis, and correcting for the possibility of serial correlation, Osenghale discovered that while the impact of the first two variables on the flow of US direct investment was negative, and statistically significant for all countries at a 5% level or below, political instability, although inducing a negative response, was only statistically significant (at a 10%

level) in the case of Peru. By contrast, but in accordance with the author's prediction, market size and US direct investment flows were positively and significantly associated.

6.5   CONCLUSIONS

This chapter has presented some of the empirical findings on the determinants of MNE activity. They represent but the tip of an iceberg of a voluminous literature on the subject. What, if anything, can one conclude from the findings reviewed?

First, we have sought to demonstrate that the eclectic paradigm of international production offers a useful framework for identifying and evaluating the determinants of both an initial act of FDI and an increase, or restructuring, of foreign value-added activities by established MNEs. This chapter has pinpointed, and in many cases assessed, the statistical significance of the leading O-specific advantages of actual or potential foreign direct investors, the L-specific attributes of countries in which they may create or add value to these advantages, and the many I-specific characteristics of firms and markets that will determine the extent to which, and the form in which, cross-border trade and production is organized.

Second, the studies reviewed also make it clear that beyond the kind of generalizations that may be offered by the eclectic (or for that matter the internalization) paradigm, the determinants of particular kinds of MNE activity will depend critically on the *raison d'être* for that activity, the characteristics and strategies of the firms involved, and in which sectors and countries the activity is being undertaken. Similarly, even given a particular type of MNE activity, such as natural resource or market-seeking investment, the significance of the particular explanatory variables will depend on the stage of development and ESP configurations of the investing and recipient countries. *Inter alia*, for example, the role of labour costs as a determinant of FDI is likely to differ according to its geographical and industrial composition and to the employment-related policies pursued by home and host governments, and the willingness of MNEs to adapt their products and production processes to the requirements and needs of the countries in which they operate. The relevance of the O advantages associated with multinationality *per se* (Ot) will clearly depend on the pattern and extent of the MNE's foreign commitments and whether or not it operates a globally integrated strategy towards these commitments. The significance of tax and other incentives may be a negligible influence on some kinds of MNE activity in some countries, but critically affect other kinds in other countries. We have also seen that the structure of the OLI configuration facing firms of different nationalities or those of similar nationalities producing in different countries is quite difficult. In addition, because firms differ in size, experience, attitudes to uncertainties and strategic perspectives, it may be exceedingly difficult to generalize about levels and patterns of MNE conduct and behaviour.

What, then, is the scholar to make of this plethora of sometimes conflicting research findings? Beyond the paradigmatic generalizations, other conclusions are possible. First, research has clearly demonstrated that at least some kinds of O-specific advantages of MNEs are strongly related to the competitive characteristics of their country of origin; this is broadly in line with traditional trade theory, which suggests that the distribution of location bound resources, capabilities and markets is not evenly distributed across the globe. Second, an increasing body of research is showing that other kinds of O-specific advantages, for example, those to do with the common governance of cross-border activities, are less likely to be country specific and more likely to be related to the size and strategies of firms. In other words, the appropriate 'strategic' group for the analysis of O-specific advantages depends very much on the types of advantages being considered.

Third, it is possible to offer some generalizations about the types of L advantages of countries most likely to influence different types of MNE activity as well as how, and in what situations, these may differ between Nation States. Thus, for example, the role of government policy in either encouraging or inhibiting inward direct investment may be very different in a poor resource-based developing country than in a mature, but intensively competitive, industrialized nation. This particular L-specific variable may also depend on the government's success in negotiating favourable terms with foreign direct investors (Fagre and Wells, 1982; Lecraw, 1984;

Behrman and Grosse, 1990).

Fourth, the empirical research of scholars has offered some useful pointers as to the kinds of cross-border market failure that different kinds of MNE are likely to internalize. Here country-, industry- (or activity-) and firm-specific factors all appear to be critical. Thus, while UK glass manufacturing firms contemplating an FDI in Nigeria or licensing agreement with a Nigerian firm may look at the need to maintain close quality control over the end product as a key discriminating variable, an integrated computer MNE with many foreign outlets may view its need to acquire complementary assets or to exploit the economies of geographical diversification as its critical reason for eschewing the use of external markets.

Fifth, if they have done anything at all, the empirical findings presented in the chapter must have left the reader with a sense of both the complexity of the subject under discussion and the danger of generalizations about it. At the same time, it is worth emphasizing that most of the research results described should be considered as complementary, rather than alternative, explanations of MNE activity. Each, indeed, contributes a piece of the jigsaw on the 'why', 'where' and 'how' of such activity. Often, as emphasized in Chapter 4, researchers are interested in different, but related, aspects of MNE activity. There is, then, no necessary conflict between the empirical verification of Vernon's theory of the product cycle, Knickerbocker or Graham's oligopolistic interdependence theories, or Kojima's macroeconomic analyses. Each is addressing rather different issues. Only when scholars make exaggerated claims about the generality or exclusivity of their models or theories, or when they make technical errors (e.g. in the specification of their equations or the appropriate econometric techniques), can they rightfully expect to be challenged. But for the rest, most add new light or a fresh perspective to our understanding of one or other aspect of the globalization of enterprises.

As a final point, we would observe that, notwithstanding the substantial amount of empirical research undertaken on the determinants of foreign-owned production, we still know comparatively little about the reasons for some other forms of MNE activity – notably strategic alliances and various forms of subcontracting – or about the circumstances in which one non-equity form of involvement is preferred to another.[30] Nor do we know much about the ways in which the various portfolios of international involvement by MNEs interact with each other. There has, for example, been no empirical research testing the main tenets of cross-border network analysis (see Chapter 4). This is clearly one important avenue for empirical research in the 1990s.

NOTES

1 We use the words 'associated with' rather than 'determined' as, in many cases, the direction of the causation between MNE activity and explanatory variables is uncertain. See also a study by Flowers (1975) on European direct foreign investment in the US which collected new data directly from European affiliates in the US.

2 Some of which are published as case studies by Harvard University Press.

3 See particularly UN (1992b) which we have used extensively in the writing of this chapter.

4 For the interested reader, the following are a selection of the many recent field surveys conducted on the motives and determinants of outbound or inbound MNE activity: Buckley and Mathew (1979) for first time UK investment in Australia; Bureau of Industry Economics (1983a, 1983b, 1984) for Australia FDI in various countries; Akoorie and Enderwick (1991) for outbound New Zealand FDI; Ajami and Ricks (1981) for foreign firms investing in the US; Dunning (1977) for UK firms investing in developing countries; The Long Term Credit Bank of Japan (1987) for Japanese FDI in all regions; JETRO (1990) for Japanese firms investing in Europe; Chen (1983) for Hong Kong firms investing in developing countries; Kumar and Kim (1984) for Korean outbound investment; Schive and Hsueh (1985) for Taiwanese firms investing in Asia; the Group of 30 (1984) for a survey of the motivations of 52 large MNEs which control and manage over half the world's stock of FDI; Abdel-Malek (1984) for Canadian FDI in Western Europe; Rugman (1987) for Canadian investment in the US; Artisien et al. (1991) for Yugoslavian direct investment in LDCs; and Burgenmeier (1986, 1991) for Swiss firms operating abroad.

5 Hyun and Whitmore report on a survey of 8790 Japanese direct investments carried out by the Long Term Credit Bank of Japan in 1987. Some 26.2% of the 2166 investments in the US and 23.6% of those in Europe were primarily motivated by the need to gain access to technical and market intelligence. The

corresponding proportion for Japanese firms investing elsewhere in the world was 10.6%.

6 In service sectors, for example, the chief advantage of foreign investors often lies in their detailed knowledge of how to service the needs of their domestic clients which have established overseas subsidiaries and branches (Nigh et al., 1986).

7 Overall only 12% of the 8790 Japanese firms thought this to be a major factor. However, for investments in Asia this figure rose to 22.9%.

8 See, for example, an interesting study by McAleese (1985) on the role of financial and other incentives in attracting US firms to Ireland vis à vis other countries in the EC.

9 However, a recently published study by Kogut (1992b) reveals that the role of R&D as an explanatory variable of the industrial structure of US outward investment in the inter-war years was a minor one. Far more significant was the extent to which firms in a particular sector had embraced the most up-to-date organization principles and work procedures. In another article, Hirschey (1981) questions the extent to which R&D intensity actually causes multinationality: rather he suggests analysis points to a firm's FDI as being a significant influence on the level of a firm's domestic R&D. See Chapter 11 for more details.

10 A similar conclusion was reached in respect of all non-US investment in the US by Ajami and Ricks (1981).

11 See also Chapter 11 of this book.

12 In banking, for example, several writers have emphasized the importance of product differentiation based on human capital, financial technology and the range and quality of services.

13 See, for example, Dunning and McQueen (1981) relating to hotels; Gray and Gray (1981), Sabi (1988) relating to international banking.

14 Notably data from the US Department of Commerce's benchmark survey for 1977 (US Department of Commerce, 1981).

15 The data used by Lall and Siddharthan was for 1972 and 1977.

16 Although in another study Pugel (1986) found that the number of life and physical scientists in the US as a proportion of total industrial employment to be positively and significantly related (at a 5% level) to the value of inbound direct investments.

17 In each of the five equations the value of the t-statistic was such as to suggest that the positive sign was not a statistical artefact is in excess of 98% on a one-tailed test.

18 Communality analysis is a method of variance partitioning designed to identify proportions of variance in the dependent variable which may be uniquely attributed to each of the independent variables, and proportions

of variance which are attributed to various combinations of independent variable. The unique contribution of an independent variable is defined as the variance attributed to it when it entered last in the regression equation (Veuglers, 1991, p. 375).

19 It is worth observing that most of the cross-sectional studies on the determinants of MNE activity relate to a particular point of time. One exception is that by Lecraw (1991) of the effect which *changes* in the locational variables have on *changes* of the FDI stock into 27 developing countries over the period 1976 to 1986. Among Lecraw's findings were that changes in the value of a country's natural resource endowments had a significantly positive effect on national resource seeking FDI; changes in the real exchange rate negatively affected export oriented and resource seeking FDI; adjustments in tax rates had a significant influence on market-seeking FDI but not on export oriented and national resource FDI; and alterations in the tariff rate had a positive impact on market seeking investment but not the other two types of MNE activity (Lecraw op. cit. p. 177).

20 The question of the mode of entry chosen by firms into foreign markets is further explored in Chapters 7 and 14. As Kogut's findings are corroborated by Li and Guisinger (1991) in the study of the reasons for the failure of foreign-owned firms in the US, and by Li and Guisinger (1992) in their study of the factors influencing FDI by service MNEs.

21 In other words, it is incorrect to assume that the L advantages of countries must necessarily be considered as exogenous to MNEs or the O advantages of MNEs must necessarily be considered as exogenous to countries. By their economic power and lobbying techniques, MNEs may affect the policies and strategies of home or host governments – thereby increasing or reducing the L attractions of countries – while the policies and strategies of governments (e.g. by aiding their national champions) may affect the O advantages of foreign MNEs. This point is taken up in a more general context in Chapter 10.

22 The effects of regional integration on MNE activity are explored at greater length in Chapter 17.

23 Such measures included an interest Equalization Tax which was enacted in 1964, a Voluntary Foreign Credit Program in 1965 and a Foreign Direct Investment Program (FDIP) instituted by a Presidential Executive Order (11387). By this order, companies making direct investment in certain scheduled countries had to make foreign borrowings to partially offset actual direct investment. In 1968, the proceeds of foreign borrowing used as an offset equalled 64% of direct investment; but this proportion fell in subsequent years to 14% in 1973. The program ended in 1974.

24 Those have been mainly related to the dynamics of the internationalization foreseen and the impact this might have on the methods of servicing foreign markets. Both these issues are discussed later in this book (see, for example, Chapters 7, 10 and 14).

25 Correspondence analysis is a type of factor analysis analogous to the principal component method of factoring but designed to permit the comparison of variables and objects in the same factorial space. For further details see Hill (1974).

26 Full details are set out in Dunning (1981b, 1986c, 1987 and 1988a).

27 Exceptions include foreign investment guarantee schemes and more general incentives offered by governments through the promotion of efficient macroeconomic and market facilitating macro-organizational policies – see Chapter 20 and Dunning (1991b).

28 The authors used three criteria of political instability, *viz* number of political strikes, riots and armed attacks.

29 Composite indices were computed for each of the first three independent variables and, in the case of adverse changes in government policy, which included such measures as tax discrimination, unilateral revision of contract agreements and expropriation. The variables were weighted by the author on the lines of a similar procedure used by Kobrin (1982).

30 The issues are explored in more detail in Chapter 9.

PART 2

INSIDE THE MULTINATIONAL ENTERPRISE

Throughout this volume, one recurring theme about the distinctiveness of MNE activity is the way in which resources and capabilities are organized across national boundaries. Part 2 of this volume considers some of the micro-organizational decisions which have to be made by individual MNEs. In contrast to later chapters, Chapters 7 to 9 discuss issues directly relevant to the management of international business.

Chapter 7 begins by examining the internationalization process as an extension of the domestic value (added) chain of economic activity. It then goes on to describe and evaluate attempts by business analysts to explain the evolution of international business from a firm exporting a single product to an MNE which operates a network of globally integrated and diversified value-added activities. It also shows that different kinds of FDI follow a different path towards broadening and deepening of cross-border production and that, over time, the foreign operations of an MNE develop their own momentum.

Chapter 8 considers the impact of the globalization of economic activity on the organizational structure of the globalizing firms, as well as on the locus of intra-firm decision taking. Both this chapter and Chapter 9 use the eclectic paradigm to analyse the economic and strategic determinants of the nature and character of intra-hierarchical decision taking, as well as the form which inter-firm collaborative arrangements might take. In particular, it shows that, depending on the strategic response of MNEs to any given OLI configuration, the organizational pattern of internal decision taking will vary between the hierarchical and the heterarchical, as well as being influenced by the extent to which MNEs believe they need to own assets located in foreign countries in order to deploy them to meet their global objectives.

Chapter 9 considers some of the alternative forms of cross-border activity undertaken by MNEs to that of the fully owned foreign affiliate. Again it argues that much of the theory set out in Chapter 4 can be usefully extended to explain the propensity of firms to conclude both joint and non-equity ventures (e.g. strategic alliances). This is because most economists and business analysts have been interested in explaining the extension of the *control* exercised by firms outside their national boundaries rather than the extension of their ownership. Chapter 9 shows that control may be acquired from various sources and exercised in various ways. Indeed, Part 2 concludes by suggesting that, in the past decade or so, the MNE has become the nexus of a plurality of cross-border control mechanisms, and that the way in which it organizes these to achieve its global objectives will substantially determine the extent to which it can sustain or advance its long-term competitive (or O-specific) advantages.

Finally we would urge the reader to consider Part 2 of this volume as a bridge between Part 1 and Part 3. It does not claim to be a comprehensive analysis of the internal workings of MNEs. Little attention, for example, is given to critical financial or marketing management issues. Its purpose is a different one. Together with Part 1, its aim is to prepare the reader for the analysis which follows in Parts 3 and 4. In our examination of the impact of MNEs on the economies in which they operate, we will repeatedly argue that this will critically depend on two main variables. The first are the macro-economic and organizational policies pursued by the governments of the countries (or regions) in which the MNE activity takes place. The second is the way in which MNEs, themselves, organize the cross-border governance of these activities. Part 2 will have succeeded in its objective if it identifies the main determinants of this latter variable and how these have responded over time to technological advances and changes in the global economic and political environment.

CHAPTER 7

ENTRY AND EXPANSION STRATEGIES OF MNEs

7.1 INTRODUCTION

In Part 1 of this book we sought to identify the motives for, and determinants of, international production, and to explain the historical evolution of MNE activity. In this chapter we consider foreign direct investment as part of the entrepreneurial and organizational strategy of firms. In doing so, we take a more micro-oriented and behavioural perspective of our subject matter, and consider the reasons why, and the situations in which, particular enterprises become foreign producers and/or increase, or change the pattern of, their global economic involvement. We also seek to identify the main determinants of the way in which such international production is owned and organized.

In Chapter 1 we defined an MNE as a firm that owned and controlled value-adding activities in more than one country. In Chapter 3 we suggested that MNEs engaged in foreign production to increase the value of the income generating assets of their owners. Chapter 4 argued that this goal was achieved by coordinating their existing assets (together with those which they might acquire or lease) – their so-called O advantages – with the L configurations of countries. Chapter 4 further suggested that the value-added activities of MNEs incurred two kinds of costs – *viz production* and *transaction* costs – which were likely to vary according to the nature and extent of these activities, the way in which they are coordinated and their location. Thus, for example, depending on whether production (the process by which less valuable inputs are organized to produce more valuable outputs) is undertaken by several firms or by just one, the costs of that production may be higher or lower. Similarly, where the production

of goods or service involves the use of intermediate products at different stages of its value-added chain – as it usually does – the transaction costs (i.e. the costs of organizing these separate activities) are likely to vary according to whether this function is undertaken by the market, by a single administrative hierarchy, by some kind of a cooperative alliance or by a network of firms. MNEs are likely to flourish wherever the production of two or more value-added activities are best coordinated under the same, rather than separate, ownership and where the entrepreneurs and managers of the organizing enterprises perceive it to be in their best interests to locate at least some of these activities in a foreign country.

Chapter 5 further suggested that the historical growth of the MNE reflected the interaction between three sets of forces. The first was the extent to which the resources and capabilities necessary for the efficient production and marketing of goods and services are the privileged right of particular firms. As Chapter 4 argued, it is the possession of such rights that gives a firm a competitive edge over its rivals. The second was the extent to which firms found it profitable to organize the transactions relating to the acquisition and use of these property rights themselves or to employ some other modality for this purpose, and why, along with these transactions, the organization of production within and between firms was becoming increasingly concentrated in the hands of a relatively few MNEs, rather than being shared among many. The third factor influencing the growth of foreign production was that, for a variety of reasons, firms were finding it increasingly to their advantage to produce goods and services outside rather than inside their national boundaries.

Chapter 5 also highlighted the interaction

between the growth of the human and physical assets, and the macro organization of value-added activity. It emphasized that the expansion of MNE activity must be seen as part and parcel of the growth and spread of international capitalism, technological and organizational change, the discovery of new lands and materials, the emergence of new political and economic systems, the creation of a strong and effective legal framework and capital markets, and a substantial lowering of the costs of the cross-border movement of goods, assets and people. All of these events have dramatically affected not only the availability and quality of goods and services together with their associated costs of production and transactions, but the way in which that production and those transactions are owned and organized.

This chapter – indeed, this part of the book – looks at these and related issues from the viewpoint of the entrepreneurs and managers of individual firms. It focuses rather more than did the previous chapters on the strategic management of the resources and competencies, owned or acquired by individual business enterprises, to achieve specified goals, wherever and whenever this involves the enterprises in value-added activities outside their national boundaries. This chapter, in particular, looks at the determinants of the nature, timing and form of the internationalization process.

7.2   THE CONCEPT OF BUSINESS STRATEGY

By strategy, we mean a deliberate choice taken by the entrepreneurs or managers of firms to organize the resources and capabilities within their control (i.e. their O advantages) to achieve an objective or set of objectives over a specified time period. In the economist's world of perfect competition, neither strategy nor management or entrepreneurship plays a significant role. Resources and capabilities are generally assumed to be immobile, fungible and heterogeneous. The firm is presumed to be a rational, but passive, economic agent with little or no freedom for strategic manoeuvre. In order for it both to cover its opportunity costs and to maximize the value of its assets, the output and price of whatever it supplies are predetermined. Moreover, in equilibrium, all the

stakeholders in the firm, including the main decision takers, earn only the opportunity cost of their resources.

Once market imperfections are introduced into the picture, the firm's behavioural options are widened and the entrepreneur and manager have positive and strategic roles to play. Their roles will vary according to the nature and extent of the market imperfections, the coincidence of interest between the strategist and the stakeholders in the business, the strategist's judgement of the probability and time profile of the outcome of alternative courses of action, and his attitude to risk taking.

Neo-classical economics initially analysed market imperfections by reference to their affect on the behaviour of participants in the market. In particular, three kinds of structural market distortions were identified. The first was the power of the participants in the market to influence price by adding or withdrawing output from the total amount being sold (or purchased). The second were those arising from the ability of firms to differentiate their products from those of their competitors. The third were those arising from the presence (or creation) of barriers to competition. Except in the case of oligopolistic market situations, the neo-classical economists took these imperfections as exogenous and continued to assume that firms acted as profit maximizers.

However, as we have seen, the introduction of market imperfections also opens up the possibility of firms making strategic choices. First, once it is accepted that a firm does not *have* to maximize profits to stay in business, then the *possibility* of alternative objectives and strategies to achieve these objectives arise. Initially economists and organizational scholars tended to focus on the output and pricing decisions of firms pursuing a range of non-profit maximizing objectives, for example, sales or wealth maximization or of some form of utility or constrained profit maximization.[1] Eventually they came to recognize that a more fundamental reappraisal of the firm was required as any movement away from perfect competition was liable to increase the costs of using this particular exchange mechanism. *Both* transactional cost economics and strategic behaviour arise out of market imperfections.

Second, firms may themselves attempt to create new structural imperfections in anticipation of gaining larger profits. The traditional economics of the firm skirts this particular issue – mainly because it is not interested in organizational issues and, for the most part, assumes either that the transaction costs of using markets are zero or that they are always less than that of any other organizational firm. The theory of market failure and of relational contracting (Williamson, 1979) suggests this is not necessarily the case. As Teece elegantly puts it 'By neglecting the institutional foundations of market structure, the conventional tools of economic analysis are rendered impotent before many strategic management problems' (Teece, 1984).

When orthodox economists have tried to grapple with these issues, they have been primarily concerned with identifying the possible outcome of alternative behavioural strategies. As a result, the whole of the literature on oligopoly assumes a game-theoretic perspective which yields an indeterminate solution simply because of cognitive market failure. For example, one particular oligopolist may not only be uncertain as to how its behaviour (with respect to such decisions as price, output, range and type of products supplied, innovatory activities, types of markets served, etc) will affect its competitors, but also how they will, in turn, react to this behaviour. Most economic models then seek to identify the consequences of certain types of behaviour without explicitly examining the strategies that might determine that behaviour.

A similar approach is taken to analysing information asymmetries, or inadequacies, uncertainty and time. Most economics (as opposed to finance) textbooks pay little attention to the first, while the second and third tend to be treated as a cost (though the term transaction cost is not usually used), which requires to be covered by higher receipts. Thus net income earned in five years' time has a cost of not being earned today, which is equal to the interest that would have been earned today if reinvested over four years. Similarly, a project with a 50% chance of earning £5 million and a 50% chance of earning £4 million might be treated of equal value to a project with a 100% chance of earning £4.5 million.

These, of course, are simple illustrations of the inadequacy of the market as a deterministic resource-allocative mechanism, the replacement of which opens a variety of strategic options to decision takers. In fact, not only do most decisions set in train a whole set of interrelated outcomes, each of which is uncertain, but almost every decision, whether it is concerned with the best way to organize innovatory activities, reduce inventory costs or introduce a wage incentive scheme, impinges on the level, and balance between, receipts and costs in a way that is difficult to estimate with any certainty. The options chosen, then, will depend on the strategist's estimation of the likely alternative outcomes, his assessment of the uncertainties involved and both his attitude to these uncertainties and how he evaluates that of those he delegates to take decisions on his behalf.

The approach of the business strategist is less formal and, understandably, more pragmatic than that of the economist. Instead of seeking *generalized* explanations to a particular problem, he is concerned with identifying *particular* solutions for an individual firm, or group of firms that possess similar characteristics. Though his emphasis tends to focus on specific areas of decision taking, there is an increasing recognition that successful strategists are those who adopt a systemic and integrated approach towards their value-added activities, including those which are undertaken outside their national boundaries. The following sections seek to apply some of these concepts to a number of issues concerned with the organization, ownership and operations of MNEs. First, however, we consider the very nature of a firm's economic activities.

7.3   THE VALUE-ADDED CHAIN

7.3.1   Some general principles

The main task of a business enterprise – and it is unique to this institution – is to engage in *production*. Production is defined as any value-creating or adding activity. Such added value is achieved by converting inputs of lesser economic worth to outputs of greater economic worth. Put another way, the firm owns or hires the services of a set of human, physical or financial assets for which it must pay at least their opportunity cost. In a profit maximizing model, the strategy of the owners of the firm is to coordinate and allocate these assets in such a way as to produce the maximum surplus (i.e. economic rent) over and above their opportunity cost, all of which is assumed to accrue to the owners as profits.

These profits may be distributed to shareholders or reinvested in the business in the expectation of earning future profits or increasing the net value of the firm. Alternatively, in imperfectly competitive conditions, the owners of the firm may pursue other objectives. Surplus profits may be absorbed as managerial inefficiency, or they may be wholly or partly appropriated by other stakeholders (e.g. the owners of labour services) according to their respective bargaining powers.

In order to achieve its objectives, a firm must also engage in *transactions*. Even the firm that undertakes a single economic activity has to participate in two sets of transactions. The first is with the owners of the resources it uses to produce the value added; the second is with the consumers of the goods or services which are the output of the activity. These transactions are external to the firm, that is, between it and independent economic agents (e.g. other firms and households), and they are usually organized by the market. Although these transactions involve costs, such as those identified in Chapter 4, they have to be incurred if the firm is to produce at all. Furthermore, the costs may not be independent of the benefits. The cost of coordinating labour inputs and monitoring employee performance may be directly related to the productivity of that labour. Higher transaction costs associated with the search for possible buyers may be partially or wholly offset by the additional sales generated by that search.

The objective of a firm, then, is to buy its inputs and sell its output in a way that maximizes the revenue for any given level of production plus transaction costs incurred in earning this revenue. In addition it will continue to increase its output until the marginal production and transaction costs are equal to its marginal revenue. There are various problems associated even with this apparently simple accounting exercise. One is that because it is not always possible to measure transaction costs – particularly those associated with risk and inter-personal relationships – it is difficult to judge whether or not costs *are* being minimized or revenue being maximized at a given level of output, or, indeed, if the right level of output *is* being produced. Another is that some transaction costs are not easily allocable to particular inputs, for example, the costs of monitoring labour performance so as to minimize

shirking or opportunism by workers, or those of ensuring that subcontractors adhere to the terms of their contract.

As soon as a firm chooses to engage in more than one value-added activity, not only do its transaction costs increase, but also it begins to assume a role which, in theory at least, may be accomplished by other organizational modalities. By engaging in upstream or downstream value activities in addition to the one which it is already undertaking, a firm internalizes the market for what is being bought or sold. In so doing, it brings, under a single ownership, activities which were previously (or, in the case of a new activity, might have been) produced by two (or more) separate producers. A firm that diversifies its output (e.g. from being a producer of refrigerators to being a producer of refrigerators and washing machines) also incurs transaction costs through the common governance of both activities. Presumably it believes that these are either less than those which would be incurred by using the market, or that there are other gains to be reaped, such as economies of scope of internalizing the market for refrigerators. Diversifying the location of production most certainly adds to a firm's transaction costs, for example, those to do with hierarchical control and intra-firm communications (Hirsch, 1976). However, these may be more than outweighed by the revenue gained from new markets, a reduction in the unit cost of transactions common to foreign and domestic production, the benefits of output specialization, the cross-border arbitraging of factor prices and the spreading of environmental volatility (Kogut, 1985b).

The above analysis provides the setting for analysing the decision of a firm to produce outside its national boundaries. This will occur when the firm perceives the net benefits of supplying any given market, or set of markets, is best achieved by engaging in foreign production relative to some other modality of supplying that (or those) market(s). It could be, for example, that the firm believes that the costs of engaging in any activity plus the cross-border transaction costs of internalizing the market for the intermediate product used in that activity are higher than either those of engaging in the same activity in the home country and exporting its output from there, or of concluding the transaction with an independent firm in the foreign country.

7.3.2 Value-added networks and MNE activity

Let us now look at the process of the multi-nationalization of a firm. Here we introduce the concept of the value-added chain (or, as some writers (Porter, 1980, 1985) prefer to call it, the value chain) which identifies the various stages of economic activity that make up a production sequence of a specific product or service from start to finish. At each stage up to the point at which the product or service is sold to the final consumer, an intermediate product is produced which then becomes an input into the next stage of the process.[2] The value-added chain of a cotton shirt, for example, would include the design of the shirt, the growing of the raw cotton, the spinning of the yarn, the weaving or knitting of the yarn into cloth, the manufacture of the garment (e.g. cutting, sewing and packaging) and finally marketing of the final product and its distribution to wholesalers and retailers.

Figure 7.1 illustrates a value-added chain for the production of textile products. At each stage, value is added to that created previously such that the gross value (of output) of the end product is equal to the value added (or net output) of each of the separate stages. Thus if R_A is the gross receipts from the sales of the final product A and $N_{Ai}, \ldots, N_{Av}$ are the value added at stages i, ii . . . v of the chain then:

$$R_A = (N_{Ai} + N_{Aii} + N_{Aiii} + N_{Aiv} + N_{Av}) \qquad 7.1$$

However, the concept of a chain is not entirely appropriate for describing the production process. Indeed, as we shall see later, this is becoming less so over time because some intermediate products are not used by firms sequentially but jointly at various stages of the production process. These include common administrative, financial and advisory services, transport services and public utilities, management and administrative inputs, and some professional (e.g. auditing, advertising and legal) services. Although, in theory, it may be possible to assign such complementary value-adding activities to particular stages of production (we illustrate how this might be done in Figure 7.2), in practice it might be exceedingly difficult to do. Nevertheless, they are part of the value-added network of activities.

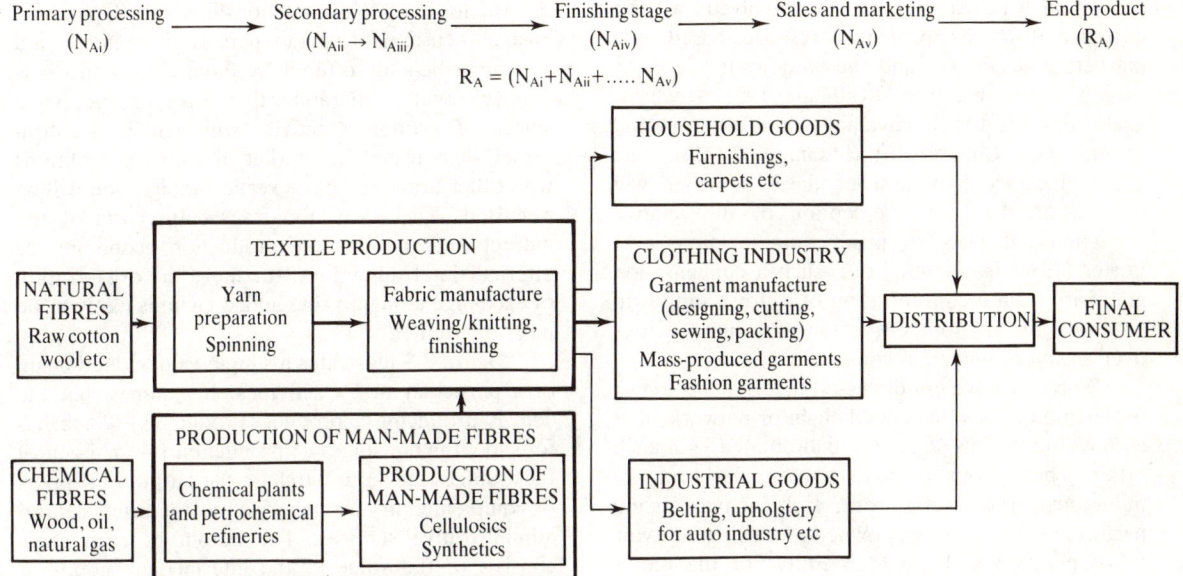

Figure 7.1 Source: derived from Dicken (1992).

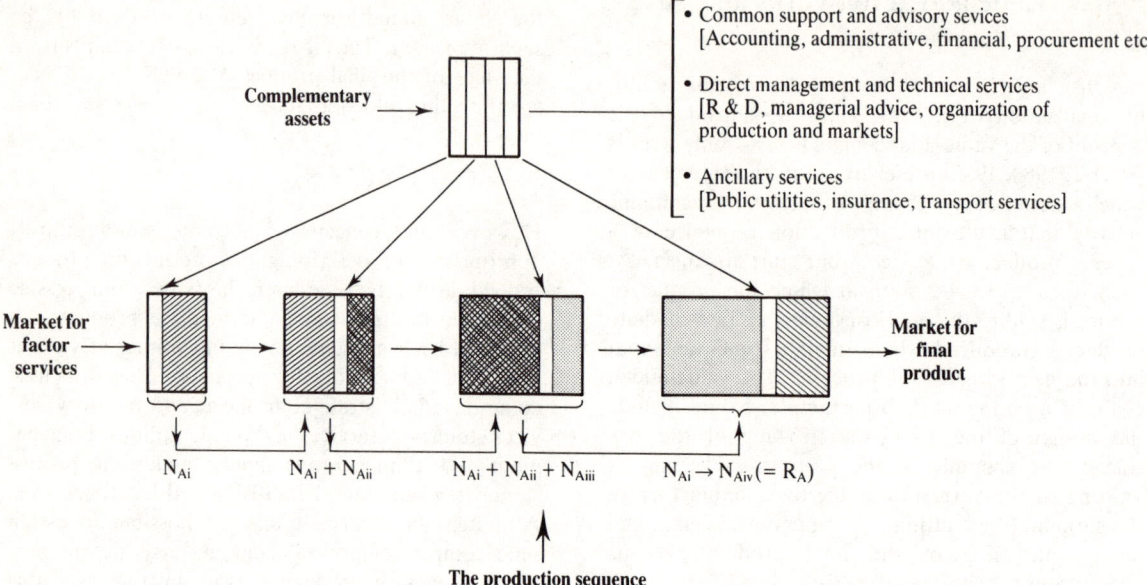

Figure 7.2   The value chain: complementary assets and the production sequence.

The choice of the particular value-added chain (or chains) and the stage (or stages of the chain, or chains) in which a firm may be involved, will be determined by its perceived resource-based and marketing advantages and the strategy it adopts to exploit these advantages (Tallman, 1991) – which, itself, may affect its O advantages in a future period of time (see Chapter 10) (Dunning, 1992b). The geographical configuration of these activities will depend on the firm's perception of the relative attractions of possible production locations. As Porter (1986) has pointed out, such a configuration may vary from a concentration of a firm's output in only one country to a dispersion of value activities over a larger number of countries.

So far we have not discussed the organization or ownership of the value-added chain or network, that is, how the various stages are coordinated with each other. The options open to a particular firm are numerous. They vary from each activity being performed by a separately owned producing entity or in cooperation with another entity, to the entire network being under the common ownership of a single hierarchy. However they are organized, the

activities in the network are linked by a series of vertical and lateral transactional relationships. The precise form of these relationships will depend on business customs and the perceived strategic and economic benefits offered by them. The more it is believed that a hierarchical control of successive stages of economic activity will benefit the firm rather than using the market or forming coalitions with other firms, the more vertical integration will be practised. The lower the transaction costs of the market and the less the production economies of internalizing transactions, the more the organization of exchange along a value-added chain is likely to be market oriented.

Figure 7.3 illustrates a simple value-added chain of a particular firm's activities. It assumes that the firm is producing a product (Product A) which has four identifiable stages of production (i–iv). Each of these stages may also purchase the output of support or complementary assets as well as the firm's central administrative services. The output of each stage consists of the value of the intermediate goods or services which are either produced by the firm itself or bought from other firms, plus the value added by

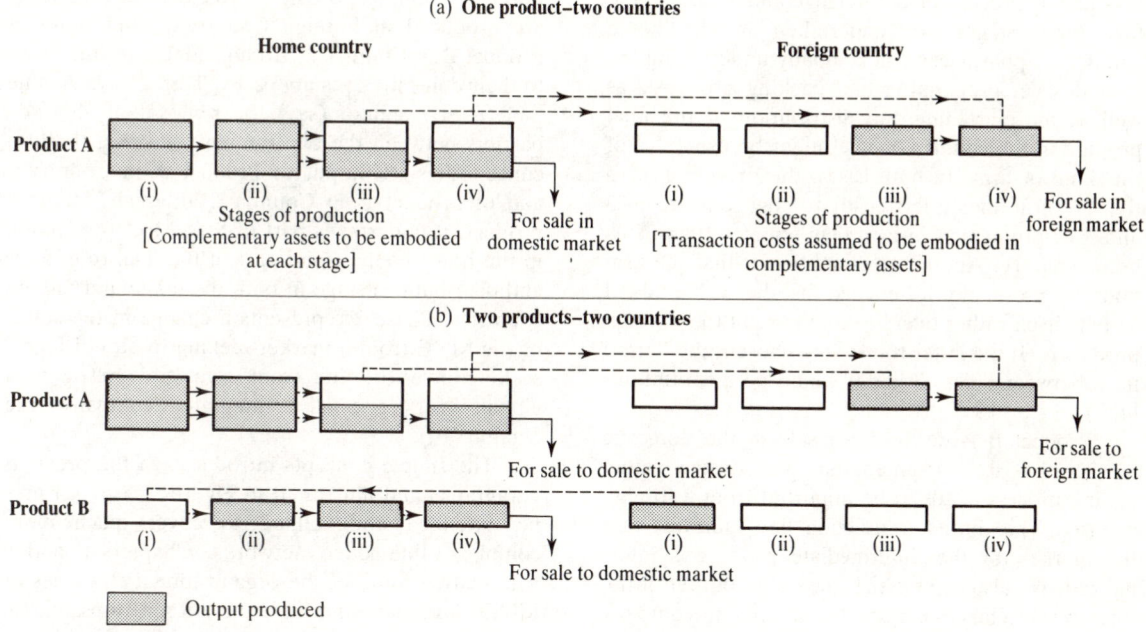

Figure 7.3   The value chain: Two possible phases of an MNE producing in two countries.

that firm. Such value added includes the payment for both production- and transaction-related activities; it also contains a residue of profit (which might be negative) which accrues to the owners of the firm. For the sake of exposition, we shall assume that all transaction costs are included in the costs of complementary assets. No attempt is made to break down the various components of value added (wages, interest, rent, etc). However, these and the prices of intermediate products may vary *inter alia* according to the quantity of the products bought and sold and the efficiency with which they are used to create value-added activities.

A dotted line between the boxes indicates that the two activities are under common ownership and that the transactions are internalized. A continuous line indicates that they are undertaken by independently owned firms and that exchange takes place through the intermediate product market. In Figure 7.3(a), the firm is assumed to be a multi-activity firm (even though it sells only one final product) in that it engages in four stages of the production process. In

stages i and ii a firm produces only in its home country, although part of this output may be exported. In stages iii and iv it produces part of its value added in a foreign country and part in the home country. The firm is also assumed to buy its factor inputs from and to sell its final product to the market.

Figure 7.3(b) takes the analysis a step further. It now assumes that the firm produces two end products (A and B) and that, in each case, it engages in four stages of production. In other words, it is a horizontally diversified and a vertically integrated multi-activity firm. Second, it assumes that at least two of the value-adding stages in the production of both products are located in a foreign country. Third, as well as buying inputs from the factor services market, the firm is assumed to engage in two external transactions between the appropriate boxes.

Figure 7.3 also illustrates the location of the various stages of value-added activity. Product A is intended for sale in a foreign market. The firm is assumed to produce the final two stages of the production process in a foreign country, while the first three stages are undertaken in the home country. A pharmaceutical company undertaking the final dosage, preparation and packing processes as well as the marketing and distribution of the final product in the country of sale might be examples of this kind of firm. In both cases, the presumption is that the firm finds it less costly to engage in stages 3 and 4 of production in a foreign country than in its home country. Another presumption is that the firm finds it profitable to engage in the value-added activity itself rather than license the right to a foreign producer. (If the latter route were chosen, the dotted lines between stages 3 and 4 would be a continuous line.)

Product B is destined for sale in the domestic market, but it is assumed that part of the value-adding process needs to be imported from a foreign country. The dotted transaction line indicates that the market for that intermediate product is internalized. We also assume that the entire output of the foreign subsidiary is exported to the parent company and that the latter relies exclusively on its foreign subsidiary for stage 1 of the production process. In Figure 7.3(b), the fact that the first part of the value-added process is assumed to be undertaken abroad suggests that the MNE is a resource seeker, for example, an aluminium company investing in a bauxite mine in the Caribbean or a rubber company seeking to own plantations in Liberia. However, an MNE might no less invest abroad to take advantage of relatively cheap labour in the later stages of the production process (e.g. investment by a German MNE in the Malaysian semiconductor industry or by a Japanese firm in the Thai textile industry, which might both import intermediate products from and export final products to the parent company or home country).

A final situation is illustrated in Figure 7.4. Here, an MNE is assumed to produce two products (A and B) in four stages of production which are intended for sale in two foreign countries (1 and 2). Consider the possible dynamics of foreign production. In Phase 1*,[3] we assume that the firm undertakes the first stage of production, for example, the research development and design work of each of the products in the home country. Thus it is a multi-domestic MNE (see Section 7.4). The next stage of production of both products is concentrated in

Foreign Country 1; the final two stages of Product A are produced in Foreign Country 1, and those of Product B in Country 2. Both products are then sold to their domestic consumers. In Phase 2*, we assume that, as a result of (say) the removal of all trade barriers between the two foreign countries, the firm concentrates its output of Product A in Country 1 and of Product B in Country 2 although, for each product, it undertakes part of Stage 1 of production in the home country and part of the final (e.g. sales and distribution) stage in both the home and foreign countries. Phase 2 represents a change in the status of the MNE from a market-seeking to an efficiency-seeking investor, and from a multi-domestic to a globally (or regionally) integrated company (see Section 7.4).

The simple concepts introduced in the previous paragraphs and illustrated in Figures 7.2 to 7.4 may be extended and refined to cover much more complex value-added networks. Chapters 8 and 9 will analyse some of the organizational strategies of MNEs and the kind of cross-border transactional relationships that they may form with their affiliates and/or with other firms supplying intermediate products as well as with their other stakeholders (e.g. suppliers of factor services). In most large MNEs, these relationships range from spot-market transactions, through a large range of collaborative arrangements with other firms, to joint ventures and 100% owned affiliates. Thus two firms producing similar products may cooperate on their research and development programmes. An example is the liaison between Philips of Eindhoven and Siemens to fund joint research on the next generation of microchips (UNCTC, 1988; Gugler, 1991). Alternatively, in order to break into a new foreign market a firm may form a joint liaison with a local company more familiar with conditions in that market.

As more firms become globally oriented and more countries generate their own MNEs, we are observing that even the terms and conditions of non-equity transactional relationships are increasingly reflecting the different legal, cultural and business norms of the countries in, or between, which they are conducted. Cross-licensing agreements – a kind of barter or counter-trade in technology – have been commonly practised for many years, as has the sharing of human capabilities or physical resource capacities between firms. What is, however, notice-

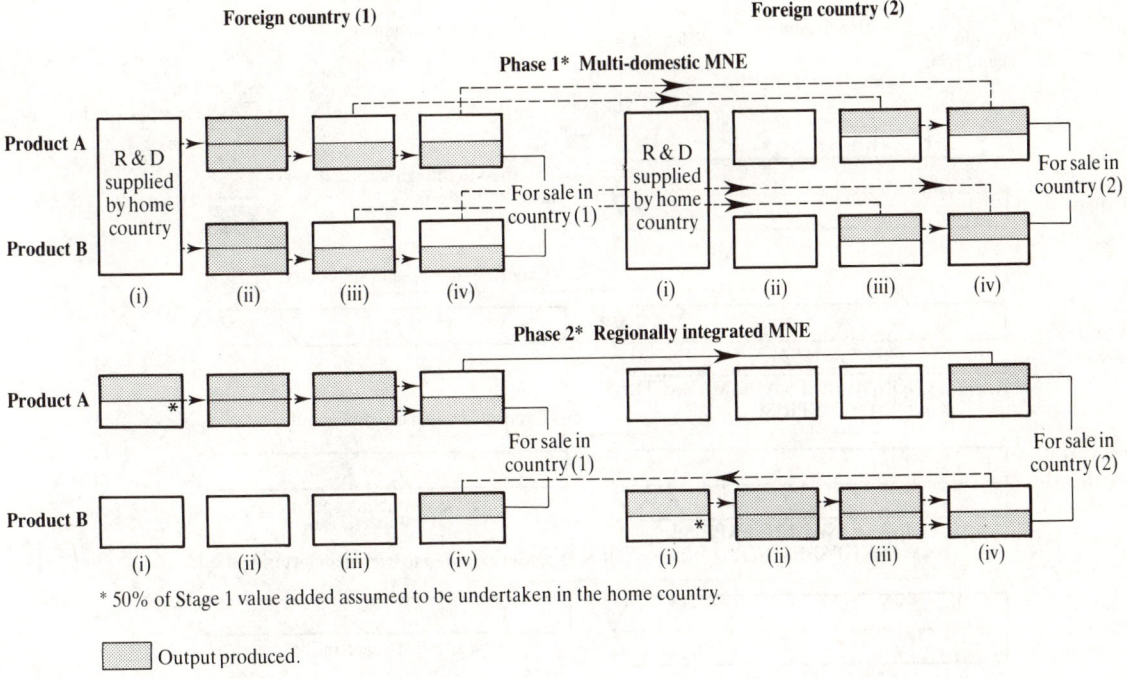

Figure 7.4 The value chain: two possible phases of an MNE producing two products in two countries.

able is the dramatic increase in the number of such collaborative arrangements and the complexity and ingenuity of them. We shall take up these issues in more detail in Chapter 9. The point we wish to emphasize here is that the value-added network of particular products and/or of the total activities of firms is to be explained partly by the value of the OLI variables likely to influence the extent and pattern of foreign production, as identified in Chapter 4, and partly by the strategic responses of firms to these variables.

The following section considers some of the possible phases[4] in the evolution of an MNE from the one prior to the initial act of FDI through to a globally integrated network of cross-border value-added activities. In so doing, it also looks at the alternative strategies open to a firm at each phase of its internationalization process.

7.4 ANALYSIS OF THE INTERNATIONALIZATION PROCESS

7.4.1 Introduction

Let us now briefly review some of the main phases of the internationalization of value-added activities by firms.[5] The following paragraphs take an incremental approach to this process, but it should be stated at the outset that the sequence of events to be described, and illustrated in Figure 7.5, is not necessarily that which firms will follow. While some firms may well go through the five phases identified, others, depending *inter alia* on their motives for foreign economic involvement, may leapfrog over one or more phases. As a final section of this chapter will show, established and globally oriented MNEs are likely to adopt a pluralistic and integrated

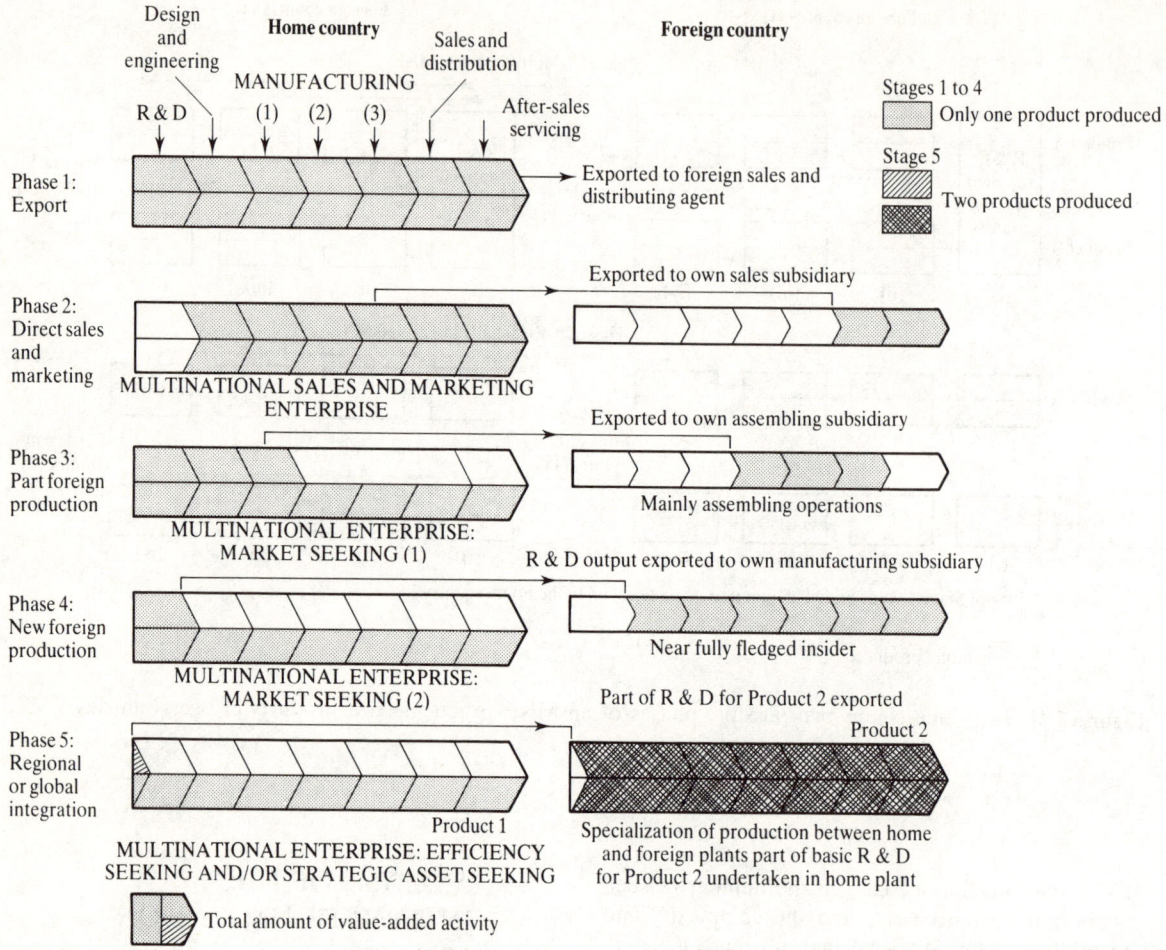

Figure 7.5 The possible evolution of manufacturing multinational enterprise. Source: Adapted from Ohmae (1985, 1987).

approach to their modalities of entering new markets or responding to changes in the world economic environment.

7.4.2   Phase 1: a firm's initial entry into foreign markets

Firms initially engage in transactions across national boundaries for one or two reasons. The first is to acquire inputs (intermediate products) at a lower real cost than they can from domestic sources, or to pre-empt their competitors from gaining access to these inputs. The second is to protect existing or seek out new markets for the output of their domestic value-adding activities. In both cases, however, the decision to become international is just one of several strategic options a firm may pursue. For example, the resources and capabilities which a firm uses in seeking and servicing foreign markets might be better spent on diversifying into new lines of activity in the home market, upgrading its supply capabilities, improving productivity in its domestic factories, or acquiring other domestic companies. At the same time, there is always some uncertainty about the costs involved in entering into a foreign market and the likely size, stability and future prospects of that market. For this reason, the strategic choice of foreign market entry is an important one for any firm.

The mode of a firm's initial entry into foreign production will differ according to the reason for that entry. Consider just three cases. The first is where a firm wishes to export its goods to a new foreign market. On the one hand, because of its relative ignorance or the uncertainties about the local demand conditions, a new entrant – particularly if it is a relatively small firm – might wish to avoid the risks involved in making an investment in a foreign sales or purchasing outlet. Instead, it may prefer to buy the services of a local sales agent, that is, make use of the external market. On the other hand, where a market has to be created for a product, where the product needs to be adapted to the requirements of the buyers, or where multiple products are being marketed and there are advantages of coordinating the sales of these products, or where an efficient after-sales usage, repair and maintenance service is a key ingredient of the product's appeal, a firm may decide that the risk that a foreign sales agent will not meet its needs adequately, outweighs any capital loss of setting up marketing and distribution facilities from the start. Chapter 5 gave some historical illustrations of this form of entry by British MNEs into foreign markets.

The second kind of value-adding activity consists of the production of goods or a service, the buying or selling of which requires a continuing association between the parties to the exchange. This is also the case where the product is idiosyncratic, is sold in small quantities, or is irregularly traded. Here, an initial market entry might take place directly with a supplier or a customer, even though the firm may use the services of a foreign broker to help it search for, or negotiate with, such suppliers or customers. Thus firms selling non-standardized intermediate products (including proprietary rights and managerial services) will tend to sell these products (e.g. license the rights to their use) to other firms which they perceive will best advance their own interests. By contrast, firms buying 'custom made' products from foreign suppliers will tend to develop ongoing contractual relationships with their suppliers.

The third type of FDI is one that generates an output which it is difficult or impossible to trade across space. Examples include goods which are costly to handle or transport, and services which need the instantaneous and joint presence of producers and consumers (e.g. a medical consultancy, wholesale or retail distribution, import merchanting, a theatre performance). In such cases, the seller of the goods or service has to produce it in the country of consumption – an example is the construction of a multi-million-dollar highway in Brazil by foreign construction companies – or the buyer has to travel to the country in which the good or service is produced, as in the case of an Australian tourist seeking to purchase the services of a hotel in Fiji. In the former case, the firm earns income from its investment or the exchange of an intermediate product (e.g. codifiable knowledge). In the second, it earns invisible exports as the service is paid for in foreign currency. The point at issue, however, is that since some products and services cannot be transported over space, a foreign entry must either take the form of a foreign investment or, if the intermediate products are tradeable, of a contractual agreement with a producing firm in that country.

There is, then, no single initial mode of entry into a foreign country. Much will depend on the characteristics of the targeted market, the kinds of goods and services being produced and traded, the market structures in which firms compete and the nature of the cross-border transactional mechanisms. The literature suggests that the value and significance of these variables will be strongly influenced by country-specific economic, legal, political, institutional and cultural considerations.[6] Firm-specific factors, such as the technical capabilities of the trading firm, its experience of foreign markets, its potential stake in the new market, its knowledge about potential buyers and sellers, and the characteristics of these buyers and sellers, will also be relevant. Indeed, as it influences the determinants of trade and production, so the configuration of OLI advantages facing firms will affect their initial entry strategies into foreign markets. Some of these variables are identified in Exhibit 7.1 which might also be used to help explain the dynamics of entry strategy by firms.[7]

Exhibit 7.1 Location and ownership specific factors influencing the strategy of entry mode into foreign markets.

	Generally favours				
	Exporting (through foreign agent)	Licensing	Sales or marketing subsidiary	Production subsidiary	Service contracts
L-specific factors (Foreign country):					
Low sales potential	X	X			
High sales potential			X	X	
Atomistic competition	X		X		
Oligopolistic competition				X	
Poor marketing infrastructure			X		
Good marketing infrastructure	X				
Low production cost				X	
High production cost	X		X		
Restrictive import policies		X		X	X
Liberal import policies	X		X		
Restrictive investment policies	X	X	X		X
Liberal investment policies				X	
Small geographical distance	X		X		
Great geographical distance		X		X	X
Dynamic economy				X	
Stagnant economy	X	X			X
Restrictive exchange controls	X	X			X
Liberal exchange controls				X	
Exchange rate depreciation				X	
Exchange rate appreciation	X		X		
Small cultural distance			X	X	
Large cultural distance	X	X			X
Low political risk			X	X	
High political risk	X	X			X
L-specific factors (Home country):					
Large market				X	
Small market	X		X		
Atomistic competition	X		X		
Oligopolistic competition				X	
Low production cost	X		X		
High production cost		X		X	X
Strong export promotion	X		X		
Restrictions on investment abroad	X	X			X

Exhibit 7.1 continued.

	Generally favours				
	Exporting (through foreign agent)	Licensing	Sales or marketing subsidiary	Production subsidiary	Service contracts
O-specific factors					
Differentiated products	X		X		
Standard products				X	
Service-intensive products			X	X	
Service products		X		X	X
Technology-intensive products		X			
Low product adaptation	X				
High product adaptation		X	X	X	
Limited resources	X	X			
Substantial resources			X	X	
Low commitment	X	X			X
High commitment			X	X	

Source: Adapted from Root (1987).

7.4.3 Phase 2: investment in trade-related facilities

Apart from firms for whom the purchasing or selling of their products can only be accomplished through some kind of physical presence in a foreign market or those who acquire an existing foreign company or those who are selling or buying in specialized or unfamiliar markets where local expertise is especially valuable, most firms regard the use of foreign agents and distributors as a first step towards both market-seeking and resource-seeking FDI. The reasons why firms might wish to internalize the market for both purchasing and selling value-added activities have been explored in Chapters 4 and 5. Essentially, these reduce to a tradeoff between the advantages of securing control over the form, quality and terms of those activities, and the risks associated with the commitment of resources. To the economist, it is primarily a matter of the efficiency of the alternative organizational modes in maximizing revenues and minimizing costs; the costs include both production and transaction costs. The two obvious advantages of using foreign brokers are first their familiarity and experience of local demand or supply conditions, and second their ability to exploit economies of scale and scope of trade-related activities. The most familiar drawbacks are those commonly associated with the principal/agent paradigm, especially where a particular agent serves many principals. These include the costs of ensuring that the distributor or import merchant operates in the best interests of the exporting or importing company (which may include *not* advancing the interests of the latters competitors).

Again it is not difficult to identify the internal and external factors affecting the strategy of firms which might cause them to switch from using foreign sales or purchasing agents to setting up or acquiring marketing or purchasing facilities of their own. Clearly, if a firm did not choose the latter route in the first place, its post-entry country-specific learning experiences and its growth in sales might cause the balance of advantages between using an internal and external market to shift in favour of the former. While there is nothing inevitable about this process, it is likely that the more familiar and experienced a firm is and the larger the buying or selling stake it has in a particular country (e.g. with respect to the volume and type of products traded), the more it will prefer to own its distribution and selling networks. At the same time trade-related FDI may be undertaken by specialist trading companies, the larger of which may also perform a wide range of business services germane to both imports and exports.[8] However, for companies of all nationalities, FDI in trade-related activities is also important. Indeed, in 1985 they accounted for around one-third of the worldwide foreign direct capital stake in services (UNCTC, 1988). Often these trade-related subsidiaries are parts of primary or secondary producing firms. In 1982, for example, 52% of all US-owned trade-related foreign investments were owned by non-service (mainly manufacturing) companies (UNCTC, 1988).

Trade- and marketing-related activities, of course, cover a wide spectrum of functions,[9] and a firm may choose different entry routes for organizing different functions. Advertising responsibilities, for example, might be subcontracted to a specialist foreign firm while after-sales servicing markets might be internalized. The larger European and US retail outlets organize their own multinational buying outlets for their major product lines, but rely on overseas agents for others. The major international airline companies own their own maintenance and repair facilities at some airports, while at others they buy these services from independent local firms. While Japan's Soga Sosha offer a synergistic and tightly controlled package of trading activities,[10] the marketing of Hong Kong products is dispersed among a large number of independent trading firms. In Indonesia, Sri Lanka and Pakistan, state-owned trading companies play a dominant role in both import and export merchanting (Ozawa, 1987b). As in the goods producing sector, the form of organization chosen will depend on its perceived impact on

the revenue-earning capacity of the MNE and the relevant production and transactional costs involved. Broadly speaking, the greater the presence or likelihood of market failure in the various trading functions, the more likely these will be internalized within private or state-owned MNEs.

It should also be recalled that investment in foreign trade-related activities might sometimes be thought of as a first step to the production of goods and services. Indeed, the firm may already be engaged in such activities in other countries. Warehousing is an example. It is only a small step from the storage of finished goods to the holding of intermediate products or kits of parts, which require some inspection, assembling and packaging before being sold to the domestic or export market.

7.4.4   Phase 3: moving forwards or backwards along the value chain

While Phase 2 is a critical step in the evolution of an MNE, both in its own right and because it can lead to further FDI, the amount of resources committed are usually quite small. This is likely to change dramatically as and when a firm starts to engage in the foreign production of goods or services, as opposed to facilitating the sale or purchase of goods and services already produced.

In Figure 7.5 this is depicted as Phase 3 in the evolutionary process. Here, a particular part of the manufacturing process is transferred from the home country to a foreign country. This foreign production might take the place of exports, or of domestic production where the FDI is intended to supply products to the domestic market either in place of domestic production or of production which might be undertaken by local firms in the foreign country. On the other hand, foreign production might supplement or be quite independent of domestic production. In any, or all, of these cases, either a completely new (i.e. greenfield) value-added facility may be set up or an existing facility acquired. We have earlier suggested that the initial entry might be of the Phase 3 variety, or indeed a Phase 1 entry may translate into Phase 2 and cease there.

This model assumes there is a progression from the ownership of mainly transacting facilities to the ownership of both transacting and producing facilities. Where does 'licensing' the property rights of the internationalizing firm to a foreign producer to engage in production enter into the picture? The answer is that so far in our analysis we have treated the export of property rights in the same way as the export of other intermediate products or of final goods. If a company previously exporting final goods to its own marketing affiliates now finds, for one reason or another, that it is strategically or economically desirable to produce part or all of these goods in a foreign country, but it is advantageous to do so by concluding a licensing agreement with a foreign firm rather than undertaking the production itself, then the firm will replace the export of the final product by export of the intermediate product. The final product will then be produced locally and sold to the marketing affiliate.

The scenario of Firm A exporting an intermediate product to Firm B which adds value to it and sells the finished product to Firm A's marketing subsidiary is just one possibility. Where, however, the export of an intermediate product is chosen as an alternative to direct export of the final product, then, depending on the terms of the contract for the sale of the intermediate product, the responsibility for its marketing and distribution could well pass to the licensee. Should a time arise when a firm chooses to engage in foreign production itself, rather than license a foreign firm, then presumably it has to consider the implications for marketing that output. The same argument applies to a possible progression from cross-border subcontracting to backward and vertical integration, as compared with moving directly from multinational buying activities to direct production for export to the investing company.

The literature on the choice between producing a particular goods or service in a domestic production facility and exporting it from there and of producing it in the country in which it is sold (or in a third country) is extensive. Reference may be made to the work of Aliber (1970), Horst (1972b), Hirsch (1976), Swedenborg (1979, 1990), Lipsey and Weiss (1981, 1984), Buckley and Casson (1981), Rugman *et al.* (1985), Grosse (1985), Vernon and Wells (1986), Anderson and Gatignon (1986), Anderson and Coughlan (1987) and Kogut (1988). Chapter 14 looks specifically at the economics of the export *versus* foreign production choice. Most of these studies emphasize the role of comparative manufacturing,

organizational and marketing costs of exporting and local production, as well as expectations about future market size and growth and transport, government-related trade barriers, and incentives and/or disincentives offered to foreign direct investors. In the main, however, the models are static, or comparatively static, rather than dynamic in as much as they compare the economics of production in alternative locations at, or between, particular points of time.

Exceptions include the product cycle model described in Chapter 4, and the work of Aliber (1970) and Buckley and Casson (1981). Aliber, for example, asserted that, as the size of foreign markets grew, FDI would be increasingly favoured relative to exports, especially in countries whose currencies were relatively weak compared with those of the exporting country. Buckley and Casson suggested that the point of switching would be negatively correlated with the relative importance of setup and recurrent fixed costs to the total production costs of the investing firms as well as the way in which increasing familiarization of foreign markets affected the various modes of servicing that market. In addition, they argued that licensing was likely to be the preferred servicing mode whenever both cross-border transport and tariff costs, and the intra-firm governance costs of FDI, were high. As and when these latter costs fall, firms might well be tempted to switch their foreign involvement from licensing to FDI.

Taking a longer-term perspective, the investment development cycle or path (Dunning, 1981b, 1988a) and Ozawa's dynamic paradigm of economic development (1991a) offer an interesting insight into the changing propensity of countries to be outward or inward direct investors according, for example, to their stages of economic development and the structure of their economic activities. While there is no attempt in this model to consider the timing of the switch from one modality of servicing a market to another, the analysis, like that of Farok Contractor (1980), does suggest some reasons why, as the income levels and economic structure of a country changes, the role played by FDI compared with licensing may also change. Chapter 10 takes up this theme in more detail.

In all of these models, trade and licensing are assumed to precede foreign production, rather than being perceived as a learning experience of the input and output markets in foreign countries, or, in the case of trade in intermediate products (e.g. licensing or subcontracting) of foreign production as well. However, this 'experience' value of non-equity forms of cross-border transactions has been noted in various empirical studies. Root (1987), for example, has observed that a firm's knowledge of foreign markets and production conditions is usually a function of time and the extent and form of foreign involvement. But other variables, such as the size of the firm and its interaction with local trading and other enterprises, which may also vary over time, may be no less important. The literature (and this is best typified by the product cycle model) mainly deals with the factors influencing the transition from exports to FDI. The variables influencing the choice between these two modalities are well known. The question is whether or not there is a natural progression from one form of internationalization to another. There are a number of reasons to suggest there are – at least in the case of newly inter-nationalizing firms (Luostarinen, 1987; Luostarinen and Welch, 1990) – but the fact that only a minority of firms which engage in trade also produce abroad suggests that, for the most part, the economics and political economy of production still favour a domestic location. However, the recent growth of all forms of efficiency and strategic asset seeking FDI (see Chapter 2) by well established MNEs or those wishing to complement their assets or governance advantages with those of other (and foreign) firms, suggests that some of the earlier explanations of the ways in which firms internalize their value-added activities may be less relevant than once they were.

Let us now consider some of the variables influencing the form of the internationalization process of firms. The relevance of these variables is likely to be country, industry and firm specific.

(i) *The experience factor* While this is obviously of greater relevance where some foreign production has already occurred, even experience accumulated in trade-related activities may be helpful to the decision as to whether or not to engage in FDI or some collaborative production arrangement with a foreign firm. Such experience includes that acquired as a result of exchange relationships with suppliers, customers, competitors and governments. Moreover, a trade-related presence may provide a firm with a

better idea of its own capacity for foreign pro-duction, or that of local firms to supply its inter-mediate inputs. It might also provide it with an insight into foreign technology and organizational structures and the kind of product adaptations may need to be made to meet the needs of foreign customers. In short, a trade-related or marketing subsidiary may provide a potential foreign investor with a useful insight into the prospects and oppor-tunities for foreign production and, in so doing, reduce the setup and transaction costs associated with that production.

(ii) *Economies of size* As and when local or regional markets enlarge, the economic viability of setting up or acquiring a foreign production facility is likely to increase. The extent to which this actually leads to FDI depends largely on the types of intermediate or final products supplied, the nature of production processes utilized and the quality of the local supply capabilities. If the domestic production process is capital intensive, or demands a lot of specialized equipment and highly trained labour, and if it cannot be easily scaled down, then it may be a long time before local production is started. If the optimum scale of plant is small and local inputs are readily and cheaply available, then foreign pro-duction may not simply replace exports at an early stage; it may be the initial modality of entry into the foreign market. It should be observed that the optimum level and locational requirements of pro-duction are likely to vary between the different stages of value-added activity, as, indeed, may the cross-border transport and transaction costs associated with these and other value-added activities. Thus some activities (e.g. dosage preparation for pharma-ceutical products) can be more easily scaled down and adapted to local factor endowments (see Section (iii) below), while others (e.g. the preparation of pharmaceutical chemicals), which are subject to the economies of scale of production or where pro-duction needs to be closely linked to other activities carried on in the home plant, may be less locationally mobile.

(iii) *The dynamics of supply capabilities and flexi-bility of production process* The more value-added activities can be adapted to the supply capabilities and market needs of the foreign country, then the more foreign production is likely to be started earlier than it would otherwise be. Moreover, over time many of these capabilities can be elevated by improved training and education, upgrading the quality of resources and stimulating local entrepreneurship, as well as by the provision of appropriate support facilities (e.g. roads, utilities, telecommunications) and the development of more efficient production methods and organizational techniques. Sometimes, these improvements may be undertaken by the firms themselves, whereas in some countries, they are likely to be provided by national or regional governments financed by regional or international agencies, such as the World Bank and Asian Development Bank. As Chapter 4 showed, as countries move through various stages of the development process, their capacity to attract inward investment changes. The question as to how far MNEs may be able or willing to behave differently abroad than at home is dependent on the variables affecting that behaviour and their strategic reactions to these variables. Both positive incentives (e.g. tax concessions, investment allowances, regional subsidies) and negative incentives (e.g. threat of loss of markets as a result of government procurement schemes designed to favour local producers, import controls, and the adverse actions of competitors) could encourage or impel firms to find acceptable ways of producing locally and of incurring the relevant structural adjustment costs. On the other hand, where the O advantages of potential investors are home-country specific and cannot easily be transferred across national boundaries, this may inhibit foreign production. For example, the jury is still out on whether or not the Keiretsu type advantages enjoyed by Japanese firms in Japan can be successfully transplanted, or adapted, to foreign cultures.

(iv) *Import barriers and/or export incentives* As a market for a particular product currently being imported expands, the government of the importing country may wish to encourage its local production. To do so, it might impose a variety of import restrictions (e.g. tariff, non-tariff barriers, quotas) which, in effect, will raise the transfer or spatial transaction costs of the exporting firms. Alternatively, to promote exports it may not only give various incentives (identified in part in Section (iii))

to attract export-oriented subsidiaries in their country, but to offer export subsidies to existing foreign affiliates. The effect is clearly to raise the cost of importing or lower the cost of exporting to the extent that local production will be encouraged. Whether this will be an economically viable alternative to importing or alternative patterns of production depends on whether the firm can cover its opportunity costs (suitably discounted for risk) either at the time of its initial entry into a foreign market or in the foreseeable future. It will also depend on whether the firm believes that a presence in the market is necessary to achieve its strategic objectives. In either case, import restrictions are rarely the only (and, even more rarely, the most appropriate) instrument used by governments to promote inward investment. More often than not they are accompanied by a gamut of trade-related investment measures (TRIMs) and/or performance requirements. The efficiency of these and other government actions to encourage or discourage FDI are dealt with in Chapter 20.

(v) *Behaviour of competitors* In Chapter 4 we discussed the 'follow my leader' and 'exchange of threats' international strategies of firms competing in international oligopolistic markets. We suggested that the securing of incremental markets might not only help to lower the average fixed costs of the investing firm (e.g. by spreading R&D and marketing outlays over larger volumes of output) but that it might also prevent a competitor from taking advantage of these economies of size or scope. In such a situation, it follows that once foreign production becomes worthwhile, a group of MNEs might set up production units even though it might not be profitable for some or all, since it would be even less profitable if they stayed out of the market altogether. Naturally, this bunching of FDI will not always occur; in some instances the size of the local or regional market may just not be sufficient to accommodate more than one or two producers. Moreover, even if and when it does take place, it need not do so in the same countries, particularly where the investment is designed to produce products for the export market.

(vi) *Cross-border transport costs* It is fairly obvious that the transport costs of shipping intermediate and final products will influence the optimum location of value-added activity. In general, the more significant the transport costs of intermediate products, which lose their weight in subsequent value-added activities (e.g. energy and some minerals), the more likely production will be sited near to the source of these inputs; while the more ubiquitous the location of intermediate products and the higher the cost of transporting the finished products to the ultimate consumers, the more likely it is that the location of production will be nearer the market. The relative significance of transport to other costs of production is also a relevant consideration.

(vii) *Cross-border administration costs* As Hirsch (1976) pointed out several years ago, FDI involves its own cross-border administrative (and other transaction) costs which are in addition to those incurred in exporting or importing from independent firms. The significance of such intra-firm organizational costs, which are mainly borne at the time of the initial FDI made in a particular market, are likely to be highly country (or culture) specific (compare those associated with US investment in Canada to Italian investment in Australia and Japanese investment in Ireland). They will also vary according to the size of the investing firm and its experience in foreign markets as well as to the kind of foreign value activities being contemplated. For example, the frequency and nature of intra-firm transactions will be very different in the case of a 'stand-alone' FDI designed to meet the very specific needs of the local market, than in one which is closely controlled by the parent company and which is intended to supply intermediate products for sale to other subsidiaries of the MNE. Cross-border administration costs are also likely to be positively related to the psychic distance between the investing and recipient countries.

7.4.5   Phase 4: deepening and widening of the value-added network

The literature suggests that most initial greenfield (but not acquired) market-seeking MNE activity tends to be in comparatively low value-adding activities – which are usually at the final assembling or initial processing stage of the value-adding chain.

These activities usually require the least investment in human competencies and physical capital, and hence involve the least risk. If successful, and, if and when markets expand, local supply capabilities improve or host governments offer more incentives, then more of the upstream higher value-added activities set out in Figure 7.5 may be transferred from the home to the host country. This is precisely what is currently happening in the case of Japanese FDI in auto production in both the US and the EC. Increasingly, such firms have become 'insiders', either by undertaking an increasing proportion of their sales themselves or, depending on the relative production and transaction costs, by buying them from local firms in the local market. In Figure 7.5, we assume that all but the R&D stage of production of a market-seeking MNE is transferred to the country of marketing (or another foreign country).

In the case of resource-based FDI, which is primarily prompted by the presence of location-bound endowments, the initial entry is intended less to replace existing import markets than to internalize them. While the locational options for the secondary processing of the natural resources are often wider, these downstream operations frequently require more sophisticated human and physical assets than are initially possessed by many of the countries that own the resources. Again, as economic development proceeds and the experience of the foreign affiliates engaged in primary production increases, the parent companies may be willing to invest more in secondary processing operations, particularly if prompted by host governments. Examples include forward vertical integration by US crude oil producers in Canada into refining and petrochemical operations, UK gold mining MNEs in Southern Africa moving into the manufacturing of ingots, and Korean-owned fishing companies in Canada and the US going into fish processing operations.

The sequential growth of MNE activity may take several other forms. One is a widening of the range of products produced by foreign subsidiaries. In this case, the number of value-added chains in which there is a component of foreign production is increased. At first, the value-added activities of a greenfield are likely to be a truncated version of those undertaken in the home country. The foreign subsidiary is likely to produce the products that offer the best (and most secure) rates of return, while other products supplied by the MNE may continue to be imported from the parent company or another foreign subsidiary. This could (though not necessarily) lead to other products being produced. One example is a UK-owned biscuit subsidiary in Canada, which initially supplied its standard lines of shortcake biscuit and imported specialized product lines from its parent company, but now produces a more comprehensive range of biscuits in Ontario. Another is Japanese electronic MNEs initiating their production in the UK with colour TV sets but later branching out to produce video recorders, microwave ovens and refrigerators.

More generally, such a widening of the product base (i.e. horizontal diversification of the subsidiary) is likely to occur either where there are opportunities of economies of scope to the subsidiary as well as to the parent company, or where for offensive or defensive strategic reasons an MNE perceives a need to diversify its foreign asset base. In this latter case, such sequential investment will normally take place through an acquisition, merger or strategic alliance.

Another form of sequential involvement is for an MNE, which has successfully penetrated one foreign market, to move into another (usually adjacent) market. In her historical analysis, Wilkins (1970, 1974) tells how the markets in successive Latin American countries were penetrated by American MNEs. Investment by leading European MNEs in sub-Saharan Africa before the First World War followed a similar pattern (Franko, 1976; Archer, 1986). More recently the geographical structure of Japanese MNE activity in Western Europe has considerably widened since the first foray by Japanese firms into the UK in the early 1970s. Much incremental FDI by Hong Kong and Taiwanese firms in South East Asia has taken the form of setting up greenfield ventures or acquiring existing firms in an increasing number of countries.

Finally, it is often the case that both resource- and market-seeking foreign investment by one group of firms might encourage investment by others. These include not only competitors, as previously described, but also suppliers and customers. Thus the substantial investments in the UK by Ford and General Motors in the UK in the inter-war years led to a large number of US component suppliers following them. Similarly, the presence of local resource-producing companies (e.g. oil exploration

companies) may lead to investment by foreign downstream specialists, such as petrochemical or synthetic fibre companies. In the past, FDI by primary or manufacturing companies has prompted supporting investment by service companies, including construction companies, banks, insurance companies, advertising agencies, hotels, car rentals and restaurants (UNCTC, 1988). Such investment is rarely trade replacing; the major question is whether the potential investors choose to undertake the value-adding activities, based on their O-specific advantages, themselves, or sell the right to do so (e.g. via licensing, franchising, management contracts) to independent foreign producers. This particular issue is taken up in Chapter 8.

In summary, if successful, an initial act of foreign production creates its own momentum and is likely to lead to sequential investment either (or both) in the form of vertical integration or horizontal diversification, as well as to the encouragement of related and supportive activities. A possible exception to this general statement is where one firm acquires another to gain certain assets, but sheds others which add little to its existing competitive advantages. Since this kind of FDI – along with the conclusion of cross-border strategic alliances – is becoming a more important component of MNE activity, the dynamics of the internationalization set out in the previous paragraphs may need some reappraisal. However, there can be no doubt of the growing plurality of the routes towards the globalization of production and markets. Neither can it be disputed that changes in the external economic and technological environment facing MNEs or potential MNEs are causing existing routes to be reappraised and new routes to be fashioned.

The dynamic relationship between the equity and non-equity modalities of foreign involvement is equally difficult to generalize about. On the one hand, licensing and other cooperative arrangements might be used by a firm as a means of testing the strengths and prospects of a foreign market – which, if proven, might subsequently lead to FDI. On the other, as development proceeds and local supply capabilities improve, or as and when the O-specific advantages of an inward investor are dissipated, foreign-owned production may give way to some form of cross-border licensing, management or marketing service agreement.

7.4.6 Phase 5: towards the regional or global integration of the value network

In their foreign market entry and expansion strategies, most MNEs coordinate, at least to some extent, their foreign and domestic operations. If they did not, there would be no point in their making the FDI in the first place. Chapter 9 will examine in more detail some of the cross-border organizational mechanisms which an MNE might adopt. For the moment, we would observe that it is possible to conceive of a continuum of control over foreign production which ranges from zero to complete; that this control may be exercised for a variety of reasons, only one of which is to coordinate foreign and domestic activities; and that the degree of control and coordination exercised will vary over time (e.g. with learning and experience) according to industry-, firm- and country-specific factors.

In its discussion of efficiency seeking or rationalized investment, Chapter 3 was mainly concerned with the kinds of value-added *activities* in which MNEs engage. But well before such foreign production takes place, there are certain decisions which affect the prosperity of resource-seeking or market-seeking affiliates, which are likely to be centrally controlled and coordinated by the parent company. Examples include those related to R&D and capital expenditure, accounting procedures and market servicing. The rationalization of international production is but one step in the process towards the regional or global integration of intra-firm production and transactions.

Phase 5 in the evolution of an MNE investment envisages a distribution of value-added activities between the home and foreign countries rather similar to that described between two foreign countries in Figure 7.4 (Phase 2*). In this phase, the parent and the subsidiary produce different products, each of which is sold in world or regional markets, and, in practice, frequently traded within the MNE. Part of the R&D for each product is also undertaken at the location of the subsequent stages of production. This phase is then different from the preceeding four, each of which was concerned with the geographical allocation of the stages of production of a particular product along the value chain.[11]

Clearly, if and when this fifth phase in the evolution of an MNE (illustrated in Figure 7.5) is reached, will depend on a variety of factors, including the range and types of products it is supplying, the extent to which product or process specialization may lead to economies of plant size or scope, the countries in which the investment is currently being made, the ease with which intermediate or final products can be traded across national boundaries, the intra-firm transaction costs involved and the attitude and strategy of the MNE towards the management of its foreign value-added activities. Such intra-firm product specialization and integration of markets is likely to be accompanied by a sharp increase in the trade between the production units and/or between the affiliates and their parent companies. Chapter 14 will show that the kinds of activities associated with intra-firm trade have a number of industry-, country- and firm-specific characteristics. Among the activity-specific characteristics are the opportunities to exploit plant economies of scale and the importance of intra-firm transport and other transfer costs. The most important country characteristic is that there are few or no physical barriers to trade. Only MNEs that take a geocentric view of their foreign operations and which believe that they have to coordinate their domestic and foreign operations are likely to practise a strategy of cross-border plant specialization.

There are still comparatively few MNEs that practise a globally integrated product and/or process strategy of a Phase 5 kind, and hardly any of them have developed a genuine reciprocal resource and organizational relationship between their various production units (Hedlund, 1986; Bartlett and Ghoshal, 1989). The handful that have evolved to this phase include some of the larger motor vehicle, consumer electronics and computer companies, such as Ford, Philips, IBM and Fujitsu. Yet even these may not be prepared to allow the management of all their subsidiaries to participate in decisions about the configuration of all their value-added activities, notably R&D. More often, product strategies are likely to be based on an intra- rather than inter-regional allocation of resources. Thus Kenichi Ohmae (1985, 1987) believes that an increasing number of MNEs in the technologically advanced sectors will be forced to adopt global marketing and/or production strategies to cover the increasing costs of R&D, and, for economic protectionist reasons, be required to establish a sizeable presence in the US, Western Europe and Japan – the so-called Triad. There may be some specialization of activity *between* countries in the Triad but there may also be such specialization between countries *within* the Triad, for example, within the EC. The question of whether regionalization of production by MNEs is a step towards globalization, or is a substitute for it in the presence, or likelihood of intra-regional trade and investment barriers is yet to be resolved.[12]

As the following chapter will show, the organization of foreign production is currently undergoing considerable change. It is not just the activities of the fully owned affiliates of MNEs which are being restructured, but all cross-border transactional relationships, including exporting and all forms of cooperative alliances. International joint ventures and non-equity alliances are an integral part of the strategy of efficiency- and asset-seeking MNEs. In some instances, they may serve their interests better than FDI. These changes are affecting both the route towards and the form of internationalization. Contemporary thinking about the MNEs of the 1990s – and we shall explore this subject in greater detail in Chapter 22 – suggests that they will come to resemble the nerve centres of clusters of inter- and intra-firm relationships, bound together by common entrepreneurial vision and organizational technological expertise in each of the markets in which they operate. The value network relationship, however, will be much more multi-pronged and varied than in the past, partly because technological and organizational advances have opened up new forms of transnational relationships and partly because the costs and benefits of these relationships differ so much according to the activities and the parties involved in the exchange. At the same time, depending on the nature of the non-equity inter-firm linkages, there may be no reason why they cannot be fully integrated into a network of cross-border equity relationships already forged by MNEs.

7.5 ENTRY AND EXPANSION STRATEGIES: TOWARDS A MORE PLURALISTIC AND INTEGRATED APPROACH

7.5.1 Introduction

Previous sections have shown that while a sequential approach to the internationalization of business activity has considerable merit, particularly as it describes the initial stages of entry into foreign markets, a more pluralistic and integrated approach is needed when viewed from the perspective of the growth of MNE activity and the changing organizational form of such activity. Most contemporary multinationals engage in a wide variety of cross-border transactions, each of which is related to the other, yet is part of the international strategy of the firm. For example, trade in goods and services of MNEs might be independent of investment and contractual agreements, but usually it will be dependent on, or influence, these activities. The extent to which licensing may be preferred to equity investment will be affected by the balance between control needs, resource commitments and the perceived risks of the two alternatives, as well as by the experience the choosing company has in FDI and related activities. The kind of strategic alliances concluded by MNEs is also likely to depend on the structure of the equity and non-equity linkages they already possess.

A review of the most recent literature of the strategies of MNEs towards their entry into new markets and of their expansion in existing markets suggests that two main theoretical strands are now emerging. The first is an eclectic approach based primarily on the dynamics of the cross-border organization and exploiting of the O advantages of a firm. The second looks on the firm as part of a network of cross-border value-added activities. It seeks to view the internationalization of the firm as an interactive process between its own competitive advantages and that of the rest of the network, and also between both these advantages and the L attractions of countries. The general characteristics of each have been described in Chapter 4 in so far as they were relevant to the understanding of the determinants of FDI. We now consider the relevance of the eclectic paradigm to our understanding of the internationalization strategies of MNEs.

7.5.2   An eclectic approach

This approach, which is identified with the work of Anderson and Gatignon (1986, 1987), Kogut (1989b), Contractor (1990) and Hill *et al*. (1990) attempts to identify the main country-, industry- and firm-specific determinants (the contextual variables influencing the configuration of OLI variables identified in Chapter 4) that are likely to determine the mode of a firm's entry and growth in foreign value-added activities. Each of the above scholars tends to take as given the competitive or O advantages of firms and the competitive or L attractions of countries, and seeks to identify and evaluate determinants of the way in which a firm will utilize and coordinate these advantages. Anderson and Gatignon (1986), for example, distinguish between four governance structures, *viz* a wholly owned subsidiary, a majority owned equity holding, a balanced partnership and a minority partnership. Kogut (1989b) focuses his attention on three entry modes, *viz* acquisition, joint venture and a greenfield investment. Hill *et al*. (1990) and Contractor (1990) are both interested in a different trio of factors, *viz* the choice between a 100% subsidiary, a joint venture and a licensing agreement.

Essentially, each of the scholars suggests that the determinants of the entry mode reduces to optimizing the configuration of three factors. The first is the need of firms for governance or control over the O assets at their disposal (or those which they might wish to acquire). Hill *et al*. (1990) define this need as 'authority over operational and strategic decision taking'. The second is the extent and pattern of resource commitments required by firms to exploit these advantages. These embrace the dedicated tangible and intangible assets which cannot be deployed elsewhere without some kind of loss. The third factor is the perceived risks associated with the commitment of these assets. These include the kinds of transaction costs identified in Chapter 4, most noticeably, the possibility that O-specific assets might be inappropriately used by a joint venture partner or contractee to the competitive disadvantage of the supplying firm. These alternative entry modes are then related to variables affecting the decision. Hill *et al*. (1990) group these into exogenous or environmental, and endogenous or firm-specific variables. The first include cultural distance, country-specific risks and the volatility of competition among firms. The second comprise strategic-related variables, which embrace some of the transaction costs identified in Chapter 4, as well as a range of firm-specific characteristics such as size and experience of foreign markets.

On the basis of these variables, a number of propositions can be derived which predict the type of entry modes adopted by MNEs. *Inter alia* these suggest that firms pursuing a geocentric strategy and who perceive the need for a close coordination of cross-border activities will prefer high control modes of entry. When cultural distance, resource commitments and volatility of competition are all high, a low control route is likely to be preferred. When demand conditions are unstable or uncertain and MNEs are inexperienced in foreign markets, then they will favour a route involving relatively few resource commitments and low risk. When firms find it easy to enforce contract provisions, when the technology transferred is codifiable and when there are high organizational costs, the licensing route is the one most likely to be preferred.

As yet there have been only a few attempts to test these hypotheses explicitly. Two exceptions are studies by Kogut (1990) and Anderson and Coughlan (1987). Kogut's study tested two basic propositions with respect to the modality of new ventures of some 228 entries into the US between 1976 and 1983. The first was that the greater the cultural distance of the country of the investing firm from the US, the more a joint venture was likely to be established in preference to a 100% greenfield venture or an acquisition. The second was that the more the culture of the investing firm is characterized by uncertainty avoidance, the less likely it is that a firm would choose the acquisition mode. Using a multinational logit model, Kogut established strong statistical support for the first proposition. He also demonstrated that the effect of cultural distance was to significantly increase the probability of choosing a joint venture over an acquisition.

At the same time, Kogut also found that other variables were significant discriminators. For example, the larger the size of the US partner, the more likely a firm would choose to enter the US market via a joint venture than an acquisition. Non-US firms involved in R&D-intensive activities appear to prefer joint ventures and greenfield ventures – indeed, acquisitions appear to be discouraged in high R&D intensive sectors. Advertising intensity – a proxy for O-specific advantages based on branding or product differentiation – appears to be negatively (but not significantly) related to joint ventures and greenfield investments.

In one of their studies, Anderson and Gatignon (1987) used data from the Harvard Multinational Enterprise project embracing some 1267 foreign subsidiaries set up in 87 countries by the 180 largest US MNEs between 1960 and 1975. They tested for a wide group of industry-, country- and firm-specific variables and, like Kogut, used a two-stage multinational logit model. The first stage concerned the decision of a firm regarding whether or not to integrate their cross-border activities. They found that unified governance was closely and positively related to the R&D and advertising intensity of the firm and to its experience with foreign entries. By contrast, firms contemplating investments in high risk countries or where the socio-cultural distance between the investing and recipient countries was considerable, were more likely to opt for a partnership. Legal restrictions also tended to increase the utility of partnership arrangements. The second stage was to evaluate which of the three partnership methods were likely to be chosen. In general, the findings were consistent with those of the first stage, except that R&D intensity and country risk did not appear to influence the choice of partnership modes.

We have taken examples from just two empirical studies on the determinants of entry modes, both of which seem to confirm the propositions put forward by the eclectic approach. They are also generally supportive of the empirical studies on the determinants of foreign production outlined in Chapter 6. This subject will be discussed again when considering the transfer of technology in Chapter 12.

7.5.3   A network approach

A rather different approach to the modality of entry or growth of MNE activity is currently being taken by organizational scholars who stress the firm-specific advantages which arise from being part of a network of complementary activities and who view the internationalization process as one which is dependent on the advantages of cooperative cross-border relationships – especially between buyers and sellers.

The thesis of the network scholars (e.g. Johanson and Mattson, 1987a, 1987b) is that, since firms are dependent on each other in the networks in which they operate, their activities need to be coordinated. However, rather than being affected by the market or individual hierarchies, this coordination occurs through the web of transactions forged by firms engaging in a series of bilateral exchange relationships. These relationships take time and effort to establish and develop, and their precise form will depend not just on the immediate interests of the firm, but on how it affects the efficiency of the network as a whole (and hence, in the long run, its own efficiency).

Relationships in the network are assumed to be both competitive and complementary. They are also cumulative and changing. Clearly, a firm may develop its own internal network of relationships or it may engage in some kind of external bonding. According to Johanson and Mattson, the extent to which it chooses the latter depends on its role *vis à vis* the firms with which it is most likely to establish the closest external relationships as well as on the transaction costs and benefits associated with being dependent on resources controlled by other firms. The costs are similar to those identified by the internalization economists. The benefits include the assets and opportunities to which the firm may have better access.

The network modes approach to understanding the internationalization of value-added activity is still in its infancy; its protagonists offer few predictions which the eclecticists do not. However, whereas the latter approach views inter-firm relationships as formal dyadic, short-term and combative, the network approach views them as custom-related, multi-faceted, long term and cooperative. Because of these differences, the perceptions of the transactional costs involved in the two kinds of external relationships are also likely to differ. In turn, these perceptions are partly culture specific. For example, Japanese- and French-owned firms seem more prepared to engage in the kinds of relationship (conducive to successful networking) than are US- and UK-owned firms. This is one reason why Japanese-owned auto assemblers in the US are replicating some of the domestic transactional relationships as their component suppliers set up subsidiaries in the US or engage in joint ventures or licensing agreements with US-owned firms.

Since they address somewhat different issues, it is unlikely that the network model of internationalization will replace that of the eclectic model. However, as firms become more dynamic and more pluralistic in the extent and form of their foreign value activities, it seems likely that they will take a holistic approach to the multitude of relationships they forge with foreign firms. To this extent, the network approach offers a useful variant of the traditional models of inter-firm relationships – a point to which we shall return in Chapter 9.

7.6   CONCLUSIONS

After discussing the concept of the value-added chain and its relevance for understanding the foreign activities of MNEs, this chapter has traced some of the main entry strategies into foreign value-added activities which might be pursued by firms that previously engaged only in domestic production. It has also discussed some of the phases of internationalization a firm may pursue.

We would emphasize, once again, that there is nothing inevitable about the movement of a firm's value-added activities through the phases described. Nor are these the only foreign entry and growth strategies which a firm may pursue. Indeed, we have suggested that much of the literature on the internationalization process is less relevant to much of the foreign production now being undertaken by established MNEs from developed countries than it was to explaining the early market-seeking and resource-based FDIs, or those currently being pursued by Third World or *de novo* MNEs. Clearly, too, the modality of a firm's global involvement will be related to its organizational structure, information systems and governance procedures. To understand the pattern of incremental and sequential investment by firms as well as the various cooperative alliances being forged by them, new models or conceptual frameworks are required – perhaps on the lines of the network approach earlier described. It should

also be emphasized that the form of entry by firms into new foreign markets or that of the expansion or restructuring of existing FDI will be determined by the industry- and country-specific characteristics and by the strategic response of firms to the OLI configurations with which they are faced.

NOTES

1 For a review of this literature see, for example, Putterman (1986) and Ricketts (1987).

2 Though some products may be either intermediate or final depending on whether they are sold to the final consumer or are bought by producers for further value-adding activities. A rubber tyre is an example.

3 We use the numbering 1*, 2* to distinguish these phases from those described in Section 7.4 of this chapter.

4 We use the word 'phase' rather than 'stage' as we prefer to use the latter to describe the steps in a nation's development process.

5 For a more extensive account of the internationalization process, the reader is invited to consult the writings of a number of Scandinavian business scholars, particularly those of Luostarinen (1987) and Luostarinen and Welch (1990).

6 In a study on the variables influencing the mode of market entry into a foreign country by some 250 US manufacturers, the author classified countries according to whether they were 'hot', 'moderate' or 'cold'. Hot countries were characterized by stable governments, favourable market opportunities, advanced levels of economic development and performance, and low legal, physiographical, theological and geocultural barriers. Cold countries had the opposite characteristics, while moderate countries revealed characteristics that lay in between. The findings show that as companies move from hot to cold countries they increasingly depend on export entry and decreasingly on investment in local production. For the average hot country, exporting represented 47.2% of all entry modes, investment in local production 28.5% and licensing and mixed modes 24.3%. But for the average cold country, exporting represented 82.6% of all entry modes, investment in local production represented 2.9% and licensing of mixed modes took care of the remainder (Root, 1987, quoting from Goodnow and Hansz, 1972).

7 In this volume, we devote only two or three pages to this important topic. For an excellent, in depth discussion of entry strategies, the reader is advised to consult Root (1987).

8 The general trading companies are *par excellence* examples of diversified MNEs, the O advantages of which stem both from their ability to coordinate many different kinds of complementary trade-related activities (including shipping, insurance, foreign exchange transactions and information gathering) and from their privileged access to both intermediate and final product markets. For a description of the different strategies pursued by the general trading companies from thirteen countries in Asia, see Ozawa (1987b).

9 These include commission, brokerage, wholesaling, retail distribution, consignment sales, warehousing, shipping, finance, project organizing, information gathering, marketing research, insurance and consulting.

10 Indeed, as Ozawa (1987b, p. 12) has put it, general trading companies may be described as the 'departmental store of trade services'.

11 Although, *de facto*, an MNE may produce more than one product and the geographical distribution of the activities along the value-added chain across national boundaries may differ between these products.

12 The OECD is currently undertaking some interesting work on this subject. See also Hamel and Prahalad (1985), Bartlett and Ghoshal (1989), Stopford and Strange (1991) and Morrison, Ricks and Roth (1991).

CHAPTER 8

THE ORGANIZATION OF MNE ACTIVITY: INTRA-FIRM RELATIONSHIPS

8.1 INTRODUCTION

It has long been recognized that the way in which a firm organizes and coordinates its value-added activities will not only influence the efficiency at which its competitive or O-specific advantages are utilized, but may also constitute a valued competence in its own right. It was Alfred Chandler (1962, 1977b, 1990) who first emphasized the importance of organizational innovation as a factor influencing the emergence and growth of the large US enterprise in the latter part of the 19th century, particularly those which led firms to shift their transactions of intermediate products (at dependent stages of the value-added chain) from external markets to managed hierarchies.[1]

Chandler further suggested that such organizational change, which, he accepted, was initially triggered by a series of technological innovations and the emergence of managerial capitalism earlier in the 19th century, would necessitate a fundamental restructuring of the locus and geography of decision taking. As the size of firms and the roundaboutness of production increased, so did the number and complexity of intra-firm transactions. In consequence, it became important more clearly to delineate and define the boundaries of managerial responsibility and authority and the lines of communication between the headquarters of a company, its regional and branch offices, and its operating units. Likewise, a replacement of external markets by administrative fiat meant it was necessary to construct more formalized incentive systems, control mechanisms, communication channels and administrative procedures to guide internal decision takers.

In examining the implication of these changes

for the internal governance of firms, Chandler argued that the unitary (U) structure of organization – in which decision-taking responsibility was linked to stages in the value-added chain or the transactions associated with these stages – became less suitable as a firm became more diversified along its value-added chains or in its input or output markets. He suggested that its interests were likely to be better served by a multi-divisional (M) structure, that is, a hierarchical division of labour based on the products produced or the geographical areas served, rather than on the functions performed by a firm.

We have already asserted in Chapter 1 that the distinctive feature of an MNE is that it is a geographically diversified multi-activity firm. We have further suggested – and will elaborate on this point further in this chapter – that the entry of a firm into foreign production imposes additional, and quite different, demands on its organizational structure and the distribution of its decision-taking responsibilities. These consequences are likely to be most marked in the case of globally integrated MNEs where traditional organizational norms based on vertical and unidimensional hierarchical relationships are proving increasingly ineffective.

With these introductory remarks in mind, this chapter considers the structure of the internal governance of MNEs. It suggests that the ways in which an MNE coordinates its domestic and foreign value-added activities (from the purchasing of factor services and intermediate products, through the various stages of production to the marketing and post sales servicing of the final products) and the determination of *which* activities to engage in and where to locate them, crucially affect not only its global marketing and production strategies, but also how these impact on the home and host economies in which it operates.

In this chapter, we shall address four main organizational questions.[2] First, we shall describe and evaluate some of the organizational structures that MNEs adopt and how these have changed as they have become a more important force in the world economy. Second, we shall examine some patterns of the locus of decision taking within MNEs, in particular, the extent to which decisions are taken at the headquarters of MNEs or are shared between different parts of the organization. Third, we shall offer some explanations as to why MNEs choose to organize their internal markets and decision-taking processes in the ways in which they do. In doing so, we shall pay especial attention to the importance of country-, industry- and firm-specific characteristics influencing the nature, extent and location of MNE activity and the strategies of MNEs towards international production. Fourth, we shall examine the ways in which differences in organizational structures and patterns of decision-taking procedures may affect the likely economic impact of FDI on the home and host countries in which they operate, as well as the responses of MNEs to policies pursued by the authorities of these countries.

8.2 THE ORGANIZATIONAL FUNCTION: SOME GENERAL OBSERVATIONS

8.2.1 The need for an organizational structure

The way in which a firm organizes the deployment of its competitive or O advantages, given the global political and economic environment in which it operates, and the structure of the organization required to fulfil this goal, will depend primarily upon six main factors:

(1) the ownership structure and legal status of the enterprise,

(2) its age and size,

(3) the number and character of the value-added

activities undertaken and the transactions related to these activities,

(4) the extent and form of its relationship with other firms (e.g. competitors, suppliers and customers),

(5) the geographical spread of the activities,

(6) its international product or marketing strategies.

Consider, for example, two extreme types of firms. First, take the case of a small privately-owned firm supplying a single product from one location to a perfect competitive market. Here the organizational function is confined to the minimum. Chapter 3 has already shown that in such circumstances the firm has little room for strategic manoeuverability. It undertakes few internal transactions, while the consequences of all its decisions are perfectly known.

Now, consider some possible ramifications of a growth in the output of this firm. This may be accomplished in a variety of ways (Wolf, 1977). For example, the firm might simply increase the output of its existing product. As a result, the number of its internal and external transactions will increase and place more demands on its organization. This may necessitate some delegation and/or specialization of decision-taking responsibilities by function, for example (marketing, purchasing, production, finance, personnel management and so on). Where the expansion takes the form of an acquisition, or partial acquisition, of another company, the implications for the organizational division of labour are more immediately apparent.

At the same time, or alternatively, a firm may seek to widen its range of value-added activities. This it can do by vertical integration or horizontal (or lateral) diversification. The object in each case is usually to increase sales or reduce production and/or transaction costs by capturing the economies of common governance. However, this in itself may require new or adapted forms of organization. Third, a firm may choose to expand its horizons by way of diversifying its markets and/or the location of its production. This may also require a reappraisal of its organizational structure. In each of these examples, a firm's choice under conditions of environmental uncertainty is likely to widen its strategic options, as well as enlarging the organizational function to include that of the management of uncertainty *per se*.

Now consider a firm that produces a large range of products, each of which requires different kinds of factor inputs and intermediate products, and which sells its output to national markets. Assume, too, that the firm competes in oligopolistic and high risk markets, and that its O-specific advantages rest in its ability to innovate and to manage a diverse group of assets located in several countries. Let us finally assume that the firm has a complex ownership structure. Its shares are quoted on all the leading stock exchanges. In addition to owning many foreign affiliates, it engages in many cross-border strategic alliances. In the case of such a firm, the costs of devising and maintaining an efficient organizational structure and mechanism for acquiring, deploying and monitoring factor services, intermediate inputs and markets are likely to be considerable. On the other hand, the costs of using other (e.g. external) routes of organization may well be greater.

Most multinational hierarchies fall somewhere between these extreme prototypes, although the fact that, unlike uninational firms, they produce in different countries is likely to introduce a new organizational dimension, *inter alia*, because of differences in cross-border cultures, political and economic systems, language and ideologies, and legal and business infrastructures. Moreover, the organization of particular functions may vary both according to the nature and purpose of FDI and the countries in which it is made. Thus, technology-intensive producer goods firms may have different organizational needs than resource-intensive consumer goods firms. Similarly, foreign subsidiaries producing in developing countries may need to be organized differently than firms producing exactly the same products in developed countries. The structure of intra-corporate relationships in a globally integrated MNE pursuing a geocentric product sourcing and marketing strategy is likely to be very different from that in a multi-domestic MNE practising an 'every tub on its own bottom' strategy.[3] Finally, the organizational needs may change over time, with changes in the nature of their activity, in technology and in the environment.

8.2.2   Strategic responses to organizational needs

The need for an organizational structure

Organizational structure both influences and is influenced by corporate strategy. Thus, a firm which produces a high value product designed to meet the needs of a particular and distinctive niche market (e.g. a BMW car or a Gucchi handbag) is likely to have different organizational needs to one which produces a standard product for a mass market (e.g. a standard size colour television set or a tube of Colgate toothpaste). A firm which chooses to exploit the advantages of the economies of common governance through centralized production is likely to be organized differently than one which aims to appropriate the benefits of nationally segmented or specialized markets (Ghoshal, 1987). A firm which pursues a policy of product, industrial or geographical diversification is likely to deploy a different organizational structure than one which supplies a single product to a single market. A firm which organizes its acquisition and use of technology through a web of cooperative alliances is likely to require a different form of governance than one which engages in R&D or buys and sells its technology in the open market.

The network of a firm's decision-taking apparatus is likely to reflect the values and entrepreneurial vision of its chief executive and its board of directors, as well as a complex set of historical, cultural and ideological factors that make up the competitive strengths and weaknesses. Finally, the environmental, ideological and institutional framework facing a firm may vary from country to country. To this extent, organizational structures and intra-firm relationships are, in part at least, likely to be country specific.

Let us now give two brief examples of the way in which firms faced with the same parameters described in the previous section might react differently. The first example is risk and the second technology acquisition.

Risk and the MNE

Risk may be classified in various ways. In a classic

article, Ghoshal (1987) has distinguished between four types of risks. The first he defines as *macro-economic* risks. These are risks which are normally beyond the ability of an individual firm to influence. They include such events as wars and national disasters as well as exogenous shifts in market forces (changes in wage rates, commodity prices, exchange rates). The second are *policy* risks. These risks arise because of the uncertainty about the future actions of home or host governments. They include possible changes in taxation, controls on inward or outward direct investment, performance requirements and anti-trust legislation. The third type of risks are *competitive* risks. These stem from uncertainties about competitors' behaviour, including, for example, their reaction to a change in one's own global strategy. The fourth are *resource* risks. These embrace the uncertainties surrounding the acquisition of the resource and intermediate inputs, as and when required and on the terms required. To these four kinds of risks, others might be added, including those associated with selling intermediate or final products. These include not only the uncertainty of demand, but also the behaviour of buyers who, in some sense or other, act as an 'agent' of the selling firm, or by their actions are able to affect its behaviour.[4]

Some risks are common to all firms; others are specific to those engaged in foreign-based value-adding activities; and a few are uniquely firm specific. Perhaps, the most obvious kind of risk associated with FDI is the uncertainty that surrounds the future value of foreign currencies or the domestic currency in international markets. Others may be of lesser or greater importance. They include political risks, resource risks and culturally-related risks (e.g. with respect to attitudes to work and authority, honouring contracts, etc). On the other hand, the flexibility of the geographically diversified MNE in dealing with environmental volatility may give it an advantage over competitors that engage in production in only a few countries (Kogut, 1985b).

The literature suggests a firm may respond to the presence of risk in a variety of ways, each of which may require modifications to its organizational structure. First, it may seek to avoid risk simply by reducing its exposure to risk-bearing activities. At first sight, this might seem to simplify the firm's organizational needs, but this would not be so wherever the activities previously undertaken by

other firms now have to be undertaken by the firm itself. Second, a firm may insure itself against some risk. Again, the effect is ambiguous. On the one hand, insurance reduces the need for self-protecting measures. On the other, because the firm has externalized its risk-bearing function, it may engage in more risky activities than it otherwise would have done. Third, a firm may attempt to lessen its risks by a variety of hedging devices. An obvious example is in the foreign exchange market where a firm hedges forward to protect itself against a fall (or rise) in the currency in which it is transacting goods.

The effect of risk on the multinationalization of a firm's value-added activities depends, first and foremost, on the types of risks being considered. In addition, it depends on the attitude of the main decision takers of the firm to risk bearing. Chapter 4 has shown that the risks associated with the failure of cross-border markets to take account of economies of common governance of separate but related transactions may act as an inducement to FDI. On the other hand, FDI may bring with it its own risks (e.g. the possibility of the expropriation of the assets committed and/or the normal commercial risks of an unprofitable investment). An increase in political or commercial risks which might reduce the value of a firm's foreign assets may then lead firms to prefer to share financial risks by engaging in a joint venture or concluding some other form of cooperative alliance. This point was further discussed in Chapter 7 in considering the benefits of alternative modes of entry into foreign markets.

Technology creation and acquisition

Chapter 4 has suggested that the ability of firms to create or acquire technological assets at an economic price is one of the key competitive advantages of MNEs. At the same time, the way in which an MNE organizes the generation or purchase of its technology can be a crucial ingredient in its success. For example, being self-sufficient in innovatory capacity will normally not only require the establishment of a R&D department, but also the integration of that department with the rest of the firm. On the other hand, an independent technology-purchasing capability may reduce the transaction costs of dealing with outside suppliers of technology, for example, in respect of price and quality of output. Although

Exhibit 8.1 Alternative organizational structures.

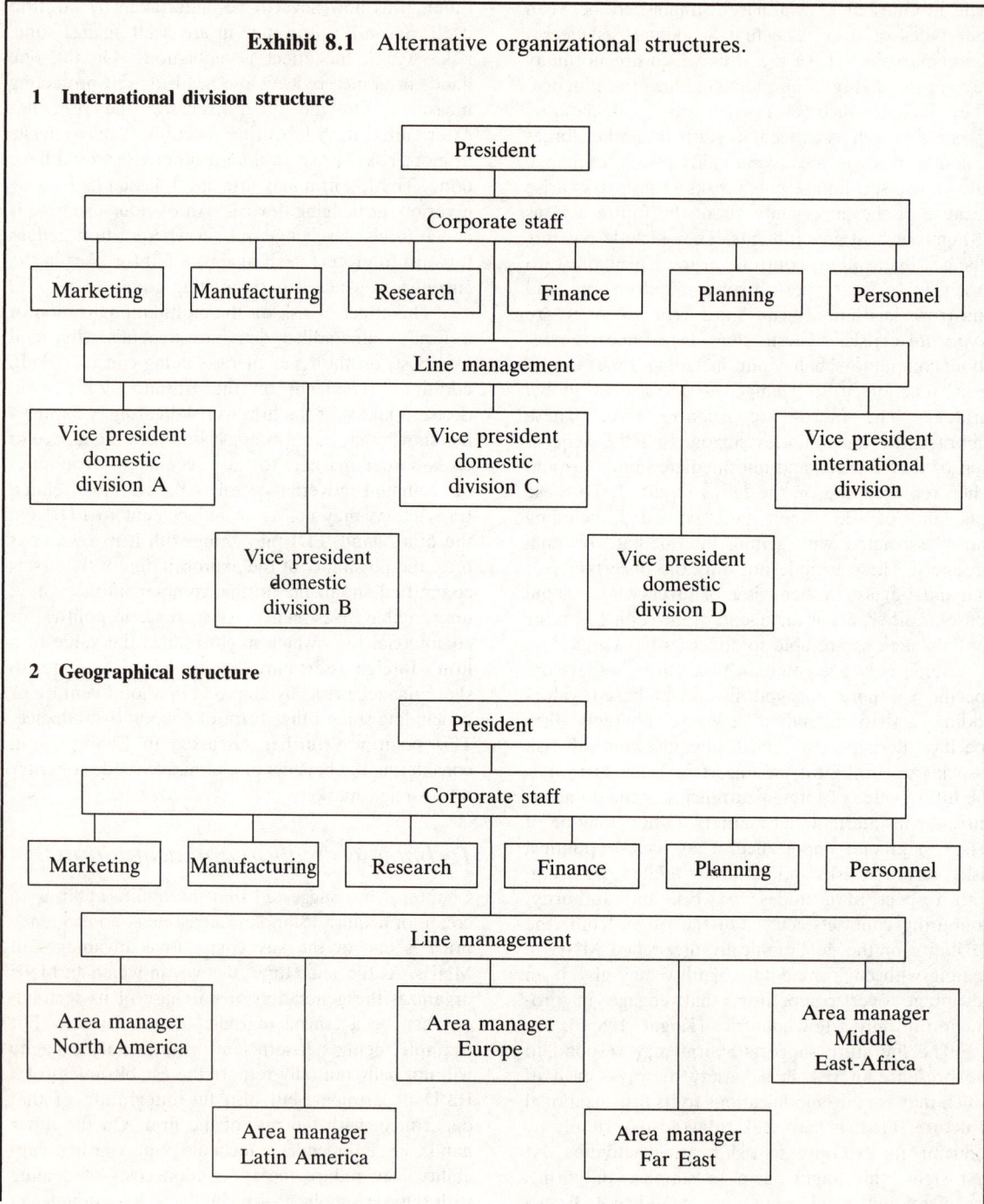

Exhibit 8.1   continued.

3   Product structure

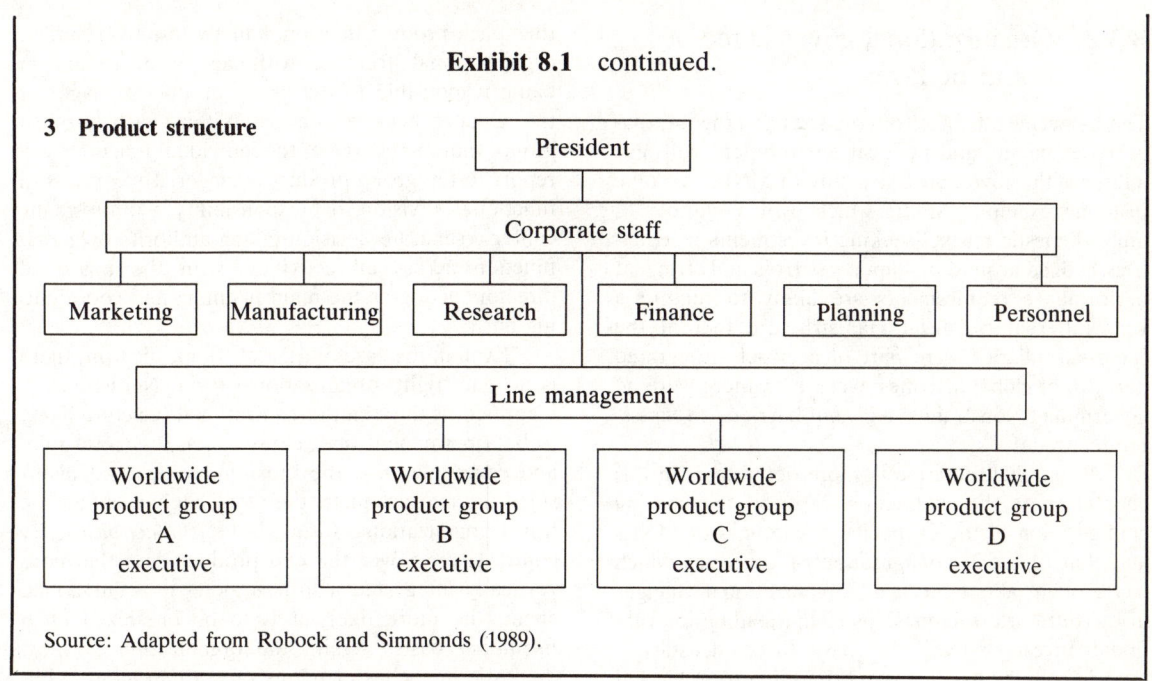

Source: Adapted from Robock and Simmonds (1989).

possibly a less risky strategy, the conclusion of collaborative alliances with other firms to finance joint R&D programmes or manufacture a wider range of products may require further internal restructuring. Buying technology on the open market or by contractual arrangement may be a third option which makes its own organizational demands.

In general, the more numerous and complex the technologies required to produce a particular product and the more products (or production processes) supplied by a firm, the more complex its organizational structure is likely to be. This being so, some authors have argued that it is the ability of the contemporary MNE to organize efficiently the acquisition, adaptation, production and use of different types of technology-related assets, which is its critical O-specific advantage (Bartlett and Ghoshal, 1989). Hence, the attention given by scholars to the structures and modes of governing this particular function – a point to which we shall return in a later section of this chapter.

8.3   ORGANIZATIONAL STRUCTURES OF MNEs

8.3.1   Some general points

We first turn to consider some organizational structures of MNEs identified in the literature. In practice, no MNE is likely to fit exactly into one or other of these typologies. Each enterprise is, to some extent, unique and usually embraces an amalgam of different organizational structures. Moreover, the optimal, or perceived optimal, organizational structure of any particular MNE may change over time as, for example, it widens or reduces its product range or increases its degree of multinationality. Indeed, in their description of formal organizational structures, at least, most textbooks on international business tend to look at these as they evolve from the point at which a firm first engages in foreign production through to when it operates an integrated network of subsidiaries in a large number of countries. Exhibit 8.1 summarizes three of these organizational structures. For further details, the reader is invited to consult specialist books on the organization of international business.[5]

8.3.2 Organizational governance of domestic firms

The L-specific attributes of countries and the international economic and political environment will also influence the governance structure of MNEs. To take just one example; MNEs which own a number of multi-domestic market-seeking investments in countries hedged around by import controls and stringent performance requirements are likely to require a very different organizational structure than if the same subsidiaries were part of a closely integrated network of global activities over which there were no government constraints and no barriers to cross-border trade.

As we shall describe in more detail later in this chapter, it is the interaction between the shifting configuration of the O-specific advantages of MNEs and that of the L configuration of countries which has brought about the main organizational changes in the intra-firm relationships of the leading international investors over the past three decades – especially in the past ten years. In doing so, it has led the more globalized MNEs to place less reliance on traditional hierarchical governance structures and dyadic relationships, and to move towards a system of lateral interfaces based on multiple centres of heterarchical decision taking.

First we consider the organizational structure of a firm prior to its engaging in FDI. Dependent on the variables identified in Exhibit 8.1, the division of responsibilities is likely to take a 'U' or 'M' form. We have already suggested that the U (or unitary) organizational structure is generally likely to be suitable for a small, single-activity firm in which the number of decisions requiring coordination is relatively small and can be adequately handled by an individual or small team of individuals. However, some large, tightly knit, family-owned firms are also likely to opt for this organizational hierarchy in which the locus of decision taking tends to be highly centralized.

The M (or multi-divisional) form allows for some specialization of responsibilities. In a firm that produces and sells only in its domestic market, the specialization is likely to be either by 'product' (or activity) or by 'function' (or area) of decision taking. It also formalizes a vertical system of intra-firm communication and decision taking. If the former,

then each product division is likely to have a similar organizational structure, with each product manager being responsible to the group product manager or the chief executive officer. Within each product group, those in charge of the individual functions will report to the group product manager. By contrast, a functional division of responsibility will normally confer a separate decision-taking authority over that function across all activities, with the board of directors acting as the main planning and coordinating body.

Even in the case of a purely domestic firm, there is no one 'right' organizational form. Neither, once identified, is the 'right' organizational structure likely to be a permanent one. However, as a general rule, and *ceteris paribus*, the more numerous and diversified the end products, the more likely it is that the firm's organizational form will be *product based*. By contrast, the fewer the end products and the more vertically integrated a firm is along its value-added chain, the more likely it is to be organized on a *functional* basis. Again, the organization of most domestic firms has elements of both structures, but with one or the other tending to be the dominant form.

8.3.3 The impact of internationalization on organizational governance

Once a firm engages in foreign transactions it is faced with new organizational challenges. These may be met in a variety of ways. Initially, the most likely response is for the firm to establish a new international division responsible for its foreign activities.[6] The *raison d'être* for such a division is that the firm perceives that, because of differences between the domestic and foreign political and economic environments and the added intra-firm communication costs (Hirsch, 1976), a new kind of arrangement is needed to organize and govern the value-added activities conducted abroad. However, where these activities become extensive and/or where a multi-product firm begins producing outside its national boundaries, then it is likely that each of the product divisions will be given responsibility for incorporating the foreign dimension into their sphere of control. This is particularly likely where firms produce a range of technically sophisticated products, and where it is essential that managers be fully familiar with the nature and performance of the goods and services for which they are responsible (Weekly and Aggarwal, 1987). Alternatively, a firm that is already governed on functional lines might take on board the international dimension for each function.

MNEs that continue to organize their foreign activities primarily by way of an international division (or divisions) include the Xerox Corporation, Bristol Myers and DuPont. MNEs that organize some or all of their activities by product divisions, each of which embraces both domestic and non-domestic business, include Rockwell International, Colgate, Sperry, Thomson Brandt and General Electric. MNEs that tend to prefer a more functionally-oriented division of organizational responsibilities – these tend to be the exception rather than the rule – include SKF, Caterpillar Tractor and Lockheed.

In deciding the appropriate organizational mode, all MNEs will need to strike a balance between adapting their products, production methods, wage policies, marketing techniques and sourcing requirements to the needs, aspirations and capabilities of foreign suppliers, customers, workers and governments. They will also have to maintain strategic flexibility while exploiting the maximum benefits from the economies of scale, scope and geographical diversification. As one pair of scholars have put it, the multinational mission involves balancing *local demands* and *global vision* (Prahalad and Doz, 1987); or in the words of the president of Coca Cola 'to think globally, but act locally' (*Miami News*, 1988).

Another way of viewing the choice of organizational strategy is to identify the nature of a firm's core competences and the motives for its foreign production, and relate these to the characteristics of the environments in which it produces. For example, where a firm contracts to buy a standard raw material, it may be appropriate for its central purchasing department to buy that material for all its production outlets so that it can obtain the maximum quantity discounts. By contrast, where a product needs to be specifically adapted to the needs of local customers and/or requires the purchase of specialized components, it may be better for these to be sourced by the foreign affiliate. Similarly, while the monitoring and arbitraging interest or exchange rate movements might best be handled centrally, negotiations with organized labour may be more properly delegated to local personnel managers. The accounting and finance function is likely to be centrally coordinated, whereas discussions involving host governments (apart from those involving a substantial commitment of resources from the parent company) will tend to be conducted by the management of local affiliates.

As a firm becomes more internationally oriented, a third form of hierarchical organizational structure, based on the geography of a firm's markets and products, becomes possible. The more countries to which a firm exports, or in which it produces, the more likely it is to set up regional divisions responsible for particular groups of countries. In some instances, this may be accompanied by the establishment of regional offices, which assume some of the organizational responsibilities of the parent company, particularly those relating to region-specific issues (e.g. monitoring and analysing the legislation and policies of host country governments). MNEs that veer towards a geographically-oriented organizational structure include the major oil, tobacco and food processing companies and branch banking. Examples are Pfizer, CPC International and Barclays Bank International.

An MNE may evolve other organizational governances as it becomes more internationalized. Vertically integrated resource-based firms (e.g. in the metals industries) might divide responsibility according to stages along the value-added chain (e.g. mineral exploration, smelting and refining). In other cases, the division of responsibility may be according to the characteristics of the major customers (e.g. consumer, industry, government).

The organizational structure adopted by an established MNE will then vary according to the *raison d'être* for its investment, the number and location of its subsidiaries, the kinds of end markets served, its experience of foreign operations, its product or process diversity and its global management strategy. As a general rule, MNEs whose foreign subsidiaries produce a limited range of products for sale to an idiosyncratic domestic market are likely to be organized on geographical lines. By contrast, the greater the product diversity of a firm and the more it pursues a rationalized investment strategy, the more it is likely to be organized on product lines. This is the case for many of the larger motor vehicle engineering and electronics MNEs. As we shall see later, other variables will also influence a firm's choice of organizational structure, including its country of origin and the countries in which it operates.

8.3.4   The organizational structure of global firms

As a firm increases its geographical scope and the value-added intensity of its foreign involvement and produces in more countries, it may need to change its organizational structure once more. Again, the choice will depend on the nature of the firm's foreign involvement, particularly on the extent to which it adopts an integrated strategy towards its foreign and domestic activities. A single-product MNE which replicates its domestic production in foreign countries and relies on essential inputs from its parent company's suppliers will have different organizational needs from one that supplies specialized products for each of the markets in which it produces. In turn, the multi-domestic MNE will have a different set of linkages with its parent company than one which is part of an integrated strategy.

The more globalized a firm becomes in its main functions, the more it is likely that adaptations will be required to any hierarchical organizational structure. Usually, this involves two types of balancing act. The first, as already described, is that between achieving the benefits of cross-border integration and those of the responsiveness of individual MNE affiliates to national capability and need. While this varies according to country-, industry- and firm-specific circumstances, the current trend seems to be towards a greater sharing of global decision taking among managers from different parts of the MNE's organization, as well as a more lateral exchange of information and ideas which act as building blocks to a professionally managed heterarchy (Hedlund and Kogut, 1992).

The second type of balancing act is that which tries to achieve the advantages, but not the disadvantages, of a geographical and product-based organizational structure. Such a mixture of structures at the primary level may, itself, take various forms. CPC, for example, divides the US by products and the rest of the world by areas. Dow Chemical has divided line responsibility for all but one of its products among five regional managers. The sixth division is a product division with global responsibility (Ball and McCulloch, 1988). However, most MNEs still tend to organize functions either by the geography of their operations or by their product lines. The greater the product diversification and the fewer the countries in which MNEs have production outlets, the more likely it is that the enterprise's organization will be product oriented. The more specialized the output and the greater the multinationality of the company, the more likely it is that the organizational structure will be geographically based. The greater the role played by foreign affiliates in the global success of an MNE, the more likely intra-firm decision taking will become lateral and multi-dimensional.

An examination of the largest and most diversified MNEs suggests a wide variety of organizational structures. Yet there are common features. All seem to group some activities according to the countries in which they are located with the appropriate managers in each subsidiary interacting with their opposite numbers in the parent company. In other functions – particularly those involving complex technical matters – the allocation of decision taking is still primarily structured on a product basis, and is more likely to be hierarchical than heterarchical. Again, the appropriate internal structure of relationships will depend on the transaction costs of the organization of the relationships. Will the common governance of product-related relationships be less or more than that of geographically-oriented relationships? Will the idiosyncrasies of country-specific resource and demand configurations outweigh, or be outweighed by, the harmonization of national policies fostered by regional customs unions? Will such regional integration lead to a strengthening of the power of the regional offices of MNEs – and if so, will this hasten the demise of MNE hierarchies? Kenichi Ohmae (1990), for example, has suggested that some MNEs have reached a stage in their organizational development which might be called global localization[7] and which, *inter alia*, requires a reappraisal of the role of the head office as a decision-taking unit. He points to the growing importance of the role of regional headquarters in Japanese MNEs, such as Nissan, Yamaha, Honda and Matsushita, and goes on to argue that 'decom-

Exhibit 8.2   Matrix organization of Ciba Geigy Limited.

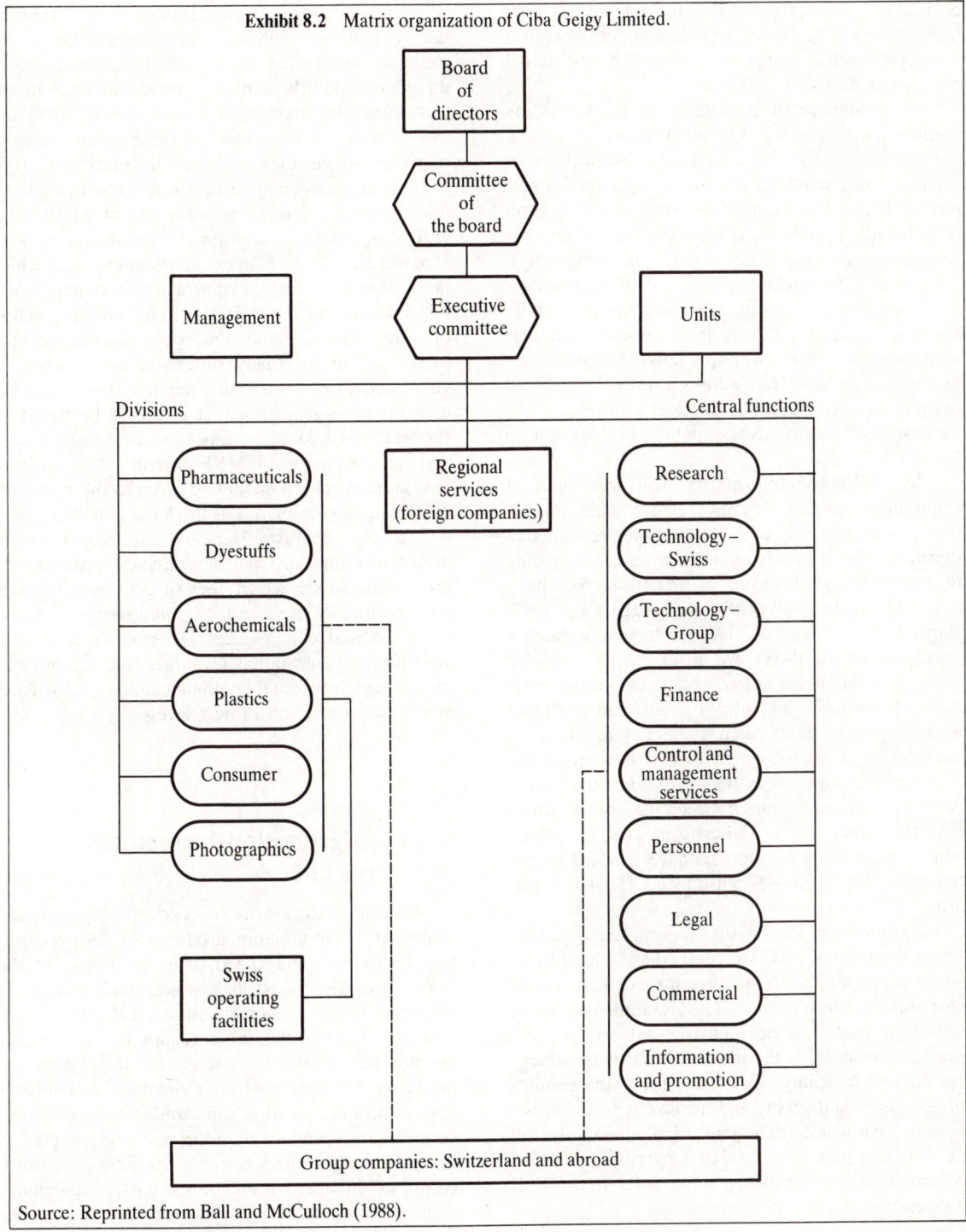

Source: Reprinted from Ball and McCulloch (1988).

posing the corporate centre into several regional headquarters is becoming an essential part of almost every successful company's transition to global competitor status' (p. 88).

In an attempt to meet some of the conflicting organizational demands identified in previous paragraphs, some MNEs have adopted a hybrid form of organizational structure known as the *matrix structure*. It is so-called because one organizational form (e.g. based on products) is superimposed on another organizational form (e.g. based on geography). Instead of a hierarchy wherein a product manager has control over various regional managers, both kinds of managers will be at the same level and their responsibilities will overlap. Ciba Geigy is an example of an MNE that adopts a three-dimensional matrix structure based on products, functions and geographical regions. Some details are set out in Exhibit 8.2.

In MNEs adopting matrix structures, lines of communication flow laterally across main dimensions; both product- and regional-specific expectations are utilized in solving problems and responding to opportunities. However, as several analysts have pointed out (e.g. Weekly and Aggarwal, 1987; Bartlett and Ghoshal, 1989), dual-responsibility structures create their own problems. To resolve competing claims for scarce resources and to minimize the conflict of interests between different interest groups, they often require some kind of managerial 'supremo' whose task it is to reconcile interpersonal differences and maintain an efficient two-way communication between the home office and the lower units. Other examples of MNEs which, at one time or another, have adopted matrix structures are Massey-Ferguson and Hewlett Packard.

Current thinking on the appropriate organizational structure of MNEs suggests that none of those so far identified can fully meet the needs of global corporations which engage in a substantial amount of intra-firm trade among industrialized and/or integrated economies. If the modern MNE is to achieve operational flexibility, yet fully capture the benefits of geographical diversity and the economies of cross-border governance, its organization's mentality will need to shift from one based on a pyramid of vertical control relationships to one based on a network of cooperative and lateral relationships.

Various authors have expressed this view in different ways. Ghoshal and Nohria (1989), for example, argue that the organizational structure of an MNE should be suited to the resources available to its operating units, their stage of development and the stability (or otherwise) of the external environment in which they operate. In particular, they distinguish between hierarchical, federative, clan-like and integrative structures – the last of which, they argue, is the most appropriate for managing subsidiaries that face complex environments and which have abundant local resources. On similar lines, Ghoshal and Bartlett (1990) plead for a reconstruction of inter-organizational theory to encompass the MNE as 'an internally differentiated network of value activities'. Doz and Prahalad (1991) put the case for an organizational structure to be based on the 'combined consequences of multi-dimensionality and heterogeneity' of MNE activity. They suggest that more emphasis should be given to the managers of individual subsidiaries as the basic unit of decision taking. By contrast, Hedlund and Kogut (1992) prefer to emphasize the heterarchical attributes of the modern MNE, which, they suggest, best illustrate the structure of decision taking in a company whose resources and competences are globally dispersed, yet whose organizational advantages increasingly rest on efficient horizontal communication – particularly at the functional and project levels.

8.3.5   Organizational structures: a resumé

To conclude, as a firm proceeds through various stages of its multinationalization, so its organizational structures may need to be modified. At the same time, technological advances and changes in the international economic and political environment have, themselves, led to a reappraisal of existing decision-taking systems. Regional integration, in particular, has necessitated a more multi-dimensional approach to the creation and transfer of cross-border financial and production information as well as to resource usage. The associated escalation of intra-corporate linkages has meant that a pyramidal multi-divisional organizational structure based on the principle of unity of command may no longer be the best for exploiting the economies of common governance. An alternative system, which allows a better circulation of information and decision-taking flows between managers responsible for particular product and geographical areas, is needed.

We have suggested that the matrix form of organization overcomes some of these problems. It does so by increasing the responsibility and decision-taking power of the head office of an MNE both to coordinate its global activities across product lines and geographical borders and to spearhead new innovatory activities, seek out new markets and adjust more readily to the demands of an ever-changing world business environment.

At the same time, because it makes for a more intensive network of intra-firm communication, the matrix structure creates its own organizational problems, notably those that arise from ambiguities over the locus of management responsibility and a conflict of goals and strategies of members of the network. These problems are most likely to arise where the foreign affiliates of the MNEs are powerful entities in their own right. In such cases, the head office becomes less a centre of control and more a means by which the constituent parts of the organization make their own inputs into the decision-making process. This is what Ghoshal and Bartlett (1990) refer to as a transnational solution, which itself demands a governance structure suited to the needs of an integrated network of distributed and inter-dependent resources and capabilities.

The clear implication of the above paragraphs is that different organizational structures will be required for different kinds of MNE activity, and for MNEs with different combinations of resources and competences. Thus, in the branded consumer goods sector, Unilever is less globally integrated and more willing to adapt its products to local needs than is Procter and Gamble, while Matsushita and NEC both follow a more globally integrated strategy than does General Electric or ITT. At the same time, the organizational structures implemented by MNEs may affect their competitiveness in world markets and their impact on the economies in which they operate. Once again, however, generalizations are difficult to make. Grant (1991) cites the case of Philips of Eindhoven whose decentralized nationally respon-

sive organizational structure encourages product innovation in its various subsidiaries, yet makes it difficult to commercialize these innovations on a global scale.

Similarly, the choice of organizational structure will also influence the response of MNEs to changes in their domestic or foreign environment. The desire to minimize the production and transaction costs of decision taking will affect the extent to which there is an integration of that decision taking within the corporation and the form of organizational governance. The greater the costs of cross-border hierarchical interaction and the less those of organizing individual affiliates to meet the goals of the parent company, the more the organizational structure of these affiliates is likely to follow that of an independent local firm. By contrast, where there are marked economies of the common governance of organizing subsidiaries, the organization of the subsidiaries is likely to be integrated into that of the MNE as a whole. Similarly, the choice of organizational structure (e.g. between a functional, product and/or geographical division of responsibilities, or a hybrid of these) will rest on the comparative production and transaction costs involved. The previous paragraphs have sought to suggest some of the variables that influence an MNE to choose one organizational form rather than another.

Finally, national and cultural differences are likely to play a major role in influencing the organizational structure of MNEs. Two examples must suffice. The first is the slower rate at which the multi-divisional (M) form of organization was adopted in Japan as compared with the US (Cable and Yasuki, 1985). The second is the differences between the way in which firms of different nationalities implement intra-firm communication and decision-taking procedures. In a study of American and Japanese subsidiaries in Taiwan, for example, Yen and Sagafi-Nejad (1990) found that the organizational structures of Japanese firms were less rigorously defined and had more group activities than their US counterparts. Moreover, the perception of the managers of both groups of subsidiaries is that American MNEs tend to prefer more formal and well documented organizational administrative procedures than Japanese MNEs, who were seen to rely more on tacit, interpersonal and behavioural control tools.

8.4   THE LOCUS OF DECISION TAKING

8.4.1   Introduction

While the organizational structure of a firm partly determines the locus of decision taking, no less important is the strategy of the MNE towards its foreign operations, which, in turn, will relate to factors identified earlier in this chapter and in Chapter 6. Recalling that we are primarily interested in this issue to improve our understanding of the determinants of MNE activity and its interaction with the Nation States in which it is located, we shall discuss the issue of the locus of decision taking under four headings. First, what exactly is meant by it? Second, what determines the allocation of decision-taking responsibility within an MNE? Third, how, in practice, do MNEs allocate decisions among their separate operating and administrative units? And fourth, what are the likely repercussions of this for the spatial distribution and economic impact on MNE activity?

Taken literally, the locus of decision taking refers to *who* has the responsibility for making decisions within an MNE. Clearly, in reaching any decision, the decision taker is dependent upon, and influenced by, the information, experience and advice of many individuals. Consequently, the pattern of decision making in any firm represents the input of a network of decision takers across activities, functions and countries.

It is fair to say that, over the years, most of the interests of organizational scholars have focused on two kinds of issues. The first is the extent to which the locus of decision taking is centralized in the headquarters of an MNE or is delegated (i.e. decentralized) to its regional offices or branch affiliates and how this locus varies according to the kinds of decisions that have to be taken. The second concerns the nationality of the decision takers and whether they are appointed by the MNE or one of its affiliates. Empirical research suggests that the answers to these questions vary substantially according to the OLI configuration facing MNEs and their strategic response to that configuration.

8.4.2   An economic approach to decision taking

Any explanation of the locus of decision taking within a firm must relate to the number and character of the decisions that have to be made. Within the small single-activity firm, decisions may be taken solely by the owner-cum-entrepreneur. As a firm grows, the responsibility for at least some decisions may have to be delegated to 'agents' appointed by the owner. Usually these agents are 'functional' decision takers. As the firm becomes multi-activity, so the network of decision takers increases. As well as functional decision takers, there may be others who are product specialists.

The setting up of a foreign or domestic subsidiary requires a new team or network of decision takers who not only have to relate to each other, but also to those in the parent company. It is at this point that the locus of decision taking becomes an important issue. It is because the economic, legal and cultural environment facing foreign subsidiaries is different from that facing the parent company, or its domestic subsidiaries, that the delegation of decision taking may be different in an MNE than in a uninational firm.

Why should any decisions taken within an MNE not be centralized? Why should the owners or senior management located in the head offices of such enterprises choose to delegate at least some decisions to the managers of their subsidiaries? In answering these questions, we shall turn once again to the framework of the eclectic paradigm. More particularly, we shall argue that the structure of decision taking within hierarchies or heterarchies depends firstly on the willingness and capabilities of the managers and administrators of the subsidiaries to take the kind of decisions which are perceived, by those at the head office, to be in the best interests of the MNE as a whole. Secondly it depends on the comparative costs of siting decision-taking units in one country rather than another. We shall now elaborate on these two points.

Economic theory suggests that there are three main reasons why MNEs should not wish to delegate decision taking to their affiliates. First, when viewed as self-contained profit centres, the objectives of the affiliates may not always be in accord with those of the MNE of which they are a part. Such a conflict of interest will be most pronounced where:

(1) there are differences in the perceived objectives of the affiliates and those of their parent company and/or of the strategy required to best advance these goals;

(2) there are costs or benefits arising from the decisions taken by, or on behalf of, the affiliates, which are external to those affiliates, but internal to the MNE of which they are a part.

Second, the real costs of decision making and/or related support services may be higher in the host than in the home country. Third, for one reason or another the parent company may be more efficient at undertaking these activities than its regional or branch affiliates.

Applying the eclectic paradigm to these criteria, the first and third reasons suggest that the choice between the centralization and delegation of decision taking, and also the nationality of the main decision makers, may be likened to that between the hierarchical and market route of organizing the disposition of O-specific advantages. For example, it might be hypothesized that the more the O advantages of an MNE stem from the common governance of geographically dispersed activities and/or from proprietary knowledge which is idiosyncratic, uncodifiable, costly to transmit and liable to be inefficiently or inappropriately used, the more likely it is that either the top decision takers of the affiliate will be nationals of the home country, or that their decisions will be most closely guided or controlled by the management of the parent company.

The second reason for MNEs to centralize decision making has to do with the distribution of decision-making resources and competences across national boundaries, where the views of the management of the parent company differ from that of its subsidiaries on the best way to utilise these resources and competencies. Given the same 'output', then, wherever the (marginal) cost of decision making is less in the home country than in the host country, such decisions are unlikely to be delegated. Quite apart from economies of scale and scope in decision making, management support costs may vary between countries. In some cases it may be desirable for

management to be in close proximity to the market and for decisions to be customized to local requirements. In others it may need to be close to the core of the firm's value-added activities.

Using the above framework, it is possible to offer some general hypotheses about the locus of decision taking. First, centralization is most likely where the O advantages of the MNE are highly idiosyncratic and need specialized and experienced support services, or when they arise from the common ownership of geographically diversified activities. Second, centralization is likely to be preferred when the relative real costs of decision-taking services are higher in a foreign location. Third, centralization may be preferred where intra-firm market failure means that the transaction costs of delegating decisions to the management of the subsidiary are perceived to be unacceptable to the management of the parent company.

A somewhat different, though related, economic approach to analysing the locus of decision taking has been taken by scholars who view organization in hierarchies as paralleling that of a metropolitan–hinterland relationship of countries, with levels or tiers of decision-taking activities (Cohen et al., 1979; Hymer, 1970). The top level of decision taking is responsible for identifying the objectives of the firm, determining its long-term strategy, coordinating information flows and setting organizational control and procedures. The next tier is likely to be concerned with translating this strategy into operational production and sales targets, and assigning the necessary tasks and duties to accomplish these targets. The bottom tier has the responsibility for executing the plans laid down by the second level of decision takers.

The suggestion here is that as a firm becomes an MNE and/or increases its multinationality, the division of responsibilities and tasks between the headquarters, regional offices and affiliates changes. Where the need to coordinate the global activities of the firm is most obvious, the locus of decision taking remains at the centre. Where the emphasis is on regional coordination, but the managers of operating units need a great deal of local information and contacts with local firms to fulfil the function efficiently, the locus of decision taking may be largely decentralized to regional offices and/or local affiliates.

8.4.3   A strategic approach to decision taking

Perhaps the most significant strategic factor affecting both the organizational structure and locus of decision taking within an MNE is the firm's philosophy or ethos towards its foreign value-added activities. In 1969, Howard Perlmutter wrote a classic article in which he identified three orientations an MNE might take, *viz ethnocentric, polycentric* and *geocentric*. In a later contribution, jointly authored with Balaji Chakravarthy (1985), he added a fourth, *viz regiocentric* orientation. Perlmutter argued that the locus of decision taking in an MNE was likely to vary with these orientations, which, in turn, reflected its country of origin as well as its size and degree of multinationalization.

The *ethnocentric* firm, whose attitude towards its foreign affiliates is rather like that of a mother country towards its colonies, is likely to permit little decentralization of decision taking. Where it does, it will do its best to ensure that such decisions conform with the wishes of the parent firm. More often than not, it will be a market- or resource-seeking MNE in the early days of its internationalization process. Product development is determined primarily by the needs of home-country customers, and the organizational structure is likely to be based on hierarchical product divisions. R&D is highly centralized, while the chief executive officers of the affiliates of ethnocentric MNEs tend to be expatriates appointed by the parent organization.

By contrast, a *polycentric* MNE is best described as a federation of loosely linked multi-domestic affiliates. Its strategic decision taking is tailored to suit the needs and cultures of the countries in which it operates. In consequence, it is likely to be highly decentralized in its decision-taking procedures, although critical decisions affecting the allocation of the core assets of the MNE may continue to be centralized.

A *regiocentric* MNE is one which tries to blend its own strategic interests with those of its subsidiaries on a regional basis. More often than not, such MNEs are likely to operate regional offices (Dunning and Norman, 1987). The governance of regiocentric MNEs is likely to be mutually negotiated between the headquarters and the regional offices and to be geared towards balancing the advantages of regional integration and responding to national needs and aspirations. Marketing is likely to be standardized within the regions, but not across regions. Also firms pursuing a regiocentric philosophy are likely to adopt a matrix structure of decision taking in which product and regional orientations are juxtaposed.

A *geocentric* MNE is one which tries to adopt a globally integrated approach to decision taking. Such an approach will adopt a mixed strategy towards the locus of decision taking. This will, essentially, depend upon the location of individuals with whom the decision taker has the most transactions. On technical matters (e.g. those relating to R&D, product and market development, finance and capital expenditure) the decisions are likely to be centralized simply because most discussions and transactions are likely to be undertaken between the different units of the MNEs. By contrast, those having to do with personnel recruitment and purchasing are apt to be decentralized, because most exchanges of information, goods and services are likely to be between firms or individuals in the host country (i.e. external to the MNE). In all cases, however, the influence of the parent company (which may extend to guidelines on philosophy and strategy, even on matters which are decentralized) is much greater than in the first case.

Geocentric MNEs are more likely to be heterarchical, rather than hierarchical, in their approach to decision taking. Their organizational structure comprises a network of affiliate companies and strategic alliances. Governance is likely to be multi-dimensional, lateral and negotiated at levels of the business corporation. The culture of the geocentric MNE is transnational, yet sensitive to the attitudes and ideologies of countries in which it operates. The geocentric MNE is also likely to practise a global procurement and human resources management strategy – both of intermediate products and people.

8.4.4   Some empirical findings on the locus of decision taking

An excellent review of the literature is contained in Martinez (1987) and Martinez and Jarillo (1989). Among the findings of these authors, one might mention especially that the overall degree of centralization or autonomy is seen to vary with the functional areas of decision taking. Also it seems that over the past half century or more decision taking has tended to become more centralized. Several of the contributions considered, such as those of Otterbeck (1982), Negandhi and Baliga (1981), Negandhi (1982) and Negandhi and Welge (1984), found that US MNEs exercised more influence on the decision taking of their subsidiaries and relied on more formal or bureaucratic control procedures than their European or Japanese counterparts. They also discovered that subsidiaries in developing countries tended to be allowed less autonomy than those in developed countries, while centralized control over decision taking was most pronounced among MNEs which engaged in a substantial amount of inter-firm trade. By contrast, subsidiaries operating in competitive markets were likely to be granted more autonomy than those operating in monopolistic markets (Negandhi, 1982).

At the same time, it would appear that informal and more subtle control and coordination procedures have increased over the past decade. Clinical studies

by Doz and Prahalad (1981, 1984), Doz (1986), Bartlett (1986), and Bartlett and Ghoshal (1987a, 1987b, 1989) all point to a more pluralistic or multi-dimensional approach to decision taking in contemporary MNEs, with less emphasis being given to rigidly defined hierarchical channels and more to the sharing of heterarchical values and systems.

Rather than attempt to summarize or to reproduce the findings of Martinez (1987), and Martinez and Jarillo (1989), we shall illustrate the points made in the previous paragraph by detailed reference to two field studies conducted in the United Kingdom. The first is by a group of economists (Young et al., 1985) who examined the locus of decision taking in some 154 US and other (mainly European) foreign-owned MNEs which had production facilities in the UK in the mid 1970s.[8] Two aspects of their findings are of particular interest. The first concerns the main influences on the locus of decision taking and the direction of those influences. We believe that Table 8.1 is self-explanatory on this point.[9] Exhibit 8.3 sets out the consensus of findings of these and other scholars.

Table 8.1 Influence on the degree of centralization/decentralization of decision-making within the MNE.

Characteristics of subsidiary and parent	Direction of influence
Nationality of ownership	United States firms more centralized than non-United States firms
Proportion of equity stock held by parent	Wholly-owned subsidiaries more centralized than partially-owned subsidiaries
Date of establishment in the host country	Centralization decreases over time
Method of establishment in the host country	Greenfield entrants more centralized than acquisitions
Absolute size of subsidiary	Large subsidiaries more autonomous than small subsidiaries
Size of subsidiary relative to parent company	Centralization increases with relative size of subsidiary
Industry factors	Subsidiaries in some industries (e.g. chemicals; mechanical and electrical engineering) more centralized than others (e.g. food and papers)
Degree of inter-subsidiary production integration	Centralization increases with the degree of intra-group trade
Subsidiary performance	Poor performance reduces subsidiary autonomy
Multinationality of parent company	Centralization increases with degree of multinationality
Organizational structure of parent company	Geographically organized MNEs less centralized than functional, product or matrix-organized companies

Note: The directions of influence indicated here have been derived from hypotheses in the literature and various empirical studies.

Source: Young, Hood and Hamill (1985).

Exhibit 8.3   Centralization vs decentralization in decision taking.

Pressures towards centralization	Pressures towards decentralization
Need to take global view of resources	Where ownership is shared
Need to obtain and monitor global data	Desire by affiliate for independence
Where rationalized production is necessary	Where speed of decision taking is crucial
Where level of expertise at centre makes delegation inexpedient	Where knowledge of local setup is important (labour relations)
Where economies of scale/scope in centralized decision taking	Where cost of centralization is high
Where conflicts of interest likely to arise between affiliate and parent	Need to encourage local participation in decision taking
Strategically sensitive areas	Need to recruit good staff locally and provide good career structures
Inexperience of local affiliates	Pressure from host governments
	Size and experience of local affiliates

Source: A variety of studies, including those identified by Martinez (1987) and Martinez and Jarillo (1989).

The second aspect concerns the extent to which decisions taken on a wide variety of matters affecting the operations of the affiliates are strongly or decisively influenced by the parent company (n.b. irrespective of who takes the final decision). Table 8.2 shows quite clearly that there are major differences according to the area of decision taking and the country of origin of the MNE. In particular, it reveals that the influence of the parent company on the kind of decisions taken by, or on behalf of, the affiliate is likely to be the most pronounced in the functional areas which are perceived to be culture free, in those which offer substantial economies of common governance, and in those which are likely to be more efficiently implemented by the parent firm. R&D, capital expenditure plans and dividend policy are examples. On the other hand, decisions the consequences of which are confined to the decision-taking entity, or which involve culture-specific relationships either within the foreign affiliate or between them and local firms and customers may well be taken without much guidance from the parent company. The organization of personnel matters and sales promotion fall into this category.

Other research suggests that in the case of host-country-specific factors, decisions are more likely to

be centralized when the subsidiary is lacking in experience, knowledge and organizational capabilities. On the other hand, in some strategically- or culturally-sensitive areas (e.g. government–industry and labour–management relations, and environmental protection) local management may well be allowed more decision-making powers. Decisions are also more likely to be centralized in the formative years of an MNE's foreign experience, and the smaller the size of the foreign affiliates, both absolutely and relative to their parent companies.

The second study is based upon some field work of the author (Dunning, 1958, 1986; Hood et al., 1983). The results, which are set out in Table 8.3, give further examples of the way in which the locus of decision taking may vary according to the nationality of the investing firm and the functions performed. They also show that the allocation of responsibility may vary within the same group of firms over time. While the contents of the table are reasonably self-explanatory, the conclusions of the studies on which they are based are, perhaps, worth summarizing.[10]

There are several important differences between the decision-making structures and processes of US manufacturing subsidiaries in the 1950s and those in

Table 8.2 Nationality of ownership, types of decision taking and locus of decision-making.

	Per cent of subsidiaries in which headquarters influence on decision is strong or decisive	
	North American[1]	*Continental European and other[1]*
Financial decisions		
Setting of financial targets	51	29
Preparation of yearly budget	20	11
Acquisition of funds for working capital	44	16
Choice of capital investment projects	33	13
Financing of investment projects	46	16
Target rate of return on investment	68	32
Sale of fixed assets	30	16
Dividend policy	82	76
Royalty payments to parent company	82	66
Production/marketing decisions		
Output volume	17	13
Product range	22	26
Introduction of new products	29	29
Withdrawal of products	24	24
Markets supplied by UK subsidiary	42	39
Entering new UK markets	16	8
Entering new non-UK markets	46	50
Price policy	13	10
Advertising and sales promotion	4	8
Distribution	6	3
Employment/personnel decisions		
Union recognition	4	–
Collective bargaining	1	–
Wage increases	8	–
Numbers employed	13	–
Lay-offs/redundancies	10	–
Hiring of workers	10	3
Recruitment of executives	16	–
Recruitment of senior managers	13	3
Other decisions		
R&D	49	45
Technology employed	37	42

1 The sample comprised 116 North American companies
   and 38 Continental European and other.
Source: Young, Hood and Hamill (1985).

Table 8.3 Comparative managerial influence and control exerted by United States and Japanese parent companies over United Kingdom Affiliates.

Area of management	US affiliates (c. 1953)	US affiliates (c. 1982)	Japanese affiliates (c. 1982)
Overall managerial philosophy and strategy	Affiliates mainly nationally responsive (Doz, 1986) or part of multi-domestic operations of MNEs. Moderately reflects that of US parent company (though varies between sectors). US nationals or expatriates mostly a minority on board of directors of affiliates.	In some sectors (motor vehicles, pharmaceuticals, computers, etc) UK affiliates part of the integrated network of European operations. Decision taking more centralized.	Strongly influenced and moderately controlled by parent company. Chief executive of affiliate normally a Japanese national. Japanese nationals or expatriates comprise majority of local board of directors.
Product and pricing policy	Truncated range of product supplies by parent companies. Minor modifications and adaptations to UK customer requirements. Pricing policy mainly determined by local management.	Move towards more multi-site rationalized and/or product specialized production and European branded consumer goods. Fuller range of products produced in Europe.	Affiliates supply only one major product line which, when adapted to local needs, is of the same quality as that produced by parent companies. Product policy decided centrally. Pricing policy also influenced by parent companies.
Production methods	Less automated, particularly in ancillary (e.g. mechanical handling) equipment.	Increasingly approaching those of US parent companies.	Mainly same as in Japanese parent companies, but in some cases scaled down to suit lower volumes produced.
Procurement policy	Left mainly to UK purchasing managers, but stricter tolerances and standards required (cf those demanded by UK firms).	More attention given to quality of intermediate products subcontracted, particularly where final product is destined for export market.	Strongly influenced and controlled by parent company. Very rigorous quality control procedures. Considerable help given by affiliates to suppliers in upgrading quality.
Wages and salaries	Loosely controlled; tendency to pay well above average rates; many incentives and bonuses.	Now more in line with practices and procedures adopted by UK companies. Employer compensation differences between US subsidiaries and UK firms less than in 1952, but former still often lead UK industry in working conditions.	Moderately influenced and loosely controlled. Pay slightly above average rates. Few incentives. Time rates disliked.
Training and industrial relations	A good deal of training given at all levels. Loosely influenced and controlled, but bargaining conducted at plant level. Majority of affiliates unionized; some just one union.	A movement towards one union.	Expected to conform to overall managerial philosophy; hiring and firing policy decided centrally. No, or only one, union preferred. Appointment of senior management personnel requires approval of parent company. Substantial training given at all levels.

Table 8.3 continued.

Area of management	US affiliates (c. 1953)	US affiliates (c. 1982)	Japanese affiliates (c. 1982)
Marketing	Strongly influenced and controlled by parent company. Marketing methods replicate US practices. A lot of attention given to after-sales servicing.	For nationally responsive affiliates less influenced and controlled by parent company. Most integrated affiliates adopt a common European marketing policy. Advertising generally follows US practices. Export markets generally controlled by parent companies.	Destination of output decided and controlled by parent company. Most output sold to separate marketing affiliates. Nothing especially noticeable in marketing methods, except Japanese are tough negotiators over price and salesmen maintain more face-to-face contact with clients than in normal UK practice.
Innovation policy	Strongly influenced and controlled by head office. Some R&D in UK mainly to do with machinery design, product and materials adaptation. Some development research in industrial instruments, pharmaceuticals and vehicles.	As in 1952, but more fundamental to specialized R&D undertaken in UK by US affiliates in pharmaceuticals, information, processing and electronics sectors. Less R&D is now undertaken in tyre and motor vehicle industries.	Strongly influenced and controlled by parent company. Little R&D in UK, but some product design and research starting in colour TV sector.
Accounting and financial control	Moderately influenced, especially in new methods of production planning and control. Accounting usually standardized on US lines. Dividend policy determined by parent company (Dunning, 1986).	As in 1952.	Strongly controlled by parent company. Usually a Japanese is in charge of this managerial area. All decisions relating to financial targets, choice of investment projects and dividend remission determined by parent companies.
Organization of affiliates	Few regional offices. Most subsidiaries organized as part of an M structure of organization – either on geographical or product lines. Locational decisions taken at head office or regional office.	More regional offices. Otherwise as in 1952.	No regional offices. Some Japanese MNEs organize their subsidiaries on M lines, but many have gone no further than setting up an international division.

Sources: Data derived from Chapters 4 and 9 of Dunning (1958), Chapter 4 of Dunning (1986b) and Dunning (1991). See also Young *et al.* (1985). An earlier version of this table was originally prepared for the ILO.

the early 1980s, as well as between Japanese and US affiliates in the early 1980s. In general, decisions are likely to be more centralized yet less formalized in Japanese MNEs. Where they are decentralized, a Japanese expatriate is usually in charge. At the same time, over the past 30 years, decisions relating to the UK operations of US MNEs would seem to have become more centralized.

The table suggests that differences in the locus of decision taking varies across functional groups, according, for example, to the transaction costs of transferring intermediate goods and services (and especially technical knowledge and organization skills) from the US and Japan to the UK, as well as those related to the delegation of decision taking to local affiliates. These transaction costs are likely to be greater:

(1) the larger the number of intra- and inter-firm transactions;

(2) the more pronounced the difference between the normal operational practices of firms in the investing countries (i.e. US or Japan) and those in the UK;

(3) the greater the obstacles to successfully transferring and/or adapting these practices to and within a UK environment.

In turn, these obstacles are likely to be least evident in the more technically-oriented functional areas (e.g. R&D, accounting and financial practices) and/or where learning costs are small. They are likely to be most evident when marked changes of existing institutional arrangements, social mores, and human relationships are required.

In essence this conclusion supports the findings of other scholars who have found that new organizational practices, institutional structures and work methods take longer to diffuse across national boundaries – particularly between markedly different cultures – than do technological innovations (Kogut, 1990). However, it is possible to go a step further and hypothesize that, once transferred to a foreign country, not only are organizational advances more likely to be 'internalized' within the transferring company, but that their implementation will be centralized.

Earlier in this chapter (p. 222) we suggested three reasons why decisions over the resource allocation within an MNE might be centralized. Each

of these is reflected in the different attitudes of American and Japanese MNEs towards the organization of their UK affiliates. For example, to ensure maximum efficiency of their affiliates, the Japanese currently believe that they must have centralized control over R&D, product design, production management and procurement, finance and accounting procedures, work organization and export marketing. By contrast, in the 1950s the Americans believed that the UK's competitive weakness lay in its unprofessional management, lack of marketing expertise and unfamiliarity with the latest generation of products and production methods. Decisions relating to these matters then tended to be centralized and/or taken by US expatriates. However, in the 1980s parental control by US parent companies was enforced less to compensate for a lack of knowledge or competence of local decision takers and more to ensure that their decisions were consistent with the global goals of the parent organization.

We have asserted that the conflicts arising between the interests of UK affiliates and those of the organization of which they are a part arise particularly in the case of MNEs pursuing a geocentric or regiocentric product or marketing strategies. In the 1950s, very few US affiliates in the UK were part of MNEs operating such a strategy. Many were treated by their parent companies as self-contained profit centres. This is no longer the case, at least in the case of efficiency or strategic asset seeking investors. In several strategic areas, notably R&D, allocation of markets, recruitment of top executives and sourcing policies, decision making in US MNEs, such as Ford, IBM, Caterpillar and 3M, has become increasingly centralized. By contrast, the entry of Japanese MNEs into the UK is part of their long-term European development strategy. From the start, the tasks assigned to the affiliate have been designed to promote the goals of the parent company rather than the welfare of the British subsidiary. With this vision in mind, it is then not surprising that important decisions tend to be taken in Tokyo or Osaka rather than in Cardiff or Washington, Tyne and Wear.

At the same time, it is important not to neglect differences in cultures and ideologies between the two investing economies. The consensus approach to decision taking by Japanese managers makes for a good deal more discussion among the parties affected by any decision than was (or is) evident in US subsidiaries – for all the emphasis in US culture on industrial democracy. *Inter alia*, this means that the decision-making process is less formal, but more protracted, in the case of Japanese MNEs. However, in the last resort they have an even clearer recognition of the role of the manager as a decision taker.

On the third reason for the decentralization of decision making (i.e. lower decision-making costs in the country of the affiliates than in that of the parent company), there was considerably more pressure for US enterprises to relocate managers in the 1950s than in either these same enterprises or Japanese enterprises in the 1980s. However, in both instances the cost of employing expatriates is (and was) between 50% and 150% higher than their domestic cost, with additional costs for housing, education, travel, resettlement, etc.

In the 1950s the average salaries of UK managers and management-related staff would have been about one-half that of their US counterparts. Currently (1992) it is nearer three-quarters. By contrast, UK and Japanese managerial and related costs were about the same in the early 1980s. Consequently Japanese MNEs had less incentive to decentralize the decision-making function. On the other hand, the greater unfamiliarity of the Japanese with the English language and with business norms and customs, together with their lack of knowledge about United Kingdom suppliers, laws and regulations, and ways of dealing with central and local government, make it more likely that they would favour decentralizing many decisions to 'on-the-spot' line managers. Thus Japanese affiliates were, almost without exception, fully unionized and inclined to adapt their labour relations to local practices.

Finally we examine some of the other differences between the two groups of decision makers, which cannot be attributed to their country of origin, and see how these might affect their decision-making structures and procedures.

(1) *Age*. We have already touched on the likely influence of this variable. Since younger and less experienced affiliates are more likely to be subjugated to their parents in decision taking than their older counterparts, for this reason we would expect decision-taking to be more strongly centralized in Japanese MNEs. How-

ever, while recently established US subsidiaries in the 1950s were less autonomous in their decision making than those set up prior to the Second World War, they were considerably more autonomous than their Japanese counterparts in the 1980s. Exceptions include those which were part of an integrated network of value-added activities in the EC.

(2) *Size of affiliates*. After taking age and industry differences into account, there appears to be no significant difference between the average size of US affiliates in the 1950s and that of their Japanese counterparts 30 years later.[11] However, relative to their parent companies, the Japanese affiliates were considerably smaller, hence their economic influence in the multinational hierarchy of which they are part may well be that much less.

(3) *Product diversification*. We have indicated that in 1982 almost all Japanese affiliates were single-product firms. This is in contrast to US firms in the 1950s – even those that had just been established. In the 1980s the perceived need to adapt products to local customer requirements made for more local decision making. On the other hand, there is currently much more intra-plant specialization among US affiliates in the EC than there was in the 1950s, particularly in the motor vehicle, earth moving equipment, computer and electronics sectors.[12]

(4) *Regional or global product market strategy*. In our view, this is one of the most important factors leading to centralized control. The evidence strongly suggests that such a strategy is being practised by Japanese MNEs with investments in the UK, in fairly marked contrast to the 'controlled autonomy' allowed to US subsidiaries in the 1950s. New United States subsidiaries now entering the UK to supply the European market might well be persuaded to follow the Japanese strategy, which is partly industry specific and partly a reflection of the UK's membership of the EC. Such a strategy affects the structure and process of decision making in almost all functional areas, especially where the MNE is promoting a world product (e.g. of the Coca Cola variety) and is geocentric in its approach to resource management.

At the end of the day then, it is our judgement that while the general *level* of control exercised over decision making in US and Japanese affiliates is associated more with the firm or industry characteristics, such as the age and industry of the affiliate and the degree of multinationalization and strategy of the parent company, the *direction* (or emphasis) of control and the manner in which it is exercised strongly reflects the country of origin of the parent company. In its turn, of course, this may have a time dimension. As Japanese firms become more multinational, as they compete with US and European MNEs on equal terms, as they become more immersed in different cultures and as their competitors adopt their more successful managerial and other styles, then they may lose some of their cultural idiosyncrasies, as indeed have US affiliates in the UK in the past 30 years.

But, for the moment, these unique country-specific characteristics do help to explain many of the differences in the structure and processes of the decision-taking pattern of the two groups of firms studied in this chapter.

8.4.5   The relevance of the locus of decision taking

Finally, what does it matter *who* takes the decisions in an MNE? Obviously, in so far as the long-term goals of the firm are affected, it *does* matter. If the organizational structure and the allocation of decision taking are inappropriate, both the firm and the countries in which it operates lose. In other instances, in so far as the source of decision taking may affect the quality of the decisions made, the question then arises as to whether some decision takers are more likely to act in accord with the interests of the host countries than those of the MNE as a whole.

The answer is almost certainly 'yes'. Centralized decisions made by geocentric or regiocentric MNEs are likely to be taken more with the global interests of the MNE, and occasionally those of the home country, in mind. By contrast, decentralized decisions by polycentric or multi-domestic MNEs are likely to be taken more with the interests of the host country in mind. Particularly, this would seem to be the case in respect of decisions relating to product development, production methods, local sourcing

policy, wages policy, personnel management and marketing. Surveys have also suggested that the nationality of the chief decision takers in subsidiaries will also affect the extent to which the subsidiary is more likely to be integrated into the economy of the home or host country.

Clearly, in their policies towards outward and inward MNE activity, host governments do pay considerable attention to the locus of decision taking. Indeed, it may be argued that performance requirements imposed by governments would be unnecessary, or less necessary, if the affiliates acted as free-standing economic units and decisions were taken by local managers rather than by those in parent companies.

The other aspect of the locus of decision taking concerns the power of the host government to modify the behaviour of MNE affiliates. This is critical when considering the relationships between organized labour and the MNE, since the local union negotiatiors may know very little about the economic viability of the affiliate or of the MNE of which it is part. It is shown in such areas as transfer pricing, dividend and capital repatriation and the location of technological capacity. We shall address our attention to these, and other matters, in Parts 4 and 5 of this volume.

8.5   CONCLUSIONS

The organizational structure of the cross-border activities of MNEs reflects not only the configuration of their O-specific advantages and that of the L characteristics of the countries in which they operate. However, it is also contingent on the degree and character of their multinationalization. The past half century has witnessed an increasing complexity both of the structure of multi-unit enterprises and of the global environment in which they operate. As a consequence, the organizational structure of MNEs has undergone considerable change and increasing differentiation. From a comparatively simple vertical and unidimensional set of control procedures designed to promote the ethnocentric or polycentric orientation of market- or resource-seeking foreign investors, the MNE has evolved into a complex hierarchy (or, in some cases, a heterarchy) of a network of vertical and lateral intra- and inter-firm relationships geared to advance its geocentric or regiocentric objectives.

In a recent article, Ghoshal and Nohria (1990) have used the expression 'requisite complexity' to suggest that the character of a firm's organizational structure must match that of the environment in which it operates. They assert that as the technological, economic and political content of the global environment has become more integrated and multi-faceted, yet at the same time more integrated, it has become necessary for MNEs to replace their archetype organizational systems, based on functional geographical, product or matrix structures by others that enable them both to be more responsive to national contingencies, yet exploit the benefits of cross-border linkages. Bartlett and Ghoshal identify such a structure as 'integrated variety', which they distinguish from a 'differentiated fit' structure, which, as its name implies, suggests a governance of headquarters–subsidiary relationships, which are adapted to the contingency of its environment.[13] In an examination of the organizational structure of some 41 MNEs, Ghoshal and Nohria found some support for the idea that companies that adhered to the principle of requisite complexity were those which, in the period 1982–86, achieved the best economic performance.[14] If anything, organizational developments since then have strengthened, rather than weakened, that principle.

NOTES

1 To quote from Chandler (1977b) 'If changes in business procedures and practices were patentable, the contribution of business change to the economic growth of the (US) nation would be as widely recognized as the influence of mechanical inventions or the inflow of capital from abroad'. In a similar vein, and some years earlier, Arrow (1970) had observed that 'truly among men's innovations, the use of organization to accomplish his ends is among his greatest and his earliest'.

2 We should emphasize that this chapter will deal with only very selective issues relating to the organization of MNEs and their affiliates. For a more comprehensive analysis, the reader is referred to international business textbooks, such as Beamish *et al.* (1991), Daniels and Radebaugh (1989), Grosse and Kujawa (1992), Robock and Simmonds (1989), Vernon and Wells (1987) and Weekly and Aggarwal (1987). For a more specialist treatment of organizational issues and the MNE, see three recently published volumes of collected writers, *viz* Bartlett *et al.* (1990), Hedlund (1992) and Westney and Ghoshal (1992).

3 For further details see p. 224 of this chapter.

4 The reader will observe that these risks are all aspects of market failure, dealt with in Chapter 4.

5 As identified in Note 2.

6 Some commentators describe a prior stage to the international division as the 'mother–daughter' structure in which the corporate headquarters is in charge of each and every foreign unit serving its own market, and which, for the most part, is given a fairly free hand in the operation of the business.

7 A term originally coined by Akio Morita of Sony.

8 Or, more particularly, of the perceptions of the local managers of these subsidiaries. It is quite possible, of course, that the perceptions of managers at the headquarters of the MNEs might have been rather different.

9 It should be observed that the authors' conclusions are based upon an examination of the tabulation results rather than by any formal statistical testing.

10 The following two pages are based upon Dunning (1986) and Dunning (1992c). We acknowledge that the data contained in this part of the chapter was initially prepared for the International Labour Organization (ILO).

11 In 1953 the average number of employees of the 59 US affiliates set up since 1940 was 361; the average number employed by Japanese affiliates in 1982 was 205 and in 1988 290.

12 See Chapter 17 for more details.

13 These structures follow the dimensions of differentiation and integration first introduced by Lawrence and Lorsch (1967).

14 Operationalized in terms of average return on net assets, average revenue growth and average annual growth of return on net assets.

CHAPTER 9

THE ORGANIZATION OF MNE ACTIVITY: INTER-FIRM RELATIONSHIPS

9.1 INTRODUCTION

We now turn to examine the ways in which MNEs may exert influence over the form and outcome of the transactions concluded between themselves and other firms. As in the previous chapter, we shall consider this aspect of the organization of resources, capabilities and markets from the perspective of the competitive advantages of firms and countries, as well as the ways in which these interact with each other. In particular, we shall argue that not only can the determinants of external relationships be analysed by use of the eclectic framework of international production, but also that the strategic choice as to the structure and pattern of these transactions is likely to be an important influence on the future OLI configuration of MNEs.

The chapter proceeds in the following way. First, it describes the kind of relationships an MNE may forge with other firms located outside its national boundaries. In doing so it considers all kinds of external relationships other than those which are purely arm's length. Second, it pays especial attention to two particular trans-border cooperative relationships, *viz* joint ventures and strategic alliances.

9.2 THE SPECTRUM OF ORGANIZATIONAL MODES: COOPERATION AND COMPETITION

In principle, any set or network of value-added activities may be organized in a variety of ways. Indeed, one can imagine a spectrum of organizational modes. At the one end of the spectrum, each activity along the chain may be undertaken by a separate (i.e. a single-product) firm, which will buy and sell its intermediate products from and to the open market. At the other end, all the activities may be undertaken by the same firm, which means that each of the intermediate product markets is internalized. In the former case, ownership, and hence the right to control the use of the products being bought or sold, is transferred at the point at which the transaction is made. In the latter, there is no change in *ownership*, hence *control* over the products transacted remains within the jurisdiction of the one and the same firm.

In between these two extreme forms of organization, a firm may engage in a variety of organizational relationships, each of which involves a different combination of resource and capability commitment, risk bearing and control sharing. In a command, or mixed economy, government fiat may also be considered a transactional mechanism. Most larger MNEs, and diversified MNEs, particularly those whose organizational structure is heterarchical rather than hierarchical, are likely to be simultaneously involved in a matrix of interdependent bilateral relationships, the character of each of which is likely to affect, and be affected by, the complex of relationships of which it is part.

A rather different (but complementary) approach to analysing the organization of business transactions is based on the extent to which economic agents perceive that it is better to compete or cooperate with each other to achieve their objectives. Most neo-classical economists view firms as vying with each other for resources, capabilities and markets, and for buyers and sellers as adversarial parties in any transaction. Moreover, while the invisible hand of the market is assumed to serve to organize transactions in such a way as to benefit all parties, it is also presumed that, except at the point of the exchange, the parties have no contact with one another.

In reality, there is a great deal of collaboration between enterprises, both as producers and as transactors, and there is every reason to suppose that in the modern global economy, this collaboration is increasing (Contractor and Lorange, 1988; Mowery, 1988, 1989). Indeed, apart from the two organizational extremes, all other relationships implicitly or explicitly assume that some degree of cooperation is beneficial for the participants. It is the perceived net advantages of the different kinds of cooperation, as compared with those of external markets or self-contained hierarchies or heterarchies, that will decide the mode employed. This will naturally vary according to the types of transactions undertaken, the organizational options open to the transactors and the characteristics of the firms, industries and countries participating in the transactions. In some cases, firms may work together to achieve specific and well articulated goals and for a limited period of time. In others, they may form joint ventures or non-equity alliances to promote and organize a large number of activities over a much longer period of time. Some firms, when faced with a particular market failure, may react by internalizing the market. Others might respond by working to lower the transaction costs of using it.

Until comparatively recently, most of the literature on MNE activity and international production has concentrated on the nature of *ownership* relationships rather than on *transactional* relationships between firms. Even today, most international business text books separate the issue of whether a firm that wishes to invest in a foreign country should do by acquiring or setting up a joint venture or a 100% owned affiliate, from that of the operational relationships it has both within its ambiance of governance (e.g. selling management services from the parent firm to one of its foreign affiliates) and between itself and independent firms. Network analysis suggests the *form* of these latter relationships may be no less important to the global competitiveness of the firm than the former, and that their determinants have much in common with ownership-related issues. While accepting this point,

we shall confine this chapter to describing and analysing the options to the complete ownership of firms. At the same time, we acknowledge that MNEs frequently engage in a myriad of cross-border transaction relationships with foreign firms and that the common governance over each may confer an O advantage in its own right.

9.3 COLLABORATIVE AGREEMENTS: SOME THEORETICAL CONSIDERATIONS

The choice of ownership by a firm of multiple value-added activities will be primarily decided on economic and strategic grounds; it will basically represent a tradeoff between its desire to control and manage these activities and that of minimizing resource commitments to achieve its objectives. Chapter 4 demonstrated that, if and when markets worked perfectly, there is no incentive for one firm to own or control[1] other than a single value-added activity. In imperfect markets, a firm may seek the ownership or control over multiple activities for three reasons. The first is that it believes such a governance is more likely to advance its goals than if the activities were under separate ownership. The second is to reduce the perceived transaction costs (including risk) of organizing the activities in a way that best advances its objectives. The third is to increase the economic rent earned on the activities and/or to control the use made of the final output.

The main costs of internalizing intermediate product markets are, first, the additional communications and organizational costs involved; second (in some instances), the additional production costs; and third, the uncertainty surrounding the commitment of additional resources and capabilities required to undertake the value-adding activities.

Let us give one or two examples of the kinds of tradeoffs involved in a control *versus* a no control situation:

(1) A Canadian aluminium fabricating company buys out a bauxite mine from a Jamaican mining company previously supplying it with bauxite. In doing so, it will incur capital costs in

acquiring the mine and, almost certainly, additional intra-firm communication and organizational costs in operating and managing the company. *De facto*, it is also likely to reduce its options for buying bauxite from alternative sources. On the other hand, it may reduce the transaction costs of procuring the product from an external supplier. These include the possibility of supply disruptions, the costs of not being able or willing to supply raw material of the right quality, the chance of price hikes and the possibility of a supplier concluding a relationship with a competitor to the firm's disadvantage.

(2) A Swiss pharmaceutical company decides to set up a foreign subsidiary in Australia to produce a new drug to cure AIDS from a formula developed in the Swiss laboratories. Again, it will incur capital costs in setting up a foreign subsidiary and coordinating its operations with those of other parts of its network of activities. At the same time, by internalizing the market for the drug formula, the Swiss firm may not only be able to control its use better than if it licensed the production rights to a foreign firm, but it also lessens the likelihood of any infringement or dissipation of its property rights.

(3) A US auto firm which, up to now, has licensed five manufacturing companies in Europe to produce a range of auto components to its specifications, decides to acquire the full ownership of each of these affiliates. It does so in order to promote better rationalization of its motor vehicle production, thereby lowering its production and transaction costs. Without such control, there might be resistance from the individual licensees as their goals may not coincide with that of the licensor. The capital costs and extra common governance costs incurred are among the additional resource costs which may require to be committed.

(4) A Singaporean-owned hotel chain wishes to extend its sphere of operations into the Japanese market. It has a choice of entering this market by setting up a joint equity venture or concluding a franchising agreement with a Japanese hotelier. In the former case, it may 'buy the right' to exert a critical influence over the design and building of the hotel and over its day-to-day management. In the latter case, though committing fewer resources, it is reliant on the terms of the franchise agreement to gain the maximum economic rent on its O advantages.

The above examples illustrate some of the advantages and disadvantages of not using both the market and the hierarchical organizational mode. According to Richardson (1972), firms do not abrogate their organizational territory at their boundaries of ownership. Indeed, their interests may embrace the whole of the value-added chain that affects their own wealth-creating capabilities. However, Richardson argues that firms are most likely to conclude alliances when they engage in complementary but dissimilar activities. He defines dissimilar activities as those requiring different technological capabilities and organizational skills, and complementary activities as those requiring different capabilities which need to be coordinated if a successful end product is to be produced. In such instances, coordination by co-operation may well be preferred to that by a single hierarchy, as the transactional costs of the latter in organizing dissimilar activities may be unacceptable. It may also be thought better than the market, as it is the plans of separate enterprises that need to be coordinated rather than the matching of aggregate supply to aggregate demand (Richardson, 1972). Indeed, Richardson goes on to suggest that any spectrum of inter-firm relationships ought to be based on the matching of activities to capabilities rather than on whether the constituent firms are producing complementary or substitutable products or processes.

The question then arises as to what extent it is possible to identify the determinants of the various type of inter-firm relationships and to suggest the appropriate relationships for a firm to pursue in its cross-border activities. Chapter 7 has suggested that such relationships embrace activities that might otherwise have been undertaken by separately owned firms along the value-added chains.[2] We will describe briefly each of the main forms of cooperative ventures and summarize the advantages and disadvantages of each. In doing so, we shall take both an economic (e.g. transactions cost minimizing) and a strategic perspective.[3]

9.4   JOINT EQUITY VENTURES

9.4.1   Forms of joint venture

We shall define a joint equity venture as any long-term alliance which falls short of a merger and in which two or more economic entities own a sufficiently large proportion of the equity capital to give each of them some degree of control or influence over key areas of decision taking. The participating owners in a joint venture may be business enterprises, public bodies, international agencies, charitable foundations or individuals. A cross-border joint venture is one in which economic entities from at least two countries are involved. When any one economic entity owns the majority (i.e. 51% or above) of the equity stake in a joint venture, it is *de jure* able to control the decision taking in the venture. *De facto*, however, the extent to which control or influence is exerted by a majority shareholder depends on the relative contribution which each of the shareholders can, and does, make to the venture other than the capital investment,[4] as well as on the transaction costs which may have to be incurred before a mutually acceptable decision is reached, for example, in respect of location of new investments, repatriation of profits, allocation of export markets etc.

In other cases, although an MNE may own a majority equity stake in a foreign-based venture, it may choose to devolve decision taking to that venture. It will do this whenever it is perceived that the local partner, for whatever reason, is likely to take the optimal organizational and operational decisions, and where there is a complete congruence of goals and managerial philosophy between the foreign and domestic shareholders. By the same reasoning, a firm with a minority interest (i.e. less than 50%) may not have *de jure* control, but because of its size and reputation and the nature of its contributions to the joint venture, may still exercise a good deal of influence (Prahalad and Hamel, 1990). Moreover, such influence may vary according to the structure of the equity stake. A joint venture in which there are just two active equity shareholders – one holding a 51% and the other a 49% stake – is likely to be organized and managed very differently from one in which there is no majority shareholder but several substantial minority shareholders, or, indeed, from one in which two firms each own one-half of the equity capital.

Much will also rest on the identity of the other partners and what each brings to, and expects of, the partnership. For example, it is quite possible for the majority shares of a foreign affiliate to be owned by the host government, yet for it to have no active role in its management. Often, the function of such passive partners is to ensure that, as far as possible, the local shareholders or other stakeholders get a fair share of the value added by the subsidiary, and that the decisions taken by the board of directors are not against the interests of the majority stakeholder. In other instances, a joint venture may involve both a financial and an active participatory input from each of the partners.

9.4.2   Origin of a joint venture

A joint equity venture may be initiated by two or more parties to the venture setting up a new enterprise to supply a particular range of goods and services. Or it might come about by one, or more, of the participants partially acquiring the assets of the other. A cross-border joint venture may be owned by shareholders from one or more countries. It may be the only FDI which one or more of the parties to the venture may have. Alternatively – and this is increasingly the case in the early 1990s – it may be part of a network of international value-added activities.

Like fully-owned affiliates, joint ventures may be set up to service, or better service, markets, to acquire resources or capabilities, or to promote a more efficient deployment of existing foreign-based assets. To this extent, the motives underlying joint ventures are exactly the same as those for MNE activity set out in Chapter 3. Conglomerate companies might also engage in joint venture activities as part of their portfolio restructuring strategies. In some cases, the initiative for setting up a transnational joint venture may come from sources in the host country. Examples would be the Indian government seeking a UK partner to help it develop a line of machine tools for sale to the Indian market, or a Thai clothing firm wishing to arrange a joint venture with a Japanese trading company to help it market its products in Japan. In others, the impetus will come from a foreign firm. More recently the setting up of a new joint venture by two or more established MNEs to fulfil a specific objective which neither can (or is prepared to) achieve on its own has become an increasingly important vehicle of entry.[5] Other joint ventures may arise as the result of partial acquisitions or by merger. This may also be encouraged, and sometimes partially financed by, international financial agencies, such as the International Finance Corporation, the World Bank, the European Investment Bank and the Asian Development Bank.

9.4.3   Under what conditions are joint equity ventures likely to be concluded?

In organizing its foreign production, a firm may choose to share its ownership with another firm for a variety of economic or strategic reasons. In some cases, of course, a host government may not allow a foreign entity complete ownership of a local firm. Should this happen, a joint venture may be the second-best option open to it. In others, however, joint ventures may be perceived as a first-best cross-border ownership and organizational strategy. This is particularly likely where each partner brings to the venture a different, but complementary, set of resources, capabilities and markets, where the resource commitments are substantial and where the outcome of the venture is highly uncertain. In such a situation, the transaction costs of partly owning and managing a joint venture are likely to be less than those of fully owning and controlling that venture. This, in turn, would suggest that the expected returns (discounted for risk) perceived to arise from the additional capital necessary to acquire a full ownership are less than the marginal opportunity costs of that capital.

The literature identifies characteristics of, and reasons why, firms conclude joint ventures. Some of these are set out in Exhibit 9.1. As Tallman and Shenkar (1990) observe, any full explanation requires an integration of both economic and sociological theories. In this chapter, we shall concentrate on the former. Sometimes such ventures are used as the

---

Exhibit 9.1   The changing characteristics of joint ventures.

1960s–70s	1980s–90s
Transitional: 'testing the water' entry strategy; a hybrid ownership form between a non-equity alliance and full equity participation.	Frequently non-transitional or complementary to other entry strategies.
Second-best to other organizational modalities.	As a first-best entry strategy.
Freestanding as part of a polycentric or multi-domestic strategy of MNEs.	Integrated with a geocentric or global strategy of MNEs.
Mainly undertaken by medium or smaller MNEs, especially from smaller home countries.	Increasingly undertaken by larger MNEs from leading capital exporting countries.
Especially favoured by firms engaging in *market-seeking* or *natural resource* seeking investment.	Also favoured by firms engaging in *strategic asset seeking* investment.
Especially favoured by developing countries.	Spread throughout both developed and developing countries.
Especially prevalent in mature sectors or in those producing standard goods.	Spread throughout sectors, including technology and information intensive sectors, in which economies of scale are prevalent.
Designed primarily to reduce risks of 100% commitment.	Intended mainly to acquire complementary assets and capture economies of synergy.

initial mode of entry into a foreign market, or as a way of acquiring intangible assets or knowledge about local supply capabilities and labour conditions. Sometimes a foreign affiliate may find it easier to deal with a host government, or gain contracts from public authorities if it is locally financed and/or managed. Sometimes a foreign company may not have the capital (or the credit rating) to form a subsidiary by itself.

The extent to which a joint venture is integrated into one or the other partner's overall strategy and plans may crucially affect the attitudes of each partner to it. In general, a self-contained and free-standing joint venture set up to supply goods and services for the local market is likely to give rise to fewer and less serious conflicts of interest between the parties than one which is part of a global network of the foreign investor. There is also some evidence to suggest that joint ventures involving partners of equal size and importance are less likely to be successful than those involving partners of different size and significance (Mowery, 1990).

Joint ventures will be preferred to non-equity contractual arrangements for exactly the same reasons as will fully-owned subsidiaries, *viz* to reduce production or transaction costs and advance the strategic objectives of the participating firms. The exact nature of the market failure will depend on the kinds of products being traded and on the bargaining relationship between the trading parties. Thus, some joint ventures are *vertical* and essentially replace subcontracting and/or licensing relationships *along* the value-adding chain of a particular product. Others are *lateral* or *horizontal* and are concluded primarily to exploit the economies of scope and scale of at least one of the investing parties *across* value-added chains. Both may be undertaken to protect or advance the competitive positions of the participating firms and to assist them in the restructuring of their portfolio of assets. Joint ventures may be used both as an entry into unfamiliar markets and as a way of acquiring or monitoring new technological and organizational developments.

The joint equity venture, then, is an enterprise that attempts to capture the general benefits of internalizing the market for the proprietary rights of the participants and any specific benefits associated with shared joint ownership. At the same time, it makes it possible to spread some of the transaction costs associated with the indivisibility of scale and scope economies. Hennart (1988) has termed joint ventures motivated by this objective as 'scale' ventures and distinguished them from 'link' joint ventures which are prompted by the simultaneous failure of at least two intermediate product markets. In both cases, as long as the expected economic and strategic gains are sufficient to offset the organizational costs involved and the economic rent foregone, joint ownership will be the preferred modality of foreign participation.

9.4.4   When are joint equity ventures likely to succeed?

The simple answer to this question is when the parties are in complete accord about:

(1) the objectives of the joint venture,

(2) the amount and type of resources which each partner should commit to the venture,

(3) the way in which the venture is organized and managerial responsibility is divided,

(4) the distribution of benefits of the venture,

(5) the form and direction of the venture's growth and/or its pattern of diversification.

There are many reasons why such an accord may be difficult to achieve or maintain among the partners to a joint venture. Also the transaction costs associated with reconciling or settling such differences as and when they occur may sometimes cause a joint venture to flounder or fail.

Some issues surrounding the formation and operation of an international joint venture which may need to be resolved are identified in Exhibit 9.2. Sometimes these may be explicitly addressed in any contract. At other times the understanding reached by the partners may be more tacit or implicit. Can one identify such situations in which this is likely to occur?

First, as a general rule, free-standing or self-contained co-operative ventures are less likely to give rise to conflict situations than those which are intended to advance the global strategy of the foreign investor. The expectation of gains to the rest of the MNE of which a joint venture is part may considerably influence operational decisions with

Exhibit 9.2   Partnerships involving MNEs: management and organizational issues.

Nature	Who with?
Objectives	What for?
Strategy	How does it fit in with TNCs goals?
Bargaining	Who gains what?
Verticality	How are risks shared?
Behaviour	What is expected of venture by governments?

respect to such functions as the sourcing of components, distribution of assets, marketing, movement of personnel and transfer pricing. These may not accord with the interests of the local partner. The external costs and benefits of joint ventures[6] are likely to vary between the parties. Indeed, a benefit to one party may be a cost to another. In consequence, a consensus will be more difficult to reach. Second, there is likely to be some conflict where the parties operate radically different managerial styles and philosophies and the division of executive responsibility is unclear. This was dramatically demonstrated by the very different managerial approaches adopted by GEC (UK) and Siemens (Germany) at the time of their joint bid for Plessey in 1989. Successful joint ventures require partners to have a congruence of goals and empathetic corporate personalities.

Third, the more idiosyncratic and less saleable the assets provided by each partner, the greater the problem of costing these contributions. Fourth, and this may occur particularly in cases in which government has a substantial equity stake, disagreements may arise on operational questions, such as production methods, sourcing, employment and training of nationals, and export strategies. What the local partner perceives to be in its best interests will not necessarily be that which the foreign firm aims to achieve. An extreme example is the closure of a plant which, although viable, is not perceived to advance the goals of the foreign MNE. However, there are many day-to-day decisions which may constrain the freedom of the partners to a joint venture.

By contrast, it is possible to establish situations in which the economic or strategic interests of firms are closely aligned to each other. These include those identified by Richardson (1972) where there are pronounced organizational, market and technological synergies, and where the combined strengths of the partners help each to compete more effectively against a larger or more aggressive competitor (Contractor and Lorange, 1988), and/or to negotiate more effectively with suppliers, customers, labour unions and governments. In each case, however, it is possible that one or other of these objectives could also be accomplished through a non-equity alliance. The subject of strategic alliances will be discussed later in the chapter.

One of the factors influencing the viability and success of cross-border joint ventures concerns the choice of partner. Several writers from Tomlinson (1970) onwards have sought to identify the criteria by which a partner may be selected. These include the opportunity for reciprocal benefits, a tight appropriability regime to minimize undesirable spill-over effects of shared assets and competences, a favourable past association, an ability to negotiate with foreign governments and local labour unions, compatible goals, and mutual trust and forebearance. Geringer (1991) makes the distinction between task-related criteria, which he defines as 'operational skills and resources which a venture requires for its competitive success', and partner-related criteria, which he defines as 'the efficiency and effectiveness of partners' cooperation'.[7] Both criteria are normally related to the extent to which each partner can contribute to the core assets or critical success factors of the joint venture.

In a wide ranging field study embracing a random sample of 81 international joint ventures selected from a list of ventures concluded between 1980 and 1985, Geringer sought to relate some 15 variables which might influence partner selection to the significance attached to these variables as advancing the Critical Success Factors (CSF) of firms. Responses of firms were assessed using a 5-point Likert-type scale (0 = 'not important', 4 = 'very important'). The results of the study suggested that the association between CSFs and the importance attached to the variables influencing partner

Table 9.1 Characteristics affecting the choice of contractual arrangements.

Characteristic	Outright control		Contractual arrangement				
	Green-field	Merger	Joint venture	Industrial collabor-ation	Subcon-tracting	Sales fran-chising	Licensing
Nature of advantage							
Involves work organization and management	+	0	0	0	−	0	−
Protection and codification difficult	+	+	0	0	−	−	−
Further improvements likely from experience	+	+	0	−	−	−	−
Nature of firm							
Capital is difficult to obtain	−	−	0	0	0	0	+
Management skills are narrow	−	−	0	0	+	+	0
Nature of industry							
Output mobile and demand very inelastic	+	+	0	0	+	−	−
Inputs mobile and supply very inelastic	+	+	0	0	−	+	−
Quality very variable	+	0	0	0	−	+	−
Quality difficult to judge by inspection	+	+	+	+	−	−	−
Perishable or delicate output	+	+	+	+	−	−	+
Monopolized distribution channel	+	+	0	0	−	−	+
Economies of scope in marketing	−	−	0	0	−	+	0
Nature of countries (and industry)							
Large difference in production environment	−	+	+	+	+	−	+
Large difference in marketing environment	−	+	+	+	−	+	+
Large scope for transfer pricing gains	+	+	0	0	−	−	−
Host government dislikes foreign control	−	−	0	+	0	0	0
Political relations make expropriation risk high	−	−	0	+	0	0	+
Difficult communications	−	−	−	−	0	0	+

+ joint venture is likely to be able to resolve these issues.
0 joint venture may make only a modest contribution.
− joint venture is unlikely to be able to resolve these issues.

Source: Casson (1987).

selection were positive and significant. Also, the greater the perceived difficulties of the partner firms in maintaining or advancing their CSFs, the higher the relative weighting of selection criteria associated with these factors.[8]

Finally, it should be observed that the costs and benefits of joint ventures (compared with those of contractual arrangements) may differ according to a variety of economic or strategic characteristics which may themselves be industry, country and firm specific. Table 9.1, adapted from Casson (1987), identifies some of these and the extent to which a joint venture is likely to be a potentially satisfying organizational arrangement for dealing with each of

them. A positive sign indicates this to be so; a negative sign that it is unlikely to do so, or to bring net costs; and a zero suggests a joint venture may make only a modest contribution to the strategies of the partners involved.

9.4.5 Minority and majority joint ventures

The factors influencing the extent of a firm's ownership in a foreign joint venture are usually discussed in the literature in terms of the advantages of a majority versus a minority stake. The argument is that a majority stake will be preferred when control over a resource commitment is highly valued and where the firm perceives that it can absorb the transaction costs of acquiring and monitoring that control. On the other hand, where, for example, the contribution of the minority partner is a unique and highly valued competence, its bargaining strength derives from that capability rather than from any equity capital it may supply. Assuming that it can effectively control the use of its assets and can appropriate the full economic rent from them, the firm needs no equity participation in the value-added activity arising from it. This is especially likely to be the case if the minority investor is more efficient in the utilization of the technology and there are no benefits to be derived from integrating the joint venture with the rest of the foreign firm's operations.

In such cases, a non-equity cooperative venture may well serve the interests of the foreign firm. We shall see, in the following section, that where the quality and use made of the intermediate product being traded can be controlled through a contract or some kind of less formal (but no less binding) agreement between the partners, this modality of transference may be acceptable. A minority equity stake as a first-best solution is only likely to occur when a firm wishes to influence the general management philosophy or operational strategy of a firm to which it is selling, or from which it is buying particular intermediate products, and where it believes that it can best achieve this by being represented on its board of directors and other decision-taking bodies.

However, it might not be able to do this without owning a majority equity stake. How much equity stake the foreign investor may feel it *needs* will vary according to the distribution of the other shareholdings and the extent to which it wishes to influence the activities of the firm which are complementary to those in which it is directly involved. How much equity stake a foreign investor may be *allowed* will depend on its bargaining strength relative to that of the other partners. As the literature points out, the set of factors influencing the balance of bargaining power among the participants in a joint venture are not the same as those influencing the optimum balance of incentives. Hence, the prevalence of side payments (e.g. licence fees) particularly in cases where there are transaction

costs or moral hazard or adverse selection (Chi and Roehl, 1989).

9.4.6   Empirical evidence on joint ventures

Introduction

Many studies have been undertaken which attempt to evaluate the reasons why, or the circumstances in which, joint ventures are concluded and the factors influencing their success. Though they vary by industry, country and type of firm, they all present a consistent picture. Joint ventures are most likely to be undertaken when the benefits of inter-firm interdependence are the most pronounced (Pfeffer and Nowak, 1976); where the financial risks of innovation and foreign marketing are particularly high (Mowery, 1990); and where there is likely to be strong trust and mutual forebearance among partners to the venture (Buckley and Casson, 1988; Casson, 1987). By contrast, joint ventures are generally more difficult to manage and coordinate than single-firm hierarchies and heterarchies. Also, the transaction costs associated with resolving these difficulties – particularly those to do with differences in cultural and attitudinal perspectives and organizational structures – are often underestimated by the partner firms. Nor can the problems always be anticipated or evaluated prior to the formation of the partnership. Some are 'experience' rather than 'inspection' disbenefits.

As might be expected, the problems tend to be most pronounced between partners of joint ventures from different industries and countries, as well as between firms of different sizes, entrepreneurial vision and managerial ideologies. They are greatest in sectors where the competitive advantages of at least one of the partners are highly transaction idiosyncratic and where the risk of dissipation or misuse of property rights is high. Until the 1980s, cross-border joint ventures were more likely to be preferred by firms producing mature or standard products; by enterprises from developing rather from developed countries; by inexperienced rather than experienced foreign investors; by firms investing in unfamiliar organizational and/or political unstable regimes; and by MNEs pursuing multi-domestic rather than globally-oriented production or marketing strategies.

Some illustrations

The earliest empirical studies on joint ventures were mainly concerned with identifying their *raison d'être* and structures. These studies found that joint ventures tended to occur between firms in the same or similar industries as a 2-digit (US) SIC[9] level (Fusfeld, 1958; Pate, 1969), and that the majority were either horizontally or vertically integrated. Their incidence was especially noteworthy in mining, petroleum refining and technology-intensive sectors, and among larger and diversified firms (Boyle, 1968; Pate, 1969). There is also some suggestion that joint ventures were motivated more to capture the gains of synergy and reduce uncertainty in oligopolistic sectors than to advance market power[10] (Pfeffer and Nowak, 1976; Berg and Freidman, 1977, 1981; McConnell and Nantell, 1985).

Chapter 6 (Sections 6.2.5 and 6.3.4) has already surveyed some of the attempts by economists and marketing scholars to identify the main variables influencing the choice of entry into a foreign market. Most have indicated that, until the mid 1980s, joint ventures served as a substitute for other modes of entry, but that the preference for them varied according to the country of origin of the partner firms (Franko, 1976; Kogut and Singh, 1988) and the perceived need for cross-border collaboration (Hladik, 1985).

The following section amplifies this evidence by considering two other areas of research. The first seeks to explain the ownership structure of MNEs; the second deals with some behavioural characteristics of joint ventures.

(i) *Ownership patterns* Using the extensive database compiled for the Harvard Multinational Enterprise Study, Stopford and Wells (1972) found that the preference of MNEs for full ownership of their foreign affiliates rested on their perceived need to protect their proprietary rights and to control decision taking. The authors established that the propensity of firms to conclude joint ventures was lowest in R&D-intensive industries and where they practised:

(1) a centralized market strategy and standardized production methods,

(2) produced high income differentiated products,

(3) were dependent on critical raw materials.

Joint ventures were most likely to be undertaken when the investing firm had little knowledge of the local company and politics and where speed of entry was essential. Of the areas of conflict identified by Stopford and Wells, those to do with the retention of earnings, export market allocation and intra-firm pricing were the most frequently cited.

It is only comparatively recently that the same data has been econometrically analysed. Using such data supplemented from other sources, including the PIMS database, Gomes-Casseres (1989b) tested the ownership choice between a fully-owned and joint venture by using binomial logit analysis. Controlling for government influences on ownership patterns, Gomes-Casseres discovered that the probability of an MNE concluding a joint venture was *negatively* correlated with its previous experience of operating foreign subsidiaries in the same sector and with its familiarity of the country in which the joint venture was being contemplated. Subsidiaries in marketing-intensive industries were less likely to be jointly owned than others, while the odds of shared ownership were 'about one-third lower for a subsidiary that sold more than 10% of its output to the MNE system than for one that sold less' (p. 16). On the other hand, the size of the host country's industrial sector was positively correlated with the propensity of MNEs to conclude market-seeking joint ventures, particularly when the investing firm depended on the input of raw materials and the local partner could contribute marketing knowledge and skills. It was also established that the probability of concluding joint ventures was greater in technology-intensive sectors in which process technologies were more critical than in product industries. Gomes-Casseres suggests that this reflected the lower transaction costs in process technology. In both cases, the presence of local supplier capability was found to be important.

In another contribution, the same author (1990) demonstrated that the role of host governments was often critical in affecting the ownership structure of FDI, and that in part, at least, its willingness and capability to do so reflected its bargaining and negotiating ability *vis à vis* the MNE. Building on some earlier work by Fagre and Wells (1982) and Lecraw (1984), Gomes-Casseres showed that, normalizing for other variables and assuming that, from a host government's viewpoint, it was desirable for there to be some local ownership of foreign affiliates, that the greater the bargaining power of governments, the more likely that joint ventures would be concluded. In this same piece of research, Gomes-Casseres also established that MNEs which owned relatively large subsidiaries and were faced with intensive competition were most likely to conclude joint ventures, as were smaller-sized foreign investors. However, both these latter variables lost much of their statistical significance once the bargaining strength of the host government was introduced as an explanatory variable.[11]

(ii) *Characteristics of joint ventures* Most of the empirical work on joint ventures has not distinguished between those involving both domestic and foreign companies. Typical of such studies is one by Berg and Friedman (1980) who examined the incidence and characteristics of 796 US joint ventures concluded between 1964 and 1975. In an OLS multivariate analysis, the authors found that the incidence of joint ventures was positively related to the size of firm and that industry R&D intensity was a significant determinant of the sectoral mix of joint ventures. There was little or no evidence that joint ventures led to higher rates of profitability, but some suggestion that innovatory collaborative arrangements substituted for hierarchical R&D expenditures.

There have been several field studies of the attributes of cross-border joint ventures. Some of these are summarized by Beamish (1984, 1985) and Beamish and Banks (1987). Most, however, are dyadic by nature. While transaction costs analysis provides a powerful analytical tool, it needs to be supplemented by a bargaining model in the case of joint ventures in developing countries and a strategic model in the case of those in industrialized economies. The distinction between the motives for investing in developed and developing countries is further emphasized by Beamish (1985). In his field research, he established that while 64% of foreign firms questioned gave the need for partner skills as their main reason 'for concluding joint ventures', and

17% 'government restrictions', some 57% of those seeking partners in developing countries thought 'government restrictions' and 38% the need for local skills to be the most important determinants.

In a study of 141 joint ventures formed in China between 1980 and 1987 and involving US partners, Shan (1991) discovered some support for the proposition that the parent company's share in a joint venture was inversely correlated with the amount of uncertainties and risks involved, and the dependency of the venture on the contextual and transactional relationships within the host country. Using a truncated Tobit model (Maddala, 1983) an performing a two-tail significance test, he also established that a larger share of foreign ownership is associated with a lower level of operational dependence in resource-based, but not in manufacturing and services, sectors. Also, the dependence of joint ventures on local cf. export, markets is inversely correlated with the foreign share of ownership. The study gives some credence to the view that committing the local partner to a larger share of the joint venture aligns it to the interests of the managing partner and reduces its incentive to pursue goals which may work against the interests of the venture.

In an examination of the determinants of majority (as opposed to minority) ownership in 497 foreign affiliates of Swedish MNEs in 1974, and using a model of dichotonomous choice,[12] Blomström and Zejan (1991) ascertained that firms with only brief experience of foreign production and with highly diversified product lines were the most likely to choose minority ventures. After a certain point, the size of a host country's market was positively related to the propensity of a firm to conclude minority joint ventures. Such ventures were also found to be a preferable mode of investment in developing countries. Rather surprisingly, the probability of including a minority ownership was positively correlated with the size of the parent companies, while the R&D variable was found to be insignificant.[13]

In another study,[14] Kogut (1989b) demonstrated that dissolutions among the US joint ventures in manufacturing are least likely to occur where the opportunities for reciprocal gains and 'tit for tat' behaviour are most pronounced. One example was in R&D ventures concluded by firms in technologically-intensive industries. The hazard of unwanted termination was also seen to be statistically significant in cases where the partners to the ventures had other horizontal ties with eachother, for example, via licensing or other joint venture agreements.

In a careful econometric analysis of the ownership structures of Japanese manufacturing affiliates in the US in 1985, Hennart (1991) concluded that joint ventures were likely to be the preferred ownership mode wherever the transaction costs of acquiring intermediate products in the US market were particularly high. *Inter alia* Hennart found that the propensity to conclude joint ventures was highest when Japanese firms were entering the US market for the first time and when they needed complementary local resources and capabilities to exploit fully their own O-specific advantages. Contrary to other empirical research described in Chapter 6, Hennart did not discover any statistical relationship between the R&D intensity of a sector and the preference of Japanese investors for full equity ownership. This, Hennart speculated, was because the particular proprietary advantages of Japanese MNEs manufacturing in the 1980s did not rest in their innovating prowess.

Other empirical studies pay some attention to the instability of joint ventures (Killing, 1982, 1983; Harrigan, 1985). Most of these reduce to a conflict of goals and managerial strategies between the participating partners. As Kogut (1988b) has shown using data from a variety of field studies, these are likely to be significantly higher between partners of disparate size. Apart from these studies, however, many of the hypotheses about the character and behaviour of joint ventures put forward by Harrigan (1985), for example, still await rigorous empirical testing. However, what does seem to be emerging from the literature is that it is increasingly difficult to take a unidimensional approach to understanding the 'whys' and 'wherefores' of joint ventures. For example, only limited progress has been made in examining the impact of the changing form of inter-firm governance on the thinking about the organizational structure of MNEs, yet an MNE that owns an integrated network of activities is likely to view the role of joint ventures very differently from a multi-domestic MNE that operates a group of 'stand-alone' affiliates. Similarly, a local partner of a joint venture will evaluate the costs and benefits of a joint venture according to its own organizational strategy and positioning in other networks of value-added activities.

It is these issues, which require a multi-dimensional approach, which are still awaiting serious analysis by scholars.

The dynamics of joint ventures

A review of the literature quite clearly suggests that both the propensity to conclude joint ventures and the motives for such joint ventures have changed over the past 30 years. In a study of the ownership patterns of foreign direct investments of large MNEs between 1961 and 1975, Gomes-Casseres (1988, 1989b) identifies an ownership cycle by which the proportion of joint ventures to all new investments by large US MNEs rose from 28% in 1955 to 55% in 1961, then fell back to only 31% in 1969. This cycle was repeated in the following two decades. The fact that the proportion of jointly owned US affiliates in developing countries had remained between 34% and 38% between 1966 and 1985 (Kobrin, 1988) is entirely consistent with the findings of Gomes-Casseres.

Taking a longer perspective, it may be more appropriate to view these changing ownership patterns rather differently and, in particular, relate them to the interface between the gradual globalization of business activity and the world economic and political environment. In the first three decades of the post-war period, most MNE activity took the form of market-seeking or resource-based FDI. Frequently the strategies of MNEs were polycentric, while in the main, host governments favoured the shared ownership of inbound direct investment.

In the last decade, for both internal and external reasons, the factors making for joint ventures have undergone quite dramatic changes. With the growth of efficiency and strategic asset seeking investment, the organization of MNEs has become more geocentric in character. At the same time, the more liberal stance adopted by many host governments towards inbound FDI since the late 1970s has, in the words of Contractor (1990), 'resulted in a small but unequivocal reduction in the proportion and share of sales of 50–50 and minority affiliates (as a fraction of all US affiliates) in all but a handful of countries' (p. 71). Both these factors might have been expected to lead to a decline in the role of joint ventures.

Counteracting this tendency have been the escalating costs of innovatory and marketing activities, the shortening of product cycles, the increase in speed of technical obsolescence, the technological convergence of the leading industrialized countries and the opening up of territories previously closed to all forms of FDI. These factors, together with the need for firms to concentrate their areas of control over their core assets and the reduction in some kinds of cross-border market failure, have led to more coalitions of all kinds.[15] Indeed, it may be fair to say that many contemporary MNEs regard markets, joint ventures and hierarchies less as antithetic organizational forms and more as complementary transactional relationships within a network of heterarchically governed activities.

The evolutionary approach expressed in the previous paragraphs has been more explicitly examined by Jacques (1985) with reference to the changing ownership pattern of Japanese firms. Jacques shows that over the past 30 years, Japan has moved from a relatively closed economy which favoured inbound market-seeking joint ventures, aimed primarily at overcoming indigenous marketing and distribution facilities, towards a more open economy in which the Japanese aspire to become world-class industrial leaders. To do so, however, Japanese firms needed to supplement their own assets with those of foreign firms and to move higher up their value-added chains. Sometimes they did this by cross-border A&Ms or by setting up fully-owned subsidiaries. However, more often than not they did so by fostering a new breed of partnership in high value activities. Jacques shows that between 1973 and 1984, the percentage of Japanese joint venture entries into the US in marketing fell from 55% to 25%, while those in R&D rose from 8% to 38%.

A final example of the metamorphic character of the ownership structure of MNEs is given by Cainarca *et al.* (1988) who, in an examination of 2014 agreements in the information technology industry, revealed that according to the stage of the technological life cycle of the industry, O-specific assets tend either to be internalized within hierarchies or be exploited jointly with those of other firms. According to the authors, the propensity to enter into cooperative arrangements is most likely in two of the five stages of development identified. The first is where the innovatory firm is in need of complementary assets to exploit its own competitive advantages properly; the second is where the industry is in its mature and experienced stage in which market structures have stabilized and there are few barriers to entry for new firms. Somewhat surprisingly, in the light of the growth of R&D-oriented joint ventures, the authors concluded that only a relatively small proportion of agreements in the pre-production stage did not involve equity participation.

9.5   NON-EQUITY CROSS-BORDER COOPERATIVE VENTURES

We now turn briefly to discuss inter-firm agreements and cooperative relationships that do not involve equity capital. There are a large number of these. Each reflects the outcome of a bargaining process. Each involves varying degrees of resource commitment and division-of-responsibilities risk sharing between the parties to the relationship. They may range from one-off, time limited agreements (e.g. turnkey ventures) to continuing, space limited contracts (e.g. franchising agreements). However, for the purposes of this discussion, it may be helpful to distinguish between two main types of organizational form: buyer/seller relationships and strategic business alliances.

9.5.1   Buyer/seller ventures

These mainly involve relationships *along* a value-added chain between a firm in one country and that in another. They include cross-border procurement ventures as an alternative to backward vertical integration or buying in the open market, as well as licensing agreements, franchising and management contracts as an alternative to forward vertical integration or selling in the open market.

Each of these arrangements may involve varying degrees of cooperation between the parties to the agreement, together with a range of formulae by which rights and duties are assigned, and risks, responsibilities and returns are shared. Let us give some examples. First, consider some kinds of backward cooperative or forms of buying relationships. These may consist of a one-off transaction in which the contractor simply specifies what he needs from the supplier and accepts or rejects the product according to whether or not it meets that specification. Alternatively, they may involve a detailed and continuing interface between customer and supplier. Such interaction may include the provision of information or financial assistance by the contractor, and/or advice on methods, pricing, component sourcing, testing procedures, costing and so on (UNCTC, 1981; Lall, 1980b). These issues are taken up more fully in Chapters 11 and 16.

A different sort of agreement is the *risk service* contract in which a foreign firm is subcontracted to carry out exploration development and operations for which the contractor provides the risk capital. In this case, the capital plus interest is usually reimbursed once production begins. In addition, the foreign enterprise may be entitled to purchase part of the product at an agreed discounted price, or indeed share in the profits of the enterprise. A *production sharing agreement* is another variant of subcontracting. Here, the foreign enterprise bears the production expenses in return for which it receives a stipulated percentage of the gross output plus a share of the remaining output and/or profits, as agreed by the two parties. In this case, the risk is almost entirely borne by the foreign investor without any formal equity participation.

Forward cooperative or selling agreements are even more numerous and complex. The literature usually makes a distinction between four main kinds of arrangements, *viz licensing, franchising, management* and *turnkey contract* agreements. In each case some kind of proprietary advantage is leased by the contractor to the contractee for an agreed and specified period of time. It is the contractee (rather than the contractor) that then owns the value added to this advantage. The agreements, however, may differ in the kinds of advantage transferred, the allocation of rights and responsibilities between the contractor and contractee, the timing of the contract and the nature and distribution of the benefits conferred by it.

Licensing agreements, for example, typically involve the transfer of a right to use a specific piece of proprietary technology (e.g. the exploitation of a patent) relevant to the production of a physical product. Though the licensee is usually responsible for that production, the agreement may allow the contractor some control over the use made of the

rights to ensure that his own competitive position is protected. In some cases, such control may embrace a wide range of decisions, for example, sourcing of inputs, production methods, employment of foreign nationals and export markets served. Such control is frequently a cause for conflict between MNE and host governments; this point is taken up at some length in Chapter 15. The usual payment for a licence is a fee or royalty based on the value or quantity of the output which embodies the information and knowledge provided by the licensor. Occasionally it may also be related to the profits earned by the licensee.

Franchise agreements, which are most common in service sectors, may contain extremely detailed requirements and conditions, for example, with respect to quality control, which the franchisor may expect the franchisee to observe. MacDonald's, the fast food chain, lays down 35 steps in the cooking and marketing of a hamburger, which each of its franchisees must scrupulously follow. In other cases, however, the only service provided may be the marketing, distribution or selling of a product, for example, hotel reservation systems. As in licensing, the terms of the agreement will normally allow the contractor some governance over the deployment of the transferred rights. They are also likely to permit the contractor to make regular inspections of the franchisee's facilities, and sometimes to have a voice over critical areas of decision taking and the recruitment of key personnel. Consideration typically takes the form of a lump sum payment from the franchisee to the franchisor for the franchising right, plus a fee based upon unit sales.

In the case of *management contracts*, the 'know-how' of the management of the contractor is transferred to the contractee, who then has the responsibility for undertaking the normal management services according to the terms of the contract. However, *de facto*, management contracts are rarely concerned with transferring management skills alone. In the international hotel industry, for example, it is common for the contractor – normally a hotel chain – to inject a particular corporate philosophy, provide managerial and personnel skills, offer access to funds, train local personnel, provide worldwide procurement capabilities, and – through a global reservation system – tap the local hotel into an international marketing network. Management contracts usually allow for a considerable amount of direction by the contractor over the contractee's operations, including the appointment of senior staff. At the same time, the contractor is relieved of any capital responsibility, which may be substantial (e.g. in the construction and airline industries). Successful management contracts do, however, require a close understanding between contractor and contractee, as well as clearly defined lines of responsibility. Payment usually consists of a lump sum managerial fee plus a variable royalty based on turnover and/or profits.

The *turnkey contract* is a 'one-off' agreement by which a foreign enterprise agrees to design, build and equip a complete unit of production, such as a petrochemical plant or a motor car factory, and then turn it over to a local enterprise after a 'running in' period during which the staff of the foreign enterprise manages the establishment while training local personnel. The turnkey normally involves a comprehensive and integrated package of foreign assistance, covering feasibility studies, basic design, engineering, procurement, construction, technical assistance, training, finance and management, all of which are laid down in the initial agreement. The payment to the enterprise is usually based on a formula which might include a lump sum fee plus a royalty on the output produced. In East–West cooperative agreements, it is common for such agreements to be associated with a counter-trade arrangement.

In some respects, the turnkey agreement is like a subcontracting arrangement, but with most of the product specification being determined by the contractee rather than the contractor. In other respects, it is an amalgam of a 'one-off' licensing and management contract, in so far as it is really these services which are being provided by the foreign firm. The risk for the venture is borne by the foreign firm; the amount of ongoing cooperation between buyer and seller is usually quite limited.

The above arrangements represent the main forms of buying/selling cooperative agreements in which there is usually a one-way flow of knowledge between the partner who otherwise would be the foreign direct investor, to the one who would otherwise be the subsidiary of the investor. The extent and form of cooperation, or as Buckley and Casson (1988) prefer to put it, 'coordination through mutual forebearance', will depend on the options open to and the negotiating strengths of the two parties and how important each is to the other as a trading partner. To the *seller*, a non-equity arrangement alleviates the risks of ownership, but increases the transaction costs associated with the misuse or dissipation of property rights whenever these cannot be fully protected through the contract and/or where the litigation procedure is costly or ineffective. The need to seek out 'agents' who are efficient, whose interests and reputation coincide with those of their principals and who can be trusted not to cheat (i.e. be opportunistic in their behaviour) becomes more pronounced the less formal the control mechanism of the contractor and the greater the options open to the contractee. Different cultures and economic and legal systems offer different incentives and penalties to encourage cooperation and reduce opportunism. There is, for example, a marked contrast between a business relationship built on forebearance, reputation, commitment and trust, as is common in many Far Eastern countries, and that of the US which relies almost solely on the formal contract and the threat of litigation if such a contract is broken. Moreover, buyers will be more readily induced to cooperate with sellers where there are good opportunities for sellers to switch to other buyers and/or where the sellers are particularly dependent on them for their economic prosperity.

To the *buyer*, subcontracting poses some similar and some different risks. Availability, price, quality and timing of delivery of the products being purchased are some of the areas in which a buying firm may fear that the kind of cooperation they require is not easily guaranteed by a contractual relationship. Again, as has just been described, the transaction costs of cooperation are likely to be least where the benefits of non-cooperation are small and/ or where the penalties for non-cooperation are great.

Table 9.2 highlights the characteristics of the industrial cooperation modes just described. For the most part, non-equity cooperative agreements are neither economic nor strategic alternatives to each other, but to some kind of equity-based relationships or spot-market transactions. Such collaborative arrangements range from the general to the particular. They might involve one-off or regular transactions, and be of varying time durations. Many non-equity agreements, however, are pluralistic in

Table 9.2 A typology of international industrial cooperation modes.

Form of cooperation	Equity or non-equity	Time limited or unlimited	Space limited	Transfer of resources and rights	Mode of transfer
Wholly owned foreign subsidiaries	Equity	Unlimited	At discretion of MNE	Whole range?	Internal
Joint ventures	Equity	Unlimited	Agreed	Whole range?	Internal
Foreign minority holdings	Equity	Unlimited	Limited	Whole range?	Internal
'Fade out' agreements	Equity	Limited	Nature of agreement	Whole range? for limited period	Internal changing to market
Licensing	Non-equity	Limited by contract	May include limitation in contract	Limited range	Market
Franchising	Non-equity	Limited by contract	Yes	Limited+ support	Market
Management contracts	Non-equity	Limited by contract	May be specified	Limited	Market
Turnkey ventures	Non-equity	Limited	Not usually	Limited in time	Market
Contractual joint ventures	Non-equity	Limited	May be agreed	Specified by contract	Mixed
International subcontracting	Non-equity	Limited	Yes	Small	Market

Notes: See text for full explanation. This table is derived from Buckley and Casson (1985).

that they embrace some of the attributes of other agreements, and indeed of FDI. For example, management contracts might lead both to a technology service agreement and to the transfer of marketing expertise, which has all the features of a franchise arrangement. Likewise, licensing agreements might contain restrictions on the use made of the technology and/or the kind of markets served by the products embodying it. *De facto*, this gives the licensor as much control over management and marketing decisions as if it owned the licensee. Finally, turnkey agreements may incorporate a series of engineering, licensing and technical services agreements under which the local firm can obtain specific pieces of knowledge.

The above paragraphs have discussed the economic costs and benefits of cross-border non-equity coalitions from the perception of the individual parties to the venture. In many respects, these costs and benefits are similar to those involved in any buyer–seller agreement concluded by firms in the same country. However, international agreements often expose the parties to additional economic and political risk, as well as to the transaction costs of concluding and monitoring contracts where the participants operate in very different business environments. Later chapters in this book will evaluate these same costs and benefits from the viewpoint of the home and host countries of the partners to the cooperation agreement.

9.5.2   Strategic business alliances

Introduction

Just as FDI may take the form of international vertical or horizontal integration, so non-equity agreements may be between firms at different stages of the same value-added chain or between firms producing on different value-added chains. The previous section mostly dealt with vertical non-equity relationships. This section extends that analysis and widens it in two ways. First, it gives consideration to a rapidly growing form of cooperative agreement, *viz* between firms supplying different products but engaging in broadly similar activities. Second, it focuses on a particular form of alliance which has become particularly prevalent in recent years. Prior to the late 1970s, most cross-border non-equity alliances concluded between firms were part of a multi-domestic strategy of the participants. They tended to be self-contained entities, and their success was largely judged in terms of their contribution to the profits of the enterprise of which they were part. In the past two decades, however, alliances have increasingly been used by enterprises as a tool to promote their global product and marketing strategies. Hence the expression 'strategic business alliances' (SBAs). *SBAs are alliances deliberately designed to advance the sustainable competitive advantage of the participating firms*.

The reason for the growth of strategic business alliances

In a volume *Cooperative Alliances and International Business*, published in 1988, Contractor identifies several reasons why firms might wish to cooperate with each other to promote their strategic objectives. Some of these are set out in Exhibit 9.3. A closer examination of many of the motives reveals that over the past decade or so economic, technological and political events, both exogenous and endogenous to firms, have contributed towards the growth of SBAs. Like other forms of cooperative ventures, such alliances may be between firms producing on the same value-added chain or on different value-added chains.

We might identify four main reasons for the growth of SBAs. The first is the increasing cost of

Exhibit 9.3   Some reasons for concluding cross-border strategic business alliances.

NB. These may be *aggressive* or *defensive*; they may be market facilitating or collusory; they may be between firms along a value chain or between value chains.

To capture economies of synergy (e.g. by pooling resources and capabilities, and by rationalizing production).

To lower capital investment; to disperse or reduce fixed costs; to better exploit scale and/or scope economies; to lower unit costs by using the comparative production advantages of each partner.

As a consequence of the convergence of technologies and interdependencies among innovation processes; to spread R&D costs; to gain speedy access to new technologies.

As a response by firms to growing competition, a shorter product cycle and a faster rate of technological obsolescence.

To obtain reciprocal benefits from the combined use of complementary assets; to exchange patents and territories.

To overcome government-mandated trade or investment barriers.

As a means of promoting joint R&D and design efforts with suppliers and/or customers.

To assist the entry process of small firms into high risk, entrepreneurial ventures, especially in emerging technology sectors.

To gain new knowledge about, or achieve quicker access to, markets and/or to spread marketing and distribution costs; to widen market sources.

To pre-empt or neutralize the strategy of competitors or to advance monopoly power; as a defensive strategy to reduce competition.

To better secure contracts from foreign governments who favour local firms; to better deal with local suppliers and/or labour unions.

As an initial entry strategy to unfamiliar markets.

To reduce cross-border political risks.

Table 9.3 Forms of cooperative R&D and joint technology development; some illustrations.

Description	Examples
Pre-competitive R&D	
University research funded jointly by industry.	Semiconductor Research Corporation; Stanford Center for Integrated Systems.
R&D conducted or sponsored by industry associations; contract R&D performed for multiple clients by non-profit organizations.	Electric Power Research Institute: Welding Research Institute (UK).
Jointly funded government–industry R&D.	ESPRIT (European Strategic Program of Research in Information Technology); Fraunhofer Gesellschaft (Federal Republic of Germany); International Super Conductivity Technology Center (Japan).
Private sector R&D joint ventures.	Microelectronics and Computer Technology Corporation (MCC); Bellcore (Bell Communications Research); Rolls Royce (UK) and Snecma (France) signed a cooperative agreement in 1989 to develop jointly a new generation of supersonic engines.
Feasibility studies	Five-year study (announced in 1990) by British Aerospace (UK) and Aerospatiale (France) on a supersonic commercial aeroplane to replace Concorde.
Downstream technology development	
Shared venture capital investments.	Biotechnology (many cases); high temperature super-conductivity.
Project-specific R&D and/or technology development, either horizontal (linking competitors) or vertical (linking suppliers and customers), with or without government funding.	Eureka (Europe); VHSIC; joint development agreements in micro-electronics, robotics, etc.; technical standards (Manufacturing Automation Protocol, MAP). In 1990, Waferscale Integration signed an agreement with National Semi Conductor Corporation to produce higher speed and higher-density semiconductors. In 1992, Olivetti (Italy) formed an alliance with Canon (Japan) to produce bubble ink-jet printers.
Cross-licensing and other agreements to share independently developed technologies.	Many international arrangements in industries like micro-electronics. For example, in 1990, AT&T and NEC signed an agreement by which the former company has the right to market, design and produce chips licensed by NEC; in return, the Japanese firm will receive computer-assisted design tools developed by AT&T. An agreement by AT&T (US) and Mitsubishi was concluded in 1989 covering technology sharing, marketing and manufacturing of static random memory (SRAM) chips. In 1992, IBM, Toshiba and Siemens formed a joint project worth more than $1 billion to develop 256 D-RAM chips; while Philips is joining forces with Motorola to develop semiconductor chips for compact disc interactive (a new CD medium).
Joint ventures (with or without government funding).	Sematech; Megachip (Philips–Siemens) (1988). Also in 1988, Motorola and Toshiba created a joint venture in order to swap Motorola's microprocessor design for Toshiba's know-how in producing computer memory chips.
Production and/or marketing, as well as technology development	
Customer–supplier agreements, including co-production or contract production; equity affiliations linking firms that do not compete directly.	Joint development of products or production equipment; shared engineering databases (e.g. automakers and parts suppliers); subcontracting on defence or aerospace systems (including commercial aircraft) to second tier firms.

Table 9.3   continued.

Description	Examples
One-way licensing and second-sourcing agreements; contract production or co-production linking direct competitors (including military offset and co-production agreements).	Subcontracting on major defence or aerospace systems (FSX) (General Dynamics–Mitsubishi Heavy Industries).
Joint ventures among nominal competitors.	Airbus Industrie (Europe); International Aero Engines (Europe, Japan, US); NUMMI (GM–Toyota); Boeing Mitsubishi Heavy Industries and Kawasaki Heavy Industries (aircraft design and manufacture); Advanced Micro Devices (US) and Fujitsu (Japan) ('flash' memory chips).

Source: Adapted and updated from Chesnais (1988) and Gugler (1991). See also Nakamoto (1992).

R&D in technologically advanced industries,[16] and the global competitive pressures that have forced even the largest MNEs to collaborate in innovatory activities. A classic example of a cross-border R&D agreement is that of Siemens and IBM to develop a new generation of microchips. Each company will share both the R&D costs and the results. Other reasons prompting firms to conclude technological alliances include their need to access or to monitor the progress of complementary technologies, to spread capital risks, to share the uncertainties of R&D and to counteract the shortening of the product life cycle, as well as to capture the partner's tacit knowledge, innovatory capabilities or organizational competences (Hagedoorn and Schakenraad, 1990a, 1990b; Gugler and Dunning, 1992). Some examples of collaborative R&D and joint technology projects are set out in Table 9.3.

Second, firms may collaborate to exploit better O advantages arising from the economies of large scale production, scope, specialization and rationalization. These benefits are particularly likely to occur in sectors where the optimum scale of plant or firm is very large, as well as in cross-border alliances where differences in the resources and capabilities of the partners may be fruitfully explored. Additional economies of scale may arise from the sourcing of components and marketing of the end product. Such prospective gains have led both to transnational A&Ms and production-sharing contractual arrangements in sectors such as autos, rubber tyres, pharmaceuticals and computers.

Third, firms may form SBAs to co-opt or counteract the O advantages of competitors deemed to work against their interests. Such alliances may be both reactive and proactive.[17] Typical of the former are the deals struck between several US and Japanese auto producers to gain better access to the Japanese market following the entry of Japanese MNEs into the US market. An example of the latter, given by Hout *et al.* (1986), is the case of the link-up between Caterpillar Tractor and Mitsubishi to reduce the profits and market share of their common competitor Komatsu. SBAs may also be formed as a competition-reducing measure.

Each of the reasons so far given for the growth of SBAs concerns the need of firms to make better use of their existing O advantages, gain new advantages or to protect or sustain their global competitive positions. However, two questions remain to be answered. Why do firms prefer to conclude SBAs rather than some other organizational form to achieve the same result? Why should firms wish to cooperate with each other rather than pursue a solo strategy?

The fourth reason for the growth in SBAs is that the relative attraction of other organizational forms of multiple activities (including MNE hierarchies) has fallen. According to Bruce Kogut (1988b), the 'critical dimension of a joint venture is its resolution of higher levels of uncertainty over the behaviour of the contracting parties when the assets of one or both parties are specialized to the transaction and the hazards of joint cooperation are outweighed by higher production or acquisition costs of 100% ownership'. It follows that if the latter increase relative to the former, SBAs will tend to be the preferred organizational route for exploiting or acquiring the kind of O-specific advantages that the participating firms believe are necessary to sustain or advance their competitiveness. In their review, Lado and Kedia (1990) conclude that firms are most likely to conclude alliances when there is a close degree of goal congruence among the prospective partners; where there is a substantial amount of resource complementarity; where there is a low degree of fiduciary risk; and where there is a high degree of environmental risk.[18] The joint venture, Cereal Partner World Wide, set up in 1990 by Nestlé and General Mills, is an example of a synergy of interests between two large MNEs[19] to counteract the growing domination of Kellogg in non-US markets.

Contractor (1986) suggests that SBAs should be considered as a mode of quasi-integration between firms. The relationships established between the participants is neither purely contractual nor entirely integrative. They also tend to be very industry specific and related to a limited area of the collaborating firms activities. Essentially, SBAs are to do with the cooperation along or between the value-added chains up to the point at which the product is sold to the final consumer. At this point, the relationship between firms tends to be at its most competitive.

Up to now, few scholars appear to have given much attention to the locational characteristics of SBAs. In many respects, there is little which can be added to our analysis of the 'where' of FDI (see Chapters 4 and 6). But it is clear that the pattern of created factor endowments and government policies may critically affect a firm's choice of SBA partners. Much, of course, depends on *raison d'être* for SBAs and how they relate to the other cross-border activities of the participants. Horizontal agreements (e.g. in R&D), which are intended to promote efficiency-seeking production or sustain or advance the global competitive advantages of firms, tend to be concluded between firms located in advanced industrial countries.[20] Agreements intended to gain entry to foreign markets or to exploit the availability or lower cost of natural resources, will be influenced by similar L factors to those determining market- or resource-seeking FDI. However, culturally-sensitive

transaction costs may play a particularly important role in determining the pattern of SBAs for, as we have already seen, their successful outcome rests on mutuality of interest between the goals and organizational philosophies of the local and foreign partners.

Data on strategic business alliances

Comprehensive and reliable data on cross-border SBAs is hard to obtain. Quite apart from identifying an SBA from other forms of cooperative agreements, it is virtually impossible to attach a value to a particular alliance. Most information so far published has been the result of painstaking research into the number of SBAs. These have been largely culled from reports in magazines, professional trade journals and newspapers, as well as from data provided by accountants, specialized consultants and governments. Often the collected information reflects the bias of interest of the investigators. Most relates to both intra-national and transnational SBAs. The data we present on SBAs is illustrative rather than exhaustive, although it does accord well with that collated by other researchers.

Among the most widely used databases of SBAs, we might mention those of INSEAD and FOR. Using the INSEAD data, Ghemawat et al. (1986) showed that during the period 1970–82, the majority of 1546 SBAs were concentrated in the high technology manufacturing and information-intensive service sectors.[21] Firms in other sectors, though sometimes no less globally oriented, appear to favour the A&M and joint equity routes in pursuance of their strategic goals.[22] Ghemawat et al. also found that three-quarters of SBAs were motivated by three factors – the promotion of technological cooperation, the integration of production and to better access distribution and marketing networks.

In his analysis of 1883 cooperative agreements concluded in the manufacturing sector between 1982 and 1986, Ricotta (1987), using FOR data, found that 69.6% were concentrated in the most R&D-intensive industries, with only 8.9% in traditional processing industries. Of these agreements, 64.2% were transnational – 21.9% between the US and the EC, 8.6% between the US and Japan, and 10.8% between the EC and Japan. Ricotta also discovered that 39.8% of all agreements were intended to

Table 9.4   Distribution of strategic alliances, by sectors and fields of technology, 1980–89.

	Number of alliances	Main reason for alliances						
		High cost risks	Lack of financial resources	Technology complementarity	Reduction innovation time span	To share basic R&D	Market access/ structure	Monitoring technology/ market entry
Biotechnology	847	1%	13%	35%	31%	10%	13%	15%
New materials technology	430	1%	3%	38%	32%	11%	31%	16%
Information technology	1660	4%	2%	33%	31%	3%	38%	11%
Computers	198	1%	2%	28%	22%	2%	51%	10%
Industrial automation	278	0%	3%	41%	32%	4%	31%	7%
Microelectronics	383	3%	3%	33%	33%	5%	52%	6%
Software	344	1%	4%	38%	36%	2%	24%	11%
Telecommunications	366	11%	2%	28%	28%	1%	35%	16%
Other	91	1%	0%	29%	28%	2%	35%	24%
Automotive	205	4%	2%	27%	22%	2%	52%	4%
Aviation/defence	228	36%	1%	34%	26%	0%	13%	8%
Chemicals	410	7%	1%	16%	13%	1%	51%	8%
Consumer electronics	58	2%	0%	19%	19%	0%	53%	9%
Food and beverages	42	1%	0%	17%	10%	0%	43%	7%
Heavy electric/power	141	36%	1%	31%	10%	4%	23%	11%
Instruments/medical technology	95	0%	4%	35%	40%	2%	28%	10%
Other	66	35%	0%	9%	6%	0%	23%	8%
Total	4182	6%	4%	31%	28%	5%	32%	11%

Source: Hagedoorn and Schakenraad (1990a).

promote R&D integration or technology transfer, 26.4% to improve production efficiency and 21.4% to gain access to new markets.

A rather more detailed analysis of SBAs in the technologically advanced industries has been made by the Maastricht Economic Research Institute in Innovation and Technology (MERIT). Table 9.4 reproduces some interesting data on 4182 strategic inter-firm partnering between 1980 and 1989. Not only does this data reveal a heavy concentration of SBAs in the biotechnology and information technology sectors, but also points to the importance of technological complementarity, the acceleration of the innovatory process and a gaining of market access as the predominant reasons for concluding SBAs. R&D-centred alliances are most apparent in

intra-US collaborations and in partnering between European and US companies and intra-European alliances. By contrast, alliances between US and Japanese firms tend to be more geared towards gaining market access (Hagedoorn and Schakenraad, 1991).

Most SBAs involve large firms. In the computer industry, 67% of the agreements identified by FOR for the period 1982–86 were concluded by the top producers. Indeed, the leading six firms concluding agreements in electronics accounted for 30% of the total (Ricotta, 1987). As might be expected, MNEs are particularly active in strategic partnering.

Enterprises engaging in cross-border alliances may do so in pursuance of regional, international or global partnering strategies. Hagedoorn and Schakenraad (1991) found that during the 1980s, about one-third of European companies followed a regional strategy in their technology partnering, while their Japanese and US counterparts were more inclined to favour an international or global strategy. Hagedoorn and Schakenraad also discovered that there has been a marginal increase in the globalization of strategic alliances in the second half of the 1980s, particularly by Japanese MNEs, and by firms of all nationalities in the chemical and automobile sectors. Nevertheless, according to the MERIT/CATI database, only 6% of the several thousands of firms which engaged in SBAs in the late 1980s actually did so as part of a clearly identifiable global strategy.

According to the same authors (Hagedoorn and Schakenraad, 1990a), at least 21 MNEs had each concluded more than 100 technology related SBAs in the 1980s.[23] Between them they accounted for 3805 or 76.3% of the total alliances identified by the authors. The Japanese have the highest propensity to conclude SBAs. Indeed, for some time now it has been part of the Japanese government's strategy to foster such alliances – mainly, it should be said, as a means of gaining an entry to window-edge technology (Reich and Markin, 1986) and of penetrating new markets. Of the 3805 SBAs identified by Hagedoorn and Schakenraad, Japanese MNEs accounted for 41.5% – the Europeans came second with 37.4% and the Americans third with 21.1%.

However, not all of the above alliances were cross-border. Another piece of research which identified 2014 agreements in the information technology sector between 1980 and 1986 found that 1149 or 57.1% were cross-continental[24] (Cainarca et al., 1988).

Are SBAs successful?

It is too early to judge the success or failure of SBAs. Although over the past decade they have been the fastest growing form of trans-border inter-firm collaboration, economists and business analysts remain skeptical about their long-term viability. The history of other forms of cooperative relationships suggest that many have been terminated within two to five years of their initiation. Sometimes they may outrun their 'natural' life. Sometimes they may be replaced by mergers, acquisitions or market transactions. Sometimes they are disbanded because they are unsuccessful. One thing seems clear, however. SBAs are generally likely to be an unstable form of partnering – and one in which the outcomes are highly uncertain. Foremost among the reasons for this is that both the international competitive environment and the strategic preferences of firms change over time. Often so does the efficiency of this mode of governance and, indeed, the very rationale for the cooperation in the first place. Moreover, since there tends to be less resource commitment on the part of the partners than there is in a joint equity venture, it is less costly to 'exit' from an alliance.

For the scholar of international business, SBAs are best thought of as one kind of collaborative venture which is a hybrid between the intra- and inter-firm modes of governance (Mowery, 1990). They are likely to flourish whenever firms perceive that their global strategies are best perceived by an ongoing relationship with another firm to fulfil a very specific function or set of functions. As a means of pooling assets, of risk spreading, of speeding up innovation and of gaining access to markets, they offer advantages that neither a market nor a purely hierarchical venture can provide.

At the same time, they pose various challenges to management. We have already referred to their dynamic character. They also bring their own particular risks, learning and organizational problems. Though, from chairmen's statements and press reports their objectives may appear straightforward, in fact SBAs offer considerably more room for interpretation and misunderstanding than a simple profit-seeking joint venture. Almost inevitably, all the features that analysts suggest should make for a successful business partnership are uncertain and fuzzy in an SBA. What, in fact, are the strategic motives of the partners? How, in fact, does one identify the most suitable partners? How are decision-taking responsibilities shared out? How are the financial implications resolved? How are the benefits distributed? What, indeed, are the benefits? What are the implications for the competitive or O advantages or global positioning of the participating parties? And so on. All these questions need to be resolved before the business scholar can make a proper comparison between the merits and demerits of SBAs as a form of cross-border transactional relationship.

Some interesting work by Doz (1988) and by

Doz and Hamel (1993) is beginning to provide us with some answers. In a study of the collaboration process of 12 firms from different countries, Doz found that the most successful partnering occurred when each partner was clear about the intent of the other; where the partners accepted that the relationship was an evolving one and involved a continual learning process; where there was a match between the governance structure of the parties and the tasks of the alliance; where cultural differences were respected and understood; and where each participating firm was able to balance its needs for a focused strategy with its multi-dimensional interests outside the partnership.

In a more comprehensive review of strategic alliances, Doz and Hamel (1993) identify successful partnerships as being those which are best able to manage a compromise between the gains to be achieved from reduced capital risks, opportunities for skill internalization, task and partner learning, accessing complementary competences and information about industry futures, on the one hand, and the reconciliation of differences between different organizational structures, value creation and appropriation, learning patterns mismatches, and the costs of the new dependency structures created by the alliances on the other.[25]

9.6   A NOTE ON CROSS-BORDER CARTELS

Our analysis of cooperative agreements would be incomplete without at least a brief consideration of cross-border cartels. Unlike most of the collaborative agreements considered in this chapter, cartels usually represent a collaboration of several firms producing similar products, which are intended to fulfil a particular purpose. Sometimes the agreement is benign, such as an exchange of patents, technical know-how and information. In others it is more restrictive or exploitative, as is the case with agreements on output or export quotas, consultation on bidding for contracts, price maintenance and stabilization schemes etc.

One dictionary definition of a cross-border cartel is 'an international syndicate, combine or trust formed especially to regulate prices and output in some field of business'. Most cartels are formed by producers; usually they are industry specific. They are particularly common among oligopolists in the primary product sectors, such as oil, copper, aluminium, lead, zinc and iron ore, as well as among those supplying fairly standard manufacturing products, such as steel and basic chemicals. In recent years, they have been supported by some governments in an attempt to stabilize raw material prices, to tilt the terms of trade in favour of exporting countries and to control the rates of exploitation of non-renewable resources. Examples include cartels formed in oil, copper, bauxite and phosphate.

International cartels have almost as long a history as that of MNEs.[26] Indeed, the two are often alternative ways of overcoming cross-border market failure. However, cartels tend to flourish where products are homogeneous and subject to cyclical patterns of demand, where there are few economies of scale, where technology is static, and where international markets are structurally distorted. In contrast, MNE activity is most pronounced in free and growing markets, in dynamic innovatory sectors or those producing high income differential products, and where there are marked economies of common governance.

The propensity of firms to conclude cartels also varies according to their country of origin. Because of cultural, geographical and institutional differences, a somewhat more relaxed attitude by the European authorities towards monopolies, mergers and restrictive practices, and their acceptance of a 'negotiated environment',[27] cross-border cartelization involving European firms has been more common than that involving US firms.[28] Indeed, at one time or another, national governments have actively supported cross-border cartelization. This is one reason why, during the inter-war years, the number of foreign subsidiaries established by European MNEs fell more than did those set up by US MNEs (Vaupel and Curhan, 1974; Franko, 1976). Not infrequently, the cartels established in these years controlled both the amount and geographical distribution of FDI of their members.[29]

The history of cartels suggests that there are certain common features between them and other forms of cooperative arrangements, and also regional integration. To be successful, the participants must be in agreement about the aims and strategies of the association, and the distribution of the benefits. They tend to be more successful where there are many buyers and few sellers; where there would otherwise be intensive price competition among the member firms; and where the products involved have few substitutes or potential substitutes. They are less likely to flourish where there are distinct and substantial differences between the O-specific advantages of the participating firms and where, in order to exploit these advantages, firms need to internalize the markets for them. In particular, there is sometimes a tradeoff between the gains of the common governance of intra-firm integration and those arising from inter-firm cooperation. As with any grouping of institutions or countries, much depends on the gains anticipated from cooperative action and the way in which these gains are distributed among the members, compared with some other modality of achieving the same result.

Cartels are sometimes preferred to FDI where it is felt that action may need to be taken at an industry level, where collective action will help improve a particular aspect of a firm's performance, or where it does not wish to make a substantial resource commitment. In the world economic climate of the 1990s, cartels are tending to be replaced by cross-border strategic alliances, consortia of MNEs and less formal market sharing and price agreements.

9.7   CONCLUSIONS

International cooperative agreements make up the organizational space between multinational hierarchies on the one hand, and arm's length markets on the other. While some forms of collaborative arrangements (e.g. joint ventures) veer towards hierarchies, except that they involve the sharing of risks and resource commitments, others (e.g. non-equity strategic alliances) veer towards market transactions, except that they involve a continuing relationship between the contracting parties, in which there is usually an exchange or sharing of assets and responsibilities.

In the last decade, inter-firm agreements have become an increasingly important form of cross-border economic involvement. Indeed it is probably true to say that they account for a proportionately higher number of transactions along and between

value chains of MNE hierarchies than ever before. Especially since the mid 1980s, there have been powerful forces at work leading both to the disinternalization of the peripheral activities of hierarchies and to the formation of new kinds of cooperative ventures. Foremost among these forces has been the impact of technological advances on the fixed costs (especially R&D and marketing costs) of firms. Second has been the growing impetus (as perceived by firms) to focus their value activities on their core competences (Prahalad and Doz, 1990). The increasing speed of technological obsolescence and the need for firms to respond ever more quickly to the actions of competitors have also forced them to collaborate to maintain or advance their competitive positions.

These events, together with a more relaxed stance taken by governments on the kinds of inter-firm collaboration thought likely to advance national competitiveness, have brought about a change in the strategy of firms towards such ventures. In the 1950s and 1960s cross-border joint ventures and non-equity agreements were primarily viewed as a way of entering into a foreign market to promote either the market-seeking or resource-seeking goals of ethnocentric or geocentric MNEs. Alternatively they were considered as a second-best organizational strategy to satisfy the demands of governments who were not in favour of 100% equity investment. In the 1990s cooperative ventures are increasingly seen as a first-best organizational form designed to spread financial risks, promote the efficient use of resources and to acquire new assets and capabilities. More generally, they are seen as part of a geocentric or regiocentric strategy of MNEs. In examining the motives and consequences of modern collaborative ventures, it is important to take an organic and a holistic approach to the management of cross-border activities and to an evaluation of their contribution to the global goals of enterprises. We have also seen that the appropriateness of international collaborative ventures will vary according to the stages of the value-added chain undertaken by the firms.

In any explanation of cooperative ventures, it is becoming increasingly necessary not only to take an integrated and evolutionary approach, but also an interdisciplinary one (Tallman and Shenkar, 1990). The choice between the relative net advantages of a self-contained 100% owned subsidiary, a joint venture and a non-equity agreement was (and still is) largely based on economic calculations. However, just as business strategy has become a more important ingredient of the decision of MNEs – particularly in international oligopolistic sectors – so is it affecting the mode of organizing these ventures. As a result both of the growth in the size and diversity of firms and the number of countries in which they compete, transnational relationships have become more complex. Consequently, sociological theories[30] have been developed to explain the different forms of cooperative ventures (Tallman and Shenkar, 1990) and the extent to which the success of such ventures might depend upon the structure of the resources and skills possessed by the participating firms, their respective management cultures and previous organizational interdependencies (Hladik, 1988), as well as the way in which they respond to environmental change.

The emergence of the globally integrated or transnational heterarchy (see Chapter 7) has both blurred the boundaries of the firm and *de facto* rendered meaningless several of the distinctions between internal and external transactional relationships. Network analysis has shown that many relationships between firms in the network are both heterarchical and multi-dimensional. That is to say, Firm A may have a reciprocal relationship (rather than a subservient relationship) with Firm B, which has another set of relationships with Firm C, which, in turn, has dealings with Firm A. Moreover, the way in which MNEs organize their inter-firm transactions and integrate them with their intra-firm transactions, may itself be an important O advantage. For example, the cooperative relationships which many Japanese firms enjoy with their subcontractors not only assures them of a reliable and speedy delivery of high quality, fault-free products, but often of valuable research, design and processing knowledge as well. Taken as a whole, and over time, these assets become embodied into the O advantages of the contracting firms. Hence it is important to take a systemic view of both the inter- and intra-firm transactional advantages of MNEs.[31]

The literature has hardly addressed these aspects of inter-firm relationships; perhaps it is a major subject for research in the 1990s. But what does seem crystal clear is that many of our earlier preconceptions about the motives and consequences of collaborative ventures are no longer appropriate

in the global economy of the 1990s. At the same time, some of the analytical tools now being developed by economists, strategic business analysts and organizational scholars to explain the extent, and pattern of MNE activity and the implication of these changes for the organizational structure of firms and hierarchical transactional relationships can also be used to explain inter-firm arrangements. It is also evident that, while a general organizational framework might be used to explain the situation in which such arrangements might flourish, the precise values of the variables identified will – as in the case of FDI theory – vary according to the motives underlying the arrangements, as well as to the countries, industries and firms involved.

NOTES

1   We would emphasize that ownership and control are by no means the same thing. *De facto*, each may be present without the other. However, the right of control does rest with the majority equity shareholder in any joint venture. This right can, of course, be abrogated or delegated by the majority shareholder; while in any contractual agreements, rights and responsibilities (including the right to control the use of value-added activities) can be distributed in any way acceptable to the contracting parties.

2   See pages 187–193.

3   For a discussion of other conceptual frameworks see Pfeffer and Nowak (1976) and Tallman and Shenkar (1990).

4   Or, putting it another way, the cost to one group of shareholders if another shareholder withdraws from the venture.

5   Examples include joint ventures set up in 1990 between Nestlé (Swiss) and Coca Cola (US) to distribute chilled Nestlé products in Coca Cola's vending machines; by Thomson Sintra ASM (French) and Ferranti (UK) to make sonar systems; by Philips (Dutch) and JVC (Japanese) to produce video cassette recorders in Malaysia; by Fiat (Italian) and Ford (US) to produce tractors, and farm and earth moving equipment; by Alcatel (French) and Quelcomm (US) to market and service long-range mobile message systems; by Rhone Poulenc (French) and BVK (Hungarian) to produce and market chemicals for crop protection in Eastern Europe; and by Daimler Benz (German) and Aerospatiale (French) to produce helicopters.

6   By which is meant the costs and benefits affecting the

prosperity of the partners to the joint ventures, outside of the joint venture. In some cases, of course, there may be no such costs and benefits.

7 See, for example, studies by Daniels (1971), Renforth (1974), Tomlinson and Thompson (1977) and Awadzi (1987) reviewed in Geringer (1991).

8 To take Geringer's own example, and quoting from his words, 'the greater the perceived difficulty of the parent firm's efforts to obtain access to a well developed distribution system increases, the relative importance of selecting a partner with access to such a distribution system will also increase' (p. 49).

9 Standard Industrial Classification.

10 An exception is that of Fusfeld, who discovered that out of 70 joint ventures in the iron and steel industry, 53 were supply agreements between firms within the industry.

11 This point is taken up in more detail in Chapter 20.

12 That is, where firms choose between majority or minority ownership.

13 A fact the authors attribute to the probability that the most technologically intensive MNEs prefer to accept no ownership sharing at all.

14 Kogut's sample consisted of 92 joint ventures in manufacturing industry which replied to a questionnaire sent to 475 firms which concluded joint ventures between 1975 and 1983.

15 For further details see Prahalad and Doz (1990).

16 Examples include £1 billion for a telecommunications switching system, £2 billion for a new global car and £500 million for a mainframe computer (Clarke and Brennan, 1988).

17 At the same time, as Contractor points out, a patent is not merely a right to process a design; it is also a right to a territory. By swapping or pooling patents, companies may also be swapping or pooling territories.

18 Root (1987) defines fiduciary risk as the probability that a prospective partner to an alliance will fail to carry out its responsibility for an arrangement. This risk will be lower the less the alliance complexity, volume unpredictability and performance ambiguity. Environmental risk embraces political, cultural and technological risks.

19 With General Mills providing the knowledge in cereal technology, including some of its proprietary equipment, its range of proven cereal brands and it's knack for pitching these products to consumers, Nestlé is supplying the name on the box, access to retailers and the production capacity that will be used to make General Mills cereal (*Fortune*, 1990).

20 The exception may be alliances sponsored by Third World MNEs in the First World.

21 Others include those of Morris and Hergert (1988), which was biased towards alliances involving European firms, and the ARPAN data based on cooperative agreements in the information technology sectors.

22 Notable examples include Nestlé and Unilever, both of whom, since the mid 1980s, have embarked on a systematic and strategically related series of cross-border A&Ms.

23 The companies that concluded the largest number of alliances were identified by Hagedoorn and Schakenraad as the Mitsubishi Group (335), Siemens AG (316), Dai-Ichi Kangyo Group (291), Sumitomo Group (268), Philips NV (229) and the Mitsui Group (215). IBM with 179 links and GEC with 151 links were top of the US MNEs including alliances.

24 In other words, of the remaining 859 some (unknown) proportion may have been cross-border (e.g. within the EC).

25 Examples of SBAs being dissolved include that between Ciba Geigy and Alza after four years as a result of the conflicting interests between that alliance and others which Alza wished to form with pharmaceutical companies. By contrast, Doz (1988, p. 179) quotes the case of a partnership between a European nuclear medicines product supplier and a US radio-pharmacy company coming to an end because, over time, the areas of mutual interest of the two parties shrank to a 'fraction of their respective activities'. Cases of partnerships breaking up because the expected outcomes did not materialize include that between two biotechnology firms – the GENE Corporation and BioHelix – while a learning pattern mismatch between XYZ Corporation and Polytek ended collaboration between the two companies (Doz *et al.*, 1992).

26 See Chapter 5 for a historical perspective.

27 Quoted in Wilkins (1970, p. 96) as meaning an environment protected from the free play of competitive forces.

28 Exceptions include a copper cartel initiated by the Americans in the 1920s.

29 Franko (1976), in particular, cites the case of the agreements between IG Farben and members of the Swiss Interest Association.

30 In particular, Tallman and Shenkar consider three groups of sociological theories. These are (i) resource dependence theory – which attributes organizational motivations to dependencies on the environment to include mutual dependencies with other organizations; (ii) population ecology theory – which holds that organizational births and deaths are determined through a national selection process, with survival depending upon the existence of suitable niches in the environment (Aldrich, 1979); and (iii) the theory of the inter-organizational relationships seeks to analyse patterns of interaction and exchange among organizations by using the concepts of interdependence awareness, the

uniformity of transacted events and intra-organizational linkages (Litvak and Rothman, 1970).

31 For a discussion of the governance of inter-firm cooperative arrangements involving Japanese firms, see Okada (1991). One interesting question is the extent to which such cooperative arrangements which exist in Japan, and which may give Japanese firms a competitive edge in supplying world markets, can be successfully transferred to foreign cultures in which competition rather than cooperation between firms is the norm.

PART 3

THE IMPACT OF MNE ACTIVITY

Part 3 is the longest part of this volume. Its task is to present the main findings of academic scholars and business analysts of the ways in which MNEs have impacted both on the global economy and on the individual Nation States in which they operate. Chapter 10, which should be regarded as an extension of Chapters 4 and 7, sets the analytical framework for Chapters 11 to 19. Basically, it argues that the likely effects of MNE activity will depend on the nature and form of the unique assets of the investing companies (*vis à vis* those of their domestic competitors) and the location-bound resources and capabilities of the countries, which generate or receive the investment, and on the organizational mechanism by which each interacts with the other, both at a given moment of time and over time.

Most of the following chapters are issue oriented. They follow a certain logic in their ordering. Chapters 11 to 13 are concerned with the role played by MNEs as generators, transferors, disseminators and upgraders of natural resources and created capabilities. The emphasis of Chapters 11 and 12 is on the competence of a country to upgrade its *physical* assets, and, by so doing, innovate new goods and services and produce existing goods and services more effectively. Chapter 13, on the other hand, is concerned with the impact of MNE activity on the use and upgrading of *human* resources and competences, without which very little economic progress can be achieved. Both chapters review and analyse a very extensive literature on the ways in which MNE activity may advance or retard a nation's wealth-creating ability – be that nation a capital-exporting (home) country or a capital-importing (host) country.

Chapters 14 to 17 then turn to examine some of the consequences of MNE activity, which follow from the findings of the previous chapters. Chapter 14 looks at the impact of FDI on the allocation of a particular country's resources and capabilities *in relation to that of other countries with which the country trades*. The chapter acknowledges that, in some cases at least – especially in developing countries – the extent to which a country can balance its external payments may be a critical factor influencing the rate and trajectory of its economic development. By contrast, Chapter 15 deals with the consequences of inbound and outbound direct investment on the structure and efficiency of resource allocation *within home and host countries*. In doing so, it considers the effect of MNEs or their affiliates on the efficiency of producing a particular product or range of products (technical efficiency); on the efficiency of allocating resources and capabilities between different value-added activities (allocative efficiency); on the efficiency with which firms in particular sectors can fully exploit the economies of size (scale and scope efficiencies); and on the efficiency with which resources and capabilities are reallocated between uses to meet changing supply and demand needs (structural adjustment efficiency). *Inter alia*, this chapter touches upon some of the most sensitive issues about the operations of MNEs e.g. their impact on market structures, and industrial concentration, and on the extent to which, in pursuance of their global strategies, they may engage in business practices unacceptable to home or host governments.

Chapter 16 then proceeds to examine some of the consequences of MNE investment on economic activities other than those which they own or control. These are essentially of two kinds. First, there are those of other firms which produce further up or down on the value chain on which the MNE or its affiliates also produce (e.g. its suppliers or industrial customers).

Second, there are those undertaken on different value chains, which might be either competitive or complementary to those pursued by MNEs. These include the activities of competitors to MNEs in product or factor markets, and those which are supportive to MNE activity as members of a cluster or network of interdependent activities. These spill-over effects are sometimes more important than the direct effects, and are often those to which governments pay special attention when framing their economic strategies.

Chapter 17 examines the interaction between MNE activity and the international division of labour. It is, in some respects, an extension of Chapter 14 and asks the question: 'To what extent does the cross-border internalization of intermediate product markets affect the way in which resources and capabilities are allocated between countries'? In other words, does the *ownership* of nationally generated resources and capabilities matter? The chapter goes on to examine the relationship between the regional integration of countries and that of the governance of corporations. Paying especial attention to the European Community (EC) it shows how regional integration has affected the kind of FDI undertaken, the geographical and industrial composition of such investment, its organization and its economic consequences both for Member States and for the region as a whole. The chapter concludes by examining the prospects for further integration in the world economy and the resulting implications for MNE activity.

After considering how MNEs affect the level and composition of international production, Chapter 18 turns to analyse some of the distributional consequences of such production. In doing so it pays especial attention to the ways in which the share of value added created by MNEs or their affiliates may be retained by the countries in which the value is created. This subject is worthy of a monograph in itself. However, in this volume we shall limit our attention to two main issues affecting the distribution of value added by MNEs, *viz* taxation and transfer pricing.

Chapter 19 completes our review of the consequences of MNE activity by giving some attention to issues, which, while not directly related to economic welfare, are critically important for sustaining and promoting sustainable economic development and growth. Again, space precludes us from considering more than four issues, which as well as being of contemporary interest are likely to command increasing attention in the future. These are, first, economic and political autonomy, second, cultural identity, third, national security, and fourth, environmental protection. Each of these issues involves the use of real resources, and each affects the total welfare of a country's citizens. In so far as MNE activity might increase or reduce the level and quality of these goods and services, and the efficiency with which they are supplied, it is appropriate that these issues should be included in our analysis.

CHAPTER 10

ASSESSING THE CONSEQUENCES OF MNE ACTIVITY: A CONCEPTUAL FRAMEWORK

10.1 INTRODUCTION

Perhaps the most frequent and persistent question asked about MNE activity, both by ordinary citizens and policy makers of the Nation States in which they operate, is 'It its impact on economic welfare a good or bad thing?' This question is usually followed by a second, *viz* 'If it is good, how can it be made even better?', and sometimes a third 'Do we wish our country to be tied in to an international division of labour fashioned or influenced by foreign MNE activity?'

Yet if there is one lesson to be drawn from a plethora of empirical studies on the economic consequences of FDI and the behaviour of MNEs, it is that there is no satisfactory general answer to these questions. In the formation of government policy towards MNEs, or as a result of their activities, so much depends on country-, industry- and firm-specific characteristics and the kind of FDI being undertaken. It also rests on the particular effects of MNE activity with which one is concerned; the time period in which one is interested; and from whose, or which, perspective one is trying to assess the impact. For example, the long-term consequences of US direct investment in a Chilean copper mine are likely to be quite different from the short-term impact of a French takeover of a Canadian-owned hotel. The consequences for local employment of a UK investment in a Jamaican sugar plantation are likely to be different from those of a Japanese investment in a German electronics firm, or that of an Indonesian investment in a US fish canning factory. The purchase of an R&D facility in the US by a Korean firm is likely to have very different consequences on the home country's technological capacity than that of the restructuring of a Swedish MNE's value-added activities between its parent plant and its foreign subsidiaries in South East Asia. Questions relating to the effects of outbound or inbound investment on such non-economic variables as political autonomy, cultural identity, industrial safety and environmental protection are no less pertinent.[1]

To the academic researcher, such a finding is frustrating; to the policy maker it may appear unhelpful or even irrelevant. Yet in Part 2 of this volume, we also suggested that no general conclusions could be drawn about the causes or determinants of FDI and MNE activity. Different kinds of international production demanded different kinds of explanations as, indeed, did the same value-added activity undertaken by MNEs of different nationalities. In particular, we found it useful to make a distinction between the 'why', 'where' and 'how' of international production.

At the same time, we argued that while no one set of explanatory variables could explain all kinds of foreign production, the economic theorist or business analyst was able to offer a useful conceptual framework for understanding the reasons for MNE activity *in toto*. In particular, this framework was based on a number of economic and organizational propositions. The key analytical tools were a macro-economic theory of factor endowments and a micro-organizational theory of market failure and strategic management. In particular, the idea of the eclectic, or OLI, paradigm was to provide an analytical structure within which specific explanations of MNEs, or MNE activities, could be accommodated. In this and the next part of the book, we switch our attention from a firm, or group of firms, as the unit of analysis, to a country, or group of countries. Specifically we shall consider some of the consequences of the actions of MNEs for the economic and social well-being of the countries in which they operate, as well as the response by those institutions and individuals or groups of individuals most affected by their presence, *viz* national governments, labour organizations, consumers, regional authorities and the international community.

In the following chapters we shall discuss the effects of MNE activity on a number of policy-oriented areas. In this chapter we shall offer a schema for analysing these consequences, which might apply to all kinds of FDI and embrace all kinds of impacts. Can one identify the key analytical variables by which the actions of MNEs can be studied and evaluated? To what extent can the OLI framework be extended to help our understanding of the consequences, as well as the causes, of international production? Is it possible to offer any general conclusions about the likely impact of outbound or inbound investment on the goals of Nation States?

10.2   A FRAMEWORK FOR ANALYSIS

We first address some methodological issues underpinning any attempt to evaluate the impact of MNE activity. Let us first seek to establish a general framework within which it may be possible to evaluate such an impact.

The literature usually distinguishes between the effects of outward investment by domestic or own MNEs on the home (i.e. source) country and that of inward investment (i.e. activities of affiliates) by foreign-based MNEs on the host (i.e. recipient) country. For the most part we shall also adopt this distinction, while acknowledging that increasingly, especially among countries within the Triad, the determinants and impact of outbound and inbound investment are becoming interdependent of each other.

Any evaluation of the economic impact of MNE activity must address itself to the question 'What are the unique features about such activity?' Chapter 1 suggested that MNEs were multi-activity firms which internalized cross-border intermediate product markets. Because of this, we argued, the resources and capabilities owned by them and traded across the

exchanges, the control exerted over such resources and capabilities – and any others which might be acquired on the open market – and the distribution of the value added created by their foreign-based activities, were likely to generate distinctive consequences.

The literature has identified two main ways in which these distinctive features can be identified. The first is to compare or contrast the behaviour and performance of MNEs (or their affiliates) with those of their uninational or local competitors. The important question here is to identify the unique contribution of outbound investment to a home country and of inbound investment to the host country. While, in practice, much FDI is valued for its general characteristics, it is the purpose of this volume to try and identify and evaluate the *differences* between the impact of MNE and non-MNE activity, as well as between different kinds of FDI. The second is to compare the effects of FDI with those of other modalities that are open to home or host countries for obtaining the benefits of such investment. In Chapters 4 and 7 we observed that firms had a choice in the exploitation of their O advantages between:

(1)   exporting (or importing) products,

(2)   contracting foreign firms to produce the products which might be exported or imported,

(3)   engaging in foreign production to replace exports or imports.

We suggested that any satisfactory general paradigm of foreign production must seek to explain why, and in what circumstances, this third form of international economic activity is to be preferred to the other two.

Following along the lines of Chapters 3 and 4, it might also be hypothesized that the consequences of MNE activity will also vary according to country-, industry- and firm-specific circumstances. The consequences of an investment by a US electronics company on a small industrializing country in which there is little local competition or supply capability, and where the host government engages in an import-substituting policy and makes stringent demands on the behaviour of foreign affiliates, is likely to be very different from that of the same investment in a large advanced industrial country where there is a thriving indigenous sector, good supply capabilities and the government allows foreign investors complete operational freedom. It is also worth recalling that these examples of country-specific characteristics will also influence the incentive of firms to engage in FDI, for example, compared with licensing and exports, in the first place.

Another aspect of L-specific factors relates to the target of the impact. For example, in considering the investment by a US bank or Italian footwear company in the Philippines, is one primarily concerned about its consequences for the general economic welfare of the host country or a particular aspect of that welfare, such as the global competitiveness of its resources and capabilities? Or is one concerned with the wider social, political and cultural goals that embrace the company's political and cultural goals? Is one interested in the impact of the investment on all its citizens or on particular sectoral interests? The impact of inbound MNE activity on organized labour, for example, may be quite different from that on consumers, competitors or suppliers. The attitude of regions with high unemployment to the presence of foreign-owned firms may be quite different from that of those with acute labour shortages. The impact of MNEs on the market structure and technological capability of a particular industry may be strongly dependent on the rivalry in, and efficiency of, that industry prior to the investment being made. The consequences of the injection of new technological assets or managerial skills to a natural resource-based economy in the early stages of its development may be entirely different from those in an advanced industrial economy.

Various analytical frameworks might be used to identify and assess the impact of MNEs on the countries in which they operate. As our 'generic' framework we shall use the eclectic paradigm, which was adopted in the two previous parts of this book. We shall then amplify or 'flush out' some of the more important ingredients of this paradigm by reference to four 'supplementary' paradigms or supportive frameworks. The eclectic paradigm suggests that the consequences of multinational investment will vary according to the nature and extent of the O-specific characteristics of the investing firms, and the L-specific characteristics of the countries in which the MNE activity is being (or could be) undertaken. In the light of these O and L characteristics, it considers the extent to which firms will choose to internalize the cross-border markets for intermediate products (i.e. their propensity to internalize (I) market failure). The paradigm further avers that each of these characteristics is likely to vary according to the countries and sectors of activity in which MNE activity occurs and the attributes (including the strategies) of the investing firms. We now turn to consider the four supplementary paradigms:

(1) The first is the so-called **Environmental/Systems/ Policy (ESP)** paradigm of country-specific characteristics devised by Koopman and Montias (1971) a decade ago. We shall see (in Section 10.3.2) that the components of this paradigm can be used not only to help explain the location of production by both foreign- and home-based MNEs, but also the competitive advantages of these companies and the way in which they organize their cross-border activities.

(2) The second (and related) paradigm is Michael Porter's **Diamond of Competitive Advantages**, as set out in his 1990 book *The Competitive Advantages of Nations*. Porter argues that the competitive (or O-specific) advantages of the firms located in a particular country (hence, those of the country as a whole) are determined by certain attributes which are unique to that country (in our terminology, L-specific assets). Porter identifies four of these attributes:
   (i) the natural resources, and created capabilities (especially human and innovatory capital, and the wealth facilitating infrastructure of a country);
   (ii) the level, variation, composition and quality of output demanded by domestic consumers;
   (iii) the presence of 'clusters' of suppliers or supporting industries;
   (iv) the extent and pattern of inter-firm rivalry and the effect this has on the innovatory and competitive strategies of domestic firms.[2]

Surrounding and interacting with these four attributes is the role of national governments and also that of chance. Each of these facets of the diamond are, to some extent, interdependent. Although the relative significance of each is likely to vary between countries and between particular industries or segments of industries, it is Porter's contention that only when they are systemically organized will they be fully effective.

(3) The third paradigm is what we shall call the **Asset Accumulation and Restructuring** paradigm. It is an extension of the model of cumulative technological change, developed *inter alia* by Pavitt (1987) and Cantwell (1989c), and extended to embrace organizational resources and the restructuring (and accumulation) of assets. Its propositions are threefold. The first is that a change in the human and physical assets within the jurisdiction of a firm or industry is both cumulative and interdependent over time. For example, a change in a firm's R&D capability between time t and $t + 1$ will affect not only its performance at time $t + 1$, but also, to a greater or lesser extent, in later time periods.[3] Since the process is a cumulative one, it may lead to 'virtuous' or 'vicious' circles of asset capabilities. The second proposition is that a firm's or industry's capabilities tend to develop incrementally so that the full impact of any discrete acceleration or deceleration in innovatory capability, asset productivity, or inter- or intra-firm organizational change will not be immediately apparent. The third proposition is that the path of asset development and restructuring will be characterized by elements which are specific to particular firms, industries or countries. It is this proposition which is particularly relevant in helping to explain the extent to which a country's capability to use, upgrade or restructure assets efficiently may be affected by the activities of its own or foreign-based MNEs, as well as the ways in which the development of a firm's own capabilities may be affected by the level and character of its foreign involvement. While the application of the paradigm is usually sectorally oriented, it can also be used to consider the impact of FDI on macro-asset accumulation or restructuring.

(4) The fourth paradigm is particularly appropriate for analysing the interaction between MNE activity and the economic development and/or restructuring of countries. It may be called the **Stages of Growth** paradigm. Its lineage can be traced back to the classic work of Rostow (1959a). In its most general form, this paradigm is identified with the work of Hollis Chenery and Bela Balassa,[4] both of whom, over the past two decades, have sought to explain the developmental trajectories of countries and the reasons why some countries are more successful in their development strategies than others. More recently, Teretomo Ozawa (1991c, 1992) has used a stages-of-growth model to explain the changing role of inward and outward direct investment as a shaper and influencer of economic development. Such a model may be extended to analysing the contribution of MNE activity in assisting or inhibiting the structural adjustment of developed countries to technological and other changes in the world economy. Coupled with the concept of the investment development path analysed in Chapter 4,[5] the stages-of-growth paradigm can usefully add to our understanding of the role of FDI as an engine of growth and structural adjustment.

Each of these paradigms offers useful insights into the likely consequences of MNE activity on the economic welfare of both home and host countries. Take, for example, the impact of inward direct investment by Country A's firms on the competitiveness of Country A's resources and capabilities. The eclectic paradigm suggests that Country A's firms will invest in Country B only in so far as they perceive that they possess the necessary O advantages to do so, and that the L advantages of Country B and the I advantages for internalizing cross-border markets for the intermediate products traded between Countries A and B favour FDI. Clearly, the exogenous variables affecting this decision are influenced by the relative ESP configurations of both Country A and Country B – which include the competitive advantages identified by Porter (1990) – and by the positioning of the two groups of firms in the asset accumulation circles of their respective industries and countries. At the same time, inbound MNE activity will, over time, affect the L-specific assets of the recipient country. It will do this initially via its impact on the structure and components of its diamond of competitive advantage and on the actions of the host government. Next, depending on the sectors and countries in which the investment is made and the presence, or absence, of effective competition and supply capabilities, the cumulative assets of the country may be beneficially or adversely affected in a way identified earlier. This, in turn, will change both the configuration of the ESP of the host country and the OLI configuration facing both foreign and domestic firms. Depending on its share of economic activity and its influence on government policy, inward investment may affect the developmental trajectory of the host country.

The dynamics of the interplay between outward direct investment and a home country's competitiveness can be similarly analysed. An investment by Country B's firms in Country A will impact on the diamond of competitive advantage of Country B which will set in train a series of events which, by increasing or decreasing asset capability in particular sectors, will affect both the ESP configuration of the home country – making it more or less attractive to both foreign and domestic investors – and the OLI configuration affecting Country B's MNEs or potential MNEs. Depending upon their strategic reaction to these changes, MNEs will then increase, decrease or restructure their foreign value-added activities and the programme of events starts all over again. Equilibrium will only be restored when the outward direct investment causes no further change in the L- or I-specific variables, which themselves affect such investment.

A possible sequence of events following an initial or sequential change in MNE activity is set out in Exhibit 10.1. Though, to the best of our knowledge, this kind of approach to examining the dynamics of MNE activity has not yet been rigorously tested,[6] implicitly, a lot of the literature – which we shall be reviewing in later chapters – has some of its ingredients. At the same time, it is not enough for the scholar to hypothesize about the *nature* of the linkages between inward and outward FDI and economic welfare. He should also be able to hypothesize about their direction and significance. Under what circumstances, for example, will the chain of reactions just described lead to a beneficial impact of MNE activity on the home and host countries? How far does this vary according to the type of investment and the stage of a country's development? In what industrial sectors will this beneficial impact occur? How substantial will the benefit be? Is FDI the 'best' way of obtaining these benefits? And what are its costs?

The following section of this chapter suggests that the answers to these questions must lie firstly in the distinctiveness of the MNE, *qua* MNE, as an acquirer, provider, user and controller of income-generating assets; secondly on the characteristics of the home and host countries, including the policies pursued by their governments; and thirdly on the ability of their own firms not only to assimilate and effectively deploy these assets, but also to advance their own competitive capabilities.

10.3   THE OLI PARADIGM REVISITED

Let us now seek to apply the kind of integrated framework we have suggested for analysing the economic impact of MNEs on the countries in which they operate.

10.3.1   The impact of O-specific advantages

In so far as the assets owned and organized by MNEs are different from those of their uninational competitors, then it may reasonably be hypothesized that the distinctive impact of inward direct investment will reflect the nature and extent of these assets. However, depending upon the stage of development of a country, there are some advantages likely to be enjoyed by foreign-based MNEs which may also be possessed to a greater or lesser extent by the host country's own MNEs. These include the advantages that arise from multinationality *per se*. In such cases, the *distinctive* advantages of *foreign-based* MNEs may rest more in the kind of proprietary assets they possess or any favoured access they might have to input or output markets. However, as stated in Chapter 4, the ownership of these advantages does not necessarily imply that a firm will actually engage in FDI. To some extent, at least, the impact of these advantages may be similar to those which arise from exports or from cross-border cooperative ventures.

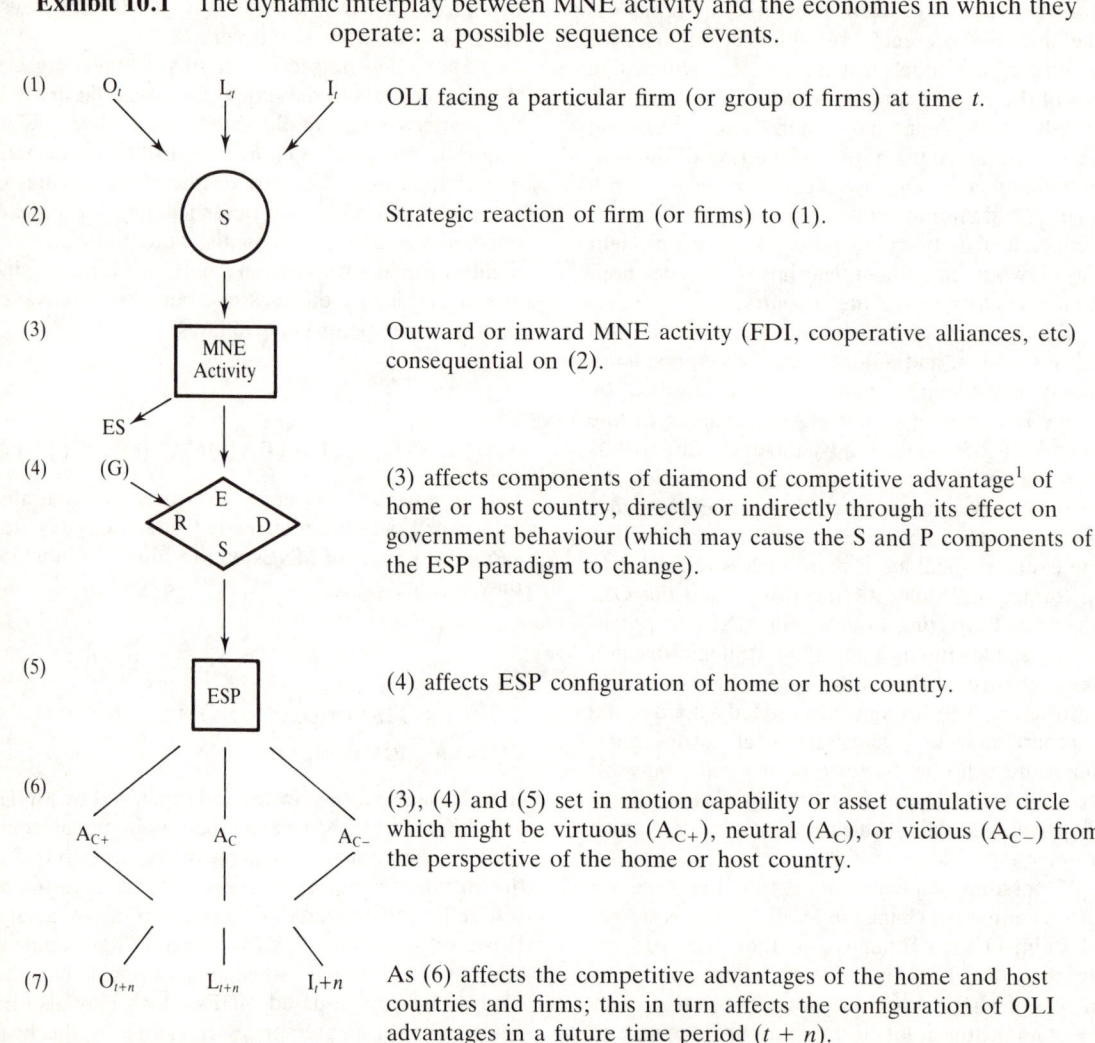

Exhibit 10.1   The dynamic interplay between MNE activity and the economies in which they operate: a possible sequence of events.

(1) O_t L_t I_t OLI facing a particular firm (or group of firms) at time t.

(2)   S   Strategic reaction of firm (or firms) to (1).

(3)   MNE Activity   Outward or inward MNE activity (FDI, cooperative alliances, etc) consequential on (2).

(4)   (G)   E R D S   (3) affects components of diamond of competitive advantage[1] of home or host country, directly or indirectly through its effect on government behaviour (which may cause the S and P components of the ESP paradigm to change).

(5)   ESP   (4) affects ESP configuration of home or host country.

(6) A_{C+} A_C A_{C-} (3), (4) and (5) set in motion capability or asset cumulative circle which might be virtuous (A_{C+}), neutral (A_C), or vicious (A_{C-}) from the perspective of the home or host country.

(7) O_{t+n} L_{t+n} I_{t+n} As (6) affects the competitive advantages of the home and host countries and firms; this in turn affects the configuration of OLI advantages in a future time period ($t + n$).

Key: 1   R – indigenous resources and capabilities; E – market structure; D – indigenous demand characteristics; S – availability of support or related sectors.

In many instances, however, MNEs are likely to compete alongside uninational indigenous firms. This impact is likely to be doubly distinctive, that is, it arises from their privileged possession of both asset-specific (Oa) and transaction-cost-minimizing (Ot) advantages.

The nature and extent of a firm's O-specific advantages will also affect its impact on the economic welfare of the home country. For example, a firm with an important cutting edge technology which it transfers to a foreign country via its subsidiaries is likely to have different economic implications for the home country's employment and technological competitiveness than one whose advantages rest primarily in the ownership of a particular trademark or marketing technique. A firm whose main capabilities lie in its ability to utilize more efficient, but capital-intensive, production techniques is likely to affect the employment goals of a home country differently from one that is able to raise the quality of, or provide new markets for, labour-intensive products. The impact of a firm whose foreign activities are geared to exploiting a particular natural resource is likely to have a very different impact on the consequences for the trading structure of the home country from one whose activities are designed to substitute for exports from the home country. An MNE which derives substantial economies of common governance through closely integrating the product and sourcing strategies of its foreign and domestic operating units may affect the industrialization policy of a capital-exporting country very differently than one which has a monopoly of the product it supplies, but which seeks to serve only its domestic market.

Our first proposition, then, is that the more distinct and the greater the number and extent of O-specific advantages possessed by MNEs relative to those of their indigenous competitors, and the more the countries in which the MNEs operate, then the more pronounced the economic and social impact of their presence, *for good or bad*, is likely to be on the host country. Thus, *ceteris paribus* a firm that offers access to completely new intermediate or final goods markets is likely to increase the host economy's exports more than one that does not. A firm which sets up R&D facilities in its foreign subsidiary is likely to affect the host country's innovatory abilities more than one which does not. A firm with distinctive managerial skills and new approaches to industrial relations is likely to have a greater impact on the local labour market than one that does not. An MNE which is large, diversified and operates in several countries is likely to have more pronounced consequences on the economy of its home country than a small specialized firm with only one foreign subsidiary.

All the above O advantages stem from the favoured possession of particular intangible assets. Others referred to in Chapter 4 arise from the ability of the firm to coordinate a set of interrelated assets more effectively. This ability essentially reflects the investing firm's opportunities and ability to internalize cross-border intermediate product markets and/or to coordinate its assets and competences better than can some alternative organizational form (e.g. joint ventures or cooperative agreements). These Ot advantages all arise from the common governance of similar or diversified cross-border value-added activities. As Chapter 4 has shown, such benefits include the sharing of overheads, the arbitraging of differential factor costs, the balancing of country-specific environmental turbulences, and the exploitation of scope and scale economies. Thus it may be hypothesized that the more diversified a firm and the more countries in which it produces, the greater the impact of these assets is likely to be. However, in order for such advantages to be properly exploited, they have to be organized by the firm owning them, that is, the market or potential market for them has to be internalized.

Before turning to consider the L advantages of countries, it is worth observing that the O-specific assets of a country's firms (in relation to those of its foreign competitors) is likely to be strongly linked to its stage of development and particularly its degree of industrialization. Empirical work on the investment development path (Dunning, 1988a; Tolentino, 1992) has shown that the propensity of a country to engage in outward direct investment is positively and significantly correlated with its stock of innovatory capacity and human capital which, in turn, reflects the willingness and ability of its government to upgrade and make better use of its natural resources. It is also the case that as a country develops and its firms become more internationalized, the Ot advantages of MNEs become *relatively* more significant than their Oa advantages.

10.3.2   L-specific advantages

As identified by the received literature

In Chapter 4 it was suggested that a firm's propensity to invest in a particular country is often strongly influenced by the factor endowments, created capabilities and markets available in that country relative to others, as well as the extent to which it is perceived that the economic system and policies of a country enable it to exploit its O advantages profitably. Similarly, the consequences of the presence of an MNE on the economic welfare of a particular country will vary according to these same characteristics. For example, an investment by a computer producing company on a developing country with little indigenous technological capability will have a very different impact than the same investment in West Germany or the US. Production and marketing of some consumer goods products (e.g. dried milk, microwave ovens and many medicines) is likely to have different consequences in countries familiar with the contents of those products and the proper conditions for their use, than in one where they are being produced for the first time. Country-specific cultural factors explain why investment by US and French MNEs in the tourist sector may have a very different impact in Fiji, Nigeria or Japan than in Canada or Germany. Production of minerals, such as bauxite, copper and phosphate, or agricultural cash crops, such as tobacco, sugar and bananas, will have markedly different consequences in a country that is entirely dependent on those products for its economic prosperity than on one whose economic structure is more diversified.

We have already suggested that scholars interested in making comparisons between the economic and social characteristics of countries have found it helpful to classify countries according to their configuration of ESP characteristics. Countries differ from each other in respect of their stage of development and propensity to attract international business, according to their economic *environment* (E), economic *systems* (S) and government *policies* (P). Here *environment* encompasses the resources and capabilities, including a wide range of intangible assets to a particular country, as well as the ability of its enterprises to use these to service domestic or foreign markets. *System* means the macro-organiza-

tional mechanism within which the allocation of these resources and capabilities is decided. For example, does the market primarily perform the task or is it decided by government fiat or by some combination of the two? What is the role of commercial hierarchies in affecting the transaction costs of different organizational forms? *Policy* means the strategic objectives of governments and the macro or micro measures taken by them, or related institutions, to implement and advance these objectives, within the system and environment of which they are part. Exhibit 10.2 sets out the main attributes of the ESP configuration and their respective outcomes.

Clearly, the three elements of the paradigm are interlinked; each affects and is affected by the other. A change in government policy may dramatically recast the economic system, as recent events in the People's Republic of China and Eastern Europe have vividly shown. Over a longer period, government involvement in education and in R&D programmes may impinge on the environment in a way that is no less significant. A detailed appraisal of the ESP characteristics of countries takes us a long way to understanding the likely interaction between MNEs and the Nation States in which they operate.

Most of the extant literature on international economics tends to concentrate its attention on the E influences on trade and FDI. For example, both the classical and neo-classical trade models assume a market system in which there is atomistic competition and all resources are immobile between countries. The models also assume no government intervention, zero economic or psychic distance, and the free and instantaneous transfer of all kinds of technology across national boundaries. More recent trade theories have acknowledged the existence of market imperfections and, implicitly at least, the characteristics of a mixed economy by accepting that firms may possess proprietary assets yet incur positive transaction costs in their usage. From the start, explanations of international production have more explicitly taken the S and P variables into account. For example, in a survey of the 44 most commonly quoted factors said to determine the investments by MNEs in developing countries, one-half were found to be directly related to S or P variables and the remainder to E variables (Root and Ahmed, 1978). Although the survey was primarily

Exhibit 10.2   The ESP paradigm.

ENVIRONMENT (E)

Components:
Human resources
Natural resources
Stage of economic development
Cultural/historical background

Outcomes:
Level and structure of output (primary, industrial services, specializations)
Attitudes to work, wealth, foreigners, etc.

SYSTEM (S)

Capitalist (free enterprise)
Socialist
Mixed
Alliance with other countries

Structure of decision taking
Propensity to engage in international commerce
Resource allocation controlled by market
Nationalization

POLICIES (P)

Macro-economic (fiscal, monetary, exchange rate)
Micro-economic (industry, trade, competition)
General (education, consumer protection)
Specific to FDI

Extent and form of government intervention
Controls
Performance requirements

Source: Adapted from Koopman and Montias (1971). See also Dunning (1988b, p.14)

concerned with identifying the determinants of the locational choice of companies, the ESP paradigm is no less relevant in explaining differences in the O advantages of MNEs of different nationalities and the modalities by which these advantages may be organized.

Viewed from a dynamic perspective, perhaps the most important L factors influencing the likely impact of MNEs are the macro-organizational policies and development strategies pursued by host countries together with the structure of the diamond of competitive advantages identified by Porter (1990). In the case of industrialized developed countries, these factors usually reduce to the extent to which governments are likely to intervene in the systemic

process of resource allocation. In the mid to late 1970s, for example, there were considerable differences in the macro- and micro-organizational strategies pursued by the French and the British, on the one hand, and the US on the other. In the early 1990s, the variations are fewer, but in certain policy areas, for example, education, R&D, industrial restructuring and anti-trust legislation, there are still substantial differences in the actions taken and influence exerted, by the East Asian, as compared with the US and most Western European governments. These differences impinge both on the structure of the diamond of competitive advantage and, through the diamond, on the asset accumulation of particular firms or sectors. In turn, they affect the ability of domestic producers to compete in world markets through FDI and the likely impact of such investment, and that of foreign firms, on the competitiveness of location-bound resources.

In the case of developing countries, economists tend to use a classificatory scheme based on either *levels* or *types* of economic development. À *propos* the former, the World Bank uses such indices as income per head, economic structure, education, degree of urbanization, housing, health care, etc, and changes in these variables over time. Another measure, recently compiled by the United Nations Development Programme (UNDP) (1990), is the Human Development Index (HDI) which comprises an amalgam of life expectancy, adult literacy and real purchasing power.[7]

As regards the types of development paths, perhaps the most widely used classification is that of Hollis Chenery (1979). Chenery grouped developing countries according to the four main development strategies they might pursue. These are:

(1) primary goods specialization,

(2) import substitution,

(3) balanced production and trade,

(4) industrial specialization.

The World Bank (1987) has suggested a similar typology of strategies based on the orientation of trade, *viz* 'a strongly or moderately outward oriented' strategy and a 'strongly or moderately inward oriented' strategy. To be successful, each of these development strategies requires several conditions to be met, although their exact configuration and the role MNE activity might play in advancing them, is likely to depend on the actual development strategy being pursued. These conditions include:

(1) an adequate legal, administrative and commercial infrastructure,

(2) an efficient economic system,

(3) expanding domestic demand,

(4) an increase in savings and domestic capital,

(5) the creation of or ready access to technological and organizational capacity,

(6) a cadre of indigenous entrepreneurs and a work culture which favours wealth-creating activities,

(7) access to foreign inputs and markets for outputs.

The ability of a country to meet these requirements rests on its social objectives and policies, its indigenous resources and capabilities, its institutional structures, its attitude toward transactional relationships and the role of government, and the extent and form of the kind of foreign resources it needs.

A *stages approach*

A rather different, but complementary, approach to those just outlined is to look at the interaction between MNE activity and the economic development and/or restructuring of a country. It is here we believe that a 'stages of development cum restructuring model' is especially appropriate. This is first because it links the development of a country to its positioning in the world economy; second because it can most easily accommodate and evaluate the role of inward and outward investment at different stages of that development; and third because it introduces a dynamic element into the other paradigms which form the analytical underpinning of this part of the book. The approach is best exemplified by the present author's investment development path, by Ozawa's stages of economic development (Ozawa, 1992) and by Porter's approach to the competitive evolution of national economies (Porter, 1990).

While it is possible to distinguish between many stages of development and to group these according to a broad range of criteria, we shall concentrate on just four, and classify them according to their main driving forces which are likely to influence both inbound and outbound MNE activity.

(i) *Stage 1*   In this phase, a country's diamond of competitive advantages rests mainly on the possession of **natural resources**. In so far as inward investment is likely to be attracted by the (ESP) assets of the country, it is likely to be directed to the primary product sector and to labour-intensive manufacturing sectors supplying relatively simple consumer goods, either to the local or to export markets. In this phase, the country is likely to have few created capabilities or competences apart, perhaps, from an accumulation of human skills in craft industries and in specialized mining, agribusiness and fishing activities. Because of this, outbound MNE activity is likely to be small and of either the trade-supporting and/or the asset-seeking kind.

Countries in this stage of development – which approximates to Rostow's two pre-take-off stages of growth – are likely to take a reasonably relaxed view to inward direct investment and to impose few performance requirements on foreign affiliates (see Chapter 20). Asset accumulation is likely to be limited and largely dependent on whether or not the supply capabilities or markets of the host country are sufficient to induce forward processing of primary activities. Without such capabilities, there is a danger that inward investment may simply lead to the establishment of enclaves of economic activity and the promotion of a dual economy (see Chapter 16).

(ii) *Stage 2*   This stage of development is marked by the growing importance of **investment capital** in value-added activity and, in some cases, by the size and quality of the domestic market. It represents the equivalent of Rostow's take-off stage of development where the percentage of gross domestic investment to gross domestic product (GDP) may rise from between 5% and 8% to between 15% and 20% (World Bank, 1991, Table 9). At the same time, depending on its ability to accumulate and disseminate assets, a country may develop clusters of economic activity. Stage 2 is also likely to be marked by a sharp increase in expenditure on secondary education, public utilities, transport and communications. By upgrading the capabilities and productivity of local resources, and by stimulating competition, inward investment may play an important tutorial role in steering a country through this stage of development, particularly if it is pursuing an export-led development strategy. On the other hand, a country may prefer to develop its own asset capabilities and restrict the amount of inward investment. This was the initial post-1952 strategy of Japan and Korea.

During the investment-led stage of development, the structure of a country's revealed comparative advantage is likely to shift towards medium to large scale, capital-intensive sectors, such as basic chemicals, iron and steel, and shipbuilding; some smaller scale and specialized mechanical engineering activities; and the production of labour-intensive, but moderately knowledge-intensive consumer goods, such as electrical products, clothing, leather goods, processed foods and cigarettes. The propensity for inward investment to generate 'vicious' or 'virtuous' circles of asset accumulation is likely to be strongly dependent on the extent to which host governments are able to foster the requisite domestic infrastructure and supply capacities, successfully design and implement the appropriate macro-economic and organizational policies, and provide the necessary impetus for their own firms to upgrade the quality of their output to internationally acceptable standards.

(iii) *Stage 3*   In this stage, a developing country is approaching economic maturity and its income level and industrial structure are beginning to resemble those of a developed country. Depending on its size and the structure of its resources and capabilities, the country will be moving towards a purely industrialized or mixed economy. In either event, but especially so in the former case, the third stage is marked by a switch of emphasis from **investment-led** to **innovation-led** growth, as shown by a sharp increase in urbanization and expenditure on innovatory activities.

As living standards improve, consumers favour high quality and differentiated products, while low cost resource-intensive goods become less competitive in world markets. Stage 3 economies are marked by a noticeable increase in government expenditure on tertiary education and communication facilities. At the same time, the competitiveness of their firms begins to rely less on their possession of indigenous natural resources and more on their managerial and organizational competences, and on the quality of their entrepreneurship.

The role of inward investment continues to be valued for the provision of O-specific assets in which the country has a comparative disadvantage, and for assisting the host country to upgrade its indigenous capabilities. In addition it will help the host country to restructure its activities away from natural resource- and/or physical capital-intensive sectors, to innovatory-intensive sectors or those producing high quality differentiated products. Inward investment is likely to be less welcome when it drives out indigenous competitors and promotes a vicious circle of asset decumulation – except where this occurs in sectors in which the country is losing its comparative dynamic advantage.

Outward investment may aid a 'virtuous' circle of asset accumulation wherever it adds to the competitiveness of domestic firms and enables them to secure new foreign markets more remuneratively than by other means. Such investment may either be of a resource-seeking or market-seeking kind. However, Stage 3 may also see the beginning of rationalized and strategic asset acquiring MNE activity, which is designed to tap into, and benefit from, the diamonds of competitive advantage of foreign countries.

During Stage 3, the key attributes of the ESP paradigm in determining competitiveness are likely to shift from the E and S to the S and P. Devising the right economic system and the optimum policies to support and, as necessary, modify the system becomes an increasingly important ingredient of competitiveness. In so far as these variables are strongly influenced by governments – especially in the way they affect the efficiency of markets and the transaction costs of wealth-creating agents – the role of government as a facilitator of efficient resource allocation is likely to become more rather than less significant (Dunning, 1991a).

(iv) *Stage 4* Stage 4 – which we shall call the **information processing** stage – is the final and most advanced stage of economic development. So far it has been reached by only a small number of advanced industrial countries. This stage has also been called the **post-industrial** or **services stage of development**. However, a closer examination of economies like the US, Japan, Norway and Germany, which make up this group, reveals that these also remain the leading spenders on R&D, which, for the most part, is directed towards the innovation of new products and production methods. What is true, however, is that radical advances in computing and telecommunications technology have hastened the blurring of the traditional frontiers between manufacturing and services, particularly the service content of innovatory activities. It is also the case that a larger percentage of finished output consists either of direct services or of goods which have a high content of services embodied in them.[8]

The role of government continues to be important, but its emphasis is now less directed to minimizing structural market distortions and more to assisting firms to circumvent or overcome endemic market failure. Such market failure arises because of the increasingly technological complexity of the goods and services traded and the interdependence of markets. Both features lead to a more uncertain

outcome of transactions concluded and to more externalities associated with them.[9]

Stage 4 in the development process is one in which there are more national and cross-border inter- and intra-firm linkages, and the success of countries in accumulating assets depends increasingly on the ability of their firms to coordinate their resources and capabilities at regional and global levels. With a broadly similar structure of natural resource endowments, the comparative advantage of countries in Stage 4 is likely to be based more on the efficiency of their macro-economic and macro-organizational systems. Hence, the value of inward or outward MNE activity is judged not only by the provision of foreign resources and capabilities, but also by the way in which these may be organized and their spillover affects the efficiency and competences of local competitors, suppliers and customers. Because organization is itself an asset that is strongly influenced by a country's culture, by linking cultures, MNE activity can materially affect, for good or bad, the ability of Stage 4 economies to retain or advance their global competitive positions.

This is particularly well demonstrated in the interaction between an MNE's location of innovatory capacity and the asset-accumulating goals of particular economies. Chapters 11 and 12 will give some attention to this important subject. Here, we would simply observe that a country's diamond of competitive advantage and its likely future configuration in high technology sectors will strongly influence whether or not, and how far, MNEs choose to locate their high value activities in the country in question. This, in turn, may well influence the future national and international competitiveness of those sectors.

Comment on the stages approach

There is, of course, no presumption that all countries will progress through each of these stages of development, or, if they do, that the trajectory of their developmental paths will be the same. Moreover, countries may well straddle more than one stage at the same time. Attitudes towards the role of FDI as an engine of development may not only vary between countries, but in the same country at different periods of time. Within a country, different regions may be at different stages of development. To some extent, at least, the phasing of a country's development is also likely to be industry specific – as is the likely impact of inward investment on the character of 'vicious' or 'virtuous' asset-accumulation circles.

Certainly, it is difficult to generalize on the optimum role of FDI in economic development. In the 19th century, foreign capital, technology, human skills and entrepreneurship played a variable role in the 'take-off' of the development of Western European economies, the US and Japan. The experience of the 20th century equivalents of these economies is even more diffuse. One needs look no further than the post World War II history of Japan and Germany, or Korea and Brazil, to see that economic development and success do not necessarily rest on a substantial injection of MNE activity. At the same time, the Indian, Chinese and East European experiences also show that the absence of MNE activity does not guarantee economic well-being either! In the developing world, there is no direct correlation between the share of foreign investment and economic development. Where this does seem to be the case, the causal relationship is a difficult one to establish (Bornshier, 1980; O'Hearn, 1990).[10] This does not mean that MNE activity has no effect on economic development, but simply that the *raison d'être* for that activity, and the conditions leading to it, are of critical importance in determining what the consequences are and whether or not the resources and capabilities it provides might not have been better obtained by other routes.

At the same time, the data on international direct investment does seem strongly to suggest that countries do go through an identifiable development path – at least up to the point of industrial maturity. Subsequently, their net international investment positions would seem to fluctuate according, *inter alia*, to their *relative* economic prosperity. We have already described the nature of the investment development path in Chapter 4, but essentially its trajectory begins with a country undertaking little or no inward or outward investment. As development proceeds, inward investment increases (in relation to GNP); this is followed by the emergence and growth of outward investment, which may eventually exceed that of inward investment. A final phase is where, allowing for year-to-year fluctuations, inward and outward investment are more nearly balanced, although how nearly and whether the country is a net outward or inward investor will depend on the configuration of its diamond of competitive advantage relative to that of its major competitors.

As with the 'stages' approach, it cannot be assumed that all countries will necessarily travel through all phases of the investment development path. Moreover, each country's trajectory will differ according, *inter alia*, to its size, economic structure, propensity to engage in international commerce and government policy. In particular, the willingness and capabilities of a country to identify and promote its own dynamic comparative advantage, and to use effectively both inward direct investment, and the activities of its own companies outside their national boundaries, to help achieve this end, will be strongly country specific and closely dependent on the type of the macro-organizational system it pursues.

In each of these scenarios, the impact of MNEs may then be judged by their contribution to the speed and direction of the development process. Moreover, each of these scenarios tends to be associated with very different economic policies (P) and attitudes towards FDI. Chapter 20 will show, for example, that governments of countries pursuing export-led industrialization are likely to impose relatively few restrictions on inward investment or the activities of foreign-owned firms. Also, import protection is generally low or non existent. By contrast, authorities pursuing import substitution developing strategies are prone to impose moderate to severe disincentives to imports, keep the exchange rate at an overvalued level, operate rigorous price controls and maintain close supervision over all forms of inward investment and the behaviour of foreign affiliates. Countries adopting the former strategies will seek to participate fully in the international division of labour in order to strengthen their diamonds of competitive advantage in sectors in which they perceive they have a comparative trading advantage. Those following the latter strategies will attempt to build their own economic destinies; they tend to value economic sovereignty over the most efficient resource allocation, and the preservation of cultural values over the gains of economic specialization.[11]

It is, then, not difficult to understand that the impact of MNEs on economies that pursue, or have pursued, inward-looking import-substituting or quasi-socialist economic policies, is likely to be very different from that on countries that pursue outward-looking export-oriented and free market strategies. So will the nature of their diamonds of competitive advantage and their ability to assimilate, and fully benefit from, the resources, capabilities and organizational strategies provided by MNEs. The impact of inward direct investment will also vary according to the economic signals provided by host governments. An economy strongly protected by tariffs or non-tariff barriers, such as Canada in the 1960s, Brazil in the 1970s, India until very recently and Japan even in the 1990s, will be affected differently than one in which there are no or few trade restrictions, for example, Singapore, Hong Kong, Switzerland or the UK. Similarly, an economy that believes in the virtues of the free market is likely to attract a different kind of FDI and be differently affected by it than one in which prices and output are determined or strongly influenced by some central planning authority. Countries which ensure that their factor prices reflect their true opportunity cost are likely to judge FDI differently than those whose factor prices are distorted by non-market forces. Finally, and perhaps most important of all, countries will differ according to the expectations they have of foreign firms, as well as according to their goals and their order of priority in achieving these goals.

In practice, although most democratic countries have broadly similar objectives for their citizens, the priority accorded to these objectives – particularly when they compete with each other – will differ considerably. As we suggested in Chapter 3, the goal of most MNEs is to earn profits or to create wealth for their stakeholders – their shareholders in particular. Nation States, on the other hand, seek to achieve a variety of goals. These include not only maximizing GNP, or growth of GNP, but a range of social and strategic goals to do with income distribution, economic and political sovereignty, cultural identity, technological capability, environmental protection and so on. According to the particular mix of the objectives that governments seek to achieve, the perceived value of outbound and inbound MNE activity will differ. At the same time, by their actions and influence, MNEs may affect the priority assigned to these goals and the extent to which they are achieved.

To summarize, just as individual MNEs will affect countries differently, so individual countries will find that the same MNE activity may have different economic and social consequences. Partly this is because their goals or priority in achieving these goals is different, and partly because the structure of their ESP configuration or competitive advantages is different. The task of this chapter is to offer an analytical framework within which it is possible to theorize on the impact of MNE activity according to their distinctive characteristics and those of the countries in which they choose to operate.

10.3.3   I-related advantages

Finally, MNEs that possess similar O-specific advantages and are faced with broadly comparable L-specific characteristics of countries[12] may still have different impacts on the countries in which they operate because they organize and control the use of these assets differently. Chapter 3 has shown that the price and output decisions of a single-activity firm producing in a perfectly competitive market are confined to those which are consistent with profit maximization. In an imperfect market structure, especially in the presence of uncertainty and where the economies of scope encourage a firm to diversify its products and production outlets, the firm has more options. This being so, it could well be that the governance exerted over any one activity may be different from that exerted over the same activity if it is one of many (Caves, 1981). In other words, the ownership of assets may affect the way in which they are organized; this, in turn, may affect the consequences of their usage.

Basically, the MNE seeks to ensure that it controls its value-added activities in such a way as to advance the interests of the company as a whole. Because of differences in the common governance between a firm with many subsidiaries and one with only one, it follows that the impact on the host country will be different. In fact, as later chapters will show, it is the different strategies of MNEs towards their purchase and use of intermediate products and the way in which they organize their marketing and distribution, which many governments consider as their main distinguishing characteristics *vis à vis* uninational firms. While it is recognized that foreign MNEs provide new resources, capabilities and markets, and home-based MNEs export technology and human capital, the unique contribution of MNE activity is the way in which the resources transferred and the markets accessed are organized.

The hypothesis is that the greater the likely difference between the impact of the alternative modalities of the market and cooperative agreements and that of multinational hierarchies, the greater, for good or bad, the distinctive impact of outward and inward FDI will be. Moreover, the propensity of MNEs to internalize cross-border markets will also vary according to the stages of development of a country. In Stages 1 and 2, since the markets for intermediate products produced by foreign firms are likely to be highly imperfect, the modality of supply is likely to be FDI. In Stages 3 and 4, as the business infrastructure and capabilities of indigenous firms improve, some FDI will be replaced by inter-firm agreements. At the same time, as firms, particularly in technology or information intensive sectors, become more of an efficiency or strategic asset seeking variety, the need to exploit the economies of synergy and common governance tend to favour either FDI or FDI coupled with a network of cross-border collaborative agreements, as the main vehicles of cross-border involvement.

A glance at the financial press provides ample evidence that individual firms in a particular industry or country do adopt distinctive strategies in pursuance of their global markets. Hence, their impact on the countries in which they operate is likely to be different. Sometimes, differences in behaviour reflect the country of origin of the MNE (e.g. Japanese industrial relations and procurement practices are not the same as those of the Americans), as a result of which their impact on the countries in which they operate will be different. Sometimes it reflects the size, age or experience of MNEs, and at other times, the country-specific characteristics of the external markets for the intermediate products being transferred. In some countries, for example, there is an adequate market for technology acquisition and dissemination; in others it may be non-existent. But the key point is that, just as the propensity of individual firms to prefer international production to licensing or collaborative agreements varies according to the characteristics of those firms, so the economic and social impact of these modalities will differ, as indeed it will between different MNEs. It is the purpose of the following chapters to try and set down some general principles by which one can establish the main factors that are likely to influence the distinctive impact of MNEs, in terms of the control exercised over resources, capabilities and markets by such hierarchies, as compared with that of other organizational forms.

10.3.4 The interaction between MNE activity and economic development: a resumé

The process of the interaction

We illustrate the main conclusions of the previous paragraphs by reference to Exhibit 10.3 which charts the possible impact of an inward MNE activity on the recipient country and how it may, in turn, affect the competitiveness of the investing companies. It also considers how autonomous (i.e. non-FDI-induced) changes may also impact on the O advantages of these same enterprises and countries. In this exhibit, we consider just two stages of development of a particular country, t1 and tn. In practice, these may refer to any two of the stages described earlier.

Consider first the top half of the chart. In stage t1, existing and potential foreign investors are faced with a given set of OLI configurations. These, we assume, will lead to new FDI. As a direct consequence of this investment (identified as an FDI-led change), a train of events is set in motion which affects the trajectory of the development path of the recipient country (or countries), as well as the future OLI configuration of the investing firms. Some of the determinants of these changes are illustrated in the exhibit. They have been fully described either earlier in this chapter or in previous chapters.

The chart makes no *a priori* assumption as to *how* a country's development or the OLI configuration of investing firms will be affected. We have already emphasized that this will depend on the kind of FDI undertaken, as well as on country-, industry- and firm-specific variables leading to it, and resulting from it. The nature of the impact will also vary according to the stages of development being considered. What the chart does show, however, is

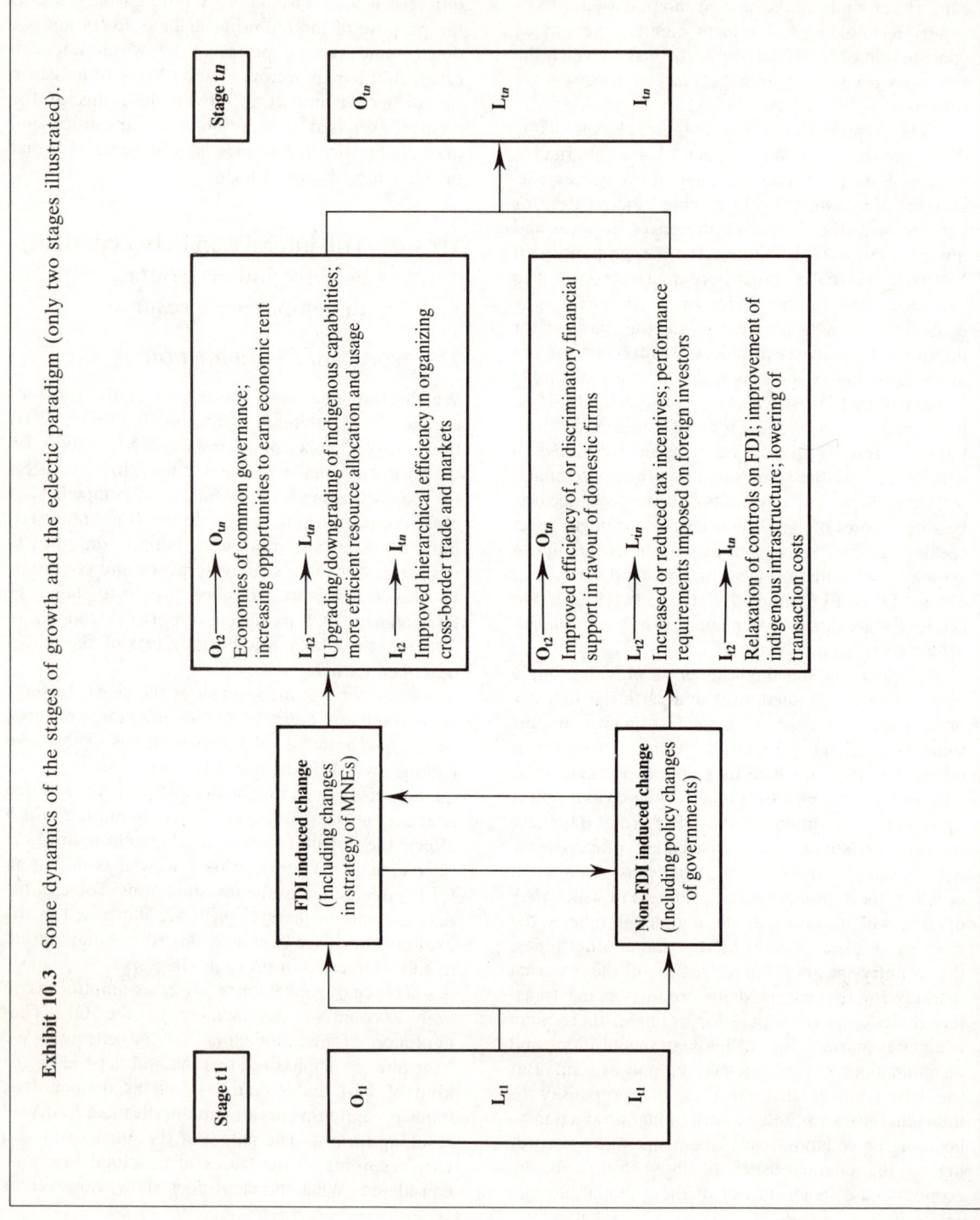

Exhibit 10.3   Some dynamics of the stages of growth and the eclectic paradigm (only two stages illustrated).

the kind of iterative interaction which might occur between foreign MNEs and the host countries in which they operate, the outcome of which will influence, to some extent at least, the form and character of the latters' next stage of development.

The lower part of the exhibit identifies some non-FDI-induced changes which might affect the O advantages of firms and the L advantages of countries, and, in the light of these, the relative merits of markets, hierarchies, and cooperative ventures as modalities for the cross-border organization of the former. It is the combination of these two kinds of changes that will determine the configuration of the OLI variables facing foreign investors in stage tn, as well as the ESP of host countries, the extent and structure of which will identify its trajectory of development.

It would be possible to produce a similar chart considering the interaction between outward investment and a home country's economic development. One could also incorporate other variables influencing changes in the OLI t2 configuration into the existing chart.[13] In the former case, the kind of outward investment, the extent to which it is substitutable for, or complementary to, domestic investment and the conditions in which it is made, are among the critical factors likely to determine the extent to which it impacts favourably or unfavourably on domestic economic welfare. Again, it may be demonstrated – as later chapters will seek to do – that the contribution of MNE activity to a nation's economic and social objectives will not only depend on the nature of these objectives, but also on its stage of economic development. For example, while in the earlier stages of development, some kinds of outbound MNE activity may be at the expense of upgrading domestic technological capability and may lead to a reduction in the competitive advantages of both investing firms and countries, in Stage 4, the globalization of value-added activity is often essential to maintain or advance those same advantages.

However, if the diagram illustrates the points made in the earlier sections it will have served its purpose. Table 10.1 sets out an alternative way of depicting the interaction between the competitive advantages of domestic firms and countries at the four stages of development earlier identified. We present this table without comment, as we believe it is self-explanatory.

Asset accumulation and restructuring

We would make one further observation. Earlier (in Section 10.2) we outlined the way in which the asset-accumulation paradigm might be used to improve our understanding of the dynamic interplay between FDI and economic development. What exactly is the process of this interaction? How might inward and outward investment affect the direction, pace and structure of a country's ability to create and sustain wealth? Let us give just two examples by considering the dynamic repercussions of inbound MNE activity.

Take first the acquisition of a domestic firm in a high technology fabricating sector by a foreign MNE. Assume that this industry (in the host country) is moderately competitive in international markets, has reasonable support facilities, is subsidized by the government and is protected from foreign competition. Assume, next, that the purpose of the acquisition by the foreign company is to gain access to local or adjacent markets for its products. And finally, assume that the foreign company transfers the R&D facilities of the acquired firm back to the parent company and undertakes only local assembling operations on imported intermediate products.

Assuming all these things, and tracing through the repercussions on the diamond of competitive advantage of the host economy and on the future competitive position of the investing firms, it may be that the net result of the inward investment is to reduce the international competitiveness of the industry and to accelerate a vicious circle of asset decumulation and a restructuring of assets away from that sector to others in the host country.

Take, however, a second scenario. Assume in this case that the inbound investment is directed to an expanding sector which requires resources in which the country is developing (or could develop) a dynamic comparative advantage. Assume also that there are already strong indigenous rivals in that sector and that the government is promoting market-facilitating measures and working with its own firms to upgrade skills and capabilities, as well as to build up a network or cluster of supply capabilities. Assume that the foreign company foresees the host country as a major base for supplying regional or global markets, and for innovatory activities, and that it plans to assist the development of local supply capabilities. Assume finally that the inward investor

Table 10.1 Stages of economic development and characteristics of the O advantages of domestic firm and L advantages of its countries.

	Nature of development	Characteristics of inward (I) or outward (O) investment	O	L	I	Sectors of outbound MNE activity
Stage I	Natural resource	I. Resource based. O. Export supporting; limited resource seeking. .... Little I and negligible O FDI.	Limited to small entrepreneurs producing specialized products for sale in neighbouring territories or niche markets.	Mainly presence of natural resources. Infrastructural support also important. Governments role in setting up legal and commercial system.	Except in export and import merchanting-oriented sectors, only markets tend to be imperfect, but generally foreign participation either by exports or FDI.	Most agricultural and primary good sectors. Small-scale craft and labour-intensive manufacturers, especially textiles and clothing.
Stage II	Investment driven	I. Still resource based but in more capital-intensive sectors; low cost labour market. O. Market seeking; mainly market but some resource or asset seeking. .... I increasing and limited O FDI.	Related to ability to produce low cost, standardized products, or those based on natural resources of home country.	Low real wage costs. Natural resources. Supply capacity. Clusters of local industry. Education, transport and communications infrastructure.	Depends strongly on government policy and adequacy of local infrastructure but, on balance, rather more licensing likely.	Capital-intensive producer sectors (chemicals, machinery, steel, etc). Fairly standardized consumer good sectors, requiring little adaptations to imported technology.
Stage III	Innovation driven	I. In activities supplying more sophisticated products for domestic market, or requiring more skilled labour. O. All kinds of investment including some rationalized. .... O increasing faster than I FDI.	The ability to differentiate products and/or adapt to local consumer tastes. Some limited product and process innovation-based (home) country-specific assets.	Entrepreneurship. Larger and more sophisticated markets. Competition between firms. Ability to offer conditions for rationalized investment.	Tendency for firms to prefer more equity ownership so as to protect proprietary knowledge and control markets.	Mass produced highly differentiated consumer durable products (cars, electrical products, cameras, etc).

Table 10.1   continued.

	Nature of development	Characteristics of inward (I) or outward (O) investment	O	L	I	Sectors of outbound MNE activity
Stage IV	Information and service intensity	I. Increasingly rationalized and asset seeking. O. Increasingly rationalized and asset seeking. .... Substantial I and O FDI. Balance between I and O FDI fluctuates.	Substantial, but often fluctuating in relative significance. Country-specific $O_a + O_t$ advantages continue to be of some importance. Organizational ability to manage clusters of O_a advantages; also flexible, multi-variety production.	Increasing importance of supply capabilities, support services and market facilitating services. Government role in minimizing transaction costs of both own firms and foreign MNEs.	Linkages between activities on value chains at its peak; though non-equity alliances growing in importance. Some hiving off of some activities as firms reappraise the benefits of the common governance of 'core' assets.	Biotechnology, information, mechatronics, high value service activities (consultancy). Sectors servicing global markets.

has an international reputation for supplying high quality products at competitive prices.

In this scenario, FDI may set in motion a train of events which could lead to, or enhance, a virtuous circle of asset accumulation in the particular sector in question, and that would directly assist in a beneficial restructuring of the assets of the host country.

We accept, of course, that these scenarios are extreme cases. We also accept that from a national (rather than a sectoral) perspective, a vicious circle may not necessarily be a bad thing, as it is quite possible that the resources released might be capable of being put to more productive uses elsewhere in the economy. Finally, it could well be that the inbound investment could turn a movement towards asset decumulation into asset accumulation, or vice versa. We shall give some further illustration of these possibilities in the following chapter.

Likewise, outbound MNE activity might encourage either virtuous or vicious innovatory circles, and welcome or unwelcome asset restructuring. Where, for example, it stimulates effective rivalry and builds up a strong domestic innovatory base in a

sector in which the home country has (or could have) a dynamic comparative advantage, it could promote welfare-enhancing asset accumulation and restructuring. Where it destroys competition, weakens indigenous support and causes governments to behave in a structurally distorting fashion, it may result in asset decumulation and welfare-reducing asset restructuring.

10.4   SOME FURTHER METHODOLOGICAL POINTS

The previous sections have indicated that no sensible assessment may be made of the impact of MNE activity without first identifying the criteria by which this impact is judged. Furthermore, any explanation of the impact must take account of the country-specific factors influencing the decisions of MNEs, including the level and patterns of demand, the structure of resources and capabilities, and the actions taken by policy makers to pursue their economic and other objectives.

It follows that, while it may be possible to suggest a general paradigm for evaluating the kinds of economic and social impact of MNEs on the countries in which they operate, any operationally testable theory of this impact must be conditioned by the types of MNE activity, the strategies of MNEs and the ESP configurations of the countries in which they operate. As in such policy-related research, the *ex ante* 'if . . . then' approach rather than the *ex post* 'because . . . then' approach has some merit. This is almost inevitable for countries seeking to design strategies towards both outward and inward MNE activity. Indeed, we believe that enough is now known about the economic impact of MNEs in different sectors and in different ESP configurations, to guide the formation of general policies which can optimize the value of their presence. At the same time, each country is unique and needs to evolve its own *specific* policies towards, or as a result of, MNE activity. In other words, while there are general lessons to be learned about the impact of foreign MNEs in (say) the pharmaceutical industry for a country like France or Thailand, there will also be factors that are specific to France or Thailand which will make any such impact different than in (say) Germany and Italy on the one hand, or Malaysia and Brazil on the other.

We now return to one important methodological issue concerning the assessment of the impact of MNE enterprise *qua* MNE. It concerns the question of attribution. Suppose it is possible to identify the transactions and performance of MNEs or that of their affiliates. For example, suppose it can be shown that German-owned affiliates in Brazil record a good export performance, or that Japanese affiliates in the UK are highly productive, or that Swedish subsidiaries in Malaysia pay their workers above the national average wages, or that French-owned hotels in Jamaica import most of their food, or that UK mining companies in New Guinea limit the markets to which their affiliates can sell, or that US subsidiaries in Canada carry out only a limited amount of R&D; or that, as a result of a takeover of a Thai textile company by a Hong Kong foreign investor, a large number of redundancies occur; or that in order to obtain a permit for building a petrochemical plant an Italian construction company is found guilty of bribing a Nigerian government

official; or that a Dutch and Indian food processing firm concluded a strategic alliance to drive out a powerful US competitor; or that, by a variety of questionable tactics, an Australian wholesale trader has managed to gain control over most of the leading retail outlets in Fiji.

Suppose all these things. To what extent may it be said that these events are a result of specifically the *foreignness* or the *multinationality* of these companies, and to what extent to other attributes they may possess, but which may have little, if anything, to do with their nationality of ownership or degree of multinationality? For it is a fact that, as well as engaging in foreign production, MNEs are often big and diversified – but so are many uninational firms. They may also influence, if not control, sources of supply or marketing outlets – so might some of their local competitors. Their marketing and advertising practices may, for good or bad, affect the purchasing habits and values of consumers – so might indigenous firms or foreign firms exporting to the countries in question! In assessing the unique contributions of MNEs, the scholar needs to be constantly careful only to attribute factors that are a consequence of their foreignness and/or their degree of multinationality.

There is another, but related, problem. Let us take just one example which will be explored in some detail in Chapter 14. How does one measure the impact of the operations of a foreign affiliate of an MNE on the balance of payments of a host country? We shall demonstrate that it is not sufficient to calculate the external transactions on capital and current account of MNEs or their foreign affiliates, for these must be set against some estimate of the transactions that would have occurred in the absence of such foreign affiliates – the so-called *alternative* or *counterfactual* position. For example, suppose that a Dutch MNE company finds that after two years of operating a foreign affiliate in Pakistan, its exports to that country are only one-half of those before the affiliate was set up? How far can this decline in exports be ascribed to the foreign investment? The answer depends very much on what would have happened had the investment not taken place. There is also the question of what happens to the resources (e.g. capital and labour) displaced by exports. Will these be employed elsewhere in the economy where exports might be earned, or will they remain unused? Much in this instance rests on the supply capacity of the home country and the kinds of macro-economic, fiscal and employment policies pursued by the home government. Depending on the answer to these questions, the net balance of payments effects of outward investment may vary from being strongly negative to strongly positive.

Naturally, any alternative or counterfactual position is bound to be hypothetical as one cannot be sure what would actually have happened in the absence of the foreign investment. For this reason, some researchers have argued that it is more helpful to try to identify the specific characteristics of the *ownership* of foreign affiliates by making comparisons between the conduct and performance of foreign and indigenous firms or between foreign firms according to the nationality of their ownership or degree of multinationality. Any differences that are revealed may then be reasonably attributable to the nationality or multinationality of the firm. This is an interesting estimating procedure. At the same time, it does make the implicit assumption that in the absence of FDI, the output gap would be met by other firms, that is to say, that the resources released by the foreign firms would be utilized.

Such methodological points are critical if the distinctive impact of MNEs is to be properly appreciated and evaluated. Of course, it is quite possible that the main contribution of inbound investment to a particular country may have little to do with country of origin. One suspects that this particularly applies in the case of intra-OECD investment in international industries where the main competitors of foreign MNEs are domestic MNEs. On the other hand, in some cutting-edge technology and information-intensive sectors (e.g. biotechnology, banking and financial services), the nationality of ownership may be a decisive variable affecting technological or organizational competences. Even in other sectors, since foreign-owned firms are often more efficient than domestic firms, their marginal impact on the competitiveness of indigenous resources may be quite substantial.

10.5 FDI AND ECONOMIC DEVELOPMENT: SOME ALTERNATIVE APPROACHES

In assessing the distinctive impact of MNE activity on the economies of both home and host countries, the scholar has various procedures open to him. The first is to look at the impact of such activity on just one variable, for example, output, and then to view this from different viewpoints, such as countries, industries, firms and sectoral interests.

The second is to look at the impact of MNE activity in terms of the specific goals of countries. Some years ago, for example, Streeten (1974) suggested that the impact of MNEs on the development policies of developing countries could best be analysed by their contribution to filling a number of gaps or lacunae in a country's economic armoury and/or by their effects on other variables relevant to the development objectives. In particular, Streeten identified four major lacunae which MNEs might help fill. These were:

(1) the *resource gap* between desired investment and locally mobilized savings;

(2) the *foreign exchange* or *trade gap* between foreign exchange requirements and foreign exchange earnings plus official net aid;

(3) the *budgetary gap* between target revenue and locally raised taxes;

(4) the *management and skill gap* by providing foreign management and the training of local managers and workers.

He also suggested that MNEs might aid or inhibit other objectives of recipient countries, for example, in respect of the development of indigenous technological capability and environmentally favoured growth.

The third possible way to analyse the impact of MNEs is to examine its impact on certain attributes of economic and social prosperity. Among those most frequently considered are the impacts on gross national product, labour productivity, competitiveness, quality of output, investment, upgrading of human capital, technological capability, exports, industrial relations and the environment.

As and when appropriate, and depending on the data available, each of these kinds of impact will be considered in the following chapters. However, in general we shall concentrate on the third approach; in particular, we shall consider the ways in which the unique characteristics of MNEs interact with the unique characteristics of countries. In Chapters 11 to 14 we shall examine the direct consequences of MNE activity in terms of the resources, capabilities and markets it creates and provides, and the control it exercises over the use of these and other assets it acquires. Chapters 11 and 12 deal with the MNE as a creator and organizer of technological capacity, and the transferor and disseminator of technology. Chapter 13 examines its contribution as a provider, controller and upgrader of human resources, including entrepreneurship. Chapter 14 then examines the possible contribution MNEs may make to the trade and balance of payments of home and host countries. Chapter 15 considers the way in which MNEs *use* the resources and capabilities under their control. What impact do they have on the economic structure of home and host countries? Are they more or less productive than indigenous firms? Do they stimulate or inhibit indigenous competition?

Having analysed the direct transfer and usage of resources by MNEs, the next group of chapters look at the consequences of their activities on the rest of the economies of which they are part. We shall see that these may sometimes be more important than the direct effects. Chapter 16 looks at the spillover or linkage effects of MNE activity on suppliers, customers and competitors in home and host countries. Chapter 17 widens the discussion and considers the extent to which MNE activity fashions, or is fashioned by, economic integration and the changing international division of labour. Chapter 18 then turns to some aspects of the distribution of a country's output and wealth which might be affected by MNEs. In particular, the chapter considers the role played by transfer pricing as an instrument affecting the value of cross-border transactions internalized by the MNE. Finally, Chapter 19 addresses itself to the impact of FDI on some strategic, cultural and environmental goals.

10.6   CONCLUSIONS

As a prelude to a more detailed examination of the impact of MNEs on the economies in which they

operate, the first part of this chapter has set out a conceptual framework by which this impact can be studied. In doing so, it has suggested a number of hypotheses concerning the likely impact of outward and inward direct investment on home and host countries, and how these are likely to vary according to the nature of the OLI configuration affecting the investing firms and the ESP configuration of countries. The second part of the chapter discussed some alternative methodologies for estimating the impact of the activity. The third and final part of the chapter set out the framework of the subsequent chapters in this part of the book. It also identified some of the alternative interpretations of the nature of the impact and the difficulties of evaluating that impact in any rigorous way.

Appendix

The effects of MNEs on national economic prosperity: a resumé

1 MNEs are important agents in many home and host countries, in so far as they are able to affect substantially, the attainment of economic and other goals, and sometimes the nature of the goals pursued. Many countries in the world are dependent on MNEs as *providers of resources, capabilities and markets*, as *creators of jobs and wealth*, as *suppliers of foreign currency*, as *stimulators of entrepreneurship and worker motivation* and as *raisers of demand expectancies*.

2 Why should Nation States (NSs) concern themselves with the activities of MNEs? There are basically two reasons. First, MNEs and NSs pursue different objectives or a different mix of objectives. For example, MNEs are interested in a limited number of private economic goals (e.g. profits, growth) while NSs are interested in a wide range of social goals. *Economic* objectives include maximization/stability of GNP or growth in GNP, full employment, currency stability; *non-economic* objectives (which may be affected by economic policy) include a 'right' distribution of income and wealth, sovereignty over decision taking, political and cultural identity. Also, MNEs are interested in maximizing *global* profits, sales, etc, irrespective of where they are made, whereas NSs are interested in maximizing the welfare *of their own citizens*. Secondly, MNEs often have sufficient economic power to thwart NSs in achieving their goals as much as they might like. In a few cases, this may mean that NSs are worse off as a result of MNE activity, but mostly, that they are not as well off as they could be. This is a question of the

distribution of costs and benefits arising from the presence of MNEs (cf. those which would have occurred in their absence).

3 In what ways, then, do MNEs affect the goals of NSs *differently* from that of uninational enterprises? These may be discussed under six main headings:

- MNEs as *transferers* of resources and capabilities between countries. The questions here are *what kinds* of resources and capabilities are transferred and at *what cost*? These questions are particularly important in the case of technological capacity, organizational competences and the upgrading of human competences.
- MNEs as *controllers* of the use of these, and local resources and capabilities. This concerns such questions as *what* products or processes are produced by *which* methods of production, using *which* kinds of inputs (skills, materials, machinery, components). Resource usage by MNEs may be different from that of indigenous firms in NSs partly because of differences in efficiency and partly because of differences in product and market process structure.
- MNEs as *providers* of both sourcing capabilities and of markets. Here, the question is the extent and kind of input and output markets supplied by MNEs, and/or the way in which MNEs divide markets within their organization. Moreover, to what extent do MNEs affect the quality and type of demand both by their own purchasing or marketing practices, and by setting examples to other firms?
- MNEs as *stimulators* of competitiveness, entrepreneurship and good industrial relations. Here, the questions are whether MNEs enhance or reduce the ability and willingness of their competitors and suppliers to be competitive, and how far foreign-based organizational and work practices can be successfully transferred into a foreign institutional and relationship culture.
- MNEs as *distributors* of the benefits of value-added activity. This concerns matters to do with pricing of inputs and outputs, and the share of interest, profits, royalties, fees, credited to the investing company compared with that gained by the host country.
- MNEs are *institutions* affecting the *international allocation of resources* (i) in the short run, for example, by currency movements, and (ii) in the long run, by affecting the structure of output (e.g. between developed and developing countries) and the terms of trade.

4 As well as the impact of MNEs on NSs, one also has to consider their impact on particular groupings of NSs (e.g. customs unions and free trade areas) and on the international economy as a whole. What, for example, is the relationship between MNEs and the New International Economic Order? At a more micro level, one is interested in evaluating the effects of MNEs on particular sectors or interest groups in home or host countries (e.g. workers in a particular industry or region, the consumer protectionist movement, the environmental lobby, small firms).

NOTES

1 See Chapter 20 for more details.
2 In Exhibit 10.2 (p. 271) these four attributes are notated as R, D, S and E, respectively.
3 For a further elaboration see Cantwell (1987, pp. 18–19 and 139–41).
4 See, for example, Chenery (1979), Chenery *et al.* (1986) and Balassa (1980).
5 The investment development path suggests that as countries upgrade their asset capabilities and increase their living standards, their propensity to be net outward investors changes. For further details, see pp. 87–9 of Chapter 4.
6 See Dunning (1993b) for a review of the attempts which have so far been made.
7 For example, as described in *The Economist* (1990).
8 For further details see, for example, UNCTC (1988) and Dunning (1989).
9 In other words, markets are much less self-contained and generally involve more transactional costs and benefits than they used to. The distinction between 'social' and 'private' markets is also a more important one, as actions taken by participants of the market may affect economic players other than themselves.
10 The UNCTC is currently undertaking a project to evaluate the linkages between inward FDI exports and output growth. Preliminary results suggest that in Korea, Taiwan and Singapore, FDI has promoted exports and growth, while in Mexico, Malaysia and Thailand, export-led growth appears to have prompted FDI. See also UN (1992b). In some earlier work by Bornschier (1980), which tested the relationship between foreign investment and economic growth in some 90 developing countries, the author found that while the *flow* of inward investment was positively associated with economic growth, there was a negative relationship between the degree of foreign participation (measured by the stock of capital controlled by MNEs to total capital stock) and economic growth. In a longitudinal study of Ireland, O'Hearn confirmed these results, but argued that one of the reasons for them was the inability of domestic firms to respond to the rigours of the free market which often accom-

panied the opening of a country's border to inbound MNE activity.

11 Not that these are necessarily competitive with each other. One of the main goals of the EC, for example, is to achieve the benefits of regional economic integration while giving full expression to national cultural diversities.

12 One country-specific difference of L-specific advantages faced by MNEs concerns differences in home–host country transport and communication costs. See Chapter 6 for some empirical research on this question.

13 These might include new O advantages generated by MNEs, such as changes in government policies in other countries in which the MNE is operating.

CHAPTER 11

MNEs, Technology and Innovatory Capacity: A Host Country Perspective

11.1 INTRODUCTION

In its generic sense, technology embraces all forms of physical assets, knowledge and human learning and capabilities that enable the efficient organization and production of goods and services within a particular ESP configuration or 'diamond' of competitive advantage. It determines the way in which natural resources and created assets are managed and utilized to produce valued outputs. It affects all activities along the value chain, from the production of primary products and the undertaking of research, design and development, through the various stages of manufacturing, to the marketing and after-sales servicing of the finished product. It is no less relevant in influencing the way in which decisions on accounting, financial and industrial relations matters are made, than it is in affecting the techniques of mineral extraction, manufacturing methods and the logistics of distribution.

More often, of course, the role of technology or knowledge-related capital is discussed with respect to a particular activity or function of a firm. Random examples include the innovation of a new drug, a new technique of crop rotation, the design of an integrated circuit board, the manufacture of a window or cigarettes, the construction of a school, devising a new organizational structure, the preparation of a bank statement, the marketing of rubber tyres, the planning of a TV commercial or the booking of a theatre or airline ticket.

In this chapter, we shall define technology as the output of technological and organizational capacity, which determines the way (or ways) in which tangible and intangible resources may be physically converted into intermediate and finished goods and services. However, we shall recognize that the total impact of MNEs comprises a myriad of both generic and specific technologies and organizational competences associated with the management of human and physical assets and the learning process, which is an inherent part of technological progress (Stiglitz, 1987).

Whatever the definition chosen, it is widely accepted that the ability to create, acquire, learn how to use and effectively deploy technological capacity is one of the key ingredients of economic success in virtually all societies. It is also acknowledged that advances in product, production, information and organizational technology have accounted for much of the economic growth of nations over the past century (Denison, 1967). Prior to the industrial revolution, it was the possession of natural factor endowments together with entrepreneurship and the facilitating role of the state (e.g. with respect to the establishment of a satisfactory legal and taxation system) which determined economic progress. Since the invention of the spinning jenny and steam power, and later managerial capitalism, a stream of technological and organizational innovations have led to a gradual replacement of natural resources by man-made created assets[1] as the key determinants of economic progress – at least among the industrially advanced countries. Moreover, the literature strongly suggests that, in the past, both inward and outward FDI has often (though not always) been a significant contributory factor to the level and structure of a country's technological capacity. While accepting that several nations (e.g. New Guinea, Saudi Arabia, Botswana and Jamaica) still obtain a large part of their wealth from primary production (World Bank, 1991), some of the world's most rapidly growing economies (e.g. Japan, Hong Kong, Singapore and Korea) almost entirely rely on their ability to obtain or produce the necessary technological capabilities in order to be competitive in world markets.

This point is further emphasized by the fact that both unskilled labour and natural resources are accounting for a decreasing proportion of the costs of production of many goods and services. In 1984, for example, for every unit of industrial production, Japan consumed only 60% of the raw materials it consumed in 1973 (Drucker, 1986). Another study suggests that the labour content of traditional assembly operations has dropped 'from 25% to somewhere between 5% and 10% of the total cost of production' (Ohmae, 1985, p. 3). By contrast, in high technology industries, the ratio of pre- and post-manufacturing activity has steadily increased. In the UK pharmaceutical industry, for example, the ratio of non-operative to operative workers rose from 0.79% in 1963 to 1.20% in 1988; R&D expenditure (as a proportion of net output) in the Japanese and US semiconductor industries has trebled over the same period.

At this point we would make three other observations. The first is that technological capacity, that is, the human and physical assets necessary efficiently to produce, deploy and organize technology, is highly concentrated in the wealthier industrial economies. Further details will be given in Section 11.6.1. Suffice it to note here that in 1986–87 only 4.3% of worldwide R&D expenditure was accounted for by developing countries (National Science Foundation, 1989). Data on the output of graduates and/or professionally trained managers and administrators, though less comprehensive, tells a similar story (UNESCO, 1987). It follows that many – indeed most countries in the world – must import the bulk of their technology in the form of intermediate or finished goods, capital equipment and machinery and intermediate services. Moreover, since the production of technology is an expensive business, it tends to be concentrated among large or specialized enterprises, which can attract global markets to finance the necessary R&D.[2] Thus it is these enterprises that dominate the organization and production of technology. In so doing, they use both the market and their own network of subsidiaries and cooperative alliances as vehicles for technology creation and dissemination.

Second, and this partly follows from the first observation, there is a very considerable amount of cross-border trade in technology. Moreover, not all of this trade is one way. Increasingly, countries – especially industrialized countries in the Triad – are both exporters and importers of technology. For example, in 1988 the US received $2.8 billion in royalties and management fees from foreign-based companies (including their own affiliates). However, it also paid out $1.69 billion in royalties and fees to foreign-based licensors. The corresponding figures for the UK (1987), France (1987), Germany and the Netherlands were £1.10 billion, FF 5.4 billion, DM 1.94 billion and NFR $1.64 billion, and £1.07 billion, FF 9.6 billion, DM 4.39 billion and NFR $3.40 billion.[3]

Third, MNEs account for the great bulk of expenditure on knowledge-creating and skill-enhancing activities, and for trade in technology or technology-intensive products. Reliable figures are difficult to obtain, but from an examination of the company accounts of the leading industrial companies, it would seem that MNEs account for about three-quarters of civilian R&D undertaken in market economies, and as much as 90% of the trade in technology or technology-intensive products. More especially, about 80% of the cross-border receipts and payments of royalties and fees of the US and Germany represented intra-MNE transactions.

This data underlies the interest and concern of policy makers in all countries in the generation and acquisition of technological capacity, and the role which their own and foreign-based MNEs may play in its ownership, organization and disposition. Possession and control of technological capacity is indeed one of the main O-specific advantages of enterprises and the L-specific advantages of countries.

11.2   THE TAXONOMY OF TECHNOLOGY

The taxonomy of technology is a subject in itself,[4] but because the word is loosely used to cover different meanings it is necessary to identify some of the concepts in common use. The following are some of the main distinctions made by scholars:

(1) Between *technological capacity*, which represents the stock of technology producing assets (e.g. R&D laboratories, higher educational institutions, scientists and engineers, information of all kinds, the accumulated experience of private and public institutions, and the knowledge of managers and administrative workers) and *technology*, that is, the output of technological capacity (e.g. new products, organizational improvements, more efficient inventory control techniques, new forms of transport and communication).

(2) Between human and physical technological assets (and their output). The former include the stock of scientists and engineers, designers, managers, etc, and the services flowing from them. The latter embrace buildings, plant and equipment, drawings, specifications, etc, and their output, including patents and capital goods which contain the output of technological capacity. A different but related distinction is between 'hard' and 'soft' technology (UNCTC, 1988). The former mainly represents equipment, machinery and R&D laboratories (or the output of same), and the latter, drawings, blueprints, formulae, specifications, training manuals, technical skills, organizational management techniques, systems of quality control, inventory management, industrial relations procedures and so on.

(3) Between levels or 'rungs' of technological competence. Sanjaya Lall (1987), for example, suggests that there are various degrees of technological capability, according to its contribution towards raising productivity or advancing economic autonomy. In particular, Lall distinguishes between *know-how* and *know-why* technology. The former comprises the knowledge of how to make the best use of the technology or technological capacity acquired. Much production technology is of this kind. The application of know-how may also lead to improving plant layout, upgrading quality control and inspection procedures, and the modification of equipment, products or marketing methods. By contrast, know-why involves the understanding of the nature of the underlying materials, process and product technologies, and leads to a substantial adaptation, improvement and even replacement of existing materials, processes and products. Such technological development arises partly as a natural extension and deepening of know-how capabilities and partly as a result of conscious efforts to develop design testing, pilot plant and similar activities (Lall, 1987, p. 196). Lall argues that the next stage of technological development is applied research, that is, the application of given scientific knowledge to the process of commercial innovation. The final strata of technological capability is the ability of countries and firms to undertake basic research, pushing back the frontiers of knowledge without regard to specific commercial applications.

(4) Between technology transfer, dissemination and absorption. *Technology transfer* usually means the transfer of technology within or between firms across national borders, but it could equally be between other institutions in the same country. Such a transfer will not necessarily deprive the sender of the technology transferred. Consequently, *transmission* may be a more appropriate term than transfer. The term *dissemination* implies the diffusion of technology away from the firm or institution possessing or acquiring it to other firms, that is, externalizing its ownership or use. Later in this chapter we shall see that most dissemination is likely to occur between firms along the same value-added chain (e.g. to suppliers or industrial consumers) or across value-added chains (e.g. to competitors or non-competing firms in the same locality). Host countries may be especially interested in the diffusion of technology initially imported by affiliates or foreign MNEs to the rest of the economy. *Absorption* indicates the competence of an economy which acquires technology to utilize or adapt it to its advantage. The lack of complementary assets, particularly administrative and organizational capabilities of some countries to assimilate foreign technology efficiently, is often as important an obstacle to economic development as the failure of these countries to acquire or obtain the technology in the first place.

It is almost self-evident that the location of technological capacity and technology, and how, and at
what cost, technology is disseminated across national
boundaries, will influence the competence of any
particular country to advance its own economic,
social and strategic goals. No less important, especially in a world in which production is becoming
increasingly internationalized, is the nationality of
ownership of the technology. Depending, for example,
on whether the technological capacity in a particular
country is owned by domestic or foreign firms and, if
the latter, by multi-domestic or globally-integrated
MNEs, the ability of that country to direct and
control its wealth-producing capacity may be affected.
It will also influence the extent to which a country is
able to accumulate technological capacity. By so
doing, it may critically affect the macro-economic
organization and diamond of competitive advantage
of a country.

MNEs, in particular, may strongly influence the
creation and distribution of the world's technological
assets. Later in this chapter we shall present some
statistical data. For the moment we would observe
that in the late 1980s MNEs were accounting for
between 75% and 80% of the privately undertaken
R&D in the world. While it is true that the R&D
undertaken by their foreign subsidiaries (as a
proportion of sales) is generally the same as, or less
than, their indigenous competitors, the situation is
changing as an increasing amount of R&D is being
cross-traded between the most advanced industrialized countries. Moreover, viewed from a host
country perspective, the innovatory activities of
MNE affiliates are often *relatively* quite important.
Again the data is fragmentary, but in Australia,
Belgium, Canada, the UK, West Germany, South
Korea, India and Singapore, the share of national
R&D expenditure accounted for by foreign-owned
firms exceeded 15% in the mid 1980s. In Belgium
and South Korea, foreign affiliates spent a higher
proportion of their sales on R&D than did their
domestic competitors (Dunning, 1992d). But even
where foreign affiliates do not undertake much
innovatory activity, this does not mean that MNEs
do not have an impact on the location of innovatory
activities. In fact, for reasons to be discussed in
Section 11.6, they do exert a very considerable
influence.

11.3 THE ISSUES TO BE ADDRESSED

What, then, are the issues of concern to host
countries concerning the impact of inbound MNE
activity on their indigenous technological assets and
organizational competences. We will discuss these
under six headings:

(1) To what extent do MNEs influence the supply
of technological capacity or technology to which
host countries desire access?

(2) When MNEs own or control technologies, how
far are they prepared to adapt such technologies to the perceived needs of recipient
countries? Putting it slightly differently, to what
extent is the technology transferred by MNEs
appropriate to the needs and aspirations of host
countries?

(3) To what extent can and do MNEs affect the
location and organization of innovatory activities, and thereby influence a host nation's
technological capacity and long-term competitiveness?

(4) How far, and in what ways, do MNEs control
or influence the terms of the cross-border
production and marketing of technology?

(5) To what extent and in what ways do MNEs or
their affiliates affect the diffusion of technology
both between and within countries (e.g. by
their linkages with suppliers, customers and so
on)?

(6) What should the policies of host countries be
towards MNEs as agents for upgrading and
restructuring indigenous technological capacity?

11.4 THE PRODUCTION OF
TECHNOLOGY

It is generally agreed that one of the main O-specific
advantages of MNEs is their ability to produce,
acquire, master the understanding of and organize
the use of technological assets across national
boundaries. Partly this reflects other O advantages of
these companies, in particular their size and experience, as well as their ability to tap the global market
for scientific managerial and professional personnel,

and to capture the cross-border economies of the joint governance of related technologies, or of the same technologies which may be differently used (Bartlett and Ghoshal, 1989). While much research is still undertaken by universities, cooperative research institutions and small uninational firms, the commercialization of new generic technologies is increasingly requiring a network of physical facilities and organizational and management capabilities which global companies are best equipped to supply. In the early 1990s even the largest MNEs are being forced to conclude collaborative arrangements with other firms to gain access to new technologies and exploit efficiently and speedily the latest technological advances. As Chapter 9 has shown, such alliances are particularly common in the telecommunications, electronics, aircraft and banking sectors. One example of an inter-firm consortium is that organized by the Kennecott Mining Company to prospect the seabed for mineral wealth. The venture brings together a large number of technological disciplines and firms from many different sectors and four industrial nations.

It is then probable that large diversified and global firms will continue to control the supply and use of most of the privately-generated advanced technology in the foreseeable future. This is because they are most likely to possess or be able to acquire and efficiently organize the range of entrepreneurial, financial and managerial assets necessary to promote and sustain this capability. It is also fair to say that as 80–90% of the sales of such technology are within the advanced industrial economies, that it will not necessarily be appropriate for the rest of the world. At the same time, an increasing number of companies from the Third World are themselves accruing technological competences and improving their mastery over imported technology, particularly in those areas most in demand by other developing countries. For some years now, India, Brazil, Mexico and South Korea have been important exporters of technology and of knowledge-intensive products. Moreover, these countries, together with Taiwan, Indonesia, Singapore, China and Hong Kong, are generating their own MNEs, which not only helps them to compete better in global markets, but also to gain access to new technological strengths. Third

World MNEs are also being increasingly drawn into the cross-border networks of First World MNEs, not only in developing countries but also in developed countries. Examples include the setting up or acquisition of R&D 'listening' posts and the formation of collaborative agreements by Indian, Brazilian, Mexican, Korean and Taiwanese companies in the US, Europe and Japan (World Bank, 1989).

We conclude. For some time now, large industrialized firms have been the main producers, organizers and users of technological capacity. This partly reflects the competitive advantages of their home countries, and partly the fact that the economics of managing the production and use of technology favours large firms. The globalization of markets and production and the tendency for technologies to become more generic and systemic have tended to strengthen the O advantages of large MNEs. However, small and medium sized firms continue to be a prolific source of new inventions and design capabilities, while the upgrading of human and physical capital in many developing countries has enabled them to improve their technological capabilities over the past two decades. Nevertheless, with few exceptions, directly or indirectly, MNEs are increasingly affecting this progress. This they do by internationalizing the production and dissemination of the technology and by concluding technology leasing or collaborative arrangements with other firms.

The literature has so far given little attention to the macro-organizational costs and benefits of organizing cross-border technological activities by alternative means. It is true that in collectivist economies, such as China, it is the state that determines the amount of technology produced and how it is used and disseminated. Also, in other countries, such as Japan, the role of foreign MNEs is relatively insignificant. The innovating proclivities of small or medium sized firms and those of other institutions, for example, universities, varies between countries. Clearly, much depends on the ESP configuration of countries and, in particular, how much they need the kind of innovatory activity that MNEs are best able to provide and how well they are able to attract and absorb it.

11.5 APPROPRIABILITY OF TECHNOLOGY

11.5.1 Introduction

There are several choices open to countries that wish to take advantage of the world's stock of physical and human capital. At one extreme, a country can rely entirely on other countries to produce technology, only importing it when it is embodied in human capital or in intermediate or final products. Some smaller natural resource rich countries, such as Brunei, Kuwait, Jamaica and Papua New Guinea, are almost completely dependent on foreign-sourced technology. At the other extreme, a country may attempt to be completely self-sufficient in the technology it needs. In the past, some larger socialist countries (e.g. the Soviet Union, India and China) have followed this strategy. In between these extremes are a host of possible scenarios of knowledge 'dependence' or 'interdependence'. Each scenario encompasses a large number of modalities by which foreign-owned technological capacity or technology may be acquired, adapted, absorbed and disseminated.

In choosing between the different sources of foreign-owned technology, the extent to which the technology is appropriate, or can be adapted to the particular needs of the host country – and at what social cost – may be, and often is, of critical importance. This is because a production or marketing technology that is suitable to one country's ESP configuration, or its diamond of competitive advantage, might not be so for another. In particular, a country's needs are likely to vary according to its industrial structure and stage of economic development. Take, for example, the composition of its supply capabilities. The production of a cotton shirt in a cheap labour but dear capital and technologically backward economy, such as Mali, is likely to be very different from that in a dear labour but cheap capital and technologically intensive country, such as Belgium. A product (e.g. a washing machine) designed to meet the tastes of households in Italy may not suit the requirements of consumers in Brazil or Canada. The ingredients of canned soups traded under the same brand name may be very different in New Zealand, Finland and Mexico. Cultural differences may require different wage incentives and industrial relations procedures in India, South Africa and Ireland. Legal requirements and business customs may make more demands on computerized accounting systems in some countries than others. Cross-border differences in attitudes towards environmental protection (e.g. Germany compared with Taiwan) may affect the innovation of environmentally-sensitive products and production processes.

It might be argued that if the private costs and benefits of adapting technology supplied by MNEs were the same as the social costs and benefits to the host countries, and if the MNEs were operating at optimum efficiency, then inbound investment would automatically provide the right kind of technology for the host country. However, there are at least three reasons why this may not be the case. The first is that the goals of MNEs may be different from that of the countries in which they operate; hence their response to a given configuration of L-specific attractions may be different. The second is that, where structural market imperfections exist, the strategic behaviour of MNEs or their affiliates may not accord with the best interests of the recipient country. The third is that the private and social costs and benefits of adaptation – particularly of soft technologies – may be very different. To the firm, the costs of adaptation may be considerable in relation to the perceived costs to the host country. For example, because of their consequences on employment, linkages and market structure, there may be substantial net social gains from such adaptation.

On the other hand, a host country's preference for technology adaptation may be linked to the macro-organization policies it pursues. Certainly, a firm's readiness to transfer, utilize and organize foreign technology will depend on the economic and other signals set by the host government. An economy which pursues a market-oriented and export-led growth development strategy may promote policies that necessitate fewer process or product adaptations by MNEs than one which pursues a protectionist import-substitution strategy. Similarly, a country which aims at technological self-sufficiency is likely to make different demands on both its own firms and inward direct investors than one which accepts that its technological strengths will be determined by its (dynamic) comparative trading advantages.

The questions now arise: To what extent do MNEs help to provide host countries with the technological assets they need to upgrade their indigenous resources and capabilities? How far, in practice, are they prepared to adapt their technologies to meet the particular supply and demand requirements of host countries?

While it is difficult to give general answers to these questions, research so far conducted suggests that there are four main determinants of the willingness of MNEs to adapt their O-specific technologies to different country-specific circumstances:

(1) size and characteristics of the markets served,

(2) differences in factor costs,

(3) differences in the availability of factor inputs and materials,

(4) differences in organizational cultures and the form of inter-firm relationships.

Furthermore, such adaptations may either take the form of modifications of the methods by which particular products are produced (e.g. process or fabricating technology) or the types of products produced (product technology). We shall discuss each of these kinds of technology adaptation in turn.

11.5.2 Market size and characteristics

Process technology

We have seen that one of the most frequently cited O-specific advantages of MNEs – which are sometimes a cause and sometimes an effect of their multinationality – is that they are able to select production and organizational techniques to take advantage of size and/or scope economies.[5] *Inter alia* this enables them to develop and exploit not only new 'hard' or direct production technologies, but also new soft technologies (e.g. in purchasing, inventory control, work organization, budgetary control and strategic planning procedures).

In terms of private costs and benefits this may have two effects on host countries. The first is that some functions will be performed differently by foreign affiliates than by indigenous firms. This is because the former are part of larger, and often

more diversified hierarchies, whose management, in pursuance of economic or strategic goals, may choose to internalize cross-border markets for intermediate products. Suppose, for example, that a small UK biscuit manufacturer is taken over by a large US biscuit MNE. What effect might this have on the technological capacity of the acquired firm? Well, one effect may be to centralize certain functions or activities which had previously been performed locally, in order to exploit the economies of size that accrue to the investing firm. An example might be the purchasing function – the larger company may be able to obtain larger discounts on flour, sugar and fats than the smaller company (indeed, it might have its own supplying companies). Another might be the accounting and finance function which may need to be standardized to meet the technology utilized by the various parts of the acquiring organization. The first consequence of the change in ownership is, then, that the production functions of a whole range of activities may be different because the foreign affiliate is part of a larger network of activities. The ownership effect may also affect the location and form of control of such activities. On balance, the acquisition is likely to draw the host country more into the division of labour of the MNE (and, indirectly, that of the global economy) than it would otherwise be.

The second effect is on the activities which have to be undertaken in the host country – be they in the production of primary, secondary or tertiary goods. The evidence suggests that, *ceteris paribus*, MNEs would prefer to standardize their technologies in all their production outlets, thus avoiding the costs of adaptation. In some cases, for example, where the affiliates are producing goods and services for sale to international markets, there may be a positive disincentive to modify production methods lest product quality be adversely affected. A lot of efficiency-seeking investment is of this kind. In others, such as import-substituting investment where the product is sold only to the local market, which is less developed or smaller than that of the investing country, the cost of 'scaling down' production processes may be considerable (Parry, 1980). In some high technology sectors, it may not be feasible at all.

Nevertheless, empirical research suggests that the main reason why MNEs choose to adapt their process technologies in their foreign subsidiaries is because of the smaller output produced by the latter. Clearly, the extent to which such adaptation takes place depends upon the substitutability of production processes. In general, extractive firms find it difficult to modify their value-added activities, as do capital intensive and high technology firms. Morley and Smith (1977a), for example, argued that the major reason for the substantial adaptation of US production methods by US subsidiaries in Brazil was the smaller output which they produced. In a classic and far ranging study by Grant Reuber and colleagues (Reuber *et al.*, 1973), the authors not only confirmed that technology adaptation by affiliates in developing countries was more common in market-seeking than in resource-seeking or rationalized FDI,[6] but also that by far the most important stated reason for such adaptation was the idiosyncratic demands of the domestic market. Reuber's findings have been confirmed by several later studies, including those of Helfgott (1973), White (1978, quoted in Jenkins, 1987b, p. 218) and Lipsey *et al.* (1982). However, Isaiah Frank (1980), in his field survey of 402 foreign-owned subsidiaries in developing countries, found that the most common reason for the adaptation of imported production processes by foreign firms was to take advantage of comparatively cheap labour. Moreover, some scale-motivated adaptation may well be a response to a different structure of factor prices, since the smaller plants may only be competitive where labour costs are lower. It may also be influenced by fiscal and other incentives offered to foreign affiliates to remodel their production processes in a way which governments perceive will most advance their economic or social objectives.

While there may be a tendency for host governments to overstress the need for process adaptation, so some MNEs are inclined to underestimate the importance of such adaptation. In a study referred to earlier, Frank (1980) found that while most MNEs adapt their production processes to some extent or other – noticeable exceptions include MNEs who argue that it is necessary to duplicate the processes of their parent companies to ensure uniform quality standards – few believe that it is necessary to make radical alterations. At the same time, Frank cites the case of four US subsidiaries in Latin America which used the same technology as

that employed by their parent company. Two of the subsidiaries went bankrupt and one ran its machinery only three days a year! (Frank, 1980, p. 75).

Product technology

Market characteristics also affect the willingness of MNEs to adapt their products to meet local needs. Again, it is worth observing that one of the main asset-based advantages of MNEs is that they are frequently in the van of product development and help to upgrade the quality of consumer demand. At the same time, it has to be accepted that the majority of their products tend to be sold to relatively high income consumers and technologically sophisticated or scale intensive producers. This may mean that an automobile made to meet the needs of mid-western US consumers may not ideally meet the needs of Finnish, Indian or Nigerian consumers; or that food products primarily destined to meet the tastes of German households will not necessarily satisfy those of Japanese or Brazilian consumers; or that electrical appliances suitable for the British market cannot be manufactured without modification for sale in Indonesia, Italy or Mexico. On the other hand, certain products seem to translate across national boundaries with only minor modifications. Examples include Gillette razor blades, Coca Cola, MacDonald's hamburgers, Kellogg's cornflakes, Holiday Inn hotels and civilian airplanes. Indeed, one of the appeals of some MNEs to consumers is that they offer standard quality controlled goods.

In some cases, product technology has to be modified to meet local supply capabilities. Frequently, governments may intervene to encourage the upgrading or scaling down of quality. Such evidence as may be adduced from field studies suggests that MNEs are generally less inclined to alter their product than their process technology (Frank, 1980, p. 74). A survey of 19 foreign affiliates in Nigeria by Biersteker (1978) reported that only five had made any adaptation to the local environmental regulations, employment conditions, raw material or marketing needs. Langdon (1981) unearthed only minimal evidence of product modification by 48 multinational subsidiaries in Kenya. Chen (1983a) concluded that the amount of product adjustment by foreign-owned firms in Hong Kong was largely industry specific. He found, for example, much less product differentiation in textile and electronic products than in garments and toys. In other instances (e.g. drugs and constructional services), firms appeared reluctant to downgrade quality as this might result in bad publicity for them. Japanese MNEs, which set up subsidiaries in Asian developing countries in the 1970s to supply European markets, asserted that their products had to be identical to those produced in their home factories (Frank, 1980). Other MNEs have maintained that product uniformity is critical if they are to offer a flexible and internationally acceptable sourcing network for their customers. For their part, governments – particularly those from South and East Asia – have frequently used MNEs to promote the image of their countries as producers of high quality and prestige products.[7]

Finally, it should be noted that some writers (Griffin, 1978, quoted in Jenkins, 1986, p. 76; and Helleiner, 1975a) argue that MNEs are reluctant to adapt their products to the economic and cultural needs of consumers in host countries, and that they encourage a global uniformity of purchasing patterns. Such patterns, so it is argued, are further influenced by intensive advertising by MNEs.

The evidence for or against these assertions is mixed. On the one hand, one of the main O advantages of some MNEs rests in the quality and uniformity of the products supplied to their main markets. They may perceive that the costs of adapting these products to meet the needs of particular markets are greater than the costs of persuading consumers in these markets to buy these products. This and similar perceptions have led to the development of world or regional (European, Asian, etc) product mandates. On the other hand, an increasing number of MNEs are perceiving their ability to localize their products to country-specific customer needs as a competitive advantage in its own right. Thus, although all the glass products of Corning Glass Works are derived from a common set of core technologies in heat resistant glass, most of them (e.g. Corningware, technical materials and some chemical systems) are tailor-made to the specific needs of customers in industrial countries (Prahalad and Doz, 1987). This, in part, has been made possible by the introduction of flexible manufacturing methods. So far, such localization is more

in evidence in developed countries. In any event, it is country-specific characteristics (e.g. income levels and income distribution) which largely determine demand patterns in most countries.

11.5.3 Factor availability and price differentials

Process technology

Neo-classical economic theory predicts that a firm will select the technology which, given the availability and price of factor inputs and intermediate products, will minimize the costs of producing any given level of output. Where real labour and raw material or energy costs are low and real capital costs are high, the production technology employed is likely to be capital saving. By contrast, where real capital and raw material or energy costs and real labour costs are high, then technology is likely to be labour saving.[8] And where real labour and real capital costs are low and raw material costs or energy costs are high, technology is likely to be materials or energy saving.

Where demand standards are high and there is a sophisticated supply capability of components, parts and raw materials, as well as a supportive technological and communications infrastructure, the manufacturing methods pursued by MNE affiliates are likely to be more technologically intensive than in the absence of these conditions. They will also differ according to the structure of natural resources and created assets in a country. Thus the production of soap, textiles, light bulbs or cigarettes in Sri Lanka or Kenya is likely to be different from that in the US or Sweden, irrespective of the ownership of firms, simply because the ESP configurations or diamonds of competitive advantage of the countries are so different. There is ample evidence to suggest that the factor input ratios of value-added activities do vary across countries to some degree or another. Moreover, as Chapters 4 and 6 have shown, much export processing manufacturing investment in developing countries is prompted by the desire to economize on real labour costs. Some value-added activities (e.g. tobacco growing, many chemical processes and long-distance airline journeys) can only be economically undertaken in a particular way; the introduction of computerized design and manufacturing techniques is increasing the number and range of these activities. In others (e.g. coal mining, drug dosage preparations, textile finishing, lamp bulb manufacturing, materials handling, accounting procedures, building and construction, dental services), there remains some latitude in production techniques. Indeed, there are few value-added activities or organizations which at the margin do not respond to real factor price differentials. In general, it would seem that the greater the specificity of assets required in the production process, the less room there is for product adaptation. The more idiosyncratic the end products and the greater the possibility of varying the amount of natural resource inputs, the more flexible production methods are likely to be.

To what extent, then, do MNEs adapt their process technologies to take account of differences in country-specific factor costs and availability? How do the process techniques of their affiliates compare with those of their parent companies or that of their indigenous competitors?

The consensus of research findings[9] is that a substantial modification in production processes is only likely to occur in medium to low technology import-substituting industries in developing countries. The degree of such adaptation would appear to vary between country, sector and firm. For example, whereas in Kenya an International Labour Organization (ILO) team of researchers discovered that all of the eight foreign-owned firms visited were using more labour-intensive production methods than they employed in their home factories (ILO, 1972), Reuber and his colleagues found that in only four of the market-oriented projects analysed did low labour costs or lack of skilled labour contribute to adaptation (Reuber, 1973, p. 195). At the same time, it is quite common for production processes to be revamped following a modification to product or plant design, while, as suggested earlier, some parts of the value-added chain might lend themselves to more adaptation than others.

Work done on comparing the technology of affiliates of MNEs with indigenous companies is fraught with conceptual and statistical pitfalls. Chief among these is the difficulty of separating the ownership effect from other attributes of the foreign affiliates, and of making comparisons between firms that engage in a similar set of value-added activities. Several studies, including ILO (1972), have shown that foreign affiliates of MNEs employ more capital- or technologically-intensive methods than their indigenous competitors. However, on closer inspection this is found to be because the former are more concentrated in capital- and technology-intensive sectors than the latter. Even within sectors, the product composition and degree of vertical integration may differ between firms and regions, and thus cause differences in capital intensity.

What, then, is the evidence? In a nutshell, it is mixed. Meller and Mizala (1982), for example, compared the capital intensities of US subsidiaries and local firms in 13 manufacturing industries in seven Latin American countries in the late 1970s. Their conclusions were that the US affiliates utilized production techniques that, in general, were more capital- and technologically-intensive than those employed by local manufacturing establishments of a similar size in the same industry. Similar conclusions were reached by Agarwal (1976), who, in a study of the large-scale manufacturing sector of India, found that foreign-owned firms recorded a higher capital per employee ratio in 22 out of 34 industries. In an examination of 22 industries in Indonesia, Balasubramanyam (1984) discovered that foreign-owned firms were 40% more capital intensive in their production processes than local private firms and 30% more capital intensive than local public sector firms. Newfarmer and Marsh (1981b) found that foreign subsidiaries were relatively more capital intensive than their indigenous competitors in Brazilian manufacturing industry, as did Forsyth and Solomon (1977) in a similar study in Ghana. In Nigeria, Biersteker (1978) concluded that foreign affiliates were more capital intensive than their domestic counterparts in the textile industry but not in the cement or saw milling industries.

By contrast, other studies, for example, Chee and Lim (1976) for Malaysia, Chung and Lee (1980) for Korea, and Willmore (1976) for Costa Rica, found that there was no consistent tendency for the production methods utilized by foreign and domestic firms to be different. Using a rather different estimating procedure[10] in a study of 400 firms in Thailand, Lecraw (1977, 1979) came to the same conclusion with respect to local Thai and foreign affiliates of MNEs from developed countries. However, he found that affiliates of MNEs from developing countries were, on average, 39% less capital intensive than both groups of firms. Lecraw also discovered that these latter firms were also more efficient in their use of indigenous factor services.

The above data is subject to widely different interpretations. On the one hand, it tends to confirm that foreign firms – especially in export-oriented sectors – do not always choose to adapt to differences in ESP conditions. On the other, it could mean that, relative to indigenous firms, foreign affiliates are better organizers or managers of the local labour force. Wells (1973) suggested that this was particularly true for MNEs that operated in unfamiliar cultural settings and were uncertain about how to manage people. Forsyth and Solomon (1977) argued that MNEs are particularly adept at 'deskilling' existing technology, and that this explained why their affiliates used a lower proportion of skilled labour than their indigenous competitors. However, it was also the case that, as offshoots of a foreign domiciled company, they tended to undertake fewer higher value activities (R&D, general administration, etc) than their local rivals.

There is, however, a general consensus among researchers that because of the asset-specific advantages of MNEs and the differential response of foreign affiliates and domestic firms to the ESP characteristics of the countries in which they operate, there are important differences in the selection of all forms of technologically related inputs. On balance, the inducement for non-resident firms to be more capital intensive than their indigenous competitors seems likely to outweigh the incentives for them to be more labour-intensive. In particular, there is a tendency for MNEs operating in culturally unfamiliar or politically uncertain environments to prefer machine power (even secondhand machine power) to manpower, and to avoid the transaction costs of organizing and training a labour force whose work ethos is different from theirs. The result is that MNEs may well inject a deskilling element in the sectors in which they operate, simply because their competitive advantages lie in the possession and organization of machine power rather than of manpower.

There are, however, exceptions to this generalization. Japanese direct investment in Western Europe has led to an upgrading of human assets, simply because the Japanese believe that one of their O-specific advantages lies in their ability efficiently to organize and motivate labour – even within an unaccustomed working environment. Moreover, as Chapter 13 will demonstrate, MNEs have made significant contributions to the training and upgrading of human skills, particularly in upper middle developing and advanced industrial countries. Much depends on the kind of value-added activities undertaken by MNEs. At the one extreme, they might find it beneficial to substitute machine power for manpower; at the other, they may introduce new and higher value-added kinds of activities and make a major contribution to economic development and the upgrading of human capital. Once again, it is not only the choice of technology of what best suits the O advantages of the investing firms that is important, but also the L advantages associated with the stage of development and the government policies of the host economies.

Product technology

Most of the discussion about the appropriability of the products supplied by foreign affiliates of MNEs (i.e. consumption technology) has centred on market needs, as dealt with on p. 293. But it might also be supposed that since different products require a different mix of factor inputs, then the composition of output supplied by companies in different countries might also be different.

There is some reason to suppose that in the case of some consumer good products, MNEs have made some design et al. modifications to take account of different factor costs, especially where host governments have encouraged this by employment premiums etc, or where the local market is a large one. Usually, this has resulted in a more customized and, in developing countries, a sometimes inferior product to that supplied in home factories. More often, the kind and quality of products supplied by MNEs will be market driven or influenced by the price and availability of factor inputs. Where, however, the products are geared to the needs of the international market, no such adaptation is likely to be made; in this case the consumption technology will be entirely market driven.

11.5.4   Materials availability

The third reason why MNEs might wish to adapt their production technology in foreign countries is to take account of the differences in the availability and quality of local materials and intermediate products. Such differences are likely to be most pronounced in the least developed host countries. While foreign affiliates may wish to import some of these inputs, transport costs, tariffs, non-tariff barriers and government import controls may induce local procurement. Usually, materials availability tends to affect the kinds of products supplied rather than the process technology employed. Occasionally, however, it may influence the kind of capital equipment utilized. This is likely to be the case where synthetic materials (the use of which is likely to be relatively capital intensive) are used in place of natural materials (the use of which is likely to be relatively labour intensive). The need to economize on materials and/or components in some countries more than others (because of availability or higher real prices) may also affect the organization of their deployment, including inventory control, testing and inspection procedures, and the policy towards wastage.

11.5.5   Organizational and cultural differences

Most of the literature on the costs and benefits of technology transferred by MNEs to host countries has been concerned with hard technology. No less important is their willingness and ability to transfer and/or adapt soft technology and, in particular, organizational structures and work practices. There is some suggestion that in the services sector, these soft technologies are at least as important as hard technologies (UNCTC, 1988), and that the resources and capabilities of developing countries are better able to absorb and modify such assets than they are for more advanced machinery and equipment (UNCTC, 1990d).

At the same time, the evidence suggests that, because of differences in organizational cultures, it is often more difficult for MNEs successfully to transfer unadapted soft technologies across national boundaries. Certainly, it is likely to take longer. Kogut (1990) has demonstrated that whereas European firms were fairly quick to introduce the mass production methods of the auto and other industries in the early 20th century, it took them much longer to adopt the M form of organization. It would seem that it is easier to introduce new products and machinery than new means of managing people! The transaction costs of overcoming the rigidities of ingrained tradition and business practices are considerably higher than those of replacing a faulty machine or introducing new products. This is primarily because of the higher human intensity of the former than the latter, and also because people are likely to be more resistant to change and adaptation than are machines!

The willingness and ability of a country to reconcile the need to adapt its culture to meet the changing needs of world markets – and the speed with which it can do so – is itself a competitive advantage (Porter, 1990). Such cultural fluidity is shown in various ways, from product labelling in foreign languages, exposure to foreign ideas and concepts, and standardization of weights and measures, to full blown membership of a regional community. History suggests that some countries – particularly those which are highly dependent on international commerce for their prosperity – are much better at doing this than others. Moreover, some nations have much more distinctive business cultures than others. Japan is one of these and is only just beginning to integrate herself fully into the world economy. In doing so, the question as to whether she can transfer those competitive advantages that arise specifically from her organizational culture is still to be resolved. One example is the kind of relationship that Japanese firms have with their suppliers, which explains much of the success of the Japanese auto and electronics industries. When these sectors are transplanted into an alien culture, can they succeed?

Once again, for good or bad, the MNE is one of the key channels for the cross-border transfer of culture and business customs. Chapter 19 will take up this point in more detail. At the same time, in the past it has been the failure of MNEs to appreciate the significance of cultural differences and the difficulties of overcoming or coming to terms with them, which has so frequently led to inappropriate decisions on technology transfer and usage. It has also caused much friction between MNEs and the citizens and governments of the countries in which they operate (Buckley and Casson, 1991).

Travel, technical advances in all kinds of communication and the emergence of the global corporation are all leading to a greater uniformity of business culture. Yet substantial differences in 'doing business' remain. Given a proper sensitivity and respect for national and regional traditions and habits, the MNE can play an important role in introducing new organizational forms and relationships. Three brief examples must suffice. The first is the role of US MNEs in introducing new organizational and financial control systems into their European subsidiaries in the 1920s and 1930s, and a range of new marketing techniques in the 1950s and 1960s. The second is the successful implantation of Japanese work practices and quality control procedures (the latter, at least, pioneered in the US by Taylor half a century earlier) into the US and Western Europe. The third example is typified by the current debate about the merits of two quite distinct organizational philosophies, *viz* Fordism and Toyotaism. To some extent, each philosophy is a creature of its time and reflects its country of origin. Yet each is meeting with a certain measure of success when translated into a foreign ESP configuration.

11.5.6 Some conclusions on the adaptation and appropriability of MNE-owned technology

Too often the costs of technology transfer and adaptation are underestimated. In a pioneering study, Teece (1976) showed that depending on the production and product-specific characteristics of the foreign investors, the costs of the adaptations to product, process and materials made necessary by a different production and marketing environment might be considerable. Clearly, the extent of both product and process adaptation is likely to vary according to the stages of a country's development (see Chapter 10) and the *raison d'être* for the FDI. In general, it is likely to be greatest in the early stages of development and in the case of market-seeking

FDI. It is likely to be least in the case of efficiency-seeking or asset-acquiring investment undertaken by MNEs within the industrialized world. Technology transferred by Third World MNEs to other developing countries is also likely to require rather less adaptation than that transferred by First World MNEs (Lall, 1992).

Finally, from a policy perspective it is important to know the reasons for the ESP conditions and the configuration of the diamond of competitive advantage which might affect the choice of technology by MNEs. Are they, for example, the result of market forces, or do they represent distortions brought about by monopolistic behaviour on the part of participants in the market or government action? The evidence is mixed. Clearly, where it is shown that the choice of technology is affected by the subsidization of capital, then the appropriate policy measures towards the technology choice by MNEs may be different than when it is in response to a market situation. We shall return to this point later in the chapter.

11.6 THE LOCATION OF TECHNOLOGICAL CAPACITY

11.6.1 Introduction

The third issue to be addressed in this chapter concerns the uniqueness of MNEs as generators and organizers of technology-related assets, and the location of these activities. This issue is of interest to both developing and developed countries, as it is the ability to improve the human and physical capabilities to produce technology, on which the advances in living standards of most industrialized and many newly industrialized economies rests. Of course, it is perfectly possible, and sometimes desirable, for countries to import the output of technological capacity located elsewhere. However, unless the recipient country can offer the complementary assets to make the best use of that output, it cannot expect to sustain, let alone improve, its competitive advantages. In addition, many countries welcome a degree of technological autonomy, at least in key sectors, for strategic-cum-security reasons.

11.6.2   Some macro-data on the location of technological capacity[11]

Some statistics on the distribution of technological capacity between countries are set out in Table 11.1. All the usual cautions apply to this data, which is fragmentary and rarely directly comparable. Nevertheless, the general picture it portrays is a fairly clear one. In 1986–87, 82% of the world's expenditure on R&D and 69% of the scientists and engineers engaged in R&D was accounted for by five innovation-driven countries, *viz* the US, Japan, France, the UK and West Germany; 91% and 84%, respectively, were accounted for by ten countries. Only 4.3% of worldwide R&D expenditure was undertaken in developing countries. Because, however, of the greater labour intensity of R&D activities in the Third World, developing countries were responsible

Table 11.1   Geographical distribution of R&D expenditure in constant (1982) $ billions, 1986–87.

	$b	%	$b	%
Developed countries				
North America			105.6	46.3
of which:				
US	100.8	44.2		
Western Europe			71.1	31.2
of which:				
West Germany	19.4	8.5		
United Kingdom	13.8	6.1		
France	13.7	6.0		
Italy	7.4	3.2		
Sweden	4.0	1.8		
Japan			39.1	17.2
Other developed countries			2.2	1.0
Developing countries[1]			9.9	4.3
of which:				
India	1.5	0.7		
Brazil	1.4	0.6		
South Korea	1.3	0.6		
Argentina	1.1	0.5		
All countries			227.9	100.0

1   Including Yugoslavia.
Source: National Science Foundation (1989).

for a higher proportion – 12.6% – of the personnel employed in such activities.

Output data presents a broadly similar picture. Of all the patents registered in the US in the period 1978–88, 90% were accounted for by firms which had their headquarters in the US, Japan, France, Switzerland, the Netherlands and West Germany; less than 1% were from developing countries. Of the developing countries, South Korea, Taiwan, Brazil, Mexico, Hong Kong and India were among the leading registers of patents.

Table 11.2 suggests that there has been some movement towards a geographical dispersion of innovatory capacity since 1970. In that year, for example, the US and the UK accounted for 71.8% of R&D expenditure, 65.6% of R&D personnel and 85.0% of the US registered patents of the five leading industrial countries. The corresponding proportions for 1987 were 61.4%, 57.2% and 61.2%. The growth in technological competence has been particularly spectacular in the case of Japan, where real R&D expenditure increased by over three times between 1970 and 1987, the number of R&D personnel more than doubled, and there was a sixfold increase in the number of patents registered (National Science Foundation, 1989). Between 1988 and 1990 Japanese firms registered more patents in the US than those of any other foreign nationality. In the period 1978–86, Japan's share of the patents registered in the US by non-US firms was 34.6%, compared with 13% in the period 1963–70 (Cantwell, 1991b).[12] There was also a noticeable increase in the technological capacity of developing countries. Their share of world R&D expenditure rose from 2.5% to 6.2% and that of R&D scientists and engineers from 8.5% to 11.2% (UNESCO, 1987). They also more than doubled their participation in world patenting between 1963–70 and 1974–84. Some of the newly industrializing countries are also gaining an increasing share of new patents registered in some (mainly fabricating) industries.

Data set out in Table 11.3 suggests that the industrial pattern of technological capacity differs between countries. For example, in the period 1978–86 the US had a particularly strong patenting advantage[13] in several resource-based activities, such as food processing, textiles, clothing and leather goods, coal and petroleum, and in aircraft.[14] Japan's innovatory performance was especially impressive in

Table 11.2 Distribution of innovating capability between five leading innovating countries 1970–87.

	R&D expenditure Constant 1982 $ (billion)				R&D personnel (thousands)				Patents (number)			
	1970		1987		1970		1987		1970		1987	
		%		%		%		%		%		%
US	62.4	61.7	100.8	54.0	543.8	59.8	791.1	50.9	47 077	80.0	40 496	58.5
Japan	12.4	12.3	39.1	20.9	172.0	18.9	405.6	26.1	2 625	4.5	16 158	23.3
West Germany	9.9	9.8	19.4	10.4	82.5	9.1	151.5	9.7	4 435	7.5	7 307	10.6
France	7.1	7.0	13.7	7.3	58.5	6.4	108.2	7.0	1 731	2.9	2 661	3.8
UK	9.4[1]	9.3	13.8	7.4	52.8[1]	5.8	98.7[2]	6.3	2 954	5.0	2 583	3.7
	101.2	100.0	186.8	100.0	909.6	100.0	1555.1	100.0	58 822	100.0	69 205	100.0

1 1969.
2 1986.
Source: National Science Foundation (1989).

photographic equipment, office equipment and semi-conductors.[15] The UK registered an above average number of patents in tobacco processing, pharmaceuticals and aircraft. Germany's prowess lay in drink products, nuclear reactors and a wide range of chemicals; while Italy's comparative advantage was most noticeable in footwear, textiles and clothing, and rubber products.[16] Developing countries (as a group) appear to have revealed a patenting advantage in food products, textiles and clothing, leather goods and, in the case of Brazil, in aircraft (Cantwell and Hodson, 1991).

Table 11.4 presents some details on the distribution, by subject area, of students enrolled for graduate courses in colleges and universities in selected countries. The data suggests that relative to other nations, the US, Mexico and Korea place particular emphasis on business and organizational studies, while Japan and West Germany have a 'revealed' educational advantage in engineering and in arts and humanities. Mexico and Egypt are particularly strong in medical science, the UK, Canada and Korea in educational studies, India in arts and the humanities, and West Germany in law and the social sciences. At the same time, other data suggests there is a strong resistance by Japanese companies to hiring university trained PhDs into their organizations. In engineering, for example,

whereas in 1986 Japan produced about the same number of first degree graduates as did the US, it produced only 588 doctoral graduates compared to 3376 in the US (Westney, 1992). It is to be noted that these statistics take no account of 'on the job' training. Here the data suggests that German, Japanese and Swiss firms allocate considerably more resources, particularly in the areas of their comparative patenting advantages, than their counterparts in the UK, France and Italy.[17]

11.6.3 The ownership of innovatory capacity

There is no comprehensive data on the innovating capacity of firms by country of ownership. It is, however, known that with the exception of some European-based companies, the proportion of R&D activity by MNEs undertaken outside their home countries is generally quite small and, in the case of Japanese firms, negligible. Moreover, the majority of FDI originates from countries which spend the most on R&D, register the largest number of patents and record the highest enrollment in higher education. This would suggest that the geographical distribution of innovatory capacity by country of location and of firms should be broadly similar. However, this is not

Table 11.3 The revealed technological advantage[1] of locations in innovation, classified by technological activity, 1978–86. Some selected countries and areas.

Sector	Country						
	US	Japan	Germany	UK	Italy	Switzerland	Others[2]
Food products	1.07	0.69	0.75	1.43	1.36	1.77	1.27
Chemicals (not specified elsewhere)	0.99	0.87	1.27	1.03	1.05	1.50	0.76
Inorganic	0.97	0.74	1.26	0.89	0.62	0.28	1.47
Organic	0.97	0.91	1.35	0.90	1.31	1.69	0.61
Pharmaceuticals	0.83	0.74	0.96	1.72	1.84	1.48	0.77
Metals	1.11	0.74	1.00	1.06	1.02	0.95	1.53
Mechanical engineering	1.00	0.69	1.18	1.01	1.31	1.09	1.30
Chemical equipment	1.00	0.69	1.18	0.94	1.49	1.03	1.35
Construction equipment	1.03	0.77	1.15	0.91	1.32	1.14	1.20
Mining equipment	1.21	0.30	1.10	1.74	0.71	0.30	1.98
General equipment	1.01	0.77	1.18	1.20	0.84	0.75	1.10
Electrical equipment	1.03	1.21	0.79	0.95	0.74	0.76	0.81
Telecommunications	1.07	1.12	0.65	1.17	0.98	0.64	0.91
Semiconductors	0.99	1.72	0.70	0.68	0.34	0.39	0.31
Systems	1.06	1.15	0.87	0.97	0.77	0.74	0.73
General equipment	0.94	1.19	0.83	0.85	0.66	0.99	1.00
Office equipment	0.95	1.80	0.53	0.64	0.78	0.40	0.37
Motor vehicles	0.69	1.54	1.06	0.68	0.71	0.31	0.54
Aircraft	1.24	0.18	1.06	2.10	0.35	0.05	1.32
Textiles	1.18	0.61	0.93	0.94	2.65	0.88	1.81
Rubber products	0.91	0.98	1.01	1.22	1.51	0.48	0.84
Non-metallic minerals	1.01	1.11	0.88	1.00	0.73	0.68	1.11
Coal and petroleum products	1.35	0.81	0.71	1.13	0.81	0.16	1.55
Professional instruments	0.92	1.44	0.80	0.83	0.56	0.85	0.70
Image equipment[3]	0.89	1.77	0.50	0.79	0.37	0.51	0.46
Photographic	0.63	2.14	0.56	0.38	0.24	0.44	0.25
Other instruments	0.99	1.11	0.96	1.00	0.71	1.08	0.91
Other manufacturing	1.29	0.51	0.84	1.09	0.89	1.03	2.39

1   Revealed technological advantage is defined as

$$RTA_{ij} = \frac{P_{ij}/E_i P}{E_j P_{ij}/E_i E_j P_{ij}}$$

where j is industry and i is country.
It represents the share of world patenting (in the US) of a particular country in a particular industry divided by its share of world patenting (in the US) in all industries over the period 1978–86.

2   Other countries, outside Europe.
3   Including television and ratio sets.

Source: Adapted from Cantwell and Hodson (1991).

Table 11.4 Percentage distribution by field of study of graduate students[1] in selected countries.

Subject	Developed countries					Developing countries			
	Canada	US	West Germany[2]	UK	Japan	Mexico	India	Republic of Korea	Egypt
	(1988)	(1985)	(1988)	(1987)	(1983)	(1988)	(1985)	(1988)	(1987)
Arts and humanities	12.5	7.8	17.4	11.5	13.0	2.5	50.1	15.4	11.9
Education	15.2	9.8	4.6	19.2	5.7	6.8	1.8	16.7	14.0
Law and social sciences	12.3	11.2	29.3	26.6	9.6	12.4	1.2	8.3	14.5
Business studies	15.1	23.2	1.8			24.6	16.2	19.2	13.9
Natural sciences and mathematics	10.7	8.8	13.9	17.4	10.5	10.5	18.4	8.0	6.8
Medical science and health related	13.2	10.0	7.6	6.4	16.3	29.1	4.6	9.2	18.0
Engineering	9.6	5.5	17.4	11.1	35.7	7.8	3.5	13.2	9.4
Other	8.9	23.7	8.0	7.8	9.2	6.3	4.2	10.2	11.5
	100.0	100.0	100.0	100.0	100.0	100.0	100.0	100.0	100.0

1 Programmes leading to a graduate university degree or its equivalent.
2 Including programmes leading to first university degree or its equivalent.

Source: UNESCO (1987) Table 3.14 and UNESCO (1990) Table 3.13.

necessarily the case. Moreover, if it were, it would be incorrect to assume that the impact of MNE-related activity was negligible. Far from it; in a variety of ways, the strategies and policies of foreign direct investors can, and do, markedly affect the capacity of indigenous firms in the countries in which they operate.

Data compiled on the world's largest industrial companies suggests that while, in 1982, about 30% of the production of the world's largest industrial companies was undertaken outside their national boundaries, only about 12% of their innovatory activities were (Dunning and Pearce, 1985). In the US case, where the data is the most comprehensive, 26% of production and 7% of R&D was undertaken outside the US in 1982. In the same year, corresponding figures for the leading European MNEs were 37% and 23%. By 1989, the proportion of foreign-based R&D undertaken by US MNEs had risen to 9% (US Department of Commerce, 1991). This was just one-half the percentage of the worldwide R&D employees of 33 large German MNEs accounted for by their foreign affiliates in that year (Wortmann, 1990). In 1987, some 22.8% of the

R&D expenditure by 20 of the largest Swedish MNEs in the chemical and engineering industries was undertaken outside Sweden – a slight increase on the 20.6% recorded by the same firms in 1980 (Hakanson and Nobel, 1989). In 1980, Swiss industry spent 2.8 billion francs in Switzerland and 1.7 billion francs abroad on R&D activities. In the previous decade, R&D expenditure rose by 19% in Switzerland but 50% in other countries (Swiss Association of Entrepreneurs, 1982). Between 1966 and 1989, the proportion of the global R&D undertaken by US MNEs in foreign countries increased from 6.5% to 9.0%, whereas R&D expenditure by foreign manufacturing affiliates in the US as a percentage of their sales rose from 1.5% in 1977 to 3.5% in 1988 (US Department of Commerce, vd). In 1989, Japanese MNEs were thought to have spent less than 5% of their research funds abroad (Peters, 1991). Taken as a whole, then, in the late 1980s the foreign affiliates of MNEs would appear primarily to be producers of goods and services rather than of technology.

However, this data conceals important country and industry differences. For example, in 1989, some 95% of the foreign R&D expenditure of US firms was concentrated in developed countries, whereas only 78% of the output of goods was. In the same year, the R&D intensity of the value-added activity of US affiliates was well above average in the case of Germany and the UK (which between them accounted for one-half of all R&D by US manufacturing affiliates) and zero or very low in most developing countries. While the average share of global R&D expenditure of US firms accounted for by their foreign affiliates was 9.1%, the ratio varied between 30.8% in household appliances, 20.2% in textiles, and 14.1% in drugs, to 5.6% in transportation equipment and 3.3% in primary and fabricated metals.

This data is largely corroborated by a 1989 field study of the geographical distribution of the innovatory activities of 167 of the world's largest industrial enterprises (Pearce and Singh, 1992). The survey found that although 44% of these companies undertook no foreign R&D, 21% allocated more than 20% of their global R&D budget to their overseas activities. The propensity to engage in foreign R&D was most pronounced in the case of food, drink and pharmaceutical MNEs, and among those of European origin. Most of the foreign R&D units were relatively new, 42% having been set up after 1980. About two-thirds of all R&D facilities established since 1980 had been located in foreign countries, compared with only one-third of those set up prior to 1980.[18]

At the same time, cross-border A&Ms are changing the relative significance of the foreign-based R&D activities of MNEs. The most dramatic example of this was the $8.3 billion merger between the US pharmaceutical company Smith–Kline–Beckman and Beecham of the UK in 1990. In like manner, Japanese pharmaceutical companies are raising their foreign R&D profile by acquiring young US and European owned biotechnology ventures. Finally, it is worth observing that data on the foreign R&D activities of MNEs takes no account of the spate of intra-Triad technology-based strategic alliances, which have occurred since the mid 1980s. As Chapter 9 has described, these have been especially prolific between electronics and information technology companies. To give just two examples, Hagedoorn and Schakenraad (1990a) estimate that by the end of the 1980s, Siemens had established over 300 technical links with other firms, many of whom were

non-German. Peters (1991) gives details of the extensive network of non-equity innovatory activities recently forged by the Japanese-owned NEC in both Europe and the US.

With this data in mind, it is not surprising that, viewed from a host-country perspective, the R&D activities of multinational affiliates are often *relatively* quite important. Again the data is fragmentary, but in the mid 1980s, in Australia, Belgium, Canada, the UK, Germany, South Korea, Singapore and India (to give some examples), the share of R&D activity accounted for by foreign-owned firms exceeded 15%. Moreover, there are suggestions that this share is increasing at a faster rate than that of the other value-added activities of MNE affiliates. In other words, FDI is becoming more R&D intensive.[19]

At the same time, in most countries foreign affiliates tend to spend less on technology-creating activities than do indigenous firms (Pearce, 1989). In 1981, foreign manufacturing affiliates in the UK spent 1.8% of their sales on R&D compared with 2.1% for all firms (including foreign affiliates). In Sweden, in 1977, the average R&D costs of indigenous manufacturing companies, as a percentage of their net output, was estimated by Hakanson (1981) to be 4.3%, and that of foreign subsidiaries to be 3.2%. In Canada, Rangachand (1981) demonstrated that US affiliates in Canada consistently spent less on technology-creating activities than did their indigenous counterparts. Other Canadian studies (Globerman, 1973; Alexander, 1983; McGuinness, 1983) have found that foreign ownership is either not significantly or is negatively correlated to R&D performance. In Hong Kong, a survey by Chen (1983a) revealed that, with the exception of the garments industry, foreign affiliates were less likely to perform R&D than were local firms. Chen put this down to the fact that most foreign affiliates were export-oriented.

A matched-pair analysis of domestic and foreign-owned firms in 43 sectors of Indian industry by Kumar (1990) concluded that, in the early 1980s, MNEs spent a smaller proportion of their income on R&D than did their local counterparts. However, relative to other variables explaining the distinctiveness of inward FDI, R&D intensity was insignificant. A study by Van den Bulcke (1985) of foreign subsidiaries and indigenous firms in Belgium came to a similar conclusion. In Brazil, a survey of 183 firms in the San Paulo region in 1967 led Evans (1979) to assert that there was a negative correlation between the extent of foreign ownership and the propensity to undertake R&D. A similar finding was reached by Cooper (1975) with respect to the impact of foreign-owned firms on R&D activity in Ireland. He argued that while inward direct investment had compensated for a lack of Irish technological capacity, it had not been applied in a way that helped build up such capacity.

There are, however, exceptions to this general picture. Most noticeably as a group, foreign manufacturing affiliates in the US spent relatively more on R&D than all US firms – $3,880 compared with $3,360 per worker in 1989 (Graham, 1991a). One possible reason for this is that foreign MNEs sometimes invest in the US specifically to acquire R&D facilities. Most certainly, the recent acquisitions of foreign companies by foreign MNEs have resulted in a foreign transfer of technological assets into foreign hands. Moreover, the share of US R&D accounted for by foreign subsidiaries is increasing. Between 1982 and 1989, for example, the share of company-funded R&D accounted for by Japanese affiliates alone rose from under 0.4% to nearly 1.1% (Graham, 1991a). In the UK, the proportion of industrial R&D funded from overseas rose from 6.4% in 1972 to 12.4% in 1987 (Stoneman, 1989). In South Korea, foreign affiliates spent 1.8% of their sales on R&D in 1980; this compared with an expenditure of 0.5% for indigenous firms. A more extensive survey by Lecraw (1983) of 153 foreign subsidiaries in six manufacturing sectors in five ASEAN countries in the late 1970s revealed a R&D intensity of 2.5% for US-owned firms and 2.3% for European-owned firms, which compared very favourably with that of Asian-owned firms.

One problem with most of these general comparisons is that they take no account of differences in the industrial or size composition of foreign and domestic firms. However, sectoral studies yield mixed results. In the UK, for example, government statistics published in the early 1980s showed that US subsidiaries recorded a higher R&D propensity in the mechanical engineering sector than did UK-owned companies. On the other hand, Gordon and Fowler (1983) found that the R&D intensity of foreign-controlled firms in the Canadian pharmaceutical industry was less than that of their locally-controlled counterparts – a conclusion echoed by Subramaniam (1972) in his study of the Indian chemicals industry and by UNCTAD (1983a) in a study of the Indian capital goods industry.

Other scholars have suggested that the propensity of foreign affiliates to engage in innovatory activities might vary according to the nationality of the parent company. In Belgium, Van den Bulcke (1985) found that US-owned subsidiaries spent 2.2% of their sales on R&D activities in 1976, compared with an expenditure of only 1.1% of EC-owned subsidiaries. Other studies (e.g. Pearce and Singh, 1992) show the generally low R&D intensity of Japanese multinational investors. However, this as much as anything else, almost certainly reflects their relatively early stage of internationalization.

11.6.4 Types of technological capacity created by MNEs

There are several kinds of technology-creating capacity. The extent to which a firm is willing to disperse these activities geographically and its choice of mode of technology transfer (e.g. by FDI, licensing or strategic alliance) varies between these activities.

It is perfectly clear from a variety of studies (e.g. Pearce, 1989; Casson, 1991; Pearce and Singh, 1992) that the great majority of R&D undertaken by the foreign affiliates of MNEs is directed to the adaptation of particular products, processes or functions and procedures of the firm rather than to basic or fundamental research. At the same time, the evidence on the effects of foreign ownership on the kinds of research undertaken is ambiguous. In the UK in the 1950s, around 56% of 205 US manufacturing affiliates claimed they did some development or adaptive research and only 19% did basic research; at the time there was little rationalized research (Dunning, 1958). These findings were largely confirmed by a later survey of US subsidiaries in Scotland (Hood and Young, 1982a), which revealed that, although 26% of 88 foreign-owned firms performed some fundamental product and process development, there was little basic research of a more general nature. A more detailed study by Haug et al. (1983) of 15 US electronics affiliates in Scotland concluded that none were involved in basic research and only two were producing results of value to the MNE of which they were part. In a survey of the R&D activities by 108 foreign subsidiaries in Greece in 1981, Dokopoulou (1987) found that only nine undertook any original research.

In Canada, one of the earliest surveys (Safarian, 1966) concluded that although only about 13% of foreign affiliates undertook basic research, there was no reason to suppose that the percentage was any different than that for Canadian firms. However, this and other studies show that there is a substantial difference in both the amount and kind of R&D undertaken by parent companies of MNEs and their affiliates. US data reveals that, in 1989, US manufacturing MNEs spent 2.6% of their sales on R&D, whereas their foreign affiliates spent only 0.8% (US Department of Commerce, 1991). An earlier study based on 122 of the world's largest corporations came to a similar conclusion. However, the data also shows that European-based MNEs generally spend proportionately more on foreign-based R&D activities than do their US counterparts (Dunning and Pearce, 1985). Some of the relevant statistics are set

Table 11.5 Research and development expenditure as a percentage of sales, 1982, for parent country and overseas operations.[1]

	USA		Europe		Total[4]	
	Home country[2]	Overseas[3]	Home country[2]	Overseas[3]	Home country[2]	Overseas[3]
Aerospace	4.9	0.0	10.7	0.0	5.9	0.0
Office equipment (inc. computers)	9.0	2.3	12.4	3.6	9.2	2.4
Electronics and electrical appliances	1.8	0.8	9.3	4.4	8.1	3.9
Industrial and agricultural chemicals	4.6	2.6	5.0	3.2	4.6	3.0
Pharmaceuticals and consumer chemicals	5.9	3.6	13.4	4.2	8.9	4.3
Motor vehicles (inc. components)	4.8	3.2	3.8	1.2	4.1	2.2
Total high research intensity	5.4	2.9	5.9	3.2	5.6	3.0
Industrial and farm equipment	5.2	1.5	5.2	1.1	4.7	1.4
Building materials	3.9	0.7	1.8	0.8	1.7	0.8
Metal manufacturing and products	1.6	0.7	1.4	0.4	1.5	0.5
Total medium research intensity	3.2	1.2	1.9	0.6	2.4	0.9
Paper and wood products	1.2	0.1	0.6	0.1	1.0	0.1
Food	0.9	0.6	2.0	0.9	1.2	0.8
Total low research intensity	1.0	0.5	1.1	0.8	1.0	0.7
Petroleum	1.3	0.1	0.6	0.4	1.1	0.2
Total	3.1	0.8	3.6	1.8	3.3	1.2

1 Sample covers 122 firms of the world's largest industrial companies for which information on overseas R&D in 1982 was available. These 122 firms accounted for 22% of the sales of the 792 firms about which data on global production was available.

2 R&D expenditure in parent company divided by parent country production (percentage).

3 R&D expenditure overseas divided by foreign production (percentage).

4 Includes Japan and other countries.

Source: Dunning and Pearce (1985).

out in Table 11.5.

More recent data shows that in the case of some European firms, especially in the pharmaceuticals, food, drink and tobacco sectors, foreign R&D expenditure exceeds that undertaken in the home country. Examples include one large UK brewery company, which, in 1988, undertook four-fifths of its R&D outside its home country, and a leading tobacco MNE which did three-quarters of its R&D abroad. Among the leading European MNEs, Ciba Geigy, Royal Dutch Shell, Bull, Philips, Olivetti, ABB, SKF and Norsk Hydro all undertake more than one-third of their R&D expenditure outside their home countries. Among the US MNEs, IBM has long decentralized a high proportion of its R&D activities, while one of the newest elevators of Otis Elevator (the Elevonic 411) was the combined design and development effort of six research centres in five countries (*Business Week*, 1990). Most of the large Japanese auto companies have expressed intentions to set up regional R&D centres in Europe and North America. Finally, while regional integration in Europe and North America is causing MNEs to restructure their foreign R&D operations, global competition is forcing more strategic asset acquiring FDI – particularly in technology-intensive sectors.

11.6.5 Under what circumstances will MNEs engage in foreign-based R&D?

Introduction

R&D activities represent a particular form of value-added activity by firms. While these activities are usually perceived to precede the manufacturing of a product, post-manufacturing product modifications and improvements make it desirable to link innovatory activities with both past and future output.

Chapter 4 has shown that firms will normally engage in FDI whenever they perceive that they possess technological or organizational O advantages which are best exploited internally from a foreign location. However, as we have also seen, the MNE activity may be prompted by the need to acquire intangible assets, which, coupled with those it already possesses, are expected to sustain or improve its global competitive position. Firms choosing to acquire or engage in foreign innovatory activities do so for several reasons. Basically, however, we might identify four types of R&D.[20]

Product, material or process modifications and improvements

The bulk of the innovatory activities of MNEs outside their national boundaries takes the form of technical and organizational support facilities. Such activities are made necessary by country-specific differences in materials availability, supply capabilities and consumer needs, as well as differences in work practices and organizational customs. Such innovatory activities may be resource based, market oriented, rationalized or asset seeking. They frequently require many kinds of skills and expertise, but particularly those of applied scientists, development engineers, technicians and professionals. External contact is mainly with suppliers of intermediate products and with final customers.

This type of R&D both depends on and affects the *know-how* rather than the *know-why* capabilities of the country in which it is located. Occasionally, the absence of particular materials or host government policies may necessitate a complete reappraisal of production methods and/or products, in which case R&D becomes of the next category. R&D of this type both depends on, and affects, the local technological capacity. Much of the initial innovating activities undertaken by MNEs in their foreign subsidiaries are of this kind. For example, 57% of a sample of 218 Japanese MNEs questioned in 1990 by the Export–Import Bank of Japan said that the main objective of their foreign R&D facilities was to develop products tailored to meet local needs. The major exception is where MNEs acquire foreign firms with existing R&D facilities. Moreover, except in a few sectors, notably agribusiness, food processing, textiles and clothing, pharmaceuticals, advertising and management consultancy, and in a few countries, such as Brazil, India, Korea, Mexico, Singapore and Taiwan, it is the only R&D carried out in developing countries. However, in some cases the R&D consequent upon MNE activity is externalized to upstream sellers or downstream buyers.

Basic materials or product research

This kind of research is most likely to be located in the MNE's home country, although in the survey undertaken by Pearce and Singh (1992), 22% of the sample companies indicated that basic or original research was, at least as, if not more important to the subsidiary than to the parent units. Where this research is undertaken abroad, it is likely to be of two main kinds. The first is where the inputs required for the research are themselves immobile (e.g. tea plantations, bauxite mining, a particular climate or ecological condition, quality improvement techniques for agribusiness). The second is that the need for continual testing and interaction with customer needs requires a local R&D facility. The latter requirement is similar to that for a close proximity between R&D and production in the first stage of the product cycle. The output of this research may be used for products supplied to local or export markets.

This latter type of research is likely to make more demands on the local innovatory infrastructure. It is more of a *know-why* than a *know-how* variety, and is most likely to flourish where it is part of a cluster of similar R&D activities and/or has access to university or cooperative research facilities. At the same time, MNE activity might itself influence, for good or bad, the development of innovatory clusters.

11.6.4   Efficiency-seeking research

This research is the equivalent of rationalized or efficiency-seeking production. To gain economies of scale and scope, MNEs may choose to concentrate certain types of R&D in particular foreign countries, the output of which they export to other parts of their organization. Like the second type of R&D, specialized or rationalized research will usually be attracted to countries with a sophisticated technological and educational infrastructure, and which are host to related or supportive industries (Porter, 1990). There is some evidence to suggest that this type of R&D is increasing the fastest, particularly among the developed countries and in those sectors in which the degree of multinationalization is most marked and where intra-firm speculation is the most pronounced (Pearce and Singh, 1992).

11.6.5   To acquire technological assets or gain an insight into foreign innovating activities

As the ownership of R&D becomes increasingly concentrated but its location becomes more dispersed, many MNEs, particularly in the technologically-intensive sectors, are finding it desirable to have an innovating, as well as a manufacturing presence in the main industrialized countries. Competitive pressures and the escalating costs of R&D are also leading an increasing number of companies to conclude cross-border research alliances.[21] Companies like IBM, Philips, Siemens, Sony, ICI, SKF and Dupont all have R&D facilities in Western Europe, the US and Japan. Countries anxious to attract high value activities of firms are attempting to create centres of innovatory excellence.[22] Some MNEs from investment-driven developing countries are also investing in Europe and North America to acquire innovating capabilities in the same way as firms from industrialized countries invest in some developing countries to acquire raw materials or low cost labour.

The extent to which R&D is undertaken by MNE affiliates will depend, first, on whether it is undertaken at all, and second, on the relative advantages of locating the activities in the home country. Unlike foreign production, which requires some kind of O-specific advantage on the part of the investing firm, research is undertaken to create or acquire an advantage. However, new R&D activity is not independent of the existing technological capacity (including the learning experience) of the firm and/or the availability of complementary assets. To the extent that the possession of these complementary assets may lower the marginal costs of R&D, the MNE may have an advantage in seeking out, monitoring and incorporating the research output of other firms into its own research portfolio. Hence, the desire of US corporations to have an innovatory presence in Western Europe, and of European and Japanese MNEs to have a research base in the US. Research listening or monitoring posts are also common in all research-intensive economies – particularly by MNEs from low-research-intensive countries, including some developing economies.

Finally, it is worth recalling that the market for

innovatory resources is generally considered most imperfect. When such imperfections lead to the price of such resources being relatively lower in foreign countries (in relation to their opportunity and replacement costs) than in home countries, the MNE may have an additional reason for engaging in foreign-based R&D.[23]

11.6.6 The strategy of MNEs towards foreign innovatory activities

The literature identifies several industry-, firm- and country-specific characteristics influencing the extent of the technology-creating activities undertaken by MNE affiliates. In addition, the age, size and experience of the investing firm and the extent and location of its other foreign value-adding activities are relevant variables. Generally speaking, apart from where MNEs acquire foreign firms or set up an R&D faculty to gain an insight into local innovatory capacity, R&D tends to follow downstream production. A current example is Japanese investment in the European electronics and motor vehicle industries.[24] It is also related to the strategy of the MNE towards its foreign operations. For example, where the R&D of an MNE is broadly based rather than being product or process specific, then it is unlikely to follow rationalized investment. Indeed, Hakanson (1981) suggests that the R&D intensity of foreign subsidiaries is negatively related to the firm's level of global integration (proxied by measures of intra-firm trade). At the same time, it appears to be positively related to its export orientation. Brash (1966) and others have concluded that the propensity of MNE affiliates to engage in R&D (but not the extent of R&D) is positively related to the age of the subsidiary (itself often a reflection of experience and standing) and its degree of vertical integration. This is confirmed by Hakanson and Zander (1986) who also found that affiliate size was positively related to R&D intensity. Blomström (1990) suggests that both the incentive for the impact of intra-Triad R&D activities by MNEs are likely to be more pronounced than the North–South equivalent.

More generally, it should be recalled that there are powerful locational reasons for both the centralization and decentralization of R&D. Some of these are set out in Exhibit 11.1. The most powerful

motive for decentralizing R&D is the desire to exploit the pool of research talents of another country 'to tap into another scientific culture', as one research director has put it. In a comment on the setting up of Hoechst's overseas R&D activities, Garies (1971) noted that although economies of scale dictated a centralized R&D function, the desire to profit from the talents of foreign chemists and pharmacologists and the need to be part of the communities at the forefront of pharmaceutical research were strong decentralizing forces. In operational terms, this means forming close relationships with local universities and other public research centres and using the special skills and insights of local scientists. This is currently being actively pursued by Japanese affiliates in the UK (Japan, 1991). It cannot be done at a distance or second hand. It is best achieved by creating a local research centre of genuine innovative capacity which can interact fruitfully with the local or national scientific community. Clearly, this is an expensive course of action which only a few companies and innovation-driven countries can afford.

Commercial reasons often play a part in the decision to begin R&D abroad. Availability and cost of scientists and engineers is obviously a critical consideration, while a large national market may require particular products in particular forms. Generally it is best to develop these products on the spot and in close association with the local production and sales personnel. There is an obvious analogy here with the product cycle (Vernon, 1966, 1979).

Pressure and/or support from host governments are also relevant factors. Many national administrations are anxious to build up their national technological capacities for innovation, in effect, as a form of import substitution. They use a variety of instruments for this purpose, such as cash or in-kind grants for R&D, procurement preferences and domestic content requirements. Other forms of government action are less important. In the case of the drug industry, for example, controls over the introduction of new medicines vary considerably in extent and content from country to country. At the present time, however, many products have to be sold worldwide to recoup their large development costs, reducing the incentive to shift research to permissive nations. Nevertheless, in recent years US

Exhibit 11.1   Forces making for the centralization or decentralization of R&D by MNEs.

Centralization forces

Need for critical mass to gain economies of scale.

The presence of supporting industries and agglomerative economies.

Need to be adjacent to downstream operations.

Availability of resources and capabilities (e.g. R&D facilities, skilled manpower).

Accumulated experience of R&D know-how and organization of innovating, generating activities.

Avoidance of cross-border communications and coordination problems.

Decentralizing forces

Need to cater for local market needs (autos, tractors, food products, toiletries, etc).

'On the spot' R&D desirable (e.g. into tropical diseases, pesticides and new varieties of seeds and crops).

Differences in local materials and need to test products locally.

Need to be where there are clusters of cutting-edge R&D activity.

Need to acquire new technological assets or specialized skills and talents.

To scan and monitor R&D activities of foreign firms.

To take advantage of differences in cross-border location-bound resources and capabilities, and markets.

To satisfy host government pressures or regulatory instruments; or as part of a regional or global strategy to raise the quality of the output of at least some subsidiaries.

To defend a competitive position in R&D-intensive sectors.

MNEs have often chosen to introduce their latest drugs in Europe rather than in the more demanding regulatory environment of the USA, and this has undoubtedly influenced their levels of spending abroad. Although sometimes appreciable, tax concessions and subsidies do not seem to have played much part in decisions to move research to other countries.

MNEs may pursue various strategies towards the international organization of their research activities. Hood and Young (1982a) distinguish between three main types of R&D laboratories which a foreign subsidiary might house. These are:

(1) laboratories whose primary function is to assist the production and marketing facilities in a host country to make effective use of technology and ideas imported from the parent company;

(2) locally integrated laboratories which, while remaining predominantly oriented towards the requirements and needs of the host country, undertake some product or process adaptation, development and design work;

(3) the international interdependent laboratory which, though located in a particular host country, undertakes R&D as part of a coordinated global R&D programme of the parent firm.

A related classification to that of Hood and Young is made by Bartlett and Ghoshal (1988) who delineate the innovatory activities of MNEs according to where the R&D is undertaken and for what purpose. Thus they define local-for-local R&D activities as those in which a particular national subsidiary of the MNE creates and complements innovations entirely at a national level. Where these innovations are found to be applicable in multiple locations, they become local-for-global activities. By contrast, a centre-for-global innovatory strategy is that in which a central R&D laboratory creates a product, process or system for worldwide use, while global-for-global innovations are those which are created by pooling the resources and capabilities of many different R&D units to arrive at a jointly developed general solution to a worldwide problem (Ghoshal and Bartlett, 1990).

Returning to our example of the pharmaceutical industry, the great majority of the leading MNEs still undertake most of their basic R&D activities in their home countries and operate or support locally-integrated laboratories in other developed countries, and in India and Brazil. The European MNEs tend to be less ethnocentric in their R&D strategies than either the American or the Japanese. A number, for example, Ciba Geigy, Welcome, Merck, Rhone Poulenc and Hoechst, undertake some fundamental (and usually specialized) research in at least some of their foreign R&D laboratories. Welcome, for example, has set up four laboratories in developing countries to develop new drugs for treating tropical diseases. At least four Dutch MNEs are currently undertaking a significant amount of R&D in India (UN, 1992b). Increasingly, however, there appears to be a shift in the organization of R&D among pharmaceutical MNEs of all nationalities from a local-for-local to a local-to-global stance, and from a centre-for-global to a global-to-global stance. Among the reasons for this are the continued growth of world demand for drugs and an increasing inter-nationalization of their production; the steeply rising cost of R&D; the trend towards cross-border corporate alliances (particularly in the more complex area of physio-chemical and biotechnology research); improvements in the protection of intellectual property rights; the convergence of scientific and technological capacity and skilled personnel, particularly in the Triad countries; and advances in trans-border data transmitting facilities. For further details of the determinants of the location of R&D by pharmaceutical MNEs see, for example, Dunning (1988b) and Taggart (1989).

To summarize some of the reasons for the decentralization of R&D activities by MNEs, we can do no better than reproduce a table from Pearce and Singh (1992). Table 11.6 contains the results of the opinions of the directors of research (or the nearest

equivalent executive) of some 133 parent companies and subsidiaries of industrial MNEs, who, in 1989, were asked to rank the significance (on a 1 to 3 scale) of a number of the factors thought likely to influence the location of R&D activities.

The data in the table is largely self-explanatory. The primary reasons for engaging in foreign R&D appear to be market oriented, although supply capabilities (e.g. availability of research professionals and a distinctive local scientific, educational and technological tradition) are important in some sectors. They also appear to assume greater significance in the case of Japanese MNEs than those of other nationalities. MNEs from developing countries appear to place especial emphasis on the need to provide technical support to the MNE group.

11.7   THE ORGANIZATION OF TECHNOLOGY TRANSFER

11.7.1   Modes of technology transfer

From the viewpoint of the MNE, there may be several different ways in which technology can be transferred from one country to another, assuming that it is profitable to do so. There have been several attempts by economists and business scholars to identify some of the key characteristics in the mode of technology transfer. These modes vary, along a spectrum, from arm's length sales of technology to independent purchasers (e.g. as with a technical service or licensing agreement) through a range of cooperative alliances to equity investments. The markets and hierarchies literature offers some explanations as to the factors influencing the choice.[25] Basically it depends on the nature of the technology or technological capacity being transferred and the characteristics of the sellers and buyers to the exchange.

Transaction cost theory suggests that, *ceteris paribus*, newer technologies, those which represent a radical change in the state of the art, those which require the presence of related industries and sophisticated supply capabilities if they are to be used properly, and those where the perceived risk of loss of proprietary rights is the highest, are most likely to be internalized. On the other hand, as has

Table 11.6 Conditions and circumstances considered to have most influenced[1] recent decisions with regard to development of subsidiary R&D units by industry.

Types of influence: average response[2]	Food, drink, tobacco	Petroleum	Metal manufacture and products	Industrial and agricultural chemicals	Pharmaceuticals and consumer chemicals	Motor vehicles (incl. components)	Industrial and farm equipment	Electronics and electrical appliances	Office equipment (incl. computers)	Other manufacturing	Total
A distinctive local scientific, educational or technological tradition conducive to certain types of research	1.60	2.00	1.20	1.83	2.07	1.00	1.50	1.83	1.86	1.67	1.78
Presence of a helpful local scientific environment and adequate technical infrastructure	1.54	2.17	1.18	1.65	2.03	1.40	1.50	1.77	1.75	1.83	1.73
Availability of research professionals	1.82	2.50	1.46	2.05	2.20	1.80	1.50	1.92	1.88	2.17	1.99
Favourable wage rates for research professionals	1.27	1.50	1.46	1.42	1.53	1.80	1.75	1.31	1.25	1.33	1.44
Need to provide technical services to local production unit	2.46	2.17	2.36	2.22	1.77	3.00	2.50	2.21	1.50	2.33	2.14
To help modify/standardize products for the local market	2.82	2.00	2.36	2.69	2.07	2.50	2.25	2.38	1.37	2.17	2.34
To help modify/standardize products for overseas markets	2.36	2.17	2.00	2.11	1.79	1.75	2.00	2.00	1.75	2.00	1.97
To help develop new products for the local market	2.91	2.33	2.82	2.73	2.47	3.00	2.50	2.31	2.38	2.50	2.60
To help develop new products for overseas markets	1.91	2.33	2.36	2.19	2.34	2.25	2.25	2.15	2.75	1.83	2.24
To provide technical support to other parts of the multinational group	1.91	2.83	1.91	2.14	2.03	2.75	1.76	1.77	1.87	1.83	2.05
A large and growing local market where R&D is seen to play a critical role	1.91	2.00	1.46	1.97	2.30	2.26	1.50	1.92	1.50	2.00	1.96
To forestall entry of another firm	1.18	1.00	1.00	1.19	1.07	1.00	1.00	1.17	1.00	1.17	1.11
To match local R&D of competitor firm	1.46	1.33	1.27	1.44	1.31	2.00	1.50	1.67	1.25	1.17	1.41

1 Respondents were asked to grade each condition or circumstance on the scale, (1) irrelevant to decisions, (2) of some influence on decisions, (3) a major factor contributing to decisions.

2 The average derived by allocating values to the responses of (1) for 'irrelevant', (2) for 'some influence', (3) for 'major factor'.

Source: Pearce and Singh (1992).

already been suggested, sometimes there are substantial fixed costs associated with intra-firm technology transfer (Teece, 1976). These include the costs of providing legal, administrative and operating infrastructures, as well as those of monitoring and controlling performance. *Inter alia* this suggests that single or infrequent transfers of technology, and those which have a speedy rate of obsolescence or are peripheral to the firm's core O advantages, are less likely to be internalized. This is particularly likely to be the case with *de novo* investments.

No less important are country-specific characteristics which affect the extent of market failure in the markets for technology and technological capa-

city. These are likely to be of two kinds. The first reflect national policies towards inward direct investment. As later chapters will describe, such investment may be subject to widely varying degrees of review, regulation and monitoring procedures. In the extreme, receiving governments may preclude the internalization of technology altogether by disallowing inbound MNE activity altogether. By contrast, they may encourage FDI by appropriate policies and incentives which are sufficient to overcome some of the risks associated with equity ownerships. Joint ventures are another modality for technology transfer which allow a sharing of risks among the shareholders.

The second type of market failure, which may also be influenced by government action (or non-action), concerns the conditions of the market for technology between the sending and recipient countries. Contractor (1980) has argued that the market for technology between developed and developing countries is likely to be more imperfect than that among developed countries. For example, where there are inadequate technological supply capabilities, back-up services, or an inability to absorb new technologies, foreign firms may prefer to internalize technology transfers. If these are satisfactory, however, they may choose to license rather than own technology. At the same time, the risks of investing in developing countries is greater than that in developed countries, so to avoid such risks firms may choose to license or engage in joint ventures in developing countries rather more than in developed countries.

There have been various attempts to evaluate the role of market characteristics affecting modes of technology transfer. Davidson and McFetridge (1984), for example, in a study of 1226 technology transfers carried out by 32 US-based multinationals between 1945 and 1978, found that the transaction costs of using markets, together with the experience of firms, were the most powerful explanatory factors of the modality of the transfer. In particular, the age of the technology, the number of prior transfers of technology, and the transferor's R&D intensity were all strongly and positively related to the propensity to internalize technology markets. By contrast, the relationship between market size, the technological sophistication of the receiving country and the profitability of internal markets were not supported by the evidence. The role of government policy appeared to play a modest role in influencing the form of technology transfer.

In another study, Dunning (1984) showed that among the country-specific characteristics determining the propensity of UK firms to export technology to their subsidiaries or to license it to third-party firms, the extent to which host countries engaged in international trade, government economic policy (both generally and towards inward investment) and the quality of technological and educational infrastructure were among the most significant factors. The more open the economy and the less restrictive the government policy towards FDI, the more likely transfers of technology will be internalized within the sending firm. Unlike Contractor (who used US data), Dunning did not find any correlation between the mode of transfer and income levels. The reason for this, he concluded, was that while a reduction in market failure – which often reflected the enhanced ability of a host country to use imported technology properly – lessened the need for hierarchical control over the development of technological assets, economic growth was sometimes accompanied by economic integration which tended to prompt more efficiency or strategic asset seeking FDI which was often handled better through an internalized system of governance.

One of the fastest growing forms of cross-border technology transference (perhaps 'sharing' is the better word) is the strategic alliance. The reasons for such alliances have been described in Chapter 9 and in Gugler and Dunning (1992). Here we would simply point out that about two-fifths of all such alliances are knowledge related, and usually by firms in similar sectors (Cainarca et al., 1989). Between 1976 and 1987, the proportion of US cross-border joint ventures with R&D activity rose from 7% to 23% (Hladik and Linden, 1989). The desire to pool R&D facilities in order to speed up technological development, reduce resource commitment share risks, or to forestall the actions of competitors are particularly noticeable in the case of firms utilizing generic and cutting edge technologies[26] and/or those which are subject to rapid obsolescence. Strategic alliances are also favoured by large international oligopolists seeking to establish or maintain their global competitive positions.

11.7.2 The emergence of technological systems

Chapter 5 has shown that advances in the deployment of technological and organizational capacity have been at the root of much of the growth of MNE activity. Historically, product and process innovations have been a critical source of the competitive advantages of firms. There is considerable evidence that many MNEs which maintained successful foreign value-added facilities abroad before 1914 depended upon specialized product or process innovative strengths (Wilkins, 1970, 1974; Franko, 1976; Stopford, 1974). More recently, field research by Wyatt *et al.* (1985) and Archer (1986) has revealed that many MNEs still believe that technological superiority is the major means by which they can maintain their global competitive advantages.

At the same time, as Chapter 4 has demonstrated, the success of the modern MNE also rests on its ability to create, or acquire, advantages of a transaction cost minimizing kind. In the present context, this type of advantage arises from the role of the firm as a coordinator of a number of separate value-added activities, each of which requires different (but often related) technologies, rather than as a producer of a single product using one particular technology. Such an advantage can only be exploited by it producing at different points of the value-added chain or on different value-added chains. The technological complementarity which exists between certain groups of products and processes is a case in point. Rosenberg (1981), for example, has demonstrated that innovative success in related activities and the opportunity for new applications of particular innovation may often stimulate complementary innovations. However, close links are required between the creation and use of technology (which is an iterative and cumulative process). These links are often maintained more efficiently within, rather than between hierarchies. Historically, MNEs have been able to provide such linkages and, as a result, have been in a particularly favourable position to exploit the economies of common governance associated with managing larger and more complex firms.

In more recent years, the development of integrated technological systems by MNEs and other firms has led to a further internalization of cross-border technology markets. In part, this is the natural outcome of the decentralization of technological capacity, as well as of a new generation of technological advances which have helped forge new links between established production procedures and potential new applications for the underlying skills and technologies. Moreover, not only has technology become less activity specific, but has also increasingly affected the capacity of firms to coordinate different and/or geographically diversified activities. In other words, the organization of technology has become a generic competitive advantage in its own right (Bartlett, 1986; Bartlett and Ghoshal, 1988).

This transformation in the extent to which technological innovation is organized within the firm has also been influenced by changes in the international economic and political environment. In a purely technological sense, there may well have been benefits from a closer international integration of production in the inter-war period, especially between Europe and the USA. However, in these years, such a development was inhibited by the height of protectionist barriers as well as by the political and exchange risks encountered by any MNE that sought to coordinate production across potentially hostile countries. Since 1945, the liberalization of trade in manufactured goods between the industrialized countries (particularly within the EC), aided and abetted by their relative political stability, has encouraged the establishment of global networks of trade and production covering both the industrialized and the newly industrialized world. Chapter 17 will explore this point in more detail.

Recent changes in the international economic environment have further aided the development of integrated technological systems. The advantages that stem from such centralized coordination have helped to strengthen the position of many MNEs *vis à vis* uninational firms, which are constrained to pursue seriously only those activities in which their own countries have an existing or potential locational advantage. In turn, MNEs that have remained strongest in the creation of new technologies, as well as in their use and dissemination, have generally been those which have recorded the fastest growth rates of all. The most potent illustration of this is the emergence of many Japanese MNEs, which have developed a unique capacity for linking the import and dissemination of foreign technology to the creation and transfer of new indigenous technology. While Japanese firms accounted for 9.1% of all patents granted in the USA to foreign residents in the period 1963–69, they accounted for a massive 36.5% in 1983. This improvement was matched by an increase in the Japanese share of the sales of the world's largest 483 industrial firms, from 6.0% in 1962 to 12.1% in 1982 (Dunning and Pearce, 1985). The innovatory capability of a firm must embrace its ability to create and accumulate technological assets and the efficiency with which it organizes the dissemination and use of these assets.

11.8   MNES, TECHNOLOGICAL ACCUMULATION AND COMPETITIVE ADVANTAGES

So far in this chapter we have identified and evaluated some of the ways in which MNEs might affect the technological capacity of the foreign countries in which they operate. We have concluded that the O-specific advantages of MNEs offer opportunities for the upgrading of this capacity, together with a more efficient usage of indigenous resources. However, whether or not this occurs depends on the extent to which any such upgrading is consistent with the goals of the MNEs and the ESP configuration of the countries concerned.

Chapter 16 will consider, in some detail, the possible spillover effects of the presence of MNEs on the rest of the economy of which they are part. In particular, it will discuss the impact of inbound and outbound FDI on the technological capacity and competitiveness of suppliers and competitors, as well as on the development of clusters of related and supporting industries – one of the facets of Porter's diamond of competitive advantage. Appropriate advertising and marketing procedures may enable foreign firms to raise the quality of domestic demand, as the Japanese have successfully done in the European auto and consumer electronics sectors, which may, in turn, stimulate a more efficient use of resources and capabilities by competitors. Inward direct investment may further encourage a more dynamic entrepreneurial attitude by indigenous firms to the creation and upgrading of their human and physical assets.

In this section, however, we will confine our attention to the dynamic interaction between MNEs and the economies of which they are part in terms of the asset cumulative causation model set out in Chapter 10. The proposition we wish to advance is that the increasingly footloose nature of international production and innovatory activities is likely to reinforce patterns of asset cumulative causation both within and between countries. The precise nature of these patterns will depend on a range of specific factors, as identified by the ESP paradigm, and the kind of investment undertaken by MNEs.

The impact of inward investment is also likely to vary according to both its source and the stage of economic development of the recipient country. For example, in the case of poorer developing countries, whose engine for growth is essentially factor-driven, the most foreign MNEs can do is to help enhance the quality of their natural resources and labour force, and to provide additional assets of capital and technology by which existing products may be produced more efficiently. However, the extent to which this leads to a cumulative improvement in domestic resource capabilities rests on the structure of inter-firm competition and whether the presence of foreign firms helps or inhibits the development of indigenous clusters of related activities. It also depends on the efficacy of the macro-organizational policies of governments, particularly with respect to upgrading the educational and technological infrastructure.

In the case of investment-driven economic development, market-seeking FDI is likely to play a more important role than resource-seeking FDI in all but the smaller resource-intensive developing countries. Here, the impact of MNEs on cumulative asset creation will very much depend on the size of domestic and adjacent markets, the supply capabilities of indigenous producers and the structure of competition. Any impact is likely to be both product and process specific, but in as far as MNEs can act as 'tutors' to a country in the creation and sustainment of its dynamic comparative advantage, they can (and do) play a useful role. Such upgrading from a factor-driven to an investment-driven stage of development will normally show itself in a raising of the capital/labour ratio and, at least in some sectors, an increase in the skilled labour content. MNEs may also assist factor-driven sectors to engage in more high value activities, for example, by appropriate on-the-job training and technological guidance on product development and process adaptation. Where, however, MNEs set up offshore enclaves of activity to produce low value products for other parts of their organizations, far from encouraging indigenous asset cumulation, they may inhibit a country from developing its full economic and technological potential.

It is, however, as a country approaches the innovation-driven stage of its development that the impact of inbound MNE activity on its long-term technological viability is likely to be critical. It is possible to identify both beneficial and unwelcome scenarios. Although much will depend on country- and industry-specific variables, some generalizations are possible. Thus, countries with a large domestic market which are achieving good productivity records and rates of growth, and are allocating an above average proportion of their resources to upgrading their human and physical capital, are more likely to attract inward MNE investment in technology-intensive activities. They will also be in a good position to absorb, disseminate and improve on that technology. By contrast, smaller industrial countries which pursue inefficient structural adjustment policies and are less competitive in world markets, are more likely to attract MNE satellites concentrated in assembling and low value-added activities. However, since these affiliates are able to import the O advantages of their parent companies, they may still be able to drive out their local competitors. In doing so, they may well reduce the technological capabilities of indigenous competitors (and that of their suppliers), thereby lessening their capacity to accumulate new technology. It is this possibility which, in the case of recent Japanese direct investment in the UK and the US, has been labelled the 'Trojan horse' effect (Dunning, 1986b).

Considering the role of outward direct investment, where domestic firms hold a strong position in global markets, they can usually afford to invest more in domestic innovatory activities, which, through backward linkages, may benefit their domestic suppliers. This, in turn, will strengthen the latter's competitive capacity to supply the affiliates of foreign firms requiring their products. More subcontracting work is then given to domestic suppliers by foreign affiliates which further strengthens indigenous technological capacity. In this scenario, outward and inward investment complement each other in making for an improved diamond of competitive advantage of the country concerned. An important component of this success is the technology creation and dissemination made possible by the MNE.

In summary, then, as and when national economies become convergent in their technological capabilities – aided and abetted by intra-industry trade and production – MNEs may assist the transfer and diffusion of technology between them. Cross-investments and spillover effects increase the international diffusion of technology, while technology creation in each country becomes more closely intertwined. Thus, in the context of national economic

policy, MNEs may play a dual role. On the one hand, they may help to advance the technological capacities of particular home and host countries; on the other, they may strengthen the technological linkages between them. Whether countries are brought closer together or pushed further apart, the interdependence between them is increased and the development of technological systems or galaxies within MNEs reinforces such interdependence.

We now consider how the technological activities of MNEs may intensify the cumulative causation of independently-owned technological capacity, but do so in different directions in different industries. Cantwell (1987) and Cantwell and Dunning (1991) have shown that high value inbound MNE activity is likely to be attracted into innovative and productive sectors caught up in a virtuous circle of asset accumulation. In doing so, it may well further increase local capacity, assist the dissemination of new knowledge to suppliers and customers, raise the quality of output, and spur local rivals to a more efficient rate of innovation. Indeed, this type of sector is probably home to outward MNE investors which, in turn, is likely to strengthen the position of local component suppliers. The technological activity of MNEs, and its local dissemination, then reinforces the industry's virtuous cycle.

At the same time, inward direct investment may still take place in declining sectors, but it is likely to be in low value-added subsectors of the industry, importing the more high value-added intermediate products. By dint of their higher efficiency, or by deliberate strategy, foreign affiliates may encroach on the markets of local competitors. Indeed, the foreign MNE may be able to finance an increased level of R&D within its parent company from its increased global sales. Meanwhile local firms whose markets are cut back may lack the resources to 'go global' themselves and, as a result, be compelled to cut back their R&D expenditures. If, in addition, the government of the home country of the MNE prohibits, or creates obstacles to investment by foreign firms in its own domestic market, then this constitutes the type of 'technological protectionism' of which the Japanese are sometimes accused (Spencer and Brander, 1983). In these circumstances, inward direct investment may not only drive out local competitors, but also restrict the creation of new technology by local suppliers, even if more technology disseminates to them from the MNE.[27] For both these reasons, domestic technological capacity is reduced.

Several studies of US direct investment in Europe provide evidence both of cases where it has helped to set in motion or intensify a virtuous circle, and of those where it has helped to drive out local firms and set in motion a vicious circle of increasing dependency on external sources of supply.[28] Much depends on the initial technological capacity and international competitiveness of the country and sector in question, and how this influences the motivation underlying the MNE investment. Until now, the literature on MNEs and international technology dissemination has not paid much attention to this issue. Instead it has preferred to concern itself with the immediate form or impact of technology transfer in a static framework, rather than the unfolding dynamic process which it opens up.

11.9   THE ROLE OF GOVERNMENT ACTION

11.9.1   The ability of governments to affect indigenous technological capacity

Of all the exogenous factors influencing the impact of MNEs on the creation and location of innovatory capacity, and of the dissemination of its output, perhaps none is more important than the attitudes and actions of the governments of the countries in which they operate. It is well known that, by regulation, commissioning or funding R&D activities, national governments and regional authorities may *directly* influence the level and structure of innovatory-related activities. Somewhat less appreciated is the *indirect* role which governments may play in fashioning the ecostructural dimension within which firms (including MNEs) are induced to undertake such activities and, in some cases, in determining *which* firms undertake these activities.

Numerous studies have identified the multifaceted role of government in influencing the supply of trained manpower through educational and vocational training programmes; through the availability of finance capital, interest rates and fiscal policies (especially towards savings); the provision of transportation and communications infrastructure; the degree of rivalry between innovating, or potentially innovating, firms; the market structures within which firms operate, including the ease or difficulty with which they may conclude cooperative alliances; environmental regulations; purchasing standards; entrepreneurial incentives and the work ethos; the protection of intellectual property rights; and so on. Each of these policies, in its own way, may influence the ability and motivation of both domestic and foreign-owned firms to enhance their value-adding activities. However, of no less importance is the way in which these policies are implemented and integrated with each other. Let us explain what we mean.

For the most part, in advanced industrial societies, at least, government policies are geared towards achieving a different mix of economic and social objectives. Seldom, in the past, have the upgrading of national resources and the promotion of competitiveness been key strategic objectives. In other words, although it may be recognized that competition, education, fiscal, environmental and other policies may affect the innovatory capabilities of the country, this is rarely the main focus of such policies. Viewed from the perspective of advancing competitiveness, then, such policies often appear piecemeal, uncoordinated and inefficient. Moreover, government policies aimed at *directly* influencing innovatory capacity are often less successful than they might be simply because the rest of government policy is not conducive to this objective!

It is not the purpose of this chapter to make a comparison between the attitudes and policy measures of different governments that directly and indirectly impinge upon innovating capacity and the role played by MNEs. However, there can be little doubt of the diversity of such attitudes and policies, and their effectiveness. The contrast between the holistic and coordinated economic strategies of the Japanese and Koreans – geared towards a systematic upgrading of their resources and innovatory capabilities – and the fragmented and uncoordinated micro-economic policies of many Western nations, has been well documented, for example, by Porter (1990).[29] Even the organization of R&D policies may differ. Henry Ergas (1988), for example, distinguishes between the 'mission' oriented technological policies of the US, UK and France, with the 'diffusion' oriented policies of Germany, Switzerland and Sweden, which he suggests will have very different effects on the types and structures of innovatory capacity.

Much less attention has been paid to policies towards the creation or diffusion of innovatory capabilities by foreign firms, or indeed to the location of R&D by domestic MNEs. Yet we have seen that for the leading innovatory countries, at least, both the proportion of registered US patents accounted for by foreign-owned firms and the proportion of patents registered by their own firms attributable to research outside their home countries, is rising (Cantwell and Hodson, 1991).

Why should it matter who owns or controls the innovatory capacity of a country? Consider, first, the case of inward investment. The simple economic answer is that as long as the social rate of return from inward investment (which is equal to the value added less profits accruing to the foreign owners) is greater than the opportunity cost of the resources used, it is likely to be beneficial. This condition is easier to identify than to measure, particularly over any length of time. The critical issue is not so much the extent to which the investment of foreign affiliates yields a higher domestic value added than that of indigenous firms, or to whether outward investment yields a higher rate of return than that of domestic investment, but of how, through their product and innovatory policies, contacts with suppliers and customers, competitive stimuli and entrepreneurial example, foreign and domestic MNEs may better upgrade indigenous resources and advance economic welfare, as compared with domestic or uninational firms.

The basic concern over the impact of inward investment on innovatory capacity may be illustrated with reference to the current wave of Japanese manufacturing investment in the UK – although in many ways this is a 'reprise' of some of the anxieties that have been articulated by developing countries for many years now. Here there appear to be two main worries. The first is lest the Japanese undertake only low value-added activities in the UK and centralize their innovatory activities in Japan. The argument then goes on to assume that, by their competitive strategies, they will drive out local firms

which perform higher value-added activities. The innovatory base of the UK then becomes eroded, helping the Japanese economy further to strengthen their indigenous capacity and Japanese MNEs better to penetrate global markets. One country's vicious circle of asset decumulation then becomes another's virtuous circle of asset accumulation. The second anxiety has less to do with the way in which Japanese MNEs may or may not control the amount and kind of resources transferred and more with the way in which these are used. The argument is that what is perceived good for the global objectives of Japanese multinationals is not necessarily good for the development of the UK economy.

Now, there is nothing new about these concerns. However, because of the increasing importance attributed by countries (particularly advanced industrialized countries) to upgrading the productivity of their resources and the way these are used, the contribution of MNEs to innovatory capacity is being more and more judged from this viewpoint (Inman and Burton, 1990).

However, while these anxieties are understandable, they are based on a whole set of assumptions which may or may not be justified. First, it is virtually certain that, had not the greater part of Japanese manufacturing investment come to the UK, it would have been directed elsewhere in the EC and the UK would have been faced with the same competitive pressure. Second, it cannot be assumed that the UK resources used by Japanese investors would have been put to better use elsewhere in the economy, for example, by indigenous firms. In this instance, much depends on the macro-economic and organizational policies pursued by the UK government and the relative efficiency of resource usage by UK and Japanese firms.

Third, we have seen that the presence of foreign-owned firms may not only stimulate indigenous firms to be more efficient, but may also help to create and sustain centres of R&D activity which yield agglomerative economies of benefit to competitors. Fourth, even if it could be demonstrated that Japanese investment weakens the innovatory capacity of the sectors in which it invests, it might well be that the resources would be of even greater value if they were used elsewhere in the host economy and that inward investment performs a useful restructuring function.

Much, of course, depends on the assumptions made about the adequacy of the existing eco-structure for innovatory capacity and the role of government in implementing resource-allocative mechanisms which best lead to the improvement of the quality and use of human, physical and financial resources at the lowest possible cost. Such policies do not only relate to innovatory activities *per se*, but also to those that affect these activities (e.g. anti-trust, interest rates, public procurement, education and training, fiscal, transport and communications, and trade and investment policies). Innovatory competitiveness in a modern global economy depends, first and foremost, on the pursuance of pro-competitive public policies and on the provision of adequate supportive infrastructures (Davidson, 1988).

One of the difficulties in evaluating the economic impact of inbound MNE activity on technological capacity where intermediate product markets are imperfect and distorted is that it is difficult to evaluate the true economic worth of the resources used. Almost all the markets identified contain elements of imperfection. Sometimes, governments add to these imperfections by imposing import quotas, offering regional subsidies, regulating prices, and so on. Sometimes they may help eradicate them (e.g. by anti-trust policies and reducing uncertainties). However, when assessing the response of policy makers to inward and outward direct investment, it is entirely possible that the effects are not as beneficial as they might be, either because of market distortions or because of the failure of markets correctly to signal the need for socially beneficial innovatory-related activities. Rather than controlling the activities, it is far better to enact policies, which, taking cognizance of the globalization of markets, will best enable them to upgrade and restructure their resources, to meet the needs of both domestic and international consumers (World Bank, 1991).

We accept, of course, that however much governments may seek to put their internal economic affairs in order, they may still be faced with structural distortions in international markets caused by other governments seeking to advance the interests of their own national champions. Where these cannot be regulated or neutralized by international action or negotiation, it is entirely understandable that the disadvantaged governments may wish to respond by some kind of retaliatory action, such as trade or industrial strategies which may directly affect the innovatory capacity of domestic and foreign-owned firms.

11.9.2 Specific policies of governments to influence the technological impact of MNEs

We turn finally to consider how the impact of inbound MNE activity directly affects the objectives of host countries and, given these objectives, how they fit into the wider goals of government policy. What might or what should countries do about it? Is it possible to identify an optimum policy or set of policies of government?

We might break down these questions into three parts. The first is to identify the attitude of host governments to the foreign ownership and control of technology and/or technological capacity. The second is to identify the options open to policy makers. The third is to indicate the conditions under which one or more of these options might be the most appropriate. In turn, these conditions are likely to depend on the nature of the interaction between the technological advantages of MNEs and the specific characteristics of the countries involved, as well as the extent to which firms perceive that these advantages can best be organized by internalizing the market for them.

A somewhat different, but related, approach is to suggest that host government policies reflect the relative bargaining strengths of the MNEs and the host countries, which, in turn, will depend on their respective opportunity costs. Thus, a country that badly needs a particular technology or technological capacity which a particular foreign firm is uniquely able to supply, but which can be exploited from a variety of foreign locations, is in a much weaker position than one that has a strong indigenous capacity to disseminate and absorb the foreign technology, and, if needs be, can produce the technology itself or buy it from the open market. Once again, the relevant bargaining model is one which assesses the role of MNEs as creators, transferers and disseminators of technology in terms of its impact on general economic and social welfare, and not just that of its technological goals. We take up the issue of the influence of bargaining outcomes on the policies of home and host countries in more detail in Chapter 20.

11.9.3   Attitudes and strategies of host governments

We have suggested that host countries may differ considerably in their attitudes towards the foreign ownership of technology and technological capacity and that this may affect their ability to attract new inward investment. Even governments that believe in the virtues of free trade and economic interdependence are uncomfortable if certain technologies and organizational competences (notably those considered necessary for it to fulfil its strategic and political objectives) are not within their own ambience of control. To the extent, too, that the political power or influence of a country is strongly dependent on its economic strength, and that this largely rests on its technological capabilities, a government may be reluctant to surrender an undue amount of this capability to foreign ownership. In this respect, an industrial country is likely to protect its technology-related assets jealously in the same way a resource rich country might not wish to surrender ownership or control of its key resources to foreign investors.

Finally a country's strategies and policies towards its technological capacity will depend not only on how it perceives that actual or potential foreign direct investors will react, but also on the policies and strategies of other countries. This will especially be the case where technology is used to promote export-oriented value-added activities.

Let us now consider some actions which a government might pursue towards inward technology transfer, owned or controlled by foreign MNEs, and the conditions under which these are most likely to be successful. Exhibit 11.2 identifies some options open to it. It should be observed that the policies are not necessarily mutually exclusive. For example, a government may decide to eliminate restrictions on the use of transferred technology while encouraging the development of its own technological capabilities.

(i)   *Do nothing*   Such a policy may be favoured by two kinds of countries. The first are those that are strong and confident that their macro-economic and organizational strategies are adequate both to attract the right kind of foreign technology and to ensure the benefits accruing from it are optimized or near optimized. Such countries are likely to be large and

innovation driven. More often than not, they will be substantial foreign direct investors and exporters of technology in their own right.

Alternatively, countries may adopt a 'do nothing' policy from a position of weakness. Such weakness may reflect ignorance as to the effects of inward foreign investment, or the inability to implement appropriate policies to deal with it. It may also reflect a lack of bargaining power to force the MNE to adapt its technology to local needs, or an inadequacy of indigenous capability to develop an alternative to inbound investment. This position applies to most of the smaller natural resource driven developing countries as well as to other host countries, in sectors in which foreign MNEs possess key O-specific advantages, who are competing intensively among themselves for the same investment.

A variant of the 'do nothing' policy is to give a variety of fiscal incentives to promote inward MNE activities but impose no penalties or requirements. The sole aim of such a policy is to attract investment away from other countries. Such a policy is more likely to be pursued by relatively weak countries in the investment-driven stage of development. Strong countries usually combine an integrated and market-supporting package of incentives and disincentives.

(ii)   *Limit certain sectors to domestic ownership*   All countries disallow the ownership or control of some sectors to fall into foreign hands. In the past, such control has usually been introduced to achieve strategic and cultural objectives, rather than to reduce or limit the country's technological dependence (see Chapter 19). The increasing role of technology as a force influencing economic prosperity has, however, added to the need of countries to protect their interests in this area. This has led to more industries being identified as technologically sensitive. At the same time, the costs of technological self-reliance have risen, as have the opportunities for trade in technology or technologically-based products. Moreover, the movement towards regional integration has led to a reduction of controls over intra-regional investment and technological transfers. The net result of these forces has been an increase in the division of labour in the production of many kinds of technology; yet, with some countries becoming even more sensitive of the need to be at least partially self-sufficient in the production of

---

Exhibit 11.2 How to maximize benefits from technology transfer: some options available to host governments.

Do nothing.

Identify and set entry conditions for new and/or existing foreign investors.

Reserve certain sectors for local producers.

Specific performance requirements from MNE affiliates.

Try and eliminate restrictions on use of technology supplied by MNEs.

Limit technology payments (royalties) to foreign firms.

Improve understanding of costs and benefits of technology: improve negotiating abilities.

Solicit competitive bids from alternative technology suppliers.

Encourage MNEs to sell technology on contractual basis.

Limit duration of technology contracts.

Encourage indigenous production of technology.

Encourage market structure most conducive to an efficient inflow and dissemination of technology.

Impose training obligations on MNEs.

Give more incentives to MNEs to set up R&D facilities in host countries.

Encourage development of state-owned enterprises (as in Brazil and India).

Provide fiscal and other incentives to encourage privately financed R&D to the point where its marginal social benefits equate with its marginal costs.

Reconsider macro-economic and macro-organization policies so as to remove structural distortions in cross-border technology markets.

Encourage development of clusters of supporting or related activities, and also interaction between universities, cooperative research associations and private firms.

Support industrial restructuring and by general educational and other policies facilitate the upgrading of indigenous human capital.

Liberalize technology and other markets which distort terms of technology transfer and diffusion.

---

some key technologies. Often, MNEs may play an important role in a country's technological strategies through their policies towards the location of technological capacity (see Section (iv) below).

(iii) *Limit the amount of inward investment* This is a variant of the previous policy: some direct investment is freely permitted, but only so long as there remains a viable domestic alternative. In practice, several industrial countries, which pursue basically liberal policies towards investment, deploy this kind of strategy. Three arguments are usually put forward in its justification. The first is that without some limitation on inward investment there would be little hope of the indigenous sector reaching its full innovation-driven potential and becoming competitive in international markets, either as a producer of technology (know-why) or of the goods the technology embodies (know-how). This is essentially a variant of the infant industry argument as applied to technology as a commodity in its own right. The second argument is that the foreign MNEs are supported by their own governments or are pursuing anti-competitive practices. This is essentially the argument of the strategic trade economists (Krugman, 1986; Stegeman, 1989). The third is the concern that the withdrawal of inbound direct investment would leave the sector bereft of any indigenous capability in a defence or strategically-sensitive sector (see Chapter 19).

Again, while there is some force in these arguments, particularly where governments are actively seeking to promote the dynamic comparative advantage of their location-bound resources in a world of rapidly increasing technological costs and interdependence, there is a danger that anything approaching an isolationist or self-sufficient policy will be too costly to make any economic sense. This, of course, has long since been recognized by small industrialized or industrializing economies, such as Belgium, Switzerland and Singapore. Increasingly, even the largest and most prosperous economies (e.g. the US) and the most nationalistic (e.g. India and China) are accepting that, to paraphrase John Donne's words, 'no country is a technological island' – especially in respect of advanced or cutting-edge technologies. Of course, a reliance on foreign technology does not necessarily mean that the use of that technology will be controlled by foreign companies, but in practice, most technologies required by other than the least advanced (e.g. some African) economies, is supplied by MNEs either via foreign direct investment or by non-equity contractual arrangements and strategic alliances.

(iv) *Specify performance requirements for foreign investors* To some extent or another, explicitly or implicitly, most governments either encourage or insist on foreign affiliates fulfilling some performance requirements. Until the early 1970s, these require-ments were mainly directed to saving foreign cur-rency and increasing domestic employment. Since then they have widened to embrace the discourage-ment of the setting up of purely assembling or 'screwdriver' plants by foreign firms, both in de-veloped and developing countries, the promotion of the transfer of 'state of the art' technology and the creation or upgrading of technological capacity. The debate over the local content of Japanese auto affiliates in the EC is not only driven by employment considerations, but by concern over the technological competitiveness of the European motor component industry *vis à vis* its Japanese counterpart. To avoid

being dubbed Trojan horses, Japanese MNEs are having to accelerate their establishment of innova-tory facilities and to demonstrate their support for, and participation in, university-funded research and science parks.

How far governments of host countries are right to encourage or insist on such technological perfor-mance requirements is another question. Like any other market intervention, much depends on the extent to which the actions of government are likely to enhance long-term allocative and technical effi-ciency and lower social transaction costs, or whether they are simply another form of market-distorting protectionism. Clearly, as Japan, Taiwan, South Korea and France have shown, there is a case for government playing its role in facilitating the devel-opment of a technological base by providing, or offering incentives for others to provide, the neces-sary infrastructural services, by raising technical standards, and by prompting both public and private institutions to upgrade the level of technological capacity up to a point where its marginal social benefits are equal to its marginal social costs (Dunning, 1991a).

In parallel with performance requirements, many countries offer foreign companies incentives to engage in particular kinds of value-added activity. By such means as tax concessions, patent protection, R&D, subsidies or grants, government procurement policies, the funding of research councils, the finance of higher education, and the initiation and funding of vocational training or retraining schemes, govern-ments can play a key role in affecting the level and structure of technology-related activities. Like in-digenous firms, foreign subsidiaries can and do take advantage of these provisions. In addition, some countries might give special inducements to foreign investors, such as the relaxation of performance requirements (e.g. with respect to access to local capital markets and the sourcing of components).

Once again, evidence on the effects of such schemes is inconclusive and the debate as to whether it is preferable to encourage foreign affiliates to undertake R&D or to develop indigenous tech-nological capability (see option (vi)) is a matter unresolved in the literature.[30]

(v) *Discourage restrictive clauses on technology transfer* For a variety of reasons, it may be in the best interests of foreign MNEs to attach terms and conditions to technology transferred to their subsidiaries. Many of these accord with normal commercial practice and would be quite acceptable to a government if imposed by the head office of a domestic firm on one of its branch plants located elsewhere in the same country. The difference is that while, in the latter case, the benefits resulting from the imposed conditions may redound to the good of both firm and country, decisions taken by a foreign-owned firm which affect the allocation of its output between the countries in which it operates, are likely to have mixed consequences on the cross-border distribution of economic welfare. For example, to the extent that a host country may be adversely affected by a decision by a foreign MNE to limit the R&D activities of its subsidiary in that country, to restrict the output it may produce, or the markets it may serve from the technology it transfers, such provisions may be deemed 'restrictive' to advancing its own welfare. However, *de facto* it may be exceedingly difficult to distinguish between the act of controlling the use made of technology resulting from FDI, which may be interpreted as a restrictive practice, and the act of not transferring technological capacity in the first place, which, while no less damaging, may not be regarded as a restrictive practice *per se*.

Nevertheless, by a variety of means, host governments may be able to discourage MNEs from imposing unwelcome restrictions on the first kind on subsidiaries. Foremost among these is to make it economically worthwhile for the foreign MNEs *not* to wish to impose such restrictions (e.g. by the removal of some kinds of performance requirements and improving the attractions of their indigenous resources or markets). Such actions may include a reduction in transaction costs, for example, those arising from political uncertainty, insufficient protection against abuse of property rights and an ineffective science and technology policy. A development strategy designed to protect domestic firms from foreign competition rather than encouraging them to develop their comparative advantage in world markets is unlikely to induce foreign-owned firms to develop new technologies for use in products intended for export markets. Moreover, while several studies have shown that the setting up of export enclaves by MNEs may do little to promote indigenous technological development, a healthy home market may be a precursor to innovating new products and processes specific to the needs of domestic consumers, but which may later be exported to foreign markets.[31]

(vi) *Influence terms and conditions of technology transfer* It is obviously in the interests of host countries to acquire technology from foreign sources at the minimum real cost. At the same time, it may wish to obtain the level and type of technology that will best contribute to its long-term economic and other goals. The two objectives need not be inconsistent with each other, but if a host government presses a foreign firm (already producing in the country) to accept a lower return for its technology than its opportunity cost, the latter is likely both to reduce its flow of future technology and lessen its inducement to transfer (or create new) technological capacity, which otherwise would have benefited the host country.

The extent to which a host country has any latitude to influence the terms on which it obtains foreign-owned or sourced technology will depend firstly on the market conditions in which it supplied, and secondly on its ability to extract the highest possible share of economic rent (or consumers' surplus) generated by the transaction. Where technology is standardized and supplied by several producers on the open market, then its price is likely to reflect its true opportunity cost. At the other extreme, technology may be highly idiosyncratic and owned by only one firm. Moreover, because of market failure, the firm may wish to add value to this technology itself. In so far as it wishes to do so from a foreign location, it will then seek to transfer it internally. Assume, finally, that the technology and/or the technological capacity associated with it is highly sought after by several host countries, but cannot be economically utilized by more than one or two of these. In such a situation, not only is the value of the technology likely to be well above its competitive price, but the selling firm may be in a strong bargaining position *vis à vis* the host country because its options are so much wider. Most types of technology transfer by MNEs involve trading situations somewhere in between these two extremes.

Even accepting some of the exogenous factors making for a high price for some technologies, host countries may still not be obtaining their technology on the most favourable conditions. This is because their competitive advantage or bargaining power is weak. Chapter 20 will discuss the issues of negotiating and bargaining in some detail. For the moment we would simply observe that countries may not be optimizing the terms on which they acquire technology from MNEs for two reasons. The first is lack of information or understanding about:

(1) the technology being supplied (e.g. how valuable it is to the host country, how easy or difficult it is to obtain from other sources, how costly it is to produce);

(2) the production and transaction costs facing supplying firms and their opportunities for selling the technology or engaging in technological capacity in other countries;

(3) the terms and conditions offered by other countries for the same technology.

The second reason concerns the bargaining capabilities of the host administration of the country. This is partly a matter of negotiating competence *per se* and partly a question of the inducements a host country can offer foreign MNEs to supply the technology or create the technological capacity it needs. Foremost among these inducements are a good supply of professional and skilled manpower, a well motivated labour force, an adequate local supplier capability and an appreciation, by the regulatory authorities, of the need for some MNEs to engage in acts of resource allocation and organizational methods which may not be perceived to be in the best interests of the host country. Finally, the extent to which a country may be able to purchase similar technology or to buy (or create) a similar technology by another route (e.g. licensing or local production) will also affect its bargaining position.

Improving the terms of technology transfer, then, may require changes in policies, institutional mechanisms and administrative procedures, which may affect the wider costs and benefits of FDI. Indeed, this is a general conclusion on the possible reactions to all aspects of FDI. All too frequently, economic policy is viewed in a fragmented, issue-specific way, when what is required is a holistic and integrated policy towards foreign direct investment (which may well be the same as that towards *all*

investment into which specific areas of policy fit like pieces of a jigsaw). We shall amplify on this point in Part 4 of this volume.

(vii) *Encouraging indigenous technological development* An alternative to importing technology is for a country to produce it itself. This may be more costly, at least in the short run, but if it eventually leads to a more efficient allocation of resources, it may be a sensible thing to do. The economic justification for non-market intervention by governments to develop technological and organizational capacity essentially rests on the reasons why markets fail to fulfil this task. The fact that technology is supplied under conditions of monopoly and that there are costs involved in promoting dynamic comparative advantage, suggests that the market mechanism, by itself, may not always ensure an optimum supply of technology. Often individual enterprises (or the capital market in general) may view the risks of investment differently from that of the community of which they are part. Also, where the potential technology producers are sheltered from competition, they may lack the initiative or the imperative to develop their full potential.

Governments have long accepted that the social costs and benefits of innovating activity are not the same as the private costs and benefits, and that extra market incentives may be necessary to induce the socially optimum level of activity. At the same time, governments may be tempted to go beyond this level of encouragement, without properly evaluating the net benefits of the expenditure involved. Sometimes they may subsidize R&D by their own firms to avoid undue domination by companies who, for the most part, are not under their jurisdiction.

Indigenous R&D might also be inhibited because of an inappropriate industrial structure and the unwillingness of the participants in the market – perhaps because of higher adjustment costs or of anti-monopoly legislation – to create production units of a size and technological strength capable of undertaking R&D. Here, governments may assist by facilitating (or not prohibiting) mergers, acquisitions or cooperative alliances, or, indeed, by establishing or strengthening state-owned corporations. This, again, is a strategy not specifically or necessarily intended to achieve only technological goals, and is widespread in some developing countries, particularly in resource-based sectors (e.g. oil) and service industries (e.g. banking, insurance, hotels and wholesale trade). Among the developing countries, India, Korea, Brazil and Mexico have been most prone to follow this route. In the industrialized world, for many years and by a variety of means, including the outright nationalization of private companies, both the UK and French governments have sought to encourage and promote their own national champions against the inroads made by the large US MNEs, particularly IBM. In several other sectors (e.g. biotechnology, consumer electronics and motor vehicles), contemporary reaction to the *Le Defi Japanaise*[32] is causing European governments to look more favourably at national and cross-border mergers and alliances.

Again, it is difficult to identify the conditions in which governments *should* intervene to ensure that the best of some sectors of activity remains in indigenous hands. Similarly, it is difficult to suggest the optimum modality of that intervention. Partly this is because a mixture of economic and non-economic motives are involved, and partly because any such social cost–benefit analysis must involve a set of heroic hypotheses and assumptions. On economic grounds, however, it might be argued that this is only relevant if and when the foreign ownership of value-added activity leads to a less desirable pattern of resource allocation or industrial restructuring than would have occurred under domestic ownership. Often, at the end of the day, it is the uncertainty over, or inability to control, the behaviour of foreign affiliates which is perceived to be less compatible with national economic interests than that of domestically-owned firms, which host governments may attempt to counteract by limiting the dependence on foreign-owned technology. However, it is also possible to argue that this position is becoming less tenable as an increasing number of countries are participating in regional trading blocs, and where firms from within the region may influence, for good or bad, the technological capabilities of a country within the region, no less than can foreign firms from outside the region.

(viii) *Encouraging cross-border collaborative R&D*
Competition from foreign MNEs might also encourage governments to engage in cross-border technological cooperation. Nowhere is this more

clearly an issue than in Western Europe. At the initiative of the European Commission, several inter-country research programmes have been set up, which have been wholly or partly financed by the European Community (EC). Among the best known of these programmes is the European Strategic Project on Information Technology (ESPRIT) which was initiated in 1984 by Etienne Davignon, an EC commissioner who had earlier helped to revitalize and rationalize the European steel industry.

ESPRIT is a ten year, multibillion dollar research programme which is targeting the R&D-intensive sectors of the information technology industry, in which the challenge of US and Japanese competition is especially fierce. The programme has three main objectives. First, to help provide European-owned firms with the technologies they need to be competitive in the 1990s. Second, to promote intra-European cooperation among these firms. And third, to develop internationally acceptable standards.

From the outset, there was a conflict among European policy makers as to whether subsidiaries of non-EC owned firms should be allowed to participate in ESPRIT. In the end a compromise was struck, by which in Phase 1 of ESPRIT, which lasted until the end of 1987, membership was reserved for firms based in EC countries; in Phase 2 it was to be open to partners from other European countries. Non-European firms were only allowed to participate in a limited way through their EC subsidiaries. Up to the time Fujitsu gained control of ICL in 1990, they had been involved in less than 10% of the projects involved.

There is general agreement that ESPRIT has been successful in promoting the exchange of information and developing standards, but judgement is more cautious regarding the extent to which it is achieving the first of its three objectives. There is more general disquiet as to whether the principle of using government subsidiaries to finance technological development – particularly start-up ventures of small entrepreneurial firms – is the most cost-effective way of creating and sustaining technological capability, even in the 'pre-competitive' stage of R&D activity. In this regard, the removal of all remaining barriers to the flow of people, assets, goods and services, within the EC consequent upon the completion of the internal market at the end of

1992, may act as a no less powerful incentive to achieving the balance of collaboration and competition among EC firms, and between EC and non-EC firms, which is best able to promote indigenous innovatory capacity.

One other collaborative research programme which deserves brief mention[33] is that of the European Research Coordinating Agency (EUREKA) which was set up in 1985 as a European response to the US Strategic Defense Initiative programme (SDI). EUREKA's objective is to facilitate cooperative R&D with commercial applications, rather than basic research, which is the focus of ESPRIT. EUREKA is a pan-European initiative, which by the end of the 1980s had funded – to the tune of $6 billion – more than a thousand European companies to cooperate on projects ranging from biotechnology and energy to machine tools and robotics.

(ix) *Attempt to obtain knowledge through alternative routes; unbundling the package* The previous paragraphs have shown that host countries have two major concerns over importing technology or technological capability through the good offices of MNEs. The first relates to the extent, pattern and terms of technology transfer, and the second to the control exerted over the way in which the technology is used. One way in which host countries may try and overcome the second concern is to try and buy technology on the open market, and in so doing separate this capability from the other resources associated with FDI and the control exercised over their deployment. Both concerns relate to the effect such reliance on foreign-owned technology has on the current ESP configuration of the recipient country and on its future asset accumulation and diamond of competitive advantage.

The question at issue is whether such a strategy is likely to reduce or increase the net benefits of obtaining technology from foreign-owned firms. The argument that a country may pay less for its technology by buying it from the open market than through inbound investment presupposes that, in the absence of government intervention or encouragement, this would not have occurred. However, where technology is currently, or is likely to be, supplied through a 100% owned subsidiary, it may be appropriate for the government to consider forcing the foreign firm to shed part of its ownership

and the control over the technology it supplies. Where this does happen, there is an implicit assumption that the country can obtain its technology at a lower real cost and/or without as many strings attached to it. Whether or not this is the case depends on the composition of the market for technology. Where there is only one supplier, it may make little difference to the purchaser *how* it is provided. Indeed, if the supplying firm is forced to relinquish some of the external benefits of controlling the use of the technology, it may charge the purchaser a higher price for it. This, of course, may still be considered worthwhile by the host nation if domestic ownership offers other benefits.

Where there are many sellers, then, a host country may well benefit from getting the technology from the market if the MNE charges a higher price. However, if this is the case, the MNE is likely to have already adjusted its price accordingly. On the other hand, there may be considerable benefits or externalities to the host country in buying its technology along with other ingredients of the package of FDI. Indeed, there is reason to suppose that host governments frequently underestimate the transaction costs associated with the management and absorption of technology bought from independent firms. Rarely does an MNE supply *only* technical knowledge to its affiliates. Along with the hardware usually comes installation, operating and servicing advice. Where a system is based on several different techniques, the MNE will provide guidance as to the organization and management of the system. In addition, an affiliate may receive regular modifications and updating of technology from the investing firm, which may also allow scientists and technicians from the subsidiary to visit its own R&D laboratories and training facilities. Thus, being part of a global family unit may offer considerable benefits to the local affiliate (and the country in which it is situated).

The extent to which there are likely to be alternatives to FDI by which a host country can acquire technology will clearly depend on the type of technology being considered, the need to adapt it to local resources and the capabilities of host countries to provide the technological infrastructure to assimilate and manage it. We have already suggested that firms are often reluctant to externalize cross-border transfers of technology where the transaction costs of the market are high and there are worthwhile production or transactional benefits of hierarchical control. The evidence further suggests that the technology and organizational skills associated with market-seeking investment directed to national resource or investment-driven economies is more likely to be available from external sources than is that associated with efficiency-seeking investment directed to innovation-driven economies. Similarly, countries are most likely to want to externalize their technology flows where they perceive the advantages of integrating or forming alliances with local firms, relative to those within a multinational network, are likely to be powerful. These, too, may be greater in the case of market-seeking MNE activity, but as a long-term strategy, the sensible integration of all forms of resource acquisition may be preferable. However, it is the non-technological benefits of the presence of multinational affiliates (e.g. access to markets) which make such alternative modalities (which do not provide these externalities) less attractive than they might otherwise be.

In conclusion, it would seem that there is a tendency for governments of host countries to overestimate the availability of, and cost of seeking out and acquiring, foreign technology not owned by MNEs, as well as their own capabilities to assimilate and manage this technology. Governments are also prone to undervalue the benefits of technology being supplied by MNEs as part of a package of resources, while underestimating the costs of obtaining technology from other sources and of supplying the back-up resources for unbundled technology. On the other hand, there is no denying that the control of technology and technological capacity by MNEs will not always optimize the asset-accumulation or economic-restructuring programmes of host countries. The Japanese case of limiting inward MNE activity, while making full use of other routes to acquire foreign technology, is particularly instructive. It shows that it is possible for a country to move through the initial stages of its investment development path without undue reliance on FDI. However, it also shows that it can only do so if it has the right ESP configuration, and particularly a strong technological back up and an entrepreneurial and work ethic dedicated to the improvement of product quality and consumer satisfaction. The Indian example demonstrates that economic progress can be made with little or no FDI, but in this case the pace

of change has been very much slower. Although India has one of the best educational and technological infrastructures of all developing countries, much of it is inefficiently organized and several facets of its diamond of competitive advantage are weak (Lall, 1985). If it were permitted to do so, FDI could play a valuable role, both directly, by contributing to the technological base, and indirectly, by providing the stimulus for a more efficient organization of resources.[34]

11.10   CONCLUSIONS

It is difficult to generalize on the direct or indirect effects of MNEs on the innovatory capacity of host countries. So much depends on the reasons for the ownership and cross-border location of value-added activities of MNEs, and on the response of indigenous firms to them. This, in turn, will depend upon the eco-structure and institutional environment in which R&D is organized and located, and on the role of government in shaping this environment and facilitating the upgrading of its resources.

In the past, countries have adopted different policies towards inward direct investment according to how they have perceived that such investment might affect national economic objectives. Two main views have been expressed. The first is that FDI speeds up the process of economic development and restructuring. It does so both by providing technology, entrepreneurship and organizational skills at a lower cost than any alternative usage of resources, and by its competitive stimulus and spill-over effects on the rest of the economy. The alternative view is that, while in the short run this may, or may not, be the case, in the long run it is only likely to happen if MNEs do not distort (or add to the distortion) of asset or product markets, and as long as the control exerted over their affiliates' activities is consistent with the innovatory goals of the countries in which they operate. To a certain extent, the globalization of markets and the growth of intra-industry trade and investment is helping to bridge these views by directing more attention to the macro-organizational actions of governments in setting the conditions in which MNEs are able efficiently to perform the role required of them.[35]

The perception that, because they are faced with market distortions and failures, MNEs will not, left to themselves, ensure the best cross-border distribution of innovatory capacity has dominated the thinking of countries like Korea and Japan. In these cases, not only has government policy towards outward direct investment been geared to sustaining the domestic innovatory capacity of the home country (Ozawa, 1990), but it has deliberately limited inward investment until indigenous technological capability is sufficiently strong for such investment to interact with it in a mutually beneficial way. Germany and Singapore have followed a different strategy. They appear to believe that inward investment is the quickest (and often the cheapest) way of upgrading local technological capability, and that the opportunity cost of such investment is more than covered by the increases in social productivity it brings about. The debate is by no means resolved, and is being increasingly complicated by the fact that the avenues of creating or obtaining innovatory capacity are widening both for firms and countries. Joint ventures, strategic alliances, subcontracting arrangements and inter-government cooperation are some of these ways, each of which has its own particular costs and benefits for the participating partners and for the countries involved.

We would make three final points. The first is that, however understandable it may be that countries wish to advance their technological prowess, and however much one might judge the success of inward and outward investment in these terms, all countries cannot expect to be technologically competent in all sectors. The principle of comparative advantage is no less applicable in explaining the international allocation of R&D than it is in explaining the trade in final goods and services. Unless it is prepared to sacrifice economic welfare for other goals, no country can expect to be entirely self-sufficient in its innovatory capabilities any more than it can expect to be self-sufficient in all goods and services. So the role of the MNE must be judged not only in the light of the effect it has on the *generation* of innovatory capacity, but also on the *allocation* of that capacity; and this, in turn, on the long-term economic interests of the country concerned. Indeed, it is possible to conceive of an MNE doing a country a service by transferring R&D out of that country whenever this opens the door to more productive R&D – or, for that matter, non R&D – activities.

The second point is that, to be able to utilize efficiently the accumulated technological expertise of foreign MNEs, host governments need to pursue a positive and well defined technological strategy. Such a strategy should be part of a wider macro-organizational strategy, and be directed not only to promoting the upgrading of human skills and innovatory capacity, but also to providing the scientific and communications infrastructure that high technology MNEs regard as the *sine qua non* for their full participation in the countries in which they invest. In the case of developing countries, it has been suggested that one of the most cost-effective ways of assimilating and disseminating imported technology is to ensure there are adequate local design engineering and organizing capabilities. It is these capabilities which so often provide the critical bridge between the technology provided by the MNE, and the local innovatory capabilities and consumer needs (Huss, 1991).

The third point is this. This chapter has demonstrated that some countries may have limited power to influence the kind of technology they receive from MNEs or the terms of the technology creation or transfer. In such instances, countries may find it beneficial to group together to exchange information *inter alia* about each other's bargaining and negotiating strategies and/or to formulate common policies towards technology acquisition or the creation of technological capacity by MNEs. Chapter 21 will describe some of the multilateral strategies which countries might pursue, and such attempts as have been made by international agencies (e.g. OECD, UNCTC) to formulate codes of practice or guidelines to both MNEs and governments about the form and terms of technology transfer and/or local technology production, and the kinds of action host governments might take to ensure that such transfers will be in the best interests of their economic and other objectives.

NOTES

1 Such created assets include that of government itself, which some might perceive to be a negative asset!
2 See also Chapter 9 for a discussion of global markets and strategic alliances.
3 See UN (1992a).

4   Unless otherwise indicated, our use of the word technology in this chapter embraces both the capacity to generate technology and the technology generated by the capacity.

5   As set out more fully in Chapters 5 and 6.

6   They found, for example, that of 24 export-oriented projects examined in a number of developing countries, only two adapted product design, four adapted production equipment and four adapted production techniques. By contrast, of 53 import-substituting projects, 18 adapted product design, 18 adapted equipment and 23 adapted operating methods.

7   In the words of one manufacturer who participated in the Frank study 'we respond to income growth by offering products to people ascending the consumer products "ladder" ' (Frank, 1980, p. 74).

8   Real labour and capital costs are the costs of labour and capital adjusted for the quality of the two inputs. Thus, low wages do not necessarily mean low real labour costs. It is quite possible that a higher wage cost might be more than outweighed by higher productivity of the labour (Moxon, 1979; Pack, 1976). At the same time, it would be wrong to conclude that because some kinds of labour are inexpensive, all labour is inexpensive. An ILO report (ILO, 1984, p. 23) cites the case of foreign affiliates in Nigeria using more automated processes than in developed countries in order to economize on skilled labour.

9   See especially those of ILO (1972), Langdon (1978), and Morley and Smith (1977a).

10   Lecraw estimated production functions for each industry and the factor prices paced by each firm, and then calculated an optimum cost-minimizing technique for each firm. Finally he compared this with the actual technique adopted.

11   This section draws substantially on Dunning (1992d) and Dunning (1988b).

12   Over the same period, the UK's share of patents registered in the US fell from 17.8% to 8.8%, that of France from 10.3% to 8.0% and that of Germany from 26.0% to 22.4% (Cantwell, 1991b).

13   Defined as the share of world patenting (in the US) of a particular country in a particular industry divided by its share of world patenting (in the US) in all industries over the period 1978–84. For a discussion of the appropriability of patent data as a measurement of technological capacity, see Cantwell (1989c) and Archibugi and Pianta (1989).

14   According to Wright (1989), the fact that the technological competence of US industry is especially marked in resource-based sectors dates back to the last century, when the first technological advances were designed to promote the efficiency of US agribusiness

sectors. A rather different approach is taken by Nelson (1991) who argues that the US innovatory advantage in mass produced goods reflects the size and characteristics of the US domestic market a century ago, while her lead for most of the post-war period in higher technology sectors reflected the massive public and private investments in R&D during and after the Second World War.

15   Considering products rather than activities, the Japanese share of patents granted in the US *relative to US firms* has risen most spectacularly in the case of lasers, robots, internal combustion engines and digital computer systems (National Science Foundation, 1988). For a recent analysis of Japan's growing technological capability see Teece and Mowery (1991).

16   Other data presented by Archibugi and Pianta (1989) and based on data compiled by the World Intellectual Property Organization (WIRO) from national patent offices shows that Sweden had a marked patenting advantage in paper products, Canada and Belgium in agricultural products, the Netherlands in foodstuffs, Switzerland in textiles and chemicals, and France in nuclear engineering.

17   In a survey conducted by IMD and the World Economic Forum (1989), a group of international business executives were asked to rank (on a scale of 0 = inadequate to 100 = adequate) the vocational training facilities offered by some 32 countries. Of these, Germany was ranked highest with a score of (77.2), followed by Japan (73.9) and Switzerland (70.8). Among the lowest scorers (among developed countries) were the UK (35.7), Italy (35.1) and France (43.9). According to Tom Peters (quoted in Lincoln, 1990), Japanese companies, on average, spend three times the amount on worker training programmes than do US companies. No less significant is the fact that Japanese companies place more emphasis on training their workers to develop a broad range of skills which can be adapted to variations in the tasks required of them. By contrast, US training is much more sector or skill specific. Moreover, 57% of the PhDs in natural sciences and engineering in Japan were earned by industrial researchers submitting papers based upon their work for companies, rather than as a result of any formal training at Japanese universities (Westney, 1990).

18   This data is supported by a study by Peters (1991) of the 400 top world corporate spenders on R&D. Peters found that in the 1980s, there was a substantial growth in the number of new foreign sites in which R&D was undertaken. In particular, she cites the case of Dow who in 1990 had at least 14 overseas R&D laboratories compared with only one in 1990, while 3M had an

estimated 50 such facilities outside the US in 1979 and one hundred in 1990 (Peters, 1991, p. 9).

19 However, in six of seven industrialized countries identified by the OECD (1991), *viz* Australia, France, Japan, Netherlands, Sweden, the UK and the US, the share of the total R&D expenditures by business enterprises accounted for by foreign-controlled firms in 1987 was lower than that of the share of total manufacturing sales accounted for by such firms.

20 For an elaboration of these activities see Pearce (1989), Ghoshal and Bartlett (1990) and Pearce and Singh (1992).

21 Noticeable examples include the collaboration between Siemens and IBM (in 1990) to jointly develop a memory chip capable of storing 64 million bits of information; that between Ciba Geigy and Tanox Biosystems (1989) to develop a therapeutic agent against AIDS; that between Ciba Geigy and Nestlé (in 1988) to undertake basic research in microbial genetics; that between Aerospatiale and British Aerospace (in 1990) for the development of a second generation of supersonic airliners; and that between Thomson and Philips (in 1990) to develop a European system of high definition television (HDTV). Other examples are given by Gugler (1991) and Gugler and Dunning (1992).

22 A recent example is the setting up of Tsukuba Science City in the Ibaragi Prefecture of Japan as an international centre for R&D. Already, several government research industries and colleges are concentrated in Tsukuba; at least eleven foreign chemical companies have established R&D laboratories. According to the president of one of these companies – Bayer – 'the importance of a corporate R&D triad stretching between Japan, the US and Europe, is an essential part of a successful international strategy of any large MNE' (*Japan Update*, 1990).

23 It is claimed, for example, that this is particularly the case in the UK, which results in the words of one scholar (Stoneman, 1989) 'in the use of (technological) resources by an MNE representing a subsidy to the research of the MNE by the UK taxpayer'.

24 Some examples of the setting up of R&D facilities in the UK, see *Japan*, No. 507, 19/2/91. Nissan, Canon, Kobe Steel, Sharp, Yamouchi Pharmaceutical and Hitachi are among the Japanese MNEs active in UK science and technical parks.

25 See, for example, Chapters 4 and 7.

26 Some examples are set out in Gugler and Dunning (1992). See also Note 22. They include a five-year technology exchange agreement, signed in 1990 between Waferseale Integration with the National Semi Conductor Corporation to produce high-speed, high-density semiconductors; an agreement signed in 1990 between AT&T and Mitsubishi covering technology sharing of static random access memory (SRAM) chips; and a whole series of R&D links between the major pharmaceutical companies and the smaller biotechnology firms (e.g. Genetech and Cetus, Centocor and Synergen).

27 In the language of the eclectic paradigm, inward investment will be attracted where there are strong L-specific advantages of the host country, both for the generation of technologically-oriented O-specific advantages possessed by foreign-owned MNEs. Inward direct investment will help create or sustain a virtuous circle when it interacts with local competitors to add to indigenous production and technological capacity; it will intensify a vicious circle, which not only drives out local competitors, but, by concentrating the high value activities (e.g. innovatory) in the home countries, reduces the production capabilities and hence the L advantages of the host country.

28 As reviewed for example by Dunning (1988b) and Cantwell (1989).

29 This point is again taken up in Chapters 20 and 22.

30 Of these, the literature on Canada (see Gray, 1972; Rugman, 1981), the UK (see Dunning, 1986) and Australia (see Brash, 1966; Parry and Watson, 1978). See also Pearce *op. cit* (1987).

31 Particularly this is the case where products or production methods are adapted to meet the needs of a particular host country, which are then suitable for consumption or use in countries with similar ESP configurations. See, for example, Parry (1974).

32 *The American Challenge* written by Jacques Servan Schreiber, which pictured the possibility of US technological domination of a wide range of European industry.

33 There are several others, including RACE, a programme which is designed to promote technical collaboration and common technical standards among European companies in the field of telecommunications. For a detailed analysis of these programmes, see Mytelka and Delapierre (1990) and Mytelka (1991), as well as a very useful Harvard Business Case Study (9–389–130) prepared by Levy and Gomes-Casseres on 'Technology Collaboration in Europe'.

34 There is evidence that this is now recognized by the current (1992) Indian Administration which has considerably liberalized its policies towards inward investment. The improved investment climate and some of the recent changes introduced by the government of India to attract more FDI are described in UNCTC (1992). In spite of these changes, however, the normal limit of foreign equity participation in Indian companies remains at 40% (74% in the case of companies making substantial exports or providing sophisticated or advanced technology).

CHAPTER 12

MNEs, Technology and Innovatory Capacity: A Home Country Perspective

12.1 INTRODUCTION

Later chapters in this volume will deal with a variety of ways in which MNEs interact with both the home and host countries in which they operate. However, as technology is of such critical importance to the sustained competitiveness of modern Nation States, and the main producers and disseminators of technology are MNEs, we consider that the subject of the technological impact of MNE activity warrants two separate chapters. This is especially so since, for the great majority of capital-exporting countries, their competitive strength rests on their ability to create and effectively deploy human and physical assets. Any unwelcome erosion of such an advantage is, to them, as serious as any unacceptable exploitation of non-renewable resources is to the resource-rich developing countries.

Since technology first became an important engine of economic development and growth, governments have attempted to protect their proprietary rights. Compared with natural resources (untrained labour, land, etc), technology and technological capacity have four unique features. First, they have to be created, which costs resources.[1] Second, once created, the marginal cost of replication and usage is often very much less than that of natural resources, that is, technology has the characteristics of a public good. Third, both technological capacity and technology are mobile across space. Fourth, because of these characteristics, society has devised a variety of measures and instruments, including the patent system, both to encourage the production of technology and to protect the innovators against the dissipation of its use. In this way, technology becomes O specific, yet locationally flexible, both in its creation and use.

Nations have always sought to protect themselves against the perceived erosion of their competitive advantages. In the early 19th century, the UK, for example, disallowed or strongly discouraged its overseas possessions from producing the first generation of modern technology-embodied goods (e.g. textiles, iron and steel products). Fearful of the emergence of rivals from later industrializing nations, it tried to bar the export of knowledge, machinery, drawings and patterns. Yet such legislation failed to stop either the smuggling of technology or the emigration of well qualified technicians, managers and entrepreneurs. Indeed, it is not too much to say that in one form or another, non-resident (and especially UK) technology helped create and sustain the basis of secondary industry on which the future wealth of the US and Canada was built.[2]

As Chapter 5 has shown, until the late 19th century, the export of technology and capital were largely independent of each other; both were transacted through the market. The exception was *expatriate* investment. With the emergence of the MNE, first to seek out and control natural resources and later to seek out and control local markets, the export of technology became increasingly internalized to the point at which, as the previous chapter has shown, the great majority of commercial technological capacity is now owned by MNEs. As a consequence, in their policies towards technological exports, home governments have had to take account of the unique and special role of MNEs as cross-border carriers of technology.

We have already suggested that technology is an increasingly important component of economic growth. No less critical is the way in which it is transferred and disseminated across national boundaries and the location of technological capacity. It is also clear that the efficient creation and organization of physical and human capabilities by firms and sectors is becoming an important competitive advantage in its own right (Ghoshal and Bartlett, 1990).

The impact of MNEs on these variables is likely to be different according to the home and host countries involved and the extent and pattern of their global networking. For example, most large industrial countries, at similar stages of economic development and producing a similar range of goods and services, will engage in cross-border technological transactions to sustain, or advance, their competitive positions *vis à vis* each other. In the case of countries at different stages of development and producing different goods and services, the kind of technological capabilities each is prone to produce and use are more likely to be complementary to each other. Chapter 11 has shown how the cross-border organization of technological assets and technology may critically affect the O-specific advantages of home country firms and the dynamic comparative advantages of host countries. By the same token, it may also have an impact on the configuration of the diamonds of competitive advantage of home countries and, in particular, their ability to accumulate technological assets.

We have also indicated (in Chapter 11) that the effects of MNEs on the technological competitiveness of recipient countries depends very much on the type of the FDI undertaken; on the existing technological competences and entrepreneurial initiatives of these countries; and on the extent to which their wealth-creating institutions can efficiently absorb and build upon the assets and capabilities transferred. In particular, we considered the case of 'virtuous' and 'vicious' technology circles and used these to illustrate how, in the right circumstances, MNEs could aid a country in its pursuit of technological excellence, but in the wrong circumstances they could bring about the opposite effect.

In Chapter 4 we also suggested that MNEs may sometimes engage in FDI to exploit a technological-based O-specific advantage and sometimes to acquire new technological assets. Depending, again, on the circumstances in which both kinds of investment are made, MNEs may help raise or reduce economic welfare in the home country. Several economists,

including Caves (1982) and Teece (1985), have suggested that where MNEs operate in an efficiency-enhancing way (e.g. by overcoming 'natural' market failure in cross-border technology markets), they will enhance the long-term competitiveness of the home countries. They will do so both by promoting a more efficient international division of labour and by better exploiting the economies of common governance of cross-border activities.

By contrast, other economists (e.g. Kojima, 1978, 1990) and political scientists (e.g. Gilpin, 1975, 1981) have argued that where MNEs engage in defensive oligopolistic tactics and where governments distort prices for the technology creating and using products, such activities of MNEs are likely to be welfare reducing. In addition, it is frequently asserted that, since technology has some of the characteristics of a public good, by transferring it to a foreign country at low marginal cost, the MNE may help to erode the competitive advantage of the home country. Put another way, the recipients of the technology are not paying the full (marginal) social cost of that technology, which *inter alia* should include the possible erosion of the benefits of technological cumulation of the exporting country.

Robert Gilpin (1987) adds a political dimension to this argument. While accepting that in some circumstances the transfer of technology may be economically good for the exporting country, if the importing country should gain the higher share of the benefits, then it could well be at the expense of the political power of the exporting country. Clearly it would be foolish to push this argument to the extreme, otherwise countries which are currently industrial leaders in the world would never foster the development of their poorer counterparts. However, there can be little doubt that in today's acutely competitive environment that some kind of tradeoff between absolute economic well-being and relative political power is inevitable.

Nevertheless, perceptions change and yesterday's political 'enemies' may be tomorrow's friends. If one did not believe this, one would be highly sceptical of the current efforts of the US and European administrations to offer technical assistance to the Soviet Union. For almost certainly, because of the backwardness of the Soviet Union, if such schemes were successful her *relative* economic progress and rate of asset accumulation will outstrip

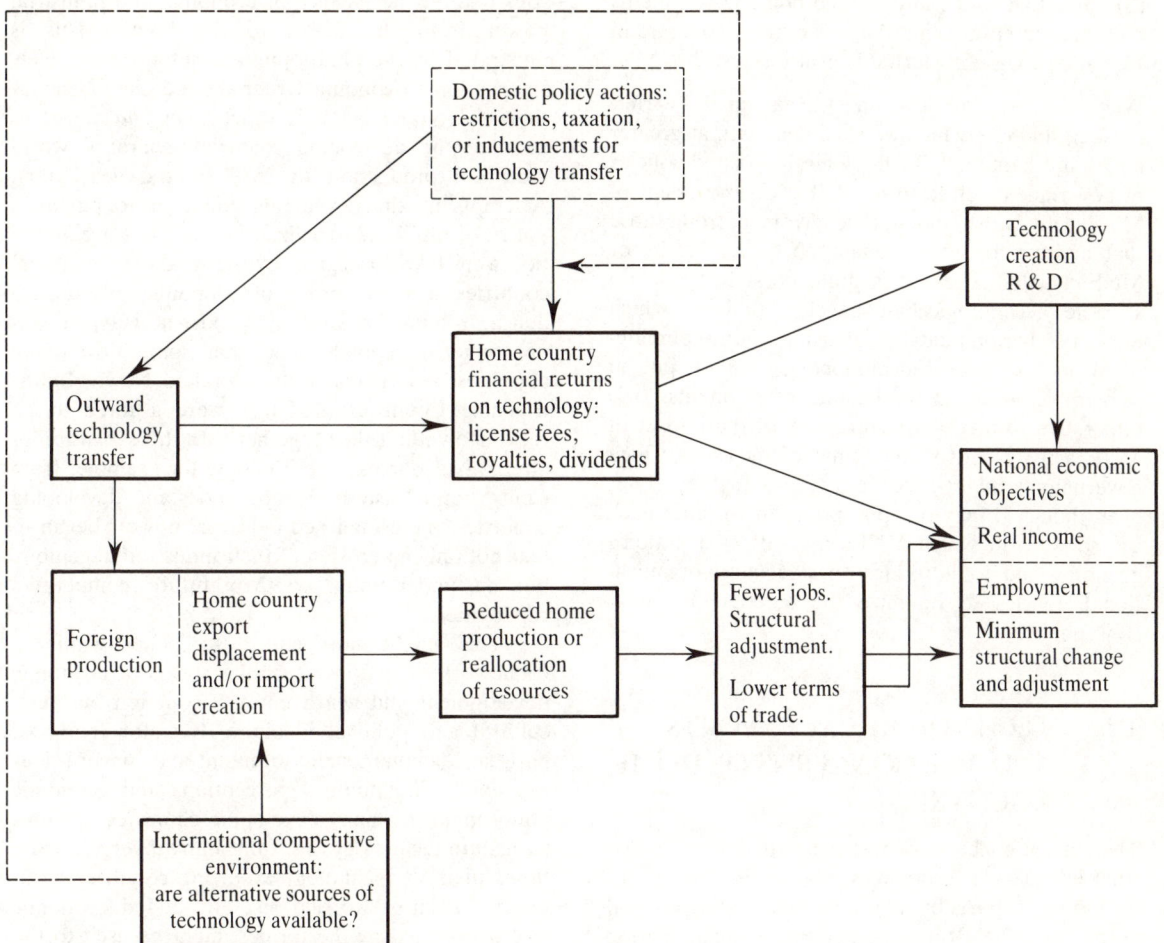

Figure 12.1 Linkages between technology transfer and home country economic objectives.
Source: Hawkins and Gladwin (1981).

that of the US, just as that of Japan has done *vis à vis* the US (to whom it owes a great technological debt) since the mid 1960s.

Figure 12.1 (reproduced from Hawkins and Gladwin, 1981) identifies some of the concerns only expressed by home countries over the export of technology. Some of them are primarily non-economic; they are considered more fully in Chapter 19. Some are to do with the more general effects of MNE activity (though made possible by exports of technology) on jobs, the balance of payments and industrial structure. Some of these effects are dealt with in later chapters. Although it may be difficult to separate the various effects of technology transfer, as far as possible the chapter will focus its attention on the consequences of outward FDI for the technological capacity of the home country.

In particular, it will address three main issues:

(1) Under what circumstances will the foreign technology-related activities of MNEs be to the benefit of home countries?

(2) What is the evidence that home countries have so benefited?

(3)   What action (if any) should home governments take to ensure that their own MNEs operate in their long-term technological interests?

We would repeat just one caveat made earlier (p. 328) and one which we shall deal with at greater length in Chapter 20. Technologically-related policies of governments directed to MNEs, or as a result of MNE activity, should not be divorced from those that address the total welfare effects of MNEs or MNE activity. Thus, it is quite possible to devise sensible technologically-enhancing policies which might be environmentally damaging, reduce employment, lead to increased monopoly power or put an intolerable strain on the balance of payments. It is imperative to take a systemic view of the impact of MNE activity and of the gamut of measures which governments might take in response to that input, even though it may be appropriate to consider each of the ways in which MNEs may affect a nation's economy and to introduce specific micro-organizational policies to optimize the outcome of these consequences.

12.2   TECHNOLOGICAL EXPORTS AND THE CONCERNS OF HOME COUNTRIES

The current concern of most policy makers in industrialized market economies about the effects of technology exports by their own MNEs first surfaced in the late 1970s. It was sparked by two main factors. The first was a marked slowing down of international economic growth – itself a result of the second oil crisis of the 1970s – which coincided with a downswing in technological innovation, rising domestic unemployment, stagnant industrial productivity and widespread inflation. Later in the 1980s, these concerns became crystalized into a broader-based anxiety about international competitiveness. Such concern has been most often voiced in Sweden, the US and the UK, the three industrialized economies that have experienced the most dramatic fall in their share of world trade in manufactured goods and relative technological status *vis à vis* both other industrialized countries and the rest of the world.[3]

Second, and partly related to this first concern, has been the increasing effort of developing countries to shift the balance of economic and industrial power from the North to the South. This is illustrated by the philosophy and intent of the New International Economic Order and the Lima Declaration of UNIDO in 1975, which *inter alia* aimed to increase the developing countries' share of world industrial production to 25% by the year 2000. Attempts by the developing countries to pursue a policy of rapid industrialization and asset accumulation were taken as signals by the wealthier industrial countries that the order of economic interdependence, fashioned at Bretton Woods and Havana, was no longer acceptable, and that some developing countries – particularly the so-called Newly Industrializing Countries (NICs) – were a force to be reckoned with. Taken together with the expansion of alternative sources of technology, for example, from Central and Eastern Europe and some developing countries, the established industrial powers began to fear not only an erosion of their industrial hegemony but an undermining of their future competitive capabilities.

This might not matter so much within a framework of nations at similar stages of economic development and which enjoy a common business, cultural and political ideology. But, for the most part, such a commonality of intent and concern does not exist. The political perceptions and economic philosophies of many developing countries, anxious to acquire technology, are sufficiently divergent from those of most technology-exporting countries as to make the latter worried lest any added economic leverage gained by the former might be used to the detriment of their strategic and other aspirations. Here, as has been pointed out by Hawkins and Gladwin (1981), a conflict may arise between the humanitarian, economic and political goals of the home countries.

The matter is further complicated by the effects which some kinds of non-commercial technology transfers or sharing may have on the home country's commercial technological capacity. The export of defence-related goods and services by the US may help support innovation in the military aircraft and missile industries, with consequential spillover effects on the domestic aerospace and electronics industries. Just as the cut-back in the US space research programme has reduced the flow of commercially useful technology, so the current retrenchment of defence spending, including arms exports to friendly nations, could have similar effects.

While no commentator would go as far as to ascribe the relative decline in the competitiveness of some of the older industrial powers solely to the export of technology by some MNEs, Baranson (1979) and Scott and Lodge (1985), for example, as well as many of the labour leaders, assign it a major role, at least from a US perspective. There are two main thrusts to this allegation. The first is that MNEs, by engaging in FDI, have diverted their energies away from technology-innovating activities in their home countries. The second is that technological exports – most of which are international within MNEs – improve the international competitiveness of firms in the recipient country at the expense of those in the sending country. Thus, while over the past two decades, the US's trade balance in R&D-intensive manufactured goods has increased, her share of world high technology exports – notably electrical and electronics components – has been substantially reduced. A similar picture emerges for most Western European countries (but not Japan). This, in turn (so the argument goes), erodes the market base of the technology-exporting firms and makes the rising costs of R&D more difficult to recoup. In the case of labour-intensive industries, the effect is more dramatically and immediately felt on domestic employment. In the context of North/South technology transfers, the debate has been less to do with falling export shares of industrial nations and more with the increasing import competition faced by them. Nonetheless, it is a variant of the 'we want to sell more milk and fewer cows' type of argument.

These, then, are some of the main concerns currently felt to a greater or lesser degree by all developed countries. To what extent are they justified? How far can they be attributed to the activities of MNEs? What, if anything, can be done about them? And how far are the possible social costs of technology transfer outweighed by reverse transfers of strategic asset acquiring investments?

12.3   THE CONDITIONS OF TECHNOLOGY TRANSFER

Let us take, as our starting point, the proposition that firms will sell or transfer proprietary technology if they believe it is in the interest of their global strategy. Where a firm sells or leases technology to a foreign supplier or customer, it is presumed that the terms and conditions of the exchange will fully compensate it for the opportunity costs of supplying that technology. In some cases, a transfer will only take place subject to the transferee agreeing to some restriction on its use. Thus, a license to exploit a patent may only be granted on the understanding that the licensee will only market the product embodying the technology in his own country, if certain production methods and material specifications are adhered to, if a satisfactory standard of maintenance and after-sales servicing is assured, or if specific tie-in arrangements are accepted. Where a firm owns the technology produced in, or transferred to, one of its foreign affiliates, then, subject to the regulations and policies of the host government, it has full and continuing control over its use. *A priori* one may assume that from the transferring firm's perspective, in the short and medium run, at least, the transfer is expected to be beneficial. In the long run the matter is less certain since it is possible that, as a result of the competitive stimulus of FDI, indigenous firms may upgrade their own technological capabilities and out-compete the foreign affiliate or, indeed, the investing MNE.

Depending on the modality of cross-border technological transfer, various gains may be expected to accrue both to the transferor and the transferee or, in the case of strategic alliances, each of the participating firms. To the firm selling under contract, these primarily comprise the revenue it receives from the sale of technology. As long as the marginal revenue exceeds the marginal opportunity costs (including externalities) of supplying the technology, the firm will find the transfer worthwhile. In practice, for many firms selling technology that would have been produced in any case for sale or use in the domestic market, the costs reduce the marginal negotiating and transaction costs. In other cases, particularly for technology-supplying specialists such as construction contractors, project engineers, systems analysts and petrochemical consultants, the resource costs of producing the technology are relevant (Graham, 1981; Teece, 1977, 1981b). To the MNE, transferring (or sharing) technology by FDI is frequently the preferred means of appropriating the full economic rent of the technology and unique O-specific advantages transferred with it.[5] The gains from the transfer are those that accrue to the enterprise as a whole. They include not only the profits earned on the capital invested but also all the other benefits that arise from foreign production, including the securing of new markets which help spread the R&D and other overhead costs of the parent company, thus helping the MNE to maintain and extend its competitive strength.

MNEs may also transfer technological capacity and, by so doing, foster the capabilities and competences of the recipient country to produce technology for itself. Chapter 11 has shown that this may be done either because it is cheaper to set up or acquire new R&D facilities abroad, rather than expand facilities in the home country, or because differences in factor endowments and/or markets enable the host country to specialize in particular kinds of innovatory capabilities in different countries.

Excepting, then, cases of business misjudgment, to suggest that a home country may not benefit from an export of technology on the part of its firms is to suggest the social opportunity costs of such exports transfer exceeded the private opportunity costs. This may be so if only because MNEs and home countries are not pursuing the same goals. MNEs are primarily interested in making profits independently of *where* those profits are earned. Consequently they will engage in foreign production and transfer the necessary technology with this objective in mind. Investing countries, on the other hand, are interested in the activities of their MNEs from a wider perspective. Their goals include the growth of GNP, maintaining full employment, controlling inflation, building up indigenous technological capacity, promoting the most efficient structure of resource allocation and so on. There is no presumption that, in pursuing their own objectives, firms will necessarily advance those of their home countries.

At the same time, it would be wrong to judge the macro-economic consequences of a transfer of technology by an MNE by its micro-economic opportunity costs, or to attribute such costs solely to the MNE. Suppose, for example, that as a result of the transfer of technology by their parent companies, US affiliates in South Korea are able to out-compete domestic producers in the supply of colour television to the US market and that jobs are displaced in the

US television set industry. Suppose also that the people who are made unemployed do not find other work. Then the immediate gains to the USA of the transfer of technology will be the profits, net of foreign tax, earned by the foreign affiliates together with any reduction in the price of television sets passed on to the US consumers, while the opportunity cost will be any loss in the GNP caused by unemployment. To the MNE, on the other hand, the effect of the transfer may be higher sales and profits than otherwise would have been possible.

It is obvious that this conclusion may be entirely false. It may be quite wrong to attribute any fall in domestic employment to a foreign capital outflow. This is because, in its absence, the investment might have been made by other firms. This would not only have resulted in the same fall in domestic jobs and output but would also have meant that the US economy would have lost the profits and other benefits which it otherwise would have achieved from the foreign operations of its own MNEs. Moreover, the resulting unemployment may only be temporary and, over time, the labour displaced may be employed in more productive activities, either in the same firm or elsewhere in the economy, so raising rather than lowering the GNP.

All this, of course, approaches the question from a micro-economic standpoint. Depending on their consequences for the host countries, however, it is not only the costs and benefits of the investing firms that have to be taken into account. Studies carried out in the UK and USA[6] suggest that the main beneficiaries of outbound MNE activity are often the suppliers of capital equipment and intermediary products to the foreign affiliates.[7] All, or part, of these exports would have been lost without the FDI, as investment by firms of other nationalities may well have bought these same goods from their home countries. On the other hand, the extra output produced abroad may not only replace domestic output by the investing MNEs but that of its domestic competitors as well. Again, the effects depend critically on the assumptions made about what would have happened in the absence of such a transfer of technology, or as a consequence of it.

It is worth observing that in the neo-classical literature, provided that there are no market distortions, a transfer or dissemination of technology between countries will normally be expected to increase world real output by raising both allocative and technical efficiency. Moreover, both technology exporting and importing countries would benefit, although some redeployment of resources may be necessary. The difficulty of using this approach in the current context is that the assumptions underlying it are unrealistic. MNEs do not normally transfer technology in a competitive market situation, neither are governments always able to ensure that, come what may, full employment is achieved. Moreover, the welfare functions of countries embrace goals other than the maximization of output or growth of output, which could be adversely affected by the transfer of technology. It may be that the transfer of technology is not as beneficial to the home country as it could be, precisely because of market distortions. In such an event, rather than controlling the outflow of technology, policy might be better directed to removing the distortions that gave rise to it in the first place.

So far, much of this argument has implied that the technology being transferred by MNEs will be used to produce competitive products to those produced by the transferring firm or country. With market-seeking investment, a lot of technology will be of this kind. But even here, experience has shown that where a foreign affiliate is set up to produce one line of goods, its presence may stimulate the imports of other lines of goods from the home firm or country. This has proved to be especially common in the case of firms producing consumer goods, for example, colour television sets, motor vehicles, man-made textiles, processed food products, cosmetics and pharmaceuticals.[8]

With other kinds of FDI (e.g. resource-based or rationalized or strategic asset seeking investment), technology may be used to produce complementary, or even quite unrelated, goods to those produced by the transferring firm or country. In such cases, output and employment in the home country may be increased and its technology base strengthened. Investment by MNEs in trade and distributive activities is of this kind. While it may improve the marketing competence of recipient firms, it may directly increase the exports of goods from the home country. Investment in building and construction, capital equipment and energy ventures, and by chemical and engineering consultancies, may have the same effect. It is, of course, a moot point how far

technology is transferred through physical assets and goods, but, for the purpose of this analysis, we shall treat such exports as a benefit to the home firm and country.

The transfer of technology through international backward integration by MNEs in resource-based industries may also result in a spin-off in technological capacity in the home country, depending on the extent to which secondary processing activities are undertaken in the host or the home country. Even if there is a transfer of technological capacity, imports of capital equipment are likely to take place. These are more likely to be obtained from the home rather than from other countries. In some service industries, such as banking and international tourism, similar externalities are likely.

Finally, there are multiplier effects of the income generated from the transfer of technology, whatever its kind. In the 19th century, these yielded substantial benefits to the UK economy. Rising incomes of recipient countries generated by the exports of British capital and expertise provided markets for UK-manufactured goods which helped to finance new investment and, through the economies of firm size, reduce the prices of goods supplied to home markets. Although there is no economy currently as internationally dominant as the UK once was, it is nevertheless the case that, depending on the value added by the foreign affiliates and the recipient country's marginal propensity to import from the investing country, gains may accrue to the latter. Work done by Hufbauer and Adler (1968) and Bergsten et al. (1978) suggests that these consequences may often be significant for the US economy.

It must be admitted that some of the effects on the home country attributed to the transfer of technology by particular MNEs would be better ascribed to FDI in general. Our defence of the present approach is that the unique ingredient of most kinds of MNE activity is technology, be it the technology of product, materials, production, management, organization or marketing. Without this component, direct investment would become portfolio investment. The main incentive for a firm to internalize its cross-border flow of resources and capabilities is to control their organization and to capture the full economic rent on them.

Nevertheless, accepting that the focus of interest

is often on the effects of transfer of technology *per se*, it is reasonable to examine the likely repercussions of any transfer of technology by MNEs on the exporting countries. The previous paragraphs have suggested certain principles which will determine these effects. These include, first, the market conditions in which the transfer of technology takes place. Second, the form of technological transfer and, in particular, whether it is likely to complement or substitute that produced at home. Third, the strategies of the investing or technological-exporting firms. And fourth, the goals of home and host governments, and the policies pursued by them to achieve these goals.

12.4 SOME EFFECTS OF TECHNOLOGY TRANSFER

12.4.1 Some general points

Chapter 2 has revealed that both the home and foreign activities of MNEs tend to be concentrated in sectors that are technology or information intensive, or in those supplying differentiated consumer goods and services. It also indicated that their share of the output and trade of these sectors tends to be well above average.[9] However, the fact that most published statistics are confined to sales (or gross output) rather than value added (or net output) means that its technological content cannot be calculated without further knowledge about the nature and form of that activity.

The pharmaceutical industry provides a good illustration of this. In most larger developed countries, the R&D content of the sales of MNEs is quite high, averaging around 15%. By contrast, with the exception of a limited amount of R&D on tropical diseases and animal feed supplements, pharmaceutical affiliates in developing economies undertake few innovatory activities, and in only a few of the larger Latin American and Asian countries are pharmaceutical chemicals produced in any quantity. By far the greater part of the sales of foreign affiliates of MNEs consists of labour-intensive formulae or dosage preparations and the packaging of the final product. It could well be that within the sectors dominated by MNEs, the operations actually carried out in developing countries are labour intensive,

while in the developed countries they may be capital or technology intensive.

Much, of course, will depend on the type of FDI undertaken, its position in the product cycle and the policies pursued by host governments. Greenfield market-seeking MNE activity normally starts with simple finishing operations to a product which is mainly made elsewhere, and gradually work backwards to other, more technologically intensive, manufacturing stages. By contrast, investment in resource-based industries usually begins with extractive activities but later extends forward to secondary processing operations. Investments intended to take advantage of cheap and abundant supplies of semi-skilled labour may initially be directed to labour-intensive production processes, and later embrace the more capital- or technology-intensive processes. Investment specifically designed to acquire R&D facilities is the most technologically intensive of all. Nevertheless, although the particular processes undertaken by MNEs may not be technology intensive, the final output produced may be classified to an industrial sector which is defined as technology intensive. Technology affects the way all factor inputs are organized, but it does not necessarily make for a more technology-intensive industrial structure.

As far as the transfer of technological capacity is concerned, Chapter 11 has shown that there is some suggestion that First World MNEs are beginning to decentralize and rationalize their R&D activities, and that this is leading to more two-way internalized trade in technology within the Triad. By contrast, most R&D carried out in developing countries is specifically designed to cater for the needs of those, or adjacent, countries. Of all the R&D undertaken by MNEs outside the US in 1989, only 2.8% was located in developing countries (US Department of Commerce, 1991). Other estimates suggest that the developing countries only account for 2% of the world's R&D compared with 12% of world manufacturing production and 10% of manufacturing exports (Dunning, 1992d). MNEs may also advance foreign technological capacity by training programmes and skill development.[10] OECD, ILO and academic studies suggest that this has been quite important in some industries (e.g. rubber tyres, petrochemicals, pharmaceuticals, constructional engineering and hotels), while in others (e.g. textiles and clothing) the development of indigenous skills, at least in East Africa, has been largely a result of the efforts of local institutions.

The main conclusion to be drawn from this data is that although MNEs may transfer most of their technology within industries classified as high or medium technology intensive, in some cases, particularly in developing countries, the technology will be used to improve the efficiency of labour-intensive processes of production rather than the promotion of high-value production or innovatory activities. This is most likely to occur in the so-called high technology industries, in which some form of vertical international specialization of products or processes is practised, and in which cross-border intra-firm transactions tend to be concentrated.

Chapter 4 identified four main categories of MNE activity, *viz* market seeking, (natural) resource seeking, efficiency seeking (or rationalized) and strategic asset seeking. In this chapter, we have further distinguished between outward investment directed to countries whose specific attributes are similar to those of the investing country, and those whose attributes are quite different.

12.4.2 Investment to supply the local market

Elsewhere in this volume, we have suggested that for firms of one nationality to supply foreign markets they must have, or be able to acquire, some competitive or O-specific advantages over and above those possessed by local or other foreign firms. If they choose to supply that market from a local production base rather than by exports, then it is assumed this is because L advantages favour the host country rather than the home country. The product cycle theory of investment suggests there is a natural progression from exports to foreign production, and that the technology intensity of FDI is likely to increase as the MNE affiliates become more experienced and more productive, or as local supply capabilities improve. However, once a network of subsidiaries has been established, new products are often launched simultaneously in both home and overseas markets.

Market-seeking investment may affect the technological capacity of the home country in various ways. An increase in demand for a firm's products may allow it to exploit economies of size and scope, and to finance new marketing and innovatory activities. Where there are pressures on the firm's domestic operations, foreign production may release resources and competences for more productive use at home. There may be technological feedback from the foreign affiliates to the parent company, especially where investment is made in a more advanced industrial country, or where the affiliates undertake R&D on behalf of the MNE of which it is part. Firms may be better able to take advantage of the geographical diversification of activities in their purchasing arrangements, fund raising and management recruitment.

By having their assets spread over many countries and denominated in different currencies, they can better cover their risks, take advantage of leads and lags, protect themselves against exchange rate changes and so on. As a consequence of the transfer (or sharing) of the technology of production, the investing enterprise almost always strengthens its technology of information and choice and, in some cases, its technological capacity as well. MNEs provide an excellent example of how domestic capacity released by FDI may be used to produce new or upgraded product lines, and/or be given over to technologically more advanced or complex production processes.

Much, of course, depends on whether the market-seeking FDI replaces or adds to domestic production, and whether it is part of a defensive oligopolistic strategy or an aggressive competitive strategy on the part of MNEs. We have already referred to Kojima's argument that much of US foreign investment in technology-intensive industries has been of an anti-trade kind, and operates to the disadvantage of both host and home countries.[11] In so far as his criticism is correct, it would be better directed to the activities of MNEs, of all nationalities, operating in large advanced industrial countries, as a much smaller percentage of FDI in developing countries is undertaken for defensive oligopolistic reasons. On the other hand, investment by MNEs to take advantage of resource or labour cost differentials has probably benefited the investing country, as it has freed the flow of technology which might otherwise not have taken place, or not have taken place to the same extent. Professor Kojima regards the technology exported by MNEs to promote this kind of activity as trade promoting and in accord with the principle of comparative advantage.

12.4.3   Resource-based investment

The purpose of this investment is usually to supply the home firm or country and other countries with natural resources. Possession of the technology required for the exploration, extraction and processing of mineral resources, together with a favoured access to international capital required, markets and to final goods markets, gives MNEs O advantages over their domestic competitors in a number of industries. In such cases, there is no substitution between foreign and domestic investment; the purpose of the technological transfer is to increase or protect the existing supply of primary products or to improve the terms of trade for the importing country. It may also strengthen the technological capacity of the capital-exporting countries in engineering, chemical design and consultancy, and maintenance work.

In some cases, technology transfer to promote foreign secondary processing activities may be at the expense of similar activities in domestic markets. Again, it may be that the firm has little choice but to locate or relocate the processing operations in host countries in response to the policies pursued by their governments. However, the basic equation is the relationship between social and private opportunity costs. The amount or kind of technology transferred may be too high because FDI confers lower net benefits from a social, rather than a private, viewpoint.

12.4.4   Efficiency-seeking (rationalized) investment

(i)   *Between countries with dissimilar economic structures* We have suggested that it is the transfer of technology associated with this kind to facilitate investment which is likely to have the greatest effect on domestic employment as they are labour-intensive activities. Unlike import-substituting investment, where if an MNE wishes to supply a foreign market it must produce in that market, rationalized invest-

ment usually allows the investing firm much greater latitude of locational choice.

Chapter 3 identified two forms of this kind of investment. The one is to produce complete goods and/or services which require substantial inputs of labour. Here the advantages of specialization and division of labour would seem to dictate that MNEs should concentrate their production of labour-intensive goods in labour-rich countries, and of capital- or technology-intensive goods in countries that are rich in capital and technology.

The second kind of export platform investment is in labour-intensive parts of a production process for sale in world markets, the capital- or technology-intensive part of the production being produced in the capital- or technology-rich countries. Again, this conforms to the principle of the international division of labour, except in so far as the action may sometimes be prompted by distorted markets or government policies.

Perhaps the reason why this kind of investment is strongly criticized is that it is believed that, without it, the adverse effects on domestic employment can more easily be arrested. The fact that other firms might have invested if the home country's MNEs had not done so – thus competing with the home firms in these markets – is generally ignored because it is also argued that this can be prevented by import controls. The fact that consumers may have to pay a higher price for their products and that domestic firms will earn lower profits is regarded as an acceptable cost for avoiding more unemployment. However, to repeat an earlier point, it is not the transfer of technology by MNEs *per se* which is the root of the concern, but the general dissemination of technology from developed countries to developing countries, coupled with the consequences of free trade.

(ii)   *Between countries with similar economic structures* Efficiency-seeking FDI – like efficiency-seeking trade between countries with similar economic structures – is likely to promote a cross-border division of labour, provided that it is undertaken to overcome endemic market failure rather than to advance the market power of the investing firm or to take advantage of government-induced price and other distortions.

The classic example of such investment is that which has occurred within the EC since 1958, and which is now accelerating between Canada and the US as a result of the Canada–US Free Trade Agreement. Both types of regional economic integration are examined at some length in Chapter 17. For the moment, we are interested in the likely consequences of such investment for the technological capacity of the home country – whether it is in or outside the integrated area.

Unlike the previous section, efficiency-seeking investment between countries with similar economic structures is intended to exploit the benefits of *intra*-sectoral (rather than *inter*-sectoral) product specialization and the economies of scale and scope. Such a division of labour is normally horizontal rather than vertical, although it may occur in both intermediate products (carburettors, wheels, electrical equipment, automobile engines) and final products (refrigerators, hair dryers, microwave ovens). Companies may also choose to specialize their innovatory R&D facilities.[12] IBM, for example, has some eight laboratories in different countries which operate on behalf of the group as a whole – or one of its operational regions. ABB (the Swedish MNE) operates foreign R&D units in five different countries, with each unit being responsible for research in specialized product areas (Solvell *et al.*, 1991).

With such specialization, then, depending on the nature of the products and processes produced, the production technology and technological capacity related to these activities is likely to be dispersed at the same time. Both the organization of the technologies employed in the various affiliates and the development of the new technologies essential to the competitive advantage of the MNE may continue to be centralized. Put another way, rationalized MNE may lead to a 'hollowing out' of some of the technological functions of the home country, but, in its place, a cadre of high-powered technological managers may concern themselves with the organization of the global technological system.

12.4.5 Strategic asset acquiring investment

When a firm – for whatever reason – acquires the assets of another firm, it buys its stock of technological assets as well. While this will increase its global technological capability, the extent to which the home country gains will depend, in the short run, on the effect of the acquisition on the form and distribution of the technological capacity. In the long run, it will depend on the global competitiveness of the acquiring firm.

An obvious example of a home country gaining technological capability from a foreign acquisition is where the assets acquired are either physically shipped back to the investing company or used to enhance the technological competence of the parent company. Though relatively uncommon, there are several examples of an MNE shutting down the R&D laboratory of a recently acquired subsidiary and shipping the assets (or knowledge) gained back to the parent company.[13]

In theory, of course, the transference could go the other way, although this, perhaps, is more likely in the case of a merger than a takeover. In the event of a strategic alliance (see Chapter 9) the short and medium run benefits are uncertain, and are likely to depend on the relative technological strengths of the partners to the exchange. Moreover, while most cross-border collaborative ventures in R&D or in technologically-advanced industries are designed to strengthen the overall innovatory capacity of the participating companies, whether or not this also benefits the home countries depends on the geographical distribution of the innovatory capacity. In the long run, the benefits will rest on how the coalition affects the global competitive positions of the competing firms.[14]

12.4.6 FDI as a means of domestic technological restructuring

(i) *As a result of exports to developed countries* The above paragraphs suggest that the impact of FDI on the technological capacity of the home country will depend on the type of foreign investment, the conditions under which it occurs, the home and host countries involved and the time horizon being considered. Gains include any feedback in technology resulting from the FDI (particularly important where the investment is in a technologically more advanced economy); extra business to technology suppliers in the home country; and (unique to FDI compared with other forms of technology exports) control over the use of technology.

The possible costs to the home country include an erosion of its long-term competitive advantage and a weakening of its balance of payments position. At the same time, it is important both to take account of the (opportunity) costs of not exporting technology; and of the opportunities FDI might provide for a restructuring of domestic technological activities. On the first point, it is quite possible that if (say) US MNEs did not export technology or relocate technological capacity to another country, German or UK MNEs would have done so[15] – and the effects on the US economy would be even less welcome. Clearly, the 'alternatives' or 'counterfactual' position one assumes is very important.[16] On the second point, it is quite possible that the foreign activities of MNEs might replace similar activities in the home country. But, this may release resources for the undertaking of different (and higher grade) technological activities.

At a macro-level, the product cycle was predicated on the assumption that as one product nears the end of its cycle, a new product takes its place. As we have seen, the whole philosophy of the Japanese government towards outward FDI is to use it as a mechanism for restructuring the allocation of domestic resources.

If one applies this analysis to technological restructuring, it can be seen that a home country need have little concern about outward investment on *economic* grounds where it helps to improve the efficiency of international resource allocation and is able to devise realistic and cost-effective policies of technological structural adjustment. This is not to deny that there would be some technological hardship – particularly in the sectors adversely affected – but these should be outweighed by the longer-term gains resulting from the upgrading and higher productivity of human and physical capabilities.

The difficulty arises when governments, either as a deliberate strategy or as an outcome of other policies, distort domestic and cross-border markets and cause MNEs either to relocate their technological capacities or to export technology at below the socially optimum price to the source country. This problem is likely to be the most acute in the high technology sectors dominated by international oligopolists seeking to protect or advance their own market positions, and also where opportunities for domestic restructuring are the least. In these situations, MNEs may be the instruments for either reducing domestic technological capabilities or restructuring them in a sub-optimal way. In these circumstances, home governments may well be driven to pursue counteractive technological strategies or to be more strict in enforcing anti-trust *et al.* regulations to combat the unacceptable oligopolistic tactics of MNEs.

Of course, the export of technological capacity by its own MNEs, like the reluctance of foreign MNEs to engage in technology-creating activities in its midst, may reflect the inadequate L attractions of the country in question. Several writers, including Porter (1990), Driscoll and Wallender (1987), and Inman and Burton (1990), have emphasized this point. A poor educational system, inappropriate or inferior government policies, ineffective institutions to facilitate commercial innovation, a discouraging entrepreneurial and work ethos, an inadequate transport and communications infrastructure and a lack of effective competition are a few examples. Rather than blame MNEs for exporting technology, their home countries would do well to recognize the market for technology as a highly imperfect one and to revise their own policies to make it economically worthwhile for MNEs both to produce and use more of their technology in their home countries.

(ii) *As a result of exports to developing countries* A different kind of problem of technological restructuring occurs in the case of technology exports from sectors whose domestic markets are static or declining, and in which there is little product or process innovation, output is specialized and production methods are labour intensive. Often the difficulties of these industries are exacerbated by the fact that they tend to be located in the less prosperous regions of the home economies and use the types of labour that cannot easily find alternative employment or be retained. The new jobs being created require different skills to those which are being replaced. In such cases, without effective retraining programmes, structural unemployment is likely to persist. Most unemployment of this kind has occurred in the labour-intensive sectors, notably textiles and clothing, consumer electronics and light engineering. The European Commission has estimated that more than two million jobs in Europe have been lost as a result of import competition from developing (mainly Asian) countries, and that the figure would have been considerably higher had not agreements, like the multi-fibre agreement, restricted imports from the developing countries.

That this is an old problem, and the inevitable outcome of a changing and international division of labour, and the emergence of newly industrializing economies, is of little comfort to those adversely affected. Neither is the fact that MNEs are not always actively involved in these industries. The fear is that import competition from a comparatively few industries today will spread to many others tomorrow. As newly industrializing countries climb up the economic ladder, will they not attract more markets away from the developed countries? And if they do, will not the MNEs become increasingly involved? In this respect, the participation of MNEs in audio and video equipment, in synthetic fibres, in pharmaceuticals, auto components and telecommunications equipment in some countries in East Asia and Latin America is cited as a foretaste of the pattern of the future. Here the economic renaissance of Japan provides a salutary experience. Japan increased her share of world exports in manufactured goods from 6.9% in 1960 to 11.3% in 1990 with the minimum contribution from foreign MNEs. Yet to achieve this resurgence in her industrial capabilities, she imported a very substantial amount of foreign technology, while building up an indigenous strength in the ability to absorb, alter and adapt that technology. For example, between 1950 and 1983 alone, the Japanese government approved 2212 contracts made by Japanese concerns involving purchases of technology from Western enterprises.[17]

It is a debatable point whether Europe and the US would have been better off without the Japanese economic miracle, but the point at issue is that it would have been difficult, if not impossible, for these countries to have used normal commercial channels to have arrested that miracle. At the same time, it is at least arguable that the US and Europe would have benefited had they been allowed a stake in the Japanese developmental process. The contrast to Japan is Brazil and Mexico, whose rates of growth of industrial production since the late 1960s have paralleled that of Japan, but in whose prosperity foreign-based (particularly US) MNEs have fully participated.

At the same time, in the past two decades, the exports of manufactured goods, particularly intermediate products and capital goods, from industrialized countries to developing countries has sharply increased, as has the proportion of those shipped between MNEs and their foreign affiliates (US Department of Commerce, vd). It would also seem that while MNEs have played an important role in fashioning the realignment of international economic activity, government policy – particularly with respect to structural adjustment – may determine the success of both developed and developing countries in responding to the changing international division of labour.

The evidence suggests, however, that the type of technology required by developing countries for upgrading their value-added activities is fairly readily obtainable in the open market, and that, far from reducing their domestic technological capacity, the additional markets created by MNEs from their investments in developing countries help sustain that technological capacity. Indeed, the alternative proposition that developing countries are not inducing MNEs to transfer high value-added activities seems to us to warrant more consideration. In this connection, it is important to distinguish between the consequences, for technology exporting countries, of transfers of technology to developing countries and those of the transfer of technological capabilities to developed countries. While the former is likely to give considerable cause for concern among labour leaders in advanced countries, the latter is more likely to have more far reaching significance to the long-term competitiveness of the exporting countries (Ohmae, 1985).

One final question remains to be asked. Even if MNEs do relocate technological capacity or export technology, which *prima facie* results in a reduction in the technological competitiveness of the home country, does this really matter if the *terms* (i.e. the price) of the sale or relocation are adequate to cover its costs (to the home country). Here we return to the difficult question of the difference between social and private costs and benefits, as well as to the sometimes controversial issues surrounding the payment of royalties and fees for exported technological services (including patents).

Clearly, there are divergences of interest between home and host countries as to the technological impact of MNE activity. To the host country, the opportunity cost of obtaining technology via inward investment is the cost of obtaining it by other routes or by the internal generation of that technology. To the home country, the cost is essentially the impact – beneficial or otherwise – which the sale might make to its overall competitive position. In the last resort, and in the absence of market forces that adequately take account of the extra-market consequences of technology transfer, it is difficult to see how these issues can be resolved except by the acceptance of general principles on the way in which successful innovation is rewarded, and on an *ad hoc* basis around the negotiations table.

12.5   EMPIRICAL EVIDENCE

Frustratingly little empirical research has been undertaken on the extent to which the export of technology, or the relocation of technological capacity, affects the technological capability of the home countries. Data on the domestic and foreign R&D activities of MNEs gives little guidance as to whether the one substitutes for or complements the other. In most industrial sectors, US MNEs continue to spend more on R&D (as a per cent of sales) in their home countries than their uninational competitors. There is no suggestion that as their expenditure on overseas R&D has increased, it has fallen at home.

We might identify three approaches to evaluating the effect of outbound MNE activity on domestic technological capability. First there have been several empirical studies since the 1960s (for example, Reddaway *et al.*, 1968, and Mansfield and Romeo, 1984) which have demonstrated that the technological feedback from outbound FDI can be considerable. This is obviously most likely in the case of intra-Triad MNE activity, and in the case of cross-border A&Ms specifically designed to acquire foreign technology or to scan and monitor foreign innovatory developments. As Cantwell and Hodson (1991) have shown, quite a high proportion of patents registered by MNEs originated from their foreign subsidiaries. More generally, it is only by undertaking investments in the most competitive locations that many high technology firms can secure the global markets which are needed to finance their innovatory activities, which themselves are critical to their survival.

Second, some recent research by Kotabe (1990a, 1990b) has sought to establish the linkages between offshore production by US MNEs and their domestic innovatory capacity. Taking the imports of duty free products, under items 806.30 and 807.00 of the US Tariff Schedules, and relating them to a range of explanatory variables, including the number of product innovations to total employment in each of 30 manufacturing sectors, Kotabe obtained a positive and significant relationship between import propensity and R&D intensity. Though he was careful not to impute a causal relationship between these two variables, Kotabe rightly concluded that his research findings tended to support the proposition that the strategic readiness of US MNEs to use their corporate resources to exploit the locational advantages of various locations did not impair their domestic innovatory capabilities. However, other analysts (e.g. Porter, 1990) have suggested that in some sectors, such as semiconductors, the readiness of US MNEs to switch locations to lower their production costs may have been a misplaced strategy, in so far as it reduced their incentive to invest in product innovations and improvements.

Third, there is some evidence to suggest that some Swedish, North American and UK MNEs have relocated some of their R&D activities outside their national boundaries to gain access to more plentiful and better qualified personnel[18] or to tap into a more virile and sympathetic innovatory environment.[19] Such an environment not only requires the active support by national governments of innovatory activities and cross-border collaborative research programmes,[20] but, for the international community to establish rules for the game by which government-distorting actions favouring or discriminating against technology-creating activities or cross-border technology transfer are, as far as possible, eliminated.[21]

12.6   A POLICY FOOTNOTE

Throughout this chapter, a variety of policy options have been identified which are open to government to maximize the technology-related benefits or minimize the technology-related costs of FDI. We have also argued against any measure specifically directed to maximizing the technology-related net benefits without taking into account the wider economic effects of outward FDI investment.

We have also cautioned against generalizing about the technological consequences of MNE activity. As we have asserted, much depends on the motives for the investment and the conditions under which it is made. We have tried, too, to identify some of the unique characteristics and effects of technological exports and the relocation of technological capacity which is internalized by MNEs. We have suggested that, apart from the scale and speed of the domestic restructuring involved as a result of their foreign activities, and except in cases where MNEs add to market imperfections, home countries are likely to benefit more from intra-hierarchical than open market transactions.[22]

One thing does seem crystal clear. Because of the globalization of economic activity and the role of MNEs as exporters of technology and relocators of technological capacity, home governments are being forced to appraise their policies towards technological creation and productivity. In particular, it demands a new emphasis on measures to enhance the quality of human capital, improve the motives for, and the capabilities of, firms to undertake innovatory activities and to stimulate competition and entrepreneurship. It requires, too, a generally liberal stance towards trade and investment and a refusal to enter into sheltering agreements with its own firms (Rugman and Verbeke, 1990b) – except, perhaps, those intended to counteract strategically-distorting policies on the part of foreign competitors or governments.[23]

Among the developed countries, the US is the most overtly concerned about the impact of both outbound and inbound MNE activity on its own technological capacity. In the early 1990s, there is a strong 'mercantilistic' air about some of the actions being urged on the legislature, and little appreciation of the fact that in the emerging global economy, restrictions on trade in technology, whether it be at arm's length or within MNEs, can be as economically damaging – at least in the long run – as tariffs and non-tariff barriers on finished goods and services. While at the time of America's technological hegemony, there may have been a case for outlawing the affiliates of foreign firms from participating in officially sponsored discussions and symposia on innovation strategy in high-technology industries or not permitting them to be members of R&D

consortia funded with government money,[24] in the contemporary situation, characterized by an increasing interdependence of US and foreign scientific and technological research, there is no such case today. Undoubtedly such restrictions would lead to retaliatory measures by competitive nations and US companies with major R&D interests in those countries would be the first to suffer. Issues such as these are explored in some detail by Mowery (1990) and Mowery and Rosenberg (1989a, 1989b).

This, however, is not to deny that there may be genuine strategic or defence-related arguments for controlling the outflow of technology or for limiting some kinds of inbound investment, including some A&Ms. We discuss some of these arguments in Chapter 19. Nor does it argue for a 'hands off' policy by governments towards upgrading technological capability. Indeed, the thrust of this chapter has been to argue that the inability or unwillingness of liberal governments to correct, or assist firms to overcome, an endemic failure in the supply of technology, at a time when less liberal governments have no such inhibition, is likely to lead to vicious rather than virtuous competitive circles in key industrial sectors.

We have already suggested some policies which governments might pursue towards inward technology transfer. If these are adopted, then it is likely that many of the problems associated with outbound MNE activity will also disappear. For concern over technology exports usually reflects not economic strength but economic weakness. Policies to enhance the manufacturing base, encourage more cooperative R&D programmes, better motivate firms to upgrade their resources and invest more in innovatory activities, rebuild the technological infrastructure and improve the policy-making machinery will not only aid competitiveness in domestic markets, but better enable MNEs to exploit foreign markets through FDI and strategic alliances (Inman and Burton, 1990).

As far as MNE activities in developing countries are concerned, it is worth recalling that only a small amount of the innovatory activity undertaken in the Triad is directly or immediately relevant to the *present* industrialization programmes of most developing countries. Much of the product, process, materials, marketing and organizational know-how currently required to meet the needs of these countries is not proprietary to individual firms but is generally available in the marketplace.

However, in the next decade the picture may change quite dramatically as the newly industrializing countries become increasingly sophisticated in their product structure and production techniques. The first question that industrializing nations have to address – provided they are allowed to – is how far they wish to be involved in this industrialization programme. This chapter has hinted that, in the short to medium term, the net social benefits of being involved through technology transfer by their own MNEs may be higher than any alternative course of action they might pursue.

In the longer run, there are basically four policies open to governments of the capital-exporting nations. First, they can resort to some form of technological protectionism. Second, they can enter into agreements with their newly industrialized competitors to control their increase in manufacturing exports or to insist that they should import from industrial countries as much as they export to them (the assurance of fair trading comes into this category). Third, they can encourage their firms to differentiate their products and introduce new production techniques more suited to their supply capabilities.[25] Fourth, they can seek to identify emerging patterns of dynamic comparative advantage and introduce policies to help firms and individuals to move into the appropriate value-added activities.

Assuming the last is judged the first-best solution, then, this would require more decisive and far-reaching strategies to stimulate productivity, encourage innovation and promote the development of technology and information intensive activities than those which have so far been introduced by most OECD countries. In the interim, however, the problem is how to minimize the adjustment costs of market disruptions and maximize the smoothness of the adaptation and restructuring. Where appropriate, it is necessary to encourage firms affected by competi-tion from newly industrializing countries to be more efficient. To solve these problems, which may well mean controlling the character and pace of the restructuring process, some form of phased import restrictions cannot be completely ruled out.[26]

It is, however, difficult to understand how regulating the activities of manufacturing MNEs in developing countries can advance these goals, any more than the controls exerted by the UK on the export of technology in the nineteenth century helped its objectives (Rosenberg, 1981).[27] If any attention at all is needed in this direction, it should be towards removing any distorting influences which might encourage MNEs to transfer different amounts or types of technology than they might otherwise have done, or which might interfere with their returning the maximum benefits to the home country. Again, action may involve changes to international patent, monetary or tax systems, at least some of which would operate against the interests of the technology-receiving countries.

The area to which home governments need to pay most attention, apart from that of defence and national security which we discuss in Chapter 19, is where their own firms, acting in a mainly consultative capacity, are transferring technology that cannot be obtained from other sources. Here, the social opportunity costs of transfer may be considerably greater than the private opportunity costs, and ways may need to be found of redressing this difference.

Individual industrialized countries are likely to be differently affected by the improved technological capacity in the developing world.[28] The role of their own MNEs in this process and the attitudes of their governments (compare the US and Japanese cases) also differ. We have asserted that one reason why a particular firm or country may be reluctant to control technology exports is that its competitors may *not* do so. This suggests that the main area of international competition will continue to be *between* countries of the developed world. Only if the leading Triad countries should choose to adopt a common policy towards the actions of their MNEs would it be feasible to control the outflow of technology specific to MNEs, without any one country perceiving it was worse off as a result. While such a strategy, at least on economic grounds, seems very unlikely, the efforts of the developing countries, including the newly industrializing countries, to strengthen their bargaining power *vis à vis* MNEs from the developed world, may eventually provoke a countervailing reaction on the part of the newly industrializing countries to redress the balance which they believe to be against their own interests (Bergsten, 1974). A less controversial route to follow might be a search for harmonized policies between North and South designed to smooth the adjustment process, which might be of benefit to both older and newer industrialized countries.

We would make one final observation. This chapter began with the expression of concern of developed countries about the possible adverse effects of exporting technology to developing countries through their own MNEs. It ends by asking the question: Can developed countries afford *not* to export technology to developing countries through their own MNEs? If the activities of MNEs are seen not as a threat to domestic investment, jobs and technological capacity, but as a means of:

(1) gaining or protecting access to foreign markets,

(2) acquiring resources and capabilities vital to the competitiveness of the capital-exporting country,

(3) ensuring a stake in the prosperity of developing countries,

(4) protecting or advancing the *international* competitive position of one industrialized country relative to another,

the question of whether the export of technology is a 'good' or a 'bad' thing takes on a completely new meaning. The case presented in this chapter is not that the latter proposition is in any way proven, but that it deserves at least as much attention as the alternative thesis which, for some years now, has been more forcibly presented and actively researched.

NOTES

1   That is to say, technology is the output of natural resources. It is a capability and is a secondary, rather than primary, resource. However, once produced it will gradually affect the efficiency of natural resource usage.

2   Notably, in the cotton and woollen textiles, metal, canning and brewing, carpet, pottery, jute, silk and cutlery industries. For a more detailed examination of the role of European technology in the pre-Civil War development of the US, see Coram (1967) and Wilkins (1989).

3   These countries' share of world manufacturing exports fell from 36.5% in 1967 to 23.0% in 1985. Of the other industrialized nations, Japan has increased her share from 9.8% to 15.7% while France and Germany have maintained theirs at around 8% and 15%, respectively.

4   Data on the royalties and fees paid by the US, UK and West Germany to other countries and received by them from other countries suggest that on average about four-fifths were internal to MNEs.

5   For a discussion of the conditions under which the enterprise may prefer to externalize technology transfers, see Telesio (1979), Robinson (1978) and Teece (1981b).

6   See especially Reddaway *et al.* (1968), Hufbauer and Adler (1968) and Stopford and Turner (1985).

7   The study by Kawaguchi (1978) suggested that Japanese joint ventures and subsidiaries in South East Asia buy between 30% and 100% of their inputs (in value terms) from Japan (see especially his Table V3, p. 31). In our own study of Japanese manufacturing affiliates in British industry, it was found that 50% of equipment and machinery purchased by the affiliates in 1982 was imported from Japan (Dunning, 1986a).

8   See Chapter 13 for further details.

9   See also Chapter 8 of Dunning (1988b).

10   See Chapter 13 for further details.

11   In Chapter 4, pp. 89–90.

12   For an examination of the different kinds of R&D undertaken by the MNE affiliate, see Pearce (1990) and Casson (1991).

13   Especially in the 1960s and 1970s, at which time European R&D facilities were relatively inexpensive for US firms to acquire.

14   Thus it is quite possible that both parties to an alliance may benefit in the short run, but if one benefits *relative* to the other, in the long run the one who benefits the least may see its overall competitive position reduced.

15   For examples of the competitive position of MNEs from different nationalities in various industries, see Inman and Burton (1990). See also Harvard Business School (1989).

16   See Chapters 11 and 13 for more details.

17   For further details of the role of Japan as a technology importer and exporter see Ozawa (1985).

18   This argument, however, was put forward in the 1960s and 1970s much more than it is today, as the differential in real salary costs between, for example, the US and Europe, has narrowed.

19   Which may be very industry specific. For an examination of factors influencing the location of R&D activities by MNEs in the pharmaceutical industry see Dunning (1988b) and Casson (1991).

20   For some examples of both cross-border technological and international cooperation in export control support programmes, see Inman and Burton (1990) and Harvard Business School (1989).

21   The Reagan administration was particularly active in these efforts in a variety of trade negotiations (Nau, 1986).

22 This is predicated on the assumption that *ceteris paribus* firms with headquarters in a particular country are more likely to behave in the interests of that country than are firms based in another country.

23 Some of the issues are discussed by Vernon (1987b).

24 Examples are the exclusion of foreign-owned firms from the symposium on high temperature superconductivity (NTS) organized by the White House Office of Science and Technology Policy and the National Science Foundation, and the restricted membership of foreign firms, including those with US subsidiaries, in the Sematech initiative and DARPA (Defense Advanced Research Projects Agency).

25 Which, in fact, is what has happened, though one suspects accidentally, more than deliberately, as a result of the introduction of robotics and computer-aided design and manufacturing equipment.

26 As was agreed by the Japanese government in July 1991 to limit Japan's share of the EC market for cars and light vans after which there will be restrictions (*Economist*, 1991).

27 The sluggishness of the UK to adapt to the structural changes required of her industrial economy in the late 19th century is an object lesson to industrialized countries faced with the competition from the newly industrializing countries.

28 See the OECD (1981) and studies quoted therein (e.g. in Chapters 3 and 4).

CHAPTER 13

MNEs, EMPLOYMENT AND HUMAN RESOURCE MANAGEMENT

13.1 INTRODUCTION

Almost all actions by MNEs, or their affiliates considered in Part 3 of this volume, are likely to directly or indirectly impinge on the level, growth, stability, quality and rewards of the labour force. For the most part, however, these issues have been addressed from the perspective of Nation States rather than from that of particular sectoral interests (e.g. consumers, workers or capitalists).

However, at the end of the day, economic activity is designed to promote human welfare. In so far as the content and quality of that welfare is affected by income earned from employment and the work environment,[1] it is appropriate this volume should give some attention to the interaction between these variables and MNE activity.

There is another reason too. Chapter 11 emphasized the fact that, in the modern global economy, the competitiveness of most industrial countries rests on their ability both to upgrade and more effectively utilize their income-creating assets. Such assets we identified as physical capital (e.g. R&D laboratories, university buildings, machines, equipment) and their supporting infrastructures, and trained human resources, such as scientists, engineers, skilled craftsmen, managers, administrators and salesmen. It is a fact that, over the past two or more decades, the industrial countries that have devoted the most attention to upgrading these assets and motivating their citizens to produce more wealth are those which have recorded the fastest rates of economic growth (World Economic Forum, 1991). Indeed, it is almost a truism that a country's economic progress must largely rest on the entrepreneurship, ingenuity and intelligent work of its people. New products and new ways of producing goods and services stem from the initiatives and intelligence of individuals. Work and working practices are organized by individuals. New advertising slogans and marketing techniques are conceived by individuals. The service economy, as its name implies, comprises the services provided by one group of individuals to another. The success of inter-firm alliances rests on the willingness and ability of the people involved to cooperate with each other. Even in our modern age, science, technology and commerce are the servants of man, not vice versa.

For these two reasons, then, this chapter will review some of the scholarly research which has sought to identify and evaluate the role MNEs and their affiliates with regard to:

(1) the level, structure and composition of employment, wages and working conditions of individuals;

(2) the productivity and upgrading of human skills and capabilities in the context of the human resource strategies of MNEs;

(3) the motivation of human beings to create wealth;

(4) the role of government in fashioning the ESP environment as it influences factors (1)–(3).

While these topics are interrelated in the sense that a worker's productivity and satisfaction may be linked to the quality of the work he or she performs, we shall treat the first more from the perspective of the welfare of the worker, *qua* worker, and the other three primarily from that of the competitiveness of the firm, industry or nation of which the worker is part.

We would make one further introductory point.

Over the past 15 years numerous monographs and reports on MNEs and labour-related issues have been published by the International Labour Office (ILO). By the end of 1990, these had included 49 working papers on the employment effects of MNE activity in developed and developing economies and a further six on the relationship between technological change, employment generation and FDI. In addition, the ILO has published 12 books which embrace both of these issues and those relating to the training, social, labour and safety practices of MNEs.[2]

With this in mind, this chapter can hardly be expected to cover more than the tip of the iceberg on employment and human resource related issues. Readers who are interested in this topic would be well advised to consult the various ILO studies. A thorough and well balanced analysis of the impact of MNE activity on labour markets, labour utilization practices and industrial relations is also contained in Enderwick (1985, 1993). Rather, then, simply cataloguing the findings of these studies, we shall attempt to present our own particular gloss on the issues to be discussed. First, we shall examine the predictions of the OLI paradigm as to the likely consequences of MNE activity for employment and human resource management; second, we shall review some of the empirical evidence relating to these predictions and the relevance of industry-, country- and firm-specific factors; third, we shall consider the interaction between these findings and the ESP configuration of countries; fourth, we shall touch upon some of the policy issues arising from these interactions.

13.2   THEORETICAL UNDERPINNINGS

13.2.1   What is distinctive about MNEs: a reprise!

What, if any, is the distinctive impact of MNE activity on the use, location and compensation of human resources and capabilities? The answer must lie essentially in the extent and pattern of the O assets possessed by these companies, and how and where these are utilized to generate employment. In this respect, by their innovating strategies, their product profiles, the nature of their production processes and their flexibility in siting their production units, MNEs may affect the amount and kind of labour they employ, the extent to which they are willing to upgrade the skills and competences of such labour, the conditions of its employment and the location of that employment.

Chapter 11 demonstrated that MNEs account for most of the innovating capacity in the free market economies, and that increasingly they are locating this capacity outside their home countries. To the extent that these innovating advantages stem, at least in part, from their foreign activities, MNEs, both by their opportunities to scan and recruit from global labour markets and by their ability to motivate better and train labour, are likely to play an extremely influential role in human resource development.

Chapter 11 also suggested that, because of the activities in which they engage and the production techniques they employ, MNEs are likely to affect both the amount and composition of the global labour force and its productivity. Since, as Chapter 2 has shown, MNEs tend to engage in capital- or information-intensive and high value activity, it might be expected that not only would their impact on the level of employment in the countries in which they operate be quite small, but in cases where they replace uninational firms using more labour-intensive techniques, it might be negative. On the other hand, in so far as, by their access to superior resources and capabilities, MNEs may help to lower production costs and/or raise product quality, they may increase demand for certain kinds of labour, while the indirect or spin-off effects on component and raw material suppliers (which might use more labour-intensive production processes) could be quite positive.

The likely effects of MNE activity on the skill mix and quality of labour are equally ambiguous. Where foreign production helps to improve the competitive position of the investing companies and allows the international division of labour, this may well lead to an upgrading of human resources (especially those associated with R&D and administrative activities) in the home country. From a host country's viewpoint, depending on the nature of the production processes introduced by MNEs, the skill content of labour might be lowered (e.g. where its task is essentially reduced to that of a machine minder) or raised (e.g. in the case of the introduction of a sophisticated multi-purpose piece of equipment which may require the services of a skilled operator). In some cases, the design of components, machinery and equipment might have to be modified to meet the availability of local resources and customer needs. Some indigenous manpower enhancement and training may be required to accomplish this task.

It is also a feature of MNE activity – particularly in situations of rapid environmental and technological change – that it is likely to be more locationally footloose than uninational activity. Over the past 20 years there have been substantial relocations of all kinds of value-added activities by MNEs. Sometimes – perhaps on most occasions – the triggering factor has been the actions of host governments (e.g. the imposition of tariffs or import quotas). Sometimes it has been a shift in the comparative advantage of countries in the production of mineral and agricultural products. Such shifts might include those brought about both by pro- and anti-market forces. An example of the latter would be actions by international cartels to raise prices or control production.

In manufacturing, too, rising real wages – themselves a consequence of rising levels of economic prosperity – may affect a country's ability to produce labour-intensive products. Over recent years, there has been a steady resiting of labour-intensive activities by MNEs away from the more advanced industrializing countries like Singapore, Hong Kong, Taiwan, South Korea and Brazil to those one or two steps behind in the industrialization chain, such as Thailand, Malaysia and the Philippines, or even those three or four steps behind, such as Sri Lanka, Pakistan, Bangladesh and Morocco. On the other hand – again Chapter 11 gave examples of this – advances in computer, communications and design technologies together with the introduction of flexible manufacturing processes have caused a relocation of previously labour-intensive subcontracting activities in such industries as textiles, clothing and semiconductors from Asian to European sites.[3]

The extent to which the impact of MNEs on employment levels and patterns is different from that of uninational firms is also likely to vary according to the type of FDI in which they are engaged and the organizational strategies they pursue. Market-seeking affiliates, which are part of a multi-domestic-oriented parent company, are less likely to impact dramatically on domestic or international labour markets than those which engage in rationalized or strategic asset acquiring investment, and whose recruitment, employment and training programmes are part of a globally-integrated human resource management strategy. As Chapter 9 has pointed out, with the relaxation of some national labour laws and employment regulations (e.g. in the EC) and the falling real cost of air transport, labour – even unskilled labour – is becoming an increasingly mobile resource across countries.

Globally-integrated MNEs frequently draw their managerial, professional and technical work force from a worldwide employment pool – sometimes from within and sometimes from outside their organizations. Some MNEs have even been able to create new O advantages by recruiting substantial numbers of unskilled or semi-skilled workers in one country and transporting them for employment in another. Examples include Korean, Turkish and Philippine workers employed in construction projects in the Middle East. In these and similar ways, MNEs are performing an arbitrage function which the international labour market is apparently unable to do. By so doing, they affect both the international division of labour and the conditions of the labour market in individual countries.

An MNE may also affect cross-border employment conditions and wage bargaining. There are two particular aspects which deserve attention. The first concerns the greater experience of, and information available to, MNEs about employee compensation, working practices and personnel management in different parts of the world. This means that, as and when appropriate, the MNE can draw upon and implement 'best' practices to stimulate employee motivation and productivity in any one of its subsidiaries. As we shall describe later in this chapter, there are many instances in which MNEs have tried to transfer the work methods and personnel-related procedures of their home countries to their foreign subsidiaries. Some, notably those recently introduced by Japanese affiliates in Europe and the United States, have been outstandingly successful. Others, like some US and European MNEs operating in developing countries, have failed miserably because of a lack of appreciation for culture-specific attitudes to work, rewards, authority and management–labour relations (Buckley and Casson, 1991).

Secondly, the management of an MNE is likely to have greater power and flexibility in negotiating work practices, employment conditions and human resource development with labour unions (and sometimes with governments) in the countries in which its affiliates operate, than its uninational counterpart will have. Some MNEs, of course, may choose to delegate part of this power to the management of their affiliates. However, even then the philosophy and influence of the parent company may permeate the local management's thinking and actions. An outstanding example here is the insistence, by many Japanese MNEs, that only one union should represent the workers in each of their subsidiaries. Yet, even if decisions are not centrally controlled or influenced, the local labour representatives may still be at a negotiating disadvantage, simply because they lack the necessary information about the real economic strengths (or weaknesses) of the affiliate and the organization of which it is part. This asymmetry in bargaining capacity between the management and local work force of the MNE is one which has caused much unease and dissatisfaction among labour unions. We shall take this issue up later in this chapter.

Finally, the interaction between the foreign affiliates of MNEs and host governments on labour-related issues may be different from that involving their own firms. Partly this is because of the differences in labour practices already described, which may affect government policies (e.g. towards wage increases, industrial training and collective bargaining). Partly, too, the response of MNEs to the introduction of new labour laws and regulations may be different from that of national firms. Basically, this reflects the greater options open to MNEs, *qua* MNEs, to site their value-added activities. It applies particularly to firms whose subsidiaries are supplying, or are intending to supply, regional or global markets, and who are pursuing efficiency-seeking investment strategies. Throughout most of the 1970s, the poor industrial relations environment in the UK led some UK- and foreign-based MNEs to eschew new production facilities in the UK. By contrast, in the 1980s and early 1990s, foreign firms have responded to the dramatic improvement in this environment[4] by favouring the UK for their EC-based operations.[5] Similarly, in Latin America, Asia and the Far East, MNEs have more readily reacted to political unrest and unwelcome economic policies by governments than have indigenous firms.[6] Section 13.7 will give further examples of the interaction between government policy and multinational human resource management.

13.2.2   A methodological note

Attempts to identify the distinctive features of the strategies of MNEs (or their foreign affiliates) towards the management or deployment of human resources have been only partially successful. This has been especially the case where there are no comparable domestic competitors. In such instances, economists have been forced to fall back on an assumed alternative position or counterfactual situation to measure the effects of MNE activity. Essentially, this seeks to estimate the most probable consequence on such variables as employment, employee compensation, working conditions, training, health and safety regulations in the absence of such activity. Clearly, these effects are likely to depend as much on the particular alternative situation assumed (as there are likely to be more than one) as on the actual labour-related practices of MNEs. However, in the absence of any comparable data on uninational or indigenous firms, some estimate of this kind has to be made in order to separate the impact of the foreignness or multinationality of firms from that resulting from their other characteristics.

The reader may have observed that in Chapter 10 we identified this problem as one which is common to all attempts to measure the distinct impact of FDI- and MNE-related activity. But, because of the priority attached to minimizing unemployment and upgrading human resource capabilities by most countries, it is particularly important that the specific and particular role of MNEs in the attainment of these goals be properly understood.[7] This issue will be further addressed in Section 13.4.

13.3   EMPLOYMENT IN MNEs

13.3.1   Numbers employed[8]

Let us now examine some facts about MNEs as employers of labour. Conservative estimates suggest that worldwide employment by, and within, MNEs was around 65 million in 1986. Of this, 43 million (or 66.2%) was in the home countries of these companies and 22 million (or 33.8%) in their foreign affiliates. Of the latter figure, seven million (or about one-third) was accounted for by affiliates in developing countries (Bailey and Parisotto, 1991).

Since, in 1986, the world's labour force numbered around 2160 million, it can be seen that the share of MNE employment is very small, *viz* about 3%. In developed countries, the share is rather greater – about 10% – while in developing countries

it is less than 1%. Moreover, these figures represent the actual numbers employed, *not* the net employment attributable to MNE activity.

Of course, as Chapter 2 has shown, since the contribution of MNEs to the output of particular sectors and countries varies a great deal, so it might be expected, would their participation in labour markets. This, indeed, is the case, as is the relative significance of foreign to domestic employment by MNEs from different countries. Some estimates are given in Tables 13.1 to 13.3.

Table 13.1 shows that the contribution of the domestic employment of home-based MNEs to total domestic employment in the mid 1980s varied from 4.3% in Belgium to 15.7% in Sweden, while the ratio of the foreign to the total employment of MNEs ranged from 20.1% in France to 75.7% in Switzerland. Table 13.2 presents some data on the

Table 13.1   Estimates of direct employment by MNEs from selected countries by country of origin (mid 1980s).

Country of origin of enterprises	Year	Type of estimate	Employment (millions)					
			1 All domestic employment	2 Total	3 Domestic MNE employment	4 Foreign MNE employment	5 3 as percentage of 1	6 4 as percentage of 2
Austria	1983	(c)	3.16	0.40	0.30	0.10	9.49	25.0
Belgium	1975	(b)	3.74	0.35	0.16	0.18	4.28	52.8
Canada	1984	(b)+(c)	10.95	1.76	1.06	0.71	9.68	40.3
France	1981	(b)+(c)	20.96	3.93	3.14	0.79	14.98	20.1
Germany (Fed Rep)	1983	(a)+(b)	24.65	9.63	7.22	2.41	12.74	33.4
Italy	1981	(b)+(c)	20.62	1.00	0.75	0.25	3.64	25.0
Netherlands	1987	(a)+(b)	5.25	1.29	0.51	0.78	9.71	60.5
Sweden	1984	(b)	4.26	0.95	0.67	0.29	15.73	30.5
Switzerland	1986	(b)	3.22	0.74	0.17	0.56	5.28	75.7
United Kingdom	1981	(b)+(c)	23.82	5.25	3.17	2.08	13.31	39.8
United States	1987	(a)	112.44	17.85	11.62	6.23	10.33	34.9
All countries			233.07	43.15	28.77	14.38	12.34	33.3

Type of estimate:
(a) Comprehensive official data and/or comprehensive survey of companies.
(b) Incomplete official data and/or incomplete company surveys (extrapolated where reasonably possible).

(c) Rough estimate based on incomplete information and specific assumptions.

Source: Derived from Kreye, Heinrichs and Frobel (1988), National Employment Agencies and UNCTC UN Statistical Yearbook (various editions) and Bailey and Parisotto (1991).

Table 13.2 Share of employment accounted for by foreign subsidiaries in selected host countries.

	Year	All Sectors		Manufacturing	
		Labour force[1] (000s)	Per cent of total	Labour force (000s)	Per cent of total
Developed countries					
North America					
Canada	1976	778.0	41	na	45
US	1987	3224.3	4	1377.8	7
Europe					
Austria	1987	265.3	12(1982)	na	22(1982)
Belgium	1975	331.4	na	na	33
Denmark	1984	86.7	4	na	15
France	1984	2798.0	12	1010.0	19(1981)
West Germany	1982	1485.0	10	na	16
Greece	1977	75.7	na	na	21
Ireland	1987	na	na	85.7	43
Italy	1986	445.9	5	na	83(1981)
Netherlands	1987	196.0	4	na	14
Portugal	1982	136.6	8	na	13
Spain	1987	1244.7	9	na	46(1977)
Sweden	1983	150.0	4	74.2	6
United Kingdom	1987	na	na	1050.0	13
Far East and Pacific					
Australia	1983	na	na	266.2	22
Japan	1984	511.0	1	na	na
Developing countries					
Latin America and the Caribbean					
Argentina	1981	na	na	185.0	19
Bolivia	1983	5.2	0	4.4	11
Brazil	1984	1285.6	3	908.7	23(1981)
Chile	1979	39.9	15	na	na
Mexico	1984	629.2	2	na	20
Peru	1984	43.5	1	na	7
Uruguay	1978	na	na	14.7	5
Asia and the Pacific					
Fiji	1980	14.8	18	na	22(1985)
Hong Kong	1988	na	na	108.1	12(1987)
Indonesia	1977	380.0	1	na	11(1980)
Korea	1986	416.0	3	na	10
Malaysia	1988	251.8	32	133.7	45(1984)
Singapore	1988	na	na	235.1	60
Taiwan	1986	266.8	5(1981)	na	17(1981)
Thailand	1985	182.7	na	na	9
Africa					
Cameroon	1984	35.0	1	na	>20
Gabon	1984	17.0	3	na	na
Kenya	1976	49.8	6	na	55

Table 13.2 continued.

	Year	All Sectors		Manufacturing	
		Labour force[1] (000s)	Per cent of total	Labour force (000s)	Per cent of total
Africa					
Liberia	1981	124.4	65[2]	na	>20
Nigeria	1977	166.0	na	na	na
Sierra Leone	1981	39.0	17	na	13

1 Of foreign subsidiaries.
2 Of paid employment.
Source: Dunning and Cantwell (1987); Kreye, Heinrichs and Frobel (1988); UNCTC (1992b, 1993). These are all secondary sources; the original data is primarily based on statistics published by, or provided to, ILO and UNCTC by national authorities.

share of the total labour force in selected host countries accounted for by foreign-owned firms. It reveals that, in the mid 1980s, in at least seven countries, *viz* Brazil, Canada, China, France, the Federal Republic of Germany, the United Kingdom, and the United States, foreign-owned firms employed more than 1 million. The percentage share of total domestic employment in the manufacturing sector (where data is more complete) exceeded 15% in at least 20 countries (e.g. Argentina, Austria, Australia, Belgium, Brazil, Cameroon, Canada, Columbia, Fiji, France, Germany, Greece, Ireland, Liberia, Malaysia, Mexico, Taiwan, Singapore, Spain and Zaire) and 10% or more in at least another eight countries.

Table 13.3 sets out some data on the percentage of host country employment accounted for by foreign affiliates in some leading manufacturing industries. As expected, the contribution is highest in the technology-intensive sectors and those supplying consumer goods with a relatively high income elasticity of demand. In the past decade, the growth of foreign employment by MNEs has been particularly noticeable in offshore assembling and processing facilities in Latin America and the Asia–Pacific region. In most countries and sectors, the contribution of foreign-owned firms has been increasing over the past decade – Canada and Australia are notable exceptions – as has the percentage of foreign to local employment of most of the leading MNEs (Dunning and Pearce, 1985; UNCTC, 1988). This data is

further confirmation of the globalization of economic activity and of its consequences for the structure and ownership of domestic employment. Perhaps nowhere is this better illustrated than in the case of the UK, where in 1987 the foreign manufacturing employment of UK companies' overseas and foreign affiliates in the United Kingdom was 45% of domestic employment.

Data on the distribution of employment by MNEs in the non-manufacturing sector is extremely fragmentary. In the mid 1980s, MNEs from three of the largest outward investing countries, *viz* the United States, Japan and the Federal Republic of Germany, employed just 119 thousand (or 1.3% of their total foreign labour force) in foreign agricultural and forestry activities, 391 thousand (or 4.3% of their labour force) in mining, 1379 thousand (or 15.2% of their labour force) in wholesale and retail trade, 123 thousand (or 1.4% of their labour force) in construction and 634 thousand (or 1.0% of their labour force) in other services.

From a recipient country's standpoint, in some agribusiness, forestry and mineral sectors in the smaller developing countries, MNEs account for the greater part of the local labour force. Most of the larger forestry, banana, tea, coffee, tobacco and pineapple plantations are foreign owned. Also, despite the nationalization of many petroleum and hard mineral foreign affiliates, MNEs continue to be the leading employers in the diamond mines of the Transvaal, the copper mines in New Guinea and

Table 13.3 Share of foreign affiliates of manufacturing employment in selected host countries.

| | Developed countries | | | | | | | | Developing countries | | | | | |
| | Australia | Germany | Japan | Netherlands | Ireland | Sweden | UK | USA | Thailand | Mexico | Hong Kong | Indonesia | Peru | Fiji |
	1983	1982	1986	1980	1987	1978	1988	1987	1986	1985	1987	1980	1988	1985
Food and drink products	25.5	17.7	0.2	19.7	27.7	13.8	8.2	8.8	6.0	6.52	19.5	4.7	10.6	16.9
Chemicals and allied products	59.6	21.8	1.9	36.9	75.7	22.1	28.9	23.5	23.2	44.7	26.1	16.7	20.1	41.3
Metals	22.5	30.4	0.1	nsa	24.0	11.4	11.3	6.7	9.9	10.6	5.2	22.2	4.2	50.0
Mechanical engineering	25.1	16.3	1.4	2.3	74.6	nsa	16.2	5.8	38.4	32.1	7.2	24.4	neg	neg
Electrical engineering	nsa	nsa	nsa	23.6	nsa	16.4	nsa	nsa	nsa	nsa	nsa	nsa	nsa	nsa
Motor vehicles	43.0	18.9	0.3	17.5	17.9	9.1	32.0	6.5	4.9	96.4	neg	neg	13.5	11.1
Textiles and clothing	18.7	4.8	neg	7.9	42.2	7.2	3.3	3.2	11.4	5.66	5.4	8.6	2.1	neg
Paper and allied products	12.2	7.6	0.2	11.8	10.8	3.8	13.9	5.5	4.3	8.38	7.2	9.4	neg	38.3
Rubber products	37.3	20.4	neg	nsa	56.9	nsa	18.2	6.5	22.0	neg	neg	neg	10.7	neg
Coal and petroleum products	80.8	61.0	14.5	nsa	nsa	nsa	nsa	39.5	nsa	3.2	6.5	nsa	2.9	neg
Other manufacturing	10.1	15.0	0.2	nsa	51.8	11.9	9.5	4.4	3.9	35.2	5.4	nsa	1.0	41.5
All manufacturing	21.6	15.8	0.8	nsa	42.8	5.7	12.9	7.3	8.8	20.2	11.9	10.9	6.5	21.5

Source: As for Tables 13.1 and 13.2.

Peru, the bauxite mines of Jamaica and the uranium mines of Namibia.

In the services sectors, the huge Japanese and Korean trading companies dominate the import–export merchanting business in Asia, while the largest wholesale distribution outlets in Fiji are Australian owned. Foreign-owned banks account for the majority of employment in banking and finance, insurance, computer software, management consultancy and advertising in most developing and in some smaller developed countries. The labour force engaged in the large-scale construction industry in the Middle East is mainly employed by Turkish, Korean or Philippine MNEs, while the numbers employed in foreign-owned or managed hotels far exceeds that employed in indigenous hotels in the Caribbean and Bahamian islands, the Seychelles, Mauritius and Fiji.

13.3.2 The skill mix

Only fragmentary data is available on the skill mix of employment in MNEs at home or abroad; neither is it easy to obtain a breakdown of the labour force along the value chain for particular products. However, elsewhere in this book, especially in Chapters 11 and 15, we have suggested that the proportion of the higher value-added activities undertaken by MNEs is likely to be considerably more in their home countries than in their subsidiaries; although, in some larger developed countries, foreign affiliates either fully replicate the activities of their parent companies or produce a specialized range of products as part of a globally-integrated strategy. Furthermore, both US and European data suggests that there is a positive correlation between the degree of multinationalization of enterprises and the skill content of their labour forces, both in their domestic and foreign operations.[9]

Data on the comparative labour skill mix of the subsidiaries of foreign-owned affiliates compared with that of their domestic competitors reveals a mixed picture. In the UK and West Germany, both of which are highly favoured venues for the technology-intensive production of foreign affiliates, the proportion of pre- and post-production personnel to the total numbers employed by such firms is about the same as that of their indigenous competitors. In Canada, Belgium and the US, the numbers employed by foreign subsidiaries in innovative activities compares favourably with that of indigenous firms, although data on R&D expenditure suggests that the former undertake relatively less basic or fundamental research than the latter.

In developing countries, some data obtained from an ILO survey (1981) on the employment structure of foreign manufacturing affiliates in Kenya, Libya, India, Pakistan, Chile and Mexico found that, in the late 1970s, workers engaged in direct production accounted for the highest percentage (in most cases 60% to 75%) of the total personnel of foreign affiliates (ILO, p. 33). Clerical and administrative staff accounted for between 12% and 25%, technical and professional employees 3% to 11% and managerial staff from 4% to 6%. The ILO study further concluded that between 1960 and 1977 there had been a noticeable increase in the proportion of workers with above average skills employed by foreign affiliates.

Data on the comparative skill mix of foreign-owned and indigenous firms also shows that this varies between host countries. In Nigeria in 1979, for example, foreign-owned firms employed a much higher proportion of managerial, skilled and clerical labour than did indigenous firms, although one suspects this was as much a result of the kinds of activities engaged in by foreign affiliates as their nationality of ownership. In Malaysian manufacturing industry in 1983, MNEs employed a slightly higher percentage of professional and technical staff and a considerably higher percentage of managerial staff than did their indigenous competitors (Yong, 1988). A similar employment structure was observed in Thailand, but there were also substantial differences in the skill mixes of foreign-owned firms. In 1985, for example, unskilled workers accounted for 49.6% of the manufacturing labour force of Thai-owned firms, 29% of US affiliates, 40% of European affiliates and 55% of Japanese affiliates (Sibunruang and Brimble, 1988).

In Indian industry, Kumar (1991) found that in the late 1970s the proportion of high income employees was significantly higher in foreign-owned than in domestic firms, although whether this was because the foreign-owned companies employed more talented personnel or paid their employees

better was unclear. Balasubramanyam (1984), in the case of Indonesia, and Willmore (1986), in the case of Brazil, both attribute the higher wages paid by foreign affiliates to differences in the quality of the labour force. In UK manufacturing industry, for some years now, except in the case of Japanese-owned firms, the proportion of non-operatives to all workers employed by foreign affiliates has been consistently higher than that of domestic firms, although this is partly because the former tend to concentrate in sectors where this ratio is above the average (Dunning, 1986a).

The impact of multinational affiliates on both the level and skill content of employment is also likely to depend on the nature of the activity undertaken by them. Chapter 11 suggested that in both the goods and service sectors there is evidence to suggest that MNEs use more capital-intensive techniques than do indigenous firms. At the same time, foreign firms have frequently played an important role in upgrading labour aptitudes in several developing countries (notably Thailand, Taiwan, Malaysia and Singapore) by producing goods and services that require a higher than average skill input.

Studies of the initial impact of MNEs undertaking greenfield market-seeking investments in developing and developed countries suggest that this will be felt mainly by unskilled and semi-skilled workers. However, providing the venture is a success, backward integration along the value-added chain is likely to lead to the employment of workers with higher skill levels. For example, the 'competence' content of the labour force employed by Japanese affiliates in the European motor vehicles and consumer electronics industry is considerably lower than that of their longer-established American counterparts. In the US, some Japanese affiliates are already as skill intensive in their labour content as their local competitors.

However, perhaps the most contentious issue about the impact of MNEs on the structure of employment in developing countries is that to do with export-processing investment. Here, the assertion is often made that, while as part of their global sourcing policies, MNEs may create new jobs in countries with plentiful supplies of cheap and well motivated labour, this is unlikely to be of permanent benefit to these countries, since, as and when wages rise, production will be shifted to countries one or

two stages back in the investment development path.
Moreover, according to the critics, export-processing
affiliates will rarely employ other than unskilled or
semi-skilled workers.

The evidence for these assertions is inconclusive.[10] In any event, employment in export-
processing or free trade zones in the majority of
industrializing, developing countries has continued to
increase since the early 1970s. Several of these zones
are now being set up in Eastern Europe (UNCTC,
1990e). In the Maquiladora plants in Mexico, for
example, employment trebled between mid-1982 and
the end of 1989 to over 400 000, and is likely to
increase further if and when the North American
Free Trade Agreement (NAFTA) comes into effect.
More generally, the change in emphasis of many host
developing governments from an import-substituting
to an export-led industrialization strategy has
prompted more investment by foreign firms, even in
African countries, like Kenya and Zimbabwe, where
inbound investment has been dormant for many
years.

Generally speaking, activities which are intended
to promote a country's dynamic comparative advantage rest less on the availability of cheap labour and
more on the opportunities for upgrading human
skills and technological capabilities. In so far as
foreign-based MNEs choose to use their O-specific
advantages in a way that helps advance the host
country's international competitiveness, the long-
term employment effects are likely to be favourable.
Indeed, there is evidence of completely integrated
production lines for the manufacture of quite sophisticated products (e.g. motorcycles, engines, cameras,
TV sets and machine tools) being located in
countries like Korea, Taiwan, Singapore, Mexico
and Brazil. In all cases, the consequential improvement of occupational skills has been aided by the
presence of the foreign affiliates.

In developed countries, the role of MNEs in
influencing labour skills and productivity has largely
depended on the existing competitive advantages of
the countries in question, as well as on how
indigenous firms and governments have reacted to
the presence of MNEs. In sectors that can boast a
strong innovative capability, where rivalry is strong
(but not destructive), which produce goods for a
sophisticated market and where government action
helps to strengthen the competitive position of its

own firms, MNE activity is likely to stimulate further
the upgrading of human capital. Section 13.5 and
Chapters 16 and 19 will take up these points in more
detail.

Inbound direct investment may also have beneficial affects in raising skill levels by injecting
entrepreneurship and rivalry into a sector which has
the potential to be internationally efficient, but is
currently insulated from foreign competition. Moreover, where it is first in a completely new industry, it
may pioneer entirely new aptitudes and talents.
Examples include the entry of US computer, semiconductor and pharmaceutical companies in the UK
in the 1960s; that of European lighting and electrical
equipment firms into Pakistan and Kenya in the
1970s; and that of US and European computer
software and business service firms into Barbados in
the 1980s. Finally, as Section 13.6 will describe,
many foreign-owned firms – particularly those which
are leaders in their industries – have done much to
advance the skills and capabilities of their workers by
in-house training.

On the other hand, in the absence of strong (or
potentially strong) indigenous supply capabilities, a
market structure that is conducive to innovation and
change, and appropriate government macro-organizational policies, inbound direct investment is less
likely to promote the upgrading of human skills and
competences. Indeed, it may reduce or inhibit them,
either by out-competing a local company that does
have such capabilities, or by thwarting the entry of
others. This happened in the UK motor vehicle
industry in the 1960s and 1970s (the situation is now
changing as a result of the entry of Japanese auto
affiliates), in the pharmaceutical industry in Denmark
and in several various branches of the agri-business
sector in resource-rich developing countries. However, whether or not this acts to the disadvantage of
the host country depends upon the configuration of
its diamond of competitive advantage. It could well
be, for example, that technological advances dictate
a restructuring of skills, and that the sectors in which
foreign affiliates operate are not those in which a
country has (or could have) a dynamic comparative
advantage.

As far as outbound MNE activity is concerned,
there is a strong presumption that it may help to
raise the quality of the domestic labour force though,
as we shall see later, it does not necessarily lead to

more employment. This presumption is based on the perception that to be competitive in world markets many firms need not only to sell, but to produce, abroad. The foreign markets so captured help these firms to finance the innovatory activities necessary to sustain and/or upgrade their technological and other O-specific assets. Yet, though some of these latter activities will be undertaken in foreign subsidiaries, the bulk will continue to be conducted at home. One possible exception is where an FDI is specifically made to acquire higher value activities. Even in this case, the additional knowledge and experience gained is likely to enhance the quality of the domestic labour force. A reading of the company reports of the major innovating MNEs suggests that, in spite of the gradual decentralization of innovating activities (see Chapter 11), most important new products (which are usually the most skill intensive) still tend to be produced first in home-based factories.

Here again, however, it is worth emphasizing that only the most successful home-based MNEs will help to upgrade domestic skills. Also, the extent to which they do will at least partly depend on the domestic competitive advantages of, and pressures to create and use these advances in, the capital-exporting countries.

13.3.3   Indirect employment associated with MNE activity

We propose to deal with the indirect or spill-over consequences of the value activities of MNEs or their affiliates on the rest of the economy in which they operate in Chapter 16. Much of what we write there can be translated into the effects on employment or human resource capability. To avoid repetition in this section, we will simply highlight the conclusions of some of the studies which have specifically addressed this question.

Exhibit 13.1 divides the indirect employment generated by MNE activity effects into: general macro-economic, horizontal and vertical consequences. Macro-economic consequences include any employment brought about by changes in macro-economic related variables (e.g. monetary and/or fiscal policy, exchange rate) which might be induced by inward investment. Horizontal consequences

include those on the competitors of foreign affiliates and also on firms that compete with them in the labour market. Vertical consequences relate primarily to the linkages along the value chains on which the affiliates are producing.

Clearly, the magnitude of the indirect employment associated with inward direct investment will depend on the size of output produced by foreign affiliates, their propensity to acquire their intermediate products from domestic suppliers and the choice of technologies facing both the suppliers and the affiliates. The size of the output is self-explanatory. The propensity of foreign affiliates to buy from local firms will rest on their supply capabilities *vis à vis* those of their foreign competitors, the role of government (e.g. in limiting imports and/or influencing the competences of the local supplying industry) and the sourcing strategy of the foreign investors. Such a strategy may involve the affiliate providing assistance to suppliers to improve the quality or lower the prices of their products.[11] The kind of technology choice will influence the level and skill content of the labour employed by the affiliates, their competitors and supplying firms. In some sectors (e.g. oil exploration and refining) the direct employment impact will be limited, but the effect on suppliers (e.g. of oil drilling equipment) may be quite considerable. The significance of each of these variables will also depend on the stage of a country's economic development and the developmental strategies it is pursuing.

It is even more difficult to predict how MNEs might impinge upon the employment of their competitors. On the one hand, if they gain domestic or foreign markets at their competitors' expense (see Section 13.4) or force them to adopt labour-saving production processes, the impact on employment may be negative. On the other, if they increase consumer demand and stimulate their competitors to be more innovatory or efficient, the employment impact may be positive. Again, much will depend on the structure of the labour market prior to entry of the MNE.

It is also important to distinguish between the short-run and long-run impact of MNE activity. This is because it is possible to conceive of an employment-accumulation model corresponding to the asset-accumulation model set out in Chapters 10 and 11. Given the right conditions, inward direct investment

---

Exhibit 13.1   Direct and indirect employment effects associated with MNE activity.

	Definition or illustration
Direct employment	Total number of people employed within the MNE subsidiary.
Indirect employment	All types of employment indirectly generated throughout the local economy by the MNE subsidiary.
1. Macro-economic	Employment indirectly generated throughout the local economy as a result of spending by the MNE subsidiary's workers or shareholders.
2. Horizontal	Employment indirectly generated among other local enterprises as a result of competition with the MNE subsidiary.
a. Narrow horizontal effects	Employment indirectly generated among local enterprises competing in the same industry as the MNE subsidiary.
b. Broad horizontal effects	Employment indirectly generated among local enterprises competing in the same industry as the MNE subsidiary.
3. Vertical	Employment indirectly generated by the MNE subsidiary among its local suppliers and customers.
a. Backward effects (or linkages)	Employment indirectly generated by the MNE subsidiary among its local suppliers (of raw materials, parts, components, services, etc).
b. Forward effects (or linkages)	Employment indirectly generated by the MNE subsidiary among its local customers (e.g. distributors, service agents).

Note 1   The above employment effects, if they could be measured, should be calculated to net terms (i.e. gross employment directly or indirectly generated minus total employment displacement).

Note 2   Item 3a comprises contract-related MNE employment for contracts with a local economy.

Source: Exhibit based on Chapter 3 of ILO: *Employment effects of multinational enterprises in developing countries* (Geneva, 1981) and Susumu Watanabe: *Multinational enterprises and employment-oriented 'appropriate' technologies in developing countries*, Multinational Enterprises Programme Working Paper No 14 (ILO, Geneva, 1981).

---

may set in train or contribute towards a virtuous employment circle in a particular sector. In time, this will lead to an improvement in labour quality and productivity, and possibly an increase in employment. However, if the sector is losing its competitiveness in world markets, there is a real possibility that the presence of foreign affiliates may aggravate a vicious employment circle, leading to a fall in both the quality and quantity of domestic employment. At the same time, the current experience of the UK auto industry suggests that inward direct investment can reverse a vicious employment circle.[12] There is also ample evidence, both from developed and developing countries, to suggest that inappropriate govern-

ment action (e.g. as it affects education and training, innovation, industrial relations, the environment and acquisitions and mergers) can reduce or halt the momentum of a virtuous circle.

The consequences of MNE activity for local labour markets are also likely to be mixed. First – particularly in the case of greenfield investments – it depends on whether the labour is recruited from other firms or from the ranks of the unemployed. Second, and scarcely less important, are the training policies of the investing firms and the support they may (or may not) give to local higher educational and training institutions, as well as to university and other research programmes. If, by their human resource strategies, MNEs create a demand for new labour skills and competences, then this could have beneficial effects on the quality of the labour market. However, if they simply add to the pressures of demand for a fixed supply of labour, their presence may either lead to inflationary wage settlements or force competitors to make better use of their existing labour.[13]

What is the evidence on the direct and indirect employment consequences associated with MNE activity? The results of a series of country case studies conducted by the ILO show clearly that the indirect employment effects associated with inward direct investment may sometimes be as, if not more, important than the direct effects. The authors of the studies confirm that country-, industry- and firm-specific factors (such as the level of tariff protection, local content requirements, the nature of the products produced, the age and size of the foreign affiliate, the sourcing strategy of the MNE, the technological competence of both suppliers and customers, and the willingness of the foreign affiliates to help train their distributors and service agents) make it difficult to generalize about the extent and form of these effects.

Since well over four-fifths of the total employment by MNEs is in developed countries, it might be expected that the indirect employment generated by such companies would be much greater than that of their counterparts in developing countries. We need not concern ourselves about the impact of home-based MNEs on vertical or horizontal indirect employment, except to make just one point; because of their greater flexibility in global sourcing policies, it might be reasonable to hypothesize that foreign-owned companies should buy a larger proportion of their inputs from foreign suppliers than domestic firms. Such evidence as can be gleaned from US and Japanese data supports this hypothesis (US Department of Commerce, 1991; JETRO, 1990). Both Japanese and US MNEs tend to import a higher proportion of their sales than their uninational competitors. However, these additional imports are more than offset by the purchases made by their foreign-owned distributors from their parent companies or home countries.

To what extent can it be said that the affiliates of foreign firms generate different employment effects than their indigenous competitors? Here the evidence is inconclusive. For well established manufacturing affiliates supplying large domestic markets, the impact on employment in the intermediate product sectors is likely to be strongly positive. By contrast, newly established affiliates and those producing specialized products requiring intermediate products that are not yet produced locally, are likely to have a more limited impact on domestic employment.

However, one of the expectations that most governments of advanced countries have of inward investment is that it will help economic restructuring and the development of industrial clusters. Whether or not this is achieved depends, in part, on the ability of the host country to provide the necessary economic and technological milieu for such productivity improvements. In the case of some Japanese MNE investments in the United States and Europe, new networks of supporting producers are being formed. In the United States auto industry, for example, there are now some 300 Japanese affiliates or joint US–Japanese ventures supplying parts and components both to Japanese and US auto producers. By the end of 1990, these firms were employing at least the number of people employed in the Japanese-owned auto assembling subsidiaries.

13.4 MEASURING THE EMPLOYMENT EFFECTS OF MNE ACTIVITY

13.4.1 Introduction

So far in this chapter we have focused on the actual numbers employed and skill mix of MNEs and their affiliates, and of other firms which might be affected by their presence. In doing so, we also paid some attention to the distinguishing characteristics of MNEs as employers. However, any amount of data about the human resource management of MNEs can tell us very little about the extent to which their employment may be attributed specifically to their ownership or degree of multinationality. To take an extreme example, suppose there were no MNEs; what proportion of the 65 million people currently employed by them would still be employed? If, as some authors claim (ILO, 1984), the indirect employment associated with MNE activity is at least equal to the numbers employed by them, is that figure greater or less than one would have expected in their absence? If MNEs are shown not to employ many personnel in managerial, administrative or innovating activities in developing countries, can one presume that, in their absence, more would have been employed by indigenous firms? And, had not MNEs from (say) the United States been permitted to invest in export processing zones in (say) Korea or Malaysia, would not the employment in US factories still have occurred, because (say) Japanese MNEs would have invested in their place?

Such questions as these have plagued economists and business analysts for many years. For, as we have already seen, the answers will rest substantially on the assumptions one makes about the alternative or counterfactual situation. Also, even the most realistic of these situations will vary according to the types of FDI made, the response of competitors and the policies pursued by home and host governments. Yet, whether or not a particular investment is made may have considerable employment consequences. The analyst is then perforce required to make some estimates of the employment consequences of alternative scenarios.

13.4.2 A home country perspective

Let us, first, look at some surveys conducted on the domestic employment consequences of the foreign activities of home-based MNEs. Studies conducted by US and European economists in the late 1960s identified four possible consequences:

- *The production or job displacement effect*: This effect attempts to assess the extent to which foreign production from the investing country replaces exports and, where that output is imported back into the investing country, the domestic employment required to supply that output.

- *The export stimulation effect*: This follows from the possibility that foreign affiliates will buy some of their raw materials, capital equipment, intermediate products and finished goods and services from their parent companies and/or home countries, thus helping to create new employment opportunities.

- *The home office employment effect*: This suggests that, as foreign production is increased, the innovating, management and other 'white collar' activities, which are usually undertaken by the investing company on behalf of the foreign operating units of the MNE, will also increase.

- *The supporting firm employment effect*: This is the indirect employment effect of foreign production. It arises from the change in employment in home country firms and institutions (e.g. accounting, consultancy, banking and engineering firms) which provide supporting services for the affiliates of home-based MNEs. Of course, it is possible that this effect may be negative if the supporting firms follow their customers overseas.[14]

In turn, these four effects will partly depend on the macro-economic policies pursued by home and host governments in response to the foreign activities of home-based MNEs. We shall discuss these in more detail in the next chapter when analysing the balance of payments consequences of outward and inward direct investment. However, the kinds of questions which need to be answered are:

- How successful are home governments in pursuing structural adjustment employment policies? How far will any labour displaced by the export of value-added activities find alternative work in the home country? Clearly the answers to these questions are partly country specific. For example, any adverse effects of Japanese outward investment on domestic employment may be mitigated by the fact that many Japanese MNEs pursue a policy of lifetime employment, and because the Japanese government works together with private employers to ensure that, as far as possible, any labour displaced by outward direct investment is productively redeployed. By contrast, countries without positive structural adjustment policies, and which already have a high unemployment ratio, may find any absorption of the released labour a difficult task.

- In the case of a greenfield export-substituting investment, what would have happened to employment and output in the recipient country had not the investment been made? Would other foreign or domestic firms have filled that lacunae, or would the host economy have continued to import the goods and services from the investing country?

- Assuming that some domestic capacity is released by the transfer of value-added activities to a foreign location, to what extent is the investing firm likely to utilize that capacity by, for example, diversifying its product portfolio, upgrading its profit range, innovating new products and so on? Historical evidence (Jones, 1991) suggests that domestic and foreign investment are as much likely to be complementary to, as substitutable for, each other – particularly in technology-intensive growth sectors. Again, the Japanese have deliberately used outward direct investment as a means of upgrading domestic value-added activities and the quality of work and employment conditions (Ozawa, 1990).[15]

- Assuming that outward FDI is designed to produce goods more cheaply for export back to the investing country (as in the case of low wage cost investment in developing countries by European, US and Japanese firms), what is the policy of home country governments towards these imports? Will they be freely permitted – or will import controls of one kind or another be imposed?

- What will be the international repercussions of actions taken by the government of one country to restrict outward investment to protect domestic jobs? Will similar measures be taken by other countries and, if so, what are the likely consequences for jobs in the first country?

- Assuming the wage bill of the host country is increased as a result of the new foreign investment, what percentage of that increase might be spent on goods imported from the investing country?

It is answers to questions like these that will determine the direction and value of the four employment effects identified and, therefore, the consequences of outward direct investment for the domestic labour force. At the same time, while it may be difficult to generalize on these effects, it is possible to identify the situations in which, relative to some assumed alternative use of resources, MNE activity is likely to protect, generate, restructure or affect domestic employment. Consider, for example, the most favourable scenario from the viewpoint of the home country. This is likely to include the following conditions:

- The investing company wishes to release domestic capacity to expand or upgrade its activities in the domestic market.

- There is full (or nearly full) employment and an effective structural adjustment programme operating in the home country.

- The outward investment is likely to advance the competitiveness of the home firm or economy (e.g. by providing access to cheaper or better quality intermediate products, gaining a window to the latest technological developments by helping to advance the global strategy of the investing firms, and by generating additional exports (e.g. of intermediate products or finished goods) from the home country.

- The home government is not prepared to restrict the import of goods and services by the investing company from its foreign affiliates.

- In the absence of the outward investment, the host country would have reduced its purchases from the home country in any event; for example, by imposing import restrictions of one kind or another.

- The advantages of the home country as an export base are declining.

Most investments in trade and distribution, in resource exploitation, in manufacturing sectors in which the home country's competitive advantage is declining, as well as those designed to protect, sustain or advance a global competitive position fall into this category.

By contrast, where the pressures of oligopolistic competition cause firms to engage in or increase their foreign output of products in which the home country has a comparative locational advantage; where there is high domestic unemployment; or where there are inadequate provisions or incentives for structural adjustment and retraining, then – at least in the short run – both the level and skill content of domestic employment could be adversely affected by outward investment. At the same time, some of these effects may as much be the outcome of structural market distortions or inappropriate macroeconomic policies by home or host governments as any misallocation of resources on the part of MNEs.[16]

Let us now consider some of the empirical evidence on the job implications of outbound direct investment. The most comprehensive studies have been carried out in the United States. They have yielded very different results according to the counterfactual positions assumed. In a survey of 74 manufacturing MNEs carried out by the Emergency Committee on America (1972), the authors estimated that US outward direct investment in the 1960s led to an increase of 550 000 American jobs, mainly, it seems, because of its beneficial effects on exports and home office activity in the investing companies. A similar conclusion was reached by Robert Stobaugh et al. (1976). Based on case study data, Stobaugh put the net (domestic) employment gain of US MNE activity at 600 000 (including 100 000 for support firm employment).

About the same time, a contrasting view was expressed by Stanley Rutenberg (1971) who, in an investigation for the AFL–CIO, calculated that US FDI in the 1960s had cost the US economy 500 000 jobs. However, not only did Rutenberg assume a counterfactual situation of no alternative investment, but he ignored both the home office and supporting firm employment effects. Most academic studies (e.g. US Tariff Commission, 1970; Hawkins, 1972; Frank and Freeman, 1978; Magee, 1979) emphasize the differential employment consequences of outward direct investment according to the ability of other firms to supply the market, which is (or might have been) serviced by US firms. Again, the estimates of these scholars ranged from a net job loss of over 1 million to a net job gain of 629 000.

With all these estimates in mind together with those of his own study, which was based on US Department of Commerce data for 1966 and 1970, Hawkins concluded that, apart from the job displacement effects, US outward investment created between 469 000 and 534 000 extra US jobs. According to the assumed counterfactual position, the job displacement effects varied from 190 000 to 1.2 million. Thus, the net employment effect ranged from +279 000 to −666 000.

In a later study – but for the same time period – Hawkins, in making a comparison between the employment effects of foreign production and those of US exports, sales by non-US producers and imports from third countries (both to foreign and US markets) concluded that foreign production led to a gain of about 260 000 US jobs (Hawkins, 1976). However, he also found that the likely employment effects of US outward investment were highly industry specific. While the main gains were recorded by the drug, cosmetic, soap, office machinery, electrical equipment and 'other' manufacturing firms, the industries suffering the largest loss of jobs were industrial and other chemicals, lumber, wood and furniture, and textile and apparel. Finally, the industrial structure of the gains and losses revealed that the main job beneficiaries were the higher paid, more skilled workers, while the main losers were the lower paid, less skilled workers. Hawkins concluded that because of this, not only should MNEs be required to give as much advance warning as possible about their foreign investment intentions, but that governments should offer more, and more effective, adjustment assistance to displaced workers.

The 'neutral' to 'marginally favourable' employment effects of US foreign investment have been confirmed by some later studies which have compared the domestic job performance of US MNEs with those of uninational firms. Kujawa (1980) found that in the years 1973–78, US MNEs expanded their employment by an average of 4.8% per annum, while in the latter employment fell by 2.6% per annum. Over a slightly longer period, viz 1970–78, the export growth rates of US MNEs were nearly 50% above the average for all manufacturing industry[17] (Enderwick, 1985). Similar conclusions were reached in a study of 118 large UK MNEs by Stopford (1979), who discovered that in the early 1970s, except in the auto industry, these firms had either increased their domestic employment by more, or reduced it by less, than uninational UK firms. Later research into the effects of foreign investment by 22 of the largest UK MNEs on the British economy concluded that while, in the short run, such investment probably led to a fall in UK exports, in the long run FDI and domestic employment were likely to be complementary to each other (Shepherd et al., 1985).

A different kind of analysis, which will be

discussed in more detail in Chapter 14, reveals that US export sales (and, by implication, domestic employment) tend to be positively related to the sales of US foreign affiliates (and, by implication, foreign employment).[18] However, Kravis and Lipsey (1988) concluded that, given the size of parent operations in the US, a firm that produces abroad tends to have fewer employees in the US and pays slightly higher wages to them. The authors suggested this was because foreign production frequently replaced the more labour-intensive activities in the home country. One exception to the apparent negative effect of foreign production on domestic employment (which was found to be most pronounced in the labour-intensive sectors) was the case of minority-owned manufacturing affiliates. Often this kind of investment led to strong positive effects on the exports of the parent company.[19]

The US and UK findings are broadly corroborated by European and Japanese studies. Van den Bulcke and Halsberghe (1979) concluded that in the 1970s, Belgian outward direct investment had a positive effect on employment in Belgium, in spite of some loss of jobs arising from the production displacement effect. In Sweden, a detailed examination of two large MNEs concluded that while, in the short run, their foreign activities had replaced products which might otherwise have been domestically made and exported, in the long term the global competitive position of the investing firms had been advanced and, with it, the employment security of the domestic labour force (Jordan and Vahlne, 1981). In a review of German firms abroad, the author (Bailey, 1979) observed that since a substantial amount of their FDI occurred by way of acquisition or merger, or was specifically designed to overcome trade barriers, it was unlikely to have had an adverse effect on home employment. The growing share of both US and European investment accounted for by trans-Atlantic and intra-European rationalized and strategic asset seeking MNE activity also suggests that, far from being substitutable for each other, foreign and domestic employment are likely to be complementary (Campbell and McElrath, 1990).

In Japan, a study by Koshiro (1982) found that the reaction of Japanese producers to the switch of production of 875 000 colour television sets from Japan to the US in the period 1977–80 under the orderly marketing agreement was to 'absorb the

shock without direct personnel reductions'. They did so by 'boosting production and exports of newly innovated high value-added products, increased exports of parts and components and switching their (displaced) export markets to other areas' (Koshiro, 1982, p. 35). The author concluded that while the relocation of production by Japanese MNEs had probably led to some loss of jobs, this was more than outweighed by the increased exports of parts, components and capital goods and the extra expenditure by US workers on Japanese imports. Koshiro also found that, as a result of (or parallel with) Japanese investment in the US, the quality of employment in Japan had been upgraded.

Whatever the uncertainties or approximations attached to the results just described, the balance of evidence seems to suggest that the overall effects of outward MNE activity on the level of employment in the home country are likely to be marginally positive. This is not to deny that, in some sectors, it may be very negative. Moreover, there is evidence both from Swedish and US research to suggest that multinationalization does lead to a change in the skill mix within the investing industry. The jobs lost in the source country tend to be production related, while those gained are primarily of a skilled, professional and managerial kind (Jordan and Vahlne, 1981; Hawkins and Jedel, 1975). At the same time, as another writer (Magee, 1979) has argued, the kind of job losses experienced by MNEs are rarely very different from those experienced by non-multinationals. Fundamentally, they both arise from the declining competitiveness of the exporting country in international markets, and, in some cases, an overvalued exchange rate.

Here, in so far as the case for a restriction of direct capital exports has any merit at all, it is that the resources and capabilities invested overseas would be better allocated to improving domestic competitiveness. Porter (1990) cites the case of the US-based semiconductor companies who responded to their loss of markets to Japanese competitors by going offshore to produce the same products. By contrast, when faced with the same problem, Japanese producers chose to upgrade their domestic technological capacities. Porter argues that US firms would have achieved greater long-term success had they adopted the latter strategy. At the same time, there is no denying the imperative for some firms to become global producers. Assuming they are successful, their foreign activities are likely to improve the security of jobs in the home country, especially in supervisory and white collar occupations.

13.4.3   A host country perspective

Much of what has been written about evaluating the domestic employment effects of outbound MNE activity also applies to assessing the employment consequences of inward investment on the recipient country. Once again, it is necessary, first, to estimate the direct and indirect employment associated with the operation of the foreign affiliates, and second, to identify the next best alternative to such investment[20] and estimate the employment associated with this alternative. The difference between the two is the employment effect of inward investment.

Other chapters in this volume have given (or will give) some illustrations of the differences in the sectoral composition of foreign and indigenously-owned output, as well as of the structure and productivity of labour inputs which help generate that output. According to the assumption one makes about the proportion of output produced by foreign affiliates that would otherwise have been produced by domestic firms, rather than imported, the consequences for employment may be very different.

Take, for example, Nissan's participation in the UK auto industry. Is this beneficial for the United Kingdom's level and quality of employment or not? It is easy enough to obtain data on Nissan's labour force and on the employment of its suppliers, distributors, etc. However, according to the assumptions made about what both Nissan and competitors might have done had Nissan not chosen to invest in the United Kingdom (in the 1980s), the employment effects are very different. Possibly the most realistic alternative scenario is that Nissan would have set up production facilities elsewhere in Europe and exported to the United Kingdom from there, and that the position of the rest of the auto industry would have been unaffected. In this scenario, the employment consequences of Nissan's investment are clearly beneficial to the UK as the jobs created would otherwise have been lost to the UK's competitors. An alternative is that UK-based auto companies would have produced the output instead

of Nissan and at the same efficiency, so that UK employment would have been largely unaffected. Indeed, depending on whether the output was produced by UK or other foreign-owned companies, its skill content and long-term competitiveness may have been improved as a larger output would have enabled these firms to spread their innovatory and administrative activities more effectively.

Similar exercises can, and have been, conducted for other kinds of inward investment in both developed and developing countries. Depending on the extent of the local innovating and production capacity, the policies of host governments, the kind of inward direct investment (is it market seeking, rationalized or asset acquiring?), the form of the investment (is it a greenfield venture or the acquisition of an existing firm?), and the age, experience and the kinds of strategies of the MNEs themselves, the domestic employment effects may vary from being strongly positive to strongly negative. What, then, is the evidence on this score?

First, for reasons documented in Chapter 2, it is likely that the employment impact of inward direct investment on host countries will be greater than that of outward investment on home countries. In view of this, it is surprising that remarkably few studies have used the alternative position approach to assess the job consequences of MNE activity on host countries. In most resource-based sectors, the question is not so much whether MNEs have or have not created jobs, but how many and what kinds of jobs have they created? Exceptions are in some agribusiness sectors where the replacement of large-scale capital-intensive farming techniques for small-scale peasant farming has led to some fall in the agricultural labour force. In manufacturing industry, spurred on by import barriers and/or tax incentives, foreign-owned firms have often led the way in creating new jobs.

In developing countries, in particular, both import-substituting and export-oriented value-added activities have been founded by foreign affiliates, simply because the local firms did not have the necessary O-specific advantages. In some cases, of course, these assets have been obtained by other routes. In South Korea, for example, foreign-owned firms have played only a limited role in domestic economic development as, following the strategy of its Japanese counterpart, the Korean government has encouraged the import of technological and managerial skills through licensing arrangements, while promoting an extensive programme of indigenous R&D, education and training. However, even today there are some kinds of assets that Korea and Japan can obtain only by way of inward direct investment. In both countries, employment in some of the sectors in which the two countries are relatively disadvantaged is still dominated by foreign companies (e.g. IBM in computers, and several large US and European MNEs in chemicals and pharmaceuticals).

In the service sector, too, foreign-owned banks, insurance companies, business and engineering consultancies, trading houses, hotels and construction have often helped create or upgrade local employment, in so far as these firms either serve more sophisticated and demanding groups of customers than do their indigenous competitors, or they have opened up new market opportunities for both domestic and foreign-owned firms.

In their study of the likely employment impact of some 19 foreign firms investing in the chemicals, engineering and auto sectors of Spain, Portugal and Greece, Buckley and Artisien (1987) found that, in all instances, except where pan-European rationalization had taken place, inward investment had resulted in positive employment gains. The authors concluded that in most sectors the extent of output displacement by indigenous firms was small, mainly because there were so few indigenous competitors. The indirect effects on employment were judged to be variable and strongly industry specific

> 'In the case of greenfield investment they tended to be highest in the period of construction of the plant where a ratio of one external job for each internal job was observed' (Ibid, p. 125).[21]

At the same time, the authors found that the 19 investing firms had helped to upgrade indigenous skill levels through the injection of new technology and the provision of training programmes. In each of the affiliates, the participation of local management 'was very close to 100%' (p. 125). The German study referred to earlier (Bailey, 1979) suggested that the impact of MNEs on job creation in Germany was largely dependent on the competitiveness and market structure of the industry in which the investment was made prior to the entry of the foreign firms. In particular, he contrasted the situation in the chemical

industry where, in the absence of inward investment, German producers would, in his words, 'probably have been capable, sooner or later, of stepping into the market', with that in the computer industry where, without the investment of IBM and other US producers, the products supplied by them would have had to have been imported.

On the other hand, the Japanese case, about which there is little hard and fast information, would seem to challenge this conclusion. For, notwithstanding the limited role played by inbound MNE activity for most of the post-war period,[22] Japan has managed to become the second most powerful industrial nation in the world and, arguably, the most competitive over a wide range of industries. Clearly, inward investment is not a prerequisite for increasing the level, or upgrading the quality, of domestic employment.

At the same time, it is equally erroneous to generalize from the Japanese experience. An extreme example of a country whose government has consciously and systematically used inward direct investment to restructure and improve the quality of its employment base is Singapore. In some sectors in other developing countries, foreign affiliates also enjoy the lion's share of the output produced.[23] Yet, the great majority of developing countries – particularly the poorer African countries – could never hope to emulate the Japanese experience, based as it has been on a well trained and highly motivated labour force, a strongly cohesive social structure and a quite unique entrepreneurial and work ethos.

Most studies of the consequences of foreign MNE activity in the US on domestic employment have been directed at assessing whether new jobs have been created or simply transferred into foreign ownership. Glickman and Woodward (1989), for example, have estimated that although the net employment of foreign-owned firms in the US increased by 548 000 between 1982 and 1986, there was a net loss of jobs actually created by foreign investors of 56 000. On the other hand, Little (1986), while accepting that foreign-owned employment fell in the recession years of the 1980s, argued that since domestic firms cut back their labour by a proportionately greater amount, the net employment effect of inbound investment was positive. Neither of these studies, however, made any real attempt to assess the employment consequences of the next best alternative to foreign investment.

A rather different approach is to compare the growth of employment of foreign affiliates with that of indigenous firms. Unfortunately, this procedure is also fraught with difficulties, as demonstrated by Ray (1990) in his examination of the effects of inward investment on the growth of Canadian employment between 1978 and 1986. Ray found that when the crude rates of growth were examined, foreign firms grew at a slower rate than Canadian firms in eight of nine industrial sectors. Indeed, in aggregate, their crude growth rate was −1.1% compared with the equivalent growth rate for Canadian firms of +18.4%. However, when this data was recalculated by region, industry and size for Canadian and foreign firms, very different results were obtained. In short, normalizing for inter-firm structural differences, the employment performance of foreign-owned firms was found to be broadly comparable to that of domestic-owned firms.

There have been no real attempts to evaluate the net employment contribution of foreign-owned firms in developing countries. Indeed, an ILO report (ILO, 1981), which summarized the studies commissioned on this subject, casts doubt on whether this question can be answered in any meaningful way! However, several studies have identified some very specific employment-related practices of foreign-owned firms. Most of these relate to training procedures and working conditions, but there is also general agreement that foreign employers do make use of their labour more productively and tend to employ more capital- and technologically-intensive production methods. However, only in the case of protected sectors supplying fairly standard and mature products for the domestic market is it likely that labour will be displaced by the foreign affiliates. In other instances, by lowering costs and prices or raising the quality of output, consumer demand is stimulated, and with it employment.

In conclusion, although there has been no definitive or fully satisfactory study on the effects of MNE activity in employment, the assembled evidence does, at least, point in a number of directions, some of which are set out in Exhibit 13.2. The primary impact of both inward and outward direct investment in employment is likely to be on its industrial composition, its skill mix, its quality and its productivity, rather than on its amount. The last variable is, in any case, determined by macro-economic policies. MNEs affect the structure and usage of human resources mainly as a result of their unique O-specific advantages and by the distinctive way in which they respond to the advantages offered by countries. The extent to which these actions are in accord with the employment needs of home or host countries will very much depend on the market structure and competitive strength of the sectors in which the foreign firms participate. It will also depend on the policies pursued by governments, which affect both the quantity and quality of the human resources available and the ease and speed with which such resources can be upgraded and restructured.

We would make one further observation. For obvious reasons, it is tempting to take a very partial view on employment issues, but in the contemporary global economy, such a view is likely to lead to erroneous conclusions and inappropriate policies. Technological and other forces of change are continually requiring a reallocation of resources – including human resources. To resist or impede such a reallocation is a luxury which no country can afford because, while jobs might be protected in the short run, in the longer term they will be lost to more entrepreneurial and aggressive competitors. It is here that MNEs can play a major role in helping both home and host countries in their restructuring and enhancing of human capabilities. We say *can*. Whether they actually *do* or not, depends on whether they can be induced to act in a way which best suits the economic and social objectives of the countries in which they operate and whether the ESP configurations or diamonds of competitive advantage of these countries enable them to pursue these objectives effectively.

13.5   EMPLOYMENT STABILITY

13.5.1   Some analytical considerations

MNEs and/or their affiliates have often been accused of being less stable employers than their indigenous

Exhibit 13.2   Summary of findings of ILO studies on the employment effects of MNE activities in developing countries.

1   When evaluating the employment effects of MNE subsidiaries in developing countries, account should be taken not only of employment creation (i.e. the creation of clearly identifiable new jobs, mostly within the enterprise) but of the much broader process of employment generation throughout the economy of the host country.

2   These employment effects should be evaluated in net terms (number of new jobs created or generated minus existing jobs displaced or destroyed) over a certain period of time.

3   The total number of jobs in an MNE subsidiary depends first and foremost on the subsidiary's total output; if an enterprise has succeeded in becoming big, it is generally because it has managed to make the right technological decisions over a long period of time. These decisions are the result of good management.

4   Technology choices and technological decisions in small enterprises are even more important than in large firms; the economic penalties for errors are comparatively much larger, and a small enterprise cannot rely on strong internal financial resources.

5   Industrial enterprises, whether domestically owned or foreign owned, do not choose their technologies on the basis of capital intensity or labour intensity, but on the basis of their anticipated contribution to the enterprise's growth and profitability.

6   In so far as employment effects are concerned, an MNE subsidiary's technology choices as such are less important than its innovative ability and its technological drive.

7   The complexity of the decision-making mechanisms relating to technology within an enterprise, as well as the risks involved, make it very difficult for a government to intervene effectively in this process or substitute itself for the enterprise's management.

8   The macro-economic employment effects of a subsidiary's activities (i.e. the effects attributable to the overall increase in economic activity in the host country as a result of the subsidiary's presence) are practically impossible to quantify and only very indirectly connected with the subsidiary's technology choices and decisions.

9   The broad horizontal employment effects (i.e. the effects on local enterprises in other industrial sectors) are equally difficult to quantify, and are only very indirectly connected with the MNE subsidiary's technology choices.

10   The technology choices and decisions of an MNE subsidiary have three types of clearly identifiable indirect employment effects in the host country. These are: the 'backward' effects on, or linkages with, local suppliers and subcontractors; the 'forward' effects on local distributors and customers; and the 'narrow horizontal' effects on local enterprises in the same industry.

Source: ILO, 1984.

or uninational counterparts. It is frequently asserted that by relocating activities between their various production units to meet global goals, they may cause unemployment in particular home or host countries. It is also claimed that in times of recession they will cut back production in their foreign affiliates before that in their domestic plants.

These concerns are understandable, but there is little evidence to substantiate them. Indeed, in the case of Japanese-owned affiliates there is reason to suppose that they ensure their employees more job security than do indigenous companies (Dunning, 1986a; Kujawa, 1988). Of course, there are plenty of examples of MNEs resiting value-added activities or even closing factories[24] – but so there are of uninational companies. In a world in which the supply and demand conditions for particular products and kinds of value-added activities are constantly changing, so must the structure, composition and location of employment. To the extent that MNEs tend to be concentrated in the sectors which are most susceptible to change, their actions are subject to more exposure. To the extent, too, that they can better anticipate or respond to these changes than can indigenous firms – and an OECD study (1985) suggests that this was certainly the case in the recession of the early 1980s – they could exacerbate the structural adjustment process. On the other hand, the willingness and ability of any company to react positively and speedily to change may enable it (and the country in which it is located) to better sustain or advance its competitive position.

It would be foolish to argue that the activities of MNEs add employment stability to the countries in which they operate any more than does the opening up of a country's borders to external trade. Indeed, we have suggested that one of the main benefits of FDI is that it often helps to restructure economic activities and upgrade human resources in a way which promotes balanced growth and rising living standards. In doing so, it must inevitably cause some unemployment – at least in the short run. At the same time, it might be plausibly argued that, without such restructuring, the level and stability of long-run employment would be threatened.

The adverse effects of structural adjustment, which tend to be highly industry specific, may be mitigated partly by retraining or job reallocation of the workers who would otherwise be laid off; partly

by early retirement and/or generous redundancy payments; and partly through the normal course of labour turnover. In general, MNEs (especially Japanese MNEs) have a good record in recognizing their responsibility to their workers in these ways (ILO, 1984). However, in the past there have been several cases of MNEs failing to give the employees in their affiliates sufficient information or notice about these (adverse) investment intentions.

Yet, at the end of the day, it is the responsibility of governments in their overall management of the economies over which they have jurisdiction to make the structural adjustment process as painless as possible. Some examples of these efforts in respect to job losses in the textile and clothing sections are contained in an ILO report (1984). In another study, Ozawa (1987a) showed that the Japanese government has eased the difficulties of structural adjustment by promoting the dynamic comparative advantage of its resources and capabilities. Measures include the promotion of business reconversions and an extension of the entitlement period for unemployment benefits.

There is some evidence that the degree of marketing autonomy a foreign subsidiary enjoys is positively related to its employment stability over the product cycle (McAleese and Counahan, 1979). Also, as we will show in Chapter 16, the most vulnerable of all FDIs tend to be those located in Export-Processing Zones (EPZs). Although host governments can lessen the adverse effects of such instability by implementing appropriate macro-economic policies, they can do little to influence the policies of home governments and how they react to economic change. Certainly during the US recession of the early 1980s, not only were new US direct investments in Europe drastically cut back,[25] but also there were instances of US firms shutting down their European affiliates to provide funds for support or rationalization of their domestic activities.[26] In the past, too, employment in the Canadian subsidiaries of US MNEs has fluctuated with the prosperity of the US parent company (Safarian, 1969; Government of Canada, 1972).

We have suggested that employment instability chiefly arises because of changing market patterns and supply conditions for the items being produced. However, the locational consequences of these changes are likely to vary between industry and country. Much resource- and market-seeking FDI is, for example, location bound. By contrast, the response by MNEs to a change in demand or supply conditions affecting efficiency-seeking investment may be to change the location of that investment. Thus, countries dependent upon MNEs which are fairly footloose in their locational requirements may be particularly susceptible to employment instability. The best examples are export-processing activities and regional offices, where there have been frequent switches of location by MNEs.[27] Again, domestic firms are no less vulnerable to changes in market conditions, but, because their locational opportunity costs tend to be lower, they are likely to be less responsive to such changes.

At the same time, both inward and outward direct investment may help cushion domestic employment instability associated with cyclical change. This is particularly likely where the affiliates of foreign investors are serving global markets. The effects of an economic recession in France, for example, may be partially offset by the presence of foreign affiliates in France producing for the export market.

13.5.2   Some empirical findings

Empirical research on the effects of MNE activity on employment stability is extremely patchy, although there is some casual evidence on the activities of particular MNEs. Earlier, we cited an OECD study which concluded that there were reasons to suggest that job security in foreign affiliates in Europe was less than that in indigenous firms in the 1970s. This finding was supported by Van den Bulcke and Halsberghe (1979) in their analysis of the employment stability of foreign and domestic firms in Belgium. At the same time, the authors asserted that any adverse employment effects of a branch plant of a foreign-owned company were more than outweighed by the higher productivity arising from that ownership. Killick (1982), quoted in Hood et al. (1983), found that between 1975 and 1981, employment lost through plant closures in the UK was about 5% for both the UK- and foreign-owned plants. In the case of survivor plants, the job loss was 4.5% for foreign-owned firms and 8% for indigenous firms. In Canada, employment in foreign-owned firms in 14 of 21 industrial sectors fell more sharply than that of domestic firms in the 1980–82 recession, while in the subsequent period of recovery (1982–85), the employment of domestic firms rose more quickly (or declined less rapidly) than that of foreign firms in sixteen of the twenty-one sectors[28] (Dow and Kumar, 1990). Finally, a study of employment trends in Irish industry between 1973 and 1980 concluded that foreign and domestic firms recorded almost identical job loss rates (O'Suilleabhain, 1982) – the average annual loss rate being 4.1% for the former and 4.5% for the latter. At the same time, since the growth of new employment by foreign affiliates exceeded that of Irish firms, it would seem that the overall changes in the employment scene associated with inward investment were greater. These facts would tend to support the proposition that MNE-related activity is likely to be more dynamic than that of uninational firms.

Not all – or even the greater part of – the employment losses can be put down to cyclical fluctuations. The 1970s and 1980s were a time of restructuring and rationalization in a large number of internationally oriented industries. Nowhere is this better demonstrated than in the EC, where foreign-based companies have been regrouping their activities since the early 1960s to take advantage of the Common Market.[29] In their book, Hood et al. (1988) cite the cases of Caterpillar Tractor, Massey Ferguson, Vauxhall (General Motors), Chrysler, Firestone, Uniroyal, Goodyear, Singer, International Harvester and Cummings Engine, all of whom engaged in pan-European corporate rationalization in the 1970s which cut their combined employment by one-half.

In an earlier study, two of the authors, Hood and Young (1980), concluded that because it was removed from the centre of the EC, Scotland was particularly vulnerable to some of these changes. However, partly as a result of the enthusiastic efforts of the Scottish Development Council, the Scottish economy has continued to attract substantial amounts of inward investment, particularly in high technology sectors like semiconductors. The Canada–US Free Trade Agreement is also likely to have substantial ramifications on both the direct and indirect employment of foreign firms in Canada. While, on balance, the effects are likely to be positive, much will rest on the ability of both firms and governments to cope with the inevitable structural dislocations caused by the new trade regime (Dow and Kumar, 1990).

13.6   THE TRAINING PRACTICES OF MNEs

One of the key O-specific advantages which MNEs enjoy, and can utilize in the countries in which they produce, is their ability to train and upgrade human resources. They derive this advantage, in part at least, from their cross-border experiences in manpower management. This is particularly the case where labour is in short supply in the country where it is needed and cannot easily be acquired on the open market. If an MNE, or any other firm for that matter, is to be competitive, it must be able to recruit the labour it needs or undertake its own training programmes. Of course, if there are no suitable locally-trained resources and no likelihood of these being available, the foreign firm will simply not engage in activities that require these resources. This is one of the reasons why most high value-added activity by MNEs is undertaken in the advanced industrial countries. However, in most cases, it is a question of incremental training or education that is required for new products to be efficiently produced, as well as for new production or marketing techniques to be mastered. Frequently, the rewards for the training firm can be considerable.

There is now a substantial body of literature which documents the array of formal and informal training facilities undertaken by MNEs and their affiliates in both developed and developing countries (ILO, 1984). The evidence suggests that, while the amount and character of training varies considerably between firms, as a general rule it is fairly narrowly focused on the specific manpower needs of the investing enterprises, rather than on the wider economic and social goals of the countries in which they operate. This sometimes results in uneven and sub-optimal manpower development. It follows that if foreign firms deploy their O advantages in a way that is acceptable to host countries, they may require extra market inducements to do so (e.g. training grants, structural adjustment assistance). As long as the resulting social benefits exceed the social costs involved, this is a perfectly legitimate use of resources.

The extent and pattern of human resource management by MNEs in a particular country is likely to depend upon its philosophy and general strategy towards its foreign operations; the nature of its long-term resource commitments and the length of its involvement in that country; the nature of the activities in which it is engaged, and particularly the demands they make on human resources; the availability and quality of local training institutions; the attitude and competence of the investing firms to in-house training; its market (or expected market) share; and the role played by government in promoting in-house or other kinds of training programmes.[30]

Each of these variables is, in part at least, country, industry and firm specific. Each will also depend upon the role of the affiliate in the global strategy of the investing enterprise. Such enterprises are likely to contribute most of the training (or retraining) requirements of the host country where there is a synergy of interests between their own goals and those of the host countries; where there is a domestic manpower base on which to build; and where there are incentives for the MNE to bear the training costs as well as for individual workers to undergo such training. The extent to which such conditions are met will depend on both the type of instruction required and the work ethos and capabilities of the labour force. Some countries (e.g. India, Japan, South Korea, Taiwan, Israel, Kenya and Singapore) provide an excellent environment for manpower development. Others, such as some smaller African and Latin American countries, much less so.

In what way is the manpower training of MNEs different from that of uninational firms? First, and perhaps most important, because they operate in different cultural environments, MNEs are able to draw upon and utilize, as and where appropriate, a range of value systems, attitudinal perspectives and training systems relevant to the enhancement of human resources. Put rather differently, and in the words of an executive from Unilever 'In all our specialized courses, the general objective is the building of understanding, supportive, helping and trusting relationships within the enterprise' (ILO, 1984). At the same time, the form and focus of training may depend on the nationality of the trainer. The US inclination for technical, yet individual-oriented training programmes, spurred on by promotion and monetary rewards, contrasts sharply with the emphasis of Japanese MNEs on group training, motivated by peer pressure on individual workers continually to upgrade their talents and skills. Each, when introduced into a foreign (e.g. European) culture, brings its own slant to training methods and goals. The more globally oriented a company is, the wider the experience it can bring to bear on training practices.

Second, an MNE is likely to impart its experience of training techniques in different countries. In many cases, learning by doing is one of the best forms of instruction. Lessons learned from this experience and from the direct tutelage of workers and staff at all levels may provide an important O advantage in its own right.

Third, because of the economies of scope and scale in personnel management, large and geographically diversified firms can often afford to engage in more systematic and specialized training programmes more than can their smaller uninational competitors. In its 1984 study, the ILO (1984) observed that several large MNEs[31] offered a wide variety of training programmes – particularly for senior executives, management and professional staff. In other cases, training is organized on a regional basis. One example is Nestlé's local professional training centre INDEC in Mexico which provides instruction for Nestlé personnel in Latin America. Another is a series of regional marketing courses which Unilever runs in Asia and Latin America for senior personnel from each of its subsidiaries in the regions.

There appear to be some country-specific differences in the kinds of training undertaken in the home countries of MNEs. Perhaps the most extensive headquarter management and technical training programmes are carried out by the Japanese MNEs setting up in Europe and the US. Nissan, Canon, Sony, Komatsu and NEC have all sent cadres of line managers, technicians and foremen back to their parent companies for quite extensive programmes.

Fourth, MNEs can provide face to face training by in-house expatriates. Though such training is likely to be most critical at a general or line management level, it frequently extends to the factory floor – particularly in high technology sectors. In their efforts to indigenize or localize senior staff and workers, host (and particularly host developing) countries are often anxious for MNEs to complete such training as soon as possible. In general, MNEs are sensitive to these needs and aspirations, not least because of the high costs of maintaining expatriates abroad and because local

nationals can often bring to the MNE network useful knowledge and experience of the country's business culture and institutions, and of negotiating practices with labour unions and government.

Training may take different forms. It may be formal or informal; knowledge may be transmitted by the printed word, lectures and seminars, formal or informal consultations, quality-control circles, intra-firm visits and inspections, example and experience. It may be focused on the improvement of professional and technical skills or on worker motivation. It may be geared to raising the productivity of the least skilled workers or the senior management of the company. It may be oriented towards enhancing the quality of services (e.g. in hotels or advertising), raising the level of professional competence, or improving testing and inspection procedures. Training may spread beyond the boundaries of the MNEs to their suppliers and customers, and may include that offered by local educational and training institutions. According to the industry and type of firm undertaking the training, its form and substance will differ. Likewise, so will the particular role of inbound foreign investment in the training programmes of host countries.

How might MNEs contribute the most to local training needs and aspirations of the countries in which they operate? We have already suggested that such enterprises will only spend money on training if they expect to recoup the costs of that training, *or*, should host governments insist upon their undertaking certain training, as long as the net costs involved do not reduce a firm's profits below its opportunity costs. If, however, governments are prepared to subsidize these costs, either directly or indirectly, then both foreign and domestic firms may be prepared to invest more resources in in-house training.

The issues in question are, first, to identify the extent and form of market failure in the supply of training or retraining facilities and, second, to decide on the best way to overcome that failure. As regards the former, there seems to be general agreement that the social net benefits of upgrading the *general* skills and competences of a country's human resources are likely to exceed the private net benefits. This excess will vary according to the ESP configuration of a country and its stage of development. There is, however, much less consensus on how market failure in the labour market may be overcome and *how much* and *what kind* of non-market intervention is required.[33] In some economies (e.g. the US, UK and Hong Kong) the onus for training is firmly delegated to the private sector – albeit with some encouragement and support from the public authorities. In others (e.g. Japan, France and Brazil) the government accepts a larger share of direct responsibility, even though the actions taken to implement its training programmes may be entrusted to private corporations.

This difference of approach results in different priorities being given to education and training, as well as to the incentives to firms to undertake training programmes. The amount spent on vocational training and the role of government varies greatly between countries and between sectors within countries. Switzerland, Japan, Germany and the US, among the developed countries, and Singapore, Taiwan and Korea, among the developing countries, spend the most on training as a proportion of GNP. While there is little correspondence between the proportion of direct government expenditure on training and a country's total expenditure on training, a survey conducted by the World Economic Forum and IMEDE (1990) reveals that the latter figure is quite strongly correlated, both to the extent to which complementary activities are perceived to exist between state and private training and R&D efforts,[34] and the extent to which firms take a long-term view of their innovatory strategies. Two noteworthy exceptions among the leading spenders on human resource development were the US and the UK, both of which were thought to be relatively shortsighted in their innovatory strategies and ineffectual in integrating public and commercial retraining programmes.

Empirical research aimed at identifying the unique contributions of inward direct investment to the upgrading of human skills has yielded mixed results. In a study of 41 foreign-owned and national manufacturing processing firms in Kenya, the author concluded that only those foreign affiliates in which there was some equity participation by the host government had made 'a truly significant contribution to the training of indigenous management' (Gershenberg, 1987). This view was confirmed in a comparison of the training programmes of MNE affiliates and indigenous Brazilian firms, except that

the former were found to be more active in their external training and assistance activities (Goncalves, 1986). This latter caveat is an important one, as part of the training of employees of foreign firms is undertaken outside the host economy and is frequently paid for by the parent firm. In addition, MNE-financed training may well be of a higher quality than that provided by indigenous firms – particularly in developing countries (Enderwick, 1985). In a comparison between the annual total training expenditure per employee in a group of Nigerian enterprises, Iyanda and Bello (1979) concluded that MNEs spent six times as much as their local competitors. In both Thailand and Malaysia, foreign MNEs were reported as undertaking more extensive training programmes than their domestic counterparts (Yong, 1988; Sibunruang and Brimble, 1988). In Turkey, a 1988 study concluded that in a paired sample of 30 MNE affiliates and local firms, the former spent twice as much (as a percentage of payroll) on executive training of their employees as did the latter (Erden, 1988).[32]

In a recent study of the labour practices of multinational banks, for example, the ILO (1991) concluded that while most banks took their training responsibilities very seriously, they rarely provided more than the necessary minimum required by law. On the whole, they preferred to hire already trained people on the market. To the labour movement, at least, the main O-specific advantage of foreign banks was perceived to be their ability to offer the training facilities of the entire organization of which they were part. Another study prepared by Robert Grosse for the UNCTC on the training activities of some 73 US affiliates of advertising agencies, commercial banks, computer software firms, hotel chains and management consultancy firms in Latin America concluded that the local training activities of most firms were 'fairly extensive', and that the specific MNE impact was most marked in the training of highly skilled personnel and in the training facilities provided by the MNE network (UN, 1992c).

Our final conclusion, then, about the likely impact of MNEs, *qua* MNEs, on the human resource development of both home and host countries is that much will depend on:

(1) the character of their O advantages,

(2) the ESP configuration of the countries in which they operate,

(3) the 'stick and carrot' incentives offered by governments for MNEs to provide the kind of training which they perceive can best advance their own economic and social goals.

MNEs are likely to make their most positive contribution in an economic, cultural and organizational environment that possesses a good supply of well educated and motivated manpower, and acknowledges the value of a continual restructuring and upgrading of manpower capabilities; where there are clusters of private or public institutions requiring similar training facilities; and where the forces of demand and supply both tempt and/or cajole MNEs (and, for that matter, uninational firms) to invest judiciously in the training and further education of their employees.

13.7   TERMS AND CONDITIONS OF EMPLOYMENT

13.7.1   Introduction

Having discussed the impact of MNEs on the level, structure and quality of human resources, we now turn to consider their effects on the terms and conditions of employment and on the industrial relations in the countries in which they operate.

13.7.2   Employee compensation

Many problems arise in any attempt to make accurate comparisons of employee compensation between different groups of firms. Ideally, one would wish to compare the total real remuneration (including fringe benefits) made to workers performing the same tasks in an identical working environment. However, difficulties occur both in evaluating the comparability of jobs in particular occupations and in calculating the value of non-monetary benefits received in addition to, or as a substitute for, wages. When payments to workers in different countries are being considered, a further problem arises in converting them into a common unit of measurement. Although exchange rates are often used for this purpose, such rates may not always accurately reflect the real value of money in different countries; neither do they fully take into account variations in working conditions or consumption patterns.

However, with these caveats in mind, there is considerable evidence that in most countries and sectors in which MNEs or their affiliates compete alongside uninational or indigenous firms, the former do pay higher rates of employee compensation (wages, salaries, bonuses, and monetary and non-pecuniary fringe benefits) than the latter. However, these variations are generally not as great as is commonly supposed and there are noticeable country-, industry- and firm-specific differences. A summary of the findings of some of the leading studies is set out in the appendix to this chapter.

Apart from differences in the distribution of their activities between (relatively high and low) wage sectors, the principal explanation for the higher employee compensation paid by MNEs and their affiliates is that they record higher labour productivities and capital intensities than their uninational and local competitors.[35] In some cases, these higher levels of productivity reflect a higher capital/labour ratio (Lim, 1977; Dunning and Morgan, 1980) and/or a higher proportion of high wage employees (Balasubramanyam, 1984; Willmore, 1986). Foreign-owned affiliates also tend to be larger than their indigenous competitors and large firms usually pay higher wages than small firms. Because of their size, superior performance or the need to 'buy' themselves into an unfamiliar labour market, foreign firms may also be tempted to pay above average wages to tempt workers away from competing employers.

As might be expected, differences in employee compensation paid by foreign and indigenous firms vary both between countries and sectors, according *inter alia* to the relative O advantages and the skill composition of the two groups of firms and the market structure of the industries in question. There is some suggestion that MNEs, *relative to their competitors*, tend to pay the highest wages in technology-intensive sectors and those producing consumer goods with a high income elasticity of demand. By contrast, they pay the lowest wages in industries in which their representation is the least (Dunning, 1976; Dunning and Morgan, 1980).

MNEs which are tempted into a country to circumvent import barriers are more likely to pay similar wages to their indigenous competitors than those producing goods and services for international markets. Foreign firms also normally pay relatively higher wages for skilled professional and managerial labour than for semi-skilled and unskilled workers (Chen, 1983a). However, this may partly reflect the greater inelasticity of supply of the former kind of manpower. In 1972, US MNEs also paid higher wages in their domestic plants than did their uninational competitors in similar industries (Dunning and Morgan, 1980).

There appear to be some differences in the philosophy towards employee compensation between Western and Japanese MNEs. For example, while the former tend to base remuneration on job-related determinants (job specification, function, type of work), the latter are likely to be more conscious of employee-related determinants (Kuwahara *et al.*, 1979). In addition, Japanese-owned affiliates are sensitive to any suggestion that they may be poaching labour from other local firms. In both Europe and the US, they normally offer a basic wage only slightly above average or average for the industry or region.

The composition of employee compensation may also reflect the nationality of the parent company. Thus, American-owned companies tend to favour monetary inducements and profit sharing schemes, while their Japanese counterparts give more emphasis to non-pecuniary incentives. Sometimes the introduction of new forms of compensation by a foreign affiliate may become common practice. In other cases they may be unsuitable to the work ethos or preferences of the local labour force. It is difficult to generalize on such matters. So much seems to rest on the way in which new methods of compensation are introduced and the attitudes of workers to different kinds of payments – and to responsibilities attached to each. In turn, these attitudes are likely to be country (or even region) specific and to vary, for example, according to the nature of the job being performed.

MNEs are sometimes on to 'a hiding to nothing' in their wage practices, particularly in developing countries and in some racially repressive regimes. On the one hand, it is argued that since they often replicate the production techniques they employ in their home countries, they should be able to pay comparable, or nearly comparable, wages. On the

other, they are sometimes accused of crowding out domestic firms, disrupting long-established industrial relations or encouraging a dual labour market by paying wages that are out of line with their competitors. Sometimes, particularly in very poor developing countries, foreign investors are welcome for the example they set to local firms in paying above-starvation wages. In other cases, they are accused of poaching labour or exacerbating inflationary wage settlements. Another assertion is that MNEs pay high wages as part of a deliberate strategy to counter allegations of monopolistic behaviour or as a means of buying good industrial relations.

13.7.3   Working practices and conditions

Most researchers agree that working conditions in MNEs compare favourably with those of the industry of which they are part, or those of other local firms. How far this is a result of their multinationality *per se* it is difficult to say. However, part of it undoubtedly is – particularly where companies follow common production methods and work practices throughout the world, or where their output is geared to the demands of the international marketplace. Examples range from Coca Cola's bottling operations and many food processing and pharmaceutical plants to multinationally owned and operated hotels. Here MNEs may, and often do, act as trailblazers for upgrading working practices and conditions.

Almost certainly, some working practices in foreign affiliates reflect the cultures of their parent companies. This is particularly likely in areas perceived to be critical to the success of the company. Japanese-owned companies, for example, operate within a very distinctive work philosophy. On the one hand, their employees are expected to identify completely with the company's goals and aspirations and accept that they are part of a team whose sole task is to help achieve these goals and aspirations. On the other, the company has a strong sense of commitment to the economic and social welfare of its workers, which extends well beyond the wages they are paid. Most of the distinctive characteristics of Japanese industrial relations are liked by Western personnel managers and workers, but there are some which are not. These latter include strict timekeeping, meticulous attention to detail, the highest standards of cleanliness and little or no socializing on the shop floor.

At the same time, it is clear from various ILO studies that there are considerable differences between the working conditions and practices of MNE affiliates across national boundaries. Indeed, these differences – particularly between developed and developing countries – are almost certainly greater than between MNE affiliates and local firms in any particular country. Also, there are probably fewer cross-border differences in employee compensation and working conditions within a particular MNE network than there are between indigenous firms operating in the same countries. It is worth emphasizing that it is not normally in the interest of MNEs to provide better working conditions than those necessary to ensure its economic success. Consequently, they will usually be fairly close to the norm for the particular country or industry. This is understandable as non-pecuniary fringe benefits are as much a production cost as the wages and salaries paid.

The extent to which working practices of one country can be successfully transferred to another culture is a matter of some dispute. Take Japanese working practices, for example. These would appear to be more in evidence in Japanese subsidiaries in the United Kingdom than elsewhere in Europe or in the US.[36] For example, the introduction of flexible working and job rotation has proven less acceptable to US workers. Plans and policies regarding lay-offs are much less specific, and the Japanese have had to adapt some of their collectivist labour policies to meet the individual needs of European and US workers. On the other hand, many Japanese-style social facilities have been widely embraced by American employees; educational training programmes are essentially the same as those adopted by European affiliates; while the philosophy of Japanese management in promoting employee loyalty, disseminating information and the introduction of quality circles has been warmly accepted by both US and European workers.

To what extent can Japanese working practices introduced into foreign economies be successfully emulated by indigenous firms? In a comparison between 31 Japanese manufacturing affiliates in the UK and 66 UK-based firms which were among the *Times 1000 largest companies* in 1987, Oliver and Wilkinson (1989) found that, in each of the six categories of practices identified (*viz* total quality control, flexible working, group working/work teams, statistical quality control, quality circles and just in time production) a considerably higher proportion of the Japanese affiliates were already using, or were planning to implement, these practices. At the same time, between 1982 and 1987, the proportion of UK firms undertaking or planning to undertake these practices increased quite dramatically. According to the Japanese managers who responded to a questionnaire prepared by Oliver and Wilkinson, virtually all Japanese-style working practices have been successfully transferred to the UK. The emulating companies, however, revealed a lower success rate partly, it seems, because these practices have not been properly synchronized with or into the wider manufacturing and human resource strategies of the firms implementing them.

Long before the Japanese began internationalizing their operations, US and European MNEs were spearheading new working and social practices across national boundaries. In the mid 1950s, the present author observed that several US subsidiaries in the UK were renowned 'for the attention given to working conditions in the office as well as the factory, canteen facilities and social amenities' (Dunning, 1958, p. 260). A higher proportion of US subsidiaries than the average for UK industry operated social security and non-contributory pension schemes. In its report on the social practices of MNEs in the textile, clothing and footwear industries in developing countries, the ILO (1984) observed that, in the 1970s, welfare and recreational facilities appeared to be more extensive in foreign subsidiaries than in local companies, although they had not reached the standards of their home country (p. 151). Furthermore, the ILO reported that 'some multinational subsidiaries granted social security schemes over and above the legal requirements' (p. 152).

13.7.4 Employee recruitment and labour-management relations

Chapter 8 has shown that decisions on many labour-related matters tend to be left to the personnel managers of the individual affiliates of MNEs.

Nowhere is this localization policy more in evidence than in the area of labour recruitment and industrial relations. In a survey of the locus of decision taking in foreign affiliates in the UK in 1984, Young *et al.* (1985) found that in only 10% to 15% of cases did the parent company exercise any strong influence on hiring policy, and only between 1% and 4% in the area of collective bargaining.[37] But even here the philosophy of the parent company is often much in evidence. US-owned companies, for example, are noted for their aggressive recruitment strategies, while the Japanese pay particular attention to the personal qualities of the applicants. American and European companies are more prone to hire experienced or trained labour from other firms than are the Japanese, who seem to prefer to recruit younger and less experienced workers who they can train in the 'Japanese' way. Head office influence is most prevalent in cases of MNEs pursuing globally- or regionally-integrated product, production and marketing strategies. Here, companies like IBM have fairly standard hiring guidelines. Such guidelines are also followed by companies who believe that one of their distinctive O advantages is the way in which they can obtain the maximum cooperation and output from their labour force.

In part, of course, the impact of foreign-owned companies on industrial relations depends on the nature of existing practices in the countries in which they operate, and these vary widely between countries. So, indeed, do the policies and strategies pursued by individual MNEs. Clearly, the most pronounced impact of inbound direct investment on the industrial relations of a host country is likely to occur when the practices of the foreign firm are superior to those of indigenous firms and the labour unions are receptive to the adoption of these practices. As it happens, both conditions were met in the UK in the 1980s, which allowed the Japanese auto and consumer electronics MNEs to insist that all labour negotiating rights should rest in a single union. The example set by the Japanese employers is having a profound impact on UK industrial relations where multiple craft unions are still the norm rather than the exception. On the other hand, European and US industrial relations procedures do not seem to translate as readily or well into the Japanese work environment.

There are also differences in the attitudes of Japanese and Western multinationals to worker participation in decision making. The Japanese tend to adopt a more open and consultative style of industrial relations. They place a great deal of store on good intra-firm communications. They insist upon work flexibility and discourage craft or status demarcations. They encourage participation in decision taking and the setting up of improvement and quality control circles. And they dislike any kind of confrontation with their workers. The British are more hierarchical in their industrial relations and most labour–management relations are dogged by craft unions. The Germans are used to worker participation on their management boards, while the Americans, though adopting a friendly and status-free policy towards their employees, prefer not to deal with unions at all!

Undoubtedly, both home- and foreign-based MNEs can and do spearhead the introduction of new or different methods of recruitment and industrial relations procedures. In the Republic of Korea, for example, foreign-owned firms are reported to have introduced advanced practices of operating joint labour-management bodies unknown to local enterprises (ILO, 1984, p. 154). Their standards of occupational safety and hygiene also compare favourably with those of other enterprises, particularly in developing countries (ILO, 1984). The fact that MNEs operate in many different working environments gives them important experience and learning advantages over and above those of their uninational competitors. At the same time, unless there is a full understanding of and sensitivity to the differences in work cultures, business customs, negotiating procedures and the rights and responsibilities of both employers and employees, bad mistakes can be made in attempting to translate hiring practices and industrial relations, which have been successfully utilized in one working environment, to that of another.

In general, MNEs have a good record for acknowledging and trying to work with local labour-related practices, while adapting these practices to meet the needs of both efficiency and equity. The key to successful human resource management requires both an understanding of the principles found in most textbooks and acknowledged by all personnel managers, and the sensitive application of these principles to the particular country and industry in which the MNE finds itself.

13.8 HUMAN RESOURCE DEVELOPMENT: SOME POLICY CONSIDERATIONS

This chapter has sought to demonstrate some of the more important employment related consequences of the activities of MNEs for the utilization and upgrading of human resources. Although local laws, customs and macro-economic policies may appear to determine the conduct of such companies more than in some other operational spheres, there is enough evidence to suggest that such companies can and do make a distinctive impact on the level and structure of employment training, wage and working conditions, labour recruitment and industrial relations. Indeed, with their experience of attitudes to work, wealth and authority, MNEs should be in a unique position to employ the best labour-related practices – that is, providing they interpret the local response to unfamiliar practices correctly!

The impact of MNEs on the level and structure of domestic employment basically arises from the output they produce and the methods they choose to produce the output. Because of their unique or O-specific advantages, this impact is likely to be different from that of uninational or indigenous firms. Whether it is in some sense 'better' depends largely on the *raison d'être* for the investment, the cultures of the source and recipient countries, the market structure in which the MNE competes, the economic conditions in the country in which it operates and the human resource management it utilizes.[38]

Of the above influences, the interaction between the strategy of the MNE towards the organization of the human resources capabilities, and the Human Resource Development (HRD) policies of the governments of the countries in which they operate, are probably the most important. As to the former, the globalization of production is necessitating a re-evaluation of the human resource strategies of MNEs. Indeed, as Adler and Ghadar (1990) have suggested, each stage in the internationalizing process of firms (e.g. as described in Chapter 7) necessitates adjustments to the way in which MNEs recruit, utilize, train and remunerate their personnel. To be successful, a geocentric MNE (see Chapter 8) needs to adopt an internationally integrated strategy towards its human resource management. This means that it hires and uses people in a way that takes account of differences in country-specific skills, attitudes and cultures, but, at the same time, as if there were no impediments to their cross-border movement. In the globally-oriented corporation, training needs to be more directed towards the understanding and management of interpersonal cultural diversities and to the acquisition of the skills necessary to harmonize the impact of these diversities when integration is needed.

If the kind of human resource management required of the globally-integrated MNE is very different from that needed by its ethnocentric and polycentric predecessors,[39] so is its impact on, and reaction to, government macro-economic and organization policies. Essentially, a global firm can only implement an efficient and welfare-enhancing human resource strategy if labour markets are free of structural distortions. National governments have an increasingly important role in ensuring this is brought about.

Government action may extend from facilitating an educational and technological infrastructure and a cultural ethos favourable to HRD, to instigating a wide range of specific economic measures designed, for example, to encourage the production of high skill products and production processes, to steer firms to set up factories in regions of high unemployment, to foster more in-house management training, to discourage inflationary pay settlements, to promote more consultation between management and workers over corporate planning, to spend more on vocational training in colleges, to fund more R&D in universities, and to lessen the transaction costs of structural adjustment.

But it is one thing to describe what might be done – another to prescribe what *should* be done. In this respect we might offer six essential ingredients for a successful HRD strategy. First, any government must be clear on the priority it assigns to employment-related policies *vis à vis* its other economic and non-economic goals. This priority is likely to vary between countries and in the same country over time, according, for example, to the overall economic climate, the current state of the domestic labour market, the perceived need for upgrading manpower and the other claims on its resources.

Second, the government has to consider whether its employment problems can be solved by appropriate macro-economic (i.e. fiscal, monetary or exchange rate) policies and the cost of doing so. As Graham and Krugman (1989) correctly point out, inward direct investment in the US has very little net affect on the level of *overall* domestic employment, simply because, at the end of the day, this variable is 'essentially determined by supply, not demand, except in the short run' (p. 48). The authors go on to assert that in the economic milieu of the late 1980s, what constrains the Federal Reserve Bank from reducing unemployment 'is not any difficulty in creating demand, but fear of inflation'. While the authors accept that inward investment may affect the level of employment *in a particular sector* as well as the quality and productivity of manpower, they found that in 1986 the value added per head for foreign affiliates in most US industrial sectors was marginally less than that of all US-based firms (Graham and Krugman, 1989, p. 57).

Third, the government has to identify the extent and pattern of market imperfections in the labour market, including those that arise from endemic market failure. It then has to decide, from a whole range of possible strategies and policies, which are most likely to be the most cost-effective in meeting both its manpower and broader economic and social goals.

Fourth, the government must seek to ensure that the domestic absorptive capacity is sufficient for it both to attract foreign firms and to benefit fully from the unique technologies, skills and experience they have to offer. Such an absorptive capacity not only requires a healthy, literate and skilled labour force (itself a tall order for some developing countries) but also a well motivated and upwardly mobile one. For if foreign affiliates are not simply to redirect skills and talents away from indigenous firms or, even worse, contribute to the international brain drain by relocating domestic high value activities in one of the foreign investors' other plants, the government has to provide them, and for that matter its own MNEs, with the necessary incentives to embed themselves firmly in the local economy.[40]

Fifth, it is essential that HRD policy is fully and efficiently integrated with the rest of government economic strategy. *Inter alia* this implies that governments should facilitate, not restrict, the restructuring of local resource capabilities to meet changing market conditions. Where possible, they should

foster the movement of labour into more productive activities.

Sixth, governments needs to recognize that in promoting their HRD strategies, they are both in competition with governments seeking to do the same thing, and that many of the MNEs they would like to help them in this task are pursuing global strategies. As Chapter 20 will describe in more detail, there are inherent conflicts of interest between the legitimate goals of MNEs and the equally legitimate goals of host country governments. However, the onus to resolve these conflicts rests primarily with national governments – sometimes unilaterally and sometimes multi-laterally. This is because it is governments that bear the ultimate responsibility for the creation and implementation of the institutional framework and economic policies which will determine the extent to which, and the ways in which, the knowledge, technology and management practices and values of MNEs are localized to fit their particular needs and aspirations for economic growth (UN, 1992a).

At the same time, in the formulation of their HRD strategies, governments need to examine the extent to which any of its other economic policies might have caused the problems they are seeking to cure. For example, import protection policies may inhibit MNEs from engaging in job-creating export-oriented activities because they cannot (or are not permitted to) obtain materials, parts and components of the quality they need to compete effectively in foreign markets. Subsidized interest rates or over-generous capital grants (or depreciation allowances) may discourage firms from seeking new and efficient labour-intensive production methods. A retrenchment in university or technical college research budgets may reduce the supply (and possibly raise the price) of scientific, engineering and professional personnel, thereby lessening the attraction of the country in question as a location for high wage activities – to both domestic and foreign MNEs. Lax sourcing standards by government purchasing agencies may give little incentive for foreign or domestic firms to upgrade the quality of their products – and hence their international competitiveness. Subsidization of 'lame duck' or inefficient industrial sectors may impede resource reallocation, manpower retraining and improved labour productivity. A penal tax system may encourage emigration or give individuals little incentive to upgrade their skills and talents. Too-high interest rates and poor rewards for entrepreneurship and innovation may discourage the setting up of small firms, which often provide the venues for new initiatives and ideas, as well as opportunities for new employment. An ineffectual or unduly rigorous anti-monopoly policy might discourage firms from concluding the kind of cross-alliances and mergers necessary to sustain or promote competitiveness and, hence, profits and employment.

Prima facie it may seem that these policies have little to do with the way in which MNEs can contribute to a nation's employment or HRD goals. This is not so. Other chapters in this book have argued, and will argue, that government policies affect not only the ability of their own companies to be competitive in the international market and the extent to which foreign MNEs wish to locate their value-added activities in their boundaries. They also determine the effect which these activities have on the government's own economic objectives. This means that to achieve full and productive employment, rising wages and salaries, better working conditions and more job satisfaction, governments have to provide its individuals and wealth-creating institutions with the right incentives and opportunities to utilize efficiently and enhance the quality of their resources and capabilities.

Because of their particular advantages, MNEs can play – but do not *have* to play – an important part in this task. However, for them to use (i.e. add value to) these advantages in one location rather than another, they must be able to obtain the necessary human and other resources at the right price. An efficient market mechanism can do a lot to achieve this goal, although some markets seem unable to give the right signals. In these cases (e.g. markets for public goods, innovations, risk capital), some alternative or supplementary system for allocating resources needs to be found so that other markets, including the labour market, can function properly. In the case of governments which currently use performance requirements to affect the behaviour of foreign affiliates, it might be entirely appropriate for them to negotiate away some of these conditions in return for offering more incentives to those same affiliates to increase their investment in HRD (UN, 1992a).

Some policy-related issues touched upon in the above paragraphs will be explored in more detail in Part 4 of this volume. The point we wish to end with is that in order to ensure that MNEs are best able to contribute to a country's HRD objectives, governments need to pursue a holistic strategy towards all kinds of resource management and upgrading. While embracing HRD policy, such a strategy relates to anything and everything which promotes the productivity of a nation's resources and the competitiveness of its firms.

Appendix

Summary of conclusions on employee compensation: differnces between foreign affiliates and indigenous firms

Several studies have attempted to establish the differences in employee compensation paid by MNEs or their affiliates and other firms. For example, an analysis of a sample of 500 US affiliates in Britain in 1973 (Dunning, 1976) found that US affiliates paid higher than average wages in 17 of 21 industries. Later data for all foreign firms, derived from Censuses of Production for 1984 and 1988, confirmed this conclusion, but suggested that in the majority of industries the differences were within 10%. In their analysis of FDI in the US, Graham and Krugman (1989) concluded that in most sectors, apart from mining, finance and insurance, the average compensation per employee in foreign-owned affiliates was about the same or less than that of their indigenous competitors.

In developing countries, a study by Mason (1973) established that in most industries foreign affiliates paid more than local firms in the Philippines and Mexico, a finding also reached by Langdon (1975) for Kenya, Sourrouville (1976) for Argentina, Jo (1976) for South Korea, Gershenberg and Ryan (1978) for Uganda, Iyanda and Bello (1979) for Nigeria, Yong (1988) for Malaysia and Kumar for India (1990). On the other hand, Cohen (1975) discovered that local firms paid higher wages in Singapore than did foreign firms, while no clear pattern emerged in Taiwan. In Latin America, while researchers found that the average wage and salary payments in the 1970s ranged from 42% above those of indigenous firms in Brazil (Possas, 1979) to 70% in Mexico (Fajnzylber and Martinez, 1975), by far the greater part of the difference was explained by the MNEs' larger size, their concentration in high wage sectors and their propensity to employ a higher ratio of skilled workers (Jenkins, 1984). In Greek manufacturing industry Papandreou (1980) estimated that, while foreign affiliates paid higher salaries than domestic employers in

1973, differences in average wages per head between the two groups of firms were not statistically significant.

One of the most detailed comparative studies of wage payments of MNEs and non-MNEs to date has been that conducted by the US Tariff Commission (1973). The data embraces the total yearly payroll costs (i.e. earnings) per employee of a sample of 298 firms and their 5237 majority-owned foreign affiliates in 1966 and 1970. Comparisons of domestic payroll costs per employee of the MNEs and of all US firms for all industries showed that the payroll costs of MNEs were significantly above the national average, mainly because of the heavier weight of manufacturing in the MNE sample, where payroll costs per capita tended to be relatively high. Mixed results were shown for the different industries, and it was suggested that this was partly a result of differences in the distribution of activity within the industrial groupings, and partly because of other influences affecting wages, including technical efficiency, profitability and the rate of company expansion.

Most of the above studies did not attempt to verify the statistical significance of their findings. One such study that did was that by Kumar (1990) who used uni- and multi-variant analysis to discriminate between the wage payments made by foreign and indigenous firms in India. Kumar's findings supported those of Balasubramanyam (1984) for Indonesia and Willmore (1986) for Brazil, that although the proportion of high income employees was a significant discriminant between the two groups of firms, the greater part of the difference lay in the fact that the MNE affiliates employed a relatively higher proportion of qualitatively superior personnel (Kumar, 1990, p. 74).

Few studies have compared the employee compensation paid by foreign affiliates according to nationality. However, from casual evidence obtained from studies on Japanese investment in Europe (Dunning, 1986a; JETRO, 1989, 1990; [UK] Census of Production, 1988), the US (Krugman and Graham, 1989) and Asia (Kuwahara et al., 1979), it would seem that US and European foreign affiliates are more likely to offer higher employee compensation than their Japanese counterparts who, in turn, are likely to pay marginally (i.e. 10% to 20%) above their local companies.

NOTES

1 Where, after all, most men and many women spend between one-third and one-half of their waking day between the time of leaving school and their retirement.
2 For full details, see *ILO Publications on Multinationals*, Geneva, ILO, 1989.
3 It should be observed that advances in technology do not always necessarily favour the labour force in

industrialized countries. The introduction of computer scanning by one well-known clothing store is enabling it to know what styles, sizes and colours of apparel are being sold in their various branches within 24 hours. This enables orders to be placed to its workshops in Korea the next day. Because of their ability to supply such apparel quickly, at competitive prices and of the right quality, these workshops can have the goods flown to the stockists in the United States, Europe or Japan in a few days. *Inter alia*, this procedure facilitates the holding of only 'just in time' inventories by the stockists, thereby reducing their inventory costs.
4 For example, in 1990 there were fewer days lost in strikes in the UK than at any time since the Second World War.
5 For example, in the period 1972–82, 31.6% of the increase in the US direct capital stake in the Economic Community was directed to the UK; in the following decade, *viz* 1982–89, the corresponding proportion was 27.9%.
6 As witnessed, for example, by the dramatic fall in new foreign investment directed to India and the Philippines in the 1980s, and the substantial increase directed to Thailand, Indonesia and Korea.
7 Although, the likely impact of MNE activity in one country may be partially estimated by comparing the performance of foreign- and domestically-owned firms in another, but similar, country.
8 This section draws heavily on a number of ILO publications, in particular, those of Kreye et al. (1988) and ILO (1981).
9 Although, most certainly, this also reflects the industries and countries in which MNE activity tends to be concentrated.
10 See Chapter 18 for more details.
11 See Chapter 16 for more details.
12 After a long period of decline, the labour force in the UK car industry has started to rise again; this improvement is almost exclusively the result of new Japanese investment in the industry.
13 This might include the introduction of more efficient production methods which could eventually reduce the demand for labour.
14 For an analysis of some employment consequences of the foreign activities of service MNEs, see Dunning (1989) and UNCTC (1989).
15 This point is taken up in Chapter 20.
16 Of course, this is not to deny that the MNE may be the instrument by which particular jobs are lost. However, more often than not, it is the change in world technological economic conditions which causes this job loss – not the MNE *per se*.
17 Other data suggests that the employment of non-bank foreign affiliates of US MNEs fell by 11.0% between

1977 and 1988, compared with a drop in the employment of their parent companies of 5.0% (Mataloni, 1990).

18 As documented, for example, by Bergsten *et al*. (1978), Lipsey and Weiss (1975, 1981) and Blomström *et al*. (1988).

19 Which is itself explained by the fact that minority investments are often a method used by companies to buy a share of a foreign market.

20 In employment or in more general terms.

21 The authors quote a study by the Netherlands Ministry of Economic Affairs (1976) which estimates that for every job established in a Dutch company by its foreign affiliates, two to three indirect jobs were created.

22 In 1989 the stock of inward direct investment in Germany was $83.6 billion, five times that in Japan (of $15.6 billion).

23 Even in a country like India where foreign firms account for only 1% of the total labour force, they account for more than 70% of the employment generated in certain sectors, for example, aluminium manufacture, automobile tyres, cigarettes, dry batteries and some chemical and pharmaceutical products (Kumar, 1990). Some Scottish examples quoted by Hood and Young (1982b) include Singer of Clydebank, Peugot of Linwood, Hoover of Cambuslang, NCAR of Dundee and Honeywell of Lanarkshire.

24 See OECD (1985) and Hood and Young (1982b).

25 Examples include Dupont (in Ireland).

26 In 1982 and 1983 there was a net reduction in the US direct investment stake in Europe of $9.4 billion, compared with an increase of $39.1 billion in the preceding five years.

27 For some examples, see *Business International* (1980).

28 At the same time, the value added per employee in both periods generally rose faster (or declined less steeply) in foreign than in domestic firms. This suggests that foreign firms were able to restructure their production methods and the location of their activities more speedily than their domestic counterparts.

29 For further details see Chapter 17.

30 For an excellent analysis of how the cross-border human resource management of a firm might vary according to the degree of a firm's multinationalization and its global strategy, see Adler and Ghadar (1990). The authors pay particular attention to the interaction between cross-border cultural differences and organizational effectiveness, and how this changes as MNEs move through their international product cycles. They show that the impact of MNE activity on the recruitment, management and career advancement, performance appraisal, working conditions, training

and compensation of employees is likely to be quite different in the case of an MNE which is in the early stages of internationalization, than in one which is pursuing a fully fledged global strategy. By implication too, a firm's philosophy towards its international operations (e.g. whether it is ethnocentric, polycentric or geocentric) is likely to affect its management of culturally diverse organizational structures, and hence the contribution to the human resource goals of the countries in which it operates.

31 Examples include Philips and Unilever (each of which, in the early 1980s, put on work and training courses in the UK for over 500 managers from overseas), Nestlé and Royal Dutch Shell, Ciba Geigy and Sandoz.

32 Often such training provided by MNEs leaks out into the rest of the host economy by way of labour turnover. Blomström (1991) provides several instances of this occurring in developing countries.

33 For a survey of the literature on this subject see, for example, Audretsch (1989) and Hauser (1989).

34 For example, which might take the form of grants, tax incentives to subsidiaries, creation of public funded training institutions, funding foreign training programmes, etc.

35 Which may include the domestic operations of indigenous MNEs in the host countries.

36 See the annual studies carried out by JETRO (in London and New York) on Japanese manufacturing operations in Europe and the US.

37 These figures compared with 49% on R&D matters, 31% on the setting of financial targets and 82% on dividend policy.

38 Compare, for example, industrial relations in the UK in the late 1970s with that in the 1980s. To give just one figure, in the period 1976–79, on average, each year more than 13.1 million working days were lost in industrial stoppages; in the comparable period between 1980 and 1983 the figure was 10.5 million; and between 1984 and 1990 it was 3.6 million.

39 Let us give just one example; in the first stages of a market-seeking FDI, its foreign employment is likely to be limited to unskilled or semi-skilled workers, while it is unlikely to engage in much local product adaptation or training of employees in foreign affiliates. Little or no language competence is needed and often the expatriates employed are marginal, rather than top performers. If and when, however, a firm produces in more countries and rationalizes its investment, it is likely to engage in more high value and culturally-sensitive foreign activities. The flow of intra-firm communication becomes more important; the quality of expatriate management and professional personnel needs to be improved; an increasing competence in

foreign languages becomes necessary; and training of local personnel becomes a more important ingredient of success. Finally, if and when a firm becomes a globally-integrated company, its foreign operations require the best possible management, training is continuous, while the opportunities to reach the top of the corporate pyramid is open to all employees. These and other points are elaborated by Adler and Ghadar (1990).

40 For some illustrations of the ways in which host governments have sought to prevent or reverse a brain drain from their countries, see UN (1992a).

CHAPTER 14

MNEs, THE BALANCE OF PAYMENTS AND THE STRUCTURE OF TRADE

14.1   INTRODUCTION

As part of their wider economic strategies, governments of most countries keep a watching brief over their external trade positions for two main reasons. The first is to ensure that the exchange rate and other macro-economic variables which may impinge upon the terms on which a country trades with the rest of the world are compatible with the achievement of its broader economic and social objectives. The second is to ensure that the structure of the cross-border transactions of its firms and individuals is consistent with the internal allocation (or reallocation) of resources and capabilities which the government wishes to promote.

To a certain extent at least, both these concerns are likely to be country specific, although as the globalization of the world economy increases, the latitude for unilateral balance of payments adjustment policies is becoming much reduced. The OECD countries, for example, accept that it is necessary to adopt broadly similar external economic policies in order to minimize the shocks of international, political, financial and monetary events. As more nations are caught up in the web of international commerce, it might be expected that their balance of payments policies will be increasingly exogenously determined. Nevertheless, there are still a gamut of domestic regulations and policies which, directly or indirectly, may affect the economic objectives of countries as a result of their impact on the balance of payments, and where the behaviour of MNEs affects the external trade balance of countries differently than does that of domestic companies. This might induce a different response on the part of governments. Generally speaking, however, the macro-economic effects of FDI are (or should) only be of concern to governments where, first, there is a persistent balance of payments deficit which is proving a constraint on the policies designed to upgrade the quality and improve the allocation of indigenous resources, or to promote growth and development; and second, where such investment accounts for a major part of all value-added activity in the home or host economy.

Policies directed towards creating an optimum structure of domestic economic activity are likely to be even more country specific, partly because of widely different attitudes of countries (or, more correctly, governments of countries) to being part of the international division of labour and, given these attitudes, because of differences in their strategies to achieve these goals. For example, countries that wish to be as autonomous as possible in the production of goods and services (e.g. India and China) will judge the contribution of firms (domestic or foreign owned) to the composition of their exports and imports very differently from those which see their prosperity as being linked to promoting their dynamic comparative advantage (e.g. Singapore, Taiwan, Germany). In so far as MNEs *do* promote a different sectoral distribution of economic activity and a different pattern of imports and exports than indigenous firms, then it might be expected that they might induce distinctive pro-active and reactive strategies by governments.

This chapter, then, will be concerned with evaluating the impact of the activities of MNEs on the balance of payments and on the structure of trade of both home and host countries. It will argue that this impact will depend on the interaction between the configuration of OLI advantages facing firms and the ESP configuration facing countries. It is the extent and nature of this interaction – particularly how it varies as countries move along their investment development paths – which will be the subject of our analysis. But first we consider facts about MNEs as cross-border traders and look at some methodological problems associated with identifying and measuring the impact of one particular group of enterprises on the external trading position of a country.

14.2   MNEs AS CROSS-BORDER TRADERS

In Chapter 2, we set out some facts about MNEs, including their propensity to engage in external capital and current transactions. Such data as is published by individual countries, suggests that MNEs or their affiliates generally enjoy a larger share of home or host country exports and imports than they do of output. As we shall discover later in this chapter, this is partly explained by their being concentrated in trade-intensive sectors, and partly because their trading propensity in any given sector tends to be greater than that of uninational or indigenous firms.

There is no comprehensive data on the comparative trading propensities of MNEs and uninational firms. However, based on statistics for 21 countries,[1] compiled by Dunning and Cantwell (1987) and UN (1992a, 1992b), the (unweighted) average share of the exports of all manufacturing goods accounted for by affiliates of MNEs was 33.0%. This compared with their share of manufacturing output of 29.1%. The average export share of MNE affiliates was also slightly higher in developed than in developing countries. Two exceptions were the US where in 1988 it was about 8% and Japan where it was less than 1%. This primarily reflects the greater degree of product rationalization and intra-industry trade among the former group of countries. For most host countries, too, the share of manufacturing exports accounted for by foreign affiliates has risen over the past two decades – sometimes very steeply (e.g. the US, Korea, Malaysia). Unfortunately, there is very little data on the comparative propensity of foreign- and indigenously-owned firms to import, but what there is suggests that the former tend to record

a higher import propensity than the latter. In the US, for example, in 1988 foreign manufacturing affiliates exported 7.8% but imported 10.9% of their total sales (Lipsey, 1991).[2]

From a home-country perspective, it is well known that a substantial proportion of both exports and imports are accounted for by large firms. What is less well appreciated is the extent to which such trade is also dominated by MNEs. In 1987, four-fifths of US merchandise exports were undertaken by US-owned MNEs or foreign affiliates in the US. In the same year, about the same proportion of UK manufacturing exports were accounted for by UK MNEs and foreign-owned affiliates in the UK (UNCTC, 1991a). In 1983, Japanese MNEs were responsible for 41% of Japanese exports and 57% of Japanese imports (Julius, 1990). Both figures have probably risen substantially since then.

In other leading capital-exporting countries, MNEs not only tend to dominate trade; their propensity to export and import goods and services is often considerably higher than that of their uninational counterparts. Sometimes the trade is undertaken directly by the MNEs themselves. Sometimes, as in the case of Japan and Korea, it is channelled through general purpose trading companies (Ozawa, 1987b). However, since, as Chapters 2 and 3 have demonstrated, quite a substantial amount of FDI is specifically directed towards promoting the imports or exports of the investing companies, care must be taken to allow for this fact when making comparisons between the trade propensities of MNEs and uninational companies.[3]

A considerable proportion of the cross-border trade of MNEs is within the same firm. Data is again fragmentary, but as an order of magnitude it would appear that about one-third of world trade in goods and services (outside the (erstwhile) socialist countries) takes place on an intra-firm basis (UNCTC, 1988). More specifically, in 1989 some 42% of US exports and 49% of imports of goods and services were transactions between US firms and their foreign affiliates or parents (US Department of Commerce, 1991). In 1984, around 29% of UK manufacturing exports and 50.6% of imports were between UK MNEs and their foreign affiliates (British Business, 1985). The corresponding proportions for Swedish firms (in 1975) were 29% and 25% (Helleiner, 1981), for Belgian firms (in 1976) they were 53% and 48%

(Van den Bulcke, 1985), for Japanese firms (in 1983) they were 30.6% and 18.4% (all exports and imports) and for Portuguese firms (in 1981) 31% and 34% (Simoes, 1985). In 1988, some 51% of the exports of Japanese manufacturing affiliates were to their parent companies or sister affiliates (MITI, 1989).

Earlier, Brash (1966) estimated that 91% of all imports of 76 US subsidiaries in Australia in 1961–62 were internalized, while Deane (1970) calculated that in 1963–64, 55% of the imports made by 109 foreign firms were from other parts of the same organization. In India, several large foreign affiliates (e.g. Modi Xerox, US; Pecco Electronics and Electricals, Netherlands; and Kimelic Honda Motors, Japan) obtain more than three-fifths of their imports from their foreign parents (Institute for Studies on International Development, 1991). In his field study of 266 MNE affiliates in Canada in 1965, Safarian calculated that the average export internalization ratio was 50.7% and the average import internalization ratio was 72.2%. These figures were considerably higher than those obtained by Forsyth (1972) for US subsidiaries in Scotland in the late 1960s – *viz* 21% and 57%, respectively – and by Dunning (1977) for some 30 large UK MNEs with substantial investments in less developed countries, *viz* 25% and 45%, respectively.

Further data on intra-firm exports between the parent companies of 172 of the world's largest industrial firms and their foreign affiliates, based on a survey conducted by Dunning and Pearce (1985), reveals that around the average of 34.0%, the percentage of intra-firm exports ranged from 71.9% for office equipment and computers, to 60.5% in the auto industry, to 1.7% for paper and wood products, and 7.9% for textiles, apparel, leather goods and wood products.[4] The propensity to engage in such trade was the highest in the case of US MNEs (some 94.9% of US motor vehicle exports were intra-firm) and least in the case of Japanese industrial multinationals (where only 5.2% of such trade was intra-firm).[5] It was also positively related to the degree of a firm's multinationality, and was highest for MNEs engaging in cross-border product or process specialization.[6]

Finally, it is worth noting that while the proportion of exports involving the parent companies of MNEs seems to be increasing, that of imports is stable or declining. Take the US and Japanese figures as an example. In 1977, the proportion of US exports despatched to the foreign subsidiaries of US MNEs was 26.7%; by 1985 this proportion had risen to 29%. The corresponding ratios of exports associated with Japanese MNEs were 24.1% in 1980 and 30.6% in 1983. At the same time, in 1985, the imports associated with both foreign and domestic MNEs into the US were 40.1%, 2.1% lower than in 1977. The corresponding percentages for Japanese intra-firm imports for 1980 and 1983 were 42.1% and 30.3% (Blomström, 1990). However, when one examines the trading patterns of some of the affiliates of MNEs, one sees a marked increase in intra-firm exports and imports. This is especially so in the case of the intra-EC trade of US affiliates in Europe, and also of intra-North American trade involving US and Canadian firms.

We shall examine the determinants and implications of intra-MNE trade in a later section of this chapter.

14.3   A METHODOLOGICAL NOTE

Earlier chapters (especially Chapters 11 and 13) have described the difficulty of attributing certain actions which are associated with the activities of MNEs to their multinationality *per se*. Nowhere is the problem of attribution more clearly seen than in the context of trade patterns and the balance of payments. For, in assessing the effects of MNE investment on the external accounts of a particular home or host country, some assumption needs to be made as to what might have happened had that investment not been made. In other words, what are the benefits which might have been obtained by allocating the same domestic real resource costs expended by inward or outward direct investors in some alternative way (Reuber, 1973)? If the answer to this question is 'nothing', then their impact will be measured by the transactions identified with their activities.

However, this is unlikely to be the case. Let us give one or two illustrations. Take first the case of the investment by the Japanese MNE NEC in Scotland. The first task is to identify the external transactions associated with this investment. The next is to estimate the transactions which otherwise would have taken place had NEC not invested in Scotland. These are of two kinds. First, those which might arise from any use of NEC-released resources in the UK either by other semiconductor companies (e.g. Motorola, Texas Instruments) or by other firms. Second, those which might result from any alternative action NEC might have taken, such as setting up a plant in France or Belgium, or exporting the replacement output from Japan or other Far Eastern plants. The *effect* of NEC's investment on the UK balance of payments and composition of trade is, then, its *actual* external transactions less those which would have occurred in its absence.

Naturally, any estimate of the alternative or counterfactual position is bound to be conjectural. *Inter alia* it also depends on a variety of behavioural assumptions, notably the reaction of competitors and governments. For example, supposing a Dutch MNE sets up an electronics factory in Singapore to produce and export back to the Netherlands microchips which have previously been supplied by the Dutch factory. As far as the Dutch company is concerned, this investment will initially lead to an increase in its net imports into the Netherlands and a worsening of the importing country's balance of payments. Now let us assume that had not the Dutch company invested in Singapore, a German competitor would have done so. Assume, too, it could supply the Dutch market more cheaply than could the Dutch firm producing in the Netherlands. In such circumstances, the net effect on the Dutch balance of payments might be zero, that is, it would make little difference whether a Dutch or a German investment took place. However, suppose that the Dutch government imposed a tariff or import quota on goods made in Singapore. In such a case, since neither the Dutch nor the German affiliate could export to the Netherlands, the effects of the outward investment on the balance of payments would be to worsen it. At the same time, much of the incentive for making the investment would be removed.

It is, of course, perfectly possible to produce scenarios which would generate positive, negative or neutral balance of payments effects arising from MNE activity. Much depends on the types of FDI considered and whether one is taking a home- or a host-country perspective. Resource-based and export-processing investment, for example, is primarily undertaken to obtain inputs more economically than

they would have been provided under different ownership. Compared with this alternative position, they may improve the balance of payments of both the host and home countries.[7] By contrast, market-seeking investment is aimed at substituting exports (or potential exports) from the home production unit (or, possibly, production units in other countries). This will probably better the balance of payments of the host country, while the effect on the home country is likely to be ambiguous. For example, by reducing exports of the home country, the balance of payments could be adversely affected. On the other hand, if the investment results in higher efficiency and/or additional purchasing power in the host country, it could benefit the home country, both by additional expenditure on imports by the former and by increased exports of materials, parts and components from the parent company. However, at the end of the day, much depends on the government's macro-economic handling of any change in the balance of payments associated with outward and inward investment.

Some scholars eschew the alternative position or counterfactual approach to assessing the impact of MNEs on the balance of payments, precisely because of the difficulty in identifying and assessing its appropriate opportunity cost. They also believe that such exercises do not, and cannot, properly take account of the macro-economic consequences of these activities.

These scholars fall into three groups. The first looks at the differences in performance (as it affects the balance of payments) of the foreign affiliates of MNEs and of indigenous firms. It is assumed that the secondary repercussions, including those sparked off by changes in government policy, of both kinds of activity will be the same. Examples of such comparative studies include those of Cohen (1975), and Lecraw (1983) for various countries in Asia, Jenkins (1979) for Brazil, Biersteker (1978) for Nigeria and Dunning (1969) for the UK. The attractions of such an approach are obvious. Actual data is available and a comparison of past and current performance and of changes in performance can be made. But the pitfalls are many. Not least among these are isolating the effects of foreign ownership and/or multinationality from other differences between the two groups of firms. Moreover, to draw any policy conclusions from this data, for example, with respect to encouraging or discouraging inward or outward direct investment, one has to assume that the marginal and average impacts are the same and that the real opportunity cost lies in the ownership of activity rather than in its direction. Finally, this approach implicitly assumes that, in the absence of FDI, the investment would be undertaken by other firms.

The second, and related, approach by scholars has been to compare the actual external transactions of MNEs or their affiliates with those of non-MNEs or indigenous firms prior to the investment being made. This approach is most likely to be useful at a micro (project) level and was, in fact, used by Grant Reuber and his colleagues in their study on FDI in developing countries in the early 1970s (Reuber, 1973).

The third group of scholars takes a very different tack. They seek to estimate – usually by means of regression analysis – the direct relationship between outward or inward direct investment and one or more of the components of the balance of payments. An example of this methodology is that used by Bergsten *et al.* (1978) who, in their study of the effects of US overseas direct investment on the US balance of payments, related the external trade performance of a number of US manufacturing sectors to a variety of industrial characteristics, each of which they cross-tabulated with the degree of outward foreign investment. The authors then went on to construct and test a series of cross-sectional multiple regression equations which attempted to relate the investment behaviour of US firms to US exports and imports. They concluded that, in sectors with a minimal foreign investment, an expansion of outward investment was likely to be matched by an expansion of American exports. However, at modest to high levels of foreign investment, this kind of complementarity was less evident. Later studies employing this approach include those of Blomström *et al.* (1988) and Pearce (1990a).

One final methodological point relates to the measurement of the balance of payments effects.[8] We have stated that, in the last resort, it is the macro-economic policies of governments rather than any actions taken by one group of firms which determine the trade balance of a country. By definition, the current account deficit is equal to the difference between domestic investment and savings.

It follows, then, that any deficit can only be cured by increasing either domestic or foreign savings. The principal mechanism through which the savings and investment identity is reconciled with the micro-economic decisions about trade is the exchange rate (Graham and Krugman, 1990). Thus, it is quite possible that the effects of FDI will be shown as much in a country's exchange rate as its balance of payments position. This does not mean the latter effect is unimportant. A weaker exchange rate associated with the financing of a greater tendency for foreign firms to source their inputs from abroad may make it more difficult for a country (especially a developing country) to grow or restructure its activities in the way it wishes.

The macro-economic approach to evaluating FDI must then clearly look at the dynamics or second-order effects of the activities of MNEs, as they may be reflected in a change in the value of the exchange rate as well as the structure of exports and imports. We shall take up this point later in this chapter.

14.4   MEASURING THE TRANSACTIONS OF MULTINATIONALS

14.4.1   Identifying the transactions

The external transactions associated with the activities of MNEs are of two kinds representing the capital and current accounts of the balance of payments. These transactions embrace both those undertaken directly by MNEs or their affiliates, and indirectly by other domestic enterprises with whom they have dealings (e.g. suppliers and customers).

Take, for example, the external transactions associated with an MNE's outward investment. First there are the initial capital transactions. Normally, outward investment is likely to lead to a purchase of foreign currency, a minus (−) on the capital account. However, in some acquisitions and mergers (A&Ms) there may be an exchange of share holdings between the parties to the exchange, as a result of which an outflow is immediately matched by an inflow. In the case of greenfield investments (e.g. most Japanese investment in Western Europe and much of US export-processing investment in South East Asia and

Mexico), part of the foreign currency loss is immediately clawed back through the purchase of machinery and capital equipment from the home country, which is a plus (+) on the capital account.

Subsequently, there may be additional capital outflows (−) or, in the case of a sale of foreign investments, a capital inflow (+). These outflows may be financed out of reinvested earnings from existing investments, or by new capital provided by the parent company. They could also be financed by funds supplied by other foreign affiliates of the MNE, but in the last resort these also represent a drain on the foreign currency reserves of home countries. Of course, MNEs have other means of financing their foreign operations, which may not immediately affect the capital account of the investing country. These include short- or long-term loans secured from institutions in the host country of the affiliates, or from the international capital market and, in the case of joint equity ventures, additional equity capital from local or other foreign partners.

Second, there are the current account transactions of an outward investor. Operating a foreign subsidiary may affect the current account of the home country in four main ways. First, the subsidiary may buy intermediate goods (e.g. materials, components, semi-finished goods) for further processing or fabrication from its parent company, or from other enterprises in the home country. Second, it may import finished goods for distribution or re-sale. Third, the parent company is likely to provide its foreign affiliates with a range of intermediate services (e.g. technical know-how, marketing information, and administrative, managerial and accounting expertise), for which it charges royalties and management *et al.* fees. Each of these transactions represents a visible or invisible export (+) to the home country.

However, as we have already seen, depending on the purpose of the FDI, the value-added activities of the foreign affiliates may increase or replace exports (or potential exports) from the parent company (or other companies in the home country), and/or increase or reduce imports by the parent company (or other companies in the home country). For example, the sales and marketing subsidiaries of manufacturing MNEs are specifically intended to promote the exports of the investing firms, while the function of foreign purchasing ventures is to secure,

for the investing company, imports of the right quality on the most favourable of terms. By contrast, a German producer of microwave ovens which sets up a plant in the US to manufacture the same product may not only cause German exports to the US to fall, but also, where the US is able to supply third markets (e.g. Canada) more efficiently than can its parent company, exports to these markets as well. A Swedish electrical appliances company which locates a manufacturing plant in Malaysia to supply electronic parts for the parent company is likely to cause a rise in the export of components and parts from the home country, but an increase in the imports of the final product to Sweden. Firms investing in the primary sector are likely to increase the exports of machinery and equipment from their parent company, or from other companies in the home country. However, depending on from where (if at all) they were purchasing their products prior to the investment, and on what terms, the investment may increase or decrease the value of their imports. Clearly, too, the balance of transactions of MNEs will be affected by the profitability of their domestic and foreign operations and their respective rates of growth.

In addition to the impact on the external transactions of the investing firms, there are likely to be second-order or spill-over impacts on other firms in the home economy. For example, if as a result of a foreign acquisition, an electronics firm finds its exports reduced by 10%, then this will reduce the import component of such exports, including that contained in any subcontracted materials, components and parts. Likewise, any increase in indirect exports associated with FDI is likely to lead to an increase in indirect imports as well.

A similar assessment may be made of the external transactions of the host country associated with inbound investment. Broadly speaking, these are the reverse of those just identified for home countries. Apart from the initial capital inflow, the import-substituting subsidiaries – at least in their initial years – will generally record more imports than exports, while those of resource-based and rationalized subsidiaries will record higher exports than imports. The trading consequences of strategic asset seeking investment are likely to be ambiguous, depending on the type and *raison d'être* for the investment. In each case, however, depending on the amount of goods and services which affiliates buy from, or sell to, local suppliers, there will also be second-order effects on the balance of payments.

14.4.2 Empirical research on the transactions of MNEs

Given the appropriate data, it is not too difficult to measure the balance of payments transactions associated with inward and outward direct investment. A review of the literature suggests this may be done in three main ways. The most comprehensive attempts include those which go on to evaluate the opportunity cost of such investment. These we will describe in the following section. A second group of researchers have limited their task to comparing the transactions of MNEs or their affiliates with those of other or all firms in the economy of which they are part. A good example of this approach is set out in Table 14.1, which is reproduced from an unpublished UNCTC study (1981). It shows the balance of payments transactions of US subsidiaries in Mexico in 1977 and relates these to those of *all* Mexican-based firms.

A third type of empirical study considers just the most important transactions of MNEs. One recent example is that of Stopford and Turner (1985) in respect of UK outward and inward investment in the 1970s.[9] A table (which is self-explanatory) drawn from their work is reproduced as Table 14.2. Though, in principle, the indirect or secondary transactions arising from inward and outward investment are not difficult to measure, the practical problems of obtaining the data from the suppliers, competitors and customers of MNE firms has, in general, daunted researchers from attempting to do so. And yet, particularly in the case of initial and trade-related investments, these can be very important. Examples, which are set out in Chapter 15 in more detail, are the effects which demand-induced external transactions may have on the suppliers or subcontractors of foreign affiliates and the consequences of greenfield investments on their competitors' external transactions.

14.5 ASSESSING THE OPPORTUNITY COST OF EXTERNAL TRANSACTIONS BY MNEs OR THEIR AFFILIATES

14.5.1 Some theoretical issues

It is a great temptation to identify and aggregate the external transactions of MNEs or their affiliates and to conclude that the resulting figure – be it a net improvement or deterioration on balance of payments account – is the consequence of their activities. Indeed, some writers have gone so far as to argue that the balance of payments consequences of inward or outward direct investment are best measured by the ratio between the profits and interest earned on FDI, and the capital outflow which generated the investment in the first place. They further argue that a 'balance of payments' return on capital may be computed, which *inter alia* identifies the number of years it might take to 'pay back' any given amount of capital exported.

Other analysts, such as Hufbauer and Adler (1968), Steuer *et al.* (1973), Lall and Streeten (1977), Reddaway *et al.* (1968) and Stopford and Turner (1985), while accepting that the inflow (or outflow) of capital and outflow (or inflow) of earnings on that capital are among the more distinctive characteristics of foreign (direct) investment, argue that the primary and secondary external transactions associated with the activities of MNEs may also be very different from those of uninational firms and, in some circumstances, may have more important consequences for the balance of payments than the capital/earnings equation.

Later in this chapter, we shall consider some of the factors influencing the extent and direction of external transactions of MNEs and how these differ from those of non-multinational companies. In this section, we are concerned with some of the conceptual questions which have puzzled researchers since the 1960s. At that time, both the UK and US were faced with (what was perceived to be) a fragile balance of payments situation. At that time, too, it was observed that outbound MNE activity was increasing and exerting a more pronounced influence on both trade and capital movements.

In the mid 1960s, two major enquiries were

Table 14.1   Transactions of affiliates of multinational enterprises in the balance of payments of Mexico, 1977. Sign indicates inflow (+) or outflow (−).

Item	Mexico total ($million)	MNE affiliates ($million)	Share of affiliates (%)
1 Income in current account	8 404	1 461	17
Export of goods	4 418	937	21
Assembly plants' net income	524	524	100
Other current account income	3 462	–	0
2 Expenditure in current account	− 10 027	−2 219	22
Import of goods	−5 890	−1 549	26
Dividends paid abroad by TNCs	−172	−172	100
Interests on foreign lending (private sector)	−437	−218*	50
Other services (technology and royalties)	−560	−280*	50
Other expenditures on current account	−2 968	–	0
3 Current account balance (1 + 2)	−1 623	−758	47
4 Long-term capital flows	4 379	541	12
Foreign direct investment equity	372	327	100
Credits to TNCs	214	214	100
Other long-term capital	3 838	–	0
5 Short-term capital flows	−2 151	−271	13
Liabilities – private sector	−323	−162*	50
Assets – private sector*	−219	−109*	50
Other flows	−1 609	–	0
6 Overall capital account (4 + 5)	+2 228	+270	12
7 Errors and omissions	−101	−33	33
8 Overall balance of payments position (3 + 6 + 7)	+504	−521	

*Estimate. See Note 33.

Source: Unpublished UNCTC study (1981). The data is based on the values of imports and exports of transnational corporations from Dirección General de Aduanas (Mexico) and on data on balance of payments from Banco de México.

commissioned by the US and UK governments to identify and evaluate the main balance of payments consequences of outward investment. Both sought to identify and measure the external transactions of home-based MNEs arising from their foreign activities, and to calculate what might have occurred in the absence of such investment. The US enquiry, undertaken by Gary Hufbauer and Michael Adler (1968), considered three possible counterfactual situations. These were called the *classical*, the *anti-classical* and the *reverse classical* substitution models.

Let us first briefly describe these models and then examine the difference they make to the balance of payments effects of MNE activity.

The *classical substitution* model postulates that a unit of capital invested abroad will cause a unit net addition to capital formation in the host country but a net decline in capital formation at home. In other words, FDI is assumed to replace investment in the exporting but not in the importing country. Under the *reverse classical* assumption, FDI fully substitutes for other investment in the recipient country, but

Table 14.2a Transactions of UK outward and inward investors 1973–83: outward investment (£ million).

	1973	1974	1975	1976	1977	1978	1979	1980	1981	1982	1983
Financing											
Net capital inflow[1]	+390	+603	+368	+258	+489	+541	+514	+1852	+342	+305	+1099
Dividends, profits, interest[2]	−363	−371	−378	−499	−595	−806	−851	−1184	−1323	−1381	−1334
Balance	+27	+232	−10	−241	−106	−265	−337	+668	−981	−1076	−235
Royalties and services											
Royalties, net[3]	−68	−97	−113	−131	−158	−187	−202	−222	−250	−244	−294
Services, net	−55	−54	−61	−100	−120	−135	−140	−50	−15	−104	−105
Balance on royalties and services	−123	−151	−174	−231	−278	−322	−342	−272	−265	−348	−399
Balance on financing, royalties and services	−96	+81	−184	−472	−384	−587	−679	+396	−1246	−1424	−634
Trade											
Exports, all[4]	+3000	+4200	+4830	+6450	+8300	+9200	+9850	+11 150	+10 900	+11 200	+12 000
Exports, related-party only[4]	+1400	+1950	+2200	+2850	+3850	+4600	+4400	+4950	+5000	+5400	+5750
Imports	na	na	na	na	na	na	na	na	na	na	na

1 Total inward investment, less unremitted profits; includes equity and loan capital.
2 Dividends remitted abroad, branch profits (assumed all remitted abroad), and interest paid on inter-company debt; includes associated companies.
3 Data for related-party royalty payments, allocated between inward and outward investment in the proportion for 1982.

4 Estimates based on 1973, 1976, 1977, and 1981 surveys in *Business Monitor M4A*.
na not available.
Source: Stopford and Turner (1985). Data derived from CSO, *United Kingdom Balance of Payments*, 1984 edition: Financing data for 1981–83 based on revised figures published in *British Business*, 17th May 1985.

causes no net decline in capital formation in the home economy. In both these models, MNE activity is assumed not to affect the global volume of investment – only its geographical composition. By contrast, a third model considered by the American economists – the *anti-classical* model – postulates that FDI increases world capital formation. Under this formulation, no substitution takes place at home or abroad: foreign investment increases plant capacity abroad but has no effect on domestic capital formation at home.

Which of the above scenarios is, *de facto*, likely to be most appropriate will depend on the further assumptions one makes about the aims and achievements of macro-economic policy in both the capital exporting and importing countries, and on the

strategic behaviour of the investing firms. If both countries are successful in maintaining full productive employment and an equilibrium exists between planned savings and investment, it follows that a change in the capital formation by an MNE must be offset by a fall in domestic expenditure elsewhere – be this investment or consumption. In this event, the *reverse classical* assumption seems to fit. If the investing country achieves this goal but there is unemployment in the host country, the *anti-classical* model would appear the more realistic. If it is assumed that MNE activity evokes no response on the part of either home or host governments, then the *classical* model would seem to be the most appropriate.

The assumptions made about the strategies of

Table 14.2b   Transactions of UK outward and inward investors 1973–83: inward investment (£ million).

	1973	1974	1975	1976	1977	1978	1979	1980	1981	1982	1983
Financing											
Net capital outflow[1]	−781	−724	−292	−691	−593	−1451	−1413	−1683	−3103	−867	−1354
Dividends, profits, interest[2]	+610	+639	+712	+929	+1001	+1087	+1221	+1300	+1524	+1452	+1951
Balance	−171	−85	+420	+238	+408	−364	−192	−383	−1580	+583	+597
Royalties and services											
Royalties, net[3]	+37	+49	+55	+72	+81	+97	+125	+145	+165	+179	+220
Services, net[4]	+59	+74	+84	+113	+72	+76	+78	+99	+72	+94	+128
Construction contractors[5]	+35	+55	+85	+81	+100	+141	+142	+131	+148	+150	+153
Total	+131	+178	+224	+266	+253	+314	+345	+375	+385	+423	+501
Balance on financing and services	−40	+93	+644	+504	+661	−50	+153	−8	−1195	+1008	+1098
Trade											
Investment-pull exports 25%[6]	+400	+525	+600	+850	+990	+975	+1100	+1240	+1360	+1450	+1550
Overall balance[7]	+360	+618	+1244	+1354	+1651	+925	+1253	+1232	+165	+2458	+2648

1 Total outward investment, less foreign unremitted profits; includes loan and equity capital.
2 Dividends remitted home, branch profits (assumed all remitted home), and interest paid on inter-company debt; includes associated companies.
3 Data for related-party royalty payments, allocated between inward and outward investment in the proportions for 1982.
4 Includes management fees, branches' share of head-office services.
5 50% of reported earnings of construction contractors' overseas earnings.

6 Calculated at 25%. In the words of the author 'Though lacking any statistical basis, we consider that one-quarter of the total (of UK exports) is a reasonable estimate of the export flows that are directly attributable to the fact of the outward investment, and that would not have been possible without an invested presence in overseas markets' (p. 175).
7 Imports are ignored; see text.
Source: As for Table 14.2a.

firms will also influence the effects of FDI. Take, for example, the reverse classical substitution model. The hypothesis is that, in the absence of investment by one company, the same investment would have been undertaken by a competitor. For example, if Goodyear had not set up a plant in (say) Australia to produce rubber tyres, Michelin would have done so. Thus the direct effect on the US balance of payments of Goodyear's investment is given by the external transactions associated with that investment less the transactions associated with the Michelin investment. Now, it is not too difficult to think of situations where this assumption is an eminently plausible one, particularly where competing firms are of comparable size and efficiency. But this is not always the case. One cannot really argue that General Motors or Toyota are in the same strategic groups as Jaguar or BMW. Also, extended to a country level, it seems improbable that if US computer firms, which account for 75% of the world's direct capital stake in computers, did not invest, the slack would be entirely taken up by the firms accounting for the remaining quarter. Much obviously depends on the amount and structure of the investment concerned.

Moreover, we have seen in Chapters 3 and 4 that some investments may encourage others and that, far from being competitive, these 'follow my leader' investments are likely to be complementary to each other.

What, then, is the most realistic alternative model to assume? Any model that postulates *all* output generated by FDI is additional to that which would have been produced in its absence is unlikely to be generally applicable. In post-war years, for example, with a few notable exceptions (e.g. Singapore), there appears to be little correlation between the rate of growth of output in particular countries and their import of foreign direct capital. Japan is the classic case of an economy that has managed very well without much investment from abroad. At the same time, the Japanese government has positively encouraged outbound direct investment in certain sectors (Ozawa, 1989).[10] Much seems to depend on whether or not host countries can obtain the employment and growth stimulating effects of MNE activity through alternative routes. Nor must one neglect the consequences of FDI on resource allocation and restructuring as well as on resource utilization.

It is doubtful if *any* one model can adequately explain the effects of not investing – unless it contains the ingredients of each of the models discussed. In most cases, a reduction in outbound foreign investment by one country is likely to lead to *some* additional imports of competitive products from the investing country as well as *some* reduction in the rate of capital formation in the host country. No generalization on the precise combination of these variables seems possible. It will vary *inter alia* according to the ESP configuration and state of development of the host country, the character of the investment and the nature of competition between the investing (or prospective investing) firms. It may also depend on the time period being considered. On the basis of information provided by 23 of the leading UK manufacturing MNEs, the authors of a field study conducted in the 1980s concluded that had not these firms engaged in FDI 'some extra (UK) investment would have occurred but it is doubtful whether the effect would have been substantial' (Shepherd *et al.*, 1985). Furthermore, they argued that any beneficial effect on the UK balance of payments (and domestic employment)

would probably have been short lived, as sooner or later, they suggest, if British firms had found the conditions attractive for outbound investment, so would other foreign (or indigenous) firms.

One possible solution to this seemingly intractable problem is to present a model which is a hybrid of the *reverse* and *anti-classical* models. This is, in fact, what Behrman (1969) sought to do over 20 years ago. Behrman argued that in conditions of international oligopoly, a FDI by one enterprise, instead of replacing an alternative investment, may actually trigger off an investment by a competitor, as oligopolists are more likely to enter than stay out of markets in which their competitors are operating. For the *initiating* firm, then, the balance of payments effects of not investing becomes the difference between the transactions involved when *both* the initiating firm and its competitors are producing in the market in question, and those which would have occurred had *neither* company invested. To the *following* firm, it is the difference between the transactions involved when both groups of firm invest and those involved when only the initiating firm invests. Both these models can be formulated, assuming that FDI does or does not affect the level of market activity in the host country. When this constraint is removed, we have a situation in which the impact of MNE activity is to *add* to the capital formation and output of the host country, but at the same time is accompanied by a similar amount of investment by a competitor.

14.5.2 Some empirical results: home countries

A summary of the initial recurrent effects of some alternative situations on the balance of payments of an investing country is set out in Table 14.3. The data represents the actual transactions of UK and US outward direct investors in the 1960s,[11] less those which are estimated would have occurred under three alternative scenarios. The assumptions underlying the anti-classical and reverse classical substitution models have already been described. The *income generating* model is a mixture of the two. It assumes that the reverse classical model is appropriate for analysing the export displacement component, but that the anti-classical model (which

Table 14.3 'Best guess' estimates of selected balance of payments returns of UK and US direct foreign investment in manufacturing industry.

	Reddaway data (UK, 1956–63)						Hufbauer/Adler data (US, 1957–64)					
	Per cent of net operating assets controlled by UK firms abroad			Per cent of UK share of net operating assets controlled			Per cent of total assets controlled by US from abroad			Per cent of US share of total assets controlled		
	AC^1	RC^2	IG^3	AC^1	RC^2	IG^3	AC^1	RC^2	IG^3	AC^1	RC^2	IG^3
Initial effect												
Capital equipment exports	14	10	14	21	15	21	27	3	27	49	5½	49
Immediate 'multiplier' effect[4]	na	na	na	na	na	na	2½	3	2½	5	5½	5
Specific recurrent effects												
Exports of parts and components	6	4½	6	8½	6½	8½	5	1	5	9	1½	9
Exports of finished goods (export displacement effect)	−20[9]	−3	−3	−30	−4½	−4½	−51	2½	2½	−93	5	5
Trade propensity effect[5]	na	na	na	na	na	na	6	–	6	11	–	11
Profits and interest	7½	7½	7½	8	8	8	12	12	12[10]	12	12	12
Royalties, fees and services[4]	½	½	½	½	½	½	1½	1½	1½	2½	2½	2½
Imports by investing country from subsidiaries[7]	na	na	na	na	na	na	−5	−4½	−5	−9	−8	−9
Total	−6	9½	11	−13	10½	12½	−31½	12½	22	−67½	13	30½
Non-specific recurrent effect												
Sustained multiplier effect[8]	na	na	na	na	na	na	7	−3	−5	15	−3	7
Total	−6	9½	11	−13	10½	12½	−24½	9½	17	−52½	10	23½
Recoupment period (approximate years)	Never	8	6½	Never	7	6	Never	8	4½	Never	7½	3½

1   Anti-classical substitution assumptions.

2   Reverse classical substitution assumptions.

3   Mixture of AC and RC assumptions – an income generating model.

4   The immediate multiplier effect attempts to measure the balance of payments repercussions (to the investing country) of an increase in income in the host country consequent upon the capital transfer. (See Hufbauer and Adler, p. 52, ff).

5   This effect acknowledges the more general trade effects which accompany any expansion of overseas sales. Under the anti-classical assumptions it is simply measured by the marginal propensity to import from the US expressed as a percentage of the capital outflow. (See Hufbauer and Adler, p. 47).

6   We have assumed that the royalties and fees are largely independent of the alternative assumptions made, taking as our estimates those contained in Table XII.4 (p. 373) of Reddaway and Table 3.9 (p. 29) of Hufbauer and Adler. Those of Reddaway are estimated *net* of royalties and fees which might have been earned in the absence of UK investment: the Hufbauer

and Adler data assumes that in the absence of US investment no royalties and fees would be earned.

7   US estimates are derived from figures on (a) US imports per unit of subsidiary sales and (b) US imports per unit of native firm sales in various recipient regions (see Hufbauer and Adler, p. 31, ff).

8   The sustained multiplier effect estimates the multiplier effect of the continuing influence of the various specific balance of payments effects on income flows in the host country. For the method of calculation see Hufbauer and Adler, p. 46, ff, and Table 4.3.

9   This figure is very much a guess. It is based on the approximate UK share of the imports of manufactured goods into countries in which the UK has a substantial investment stake. For further details in a US context see Hufbauer and Adler, p. 32, ff.

10   In the absence of other data, we assume that the return on non-US capital is the same as that on US capital in US controlled firms. In fact, it is likely to be somewhat less.

Source: Dunning (1969).

allows for an increase in capital formation in the host country) is more suitable for the other components. As revealed by the table, the effect this modification has on the time it takes a country to recoup an export of a unit of capital is to lower that calculated by the reverse classical model from 8 to 4.5 years in the case of the US, and from 8 to 6.5 years in the case of the UK.

We have used two of the earlier and most rigorous studies to illustrate the impact of outbound MNE activity on the balance of payments of the investing country. It is worth emphasizing that both were primarily concerned with *manufacturing* investment and that, at the time, most UK and US investment was of a market-seeking rather than rationalized or strategic asset seeking kind. Since the opportunity cost of the first type of investment is different from the rest, the (net) balance of payments results will be different. Similarly, since most foreign production in services does not substitute for trade in services (simply because many services are not tradeable), a different kind of model might be required to calculate the balance of payments affects of service-oriented MNE activity.

Mention must now be made of some subsequent studies carried out by economists. A study by Bergsten *et al.* (1978) concluded that the production of affiliates of US MNEs abroad over the period 1966–72 had a positive and significant impact on the exports of the US parents to their affiliates in the relevant markets. In addition, foreign-controlled value-added activities were found to be positively and significantly related to the exports of other US firms in the same industry to that market, so that both the direct effects (exports of the parent company) and the indirect effects were favourable to the host country. Both effects were in addition to other variables which affected US exports, including industry and host country characteristics.

The second study, by Lipsey and Weiss (1981), was even more conclusive about the favourable impact of US direct investment abroad on US exports. Based on US Department of Commerce data, and using an OLS multiple regression model, the authors found that US investment abroad (measured by net fixed assets of affiliates, by affiliates' total sales, by affiliates' sales in the host country, or by the number of affiliates) had a favourable impact on the parent company's exports,

on US industry exports and on total US exports. The effects on the exports of US industry and for total US exports included a variety of indirect effects over and above those affecting the exports of the parent company. The study also demonstrated that production by US affiliates abroad appeared to substitute for exports from 13 other major industrial countries, especially in developing countries' markets (i.e. it had a negative impact on the exports of countries other than the US) and that activities of US-owned manufacturing affiliates were most pronounced in countries which were host to many other foreign-owned affiliates. The study suggested that these findings lent support to the idea that direct investment abroad is a method by which oligopolistic forms compete for a share in host country markets. This was found to be particularly true of trade and investment in industrial products between developed countries.

A third study, also by Lipsey and Weiss (1984), supplemented their previous research by examining data *at an individual firm* level on the exports and foreign production of US MNEs in 1970. More particularly, they related (by use of a multi-regression equation) the value of the manufacturing exports of some 200 US firms in 14 industries in each of five areas of the world to the characteristics of the parent firms and the production of their foreign affiliates in, and the GDP of, these areas (Lipsey and Weiss, p. 305). The authors discovered that in all but three sectors, *viz* drugs, electronic components and non-auto transport equipment, there was a positive, and for the most part, significant correlation between exports and foreign production. The relationship was generally stronger between the two variables in the case of exports of intermediate goods for further processing than it was for the export of final products.

A fourth study, by Blomström *et al.* (1988), attempted to estimate the effect of foreign production on the home country's exports of manufactured goods using data supplied by the US Department of Commerce for 1982 and the Industriens Utredninginstitut (IUI) of Stockholm for 1965, 1970, 1974 and 1978. In both instances, the authors used trade equations which related exports from the home countries to the GDP, GDP per head of the host country and a foreign production proxy (usually net sales of the foreign affiliate, that is, sales minus imports from the home country). The authors used both OLS and two-stage least-squares equations to estimate the significance of the foreign production variable, and found the predominant relationship 'somewhere between neutrality and complementarity', that is, the foreign production induced some increase or no change in exports.

The relationship was most clear for Sweden for which increases in production appear positively related to exports, that is, the two variables are complementary for seven industries.[12] The study also showed that there was no evidence to suggest that the complementarity between exports and foreign production declined as the latter became a more important modality of servicing foreign markets.

The results for the US were mixed. At the most disaggregated level, there is a predominance of either a positive or nil relationship between affiliate net sales and US exports for four-fifths of the 34 industrial sectors. However, in five sectors, *viz* other foods, drugs, industrial chemicals, primary and nonferrous metals and lumber, wood, and furniture and fixtures, exports and foreign production were found to be substitutable for each other. These results are largely confirmed in an econometric study by Pearce (1990a) of the exports and foreign production of 458 of the world's largest industrial companies in 1982. However, the particularly interesting finding of this investigation was that the foreign value-added activities of MNEs were much more closely related to their *intra*-firm exports than their *inter*-firm exports. Pearce suggested that this reflected the complementarity between the relocation of the final stages of production and the export of intermediate products, which – because of imperfections in the market – were internalized within the MNE. Pearce also established that the *growth* of foreign production was more likely to stimulate *intra*-firm than *inter*-firm exports. Finally he discovered that the propensity to internalize exports and to engage in foreign production was most complementary in the case of US and Continental European MNEs and, for most industries, at a 1% or 5% level of significance. For UK firms, the relationship was weaker, possibly because a lower proportion of outbound MNE activity was directed to technology-intensive manufacturing sectors where the most pronounced complementarity between exports and FDI is likely to occur.

Finally, mention might be made of a study of Indian joint ventures abroad in which Agarwal (1987) concluded that on a transactional basis, their contribution to the Indian balance of payments position was a strongly positive one. However, once the export replacement effect was taken into account, much of this favourable effect was removed, although the net result still remained marginally positive (Agarwal, 1987).

14.5.3   Some empirical results: host countries

As a counterpart to the work on the effect on the home country's balance of payments of outward direct investment, there has been some research on the consequences of inward investment for the host country's balance of payments. Perhaps the most ambitious study was that undertaken by Lall and Streeten (1977) who collected data from 159 MNEs with investments in six developing countries[13] between 1970 and 1973. They examined the direct (or associated) balance of payments effect for each firm which they defined as:

$$Bd = (X + K - (Ck + Cr + R + D)   14.1$$

where
Bd	net surplus or deficit on balance of payments account of the foreign affiliate
X	value of its exports
K	inflows of its capital
Ck	value of capital goods imported
Cr	value of recurrent goods imported
R	royalties and technical and managerial fees paid to foreign countries
D	dividends plus interest accruing to investing countries.

Using this measurement, the authors found that, except in one country (Kenya), MNE affiliates recorded a net deficit on their external transactions which (as a percentage of their net sales) ranged from -55% for Iran to -11.7% for India.[14] The authors concluded that, given the fact that almost all the foreign affiliates were engaged in import-substituting activities, this result was to be expected. They then went on to compare the external transactions of foreign affiliates with those of their indigenous counterparts. They found that affiliates and local firms had similar propensities to import (p. 145). Also, on balance (although this varied between countries) they exported about the same, or rather less, than locally-owned firms (p. 146). The main reason for any negative balance of payments effect recorded was primarily put down to the outflow of profits, dividends and royalties exceeding that of new capital inflows. Indeed, according to the authors these servicing costs may well be understated (and in the one country, Columbia, for which data was available, by transfer pricing manipulation, a subject which we shall take up in some detail in Chapter 18).

Lall and Streeten, however, clearly recognized that a proper assessment of the contribution of inward direct investment to the external trade account of the host country required some assumption as to what might have happened in its absence. In their study, they offered a number of alternative scenarios.[15] The first – the 'import substitution' scenario – affirmed that the product would have been imported instead of being produced by the foreign firm in the host country. In this case, the appropriate comparison was between the foreign exchange which would have been spent on importing the product and that actually spent by the foreign affiliate in producing it locally. The second – the 'financial replacement' scenario – assumed that the investment by the MNEs would have been undertaken by a locally-owned firm. In this case, the relevant comparison was between the different costs of the alternative sources of capital. And the third was the 'most likely local replacement' scenario. Here an attempt was made to calculate that part of inward direct investment which could be replaced by domestic investment and that part which could not.

In determining the most appropriate of these scenarios, the authors devised a composite index of the technological and entrepreneurial capabilities of the host countries. A degree of local replacement was proposed for each of the firms analysed, with a higher degree of replacement occurring in industries with older or more easily available technology, or with greater local entrepreneurial potential. In ideal conditions, this alternative would provide an estimate of all the non-financial contributions of inward direct investment. In practice, however, no such estimate is reliable, simply because one firm may differ from another for reasons other than its ownership.

Using this method of evaluation, Lall and Streeten found that 40% of the 159 foreign-owned firms had negative net social income effects on the host countries. However – and this is a crucial point – the main determinant of these effects was the effective rate of protection imposed by the respective host governments, the consequences of which were unrelated to the nationality of ownership of the firms. In the case of Kenya, inward investment was found to be beneficial to both the direct balance of payments and GNP no matter which of the three scenarios was assumed. However, Kenya was not considered to be a typical host developing country, since an above average number of foreign firms there were export oriented.

Using the alternative of the 'most likely' replacement and on the basis of crude estimates obtained by utilizing the 'degree of local replacement', Lall and Streeten estimated that one-third of the foreign firms had negative income effects on the countries in which they operated and were replaceable by local firms. About one-half were thought to be partly replaceable and the remainder irreplaceable. However, these results were obtained on the basis of a number of simplified assumptions regarding the technological and entrepreneurial capabilities of local enterprises. Other relevant factors, such as managerial efficiency and economies of scale, were not considered.

In general, the Lall and Streeten study confirmed the findings of Reuber and his colleagues some years earlier (Reuber, 1973). The latter study found that although the net trade (net payments) transactions of foreign affiliates in developing countries were positive to the tune of $80.8m (i.e. the exports of affiliates exceeded their imports), this would have translated into a negative balance of $1.7 million if it had been assumed that in the absence of FDI domestic companies would have supplied the output in question.

A number of other empirical studies have illustrated the critical nature of the assumptions to the counterfactual situation. Dunning (1969) estimated that while the net contribution of US manufacturing subsidiaries in the UK to the UK balance of payments was £284 million[16] in 1965, the most likely counterfactual situation would give a positive figure of £272 million. However, this calculation excluded the secondary or spill-over effects arising from the presence of the US affiliates.

In his estimate of the *change* in the UK balance of payments brought about by all foreign affiliates in the UK in the 1960s, Max Steuer and his colleagues (1971) used the following equation:

$$\Delta B = \Delta P(x^1 - x(1 - f)) + yf - \Pi \frac{m^1}{1 + m^1} - ud \ YD$$

14.2

where

ΔB	change in balance of payments
P	output attributable to foreign affiliates
$x^1 - x(1 - f)$	change in exports attributable to new foreign investment
Π	pre-tax earnings of foreign affiliates
u	multiplier term
Y	term showing the proportion of output of foreign affiliates which supplements domestic output
f	proportion of output of foreign affiliate which substitutes for imports
m	imports.

After the addition of some tax variables and plugging in some estimates for the UK consumption and import propensities, Steuer estimated that, given the government policies at the time, inward direct investment had improved the UK balance of payments by about 10%.

Other scholars have attempted to measure the balance of payments impact of foreign affiliates operating in developing economies. In Latin America, Vernon (1973) found that the positive impact of inward direct investment on the balance of payments if it is assumed that the goods and services arising from the investment would otherwise be imported, becomes negative if it had replaced local production. Biersteker (1978) obtained the same results for a sample of foreign firms in Nigeria.

There has been little research to identify *what is* likely to be the alternative situation. In the Lall and Streeten study quoted earlier,[17] 30% of the foreign firms surveyed considered that in their absence indigenous firms would have no difficulty in replacing the output using local technology or easily replaced imported technology, and a further 50% could be partially replaced. Only a fifth of the firms asserted that their output was impossible to replace by a local producer either because of the complexity or the restricted availability of the relevant technology.

14.6   PREDICTING THE LIKELY EXTERNAL TRANSACTIONS OF MNEs AND THE ALTERNATIVE POSITION

14.6.1   The likely transactions

Having described the kind of transactions which arise from the activities of MNEs, to what extent is it possible to hypothesize about the extent and direction of such transactions? To what extent, too, can one accurately assess the most likely alternative position and hence the net *effects* of MNEs on the balance of payments of home and host countries?

The first and most obvious factor influencing the external transactions of an affiliate is the *raison d'être* for its existence. As we have already suggested, market-seeking foreign affiliates are likely to import more than they export, particularly in the initial stages of their foreign activities when a substantial proportion of materials, components and parts are likely to be bought from their parent companies. By contrast, depending on the amount of local processing undertaken, resource-based affiliates are likely to be major net exporters. Rationalized subsidiaries are likely to record both substantial imports and exports although, on balance, we would expect them to be net exporters. Investments designed to protect or advance the global competitiveness of the investing companies are likely to increase intra-firm trade in both intermediate and final products. More generally, the transactions of MNEs are likely to vary according to the degree of their multinationality, their size and the stage of development of the countries in which they operate.

Within these broad categories, there are likely to be considerable variations in the extent and pattern of the external transactions associated with FDI according to the home and host countries involved, the nature of the activities being undertaken by the affiliates and the characteristics and internationalization strategy of the investing firms.

For example, since the cost and availability of (say) metal-based motor car components is different in Thailand, Belgium and the US, so the import propensities of Japanese-owned auto subsidiaries in these countries will be different. Similarly, since the real costs of production of a length of cotton fabric will be considerably higher in Canada and Denmark than in Pakistan or Turkey, so will the export propensity of foreign-owned textile firms vary between these countries. Moreover, different value-added activities require different proportions of tradeable inputs and outputs. Also, as we have already seen, the activities likely to be preferred by foreign subsidiaries are those which reflect their particular O-specific advantages, including those associated with the common governance of cross-border value-added activities.

Even the determinants of the likely impact of MNE activity on capital account permit few generalizations. Certainly, one might reasonably suppose that a cross-border acquisition would bring with it a larger injection of foreign capital than most (initial) greenfield ventures. On the other hand, part of the finance for any new investment may be obtained from indigenous firms (e.g. by way of equity or loan capital), the local capital market or from local banks. When calculating the balance of payments impact, it is important to distinguish whether one is relating any recurrent exports or imports to the capital actually invested by a foreign firm or to the capital controlled by it. It is possible, for example, to conceive of a situation in which only a small foreign equity stake, backed by a substantial amount of locally-borrowed capital or short-term credit, might finance a substantial net export or import surplus arising from the day-to-day operations of multinational affiliates.

The ratio of external transactions to sales by MNEs or their affiliates is, then, likely to vary according to the type of activity in which they are engaged, the countries in which they invest and the economic signals provided by home and host countries as they influence the costs and benefits of engaging in trade. However, to the extent that MNEs may influence the composition of trade, particularly intra-firm trade, they may well exercise a decisive impact on both the level and form of that trade.

14.6.2   The alternative position

Obviously, the most probable alternative position is likely to vary according to the characteristics of the countries, sectors and firms being considered. Again, use may be made of the eclectic paradigm and ESP configurations of both home and host countries. In industrial sectors in which there are several vibrant indigenous competitors, and which are supported by strong supply capabilities and infrastructure, it is likely that domestic and inbound investment will be at least partially substitutable for each other. Countries that pursue a policy of self-reliance or those with acute balance of payments difficulties are likely to react differently to the absence of foreign-owned firms than those which are fully integrated into the global economy and which have no concerns on balance of payments account. Turning from the L advantages of countries to the O advantages of firms, it might be reasonably supposed that MNEs which produce fairly standardized medium to low technology products are more easily replaceable by indigenous producers (or other MNEs) than those supplying products which are strongly patented or which require cutting edge and idiosyncratic technology. Likewise, MNEs whose main O advantages include access to global markets (i.e. those in agribusiness and the hotel industry) may be less easily replaceable by indigenous producers, hence their balance of payments contribution may be strongly positive. Generally speaking, too, the greater the environmental volatility and market failure in cross-border intermediate product markets, the less it is likely that any positive balance of payments contribution of foreign firms will be offset by that of local producers.

14.7   MNEs AND THE STRUCTURE OF TRADE

14.7.1   Introduction

Because of their distinctive O-specific advantages, it is to be expected that MNEs and their affiliates will have a distinctive impact on the structure of trade of both home and host countries. This arises primarily because they are likely to affect the allocation of value-added activity both within a country and between countries. Moreover, MNEs are likely to affect the form of international transactions. Indeed, their very *raison d'être* stems from their ability and willingness to internalize cross-border intermediate product markets.

Chapter 15 will look further at the impact of MNEs on the competitiveness of resource usage in the countries in which they operate. It will demonstrate that this impact is essentially fourfold, *viz* on *technical* efficiency (i.e. on the productivity of resources and capabilities on a given use), on *structural* efficiency (i.e. on the distribution of resources and capabilities between uses, for example, from less to more productive value-added activities, from low to high growth sectors, from the production of labour to capital-intensive products, etc), on *scale and scope* efficiency (i.e. on the ability to reduce production and/or transaction costs by producing at larger and/or more diversified output); and on *adaptive* efficiency (i.e. on the ability of a country to speedily and efficiently adapt to changes in exogenous or endogenous supply and demand conditions).

In so far as each of these impacts affects the competitiveness of the producing firms, both in domestic and foreign markets, they will also influence their propensity to import or export assets, goods and services. In other words, MNEs may be expected to make a distinctive contribution to the structure of trade of both home and host countries whenever they operate in sectors with different trade propensities from their uninational or indigenous competitors. Alternatively, or in addition, they may export and/or import more or less of the particular goods and services that they are producing. This distinctive impact partly reflects the O advantages of MNEs (relative to uninational or indigenous firms), partly the opportunities available to such firms to internalize cross-border markets and partly differences in the disposition of resources and markets between the two groups of firms.

Let us now review some of the empirical evidence on these questions.

14.7.2   The structural effects of MNE activity

A priori it is reasonable to suppose that MNEs are likely to be more trade-oriented than their unina-

tional counterparts. Partly this is because foreign production cannot take place without some trade in intermediate products (e.g. management and technology) and partly because almost all value-added activity by MNEs is undertaken to replace or divert trade in goods and resources, or to create such trade. An examination of the sectors in which MNEs tend to concentrate suggests that they are those for which import and export propensities tend to be above average. Their contribution seems to be least in the domestically-oriented sectors and in those producing non-tradeable goods. This is partly because the O advantages of MNEs stem from their ability both to acquire, create and disseminate technology, management and skills, on a regional or global basis, as well as from their capacity to organize and control the diversification of value-added activities across national boundaries.

At the same time, to protect or advance their global interests, MNEs may curb or shut off the potential export markets of their subsidiaries. For example, suppose a French multinational firm acquires an American company currently exporting electronic products to Japan in competition with the French company. It may decide that it is in its strategic interests to disallow its newly acquired affiliate from exporting to Japan. As a consequence of this decision, the exports of electronic products from the US to Japan may fall. On the other hand, a Japanese chemical company might acquire a German producer and, as a result, switch the sourcing of its raw materials from local to Japanese-based firms. It is difficult, then, to theorize about the net trading effect of MNE activity without knowing about the kind of foreign production undertaken and the strategy and structure of the investing companies.

What, then, is the evidence? The data – some of which we have already reviewed – strongly supports the view that both in developed and developing countries, MNEs or their affiliates tend to concentrate in trade-intensive sectors (UNCTC, 1991a; UN, 1992)[18] and to engage in more trade in those sectors than do uninational or indigenous firms. The difference between the two groups of firms is most pronounced in open smaller industrialized (or industrializing) economies and in resource-based economies where MNEs are primarily engaged in export-generating activities. It is less evident in large industrialized or mixed economies that pursue a policy of economic self-reliance. Indeed, in a few cases (e.g. India, China and the Soviet Union), foreign-owned companies trade less than their domestic counterparts. Here, the main rationale of inward investment is the *reduction* of trade (mainly imports) with the rest of the world.

In a volume edited by Dunning (1985), several authors attempted to compare the industrial structure of inbound and outbound investment with that of the rest of the economy. In the UK, for example, Dunning found that in 1979 foreign-owned manufacturing affiliates were relatively more concentrated in sectors in which the UK's international *revealed competitiveness* was above average. In that year, for example, some 63% of the output of foreign affiliates was in sectors in which the UK's Revealed Comparative Advantage (RCA)[19] was greater than 1.00, compared with 44% in the case of UK firms. This finding confirmed earlier work by Dunning (1958) and Steuer (1973) that foreign-based firms do tilt the industrial structure of the UK towards more, rather than less, internationalization.

The conclusions for the UK were supported by several other studies. In his analysis of the impact of inbound investment on the Portuguese economy, Simoes (1985, p. 367) concluded that 'in the absence of an inflow of direct investment . . . the Portuguese industrial structure would be more biased towards traditional sectors' and that it had directly led a 'dynamization of Portuguese exports, particularly in sectors in which Portugal did not previously have any exporting capacity (e.g. electrical engineering, electronics, ship repairing etc)'. The average export/sales ratio of foreign-owned firms was 20% higher than that of Portuguese-owned firms. In like manner, Van den Bulcke (1985) reported that foreign affiliates in Belgium were most highly concentrated in sectors with the highest export/sales ratios; also, in 1976 the average percentage of sales exported by the former firms was 68% compared with 50% for uninational firms (p. 271).

The Japanese case is also instructive. In the early 1980s, the outbound production of Japanese MNEs was strongly directed to sectors in which the RCA of Japanese-based firms was either less than 1.00 or where, because of the rising value of the yen and artificial barriers to trade, it was declining. Today, in the early 1990s, there is some reason to suppose that in the more technologically advanced sectors Japanese, like European and US MNEs, are finding it necessary to have a value-added presence in each of the more important markets of the world. As a result, at least some outward investment is now being directed to sectors in which the Japanese comparative trading advantage is strongly positive.

The proposition that exports and FDI tend to be complementary to each other is supported by German data, which reveals that in 1981 both inward and outward investment were concentrated in sectors with an above average RCA (Juhl, 1985). Pugel (1985) demonstrated that there was a statistically significant and positive correlation between the pattern of US outward investment and that of its share of OECD exports in 1977, but found that the pattern of inward FDI intensity was 'essentially unrelated to the commodity pattern of trade' (p. 71). In her examination of Swedish data for 1970 and 1978, Swedenborg (1985) concluded that the pattern of Swedish production abroad broadly followed that of exports, except in the resource-based sectors. At the same time, she found inward direct investment to be concentrated in sectors in which Sweden had a RCA of more than 1.00. Singapore stands out among the developing countries in which the inward MNE activity is relatively more oriented towards trade-intensive sectors, Lecraw (1985a) showed that foreign-owned firms were not only strongly concentrated in export-intensive sectors, but that between 1963 and 1975, the industries in which inbound investment increased the fastest recorded the highest increase in their RCA ratio.

However, in other developed and developing countries, evidence on the impact of MNEs on the structure of trade is less conclusive. In the case of Canada, for example, several researchers, from Safarian (1966, 1969) onwards, have found no clear or consistent tendency for foreign-owned firms to export more or less than their indigenous counterparts, although it is generally agreed that the former are more intensive importers than the latter. Globerman (1985), for example, demonstrated that the correlation coefficient between the share of inward direct investment and the RCA index for a sample of 38 manufacturing sectors in 1960–61 was +0.176, but for US-owned firms alone it was +0.280. He also established that over the following two decades, while non-US inward investors significantly increased the competitiveness of comparatively advantaged sectors, US investment (which, in 1988, still accounted for nearly four-fifths of the total FDI stake in Canada) tended to favour sectors with below RCA values. These results confirm an earlier study by Brash (1966), in which he not only found that American-owned manufacturing subsidiaries in Australia were concentrated in import-substituting rather than export-generating sectors, but that, in these former sectors, they continued to import a higher proportion of their inputs than their Australian counterparts.[23]

In India, for reasons suggested earlier, the small amount of inward investment that has been allowed over the past three decades has been largely concentrated in sectors supplying goods for the domestic market (Lall, 1985; Kumar, 1990). However, using data for 1964 and 1969, Katrak (1983) found some support for the hypothesis that higher degrees of foreign ownership in an industry were associated with improved export performance. A later study by Lall and Mohammad (1983) confirmed that there was a statistically significant positive correlation between foreign ownership and Indian export performance.

In Korea, a study by Bohn Young Koo (1985) showed that the influence of inward direct investment on the host country's trading patterns was marginal, and that there was little relationship between the industrial sector of such investment and either exports or RCA. In the 1970s, Koo revealed that there was a growing positive relationship between FDI and *imports*, but in the 1980s, with the Korean government favouring an export-led growth strategy, FDI was more attracted to sectors in which Korea's RCA was increasing. However, Koo (p. 296) concluded that the reason for his findings have 'as much to do with (an interventionist) government policy towards inward investment as to the allocative efficiency of foreign affiliates in Korea'. The growing importance of free trade zones in several developing countries (e.g. Malaysia, Sri Lanka and Taiwan) and the reduced import duties on some products supplied by the foreign affiliates of US firms has fostered a closer association between inbound FDI and RCA in these countries. More recently, the reorientation of development strategies and the removal or reduction of import barriers by several African and Latin American countries has reinforced this relationship.

An econometric analysis by Morgenstern and Miller (1976) of 534 exporting firms in ten Latin American countries revealed that much of the superior export performance of MNE affiliates was explained by the fact that they were concentrated in the more export-oriented sectors. Finally, in a study on Korea's economic development, Westphal *et al.* (1979) asserted that, while foreign-owned firms appeared to contribute a relatively high share of manufacturing exports, this was largely the result of their above average representation in the principal export industries, rather than their having a higher propensity to export than local firms in the same sector.

It is difficult to draw hard and fast conclusions from these various contributions. A brave attempt to offer some generalizations is contained in a recent UNCTC (1989) study which looked at the impact of US, Swedish and Japanese investment on the export performance of developing countries. The study concluded that while, in general, foreign firms have played a positive role in assisting the restructuring of the production of developing countries towards tradeable commodities, there are important regional and industrial differences. Thus, while foreign subsidiaries in Latin America increased their share of the total exports of most products in the 1980s, the reverse was the case for US-owned firms in at least four Asian newly industrializing countries – Korea, Taiwan, Hong Kong and Singapore. On balance, however, the authors of the study suggested that one of the most important contributions that inward direct investment can make to assist a developing country is to move from a protectionist, import-substituting strategy to one based on its perceived dynamic RCA. This is because of the superior knowledge and operating experience of MNEs about the cross-border markets for factors of production, intermediate products and final goods and services.

14.7.3 The comparative trading performances of foreign and indigenous firms

Several surveys, from that of Dunning (1958) onwards, have compared the trade performance of foreign-owned firms with that of their domestic counterparts.[20] Taken as a whole, these reveal that MNE affiliates generally have a higher propensity to export than do indigenous firms, but that this is not as much or as widespread as some commentators have suggested once one normalizes for industry- and firm-specific characteristics.

We have already suggested reasons why multi-national affiliates might trade more or less than indigenous firms in the same sector. On the one hand, their O-specific advantages, which often include better access to, information about and greater experience in global markets, together with their propensity to engage in cross-border intra-firm product or process specialization[21] between their affiliates or between their parent company and affiliates, make it likely that they will record both higher export and import propensities than indigenous firms. Recently established subsidiaries are also likely to record higher import propensities than their domestic counterparts. On the other hand, in so far as MNEs sometimes engage in value-added activities in several countries, they may close or restrict particular markets to affiliates located outside these markets.

Obviously, then, it is difficult to generalize about the likely effects of MNE activity on exports. However, it may be possible to classify foreign affiliates according to whether they are likely to export less or more than indigenous firms. Thus, for example, the former are likely to record a better export performance, the greater the barriers to entry into the foreign markets which they already service. By contrast, the larger the number of countries in which MNEs operate, the lower the export/sales ratio is likely to be *unless* each production unit is specializing in intermediate or final products which are then traded across the exchanges. Certainly, empirical studies comparing the export behaviour of import-substituting foreign affiliates in developing countries (e.g. Lall and Streeten (1977), Lall and Mohammad (1983), Subramanian and Pillai (1979) and Kumar (1990)[22] for India; Jenkins (1979) for Mexico; Kirim (1986) for the Turkish pharmaceutical industry; Fairchild and Sosin (1986) and Newfarmer and Marsh (1981a, 1981b) for Latin American countries) found that multinational affiliates recorded either a lower or similar export/sales ratio than domestic firms.

The relative performance of foreign- and domestic-owned firms in export-oriented sectors is also mixed, and does not wholly accord with expectations. However, in many cases, the sectoral breakdowns are not fine enough to capture properly differences between products destined for local markets and those intended for international markets. This may give the export-processing subsidiary (e.g. in television components) an apparent exporting advantage over a local firm assembling television sets for sale to domestic consumers.

Moreover, these and similar studies reveal that the trading patterns of foreign firms vary between sectors and countries. For example, Cohen (1975), in a case study of export-oriented firms in three Asian countries, concluded that in the late 1960s foreign firms in South Korea were more likely to export than their domestic counterparts; in Singapore they were less likely to export; while in Taiwan they recorded about the same export propensities as local firms.

Riedel (1975), in a more detailed study of Taiwanese exports, found that only in the electronics sector did foreign firms outperform their domestic counterparts in export markets. Schive (1980) established that in nine of 12 manufacturing industries in Taiwan, the exports per employee ratio were higher for foreign firms than for local firms. Jenkins (1979) reported that in only four of 19 industrial sectors in Mexico did foreign affiliates export more than indigenous firms. In Morocco, although Haddad and Harrison (1993) found that foreign affiliates recorded a higher export sales ratio than their domestic counterparts in 16 of 19 manufacturing sectors, much of their superior performance disappeared[24] if size of firm was controlled for.

In developed countries, the picture is no clearer. Early studies on inward foreign investment suggested that US subsidiaries outperformed their UK and Netherlands competitors in the UK, but not in Canada and Australia. A later study of the UK by Dunning (1976) found that in 1973 US affiliates recorded a higher export/sales ratio in 23 of 37 manufacturing sectors, including motor vehicles, electrical machinery and mechanical engineering. However, subsequent analysis by Solomon and Ingham (1977) showed that the superior export performance of foreign-owned firms in the mechanical engineering sector primarily reflected the concentration of these firms in subsectors which had the highest export propensity.

Research by Panic and Joyce (1980) and Hamel (1985) has revealed that the biggest deterioration in the UK's trade balance in the 1970s and 1980s was in sectors (e.g. motor vehicles) in which the level of foreign participation was among the highest. On the other hand, since the mid 1980s Japanese affiliates in the auto sector have helped to revitalize the UK's exporting capabilities – mainly because Japanese investors have set up production units in the UK to supply the whole of the EC market. *Ceteris paribus*, countries which are part of a regionally integrated area are likely to attract (or not to attract, as the case may be) export-oriented inward investment.

An early study by Safarian (1966) found there was no consistent tendency for foreign subsidiaries in Canada to export more or less than domestic firms. By contrast, Stubenisky (1970) concluded that in almost all sectors in the Netherlands, the export/sales ratios of US firms were higher than those for indigenous firms. A later analysis of FDI in Belgium (Van den Bulcke, 1985) pointed to the same result and found that part of the reason for both the high export and import propensity of foreign subsidiaries is the substantial degree of intra-firm trade in which Belgium is involved. According to the same author, in 1976, 53% of the exports and 48% of the imports of foreign affiliates in Belgium were within the same company. In Portugal, Simoes (1985) found that in 15 of 24 sectors, foreign subsidiaries recorded a higher export performance than domestic-owned firms. He also found that the export performance of foreign affiliates was relatively the most favourable in the resource-based and some of the inward-oriented high technology sectors, and relatively the least favourable in the inward-oriented low technology sectors.

In Japan, foreign firms generally recorded lower export performances than their Japanese competitors in the 1970s (Ozawa, 1985). In Sweden, there are suggestions that foreign firms have helped to upgrade the export performance of those sectors in which local firms have a revealed comparative disadvantage. However, in sectors in which Swedish companies have a substantial competitive advantage, the export performance of foreign firms is no better than, and sometimes inferior to, that of their domestic competitors (Swedenborg, 1985). In his analysis of the impact of foreign manufacturing subsidiaries on the trading structure of French industry, Michalet and Chevallier (1985) concluded that while there was comparatively little difference

between the export propensities of foreign subsidiaries and French firms, the former had much higher import propensities. While only 11.3% of the value of engineering equipment and 15.1% of consumption goods was imported by French firms, the corresponding ratios for foreign subsidiaries were 36% and 26.9%. Finally, in their comparison of the export performance of foreign-owned manufacturing affiliates in the US with that of the parent companies of US MNEs, both Pugel (1985) and Lipsey (1991) established that, while the latter recorded higher export/sales ratios in technology and scale intensive sectors (e.g. electrical machinery, chemicals and motor vehicles), the former recorded considerably higher ratios in most of the traditional and domestically-oriented sectors (e.g. metals, textiles and apparel, lumber, wood and furniture, and paper products[25]). Lipsey also discovered that the import/sales ratio of foreign affiliates was considerably higher in all sectors than that of the parent companies of US MNEs,[26] and that the trade of foreign-owned firms fluctuated more than that of the US parent companies. Lipsey ascribes part of this latter difference to variations in the age and size composition of the two groups of firms.

One of the problems of most of the comparative studies described so far is that although they try and normalize for sectoral differences between foreign affiliates and domestic firms, they rarely do this systematically, or take account of variables other than the nationality of ownership (or degree of multinationality) which might also influence trade performance. Such variables include industry characteristics, the psychic distance between the trading countries, the extent of vertical integration of firms, the size of firms, the age of foreign affiliates and the degree of market concentration. One way to acknowledge such variables is to include them along with nationality of ownership (or degree of multinationality) as independent variables in a multiple regression equation – and then see how far the latter variables are a significant discriminator. This methodology was used by the authors of a study on the impact of inward direct investment on Brazilian trading patterns (UNCTAD, 1985). In this study, two multi-variate regression equations were offered – one to explain the import propensity and the other the export propensity of some 500 firms producing in Brazil over the period 1971–77. Some 33% of these observations were for foreign affiliates, and the balance for Brazilian state-owned or private firms.

The authors found that the overall import propensity of the affiliates of foreign-owned firms was 77% higher than Brazilian-owned firms, but that, after control-ling for industrial characteristics and market struc-ture, the former group of firms imported only 4% more of their sales than the latter firms. By contrast, the effect of foreign ownership on exports was positive, but insignificant, although US-owned affiliates did exhibit a significantly lower export propensity than other foreign affiliates. Of the other variables included in the explanatory equation, only capital intensity and degree of vertical integra-tion were found to be statistically significant. New-farmer and Marsh (1981b) also concluded that after controlling for other characteristics of the con-stituent firms and the nature of the market, foreign-owned affiliates in the Brazilian electrical industry had a higher import propensity than their local competitors in 1972 and 1974.

An alternative way of assessing the significance of industry- and firm-specific variables in affecting the comparative export performance of foreign- and domestically-owned firms is that taken by Kumar (1990) who regressed the export performance of the two groups of firms in 43 Indian industries to such independent variables as capital, skill intensity, product differentiation, competitive structure and size of firm. Kumar found that there were no significant differences in the role of these characteris-tics in explaining the export performance of the two groups of firms.

14.7.4 Summary and appraisal of empirical studies

The external transactions by MNEs and their affiliates are determined first by the value-added activities in which they are engaged; second by the efficiency with which these activities are conducted; third by the countries in which they are undertaken; and fourth, by the costs of trading these products across the exchanges, including any artificial impedi-ments or incentives initiated by government.

The effects of MNEs on the external transac-tions of the countries in which they operate depend first, on the extent to which the O advantages which influence the extent and nature of these transactions can be replicated by other firms (either in the home or host country), and second, on the macro, structural adjustment and trade-related policies pursued by governments.

We have seen that the net consequences of MNE activity on the trading structure of the global economy will depend critically on the type of FDI in which they are engaged. It will also be influenced by the age, extent and pattern of the investment, the stage of the life cycle of the goods and services being produced, and the structure of competition facing the MNEs. Without some knowledge of these variables and of the ESP configuration of the countries in which MNE production takes place (or might take place), it is exceedingly difficult to generalize about the impact of such value-added activities on trade. Indeed, the best that can be said for most empirical studies is that they have identified and evaluated some of the more significant variables influencing particular types of MNE activity under-taken under very specific conditions. Disappointingly few researchers, however, have attempted to identify the situations in which MNEs will improve or worsen the balance of payments or trade structure of home or host countries and, whatever their impact, the extent to which this is in the interests of the economic welfare of these countries.

Again, this chapter has pinpointed government policies as a vital L-specific variable. Take, for example, the replacement of exports of rubber tyres by a French MNE to Thailand by a local production subsidiary in Thailand; or the increased export of copper from a UK mining company in New Guinea; or that of computer software services from a US subsidiary in Barbados. The extent to which these actions are likely to yield beneficial effects to the host countries will depend critically on the conditions in which they were made and the alternative options open to the host governments.

The only generalization which seems to be possible is that MNEs, *qua* MNEs, generate certain O advantages, because of which, and the fact they produce in more than one country, they are likely to organize cross-border value-added activities (and hence the trade) arising from these activities dif-ferently from uninational companies. It is the extent and nature of these differences and the way in which MNEs, cf uninational firms, react to the ESP configuration of home and host countries (which themselves may be affected by MNE activity) which will determine, for good or bad, the impact of FDI on the international allocation of activities, and hence the kind of trade conducted between countries.

A priori, then, there is no presumption whatsoever that MNEs as a group of firms will affect the extent or direction of trade in one way or another. *De facto*, however, the evidence strongly suggests that the combination of the actions of MNEs and the influence of governments on these actions has, over the past 20 to 30 years, both increased the level and restructured the composition of world trade to the general benefit of the participating countries.

14.8   MNEs AND INTRA-FIRM TRADE

14.8.1   The reasons for intra-firm trade

We have seen (pp. 386–7) that a substantial and increasing proportion of cross-border trade is undertaken by and within MNEs. Undoubtedly, part of the explanation for the growth of intra-firm trade may have nothing to do with its modality *per se*, but with the growing roundaboutness of production, changes in the international division of labour and the growing role of tradeable goods in the world economy (Casson and Pearce, 1990). However, part is likely to be the direct result of the failure of cross-border markets to operate efficiently.

As this volume has frequently stressed, the distinctive feature of the MNE is that it internalizes intermediate product markets across national boundaries. Intra-firm trade, be it of raw materials, parts and components, semi-finished or finished (but not final products), is the expression of such internalization.[27] While the O advantages of firms and the L advantages of countries help to explain the level and pattern of international trade, the organization of that trade is essentially explained by the costs and benefits of the alternative transactional modes.

On p. 81 of Chapter 4 we gave some examples of the variables influencing the internalization of cross-border markets. We further asserted that the propensity of firms to replace inter-firm trade by intra-firm trade differed according to industry-, country- and firm-specific characteristics, as well as

to the strategic action or reaction of managers to any given OLI configuration with which they were faced. Clearly, one would expect a close parallel between the propensity of MNEs to participate in particular industrial sectors and their propensity to internalize cross-border trade. Several writers, for example, Lall (1978), Casson *et al.* (1986), Casson and Pearce (1988), Cho (1988) and Gray (1993), have elaborated on this kind of approach. They have sought to identify the factors most likely to generate intra-firm trade, the types of firms most likely to engage in such trade and the characteristics of countries between which trade is most likely to be internalized.

Table 14.4, extracted from Casson *et al.* (1986), identifies some of these factors. Unfortunately, few have been incorporated into any formal statistical testing. Four exceptions might be mentioned. In an examination of the cross-industry pattern of intra-firm exports by US MNEs in 1970, Lall (1978) found that the technological intensity of the products being traded, the size of the FDI involved, the divisibility of the production process and the perceived need to control after-sales service and maintenance facilities were each positively and significantly related to the share of intra-firm to total exports by US MNEs. Later studies by Siddharthan and Kumar (1990) and Cho (1988), based on 1982 data published by the US Department of Commerce, confirm the importance of the R&D variable. Both studies using OLS or least squares with a dummy variable (LSDV) models found that it was positively correlated with intra-firm trade, either at a 1% or 5% significance level. Other significant variables included the amount of selling and marketing development expenditure, the presence of scale economies and the extent to which US firms relocated pollution-intensive industries abroad, the output of which was subsequently imported into the US by the investing firms. Somewhat surprisingly, the Cho study also found that both the degree of vertical integration and the extent of international production was negatively (though not significantly) related to the propensity of MNEs to engage in intra-firm trade.

Other studies reveal the importance of regional- or country-specific L variables influencing the amount and pattern or intra-firm trade. In particular, European economic integration has substantially increased the extent of product and/or process specialization engaged in by MNEs in different parts

Table 14.4 Factors affecting the propensity to internalize intermediate product trade.

Factors	Positive or negative effect
Technical	
High fixed costs	+
Large non-recoverable investments	+
Perishable intermediate products	+
Quality, variability, coupled with a natural asymmetry of information	+
Efficient scales at adjacent stages of production vary, and their lowest common multiple is large	−
Multiplicity of joint inputs and outputs	−
Economies of scope in the utilization of assets	−
Market power	
Monopolist faces downstream substitution, or monopsonist faces upstream substitution	+
Multi-stage monopoly or monopsony	+
Entry deterrent by dominant firm	+
Dynamic	
Novelty of product and its division of labour	+
Fiscal	
Incentives for transfer pricing: differential rates of profit taxation, *ad valorem* tariffs or exchange controls	+
Statutory intervention in intermediate product markets (e.g. price regulation)	+
Restrictions on foreign equity participation; expropriation risk of foreign direct investment	−

Source: Casson *et al.* (1986) Table 1.3, p. 12.

of the Community with a subsequent increase in intra-affiliate trade. In 1982, for example, no less than 69% of EC-based exports to other EC countries by US manufacturing affiliates were to other affiliates (US Department of Commerce, 1985). Of the ESP variables likely to influence the organization of trade, the most important seem to be the extent to which the countries are, themselves, involved in the international division of labour and the kinds of actions taken by governments to affect the level and structure of trade. Helleiner and Lavergne (1979) have demonstrated that the relative importance of

intra-firm imports by US MNEs in the early 1970s was negatively related to the height of the US tariff at the time, and positively related to the reduction in tariff costs brought about by the Kennedy and Tokyo rounds. Other government-related variables include local content and sourcing requirements, both of which may reduce intra-firm trade, and the encouragement of the establishment of export processing zones, which may lead to more intra-firm trade. In so far as they may tempt MNEs to engage in cross-border transfer pricing, or dissuade them from doing so, government policies may also have a positive or negative effect on intra-firm trade in assets, goods and services.[28]

Firm-specific factors influencing intra-firm trade (which may also be country specific) include the extent of a firm's multinationality (which, in turn, may be a function of its size, product structure, age and experience in foreign production) and the associated transaction costs. For example, because they are in the early stages of their internationalization process, because of their policies of just in time deliveries, and because of the unique role played by the Soga Sosha, Japanese manufacturing MNEs have a higher propensity to internalize intermediate product trade than do US firms. According to Dunning (1986a, p. 106) no less than 84% of imports by Japanese firms into the UK in 1983 were intra-firm. A survey by Lecraw (1983) of 111 MNEs in six light manufacturing industries operating in five Asian countries in 1978 found that Japanese subsidiaries sent 79% of their exports to, and received 84% of their imports from, related units of the same organization. The corresponding percentages for US subsidiaries were 68% and 53%, for European subsidiaries 65% and 57% and for the subsidiaries of Third World MNEs, 23% and 37%. A recent study by Encarnation (1992) has shown that more than two-thirds of the exports from Japan to the US and about one-half of the imports into Japan from the US are within US or Japanese MNEs.

Finally, in seeking an explanation of the determinants of global integration, Kobrin (1991) related a measure of the intra-firm trade[29] of US MNEs to a group of four independent variables, *viz* research intensity, advertising intensity (as a proxy for the importance of market responsiveness), the percentage of total industry sales of US firms generated abroad (as a measure of the degree of internationalization) and minimum optimal or efficient scale of plant (as a measure of the economies of size).

In a cross-sectional study of 56 US manufacturing industries for 1982, using an OLS multiple regression equation, Kobrin established that of the four variables considered, the first three were positive determinants of intra-firm trade (at a 1% or 5% significance level), while the sign for the advertising variable was negative, as predicted.[30] None of the measures for plant scale, however, turned out to be significant variables. Kobrin also found that in 22 of the 30 sectors for which data was available, intra-firm ratios increased between 1982 and 1986, and that the most globally-integrated sectors tended to record the most dramatic increases in ratios.

14.8.2   The implications of intra-firm trade

Why should the way in which trade is organized matter to the participating nations? Is it correct to argue – as is often argued – that trade conducted within hierarchies is somehow less beneficial than trade organized through the market?

First, there seems little doubt that, just as MNEs influence the structure of economic activity within and between countries because of their O advantages and the way in which they organize these advantages, so they affect the structure and organization of trade – and for the same reasons. Hence, the effects of a hierarchical control of trade flows are likely to be similar to those associated with foreign production *per se*.

Second, the welfare implications of internalizing trade flows rests first on the conditions which prompted it, and second, on the assumptions made about the alternatives to that pattern or organization. In particular, in comparing intra-firm trade flows with inter-firm flows, what assumptions are made about the market conditions in which the latter are (or might be) conducted? Are there many or few structural market impediments?

Let us give just one example. Chapter 18 will concern itself with some issues related to transfer pricing of products and services traded within MNEs. Clearly, the opportunities for manipulating such

prices rests on the extent to which intra-firm trade is both possible and desirable. However, intra-firm trade may, in fact, help MNEs to exploit cross-border market failure, brought about by, for example, differential tax policies of governments, by manipulating the terms on which goods and services are traded. At the same time, foreign ownership may bring with it technological, marketing and organizational and other benefits which could not be obtained, or obtained as economically, by other means. Whether a host or home country is a net gainer or loser by such intra-firm trade – taking all costs and benefits into account – will critically depend on the particular circumstances in which it occurs.

Apart from some general speculations about the (largely) adverse affects of intra-firm trade, for example, by Murray (1981) and Helleiner (1981), there have been frustratingly few attempts in the literature to examine its welfare consequences on either the exporting or importing countries. There seems to be general agreement that intra-firm trade designed to promote structurally distorting pricing and other practices by MNEs is undesirable. It is also accepted that intra-firm trade which promotes a cross-border division of labour to achieve the global goals of the MNEs rather than the national objectives of countries may not always be welcomed, at least, by some of the participating countries. However, apart from some casual empirical studies, scholars have not so far rigorously pursued these issues. Because of this, and the failure to distinguish between the efficiency-enhancing effects of intra-firm trade arising from the internalization of imperfect markets and its possibly harmful consequences arising from an increase in monopoly power – both of which may arise from the common governance of cross-border activities by MNEs (of which intra-firm trade is an outcome rather than a cause) – there is little *a priori* reason to conclude that intra-firm trade (cf., inter-firm trade) is either welfare enhancing or welfare reducing.

At the same time, from their general knowledge of the determinants and effects of MNE activity and, in particular, the OLI configuration in which they operate and their strategic response to such a configuration, scholars are able to infer much about the likely costs and benefits of intra-firm *vis à vis* inter-firm trade. It is, for example, difficult to argue against the benefits that intra-firm trade within the EC has brought to the recipient countries, particularly in cases where there is competition between the trading firms and little inducement for these firms to engage in manipulative transfer pricing. On the other hand, some kinds of market-seeking or resource-seeking investments which are prompted, or protected, by structurally-distorting actions on the part of host governments, may induce MNEs to make more use of their internal cross-border markets and, by so doing, to affect the terms of trade, which may work against the interests of the importing or exporting countries.

14.9   A POLICY FOOTNOTE

In the light of the findings of this chapter, what actions, if any, should home and host governments pursue so that MNEs and their affiliates conduct their affairs in a way that is consistent with their balance of payments and resource allocative objectives.

We would make just three points. The first is to reiterate that, for the most part, issues relating to the balance of payments of either home or host countries to MNE activity should be dealt with as part and parcel of general macro-economic policy. Any attempt by governments to influence the state of the balance of payments or the terms of trade should take account of the consequences of such actions on other macro-economic goals which are more important in the long run. For example, if the main objective of economic policy is to increase its GNP per capita, then independently of the cause of any worsening of the balance of payments, any action taken to remedy it should be judged in terms of its effectiveness in achieving this objective. If the inward direct investment advances this goal better than indigenous firms, but worsens the balance of payments in so doing, then it may be entirely appropriate that the indigenous firms (or the consumers of their products) should pay the price of putting this situation right.

Second, and following the first point, it follows that in addition to examining the likely impact of MNE activity on the balance of payments and the structure of trade, governments ought to consider any and all of their policies that might directly or indirectly affect these variables. It might well be, for example, that inward or outward investment lays bare the deficiencies of other economic policies or

requires the implementation of new measures which may help improve the external trading position of the home or host countries. This is a general point about the impact of MNE activity which Chapter 20 will take up in more detail.

Third, where it can be shown that MNEs (because of their ownership or multinationality) worsen the balance of payments through the abuse of monopoly power, which at the same time reduces their contribution to the GNP (e.g. by transfer pricing manipulation, restrictions on exports, tied imports), it is entirely appropriate that some remedial action should be directed to modifying the behaviour of the MNEs concerned. It is also possible that, while MNE activity may lead to a higher real income over a long period, it may act as a destabilizing influence in the short run. Or it may help fashion an international division of labour which stifles the long-term comparative advantage of the host or home countries. In such cases, as well as for non-economic reasons (e.g. to maintain a degree of economic sovereignty and political independence), some intervention directed at restructuring the operation of MNEs or externalizing transactions internal to the MNE may be justifiable. However, each case must be examined on its merit. As in other areas of policy, generalizations are difficult – indeed dangerous – to make.

In the last resort, however, a government's attitude towards the impact of MNEs or their affiliates on trade and the balance of payments must rest on its perceived role in the world economy. Consider two extreme examples. Singapore, which fully accepts the costs and benefits of being part of the international division of labour, operates a *laissez faire* policy towards trade, and has little concern about the impact of MNEs on such trade. By contrast, India operates a policy of controlling trade to promote its long-term goals of (near) economic autonomy, and thus will view critically any attempt by MNEs to draw the Indian economy into the international division of labour. The ESP configuration and competitiveness of most countries normally lies somewhere between these two extremes, but the positioning and policies their governments take to protect and advance this position – much more than any specific attributes of MNEs – are likely to be the decisive determinants of their judgement on, and the actions taken towards, inward or outward direct investors in their trade-related activities.

14.10   CONCLUSIONS: THE EVOLUTION OF TRADE AND FDI LINKAGES

In Chapter 10 we set out a framework for examining the interface between MNE activity and the economics of the Nation States in which this activity occurred. *Inter alia*, we suggested that the nature and significance of this interface depended on the type of FDI undertaken by MNEs and the ESP configurations of the countries in which it was located. In turn, the significance of these variables was likely to vary according to the age, degree of multinationalization and global strategy of the MNEs involved as well as on the stages of development of the home and host countries.

Chapters 4 and 6 discussed the determinants of FDI and the extent to which it was likely to substitute for, or complement, other forms of international economic activity, particularly arm's length trade in goods, services and assets. Chapters 11 and 12 further argued that the linkages between FDI and trade were critically dependent on the cross-border transfer and dissemination of human and physical technology, and technological capability organized by the MNE. Often, as earlier sections of this chapter have shown, one of the main consequences of both outbound and inbound FDI is to restructure the trade of the countries. Throughout history, trade-related policies of governments have decisively influenced both the motivation and ability of MNEs to engage in FDI.

Applying the *stages* approach to economic development and MNE activity (see especially Table 10.4), it is possible to trace the changing interaction between trade and FDI. In the early stages of development, the two forms of international activity tend to complement each other as both are organized on the basis of Heckscher–Ohlin comparative advantage. Indeed, FDI fosters trade in (natural) resource-intensive goods wherever it provides the capabilities and markets to the exporting countries. Also, in so far as MNE activity may help upgrade the diamond of competitive advantage of both the investing and recipient countries (Porter, 1990), it may assist in the global industrialization and restructuring process. This, indeed, is the claim made by Kojima (1978, 1983, 1985, 1990) in respect of Japanese FDI in the 1960s and 1970s. Kojima applauds MNE activity

whenever and wherever it helps to overcome cross-border market failure and aids the L-specific advantages of both home and host countries. By contrast, where FDI is intended to defend or exploit a monopolistic or oligopolistic market structure, it may lead to a less efficient international division of labour and a sub-optimal pattern of international trade.

The compositions of both FDI and trade changes with the process of industrialization. As the chapter has already observed, the great majority of intra-Triad economic involvement is of an intra-industry character. Moreover, in today's global economy not only are trade and FDI increasingly linked with each other, but also a substantial portion of the former is undertaken by, and within, MNEs. As MNEs become more regionally- or internationally-integrated in their value-added activities, so trade switches from being based on traditional factor endowments to being based more on 'created' country-specific assets and capabilities, demand characteristics and actions taken by governments (Audretsch, 1989; Porter, 1990). Efficiency-seeking and strategic asset acquiring FDI each have distinctive consequences for trade. While the former tends to lead to more trade based on product specialization, differentiation and scale economies, and tends to be intra-firm rather than inter-firm in character, the latter only affects trade in so far as the changing ownership of cross-border activity itself leads to a further rationalization and/or upgrading of the L-specific attributes of countries.

Elsewhere we have examined the interaction between FDI and trading structures according to the changing OLI configurations facing MNEs as countries move along their investment development paths. In essence, it may seem that patterns of TNC activity tend to follow those of trade in as much as they gradually become more intra – and less inter – industry. At the same time, FDI impinges on the way in which trade is organized. For intermediate products, at least, intra-firm trade is increasingly replacing inter-firm trade. The role of TNC activity in affecting the trade of economies which may be innovatory or information and service driven is very different from that in most developing countries. However, within these two groups of nations, much will depend on the conditions under which TNC activity takes place and the way in which it affects the long-term asset base of both the investing and recipient countries.

Once again, generalizations are difficult to make. A recent study by Louka Katseli for the UNCTC (as yet unpublished[31]) has shown that while in several developing countries (e.g. most Asian newly industrializing countries and, more recently, Mexico) inbound investment has acted as a catalyst for industrial restructuring and cross-border economic integration, in others (e.g. Brazil and Nigeria) linkages between MNE activity and export development are much more tenuous. Katseli firmly puts the onus for ensuring an orderly and sequential evolutionary pattern of trade and investment on governments. She cites, as a role model, the strategy of the Japanese authorities in the upgrading of their postwar economy from export-oriented and labour-intensive manufacturing, to domestic capital goods and chemical industries, to assembly-based production, and finally to knowledge-intensive and globally-oriented manufacturing and service-based industries. Although, in the Japanese case, inbound MNE activity did not play a major role in this process (but outward direct investment did), in several other Asian countries it is currently playing a critical role. As Ozawa (1990) put its, MNEs are acting as 'inter-stage arbitragers of economic development'.

Clearly, there are important policy issues surrounding the interaction between MNE activity and trade. In the 1960s and 1970s, most of the emphasis of home and host governments focused on the contribution of FDI to the balance of payments. This is no longer the case, although in some developing countries, FDI is helping to alleviate (though not solve) the debt crisis. Instead, governments are viewing MNEs as vehicles for upgrading the quality of their indigenous resources and capabilities and for integrating their economies into the international marketplace. Policies designed to meet these objectives – especially as they affect trade – are likely to be very different from those which primarily view FDI as an important replacement mechanism, or as a necessary (but not always welcome) vehicle for the exploitation of natural resources. The question facing governments of the 1990s is not whether MNE activity is trade promoting or trade replacing, but whether it is an efficient instrument for the reorganization of the cross-border allocation of economic

activity in a way which is conducive to both national and international economic welfare.

NOTES

1 Collected at various dates ranging from 1975 to 1988.
2 See also Section 14.5.2 and 14.5.3 of this chapter.
3 For example, as Graham and Krugman (1989) show, the import propensity of Japanese firms in the US in 1986 was 2.5 times greater than that of other foreign affiliates. The authors partly put this higher propensity down to the preference of Japanese subsidiaries for foreign suppliers, but mainly to the 'mismeasurement of marketing firms as manufacturers and the selection bias that leads from the propensity of foreign firms to enter the US disproportionately in activities that make use of imported inputs' (p. 60).
4 Generally speaking, intra-firm trade is highest in the high technology fabricating industries and lowest in the low technology resource-based sectors.
5 These MNEs did not include the large trading companies. Moreover, data provided by Japanese manufacturing affiliates strongly suggests that until the early 1990s these firms were largely engaged in assembling intermediate products imported from their parent companies. In 1983, for example, 90% of the imports by Japanese affiliates in the UK were from their parent companies (Dunning, 1986a, p. 106).
6 For example, in 1989 some 60.8% of exports from US manufacturing subsidiaries in EC countries to non-US destinations (mostly other EC countries) were intra-firm (US Department of Commerce, 1991).
7 But worsen the balance of payments position of a third country.
8 We shall use the word 'associate' to mean the actual external transactions associated with MNE activity; the words 'effect' and 'consequence' are used to mean associated transactions less (an estimate of) those which would otherwise have occurred in the absence of these activities.
9 See also some calculations by Hood et al. (p. 84). It should be noted that neither study makes any allowance for the imports of foreign affiliates.
10 For further details, see Chapter 20.
11 In the case of US firms, data published by the US Department of Commerce was used. In the case of UK firms, data was collected directly from 60 MNEs which, between them, accounted for 15% of outward direct investment in the manufacturing and mining sectors in the 1960s.
12 This relationship was first established by Swedenborg (1979, 1985).

13   *viz* Columbia, India, Iran, Jamaica, Kenya and Malaysia.

14   The figures were 2.7% for Kenya; −11.7% for India; −25.5% for Jamaica; −35.3% for Columbia; −37.6% for Malaysia; and −55.0% for Iran.

15   The following paragraphs are derived from the report originally submitted by Lall and Streeten to UNCTAD in 1976 (UNCTAD, 1976).

16   Using a formula $B = E_{us} - (M_{us} + Y_{us} + R_{us})$, where E_{us} represents exports of US subsidiaries, M_{us} represents imports of US subsidiaries, Y_{us} is the earnings of US subsidiaries and R is the royalties and fees paid by US subsidiaries to parent companies.

17   Lall and Streeten (1977, pp. 179–80).

18   Measured, for example, in terms of the total value of foreign trade as a percentage of the gross national (or domestic) product.

19   Defined as the proportion of world exports of a particular industrial sector accounted for by UK-based firms divided by the proportion of world manufacturing exports as a whole accounted for by UK-based firms.

20   Some of these surveys are identified later in this chapter. The reader is also referred to useful summaries contained in Kumar (1990) and Gray (1992).

21   Note that this does not contradict some of the findings of Chapter 12 in which the Japanese were shown to have a strong revealed technological advantage in the sectors in which they were most actively involved in international production. However, it would seem that a higher proportion of the value-added activities from these and other O advantages of Japanese firms are being increasingly exploited from a foreign location.

22   Kumar (1990), for example, sought to explain variations in the export performance of foreign- and domestically-owned firms in 43 Indian industries.

23   A rather different kind of study by Williamson (1986) attempted to estimate whether, in their foreign investment strategies, MNEs would act as a conduit for imports in response to an increase in the competitive advantages offered by off-shore production; or whether such production might be restricted as part of any global optimizing strategy. In an econometric analysis of the responsiveness of Australian imports to price change in 36 industries over a 10-year period, the author concluded that, in the sectors in which there was a strong foreign presence, the first of his hypotheses had the greater validity.

24   Indeed, on average while recording an exports to sales ratio twice as high as their domestic counterparts, they recorded only 70% of the export propensity.

25   For all manufacturing the export/sales ratio of foreign affiliates in the US averaged 7.0% in 1979, 9.1% in 1982 and 7.8% in 1988. The corresponding ratios for the parent companies of US MNEs were 9.3%, 10.5% and 11.2% (Lipsey, 1991, Table 4, p. 12).

26   For all manufacturing, the import sales ratio of foreign affiliates in the US averaged 11.1% in 1977, 8.8% in 1982 and 10.9% in 1988. The corresponding ratios for the parent companies of US MNEs were 4.2%, 4.3% and 6.5%.

27   Finished goods are those whose physical state does not change when sold to the external purchaser. However, value added may still be created through marketing distribution and after-sales services. Final products are those which are bought directly by the consumer, for example, from a retail shop (see Gray, 1993).

28   This point is taken up further in Chapter 18.

29   *viz* the ratio of affiliate sales to *foreign* affiliates, affiliate sales to parents and parent exports to affiliates, to all foreign affiliate sales plus parent exports for majority-owned non-bank affiliates of non-bank parents (Kobrin, 1991, p. 20).

30   Indicating that the lower the advertising intensity, the less the pressure of firms to respond to differences in national demand patterns, hence the greater the incentive for integration and intra-firm trade.

31   See Katseli (1992).

CHAPTER 15

MNEs, Market Structure, Performance and Business Practices

15.1 INTRODUCTION

We now turn to consider the ways in which MNEs may affect the structure, efficiency and adaptation of resource usage in the countries in which they operate. In particular, this chapter will seek to answer five groups of questions which have particularly engaged the attention of researchers and policy makers over the past two decades or so. These are:

(1) What effects do MNEs have on the composition of value-added activities in home and host countries? Is the inter- and intra-sectoral distribution of output of the parent companies of MNEs, or that of their affiliates, different from that of uninational or indigenous firms?

(2) Given the value-added activities in which they engage, are MNEs more or less efficient in undertaking these activities than their uninational counterparts? Do they adjust more or less speedily to changes in international demand or supply conditions than their competitors? Do they perform a distinctive role in fashioning such changes? Are they more or less productive and/or profitable?

(3) To what extent do MNEs affect the organizational structure of economic activity? Do they induce more or less industrial concentration than would otherwise be the case? Do they prompt more or less product diversification? Do they foster more or less vertical integration? Do they promote or inhibit the development of clusters of related economic activities? Do they lead to more or less domestic or international rivalry? Do they stimulate or dampen entre-

preneurial initiative? Do they encourage or discourage the upgrading of consumer demand?

(4) In what ways are the conduct and behaviour of MNEs different from those of other firms in the economies in which they operate? To what extent is this explained by their governance of interrelated cross-border activities? Do they engage in more, less, or in different kinds of anti-competitive strategies? What is their particular impact on the competition and anti-trust policies of home and host governments?

(5) What are the policy implications of the kinds of effects identified in (1) to (4) above? In particular, how might home or host governments ensure that, as far as possible, that the conduct of their own MNEs and that of the affiliates of foreign MNEs is consistent with their own economic and other objectives?

These are the main issues addressed by this chapter. But first the following section sets out the conceptual framework for the analysis which follows.

15.2 A CONCEPTUAL FRAMEWORK

Why and under what circumstances should it be expected that the impact of MNEs on industrial and market structure would be different from that of uninational firms? What, in fact, are the main determinants of this impact? Once again, we believe the answers to these questions lies in the distinctive characteristics both of MNEs *qua* MNEs and of the economic and political environments in which they are operating. More particularly, we would expect the impact of MNEs on the competitiveness of home and host countries to be dependent on the nature and extent of their O-specific assets and of the ways in which they organize the deployment of these assets across national boundaries. Secondly, it will no less rest on the structure of the ESP configuration facing MNEs and how this changes as a result of the conduct and performance of MNEs.

Previous chapters have analysed some of the ways in which MNE activity impacts on the availability and quality of technological capacity, and on the upgrading of human resources, as well as on the external trade and payments of both home and host countries. This chapter and the following ones concentrate on the interaction between MNEs and such country-specific characteristics as the size and composition of markets, the pattern and quality of demand, the number, quality and effectiveness of competitors, the strength and structure of supplying industries, the ethos of entrepreneurship, the degree of openness of the economy and the influence exerted by governments on these variables. It is the way in which MNEs interact with these factors and how each affects the industrial and market structure in which they operate, which is the subject matter of this chapter. Chapter 16 will be concerned more directly with the linkages formed between MNEs or their affiliates and the value-added activities of their competitors, suppliers and customers.

The impact of MNEs will initially show itself on the level, range and composition of economic activity in which they engage *viz* (1) and (3) in Section 15.1, and on the extent to which their behaviour and performance differ from those of uninational firms *viz* (2) in Section 15.1. The outcome of the distinctive actions by MNEs will directly or indirectly influence the economic position and organizational structure of 'related' firms and the competitive position of the industries of which they are part. Such actions may also actuate a response by governments, which, in due course, may also impinge on the composition and efficiency of industrial activity (Porter, 1990).

Can one predict the direction and extent of these activities of MNEs on the industrial and market structures of home and host countries? In theory, their distinctive O advantages should improve inter-sectoral (allocative) and/or help raise technical and/or scale efficiency. Over time, these advantages should also assist the reallocation of resources to

meet new supply or marketing needs. *De facto*, however, much will rest on the nature of the O advantages, in particular, whether they are the outcome of competitive or monopolistic forces, and of the use made of these advantages. This, in turn, will be partly dependent on the country-specific ESP configurations with which the MNEs are faced.

Take, for example, the case of an MNE or uninational firm which acquires its foreign supplier of a particular raw material. The outcome of this acquisition will be very different depending on whether the acquired firm is the sole supplier of the material or one of several. In the former case, the acquiring firm could, if it so desired, crowd out any or all of its competitors, or potential competitors, in the final goods market. In the latter case, it may inject a new element of competition into the supplying industry. Similarly, by integrating forward an MNE may either reduce, or block, the marketing options of competitors, or stimulate competition in the distribution sector. Thirdly, consider the case of a firm which acquires a foreign competitor. This could restrict the purchasing choices of consumers and, by lowering the elasticity of demand for the product, enable the MNE to raise prices. Alternatively, it may save the acquired firm from extinction, thereby protecting the competitive structure of the industry. In almost every new or expanded FDI, there is a possibility of it having both positive and negative consequences for the market structure and economic welfare. Even the most obvious O advantages of MNEs (e.g. the provision of superior intangible assets, new markets and more dynamic entrepreneurship, and the benefits which arise from operating cross-border value-added activities) may have an ambivalent outcome. On the one hand, they may promote growth and competition in the industries or strategic groups in which they operate.[1] On the other, they may squeeze out their competitors and give the investing firms a monopolistic stranglehold on the industry of which they are part.

Neither does economic theory offer any clear cut prediction as to whether international production will lead to a more or less concentrated market structure, to more or less product diversification, or to more or less vertical integration than otherwise would have been the case. On the first question, as we shall argue later in this chapter, much depends on the mode of entry by the MNE and on its size and status in relation to its competitors. Moreover, the effects of MNE activity on the market structure of a particular home or host country may be different from that on the global economy. The only general point which may be made is that, where the geographical distribution of value-added activities offers further opportunities to the investing firm to exploit the economies of scope and of size, then from a global perspective FDI may foster a greater concentration of market power than otherwise would be the case. Similarly, it may offer new opportunities for product diversification, vertical integration and arbitraging, while the experience gained by internalizing cross-border markets may give MNEs a cutting edge over national firms in overcoming domestic market failure.

In short, the OLI configurations with which MNEs are faced and their strategic responses to these configurations are likely to be different from those facing indigenous or uninational firms. It is the nature of this difference and its impact on domestic and international market structure that the following sections of this chapter seek to analyse.

15.3   MNEs AND ALLOCATIVE EFFICIENCY

15.3.1   Inter-sectoral efficiency

Data set out in Chapters 2 and 6 has shown that the sectoral distribution of value-added activity by MNEs, both in their home countries and in those in which their affiliates operate, is different from that of the other firms in these countries. However, this is no more surprising than the fact that the structure of a country's imports and exports of goods and services is likely to be different from those domestically produced and consumed. For after all, the MNE is one of the main conduits for trade in intermediate products in which the exporting country has a comparative advantage, to which it adds value by utilizing resources and capabilities in which the importing country has a comparative advantage. In his macro-economic theory of foreign direct investment, Kojima (1978, 1990) explicitly recognizes the beneficial contribution that MNE activity can, and does, make to the restructuring of economic activity in both home and host countries.[2]

It is true that, among advanced industrialized countries at least, that there is some similarity in the structure of both domestic and international economic activity. *Inter alia*, this is shown by the particularly rapid growth in intra-industry trade in recent years. Similarly, there is some suggestion that the pattern of FDI and of cooperative ventures by MNEs in these same countries are beginning to converge – and with it the nature of the impact of MNE activity.

It might also be reasonable to hypothesize that the greater the structural differences between countries exporting and importing capital, the more pronounced the impact of FDI by the former on the latter is likely to be. In part, at least, this may explain why developing countries are generally more mindful of this particular consequence of MNE activity than are most developed countries.

We would make one other observation. Most analyses of the impact of MNEs on industrial structure tend to use sales rather than value-added data, and look at the composition of the output of final rather than intermediate goods. But no less important to the efficiency of an economy may be the contribution of FDI to intra-sectoral resource allocation. For example, take the case of a group of foreign MNEs which have set up subsidiaries in Pakistan to produce pharmaceutical products. Using sales data, their impact on market structure may appear to be a major one. However, if the purpose of the affiliates – unlike that of their Pakistani competitors – is simply to undertake dosage and bottling operations from imported pharmaceutical chemicals, it may be quite minor. Contrast this situation with one in which these same pharmaceutical companies transfer part of their R&D facilities and pharmaceutical chemical production to Pakistan. The total sales of the subsidiaries in Pakistan may not change, but their contribution to the value added of the drug industry could be a quite significant one.

It is quite clear that the OLI configuration influencing the type of production likely to be undertaken by affiliates of MNEs is different from that of indigenous firms – even if the latter also engage in FDI. Take innovatory capacity, for example. Chapters 2 and 11 have shown that the great majority of MNEs still undertake most of their R&D in their home countries. ICI, for example, undertakes 65% of its R&D in the UK, Dupont does

85% of its R&D in the US, Hoescht carries out 80% of its R&D in West Germany and Nissan performs 90% of its R&D in Japan. We also explained why this kind of value-added activity tends to be among the last to be transferred by MNEs from home to host countries. Within the Triad, increasingly the larger, high technology MNEs are seeking to establish or acquire some kind of innovatory presence in each other's territories. Generally speaking, however, because of local supply capabilities and the costs of coordinating and controlling the quality of foreign-based R&D, firms incline towards the centralization of innovatory capacity (Kay, 1988). This immediately suggests, then, that the impact of FDI on the structure of activities along a value-added chain is likely to be different from that on activities between value-added chains – a point which both analysts and policy makers would do well to bear in mind.

There has been a good deal of empirical research on the impact of MNE activity on *inter*-sectoral industrial structure. Early studies by Dunning (1958) for the UK, Safarian (1966) for Canada and Brash (1966) for Australia all showed that the sectoral composition of inbound direct investment in manufacturing industry was markedly different from that of indigenous firms. Dunning expressed the difference in terms of a coefficient of deviation, which measured the average difference between the percentage share of employment in US affiliates in a particular industry and that of their employment in all industry, and of an equivalent percentage for all UK firms. He calculated that this coefficient was 0.9% in 1953. (A zero figure would indicate an identical industrial distribution between the two groups of firms.) In particular, Dunning, Safarian and Brash each found that US affiliates were especially concentrated in sectors supplying three kinds of products:

(1) high capital and technology-intensive producer goods (e.g. earth moving equipment, industrial instruments and pharmaceuticals);

(2) mass production consumer or producer goods (e.g. motor vehicles);

(3) differentiated consumer goods with a high income elasticity of demand (e.g. processed foods, detergents and cosmetics).

At the same time, FDI was generally under-represented in some of the traditional sectors, such as metal manufacturing, textiles and clothing.

The first studies of the industrial structure of outward direct investment were undertaken in the US. Based upon some data collected in 1972, the US Tariff Commission (1973) showed that there was a considerable difference in the distribution of the foreign sales of US MNEs – and, indeed, the domestic sales of such firms – compared with those of their uninational competitors. Several years later, a major study of American investment overseas (Bergsten *et al.*, 1978) concluded that such activities improved the competitiveness of the investing firms, both by enabling them to intensify or upgrade their innovating activities (as R&D could be spread over a larger sales volume) and by the gains of multinationalization *per se* (e.g. the spreading of risks and overhead costs and economies of product or process specialization).

Subsequent, more sophisticated studies (see Chapter 6) have all come to the same conclusions, although they show that the degree of deviation in the inter-sectoral distribution of activity between MNEs and other firms varies according to the kind of investment undertaken between host and home countries and over time. In general, both trade and industrial organization theories suggest that the impact of MNE activity on the composition of output of host countries should be positively correlated to the differences between their industrial structure and those of the investing countries, although other factors (e.g. government policy towards inward investment) may also affect that composition. We would also expect that if, and when, economies converge in their industrial structure, the divergence between the composition of output of foreign- and domestically-owned firms should diminish.

These propositions are generally upheld by most empirical evidence. We refer particularly to a detailed study edited by the present author in 1985. The study was unique in that it presented a series of 12 country case studies. It used a common analytical framework to compare and contrast the industrial composition of outward and inward direct investment with that of domestic investment by uninational firms and to examine how far, and in what ways, any of the revealed differences affected the competitiveness of the capital exporting and importing countries. The basic propositions examined in the monograph may be stated as follows. Most inward direct investment will tend to be directed to sectors in which the O-specific advantages of the investing firms are based upon resources and capabilities in which the investing country has a comparative advantage, but need to be used with resources and capabilities in which the recipient country is comparatively well endowed. In the case of strategic asset seeking investment, those which are perceived necessary to sustain or enhance the O advantages of the investing firms and countries. Such MNE activity may, then, normally be expected to reallocate resources in the recipient country towards sectors with a higher productivity. At the same time, outbound direct investment will either be directed to those activities which require resources and capabilities in which the home country is comparatively disadvantaged, or, in the case of asset-acquiring investments, to those which will maintain or upgrade the O advantages of the investing firms and countries. In this way, resources are reallocated from sectors with low productivity to sectors with high productivity.

Using data mainly derived from national Censuses of Production,[3] these studies found that, in the absence of artificial barriers to trade or investment and other structurally distorting features in the domestic economy, MNEs have had a generally beneficial effect on resource allocation – at least in a static sense. However, in several of the 12 case studies (i.e. in Sweden, India, Canada, Korea and France), the authors concluded that the beneficial effects might have been even greater had domestic government policies been more market oriented. Given such policies, however, it was found that the impact of inward and outward investment in Canada and Germany had been mildly positive (in the sense that it had generally advanced inter-sectoral efficiency), and decisively so in Belgium, the UK, the US and Japan. In India, according to Lall (1985), the government's restrictionist policies towards inward investment had inhibited efficient restructuring.

The studies also revealed that the effects of outward investment on domestic economic structure have been primarily indirect, through the impact of MNE activity on *trade*. In the case of Korea and Japan, recent government policy has steered inward investment by MNEs into those sectors in which they were perceived to have a competitive advantage over domestic firms. Koo (1985) contends that this policy has worked well in Korea in the case of export-oriented investment, but not in the case of import-substituting investment. In Singapore, a variety of investment incentives have steered foreign-owned companies to invest in higher than average value-added activities as well as to upgrade the quality of indigenous human capital.

Another measure frequently used to evaluate the impact of MNEs on allocative efficiency is the extent to which they are concentrated in sectors that have a higher than average Revealed Comparative Advantage (RCA) or have helped to reallocate resources to sectors in which a country's RCA is growing.[4] The higher the RCA, the more a sector is assumed to be comparatively *advantaged* in international markets. With the exception of France and Canada, in all the countries studied in the Dunning volume,[5] MNEs, relative to indigenous firms, were more prone to concentrate their activities in sectors in which the RCA ratio was greater than 1, or – particularly in the case of Portugal – was increasing over time. However, there was some divergence of opinion about the interaction between outward foreign investment and a sector's RCA. The Japanese and UK data seems to support the view that such investment will favour sectors in which the home country's RCA is less than 1, or is declining, while that of the US, Sweden, Germany, France and Canada strongly suggests that exports and outbound MNE activity are likely to be complementary and in the same sector.

These apparently conflicting views may be explained by several factors. The first is that, just as much trade between countries is within similar sectors (i.e. intra-industry rather than inter-industry), so a good deal of cross-border production is also intra-industry (see Chapter 2). Such investment is likely to be based less on the O advantages of MNEs which are specific to their country of origin, and more on those which arise from their multinationality *per se*. Second, an increasing proportion of investment is trade creating in the sense that it has promoted the international division of labour within the control of the MNE. In such cases, intra-firm trade is part and parcel of FDI. And third, as Chapter 14 has shown, even much import-substituting trade may lead to a continued, and often increased, export of intermediate products, as well as of final products not manufactured by the foreign affiliates.

The growth of intra-firm, intra-industry FDI, especially between countries in the OECD area – a feature related to the growing convergence of Western European and Japanese industrial economies with that of the US – partly explains why, in recent years, there has been a less clear cut *inter-industry* impact of MNE activity on the economic structure of advanced industrial economies.

So far our analysis has confined itself to the primary and static effects of inter-sectoral structural change. This has demonstrated that MNEs tend to invest in high growth sectors and those in which the host country has a RCA or an increasing RCA. For the most part, this reflects the outcome of market forces, but in some instances the oligopolistic behaviour of investing firms and government action have induced a higher level of MNE activity than may be optimum for either home or host countries. We have also argued that sales figures may overestimate the real contribution of MNEs to value added. Moreover, through a variety of business practices, foreign-owned firms may drive out local competitors. If the contribution of the value-added component of the former is less than that of the latter – particularly in the area of R&D – this could result in a diminished competitive ability of the sector. This is an example of the vicious circle of technological causation discussed in Chapter 11.

However, even if this did occur, it should not necessarily be assumed that MNEs are the sole or even the main cause. As has been pointed out by several commentators (e.g. Scott *et al.*, 1985; Lawrence, 1987; Dunning, 1991a, 1991b; Porter, 1990), governments may strongly influence the ability of their own firms to undertake high value-added activities by their educational, scientific and technological, competitive and industrial strategies. Cantwell (1989c) has demonstrated that there is a frequently strong connection between both the causes and effects of inward direct investment and the strength of local innovatory capacity.

MNEs can only be properly integrated into the economies of which they are part and make a positive and sustainable contribution to improving industrial structure, if the ESP configuration, within which they operate, is conducive to this objective. We have already referred to Porter's diamond of competitive advantage. In the present context, this

suggests that five conditions are necessary if FDI is to make its optimum contribution to industrial restructuring. First, there must be effective competition between indigenous producers. Second, the level, pattern and quality of domestic demand must be sufficient to motivate producers both to be efficient and continually to upgrade the quality of their products. Third, there must be adequate local capabilities and competences for absorbing and building on the O advantages provided by MNEs. Fourth, there need to be strong clusters of related industries (e.g. comprising suppliers and industrial customers) to provide the support facilities that are needed to effectively utilize the resources transferred by the MNEs. Fifth, surrounding and influencing these variables, the role of government must be predisposed to facilitating the efficient operation of market forces and restructuring domestic resources and capabilities to meet the needs of global consumers.

The work of Porter and other scholars demonstrates that the likely impact of FDI on the industrial restructuring will be both *country* and *industry* specific. An example of an industry in which multinational investment has been associated with a fall in competitiveness is the UK automobile industry – although, more recently, Japanese investment has helped halt this decline. An example of a more favourable association between inward investment and an improvement in domestic competitiveness is the UK pharmaceutical industry.[6] Here the technological advantages of foreign firms combined with a strong indigenous sector and a sympathetic environment to both R&D and the clinical testing of new drugs has provided an atmosphere conducive to a virtuous circle of innovation and productivity growth, and has led to a dynamic and welfare-enhancing restructuring of resources.

15.3.2   Intra-sectoral efficiency

No less important than the impact of FDI on the inter-sectoral distribution of value-added activity is its consequence for the intra-sectoral distribution of such activity. For in many sectors, particularly the technology-intensive ones, the productivity of activities at different points on the same value-added chain may vary as much as that between similar activities across the value-added chain. Measured in terms of opportunity cost of inputs, for example, it is likely to be high in innovatory activities and manufacturing or service activities involving substantial amounts of human and physical capital, and low where the activity involves substantial amounts of unskilled labour and standard raw materials. In principle, there is no reason why the *activities* of firms should not be classified by their contribution to GNP or international competitiveness, in the same way as are the products they produce. In practice, however, data is not classified in this way, but the point at issue is that, where it is possible spatially to separate stages of the value-added chain, there is an optimum intra-sectoral structure of activity which foreign-owned firms may and do influence.

What, then, is the evidence that MNEs behave any differently than domestic-owned firms in the extent and pattern of their vertical integration? Are they more or less prone to concentrate their activities in the higher value-added stages of the production sequence?

Chapter 14 has suggested that compared with both their parent companies and their indigenous competitors, the affiliates of MNEs will produce a truncated range of goods and services, especially in the first years of their establishment. In *market-seeking* ventures, it is common for greenfield investors to start by engaging in relatively low value-added activities (e.g. assembling kits of video recorder parts imported from the parent company or other affiliates) and then to diversify into the higher value upstream manufacturing processes and innovatory activities (e.g. research, development and design work). In *resource-based* ventures, the extraction of minerals or the growing of raw materials and foodstuffs is often the initial activity, while the secondary processing of these outputs – which is usually a higher value activity – tends to follow later (if at all). For *export processing manufacturing* activities, the value-added component will again vary between countries and in a country over time, according to the nature of the products produced and the kinds of inputs, particularly human inputs, they require.

Indigenous firms may follow a similar pattern of development, but they are more likely to engage in higher value-added activities from the start. Indeed, many firms begin life as innovators. Frequently, production by them precedes that by foreign-owned firms. For example, US-owned companies were producing colour television sets in the US long before Japanese MNEs began to set up affiliates in that country. Moreover, where foreign markets were previously supplied by exports, foreign investors can, and often do, take their time in relocating their entire range of products – if they do at all! The impatience sometimes shown by host governments towards MNE affiliates who appear reluctant to reduce the import content of their sales has sometimes led to local content requirements being imposed on them. The justification for these requirements is currently a subject of intense debate in the European Community with respect to the participation of Japanese affiliates in the motor vehicle industry. Many developing countries have long since felt that foreign MNEs were treating their affiliates as hewers of wood and drawers of water, rather than helping them to develop their full value-added potential.

The conflict of interest between the activities which MNEs wish to undertake in particular countries and those which governments would like them to undertake has long been a cause for concern. To some extent, this conflict is inevitable. When one examines the list of sectors which developing countries identify as those in which the participation of foreign firms is especially welcome, it is usually the same sectors and, within those sectors, the same, *viz* the higher value, parts of the value-added chain.

From an economic perspective, such activities can only be justified up to a point at which the perceived marginal social benefits of the investment are equal to the marginal social costs. The profit maximizing firm is only interested in maximizing the private net benefits of its foreign activities. We have seen earlier why these two goals may not be compatible and why, in particular, governments may wish to influence the behaviour of MNEs or their affiliates for social, political or environmental reasons. However, the best the student of international business can do is to identify and evaluate the extent to which such a divergence of interest *does* occur and the reasons for it. Then, given the objectives of governments and the resources at their disposal, the student can suggest appropriate policies to minimize or reconcile these divergences.

Let us return, however, to the main theme of

this section, *viz* the extent to which MNEs or their foreign affiliates affect intra-sectoral resource allocation, and if so, in what way? First, there is some evidence to suggest that firms that operate subsidiaries abroad tend to engage in proportionately more high value activities in their home countries, and/or employ a higher proportion of skilled workers than their uninational counterparts. For example, the ratio between domestic R&D expenditure and domestic sales of US MNEs in 1989 was consistently higher than that of all firms producing in the US. In the leading European investing nations and in Japan, the share of the domestic output of capital, technology and information intensive goods and services accounted for by their own MNEs is considerably higher than their share of all goods and services. But beyond this, it is difficult to generalize, as the strategies of firms towards intra- and inter-sectoral diversification appear to vary with factors that have nothing to do with their multinationalization *per se*. For example, reference to UK data reveals that the propensity of firms to engage in vertical integration is positively related to their size. Other studies, for example, Jenkins (1979, 1984) and Pearce (1990a), suggest that firm-specific variables, such as age and experience, and country-specific variables, such as business customs, legal systems and market structures, are more important than the extent to which a firm is geographically diversified. In a detailed study of the development of the pharmaceutical industry in Latin America, Jenkins (1984) showed that the value added to sales ratio of foreign affiliates varied according to their age and the size of the local market.

What, however, does seem clear is that when the foreign activities of MNEs are taken into account, at least one group of these firms is more likely to be vertically integrated than its uninational competitors. This should not be surprising as the main rationale for FDI in upstream resource-based activities and downstream manufacturing or marketing activities is to circumvent, or capitalize on, the failure of intermediate product markets. The oil industry is a classic example. In an attempt both to create barriers to the entry of new competitors and to reduce the strength of existing rivals, the major oil companies first tried to gain control of markets and then supplies of crude oil. This led to the almost complete vertical integration of the oil industry. By 1992, just seven oil MNEs (the so-called seven sisters) controlled 90% of crude oil production in the Middle East and about the same proportion of refining capacity in the main consuming countries.

In many other industries, too, by engaging in multiple cross-border intra value-added chain activities, MNEs have become more integrated than their uninational counterparts. This has had considerable ramifications for their economic power and market structure in general. Section 15.7 will discuss this in more detail.

More research has been done on the vertical integration of multinational affiliates as compared with their local competitors. However, it points to no definitive conclusion. In the UK, Dunning (1985) found that although foreign affiliates tended to concentrate their activities in industrial sectors with higher than average value-added ratios,[7] there was no evidence that, on balance, such affiliates were more or less integrated than their indigenous counterparts. In Australia, in the early 1970s the value-added ratio of foreign-controlled firms was 35.9% of sales compared with 39.9% for Australian-controlled firms (Dunning and Cantwell, 1987). In Korea, Koo (1985) calculated that although the value-added ratios were generally higher in foreign affiliates than in domestic firms, the differences were significant in only 13 out of 29 cases. In a statistical multi-variate analysis, Kumar (1990) demonstrated that the degree of vertical integration of foreign affiliates in India was significantly greater than that of their local counterparts. While these and other studies suggest that well established market-seeking foreign affiliates may be more vertically integrated than their local counterparts, there is also strong evidence that export-oriented subsidiaries are likely to be less integrated than their indigenous competitors. Cohen (1975), for example, demonstrated this for Taiwan, South Korea and Singapore. Several studies of the role of MNE affiliates in the export processing zones in Malaysia, Kenya and Sri Lanka confirm his findings.[8]

An alternative measure of differences in intra-sectoral activities by foreign and domestic firms is the skilled labour content of the value added generated. In Belgium, Haex *et al.* (1979) found, in a matched pair analysis, clear evidence that foreign affiliates employed relatively more white collar workers than did domestic firms. In Portugal, Simoes (1985) discovered that the skill intensity of foreign affiliates exceeded that of indigenous firms in 16 of 22 sectors. In Singapore, both Hughes and Seng (1969) and Lecraw (1985a), for different time periods, showed that foreign-owned firms employed significantly higher ratios of skilled to unskilled workers than did Singaporean firms. Research by Balasubramanyam (1984) in the case of Indonesia, Kumar (1990) in the case of India, and Willmore (1976, 1986) in the cases of Costa Rica and Brazil, has established that foreign-owned firms tend to engage in more stages of manufacturing and employ qualitatively superior personnel than do their local counterparts.

By contrast, Helleiner (1975b) has argued that MNEs – particularly in export-processing sectors – often do little or nothing to upgrade the quality of the local labour force because they are prone to use more capital-intensive production techniques than local firms. A study conducted by ILO (1984) unearthed evidence that foreign-owned firms in Nigeria used more automated processes specifically to economize on skilled labour. Presumably it was less costly for them to do this than train Nigerian workers in the skills needed for the more labour-intensive production processes. In the Brazilian electrical industry, Newfarmer and Marsh (1981b) found that the higher capital intensity of foreign affiliates was associated with a noticeable reduction in the proportion of unskilled operatives employed, but with a noticeable increase in the maintenance and production personnel employed.

We conclude that the evidence, scant and fragmentary as it is, would seem to support the proposition that the transfer of O advantages by MNEs has generally raised inter-sectoral efficiency in both home and host countries. But there is no *a priori* presumption that this should be so. In cases where MNEs respond to inappropriate government policies or fail to adjust efficiently to market signals, then, as Kojima has argued, they may worsen the economic structures of home and host countries rather than improve them. However, it is important to judge the structural impact of international investment from a dynamic viewpoint and in terms of the particular goals and aspirations of the countries concerned.

The evidence on the impact of MNEs on intra-sectoral resource allocation is even more inconclusive. There seems little doubt that the global operations of MNEs are more vertically integrated than are the domestic operations of non-multinationals – especially in resource-based sectors; also, in relation to domestic sales, they are more capital and knowledge intensive than uninational firms. In host countries, while there is evidence that the presence of foreign affiliates has raised both the value-added component of sales of goods produced and the skill content of that value added, they are generally less vertically integrated than their indigenous competitors. Indeed, far from raising the skill level of host countries, in some developing countries, at least, they may reduce it. Which of these two scenarios is the more likely largely depends on the type of investment, the age of that investment and the economic environment and market structure in which it is made. Finally, it should be emphasized that a beneficial restructuring of economic activity does not mean that upgrading will occur in all sectors. It is quite possible – indeed probable – that while multinational activity will raise the skill content of the labour force in some sectors, some deskilling will occur in others. It is also important to distinguish between the short- and long-term structural adjustment effects of FDI, and especially its consequences for the entrepreneurial ethos, market structure and innovatory capacity of both home and host countries.

15.4   TECHNICAL EFFICIENCY

We now turn to examine the impact of multinational activity on the efficiency of any particular value-added activity. We examine this question, first, from the viewpoint of host countries.

15.4.1   Host countries

The fact that foreign-owned firms do possess unique O income-generating assets relative to indigenous firms might suggest that they should be both more productive and profitable. This, however, is a *non sequitur*. First, as several authors from Hymer (1960) onwards have pointed out, as well as possessing certain competitive advantages, foreign firms may be faced with certain competitive disadvantages *vis à vis* local firms in penetrating the latters' markets. This is particularly likely to be the case when the host country houses its own multinational enterprises. Second, and allied to the first point, it is often not necessary for an MNE to earn higher average rates of return on its capital than its competitors (either in its home or host country). Discounting for risk, all that is required is that, at the margin, it should be earning profits at least equal to its opportunity costs. Third, the fact that MNEs may be more efficient as suppliers of intermediate products does not necessarily mean that they are better at adding value to these products than are domestic firms. There are failures among MNEs just as there are among international firms.[9]

Fourth, like other firms, a firm may use its O advantages to exploit a monopolistic position rather than to improve the efficiency of resource allocation. Indeed, some firms may seek to acquire O advantages to strengthen their market power (Hymer, 1960; Newfarmer, 1979, 1985). In this event, not only might any increase in profitability or productivity take the form of monopoly rent, but any such benefits may accrue entirely to the investing company and will not be reflected in the performance of the affiliates. Much, of course, depends on the accounting and intra-firm pricing practices of the MNE, to which we will turn later in this section and in Chapter 18. Lastly, as Chapters 3 and 4 have shown, much MNE (and particularly incremental MNE) activity is motivated by the desire to acquire resources and capabilities in order to advance their global strategic goals. Here, as with some ancillary (e.g. trade-related) investments, the value of a foreign capital stake is judged by its effects on the economic well-being of the MNE *in toto*, rather than on that of the productivity or profitability of the local affiliate.[10]

But what of the evidence about the productivity and profitability of multinational affiliates compared with their indigenous competition?

This subject has fascinated researchers for more than thirty years. Most studies have been concerned with foreign manufacturing investments, primarily those of a market-seeking variety. Most have attempted either to make matched or paired comparisons between foreign-owned and indigenous firms, or to incorporate the foreign ownership variable into a multi-variate regression equation explaining productivity or profitability differences. A third approach has been to use discriminant analysis

to isolate the most distinctive characteristics about foreign affiliates *vis à vis* indigenous firms.

Each kind of analysis has produced similar results. The earlier studies of US subsidiaries in the UK, Canada and Australia,[11] based on intra-industry or matched paired comparisons, all concluded that, using either productivity or profitability indices,[12] US firms outperformed their indigenous competitors by a substantial margin. Haex *et al.* (1979) found that productivity and profitability were among the most significant variables which discriminated between domestic- and foreign-owned firms in Belgium; this result was confirmed by a matched sample survey. However, later work by Dunning (1976, 1985) observed that the productivity gap between US and other foreign firms and their UK counterparts had narrowed over the years – a result which the author suggested reflected some loss in the O-specific advantages of the former and some improvement in those of the latter group of firms. More recently this result has been confirmed by Davies and Lyons (1991) who found that although, in 1987, foreign-owned firms in UK manufacturing recorded a 48.6% productivity advantage over UK-owned enterprises, less than one-half of this advantage could be traced to their nationality of ownership – the balance reflecting the fact that they tended to be concentrated in more highly productive sectors.[13] By contrast, in 1971 all of the 30% productivity difference was attributed to the ownership effect. A more detailed study by Solomon and Ingham (1977) of the performance of foreign firms in the UK mechanical engineering industry concluded that foreign firms did no better than domestic firms.

The Belgian research also showed that there were country-specific differences in the performance of foreign-owned firms. While US-owned firms recorded consistently higher rates of return on capital and productivity, other (especially EC-based) firms did not.[14] In Canada, too, Shapiro (1983) found that while US-controlled firms earned a premium of 3.5% on their profits/net assets ratio in the late 1970s, other foreign-owned firms performed no better than their indigenous competitors. Perhaps most noteworthy of all, foreign affiliates in the US do not appear to record a higher value added per employee than indigenous firms, except in the mining and wholesale trade sectors (Graham and Krugman, 1989). Indeed, in 1986, although the average productivity of the former group of firms was marginally (4.0%) higher than the latter, the authors found that this was entirely because they were concentrated in the more highly productive sectors. Such data strongly suggests that the relative performance of MNE affiliates is likely to be both home- and host-country specific, and may well be a function of the overall and sectoral competitiveness of the investing and recipient nations.

What then of the differences in performance between foreign and domestic firms in the less advanced developed and industrializing developing countries? In his study of foreign affiliates in Portugal, Simoes (1985) found that in 17 out of 21 sectors their net output per head in 1977 was higher than that of Portuguese firms. The differences were most marked in the high to medium technology-intensive and advertising-intensive sectors where foreign affiliates were set up mainly to supply the local market. In Singapore, in 1975, foreign affiliates recorded a higher value added per worker than domestic firms in 17 of 28 industries (Lecraw, 1985a). In Brazil, using multiple regression analysis, Willmore (1986) demonstrated that foreign firms recorded an average of 20% higher value added per employee, even allowing for scale and industry differences; these differences were significant at the 1% level. Fairchild and Sosin (1986) obtained similar results for other Latin American countries, as did Kumar (1990) for India. By contrast, Koo (1985) found that in Korea there was no significant difference in the value added per capita of foreign and domestic firms. In Morocco, although MNE subsidiaries recorded a higher labour productivity than domestic firms in 13 out of 18 industries in 1985–89, when the data was controlled for firm size, not only were the subsidiaries more productive in only three sectors, but also their average productivity was 30% *below* that of their Moroccan counterparts (Haddan and Harrison, 1993).[15]

Labour productivity, of course, is not always a reliable indicator of total factor productivity, simply because it is possible that the former may be increased by substituting capital for labour to produce the same output. And, as Chapter 11 has shown, there is ample evidence to suggest that capital/labour ratios of foreign-owned firms do tend to be higher than those of their domestically-owned counterparts.[16] Nevertheless, for the most part, such

measures of total productivity (based on production function and/or operating data) that have been made, for example, in the UK, Singapore and India, do confirm the data on labour productivity. Dunning (1985), for example, reported that in 30 of 41 manufacturing sectors in the UK in 1979, foreign affiliates recorded a higher total factor productivity. Haddan and Harrison (1993) also found that, even normalizing for size differences, foreign firms in Morocco achieved the same or higher levels of multi-factor productivity in 13 of 18 manufacturing sectors.

Turning now to profitability data, while this generally shows a superior performance for multinational affiliates in developed countries, that of developing countries appears to yield mixed results. For example, the study of Newfarmer and Marsh (1981a) into Brazilian industry for 1971–77 concluded that Brazilian firms were more profitable than MNE affiliates, and that foreign-led industries were more profitable than domestic-led industries. A later study by Fairchild and Sosin (1986) found that in other Latin American countries foreign-owned firms recorded higher levels of labour productivity but not of profitability. Similar conclusions were reached by Lall (1976) in his study of the performance of foreign manufacturing affiliates in India and Columbia, by Gershenberg (1976) in his analysis of such firms in Uganda, and by Fairchild (1977) in his examination of foreign affiliates in Mexico. However, more recent studies by Kumar (1990) and Ros (1987), quoted in Nunez (1990), on the comparative profitability of foreign-owned and domestic firms in India and Mexico at the beginning of the 1980s show that the former outperform the latter by a significant margin.

The question however remains 'What does such data actually mean?' To what extent can one conclude that higher productivity or profitability means superior technical efficiency? The literature distinguishes a number of reasons for differences in inter-firm performances.[17] These include:

(1) manipulation of transfer prices of intra-firm transactions (including interest rates on loans and payments for managerial services and technology) which might be used by MNEs either to lower or to raise profits in one or other of its subsidiaries;

(2) manipulation of the asset base of subsidiaries by MNEs which may increase or lower the rate of return on capital;

(3) differences in accounting conventions (e.g. depreciation provisions, valuation of assets, currency translation adjustments, etc, between the two groups of firms);

(4) deliberate use of the financial leverage of the MNE *qua* MNE to alter the costs, revenue or profits of subsidiaries as a means of improving its long-term competitive power;

(5) profits recorded by a foreign subsidiary may be an inadequate indicator of their value to the investing firm (i.e. there may be benefits external to the subsidiary but internal to the MNE);

(6) host government tax and other policies may discriminate against or in favour of foreign affiliates;

(7) there may be other differences between local and foreign-owned firms which are not captured in any multiple regression or matching analysis that might explain differences in performance.

This last reason needs further elucidation. Fairchild (1977), Kumar (1990) and Lecraw (1983) have all hypothesized that part of the differences in profitability may be explained by the fact that foreign-owned and local firms – even within particular industries – do not always compete with each other as they belong to different strategic groups.[18] For example, MNEs may be technologically more aggressive, serve dissimilar market segments, engage in different kinds of competitive strategies and business practices, and be faced with different entry or mobility barriers (Kumar, 1990, p. 80). Sometimes these differences may reflect the different ownership of firms – sometimes not. Lecraw (1983), in his analysis of the performance of MNE activity in six light manufacturing industries in five Asian countries in the late 1970s, found that their profitability varied inversely with the degree of competition with which they or their parent companies were faced. Other studies (McGee and Thomas, 1986) have argued that intra-industry variables may account for up to one-half of the differences in profitability or price–cost margins.

Kumar (1990) found that foreign and domestic firms in India did belong to different strategic groups *within* an industry, and that the former are protected by entry barriers more than their local counterparts.

This was particularly the case in knowledge-intensive sectors (Kumar, pp. 94–5). His statistical analysis confirmed that it was these, rather than intra-group differences in efficiency, that accounted for the major part of the higher profit margins of foreign-owned firms.

Apart from the research just mentioned, economists and business analysts have paid only scant attention to identifying the importance of the factors identified on pages 425–6, though it is known that some of them – notably the first, fourth and fifth – can be extremely important.[19] (It will be observed these factors do not always work in the same direction!) One exception is a study by Brandt and Giddy (1989) which attempted to see how far differences in the profitability of foreign and indigenous firms in Brazil could be explained by structural distortions of one kind or another. Using data for 1974, the authors found little difference in the average rates of return on total assets earned by the two groups of firms – 11.8% in the case of Brazilian firms and 10.7% in the case of foreign-owned firms. (Again, it is worth noting that the range of ratios was greater among foreign subsidiaries than between them and their Brazilian competitors.)[20] However, correcting for the kinds of factors identified in (1) to (3) above, the authors estimated that, relative to the profitability of domestic firms, the profitability of the foreign subsidiaries was *understated* by 2%; moreover, they found that most of this understatement was a result of the underpricing of exports and overpricing of imports by the latter firms.

15.4.2   Home countries

It is not unreasonable to hypothesize that MNEs are likely to be more profitable than uninational firms because of the distinct O advantages they possess. On the other hand, there is no guarantee that geographical diversification of value-added activity is the most profitable strategy of growth. Indeed, some commentators have argued that FDI is often a second-best growth strategy and that the resources spent on it would be better allocated to innovatory activities or improving domestic productivity. However, foreign- and domestically-oriented strategies are probably less substitutable than they were 20 years ago. Today, it is often imperative for a firm to produce outside its national boundaries to remain competitive in global markets – even though, as a result, it only manages to earn an average or below average rate of return.

The balance of research suggests that, as a strategic group, MNEs are likely to be only marginally more profitable than their domestically-oriented competitors. Studies by Vernon (1971b) based on the *Fortune* 500 largest industrial corporations in 1964, by Haex *et al.* (1979) of 170 Belgian firms in 1976, by Kumar (1984) based on 672 UK-quoted companies between 1972 and 1976, by Yoshihara (1985) based on 118 of the largest Japanese companies, and by Grant (1987) based on 304 large UK manufacturing companies between 1968 and 1984, all found that MNEs earned modestly higher rates of return on sales and for assets than did non-MNEs, but the differences were rarely statistically significant. By contrast, in a major study of 1198 US manufacturing firms in 1967, Horst (1971) established that once size was taken into account MNEs did no better than uninational firms. Lall and Siddharthan (1982) went further and established (in the case of 74 of the largest US MNEs in the period 1976–79) that the overseas ratio had a *negative* influence on the *growth* of firms, excluding the influence of size, advertising and R&D intensity, scale economies and profitability. Finally, in a controlled study of 58 manufacturing MNEs and 43 domestic corporations, Michel and Shaked (1986) discovered that over the period 1973–82, the latter group of firms recorded a consistently higher risk-adjusted performance.[21,22]

Other studies have attempted to establish whether there is any relationship between the *degree* of multinationality of firms and their overall performance. In their survey of 523 of the world's largest industrial companies, Dunning and Pearce (1981) found that while firms with a modest degree of foreign production (i.e. between 2.5% and 22.5% of their global production) recorded higher rates of return on sales in 1977 than those with little or no foreign production, the most multinational of all companies did less well. In an econometric analysis, Buckley *et al.* (1984) established that profitability (net income/assets) was positively and significantly related to the degree of multinationality of the world's largest industrial enterprises in 1972, but not so in 1977 (except for non-US firms). The authors

also demonstrated that between 1972 and 1977 nationality of ownership had a strong influence on the rate of growth of (global) sales, but that, after the influence of the other explanatory variables (e.g. size, industry) had been removed, the degree of multinationality – though correctly signed – was only statistically significant (at a 5% level) for the total sample of firms. In a later study of 181 US and European MNEs, Geringer *et al.* (1989) found that their average annual rate of return on sales between 1981 and 1985 monotonically rose as the proportion of their foreign subsidiaries to total sales increased between 1% and 60–80%, at which point the relationship spiked and then monotonically decreased.[23] Finally, in a seminal study on the performance of US firms abroad in the period 1965–71, and using data provided by the Internal Revenue Service (IRS), Bergsten *et al.* (1978) found not only that US MNEs were more profitable than domestic firms in the same industry, but also that part of the reason for this higher profitability could be attributed to their FDI. However, the latter conclusion was later disputed by Gaspari (1983), who failed to find any significant impact of outbound MNE activity on domestic profitability.

15.5   SCALE AND SCOPE EFFICIENCY

In so far as, on average, MNEs and their affiliates tend to be larger than their uninational counterparts and are more geographically or industrially diversified, it might be hypothesized that they should be better able to take advantage of any economies of size and scope. However, there have been few attempts to identify or evaluate those benefits which are specifically a function of their multinationality. We do know that there is some propensity for MNEs to concentrate in sectors most subject to the economies of plant or firm size (Horst, 1972a; Dunning, 1976; Pugel, 1981; Kumar, 1990); while Kogut (1985b) and others have detailed the kind of O-specific advantages which MNEs might enjoy arising from the geographical economies of scope. Caves (1981) has also demonstrated that such economies are a significant discriminating feature between MNEs and uninational firms.

In recent years, as Chapter 17 will show, MNEs have helped refashion the international division of labour both between developed and developing countries and within regionally-integrated developed countries – notably the EC. To the extent that such specialization has taken place in industries in which economies of scale or scope are the most prevalent, this has often given MNEs a notable competitive edge over their uninational counterparts. MNEs, particularly established MNEs, have been able to adjust to some of the changes resulting from regional integration more speedily and effectively than indigenous firms in the region.

15.6   MNEs AND STRUCTURAL ADJUSTMENT

Finally, to what extent do MNEs adjust to exogenous changes in the global economic and political environment more speedily or effectively than their uninational competitors? On balance, evidence of the past 20 years suggests that they do. There are several reasons for this. First, as we have seen, they are likely to be concentrated in the more dynamic sectors. Second, they tend to be in the most rapidly growing economies. Third, their productivity and profitability compare favourably with their uninational competitors. Fourth, because of their industrial and geographical spread, they have more flexibility than uninational or non-diversified firms in the sourcing of their inputs, in the relocation of their investments, and in the markets they choose to serve.

The economic recession of the 1970s revealed that MNEs were generally more successful at protecting themselves against the adverse effects of environmental volatility and market failure. They did so both by adapting their products and processes to customer requirements, price changes and technical developments, and by reducing their exposure to both technological obsolescence and reductions and fluctuations in demand. They also attempted to counteract exchange risk by appropriate locational or intra-firm pricing policies. According to an OECD (1978) study, the European subsidiaries of MNEs did not generally engage in *more* restructuring than indigenous firms in the 1970s – although there were noticeable exceptions – but they did respond to exogenous events *more speedily*. Some more recent research on the response of MNE affiliates to

economic recession in Columbia in 1980 suggests that in the following four years they displayed a speedier and more pronounced recovery pattern than their indigenous competitors (Atyas and Dutz, 1993). The authors ascribe this fact to the lower agency costs and less stringent liquidity constraints incurred by the foreign affiliates.

More generally, MNEs have been among the first to anticipate or react to the major changes in the technological and economic environment in the 1980s. They have been foremost in concluding strategic alliances – particularly across national boundaries – and in exploiting the opportunities offered by the completion of the European internal market in 1992. MNEs – in particular, those of Japanese origin – have led in the introduction of lean and flexible manufacturing systems and new organizational structures, as well as in the adoption of the latest informatic equipment and devices. Possibly because of intensive global competition in the 1980s, they have been among the trailblazers in disinternalizing the less profitable parts of their businesses and focusing on their core competences. Also, they have been particularly active in globalizing their sourcing strategies. While it is possible to identify both small and large uninational firms which have followed a similar path, it has often been the capability of the MNE *qua* MNE to benefit from these changes, which has helped it reorganize its portfolio of assets and markets to meet the demands of a changing world economy.

15.7   MNEs AND MARKET STRUCTURE

We now turn to consider the impact of MNE activity on the market structures in the countries in which they operate. Market structure is a generic term which describes the extent and character of the rivalry which exists between firms engaging in broadly similar lines of value-added activity and which pursue broadly similar product and marketing strategies. In particular, we shall consider three elements of such a structure identified in the literature:

(1)   number and significance of firms in supplying a particular market,

(2)   degree of product or process differentiation,

(3)   extent to which markets are contestable.

15.7.1   MNEs and industrial concentration

The subject of the impact of FDI on the number and distribution of firms in a particular industrial sector or strategic group has fascinated economists and business analysts for the past 30 years.

In particular, two questions have intrigued researchers:

(1)   Do MNEs or their affiliates concentrate their production in sectors with different market structures than non-multinationals or indigenous firms?

(2)   In the sectors in which they do concentrate, what impact do they have on the market structure of that industry?

On the first question, the kind of O-specific advantages possessed by MNEs suggest that these are likely to be most prevalent in sectors characterized by a two-tier market structure. The first tier consists of a small group of large firms supplying similar, but differentiated, products to the leading domestic and international markets. The second tier consists of a large number of smaller producers supplying more specialized products for particular market segments and/or countries. Thus, in the motor vehicle industry, Ford, GM, Toyota and Nissan are in the first tier while Jaguar, Porsche, Mercedes and Ferrari are in the second. In the petroleum sector, there are several hundred oil producing and refining companies, but over 80% of the oil refining capacity is in the hands of seven MNEs. There are literally thousands of banks, accountancy firms and hotels, but in each case more than three-quarters of FDI and cross-border collaborative ventures is undertaken by the leading 25 companies (UNCTC, 1991a).

A market structure of perfect competition would contain no MNEs (and, for that matter, no multi-plant or multi-spatial national firms) simply because there would be no need to internalize intermediate product markets. Chapter 4 categorized market imperfections into two groups: first, those which were endemic to the particular market, *viz* risk and

uncertainty, scale economies and externalities; and second, those which arose as a result of the structurally distorting behaviour of the government or the participants in the market (e.g. barriers to access to intermediate or final product markets, product differentiation, predatory pricing). The greater these imperfections, the more the market structure is likely to veer towards oligopoly or monopoly.

Exhibit 15.1 classifies a selection of industrial sectors by degree of (world) industrial concentration and by the extent of multinationalization of firms. The data in the table is largely drawn from Table 2.21 and UNCTC (1988). It confirms the widespread opinion held among scholars that MNE activities are most pronounced in sectors where the market structure is best described as an amalgam of oligopolistic and monopolistic competition. In some sectors (e.g. oil, tobacco, aluminium, razor blades, rubber tyres and reinsurance) the output is largely in the hands of a few large firms. In others (e.g. cosmetics, pharmaceuticals, food processing, insurance and hotels) the concentration ratio[24] is not as high, but the sector is characterized by other market imperfections (e.g. extensive product differentiation and entry barriers). It is also worth noting that as a result of technological and organizational advances, rising standards of consumer demand and the entry of MNEs from Third World countries, today there is more FDI in the (so-called) traditional sectors such as iron and steel, textiles, clothing and footwear, than once there was.

Moreover, the propensity of firms to invest in industries with high concentration ratios seems to differ according to their countries of origin. In a study of four firm concentration ratios by industry in five Asian countries, Lecraw (1983) found that there was a significant positive correlation between US and European FDI and the degree of industrial concentration, but a negative correlation between industrial concentration and Japanese and developing country FDI. However, as Chapter 2 has demonstrated, the average concentration ratios of the sectors that account for the greater part of MNE activity are considerably higher than that for the rest of industry.[25]

At the same time, a high concentration ratio should not be equated with a lack of competition. Indeed, an oligopolistic market structure may *de*

Exhibit 15.1 Estimated share of production of foreign affiliates of domestic output and market structure: some illustrations.

Participation by MNE affiliates	Industrial concentration*		
	High (Concentration ratios of 67% or above)	Medium (Concentration ratios of 34–66%)	Low (Concentration ratios of 33% or under)
Dominant (over 50%)	Breakfast cereals Cinematic films Commercial vehicles Computers Detergents Motor vehicles Pet foods Petrol (gasolene) products Photocopying equipment Processed milk products Reinsurance services Sewing machines and parts Tractors	Colour TV sets Luxury hotels Investment banking Microwave ovens Office machines and parts Pharmaceutical products Rubber tyres Semiconductors Video recorders	Toilet preparations and perfumery
Substantial (30–50%)	Abrasives Canned soups Lifts and escalators Processed coffee products Razor blades and safety razors	Accounting or auditing services Advertising services Agricultural machinery Cameras Data processing services Portable power tools Refrigerators and washing machines Safes, locks, latches, etc	Fast food restaurants Management consultancy services Rental cars
Fairly important (15–29%)	Cigarettes Man-made fibres Polishes Precious metals refining Telegraph and telephone apparatus	Chemicals (general) Greeting cards Mining machinery Oil drilling equipment Ophthalmic instruments Watches and clocks	Ceramics and glass products Construction services Heating and ventilation apparatus Insurance Pumps, valves and compressors

* Estimated proportion of sales or employment accounted for by five largest enterprises.
Source: Various studies.
NB   The precise relationship between concentration ratios and shares of output accounted for by MNE affiliates will vary between countries. This being so, the data in the exhibit should be treated as indicative. We have also classified products to only one box. *De facto*, however, some differentiated products (e.g. pharmaceuticals) could realistically be classified to a number of different boxes.

facto provide the best guarantee of effective inter-firm rivalry in sectors where the optimum size of firms is large, yet there is open competition between foreign and domestic producers. Nor is it correct to assume that MNE activity will always lead to an increase in concentration ratios. Even if one takes perfect competition as a norm, one cannot infer that prices will necessarily be higher and quality lower in imperfect markets. Economies of scale and scope may offset any increase in market power resulting from an increased inelasticity in demand. As part of a rising standard of living, consumers may value a higher quality of output, or environmentally friendly products which only a small number of firms may be able to supply. Viewed from a dynamic perspective, oligopoly may be the best structure to promote innovation. In short, in some circumstances a highly concentrated market structure may offer a better guarantee of workable competition than any other practical alternative.[26] Most certainly, too, the attributes of an optimum market structure are likely to vary both between sectors and, within sectors, by countries (Porter, 1990).

On the question of the role played by MNEs in fashioning market structure, much will depend upon the kind of market one is considering. Is it the home country market, or that of the host country, or that of a region, or the worldwide market? Is it for the complete range of (similar) products produced by a firm (e.g. glassware, chemicals, rubber products or management consultancy) or a particular product line? For example, concentration ratios for the *worldwide* output of a wide variety of products, largely supplied by MNEs, generally fell in the period 1962–82 (Dunning and Pearce, 1985). In the later 1980s, as Chapter 2 showed, these ratios have tended to increase again – at least in sectors such as rubber, tyres, pharmaceuticals and hotels – as a result of a substantial number of cross-border mergers and acquisitions, and an increasing tendency for firms to hive off their less profitable activities.

However, at a country level, concentration ratios in most industrial and service sectors have risen over the past 20 years. Similarly, while it is possible that a large number of firms may produce a generic product (e.g. an anti-histamine drug), a particular variety of that product may be supplied by very few firms, or even only one firm. Moreover, while measured in terms of the *products* supplied,

there may have been a fall in concentration ratios measured in terms of the *ownership* of the resources to produce these products, it is possible that the ratios may have increased. Finally, in so far as the economies of scope may confer market power on the firm, this type of concentration should also be considered. Certainly, the evidence suggests that, at an *enterprise* (rather than product) level, and in most countries, the level of concentration has steadily increased over the past half-century or more.[27]

Most empirical research by international business scholars has centred on the effects of MNE activity on the market structure of host countries. Here there are two conflicting hypotheses. The first is that MNEs may increase competition and reduce industrial concentration by their entry into existing foreign markets. The second is that, because of their unique O-specific advantages, MNEs may either enter into new markets and create their own barriers to potential competitors or, as a result of their superior efficiency and aggressive business practices, drive out competitors from existing markets, thereby increasing industrial concentration.

Both hypotheses are eminently plausible. Which, however, is likely to be correct depends very much on the mode of entry by the MNE and its marketing strategy, as well as on industry- and country-specific circumstances. Moreover, at least part of the impact of foreign competition on the structure of a particular sector's market may be made without the physical presence of the foreign firm. The Japanese penetration of the US and European motor vehicle and colour television markets (to take but two examples) has occurred mainly through exports rather than by foreign production. The difference between the two modes of penetration is that foreign imports do not directly affect concentration ratios (as normally measured) as these relate only to the composition of *domestic* output.

This, indeed, is one of the weaknesses of such ratios. Although they may tell us something about the structure of production in a particular industry, they tell us nothing about its competitive position in international markets, nor about the power of its firms to pursue particular global strategies. Indeed, the more open an economy is, the more generic the intermediate products (e.g. technology) used by firms, and the more diversified or differentiated their output is, the less useful are national concentration ratios as a measure of (the lack of) competition.

Clearly, the modality of entry of an MNE into a foreign market is an important factor affecting concentration. Where it is by way of a greenfield investment and the subsidiary is not introducing a completely new product into the economy, competition is likely to increase and the concentration ratio will fall. The entry of US firms into the UK pharmaceutical industry in the 1960s and of Korean and Taiwanese firms into the US consumer electronics industry in the 1980s had this effect. By contrast, where the investment takes the form of an acquisition (e.g. the purchase of tyre companies in Europe and the US by Japanese MNEs in the late 1980s) there may be no immediate effect on the concentration ratio, except that which arises from any changes in output of the acquired firm consequent upon its change in ownership.[28]

Even in these cases, however, one has to consider what would have happened to the market structure in the absence of the foreign investment. The effect of a takeover of an ailing firm, which would otherwise have been acquired by a domestic company or gone out of business, may be quite different from that of an acquisition of a thriving enterprise. Examples of the first kind are Chrysler's purchase of the UK motor vehicle firm Rootes in 1970 and Sumitomo's acquisition of Dunlop in 1986. Examples of the second are Bridgestone's procurement of Firestone in 1988 and Fujitsu's acquisition of ICL in 1990. One also has to consider the rationale for any acquisition and merger (A&M). Is, for example, the new venture intended to supply domestic markets in place of imports, or to supply foreign markets previously serviced from other countries? Is it part of the acquiring and merging firm's portfolio restructuring strategy? Is it better to take advantage of the economies of synergy, scale or scope? Is it in response to changes in the market for corporate control, or to government attitudes towards takeovers (Stonehill and Dullum, 1990)? Is it prompted by the desire of the acquiring company, or merging companies, to protect or advance their global competitive position? Or is it purely a defensive act against a major competitor threatening the existence of the merging partners, as in the case of Caterpillars' alliance with Mitsubishi, which was intended to put pressure on the profits and market share of their common competitor Komatsu (Contractor and Lorange, 1988)?

The choice of the route of entry is, itself, determined by firm-, industry- and country-specific factors. As an example of the first, initial foreign entrants, especially those with strong O-specific advantages, will tend to prefer the greenfield route of entry. By contrast, followers – particularly late followers – seeing their national or international markets threatened, may prefer a speedier build-up to a foreign local production capability and opt for the acquisition and/or merger (A&M) route (Dubin, 1975; Knickerbocker, 1973).

As an example of the second, in some sectors the transaction costs (e.g. retraining the work force and injecting the resident management with a new philosophy) associated with an A&M might be perceived to be greater than the setup costs of a greenfield venture. Hence the preference of Nissan and Toyota for establishing new manufacturing subsidiaries in the UK rather than acquiring existing British auto firms. On the other hand, entry into an internationally-oriented industry, but one in which the investing company has only some of the necessary O advantages for complete global success, may invite the takeover route. Examples include Olivetti's acquisition of equity interests in more than 30 small and innovatory computer companies in the US; Nestlé's purchase of several large food and beverage companies in Europe and the US; Michelin's purchase of (US) Uniroyal in 1989; Chugai Pharmaceuticals $100 million purchase of Gen-Probe (US); and Saatchi and Saatchi's acquisition of several US advertising agencies in the 1980s. As Chapter 9 has shown, many cross-border technical alliances are formed with a similar objective in mind.[29]

Country-specific factors affecting the mode of entry include the size of market and the structure of A&Ms (compare, for example, the favourable institutional mechanisms and relaxed attitude towards mergers in the UK with the extreme reluctance to allow any foreign acquisitions in Japan), the age of the investing firm and the competitiveness of the exchange and capital markets (Walter, 1992).

There is also some suggestion that A&Ms are more common where the industry in which the multinational enters abroad is *different* from that in which it is based at home (Dubin, 1975). The relevance of this latter factor was dramatically shown in the early 1980s when the pound was markedly overvalued in relation to the US dollar. This resulted in some very substantial acquisitions of US assets by UK firms, many of which were awash with liquidity. A different reason for a speedy entry into a particular market is to pre-empt competitors from entering into it, or to avoid the (perceived) unfavourable consequences of *not* being active in that market. The current wave of cross-border A&Ms in the EC, involving both EC and non-EC firms, is largely prompted by this motive.

At the end of the day, however, it must be accepted that many A&Ms cannot easily be explained by traditional FDI theory as they are so much creatures of firm-specific strategies and the opportunities which present themselves at a particular time and place. At times, firms – particularly conglomerates – seem to behave as speculators in the market. To the economic theorist, there seems little rhyme or reason for their actions. The wave of acquisitions in the international hotel industry in the late 1980s is a case in point. Many of the major chains, *viz* Holiday Inn, Hilton International and Intercontinental, switched their nationality. Each was purchased by UK firms, although Grand Metropolitan later sold out its stake in Intercontinental to Seibu/Saison – a Japanese conglomerate – to help it fund the acquisition of the US Pillsbury Company. Such entry and exit strategies appear to make little commercial sense, although the full circumstances leading the firms to take such decisions are rarely disclosed. They also make any assessment of the impact of MNE activity on national competitiveness extremely difficult, particularly where the primary activity of the acquiring firm is different from that of the acquired firm. Increasingly, this would appear to be the case in the hotel sector where several of the leading international chains are no longer owned by hotel management specialists.

With these remarks in mind, let us now turn to review briefly the evidence on the effects of MNE activity on the number and size of firms in their home or host countries.[30] We shall consider these under the first stage or direct and the second stage or indirect effects.

(i) *First stage impact* Most empirical studies reveal that the average size of foreign affiliates (usually measured in sales or employment terms) is considerably larger than that of their indigenous competitors. Examples of such studies are: Rosenbluth (1970) and Statistics Canada (1978) for Canada; Stubenitsky (1970) for the Netherlands; Deane (1970) for New Zealand; Stonehill (1965) for Norway; Dunning (1958, 1976, 1985) and Steuer *et al.* (1973) for the UK; Haex *et al.* (1979) for Belgium; Newfarmer and Mueller (1975) and Willmore (1986) for Brazil; Lall (1979b) for Malaysia; Brash (1966) and Parry (1980) for Australia; Kidron (1965), Lall and Streeten (1977), and Kumar (1990) for India; Lecraw (1985a) for Singapore; and Haddad and Harrison (1993) for Morocco. Caves (1974a) suggests a major reason for this might be the formers' privileged access to the scale economies of their parent companies. Because of this, he argues, MNEs are less likely than *de novo* domestic firms to set up subsidiaries of below optimum size.

On the other hand, in some countries (e.g. the US and Japan) and in some sectors[31] (e.g. mainframe computers, tyres and aluminium) the main competitors of the affiliates are other foreign affiliates, domestic MNEs or multi-product domestic firms, which are of comparable or even greater size.[32] Moreover, where foreign affiliates are set up as part of a defensive oligopolistic strategy and/or are truncated versions or miniature replicas of their parent companies, they could be (and often are) much smaller than their local counterparts. This has been found to be the case in developed countries with relatively small domestic markets (e.g. Canada and Australia) as well as in several developing countries. For example, early studies by English (1964) and Safarian (1969) discovered that many US subsidiaries were not only smaller than their Canadian competitors, but that most of them produced at well below optimum (plant) capacity.[33] In a study of the pharmaceutical industry in Brazil, Jenkins (1984) disclosed that, although the industry was almost completely dominated by foreign-owned firms,[34] there was no evidence that the presence of such firms had led to an increase in concentration. Indeed, as a result of the presence of different nationalities of foreign firms, the contribution of the top firm and the top eight firms in the industry was less than that in the leading investing countries.[35]

As might be expected from the arguments so far addressed in this chapter, the effects of MNEs on the extent and form of rivalry between firms in host countries is mixed. While there is abundant evidence of a positive association between the participation of foreign firms in an industry and its degree of concentration[36] there is much less agreement about the *effects* of inbound investment on the market structure of an industry. In Malaysia (Lall, 1979b; Kalirajan, 1991). Guatemala (Willmore, 1976), Mexico (Newfarmer and Mueller, 1975; Connor, 1977; Blomström, 1986), Brazil (Willmore, 1989), inbound investment has generally been associated with an increase in seller concentration. However, no such association is discernible in most developed countries, notably the UK (Steuer *et al.*, 1973), France (Fishwick, 1982), Australia (Brash, 1966), Canada (Safarian, 1966), or the US (Knickerbocker, 1976). In several service sectors in which deregulation has occurred, the evidence strongly suggests that MNEs have intensified local competition, although they have sometimes encouraged a dualistic market structure (UNCTC, 1988; UN, 1992a).

One of the difficulties of reading too much into indices of industrial concentration is that this variable is influenced by others, which, in turn, impact on MNE activity. For example, Fishwick (1982) found that inter-industry variations in concentration levels in the UK, France and Germany could be explained largely by three variables, *viz* the average number of employees per establishment, the number of plants per enterprise and the total employment in the industry. The inclusion of foreign participation as an additional variable did little to improve the explanation. On the other hand, in a study of the determinants of FDI in the Brazilian electrical goods industry, Newfarmer (1979) found that industrial concentration was one of the most strongly positively identified explanatory variables. Lall (1979a) for Malaysia and Blomström (1986) for Mexico concluded that inbound investment not only tended to increase concentration by introducing new products and processes and raising the capital intensity of production, but it did so independently of these variables.

It is to be noted, however, that most of the studies identified in the previous paragraphs were based on cross-sectional rather than on time-series data. In other words, they sought to explain whether the presence of MNEs helped determine concentration ratios, rather than if they led to an increase or decrease in such ratios. One exception was that of Steuer *et al.* (1973) who found there was no evidence

to suggest that inbound investment had increased industrial concentration in the UK between 1963 and 1968. However, several of the industrial case studies described in Newfarmer (1985) strongly suggest that, in the smaller advanced and in several developing economies, industrial concentration had risen in sectors in which the participation of foreign firms was most pronounced. Finally, using data from the Harvard University project of the late 1960s, Knickerbocker (1976) found that industries in which no more than one or two MNE manufacturing subsidiaries of US firms operated in 1950 usually contained five or more rival affiliates in 1970. Furthermore, he found a negative association between the number of MNE affiliates set up in different sectors in the US, West Germany, France and Italy between 1960 and 1970, and the change in the four firm concentration ratios in these sectors over this period.

We would enter one further caveat. If there is some uncertainty about the effect of FDI on industrial concentration, there is no less ambiguity as to the optimum size structure of a particular industry and for groups of competing firms. Clearly, this will depend on the extent to which economies of scale are possible, the degree of competition from imports and/or related products and the positioning of the domestic firms in international markets. Each of these, and other related variables, is likely to be industry and country specific, making it exceedingly difficult, if not impossible, to generalize about the welfare consequences of FDI on the size distribution of firms. In some instances, MNE activity has most certainly increased (domestic) industrial concentration which has improved performance in international markets. In others, it has led to an abuse of monopoly power which has reduced efficiency and lowered consumer welfare. Similarly, FDI has sometimes broken up national or international cartels with beneficial effects, but at other times it has fragmented markets, created surplus capacity and fostered inefficient levels of production.

(ii) *Second stage impact* We have suggested that the likely initial consequences of MNE activity on industrial concentration will depend upon a variety of firm-, industry- and country-specific characteristics. In the long run, its impact will rest not only on the conduct and performance of the MNEs or their affiliates, but also on that of their competitors in the home and host countries. For example, in the short run a greenfield entry by a foreign company may reduce concentration, while in the long run, either by dint of the greater efficiency or anti-competitive tactics of the foreign firm, it may drive its competitors out of business, thereby increasing concentration. On the other hand, if its competitors, particularly those which are themselves MNEs, respond to the presence of inbound investors by improving their own efficiency, this could lead to a fall in industrial concentration.

Again, the effects are likely to vary between countries and sectors. In the case of countries with small domestic markets and which do not attract export-oriented investment, inbound MNE activity is more likely to drive out competitors than in countries with large internal markets with a strong technological capability (Burstall et al., 1981). The role of government may also be a decisive one, in particular, the extent to which it permits or encourages industrial rationalization of its own firms (as did the UK government in the 1970s through the National Enterprise Board), or is prepared to help them compete with foreign affiliates (e.g. by subsidized or preferential loans, as in the case of Japan and France), or counters the presence of the non-resident firms by setting up its own state-owned companies (as in the case of the sugar industry in Fiji, the hotel industry in India, the oil industry in Indonesia and the chemical industry in China). The consequences will also depend upon industry-specific characteristics, particularly the extent to which firms need to exploit the economies of scale or scope, so that they may minimize their production and/or transaction costs.

We shall take up some of these issues in more detail in Chapter 17.

15.7.2 Product range and scope

Depending upon the size and diversification of the enterprise of which it is part, the age and operating experience of the affiliate, the market structure and economic environment of the host country and whether the mode of entry is by greenfield investment or A&M, affiliates of MNEs may produce more or fewer products than indigenous companies. Once again, generalizations are becoming less easy

because some MNEs, as part of their global strategies, are seeking to establish a substantial presence in each of the main markets of the world, either through FDI or by cross-border cooperative alliances.

In Section 15.7.1, we suggested that the foreign value-added activities of MNEs, especially those designed to service relatively small local markets, are likely to be more truncated than those of their domestic counterparts. At the same time, it is worth recalling that some of the world's largest MNEs are, themselves, from smaller developed countries, and that the foreign operations of companies like Norst Hydro (of Norway), Ciba Geigy (of Switzerland) and SKF (of Sweden) in the larger industrialized nations, are likely to parallel or even exceed those in their home countries.

We have also seen how the extent and form of the value-added activities of a foreign subsidiary is dependent upon its age and experience, as well as its place in the global strategy of the parent firm. Most Japanese manufacturing affiliates in Europe, for example, only produce a limited range of products and buy out most of their intermediate products. By contrast, their competitors – both other foreign affiliates and their own parent companies – are much more horizontally diversified and vertically integrated.

Much, too, depends upon the international portfolio of, and strategies pursued by, particular MNEs. Ceteris paribus, one would expect rather more product and process specialization in affiliates of MNEs pursuing globally or regionally integrated strategies, than in those supplying mainly domestic markets. Philips of Eindhoven, for example, distinguishes between foreign subsidiaries designed to supply products for its world markets and those intended to produce products for the local market. While, for example, its Singaporean affiliate concentrates almost entirely on the production of microchips for export, its US factories produce a range of products, mainly for domestic consumption, which is considerably greater than that of most of its competitors. In the case of process specialization, it is possible that no country in which multinational affiliates operte supplies the complete product.

Of course, the presence of a strong foreign-owned sector may help increase the quality and range of products supplied to domestic consumers, even if not all these are produced locally. It has long been recognized that manufacturing affiliates may serve as a marketing bridgehead for the parent company in a way in which a pure sales operation may not. This may enable the investing company to gain easier access to the local market for its other goods. Again, this is especially likely if the MNE acquires, or collaborates with, an indigenous company experienced in marketing.

There seems little doubt that foreign-owned firms do engage in more product differentiation than local firms. This, after all, is what one might expect, as Caves (1974a) and others have shown that the ability to secure customer loyalty through cross-border product branding is one of their main O-specific advantages. *Inter alia*, this is shown by the above average advertising/sales ratio of foreign subsidiaries (*vis à vis* indigenous firms) in many countries (Dunning (1958, 1985) in the UK; Willmore (1986) in Brazil; Manrique (no date) in the Philippines; and Lall (1978) in Malaysia). However, in the case of Belgium (Van den Bulcke, 1985) and India (Kumar, 1990), it was found that the advertising intensity of foreign firms was not significantly higher than that of their domestic counterparts. In the tertiary sector, there is evidence from field research conducted in Peru, Zimbabwe, the Maghreb countries, Mexico and Thailand that MNEs have both introduced new and unique services, and have upgraded the quaity of existing services (UNCTC, 1991a).[37]

At the same time, most of the above studies rely on data about US MNEs, and it may be questioned whether these findings can be generalized to other foreign investors or, indeed, whether the higher advertising/sales ratios reflect other characteristics of MNEs, such as their size or product diversity which, while they may have been fashioned by their internationalization, are not the direct cause of it. In the US, for example, there is little evidence that Japanese or European affiliates spend more on advertising than do US indigenous firms of the same size and industry. Indeed, Lall and Siddharthan (1982), but not Pugel (1986), found a negative correlation between advertising intensity and foreign presence.

Finally, it is worth reiterating the point that the behaviour of foreign-owned affiliates is likely to be as much the outcome of the policies of host governments or the desire to achieve extra-plant economies, as anything to do with FDI *per se*. This is the conclusion of several scholars who have investigated the impact of inward investment on the market structure of highly protected economies (Safarian, 1985).

15.7.3   Barriers to entry

It is no less difficult to generalize about the effect of MNE activity on barriers to entry or the contestability of markets. On the one hand, whether set up by takeover or a greenfield venture, a foreign-owned firm may help reduce market imperfections in the host country (for example, by opening up new markets, sources of inputs, access to patents and trademarks). On the other, a valued benefit of inward investment arises from the ability of foreign affiliates to capitalize on certain services provided by the investing company, which would otherwise have to be undertaken by a *de novo* indigenous firm (Caves, 1971). Depending on the nature of these services, they may act as a deterrent to new entrants.

There are many other obstacles to competition which might be exacerbated by the strategy of the investing firm. If, for example, a foreign affiliate is restricted in its value-added activities (with respect to products produced, R&D, exports, use of technology and trademarks, etc) to meet the global needs of its parent company, barriers to competition may be raised in the event of an entry by takeover at least. In the case of vertically integrated investments or exclusive dealing arrangements concluded between MNEs, or their affiliates, and their suppliers or customers, it may become more difficult for *de novo* firms to source their inputs or to enter new markets. Finally, once established, and perhaps as a condition for its presence in a host country, a foreign affiliate may bargain with the host government for it to restrict competition from imports or, indeed, from other inward investors.

Substantive empirical research directly concerned with assessing the impact of outward or inward direct investment on entry barriers has been fragmentary. There is, however, a good deal of accumulated evidence about the strategies used by MNE oligopolists to maintain or enhance entry barriers. Some of these strategies will be described in Section 15.8. There is also reason to suppose that MNEs may influence, or collude with, home or host countries to shelter them from foreign competition.[38] On the other hand, as Chapter 6 has shown, there is a good deal of casual evidence to support the 'follow my leader' hypothesis, which suggests that an initial FDI might lower the barriers to entry to other competitors.

We have also seen that MNEs tend to be more vertically integrated than uninational firms and to conclude exclusive dealing agreements with their suppliers and/or customers. However, part of the reason for such integration or quasi-integration may be to reduce market failure rather than to lessen competition. In any event, that component of any anti-competitive behaviour which can be specifically attributable to the ownership or multinationality of an enterprise may be very small indeed.

15.8   BUSINESS PRACTICES OF MNEs

We turn, finally, to consider some of the business practices of MNEs which may affect the structure of markets and domestic rivalry. These may be different from those undertaken by non-MNEs, partly because MNEs internalize cross-border markets, and partly because, in the case of their foreign affiliates, they are part of a larger enterprise.

Such discriminating characteristics allow an MNE or its affiliates to pursue distinctive patterns of conduct or behaviour – some of which may have nothing to do with its efficiency. These include predatory pricing, the use of 'deep pocket' advantages to promote non-price competition, the provision of intra-group services at below marginal cost, a willingness by the parent company to accept zero or below normal profits and dividends from its affiliates, the manipulation of cross-border intra-group prices, and so on.

Most of these devices may be practised by diversified firms of all kinds and are not always against the public interest. However, there are two main differences in the case of MNEs. First, because they operate in a variety of economic and political environments, each with its specific characteristics, they may have more incentive to exploit these practices. Indeed, some – such as the manipulation of transfer prices – are largely (but not exclusively) undertaken by MNEs. Second, whatever the effects on the distribution of the benefits arising from the operation of uninational companies, they are retained within the country of production, whereas in the case of those arising from MNEs or their affiliates, part (or all) of the benefits may accrue to other countries.

Of course, various practices of the MNE parent companies will affect the long-run prosperity of their foreign affiliates, even though they may have no direct bearing on their day-to-day behaviour. Such practices (e.g. the raising of new capital, the management of international money, the allocation of export markets and the centralization of purchasing procedures) may benefit the enterprises of which the affiliates are part, but not always the affiliates themselves or the countries in which they operate. In some cases, too, the policies of home governments may affect the competitive positions of affiliates.

Here, we are particularly concerned with the kinds of business practices which affect market structure. As a general proposition, one might expect that affiliates of MNEs will engage in more non-price competition than indigenous firms in the same industry. This is partly because the types and range of products of the parent company are likely to be different from those of firms in the host country, and partly because one of the main O advantages of MNEs is their possession of assets which encourage product differentiation and diversification (Caves, 1971, 1980). *Inter alia* this is revealed by their above average expenditures both on innovating and promotional activities.

To what extent, however, are such practices perceived to be restrictive in the sense defined by Article 46 of the Havana Charter for International Trade (1948), *viz* 'practices which restrain competition, limit access to markets or foster monopolistic competition'? For a more extensive definition of Restrictive Business Practices (RBPs) see UNCTAD (1981). Here it is helpful to distinguish between two kinds of practices:

(1) Practices undertaken by MNEs or other affiliates which would normally be regarded as unacceptable when undertaken by indigenous firms, or by groups of independent firms of different nationality.

(2) Practices which would not normally be regarded as restrictive when undertaken by the above firms, but, when undertaken by foreign direct investors, may be so regarded.

The first type embraces the whole gamut of practices that lead to lower efficiency, higher costs, inferior quality goods, unfair competition, increased barriers to entry, wasteful advertising, excessive product differentiation, and so on. They arise largely because the market structure, in at least one area of a firm's operations, allows it to earn above competitive profits, which may be used to 'buy' these practices, any or all of which may help to protect the firm's established market position or to force out its competitors. Once identified, such conduct in MNEs or their affiliates can be dealt with in exactly the same way as if it were pursued by uninational firms. The only difficulty is that the criteria by which the performance and behaviour of indigenous firms are evaluated are not necessarily appropriate in the case of affiliates of MNEs.

However, it is the second group of business practices which are more relevant in the present context. They pose two challenges to the researcher. One is to discover whether the practices *are*, in fact, restrictive. The other is to evaluate them in the light of the *total* effects of the MNE's operations. Normally, host governments will only regard practices in this category as restrictive in so far as they are perceived to work against their long-term economic interests. Examples include restrictions on the foreign markets open to the affiliates, predatory pricing, cross-border subsidization of activities designed to drive out competitors, limitations on use of technology, patents and trademarks, control over sourcing of inputs, and the manipulation of intra-corporate transfer pricing.

Within a Nation State, such actions on the part of multi-regional firms may not be thought restrictive because the product of their activities is still retained domestically. However, once they are engaged in across national boundaries, they take on a very different complexion. Yet, the fact remains that such behaviour often arises because of distortions in the international price structure of goods and services which may inhibit the efficient division of labour, or because of differences in the incentives given by governments to MNEs to produce goods or to earn income within their boundaries. It also reflects the conduct of international economic institutions and the characteristics of the international patent, taxation and monetary systems. Some of the concerns of host countries towards MNEs could, in fact, be

removed by the rationalization or harmonization of these and other actions.

But if it is right that governments should accept the legitimacy of the conduct of MNEs, these enterprises need to accept that similar patterns of behaviour may produce different consequences in different situations. Control of an affiliate's markets by the parent company may have the same effect as a barrier to market entry; control over its sourcing of inputs may inhibit the development of related industries in the host country; control over the location of R&D activities may be a barrier of entry to innovation or to the development of local skills; control over trademarks may reduce the contestability of markets; control over production methods may lessen the opportunities of a country to exploit its comparative resource endowments.[39] At the same time, by their governance procedures MNEs can increase competition, open up new markets and upgrade indigenous resources. Moreover, an unwelcome business practice to one country may be a welcome business practice in another. Sometimes within the same country, an MNE may bring with it linked patterns of behaviour, some of which are acceptable and others which are not.

What, then, is the evidence about the business practices of MNEs? Studies conducted by UNCTAD (1973), Long (1981), Newfarmer (1979) and ESCAP-CTC (1984) reveal that MNEs and other foreign firms engage in a wide variety of practices which the host countries identify as restrictive. Broadly speaking, they may be classified into four main groups, *viz* anti-competitive pricing policies, controls on the use of transferred technology, territorial market and production allocation arrangements and boycott or enforcement measures. The literature suggests that the first three of these are frequently important ingredients of the global strategies of MNEs. Such strategies may be either defensive (e.g. to protect existing markets) or predatory (e.g. to pre-empt or corner new markets).

The history of the primary sector is replete with examples of MNEs attempting to limit competition.[40] Perhaps the best known of these are the cartel agreements, marketing alliances and price maintenance schemes set up at various times over the past century to regulate production and trade in the oil, copper, bauxite, tin, zinc, banana, rubber, cocoa, sugar, and bark (quinine) industries. Certainly,

MNEs soon came to dominate these markets as a result of their A&Ms and their strategies to forestall entry by competitors. However, it is erroneous to infer that their subsequent patterns of behaviour should be attributed solely to their transnationality *per se*, any more than to other firm-specific characteristics or, indeed, to the industry of which they are part. Cartel agreements also flourished in other sectors in which MNEs were not involved. Moreover, there seems little evidence to suggest that the nationalization of some of the sectors in which MNEs have been involved has lessened the propensity of firms or countries to engage in anticompetitive business practices – at least as far as the final consumer is concerned. The OPEC cartel is, perhaps, the best example.

In manufacturing industry, there are prolific examples of restrictive business practices. Foremost among these have been the oligopolistic tactics pursued by MNEs in the Latin American electrical equipment industry Newfarmer (1979, 1985) and Newfarmer and Marsh (1981b) found substantial evidence of cross-subsidization, control of supply channels, formal and informal collusion, interlocking directorates, predatory pricing and hostile acquisition behaviour, both among and by MNEs. While not all these practices were MNE specific, many did stem from their global financial and marketing power. At the same time, part of this power may be attributed to the protectionist policies followed by the Brazilian government. Similarly, the imposition of controls on the import of drugs by the Philippine government tempted foreign-owned firms into the country. By 1970, they had captured 70% of the local market. While this was not in itself a bad thing, the strategies of MNEs to obtain and maintain this share sometimes involved questionable business behaviour (such as tied purchases of raw materials, export restriction and transfer pricing (UNCTAD, 1973)). More generally, in the 1970s UNCTAD studies revealed that MNEs were imposing a wide range of export restrictive clauses[41] on their subsidiaries in numerous manufacturing countries. Indeed, of the total restrictive clauses in agreements in which MNEs were involved, export restrictions typically accounted for between 72% and 90%. Finally, a study by Epstein and Newfarmer (1982) showed that cartelization among the leading MNEs in the heavy electrical equipment industry had raised global prices on average by 23% compared with their competitive price.

In the 1980s, there is reason to suppose that MNEs have reduced some of their restrictions both on the conditions of technological transfer and on marketing arrangements. This has been both in response to the pressures of host governments and because of the improvement of supply capabilities in many developing countries. In a 1984 UN survey of 388 agreements concluded between foreign and Thai firms, export restrictions were identified in about 40% of cases, a much lower percentage than just a decade earlier. In the case of 340 purchasing contracts, only 8% of those for which data was available provided for tie-in purchases of machinery and raw materials. At the same time it would seem that in place of the earlier trading restrictions, there has been a marked increase in specifying guarantees with respect to quality-control procedures (Prasartset, 1990). Moreover, as MNEs have become more globally integrated, their control over 'what is produced, where and by whom', even if it has become less 'restrictive' has become tighter and more, rather than less, oriented to the needs of the parent organization, rather than one or other of its subsidiaries.

15.9   SOME POLICY IMPLICATIONS

While it is understandable that some countries (especially some developing countries) are concerned about possible adverse affects of the MNEs' business practices[42] on local competition, employment, the balance of payments and developmental goals (Long, 1981), it does not necessarily follow that the best way to eradicate such practices is to legislate against them. This is partly because the MNEs may regard some of them (e.g. allocation of markets and tied purchases) as a legitimate part of their global competitive strategies. If forced to abandon them, they might react by reducing or restricting their investments in a way that reduces the benefits that they currently provide to host countries. It is also partly because, since such practices are sometimes in response to ill-advised government economic strategies, it may make more sense if these were modified so that MNEs (and, for that matter, uninational firms) no longer had the incentive to engage in such practices.

All this is not to deny that MNEs do engage in unacceptable business practices, or that, in some cases, government action should be directed to removing the abuses of such actions. Most countries, for example, have established anti-trust and restrictive practices procedures and legislation. At a regional level, the EC has evolved its own law of competition policy. The OECD guidelines on international direct investment also pay some attention to MNE behaviour as it affects market structure and competition.

Mostly, such policies are directed to all kinds of firms, but occasionally they are modified to take account of business practices that arise specifically from the internationalization of production. In recent years, for example, the US government has taken a more relaxed attitude towards some kinds of cross-border A&Ms and strategic alliances which, while seemingly contravening its anti-trust legislation, are perceived to be in the best interests of US competitiveness in international markets.

Among the general policies of host governments which affect market structure and behaviour, some are specifically directed to this end; others affect it incidentally. Of the latter, we might mention two kinds. One relates to industrial policy as a whole; this basically concerns itself with the allocation of resources between industrial sectors. For example, which sorts of economic activity should a country be encouraged to develop? How much diversification or specialization should there be? These are the sorts of problems with which several countries and regional blocs, like the EC, are currently grappling. Industrial policy does have implications for affiliates of MNEs, since the viable size and structure of an industry will both affect, and be affected by, the composition of its firms and their product strategies. Also, the element of foreign ownership will vary between industries.

The second type of policy relates to the market structure of particular industries, which is framed to encourage both sustainable competition and an equitable distribution of the proceeds between the agents of production and final consumers. This point is taken up by Frischtak *et al.* (1989), Frischtak (1992) and Newfarmer and Frischtak (1993), who argue that many of the concerns of host governments towards inbound FDI could be removed if these same governments were to adopt more efficient and activist competition-enhancing policies. These might include removing entry deterrent mechanisms, regulatory constraints on capacity licensing, anti-competitive public procurement practices, and operating more market-facilitating industrial and trade strategies. Of course, governments may seek to achieve other goals, such as ensuring an adequate choice of products without excessive differentiation, encouraging opportunities for new and/or small firms, seeing that the greater part of production remains in the hands of indigenous firms and so on. It may be felt that such decisions are best left to private enterprise in a competitive situation and where social and private costs and benefits do not diverge a great deal. In some cases, however, this will not be so and governments may wish to modify the behaviour of firms.

When MNEs are introduced into the picture, more specific policies may be required, depending on the distinctiveness of their behaviour. These are usually of two kinds. First, governments might direct action to foreign firms by means of *persuasive* or *mandatory* policies to affect either the conditions of their entry or their conduct once they are established. On entry, certain assurances or constraints might be required of foreign investors both as to the form of their activities and their organizational behaviour. Some of these will directly affect market structure, while others will affect the ability of MNEs to avoid taxation by unacceptable pricing practices. Still other forms of decision-making might be conditioned by extra-territorial policies of home governments (e.g. anti-trust legislation). Here unilateral policies will be inadequate; the resulting problems can only be resolved by agreements or negotiations between governments.

Governments possess various options to rid themselves of these kinds of practices or to mitigate their impact. Most of them involve a cost to firms, in as much as they consider it in their own interests to engage in them. Whether or not firms are prepared to accept the costs without altering their behaviour depends on the level of profits they are earning. If they are forced to modify their conduct, this may have both direct and indirect consequences on the achievement of the primary goals of governments, and it is in this light that all policies must be assessed.

The second approach of governments is to

control the activities of foreign firms, or the distribution of the value added they produce, by encouraging more indigenous competition. Thus local firms may be favoured with government contracts or fiscal incentives; they may be helped to improve their efficiency, subsidized in their R&D, supported in management training schemes, advised on export markets, prompted to rationalize their activities by merger or engage in product specialization, and so on. In some cases, such policies may be justified, even in the absence of inward investment. In others, much will depend on the extent to which the strong position of the foreign affiliates is a result of their higher efficiency (or that of the enterprises of which they are part) or to their monopoly power (particularly that part associated with multinationality). If the former, action should be confined to gaining a larger share of the economic rent of the affiliate: if the latter, to improving their efficiency. In any event, any form of permanent protection *per se* to domestic producers may, on economic grounds, be difficult to justify.

Some commentators, however, would question this view. Bergsten *et al.* (1978), for example, argue that a 'soft' anti-trust policy in the US tends to reduce the incentive of domestic firms to innovate and be efficient, thereby reducing their competitive positions in world markets. The authors also believe that the US authorities should incorporate the foreign activities of US firms in their surveillance, as these could be used to promote unacceptable policies in the domestic market.

We would make one final observation, which we shall take up in more detail in Chapter 21. In considering government policy towards MNEs, or as a result of MNE activity in one particular area of their operations, it is important to adopt a holistic and integrated approach as far as possible. It is, for example, little use stopping one undesirable practice of an MNE or its affiliate if this results in another undesirable practice being introduced, or a reduction of some other benefit which would otherwise result from inward or outward FDI.

15.10   CONCLUSIONS

This chapter has demonstrated that although MNE activity does have distinctive consequences on market structure and on the efficiency of value-added activity, the extent of this significance is often exaggerated. Moreover, it is clear that such effects are sometimes difficult to interpret (e.g. the superior productivity and profitability of MNEs). At the same time, they very much depend on the mode of entry (or expansion) by the MNE, the existing market structure, the kind of investment being undertaken and the policies pursued by the home and host governments. Indeed, if there is one lesson to be learnt from the various empirical studies which have been undertaken, it is that it is more fruitful to identify the kind of OLI configurations facing MNEs and ESP configurations facing countries, which will lead to MNE activity bringing about certain consequences, than to generalize about the impact of such activity. Once more, this suggests that an 'if . . . then' approach may be more helpful to policy makers than the 'because . . . then' approach.

However, assuming that governments pursue market-oriented economic policies and adopt a reasonably neutral stance to FDI, it is possible to offer some general propositions. We would emphasize seven of these.

First, the activities of MNEs bind the countries in which they are involved more closely into the international division of labour. MNEs are, if nothing else, conduits of economic and technological change and of new patterns of consumer demand. They are also a powerful integrating force of business practices in the global economy. Whether or not these features are beneficial to the participating countries depends on the *raison d'être* for MNE activity and the market structures facing foreign direct investors. Certainly, however, each activity exposes countries to the volatility of world economic events and places more demands on governments to ensure that adjustments to external changes are accomplished with minimum social costs.

Second, and allied to this first point, there is some suggestion that as firms become more multinational, so do market structures. In particular, firms which face oligopolistic competition in domestic markets tend to replicate this structure abroad (Rosenbluth, 1970; Knickerbocker, 1973). Such MNE activity will have considerable implications for domestic macro-organizational policies, especially for those which directly or indirectly impinge on the allocative, technical and adaptive efficiency of indigenous resources and capabilities.

As yet, few governments seem to appreciate fully the implications of the internationalization of industries as it affects not only their domestic market structures, but also their ability to influence the activities of their own and foreign-based MNEs. The reconciliation between the desire of MNEs to minimize their cross-border transaction costs and the needs of home and host governments to promote a market structure which best meets their long-term goals is not as easy. This is because the benefits of multinationalization arise not so much from the O-specific assets of the investing firms, as from the common governance of geographically or industrially diversified activities. The dilemma is that without some kind of centralized and extra-territorial control, which may seem to threaten the sovereignty of Nation States, this benefit would not arise. It is such issues as these which many governments have still to address, let alone resolve.

Third, affiliates of MNEs gain their market power relative to uninational firms (of a similar size and degree of diversification) by being part of a larger and international organization. The greater the global orientation of MNEs, the more the possibility arises that affiliates will engage in competitive practices which differ from those they would use if they were independent firms.

Fourth, because of the market structures in which they compete, there is a temptation for MNEs to engage in excessive product or geographical diversification, and not to adapt their business practices to the needs of the markets in which they operate. While MNEs might help to overcome entry barriers to cross-border markets, they may (and frequently do) create their own barriers by dint of their ability to control the sourcing of raw materials and intermediate products, and their favoured access to finished goods markets.

Fifth, because of the specific attributes of MNEs – most noticeably, their ability and need to move goods and assets around the globe – governments are being forced to reappraise their macro-economic and organizational policies. The events of the past decade suggest that this has generally been to the benefit of the countries concerned. Nowhere is this better demonstrated than in the increasing attention now being given by governments to improving national competitiveness. In this respect, not only

are MNEs perceived to have an important role to play as a result of their distinctive O advantages, but it is also recognized that to gain the greatest benefit from these advantages and the way in which they are organized, countries must offer the appropriate L-specific attractions and ensure that their indigenous capabilities are restructured and upgraded in a way that is consistent with their long-term objectives. To achieve these objectives, governments need to ensure that the domestic market structure and their own market facilitating policies are such as to promote effective and dynamic competition.

Sixth, in any examination of the impact of MNEs on market structure and performance, it is important to take account of the secondary, as well as the primary effects. Secondary effects include the consequences of inward and outward investment for the network of value-added activities in which MNEs are involved. The evidence of several studies suggests that depending on industry- and country-specific circumstances, MNEs can both create and upgrade clusters of related activities, or weaken them. Chapter 11 introduced the concept of L-specific 'vicious' and 'virtuous' asset creating circles which might be modified (or even reversed) by the presence of foreign affiliates; Chapter 16 will pay more attention to the linkages between inbound foriegn affiliates and locally-owned firms.

Finally, and related to the last point, any consideration of the effects of the interaction between the O advantages of MNEs and the L advantages of countries on the organization of markets needs to take a dynamic and systemic perspective. Often, for example, there may be no direct and immediate relationship between inward or outward investment and the structure of inter-firm rivalry. Over time, however, through their impact on such variables as government policy, the pattern and quality of consumer demand, the creation of innovatory capacity and the upgrading of human skills, entrepreneurship and the work ethic, they may quite dramatically affect the market structures in which they compete, and the performance and business practices of indigenous firms.[43]

NOTES

1 A strategic group consists of a number of firms each
   pursuing similar competitive strategies. See, for

example, McGee and Thomas (1986).

2   See Chapter 4, pp. 89–90, for further details.

3   To normalize for industry size, the difference in each sector was divided through by the UK share of employment.

4   RCA is defined in Note 19 of Chapter 4. An alternative measure based on exports alone is the share of world exports accounted for by a country of a particular product divided by the share of total world manufacturing exports accounted for by that country.

5   The 12 countries studied by Dunning were the UK, US, France, West Germany, Japan, Canada, Sweden, Belgium, The Republic of Korea, India, Portugal and Singapore.

6   As documented, for example, in Dunning (1986a, 1988b, 1990), Cantwell and Dunning (1991) and Dunning (1991).

7   Net output as a percentage of gross output.

8   See, for example, Frobel *et al.* (1980), Cable and Persaud (1987), UNCTC (1983b) and UNCTC (1988).

9   Relatively little attention has been paid to the failure of MNEs. For a recent attempt to examine some of the consequences of their failure on the economies of host countries, see UN (1992a).

10   For example, the profitability of a marketing affiliate of an MNE may be quite unimportant compared to the effects which the presence of the affiliate has on the output and performance of the rest of the MNE. The efficiency of a bauxite mine may be of secondary concern to an aluminium processing company that wishes to safeguard its supplies of bauxite to its processing factories.

11   Dunning (1958, 1966, 1970), Safarian (1966) and Brash (1966).

12   In these studies, productivity is usually defined as gross or net output divided by numbers employed or wage bill. Occasionally (Dunning, 1976, 1985) a total productivity index is used. Profitability is defined as either the rate of return on sales or profits (before tax) as a percentage of net assets of capial employed.

13   Which, of course, might suggest that foreign firms were better resource allocators than their UK counterparts.

14   Although that of Japanese affiliates was 5.8% greater.

15   The question as to whether size is independent of foreign ownership is a tricky one as undoubtedly some of the productivity-enhancing advantages of MNE activity arise as a direct result of their size.

16   See Chapter 11.

17   Note that there may be other reasons why foreign firms may record high profitability ratios. These include the competitive environment within which they operate, the extent to which there are barriers to entry to new firms, the size and character of markets and so on. For

an elaboration of these, see Connor and Mueller (1977). For a critical analysis of various performance measures of FDI, see Larimo (1990).

18   The classification of firms into strategic groups is based on the extent to which firms are perceived to be mutually interdependent in their competitive strategies. One implication of the segmentation of industry into strategic groups is that entry barriers are partly specific to the industry and partly to the strategic groups. The latter kind of entry barriers help to explain why some firms in a particular industry may earn higher profits than others (Porter, 1979; McGee and Thomas, 1986; Kumar, 1990).

19   Further consideration is given to the implications of transfer price manipulation in Chapter 18.

20   In 1974, European-owned subsidiaries in Brazil recorded a mean rate of return on total assets of 9.4% compared with those of North American subsidiaries of 11.7% and those of Japanese affiliates of 12.4%.

21   At the same time, they found that US MNEs were significantly more capitalized than uninational firms, while the average systematic risk of MNEs was significantly lower than that of domestic US production.

22   Other research suggests that, even allowing for differences in accounting conventions, there are country specific variations in the performance of MNEs, with US MNEs doing considerably better than their European counterparts (Rugman, 1983, 1986; Dunning and Pearce, 1985). Part (but not all) of the differences are to be explained by the fact that privately-owned MNEs generally recorded higher profitability ratios than state owned MNEs (Rugman, 1986; Sullivan, 1992b).

23   In an, as yet, unpublished paper Freeman (1992b) has argued that the relationship between 'profitability' and degree of multinationality may depend on how each variable is measured. Replicating the study of Geringer *et al.* (1989) but using a composite measure of internationalization (which, *inter alia*, included foreign assets as a percent of total assets, overseas subsidiaries as a percent of total subsidiaries and the psychic dispersion of subsidiaries), Freeman found that a firm's profitability initially fell as it began to internationalize; then it rose and followed the pattern suggested by other researchers. See also Daniels and Bracker (1989).

24   The concentration ratio is the share of the *production* of an industry accounted for by the 'x' largest firms. 'X' varies in number but is usually three or four, but it might be as high as eight. The ratio usually refers to the structure of output in a particular country. It is not necessarily a good guide of the extent of competition for the product being produced as it takes no account

of competition from producers based in other countries.

25 See pp. 44–6.

26 For a discussion of the concept of workable competition, see Lawrence (1987).

27 The blurring of the boundaries of the firm, for example, by strategic alliances and the like, are making this kind of concentration very difficult to assess.

28 This may increase or lower industrial concentration, depending upon whether the acquired firm is in the top three or four firms in the industry, and the number of acquired firms in a particular sector which might be bought out by the same MNE.

29 See pp. 250–6.

30 The following paragraphs draw substantially on Dunning (1974, 1981b).

31 This is because, for technological and other reasons, an increasing number of sectors are becoming internationalized and an increasing number of countries are, themselves, spawning their own multinationals.

32 In other words, the strategic group to which the multinational affiliate belongs is higher than that of the sector of which it is part.

33 Optimum capacity is determined as that capacity where average unit costs are at their lowest point.

34 In 1979 it was estimated that 88% of the sales of the Brazilian pharmaceutical industry were accounted for by foreign-owned firms (Jenkins, 1984, Table 4.1, p. 82).

35 In 1968, for example, the share of the top four firms in Brazil was 14% compared with 22% in the US in 1969. The corresponding ratios for the top eight firms were 25% and 39%. See Evans (1977).

36 Though, as Lecraw (1983) has pointed out, the extent of the association varies according to the nationality of the investing companies. In his study of MNE activity of Asian developing countries he found that Japanese and Third World MNEs tended to operate in less concentrated sectors than did European and US MNEs.

37 Most noticeably in the hotel, financial services, engineering designing and consultancy and advertising sectors. See also a study prepared by Robert Grosse for the UNCTC which will be published in 1993.

38 For example, see particularly Rugman and Verbeke (1990b).

39 But, as we have already suggested, these practices may have the reverse effect, that is, FDI might overcome as well as create barriers.

40 For an examination of these practices see *inter alia* Penrose (1971) and Vernon (1973) for oil; UNCTAD (1974) and Read (1986) for bananas; Vernon (1972) for copper and bauxite; Hennart (1986b, 1986c) for tin; and Long (1981) for bark (quinine) and cocoa. The reader is invited to consult a series of studies jointly published by the Economic Commission for Africa (ECA) and UNCTC during the late 1970s and 1980s on the role of MNEs in a variety of industries in different African countries. See, for example, ECA/UNCTC, 1979, 1984a and 1984b.

41 Such clauses include provisions like a global ban on exports, exports prohibited (or permitted) to specified countries, restrictions on the use of trademarks in exports, tied purchases and restrictions on production patterns.

42 For example, transfer pricing (dealt with in Chapter 18), controls over technology transfer and the use made of technology (dealt with in Chapter 11), pricing policies and certain kinds of marketing and advertising procedures.

43 For an examination of the likely impact of MNE activity on that part of Porter's diamond of competitive advantage most relevant to market structure and business conduct, see Dunning (1992a).

CHAPTER 16

MNEs, Linkages and Spill-over Effects

16.1 INTRODUCTION

We now turn to consider the impact of the activities of MNEs or their affiliates on their suppliers, competitors and customers, as well as, more generally, on the home and host economies of which they are part. Previous chapters have examined the role of foreign firms as providers and controllers of resources and capabilities to host countries, and the effects of these O-specific advantages on the way in which resources and capabilities are allocated both between and within sectors in an economy.

In the following four chapters, we seek to analyse the ways in which the presence of MNEs may affect the economic performance and competitiveness of *other* firms, consumers and governments in the countries in which they operate. In doing so, we make no *a priori* judgement as to whether or not, and in what ways, their presence advances or reduces economic welfare. On the one hand, as suppliers of new or better quality products, as cross-border disseminators of information, knowledge, experience and ideas, as standard bearers of new working practices, and as stimulators of competition and entrepreneurship, MNEs might help raise the economic well-being of other producers and workers. On the other hand, by the acquisition of indigenous firms, MNEs might gain monopolistic control over a particular range of products and transfer innovatory facilities back to the parent company. They might eschew local suppliers and/or buy their high value components from foreign sources, not because it is more efficient to do so, but because it helps advance their objectives as global oligopolists. By their aggressive sales and advertising techniques, they might inveigle consumers into buying products which

may lead to cultural erosion and encourage acquisitive spending. Because of their size and cross-border locational flexibility they might add to, rather than reduce, employment stability in the countries in which they operate. In the interests of their regional or global marketing strategies, they may sometimes close sorely needed export outlets to particular developed or developing countries.

Some of these issues have been touched upon in earlier chapters. The remaining chapters in this part of the volume, however, specifically address five issues:

(1) What is the nature of the linkages which the affiliates of MNEs forge with local firms, and to what extent and under what conditions are such linkages likely to be socially beneficial?

(2) What are the effects of FDI on the competitiveness of the indigenous resources and institutions in the host country – particularly on the sectors and/or industrial clusters in which they are involved?

(3) What are the implications of the globalization of production for the international division of labour and, through that, on the structure of economic activity in which MNEs operate? In particular, what is the nature of the interaction between the regional or global integration of corporations and that of countries?

(4) What are the consequences of MNE activity on the budget of the national exchequers? On the one hand, by the taxes they pay, they provide revenue; on the other, they receive benefits from the government (e.g. tax free holidays, investment incentives). It is also possible that

by manipulating cross-border internalized prices they may add to or subtract from the sales or corporation taxes they provide to governments.

(5)   What are some of the more important non-economic consequences of MNE activity, in particular, those that impinge on the environment, on the strategic well-being and on the political sovereignty of home and host countries?

The present chapter concerns itself with the first issue and part of the second by examining the externalities or 'spill-over' effects of MNE activity, that is, those that arise as a direct consequence of the linkages forged between foreign direct investors and other economic agents in the countries in which they operate.[1] Linkages occur when, by design or not, any particular firm (in this case an MNE or its affiliates) affects the amount and/or conditions of supply of, or the demand for, other goods and services by another firm or by consumers. In our analysis, we shall be concerned with the linkages (and, in some cases, the absence of linkages) fashioned by MNEs to advance their objectives. We consider the possible consequences first for their suppliers, second for their customers, third for their competitors and fourth for other firms in the region in which they operate and for the rest of the community of which they are part.

16.2   UPSTREAM LINKAGES: LINKAGES WITH SUPPLIERS

16.2.1   The effects on suppliers

Like domestic firms, the affiliates of MNEs may affect the economic welfare of their suppliers of raw materials and intermediate products in three ways. First, by the quantity of goods and services they buy from them; second, by the influence they may exert on the terms of procurement; and third, by the impact they may have on the technological capability, managerial initiative and organizational competence of their suppliers. We shall deal with each of these issues in turn, where possible identifying those aspects of the procurement strategies and practices of foreign affiliates which may be specifically attributed to their being part of an MNE.

16.2.2   The 'how much' decision

The amount of purchases made by a multinational affiliate will depend firstly on the *range* of goods and services produced by the affiliates; secondly, on the *quantity* of each of the products produced; and thirdly, on the extent to which the affiliates *internalize* the markets for the inputs required for their value-added activities (i.e. how vertically integrated they are). The higher the proportion of value added to gross output, the less dependent a firm will be on the quality and price of raw materials and intermediate products bought from outside producers. The lower the proportion, the more dependent the firm will be on the vagaries of the open market for its purchases.

The answers to the first two questions will depend upon the volume and characteristics of the goods and services produced by the MNE, and on the contribution of its foreign affiliates to these value-added activities. Thus, for technical reasons, the production of processed goods (e.g. chemicals, metal manufacture and food products) tends to be more integrated than that of fabricated products (e.g. washing machines, computers and marine engines). At the same time, the strategy of the MNE towards its foreign operations is also a relevant consideration. Are its affiliates intended to serve local, regional or world markets? Are their activities coordinated with those of the rest of the organization of which they are part, or are they truncated replicas of their parent companies? The age and experience of the affiliate may also influence the range and quantity of goods produced, as is shown in the quite different structure of local production of the recently established Japanese auto companies in the EC *vis à vis* that of US-owned companies which have been producing for 50 years or more.

In this chapter, we propose to concentrate on two kinds of sourcing decisions a foreign affiliate (or, for that matter, any firm) has to make. The first is the 'make or buy' decision, that is, the extent to which the affiliate purchases its raw materials, intermediate or finished[2] products from outside suppliers rather than producing them itself. The second is the extent to which it chooses to produce or buy these goods or services in the host country or to import them from a foreign source, *viz* the 'produce locally or import' decision.

16.2.3   The 'make or buy' decision

The decision to produce a product in-house or buy from another producer will rest on the comparative costs of the two alternatives. These costs break down into the production and transaction costs involved. Production costs are the cost of internally producing an intermediate product of a given quality compared with the price paid to external suppliers. Transaction costs include any additional costs incurred in acquiring and utilizing the intermediate product. The costs of engaging in external transactions include many of the costs of market failure identified in previous chapters. They include the search costs for potential suppliers, the costs of negotiating with the chosen supplier (or suppliers) for the items and conditions of supply and a variety of costs associated with buyer uncertainty.

Normally, one might expect that the *production* costs of a specialist and experienced supplier would be lower than those of its customers, simply because the former is likely to be producing in greater volumes and be knowledgeable about the latest products and production techniques. Moreover, the purchasing flexibility of a firm is obviously reduced by vertical integration. In the case of relatively simple components, small outside suppliers may have the advantage of lower material and overhead costs. However, if the supplier is also a monopolist and/or is not aware of, or is unprepared to utilize the most efficient production or managerial techniques, the purchasing firm may prefer to undertake its own production or, indeed, to acquire its supplier. As we shall later suggest, it may sometimes be in the purchaser's best interest to aid the supplier to improve the quality of his products or productivity. Alternatively, the purchasing firm may wish to persuade the suppliers of its parent company to set up subsidiaries or license local producers in the host country.

We have already identified some of the transactional costs of using external suppliers. These are essentially the risks of market failure. The possibility of disruptions to supplies, unreliability of product quality, the failure to keep to delivery dates, unacceptable price hikes and the misuse of property rights can all be avoided if the supplying firm is owned by the purchasing firm (i.e. by backward vertical integration). The transactional costs of

hierarchies are essentially those of the additional intra-organizational and management costs. For example, by diversifying its activities, a firm may overextend its organizational capacity and/or reduce the efficiency and innovativeness of its mainstream activities. Risks are also likely to be attached to the additional capital investment involved, while governments may view any move towards vertical integration as a potential reduction in competition.

What will determine the balance between using markets or vertically integrating production? How might this vary between countries, sectors and firms? In particular, are multinational affiliates likely to forge more or fewer linkages with independent indigenous firms than are their local competitors?

The first and most obvious point is that the more numerous the suppliers, the greater the opportunities and benefits of product or process specialization; the fewer the synergies between different stages of the value-added chain, the less likely firms are likely to wish to engage in backward integration. Examples include most traded commodities and financial assets, where there are thriving futures markets. Similarly, strong external markets exist for standard and mature products, such as basic chemicals, iron ore and newsprint, which are produced under highly competitive conditions. By contrast, the more specialized the technology needed to produce the intermediate products, the less the competition between suppliers, the greater the possibility of variations in product quality, the greater the probability of some form of hierarchical control being exercised by the purchasing over the supplying firm. Intermediate product markets are also likely to be internalized where efficient production and innovation requires the close coordination and monitoring of input quality, specifications, inspection and testing procedures, testing and product development programmes, and where a regular exchange of information on future plans will help match the investment capacities of suppliers to those of the users.

Second, the literature on vertical integration emphasizes the role of country-specific differences, especially the way value-added chains are organized. For example, Japanese motor vehicle manufacturers, on average, buy out 70% of their components and parts. This compares with a figure of 50% to 60% for UK producers and 40% to 50% for US firms. Moreover, the linkages of Japanese firms with their suppliers tend to be much less formal than those of their counterparts in the US or Europe. The auto component industry is also different in Japan from in the West. In Japan most auto assemblers buy from a range of relatively small specialist suppliers, some of whom may service only that company or a limited number of producers. In Europe and the US, the leading component manufacturers are likely to be as large as their customers, and will normally produce a wide variety of components for several firms. The relationship between the two groups of firms is very different, and the transaction costs of outside purchasing in Europe and the US are considerably higher than in Japan. One of the reasons why Japanese auto firms are encouraging their suppliers to follow them to Europe and the US is precisely to avoid some of the culturally related transaction costs they have to incur in dealing with indigenous suppliers (Okada, 1991).

Third, it is clear that both external production and transaction costs will depend on the stage of development and ESP configuration of the country concerned. In some developing countries, for example, foreign subsidiaries may have to engage in more manufacturing operations along the value-added chain than they would normally wish, simply because of the lack of an indigenous supply capability, or inadequate safeguards against the adverse effects of market failure. Surveys both on the determinants of the location of investment by MNEs (see Chapter 6) and on the competitiveness of nations (Porter, 1990) have frequently stressed the importance of good infrastructural facilities and the presence of related or support industries. This is especially the case in some of the technologically advanced industries, which are critically dependent on the availability of highly skilled labour and good quality components and parts. Certainly, the relative L advantage Scotland has had (cf, for example, South Wales) in attracting new Japanese and US investment in the industrial electronics industry has helped to attract a cluster of component suppliers and a skilled labour force, which has further improved its locational attractiveness.

Fourth, government policy may also affect the 'make or buy' decision of MNEs. In pursuance of import substitution policies, governments sometimes offer inducements to foreign-based component manufacturers to invest in their countries. Sometimes financial and other inducements are also provided to domestic component producers to improve their supply capabilities.[3] In the past, however, the main instrument used by governments – particularly those of developing countries – to assist local suppliers has been to limit imports of competitive components and raw materials. While this has sometimes forced both domestic and foreign-owned companies to buy products they could not economically produce themselves or buy from local firms, in other cases it has deterred new investment in the purchasing sectors altogether.

16.2.4   The 'import or procure locally' decision

The previous section has discussed the choice open to a foreign-owned affiliate as to whether it produces intermediate products or buys them from outside firms in that country. In both instances, value is added in the country, although *a priori* it cannot be said which of the two is the preferred option. There is, of course, another alternative open to the affiliate, *viz* whether to import the product or buy or make it in the country in which it operates.

Imports may be sourced either from other parts of the MNE, that is, from the parent company or a sister affiliate, or from independent foreign sellers. In some cases, the parent company of the affiliates might purchase intermediate products on behalf of its affiliates. If the affiliates are billed by the parent company for these products, these are also classified as intra-firm imports.

Left to its own devices, an affiliate, like any other firm, will procure its intermediate products from the cheapest and most reliable source, that is, where the purchase price plus transaction costs are the least. In the case of imports (whether intra- or inter-firm) additional transaction costs may be involved. *Inter alia* these include longer delivery schedules, higher transport and inventory costs, increased search, negotiating and monitoring costs, and a possibility of supply disruptions from shipping delays and dock strikes, etc. Some of these costs may be reduced by the parent company (or sister affiliates) internalizing cross-border markets. However, others, such as disruptions to supply flows brought about by exogenous events, will remain.

Some intermediate products will be acquired on the open market at world prices or bought from external subcontractors at negotiated prices. Others may be supplied or procured by the parent company or one of its affiliates. Such purchases are particularly likely in the case of idiosyncratic inputs in which foreign suppliers have a unique competitive advantage, where the parent company can monitor quality and prices, where marginal costs are less than average costs, where there are economies of bulk purchase, and where a parent company may wish to use its intra-group transactions for transfer price manipulation. There may be other reasons why the parent company should wish to buy inputs for its affiliates (Jenkins, 1987b). Some of these are likely to lower the transaction costs of affiliates, for example, where the parent company crates a set of components and sends them to its affiliates. Others, while benefiting the parent company, may not be as welcomed by the host country, particularly if the internal transfer price of the input improperly reflects its real opportunity cost.

Again, the proportion of imported intermediate products will be both product and country specific. It will also vary according to the sourcing strategy of the investing company (e.g. the extent to which it engages in single or multiple sourcing), the product's marketing performance and the age of the affiliate. Previous chapters[4] have shown that most market-seeking FDI begins with the newly established affiliates undertaking simple finishing operations and importing most of their upstream intermediate products. Gradually, as and when indigenous technological and productive capacity and the prices of indigenous intermediate products become more competitive,[5] the local content ratio will increase. This is entirely confirmed by the data. In 1988, Japanese manufacturing affiliates in Europe imported 37.2% of the value of their components; this compared with a foreign procurement ratio of 52.6% at the start of their European operation (JETRO, 1989). In 1987, the first year Nissan began its operations in the UK, only 40% of the sales value of the car was produced locally; by the end of 1991 the local content ratio had risen to 75%. In the US in the mid 1980s, Japanese subsidiaries were found to import a higher proportion of their components from their home country than did European subsidiaries (Kotabe and Omura, 1989).[6]

An equally important variable is the nature of the FDI. Manufacturing affiliates established to undertake the labour-intensive operations of high technology products are likely to import most of their intermediate inputs from their parent companies or sister affiliates. Indeed, one of the concerns expressed about export processing zones is that they, like some of the natural resource-based investments which preceded them, are little more than export enclaves. Another is that the positive externalities of such investment are limited as foreign affiliates purchase few of their inputs from domestic firms and do nothing to upgrade indigenous manpower. By contrast, in large industrialized economies, MNEs may be fully integrated into the national value-added chain, producing or buying all their intermediate products, including R&D and professional services, from domestic sources.

In several developing countries, however, the evidence suggests that, over the past two decades at least, the most important determinant of the purchasing propensities of both foreign- and domestically-owned firms is the government's development strategy – and its ability to implement such a strategy successfully. In the 1960s and 1970s, many governments in Latin America, Asia and Africa vigorously restricted the import of intermediate products required by foreign affiliates, except where it could be shown that these could not be produced locally. While raising the local content ratio, this policy also frequently increased the costs of production, especially where domestic firms were protected from external competition.

The economic rationale for such a policy was clear and, on the face of it, quite plausible. With larger markets, increasing technical competence and greater experience, local suppliers would eventually become competitive with their foreign rivals, especially if foreign affiliates could help them to achieve these goals. And, in certain cases (e.g. Japan, Taiwan and South Korea), it would be difficult to argue that, in their early stages of industrialization (see Chapter 10), protectionism did not help infant industries to survive and prosper. In others, however, where the ESP configuration of a country was inappropriate to the production of the intermediate products, the pressure on firms to use local suppliers has often impeded the upgrading of quality standards and the innovation of more efficient production methods. This, in turn, has reduced the ability of the purchasing firms to penetrate international markets and slowed the pace of economic development. Although, in the short run, there may be some merit in protecting domestic suppliers or assisting them to become economically viable, in the long run, domestic linkages along a value-added chain are only desirable in so far as they help the producing firms to be more competitive in world markets.

16.2.5   Do MNEs buy more or less than indigenous firms from local suppliers?

Market-seeking MNE affiliates

There have been several kinds of empirical studies of the sourcing strategies of multinational affiliates and their indigenous competitors. The first of these concerns the procurement policies of market-seeking foreign investors. One of the earliest and most carefully documented investigations was that under-taken by Sanjaya Lall for the UNCTC, who examined the sourcing strategies of foreign affiliates in the auto industry in India, Peru and Morocco (Lall, 1980; UNCTC, 1981). He found that in India in 1977, two companies, Ashok-Leyland (AL), 60% owned by British Leyland and 40% by Tata Engineering and Locomotive Company (Telco),[7] accounted for the lion's share of commercial vehicle production. In that same year, the local content of the sales of both companies was extremely high – 94% in the case of AL and 95% in the case of Telco. However, over the previous 24 years, this ratio had increased from 35% in the case of AL and 45% in the case of Telco.

Lall argued that Indian government policy was the key variable in affecting the extent and pace of local procurement, by both firms, along with the size of the domestic market and the level of industrial development. He did not consider that the owner-ship of the companies was an important determinant of the 'import or buy locally' decision. In another part of his study, he found that the same factors also helped to explain differences in the local content ratio of automobile suppliers (all of whom were foreign subsidiaries) in Peru (35% in 1979) and Morocco (15% in 1979) (UNCTC, 1981, p. 33).

Turning to the 'make or buy' decision, Lall discovered that there were rather more differences in the percentage of materials, components and parts contracted out by the two Indian-based firms. In 1976–77, AL and Telco spent 59% and 35%, respectively, of their gross revenue on bought-out materials and parts. In examining the reasons for this difference, however, Lall concluded that the foreign ownership effect was not a major factor. Much more important was the fact that Telco was situated in an area with less developed supplier capabilities and operated its own foundry, whereas AL was in a district with good support industries and did not own its forge (UNCTC, 1980). At the same time, Telco's original collaborator (Daimler Benz) was much more integrated than AL's UK owner. Thus, there was also an historical reason for the different pro-curement strategies of the two firms.

A related study on the auto industry in Nigeria was carried out in 1985 by James Landi. Using a similar methodology to that of the UNCTC and Lall (1980), Landi (1986) found that foreign affiliates were more integrated and had a higher propensity to import their intermediate products than their indigenous counterparts. The same conclusion was reached by McAleese and McDonald (1978) and Jo (1980) in their evaluations of the import propensities of foreign affiliates in Ireland and South Korea. However, in both cases the extent of the difference varied between sectors and according to the age, experience and size of the foreign affiliates.[8] A later study by Kumar (1990), using multi-variate regres-sion analysis, showed that, compared with their indigenous competitors, the degree of vertical integra-tion by MNE affiliates in 49 Indian industries in 1980–81 was significantly higher than that of their indigenous competitors, even though both groups of firms displayed about the same import propensities.

By contrast, in a comparison of foreign- and domestically-owned firms in the Brazilian electrical industry, Newfarmer and Marsh (1981b) demon-strated that the degree of vertical integration was negatively correlated to the degree of foreign ownership; this was later confirmed by Willmore (1986).

Further analysis of some of the factors influenc-ing the extent to which foreign subsidiaries engage in local subcontracting is contained in surveys by Halbach (1988) for the ILO, and by the UNCTC

(1992c) on FDI in Mexico. The survey by Halbach (1988) made a detailed analysis of the sourcing policies of 112 foreign subsidiaries in six manufacturing sectors and in several developing countries. The overwhelming conclusion of the research was that the amount of subcontracting undertaken depended, first, on the level of the indigenous technology and the skill of the local labour force, and second, on the strategies pursued by host governments. The survey revealed major differences in the extent of subcontracting by foreign subsidiaries according to industry[9] and their experience of operating in the host countries. Import-substituting affiliates were found to generate considerably more inter-industry linkages than export-oriented affiliates. Larger subsidiaries tended to be more vertically integrated than smaller subsidiaries. Subsidiaries located in Asia or Latin America showed the greatest propensity to local subcontracting and those in Africa the least propensity.

The survey of the UNCTC (UN, 1992d) sought to examine the subcontracting practices of 63 foreign affiliates in Mexico. It confirmed many of the findings of the Lall and Halbach surveys. In addition, it emphasized that the role of sourcing obligations placed on the firms by host governments were strongly industry specific. A particularly interesting conclusion of the research was that 28.8% of the firms questioned indicated that their principal motive for engaging in subcontracting was to reduce the number of components they produced in house, whereas 23.0% cited the need to reduce production costs, and 13.5% to take advantage of the greater flexibility of small and medium sized enterprises as suppliers.

This and other fragmentary data on the backward vertical linkages established by market-seeking foreign-owned firms in developing countries tend to suggest four main conclusions:

(1) MNE affiliates have established few linkages in small or industrially backward economies, mainly because of an inadequate subcontracting infrastructure in these countries.

(2) The percentage of subcontracting by MNE affiliates is positively correlated both to the sophistication of the industrial infrastructure of the host country and the length of time the affiliates have been operating.

(3) In larger and more advanced developing economies, MNE affiliates have often forged substantial linkages, but often only as a result of government import restrictions and the imposition of local performance requirements.

(4) As a result of such government policies, the linkages established have often been excessively costly and uneconomic (Little *et al.*, 1970).

Export-oriented manufacturing affiliates

A second group of studies has been concerned with the linkages established by foreign-owned firms in export-oriented manufacturing industries. Early research (Reuber *et al.*, 1973) has noted that the backward linkages formed by non-resident investors in these sectors were far fewer than in the case of import-substituting affiliates. Also, by far the larger proportion of their purchases of intermediate products were imported – often directly from their parent companies. In their study of the consumer electronics industry in South East Asia, Lim and Pang (1982) found that these linkages were 'non-existent' in Malaysia and 'miniscule' in Singapore. Yet five years later, another survey of 30 electronics foreign affiliates in Singapore revealed that, on average, they bought out 58% of their intermediate goods and services from local suppliers, and that indigenous (i.e. Singaporean) and smaller foreign firms made the most prolific use of such services (Lim and Pang, 1982). Today (in 1992) Singapore is a high tech hub of a regionally integrated electronics industry. It is providing technical support, material inputs, marketing and other services for MNE subsidiaries elsewhere in Asia. Singapore is now the world's fifth largest semiconductor producer; both foreign and domestic producers are engaging in innovatory and design-related activities (Lim and Pang, 1991).

The findings of the earlier Lim and Pang study also seem to conflict with those of a survey by UNCTAD (1975) on the electronics industry in South East Asia, which concluded that 'a whole network of small manufacturing had been set up as a result of backward linkages created by foreign investors'. Evans *et al.* (1979), on the other hand, argued that local linkages established by foreign-owned firms in the Latin American textiles and clothing industries had diminished over the years as a result of the demand by richer countries for better quality textiles, which the latter were in a better position to supply.

The sensitivity of the results of econometric analysis to the size and composition of the sample firms and the statistical methodology used is well demonstrated by two studies on the performance of foreign and domestic firms in the Santa Cruz Electronics Export Processing Zone (SEEPZ) in India. The first, by Subramaniam and Pillai (1972), showed that the value-added component in the export of five Indian firms was significantly better than that of eleven foreign-owned firms over the period 1966–77. In their attempt to normalize for size of units, the authors used the share of value added of the cluster of firms to which the unit belonged. Imports of plant and machinery were excluded from their calculations and no attempt was made to account for net inventories when estimating gross value added. Firms that recorded negative value added were excluded. A later study by Kumar (1987a), which embraced 21 foreign-owned and 16 Indian firms over the years 1966–82, and used employment-weighted value-added estimates (which also allowed firms with negative value added to be included in the sample), found that the former (particularly those which had a majority foreign equity stake) recorded a significantly higher value added to export ratios than the latter.

All these studies confirm that the key variables influencing the propensity of both foreign and domestic firms to source locally are the types of products supplied, the quality of local supporting industries and government policy. For example, within the electronics sector the nature of the production process, the complexity of the technology, the opportunities for scale economies and the rapidity with which changes in technology or customer preferences take place, have all led to more inter-firm linkages, mainly, it seems, because purchasing firms prefer to devote their own resources to technology development and marketing efforts rather than to backward integration. Moreover, as Lall (1980) has pointed out, affiliates that have evolved from import-substituting ventures to become important international exporters (e.g. Volkswagen in Brazil and Singer in Asia), and those producing traditional products (e.g. textiles, processed foods, footwear) for the domestic market are likely to establish more linkages with local subcontractors than those set up to service foreign markets.

In so far as foreign affiliates do behave differently from indigenous firms in their 'make or buy' and 'import or produce locally' decisions, it is likely to be for one of two reasons. The first is that they, or the MNE of which they are part, have better information about worldwide prices and quality of parts and components, and are able to acquire these intermediate products on more favourable terms. The second is that in the promotion of global objectives, MNEs choose to pursue distinctive procurement strategies.

Governments that pursue export-generating rather than import-substituting policies usually impose fewer controls on the sourcing arrangements of foreign affiliates. This is mainly because they perceive that unless such firms are free to obtain intermediate products on the best possible terms, their ability to export will be adversely affected. While Asian governments have done their best to encourage local sourcing by foreign-based firms, in the export-oriented sectors, at least, market forces have prevailed. Indeed, Lim and Pang (1982) argue that the development of local suppliers in South East Asia owes much to the encouragement and patronage of the MNEs themselves, who find it in their long-term interests to foster a strong indigenous capability. At the same time, because they are likely to be more specialized in their product or process structure and to be part of a cross-border network of activities, such affiliates may engage in a lower degree of vertical integration than their indigenous competitors. Certainly, Cohen (1975) found this to be so in the case of MNE affiliates in Taiwan, Singapore and South Korea.

The buyer-seller contracting relationship

A third group of researchers has been concerned with the impact of MNEs on their suppliers in host developed countries. Usually, their focus has been less on the extent and form and more on the *quality* of such linkages, particularly on the way in which they might aid or inhibit indigenous technological capabilities. This is the subject of Section 16.4 of this chapter.[10]

In recent years, however, the debate over 'make or buy' and/or 'import or produce locally' has become one of the central questions raised over the rapid penetration of Japanese MNEs into European and US industry. While such inward investment has been generally welcomed for the jobs it creates and the reduced dependence on Japanese imports, some concern has been expressed at the low local content of the output produced by Japanese affiliates, both of their purchases from local firms and their in-house production. This concern is well illustrated by the strenuous efforts made by the French authorities in 1988 to get the European Commission to treat a Nissan car exported from the UK to France as a Japanese rather than a European car. The pretext was that there was an unacceptable local (in this context local is EC) content in the British-made car (in this case 60%). In the event, the EC Commission rejected the appeal, but accusations that the Japanese simply undertake 'screwdriver' operations in the EC and the US still abound. What is the truth in this assertion?

Earlier in this chapter we argued that, in the case of import-substituting new investments, it was to be expected that greenfield foreign-owned ventures would initially only produce part of their output in the host country, but that, depending upon the extent and speed at which indigenous producers were able to meet the required purchasing standards at competitive prices, a higher proportion would be bought from them. This certainly occurred in the early days of American investment in Europe and the Japanese are following a similar path.

At the same time, the kind of sectors in which the Japanese are most active, *viz* motor vehicles and electronics, are those in which a substantial proportion of components and parts are bought out in Japan. It is also the case that Japanese MNEs follow a very different philosophy towards subcontracting than do their European and US counterparts. For example, in the European and US context the system of subcontracting is usually mono-layered and the transactions involved are market mediated and based on contractual relationships. By contrast, the Japanese system is pyramidal and multi-layered with the final assemblers at the top of the pyramid being served by primary (first tier) subcontractors, which, in turn, are supported by their own cohorts of secondary (second tier) subcontractors. At the very bottom of the pyramid are many thousands of cottage-type, family-owned and operated small production units. In addition, the relationship between buyers and sellers,

in this filial network of related activities, is of a long-term nature and is based less on an explicit legal contract than on informal inter-firm (often inter-personal) relationships, which have been cultivated over a period of time, and built on mutual trust, forbearance and cooperation (Ozawa, 1991). Indeed, one of the very specific O advantages of Japanese MNEs in the car and electronics sectors is their ability to gain and integrate new knowledge (e.g. on the design and engineering of components and parts) acquired from their suppliers into their own products and production processes (Okada, 1991).

Finally, all the evidence (e.g. JETRO, 1989, 1990) suggests that Japanese MNE affiliates have very stringent expectancies of their subcontractors. Indeed, the zero defect concept begins with the supplier meeting the price, specification and delivery standards set by the purchasers. For these reasons, it is understandable that the local value added might be initially lower than in the case of *de novo* indigenous firms. However, *inter alia* because of their sensitivity to the criticism levelled against them, not to mention tough bargaining by host governments on local content requirements, it is noteworthy that within a comparatively short period of time, the local content ratio, which often starts about 35%, increases to 60% and then to 80%.

In an analysis of some 277 main products manufactured by Japanese affiliates in Western Europe in 1989, it was found that the local content ratio had risen from 44.7% when production first began (mostly in the late 1970s or early 1980s), to 67.2% in 1989 (JETRO, 1990). In 1984, only 23% of these same affiliates had used European subcontractors; by 1989, this proportion had risen to 52%.[11] The main reasons given for these improved ratios were:

(1) the quality of locally-produced materials, parts and components had been improved,

(2) the local manufacturing capabilities for materials, parts and components had been substantially expanded,

(3) reduced price of these inputs, because *inter alia* of increased volume of orders,

(4) a shortening of, and/or greater reliability in keeping to, delivery dates (JETRO, 1990).[12]

However, in a globally-integrated economy, it would be surprising if the import content of sales of MNE subsidiaries was not quite high. What is important is not the import content *per se*, but the total value of the net output generated per resource used. Indeed, in the UK, Nissan already has a higher domestic content than Vauxhall (a US subsidiary), while over the period 1960–80, UK-owned motor vehicle firms increased their imports of components from the rest of the EC.

Backward linkages into the primary product sector

A fourth group of studies has examined the backward linkages created by MNE affiliates in the primary product sector. It is often argued that foreign firms in this sector – especially the oil and hard mineral companies – create few vertical linkages with local producers as they import most of their inputs from their parent companies (or countries), and export their output in its raw state for processing in other (and usually their home) countries. A number of empirical studies have measured the extent of backward linkages from such enclaves using the concept of retained value (Mikesell, 1970; Jenkins, 1987). The generally accepted definition of Retained Value (RV) is:

$$RV = W + L + P + T$$

where:

W   local wages of the foreign affiliate
L   local inputs
P   profits accruing to local shareholders
T   local taxes.

By expressing retained value as a percentage of the value of exports of foreign affiliates, it is possible to get some idea of the contribution of those affiliates to local value added. If the percentage is low, then the foreign affiliates may be viewed as export enclaves. This situation is illustrated by early years of oil and mineral investments in less developed countries. For example, in the late 1920s, the RV ratio of foreign affiliates in Chilean copper mines was as low as 17% (Mamalakis, 1970 in Jenkins). However, by 1950 the RV ratio had risen to 50%. Mikesell (1970) estimated that, in the mid 1960s, the RV ratios in mineral and petroleum industries in various developing countries was averaging between 60% and 70%. Later estimates by Brown and McKern put the proportion of bauxite processed to the first stage of aluminium product in 1982 as 55%;

the corresponding figures were 81% for copper and 38% for iron. Most of the tin mined in Bolivia and South East Asia is also processed locally.

Among the many reasons cited for the reduction in the processing gap (UNIDO, 1980), perhaps the most important are the indigenization of many mineral sectors, the increase in taxation levied on the profits of foreign corporations, the reduction of tariffs on imports of processed metal, the considerable improvement in the local technological infrastructure and developmental capabilities, the development of energy saving processing methods, and the tighter environmental controls imposed by developed countries over processing activities (Radetzi, 1977; McKern, 1992). However, efforts by primary producers to develop secondary processing have not always been successful. Sometimes this is because of the inadequacy of local complementary resources and capabilities (e.g. energy and trained technologists, engineers and managers) and sometimes because it is not perceived to advance the global strategic interests of the investing companies. Sometimes it reflects the failure of government to devise the right kinds of incentives to encourage MNEs to set up local processing operations. In Ghana, for example, several successive governments have sought to establish an integrated aluminium industry with little success (UNCTC, 1987).

Moreover, technological developments do not always operate to the benefit of the primary producing countries. In the copper industry, for example, new technology has made continuous-cast copper rod a major product, but producers in developing countries have so far been unable to build the rod plants to produce this product. As a result, the state copper companies in Chile, Zaire and Zambia have all concluded joint ventures with European TNCs for the establishment of continuous-cast rod plants in Europe (UNCTC, 1987).

In the agribusiness sector, the degree of local processing rests mainly on the nature of the product and the access of producer countries to the markets of the developed countries. Such access, through the reduction of some tariff barriers and a variety of preference schemes, has improved marginally over the past two decades, leading to more local processing, packaging and branding of local tea and coffee products.[13] The updating of local skills and capabilities – sometimes by the MNEs themselves – has also advanced the secondary processing of sugar, cotton and tobacco products. Several MNEs are also actively involved in shrimp farming and experimental aquaculture in Latin America and South East Asia (Hauge, 1991).

At the same time, government policies in support of local processing have been stepped up in various countries and sectors. For example, the Brazilian government has helped to promote the development of a soluble coffee industry while the Sudanese, Indian, Tanzanian and Mexican authorities (to name just a few) have encouraged the growth and upgrading of their domestic textile sectors (UNCTC, 1987).

Backward linkages by multinational service producers

The fifth type of backward linkage, which requires some attention, is that of multinational service producers, notably trading and agribusiness companies and hotel chains. Over their long history the Japanese Soga Sosha have both invested in foreign primary and secondary value-added activities and have concluded long-term contracts with foreign producers. Multinational buying groups from Europe and the US also account for a sizable proportion of the exports of consumer electronics, cameras, textiles and clothing and leather goods produced in the Far East. One estimate, made in 1977 by the Netherlands Research Institute, was that 70% of all Hong Kong exports of clothing then passed through Western retail traders and import merchants (quoted in Dunning, 1981b).

In agribusiness, there is ample documentation that the large multinational food processing firms, such as United Fruit, Libby, Del Monte and Unilever, have dramatically affected the pattern and development of the tropical fruit, vegetable oils and ground nut industries in several developing countries. In the international cotton trade it is estimated that 15 large trading companies control 80% to 90% of the globally-traded cotton. Similarly, three MNEs control 60% of the world's imports of bananas (UNCTC, 1987). We shall discuss some of the implications of this concentration of buying power in the next section.

In tourism, too, the demand for furniture and fittings and foodstuffs by MNE associated hotels, and that for souvenirs by the foreign tourist, has also made a big impact on local craft and agricultural sectors in some tourist-dependent economies (e.g. the Bahamas, Seychelles, Fiji and Morocco) as well as in parts of larger developing countries, such as Mexico, Indonesia and Kenya (UNCTC, 1982).

16.2.6   The influence on the producing capacity and productivity of suppliers

As important as any impact that foreign affiliates have on their suppliers as a result of the *quantity* of output they buy, is their impact on the *quality* of output and the efficiency with which it is supplied. Indeed, where the activities of foreign affiliates substitute for those of their indigenous competitors, this will be their only impact. It is perfectly reasonable to expect that at least some of the O-specific advantages of MNEs will have to do with their knowledge about the latest product and production techniques and/or about the sourcing of raw materials, components and parts. These are usually readily transferable to their foreign subsidiaries, giving them a competitive edge *vis à vis* indigenous producers.

The literature (see, especially, Lall, 1980; UNCTC, 1981; Halbach, 1988) identifies nine main types of linkages which purchasing or 'lead' enterprises (be they foreign or domestically owned) may form with their suppliers. These are:

(1) **Information linkages**: These include exchanges of information on market characteristics and trends, on future investment intentions, on host government regulations, and on foreign suppliers of machinery, parts, materials and components. Information might also be provided to the suppliers, by the parent company of the MNE, about local firms with whom joint ventures or non-equity collaborative agreements might be concluded (see also (5)).

(2) **Technical assistance**: This includes help given or received on such matters as innovation and product design, proprietary product specifications, development processes, factory layout, tooling, quality control, labour training, inventory management, machine maintenance,

inspection and testing procedures and so on. It might also include the provision of used machinery and specialized tools and equipment.

(3) **Financial assistance**: This may embrace repayable loans or concessional contributions to the subcontractor's risk capital, terms, grants, prefinancing of machinery and tools, and special price agreements, and financial help to local suppliers in visiting their opposite numbers in the home country of the parent company.

(4) **Procurement assistance**: This covers help, other than noted in (1), to suppliers in obtaining capital equipment, raw materials and other intermediate products at competitive prices. In some cases, the affiliates' suppliers might receive direct assistance from the suppliers of their parent company.

(5) **Location**: This includes advice given to potential suppliers (particularly those of foreign origin) on the siting of a new plant or an existing establishment. For example, Japanese auto-assemblers in the US and UK have provided information and suggested the names of suitable contacts to the component suppliers of their parent company in case the former might set up or acquire producing facilities in the US and UK.

(6) **Managerial and organizational assistance**: This includes help given on a range of financial, accounting and general managerial control procedures.

(7) **Pricing assistance**: This covers technical advice about the costing of products; and of contractual and bargaining procedures in order to determine prices.

(8) **Other assistance**: This includes helping suppliers to obtain sales to third parties in the open market; assistance in exporting to markets, which are familiar to the MNE; advice on diversification strategies, dealing with foreign suppliers, etc.

In a perfectly functioning intermediate product market, there would be no need for firms to establish any of these linkages. In the real world of market failure, however, enterprises are faced with various kinds of transaction costs, which they perceive they can best circumvent by concluding a variety of formal or informal collaborative arrangements with their suppliers. The precise forms of these arrangements may vary in their content, scope and terms. At the one extreme, as illustrated by many Japanese firms, the supplier, to all intents and purposes, is regarded as a member of the family of the purchasing firm. At the other, the relationship is confined to a formal agreement between the two parties about the specification of the products to be provided and the terms of their supply.

Quite naturally, the dominant question of interest to host countries is the extent to which foreign affiliates are better able to overcome vertical market failure by the arrangements they make with their suppliers, than can indigenous firms. Here the evidence is mixed. On the one hand, the existing relationships which MNEs may have with suppliers in other countries (including their home country) might make them less inclined to establish new linkages, especially where the initial transaction costs of setting up these arrangements are high. On the other, they may welcome some additional diversification in their sourcing strategies (Kotabe and Omura, 1989). As we have already seen, they do have the knowledge, information and finance to either upgrade the quality of many of their suppliers' products and production methods, or to put them in touch with firms that can do this. Where the improvement of local supply capability is critical to the competitiveness of the purchasing company, and where external contracting is considered superior to either importing the product or internal production, then it may pay the company to invest resources in upgrading the efficiency of its suppliers.

In fact, over the years, this is what many multinational affiliates have done. Indeed, their ability to seek out and obtain superior quality supplies at lower prices is, itself, a competitive advantage. From the recipient country's viewpoint, the findings of a large number of studies over the past 30 years are virtually unanimous that the presence of foreign-owned firms has helped raise the standards and productivity of many domestic suppliers, and that this has often had beneficial spillover effects on the rest of their operations.[14] Almost universally, suppliers have acknowledged that their foreign customers have been more demanding in their specifications and tougher in their price negotiations and delivery targets, while being more generous in their assistance and advice.

Early research by Dunning (1958), Safarian (1966) and Brash (1966) into the operation of US affiliates in British, Canadian and Australian manufacturing industry all pointed to their having substantial linkages of the kind identified above, and particularly in areas 1, 2, 4, 6 and 8. In the majority of cases, these were perceived to work to the advantage of the suppliers, but some concerns were expressed. To quote from the conclusions of the earliest of these studies, which was based on interviews within some 45 UK suppliers of intermediate products to US affiliates:

> 'Of the forty-five component and raw material suppliers which gave us information, fourteen thought there was no reason to distinguish American owned affiliated firms from any other of their British customers. The majority, however, noted such a difference. Sixteen felt that the former's purchasing thoroughness had been to their ultimate benefit in some way or another though ten argued that too many unnecessarily rigid and impractical demands were made of them. Twenty-nine considered that some specific gain in the form of materials formulae, manufacturing or processing methods and machinery design, etc. had been acquired, and one-half of these that the knowledge in question had been applied in other directions. Twenty-eight thought that the demands of US firms had stimulated the application of new knowledge from which other, e.g. British owned, companies were now benefiting; twenty-six suppliers had visited their counterparts, or the parent companies of their US customers in America, and of them seven had subsequently concluded licensing agreements.' (Dunning, 1958, p. 224)

The findings have been echoed in numerous other surveys, notably Reuber (1973), UNCTC (1981), JETRO (1990) and Halbach (1988). However, the extent and form of the affiliations vary with the form of the investment (Lall, 1978), the size and nationality of the investing companies (Kotabe and Omura, 1989), the host country in which the investment is made, the nature of the product and the value-adding process involved (Dunning, 1986a), the age and experience of the purchasing affiliate, the characteristics of the supplying firms and the sourcing strategies of the parent company of the affiliate.

In a 1978 survey of 52 foreign affiliates and 32 Brazilian firms, which were among the top 500 manufacturing companies in Brazil, Goncalves (1986) found that normalizing for size and industrial sector there was little evidence to suggest that the former provided more technical assistance to their suppliers than the latter. In his analysis of Swedish MNE subsidiaries in India, Jansson (1982) found that the main form of knowledge transfer to their suppliers took the form of product know-how rather than process know-how. In a broader study of 112 foreign affiliates, Halbach (1988) established that the most frequent type of assistance given to subcontractors was in the supply of blueprints and support in technical production and quality-control procedures. In the food industry, however, more widespread guidance was provided in the procurement of raw materials, the purchasing of machinery and general management assistance. Financial assistance was mainly confined to the pre-payment of placed orders.

In a study of Mexican subcontracting (UNCTC, 1991a) the authors found that 86.5% of the affiliates provided some training in quality control and 67.6% gave other forms of technical assistance. Financial assistance was again limited, except in the food, beverages and computer sectors. The survey also showed that subsidiaries with a majority foreign equity stake provided substantially more technical and financial assistance than those with a minority foreign equity stake, and that the assistance was most marked in the food and beverages, and technologically advanced sectors.

At the same time, technological imperatives, regional integration and the globalization of markets are introducing new nuances into both the 'import or make locally' and the 'make internally or buy out' decisions (Kotabe and Omura, 1989). Increasingly, not only are governments being compelled to accept the fact that if their firms are to remain competitive in world markets, they must be allowed to buy their intermediate products from the cheapest and most reliable sources, but also that, as and when they establish custom unions or trading agreements, they abrogate their rights to influence the 'import or make locally' choice.

At the same time, as purchasing firms pursue more supra-national and/or centralized sourcing strategies, their component suppliers may follow in their wake. Sometimes this might mean that when a firm goes abroad its suppliers will follow. In other cases the suppliers might, themselves, take the initiative by engaging in FDI or pursuing a more global integrated marketing strategy. In the past, service companies (e.g. banks, insurance companies, accountants, advertising agencies and management consultancies) have followed their customers overseas. Indeed, the ability to offer their multinational customers a global network of capabilities and services is one of the O-specific advantages claimed by the large advertising, market research, professional service and hotel MNEs (Dunning, 1989).

More recently, Japanese auto component producers have set up (or acquired) manufacturing facilities in the EC or US, or have concluded joint ventures with EC and US companies to supply Japanese assembling affiliates with intermediate products previously supplied from Japan. Moreover, they have often done so with financial or other help from the assemblers.[15] In the US, at the end of 1989, the 300 or so Japanese-owned auto component suppliers accounted for around one-half of the local purchases of Japanese auto affiliates. Some of these firms are, themselves, part of the same Keiretsu, and are set up to supply the local and regional markets with at least some intermediate products.[16] The extent to which these suppliers displace the output of their indigenous competitors will influence their contribution to the GNP. Here, as earlier chapters[17] have explained, there could be a tradeoff between increased efficiency of production and reduced innovatory capacity. However, much again depends upon what would have happened in the absence of the inbound investment.

The point worth emphasizing, however, is that the sourcing strategies of MNEs and their affiliates are becoming increasingly internationalized, both because of the global manufacturing and marketing strategies of such companies, and because the intermediate product suppliers are themselves becoming MNEs, or are engaging in cross-border alliances. Moreover, there is increasing evidence of MNEs pursuing multiple sourcing strategies and of the cross-border standardization of intermediate products (Kotabe and Omura, 1989). In consequence, the 'make locally or import' and 'make internally or buy out' decisions – and the forms of relationships between buyers and sellers, both within

and between countries – are becoming increasingly blurred and difficult to disentangle.

We would make one other point. This stems from the observed differences in the relationships established between industrial companies and their suppliers (particularly their equipment suppliers) in different countries. A case in point is the very different procedures adopted between US and Japanese semiconductor producers and their equipment suppliers (Stowsky, 1987). In the former case, the chip-makers pursue an arm's length relationship and are critically dependent on the equipment firms for information on how best to utilize the machines they buy. In the latter, the Japanese firms encourage a filial relationship between themselves and their equipment suppliers. Design, innovation and learning processes characteristic of equipment development are shared between producer and user, and in so doing, the skills and capabilities of each are enhanced. The interesting question is the extent to which these two transactional philosophies, which essentially reflect the different business cultures of the countries concerned, can be transferred to other countries. If, for example, Japanese semiconductor firms can successfully implant their purchasing techniques into an American culture, this could radically affect the innovating capabilities of the US equipment producers.

Turning once again to the contribution of MNEs to the quality of linkages established in developing countries, we would observe this has been most marked in the agricultural sector – particularly on firms supplying plantation crops, such as pineapples, bananas, tobacco, tea and coffee, as well as on those engaged in contract–production arrangements, such as the supply of dairy products, vegetables, poultry and pigs. There is considerable evidence of the role which the multinational processing companies have played in providing information, advice and credit to their suppliers (UNCTC, 1987; Oman, 1989). Such guidance and information extends to growing techniques, the introduction of new crops or strains, the establishment and explanation of quality standards, and even the choice of land and the scheduling of harvest to minimize crop spoilage. Financial help includes the provision of capital for seeds and seedlings, loans for capital equipment, and credit to hire labour to clear, irrigate or drain land. Oman (1989, p. 260) gives some examples of 'spectacular increases in production and productivity levels' as a result of MNE-related activity in Latin America.

In some cases, because of the transaction costs involved in contractual arrangements, notably those to do with quality control and delivery reliability, the multinational processing firms prefer to internalize the markets for their primary products. In others, buyers and sellers may be bonded by less legalistic ties, *viz* trust, kinship, custom, a history of mutual reciprocity and accommodation and so on.

We would make one final observation. For the most part, this section has concentrated on the impact of MNEs on linkages with their suppliers within countries which are host to its affiliates. However, the creation and sustenance of similar linkages in home countries may be no less important for the competitiveness of the purchasing firms. This, of course, is not an MNE-specific issue. Nevertheless, since MNEs have a much greater flexibility in their sourcing strategies than their uninational counterparts,[18] the ESP configuration and, in particular, the competitiveness of related and supporting industries, is likely to play a more decisive role in fashioning the locational decision of such companies.

16.3 DOWNSTREAM LINKAGES: LINKAGES WITH CUSTOMERS

16.3.1 Some general observations

The linkages established between the affiliates of MNEs and their business customers may also affect the latters' competitiveness and innovatory capacities. These effects will depend, first, on the output produced by the affiliate and, second, on the proportion of this latter amount which is sold to external buyers rather than used by the affiliates for further value-adding activity. As in the case of backward integration, these magnitudes will vary between countries, sectors and firms, as well as over time.

Some of these reasons for forward linkages, as well as particularly those to do with the 'make or sell' decision, are similar to those of backward linkages, although the nature of the costs and benefits of internalized and external transactions may be different. For example, the assurance of markets and the maintenance of quality control are the major

motives for most kinds of forward integration. Moreover, while MNEs will normally sell their finished products whenever and wherever it is profitable to do so, in cases where the quality and price of subsequent downstream value-adding activities are likely to rebound on their own reputation, they may well wish to own their wholesale or retail outlets. Obvious cases include the location and ownership of sales and after-sales servicing, maintenance and repair facilities.

There are several kinds of forward linkages which multinational affiliates may forge with their customers. Those most commonly discussed in the literature are:

(1) The secondary processing of primary value-added activities, such as agribusiness, oil refining and metal production.

(2) Linkages established with industrial buyers of technically complicated products (where, for example, advice on how to use and maintain machinery and equipment may be valuable in influencing the products' value to the buyer).

(3) Linkages established with marketing outlets where, for example, the affiliates may provide information and offer functional guidance about the technical characteristics and usage of the products being sold and their 'software' and servicing requirements. Examples include motor vehicles, domestic electrical appliances and agricultural machinery, as well as, in the 1980s and 1990s, home computer systems.

In fact, although there is a good deal of the kind of linkages fashioned by multinational affiliates with their customers, there has been little substantive research work on this or on the extent to which such linkages are unique to MNEs. One exception is in the secondary processing of minerals and agricultural products, which we will deal with later. Chapters 4 and 5 have cited examples of the reasons why exporting companies might wish to possess their own marketing and distribution networks. Indeed, one of the earliest examples of a manufacturer integrating forward into retail sales and post-sales servicing was that of the Singer Sewing Machine Company, which did so because it was not confident that independent retailers could provide its customers with the service Singer felt they merited (Davies, 1969).

Dunning (1958) gave several other examples of the way in which US firms helped their customers make the best use of their products. He quoted the case of the British United Shoe Machinery Company which set up a shoe factory organization department in 1920 to advise its industrial customers on the layout of machinery and the introduction of production control systems (Dunning, 1958, p. 268). He also found that US affiliates were more apt to provide training facilities for their customers and for their customers' staff than were their domestic competitors. In the auto industry, the Ford Motor Company has helped to introduce new service techniques and upgrade the efficiency of their dealers (Dunning, 1958, p. 270).

There is much other casual evidence which supports the proposition that foreign affiliates maintain close linkages with their industrial users. However, it is dangerous to conclude that such linkages arise exclusively from the foreignness of the supplying company, although undoubtedly this is true to some extent. One of the advantages of inward investment is that it may bring with it management techniques and production processes which have proved successful when implemented elsewhere in the world. As we have stressed before, at least the larger and more efficient indigenous firms in developed countries should be aware of the competitive advantages associated with those linkages. This is especially the case in the industrialized nations, where the competitors to foreign affiliates are, themselves, international companies. Nevertheless, the evidence, scattered as it is, does suggest that by helping to raise the standards of downstream activities of both intermediate and final consumers, foreign firms have gained a good reputation. Again, this may be partly because they are accustomed to such standards in their home countries, and partly because they perceive that, by upgrading the quality of the output of their industrial purchasers, they can create new O advantages for themselves. Repeatedly, the emphasis on downstream quality control by Japanese auto and electronics firms in the US and Europe confirms the sense of this strategy.[19]

16.3.2 Forward linkages in processing activities

We have suggested that, at least in the fabricating sectors of manufacturing industry, it is normal for 'greenfield' foreign affiliates initially to engage in downstream lower value activities, and then either backward vertically integrate into, or subcontract to local firms, the higher value activities. We have also asserted that in some cases, notably in the auto industry, the parts and components suppliers of the parent company – not to mention a range of service companies – might follow their customers overseas. One then has additional value added created in the local economy shared by both foreign affiliates and local firms.[20]

Similarly, the local value-added chain may be extended by forward linkages forged by MNEs in the primary sector. Thus, the development of an oil refining capacity by foreign affiliates may make possible a (downstream) petrochemicals industry, the output of which might be supplied by other foreign affiliates following in the wake of the oil refining companies, or by the oil refineries themselves, or by new linkages formed with local suppliers.

The extent to which downstream processing activities follow FDI in upstream activities depends on the configuration of country-, industry- and firm-specific characteristics. Many developing countries have asserted that in the nonrenewable resource and agricultural sectors, far from assisting the development of secondary processing activities, MNE activity has impeded it. This is because MNEs find that the marginal cost of undertaking the processing in their home countries is less than that in the host country plus or minus any differential in the cross-border costs of transporting the primary and the processed product. Even though the latter costs may fall as output rises, the setting up costs (including the training of local labour) are too much for the MNE to bear.

In this instance, there is considerable evidence on the extent to which foreign affiliates in the mineral and agricultural sectors engage in, or promote, local processing activities. In the early 1970s, for example, only about one-third of the non-fuel minerals extracted in developing countries were processed in these countries (Bossom and Varon, 1977). While, in 1975, some 39.2% of the copper extracted in the world originated from developing countries, these same countries accounted for only 19.2% of the refining capacity (UNCTC, 1978). A year later, the six largest bauxite/aluminium MNEs on average mined 42.2% of their bauxite in developing countries, but only 6.3% of the production of primary aluminium was supplied by these countries (UNCTC, 1981).

The amount of secondary processing of raw materials and agricultural commodities undertaken in developing countries is highly product and country specific. Several large developing countries, for example, Brazil, Indonesia, Thailand and Zimbabwe, operate tobacco processing plants. Rubber is processed in Malaysia, India and Nigeria, and there are several pineapple canning plants in Thailand and Kenya. There is a thriving cotton textile industry in many Asian, African and Latin American countries, not to mention some R&D, design and testing facilities in several of the larger developing countries (UNCTC, 1987). Moreover, while there is little processing of bananas, coffee or tea by MNEs, more developing countries are attempting to brand their products, while there is some R&D into growing techniques and new varieties of seeds and strains in the main producing areas (Oman, 1989). Frequently, the output of agribusiness foreign affiliates is auctioned at national or international markets, although these markets are frequently dominated by a handful of large multinational traders (UNCTC, 1987).

Variations in the degree of forward integration by MNEs partly reflect the strategy of individual firms and, in particular, their desire to exploit the economies of scale in the processing of primary products, their aversion to sinking large sums of capital into high risk countries and their desire to maintain maximum flexibility over their sourcing of inputs and their systems of production. Also, any savings in transport costs – at least, for raw materials and minerals that lose weight during the production process – and lower energy and labour costs are frequently outweighed by the lack of technological competence and internal transport facilities of the host countries, and the fact that most of the customers of downstream value activities are located in the developed countries.

The real issue, however, is the extent to which, by dint of their O-specific advantages, MNEs can and do promote more or fewer local value-added activities than indigenous firms. Also, where indigenous firms do not exist, how might foreign affiliates be encouraged to develop downstream activities where and when it is in the country's long-term economic interests. Here the evidence is mixed. In developed countries (e.g. Canada, Australia, West Germany and the UK), the presence and stimulus of foreign companies has generally helped promote the emergence and growth of such sectors as petrochemicals, plastics, auto and electrical components. In some developing countries, notably the Philippines, Malaysia, Thailand, Indonesia, Cameroon, and the Congo, fish, tropical fruit, palm oil, tobacco and timber processing have followed primary production (UNCTC, 1987). Bauxite (alumina) and phosphate processing plants have been set up in Jamaica by the leading alumina companies. By contrast, because of the high investment involved and the relatively low transportation costs of the end products, the oil majors are reluctant to establish petrochemical plants in developing countries. One exception is in Saudi Arabia where several MNE oil companies (including those from Korea and Taiwan) have formed joint ventures with SABIC – a local firm – to produce a range of bulk petrochemicals and thermoplastics (Oman, 1989).

In other countries, where the nonrenewable resources are exclusively owned by local firms or state corporations, MNEs have helped initiate secondary processing facilities. Often these developments have involved government assistance. In some cases this has been wisely given, for example, where it has been accompanied by appropriate training programmes and the setting up of 'clusters' of excellence. In others, this assistance has not had the intended effects simply because the necessary 'created' factor endowments for successful processing have not been available.

Historically, one of the main O advantages of MNEs in the primary goods sectors has been that of accessing foreign markets. To a large extent MNEs still control the main marketing and distribution channels for both non-renewable and renewable resources. In effect this also gives them control over the location of the downstream activities of primary production (e.g. the boxing and ripening of bananas, the smelting of tin and the processing of hardwoods). In some cases, this has worked to the benefit of the resource producing countries, while in others the dominant position of MNEs as intermediate purchasers in the supply chain has resulted in their maintaining established processing and distribution outlets. With the lack of local technological capacity, or even the capability to absorb imported technology, it is difficult for local processors to break into the market. Where they have succeeded, as in the case of South Eastern log producers, this has usually been achieved by the formation of a producers' or exporters' association which has provided some degree of countervailing power against the large international buyers (McKern, 1993).

16.4   THE NETWORKING OF VERTICAL LINKAGES

MNEs will form external linkages with suppliers and customers whenever it is profitable to do so. In some sectors, the value-added *chain* is better perceived as a value-added *network* of activities. Thus, the production of computers and word processors is linked with a network of parts, components and software suppliers, some of whom are directly owned by the computer companies, while in others the bonding takes the form of a contract or of a less formal arrangement based on trust, commitment and mutual goodwill. The geographical configuration of different parts of the network will reflect a balance between the forces of globalization and localization of production. However, the lead MNEs in the value-added network are likely to take a global perspective both as to the sourcing of their inputs and to downstream operations, whenever and wherever they perceive the efficiency of these will affect the competitiveness of their own businesses.

MNEs are in a singularly favoured position to establish and sustain a network of cross-border linkages. It is in areas such as these that the geographical diversification of activities under common governance confers substantial benefits. Yet such intra-corporate linkages may not always foster intra-country linkages. Much will depend on the efficiency of the firms which compete with each other to be members of the network. Almost by definition, the globalization of linkage strategy puts increasing pressure on countries seeking to develop their own affiliations to offer the kind of supply facilities required both by foreign firms and their own

companies. In Chapter 21 we shall return to the role of governments in providing or facilitating the provision of these facilities.

Of course, as Chapter 8 has demonstrated, only a relatively small number of MNEs pursue global linkage strategies. Most – especially smaller and medium sized companies engaged in import-substituting manufacturing investment – are likely to limit their linkage formation to firms in the countries in which they produce, as well as to take an ethnocentric or polycentric approach to their foreign procurements. Some home-based MNEs are, however, becoming uncoupled from their domestic suppliers as they increasingly opt for multiple sourcing and adopt more geocentric sourcing strategies.

Regional integration and the cross-border liberalization of markets encourage this trend. Such opportunities as these, especially their consequences for the internalization or quasi-internalization[21] of markets, add to the linkages between firms and countries. Like horizontal linkages between firms, these may be competitive or cooperative. In both cases, they may act as disequilibrating forces. As with all such forces, it requires some structural adjustment which offers both challenges and opportunities to the countries concerned. The response to these challenges and opportunities will determine whether the corporate linkages established will lead to more or fewer intra-country linkages. Several observers (e.g. Cowling, 1986) have argued that the actions of foreign MNEs may lead to the deindustrialization of a country (or of a particular industry in a country). On the other hand, as Chapter 14 has pointed out, they might also lead to a virtuous circle of linkage forming activities and promote the competitiveness both of industries and countries (Porter, 1990).

16.5   THE EFFECTS OF MNE ACTIVITY ON COMPETITORS

16.5.1   Some general remarks

Perhaps the most widely acknowledged 'spill-over' effects of MNE activity are its impact on the competitive position of the industry (or strategic group) of which it is part and on the performance of individual rival firms. The first aspect has already been discussed both from the viewpoint of an industry's innovatory capacity (Chapter 12) and from that of market structure (Chapter 15). Provided that there is strong competition (or potential competition) from indigenous firms, inward foreign investment is likely to stimulate innovatory capacity and encourage a market structure in the host country conducive to the promotion of dynamic comparative advantage.

Without such competition, which in some countries in the contemporary global economy requires local firms to be global producers, inward investment may not only lead to more industrial concentration, but, wherever rival indigenous firms are driven out by unfair business practices, to a reduction in the innovatory capacity of the industry. This latter scenario is particularly likely in the case of smaller and/or less industrialized economies where the investing enterprises perceive that their global interests are advanced by the centralization of R&D activities in their home countries. Even in these instances, however, the presence of foreign companies may still be a better solution than any alternative. Much will depend on whether the behaviour of these companies is fashioned by competitive dynamics or monopolistic strength.

Singapore is an example of an economy which is almost totally dependent upon foreign MNEs for its economic prosperity. It is, however, unlikely that given its size and developmental status, Singapore could ever have developed an indigenous innovatory capability, except in a few very specific sectors (e.g. orchid growing or as an entrepot port). By contrast, the UK in the 1960s and 1970s is an example of a country in which foreign-based firms have driven out indigenous competitors in the motor vehicle industry; also, as companies like Ford and General Motors began to rationalize their European operations, they and their suppliers were hampered by a lack of the necessary human and physical capacity to undertake the higher value-added activities. The case of the UK auto industry is a classic example of the failure of an economy to properly marshal its resources to meet the changing needs of the global market. Both the management of indigenous firms and the government, in its macro-economic policies and as a facilitator of industrial restructuring, must bear much of the responsibility for this state of affairs (Porter, 1990).

16.5.2 How might competitors be affected?

The impact of the entry of foreign-owned firms into a particular industrial sector on the producers in that sector will depend first and foremost on the existing characteristics of the sector. These include:

(1) the number and size of these constituent firms,

(2) the composition of their output and the geography and character of the markets served,

(3) their innovatory capacity,

(4) their existing and potential economic performance,[22]

(5) their entrepreneurial ethos,

(6) the market prospects for the industry and whether or not existing firms are operating at surplus capacity,

(7) the extent to which the industry is protected from competition (by import controls, subsidies, etc).

In its turn, each of these variables will be affected by the ESP configuration, that is, the L-specific advantages of the host country.

Second, the impact will depend on the nature and extent of the O advantages of the foreign firms *vis à vis* those of local producers, and also whether or not the products of the investing companies are currently being imported and under what conditions. Obviously, the more MNEs possess O advantages which can be effectively transferred or developed in a foreign location, the greater the potential impact on competitors. But, the nature of these advantages – for example, whether they mainly arise from the possession of intangible assets or from the coordination and integration of cross-border activities – may be no less relevant. As previous chapters have shown, these advantages are likely to be country, industry and firm specific.

Third, the impact will depend on the form of entry of the MNE into the host economy. The acquisition of one or two large oligopolists in a technologically advanced and fast growing sector is likely to have a very different competitive impact on the rest of the firms in the sector than the setting-up of a completely new venture or the purchase of a small and relatively insignificant supplier in a traditional and declining sector. The formation of joint ventures or strategic alliances is likely to have different consequences on the actions of competitors not party to these ventures, than is the entry of wholly-owned investment.

One of the recurrent themes of this volume is that the impact of inward direct investments on the economies of host countries will be most felt when the O advantages of the investing firms (including those which derive from their multinationality) are the most pronounced, and where the firms possessing these advantages perceive that FDI is the best modality by which they might be protected or advanced. The nature of such O advantages has been explored at length in previous chapters. The question which arises here is by what means and under what circumstances are these advances likely to promote a positive response by their domestic rivals, and hence upgrade the competitive status of the sector?

A positive response on the part of competitors, or potential competitors, presupposes both an ability and willingness to improve economic performance. The ability rests on the existing innovatory, productive and market capacity, and the competence of human resources. The motivation rests mainly on the entrepreneurial ethos, the attitudes of the work force and how management perceives its future focus, strategy and internal and external relationships in the light of the entry by the foreign firms (Buckley *et al.*, 1988, 1991). Clearly, this reaction will vary between firms in the industry according to the features identified on page 463. Certainly, one response to inward investment – particularly if the O advantages of the foreign affiliate arise from its being part of a larger and more geographically diversified organization – is to conclude a merger or some kind of cooperative agreement with one or more of its competitors.

This was exactly the reaction of UK firms in the computer industry to the growing penetration of the UK market by the computer giant IBM. In 1970, three large domestic computer firms joined forces to form International Computers Ltd.[23] As a result of the merger, the UK industry regained some of the share it initially lost to IBM. More importantly, it has also been better able to penetrate foreign markets, thus providing it with some of the necessary funding to undertake innovatory work.

The ability of local competitors to respond to inbound investment clearly depends on their ability either to create or acquire competitive advantages similar to those of the foreign firms, or to create some unique advantages of their own. In the colour TV and motor vehicles industry, for example, European and US producers have responded to the infiltration of their markets by Japanese producers, by copying and differentiating, but, in some cases improving upon, the latters' advantages. This has been a *comparatively* easy task, partly because the reasons for the Japanese success are fairly transparent, partly because their implementation has not involved large capital outlays and partly because rising production costs in Japan have partially eroded these advantages. However, in the VCR equipment sector, the story is different. Here Japanese firms have out-competed European and US firms so comprehensively that there is little indigenous innovatory capacity left either in Europe or the US (Philips is an exception). Hence, there is little hope for a home grown VDR sector in two-thirds of the Triad.

In other cases, patent protection may inhibit a local firm from producing an identical product to a foreign (or for that matter a domestic) competitor. Instead, by reverse engineering (or its equivalent in the services sector) and its knowledge derived from its own R&D, a firm has to try to develop a substitute or break into an entirely different segment of the market. This was the strategy pursued by European pharmaceutical firms in response to the penetration of their own markets by American producers in the 1960s. Far Eastern airlines have also adopted these tactics in their attempt to compete with established European carriers.

In other cases, domestic firms, or the industry of which they are a part, may be technically so far behind foreign producers that, left to themselves, they cannot hope to respond positively or constructively. In this case, which is particularly likely in industrializing developing countries, there are three options open to them. The first is to conclude some kind of cooperative or technical service agreement with one or other of their foreign competitors. This, for example, was the response of the Metal Box Company (UK) in 1930 when, in retaliation to the American Can Company setting up a subsidiary factory in Liverpool to manufacture tin cans on US lines, the company made a licensing agreement with the Continental Can Company, the chief competitor of American Can in the US (Dunning, 1958, p. 193).

The second option is to try and obtain some kind of help from their own governments, either to reduce their production or transaction costs, or to protect or enlarge their markets. The third option is for local firms to accept a reduced share of the output of the industry or exit the industry altogether. This last option was chosen by a UK firm IMI, which preferred to leave the zip fastener industry altogether rather than compete with the entry of the Japanese-owned firm YKK.

De facto, the responses by domestic firms are likely to vary according to country-, industry- and firm-specific circumstances. Applying some of the variables identified on p. 463, indigenous firms are most likely to react positively to the presence of foreign affiliates when they already compete with these firms, and where the advantages enjoyed by the affiliates are not so unique that they cannot be acquired, copied or recreated. This suggests a market structure and competitive environment which encourages innovation by local firms and cross-border strategic A&Ms.[24] By contrast, where indigenous firms have few distinct competitive advantages or have not previously competed with MNEs, or are unable or unwilling to conclude alliances with other firms, or where the advantages of their MNE rivals stem from the economies of size and geographical scope – then it is unlikely, except by becoming MNEs themselves, that they can ever compete effectively with the inbound investors.

However, as previous chapters have shown, in cases where goods and services need to be tailored to local market needs and resource capabilities, and where these needs and capabilities are particularly idiosyncratic, indigenous firms may well be able to hold their own against foreign-based investors. In such cases, the most probable outcome of MNE activity is to stimulate local firms to upgrade their resources and capabilities, and be more aggressive in their marketing strategies. Examples include improvements in the domestic hotel and fast food restaurant sectors as a result of the growth of MNE-owned (or related) chains, and the widening range and quality of indigenous banking, advertising, market research and management consultancy and executive search firms in Western Europe, which at one time were the exclusive province of US-owned firms. Within the manufacturing sector, one of the main competitive spurs of FDI has been the introduction of a new range of products and production and organizational methods. Indeed, in the last resort, it may be that the pressures of competition to modify and improve a product range, production and/or transaction costs, and to introduce new marketing and distribution methods, are the most significant positive influences of inbound MNE activity.

16.5.3   Empirical evidence

What now of the empirical evidence of the impact of MNEs on their competitors? We shall consider briefly four groups of studies. The first are field studies usually carried out as part of a wider enquiry into the consequences of FDI on the economies of host countries. The second are econometric studies that attempt to estimate more quantitatively the ways in which competitors may have been affected. The third are industry studies which usually examine the ways in which MNEs have impacted on the leading firms of the industries of which they are part. The fourth are individual case studies of the competitors of MNEs.

(i) *Field studies* In earlier chapters we have referred to field studies undertaken since the 1950s on the economic consequences of FDI on a number of host countries. Most of these have paid some attention to the impact on, and response of, competitors to the presence of foreign firms. Some of these impacts are set out in Exhibit 16.1.

Of course, any form of new competition is likely to elicit some response from existing producers. At the same time, the substitution of local production for exports by foreign firms may be of only marginal consequence. This, indeed, was the opinion of the UK competitors to the entry of Japanese colour TV set producers into the UK in the 1980s. Moreover, the impact on competitors is likely to vary according to the nature of the competitive advantages of the investing firms. Exhibit 16.2 identifies some responses by UK competitors to the entry of Japanese manufacturing affiliates in the 1980s (Dunning, 1986a). This clearly indicates that the main reaction was to improve product quality, followed by diversification of the range of products supplied. Had such data been collected in the 1950s and 1960s from

Exhibit 16.1   Impact of multinational activity on competitors in selected industries

1 Semiconductors (UK and Continental Europe)	Squeezed out many competitors or potential competitors. Forced A&Ms and alliances
2 Video recorders (US and Europe)	As (1), except that Japanese firms now completely dominate this sector
3 Pharmaceuticals (Denmark, UK, Philippines)	Foreign firms now dominate sector Noticeably improved efficiency of indigenous sector Foreign firms now dominate sector, but there is considerable competition between these affiliates
4 Colour TVs (UK, US)	More industrial concentration. Many firms eliminated; rationalization of others
5 Rubber tyres (Europe and UK)	Generally a stimulus to competition, but, more recently, a regrouping of companies. Strengthening of a few internationally-oriented companies
6 Offshore oil supplies industry (Europe)	Caused rationalization and regrouping of domestic firms. Substantial government intervention by some countries to promote national champions
7 Autos (UK)	Until recently, a squeezing out of competitors and a vicious technological cumulation circle. Since the late 1980s, new Japanese entrants have helped revitalize the assembling in some component sectors

the UK competitors to US firms, almost certainly the thrust of the responses would have been to introduce more automated production methods and budgetary control systems, to boost R&D expenditures and to upgrade managerial and marketing techniques (Dunning, 1958, pp. 189–94, 248 ff).

At the same time, field studies have revealed some of the concerns of competitors to the presence of foreign-owned firms. Competitors to Japanese affiliates in Europe have argued that the latter engage in aggressive penetration pricing (in some cases by dumping), which, because of the inability of domestic firms to respond, may result in some destruction of local productive capacity. Another anxiety, which we identified in the previous chapter, is that driving out local competitors may lead to a diminution of innovatory capacity of the industry, which in the long run might seriously damage its economic viability. We shall return to this concern later in the chapter.

The general conclusion of the field studies is that inward FDI has acted as a stimulus to the efficiency of the industrial sectors in which it is concentrated. More often than not, it has also led to a restructuring of the sectors in which some competitors have responded positively and upgraded their own performance while others have left the industry or diversified into other product lines. The field studies have generally confirmed that the most beneficial aspects of FDI have occurred in those countries and sectors where the existing or potential innovatory and production capacity of indigenous firms is the strongest.

(ii) *Econometric studies*   There are two groups of studies to which we might refer. The first relates to some very specific attempts to measure the impact of inward direct investment on the efficiency of indigenous firms. The second concerns the externalities generated by such firms on the general

Exhibit 16.2   Responses of competitors to presence of foreign investors.

Wider appreciation of importance of R&D and rewards of productive management.

Added incentive to competitors to visit the US; awareness that it is possible to emulate US production techniques of work methods.

Conclusion of licensing agreements with other foreign firms. This reaction has also been observed in the case of competitors to component suppliers of foreign firms.

Further differentiation of existing products.

Diversification of product range.

More attention paid to management and budgetary control systems.

More intensive price or non-price competition and/or improved marketing techniques.

Upgrading of product quality and performance standards.

A more progressive and/or entrepreneurial business ethos.

---

competitiveness of the industry of which they are part.

Typical of the first group of studies are those of Caves (1974b) for Australia, Globerman (1979a) for Canada, Blomström (1986, 1989) for Mexico, and Haddad and Harrison (1993) for Morocco. Each of these hypothesize that such spill-over effects should stimulate the productivity of competitors by:

(1) increasing competition;

(2) enhancing human capital (via more and/or better training of labour and management, and/or through recruitment of such resources from foreign-owned affiliates);

(3) speeding up the cross-border transfer of technology – including organizational technology.

More particularly, they postulated that if there was a positive statistical relation between the productivity level of the domestically owned sector in an industry

and the share of foreign-owned companies in that sector, then inward direct investment may be assumed to be a productivity raising force.[25] It was further suggested that, over time, the productivity of domestic and foreign-owned firms would tend to converge.

Because of data inadequacies, the Canadian, Australian and Mexican studies take labour productivity or changes in labour productivity as the variable to be explained. The Moroccan study was able to obtain data on total factor productivity. The number of sectors for which data was obtained varied between 22 in the case of Australia, 49 for Canada, 215 for Mexico and 18 for Morocco. This variable was then regressed on a number of explanatory variables which might influence such productivity, including the presence of foreign-owned firms. These included:

(1) capital intensity,

(2) labour quality,

(3) degree of concentration in the industry,

(4) extent of scale economies.

The consensus of these cross-sectional studies was that the presence of foreign-owned firms in a particular industry (measured by the share of the local labour force or output accounted for by these firms) was positively related to the labour productivity of the industry. This relationship proved the strongest in the Blomstrom study. Indeed, when labour quality, which was strongly correlated with the degree of foreign presence, was taken together with the latter variable it was significant at the 0.01% level. In the Haddad and Harrison study, the authors found that in sectors in which there was a high foreign presence there was a lower dispersion of productivity. They also established that the main impact that inward investment had on the productivity of domestic firms was the result of more pronounced competition rather than of any transfer of new technology.

Each of these exercises, however, dealt only with intra-industry externalities and concentrated on the possible impact of only one indicator of spill-over efficiency. They did not, for example, concern themselves with the long-term competitiveness of the industry, which might well be affected by the extent to which foreign firms help to promote local technological capacity (Lall, 1980). Moreover, the studies used only cross-sectional data. Ideally, to compare the impact of one group of firms on another, one should lag the dependent variable (i.e. compare the efficiency of domestic firms in time '$t + 1$' with the foreign presence in time 't'). As an alternative to this measure, the Moroccan study tried to estimate the extent to which the presence of foreign firms influenced the growth in productivity of the sectors in which they participated. While the authors found some modest, but statistically insignificant, evidence for this hypothesis, they could not attribute this to the dynamic externalities from inward investment. Indeed, Haddad and Harrison (1993) concluded that in the Morocco manufacturing sector there was no evidence of positive externalities in either protected or unprotected sectors.

The second group of studies do introduce a time dimension. They attempt to compare *changes* in the competitive position of industries with the participation, or changes in participation, of foreign-owned firms. Several of these studies are summarized in Dunning (1985). The dependent variable usually chosen is the Revealed Comparative Advantage (RCA) of particular industries.[26] The hypothesis is that an improvement in RCA over a particular period of time should be positively related to the presence of foreign firms at the beginning of the period. Again, other factors influencing a change in RCA were included in the regression equation.

The results were mixed. For Canada, Globerman (1985) found that the extent of ownership by non-US foreign investors was positively related to changes in RCA, but that there was no association between the degree of US ownership and that variable. For the UK, Dunning (1985) discovered that, for the period 1971–79, while UK firms increased their foreign activities in areas where the UK's RCA was also increasing, there was a negative correlation between changes in inward investment and RCA. On the other hand, it appeared that foreign affiliates were redirecting their output to sectors in which the RCA was improving. For Portugal, Simoes (1985) concluded that inbound foreign investment had positively affected the dynamics of Portuguese comparative advantage, while in the case of Singapore, Lecraw (1985a) found that foreign-owned firms were the main instrument for raising the productivity of local competitors. By

contrast, Bohn Koo (1985, p. 300) concluded that in Korea, up to the late 1970s at least, inward direct investment had only a marginal impact on improving the competitiveness of Korean firms or restructuring Korean RCA. In India, Lall (1985) found that Indian government policy, by restricting the ownership, sourcing and production policies of foreign-owned firms, inhibited the beneficial impact they might have had on their competitors.

(iii)   *Industry studies*   Several studies on the changing competitiveness of specific industries in different countries have attempted to assess the extent to which this has been influenced by the presence of foreign-owned firms. Some of these have already been alluded to in Chapters 11 and 14. Here we shall be concerned with the more general impact they have had on their competitors.

Exhibit 16.2 already illustrated some of the possible responses of competitors to the presence of foreign investors. They reveal an extremely diverse picture, from which it is difficult to draw any general conclusions. However, it is possible to identify the kinds of variables which are most likely to determine the impact of MNEs on their competitors. These are set out in the concluding section of this chapter.

(iv)   *Case studies*   Several mini case studies have sought to identify and explain the linkages established by foreign-owned firms with other firms in the host country. We mention just three of these. The first is a study by Lim and Pang (1982) of three MNEs with exoport-oriented manufacturing operations in Singapore. The main conclusion to be drawn from these cases is that, although, over time, the local content of the sales generated by inward investors tends to increase, the crucial variables determining the extent of the increase are the capacity of local suppliers to meet the specification standards and prices expected by the foreign firms, the options open to the foreign affiliates to obtain their inputs from other sources, and the procurement strategies of the parent companies. The authors observed that an unusual feature of the Singaporean economy was that most of the suppliers of the three foreign affiliates were also foreign-owned firms. Consequently, they required less customer assistance than might have been expected by locally-owned firms.

The second group of case studies embraces a group of six Swedish-owned subsidiaries set up in India mainly to supply the domestic market in place of exports from Sweden (Jansson, 1982). The author observed differences in the extent to which the affiliates helped develop local supplier capability. In particular, he distinguished between products which were technologically complex to produce – and often unfamiliar to subcontractors – and those which needed relatively unsophisticated new knowledge or production capabilities on the part of the suppliers. In each of the case studies, it was the former kinds of inputs where the MNEs made the most impact on their subcontractors, although deficiencies in communication and transport infrastructure frequently inhibited the development of an efficient supply capability. Jansson also found that Indian government policy – particularly with respect to import licensing – had a considerable influence on the purchasing strategies of Swedish foreign affiliates such as Vulcan-Laval (in respect of imports of stainless steel) and Sardvik Asia (in respect of precision iron and steel castings). Each of the Swedish companies provided considerable technical and/or financial aid to at least some of their suppliers.

The third group of case studies illustrates some of the consequences of MNE activity in a number of primary sectors on local suppliers and customers in various South East Asian economies (ESCAP/UNCTC, 1984). For example, in a study of the Thai pineapple industry, it was found that local firms retained a greater percentage of their sales in the domestic economy than their foreign-owned counterparts, but that the foreign firms had a greater effect on improving productivity both of pineapple growing and of canning operations. Because of their brand names and their foreign marketing contacts, they were more successful in their export marketing strategies – although their very success often created entry barriers to Thai-owned canning companies (ESCAP/UNCTC, 1984).

Another case study in the UN volume describes the content of the contracts concluded between the main banana MNEs (e.g. Del Monte and United Brands) and their growers, as well as the extent to which, and the terms on which, they influence or control the distribution and marketing of the product. Other chapters provide fascinating glimpses into the

backward and forward linkages evolved by particular MNEs in the tropical hardwood industry in Indonesia,[27] the tin industry in Malaysia and Indonesia,[28] and the copper industry in Papua New Guinea, Indonesia and the Philippines.[29] *Inter alia*, they illustrate differences in the sourcing strategies of Japanese and US MNEs, and pinpoint firm- and country-specific influences on the outcome of bargaining on both the sourcing of inputs by MNEs and the distribution of the economic rent resulting from their activities.

16.6   SOME MORE GENERAL SPILL-OVER EFFECTS

This chapter would be incomplete without a mention of some of the other ways the presence of MNEs might affect the rest of the economy of which they are a part. Chapter 19 will deal with some of the political, cultural and environmental impacts.

We will confine our attention to three kinds of spill-over effects. The following sections will briefly describe each of them.

16.6.1   By the normal course of labour turnover from foreign affiliates

This is likely to be an important spill-over consequence of MNE activity, particularly in strongly competitive sectors. Workers and management trained or inculcated with the attitudes, philosophy and ideas of a foreign-owned affiliate, or who have worked in a foreign subsidiary or a domestic multinational, may well promulgate these attributes elsewhere in the home or host country as and when they change jobs. Several pieces of research (e.g. Reuber, 1973) have shown that government administrations in developing countries recruit employees previously employed in the affiliates of foreign firms. In both developed and developing countries, the normal movement of labour between firms should normally bring new skills and experiences to the hiring employers.[30]

One explanation for this benefit, which is an

application of the theory of externalities, is that the institution which recruits the trained worker will not pay the full costs of his training. These gains are likely to be the greatest in sectors or occupations where the O advantages of the foreign-based firm are likely to arise from the internalization of the L advantages of the home country which are transferable across national boundaries (Lall, 1978). Another explanation has its parallel in the benefits accruing to the MNE as a result of its privileged access to human resources throughout its global network. In the same way, the presence of foreign affiliates brings some of these same advantages to domestic firms by offering a pool of differently trained and experienced labour through the external market.

16.6.2   By their membership of trade associations, research consortia, etc

Where foreign firms are permitted to join, and do join, local trade associations, Chambers of Commerce and research consortia, it is likely that information and knowledge will be passed on to other members, with beneficial effects on their own competitiveness. Factory visits, seminars and trade fairs are all means of exposing some of the working practices and production methods of MNEs and their affiliates. Understandably, firms differ in their willingness to be exposed. The Japanese appear to be the most receptive to factory visits. More generally, senior managers of the larger foreign affiliates make a point of participating in industrial councils of one kind or another, or on public bodies.

Sometimes, of course, the contribution of foreign firms may be limited by the action of government and/or indigenous competitors. In the US, for example, such firms are not normally allowed to become members of collaborative research efforts, such as SEMATECH.[31] More recently, as a result of the acquisition of 80% of the share capital of ICL by Fujitsu, European-owned firms have attempted to keep the new Japanese-owned firm from becoming a member of the European research based consortia of computer equipment manufacturers.[32]

16.6.3   Public image and entrepreneurial culture

It may be reasonably argued that the impact of the recent burgeoning of Japanese direct investment in the US on the average US citizen is far out of proportion to its actual economic significance. The number of words written in newspapers and magazines, as well as the frequency of TV and radio programmes presented on the subject of Japanese style work practices and management strategy, have given the American public – which includes the workers and management of firms who buy from, sell to or compete with Japanese firms – an awareness of this phenomenon, in a way which cannot fail to influence both opinions and behavioural patterns. Of course, throughout history the subject of FDI and MNE activity has attracted attention and aroused emotions, not least by those most likely to be most affected by the strategy of such firms.

However, perhaps the most underestimated effect of the internationalization of production is that which arises through the interweaving of different business cultures and exchange relationships. Though similar, the ethos of US management practices and inter-firm transactions is not the same as the British. It is more pragmatic, professional and assertive, as well as being firmly based on the law of contract. By the same token, Japanese business philosophy is very different from either the US or the British way. It is based more on an intra-firm consensus of ideas and opinions. It is more holistic in its approach and is based on meticulous attention to detail. The spillover effects of the introduction of these different modes of thinking and doing business into an economy can be quite far-reaching – if they are allowed to be.

Such philosophies and strategies are always disseminated, in part, at least, by MNE activity. However, rather like a skin graft, they need the right conditions to succeed. This is especially the case in developing countries where differences in the entrepreneurial and business cultures between the affiliates of foreign firms and indigenous producers often explain why the impact of the former on economic development is not as widespread or beneficial as it might be (Buckley and Casson, 1989). Of course, this impact is likely to be highly country specific. The competitors of US and Japanese multinational affiliates in South East Asian industrializing countries, for example, seem able to align themselves with the entrepreneurial culture of these affiliates much more easily than can their counterparts in Africa, or in parts of Latin America and the Pacific.

16.7 SUMMARY AND CONCLUSIONS

Inter-firm linkages and externalities associated with the presence of MNE activity are likely to depend on eight main factors. They are:

(1) the extent and nature of the particular O advantage associated with MNE activity;

(2) host and home government developmental and macro-organizational strategies (including those policies specifically directed to MNEs or their affiliates);

(3) the existing supply capabilities and absorptive capabilities of indigenous firms in host economies, and their reactions to inbound direct investment;

(4) the L-specific environment for absorbing, disseminating and accumulating new knowledge, technology, management skills, etc;

(5) the competitive position and market structure of the sectors in which there is foreign participation prior to that participation;

(6) the characteristics of the markets for intermediate products;

(7) the type of foreign investment (e.g. import substitution, resource based);

(8) the global strategies of the MNEs.

In larger developing industrial economies, such as the UK, the US, France, Germany and Japan, the contribution of multinational investors to the formation of inter-firm linkages would seem to have been positive and, in some cases, substantial. For example, technical and allocative efficiency has been raised by the additional knowledge of markets and higher quality standards passed on by their suppliers through backward linkages and by entrepreneurial and competitive stimuli to competitors.

In the small developed and less developed countries, the spill-over effects have been more varied. We have seen that the competitive effects have been positive in Canada, whereas in several cases (e.g. Belgium and Singapore) foreign subsidiaries have swamped domestic producers and have led to increased concentration ratios. In Japan, India and Korea, government policy has not allowed this to happen as limits have been placed on inward investment. However, even in these countries, and in those like Brazil and Mexico, backward linkages have not been as pronounced as host governments would have liked. Most developing countries are aware of the export-enclave syndrome, and attempt to ensure that foreign affiliates in their midst produce or subcontract a good proportion of their sales to local producers.

We have seen that part of the unwillingness of MNEs to establish linkages arises from the perceived inadequacy of domestic markets or of the technological and educational infrastructure, as well as of the inability of local suppliers to meet the expectations required of them. However, as revealed by Korean, Indian and Portuguese experiences, much depends on the type of inward investment and whether the international or the domestic market is served with the final product. Moreover, in some cases, the ability of affiliates to use local suppliers rests mainly on the design requirements of the final product, which is usually under the control of the parent company. Thus, Japanese colour TV affiliates are not able to buy some electronic components from UK sources simply because the chassis design, which determines the nature of the integrated circuitry, is under the parent company's control, and is primarily related to the needs of Japanese consumers. The result is that at varying levels, many countries are worried lest the affiliates of foreign-based firms do not bring with them the hoped for spill-over benefits. Indeed, in some cases there could be negative effects.

Finally, this chapter has shown that the activities of domestic-based MNEs also affect vertical integration and horizontal spill-over effects in their home countries. In developed economies, we have argued that the types of O advantages which MNEs enjoy over their uninational competitors, and which arise specifically as a result of their foreign operations, may act either as a stimulant or a depressant to competitiveness, depending on the extent to which these spill over to the rest of the economy of which they are part. Once again, the current competitive position of the home nation and the actions taken by government to retain or advance that position by raising the productivity of its resources (particularly human capital) and by fostering the right kind of market structure to best meet this goal, are of critical importance.

NOTES

1   Who, themselves, may be MNEs or affiliates of MNEs.
2   We would reaffirm our earlier distinction between finished and final products. The former represent the physical attributes of an item or service at the completion of its production process. Such finished goods, however, may only have value added to them through a variety of services (e.g. transport, storage, merchanting and retailing). The final product is that actually purchased and used by the final consumer.
3   This may include special inducements to develop small scale sectors in regions of high unemployment or in lagging areas. In Japan, government policy is conducive to the creation of clusters of small enterprises to serve large industrial producers.
4   Chapters 4, 6 and 8.
5   Research by Williamson (1986) suggests that relative to their uninational counterparts, MNEs are more responsive in their sourcing behaviour to changes in the relative prices of domestically produced and imported goods and services.
6   Based on information provided by 43 European and 28 Japanese MNEs. In giving their reasons for the differences in the sourcing strategies of the two groups of firms, the authors give especial attention to the 'gradual transition of Japanese strategy from export orientation to direct investment orientation' (p. 123).
7   Although Daimler Benz held a 14% shareholding in 1977.
8   In all of the six manufacturing sectors considered by McAleese and McDonald, the expenditure on Irish materials by new firms – the great majority of which were foreign owned – rose between 1966 and 1974.
9   In the food and auto industry, subcontracted supplies reached 70% or more of total sales, whereas in the consumer electronics sector the maximum was 50% and in the textiles and clothing sectors 15%.
10   See also Chapter 11, pp. 315–7.
11   The percentages varied between sectors. It was highest in the transport equipment industry (89%) and machinery and equipment sector (75%), and lowest in the chemicals and material producing sectors (37%) (JETRO, 1990).
12   *Sixth Survey on Japanese Manufacturing Affiliates in Europe*, 1990.

13   It being recognized that the high value added of agricultural-based products often resides in the way in which they are packaged and branded. Mountain coffee sells in Japan for four times the price of Brazilian coffee; Koshihikari rice is 30% more expensive than normal rice, while Kobe beef is two to three times more expensive than any kind of Japanese-produced beef (Ohmae, 1990).
14   Some examples are given in Dunning (1986a, pp. 132–4). In the UK, one supplier of plastic mouldings – Kenure Plastics – is on record as asserting that, as a direct result of dealing with Japanese affiliates, it has completely revolutionized its production methods and management philosophy. Consequently, it is now a premier supplier of high quality precision mouldings. Another supplier of electronic components told the author 'The spill-over effect (resulting from our dealings with Japanese affiliates) has ensured that our quality control and process control systems has developed rapidly. Because of this pressure, it has enabled us to supply high-quality products to our other customers. We have also benefited from discussions on raw material usage and various other areas that have improved our overall business' (Dunning, 1986a, p. 133).
15   In the UK, such help was especially acknowledged by UK suppliers of the Japanese-owned colour TV producers.
16   At the time of completing this chapter, the author came across a newspaper reference to the fact that Jaguar, Britain's leading up-market auto assembler, had decided 'to buy components from Japanese firms in Britain because British and European parts are not good enough' (*Daily Mail*, 10th April 1991).
17   Especially Chapters 12, 14 and 15.
18   Which, in a survey of 55 of the largest MNEs operating in high technology sectors in Latin America, was found to be the most important competitive advantage (Grosse, 1988).
19   There is fragmentary evidence (Dunning, 1986a) that Japanese affiliates do provide more technical advice and information to their industrial users and clients in the UK than do their UK competitors. Often these O advantages are short lived, as they can readily be copied by their competitors.
20   This, of course, assumes that the output of foreign firms does not replace that of domestic firms. However, even if this is the case, additional value may be created through high productivity of the suppliers to foreign affiliates.
21   Quasi-internalization is where *de facto* there are close economic linkages between firms, even if there is no formal hierarchical (ownership) relationship between them. Examples of such linkages are those fashioned by the Japanese 'Keiretsu' or industrial group in which

the core firm usually owns a small equity holding of other members of the group, including subcontractors, but which is capable of administering them as if they were fully-owned affiliates. See Chapter 9 for more details.

22 As shown, for example, by their profitability, productivity and market share.

23 Which, in 1990, was largely acquired by Japanese interests, *viz* the Fujitsu company.

24 Such as those which have been concluded between European and US firms in the 1980s; see Chapter 4 for a discussion of the rationale for such FDI.

25 However, the authors, in particular Blomström (1986, 1989), acknowledge that, since foreign companies tend to cluster in high technology and marketing-intensive sectors, the causal relationship might operate in the reverse way!

26 RCA is defined as: $1 + (Xi - Mi) (Mi + Mi) - 1 + (Xt - Mt)/(Xt + Mt)$, where X is exports, i is a particular sector, M is imports and t is all sectors.

27 In particular, the case of the US-owned Weyerhaeuser Corporation is reviewed.

28 In particular, the growth of a light engineering industry to meet the needs of both foreign- and locally-owned mines for spare parts and capital equipment; and of a large scale smelting industry in most tin-producing countries.

29 The Bougainville Mining Company, the majority owner of which is Cozinc Rio Tinto of Australia (itself majority owned by RTZ), is a classical example of a mining company that, partly in pursuance of its own strategy and partly as a result of pressure from the government of Papua New Guinea, has established substantial linkages with firms in the domestic economy.

30 In a study of the insurance industry published in Shelp *et al.* (1984), it was suggested that the loss of trained employees to other firms was one of the main ways in which insurance technology was transferred across national boundaries. Blomström (1991) quotes from Shelp (p. 45) that in the Philippines AIG – a leading US MNE – is known as the training ground for the indigenous insurance industry.

31 SEMATECH (Semiconductor Manufacturing Technology) is a US research-based consortium financed by the Pentagon and private sources; it is intended to advance the competitiveness of the US in semiconductor innovation and manufacturing. It, and an allied consortium (National Center for Manufacturing Sciences (AIG NCMS)) currently exclude foreign-owned firms from its membership, while the export of NCMS-developed technologies by member firms to their foreign affiliates is subject to restrictions. However, neither SEMATECH nor NCMS can easily prevent US know-how from 'leaking' abroad, through joint ventures or strategic alliances concluded by the US with foreign firms. Some examples are given in Mowery (1990, 1991). By contrast to the attitude of the US authorities, one of the leading Japanese government backed consortia – the International Superconductivity Technology Center (ISTEC), established in 1988 – readily permits the participation of foreign firms; the logic being that their knowledge and expertise can help create technology 'fusion' with the competences of Japanese electronics companies (Fodama, 1992).

32 In 1990, the Japanese electronics firm Fujitsu bought 80% of ICL, a UK computer company. Following this purchase ICL lost its membership of the European Round Table of Industrialists, an organization made up of the senior officers of large European companies. In addition, ICL was forced to withdraw from three of the five projects of the European Communities' JESSI programme in advanced memory chips. ICL now participates in JESSI on the same limited basis as IBM Europe, the only other non-European firm involved in JESSI (see Hudson, 1991).

CHAPTER 17

MNEs, THE INTERNATIONAL DIVISION OF LABOUR AND ECONOMIC INTEGRATION

17.1 INTRODUCTION

One of the most significant features about the global economy of the past decade has been the acceleration of a long-term trend towards greater economic interdependence between countries. This acceleration is currently most dramatically displayed by the political and economic upheavals now taking place in Central and Eastern Europe, the completion of the internal market of the European Community (EC) at the end of 1992 and the initiation of new free trade agreements by the US with both Canada and Mexico. However, throughout the world, the early 1990s are witnessing a series of moves towards closer and more open trading and investment relationships between sovereign states. Contemporaneously, the pressure towards more protectionist stances in some developing and developed countries (e.g. as witnessed in the current round of GATT negotiations, and with respect to intra-Triad trade in some goods and services) has contained the extent and quality of such interdependence.

The nature and form of economic interdependence may vary along a spectrum which identifies the degree of spontaneous or engineered closeness among the participating nations.[1] At the very least, interdependence implies an agreement between two or more countries to reduce or remove discriminatory trade restrictions with each other. At the other extreme, it may result in an elimination of political boundaries and a unification of domestic economic policies. As one moves along the spectrum, so the impact of interdependence on the international division of labour between countries and firms becomes more significant. Indeed, the two are closely interlinked, in as much as the existence of

artificially imposed barriers to the movement of goods, people, assets and technology, prevents firms from properly exploiting the benefits of cross-border product or process specialization, or fully capturing the economies of scale, scope and risk spreading. At the same time, governments may wish to promote regional integration for their own ends – most noticeably, to advance the upgrading and restructuring of their industries, including, where appropriate, a change in their ownership.[2]

In this chapter, we shall be primarily concerned with the role played by MNEs in fashioning and responding to international or regional economic integration. Integration is a form of interdependence, which is characterized by an act of agreement among the participating nations to surrender part of their national sovereignty either to the workings of cross-border markets (which tends to make for more harmonization of costs and prices) or to some supranational authority which acts on behalf of those nations. Thus, by being a member of the EC, the UK accepts that in so far as certain areas of political and economic decision thinking is concerned, the European Commission (the parliament of the EC) has power over its British counterpart. At the same time, the EC is far from being a total economic union. There is, as yet, little or no inter-country coordination of monetary or fiscal policies, and each national government continues to exert sovereignty over most areas of economic strategy.

Like economic interdependence, economic integration may take various forms. There is currently no such thing as *de jure* global integration, though *de facto* the world is probably less economically segmented than it has ever been. All attempts to formalize the nature of associations between coun-

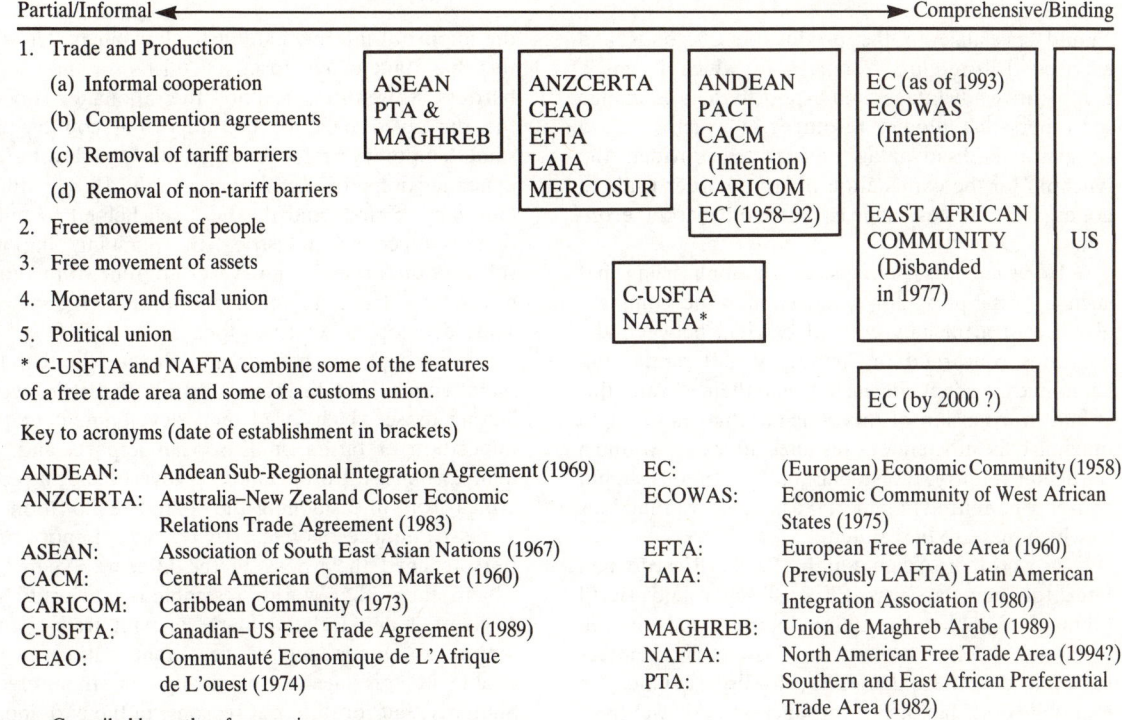

Figure 17.1 Matrix of degrees of economic integration between any geographical grouping of countries.

tries have been undertaken by groups of countries within a particular region. Hence most studies on economic integration have been concerned with regional economic integration.

Currently (March 1992), there are more than a dozen active regional cooperative and integration schemes operating in the world. The extent and character of these schemes vary along a spectrum from a relatively loose set of guidelines in the case of the Association of South East Asian Nations (ASEAN) and the Union du Maghreb Arabe (Maghreb), through a variety of free trade agreements, e.g. the Canada–US Free Trade Agreement (C–US FTA) and the European Free Trade Area (EFTA) to the more formal economic unions of the European Economic Community (EC) and the Economic Community of West African States (ECOWAS). Similarly, the effect on corporate integration and the role of MNEs on regional economy integration may, and does, differ. Figure 17.1 identifies some of these schemes. It includes the ill-fated East African Economic Community which was disbanded in 1977 after six years of gradual disintegration (Diejomaoh, 1987). The

table is self-evident. Later sections in the chapter will return to consider some of the differences identified, especially those involving developed as compared with developing countries.

17.2 THE INTERNATIONAL DIVISION OF LABOUR

17.2.1 The determinants of the international allocation of economic activity

Adam Smith (1776) was one of the first economists to explore the advantages of the specialization of economic activity. Although his analysis was couched more in terms of the division of *tasks* among individuals in a given location (e.g. in his famous pin-making example), later economists, writing after the first flush of the industrial revolution and the introduction of the factory system, took up the theme and applied it to the distribution of economic activity between firms and sectors, and over space. The well-known Ricardian concept that each country should specialize in the production of goods and services that require resources in which it has a comparative advantage, and export these in exchange for others that require resources in which it has a comparative disadvantage, has long provided the lynchpin for the explanation of cross-border trade in goods and services, at least between market economies.

However, it is, perhaps, worth emphasizing that such a prescription for trade implies the complete absence of artificially created barriers between the countries concerned or, putting it differently, full economic interdependence between them. Again, this is but an extension of the principle that, in order to maximize the efficiency of resource allocation within a particular country, individuals and institutions should be freely permitted to undertake the tasks or functions to which they are best suited.[3]

A world of Adam Smith, David Ricardo and later the neo-classicists Eli Heckscher and Bertil Ohlin thus implies the fullest international division of labour and free movement of goods and services between countries. However, it also assumes an immobility of factors of production. As we have argued elsewhere in this volume, MNEs cannot exist in such a world. Hence, all trade is conducted at arm's length prices between companies whose value-added activities take place within their national boundaries.

It is also worth observing that such an international division of labour is assumed to be based entirely on the distribution of natural endowments, *viz* labour, land, etc, and a stock of capital. Governments are assumed to exert no influence on the way these resources are used or upgraded. Technology (including organizational technology) is assumed to be a free goods and universally available across boundaries. In so far as technology enters into the picture at all, it does so by its differential impact on the quantity and quality of factor endowments, and hence on the structure of the comparative advantages of countries. However, in classical and neo-classical economies, technology is never considered as a scarce product in its own right.

In practice, such complete economic interdependence has never existed, though it came near to it in the second and third quarters of the 19th century. Since then, at one time or another, one government or another has imposed some kind of restriction on the import of intermediate or final products. Usually this has taken the form of tariffs or non-tariff barriers. More often than not, the rationale has been the perceived need of the importing country for some temporary protection to enable it to develop its dynamic competitive advantage. In the 19th century, Germany, France and the US each helped to build their indigenous industries by pursuing import-substitution strategies not very different from those utilized by Japan in the 1950s and 1960s, and by some developing countries today.

As Chapter 5 has already shown, the US tin plate, cutlery, cotton thread and silk industries were among those which owed their development to the imposition of tariffs on European imports and, in many instances, European direct investment played a critical role in fashioning the spatial reallocation of Trans-Atlantic economic activity. Such import barriers reached their peak in the inter-war years, at which time the world resembled a cluster of segmented and isolated markets, with trade being limited to goods and services that nations were unable to produce economically for themselves. Similarly, but for different reasons, in the early post-World War II period, trade and investment were restricted by currency imbalances. However, there followed a period of largely free and reasonably stable economic growth.

In the longer term, the structure of both domestic and international allocation of economic activity is primarily determined by the pace, structure and upgrading of human and physical capital. The 20th century has seen the emergence and growth of many new nations as producers and trading partners in the world economy. In the inter-war years, for example, India, Egypt, China and Japan challenged the established pre-eminence of such UK industries as cotton textile and shipbuilding industries. Today, several Far Eastern and Latin American countries are out-competing the countries of the Triad in their supply of a wide range of consumer electronic goods and photographic equipment.

Economic development is also strongly influenced by political change and by technological innovations. The discovery of new kinds and sources of minerals and raw materials has also dramatically affected the terms of trade of many developing countries. Examples include oil, bauxite, rubber, tin and synthetic fibres in the early 20th century, and the lighter speciality steels, composites and polymers, ceramics, and optic fibres in the later 20th century. Revolutionary new transport and telecommunication techniques are also affecting both the vertical and horizontal international division of labour. At the same time, advances in information and organizational technology have encouraged the concentration of the ownership and control of globally-integrated activities. *Inter alia* this is demonstrated by the growing role of FDI and cross-border alliances in the global economy, and the increasing share of trade accounted for by intra-firm transactions.

Finally, the international division of labour is critically dependent upon the extent to which participating nations wish to involve themselves in such a pattern of resource allocation, which is primarily market determined. Most nations are schizophrenic about such economic interdependence for two main reasons. First, they want the benefits of a more efficient pattern of resource allocation, without the abrogation of economic sovereignty that this implies. Second, some nations – particularly smaller and developing nations – believe that a market-driven international division of labour does not always operate to their benefit. This they attribute to the failure of the market (as an allocative device) to help them overcome the obstacles to their own participation in that division of labour. This might be partly a result of the entrenched positions of established firms (or countries) in the international market, and partly of their inability to obtain the competences without which the benefits of economic integration cannot be fully obtained.

Even in the early 1990s, it is possible to rank countries according to their acceptance of the benefits of international economic interdependence. At the top are the strongly market-oriented economies, notably the US, UK, West Germany, Switzerland, Singapore and Hong Kong. At the bottom are China, India and, until recently, most Central and Eastern European countries. In between, and favouring some degree of controlled interdependence, are most of the other nations in the world. Yet even the administrations that are most cognizant of the virtues of free trade have displayed a highly protectionist stance wherever they have perceived the actions of trading partners to be inimical to their own interests. Classic examples include the attitude of the EC towards the importation of Japanese cars and of the US authorities towards the EC's agricultural policy and the subsidization of steel exports.

By contrast, nations that tread the path of self-reliance can promote the trade of exports of goods in which they have a distinct comparative advantage (e.g. some resource-based or labour-intensive goods and services supplied by developing countries) and allow the free import of goods in which they have a profound disadvantage. Moreover, the same country, over time, may alter its stance toward engaging in world commerce. In the 1980s, this was well illustrated by an acceptance of countries like Japan, Korea, Chile and Mexico of the benefits of greater economic interdependence with the rest of the world. In the 1990s, the political reformations in Central and Eastern Europe, India, South Africa, Vietnam, the People's Republic of China and some parts of Eastern and Southern Africa are having a similar effect.

While market trends and unilateral political action have undoubtedly been the major shapers of the new international division of labour, multilateral action has played a significant role. Four examples may suffice. The first is the movement towards regional economic integration most vividly demonstrated in Western Europe, but also in East Asia (ASEAN), Latin America (Mercosur) and the Caribbean. More specialized schemes, such as the Lome Convention, cover trade in certain types of goods between developed and developing countries. We shall take up this issue in more detail in Section 17.3.

The second has been the rules of trade evolved and agreed upon by nations which are participants in GATT (General Agreement on Trade and Tariffs). Great progress has been made within GATT sponsored meetings, or 'rounds' of negotiation, over the past 30 years. For example, the Tokyo Conference in 1986 reduced tariffs on a wide range of commodities, while the Uruguay round in 1989–92 has done much to clarify the rules of establishment (of foreign subsidiaries) and to remove obstacles to the trade in services.[4] Third, have been the attempts by the leading OECD industrial nations to harmonize their macro-economic strategies, especially interest rate and exchange rate policies, in such a way as the *structure* of international economic activity, as dictated by economic and technological forces, can operate to the best interests of the trading nations.[5]

Fourth, through various UN agencies, notably UNCTAD, efforts have been made to discourage cross-border trade and unacceptable business practices, particularly in so far as they are perceived to work against the interests of poorer nations. While these UN agencies have no legislative powers, they sometimes exert considerable influence on the philosophies and actions of national governments towards trade and investment issues.

17.2.2   The role of MNEs in influencing the international allocation of activity

The main impact of the activities of MNEs on the international division of labour arises from the way in which they internalize cross-border intermediate product markets in the countries in which they operate. The nature and effects of this internalization, revealed both directly by the actions of MNEs or their affiliates and indirectly through their spill-over consequences on their competitors, suppliers and customers, has been described in some detail in the preceding chapters.[6] In so far as changes in the quality, efficiency and sectoral allocation of resources induced by MNEs affect the comparative trading advantages of the countries in which they operate, then they are also likely to impinge on the international (as well as the national) allocation of resources.

At the same time a distinction needs to be drawn between activities of MNEs designed to supply existing markets more efficiently and those intended to restructure the distribution of activities between countries. An investment by a British firm in Brazil to produce plated glass for the French market, an acquisition by a US firm of a copper mine in Brazil or an investment by a Japanese bank in the Netherlands are examples of the first kind of activity. Such import-substitution and resource-based investments may affect the international division of labour via their effect on the structure and efficiency of domestic production.

However, the reorganization of European investments of such US MNEs as Honeywell, Singer, International Harvester, Ford, National Cash Register and 3M following European integration,[7] or the restructuring of Philips' or Siemens' activities in South East Asia to exploit better the differences in factor endowments between that part of the world and their home countries, directly affects the global allocation of economic activity. There is every reason to suppose that such cross-border rationalization of production has been (and is being) spearheaded by MNEs – especially within the EC. In anticipation of the completion of the internal market in 1992, EC-based MNEs have been noticeably active in reorganizing and refocusing their European operations – sometimes in alliance with other MNEs.[8] As Chapter 14 has shown, this has resulted in the growth of intra-MNE trade, especially between subsidiaries in regionally-integrated areas. At the same time, intra-firm trade is becoming an increasingly important part of world trade.[9]

While the motives for the geographical specialization of activities among MNEs are similar to those which might be predicted among independent firms across national borders, the common ownership of such activities does, in itself, have a distinctive impact. *A priori*, it is difficult to identify the contents of this effect. However, as Behrman (1972, 1974) and others have long since observed, the international division of labour fashioned by MNEs is unlikely to be that which home or host governments perceive to be in the national economic interest.

In some instances, where MNEs can overcome entry barriers better than can independent firms, then (depending upon the reasons for such barriers) economic welfare may be increased. For example, relative to their EC competitors, US-owned firms have benefited from the removal of tariff restrictions within the EC, simply because of their superior ability (or greater incentive) to internalize intra-EC market failure arising from the presence of non-tariff barriers and protective national policies.[10] More generally, whenever MNEs are able to overcome impediments to cross-border transactions between independent parties, this is likely to be welfare enhancing.

On the other hand, MNEs may promote an international division of labour which is very much a second or third best. We suggest two situations when this might occur. The first is whenever they respond to exogenous inducements or penalties which, themselves, are structurally distorting. Examples include much defensive market-seeking FDI induced by import barriers of one kind or another. It is, for example, very doubtful whether much MNE investment in the highly protected manufacturing sector of some Latin American or African countries has advanced the efficient restructuring of these economies. It has certainly limited the geographical specialization of production between these countries and the rest of the world. In contrast, by *reducing* tariffs across the 49th parallel the current Canadian–US Free Trade agreement is resulting in a reorganization of US/Canadian investment and trade which is generally beneficial to both countries.[11] A similar outcome is likely to follow from any US/Mexico trade concord.

Second, MNEs may use their monopolistic or oligopolistic power in a way that results in an inefficient international allocation of economic activity at a given moment of time, and/or inhibits the development of the dynamic comparative advantage of a country. Examples include the fragmentation of the Canadian market by US firms anxious to protect their global oligopolistic positions, and the anti-competitive practices and transfer price manipulations of some MNEs. Sometimes such behaviour may be part of the global strategy of MNEs. Alternatively, it may simply be that the signals provided by the market fail to take account of the differences between the private and social costs and benefits of outward or inward direct investment. One illustration of these differences, which may have considerable effects on the long-term comparative advantage of the countries involved, is the possible 'Trojan horse' effects of Japanese direct investment in the EC, which we dealt with in Chapter 12.[12]

In general, and taking a long-term perspective, the evidence suggests that from a global viewpoint MNE activity has aided the international division of labour; just as in the nineteenth century the growth of national firms in the US led to an improved domestic division of labour over and above that which was generated by regional firms. The forces of technology and population growth and capital accumulation have all helped fashion the internationalization of markets and production. In so far as the common ownership of cross-border activities brings its own organizational efficiencies, this will have led to an improved allocation of resources.

17.3 ECONOMIC INTEGRATION

17.3.1 The nature of economic integration

We have already suggested that in its complete form economic integration is the political, economic and monetary unification of two or more independent national or regional authorities, in which there are no economic frontiers and the real prices of similar goods and factors of production are equalized. The United States of America is (as its name implies) a fully integrated geographical area consisting of a federation of 51 states. By contrast, the European Free Trade Association (EFTA) is a customs union of seven countries, each of which agrees to remove all tariff and quantitative restrictions on mutual trade, but which in all other respects remains autonomous in decision taking. The group of Asian countries comprising ASEAN are even more informally organized. They are bonded by the intent to pursue policies that will help enhance intra-Asian trade and they exchange information to promote this end. However, there are no formal agreements. By the end of 1992, the EC aims to abolish all non-tariff impediments to trade. This will involve the elimination of border controls, the implementation of technical standards and the harmonization of fiscal duties – each of which requires some abrogation of the economic sovereignty of the participating countries (Cechinni, 1988).

For any group of countries, economic integration may be thought of as a point on a matrix. Reference is again made to Figure 17.1. The vertical axis identifies different *degrees* of integration. Usually, as one moves down the axis, the issues assume a greater degree of political importance. The horizontal axis gauges the *nature* of the integration. This varies from an informal and limited agreement to exchange information or reach a consensus to achieve certain goals, to a comprehensive, binding and coordinated policy of action.

As the figure suggests, while the US[13] (included for the sake of illustration) is (almost) fully integrated, most other regional associations have been set up to achieve very specific goals and are far from fully integrated. One area which did approach full integration – even to the extent of having its own airline and university – was the East African

Economic Association set up in 1973. However, for political and other reasons, this floundered and was disbanded in 1977.

A country may be part of more than one integrated region. As we have already observed, the leading industrial nations try, wherever possible, to harmonize their macro-economic policies in the cause of global economic stability. There are several preferential trading agreements which exist between different groups of countries (e.g. members of the Commonwealth) and between some developing and developed countries. There are, in addition, a plethora of cross-country commodity agreements which affect the pattern of trade between the parties to the agreements, and between them and the rest of the world, although these do not always or necessarily make for freer or more efficient international markets.

One feature of such agreements is that they require some kind of coordination of economic policy by the participating governments. This, in turn, implies some kind of abrogation of national decision taking. Another is that they are generally intended to promote cross-country trade and the mobility of factor services by fostering a more market-oriented pattern of intra-regional resource allocation. The formation of the EC on 1st January 1958[14] initially led to the elimination of all tariff barriers. The completion of the internal market of the EC by 1st January 1993 is intended to remove a wide range of non-tariff obstacles. To this end, the Community is in the process of issuing 293 directives, all of which are aimed at promoting freer trade between the 12 constituent nations and ensuring a more efficient allocation of economic activity.

Economic integration may be intended to advance either the economic or political goals of the participating countries. Usually it is a mixture of the two with the political element becoming more important as one moves towards total integration. In any event, the two cannot be separated in the contemporary world as political power and influence are closely related to economic strength.[15] By agreeing to become partially or fully integrated with another Nation State, it may be presumed that the governments of the integrating countries perceive that the gains from any association will exceed the costs – including the surrender of sovereignty in one or other area of decision taking. Countries, or more

specifically governments of countries, understandingly differ in their valuations of the tradeoffs involved. Compare, for example, the attitudes of Canada and the US to the free trade agreement between them, or the attitudes of Chile and Bolivia with those of Brazil and Mexico with regard to LAFTA. There may also be genuine differences of opinions about the nature, pattern and distribution of the expected benefits from integration, as well as of the probability of these being achieved.

17.3.2   The effects of regional integration

In discussing the likely impact of regional integration on MNE activity into and out of the integrated area, it is convenient to distinguish between its *primary* or *initial* effects and its *secondary* or *consequential* effects. The response of MNEs and the net effect of regional integration on inward and outward direct investment will also depend on the particular macro-economic consequences being considered. Some of these responses and effects are summarized in Table 17.1.

Take, for example, the removal of tariff barriers, such as took place (and continued to take place) on the formation of the EC in 1958 and the conclusion of the Canada–US Free Trade Agreement of 1990. The primary consequence of this kind of integration is a change in the costs and benefits of supplying an existing market from a location inside and outside the integrated region. Thus, goods exported from France to Italy or from Canada to the US will increase their competitiveness relative to domestic firms producing in Italy and the US. Clearly, the extent to which exports will increase will depend on the relative importance of the transfer costs saved, any effect the extra sales of the exporting companies may have on its production costs and the elasticity of demand for the final products. As far as firms from countries outside the integrated market are concerned, the locational effects will depend upon the value of the common external tariff and/or non-tariff barriers relative to those previously imposed by individual countries. Like the companies within the integrated area, they should benefit from the removal of intra-country trade barriers.

Table 17.1 The effects of economic integration on foreign direct investment.

Macro-economic effect of integration	MNE response	Net trade effect	Net FDI effect
Intra-regional trade more attractive than extra-regional trade[1]	Replacement exports with foreign direct investment (defensive export-substituting investment)	*Negative* Sales by regionally based MNE affiliates replace exports to the region by MNE	*Positive* Increased investment in regionally based MNE affiliates
New configuration of L advantages among members of the region	Adjust existing investments in the region to reflect free intra-regional trade (reorganization investment)	*Neutral, perhaps positive* Intra-regional trade could rise if reorganization leads to increased plant and country specialization; extra-regional exports could rise if region's industries become more competitive in world markets	*Neutral* For the region as a whole; gains in some countries offset by losses in others
Cost reduction and efficiency gains	Increase value-adding activities within region; integrate with other offshore FDI (rationalized investment)	*Neutral, perhaps positive* Same as for reorganization but if less is imported into region	*Positive* Increase sourcing by MNEs in the region
Market expansion, demand growth and technical progress	Gain first-mover advantages via FDI (offensive export-substituting investment)	*Neutral* If demand in regional market grows faster than supply from new inwards FDI, otherwise *possibly* negative	*Positive* Same as for defensive export-substituting investment

1 Assumes that integration does not result in lower external tariffs than previously existed among individual countries and that non-tariff barriers do not prevent the growth of intra-regional trade.

Source: Adapted from UNCTC (1990c).

We have said that these primary, or initial, locational consequences (also referred to in the literature as trade diversion effects) will influence countries and sectors in different ways. They are also likely to affect different kinds of firms differently. Consider the removal of non-tariff barriers consequential upon EC 1992. The elimination of border controls, which represent a fixed cost to firms, is likely to benefit small (relative to large) firms. The cessation of favoured treatment in their procurement policies by governments towards firms located in their own country will clearly work against the uncompetitive firms in that country. Firms that already have a network of value-added activities or marketing contacts and distribution outlets within the integrated region are particularly well placed to benefit from regional integration. MNEs, particularly those which are already pursuing a polycentric strategy, are among those most likely to gain.

However, it is the secondary effects of integration which, in the long run, are likely to be of the greatest importance for the international allocation of economic activity. These arise both from the restructuring of such activity between countries, sectors and firms within the integrated area, and from the new opportunities for firms to increase their technical and scale efficiencies by reducing production and transaction costs. In so far as these gains are passed on to the owners of factor services, or to consumers, integration will lead to an increase in real income and a further exploitation of the benefits of product and plant specialization. It may also be expected to encourage innovation and technological progress. Such effects are 'dynamic' in the sense that they are likely to raise the potential growth rates of (at least some of) the integrating economies.[16]

Such gains may be substantial. The European Commission has estimated that the completion of the internal market will raise the GNP of the EC by up to 6.5% per annum. This is expected to be accomplished both by an improvement in industrial productivity and a reduction in unemployment. On average, consumer prices are expected to fall by 6.0%. About two-fifths of this gain is calculated to occur from a saving of real costs following the elimination of non-tariff barriers, another one-third from the opportunities of companies to exploit the economies of scale more fully, and the balance from a reduction in business inefficiencies and monopoly

profits resulting from more intensive competition.[17]

There are other effects of integration, which, though less quantifiable, are no less critical for both the ownership and location of economic activity. These include the policies adopted by the supervising body of the integrated region (cf those of the individual member countries) towards competition and restrictive practices, labour, the migration of labour, employment legislation, regional inequities, environmental protection, accounting and auditing procedures, deregulation or privatization of financial services, and to trade and investment negotiations with non-member countries.

It is not the purpose of this chapter to examine the possible consequences of the coordination or harmonization of such policies. It is sufficient to emphasize that these supra-government initiated measures may be as important an influence on the level and pattern of foreign-owned production both within and between the integrated region as is the reduction of market distortion. Indeed, they are often portrayed as another kind of non-tariff barrier (Robinson, 1983). More recently, the Vdreling proposal, which would have required the EC affiliates of foreign firms to disclose information about the activities of their parent companies, was bitterly opposed by many non-European MNEs.[18]

We would make one further point. Not only are the effects of economic integration likely to vary between countries, industries and firms (and history suggests that the larger, more influential, and more competitive economic units generally seem to gain the most[19]), but also they will depend on the way in which such integration affects the relationship between these units and those outside the integrated area. Currently, the prospects of EC 1992 are encouraging European firms to conclude alliances with Japanese and US firms to protect or advance not just their European but their global competitive positions. This is particularly so in the case of high technology firms whose fixed costs of innovation, production and marketing are becoming so huge that they can only survive by capturing new markets or sharing these costs with other firms. In the last resort, then, the effects of regional integration must be evaluated in terms of the costs and benefits to global economic activity and not just to that which takes place within the integrated area.

17.3.3 Regional integration and MNE activity

There are many similarities between the forces making for cross-border corporate and regional integration. In both cases, a prerequisite is a failure of markets to allocate economic activities efficiently among the units (i.e. firms or countries) being integrated, which it is envisaged that a common governance of the units will overcome or reduce. However, whereas MNEs seek to internalize cross-border markets to reduce or circumvent *inter*-firm transaction costs, the motives are arguably more complex in the case of the regional groupings of countries. While these groupings are also prompted by a desire to reduce the inter-country costs of doing business, the incentive to lower the costs of *intra*-regional government-induced market distortions or to provide a countervailing economic or political force to other countries or regional groupings may be of even greater significance.

Table 17.2 details the factors that favour corporate and regional integration. Some of these encourage both kinds of integration; others one or the other. Of course, the presence of these factors does not necessarily tell in favour of either corporate or regional integration. Nor does it follow that their operation will work in the interests of all parties. The position of established MNE producers, regions, or even countries, may mean that neither corporate nor national interests are best served by participation in regional groupings, unless there is some form of compensation for the adjustment or displacement costs likely to be entailed. For similar reasons, it is certainly not always in the interests of particular MNEs to promote regional integration if, for example, that would mean subjecting an established market to increased competition from new entrants.

17.3.4 The impact of European integration on corporate integration

Prior to the establishment of the European Common Market in 1958, there was substantial FDI in the Member States by firms from other Member States and, more particularly, by firms from other countries, notably the United States.[20] The activities of

Table 17.2 Forces influencing corporate and regional integration.

Integration of corporations	Integration of countries
Basic motive: to improve profitability and the long-term competitive position.	**Basic motive**: to increase efficiency or resource usage and to increase the economic and strategic (including political) strength of region and member countries.
• To exploit economies of the firm.	• To overcome structural market distortions (e.g. tariff barriers, subsidies) and to encourage competition.
• To reduce risk and uncertainty associated with market transactions.	• To eliminate or reduce imperfections in foreign exchange, capital and labour markets.
• To protect quality control of intermediate and final products.	• To facilitate the possibility of functional product and process specialization of firms within the region, and promote trade in intermediate products.
• To capture the economies of synergy, which result from the common ownership of separate, but interrelated activities.	• To facilitate the conduct of optimal policies and to secure gains from policy coordination in circumstances of structural and policy interdependence.
• To protect the value of proprietary assets (e.g. technology, trademarks, management skills).	• To develop economic and strategic strength by the adoption of a common policy towards non-member countries.
• To overcome the transaction costs of using markets.	• To increase market size and improve the technological capability of member countries.
• To gain competitive strength.	
• To share common overheads.	

Source: Dunning and Robson (1988).

such foreign-owned firms were primarily geared to producing goods for the domestic markets of the host countries in place of exports from the investing countries. In the main, such investment was prompted by the desire to circumvent import restrictions of one kind or another. Some investment was made for more aggressive reasons, for example, to take advantage of lower production costs in the host country or better to meet the needs of the consumers being served.

In some cases, the foreign firms operating in the EC had investments in several Member States. However, because of border and other non-tariff barriers to intra-European trade, there were few cross-border transactions either between the European affiliates of MNEs or between these and their parent companies. The competitive or O-specific advantages which made possible the FDI in the first place were usually based on the possession of specific intangible assets (Oa).[21] These were transferred to individual host countries within the same firm, rather than sold on the open market, because the former route was perceived by the foreign firm to offer a higher economic rent. Although the separate affiliates were under a common ownership, the advantages associated with this ownership could not be fully appropriated because of the high inter-country transaction costs involved.

The erosion of intra-EC trade barriers produced two opposing effects on direct investment between the Member States, and two complementary effects on inward investment from non-EC countries. By lowering the costs of exporting within the EC or from the home country of a non-EC MNE, it reduced the incentive for intra-EC MNE activity. At the same time, by reducing transfer costs between the Member States, it allowed MNEs to coordinate their European production facilities better and to serve a much wider market. This directly led to more intra-EC direct investment. In other words, the abatement of structural intra-country distortions helped both EC and foreign multinationals to exploit better the O advantages of owning and operating multiple plants.

The evidence[22] strongly suggests that the net effect of European integration has been to increase the value-added activities of both foreign-owned MNEs in the EC and of EC-owned MNEs outside the EC. Over the past three decades, not only has the EC attracted a larger increase in the share of

FDI from all countries (see Chapter 2), but a substantial proportion of this investment has been directed to the restructuring and relocation of existing activities (Cantwell, 1988, 1992; UN, 1992a). One result of this reorientation of FDI is that there has been a substantial increase in intra-industry and intra-firm trade between the Member States of the Community. Intra-EC investments have also sharply risen and are now on a par with Community investments in the rest of the world. In 1989 alone, they rose by 51% to 33 billion Ecus.

17.3.5   The distribution of MNE activities within the regionally integrated area

What of the impact of regional integration on the distribution of activities of MNEs within the integrated area? Using orthodox location theory, economists in the late 1960s (Clark *et al.*, 1969) predicted that European integration would cause FDI to become more concentrated in the central corridor of the EC to the detriment of the peripheral areas. The Community has now been in existence for more than 30 years and there have been a number of *ex post* studies on the distribution of intra-EC MNE activity, for example, Buckley and Artisien (1987, 1988). These studies do not wholly support the initial predictions. In the UK, for example, more than three-quarters of new Japanese direct investment since 1970 has been directed to regions outside the main industrial conurbations (JETRO, 1989). Similarly, between 1975 and 1985, Spain attracted more than one-third of new employment in Western European, US and Japanese-owned car plants.

Table 17.3 presents some data on the geographical and sectoral distribution of US and Japanese multinational manufacturing activity in the EC (12), in 1990. *Inter alia*, while the table shows a certain concentration of FDI in the high technology sectors in the larger and/or more technologically advanced economies, *viz* the UK, West Germany, Italy and France, investment in other sectors is more widely dispersed.

This distribution of economic activity reflects three main factors. The first is the structure of resource endowments and capabilities, and of mar-

Table 17.3 US and Japanese direct investment stake in the EC 1990. (% of total in particular countries)

	US (Stock of investment end 1990)						Japan (Cumulative investment flows 1951–March 1990)					
	France	Germany	Netherlands	UK	Other EC	All EC	France	Germany	Netherlands	UK	Other¹ EC	All Europe
Food and kindred products	2.3	4.2	7.7	3.2	6.5	100.0	14.3	0.2	0.4	0.6	0.3	100.0
Chemical and allied products	16.9	11.9	9.4	5.4	17.9	100.0	2.8	9.0	2.9	0.7	2.4	100.0
Primary and fabricated metals	2.2	4.7	nsa	1.6	2.9	100.0	1.9	0.0	2.3	0.4	1.7	100.0
Industrial machinery	21.3	14.6	4.9	4.8	14.7	100.0	8.7	6.5	2.1	2.5	1.9	100.0
Electrical and electronic equipment	2.8	2.9	4.3	2.0	2.5	100.0	4.3	9.8	11.1	8.6	2.1	100.0
Transportation equipment	3.9	12.2	nsa	4.4	4.6	100.0	1.7	0.5	1.2	4.1	4.8	100.0
Textiles and clothing	nsa	nsa	nsa	nsa	nsa	100.0	3.0	0.8	1.8	0.9	1.9	100.0
Paper and allied products							nsa	nsa	nsa	nsa	nsa	100.0
Other manufacturing	15.2	12.6	7.4	10.4	11.5	100.0	2.7	2.5	1.3	1.3	2.8	100.0
All manufacturing	64.5	63.1	35.8	31.8	59.4	100.0	32.2	29.7	22.0	18.9	18.0	100.0
All sectors	100.0	100.0	100.0	100.0	100.0	100.0	100.0	100.0	100.0	100.0	100.0	100.0

1. Other Europe.
nsa   not separately available.

Source: US Department of Commerce and Japan's Ministry of Finance.

kets in the individual member countries. Take employee compensation, for example. According to the ILO, the average auto worker in Spain earned $14.1 an hour in 1989 compared with the $25.4 an hour earned by his German equivalent. With the fall in cross-border transaction and transport costs, such direct labour costs are assuming a rather greater importance in the locational decisions of MNEs.

Second, Community policy has permitted Member States to offer relatively generous investment incentives wherever they can demonstrate that unemployment in their countries, or in particular regions of their countries, is noticeably above the average for the EC, or where they are lagging behind in growth or structural adaptation. Thus, Ireland, Southern Italy and parts of the United Kingdom, with above average unemployment, and now Spain and Portugal as part of their development programmes, receive EC regional and other grants well above the average.

At the same time, national governments, in negotiation with foreign MNEs, may differ con-siderably in their attitudes and policies to foreign investors. The attractive terms of entry offered by the UK government was one of the critical factors which drew the Nissan motor vehicle company to the UK. As part of the bargaining deal, the Japanese firm was persuaded to locate its plant in North East England, a peripheral region as far as the EC is concerned. Various studies, for example, Yannopoulos and Dunning (1976) and Young et al. (1988) have shown that foreign MNEs tend to respond rather more positively to regional incentives than do indigenous firms. Some of these incentives are provided by regional or local authorities rather than by the central or federal government. In the US, individual states actively compete with each other to obtain new inward investment (Graham and Krugman, 1989; Kline, 1989; Coughlin et al., 1991).[23] In the UK, regional development agencies, especially in Scotland, Northern Ireland and Wales, have aggressively promoted their own cases for new investment.

There is some evidence of a 'follow my leader'

geographical strategy among foreign investors, which integration helps foster. Partly this is a cultural phenomenon. In Germany, in the post-war period, a Japanese community – including a Japanese school – was established in Dusseldorf and has proved a powerful attraction to new Japanese investors.[24] In the UK, Sony was the first of the successful colour TV companies to set up a factory in South Wales; its success attracted several other colour TV companies. Rather differently, Scotland has long had a competitive advantage in the training of skilled electrical and mechanical engineers, and the clustering of related industries using this kind of labour. This, almost certainly, helped induce several US-based semiconductor companies to set up plants in the 1960s and 1970s. The Japanese followed in the 1980s. And, as mentioned earlier, Spain appears to be building a competitive advantage for itself in motor car assembling.

In conclusion, economic integration offers a wider locational choice to both domestic and foreign companies to produce within the integrated region. In so doing, it promotes both centripetal and centrifugal effects. On the one hand, in sectors where there are important economies of the clustering of related and supporting industries, it encourages centres of excellence. Mostly, but not always, these will be in towns, cities or around key arteries which are the industrial or commercial heartlands of the integrated region.[25] However, economic development and reductions in intra-firm communication and transport costs (which economic integration may, itself, promote) may sometimes help create new clusters of activity. Here, the main inducement is to gain access to cutting edge technology and the best trained scientists and engineers. Chapter 11 has already explained the growth of intra-R&D investment by MNEs in the Triad. Parallel to this is the upsurge in technical and science parks which are usually sited near first rate universities or research institutions. By the end of 1990, at least five Japanese MNEs had established R&D facilities in universities or academically-related technology and science parks in the UK.[26]

The evidence suggests that MNEs both help shape these developments and respond to them more actively than indigenous firms. This, in turn, reflects their particular O-specific advantages, including their ability to take advantage of changes in the advantages of countries. MNEs are both in the van of technological development and are generally faster growers than their uninational competitors (Dunning, 1985). They also can, and do, coordinate their activities more effectively than non-uninational firms, while an OECD study published in 1985 showed that, in response to changes in demand conditions, technology, government policies or the general economic climate, they tend to react earlier and more speedily than their indigenous counterparts. Finally, as we have seen, MNEs are likely to be more sensitive to host government policies in steering their investments to regions most in need of investment. This seems particularly to be the case with new Japanese and Korean investment in the EC and in the US.

17.3.6 Empirical evidence of the response of MNEs to economic integration

Empirical studies of the consequences of economic integration on multinational investment fall into four main groups. The first group attempts to examine the relationship between integration and the level and pattern of inward or outward direct investment. Early research by Scaperlanda (1967, 1968), Scaperlanda and White (1969), Wallis (1968), D'Arge (1969, 1971a, 1971b) and Schmitz (1970) all pointed to a structural shift of US outward direct investment towards EC countries in the decade or so after the formation of the Community.[27] Later work by O'Farrell (1983) and Walsh (1979) showed that Ireland's accession to the EC led to a substantial increase in both US and other EC investments in that country, while the UK's share of new US investment in the EC increased sharply in the years immediately before and after its accession. Other data suggests that in the 1960s US firms were substituting EC production for exports from the US (Dunning, 1991e), while their share of EC production and exports relative to that of EC-owned firms also rose.[28] However, a recent survey by Millington and Bayliss (1991) revealed that non-tariff barriers (notably discriminatory public procurement policies) were among the major factors leading to increased UK FDI in the rest of the EC in the 1980s.

A second group of studies has focused on the link between the relative tariff discriminatory effects of economic integration and the extent to which US investment in the EC is replaced by US exports to the EC.[29] The findings of these studies are mixed and often contradictory. Partly this reflects the difficulty of researchers in separating the tariff from other variables that might affect US investment in the EC; partly it is because different measures are used by researchers to identify tariff changes; and partly as a result of the differences in the specification of the models used.[30] However, even those studies which have hypothesized that the level of tariffs was a statistically significant variable influencing US direct investment in the EC (Schmitz and Bieri, 1972; Lunn, 1980; Scaperlanda and Balough, 1983), have acknowledged that a much more important driving force was the growth of the EC market. Indeed, Goldberg (1972) has estimated that about 80% of the new investment of US firms in the period 1958 to 1970 could be explained by the market growth hypothesis. Of course, part of this growth was, itself, a result of the removal of tariff barriers.

A third group of studies examined the geographical distribution of US investment in the EC, and concluded that there is some reason to suppose that such investment is attributable to the largest and fastest growing markets. However, like the first group, these studies made no attempt to evaluate the extent to which this faster growth was due to economic integration *per se*.

A fourth group of studies looked at the changing characteristics of FDI in the EC and the organizational strategies of MNEs. Here the main subject of interest has been to identify the extent to which economic integration has affected the regional division of labour within MNE affiliates. These studies have been of two kinds. The first is typified by the work of strategic business analysts such as Doz, Porter, Prahalad, Ghoshal and Bartlett, who have sought to identify and explain the ways in which regional integration may affect various components of the management strategy of MNEs, including the locus of decision taking within the MNE. The second is that of economists who have been primarily interested in the consequences of integration on the industrial structure and trading patterns of the constituent countries. We shall look at each of these in turn.

The restructuring of activity by MNEs

The literature is replete with examples of the way in which MNEs respond to, or take advantage of, regional integration. Chapter 8 paid some attention to the alternative organizational and decision-making strategies that MNEs might pursue. In particular, it distinguished between the governance of foreign affiliates that produced goods and services mainly for the local market, and were largely truncated versions of their parent companies, and those that were part of a regionally- or globally-integrated strategy. It was also suggested that the size of the regional market and the extent to which there were entry barriers to that market were among the key variables determining which of these strategies an MNE might adopt. It then follows that as and when regional integration offers new opportunities for servicing (or sourcing from) larger markets, so might the way in which an MNE organizes its affiliates' activities also change. In particular, borrowing from Porter's terminology, integration may encourage MNEs to switch from practising a multi-domestic or country-centred strategy to a regionally-oriented strategy. They will do so because integration has, itself, changed the configuration of the L advantages of the participating Member States and the O advantages of the MNEs. How, then, might regional integration affect the organization of MNE activities?

Let us again look at some examples from the experience of MNEs operating in the EC. Broadly speaking, it would seem there have been three responses to European integration. First, companies like SKF, 3M, Scott Paper and Philips of Eindhoven have adopted a pattern of more intensive product (i.e. horizontal) specialization. Sometimes, but not always, this rationalization has been accompanied by a pan-European marketing strategy. SKF, for example, is a broad range supplier of ball bearings, but each of its European plants concentrates on the production of just two or three lines which it supplies to the whole world. Philips produces electric irons and razors in its Austrian factories, colour TV sets in its Eindhoven plant and washing machines in its Antwerp facility for the entire European market. Ford produces the Fiesta car in Cologne and Dagenham and the Escort in Saarlouis. General Motors concentrates Nova production in Spain. 3M produces Scotch tape in its German factory and

'Post-it' notes in its UK factory. Previously, these companies manufactured a range of products in each country for sale mainly to consumers of that market.

Second, some MNEs have chosen to specialize their activities along a particular value-added chain (i.e. vertical specialization). The Ford Motor Company now concentrates its European production of engines in Valencia (Spain), gear boxes and differentials in Bordeaux (France) and the major body processing components in Saarlouis and Valencia. Like Ford, IBM, while practising dual sourcing, concentrates its European output of different parts and components in one or more of its EC facilities. Though fairly diversified at the final stage of production, most non-European pharmaceutical MNEs have concentrated the production of active ingredients, as well as their R&D activities, in a select number of EC locations, notably the UK, France, West Germany and Ireland.

More generally, it might be expected that integration would promote a more hierarchical division of labour, with high value activities being concentrated in one or two central locations, and lower value activities being dispersed. As indicated earlier, sometimes specialization is based on traditional factor endowments, sometimes on the need to take advantage of economies of scale and sometimes on the macro-organization policies pursued by governments. Research, however, suggests that the need to reduce transaction costs (including transport), rather than production costs, is becoming an increasingly important determinant of the locational choice (Dunning, 1991c).

Third, the pattern of specialization is likely to depend on the type of *inter*-firm competition promoted by economic integration. Thus, removing restrictions on government procurement, and encouraging the harmonization of cross-border technical standards may open up possibilities for more inter-firm specialization of similar products. In the European (and indeed global) paint industry, for example, the German firm BASF specializes in automobile paints, and the UK firms Courtaulds and ICI in marine, decorative and industrial paints.

Not all MNEs, however, have adopted a strategy of product or process specialization consequent upon regional integration. Indeed, according to one British study of 140 US and Continental European subsidiaries in the UK, although they were strongly European focused, only a minority could be said to be pursuing an integrated production or marketing strategy (Hood and Young, 1983). Those which have to meet the needs of idiosyncratic markets may find any benefits from economies of scale are outweighed by the reduced demand or additional costs of product or process adaptation. The excellent documentation of the white goods sector in the EC by Baden-Fuller and Stopford (1991) shows that, although there has been an increase in industrial concentration, there is little evidence of any trend towards the globalization of products or markets. The authors reveal that, even within Europe, there are significant differences of cross-border consumer tastes, distribution channels, production, promotion and development methods which, taken as a whole, seriously inhibit European MNEs from exploiting the benefits of regional integration.[31] Indeed, it may well be argued that despite becoming mature and having extensive cross-border trade, the European market for white goods has become less unified and the barriers to gaining access to local distribution have increased over the past decade. Other examples of the need to take account of country-specific consumer tastes outweighing the advantages of production economies include carpets and some kinds of textiles. In these cases, integration is likely to make little difference to corporate strategies. Neither will it do so where transport costs are an important component of the total costs of production or where products are strongly location bound (e.g. several building materials).

At this point it is, perhaps, worth noting that some of the obstacles to corporate integration in the EC may be removed by the end of 1992. In his writings (Doz, 1986; Doz and Prahalad, 1987), Yves Doz has classified the production and marketing strategies of MNEs with affiliates in the EC according to the influence exerted and policies pursued by host governments. Using the percentage of the sales of particular sectors to government[32] (i.e. the degree of public procurement) as a proxy for government influence, Doz (1986) concluded that in sectors where this ratio was the highest in the early 1980s (for example, it was 100% in military aircraft and 90% in electricity generating equipment), MNEs were most likely to adopt nationally-responsive strategies, that is, they behaved like multi-domestic enterprises. By contrast, in those sectors where the ratio of government purchases was the least (e.g. colour TV tubes (0%), agri-tractors (close to 0%) and motor vehicles (2%)), they tended to practise a regionally- or globally-integrated strategy. For sectors in between these extremes, MNEs were most likely to adopt a mixed or multi-focal strategy. In all instances, Doz found that there were variations in the strategies pursued *between* MNEs in particular sectors. In the early 1980s, for example, in the microelectronics and semiconductor sectors, Texas Instruments was a fully-integrated European producer while Siemens, Plessey and GEC operated purely nationally-responsive strategies (UN, 1992a).

Since, along with the privatization and deregulation of national markets, EC 1992 will reduce barriers to government procurements, it is highly likely that this will lead to a further reappraisal of the organization of transnational activities, especially of those MNEs currently pursuing nationally-responsive strategies.

For many years other factors have discouraged cross-border corporate integration. These include cross-border controls, differential technical standards and fiscal policies. Others are more 'natural' barriers, such as transport, costs and differences in buying cultures. While most of the former will disappear with EC 1992, the latter may not. In consequence, at least some MNEs will continue to be nationally, rather than regionally, oriented. As earlier chapters[33] have demonstrated, a successful locational strategy is one that balances the global advantages of exploiting the advantages of the governance of related assets and proprietary knowledge, while continuing to recognize the importance of adapting its products and production methods to the specific needs of local markets (Doz and Prahalad, 1987).[34]

Macro-economic data

Some macro-data of the extent to which product or process specialization is practised among US multinationals in the EC and LAFTA, and how this has changed over time, is provided by the US Department of Commerce. *Inter alia*, the data reveals, first, that the proportion of the sales of US manufacturing affiliates in the EC exported to other parts of Europe rose from 14.1% in 1957 to 30.5% in 1989. Second, they show that the export propensity of US affiliates

in the EC and, to a lesser extent, in the major LAFTA countries (e.g. Brazil and Mexico), is considerably greater than that in other parts of the world. However, as a result of the Canada–US Free Trade Agreement it might be reasonable to expect trade between US firms and their affiliates across the 49th parallel to increase.

Third, the proportion of exports accounted for by intra-firm transactions to countries other than the US is greater both in the case of the EC and LAFTA countries than in other parts of the world (US Department of Commerce, vd). Moreover this proportion has increased significantly since the data was first published in 1966. Fourth, the propensity of US affiliates to engage in export and intra-firm exports varies between industrial sectors. It is greatest in sectors such as motor vehicles and consumer electronics, where one would expect the benefits of product or process specialization to be most marked. It is least in sectors in which these benefits are absent or are outweighed by the localization of consumer tastes or by cross-border transportation costs.[35]

17.4 THE INTERACTION BETWEEN MNE ACTIVITY AND SOME SPECIFIC KINDS OF REGIONAL INTEGRATION

17.4.1 The European Community: Mark 1 integration

Previous chapters have shown that the connection between the activities of MNEs, or their affiliates, and the goals and policies of the individual countries, or groups of countries, in which they operate, is likely to be a wide ranging and dynamic process. In the present context, it is also highly complex in that the goals of regional integration may extend well beyond the purely economic. Let us, however, concentrate on these latter objectives which, in an EC context, might be broadly described as:

(1) a more efficient deployment of resources between Member States and sectors, and within Member States and sectors;

(2) an increase in the competitiveness of EC-owned

firms by upgrading indigenous technological, marketing and organizational capabilities, and promoting a more dynamic and aggressive entrepreneurial ethos.

To what extent has the response of MNEs to regional integration helped to accomplish these objectives? Economic theory suggests that corporate integration might have both beneficial and adverse effects. On the one hand, where the transaction costs of using the market as an exchange mechanism are reduced by intra-firm transactions, a more efficient allocation of resources may be expected. On the other, in so far as corporate integration may lead to a further concentration of economic power and to an increase in restrictive business practices, it may work against the goals of regional integration.

Both these effects, the nature, extent and balance of which have been widely discussed in the literature (e.g. Caves, 1982; Teece, 1985; Williamson, 1986), may arise from the cross-border specialization of activities by MNEs, whether or not their headquarters are located within the EC. However, two further issues arise in the case of integration which is undertaken by non-EC MNEs. The first is whether the coordination of their EC activities is, itself, part of a global production or marketing strategy. If so, what, if any, difference does this make to the extent and pattern of these activities and of their competitive postures in Europe. The second concerns the distribution of the benefits of such FDI between the EC and non-EC stakeholders.

Empirical research has, so far, provided only scattered evidence on these two questions. Although, as Chapter 15 has shown, within the EC countries in which they operate, foreign (in particular US) affiliates generally outperform their indigenous competitors and operate in the more productive, technologically advanced and growth-oriented sectors,[36] it is difficult to establish how far (if at all) these outcomes are a direct consequence of their activities. There is some suggestion that since 1958 at least some of the larger European MNEs with an extensive network of manufacturing operations in the EC have improved their competitive position vis à vis US MNEs; they may be expected to do even better following the completion of the internal market in 1992. Indicators of such competitive strengths include the recovery of the share of world

markets of European companies in several sectors (Dunning, 1988b; Franko, 1991) and the impressive growth of EC direct investment in the US.[37]

Part of the reason for the improved competitiveness of European firms has been the growth of cross-border strategic alliances and mergers – particularly in the capital-intensive and high technology manufacturing sectors and the information-intensive service sectors (Van Tulder and Junne, 1988; Gugler, 1991, 1992). Much of the attention paid to, and concern about, the process of corporate integration among non-European MNEs in the EC has been rather differently focused. Principally, interest has been directed to the extent to which such integration has aided the home countries of such MNEs to improve their global competitive position vis à vis EC firms. In other words, taking US direct investment as an example, the question addressed has been whether or not European regional integration has helped advance the competitive position of the US economy by enabling American-owned firms to derive more benefit from such integration than their European competitors?

One further aspect of the interaction between corporate and regional integration may be mentioned. Earlier in this chapter, we suggested that corporate integration may be horizontal (i.e. between activities at similar points on different value-added chains) or vertical (i.e. between activities at different points on the same value chain). In both cases, however, it leads to a division of labour between value-adding activities. There is also a vertical and horizontal division of labour over space. In this connection, Chapter 11 has shown that the location of high value-added activities – notably R&D – tends to be concentrated in the home countries of MNEs, especially in the case of US MNEs. How does this affect the distribution of the gains from corporate integration?

To some analysts, the question of who owns or controls a particular set of value-added activities in a country is irrelevant, it being argued that whoever is the more efficient coordinator and allocator of resources and capabilities ought to decide upon their use. If this should mean that the high value-added activities are better undertaken in one country than another, then, in so far as this is consistent with the dictates of dynamic comparative advantage, so much the better.

Not all governments, however, would accept this philosophy. Moreover, the justification for leaving cross-border resource allocation to the market presupposes that the mechanism is capable of inducing firms efficiently and painlessly to adjust their output to changes in supply and/or demand conditions. In a world of rapid technological change, this is a highly questionable assumption. Not only might the net private benefits of resource restructuring and upgrading be less than the net social benefits, but, since the strategies of MNEs in oligopolistic markets are not necessarily directed to optimizing resource usage or resource improvement, even the net private benefits of restructuring may be minimal.

The history of economic development is replete with examples of the preconditions for private investment, whether it be undertaken by domestic or foreign-owned enterprises. These include an adequate supportive infrastructure (e.g. power supplies, a road and rail network and efficient telecommunication facilities), a reasonably educated and well motivated labour force and a fiscal system that is conducive to entrepreneurship. To a greater or lesser extent, the role of government in helping to fashion the appropriate ESP configuration for MNE investment is generally acknowledged. It is also accepted that extra market intervention may be necessary to induce such enterprises to engage in at least some kinds of structural adjustment, particularly where these may require international relocation of some of their higher value activities. Clearly, this would only be commendable if the reallocation of activity, which was to be partially financed from public funds, were to yield a social return sufficient to recoup the costs. In some of the most successful post-war economies, where the partnership between governments and business has been a critical factor in the restructuring of industrial activity, there can be little doubt that this has been so.

In other cases, government action might be more appropriately directed to simulating or encouraging a more efficient market system than that which exists, thereby encouraging or impelling firms to adapt their international resource allocation in the desired way.

In practice, of course, national governments are not primarily concerned with promoting an international allocation of resources which adds to global economic welfare, except where they perceive that this also advances their own economic objectives. Neither the US nor the Japanese government is interested in advancing regional integration within the EC or between the EC and the US or Japan, except in so far as it is considered to be in their own long-term interests. This might imply that neither government would be prepared to advance the technological capabilities of the EC by, for example, encouraging its enterprises to locate high value activities in the community, if it thought that this would weaken the competitive position of its own firms.[38] The observed disinclination by the senior managers of MNEs to disturb the *status quo* of the geographical distribution of high value products or processes may then well be in accord with their own government's industrial strategy.

It is, therefore, left to European governments – either individually or collectively – to take the necessary action to ensure that their domestic firms are not out-competed by foreign-owned firms, where the latter have erected their own barriers to entry. The EC or its Member States can do this both by ensuring that its own firms are provided with the infrastructure they need to compete in domestic and international markets, and by facilitating structural adaptation to shifts in global demand and relative prices, to technological progress and to changing comparative advantages. This does not mean a wholesale subsidization of European industry. Indeed, it may well be desirable for European MNEs to reduce their involvement in some sectors, while, in others, foreign subsidiaries should be encouraged to engage in higher value activities. However, it certainly does demand a much more explicit recognition by European governments that if the benefits of regional integration are not to be primarily captured by foreign firms – and the countries of their origin[39] – more attention may need to be given to encouraging their own firms to protect and advance their own competitive positions.

Such encouragement might take various forms. It might be directed to the support of intra-European mergers or to cross-border cooperative alliances, including those involving non-European firms, in order to strengthen technological and productive capabilities of the European partner(s). In other cases, more public investment or assistance to private firms to improve the economic environment in which they operate might be more appropriate. In as much as this could assist the upgrading of value-added activities (e.g. R&D, training in advanced management and technology), this might favour domestic rather than foreign-owned firms. The support of more dynamic entrepreneurship, or intrapreneurship, in large firms, the reduction in innovation-impeding practices and government procurement through regional firms are other possibilities.

Such proposals as these are not new. In the past they have often been criticized as interventionist and, as likely as not, to encourage structural distortions. However, the fact cannot be ignored that European integration not only increases the incentives for non-EC firms to invest in the EC, but also spurs them to rationalize their activities both within the EC and between the EC and their home countries. Such rationalization itself adds to the O advantages of these companies *vis à vis* their European competitors. This is because the latter do not have the same incentive to internalize intra-European markets, partly because they are likely to own fewer production plants in different European countries and partly because of political, cultural or legal obstacles.

The answer to the question 'Does corporate integration contribute to the goals of regional integration in Europe?' would, therefore, seem to be 'Yes, if such corporate integration is undertaken by EC firms, and is prompted by a desire to overcome structural market distortions and transactional market failure', but only 'may be if it is undertaken by non-EC multinationals which, while operating in a structurally distorted market, use their economic power to out-compete their European rivals'. The net result of corporate integration by such firms may then be a redirection of upstream or high value activities from Europe to the United States and Japan. In turn, this would endanger the future technological capability and competitive position of European firms.

17.4.2   EC 1992: Mark 2 integration

The completion of the EC internal market at the end of 1992 will herald the end of all non-tariff barriers between the 12 Member States now comprising the Community. Many of the 293 directives of the European Commission intended to remove all intra-EC border controls, eliminate differences in technical standards, remove all restrictions from government procurement policies and reduce many differences in fiscal policies have already come into effect. A few will most certainly linger on after 1992, while complete liberalization of the capital, labour and product markets – let alone full monetary integration – will take several more years to accomplish.

The second phase of the EC will then take the EC one step forward towards complete economic union. The accession of the UK to the European Monetary System in 1990 was a significant step in that direction. Some European politicians – notably Jacques Delors – wish to bring about a United States of Europe. However, total economic union, typified by a single European central bank and an almost complete abrogation of national macro-economic policies, is vigorously opposed by several Member States, including the United Kingdom.

The abolition of non-tariff barriers is expected to have a broadly similar effect on trade and MNE activity to that of the removal of tariff barriers. Since the variable costs of exports will be lowered, then some kinds of horizontal market-seeking FDI might be expected to fall. This will be the case particularly where the existence of firm-specific fixed costs give rise to the economies of multi-plant operations (Itaki and Waterson, 1990). On the other hand, EC 1992 is likely to lead to more rationalization and restructuring of existing FDI in the EC together with more market-seeking non-EC FDI, spurred on by favourable growth prospects (i.e. offensive market-seeking investment) or the fear of a 'Fortress' Europe (defensive market-seeking investment). If, as is hoped by many European politicians and industrialists, the competitive position of EC firms improves, then one would expect more outward investment and strategic alliances by them as they seek to maintain or advance their position in global markets.

At the same time, the effects of Mark 2 integration on both trade and investment diversion and creation[40] are likely to have different effects on particular sectors and countries and, in so far as MNEs have a different propensity to invest in these sectors and countries, on MNE activity as well. Table 17.4 illustrates the kinds of sectors that are thought most likely to be affected by the completion of the internal market and the extent of

Table 17.4 Sectors most likely to be affected by EC 1992 and MNE involvement.

Impact	Sector	MNE involvement	Likely gainers*
Reduction in protection	Financial services	High	E and J
Increased competition	Pharmaceuticals	High	E and US
	Telecommunication services	Medium	E
Shift from fragmented local to	Distribution	Low	E
integrated EC-wide market	Food processing	Medium	Uncertain
	Transport (trucking)	Low	E
Gain of technical economies of scale	Electronics	High	J
through sale of standard goods	Packaging	Medium	E and US
and services	White and other consumer goods	Medium	E and J
Dependence on public procurement	Computer equipment and services	High	E and J
	Defence contractors	Low	E and US
	Telecommunication equipment	Medium	E and US
Industries where the single market	Chemicals	Medium	E and US
leads to import substitution (EC	Electrical components	High	J
goods instead of imports)	Office equipment	High	J
Industries where price exists between countries with different indirect taxation (VAT) levels			

Source: Adapted from *Business International* (1989).

* E – European firms; J – Japanese-owned firms; US – US-owned firms.

MNE involvement (whether European or non-European MNEs) in each of these.[41]

A comparable table on the *actual* effects of Mark 1 integration (i.e. the removal of tariff barriers) would have revealed that the gainers were in sectors which enjoy both economies of large scale production and *relatively* low intra-European non-tariff barriers. These include automobiles and auto components, computers, office equipment and industrial instruments, various kinds of non-electrical machinery and chemicals (including pharmaceutical chemicals). In most of these sectors, US-owned MNEs have a revealed competitive or O-specific advantage. Moreover, as we have already seen, in the early days of the EC, non-EC MNEs were better able to exploit the changing L advantages of individual Member States, chiefly because of their superior ability to internalize intra-EC market failure. Since 1975, except in the most technologically advanced sectors, there has been a resurgence in the competitive position of European-owned firms (Dunning, 1988b).

Among the sectors which seem likely to be the most affected by EC 1992 are a whole range of services, some of which (e.g. banking, telecommunications, insurance, construction and various kinds of consultancies) are strongly dominated by MNEs. Rationalization and restructuring are likely to follow in these sectors, which, because of the significance of non-tariff barriers, were *relatively* unaffected by Mark 1 of the EC integration.

The final column of Table 17.4 identifies the kinds of firms most likely to gain from EC 1992. Again, this reflects the current competitive advantages of Japanese, European and US MNEs, and their comparative abilities to exploit the gains of fuller integration. There seem to be two contrasting views of the effects of Mark 2 integration on the ownership of economic activity. The first is that, because of their relative inability to overcome non-tariff barriers, European-owned firms failed to take advantage of Mark 1 integration, so the removal of these barriers will be particularly beneficial to them. This, it is suggested, is likely to be so in the services sectors and in manufacturing sectors where the advantages of customization are especially important (e.g. white goods and telecommunication equipment).

It is further believed that, in the technologically more advanced countries, the completion of the internal market will help European firms to become more globally competitive. The opposing view is that foreign MNEs – especially Japanese MNEs – which currently have substantial O advantages, will build on these advantages. Even in international sectors in which they do not currently demonstrate such advantages (food processing, pharmaceuticals, etc), they will seek to use their financial strength and marketing opportunism to acquire European-based competitors.

There can, however, be little doubt that Europe 1992 is providing a major new catalyst to foreign investors. However, in contrast to the situation in the 1960s and 1970s, it is European and Japanese MNEs that are currently the most aggressive foreign investors, and the most prone to engage in cross-border asset restructuring (UNCTC, 1990c; Eurostat, 1991).[42] In the three years ending 31 December 1990, intra-European A&M transactions averaged $91.9 billion a year, 3½ times those of the previous three years, *viz* 1985–87. Taking the six-year period as a whole, French and Italian companies have increased their European transactions the most, even though about 58% of all intra-European A&Ms have involved British firms (Walter, 1992).[43] Since the early 1980s, Japanese MNEs sought to treat Western Europe as a single market. Most certainly, Europe 1992 is encouraging them to engage in more high value activities (i.e. deepen their European value-added chains) and to transfer their unique system of pyramidal and multi-layered subcontracting to an EC environment (Dunning, 1986a; Ozawa, 1991b).

There is also some suggestion that Third World MNEs are increasing their activities in Western Europe. Korean MNEs have been particularly active in the consumer electronics and microwave oven sectors (Young *et al.*, 1991). Brazil is one of the leading investors in the Portuguese economy with several joint ventures and recent acquisitions in industries such as construction, textiles and shoes. Indian, Taiwanese and Hong Kong firms have concluded several joint ventures and mergers with European companies. At the same time, developments in Central and Eastern Europe are causing a

reappraisal of the investment strategies of these and, indeed, of other MNEs.

Finally, it should be emphasized that there are many issues to be resolved about the policies of the Community towards third countries, for example, with respect to issues such as rules of origin, local content requirements, mutual recognition, reciprocity and membership of R&D consortia. All of these will affect not only the balance between the O advantages of MNEs and the L advantages of an EC country, but also the form of cross-border economic investment and the relative competitiveness of MNEs of different national origins.

Depending upon the future trading relationships between the EC and the rest of the world, the activities of MNEs elsewhere in the world will be affected. For example, it is possible to envisage a post-1992 scenario in which import barriers to goods originating from low wage countries were increased. This would then depress current and future export-oriented FDI located in these sectors. Alternatively, or in addition, because of their superior access to the EC markets and other advantages, MNEs may switch their investments in industries like textiles and clothing, leather products, food processing, etc, from North Africa and some Asian countries to Spain, Portugal and France (UNCTC, 1990c).

On the other hand, the dynamic effects of Mark 2 integration, for example, on rising demand, output and investment in the EC, might be expected to benefit exports to the EC from developing countries, thereby making FDI in these countries more attractive. Similarly, any intensification of competition between European, Japanese and US MNEs, consequential upon integration, is likely to force companies to become more cost conscious, thereby continuing to favour cross-border vertical integration between the Triad countries. Finally, resource-based MNE investment in developing countries could also increase if economic activity in the Community rises significantly and trade barriers between the exporting and importing countries are lowered.[44] Moreover, the expectation of increased competition between natural resource producers may prompt foreign buyers to internalize the markets for products currently imported. The UK firm Geest has recently acquired banana plantations in Costa Rica as a direct result of the likely consequences of EC 1992.[45]

17.4.3   The Canada–US Free Trade Agreement[46]

By signing the Canada–US Free Trade Agreement in January 1989, Canada and the US have partially integrated their economies by agreeing to engage in duty free trade, to remove several non-tariff barriers and to facilitate the free flow of capital and human resources across their borders. FDI is likely to be affected by the Free Trade Agreement (FTA) in two ways. First through the establishment of new rules on investment (described below), and second, through the removal of tariffs and non-tariff barriers to trade.

The Agreement liberalizes MNE activity in a number of ways, the most important of which is the acceptance by both US and Canada of the principle of national treatment between their citizens and firms so that, while each country's national policies towards inward investment will remain the same, both countries' firms will be granted equal treatment with domestic firms with respect to the establishment, acquisition and operations of a business (Safarian, 1991). Moreover, neither government will be allowed to impose performance requirements on firms from the other country in the areas of export performance, local content and minimum equity participation (although investment requirements are still allowed to be negotiated in the areas of R&D, technology transfer, product mandates and employment). Finally, the Agreement raises the asset threshold level at which Canada will review any new acquisitions by US firms from $5 million to $150 million, while Canada has waived the right to review indirect US acquisitions (i.e. purchases of firms that were previously foreign owned).

Though broad in scope, the Agreement does not represent a major shift in Canada–US economic relations. Prior to the Agreement, about 80% of bilateral trade – 70% of which was in the hands of Canadian or US MNEs – was already duty free. The Canadian acquisition review process has not been a significant obstacle to US MNE activity in Canada for several years. Furthermore, both countries are permitted to maintain their respective domestic regulatory policies, although some of Canada's industrial support policies are under review to determine whether they violate free trade principles.

According to some Canadian economists (e.g. Rugman and Verbeke, 1990), the Canadian manu-facturing industries which will be most affected following the elimination of trade barriers include petrochemicals, metal alloys, clothing and several resource-based products, all of which previously faced high or escalating tariffs in the US. US companies will primarily benefit from national treatment and larger public procurement markets, particularly in advertising and business services.

Capital expenditure plans by US manufacturing MNEs suggest that they may have increased their value-added activities in Canada as a direct result of the Canada–US Free Trade Agreement. This is in contrast to some pessimistic forecasts that US firms would react to the tariff reductions by divesting their Canadian assets and supplying the Canadian market from US factories.[47] In a survey published in June 1988, before ratification of the C–US FTA, US MNEs reported plans to decrease capital expenditures in their Canadian manufacturing affiliates by 5.4% in 1989 (*Survey of Current Business*, 1988). Six months later, in December 1988 when ratification of the Agreement appeared more certain, these plans were revised upwards to show a planned increase of 11% for 1989, 1% more than the planned revision for all countries. In June 1989, when the Agreement had been in effect for six months, plans were further revised upwards to show a 20% increase in planned 1989 expenditures – more than twice the planned increase for all countries. Plans for capital expenditure by US firms up to 1992 also show a marked increase over the period 1986–88 (*Survey of Current Business*, 1990).

This consistent upward revision of investment plans by US MNEs suggests that the C–US FTA is having a positive effect on northbound FDI flows. This prediction fits with an earlier survey on the likely reactions of 17 of the largest US subsidiaries in Canada to the FTA, which revealed that they expected their employment to increase and their workers to benefit from trade liberalization (Rugman, 1988). Part of this optimistic scenario undoubtedly reflects the fact that, in 1988, about 25% of the sales of US affiliates based in Canada was exported back to the US. This high proportion indicates that many US MNEs are already treating North America as an integrated market and are rationalizing their operations accordingly. Any divestment in import-substitution sectors seems likely to be more than compensated by an increase in the secondary processing of natural resources and by regionally or globally rationalized production (Rugman, 1990; Safarian, 1991), Much, of course, will depend on the wider effects of regional integration, including the value of the Canadian dollar.

In the case of Canadian FDI in the US, it is expected that the FTA will slow down its rate of growth. The major Canadian MNEs tend to be oriented towards the processing of natural resources (examples are Alcan, Seagrams and Noranda). Studies have shown that a major motive for them to invest in the US has been market access in the face of rising US protectionism. In so far as the C–US FTA assures such access, there is likely to be a deceleration of defensive Canadian FDI into the US. On the other hand, Rugman (1990) has argued that most large Canadian MNEs initially set up or acquired subsidiaries in the US not to circumvent tariff or non-tariff barriers, but to promote rationalized production or protect their global competitive positions.[48]

The balance of opinion among scholars is, then, that the most significant long-term impact of the FTA is likely to be an increase in FDI which is specifically directed to serving an integrated North American market. Although the Canadian market is still relatively small (with a population of 26 million in 1990), many large regional markets in the US may be profitably served from a Canadian base, given Canada's abundant natural resources, cheap energy, geographical proximity, excellent infrastructure and relatively inexpensive labour. Just as Japanese car manufacturers have chosen to locate production in Tennessee because of its central location and low labour costs, so are non-US TNCs likely to increase their stake in Canada now that they are assured duty-free access to the US market. The Korean-owned Hyundai Motor Company, for example, assembles cars in Canada for sale to the entire North American market. Although Japanese investment accounted for only 3% of total FDI stock in Canada in the 1980s, its annual growth rate between 1980 and 1988 averaged over 22%, the highest for any investing country.

Since the initiation of the C–US FTA, several US and Canadian TNCs have expanded, rationalized or reorganized their cross-border activities to create a more efficient division of labour between the two countries. Integration of the North American market

and the associated gains from more product and process specialization are expected to raise the overall strategic importance of Canadian affiliates of many US MNEs. IBM, for instance, has invested over $1 billion since the mid 1980s to upgrade its Canadian facilities, and now exports all high technology components and software manufactured in Canada to foreign markets, while importing computers to sell in the Canadian market. General Electric supplies the entire North American halogen lamp market from its Canadian subsidiary. It also plans to use its Canadian plant, which is designed to be profitable at low output levels, to supply small, but lucrative, market niches around the world.

Notable examples of the strategic response by MNEs to the C–US FTA include Procter and Gamble's decision to integrate its four Canadian plants into its existing US operations, and, in contrast, the increased investments by DuPont and Dow Chemicals in their Canadian export-oriented operations. The opening of public procurement and free trade and investment in services has intensified US acquisitions in the Canadian advertising industry. There has also been a considerable growth in the activities of US firms in the Canadian mining, pulp and paper, and communications industries.

No less interesting has been the divestment of some US MNEs in previously protected sectors. Gillette has closed down its razor and pen-making facilities in Canada. Whirlpool and Burlington also plan to cut back on Canadian production, preferring to export to Canada from US plants. The severity of the Canadian recession and the declining competitiveness of Canadian industry has also prompted some Canadian firms to move their operations south of the 49th parallel. In 1991, for example, Canada's largest industrial company – Varity Corp. (previously Massey Ferguson) – moved its corporate headquarters from Toronto to Buffalo, a US city which since 1987 is reported to have attracted 86 other Canadian companies (*New York Times*, 9 August 1991).

Finally, as a direct result of the C–US FTA, some developing country firms are shifting from exporting to investing in North America. For instance, in September 1989 the Gerdau group of Brazil purchased a Canadian steel mill for $52 million, thereby acquiring state-of-the-art steel-making technology while bypassing US quotas on Brazilian steel. Investment by Third World developing country MNEs is likely to increase further as a result of the FTA, particularly in natural resources processing and engineering industries.

17.4.4 The North American Free Trade Agreement

In February 1991, negotiations began on the establishment of a North American Free Trade Agreement (NAFTA) embracing the US, Canada and Mexico. Such an agreement has been termed a 'hub and spoke' agreement, with the US as the hub and Canada and Mexico as the two spokes. Trade linkages between Canada and Mexico are almost non-existent. On the other hand, 80% to 85% of Mexico's manufacturing exports are sold to the US (Eden, 1991). Although about one-half of the trade consists of goods produced in the maquiladoras – the inbound assembly and process factories located along the US–Mexico border[49] – some exports (e.g. automobiles, petroleum, iron and steel, paper products, textiles and apparel) compete directly with those of Canada. In the absence of a free trade agreement between Mexico and the US, one of the inevitable outcomes of the FTA is that there would be a strong trade diversion effect from Mexico to Canada (Weintraub, 1990).

In December 1988, the President of Mexico approached the US government about negotiating a separate US–Mexico free trade agreement. Clearly, such an agreement would adversely affect Canadian trade preferences negotiated under the FTA. In May 1991, the US Congress granted authority for using a 'fast-ball' procedure to negotiate a free trade agreement with Mexico and it anticipated that an agreement could be in place in late 1992. However, the triangular agreement envisaged under the NAFTA would, to a certain extent at least, compensate this adverse effect by opening up the Mexican market to Canadian exports.

Although, should it come about, NAFTA would be unlikely to have the same consequences for intra-regional FDI as EC 1992 – if for no other reason that the agreement does not include the elimination of non-tariff barriers[50] – it is likely to bring about a substantial restructuring and reorganization of MNE

activity, both within the newly integrated region and between it and other countries. This will arise both because of the changing L (or ESP) advantages of the three countries as a result of the removal of tariffs and the opportunities of MNEs to reap the advantages of cross-border corporate integration.

In their turn, these two changes are likely to affect the configuration of the O advantages of the 'insiders' in the NAFTA, relative to the 'outsiders', with the result that there could be an inflow of non-American investment into NAFTA, in exactly the same way as US and Japanese firms have been tempted into the EC. Almost certainly, part of this investment (particularly in the more labour-intensive sectors) is likely to be directed to Mexico to supply the US market. Both German and Japanese MNEs have recently expressed their intentions to increase their investments in Mexico should the Free Trade Agreement come about (Lustig, 1991). In 1989, Japanese direct investment in Mexico already totalled nearly $1.5 billion, and by 1990 there were more than 70 Japanese maquila firms compared with only eight in 1980 (Szekely, 1991). Whether or not a 'Fortress North America' might emerge to correspond to the 'Fortress Europe' may well rest on the extent to which the leading trading regimes see their interests as best advanced by the globalization of markets of production, or by the regionalization of markets and production, coupled with a controlled economic interdependence with the rest of the world.[51]

NAFTA may also be expected to lead to greater Mexican investment in the US. The major investments made in 1989 and 1990 by Vitro (a glass making company) and Cemex (a cement making company)[52] in the US may be forerunners of others.

17.4.5 Economic interaction among developing countries

In general, MNEs have been less enthusiastic about integration among developing countries than among developed countries. In some cases, they have argued the case against it (UNCTC, 1983b). Much, of course, depends upon whether firms perceive that the benefits arising from liberalized markets will exceed the costs of a reduction in a favoured position, which such companies may enjoy by selling in protected markets. Suppose, for example, that Firm A, a multinational affiliate, is the sole supplier of telecommunications equipment to the government in Country X. The opening up of X's market to competition from foreign production will probably result in a fall of its monopoly profits. At the same time, it might enable Firm A to restructure its activities in the integrated area and gain economies of scale as a result.

The balance of costs and benefits is likely to depend upon the size of markets and the structure of competition between Firm A and other firms. Because the size of markets in developing countries is likely to be smaller than in developed countries, the gains to integration by MNEs in the former are likely to be less. Earlier in this chapter we identified five regional integration schemes which are currently in operation in developing countries. These were the Andean Common Market; the Association of South East Asian Nations (ASEAN); the Caribbean Community (CARICOM); the Southern and East African Preferential Trade Area (PTA); and economic cooperation among the countries of the Maghreb.[53]

The Andean Common Market, which was set up among five Latin American countries in 1969, is the most comprehensive of these five groupings. It encompasses provisions for a common market (such as a customs union and the free movement of factors of production), as well as for an economic union (such as a regional planning of investment and the harmonization of policies related to FDI and technology transfer).

ASEAN, launched in 1967, was initially based on a loose cooperative agreement and gradually adopted provisions characteristic of a free trade area. It comprises six Member States in South East Asia, *viz* Indonesia, Malaysia, the Philippines, Singapore, Thailand and Brunei. In 1977, regional trade was selectively liberalized, although the measures taken affected only a small percentage of total intra-ASEAN trade. In 1987, regional trade was further liberalized through the lowering of tariff and non-tariff barriers and the extension of preferences to a wider range of products. Regional cooperation has mainly taken the form of common industrial projects, for example,, in the production of urea (Jovanovic, 1992). In general, ASEAN countries treat FDI in a liberal way.

The aim of CARICOM, which was established in 1973 and included 13 Member States in the Caribbean, Central and South America, was to establish a customs union, that is, a common external tariff on all commodities imported from third countries and the removal of trade barriers between the member countries. In practice, however, the scope of trade liberalization within the region has been limited as a result of many exemptions. In 1987, the member countries agreed to further liberalization by gradually reducing the list of exempted items.

The PTA Treaty of 1984 provides for cooperation and coordination in specified sectors such as agriculture, energy, industrial development and manpower planning. PTA consists of 20 African nations. Intra-regional trade is to be promoted through the removal of tariff and non-tariff barriers and the harmonization of customs procedures and regulations.

Cooperation among Maghreb countries dates back to 1964 and is currently based on loose and *ad hoc* arrangements rather than on a binding integration scheme. However, the areas of cooperation are quite wide and include coordination of national development plans, with emphasis on industrial harmonization, preferential multi-lateral trade and the adoption of a common approach towards problems of development financing.

The most comprehensive attempt in West Africa at economic integration was launched in 1975 with the formation of the Economic Community of West African States (ECOWAS). The Community comprises all sixteen states in the West African region, including the former Portuguese Colonies of Guinea Bissau and Cape Verde. It is intended that ECOWAS will eventually become a fully fledged customs union. Already trade barriers have been largely removed and many cooperative programmes have been launched. However, perhaps the major problem of ECOWAS, and one of the reasons why it has not attracted much attention from foreign MNEs, is its failure to make the necessary reforms in its administrative machinery and organizational capabilities (Diejomaoh, 1987).

Of the six integration groupings, only the Andean Pact has adopted a common policy towards FDI and technology transfer, embodied in the well-publicized Decision 24. This ruling prohibited new FDI in a number of industries in the region and placed limits on profit repatriation and majority ownership by foreign investors. Technology transfer provisions were intended to ensure that inbound MNE activity made an effective contribution to local economies. The objective of the Decision was to maximize the benefits of FDI in the region and to increase the bargaining power of the Andean Pact countries with MNEs. Although it was not intended to impede inflows of foreign investment, foreign investors considerd the decision restrictive. This led to its replacement in May 1987 by a more liberal rule (Decision 220) granting policy autonomy to member countries, albeit within a set of common guidelines.

None of the other five schemes has established a harmonized policy towards inbound foreign investment. Member States establish their own policies and investment incentives, which typically include tax holidays, free trade zones and special guarantees for foreign investors.

The economic effects of the five integration schemes under study have been generally short-lived and limited in scope. They have not had a significant influence on inward direct investment. As Table 17.5 shows, while some countries belonging to these groupings, particularly to ASEAN, have experienced substantial inflows of FDI from third countries, it would be difficult to infer that these inflows are solely, or even mainly, the result of integration.

Neither has regional integration led to a marked expansion in intra-regional trade, whether measured in absolute or relative terms, in any of the five groupings. This is in sharp contrast to an increased share of intra-EC trade of the total trade of EC countries.[54]

Table 17.5 Foreign direct investment inflows into regional integration groupings of developing countries and regions (millions of dollars and percentage).

Regional groupings and regions	1965–1970	1971–1975	1976–1980	1981–1985	1986–1988
			Value		
Andean	68.1	170.8	85.4	810.8	595.3
ASEAN	158.1	790.5	1 547.2	3 014.3	2 774.9
CARICOM	183.4	220.6	215.2	227.7	153.6
Maghreb	96.8	49.9	364.7	259.6	118.7
PTA	—	—	228.1	213.6	284.7
Developing countries	1 304.8	4 494.5	8 335.8	13 627.4	21 833.5
Latin America and Caribbean	807.6	2 654.4	4 581.2	5 837.9	9 323.5
Asia	228.1	1 083.8	2 509.8	5 378.2	9 370.4
Africa	269.1	586.1	1 055.4	2 236.3	2 992.7
		Percentage share in regional inflows			
Percentage share of Andean in Latin America	8.4	6.4	1.8	13.8	6.4
Percentage share of ASEAN in Asia	69.0	72.9	61.6	56.0	29.8
Percentage share of Maghreb in Africa	35.9	8.5	34.6	11.6	3.9
Percentage share of CARICOM in Latin America	22.7	8.3	4.7	3.9	1.6
Percentage share of PTA in Africa	—	—	21.6	9.6	9.5

Source: UNCTC (1991a), based on IMF, *Balance of Payments Tapes*, October 1989.

Given that regional cooperation and integration did not lead to the creation of large unified markets in the five analysed groupings of developing countries, foreign MNEs continue to view them as collections of small, unrelated markets. There is no real evidence to link the observed trends in FDI into these regions with economic integration. It is likely that other economic and socio-political factors not directly related to integration (such as levels of economic development, political stability, the debt crisis and the world market prices for oil and primary products) were much more important determinants of MNE-related activities within the member countries of these groupings. At the same time, there is some suggestion that MNEs, relative to indigenous firms, have been the main beneficiaries of regional integration both in Latin America and Africa. This is mainly because of their stronger production and technological capabilities, their abilities to mobilize financial needs and their more efficient cross-border organizational structures (Marton, 1986). In LAFTA, MNEs have increased their share in the output of sectors in which intra-regional complementation agreements have been conducted (UN, 1983).[55] In Central America, ten years after the formation of the CACM, MNE subsidiaries had increased their exports (Rosenthal and Cohen, 1976). At the same time, the local value added contributed by MNEs (as a percentage of gross output) has tended to fall (UNCTC, 1983b). In the Andean group, the progressive implementation of regional programmes in the metal working, auto and petrochemical sectors has resulted in a noticeable increase in the MNE activity in these sectors. By contrast, local companies do not appear to have made major efforts either to adopt local technology or to undertake R&D for local innovations in order to reduce their dependence on foreign technology (Mytelka, 1978, 1991).

There are several moves afoot to resuscitate regional integration in Latin America. In November 1988, the governments of Argentina and Brazil signed an agreement on economic integration and cooperative development, which over the following 10 years aimed to remove all trade barriers between the two countries. In March 1991 this agreement was widened to include two other South American countries – Uruguay and Paraguay. Its intention is to set up a Southern Core Common Market (Mercosur) by 1 January 1995, in which the participating

countries will remove all obstacles to the movement of goods, services and labour, and will harmonize their domestic macro-economic policies. Efforts are also being made to revive both the Central American Common Market which floundered in 1969, when war broke out between Honduras and El Salvador, and a customs union involving the CARICOM countries, which had been intended to come into being in 1991.

None of these schemes is viewed with great optimism by MNEs involved, or likely to be involved, in Latin America. The general feeling seems to be that all the prospective participants should take a leaf out of Mexico's books and get their own domestic economic houses in order prior to involving themselves in any regional programmes which might involve extremely high structural adjustment costs on their part.

17.4.6   Empirical studies: concluding remarks

The broad conclusion of the empirical studies reviewed in this chapter is that the reaction of MNEs to regional economic integration is likely to vary both according to the types of integration and to the strategic advantages they perceive may follow from it. For established foreign-based MNEs with entrenched and protected market positions, the opening up of segmented – but potentially contestable – markets might be unwelcome because of the additional competition it engenders. On the other hand, where they perceive that the economies of rationalization and specialization will outweigh any loss of market power, they might support such integration. The same logic applies for established domestic MNEs, except those which are the most efficient can reasonably anticipate that their global competitive position might be improved.

We would make one other point. Economic integration brings with it both industrial and geographical restructuring. Indeed, some commentators (e.g. Cowling and Sudgen, 1987) have asserted that the combination of regional and cross-border corporate integration may well result in more internalization of *cross-border* markets at the expense of cross-sectoral market transactions *within* a country. As an illustration, the authors claimed that as a result of a combination of the European Economic Community, an aggressive marketing policy by foreign-based companies and its own internal problems, the domestic UK auto industry had all but disappeared. Moreover, an increasing proportion of the components for cars from both UK firms and foreign subsidiaries were being bought from factories (often in UK ownership) elsewhere in the EC.

It is also suggested that the movement towards corporate integration leads to a switch in the locus of decision taking from individual host countries to the parent company of foreign-based MNEs. Because in many respects it is easier for MNEs to engage in *intra*-firm than *inter*-firm specialization, any restructuring of economic activity undertaken by such companies is likely to have a pronounced influence on both the costs and benefits of integration and the geographical distribution of these costs and benefits. This may further explain why countries that perceive they are likely to be the main beneficiaries of economic integration welcome the presence of foreign-owned firms. By contrast, countries which are struggling to establish some degree of economic autonomy in a globally interdependent world may find their task made more difficult by the operation of MNEs.

17.5   CONCLUSIONS: REGIONAL OR GLOBAL INTEGRATION?

This chapter has discussed some of the interactions between the activities of MNEs, the international division of labour and regional integration. It has shown that such enterprises both help fashion and are fashioned by such a division of labour differently than do (or are) uninational firms. These differences reflect the different ownership-specific characteristics facing such firms, and the way in which they affect, or react to, the ESP configuration of countries and to the characteristics of cross-border markets as a coordinating device in their production and marketing strategies.

The first part of this chapter set out the reasons for supposing that an international division of labour practised by MNEs would be different from that suggested either by neo-classical economic theory or that thought to be desirable by national governments (Behrman, 1972), and hence the response of the

latter to the policies pursued by MNEs or their affiliates. It also examined the main factors influencing the changing division of labour over recent years and the strategies of MNEs to these changes. In particular, it distinguished between MNEs that adopt an integrated, regional or global strategy and those which pursue an 'every tub on its bottom' strategy.

Much of the second part of the chapter addressed itself to the impact of supra-national economic integration on the level and structure of MNE activity. It distinguished between the goals of regional and corporate integration and the circumstances in which the one helped or inhibited the other. In particular, it concentrated on the effects of a number of integration schemes on the activities of MNEs, and concluded that these were significant and distinctive.

A final section of the chapter examined some of the ways in which corporate integration might affect regional integration and concluded that much depended on the extent and character of the integration, the economic and political characteristics of the integrating nations, the bargaining power of MNEs *vis à vis* both the individual governments and the supra-national authorities of the integrated region, the type of FDI and the firm-specific characteristics of the MNEs concerned. In general, however, there seems to have been a more pronounced coincidence of goals and strategies of corporations and governments in the case of regional integration in developed rather than in developing countries.

Finally the question may be asked: Is regional economic integration a substitute for global economic integration or is it an important step towards it? Or from a corporate perspective, is the regionalization of value-added activities an optional strategic choice, or is it a compromise between the multidomestic strategies traditionally pursued by MNEs and the transnational strategies now being advocated? Are the kinds of associations now being forged between nations likely to achieve a harmonious balance between advancing regional economic welfare and maintaining some degree of national political autonomy and cultural diversity? Can indeed one achieve both regional and *some* global integration at one and the same time?

The answers to these questions, like so many others raised in this book, are very much dependent on country, industry and firm specific circumstances. But in the early 1990s, we perceive that companies are being forced to pursue regional strategies because of the current pressures towards the deepening of regional integration in so many parts of the world; while contemporaneously, there remain many inter-regional tensions, for example, as shown in the current GATT negotiations. At the same time, in many functional areas, MNEs are assuming an increasingly global perspective in their decision taking. The concept of the global product mandate is very much alive. Corporations are actively pursuing global sourcing and production strategies. Many A&Ms and strategic business alliances are inter-regional. R&D activities are increasingly spanning the three most industrialized continents of the world.

On balance then, there is progress towards both regional and global economic integration. For the rest of the 1990s we suspect that the multi-regional MNE – an extension of the multi-domestic MNE of the 1960s and 1970s – will tend to be a more pervasive form of corporate internationalization than the globally integrated MNE. What is true of companies may also be true of Nation States. Throughout modern history, there has been a tension between the forces making for nationalism and those making for internationalism. Over the past 30 years this tension has been extended to embrace regionalism. We see no signs that any of these tensions will relax in the immediate future; but we do envisage that MNEs will become an increasingly potent influence in shaping both the nature of these tensions and how they are resolved.

NOTES

1 In a recently published book, Jovanovic (1992) identifies five main types of international economic integrations, *viz* a free trade area, a customs union, a common market, an economic union and a total economic union. He then proceeds to classify these according to the extent to which five criteria are met. These include the removal of tariffs or quotas on trade, the presence of a common external tariff, the freedom of movement of factors of production, the harmonization of economic policies and a total unification of economic policies.

2 One of the political motives behind the completion of the internal market, *viz* EC 92, is to allow European and other MNEs not only to treat Europe as a single market, but to reallocate and restructure their European production so they could become more competitive relative to US and Japanese firms.

3 In parenthesis, it might be noted that specialization was predicated on the basis of *existing* talents and resource capabilities, not *potential* talents or resource capabilities.

4 This point is taken up further in Chapter 22.

5 There is some debate about the success of these attempts – particularly in the early 1990s, at which time there were (and still are) considerable differences between the finance ministers of the G7 (the group of the seven leading industrial nations) about interest and exchange rate policies. Certainly, the events of the previous half decade have suggested that international markets, rather than the coordinated policies of the G7, have largely determined the structure of the trade balances and growth rates of the participating nations.

6 Notably Chapters 11, 15 and 16.

7 For further details, see Hood and Young (1982b), Cantwell (1988) and UN (1992a).

8 For a brief case study of Siemens, see UNCTC (1990c). More generally, see Eurostat (1990), which shows that intra-EC FDI is now rising much faster than non-EC inward investment. Also, see several chapters in Yannopoulos (1991).

9 Taking US statistics as a guide, intra-firm exports between non-bank US parent firms and their affiliates accounted for 40% of the total exports in 1989 compared with 32% in 1982 (US Department of Commerce, vd).

10 *Inter alia*, these advantages include the experience of operating intra-continental production facilities in the US and the reduced number of cultural and legal impediments facing EC-based firms wishing to engage in intra-EC investment. This thesis that non-EC (particularly US MNEs) helped to propel market integration and behaved more as twin communitarian businesses than their EC counterparts was first put forward by Kindleberger in 1966. For a more recent elaboration of this view, see Pelkmans (1987).

11 Though, obviously, not to all sectors, or indeed interest groups, within the two countries.

12 See pp. 315–7 in particular.

13 Lest there be any doubt, the Federal Government does not have unlimited powers over the political and economic jurisdiction of the 51 US states. Sales and real estate taxes, tax and other incentives to foreign investors, educational and hospital facilities differ between states and a variety of regulations (e.g. with respect to transport and food standards) also affect the distribution of activity.

14 The EC initially consisted of six countries – *viz*

Belgium, France, Italy, Luxembourg, the Netherlands, and West Germany. In 1973 the UK, Denmark, and Ireland acceded to the EC; in 1986 Greece joined and in 1988 so did Portugal and Spain. In June 1992, the EC consisted of 12 countries with a total population of 320 million. When the internal market is completed it will be the largest and wealthiest free trade area in the world.

15 For an examination of the relationship between economic and political power, see Gilpin (1975, 1987) and Ostry (1990).

16 That is, over what they would otherwise be.

17 For further details see Cecchini (1988).

18 See Chapter 22 for further details.

19 This has certainly been the experience of the LAFTA; indeed it was one of the original reasons behind the breakaway of the smaller Andean countries from this association.

20 For further details see Chapters 2 and 3, UNCTC (1991a) and Dunning (1991e).

21 See Chapter 4.

22 As reviewed in Dunning and Robson (1988), Dunning (1990) and UN (1992d).

23 In UNCTC (1991c, p. 74) various examples were given of the financial inducements offered by states to attract such Japanese auto-makers as Mazda, Subaru-Isuzu and Toyota. These amounted to upwards of $14 000 per job created. More recently (in 1992) South Carolina is reputed to have provided 500 acres of free land, a $40 million subsidy and tax rebates to entice BMW to set up its new US manufacturing facility in its state (*New York Times*, 19 July 1992).

24 The first Japanese investments in West Germany after the Second World War were those of Mitsubishi and Mitsui, both of whom set up sales subsidiaries in Dusseldorf in 1955.

25 For example, Silicon Valley and Highway 1 in the US (now being dubbed video valley!) and along part of the M4 in the UK.

26 These were Nissan, which had set up a technology centre in the Sunderfield and Cranfield Science Park; Canon which has located its European research centre at the University of Surrey's Science Park; Kobe Steel which undertakes R&D also in the Surrey Science Park; Sharp Laboratories of Europe which is based in Oxford University Science Park; Yamanouchi Pharmaceutical which has set up a laboratory at Oxford University; and Hitachi which has invested in a new building for micro-electronics research at Cambridge University (Japan, 1991).

27 In 1957, for example, the six founding members of the EC accounted for 54% of the outward direct capital stake of the US. By 1972, this proportion had risen to 17.1%. Of course, reasons other than economic

integration helped explain this increased share, but the consensus of the research findings is that the formation of the EC was a statistically significant factor, particularly when the impact of the EC on economic growth is taken into account. A summary of these research findings is contained in Yannopoulos (1990) and UN (1992d). See also Chapter 6 of this volume.

28 In 1957, the ratio of the sales of manufactured products by US affiliates in the EC to the exports by US firms to the EC was 2.04. By 1972 it had risen to 5.34. As a proportion of the GNP of EC countries, the US capital stake rose from 1.22% in 1957 to 2.51% in 1971. (US Department of Commerce, vd).

29 It being predicted that the common external tariff would lead to an increase in US investment in the EC. See Scaperlanda and Mauer (1969), Schmitz and Bieri (1972), Lunn (1980, 1983), and Scaperlanda and Balough (1983).

30 These are described in Yannopoulos (1990) and UN (1992d).

31 For example, Italian housewives traditionally prefer top loading machines and German and UK housewives front loading machines.

32 Doz did not distinguish between whether the sales were to the governments of the countries in which plants were located or to all governments, but it is presumed that they were mainly to the former.

33 Especially Chapters 7 and 8.

34 Thus it is quite possible that the early part of the production process be integrated, yet the final stages are not; that while a common advertising theme is adopted, parts of that theme are tailored to the cultural idiosyncrasies of particular markets; that while a common system of accounting and financial control may assist centralized control, each subsidiary may still have to meet local reporting and auditing standards; and so on.

35 For a more detailed analysis of the impact of the EC on the trading patterns of US affiliates in the EC, see UN (1992d). Other data suggests that the intra-EC export performance of US affiliates has been generally superior to that of EC firms, with the result that the former's share of all intra-EC exports has risen from 16.8% in 1966 to 19.9% in 1985 (Pelkmans, 1987; Dunning, 1991e).

36 For an examination of the impact of multinational enterprises on industrial concentration in Europe, see Fishwick (1982); for a discussion of the oligopolistic strategy of such, see Franko (1976, 1977); and for an analysis of the action taken by the authorities in Europe to minimize the anti-competitive practices of multinationals, see Robinson (1983) and Dunning (1985).

37 Between 1972 and 1988, the stake of EC FDI in the

US rose by 20 times, compared with a growth of US FDI in the EC of five times (US Department of Commerce, *Survey of Current Business*, various editions; Dunning, 1991e).

38 In this respect, a country may be likened to a firm which has the proprietary rights to a valuable intangible asset. Each will only be prepared to license the right to use that asset to another firm (country) as long as it can be reasonably sure that the lessee will not use the knowledge acquired against the interests of the lessor.

39 In the sense that the benefits of corporate integration may not necessarily accrue to the affiliates most affected by the integration but to the rest of the corporation of which they are part.

40 By its effects on economic efficiency and growth, economic integration creates new trade and investment opportunities. At the same time, by discriminating between the movement of capital goods and services *within* the integrated area and that between the integrated area and other countries, integration may lead to a realignment or division of trade and investment flows. These concepts are explored in more detail in Yannopoulos (1990) and UN (1992d).

41 Author's estimate from national statistics.

42 Until 1988, most new US investment in the EC took the form of reinvested projects by existing subsidiaries. Since that date, US MNEs have trebled the rate of acquisition of European companies. Moreover, in anticipation of EC 1992, many of the leading US MNEs, which already had substantial investments in the EC in the mid 1980s, have rationalized and restructured their existing activities. Such rationalization and restructuring, which has sometimes led US firms to divest some of their European investments, have been especially noticeable in the telecommunications, consumer electronics and appliances, banking and financial services, food processing, pharmaceuticals and motor vehicles sectors (Franko, 1991).

43 Not all of the annual growth of intra-European A&Ms of 67.4% per year can be attributed to European integration, but part of it most certainly can. Among other reasons noted by Walter (1992) for the A&M boom in Europe are (a) an overdue need for industrial restructuring in Europe, (b) the availability of financial resources, (c) the transfer to Europe of much of the A&M know-how that accumulated in the US during the 1980s and (d) the increasing liberalization of capital markets in Europe (itself an essential element of European integration).

44 For a detailed appraisal of the impact of EC 1992 on MNE activity into and out of developing countries, see UN (1992d).

45 Reported in the *London Evening Standard*, 21 June 1991.

46 This section draws heavily on UNCTC (1990c, pp. 31–2). We are grateful to the UNCTC for permission to reproduce material contained in this publication.

47 But it is not inconsistent with the received theory of international production, particularly where either the FDI is other than market seeking or where the tariff variable is swamped by other variables, such as size and growth of markets (Safarian, 1991).

48 For a detailed analysis of the reactions by some of the largest Canadian MNEs to the C–US FTA, see Rugman (1990b).

49 And often supplied by US subsidiaries in Mexico.

50 Other differences between NAFTA and EC relate to the size, economic structure and income levels of the participating countries, and the patterns of intra-regional trade investment.

51 There are certain parallels between the impact of EC 1992 on investment and trade involving non-EC firms and that of NAFTA in respect of investment and trade involving Pacific Rim countries. This latter issue is explored by Eden and Molot (1992).

52 Both investments were made not only to exploit their own competitive advantages better but also to acquire other advantages that would foster their position in world markets.

53 Member states in the regional groupings are as follows: *Andean Pact*: Bolivia, Colombia, Ecuador, Peru and Venezuela. *ASEAN*: Brunei Darusalem, Indonesia, Malaysia, Philippines, Thailand and Singapore. *CARICOM*: Antigua and Barbuda, Bahamas, Barbados, Belize, Dominica, Grenada, Guyana, Jamaica, Monteserrat, St Christopher/Nevis, St Lucia, St Vincent and the Grenadines, Trinidad and Tobago. *PTA*: Angola, Botswana, Burundi, Comoros, Djiboti, Ethiopia, Kenya, Lesotho, Madagascar, Malawi, Mauritius, Mozambique, Rwanda, Seychelles, Somalia, Swaziland, Tanzania, Uganda, Zambia and Zimbabwe. *Maghreb*: Algeria, Libya, Mauritania, Morocco and Tunisia. *ECOWAS*: All 16 states in the West African region.

54 Between 1973 and 1985, the proportion of trade of the six founder members of the EC with other EC countries rose from 51.6% to 57.1%.

55 By the mid 1970s, MNEs were responsible for 97% of the trade in office machinery created by LAFTA's industrial complementarity agreements, 80% of the trade in electronic valves and 75% of the trade in electronic components (UNCTC, 1983b). LAFTA has recently been restructured under the acronym of LAIA or ALAOI (Latin American Integration Association).

CHAPTER 18

DISTRIBUTION OF THE VALUE ADDED CREATED BY MNES

18.1 INTRODUCTION

Previous chapters have been primarily concerned with the contribution of MNEs, or their affiliates, to the output and employment of the countries in which they operate. This chapter deals with some of the factors influencing the distribution of the wealth created by MNEs between the stakeholders responsible for that creation, and in particular between the parent companies of MNEs and the countries which are hosts to their affiliates.

Elsewhere in this volume – and we shall take up the point in more detail in Chapter 20 – we have suggested that governments have a variety of expectations of MNEs. However, *ceteris paribus*, most countries welcome inward or outward FDI wherever, over a defined period of time, it raises Gross National Product (GNP), or growth in GNP, of their countries more than any alternative disposition of resources. From the viewpoint of a particular host country, the contribution of a foreign-owned affiliate to its GNP is measured by the value added generated by its activities (i.e. gross output less imports), less the amount of profits, interest and rents (net of tax) accruable to the parent company. In addition, any secondary effects on net output, resulting from the presence of foreign affiliates of MNEs, should be considered net of any payments made to its foreign stakeholders.

Thus the national value added resulting from MNE activity in any particular country may be summarized as follows:

$$R - M = DVA$$
$$DVA = F + (T - S)$$
$$NVA = DVA - Pf$$

Where

R	Receipts from the output generated
M	Imports of goods and services
DVA	Domestic value added
F	Factor payments (wages, salaries, interest, rent)
T	Payments (e.g. taxes to host governments)
S	Receipts (e.g. subsidies from governments)
Pf	Profits accruing to foreign shareholders
NVA	National value added
f	Payments made to foreigners.

Earlier we suggested that one of the major goals of any country is to maximize NVA from any given amount of resources. However, to do so requires a series of actions geared towards maximizing sales revenue (R) and minimizing the import content of those sales (M) and profits accruing to the MNE (Pf), as these represent a drain on NVA. The problem is, of course, that R, M, T, S, F and Pf are likely to be interdependent. In particular, MNEs that engage in intra-firm, inter-country specialization are likely both to import and to export a substantial share of their output; profits Pf earned may be positively correlated with R and efficiency R/F. Moreover, in some cases it may be highly desirable to import foreign factor services as, in the long run, these may help to improve gross *domestic* product more than their indigenous equivalents.

The distribution of the revenue created by a firm to the contributing stakeholders is partly determined by the real opportunity cost of the resources (as perceived by their owners) and partly by the bargaining power of the supplier of these resources.

In situations other than perfect competition, this essentially boils down to the distribution of economic rent and organizational slack[1] between the stakeholders. As far as domestic value added is concerned, the only question of importance is the distribution of that rent between foreign and local stakeholders.

The local stakeholders include the consumers of the output of the affiliate, the (domestic) suppliers of intermediate products, the suppliers of factor inputs (workers, landlords, capitalists, etc) and the government. The stronger the bargaining power of any, or all, of these stakeholders relative to that of the foreign MNE, the more likely it is that profits earned by it will approach the opportunity cost of the capital invested. The less the MNE's negotiating strength, the nearer the value added retained in the country is likely to approach the opportunity cost of the indigenous resources.

As Chapter 20 will discuss in more detail, the negotiating strength of the various stakeholders in the prosperity of the MNE is likely to be positively related to their knowledge and understanding about both their own opportunity costs and those of the MNE. There is ample casual evidence to suggest that local stakeholders in host countries, especially in the smaller developing countries, neither possess sufficient knowledge nor have the economic power to extract even a portion of any economic rent which may accrue as a result of inbound foreign investment.

In many countries, as Chapter 13 has shown, labour is comparatively plentiful and/or unorganized, and is unable to capture a wage rate above its opportunity cost. Chapter 16 has demonstrated that some suppliers, particularly of idiosyncratic or scarce resources and intermediate goods or services, may be able to charge above competitive prices for their products, while others which supply standard products in atomistic markets may not. Thus, depending upon the nature and purpose of inbound investment, its expected benefits, and the locational options open to the investing companies, host governments can offer a package of measures, which usually consists of both penalties (taxes and unwelcome performance requirements) and incentives (tax breaks, investment allowances, training grants, export subsidies, etc), which *in toto* are intended to garner some of the current (or future) economic rent earned by the foreign affiliate.[2]

In this chapter, we shall concentrate on just *two* factors influencing the distribution of the value added by MNEs or their affiliates. One is the package of government measures which determines, directly or indirectly, their share of the net output produced by these companies. This share might be negative, at least for a period of time, when the tax and other receipts of home and host governments collected from the companies, are less than the payments made to the companies. We shall not be concerned with describing or measuring the impact of investment incentives or disincentives in any detail. That topic is dealt with in Chapter 20. Here we are simply interested in recording that, by their fiscal and other policies, governments can and do affect the share of local value added created by MNEs which contributes towards their GNP.

The second determinant of the distribution of national value added we shall consider is that of disguised cross-border intra-firm payments, better known as transfer pricing. While the term 'transfer pricing' is itself a neutral one, it is often used to convey that intra-firm prices are other than those which would have been charged for goods or services had they been sold to an independent buyer or bought from an independent seller. Furthermore, since it is also (and, often, unjustifiably) assumed that arm's length prices are necessarily competitive prices, manipulated transfer prices are always seen to operate against the interests of countries. Indeed, at one and the same time, both the exporting and importing countries may argue that a price charged for goods traded within a MNE may operate against their interests – a situation which, over any period of time, is highly improbable.

In our analysis we shall describe the ways in which Transfer Price Manipulation (TPM) may affect the local value added of MNEs or their affiliates; the conditions under which firms may engage in such practices; and what (if anything) governments can do to minimize TPM wherever it is perceived to work against their own economic interests.

18.2 THE IMPACT OF GOVERNMENT POLICY ON NATIONAL VALUE ADDED BY MNEs

18.2.1 A host country perspective

The income received from the taxes or duties paid by MNEs or their affiliates represents a gain to the national value added of a host country, which might otherwise have accrued to other parts of the MNE network. While in a given country, a MNE (like a uninational firm) will seek to minimize its net tax liabilities,[3] in its attempts to minimize its worldwide liabilities, it may positively prefer to incur taxes in one country rather than another. For example, *ceteris paribus*, there are obvious incentives for MNEs to record higher sales or lower costs in countries where corporation taxes are low, and to over-price dutiable intra-firm imports from high tax countries. We have seen that one of the unique advantages of a MNE is its ability to readily switch its value-added facilities between countries, a fact which governments need to be aware of in their efforts to attract inward direct investment (and hence the tax revenue generated by it).

Chapter 4 touched upon the relevance of government-induced incentives and disincentives as L-specific variables influencing the 'where' of MNE activity. Chapter 20 will give more attention to incentives as a bargaining strategy of host governments. In the present context, this means that, if the net payments to one host government from income earned exceed those which would have to be made to another host government, then, *ceteris paribus*, a MNE would prefer not to produce in the former country. Hence all the tax revenue which might have been received by the government of that country would be lost. Where this means the national value added by the MNE is lower than that which would have been produced by the next best alternative use of resources, then the host government may be prepared to accept the situation. Where, however, there is a possibility of at least some economic rent accruing to the host government, then it may choose to reduce the net payments it receives from the MNE.[4]

Unfortunately, the matter does not end there, as the actions of host governments may affect the *level* of profits which a MNE or its affiliates may earn as well as the *share* of the pre-tax profits. Thus, a foreign affiliate may be prepared to accept an increase in tax rates (i.e. a lower share of profits) if it is able to earn higher revenues or incur lower production or transaction costs than it would if tax rates were lower. This might be facilitated by governments in various ways, including the subsidizing of energy or labour costs, lower interest rates, reduced sales taxes (to encourage demand), import protection, less stringent environmental regulations, and the promotion of a favourable industrial climate (Dunning, 1991c). In most surveys conducted on the factors influencing the location of Japanese investment in Europe, the *indirect* consequences of governments on costs and revenues have been found to be a more important consideration than those which affected the *share* of the profit earned and retained after tax (JETRO, 1989, 1990). Similarly, in studies of the role of investment incentives influencing the location of activity by MNEs, those which are government influenced or controlled appear to be among the most important.[5]

We conclude that any government policy towards inbound direct investment, which is designed to increase the share of the value added retained in the taxing country, must take into account the ability of the MNE to counteract these attempts wherever it perceives that they will adversely affect the long-term profitability of its investments. The government must also bear in mind the effect that any taxation changes may have on the level and structure of output by a MNE or its affiliates. Finally, taxation (as a policy designed to maximize the national value added of foreign affiliates) should not be considered in isolation to the various other fiscal and other measures which might be used to achieve similar goals, and of the relative effectiveness of each of these measures (Lecraw, 1991).

The reaction of MNEs to direct or indirect taxation imposed by host countries is likely to differ from that of uninational firms in three ways. First, because the former operate in multiple locations, they may have more flexibility in their choice of investment and hence are likely to be more sensitive to differential tax policies. Second, because MNEs internalize both finished and intermediate product markets, they may have more opportunity (relative to their uninational competitors) to manipulate cross-border costs and revenues in a way that enables them both to reduce, or avoid, the payment of taxes (including import duties) and to maximize their receipts of subsidies and grants of one kind or another. And third, because of their particular O advantages, MNEs may command more economic rent than non-multinationals and/or have greater opportunities to counteract or exploit taxation changes to their own benefit. These differences may prompt different responses to taxation changes by the two groups of firms. In cases where foreign investors dominate particular sectors of the economy, they may require some modification to existing tax practices and policies.

18.2.2   A home country perspective

18.2.2.1   *Introduction* There are two main concerns about the impact of outward direct investment on the national value added of the investing country. The first relates to the loss of the taxation of profits earned abroad which might have been recouped by the home country had the investment been made in that country. The second relates to the way in which the home country taxes the worldwide profits earned by its MNEs.

18.2.2.2   *Home or foreign investment?* The answer to the first question rests mainly on the opportunity cost of FDI and the reaction of the home government to that cost. From the perspective of the home government, rather than that of the MNE, outward direct investment is likely to be acceptable as long as the perceived marginal benefits which accrue to the investing country (e.g. the foreign profits of the MNE less taxes paid to the host countries plus any benefits to the competitiveness or innovatory capacity of the investing country) are at least equal to the comparable gains of domestic investment (*gross* of tax).

Research conducted on this question, for example, by Bergsten *et al.* (1978) for the US, Reddaway *et al.* (1968), Dunning (1971) for the UK, and Swedenborg (1979) for Sweden, presents a mixed picture. In the 1960s and early 1970s, the consensus of opinion was that, assuming full employment in the home countries, the marginal social rate of return on foreign MNE activity was almost certainly less than the marginal private rate of

return.[6] In the 1980s, partly as a result of the changing character of FDI and the growing complementarity between the home and foreign activities of MNEs, this was no longer the case. However, since in the late 1980s and early 1990s, the assumption of full employment in the capital-exporting countries was (and is) an inappropriate one, some commentators have argued that there is a stronger case for discouraging the foreign activities of MNEs and diverting the resources saved to stimulating domestic production and productivity.

However, irrespective of the merits of this argument, it is highly questionable whether a discriminatory policy should be used for this purpose. Far better for the national authorities to employ the appropriate macro-economic and structural adjustment policies. In so far as these affect the profitability of the domestic activities of both foreign and domestic MNEs, they are likely to be market supportive rather than market distorting. Indeed, in times of severe domestic inflation (or stagflation), a relocation of value-added activities from foreign to domestic factories could exacerbate an already difficult macro-economic situation.

18.2.2.3   *Taxation of the foreign income of MNEs* The second taxation issue of interest to home countries surrounds the tax treatment of the income and remittances of foreign MNE activity. Although the host country has priority in taxing earnings of such income, the home country determines the ultimate tax burden of the investing company. In practice, most major capital-exporting countries seek to neutralize the tax levied on foreign income by adopting methods which fall between current taxation at the home country rate, with full credit for host taxes on income and remittances, and complete exemptions from the home tax (Kopits, 1976). The first of these methods ensures *capital-export* neutrality (whereby the tax treatment of income earned by MNEs at home or abroad is identical) and the second *capital-import* neutrality (whereby foreign affiliates are taxed in exactly the same way as domestic firms). Most commonly, domestic corporation tax is payable on the foreign income earned by MNEs, but is deferred until it is repatriated to the investing country. Host taxes on income and remittances are then credited against the home taxes, the credit being limited by the home or host tax, whichever is the lower.

Such tax neutrality[7] of foreign and domestic income may be regulated by a variety of instruments employed by home and host countries. These include withholding taxes, taxes imposed on subsidiary dividends and deductible remittances by host governments, the treatment of capital cost recovery allowances and tax incentives, and the actions taken to minimize tax evasion and outlaw unacceptable tax-minimizing behaviour of regions.[8]

In addition, a number of small countries, known as tax havens, exempt either all income, or income of foreign-owned corporations channelled through them. Some MNEs can, and do, achieve substantial O advantages from the tax deferral mechanism by accumulating income in subsidiaries based in tax haven countries. However, among home countries, the US has partly offset this advantage by taxing a large portion of such foreign income of its MNEs on a current basis (Kopits, 1976).

Most of the tax policies of home countries towards the foreign income earned by their own MNEs are constructed in conjunction with those of the host countries. The result is a complex network of bilateral tax treaties, each of which is characterized by the principle of non-discrimination whereby each contracting country limits the tax liability on income earned by its foreign affiliates to the value imposed on its own firms.

Even assuming that there is agreement about the relative merits of the *residence* and the territorial or *source* method on the taxation of foreign income earned in a particular country,[9] the question remains 'How can a home government be sure that the taxable income declared by an MNE from its foreign operations represents the true income earned in that country?' The answer is 'with difficulty' – particularly where opportunities and incentives for TPM exist, and where the tax authorities in the home country have no access to the books and documents of the foreign subsidiary(ies) of their own MNEs. This has led the tax authorities of some countries, and some regions within countries (e.g. California), to adopt a global or *worldwide* taxation principle by which domestic rates of taxation are imposed on the income earned by their corporations irrespective of *where* it is earned. Credit may then be allowed against domestic tax for foreign income taxes paid, or for taxes levied in lieu of income taxes.

At the same time, the global principle of taxation does little to avoid the loss of taxation to the home country which might arise from inter-country differences in the computation of taxable income (i.e. the tax base). This has led some commentators to suggest that the geographical distribution of a MNE's tax bill should be based on the proportion of its assets, employment or value-added activities undertaken in the countries in which it operates. Naturally enough, this suggestion has been strongly resisted by the tax authorities of capital-importing countries. Consequently, the source principle remains the primary basis for taxing the income arising from outbound investment.

Finally, although much of the literature on the taxation of MNEs has tended to focus on its direct effects on the location of their investment, or the distribution of the national value added between MNEs and the countries in which they operate, there are several indirect consequences which, in the long run, may be no less important. These are usually dealt with in the finance literature. They include the impact of different systems of taxation on the methods of financing FDI (e.g. between retained earnings and long-term borrowing or between borrowing and issuing new shares), pricing policy and dividend remission.[10]

18.2.3 Tax policies of recipient countries

Chapters 4 and 6 identified and, in some cases, evaluated the significance of a number of factors influencing the location of value-added activities by MNEs. Of the non-tax variables, those to do with the stability of the political and economic environment, the institutional and regulatory framework, macro-organizational policies, and a variety of non-tax incentives (and/or disincentives) were found to be among the most important. Tax-related factors include those to do with country-specific differences in:

- the tax rate and structure (particularly in respect of corporation taxes)
- the nature of the tax base, for example, the way in which the authorities treat or value various cost items (depreciation, inventories of interest

on loans, inflationary adjustments etc)

- the treatment of capital gains, exchange rate adjustments and the system of withholding taxes.

All these were shown to play some part in influencing not only the locational decisions, but also the O-specific advantages of MNEs and the ways in which they organize their cross-border activities.

It is not the purpose of this chapter to review the ways in which and extent to which these tax-related variables vary between countries. An excellent recent summary of differential tax rates, tax jurisdiction, the corporate income tax base and the tax treatment of foreign-exchange gains and losses is contained in a paper prepared by the Tax Policy Division of the Fiscal Affairs Department of the IMF (IMF, 1990). *Inter alia*, the data in this paper reveals that although there is some movement towards tax reform and convergence, a widening of the tax base and a standardization of tax treaties among countries, by and large, capital-importing countries continue to compete rather than cooperate with each other on tax matters. So far, at least, attempts to coordinate or harmonize the tax treatment towards MNEs have achieved only limited success.[11]

18.2.4   The response of MNEs to taxation differentials

Research on the impact of country-specific taxation differences on the level and structure of MNE activity has been well surveyed by Kopits (1976a). Drawing upon studies by Moose (1968), Bergsten *et al.* (1978) and Adler and Stevens (1974) for US firms, Snoy (1975) for several leading source countries, and Mellors (1973) for UK firms, on the impact of differences in corporate taxation between either home and host countries or between host countries on the level and geographical distribution of MNE activity, Kopits confirmed that the respective elasticities were almost universally negative (i.e. as tax rates increase, the activities of MNEs decline) and often quite significant. However, since the calculated elasticities varied according to the home country of the investing firms, the host countries of their affiliates, the estimation procedures used, the nature of the data and the underlying theoretical models,[12] it is difficult to draw any firm conclusions, except

that, *in some cases*, FDI may be extremely sensitive to tax rate differentials and that governments do well to acknowledge that MNEs have more flexibility for exploiting these differences than do purely domestic firms.[13]

In another paper (Kopits, 1980), the author uses a simulated model to show that any elimination of the benefits of tax deferral by the US Government would almost certainly lead to a reduction of US outbound direct investment – particularly into low tax host countries which would no longer have an incentive to keep their corporation taxes below the US level.[14] Hartman (1981) also offers some tentative evidence that the proportion of profits reinvested abroad by US MNEs is likely to be sensitive to tax changes because of the deferral provision. At the same time, Kopits cautions countries wishing to attract inbound investment against the widespread granting of tax holidays and rebates. He goes on to suggest that the containment of inflationary pressures and a sensible use of interest rates would yield more productive results. As we have already suggested (p. 507), the level and structure of taxation of foreign income may affect both the competitive advantage of MNEs and the L advantages of countries to attract MNE activities. It may also influence the way in which MNEs choose to organize their foreign activities. The following section will deal with some of the possible interactions between country-specific differences in corporate taxation and the propensity of MNEs to engage in TPM. By influencing the structure of the financing of foreign production, the levels and rates of taxation may affect both the ownership of value-added activity in a particular country and the international distribution of capital assets. To the extent that MNEs are likely to be more responsive to changes in country-specific fiscal penalties and incentives[15] in respect of their more footloose activities, they may be afforded a further competitive edge over their domestic counterparts.

We would make one further point. Since taxation is just one variable affecting the level and distribution of MNE activity, its significance cannot be evaluated without reference to the other variables. The evidence from field and econometric studies, outlined in Chapter 6, shows that cross-border differences in corporate taxes are rarely a primary motive for MNE, but that once a decision is made to engage in FDI or increase foreign production, they may play an important discriminatory role depending upon the locational flexibility of the MNE. This is particularly likely to be the case for export platform manufacturing investment and the setting up of regional offices which are among the most footloose of all MNE activities.

18.2.5   National tax strategy in a global economy

Throughout this volume, we have argued for governments to adopt a systemic approach to MNE activity. In the present context, this means that taxation policy of both home and host governments should recognize that in the contemporary global economy many corporations have a choice of where to locate their income earning activities; and that this choice will, in part at least, be influenced by the taxation policies of the authorities. In earlier years, when there was much less mobility of corporate activity, these inter-country taxation linkages were relatively insignificant; and hence, in so far as taxation policy affected the competitiveness of a country's firms or the disposition and quality of its domestic resources it did so without much concern about the possible consequences for foreign firms or other countries.

In the world economy of the 1990s, a new dimension enters (or should enter) into taxation policy. Assuming that one of the main objectives of tax authorities is to collect revenue, then it seems appropriate to consider how a country's tax policy in time t will affect the income earning capacity of the taxed corporations in time $t + 1$. But, if one country's tax base or tax rates compares very unfavourably with that or those of its major competitors, then it is highly probable that not only will its own firms seek to earn as much taxable income as they can outside their home countries, but that as a host country to foreign investment, it will become less attractive. He and Guisinger (1992) have, in fact, demonstrated that the propensity of US MNEs to reinvest their foreign earnings is especially sensitive to a host country's tax rate as well as to the differences between home and host country tax rates. The net effect of this kind of relocation of value-added activities is to weaken competitiveness of the high tax country and earn it a lower corporate tax yield at a future date.

It is issues like these that Gary Hufbauer explores in a recent book (Hufbauer, 1992) from the viewpoint of the US economy. But his analysis could equally be applied to most other major economies of the world. Hufbauer points out that the current system of taxing the income of MNEs or their affiliates dates back to the 1920s, and is essentially concerned with the appropriate division of revenue between US and foreign taxing authorities and of upholding the principle of tax neutrality between income earned in and out of the US. But today, so Hufbauer contends, a no less important goal of tax policy should be to uphold the industrial and commercial interests of the US, partly by ensuring that the international market system is as free of distortions as it can be; but also in pursuance of a macro-organizational strategy, whenever the playing fields of national government behaviour are not level.

Chapter 20 will explore the concept of a systemic organizational strategy in more detail. For the moment, we would observe this embraces taxation policy; and it is the purpose of Hufbauer's contribution to suggest some of the components of a strategic tax policy which will best serve the long-term taxation interests of the US in a global economy. These include the adoption of a territorial approach to corporate taxation, and a repeal of foreign tax together with a series of proposals as to how best the US might work together with other leading industrial nations to harmonize the taxation of business income, and methods of settling transfer pricing and cost allocation disputes.

While the appropriate strategic tax policy for the US may not be suitable for other countries (though there will most certainly be common elements) it is clear that the globalization of value-added activity is requiring tax authorities to rethink both the principles and the practice of corporate taxation; and that whatever changes are made must be in accord with the systemic competitiveness of the economy concerned.

18.3   TRANSFER PRICING

18.3.1   Introduction

The subject of cross-border intra-firm transfer pricing has commanded a good deal of attention in the literature, mainly because it would seem that governments of both developing and developed countries perceive that, by manipulating such prices to serve their own interests, MNEs adversely affect those of the countries in which they operate. Though most attention is focused on the use of TPM to circumvent corporate taxes, governments may be no less concerned with its use to disguise the true operating costs and revenues of the MNE or its affiliates and/or to lessen some of the intended consequences of macro-economic policy (e.g. exchange and interest rate changes). Where MNEs or their affiliates play an important role in the trading activities of the economies concerned, TPM may also have some impact on the balance of payments.

Though the literature has generally focused on the consequences of TPM for the economic welfare of host countries, home countries may be no less concerned. While a loss of value added of one country will usually result in an equivalent gain of value added to another country, it is quite possible that TPM may result in a loss of value added in one country and a redistribution of value added in another, which is unacceptable to both. On the other hand, where administered prices by MNEs replace non-competitive arm's length prices, or where they are used to combat government policies which are market distorting, they may raise, rather than reduce, economic welfare (Rugman and Eden, 1985).

18.3.2   The motivation for TPM

Let us define transfer price manipulation as the action of a firm to exchange goods or services (i.e. across or along value-added chains) within its organization at a price different from that at which it would trade those goods and services to an independent firm. Again, we would emphasize that although it is often inferred that arm's length prices are competitive prices, *de facto* this may not be the case. On the other hand, without a knowledge of

why a firm may wish to manipulate market prices, there is no presumption that such prices will be higher or lower than administered prices.

MNEs engage in TPM because they perceive it advances their global interests. Thus, *ceteris paribus*, and quite understandably, a firm which is a profit maximizer will seek to shift any pre-tax profits it earns away from countries that levy high rates of corporation tax to countries that levy low rates of corporation tax. Suppose, for example, that a subsidiary of a MNE located in Country A earns $10 million of taxable income on which it has to pay a 50% tax; another subsidiary in Country B earns $10 million of taxable income, on which it has to pay a 20% tax. Suppose, too, that the subsidiary in Country A imports goods from a subsidiary in Country B worth $25 million at arm's length prices and exports goods to Country B worth $20 million at arm's length prices. Then, its total tax bill is $6 million ($4 million paid in Country A and $2 million in Country B) and its net profit is $14 million.

Clearly, in this situation, given a free choice, the MNE would prefer to declare all its profits in Country B and pay $2 million less tax. One way of achieving this (if known about and permitted by the authorities of Country A)[16] is for the subsidiary in Country A to sell goods or services to the subsidiary in Country B at a lower than arm's length price and buy goods and services from that subsidiary at a higher than arm's length price. If, for example, the subsidiary in Country A lowered its selling price by 25% and raised its buying price by 20%, this would reduce the revenue of the subsidiary in Country A by $5 million and increase its costs by $5 million, thus wiping out the profits recorded in that country. At the same time, there would be a corresponding increase in the revenue earned and/or a decrease in the costs incurred by the subsidiary in Country B, the net result of which would be to increase its taxable income to $20 million. By such TPM, the MNE is able to reduce its overall tax liability from $6 million to $4 million.

The reduction of corporation tax is only one of several reasons why MNEs may seek to engage in TPM. It might, for example, prefer to reduce declarable income in a country in which labour unions or other local stakeholders might otherwise siphon off a share of the surplus profits and transfer it to countries where its own bargaining strength is greater. Similarly, the declaration of a high rate of return on capital might be regarded by the domestic authorities as a sign of monopoly pricing. In order to save itself the possibility of investigation, the firm may seek to lower its profitability by TPM. Also, since profits earned in a country whose currency is hard (or appreciating) are likely to be worth more than those earned in a country whose currency is soft (or depreciating), there may be an incentive for firms to transfer funds from affiliates located in the latter to those in the former country. Finally, MNEs may prefer to earn their profits in low risk rather than high risk economic and political environments.

The literature on the rationale for TPM suggests that there are several motives for it, both *internal* and *external* to the firm. Some of these are summarized in Exhibit 18.1. It should be emphasized these are not, in themselves, sufficient reasons for TPM. At the same time, the taxation authorities of home or host countries may take steps to disallow, or counteract the incentives for, TPM.

The three most important *internal* incentives for TPM are first, a reduction of the global tax burden of the MNE; second, the need to improve control over the performance of and to coordinate cash and income flows from its foreign subsidiaries (Eitman and Stonehill, 1972; Lessard and Shapiro, 1973); and third, to advance the MNE's strategic objectives (Burns, 1980).

The first two of these incentives are self-evident. The third has received less attention in the literature although, in the long run, its effects on both the O advantages of MNEs and on the economic welfare of the countries in which they operate may be the most decisive. Examples of the strategic use of TPM by MNEs include the encouragement or discouragement of exports by foreign affiliates, a reduction in the (publicized) profitability of the parent company or one of its subsidiaries to mollify demands by labour unions for higher wages, the deliberate making of losses to support requests for government financial support or to justify price increases in regulated markets, the limitation of financial risk by reducing cash exposure in unstable environments, the subsidization of newly established subsidiaries to help them penetrate markets or set up distribution outlets, and the provision of disinformation to competitors about the profitability of particular ventures (Kim and Miller, 1979; Greenhill and

Herbolzheimer, 1981). When successfully employed, each of these forms of TPM may increase the O advantage of MNEs relative to those of their competitors.

Of the *external* factors making for TPM (the net effect of which may be either to *increase* or *reduce* the national value added in a particular home or host country), the most significant include the avoidance or reduction of tariffs and taxes, the diversification of economic, political or exchange risk, and the circumvention of restrictions placed on the repatriation of capital or dividends by host countries. Where domestic price increases are regulated by host governments or higher profits are treated as a sign of monopoly pricing, MNEs may engage in TPM to protect or exploit their competitive positions. One may then reasonably hypothesize that the more these internal or external factors are present in one country relative to another, the greater the incentive for firms to manipulate transfer prices on cross-border intra-firm transactions.

18.3.3   The opportunities for transfer pricing

So much for the *raison d'être* for TPM. What now of the opportunities for it? Clearly, these will hinge on the extent to which MNEs find it profitable to engage in the cross-border specialization of economic activity and, hence, exchange goods and services within their organization. Obviously, the greater the amount of trade, the more opportunities for TPM there are likely to be, even though MNEs may not always be able to take advantage of these opportunities. Much will also depend on whether the governments of the trading nations permit, or take action to negate the incentives, for cross-border TPM.

Let us illustrate these points with reference to the impact of the EC on the intra-firm trade of US affiliates. In 1957, prior to the formation of the European Economic Community, exports of US companies from their affiliates in the six founding Member States to countries other than the US (almost exclusively to other parts of Europe) were 14.1% of their total sales. By 1987, this proportion had risen to 46.5%, of which 52.4% went to other US affiliates (US Department of Commerce, vd).[17]

Other data published by the US Department of

Exhibit 18.1   Various inducements for transfer pricing.

Hypothesis: The parent company sells goods or services to its foreign subsidiary

Motivation	TPM which might be taken by MNE	Comments
External to the MNE		
To minimize global corporation tax		
• higher in home than host country	Underpricing*	
• lower in home than host country	Overpricing	
To minimize custom and import duties or export taxes	Underpricing	Affects revenue in only one country
To maximize export subsidies	Overpricing	Affects revenue in only one country
To reduce foreign exchange risks		
• claim in weak currency	Overpricing plus leading	Leading or lagging enables exchange
• claim in strong currency	Overpricing plus lagging	risks to be avoided; transfer prices
• debt in weak currency	Overpricing plus lagging	enhance the benefits of leading or
• debt in strong currency	Overpricing plus leading	lagging
To ensure repatriations of profits or capital	Overpricing	
To increase asset value of firm and raise depreciation allowances	Overpricing	Also increases the basis of depreciation allowances and of compensation in the event of expropriation
To circumvent local restrictions on capital expenditure	Underpricing	
To reduce political risks		
• in home country	Underpricing	
• in host country	Overpricing	
Internal to the MNE		
Joint ventures		
• gain maximum share of economic rent from joint ventures	Overpricing	The 'gain' from transfer pricing is, by definition, shared with the joint partner
• give support to claims for price increases	Overpricing	The 'gain' from transfer pricing is, by definition, shared with the joint partner
• avoid anti-monopoly charges	Underpricing	
• avoid anti-dumping charges	Overpricing	
• mollify claims for wage increases by showing lower profits	Overpricing	

Exhibit 18.1 (continued)   Various inducements for transfer pricing.

Hypothesis: The parent company sells goods or services to its foreign subsidiary

Motivation	TPM which might be taken by MNE	Comments
• support an infant subsidiary	Underpricing	
• intensify competitive pressure on local competitors (e.g. by predatory pricing)	Underpricing	Provided lower cost is shifted into lower price to the consumer

* Under or over pricing as compared with the prices which would have been charged on the open market.
Source: Adapted from Plasschaert (1985).

Commerce and analysed by Casson and Pearce (1987) and Gilroy (1990) confirms that the extent and pattern of intra-firm trade (and hence the opportunities for TPM) vary between types of MNE activity.[18] In particular, the literature distinguishes between vertical and horizontal intra-firm trade. The former consists of three kinds. First is trade in primary products between affiliates in developing countries and their parent companies in developed countries. This is essentially Hecksler–Ohlin type trade which is internalized within MNEs, and is based upon country-specific differences in the cost and availability of natural resources. Most investment-related trade in such commodities as oil, aluminium, copper, bananas and tea, is of this kind. Some of the fiercest critics of TPM by MNEs have been the governments of host countries which are substantially dependent upon these products for their foreign exchange earnings.

The second type of vertical trade is within the manufacturing sector, where MNEs engage in cross-border specialization along a particular value-added chain and trade products with different factor intensities. Thus, a proportion of intra-firm exports of manufacturing affiliates consists of labour-intensive intermediate or final goods from industrializing developing countries. Third, there is a substantial intra-firm trade in goods exported from MNEs to

their foreign sales and distributing outlets, or imported by MNEs from their foreign purchasing agents.

Horizontal intra-firm trade mainly occurs between manufacturing or service affiliates of MNEs located in developed countries. To take advantage of economies of scale, multi-product firms may choose to specialize their production of one or more products in one country and trade these for products produced in another country. This (as we have already seen[19]) is the main feature of rationalized or efficiency-seeking MNE activity. Strategic asset acquiring investment may also lead to intra-firm (sometimes in place of inter-firm) trade, particularly in intermediate products, such as technology, management and marketing competences. Much of this kind of intra-firm trade is also intra-industry trade. Again, it follows that the greater the incentives for specialization, the more opportunities for TPM.

18.3.4   The constraints on TPM

Given the motivation for TPM and the opportunities afforded by intra-firm trade, firms may still not actually engage in such manipulation because the costs of doing so outweigh the benefits. This, in effect, means that the incentives described in the previous section of this chapter are counteracted by disincentives. Disincentives are of two main kinds, *viz* those internal and those external to the firm.

Lecraw (1985) has observed, for example, that in multi-domestic MNEs, which largely decentralize decision taking to their subsidiaries, TPM may wreak havoc with their evaluation, control and reward systems. Even where the intra-firm transaction costs of TPM are small, those associated with justifying such manipulation to an administration bent on insisting on arm's length prices for all cross-border transactions, may make the possible gains not worthwhile. Moreover, if an MNE knows that the attitude of a particular government towards TPM is highly censorious, it may believe that it is better not to engage in the practice. IBM is an example of a MNE which, at one time at least, was particularly sensitive to being accused of TPM, and publicly stated that it always priced its traded goods as if it were buying from or selling to an independent party. Finally, although we have seen that an MNE which, as a part owner of a joint venture, might like to use TPM wherever this would increase its share of the economic rent from that venture, the local partner might vigorously oppose such a strategy.[20]

However, possibly the main constraint on TPM, particularly where there are considerable incentives and opportunities for it, are the actions taken (or the threat of actions which might be taken) by governments to prohibit it. This usually requires both a strong taxation authority and an agreement by the various arms of government to adopt a coherent and consistent policy both on the detrimental effects of TPM and what might be done to counteract it.[21]

The next section will discuss the various mechanisms open to the tax authorities to identify and minimize TPM. For the moment, we would observe that it is rarely the case that TPM is unambiguous in its impact on economic welfare. Moreover, it may affect individual government departments differently. For example, to reduce corporation taxes in a particular host country, an MNE might overprice its exports to its affiliate in that country. While this might yield less corporation tax and raise the total import bill of a country, it could well produce more import duties and, depending on the increase in domestic prices and the elasticity of demand for the finished product, realize more revenue from sales or value-added taxes.

To summarize, the extent to which MNEs engage in TPM will depend first on the motivation for shifting the geographical incidence of taxable income from where it is earned to some other country, and second on the opportunities for such TPM. The latter will depend on the extent of intra-firm trade,[22] the motivation for FDI, the transaction costs of engaging in TPM, the transparency of intra-firm trade[23] and the pricing strategies of MNEs, and the extent to which governments are willing and able to influence firms in their cross-border trading practices.

18.3.5   The evidence for TPM

18.3.5.1 *Introduction* While there is a general consensus on the determinants of transfer pricing and the conditions under which TPM is likely to occur, there is much less agreement about either the extent to which it is practised by MNEs or its consequences for economic welfare.

The evidence for TPM is largely fragmentary, circumstantial, and highly industry and/or country specific. Even the US, which has the most sophisticated system for detecting TPM, is not immune. In April 1992 there was a lively debate in the US Congress about alleged losses of several billion dollars arising from the tax avoiding tactics of foreign (especially Japanese) affiliates.[24] There can be no question that such manipulation does take place (or has done so in the past), and has made a noticeable difference to both the taxation revenue and the balance of payments of some of the countries in which MNEs operate. However, the *extent* and *significance* of TPM is still a matter of intense conjecture, although there is accumulating evidence of the kind of conditions under which it is most likely to take place. In particular, we might identify three groups of studies.

18.3.5.2 *Macro-statistical studies of MNE practices* Research by Lall (1973), Vaitsos (1974), Roumeliotis (1977), UNCTAD (1978) and the British Monopolies Commission (1973) provides numerous examples of TPM by MNEs. The UNCTAD investigation, for example, cited the case of one developing country in which the overpricing of imports of metal products and chemicals[25] by MNEs was put at 16% and 25%, respectively (UNCTAD, 1978). In his study of Colombian industry in the late 1960s, Vaitsos – using data supplied by the customs authorities – calculated that the overpricing of the imports of intermediate products ranged from 26% in the chemical industry, to 44% in the rubber industry and 54% in the electrical industry, to 155% in the pharmaceutical industry. Vaitsos further estimated that the additional cost of the imports of intermediate products for the pharmaceutical industry was $20 million a year and that the loss of government tax revenue amounted to $10 million a year.

Roumeliotis (1977), in his analysis of the transfer pricing practices of foreign affiliates in the Greek metal, chemicals and pharmaceutical sectors, found that in one-half of the 84 cases studied there was evidence of substantial overpricing of imports. Overpricing ranged from 5% to 230% of the estimated market price. In a related study, the same author discovered that the internal export prices of aluminium shipped from a subsidiary in Greece to its parent company was between 1% and 19% below the comparable world price – depending on the type of aluminium exported (Roumeliotis, 1977). In an ESCAP study (ESCAP/CTC Joint Unit, 1984) it was found that MNE pharmaceutical affiliates in Thailand were being charged above market prices for their imports of intermediate products, but by a lesser amount than that discovered by Vaitsos in Colombia. By contrast, Ellis (1981) unearthed evidence of the under-invoicing of banana exports from Central America.

A more recent study by Natke (1985) of some 141 manufacturing firms in Brazil, showed that in 76 of 127 product categories considered, the mean price of imports by MNE affiliates was higher than paid by indigenous firms; in 47 products, the price paid by the latter firms was higher. Intra-firm prices also exhibited greater variability. When a paired means test was performed, it was found that foreign affiliates consistently paid higher prices for their imports, with the degree of overpricing ranging from 21% to 39%. However, Natke also argued that such differences in pricing may have nothing to do with TPM *per se*, but may reflect differences in the quality of the goods or differences in the pricing policies or accounting practices of the firms in question. In their

investigation into the pricing practices of the Swiss MNE Hoffman-LaRoche, the British Monopolies Commission estimated that, between 1966 and 1972, some 76% of the profits earned by the UK subsidiary were remitted to the parent company by way of TPM and another 12% in the form of contributions towards R&D, for which a mark up of 71% on costs was charged (British Monopolies Commission, 1973).

18.3.5.3 *Comparative inter- and intra-firm pricing practices* A second and, in many ways, a more interesting kind of empirical research on TPM is that which seeks to test a number of hypotheses about the propensity of MNEs to engage in such manipulation and the likely extent of such price adjustments. Typical of this research is that of Lecraw (1985c), who used multiple regression analysis to test the determinants of the extent to which export and import prices of *inter*-firm and *intra*-firm exports differed. He collected data on the export and import pricing practices of 111 MNEs which operated 153 subsidiaries in six light manufacturing industries in five ASEAN countries.

Lecraw undertook two main exercises. The first was to compare the extent of the variation between the export prices of a particular product charged by 35 foreign affiliates on both inter- and intra-firm sales; and, similarly, the import prices paid by 65 foreign affiliates. Export prices paid by unaffiliated firms (i.e. market based prices) were used as the baseline for the competitive arm's length value of the product. Lecraw next hypothesized that the difference between this baseline price and the intra-firm transfer price would depend upon a number of country- and firm-specific variables. Among these were:

- tariffs (the hypothesis being that the higher the nominal tariff in the country of destination, the greater the likely difference between the prices of intra- and inter-firm exports);

- the extent to which price controls were in existence in a host country (the hypothesis being that the more rigorous such price controls, the more MNE affiliates would be tempted to reduce the price of their intra-firm exports in order to have price increases approved);

- the presence of a joint partner (the hypothesis being that the presence of such a partner would reduce the ability of MNE affiliates to set non-market based transfer prices);

- the extent to which decisions were decentralized by the MNE (the hypothesis being that the more decentralized the decision taking, the greater the problems caused by TPM, and thus the less likely there would be a deviation between inter- and intra-firm prices).

Using a multiple regression model, Lecraw found that in all cases the variables had the predicted sign, and were significant at the 95% or above level.[26] The nominal tariff in the country of destination and the extent to which control over decision taking was centralized both yielded particularly significant coefficients. As a whole, both the export and the import regression equations explained more than one-half of the variance in TPM.

The second exercise undertaken by Lecraw was to identify differences in the export and import pricing practices of MNE affiliates according to whether the goods were traded internally or exchanged between unrelated firms. Lecraw ascertained that 66% of the latter transactions were based on international or domestic market prices, or on full cost plus profit formulae. By contrast, 57% of intra-group exports and imports were traded at prices dictated by the parent company. Discriminant analysis not only helped classify 88% of the firms to the correct category; it also helped confirm the significance of such variables as nominal tariffs, relative tax rates, the prevalence of price controls, perceived country risk, and the extent of dividend and capital repatriation restrictions, as significant variables influencing the intra-firm pricing strategies of MNEs. There were, however, some interesting country-specific differences. Japanese MNEs tended to use non-market based prices for both intra-firm imports and exports more than did their US and European counterparts. Lecraw suggests that this may reflect their more centralized control procedures (Lecraw, 1985c).

In another investigation into the transfer pricing practices adopted by some leading US manufacturing firms, Benvignati (1985) established that cross-border intra-firm transactions (in this case, exports to foreign subsidiaries) were more frequently priced on a non-market basis than were intra-US transactions. He also discovered that up to 85% of variations in

the use of market pricing were firm specific, while at most 4% to 7% reflected 'industry-to-industry' differences (p. 209). Using data provided by the Federal Trade Commission of some 674 foreign transactions and 1380 domestic transactions undertaken by 466 US manufacturing firms in 1975, and applying ordinary least squares (OLS) and maximum likelihood estimation (MLE) procedures, Benvignati concluded that, of the firm-specific variables likely to lead to cross-border TPM, advertising intensity (as a proxy for product differentiation O advantages) was a statistically significant determinant. Benvignati also discovered that, except where FDI took the form of branch plant (rather than subsidiary) activity, the volume of a firm's intra-firm exports and the number of countries in which it operated, were positively related to its propensity to engage in non-market pricing. However, there was also reason to suppose that larger MNEs, possibly because of their more pronounced visibility to government tax officials and their greater need to avoid conflicting management objectives by non-market pricing, were more likely to supply exports to their foreign subsidiaries at arm's length prices than were their smaller counterparts.

A more recent study by Bernard and Weiner (1989) on intra-MNE and arm's length prices and transportation costs of crude oil imported into the US revealed that there were statistically significant differences in the case of several exporting countries. However, when multiplied by import volume and taking account of other price-related variables (e.g. quality of oil) these differences averaged only 2% over the period 1973–84.[27] Moreover, the results were inconsistent both between countries and over time.[28]

The authors also found that the relationship between TPM and differences in the corporate tax rates of the exporting countries was weak, which they suggested might be because of the watchfulness of the US regulatory authorities and the fact that to the oil companies, TPM may serve a primarily managerial, rather than a financial, role.

18.3.5.4 *Evidence of TPM from field studies* A third type of empirical research focuses on obtaining data from firms as to conditions under which, and the extent to which, they actually do engage in TPM. Illustrative of these studies is that of Roger Tang

(1979, 1981), who, in the late 1970s, used a questionnaire to ask a group of 145 US, 102 Japanese, 192 Canadian and 80 British firms about their cross-border transfer pricing practices. He found that 92% of the US, 73% of the Japanese, 85% of the Canadian and 79% of the British firms admitted they engaged in some TPM. The practice was most common in the metal manufacturing and industrial and farm equipment sectors. In general, US and Japanese firms were more prone to base their transfer prices on some kind of cost plus formula, while Canadian and British companies preferred negotiated prices.

The most frequently stated incentives for practising TPM were to minimize the global tax bill and to improve monitoring of the performance of domestic and foreign subsidiaries. The important exogenous and endogenous variables determining TPM were similar to those identified by Lecraw. In addition, the competitive position of foreign affiliates (for example, TPM was used as a means of penetration pricing or for charging below full cost to gain a competitive advantage) was consistently ranked the second or third most important variable. None of the group of firms thought 'risk of expropriation' in a foreign country or performance of inward investors to be important variables – nor, perhaps more surprisingly – 'the volume of intra-firm transfers'. Japanese firms appeared to place more emphasis on the interests of local partners than did US firms, as they did on the likely repercussions of currency fluctuations. In general, the correlation of motives was strongest between UK and Japanese firms and between Canadian and US firms. Some further details are set out in Table 18.1, which also sets out the rankings assigned by US firms in a more recent survey conducted by Tang (1992).

Table 18.2 sets out some details of the methods of transfer pricing used by the same group of firms. Clearly, not all of these are suggestive of TPM. What is especially interesting is that, when compared with the intra-country pricing methods used, all four groups of firms were less cost-oriented in their inter-country transfer pricing.[29]

The findings of Tang broadly confirm those of Arpan (1972), who also used a questionnaire to identify country-specific differences in the motivation for TPM among a sample of US, Canadian and UK MNEs. He also concluded that smaller MNEs were less prone to use administered prices and that non-US transfer pricing systems were generally less complex and more market oriented than American systems.[30] A subsequent study by Al-Eryani et al. (1990), using data obtained from 164 large industrial MNEs, found that of a number of the environmental and firm-specific variables hypothesized to influence the selection of transfer pricing strategies,[31] the most important were a cluster of legal factors and the size of the company, both of which were positively related to market-based transfer prices. However, somewhat surprisingly, government restrictions, such as exchange price and import controls, and the stage of economic development of a country, were either insignificant or secondary determinants of a market-based transfer pricing strategy.

We have illustrated a few of the empirical findings on TPM, but the subject has fascinated scholars since the late 1960s. The reader is invited to consult Tang (1979, 1981, 1992), Rugman and Eden (1985) and Plasschaert (1993) for more detailed descriptions of these studies. While each has made some contribution to our understanding of the phenomenon, it is still very difficult to form a view about the extent of TPM, how far it differs from arm's length prices or its welfare implications.

Neither does the pattern of growth of MNE activity give much guidance as to whether the practice is increasing or not, although Tang's recent survey did suggest that, in 1990, US firms were somewhat more likely to use market prices as the basis for their internal cross-border pricing than in 1977.[32] Moreover, the substantial number of foreign affiliates in some countries (e.g. the US and the UK) which report zero profits or losses is giving increasing concern to tax authorities. On the one hand, there is clear evidence that the extent of intra-firm trade is increasing. Hence so are the potential opportunities for TPM. On the other, there is reason to suppose that the incentives to engage in TPM are less in the case of firms undertaking rationalized or strategic asset seeking investment in the Triad – which, as Chapter 2 has shown, is the fastest growing form of MNE activity – than in the case of FDI in resource- or market-seeking investment in developing countries. At the same time, governments of both developed and developing countries have become much more vigilant and expert in dealing with TPM, while the improving political and social climate

Table 18.1 Ranking of some firm and country-specific variables influencing the transfer pricing strategies of MNEs, 1977 and 1990.

| Variables | Canada (N=104)* 1977 | Britain (N=47)* 1977 | US | | Japan (N=57)* 1977 |
			(N=88) 1977	(N=98)* 1990	
Firm-specific variables					
1. Overall profit to the company	1	1	1	1	1
2. The competitive position of subsidiaries in foreign countries	3	2	3	4	2
3. Maintaining good relationships with host governments	6	6	11	6,7,8	10
4. Performance evaluation of foreign subsidiaries	7	3	5	10	5
5. The need to maintain adequate cash flows in foreign subsidiaries	9	4,5	9	6,7,8	6,7
6. The need of subsidiaries in foreign countries to seek local funds	15	14	16	11	16
7. Volume of inter-divisional transfers	16	18	14	17	18
8. Restrictions imposed by foreign countries on repatriation of profits or dividends	4	4,5	2	3	4
9. Differentials in income tax rates and income tax legislation between countries	5	13	4	2	14
Country-specific variables					
10. Anti-dumping legislation of foreign countries	8	12	15	13,14	13
11. Import restrictions imposed by foreign countries	10	9	7	9	11
12. Rules and requirements of financial reporting for foreign subsidiaries	11	10	10	16	15
13. Rates of customs duties and customs legislation where the company has operations	2	11	6	5	9
14. Anti-trust legislation of foreign countries	12	16	20	13,14	19
15. Devaluation and revaluation in countries where the company has operations	13	7	12	12	3
16. Restrictions imposed by foreign countries on the amount of royalty and management fees which can be charged against foreign subsidiaries	14	15	8	6,7,8	12
17. The interests of local partners in foreign subsidiaries	17	8	17	15	6,7
18. Domestic government requirements on direct foreign investments	18	20	18	20	20
19. Rates of inflation in foreign countries	19	17	13	18	8
20. Risk of expropriation in foreign countries where the company has operations	20	19	19	19	17

Sources: Adapted from Tables 5.5 and 7.4 of Tang (1979, pp. 80–81, 1992).
*N = number of respondents.
The rankings were obtained by asking each correspondent to rank each factor listed on a scale from 1 (not important) to 5 (extremely important). The average importance score for a particular variable was computed by summing the integer values assigned to them.

Table 18.2   Transfer pricing methods for international transfers – a cross-national comparison.

Pricing methods	Canada (N=108)* %	Britain (N=71)* %	US (N=118)* %	Japan (N=63)* %
Cost-oriented methods:				
Actual variable cost of production	1.8	0.0	0.0	1.6
Actual full production cost	2.8	4.2	5.1	0.0
Standard variable cost of production	0.9	0.0	0.8	0.0
Standard full production cost	3.7	2.8	5.1	4.8
Actual variable production cost plus a lump-sum subsidy	2.8	2.8	1.7	1.6
Full production cost (actual or standard) plus some allowance for profit	19.4	22.6	32.2	33.3
Other cost-oriented methods	1.9	1.4	1.7	0.0
Subtotal for cost-oriented methods	33.3	33.8	46.6	41.3
Non-cost-oriented methods:				
Market price	26.9	23.9	20.4	22.2
Market price less selling expenses	10.2	9.9	14.4	14.3
Negotiated price	25.9	26.8	13.6	22.2
Mathematical-programming price	0.0	0.0	0.8	0.0
Other non-cost-oriented methods	3.7	5.6	4.2	0.0
Subtotal for non-cost-oriented methods	66.7	66.2	53.4	58.7
Total for all methods	100.0	100.0	100.0	100.0

Sources: Tables 5.3 and 7.1 of Tang (1979).
Note: The numbers of respondents in the four national groups are: Canada, 78; Britain, 48; the US, 85; and Japan, 42.

*N = Number of times referred to by the respondents.

towards MNE activity have lessened the *need* for MNEs to engage in TPM to counteract unacceptable risks.[33] Finally, the past two decades have witnessed a resurgence in market-oriented economic systems, a movement towards more harmonized macro-economic policies (at least between the major industrial countries) and a gradual reduction (in the EC, an elimination) of cross-border restrictions on the movements of assets, goods and people. All of these developments, by helping to erode the gains from TPM, have also reduced the impetus for it.

18.4   POLICIES OF GOVERNMENTS TOWARDS TPM

18.4.1   Unilateral policies

The reactions of governments towards TPM tend to fall into three categories. The first is to change their fiscal or economic policies so as to try to reduce the *raison d'être* for MNEs to engage in TPM. Such actions include a harmonization in income tax rates or import duties, a removal of foreign exchange and/ or dividend remission restrictions, the lifting of unwelcome performance requirements on foreign investors (e.g. with respect to import sourcing), and a greater readiness to accept the costs and benefits of economic interdependence. There is little evidence that governments have consciously taken actions of this kind – at least not to reduce TPM – mainly because, considering their effects *in toto*, they are not thought to be cost-effective.

The second, and more widespread, reaction of governments, is to seek means to encourage MNEs to engage in 'fair' or 'reasonable' transfer pricing within the framework of their (i.e. the governments') economic goals and strategies. While some developed countries (e.g. the US) have tended to rely on statutory legislation to control TPM, others (e.g. the UK and most developing countries) have preferred to settle any disagreements by discussion with the companies or by administrative or informal procedures. This latter format is especially likely to be chosen whenever and wherever the tax authorities possess bargaining leverage *vis à vis* the MNE or its affiliates (UNCTAD, 1978). Among the actions that governments may pursue to minimize unacceptable non-market based pricing, the following deserve especial mention:

- Require MNEs and/or their affiliates to provide more information about cross-border pricing practices.

- Break the internal transactional links between parent companies and affiliates, or between affiliates, by channelling imports and exports through an independent agency.

- Tax the profits of the MNEs and/or their affiliates on the basis that they charge arm's length prices for the goods and services traded internally, rather than those actually charged.

- Discourage underpricing of exports by imposing an export tariff; discourage overpricing of imports by imposing (additional) import taxes.

- Require MNEs and/or their affiliates to charge domestic or international market prices (assuming that such prices actually exist).

- Require MNEs to price goods and services internally transacted as if they were selling, or reselling, these to independent buyers. This is known as the *comparable uncontrolled price* (CUP) method, and is most suitable where there are external markets and where the goods and services exchanged are reasonably homogeneous. In respect of this and the previous policy, it is assumed that all the necessary adjustments are made for all the other variables (e.g. product quality, market characteristics) which may influence the arm's length price of a particular product (OECD, 1979).

- In cases where arm's length prices are difficult to establish, require MNEs and/or their affiliates to price their products on some pre-agreed formula. We shall identify just three of these formulae: each has its own advantages and drawbacks. The first is the *cost-plus method* by which a mark up is made on unit costs of production based on an appropriate gross profit. This method presupposes that it is possible to identify the costs for a particular product. Because of this, it may be very difficult to use in the case of products involving several stages of production and/or those jointly produced with other products. The second method is the *sales (or market) minus method* which involves deducting a discount or profit margin (customary in the branch of industry concerned) from the resale price of the end product. Quite apart from the problem of identifying the appropriate discount in a non-competitive market, this method is only suitable as long as the resale price is the market price which is not controlled by governments. The third method is the so-called *'fourth'* method[34] which consists of an arbitrary allocation of costs between the (internal) transacting parties on the basis of *ad hoc* methods relating to any intra-firm price. Such an assessment is used most frequently in judicial settlements following a disagreement between the tax authorities and MNEs about the appropriate transfer price to be charged. However, they frequently provide a yardstick to firms in the setting of future transfer prices (Alworth, 1988).

- Where none of the pricing methods identified above is practical, apportion the profits of a MNE according to the sales, geographical distribution of its assets or employment. Such a reaction to TPM is not so much to determine a fair price, but to establish a fair or proper distribution of the global profits of an enterprise without regard to how the marketplace would operate (Irish, 1987).

- Compute a transfer price on the basis of the level

of profit which the competitors of MNEs might be expected to earn in the same industry and in similar circumstances (the *comparable profits* method), or on the basis of the 'normal' expected return on capital invested by MNEs (the *net yield expectations* method).

- Conduct a series of *ad hoc* internal checks on firms to check the methods of transfer pricing and/or *raison d'être* for TPM.

- Impose restrictions on the local issue of corporate securities and on the degree of foreign ownership of local subsidiaries (Copithorne, 1971).

- Improve the means by which arm's length prices may be identified and/or calculated; for example, as spelled out by Section 482 of the Internal Revenue Code.

- Establish 'advance pricing agreements' (APAs) with MNEs, by which, for a stipulated period of time (usually two or three years), they are assured that an agreed method of transfer pricing (or TPM) is accepted by the local fiscal authority. This suggests an *ex-ante* rather than an *ex-post* interface between the tax authorities and MNEs; APA has already been introduced with some success in the Netherlands and the US (Plasschaert, 1993).

- Press for supra-national control over, or multilateral agreements on TPM (see Section 18.5.2 below). In the EC, for example, a binding settlement has been introduced to resolve transfer pricing disputes (Hufbauer, 1991).

At the same time, because TPM is often a response to cross-border market distortions, some of which may be caused by governments in the first place, actions to eliminate or minimize its adverse affects should best be considered alongside other macro-organizational strategies to promote economic efficiency and growth. Indeed, it may be argued that a systemic approach to TPM is the only way MNEs can be discouraged from reacting to specific controls by adopting countervailing measures, which, at the end of the day, are no less acceptable.[35] Moreover, the surveillance and control of TPM is both time-consuming and costly[36]; so much so that some governments believe that there is more to be gained by removing the incentive for firms to engage in non-

market pricing than to adopt legislative action to outlaw any unacceptable practices identified.

The success or failure of national governments in the pursuance of minimizing unacceptable TPM will clearly depend on their competence in identifying and implementing the appropriate unilateral actions[37] and on their bargaining power *vis à vis* MNEs engaging, or wishing to engage, in TPM. Once again, this very much depends on the balance between the O-specific advantages of MNEs and the L advantages of the countries concerned. Over the past twenty years, there is some reason to suppose that as far as cross-border TPM in most *goods* is concerned, the balance has tended to be more in favour of the countries, mostly because of the more intensive competition between MNEs and the much improved understanding by governments of the reasons for and the ways in which they might counteract undesirable TPM.[38] However, even the most knowledgeable and sophisticated governments still have some difficulty in removing TPM altogether[39] while, for their part, MNEs continue to argue that they conscientiously try to comply with the tax laws and government policies of the countries in which they operate.

18.4.2 Supra-national action

Undoubtedly, however, because there is competition for MNE activity both between home and host countries, and between different host countries, the opportunities for MNEs to play one nation against another are enhanced without the establishment of supra-national institutions and harmonized inter-government action towards TPM. Such action may take the following forms:

- The initiation of international guidelines or codes of conduct. Such guidelines have already been promulgated by the OECD and by the UN Group of Experts on Tax Treaties between developed and developing countries. Further details are set out in the Appendix to this chapter.

- The conclusion of bilateral agreements by governments on pricing new products or those which do not normally enter into trade.

- The incorporation of misuse of pricing practices

into either a restrictive practices code or a GATT-type agreement.

- The international standardization of invoicing and customs procedures of information gathering, statistical definitions and accounting procedures.

- The harmonization of cross-border corporate and value-added taxes, and of the treatment of asset valuation, depreciation and deductions from income.

- The elimination, reclassification or control of tax havens.

- The establishment of an international convention which requires MNEs to disclose publicly all prices and to outlaw price discrimination between intra- and inter-firm sales and purchases.

- The collaboration between tax authorities in the exchange of laws,[40] and simultaneously the auditing of cross-border transactions (Plasschaert, 1993).

- The introduction of arbitration procedures by which inter-country transfer pricing disputes might be resolved. The EC has recently (1990) instituted a procedure for such disputes, which may only be resorted to after all efforts to settle any disagreement at a national level have failed.

De facto, multi-lateral action is likely to be more successful at a regional level. Although little research has been conducted on this question, it seems likely that the movement towards further economic integration in Europe and North America is acting as a more powerful deterrent to intra-regional TPM than any unilateral fiscal or other policies adopted by individual host governments. Similarly, attempts by the developing nations to harmonize their policies towards restrictive business practices, trade-related investment measures and the liberalization of dividend remissions or capital repatriation, are likely to reduce the propensity of MNEs to engage in TPM which frequently were motivated by unilateral structural market distortions in the first place!

At the same time, it is unlikely that the incentive for cross-border administered prices by MNEs will entirely disappear. Indeed, it may be argued that many of the transaction costs described in Chapter 4 will become more important in influencing both the price fixing policies and strategic

management of firms, as well as the fiscal policies pursued by governments. If this is the case, the impetus for TPM may still remain in the 1990s, although its *raison d'être* and its economic implications may be quite different and require new and imaginative managerial responses by governments.

18.5   CONCLUSIONS

This chapter has examined some of the responses of MNEs to a particular set of L specific variables – especially those which are tax related – in their decisions as to *how much* and *what kind of* economic activity they might undertake in *which* countries. It has also looked at the ways in which they might influence the geographical distribution of the resulting value added. To the extent that the reactions of MNEs may affect both their O-specific advantages and the organizational mode by which these advantages are exploited, the eclectic paradigm is, once again, seen to offer a useful analytical framework.

This chapter has confirmed that a combination of inter-country tax differences and the globalization of MNE activity may afford MNEs both production- and transaction-related O advantages over and above their uninational counterparts. The precise nature of the advantages will depend on the international profile of the firms possessing them and on the ESP configuration with which they are faced. In particular, they are likely to vary according to the type of FDI undertaken by MNEs and the macro-organizational and fiscal policies pursued by government. Thus, for example, a change in the depreciation allowances or methods of controlling TPM introduced by a particular country may affect the O advantages of existing MNEs very differently than would the harmonization of tax rates, the removal of import restrictions and the relaxation of performance requirements. However, there remains a paucity of rigorous research on many of the issues identified in this chapter. Consequently, it is difficult to offer generalizations as to the kinds of action which governments might realistically take to protect or promote their national economic interests.

Appendix 18.1

Extracts from OECD guidelines to MNEs draft United Nations Code of Conduct on Transnational Corporations and on Intra-Corporate Pricing Practices

(1) **OECD Guidelines**

    (1) Upon request of the taxation authorities of the countries in which they operate, provide, in accordance with the safeguards and relevant procedures of the national laws of these countries, the information necessary to determine correctly the taxes to be assessed in connection with their operations, including relevant information concerning their operations in other countries;

    (2) Refrain from making use of the particular facilities available to them, such as transfer pricing which does not conform to any arm's length standard, for modifying in ways contrary to national laws the tax base on which members of the group are assessed.

(2) **Proposed United Nations Code of Conduct**

    (1) In respect of their intra-corporate transactions, transnational corporations should/shall not use pricing policies that are not based on relevant market prices, or in the absence of such prices, the arms's length principle, which have the effect of modifying the tax base on which their entities are assessed or of evading exchange control measures (or customs valuation regulations) or which (contrary to national laws and regulations) adversely affect economic and social conditions of the countries in which they operate.

    (2) Transnational corporations should/shall not, contrary to the laws and regulations of the countries in which they operate, use their corporate structure and modes of operation, such as the use of intra-corporate pricing which is not based on the arm's length principle, or other means, to modify the tax base on which their entities are assessed.

NOTES

1 Or X inefficiency, bearing in mind that part of the economic rent monopoly profits of a firm may be spent in 'buying' or inefficiency or other goals of the main decision takers.

2 It should be noted that governments might give incentives in period t to capture a larger tax revenue in time $t + 1$. Moreover, some of the gains might be indirect (e.g. an upgrading of human capital).

3 That is, taxes less subsidies, etc, from any given amount of taxable income earned.

4 For example, by reducing taxation or providing more incentives.

5 For more details see Guisinger (1985) and Chapter 20.

6 Grubel, for example, found that the average net rate of return on US direct investment abroad between 1960 and 1969, excluding royalties, fees and other gains (e.g. R&D feedback) was 5.9% less than the domestic equivalent.

7 The subjects of equity and neutrality in the international taxation of income and capital are extremely complex, as both concepts can be interpreted in various ways. For example, while inter-nation equity is concerned with the allocation of gains and losses from MNE activity between home and host countries, inter-individual equity implies that the home country should levy the same tax on each resident (including resident corporations) irrespective of where the income is earned. Inter-nation neutrality in taxation suggests that the MNE's choice of the location of its investment should be independent of international tax differences. Inter-nation equity from a national view requires that the source country set its tax rate so as to maximize its benefits from FDI. However, inter-individual equity from a national viewpoint defines equal treatment of taxation of the income of a company by the home country irrespective of where it is earned. For a more detailed review of these concepts and their implications for MNE activity see, for example, Alworth (1988). For an examination of some alternative assessments of the welfare implications of the nationalistic and internationalistic views of neutrality and equity see Eden (1988). Eden suggests that from the perspective of Canada, any movement away from international neutrality towards a more nationalistic stance, would work to the disadvantage of Canadian welfare because of the large amount of two-way FDI between Canada and the US.

8 Such actions might include limiting the number of designated tax haven countries and/or to limit the extent to which MNEs may accumulate undistributed earnings in closely controlled subsidiaries (Alworth, 1988).

9 The *residence* principle holds that all income is taxable by the country in which the corporation is incorporated or engages in value-added activities. The *territorial* or *source* principle holds that net income is taxable by the country in which it originates.

10 For example, whereas in the case of a tax credit system without deferral the financial policy of an MNE is likely to be the same as that of a uninational company,

with deferral, neutrality is unlikely to hold; and, dependent on the proportion of interest payments which are tax deductible, and the tax rates on undistributed earnings in the home and host countries the MNE might choose to finance its foreign operations either entirely from retained profits or only moderately so. Similarly, in instances of a tax deduction system with deferral it may be shown that a foreign affiliate will never issue new shares, in preference to financing investment by retentions when the borrowing rate of interest is higher in the home country than it is in the foreign country (Alworth, 1988).

11 As far as such coordination is desirable is a somewhat debatable point. For a defence of a more coordinated tax policy (at least among developing countries) see Musgrave (1987).

12 For example, Snoy tested a differential return hypothesis, Mellors a version of international portfolio theory, Kopits the neo-classical theory of dividend remittances and Horst the neo-classical theory of the firm. Snoy's findings were particularly interesting in that he calculated that unifying European host country tax rates would change the growth rate of US FDI in the various individual countries by one third or more.

13 Although in this section of the chapter we have largely concentrated our attention on the impact of tax policy on the costs and profits of MNEs or their affiliates, other fiscal measures may affect the revenue of MNEs. One obvious example is an increase in sales taxes. Here, there is much less reason to suppose that MNEs will be differently affected that their domestic counterparts, except in terms of their ability to adjust better to or absorb the price increase.

14 This is because with no tax deferral, any tax credit provision would immediately siphon the tax benefit which accrues to the foreign subsidiary into the US Treasury (Hartman, 1977).

15 For example, investment and depreciation allowances, regional employment premiums and subsidies for R&D or manpower training. For an elaboration on the notion of response elasticity as applied to the behaviour of MNEs and uninational firms see Dunning and Gilman (1977).

16 Presumably, Country B would not object as its tax revenue is increased.

17 The propensity of US affiliates in Europe to engage in intra-firm trade varies considerably between sectors. In 1987, such exports of office and computer equipment were 98.6% of all exports of US affiliates; those of business services 90.1% and those of banking and finance 65.7%.

18 The reader is reminded that Chapter 14 also dealt with the subject of intra-firm trade. See especially pp. 407–11.

19 See Chapters 3 and 4.

20 In any event, for this reason TPM may not be in the long-term interests of the partnership.

21 It should be emphasized that not all governments may be opposed to TPM. Indeed, governments of tax haven countries may positively welcome it!

22 Among the firm-specific factors are the size of the firm and its strategy towards both product (or process) diversification and the geography of its production and markets.

23 By which we mean the extent to which there is also an external market for the goods and services traded – or similar goods and services – and the frequency with which they are traded.

24 IRS data reveals that, in 1989, foreign-controlled enterprises earned only a 0.51% net return on their assets compared with 1.97% for US-owned enterprises (*New York Times*, 10 April 1992). For a more extensive analysis of profitability of the two groups of corporations, see Table 6.5 in Hufbauer (1992).

25 That is, above the estimated arm's length prices.

26 However, the nationality of the investing firm (Japanese and non-Japanese) was only significant once the degree of centralization of control of MNE was dropped.

27 For example, in 1981 the differences were significant, at a 5% level for Abu Dhabi, Libya, Nigeria, Saudi Arabia, Trinidad and Venezuela, and at a 10% level for Mexico.

28 For example, for four of the six years for which data is available, the arm's length price for oil imported by the US from Canada was less than the intra-firms price (about 1%), while in the remaining years it was higher – in one year by 4%.

29 Tang also found that US and Japanese MNEs were most likely to use cost-oriented methods for calculating their transfer prices. By contrast, Canadian and UK firms were more prone to base their prices on non-cost oriented methods, notably market or negotiated prices (Tang, 1981).

30 Both Tang and Arpan prefer to use the words transfer pricing rather than transfer price manipulation. Because of this it is not completely clear from the analysis – particularly that of Tang – the extent to which transfer prices actually do differ from arm's length prices.

31 Which included such variables as compliance with tax and customs regulations, anti-trust and dumping legislation, and financial reporting rules of host countries.

32 In addition, in 1990, 12.7% of firms reported that they negotiated their internal prices compared with 13.6% in 1977.

33 To take one example, the formation of the EC has lessened the significance of many ESP variables

affecting the locational choice of MNEs and has made others (e.g. the role of governments in affecting transaction costs) more important (Dunning, 1991c). The more welcoming stance taken by most developing countries in the late 1970s and 1980s has resulted in a reduction in import barriers, nationalizations and expropriations, and restrictions on the repatriation of profits and capital.

34 So-called because the other three methods include the comparable uncontrolled-price method.

35 For example, an attempt to control TPM of goods and services exported or imported within MNE networks may simply lead to an increase in TPM on cross-border service transactions.

36 As Reid and McGoldrick (1982) also point out, governments will only be vigilant in monitoring TPM if there are political advantages in doing so. Some may even have legislation that effectively prevents the transmission of information necessary to monitor such activity.

37 Such identification and implementation requires appropriate institutional mechanisms for monitoring intra-firm transactions, an audit procedure for reviewing and evaluating transactions not routinely monitored, machinery for collecting the relevant information about market and non-market prices, costs, mark-ups and the like, and to make the necessary adjustments consequent upon transfer price audits (Irish, 1987).

38 In this connection, from time to time the Internal Revenue Service (of the US) has published data on the frequency and extent of the adjustments made to the profits declared by MNEs as a result of recalculating cross-border transfer prices.

39 For example, the *New York Times* for 10th April 1992 reported that of the 45 000 foreign-owned companies filing US tax returns in 1990, only 28% pay any tax at all. In the belief that the Internal Revenue Service was losing tax revenue by TPM, in December 1989 the Federal Government gave the tax agency broad authority to assess taxes on foreign-owned companies which failed to comply promptly with demands for any records or testimony. It is generally felt that this new provision is aimed especially at the Japanese companies in the US which are strongly suspected of engaging in TPM. At the same time, the Japan Tax Association has asserted that the Internal Revenue Service is partly to blame for any loss of tax revenue which it could be receiving, simply because it had not established concrete guidelines for determining the appropriate price for transactions between units of a MNE.

40 As, for example, has been institutionalized between the member countries of the EC and the Council of Europe since 1977. More recently, a Convention on Mutual Administrative Assistance on Tax Matters by which the fiscal authorities in one signatory country will have access to information about its own taxpayers which are kept by any of the other signatory countries.

CHAPTER 19

MNEs and Nation States: Some Political, Cultural, Strategic and Environmental Issues

19.1 INTRODUCTION

While this volume is primarily concerned with the wealth-creating role of MNEs in the global economy and with the interaction between them and the nation states in which they operate, it would be foolish and erroneous to deny that the cross-border activities of enterprises are not also fashioned by legal, political, social and cultural forces, and that MNEs might influence these forces. This being so, it is appropriate that we should give attention both to some non-economic issues surrounding the determinants of MNE activity and to the ways in which firms, themselves, might impinge upon the non-economic goals of society, and on the strategies of governments to achieve these goals.

To confine our discussion to manageable proportions, we shall focus on identifying and explaining the interaction between the behaviour of MNEs and that of democratically elected governments. Though governments may choose to delegate, to private institutions, many of the responsibilities and tasks for the economic and social welfare of their citizens, in the last resort it is they who are the custodians and defenders of the heritage values, rights and ideologies of the society they represent. Previous chapters have described and analysed some of the ways in which MNEs may affect the economic well-being of the countries in which they operate, and of how this, in turn, may be influenced by the actions taken by governments. At the same time, by one means or another, MNEs may also be able to affect these actions and the ease or difficulty with which governments may implement them. They may also impinge on the broader societal objectives of governments. Indeed, in some instances these may

well be judged as more important than their economic impact.

More broadly, the achievement of most objectives other than those directed at increasing wealth, affect not only economic goals, but economic policy. Though it is possible to view many of the functions of government (e.g. defence, law and order, administration and the protection of the environment) as supportive of wealth creation, in the short to medium term they not only redirect resources away from the generation of wealth, but also they have to be paid for by the wealth generators. Sometimes the tradeoffs involved are more delicately balanced than are readily admitted. Too much expenditure on non-wealth creating activities may lower the future capacity of a nation to create output out of which the former activities are financed. The same applies to the promotion of social welfare and the protection of the less able or less privileged members of society. Here, the balance between justice, fairness and compassion on the one hand, and wealth sustainment and creation on the other, is a fine one. On the one hand, if, through the tax system, national income is redistributed too evenly, the incentive to earn additional income or be entrepreneurial may be blunted; on the other, too wide a gap between the most and least wealthy members of society may lead to a less healthy and less educated work force, and, often, to severe social unrest. Sometimes it is as much a question of inter-generational income distribution as that between the current beneficiaries of wealth and non-wealth creating activities.

The connection between the above sentiments and the activities of MNEs may seem a little distant. However, if the two main themes of this volume are correct, *viz* first that MNEs are the primary repositories of the capital, technology and organizational capabilities necessary to promote the economic welfare of societies, and second, that national governments play a critical role in influencing such enterprises, or their affiliates, in the way they utilize these assets, then the amount of resources allocated to non-wealth creating activities may directly affect the contribution of such enterprises, not just to creating additional wealth today, but to financing non-wealth activities in the future. It is also worth recalling that, in some instances, the failure of a country to attract the FDI it needs may not only reduce the competitiveness of its resources, but also increase that of its international rivals.

The fact of the globalization of business and the implications this has for the competitiveness of countries, may then force some societies to reappraise their orders of priorities of resource allocation – particularly between wealth-creating and other activities.[1] Even more significant are the likely consequences of MNE activity for the sovereignty and political autonomy of nation states. The next section of this chapter addresses itself to this issue.

19.2   SOVEREIGNTY

19.2.1   Identifying the main issues

Unless a country is completely isolated from the rest of the world, any sovereignty it enjoys is bound to be constrained, in the sense that whatever decisions it chooses to take are, to some extent, influenced by forces beyond its jurisdiction. In so far as sovereignty is the power to choose between alternative courses of action, then, in so far as a government has voluntarily abrogated its power to gain other benefits, then its sovereignty remains intact. When, however, its ability to choose future courses of action is forcibly restricted, then its sovereignty is reduced. For example, the UK's membership of the European Economic Community de facto lessens its economic and political sovereignty. However, in the last resort, absolute sovereignty rests in the choice of the UK to leave the Community. Only if that option is withdrawn is its sovereignty reduced, although as long as the UK is a member of the EC, it has to accept that decisions of the European Commission

may affect the conditions under which its firms engage in trade and investment. Cross-border financial and monetary agreements may also constrict the economic manoeuvrability of governments.

Governments, like firms, might also find it in their interests to engage in strategic alliances with other governments for specific purposes. NATO is an example of a political alliance. The collaborative actions by the heads of state of leading OECD countries to avoid the excesses of uncoordinated monetary, fiscal and exchange policies is an example of a less formal economic alliance. Each involves a voluntary surrender of proximate sovereignty for the common benefit, but as long as the right of exit exists, ultimate sovereignty remains unimpaired. There may, however, be a very considerable cost of exerting that ultimate sovereignty.

There are, of course, different kinds and degrees of sovereignty. Economic sovereignty reflects the ability of a government to choose how best to manage its resources for wealth-creating activities. Cultural sovereignty reflects the freedom of a country to determine its own way of life, including the extent to which it wishes to adopt the customs, ideologies and values of other societies. Legal sovereignty defines a country's authority to devise its own laws and regulations, independent of any outside interference. Political sovereignty embraces economic, cultural and legal sovereignty. It is the prerogative of a country to manage all its affairs as it wishes, and without any unacceptable influence from another jurisdiction. However, it is more than the sum of its constituent parts. Political sovereignty, in any meaningful sense, rests on the status, power and independence of a Nation State *in relation to* that of other Nation States which may directly or indirectly affect its own well-being (Gilpin, 1975, 1987).

In assessing the role of the MNE on a nation's sovereignty, it is necessary to examine the extent to which, and in what ways, both proximate and ultimate sovereignty are affected. Moreover, at the end of the day we are really concerned with its consequences for political autonomy. This impact may take various forms and may be directed to home or host governments. Of these, we might especially identify:

(1) Its direct impact on economic welfare, as economic power may affect the ability of a

country to defend, sustain or promote its political sovereignty.

(2) Its impact on the extent and form of a nation's economic autonomy. Does it make for more economic dependence or interdependence? And with whom?

(3) Its impact on the balance between wealth-creating and non-wealth creating activities.

(4) Its impact on the actions of governments to influence the preceding factors. This might extend from legitimate political lobbying on specific issues (e.g. the imposition of economic sanctions) to an unacceptable intervention in the electoral process (e.g. the ITT involvement in Chile). Such attempts to influence political behaviour may be addressed directly to the host and home government concerned, or indirectly, for example, by an MNE inveigling its home government to influence a host government on its behalf.[2]

In each of the above examples, it should be noted that our concern is to identify the impact of a MNE which arises specifically because of its nationality of ownership or degree of multinationality.

MNEs may also affect the sovereignty of Nation States by their actions or reactions to the policies of governments, in the political, social or cultural arena. Some of the ways this might arise are discussed in Part IV of this volume. In this chapter, we shall confine our attention to four important issues. The first concerns the impact of FDI on the sovereign power of national governments. The second addresses the role of MNEs as disseminators or fashioners of culture. The third relates to some national security issues arising from the transnationalization of business activity. The fourth discusses the interaction between MNEs and the environmental objectives of both home and host governments.

19.2.2 How might MNEs affect sovereignty

19.2.2.1 *Economic welfare and sovereignty* Since most of Part III of this volume has addressed this issue we can be brief. However, from a political perspective it is not so much the effect of MNEs on economic welfare *per se*, but of how that, in turn,

may impinge upon the political power of the Nation State – particularly as expressed in an international context. Chapter 12 identified one area of concern of some industrialized countries in respect of outward direct investment. If US MNEs, for example, by their export of high technology products to foreign subsidiaries in industrialized countries increase the economic strength of these countries relative to that of the US, might not this weaken the political clout of the US at the international bargaining table? Even more important, might it not compromise its strategic security, as some forms of advanced technology might be deployed by the recipient countries for military purposes?

However, to suggest that MNEs, *qua* MNEs, actually operate against the political interests of their home countries as exporters of technology requires at least three things to be demonstrated. First, that the importing countries would not have obtained the technology from other sources; second, that technology is disseminated in the host country outside the foreign affiliate; and third, that the costs, or possible costs, of the technology transfer outweigh the benefits. It is possible to produce a scenario in which all of these three possibilities are likely. Technology might be highly idiosyncratic, it might be disseminated through linkages and other means as described in Chapter 16 and it might be used in a potentially unfriendly way. But beyond this, the economist and business analyst – along with the political scientist – can only speculate on the balance of likely economic gains versus the uncertain loss of political power or influence.

Three things, however, may be said. First, MNEs can and do influence the relative distribution of wealth-creating capacity between countries. This volume has shown that in today's global economic environment, provided that there is adequate competition between MNEs and governments refrain from market-distorting policies, FDI is more likely than not to raise the absolute economic welfare of both home and host countries. However, there is no presumption as to *whose* economic welfare they will increase the most. For example, it is generally agreed that US FDI after the last World War helped to raise Europe's living standards relative to those of the US. By contrast, some earlier colonial-type investments by both European and US investors most surely benefited the mother country more than the host countries. Indeed, as Chapter 5 has shown, an important reason for British, French, Swedish and Dutch investments, including those of the early trading companies, was to advance the economic, and hence political, power of the investing countries relative to that of their trading competitors. At the same time,[3] a major contemporary concern of many industrializing and some industrialized countries to inward direct investment is the mirror image of that earlier identified by some home countries, *viz* that it may inhibit its own innovating capacity and strengthen that of the investing country, thus redistributing the balance of economic and political power between the countries concerned.

Second, in so far as MNEs may help bind together the trade and investment relationships between nations, they perform a useful ambassadorial act of peace. The more intertwined economies become and the more each nation's welfare is dependent on the prosperity of the others, the less likely they are to risk jeopardizing the loss of this welfare by unfriendly political acts. On the other hand, the misuse of monopoly power by MNEs – particularly where this is accompanied by political chicanery – might worsen the relations between home and host countries to the considerable disadvantage of each. Examples include the behaviour of the Belgian MNEs in the Congo prior to World War I and that of US MNEs in Chile and French MNEs in Algeria in the post World War II era.

Third, the extent to which MNEs can and do affect both absolute and relative economic welfare is very much dependent on the stimuli and pressures provided by the governments of the countries in which they operate, as well as on the bargaining power of the latter to extract the maximum net benefits from the formers' presence. Earlier chapters have stressed the complementary characteristics between the advantages MNEs have to offer countries and the advantages countries have to offer MNEs, and how, over time, these interact with each other. In particular, we discussed the role of created factor endowments and capabilities and agglomerative economies, vigorous competition and standards of demand forcing an ethos of competitiveness. We concluded that governments had an active and critical strategic and market-facilitating role to play – in ensuring that their own MNEs and the foreign affiliates of foreign MNEs were both able and willing

to upgrade their location-bound assets. Clearly, this goal is consistent with (or can be made consistent with) that of protecting or sustaining political sovereignty. No less important is the enhancement of the government's own ability to negotiate and bargain effectively with foreign-based MNEs. This ability is a country-specific asset in its own right; we shall consider its significance in Chapter 21.

19.2.2.2 *Economic autonomy and/or independence*

It is frequently asserted that inward and outward direct investment will reduce the economic autonomy of a country and increase its economic dependence on the rest of the world. We shall suggest that this is not *necessarily* the case, either in the short or in the long run. Indeed, it is possible to use unbound MNE activity to strengthen one's own wealth-creating capabilities and economic independence. This is what Kojima refers to as the tutorial role of FDI. It does, however, imply that once they have accomplished their tasks, foreign-owned MNEs will (or should!) divest their assets.

There are two obvious ways in which inbound direct investment can reduce economic autonomy. The first is that it provides resources (e.g. technology and management skills) which might be cut off at any time. This reduction in autonomy is best seen in cases of acquisitions and/or where domestic firms may be driven out of business by foreign affiliates. Secondly, the control exercised by MNEs over the resource allocation of their affiliates may not always be used in the best interests of the countries in which they are situated. However, whether or not there is a net loss of economic autonomy to the recipient countries depends on what might have happened in the absence of the investment. If it replaces imports, then it could be said to lessen dependence. In some respects at least, the foreign subsidiary is a hostage in the host country. If it replaces domestic investment, then as far as that investment is concerned, it might reduce autonomy. But again, much will depend on whether, as a direct result of the inward investment, the competitive position of the recipient country is strengthened, and how far the assets and experiences of the foreign affiliates are embedded in it.

Likewise with outward direct investment. This could clearly lessen economic dependence and uncertainty where it protects the investing firms against supply disruptions, uncertain export markets and the abuse of its reputation by foreign buyers or sellers. Moreover, if investment is diversified, it spreads the risks associated with being dependent on a limited number of markets. On the other hand, if foreign production leads to a greater geographical specialization of input sources or product markets, this might increase a country's dependence relative to (say) developing alternative inputs or new markets at home or in other parts of the world.

For both host and home countries, the question is essentially one of goals and priorities – and the tradeoff between goals and priorities. To some countries (e.g. China and India), a large measure of economic self-sufficiency is valued as an objective in its own right. Under the regime of Mrs Ghandi, for example, even if it could be shown that the presence of foreign affiliates in India would benefit the local economy considerably more than any practical alternative, they might still not have been accepted (and certainly not as a permanent feature of the Indian economy) lest they reduced the flexibility of the Indian government to pursue the policies of its choice. In the early part of the post World War II period, Japan disallowed most kinds of inward direct investment. In doing so, it was willing to sacrifice the possible short-run gains from such investment so as to (hopefully) achieve a greater degree of technological and economic autonomy in the longer run. Though rather more open-minded, Korea has followed a similar development strategy. At the other extreme, city states, such as Hong Kong and Singapore, and some small European countries, such as Switzerland and the Netherlands, are almost completely economically dependent on – they might prefer to think, interdependent with – the rest of the world. But, for most countries, the tolerance for inward direct investment varies according to its perceived economic merits, on the one hand, and the relative importance of such investment in the economy as well as the openness of the economy to trade and investment, on the other. As Chapter 20 will show, there are some strategically sensitive sectors (e.g. broadcasting, defence-related and critical resource-based sectors[4]), in which most countries require complete economic independence, while there are others for which complete economic dependence is accepted.

Again, which strategy a country will adopt depends on the resources and capabilities it possesses, how these are, or might be, galvanized to promote indigenous economic growth and the balance between its inward and outward investment. Japan's relatively restrictive policy towards investment has been more successful than that of India because of the greater emphasis it has given to vocational education and training, its more strongly motivated labour force, a higher savings ratio among its population, the higher standards of demand of its consumers and a more competitively-oriented domestic economy. As a result, Japan can now afford to open up her borders to inbound investment without the fear of being critically dependent on it. Several other countries, noticeably the UK and the US, are prepared to accept inward investment because they, themselves, are strong outward investors. Being economically interdependent is politically preferable to being economically dependent.

In some cases, the structure of dependence may be as important as its level. Diversity in dependence is generally preferable to specialization in dependence. Thus, for many years Canada tried to diversify her economic ties with other countries away from the US. The problem, however, is that throughout modern history, most of the gains to Canada's living standards have come through her association with the US. Hence the recent Canada–US free trade agreement, which is essentially geared to restructuring and strengthening Canada's trading and investment links with her Southern neighbour. Similarly, many ex-UK, French, Belgian and Dutch colonial territories have tried to diversify the geographical or industrial composition of inbound MNE activity. For many years, much of Central and Latin America has perceived the heavy hand of US MNEs – and behind that hand, US-style capitalism and culture – controlling their destinies.

There is extensive extant literature on the subject of 'dependencia'.[5] Expressed in a Latin American context, it comes over partly as a concern lest the wealth-creating activities and the direction of their economies should be controlled by foreign (in particular, US) capitalists. However, underlying this disquiet is the more profound fear of any possible loss of political sovereignty or cultural identity which might follow such economic control. The Latin Americans are particularly proud and independent people. However much they may welcome, or even envy, the living standards of the average US citizen, they value their own political systems, religious values and cultural norms more than most. In so far as inward direct investment is perceived to interfere with or emasculate these norms, it is unwelcome. Hence the desire either to obtain the resources provided by foreign investors through alternative routes or, if this is not possible, to impose strict conditions on the entry and behaviour of foreign affiliates.[6]

The Latin Americans are not alone in their views. Many Middle Eastern and African countries undoubtedly feel the same way. As regards much of the former area, notably Iran and Iraq, the contemporary resurgence of Islamic fundamentalism is dominating all trading relationships with the outside world. Their unwillingness to accept inward direct investment from countries whose economic policies and cultures are perceived to undermine these beliefs is hardly less great than that of the communist world only a decade ago. The position of most sub-Saharan African countries is one of a rich and unique cultural heritage, yet with living standards well below that of their trans-Atlantic neighbours. These, of all countries, are most surely in a 'Catch 22' situation.[7] They desperately need the direct investment which the MNEs are able to provide, but, apart from a few resource-rich countries, they have few complementary assets or markets to make such an investment profitable. They are very much in Stage 1 of the investment development path illustrated in Chapters 4, 6 and 10. In so far as dependence is an issue at all, it is a luxury which the ordinary African can ill afford to pay for.

By contrast, some East Asian countries – notably Taiwan and South Korea – have enough resources and markets of their own – including the key resource of organizational ability – to be selective in their choice of inward direct investment, while avoiding an unacceptable level of 'dependencia'. At the same time, they seem to be more confidence about their competence to protect their political sovereignty and cultural identity than are the Latin Americans, while their economic systems and policies correspond much more closely to those of Western Europe and North America. In general, the geographical origin of inbound investment is fairly diversified,[8] although most East Asian countries are well aware of being too dependent on Japan, even though, in many respects, they have a greater cultural affinity with that country than with most Western nations.[9]

There is one other point that should be made. Chapter 7 suggested that the transnationalization of production might not only affect the level and structure of a country's economic sovereignty, but also its reaction to that effect. More particularly, the movement towards regional integration in several parts of the world is, in part at least, a response to the globalization of wealth-creating activities. In essence, such globalization has increased both the costs and gains of economic independence. To reap the gains, countries have had to incur the costs of relinquishing part of their economic and political sovereignty. However, in some cases it is more a question of restructuring their existing economic dependence and sovereignty, since the costs of *not* becoming part of a customs union could be an increase of a different kind of dependence. Chapter 17 demonstrated that not all MNEs welcome such changes, particularly those which were previously producing in protected markets. But in so far as their desire for global or regional corporate integration has any influence, it is forcing countries to collaborate with each other, so that these gains can become a reality and, for the most part, be captured by the citizens of those countries.

We conclude that the impact of MNE on the economic autonomy of Nation States cannot be easily assessed. Many – and probably most – of the changes in the sovereignty of nation states which have occurred in the past 20 years have had nothing to do with the multinational firm *per se*. Instead, the main causes have been technological and political changes. At the same time, MNEs have helped fashion these changes and have been the instruments in implementing them. To this extent, they have impinged upon the economic autonomy of Nation States, sometimes increasing it, sometimes lessening it, and sometimes changing its form. But no less so have the attitudes and policies of national governments, in so far as they have affected the need or willingness of MNEs to enter into cross-border arrangements, and, by doing so impart on their own freedom of decision taking. Exceptions include some ex-European colonies (e.g. Singapore, Hong Kong and Indonesia).

19.2.2.3 *Wealth-creating versus non-wealth-creating activities* Although firms are the main instruments of wealth-creating activities in democratic societies, their activities affect – or are affected by – other objectives which society might choose to promote. This interaction comes about in various ways. First, many government-financed activities (e.g. expenditure on social services, defence, administration, law and order) are primarily paid for by direct or indirect taxes, to which the corporate sector contributes a major share.[10] In so far as corporate taxation represents a cost to firms, and this cost differs between countries, it may affect the 'where' of their FDI. Chapters 6 and 18 have already mentioned the role of both positive and negative taxes (i.e. subsidies and other incentives) in influencing the location of value-added activities by MNEs; Chapter 20 reconsiders these as a component of government policy. Here, we are simply concerned with the way in which the choices open to governments in their resource-allocative policies may be influenced by the locational options open both to domestic and foreign-based MNEs.

MNEs may impact on the level and pattern of government income and expenditure in various ways. It has long been acknowledged that one of the major potential benefits of inward direct investment is the gain (to the host government) of tax revenue through additional factor payments and consumer spending. The extent of this benefit obviously depends on whether or not inward investment replaces domestic investment, how productive foreign firms are and how far there is any leakage of income by way of transfer price manipulation.

On the other hand, MNEs may cost the exchequer resources both directly through any tax or investment incentives which may be offered, and indirectly through additional expenditure on 'support' or wealth facilitating services (e.g. education, roads, airports). The distinction between non-wealth and wealth facilitating activities – particularly those financed out of taxation – is a difficult one to draw. At the one end of the spectrum, governments provide a range of social security benefits to consumers; at the other is expenditure on assistance to small firms, R&D, airports, telecommunications, vocational training and tertiary education, and structural adjustment, which are often critical to a country's competitiveness. In between, expenditure on health, education, law and order, the environment, and so on, may be regarded as partly wealth facilitating as without them the country's GNP might be lower than it would otherwise be.[11]

Because they tend to be concentrated in the more dynamic and technology-intensive sectors and as a result of their network of cross-border operations, MNEs are likely to make more demands on modern wealth-facilitating services than are uninational firms. In the short term, these may require reductions in other government services or increases in taxation because, in shifting the balance of competitiveness between nations and redefining the role of government as a wealth facilitator, the internationalization of business may necessitate some revision to the prioritization of its non-economic goals and to its attitudes towards particular sectoral interests in society (e.g. labour unions). Certainly, the perceived need both to strengthen the competitiveness of its own MNEs and to attract more inward investment was one factor leading to a dramatic change in the industrial relations legislation of the UK in the early 1980s.

19.3 MNEs AND CULTURE

19.3.1 The concept of inter-country cultural distance

MNE activity may help refashion business culture in a particular country in two ways. The first is by the injection of cultures from its home country, and those of other countries in which it operates, into the behaviour of its affiliates and in its dealings with local firms and governments. The second is by exposing the national business culture to that of other countries.

For example, the US today is much less insular than it used to be. Undoubtedly, part of the reason for this lies in the operations of its own MNEs and those of foreign-owned subsidiaries in the US. Contrast economies like those of Belgium, Hong Kong and Switzerland, which are heavily involved in international direct investment, with those of India, China and parts of sub-Saharan Africa where the culture is very nationalistic or ethnocentric.

Although the immediate impact of MNE activity on business culture shows itself in specific functional areas, such as organization, work methods, incentives and industrial relations, in the long run it may embrace wider issues like the ethos of work and entrepreneurship, attitudes towards rewards and authority, concepts of fairness and justice, and the role of government. History is full of illustrations of the impact that foreign cultures have had on national values and patterns of behaviour through colonization, trade and migration. Franke, Hofstede and Bond (1991) have demonstrated how national differences in cultural values, and especially the contrast between Confucian dynamism and Western-style individualism may affect economic performance. At the same time, national governments have critically influenced the extent to which particular countries are open to foreign influences. However, few such changes in government policy have been so dramatic as those now occurring in Central and Eastern Europe, and to a lesser extent, in the Eastern seaboard of the South China sea. In both instances, MNEs are playing an important role as disseminators of business culture, which, over time, may shape institutional and personal values, human motivation and the social organization of production.

In a recently published volume, Terpstra and David (1991) outline some of the ways MNEs may influence culture and may be used by governments for this purpose. One of these is through education and training. Brazil, for example, has enlisted the aid of foreign MNEs to educate its citizens in technical and managerial skills. As Chapter 15 has shown, MNEs have frequently been trailblazers in upgrading vocational training. Another is about values and performance. Many years ago, Gunnar Myrdal (1970) identified the kinds of values or qualities necessary for economic development.[12] Few countries possess all these values, but most, including those which are home to the leading MNEs, enjoy at least some of them.[13]

At the same time, the translation and adaptation of these advantages to a foreign culture may be quite a costly exercise as there is often a substantial learning process on the part of both MNEs and host countries involved.[14] The successful transplant of cultures by MNEs may sometimes best be undertaken within fully-owned hierarchies, sometimes by joint ventures and sometimes by non-equity contracts. Each route of organization incurs its own transaction costs.

Buckley and Casson (1991) believe that many of the conflicts of interest between MNEs and developing countries arise from differences in the (entrepreneurial) cultural perspectives of MNEs and recipient countries. They suggest that where cultural distance (a form of psychic distance identified in Chapter 8) is great, the more likely it is that both MNEs and host governments will have difficulties in adjusting to each other's needs and aspirations. Extrapolating their thoughts, it might also be said that if and when MNEs do operate in these areas, they tend to internalize as many cross-cultural markets as possible and to establish Keiretsu type enclaves (which might extend to their suppliers and customers) over which they have as much 'cultural' control as possible.

The spill-over effects of cross-cultural differences are, however, even wider. In some ways, the social impact is comparable with that arising from the urbanization of previously agricultural communities. The MNE introduces new life styles, new patterns of work, fosters new kinds of loyalties, imposes new forms of authority and establishes new social classes. It can lead both to cooperative and knowledge sharing multi-firm relationships as well as to competitive and largely arm's length relationships.[15] The dual economy has long been a feature of developing economies. MNEs, although fashioning new industrial sectors and modernizing others, tend to exacerbate the cultural differences between these and the traditional sectors, and all the social adjustment problems arising from it.

19.3.2 The role of MNEs in culturally sensitive sectors

The culture of a country, is, of course, an amalgam of different aspects of the way of life of its citizens. Although the exposure of a country to new ways of organizing production may affect a person's life style at work (which, admittedly, may have spill-over effects on the rest of his or her life), the exposure of a country to new products, services, ideas and attitudes is, in the long run, likely to be more important.

Unlike in the first case, however, the MNE is likely to be only one of many purveyors of cultural change. Far more important influences have been technical advances, which have led to an enormous growth in international travel, tourism and all forms of trans-border communication – notably through the printed word, broadcasting and television. Whether Coca Cola is imported into Ghana or produced by a Ghanaian franchisee is not likely to make much difference to the attitudes of local consumers to the cult which has grown up around the product. Whether tourists in Thailand stay at a 5 star French managed hotel or a 5 star Thai hotel is hardly going to affect their patterns of behaviour and how that behaviour impacts on the local population. Such studies as have been conducted on the role of tourist-related MNEs on local culture (UNCTC, 1980) suggest that there is little which can specifically be attributed to their foreignness or their trans-nationality, although international airlines, tour operators, car rental companies and hotels are frequently the modality by which the foreign tourist interacts with the local culture. In any event, the amount of FDI in tourist-related activities is relatively small – especially in developing countries. It is true that such hotels, relative to their domestic counterparts, tend to be concentrated at the luxury end of the market, but if there is a 'conspicuous consumption' effect, it is the foreign tourist and, particularly, the wealthier domestic tourist, who must be held to account.

The assertion that MNEs promote income inequality and excessive product differentiation again often fails to distinguish between the presence of a foreign company and the influence it may exert through other means. Kelloggs can still advertise its processed cereal products on Brazilian or Dutch TV, whether or not it produces these products in these countries. Mercedes cars are imported into Malaysia as well as being assembled locally. Many goods sold in India, Nigeria and Mexico with the trademark of a British or Swiss firm may be produced by a locally-owned firm under licence. Culturally insensitive sales or marketing practices by foreign companies in the Philippines or Lesotho may be channelled through locally-owned distributing agents.

Of course, it is likely that the presence of MNE affiliates may have its own specific cultural impact, but it is by no means certain this will be a negative one as is so often assumed. When exports from a German or Canadian MNE to Indonesia are replaced by production undertaken in a joint venture in Indonesia, it could well be that the nature of the product and the practices surrounding its production and marketing become localized. Similarly, a 100% owned Dutch manufacturing subsidiary set up in India to supply the local market may be much more sensitive to the local tastes and work practices than the marketing department of the firm in The Netherlands. In situations where a foreign-owned firm finds it in its interest to develop a culture acceptable to the host, then its presence would be beneficial. Moreover, to the extent that MNEs are sometimes trailblazers in producing culturally friendly commodities or production methods, their presence is likely to be welcomed by host governments.

19.4   STRATEGIC INTERESTS

Though operating primarily in the economic arena, MNEs may sometimes have important strategic consequences for the countries in which they operate. By strategic capability, we essentially mean the ability of a country to pursue its political, economic and cultural goals. The fear that outward or inward investment may advance the strategic interests of another state is perhaps best articulated in the field of defence-related activities. While the participation of foreign MNEs in these activities is strictly limited by most host countries, lest this could be used to strengthen the military or political strength of the investing country, outbound investment may be disallowed or discouraged in case the defence capacity of a potentially unfriendly power is strengthened.

19.4.1   National security

Perhaps the most sensitive issue surrounding the effects of MNE activity is its perceived impact on national security. National security means the ability of a country to protect its sovereignty of action, especially in times of aggressive and hostile actions by other countries.

Even the most liberal of countries, which

otherwise practise a policy of neutrality towards inward investment, impose restrictions on the participation of foreign firms in security sensitive sectors. If anything, such restrictions are growing. In the US, for example, the Exon-Florio amendment[16] to the Omnibus Trade and Competitiveness Act of 1988 (Section 721) allows the President of the US to block a merger, acquisition or take over of US persons (sic) by foreign interests, wherever such actions are perceived to be a threat to national security.[17] Although the wording of the act is fairly specific, it does open the door to some kind of screening of inward investment, and has caused a resuscitation of the largely inactive Committee on Foreign Investment in the United States (CFIUS).[18]

In most other countries, the controls imposed on MNE activity in security sensitive sectors are more widespread and specific. Indeed, several outlaw FDI in these sectors altogether. The basic concern about the security implications of allowing domestic industries to fall into foreign hands are two fold. First, that foreign affiliates – either deliberately or unwittingly – might engage in activities which might be harmful to the security of the host country should it and the home government come into conflict with each other. Graham and Krugman (1989), who investigated this possibility in respect of activities of foreign companies in the US, concluded it was unlikely. For example, in the Second World War they found no evidence that US subsidiaries operated as a kind of fifth column on the part of their home country.[19]

Secondly, foreign affiliates might be used to impair the military efforts of a host nation. Graham and Krugman (1989) cite the example of multinational oil companies working with the US State Department in the 1930s and early 1940s to prevent Japan from building petroleum reserves.

In most cases, such overt activities by MNEs can be blocked or overcome by host governments. Exceptions include those involving direct extraterritoriality on the part of home governments. This is because they are fairly transparent. Much more difficult to deal with are those cases – often involving friendly powers – in which foreign subsidiaries engage in activities which are welcome on economic grounds, but not necessarily on security grounds. Much FDI in the electronics and telecommunications and vehicle industries falls into this category. They are liked whenever they bring new technological or organizational know-how and help to improve the host country's competitive position. They are less appreciated as suppliers of defence equipment to host governments, in so far as any knowledge gained by them may possibly be used to the benefit of the defence interests of the home country.

The host country is, then, faced with a dilemma. To exclude the foreign firm from defence-related activities may not only weaken its ability to supply products to the private sector, but (particularly where no local firms are able to supply the defence equipment) weaken the defence base itself. This dilemma is particularly acute where a foreign firm acquires a domestic firm which was previously producing defence equipment, but is no longer able to do so. Even if a foreign subsidiary is allowed to supply the host government with the equipment, its position may still not be assured wherever a home government has the power to stop it from supplying a foreign government with security sensitive products.[20]

The globalization of production and markets, and the increasing propensity of MNEs to engage in R&D outside their national boundaries, is forcing governments to reappraise their policies towards the participation of foreign subsidiaries in strategically sensitive activities. In particular, some commentators (Graham and Krugman, 1989) question the value of disallowing foreign subsidiaries membership of government-supported R&D schemes (e.g. SEMATECH in the US, and some EC-financed research consortia in Europe[21]).

The rationale for such an exclusion is partly technological and partly security related. However, the basic assumption is that the host country loses more than it gains from such a procedure. Assuming all countries adopt a similar policy, this smacks strongly of 'beggar my neighbour' type policies. In a (developed) world in which cross-border direct investment fulfils a similar role to international trade, any attempt to capture only its advantages and eliminate its disadvantages is bound to end in retaliatory action. The only case for such a restriction is where trade flows in technology are distorted by protectionist policies, or where the home government is using the R&D policies of its MNEs to advance its *strategic* objectives.

19.5   ENVIRONMENT-RELATED ISSUES

19.5.1   The impact of MNEs on the environment

Like those of any other firm, the actions of MNEs may be friendly or damaging to the national or global environment in which they operate. At the same time, many of the effects of MNE activity on the environment may have very little to do with the multinationality of the firms involved. All too frequently one reads about the MNEs being held responsible for actions which are undertaken, or may have been undertaken, by domestic firms.

The interaction between MNEs *qua* MNEs and the environmental objectives of countries arises in two ways. First, it is likely that MNEs will possess certain environment-related O advantages over their unilateral competitors, which they may or may not deploy in a way consistent with national or global environmental goals. These O advantages may arise either as a result of the environmental standards laid down by home (or other host) governments (e.g. anti-pollution controls, health and safety regulations), or they may be initiated by the company itself to secure a competitive advantage (lead free petrol, lighter weight materials, recyclable aluminium cans, smokeless fuel etc). In addition, because of its operating experience in different environments, the MNE may have acquired an advantage in environmental management or organization. Both these kinds of assets are potentially transferable across national boundaries.

The extent to which an MNE is willing to transfer environment-related practices to another country, and how far it is prepared to adapt these practices to meet the particular needs of that country, depends on what is required of the foreign subsidiary as well as on the costs and benefits involved. On the one hand, the MNE may be perceived as a pioneer of the best environmental practices. On the other, it is often accused of exporting second- or third-best practices to escape from the cost of engaging in first-best practices imposed by home governments, or of failing to adapt the practices of its parent company to suit the environmental requirements of host countries.

Not all countries, of course, value environment-related practices in the same way. Some poorer developing countries, in particular, may find that the environment-friendly products or production methods insisted upon by richer countries are unnecessary, too costly and an unacceptable form of extra-territoriality. Often the protection of the environment itself involves the use of resources which could be used to produce goods and services which are more highly valued. It is then too simplistic to argue that the MNEs should always be encouraged to transfer first-best environmental procedures, any more than they should be encouraged to transfer first-best technology or marketing practices.

This is not to deny that MNEs may sometimes have a role to play in upgrading corporate environmental behaviour and of educating those who are unaware of the long-run costs of environmental damage. However, as in other areas, any judgement of the impact of MNEs on the environment must be related to the needs and aspirations of the countries in which they operate as well as to the costs of implementing or upgrading existing environmental practices.[22]

19.5.2   Attitudes of countries to environmental issues

Most countries take a schizophrenic attitude to the environmental practices of MNEs. While they welcome their investment, they also expect MNEs to act as leaders for improving environmental customs (including the use of more environment-friendly technologies) *up to a point*, particularly where they can lead to an appropriate upgrading of domestic procedures. A problem, however, arises where there is no equivalent domestic activity of an MNE, or where the host government may have little understanding of the environmental consequences of a particular multinational (or, for that matter, domestic) activity. Past examples include deforestation, inappropriate mining practices and inadequate health and safety standards in factories (e.g. with respect to asbestos working, chemical wastages).

Most contemporary MNEs are well aware of their local responsibilities in these areas, but under competitive pressures and in their efforts to produce goods results, line managers may often take a casual attitude to (what they perceive to be) less pressing needs and less easily detectable health and safety standards. Hence, the pressure by some countries and the international community for some code of conduct of behaviour on these practices.

Disasters such as Bhopal, concern over the marketing policies of some companies which are sometimes seen as exploitative of an ignorant population (e.g. the ongoing powdered baby milk saga) and the seemingly uncaring stance taken by some MNEs about the dumping of waste materials, the uncontrolled use of chemical pesticides and the export of hazardous products have led to a barrage of criticisms against inward direct investment.[23] Equally important, but less well publicized, have been the adverse effects (sometimes unforseen) of MNE activity on more general environmental goals.[24] Yet, as we have suggested, very few such practices can be directly put at the door of the foreignness or multinationality of such companies *per se*. Usually there are a host of reasons: some are firm specific, some reflect lax industry standards and some are to do with inappropriate legislation and ineffectual controls or monitoring standards by governments. At the same time, the way in which companies deal with environmental disasters may – for good or bad – may reflect their nationality of ownership. For example, the legislative procedures following the Bhopal disaster clearly reflected the fact that the plant was US rather than Indian owned and managed.

19.5.3 The role of MNEs in environment-sensitive sectors

19.5.3.1 *Introduction* Another reason for the attention paid to MNEs is that they tend to have a significant presence in pollution- or hazard-prone sectors, notably industrial chemicals, fertilizers, pesticides and petroleum products. CFCs (chlorofluorocarbons) are both produced and bought mainly by MNEs. They are involved in activities which generate more than one-half of the greenhouse gases emitted by the six industrial sectors with the greatest impact on global warming (UNCTC, 1991d). More than this, by their dominant position in these sectors, they can, and do, have a critical impact on a whole range of environmentally-sensitive issues, such as global warming, ocean level stability, the erosion of land and the exploitation of nonrenewable resources.

Thus it is not surprising that, because of the increasing importance attached to environmental issues, the focus of attention has often been directed to MNEs – particularly as their activities may affect the international distribution of both the production and consumption of environmentally-sensitive products.

The literature has identified four main ways in which MNEs may interact with the environment of which they are part. These all arise from their ability to:

(1) affect the location of environmentally-sensitive activities,

(2) trade in hazardous products,

(3) influence the environmental content of both production and consumption (e.g. with respect to health and safety standards and, in particular, to transfer best practices across national boundaries),

(4) innovate new products and restructure activities in an environmentally-friendly way.

We shall deal briefly with each of these in turn.

19.5.3.2 *Location of MNE activities* A frequent criticism of MNEs is that they are often tempted to transfer environmentally-sensitive activities to countries which impose the least costly environmental restrictions. Empirical research suggests there is some truth in the assertion – particularly in the production of highly toxic products and some hard mineral processing. Some host countries (e.g. Ireland and Romania) have, at one time or another deliberately sought to attract such activities (Leonard, 1984). However, studies of both US and German MNEs suggests that this is not a critical consideration in their relocation policies (Duerksen and Leonard, 1980; Knodgen, 1979). Indeed, Pearson (1987) quotes a German study which demonstrated that 90% of firms surveyed claimed to use the same environmental techniques in developing countries as in West Germany.

19.5.3.3 *Exporting hazardous products* MNEs have also been accused of dumping unproven or outdated products on the open market. Examples include the export of a poisonous pesticide – leptophos, which was refused registration in the US, and methylmercury, a fungicide used to treat seed grains, which was also banned in the US and other countries – to several Third World countries, with some disastrous results, including several deaths.[25] There are also examples of hazardous or toxic waste being exported following tougher regulations in some industrialized countries. Again, however, while MNEs have often been among the worst offenders, their actions had little to do with their multinationality *per se*.

19.5.3.4 *Health and safety regulations* Perhaps a more obviously MNE-related activity concerns the protection of worker health. Here there is a great deal of evidence of double standards being practised. Castleman (1987) reports that 'extreme examples of the lack of health safeguards for Third World workers by MNEs have been reported in the asbestos, vinyl chloride, pesticide chromete, steel and chlor-alkali industries, among others'. He also cites cases of individual MNEs, for example, Johns-Manville, disregarding many or all the regulations imposed on their US operations in their Indian and Brazilian operations for many years. In a post-mortem on the Bhopal disaster, it was found that Union Carbide operated a similar chemical facility in the US but with more stringent safety standards in the design, operation and monitoring of the plant (Castleman and Purkavastha, 1985). Currently, there is some concern about the export of environmentally-unfriendly products by US MNEs to the maquiladoras (assembly) plants in Mexico.[26]

Criticism is not confined to US MNEs. Castleman (1987) documents several cases of Japanese MNEs exporting pollution-intensive products and production methods and failing properly to consider the adverse social or environmental impact of these actions. British and West German firms are also among those identified by various writers (as quoted in Castleman, 1987, pp. 161–63) as tolerating unsafe and unhealthy working conditions in countries such as India, Mexico, Nicaragua and South Korea. In 1982, for example, a Malaysian plant partially owned by the Mitsubishi Chemical company was found to be dumping radioactive thorium waste on open ground in plastic bags that easily broke up. There was a furore among the local inhabitants which *inter alia* led to a boycott of all Mitsubishi products in Malaysia. As in the Bhopal accident, the parent company argued that because the plant was under the control of local management, they accepted no responsibility. Whatever the rights and wrongs of this assertion, it is worth observing that foreign affiliates with local equity or management affiliates appear to record no better health and safety standards than 100% owned plants. At the same time, it would seem that most MNEs, at least until the mid 1980s, adopted a generally decentralized approach to environmental management in their subsidiaries. This pattern can be explained by the powerful internal and external forces that MNEs have encountered with regard to environment management. As, however, countries are now trying to work out a global strategy towards the environment, so MNEs are adopting a more unified approach, particularly at a regional level (UNCTC, 1985).

Events such as these and the Bhopal accident which claimed the lives of 2000 people, and injured 200 000 more, have sparked widespread and extremely negative views of MNEs. The World Council of Churches has expressed opinions – often with more emotion than reason – that global corporations have tended to aggravate rather than help solve the world's greatest problems. It has also called for the UN and other international agencies to act as a countervailing moral force to the ethics of power, acquisition and materialism, which they perceive to be the driving force behind MNE activity. A more balanced and persuasive view (in a case study of the Bhopal disaster, but one suspects it could be generalized) was expressed by Gladwin (1987) who argued that faults on the part of both management and the Government of India contributed towards the disaster.[27]

19.5.3.5 *Structural adjustment, environment and MNE activity* The problem of ensuring the appropriate structural reallocation of resources to meet new environmental perceptions and needs is increasingly facing national governments and the international community. It demands both national and supra-national *macro-environmental* measures – which in many ways may be thought of as paralleling *macro-economic* measures in the economic area. These measures take account of MNEs as one of the many instruments by which environmental goals may be promoted. Indeed, they may put particular emphasis on these corporations to incorporate environmental issues into the planning and execution of their international operations.

At the same time, it is the responsibility of governments to provide the appropriate regulatory machinery and facilitating measures for MNEs to behave in a way that is consistent with their own goals and aspirations. Almost certainly, this means some intervention in the market. Most environmental services are produced in conditions of considerable market failure, partly because of their externalities, partly because of their 'public good' characteristics and partly because of the huge technological risks involved. To adjust for these failures, it is encumbent on governments to create and sustain the social conditions they wish to achieve.

Governments have an armoury of instruments to achieve this end. They include legislation, for example, health and safety laws; the imposition of taxes, for example, to reduce pollution or the over-exploitation of resources; the provision of subsidies, for example, to encourage R&D into new methods of recycling waste materials, or enhancing fuel efficiency and product durability; the setting of codes of environmental practices and the granting of aid to developing countries to better audit environmental health and safety. Again, while such actions should be non-discriminatory and addressed to all firms, they must take account of both the O-specific advantages of MNEs and their locational flexibility, as well as the fact that action which causes these corporations to act in a way that is consistent with macro-environmental policies will be particularly fruitful. At the same time, there is need for some of the risk disclosure policies (for example, in respect of products, processes and the work place) adopted by developed countries to be taken up by developing countries, and for the latter to implement actions to mitigate unacceptable risks (UNCTC, 1991b).

In spite of the criticisms levelled against MNEs, there is ample evidence to suggest that they have been at the forefront of good environmental managerial practices in formulating guidelines on such practices,[28] and that the threat to publicize those corporations which blatantly abuse their environmental responsibilities is often a sufficient deterrent for them not to do so.

19.6 CONCLUSIONS

In conclusion, the interaction between MNEs and environmental issues is a complex and dynamic one. Not least this is because countries are constantly changing their views on the importance of environmental issues – particularly as it affects economic development[29] – and MNEs are developing and building environmentally-friendly acts into their competitive strategies. There is little doubt that countries do expect MNEs to be trailblazers in environmental standards. There is little doubt, too, that they have the resources and the competences both to help develop environmental management policies and programmes, and to prevent or decelerate the rate of environmental deterioration. At the same time, unfettered market forces are unlikely to motivate MNEs to use their specific attributes in a way which accords best with the macro-environmental goals of countries. In consequence, this is an area where intervention by governments to formulate standards and lessen market failure is of some importance. This may require collaborative policies both at an intra-governmental level and between governments and MNEs.[30]

NOTES

1 This reappraisal is currently being most dramatically revealed in the new political environment in Central and Eastern Europe.

2 Most notably in the case of some US agribusiness MNEs in the Caribbean and Central America in the early 1900s, which eventually led to the 'gunboat diplomacy' of the US government towards Honduras, Cuba, Nicaragua and Haiti (Wilkins, 1989).

3 See Chapter 18.

4 Which will vary between countries according *inter alia* to the significance of the resource(s) to the local economy.

5 See especially Sunkel (1972) and Hirschman (1969). For an overview and critical analysis of this literature see Jenkins (1987b).

6 For more details, see Chapter 20.

7 A 'Catch 22' situation is one in which each of the options open to solve a particular problem is equally impractical or unacceptable.

8 See Chapter 2.

9 Exceptions included some ex-European colonies, such as Singapore, Hong Kong and Indonesia.

10 To give one example, US corporate taxes accounted for 20% of all US taxes in 1989; it is estimated that US multinationals accounted for 51% of this amount.

11 The changing role of national government in the light of the globalization of economic activity is explored in Dunning (1991a, 1991b) and in Chapter 20.

12 These included efficiency, diligence, orderliness, punctuality, frugality, honesty, rationality in decisions on actions, readiness to change, alertness to opportunities, energetic enterprise, integrity, cooperativeness and willingness to take the long view.

13 For example, the Japanese tend to take a longer view of business planning than the US. They are also more cooperative, punctual, orderly and frugal, but Americans probably are more alert to opportunities, more energetic and value efficiency particularly highly. The Swiss and Italians have different values on punctuality, and the British and the Japanese different attitudes towards incentives.

14 On matters such as attitudes towards achievement, authority, wealth accumulation, interpersonal relations, security, innovation and so on. Moreover, successful MNEs recognize the adjustments which need to be made are not all one-way. This lesson has been most difficult for US MNEs to learn. So often in the past they have pursued an ethnocentric cultural attitude, as a result of which they have failed to transplant their non-cultural O-specific advantages successfully. The current evidence suggests that in their venturing overseas, the Japanese are somewhat more culturally sensitive. Coming from a wide background of cultures, European MNEs have a generally good record of cultural sensitivity.

15 Thus the suggestions that Japanese MNEs transfer (or at least would like to transfer!) the cooperative relationships, which they enjoy with their domestic suppliers, to their overseas operations. Such relationships have very different cultural implications to the less filial relationships which US firms are accustomed to having with their suppliers, although in some sectors, at least, the trend is for more collaborative linkages to be formed.

16 The version that became law.

17 For further details, see Graham and Krugman (1989) and Graham (1991a).

18 In the twelve years preceding the 1988 Act, CFIUS received fewer than 30 applications by foreign investors; in the first 12 months after, there were more than 50 cases (Tolchin and Tolchin, 1988).

19 In particular, they cite the case of Ford in Germany, which, during the Second World War, appeared to act as 'a good but somewhat ineffectual corporate citizen' (Graham and Krugman, 1989, p. 77).

20 Graham and Krugman (1989) quote the case of MITI ordering Kyocera, a Japanese producer of high technology ceramic products, not to allow its US subsidiary to supply ceramic nose cones to the US Tomahawk missile programme.

21 ICL, the leading UK computer firm was a member of such a consortium, but immediately it was taken over by Fujitsu, its involvement was strictly limited.

22 Here, there is a parallel in the role of MNEs in the upgrading of working conditions and wages of employees in developing countries. While they can often spearhead improvements, if they were to try and transfer the practices of their parent companies' wages policies and conditions of work completely, they could cause considerable disequilibrium in the local labour market.

23 Each of these and other issues are dealt with in an excellent volume edited by Charles Pearson in 1987. For more recent reviews of TNCs and the environment, see UNCTC (1985b, 1989, 1991b and 1991d).

24 The Bougainville mining development had various adverse environmental effects, including the effects of mine sediments and tailing on the adjacent river system and the social impact of mine development (Pintz, 1987).

25 Other examples include defective electrical toys and baby pacifiers, kerosene heaters, chloramphenicol, depo-provera (an injectable contraceptive), contaminated fish and mouldy flour.

26 In 1988, some 310 000 people were employed in export processing zones in Mexico under the Border Industrialization Programme initiated by the Mexican Government in 1965. It is anticipated that employment in the maquiladoras will further increase when the North American Free Trade Area comes into being (see also Chapter 17).

27 Gladwin identified five types of failure of both management and government. These were: failures to anticipate risks, failure to equip, failure to inform, failure to control and failure to comply.

28 As, for example, those set out by the International Chamber of Commerce (ICC) on the issue of industrial operations and wastes. The ICC has also evolved a Business Charter for Sustainable Development which was officially launched in Rotterdam in March 1991 at the Second World Industry Conference on Environmental Management. It is also reported (*Transnationals*, Vol. 2, December 1990, pp. 1–2) that DuPont, ICI and Rhône Poulenc are among the MNEs which are phasing out the production of CFCs, while many MNEs, including IBM, Digital Equipment, AT&T, General Motors, Nissan and Electrolux, have announced they are replacing CFCs by substitute materials.

29 The term 'eco-development' has come to mean an ecologically sound (or sustainable) development strategy.

30 Some of the internationally agreed standards and instruments so far initiated are described in UNCTC (1991d).

PART 4

IMPLICATIONS FOR POLICY

The focus of this part of the volume switches from MNEs to governments as the unit of analysis. Chapter 20 considers the changing attitudes of home and host governments towards MNE activities, and the actions taken by them to influence the level and composition of these activities and the pattern of their behaviour. It also discusses the extent to which particular home and host governments have adapted their more general macro-economic and organizational policies in the light of the internationalization of business activity and the economic strategies pursued by other governments.

The thrust of the chapter is that the interface between MNEs and governments has not only been one of the prime determinants of the way in which countries have linked themselves to, and benefited from, the globalization of economic activity over the past 30 or more years, but that the nature of that relationship has undergone a profound change. This change has been predominantly brought about by three interrelated forces: first, the emergence of new industrial nations as powerful actors on the world economic scene; second, the increasing pace of technological and organizational advance; and third, the growing liberalization of the world macro-economic environment and the movement towards closer economic interdependence between nations. While in the 1960s and 1970s, the main concern of governments was to maximize the direct economic rent from inward investment and to ensure that MNEs provided the right kinds of resources and capabilities to promote their economic development, in the 1980s and 1990s, governments are increasingly viewing MNEs as a means by which they can upgrade the competitiveness of their domestic resources and capabilities and evolve a pattern of development which is consistent with their long-term dynamic comparative advantage. To do this, the chapter argues that the economic function of government is shifting from one of intervention in particular markets to counteract the structurally distorting behaviour of firms or consumers, to one of ensuring that the market system operates at the lowest possible transaction costs to its participants. To the extent that MNEs are a key influence both in the ways in which resources are located across national boundaries and in which these activities are organized, they directly affect, and are affected by, domestic government policies.

But, as Chapter 21 shows, not always can the unilateral policies of governments achieve their objectives because of the ability of MNEs to avoid, or exploit, country-specific differences in government actions. In some cases, these may be the result of market forces; in some they might be guided by different social objectives (e.g. with respect to the environment); and in others, there may be deliberate strategies by governments to transfer the economic rent of MNE activity from one country to another, by policies which at the end of the day may prove as structurally distorting as actions taken by firms or consumers. Examples include the provision of some kinds of investment incentives and export subsidies, as well as the imposition of tariffs and import quotas. To circumvent an unacceptable distribution of rents between countries, or between particular countries and MNEs, some kind of supra-national action may be called for. The various forms of such action and their likely effectiveness in influencing the pattern of MNE activity and behaviour are identified and discussed in Chapter 21. *Inter alia* the chapter suggests that attitudes formed and action taken at a regional level (by the EC, NAFTA, etc) and at an international level by such institutions as GATT (or perhaps, a new agency concerned specifically with MNE-related matters) are likely to become relatively more important influences on the disposition of MNE activity in the 1990s.

CHAPTER 20

GOVERNMENTS AND MULTINATIONAL ACTIVITY: THE UNILATERAL RESPONSE

20.1 INTRODUCTION

Part 3 of this monograph examined some of the ways in which the value-added activities of MNEs might impact on the home and host economies in which they operated. It also dealt with some issues of policies related to specific impact areas. The next two chapters will describe and analyse the more general attitudes and reactions of national governments, regional authorities and international organizations to the perceived consequences of MNE activity. These chapters also discuss some of the measures taken by them to modify either the extent and form of this activity, or their own strategies and policies in the light of it.[1]

At the outset, however, it is worth repeating the point made earlier (Chapter 10, pp. 281–3), that the economic effects of MNE activity in particular home or host countries must be evaluated, first, in terms of the opportunity cost of the resources used, and second, by reference to the variables under the control of the policy makers which determine that activity. In other words, the structure and performance of foreign-owned firms in a particular host country in time t is partly a function of the macro- and micro-economic policies pursued by the government in the country in time $t - 1$. If the economic signalling of governments is inefficient or distorted, then the responses of MNEs will be also. In one sense at least, a government's actions towards MNEs are the outcome of its own past economic and political strategies. This lesson has only recently been learned by some governments, who are now reappraising their macro-organizational policies in the light of the globalization of markets and production.

Although the interaction between governments and MNEs is a dynamic and iterative process, it is possible to identify the main attitudes formed, and actions taken by governments, both towards, and as a consequence of, MNE activity. It is also possible to explain why such attitudes and actions differ between countries, and even in the same country towards different types of foreign investors, or towards the same foreign investors over time. Furthermore, it is possible to pinpoint the opportunities and constraints facing governments and regional authorities in their attempts to relate the level and pattern of inward and outward direct investment, and the operating behaviour of MNE's affiliates to their domestic, economic and social objectives.

In doing so, we shall not attempt even to summarize the very considerable literature which has built up over the past two decades or more on the laws, regulations and policies implemented by home and host governments towards FDI and MNEs. For the interested reader, the best sources of data are those compiled and presented by the UNCTC (v.d.), the US Department of Commerce (1985) and Business International (vd), each of which regularly publishes details of the main laws, regulations and policies pertinent to FDI. Rather, we shall attempt to offer some generalizations and illustrations about the nature of the interaction between governments and MNEs, and how this has changed over the past 30 years. In doing so, we shall continue to use the theoretical underpinning of earlier chapters. Indeed, we shall argue that the OLI and ESP paradigms offer a useful framework for understanding both the nature and outcome of government–MNE interaction.

20.2   SOME THEORETICAL ISSUES

20.2.1   A further application of the OLI paradigm

Why should national governments wish to modify their laws, regulations, policies, or even their entire economic system, either to affect the behaviour of MNEs or as a result of their increasing presence in the global economy? In terms of the eclectic paradigm, the answer rests, first, in the distinctive O-specific advantages of MNEs and the way in which they combine these assets with the indigenous resources, competences and intermediate products of the countries in which they are producing; and second, in the knowledge that, by their actions, governments may not only be able to influence the O advantages of their own MNEs (or potential MNEs), but also the attractions of their own specific assets to inward investors. Governments, by their abilities to influence market conditions and/or the efficiency of hierarchies, may also affect the capacity and willingness of both their own and foreign firms to internalize cross-border markets and to conclude collaborative alliances with foreign firms.

It is possible to formulate a number of propositions, or hypotheses, which relate the extent and form of government action to the configuration of OLI advantages facing MNEs and to its own objectives. Consider, as examples, just four propositions. *Proposition 1* is that *ceteris paribus* the fewer the distinctive O advantages of MNEs (*qua* MNEs) the less likely it is that any actions by governments will be specifically directed towards such firms. *Proposition 2* is that *ceteris paribus* the greater the inter-country competition for investment, both by foreign- and domestic-based MNEs, and the more 'footloose' such investment is, the more governments of any one country will need to ensure that their location-bound assets are at least as attractive as those of its competitors. *Proposition 3* is that the greater the attractions of a host country's resources or markets to MNEs and the more the competition between MNEs for these resources or markets, the more likely it is that the government of that country will be able to implement actions to extract the maximum benefits from such MNEs.[2] *Proposition 4* is that the more the MNE values its O-specific advantages and the more they are systemic

by nature, the less likely they are to be willing to sacrifice hierarchical control over them or to conclude joint ventures with foreign firms.

Each of these propositions suggests that government action to affect the level and pattern of value-added activities by MNEs will, first and foremost, be a function of the interaction between the configuration of the L-specific (or the ESP) assets under their jurisdiction and the O-specific advantages of MNEs. Second, it will depend upon the government's evaluation of the likely impact of this interaction on their economic and other goals, as well as on the strategies they adopt to achieve these goals. Third, the ability of governments to modify their actions successfully depends, first, on the extent to which these actions are perceived by MNEs to advance or hinder their corporate objectives, and second, on the bargaining power of governments *vis à vis* that of the MNEs.

In examining the actions taken by governments over the past three decades as they have affected or have been affected by outward and inward direct investment, we will be especially interested in the motives for these actions, and the extent to which they are *symbiotic* or *anti-symbiotic* to those which MNEs perceive to be in their best interests. Indeed, we shall suggest that for most of the post-war period, the relationship between MNEs and most governments has been more confrontational than cooperative. Usually this combative approach has reflected the different goals sought by MNEs and governments. However, even where MNEs are perceived to benefit the countries in which they operate, governments have sought to ensure that their own share of the economic rent created by the MNEs' activities is maximized.

As we have seen in previous chapters, the consequences of the globalization of markets and production for individual countries have been mixed. Usually a tradeoff is involved as some economic objectives are advanced and others inhibited. Frequently, governments have sought (not with great success, one might add) to achieve only the 'best of all possible worlds' from all kinds of MNE activity. This has led them to take a bevy of actions, most of which have failed to meet their objectives.

Unlike MNEs, which have broadly similar economic objectives, at least as far as their activities *in toto* are concerned,[3] governments have a variety of economic and other goals. Some of these goals and the priorities assigned to them are likely to be consistent with the objectives of MNEs, for example, the opening up of new markets and the upgrading of local resources and capabilities. Others, such as the advancement of environmental and safety standards, regional development, the pursuit of economic autonomy and the protection of cultural values, might require policies which could reduce the revenues or impose additional costs on MNEs or their affiliates. Obviously, the less palatable the actions of governments are perceived to be, the more the relationships between MNEs and governments are likely to be adversarial. In such cases, the final outcome will rest on the negotiating and bargaining strengths of the two parties. By contrast, the higher the priority afforded by governments to achieving goals consistent with those of MNEs, the more likely it is that the relationships will be cooperative.

We shall argue in this chapter that over the past 30 years there has been a noticeable shift in the priority of the goals of Nation States and in their appreciation of the role which MNEs can (and cannot) play in advancing these goals. The relative bargaining strength of MNEs and Nation States has also undergone some change. Chapter 2 showed that, since the 1960s, MNE activity in the manufacturing and service sectors has shifted from first-time investment to the servicing of local markets to sequential investment in pursuance of a regional or global strategy. Such a change in emphasis has considerable implications for the interface between the actions of MNEs and host government policies (Doz, 1986).

At the same time, MNEs have learned a great deal by their FDI experiences over the past 30 years, including how best to accommodate the objectives of governments with the most benefit – or least disbenefit – to themselves. This learning process on the part of both governments and MNEs, together with exogenous changes in the global political and economic environment, has helped reshape the attitudes of national and regional authorities to both inward and outward direct investment. In general, it has led to a more relaxed stance, as governments have come to appreciate the benefits of economic interdependence and to see MNEs as a means by which these benefits may be increased. Moreover, as the industrial structure of the wealthier industrial nations

has tended to converge, governments have become more competitive in their macro-organizational and trading strategies. Here, too, governments are increasingly perceiving that under the right conditions MNEs may help them to enhance the competitiveness of the resources and capabilities under their jurisdiction.

At the same time, governments have become increasingly conscious that the kinds of international economic links forged by MNEs may not always be to their long-term benefit. Chapters 11 and 12 have explored, at some length, the concerns expressed on the role played by FDI on the allocation of cross-border innovatory capabilities. Because such capabilities are being increasingly perceived as the 'seed corn' for economic growth and competitiveness, governments are viewing both outbound and inbound MNE activity in terms of their contribution to the upgrading of these capabilities.

One thing is certain. The interaction between governments and MNEs needs to be studied in the context of a constantly changing world economic and political landscape. There is no (and never has been) one set of optimum policies that governments can adopt towards, or as a result of, MNE activity, which holds good for all nations for all time. Countries differ in their need and ability to attract inward investment or to encourage outward investment. For their part, according to the nature of their value-added activities and the locational options open to them, MNEs will value a production facility in different countries differently. And, over time, as has been so well demonstrated in the case of countries like Japan, South Korea, Nigeria, Chile, France and Mexico – not to mention the whole of Central and Eastern Europe – the ESP configuration facing MNEs may quite dramatically change.

20.2.2 A schematic framework

To conclude this section, Exhibit 20.1 sets out an analytical framework for examining and evaluating the main relationships between MNEs and governments. This schema draws on some ideas set out in a paper by Lecraw and Morrison (1991), but extends their analysis by incorporating the home country. The framework is essentially based on the interaction between the O advantages of firms and the L

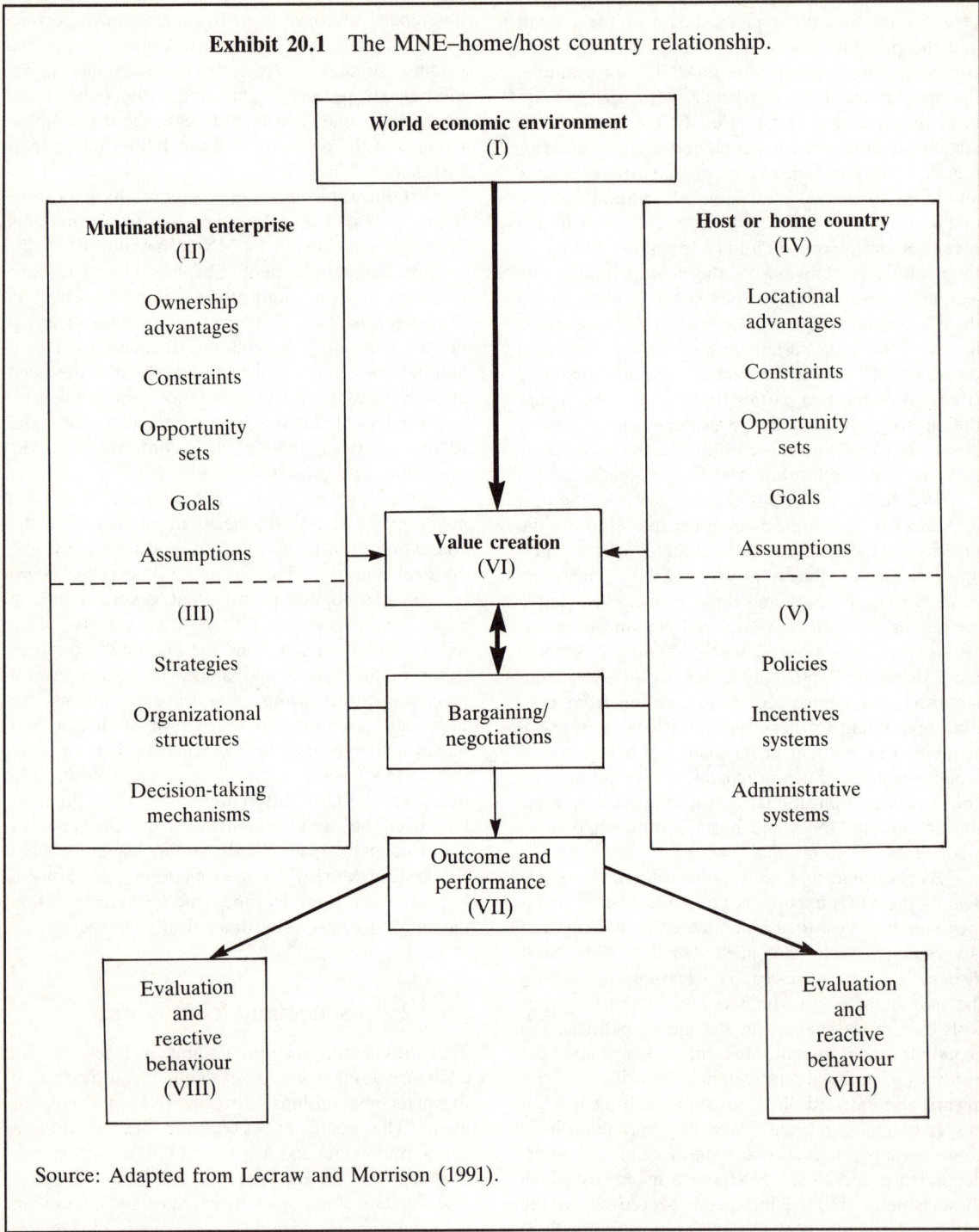

Exhibit 20.1   The MNE–home/host country relationship.

Source: Adapted from Lecraw and Morrison (1991).

advantages of countries and how these, in turn, affect the organization of cross-border, value-added activities (i.e. the I advantages of MNEs). The schema contains eight components, or steps, which may precede some course of action, or set of actions, taken by governments. Later in this chapter we shall examine some of these components in more depth.

The schema is essentially *static* in its approach. It assumes that at a given moment of time and within a particular world economic environment:

(1) MNEs possess a set of O-specific advantages and constraints and, according to their goals and opportunity sets and organizational structures, will pursue certain strategies to meet those goals.

(2) Similarly, Nation States possess a set of L- or ESP-specific advantages and constraints which, according to their goals and opportunity sets, will lead them to take certain actions.

(3) Such actions – as directed towards MNEs or one or other of their affiliates – may range from the provision of information and moral persuasion, through a gamut of entry requirements and performance regulations to the outright prohibition of FDI in certain sectors, and/or allowing foreign investors only a minority equity stake in indigenous firms.

The juxtaposition between the O advantages and strategies of MNEs and the L advantages and strategies of Nation States is potentially of economic value to both parties. The next question is how the net income resulting from MNE activity is distributed between the investing companies and the countries within which they operate. This issue is usually of less concern to capital-exporting countries as the surplus earned by their own MNEs (net of the taxes collected by the host country) accrues to it.[4] But it may critically affect the judgement of the host country of the economic viability of an inbound investment. Here, the balance of the negotiating strengths and weaknesses of the two parties enters the picture. The outcome will affect the final structure and content of MNE activity and the actions taken by governments.

20.2.3   A bargaining model

Before proceeding to a more detailed examination of the interactions between governments and MNEs, a word about the theory of bargaining may not be out of place. This is modelled in Exhibit 20.2, which is again adapted from Lecraw and Morrison (1991).[5] It is particularly apposite to MNE–host country government relationships. Such bargaining options only arise where, as a result (or an expected result) of MNE activity, an economic rent over and above the anticipated opportunity cost of the O-specific advantages of MNE activity, and the anticipated opportunity cost of the L advantages of the host countries, is earned, or thought likely to be earned. It is important to realize that unless both sets of opportunity costs are covered, no MNE activity will take place. The distribution of the surplus value or rent will then be determined by the bargaining positions and negotiating strengths of the two parties.

The bargaining outcome depends upon the value of these opportunity costs together with the MNE's perceived assessment of the L advantages offered by the country and that by the country of the O advantages offered by the MNE. Clearly, the MNE is in a strong position where its opportunity cost is low and when the government of the host country puts a high value on the MNE's contribution to its economic and social goals. By contrast, the host country's position is likely to be strongest where it has much to offer the MNE and it is able to obtain the assets and capabilities offered by the MNE from other sources (or produce them itself). As might be expected, not only do the bargaining abilities of countries vary according to the configuration of their diamonds of competitive advantage (Porter, 1990) but, so too, will those of MNEs depend on the character and uniqueness of their O-specific advantages.

Yet, even with these bargaining 'chips', the outcome rests upon the negotiating abilities of firms and countries. These, in turn, will depend on each party's knowledge about the other's options, of their perceptions of what each has to offer the other and on their respective negotiating experience and skills. Difficulties of evaluation on the part of the host country, for example, will be particularly acute where the outcome of MNE activity is multi-faceted

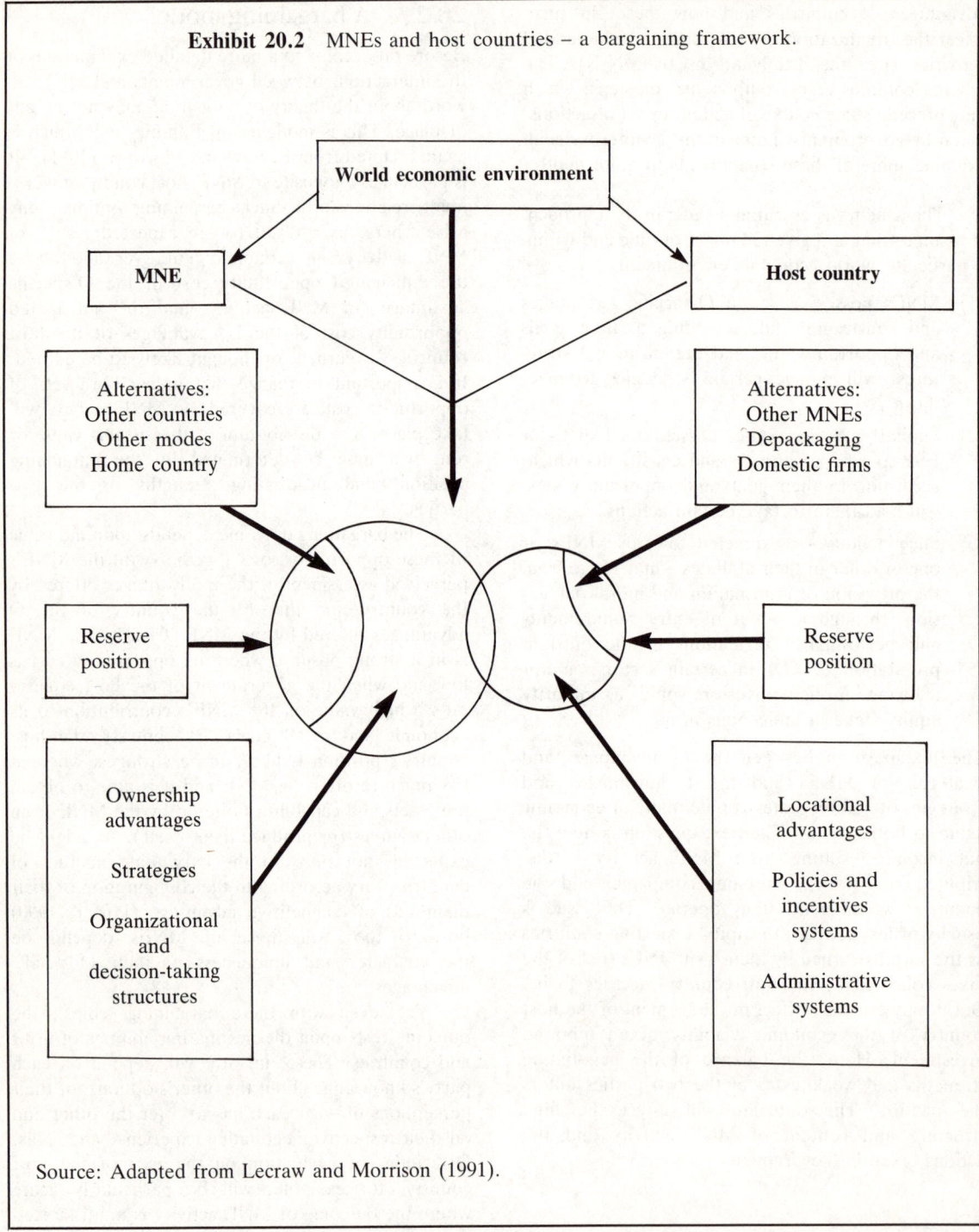

Exhibit 20.2   MNEs and host countries – a bargaining framework.

Source: Adapted from Lecraw and Morrison (1991).

and likely to yield mixed benefits. The outcome of the negotiations may depend critically on the way they are handled and on the competence of the government department or investment agency responsible for the final decision. We shall take up this point later.[6] Finally, investment proposals may be assessed either by reference to general guidelines, which, while having the advantages of efficiency, clarity and objectivity, take no account of the distinctive features of individual projects, or on a case-by-case basis, which, while acknowledging the uniqueness of each project, can be very time consuming and may send confused signals to MNEs as to how host governments are likely to evaluate their investment proposals (Encarnation and Wells, 1985).

Two other points should be noted about the bargaining process. The first is that most of the literature on the subject tends to focus on the interaction between MNEs and host countries *at the time of the proposed entry by the foreign investor*, even though the provisions sought by the host country (e.g. as in the case of the negotiations between Nissan and the UK government in 1986) may include post-entry performance requirements, or even a provision for divestment or 'fade out' after a stipulated time period. However, *de facto* both the MNE and host government may wish to renegotiate the terms of the MNE's presence at a later date. This is because the relative negotiating strengths of the MNE and host country may change once inward investment occurs. At one time it was believed that as soon as a MNE entered a country, its bargaining position began to obsolesce as a result *inter alia* of its investment in immobile plant and equipment (Vernon, 1971b) and the erosion of some of its O advantages through involuntary leakages or competition. In such cases, countries (and, for that matter, local business partners of joint ventures) might wish to renegotiate the terms originally agreed to tilt more of the value added to themselves. On the other hand, if the MNE yields more economic benefits than was originally envisaged, the host country may be tempted to give additional incentives for it to engage in more, or more high valued, production.

At the same time, if the inbound investor generates new and more valuable O advantages, or if they change the character or emphasis of their existing investments (e.g. by engaging in more R&D

or rationalized investment), it may wish to renegotiate the terms of the original agreement, particularly as regards any performance constraints which were initially imposed upon it.

The second point about the bargaining process is that the host government may be able to influence its own ability to negotiate effectively by modifying its overall economic strategy or particular economic measures to make the country more attractive to foreign investors. Examples include the relaxation of performance requirements, freeing controls on dividend remissions or capital repatriations, and the removal of structural market distortions – all of which may act as disincentives to inward direct investment. Such cases reflect a situation in which both parties may gain from the 'right' kind of government action which, as a later section in the chapter will show, have bcome more frequent in the past decade or so.

It is, then, difficult to generalize on the nature and direction of the obsolescing bargain as the O and I advantages of MNEs and the L advantages of countries are constantly shifting, as indeed are the respective opportunity costs of the bargaining parties. This, of course, presupposes a dynamic view of the upgrading of both firm- and country-specific resources and capabilities. The original concept of the obsolescing bargain was rather more static (or comparatively static) in its orientation.

Considerably less attention has been given to home country–MNE bargaining relationships. This is presumably because it is assumed that the interests of two parties are likely to be compatible, or that the home government can take whatever action it wishes without sacrificing the gains to be had from the domestic activities of its own firms. As it happens, neither view is necessarily correct. In the first case, several studies have revealed that the marginal social rate of return of foreign direct investment *may* be (but not necessarily is) less than the private rate of return[7] and that, in such circumstances, from a social viewpoint, domestic firms may over-invest overseas.

In the second case, which runs counter to the first, home governments may underestimate the gains to the competitiveness of their home economies as a direct result of the outbound MNE activity. These gains, which have been dealt with at some length in other parts of this book,[8] arise because of the complementarity of outward and domestic investment. They include a feedback of knowledge about the presence and behaviour of competitors, suppliers and customers, and any additional economies of scale and scope which foreign production makes possible.[9] Moreover, *de facto* governments have very little power to curb outward direct investment except by discriminating against foreign earnings, which they are generally loathe to do. Nevertheless, they may still exert some influence upon the timing and scale of outbound MNE activity and curb its profitability through a variety of extra-territorial controls.

20.3   INTERACTION BETWEEN HOST GOVERNMENTS AND MNEs

20.3.1   The changing scenario over the past 30 years

We have suggested that the actions taken to influence foreign MNE activity in host countries depends essentially upon the nature of the existing contribution of the investing companies to the economic objectives of the countries, as compared with the benefits of using the resources involved differently. In practice, such actions (at one time or another) have ranged along a continuum from complete *laissez-faire* to the complete outlawing of inward investment, although nowadays no government in the world takes either of these extreme positions. Moreover, since the goals of national governments are multi-faceted and their needs for inward investment differ (cf those of Botswana with those of Germany, or those of Fiji with those of Canada), it follows that their propensity to influence inbound MNE activity is likely to vary according to both the type of FDI and its perceived operational impact.

Thus a country whose prosperity rests on its possession and exploitation of a single natural resource may be very sensitive to foreign control over that resource. Also, as Chapter 19 has shown, even the most liberal countries restrict the degree of foreign participation in strategically and culturally sensitive industries. Similarly, countries with a severe balance of payments or external debt problems may be more cautious in permitting investment in those activities which will exacerbate these difficulties than

in those which are not so constrained. The different needs of host countries for technology, capital, entrepreneurship, management and organization skills, and competitive stimuli might result in liberal performance demands of MNEs in one functional area and extremely restrictive requirements in another.

We have further suggested that actions taken by host governments as a result of inward investment may be of two main kinds, *viz* those specifically directed to MNEs or their affiliates and those which may affect all kinds of firms. Each may be designed to influence the contribution of inbound investment to the short- and long-run objectives of the host country. Short-run objectives essentially relate to the immediate (net) output produced by foreign affiliates and the share of that output retained in the host country. Long-run objectives are concerned with the impact of MNE activity on the ability of the host economy to upgrade its location-bound resources and competences, and for its firms to improve their penetration of external markets.

The recent history of the interaction between host countries and MNEs is essentially that between the changing L advantages offered by the former and the O advantages of the latter. Elsewhere in this book we have used Michael Porter's classification of the competitive advantages of countries to describe the former. Here we make use of the ESP paradigm described in the introduction to this book and expanded on in Chapter 10. To recapitulate, the paradigm avers that a country's location-bound attractions are a function of the economic, political and cultural environment it offers (E), the system it adopts to organize the disposition of its indigenous resources and capabilities and any of those it may import (S), and the institutional mechanisms and policies (or strategies) it may follow to achieve its objectives.

Exhibit 10.3 set out the main attributes of the ESP configuration and their respective outcomes. In discussing this exhibit, we suggested that the three elements of the paradigm were closely interlinked.[10] A change in the political philosophy of a government may lead to a dramatic recast of its economic systems as, for example, is currently occurring in Central and Eastern Europe. Over a longer period, government involvement in educational and R&D programmes may critically affect the future economic environment as for example has occurred in Singapore over the past 20 years. A detailed appraisal of the ESP characterization of countries together with the relationship between these and the O and I advantages of firms takes us a long way to understanding the likely actions which governments might wish to take, and have the competence to take, towards their own MNEs and the affiliates of foreign MNEs operating in their countries.

Using this kind of approach, let us now consider some changes in the interaction between MNEs and host countries over the past 30 years or so. In doing so, we may identify three fairly distinct phases. While the precise timing of each has differed between companies and countries, by and large the first lasted from the early 1950s to the mid 1960s, the second from the mid 1960s to the late 1970s and the third from the late 1970s to the present. For reasons which will become apparent, we shall call them respectively *the honeymoon*, *the confrontation* and *the reconciliation* phases.[11]

(a) The honeymoon phase

Any partnership, particularly a fully fledged marriage, starts off with each partner having great expectations of what the other can offer, although this is sometimes more a matter of faith than anything else! Certainly, even if love is not blind, it does tend to wear rose-coloured spectacles which magnify the good and overlook the less desirable features of one's partner. So it was with the early post-war interface between MNEs and the governments of the countries in which they operated. From the viewpoint of both newly emerging developing nations and war-ravaged Western Europe, the capital, technology, organizational capabilities, managerial skills and entrepreneurship of foreign-owned (particularly US) firms were sorely needed. However, because of an inadequate or distorted market for these assets, they could often only be obtained via inward direct investment. During these years, US economic and technological hegemony was at its peak and American corporations dominated international production, just as UK firms had controlled much of world trade a century and a half before. At the same time, US manufacturers were seeking new markets for their products and new sources of energy and raw materials to supplement their indigenous supplies.

On the fact of it, it seemed a perfect partnership between US foreign investors and host countries, although in some cases it was Hobson's choice for the latter as, at the time, only MNEs possessed many of the assets and/or markets they needed. It was this very control of assets and markets which gave rise to the first signs of discontent with the partnership. Nevertheless, in the 1950s and early 1960s, at least, all (or most) was sweetness and light. With the international economic climate fashioned at Bretton Woods and Havana in the mid 1940s ensuring exchange rate stability and a well ordered training regime, the scenario for international business was as promising as it had been during the previous 30 years.

One other thing is worth mentioning. Most MNEs in those days were comparatively small, mono-centric and involved in many fewer countries than they are today. Most manufacturing affiliates, too, were set up as import-substituting ventures and were truncated replicas of their parent companies acting largely independently of each other. Only in the resource-based sectors had foreign corporations evolved anything like a global product or marketing mandate, or were engaging in much intra-firm trade. The main economic impact of FDI in those years was, then, in the resources, capabilities and markets they provided to the recipient countries, rather than the way in which these were organized.

(b) The confrontation stage

As a marriage passes out of its honeymoon stage and becomes more firmly established, the partners are better able to assess how far each is, in fact, able to satisfy the other's desires and aspirations. Sometimes this learning process affects the attitudes and behaviour of one or both of the partners; sometimes the character of the relationship changes; and sometimes the balance of influence on decision taking shifts. One thing is certain: after a time each partner becomes aware of the weaknesses as well as the strengths of the other, and the costs as well as the benefits of the relationship.

The most far reaching changes in the international economic climate of the 1960s and early 1970s stemmed directly from the growing political independence of many developing countries, a better identification of their economic goals and a growing

belief of governments (which was not always justified) that they had the resources, institutional
mechanisms and organization skills to achieve these
goals.

This new self-awareness or self-faith, coupled
with a Keynesian approach to economic management
and the setting up of new administrative networks,
was occurring at a time when MNEs were gaining a
substantial foothold in many host countries. As more
emphasis began to be given to such developmental
goals as satisfying basic needs, advancing self-
reliance, improving the balance of payments and
raising the level of technological capacity, so inward
investment became evaluated in these terms. Not
surprisingly, it was found wanting in one direction or
another. Gradually, it dawned on governments that
the kind of contribution which MNEs might make to
economic development was not always that which
they needed most. To be sure, foreign firms provided
technology, but was it always the appropriate kind or
at the right price? Admittedly, their affiliates might
help to save imports, but did they always buy as
much from local producers as was socially desirable?
Agreed that they created employment, but were not
their production methods more capital-intensive than
those of indigenous firms, and did they always recruit
or train local management as well as they might?
And, while they sometimes led to more exports of
primary products, what if this was at the cost of
sustainable and environmentally friendly development?

In addition, MNEs were perceived as transmitting a way of life which was not always welcomed,
while, through advertising and other promotional
means, they might adversely influence social and
cultural values. By their presence and behaviour,
they could drive out, or preclude the entry of
indigenous competitors. In continuing to locate high
value-added activities from their home countries and/
or by internalizing knowledge and information
transfers, they might lessen the chances of a host
country achieving even a modest technological
capability of its own. Finally, because of their market
power, they were perceived not only to earn high
economic rents, but also, through a variety of
devices, to minimize the host country's share of these
rents.

These were years, too, when the management
style and organizational strategy of some of the
larger MNEs were changing. As the geographical
spread of their activities increased, so did the
tendency of corporations to adopt a more centralized
and multi-divisional control structure. At the same
time, decisions about capital investment, product
range, the sourcing of inputs and the kinds of
markets served were more likely to be taken from a
regional or global perspective. The trend, too,
towards the international standardization of some
products and the specialization of processes and
markets, placed an increasing premium on quality
control, continuity of output, protection of proprietary rights and the exploitation of economies of
scale and scope, all of which prompted a more
integrated governance structure of MNE activity.

In the late 1960s, fixed exchange rates held
good, world economic growth continued apace and
inflation was generally under control. Nonetheless,
the system was under great strain, particularly when
the US balance of payments position turned sour and
the US dollar lost some of its appeal as a reserve
currency. Two events in the early 1970s – the
devaluation of the dollar and the huge price rise of
oil by the Organization of Petroleum Exporting
Countries (OPEC) – heralded a watershed in post-
war international economic relations. These events,
together with the growing frustration of many
developing countries with the inability of the existing
economic order to reduce the income gap between
themselves and the developed nations, sparked off
a period of intensive North/South confrontation.
Though much of the debate was rhetorical, it did
create an uncongenial climate for international
business.

In the first half of the 1970s, MNEs came under
increasing scrutiny and attack. Not only were they
criticized on the grounds of their unacceptable
behaviour and uneven contribution to economic
development, but also because they were perceived
to be a product of an international economic system
that was no longer acceptable. If the system could
not be changed, then at least – so the critics argued –
some redress might be taken against one of its
leading manifestations.

The early 1970s were the 'high noon' of
confrontation between the governments of several
host countries and MNEs. The measures taken by
the former to affect the behaviour of the latter are
well known and already part of history. They ranged

from the outright expropriation of foreign assets of MNEs,[12] through restricting the level and direction of new investment, to laying down comprehensive performance criteria for foreign affiliates and to aiding indigenous firms to compete more effectively in world markets. In these years, however, there was little recognition by host governments of the need to modify their economic strategies and policies in the light of the new challenges and opportunities posed by inward FDI.

The response of the MNEs – which has not been so well documented – was predictable. Where their subsidiaries were already fully integrated into the local economy (as in the case of many older import-substituting ventures) and were still earning an economic rent, they absorbed the costs of intervention – but thought twice before investing any new capital. In other cases, their options ranged from restricting the transfer of technology or technological capacity to circumventing controls on income flows through transfer pricing manipulation; and from switching – or threatening to switch – their production to another country, to trying to persuade their home governments to use their economic or political leverage to obtain a better deal from host governments.

In the main, this kind of reaction enraged host countries even more, especially where, in order to compete for the same MNE activity, they were forced to pay even higher economic rents. So countries sought to increase their bargaining power either by harmonized regional action or by obtaining the advice and guidance of such international organizations as the UNCTC, UNCTAD, UNIDO and the World Bank on how best to use inward investment to aid their development or restructuring process.[13]

(c) The reconciliation phase

As often happens, just as a particular problem is beginning to be solved, it becomes less acute or ceases to exist. The late 1970s saw governments learning from the experiences of the previous decade and refining, modifying and extending their policies to better harness the contribution of inward direct investment. At an international level, attention centred on drawing up codes of conduct or guidelines of behaviour for MNEs and improving the

flow of information about their activities. There are now encouraging signs that national governments have made progress in their knowledge and understanding not only of the costs and benefits of different types of MNE activity, but also of the implications of being integrated into the global economy, through the actions taken by MNEs. If the 1960s and the early 1970s were years of disillusionment about the net benefits of FDI, the late 1970s and 1980s brought no less dissatisfaction with the organizational strategies, institutional mechanisms and economic policies of governments.

However, the result of this learning process has been a more enlightened appraisal of the value of alternative modalities of resource importation, and the introduction of more realistic and constructive macro-economic and organization policies towards, and in the light of the activities of, MNEs. At the same time, MNEs have become more appreciative of the fact that their global strategies might not always work to the environmental and cultural benefit of each and every country in which they operate. A more sensitive and better trained breed of managers and civil servants has emerged, while the emphasis of bargaining has moved to promoting a more mutually rewarding relationship between the parties concerned and away from extracting the most economic rent out of an FDI.

These shifts in attitudes have been sparked off and shaped by changes in the ESP configurations of countries and the OLI configurations of firms. We would simply identify four such changes. First, and most important, there has been a widening of the sources of many of the assets which, in the 1960s, were largely monopolized by US and some European MNEs. The markets for many kinds of technology, management skills and capital have become less imperfect; hence the incentive to internalize them has lessened. Second, the past two decades have witnessed considerably higher levels of unemployment, more competition for the kinds of resources which MNEs have to offer and lower rates of economic growth. Consequently, host countries have become welcoming towards inward direct investment.

Third, as we have already noted in this volume, an increasing number of smaller developed and Third World countries are engaging in FDI. As a result, trade in intangible assets is increasingly resembling that of goods embodying these assets, with intra-industry international production following along the lines of intra-industry trade (Dunning, 1988a). Fourth, notwithstanding the substantial growth of cross-border strategic alliances and other kinds of non-equity ventures, we see most MNEs are adopting more integrated strategies towards their transnational operations. Integration has occurred despite the volatility of exchange rates and the unstable monetary environment of the past decade or more. This has led some countries to question the extent to which they wish to be locked into the kind of international economic division of labour fashioned by MNEs. The dilemma is that the more unique the contributions of MNEs are to economic development, the less amenable they are to control by national governments.

There is, of course, a political dimension to the events of the past decade. With a few exceptions, national administrations have become noticeably more right-wing, and have therefore placed more emphasis on market-oriented economic policies. At the same time, social priorities have changed. For example, environmental protection is now high on the political agenda of many countries. For the most part, countries which have grown the fastest in the past decade are those which are the most favourably disposed towards inward direct investment and most value the benefits of economic interdependence. Indeed, as more countries generate their own MNEs, they are beginning to view inward and outward investment as part of a more holistic economic strategy.[14]

In conclusion, the 1980s witnessed the emergence of a more mature and symbiotic relationship between MNEs and governments. Each now knows the conditions under which the one may, or may not, be expected to contribute to the other's well-being. Each better appreciates the role which mutual commitment, trust and forbearance should play in the success of any partnership. Nevertheless, because economic and social goals, and the ability to achieve these goals, differ between the two parties, it is inevitable that some differences in perception and some clashes of interest will remain. Moreover, there is nothing permanent about a particular ESP configuration or diamond of competitive advantage of a country. History is replete with examples of the rise and fall – and, sometimes, rise again – of the

economic prowess of Nation States. However, the *pace* of structural change is probably greater than it has ever been. Similarly, MNEs vary in size and strategy, and the OLI values affecting their behaviour are frequently transient.

The link between the role of MNEs in developing and developed countries lies in the interface between the global activities of the former and the development and restructuring processes of the latter. Ignoring the role of government, for the moment, factors such as the size of a country, composition of its resources, degree of urbanization, extent of inter-firm rivalry, economic distance from the main centres of technology, and the size and character of domestic markets all play critical roles in influencing the OLI configurations of both foreign and domestic firms.

However, as Chapter 10 has demonstrated, we would expect that as a country moves along its development path, its indigenous firms, often stimulated by the presence of foreign-owned affiliates, would themselves generate O advantages in the supply of those products which require the type of L-specific endowments and capabilities in which the country has, or is developing, a comparative advantage. At the same time, expanding markets and changes in a country's ESP configuration might increase the demand for new products which require the kinds of resources and capabilities which foreign firms are best able to provide, either by trade or foreign production. On balance, the evidence suggests that, as it approaches economic maturity, a country is likely to engage in relatively more international direct investment, although whether it is a net capital importer or exporter will depend upon the extent and pattern of its specific assets and advantages *vis à vis* those of its major competitors.[15]

What, then, is the role of governments in the development process? More than anything, governments have, by their impact on the relative transaction costs of markets and hierarchies, influenced the *modality* of resource transfer across national boundaries. Sometimes their educational, technological and industrial strategies have also affected the O advantages of their own firms. We have also suggested that governments may shape the climate for international business by the macro-organizational systems they operate, the entrepreneurial ethos, cultural norms, environmental values and social values they fashion, as well as by the particular economic strategies they pursue (Dunning, 1991a).

More important, perhaps, is the extent to which countries *wish* to be interdependent or independent of each other. With so many political and environmental uncertainties, but with the growing internationalization of ideas, business values and technology, most countries tend to chart an ambivalent course. They want the benefits of cross-border interdependence, but not the costs. Most noticeably, they are reluctant to forego their economic sovereignty and systems of governance, or to dilute their cultural identities. Thus, while regional integration is a recognition of the benefits of large markets, the thrust of defence, energy, and science and technology policies suggest that countries also value some degree of autonomy in matters of national security and innovatory capability.

20.3.2   Policies specifically directed to affect inward direct investment

20.3.2.1   *Greenfield investments*

(a)   Conditions of entry

Policies towards inward direct investment broadly fall into four groups. The first group relates to the conditions of entry or setting up of foreign investors. These are usually based on five main criteria. The first concerns the allowed degree of foreign ownership of indigenous resources. Is 100% – or majority – foreign ownership permitted, or are foreign firms only allowed a minority participation in indigenous enterprises? The second criterion relates to the kinds of value-added activities in which MNEs may participate. In the past, some national authorities have been very strict, not only about the sectors open to foreign investors but also as to the proportion of a sector's output they are permitted to supply.[16] Even the most liberal countries are reluctant to allow much foreign participation in strategic or culturally sensitive sectors. At the other end of the spectrum, foreign investors may also be unwelcome in sectors producing goods or services perceived (by governments) as undesirable or inessential.

The third criterion relates to the financing of the inbound investment. Countries that are short of foreign currency are likely to insist that all of the initial capital investment be financed by the foreign investor from the international capital market. The fourth criterion concerns the location of the investment within the recipient countries. Countries which pursue vigorous regional policies may require, or put strong pressure on, foreign firms to locate their activities in areas of lagging growth or above average unemployment. For example, in 1988 no less than 75% of the employment of Japanese manufacturing subsidiaries in the UK was in such regions, which at that time employed only 25% of the total labour force.

The fifth criterion relates to the pre-entry conditions for FDI, and comes within the broad heading of investment incentives. While the extent to which these incentives are fully captured by MNEs (e.g. tax holidays or rebates) may depend upon the performance of their affiliates, others are directed to aiding the start-up of new ventures. These include investment and regional development grants, subsidized loans and/or factory rents, and accelerated depreciation allowances. Such incentives can sometimes be very substantial (Guisinger, 1985, 1986).[17]

(b)   Operating requirements

The second group of government policies concerns the operating requirements demanded or expected of foreign-owned affiliates.[18] These may well be a precondition for the investment being allowed in the first place. However, we shall consider them separately as they concern the day-to-day operations of affiliates.

Performance-related measures may embrace the whole gamut of operating practices. They include behavioural guidelines or requirements in respect of the local purchases of capital goods, raw materials, intermediate goods and services; recruitment, employment and training practices, particularly at a managerial and professional level; the proportion of output exported; the type of value added (e.g. R&D) undertaken by the affiliates; information provided on intra-firm pricing practices; conditions attached by MNEs on the use of technology transferred; and even (in the case of developing countries, in particular) types of production methods utilized. In some cases, these requirements may be traded for more favoured treatment of MNEs by governments, such as the granting of additional import licences and protection from foreign competition.

Not all governments encourage or insist upon such patterns of behaviour (which in many, though not in all, cases lead to market distortions). Governments that do are inclined to focus on just a few. For example, most European governments try to obtain some assurance from Japanese manufacturing investors about the local content component of their output reaching a certain level within 4 to 5 years. Performance requirements tend to be most demanded by host governments when there is inadequate competition from local firms, or where it is clearly in the best interests of the MNE (but not necessarily that of individual foreign affiliates) to act in a way that is unacceptable to the host government.[19] They may also be used as a means of assisting industrial restructuring,[20] which may be an entirely laudable objective.

Less justifiable, however, is the practice of some governments to use performance requirements as a substitute for the adoption of more appropriate macro-organizational policies, which, though possibly more difficult to implement, might better serve their long-term objectives. Examples include using performance requirements to help reduce (or not increase) a balance of payments deficit (see Chapter 14); to stimulate employment at the cost of less efficient production methods (see Chapter 13); to insist upon R&D and training programmes by MNE affiliates that use resources which might be used better elsewhere in the economy (see Chapter 11); or to disallow the control of export markets by the investing MNE, where this might help advance its global efficiency.

(c) Exit conditions

The third group of policies is directed at the conditions for the exit of foreign investors. Few governments now impose divestment requirements at the time of a new firm's entry. However, they were quite common in the 1960s and 1970s, particularly among developing countries who viewed the role of inward investment as that of a tutor to indigenous firms and considered that as soon as the tutoring had

been successfully accomplished, the tutor should gracefully withdraw. Such conditions are likely to prove most successful in cases of market-seeking MNEs whose competitive advantages rest on the kinds of intangible assets[21] which can be most easily transferred and assimilated by the recipient economy. They also appertain to some resource-seeking FDI where the host country, by dint of its favoured possession of such resources, is in a strong bargaining position. They (and, for that matter, entry and performance requirements) can less easily be imposed on foreign affiliates which are part of a global or regional network of activities over which the parent company wishes to maintain close control.

(d) Achieving cost-effective FDI

The fourth group of policy measures encompasses the other three, but, unlike them, addresses itself to the most cost-effective way of attracting inbound direct investment. In practice, incentives, regulations and performance requirements go hand in hand. It is quite consistent for governments to limit the participation of foreign-owned firms in one sector while giving tax incentives to encourage investment by them in another; or for it to insist upon a certain local content requirement while offering export subsidies. Fiscal incentives may take various forms, but the most common are tax holidays, investment grants, accelerated depreciation allowances, employment premiums, subsidized loans or rents and regional grants. Some of the incentives impinge directly on the revenue costs of firms and sometimes on the profits earned.

Research by Root and Ahmed (1978), Lim (1983), O'Sullivan (1985), Guisinger (1985, 1986), Balasubramanyam (1991) and OECD (1989) reveals that while, in some instances, MNE-specific incentives have played an important role in influencing the location of FDI, they have not, in general, been a major determinant of such investment.[22] However, much depends on the *raison d'être* for the MNE activity and the kind of incentives offered.[23] Incentives are likely to have their greatest impact where a foreign firm is undecided about its choice of a number of economically viable locations, and where they are not counteracted by performance requirements (Siggel, 1986). They have generally been less successful in attracting the kind of investment drawn by the unique assets and competences of the host country.

Certainly, this is perceived to be the case by the individual states within the US, most of whom are currently fiercely competing with one another for foreign investment.[24] And there is some evidence (Morse and Farmer, 1986; Papke, 1987; Coughlin, Terza and Arrondee, 1991) that differences in tax rates among subnational units in the US do have a significant impact on the location of the investment. In the EC, too, for many years now there has been intensive rivalry between countries like Ireland and Belgium to attract North American and other European capital and technology, so much so, in fact, that the European Commission has tried to discourage these 'beggar my neighbour' tactics which, in the long run, almost certainly benefit the investing companies (or countries) rather than the recipient nations.

Though some attempt has been made to identify the conditions under which fiscal and other incentives[25] are likely to increase the flow of inward direct investment, surprisingly little attention has been paid to appraising the benefits resulting from the incentives or, indeed, to the opportunity cost of such incentives. As Lecraw has pointed out in an unpublished study for the UNCTC, it is one thing for countries to attract foreign investment to their borders and quite another to ensure that the benefits derived from such investment compensate for any 'buying' costs incurred. Few governments appear to have made any serious cost–benefit analysis of MNE-directed investment incentives, taken as a whole, or of different kinds of incentives.

Certainly, a review of the country-specific incentive schemes currently in operation suggests that governments still believe these *are* cost-effective. However, in recent years there has been some redirection of emphasis, particularly among industrialized countries, towards improving the economic environment for inward investment, for example, by deregulating or liberalizing markets and encouraging a more efficient use of domestic resource usage. To some extent the renewed faith in market forces is extended to limiting the use of MNE-specific regulations and performance requirements as well. We will take up this point further in Section 20.4.

(e) Summary of policies towards greenfield FDI

Summarizing up to this point, it is possible to identify three groups of countries according to the attitudes of their governments towards inward direct investment. The first group consists of countries whose governments perceive that market forces coupled with appropriate macro-economic and organizational policies are sufficient to ensure that they can obtain the level and kind of inward investment they require. They consider that the behaviour of foreign affiliates is likely to be symbiotic with their national interests. These countries include most developed nations and the more market-oriented developing countries, such as Hong Kong, Taiwan and Singapore. Most of the activities of affiliates in this first group are within the secondary and tertiary sectors; a larger than average proportion are likely to be owned by MNEs pursuing regional or globally-integrated production and marketing strategies (Doz, 1986; Porter, 1986). Finally, these countries tend to be (or aspire to become) significant outward direct investors.

Group 2 countries tend to be at an earlier stage of development than Group 1 countries, and their governments normally play a more important role as resource creators and allocators. They are inclined to rely less on external trade for their prosperity and are more prone to pursue hybrid developmental strategies. FDI in these countries is more likely to be resource based or market seeking than in Group 1 countries. Controls are likely to be more emphasized than incentives. In some of these countries, while foreign MNEs often play a dominant role, their own firms are likely to be important outward investors. Few Group 2 countries would acknowledge the need either for a systemic strategy towards MNE-related activities or to modify their general macro-organizational strategies in the light of such activities. Examples of Group 2 countries include Brazil, Thailand, Indonesia, Zimbabwe, Kenya and Morocco.

Group 3 countries are those which allow only limited freedom to market forces and who pursue (as far as it is possible to do so) a policy of economic autonomy and self-reliance. FDI may be welcome for its 'tutorial' and resource-transferring role. However, it is likely to be strongly controlled or guided by the host authority. Since domestic markets are likely to be distorted by government intervention (e.g. by import and price controls), it is very difficult to judge the costs or benefits of inward investment. Likewise, it is difficult to assess the cost-effectiveness of government measures to influence its form and impact. India and China are examples of Group 3 countries.

These three groupings are, at best, rough classifications. Most countries fall somewhere between one or the other of these patterns, while some attributes of FDI best fit into one group, and others in another. Japan is particularly difficult to categorize in this respect. For many years it rigorously limited inward direct investment, yet it has many of the characteristics of other Group 1 economies, notably West Germany. The major, and unique, feature of the Japanese attitude towards MNE activity is the belief that it is in its long-term interests to disallow foreign firms to control its key economic sectors, and that inward investment should be welcomed only in so far as it provides an added and worthwhile stimulus to its own producers to upgrade their indigenous resources and capabilities and/or opens up new foreign markets.

Up to now, Japan has been successful in achieving its goals, mainly through the strength and motivation of its skilled and professional labour force, an excellent supply of domestic savings, and its own ability to utilize, adapt and build upon foreign technology, management skills and organizational methods. However, with Japan now the second largest outward investor, and with the overseas operations of Japanese MNEs being increasingly targeted to other developed economies, it is questionable how long Western governments will tolerate any strategic actions on the part of the Japanese government which are aimed at reducing the ability of their MNEs to do what Japanese firms are allowed to do in these governments' territories.[26]

Finally, the composition of the countries classified to the three groupings and, indeed, the characteristics of the groupings themselves, have undergone considerable change over the past 20 years. In the early 1990s, far fewer countries can be classified to Group 3 than in the 1970s. For example, the Eastern European and Indo-Chinese economies are now moving into Group 2. As far as Group 1 and some Group 2 countries are concerned, the most noticeable change in attitudes and actions towards inward direct investment reflects a shift in the focus of the economic strategies of many governments towards maintaining and advancing the competitiveness of their resources and capabilities as well as an increasing appreciation of the role which MNE investment can play in their strategy. Mexico is a good example of a country which is now moving into Group 1 from Group 2.

Though, as we shall see later, this refocusing of the role of countries in the global economy has not yet been articulated in any systemic economic strategy, except in a few cases like Japan and Korea, it is resulting in a reappraisal of the merits of both inward and outward investment. In particular, inbound MNE activity is being increasingly evaluated by its likely effect on domestic innovatory capabilities, and on the upgrading of human skills and competences. This has resulted in a more conciliatory attitude by governments towards foreign MNEs, which are being increasingly viewed as partners in their pursuit of mutually consistent goals. Consequently the 1990s are seeing governments giving more emphasis to the promotion of attractive macro-economic and organization policies, and less to direct controls, performance requirements and incentives directed specifically towards MNEs (Dunning, 1991a, 1991b, 1992b).

There is just one caveat to this observation. While Group 1 and 2 countries are becoming more market oriented and regionally integrated, there are also signs of a resurgence in inter-regional protectionism – at least with respect to some kinds of inward direct investment. This is most clearly seen in the US where, in some quarters at least, Japanese investment is less welcome than it was a decade ago. The concept of 'Fortress Europe', though vigorously denied by the European Commission, has very much affected the response of non-EC investors to the completion of the internal market in 1992. Indeed, there is some concern that, although individual countries may be opening their borders to inward investment, the 1990s may witness an increase in regional protectionism, particularly of an intra-Triad kind (Bergsten, 1990; UNCTC, 1991a).

20.3.2.2 *Acquisitions and mergers* Chapter 15 has examined some of the differences between the consequences of greenfield FDI and cross-border

A&Ms on competition and market structure. However, in other ways, it has different effects. A change in the ownership of an important R&D facility may have important implications for the indigenous technological capacity of the host country. The integration of a company which was previously a substantial net balance of payments earner into the global marketing network of a MNE may reduce that benefit. A takeover followed by the sale of part of the acquired company also brings repercussions very different from that of a greenfield investment.

Most host countries deal with the distinctive effects of trans-border A&Ms as an extension of their domestic competition and anti-trust legislation. Again, policies differ. Some countries disallow acquisitions altogether, while in others (e.g. Japan) there are substantial institutional obstacles to foreign takeovers. If they so choose, governments can insist upon the foreign investor gaining approval prior to any takeover. In practice, in most developed countries at least, most slip through the net of perusal altogether. Only if the takeover threatens national security, involves a major company, is in a sector already dominated by foreign firms, or is expected to reduce domestic competition does it attract the interest of host governments.

In the period 1985–90, foreign companies acquired more than $224 billion of US assets, while US companies acquired more than $64 billion of foreign companies (Walter, 1992). These values outstripped greenfield investments in the same areas by an average ratio of 5 to 1. Intra European mergers also mushroomed in the late 1980s. Yet few of these A&Ms were referred to their national governments for approval, although some involving EC member states required the authorization of the European Commission. In developing countries, especially of the Group 3 variety, A&Ms are examined more carefully. For the most part, except for the foreign currency they bring, they are less welcome than greenfield MNE activity.

20.3.3 General policies of host governments as a consequence of the growth of inward direct investment

The growing significance of the activities of the affiliates of MNEs in most developing and developed economies, as documented in Chapter 2, has meant that governments have been increasingly forced to re-evaluate their macro-economic and organizational strategies in the light of this phenomenon. At the same time, the growing interdependence of the global economy has led to a closer harmonization and interlocking of macro-economic policies pursued by the leading industrial nations, particularly the so-called Group of 7.[27] At a macro-organizational level there is far less cross-border collaboration. Indeed, such policy convergence as there is is being achieved by the forces of competition, rather than by any deliberate act of cooperation between national governments.

Of the changes that have occurred as a result of these forces, together with a cluster of new technological breakthroughs in the 1970s and 1980s,[28] none have been as far reaching as the widespread renewal of faith in the market as a resource allocator and stimulator, and the disillusionment of the role of the state as an owner and organizer of economic activity. Undoubtedly, this change in attitude is a reflection of the favourable growth rates achieved by the more market-oriented economies. However, it is also a testimony to the failure of political regimes which had pursued alternative organizational systems or have so abused the market system as to make it unworkable.

Yet, accompanying the renaissance of the market system, has come a growing realization that it cannot, by itself, always create or sustain the conditions necessary to guarantee its own success. Nor can individual markets cope with some of the spill-over or external effects of the transactions they organize. Most particularly, and through no fault of its own, the market cannot provide the requisite supply and demand conditions to ensure socially optimal investment in education or commercial innovatory activities – the main engines of a country's future wealth.

The combination of renewed confidence in the

market to perform a wide range of functions and a growing appreciation of its endemic limitations as a generator and allocator of human and technological assets and human competences in an uncertain, interdependent and environmentally-conscious global economy, is causing national governments to reappraise their macro-organizational strategies. In a Ricardian or Heckscher–Ohlin world, nations perfectly complement each other in their value-added activities. Each country produces the goods and services that require factor inputs in which it has a comparative advantage and trades these for others which require inputs in which it has a comparative disadvantage. Though the principle of comparative advantage remains valid today, it is nonetheless the case that most of the leading industrialized countries (especially those located in the Triad of North America, Western Europe and Japan) produce and trade similar goods and services.

It is also true that the competitive advantages of these countries are becoming increasingly based on the level and structure of the assets and capabilities they create for themselves rather than on their natural factor endowments. While markets play an important role in the production of such assets and capabilities, they are generally highly imperfect. This, however, is not primarily a result of the presence of structural distortions imposed by the participants in the market, but because of the inability of the market *per se* to cope adequately with such variables as uncertainty, economies of scale and scope, externalities and the production and distribution of public goods.[29] In other words, markets may not be able to 'shape' the production and transactions of products – like technological knowledge, organizational techniques, airports and universities – as successfully as they previously shaped those based on purely natural resources. In such cases, governments, acting as custodians of the citizens under their governance, may be required to step in either to compensate for market impurities or to help create a 'social' market system by which production and transactions are organized in a way which benefits the community as a whole.

Although the above paragraphs may seem a digression from our main theme, they are not. The opening up of national economies to the winds of global competition, and the role which MNEs play both as actors in global markets and as brokers in the allocation of economic activity between Nation States, has meant that host governments are now evaluating inward investment less for the new resources it provides and more for the way in which it can integrate their economies into the global market place and help upgrade the quality of indigenous human and physical capital. At the same time, to promote the right kind of MNE activity, governments have had to reappraise the efficiency of the markets under their jurisdiction and, where necessary, to help create the conditions under which they might work to the social good. Although negotiation and bargaining over the share of the benefits from inward investment may remain as fierce as ever, the primary focus is being directed increasingly towards obtaining the right kind of MNE activity in the first place, and then to ensuring that the activity fulfils its proper role in advancing domestic competitiveness.

To what extent, then, have the policies of governments towards MNE activity changed over the years? The answer is that in some countries, particularly Group 3 and 2 countries, they have changed a great deal. The most dramatic examples include the sweeping changes to the political and economic systems currently occurring in different parts of the world. As Chapter 14 showed, in many developing countries in Latin America, sub-Saharan Africa and Indo-China there has been a distinct realignment of development policies away from an import substitution to either an export-generating or a balanced development strategy.

In Western Europe, North America, and to a lesser extent in East Asia, there has been a parallel thrust towards regional economic integration. Consequently, there has been a removal or reduction in the barriers to the movement of goods, people and assets between the countries in these integrated regions. Throughout the world, the movement towards market-oriented economies has forced a reappraisal of macro-economic control mechanisms, on the one hand, and that of the direct managerial role of the state on the other. In a nutshell, over the past two decades, macro-economic policies have become somewhat less Keynesian and micro-economic strategies less (directly) interventionist in affecting the structure and restructuring of resource allocation.

At the same time, the role of governments in a variety of areas (e.g. health, safety and the environ-

Table 20.1 Classification of countries according to policies likely to be adopted towards MNE activity in the 1990s.

Pattern 1:   **Non-interventionist scenario**

General encouragement to inward direct investment, particularly where it is seen to promote industrial competitiveness. Few performance requirements or controls. Outbound MNE investment increasingly seen as part and parcel of the need to penetrate foreign markets and gain assets to protect or advance the global market position of investing companies. Examples of countries pursuing such policies include most OECD countries and a few Asian developing nations.

Pattern 2:   **Structural adjustment and upgrading scenario**

Deliberate attempt by governments to incorporate both inward and outward direct investment policies into general micro-organizational strategies – particularly as far as the restructuring of economic activity and upgrading of domestic resources and capabilities is concerned. Examples of countries pursuing such policies are Japan, Korea and Taiwan.

Pattern 3:   **A selective investment scenario**

Mostly adopted by developing countries which pursued import-substituting FDI policies in the 1960s and 1970s. Inbound FDI confined to certain sectors; incentives and regulations imposed to ensure that such investment accords with national economic political and cultural goals. Most of economies pursuing Pattern 3 policies, which include the majority of Latin American (except Mexico) and sub-Saharan African countries, still operate a largely managed economy, though in the 1980s their macro-organizational policies have become more (internationally) market oriented.

Pattern 4:   **A controlled investment scenario**

As for Pattern 3 but inbound and outbound investment much more stringently controlled, with many more authorization procedures involved in the setting up of new foreign subsidiaries or the acquisition of existing firms. Usually, Pattern 4 countries still prefer foreign investors to own only a minority direct investment stake in domestic companies. Examples of countries pursuing controlled investment strategies are India, China and some Latin American and African countries. Central and East European countries and parts of Indo-China are now moving out of a Pattern 4 scenario to one between Patterns 2 and 3.

---

ment) has become more interventionist. Increasingly, policies towards education, science and technology, transportation and communications are determining the ability of countries both to attract inward investment and of their own firms to penetrate global markets. It is not so much that the role of government in influencing MNE activity has become less important over the years, but that the *nature* of that influence has undergone a profound change. One expression of this change is the greater emphasis given by governments to general rather than specific instruments of policy in their efforts to obtain the right amount and quality of inward investment. Another is that governments are beginning to think strategically about their economic actions. Governments, like firms, are operating in an oligopolistic environment. Their actions may lead to a reaction by other governments which may negate the intended effects of the first action – or even worsen the original situation.

The continuation of the events just described together with the changes in the world economic scenarios and the evolution of the global strategies of MNEs, would suggest a modification to the grouping of countries described earlier. Table 20.1 suggests four scenarios likely to dominate the 1990s. Pattern 1 might be described as the non-interventionist scenario, which, in spite of much rhetoric about the possible disbenefits of inward investment, still best describes the attitudes and actions of most OECD countries and a few Asian developing countries. Countries conforming to this pattern also tend to implement very simple authorization procedures. A review of national policies undertaken by the OECD member countries (OECD, 1991c) reveals a steady removal of government-imposed obstacles to both outward and inward direct investment over the past decade as well as a relaxation in the performance expectations of foreign affiliates. At the same time, there remain some sharp differences about the *kind* of inward investment that is most welcome by the industrialized countries. These differences are particularly marked as between the smaller and larger, and the more and less developed Member States. There is also a growing divergence of attitudes – particularly on the part of France and Italy – towards inward investment according to its country of origin. Japanese inward investment, for example, is often viewed with more disquiet than is either intra-EC investment or North American investment. Some of the recent changes in attitudes and actions towards inbound MNE activity in a selection of OECD countries is set out in the Appendix to this chapter.

Pattern 2 is followed by those countries which use a mixture of incentives and controls to attract inward direct investment. At the same time, such policies are an integral part of a dynamic macro-organizational development or wealth-creating strategy. We may call this the *structural adjustment and upgrading* scenario. It is best characterized by the attitudes and actions of the Japanese, Taiwanese and Korean governments towards MNE activity, although in the past these governments pursued a much more restrictive policy.[30]

Pattern 3 is a *selective investment* scenario. It is similar to the old Group 2 strategy, except that measures to encourage or restrict inbound direct investment are now more systemically related to macro-economic and organizational policies, which are themselves geared towards promoting dynamic comparative advantage. Most of the more advanced developing countries and some African countries, which have sought to liberalize the investment codes in the 1980s fall in this category;[31] some Central Eastern European countries are moving into it from Pattern 4.

Pattern 4 – the *controlled investment strategy* – remains the dominant pattern of India, The People's Republic of China and several larger Latin American countries who continue to pursue policies of economic self-reliance, welcoming inward MNE activity only in so far as it is perceived to contribute to these goals. It is also the policy implemented by some African, Caribbean and Pacific resource-based countries that wish to protect their critical assets from being controlled by foreign companies whose objectives may not coincide with their own. Although in the case of smaller economies, where FDI plays a dominating role, there is little attempt of Pattern 4

countries to systematically modify their general economic policies, even in these countries, the learning and experience of inbound investment has caused them to make some adjustments – particularly in their employment, manpower, taxation and balance of payments policies.

20.3.4   A note about the administration of policies toward inward direct investment

At the end of the day, the success of government policy towards, or as a consequence of, inward direct investment depends upon the effectiveness of the administrative machinery set up to implement and monitor the policies decided upon. Take first the instruments designed to affect the policies specifically directed towards inbound MNE activity. In the 1970s, few host countries had a centralized coordinating mechanism for screening prospective inward investors or administering new investment projects. This was primarily because the responsibility for macro-organizational policy was shared between several government ministries as, indeed, were decisions over the policy measures intended to achieve this goal.

As several writers, notably Lecraw and Morrison (1991), have pointed out, such an administrative system may have two consequences. The first is that foreign investors receive a variety of conflicting signals as to what is expected of them. The Ministry of Labour, for example, may be primarily interested in attracting the kind of MNE activity which reduces unemployment. However, this goal may not always be consistent with that of the Ministry of Science and Technology to upgrade domestic innovatory capacity, or that of the Ministry of Trade to improve the balance of payments. The Ministry of Regional Development might provide incentives to foreign firms to locate their activities in areas of high unemployment, but unless the Ministry of Transportation provides the necessary roads and the Ministry of Telecommunications the requisite telecommunications facilities, these efforts will be to little avail. While the Ministries of Labour and Regional Development might encourage foreign affiliates to buy their inputs from local sources, the

Ministry of Trade, in its desire to promote exports, might wish to encourage efficiency-seeking production, the domestic content of which is lower. The Ministry of Industry might applaud a merger between a domestic and foreign-owned firm if it improves the competitive position of the new enterprise in world markets. By contrast, to the extent to which it might lead to more industrial concentration, the minister in charge of anti-trust legislation might perceive it to be against the public interest.

While such intra-government conflicts are not confined to inward direct investment, they are particularly well highlighted in this area. Yet, without some sense of a systemic strategy towards MNE activity, it is difficult to evaluate the contribution of these micro-policies to maximizing the benefits of such activity. At best, it seems highly doubtful if such fragmentary policies are cost-effective. At worst, they could reinforce structural distortions as one government department seeks to offset any adverse effects of another government department's actions on its own policies.

The piecemeal administrative approach to FDI leads to a lopsided macro-organizational strategy, the success of which is largely dependent on the negotiating and bargaining strengths of the government ministries involved. This may not matter too much in a large economy which does not engage in much trade with the outside world and in which FDI plays a relatively unimportant role. However, it is a luxury which few countries can afford in their efforts to identify and fashion their competitive advantages in a world increasingly dominated by cross-border transactions. More generally, the inability or unwillingness of governments to properly coordinate their policies towards, or as a consequence of, inward direct investment, is *de facto* a microcosm of their failure to restructure their modes of governance to meet the challenges of the global economy.

In revamping their administrative machinery in the light of their learning experiences, host governments have mostly adopted two strategies. The first is to lodge administrative authority over the nature and form of MNE–host country interaction in one decision-taking unit. Such a structure is designed to reduce the transaction costs of both governments and MNEs in the approval and monitoring of inward investment. This structure is likely to succeed only as long as the objectives of the decision-taking author-

ity are compatible with those of the wider goals of the host country. The danger is that it might take on a life of its own and seek to maximize the amount of inward investment without a proper evaluation of its net benefits. Its success will also depend upon its ability to harmonize and coordinate the widely different interests of the participating government departments.

The second strategy is formally to rationalize authority between the many administrative units of governments, giving each a coherent set of criteria by which the efficacy of FDI may be judged. Such a policy, however, almost invariably results in an increase in the negotiating power of foreign investors and carries with it a danger that the stronger ministries will determine the kinds and conditions of investment made, which may not result in the mix of policies which will optimize the benefits from inward investment.

There is some suggestion that host governments – particularly those which have previously pursued fragmented policies towards inward investment – have begun to coordinate their administrative frameworks. Indeed, the majority of the governments of the leading recipient nations have now set up Ministries of Foreign Investment, or have assigned a specific department, bureau or agency the responsibility for overseeing the administration of inbound MNE activity. Examples include Malaysia, Thailand, Brazil, Indonesia, Kenya and South Korea. At the same time, except in the cases of South Korea, Taiwan, Japan and Singapore, it is unclear, in many of these countries, the extent to which the policy towards inward investment is related to, or reflected in, their general macro-organizational policies.

Earlier in Chapter 6 we examined some of the determinants of MNE activity and suggested that the role of national governments as a factor influencing the location of FDI was probably increasing, rather than decreasing. This view was based on the growing significance of created assets and competences as locational determinants, and the part played by governments in their production and organization. Unfortunately, however, there have been few attempts to test this proposition formally. In his study of the effects of policy changes implemented by some 46 countries towards inbound FDI over the period 1977–87, Contractor (for the UNCTC, 1991e) found that, relative to other possible factors hypothesized, for example the size and growth of the host economy, the overall influence of these changes was generally insignificant. At the same time, it is also a fact that those countries that have pursued the most market oriented policies over the past decade and whose governments have actively sought to upgrade their indigenous physical and human capabilities and to lower the transaction costs of doing business in their countries are those which have attracted the fastest rate of growth of both domestic and foreign investment (World Bank, 1991). Other research, for example by McFetridge (1987) and Kokko (1990), has shown that technology imports by MNE affiliates tend to increase as the level of performance requirements imposed by host governments falls.

20.4   ACTIONS OF HOME GOVERNMENTS TOWARDS OUTWARD DIRECT INVESTMENT

Chapter 2 has shown that, until the mid 1960s, the US and the UK accounted for one-half of the world's outward direct investment stock. At the time, the *relative* economic significance of this investment was even greater in the case of several European countries, notably the UK, the Netherlands and Switzerland.[32] Not until the late 1960s did West Germany begin to be an important outward investor, while Japan's contribution to the world's investment stock only became of real significance in the 1980s.

We have argued elsewhere that the main reasons for the concentration of outward investment in the 1960s were, first, that the O advantages necessary for such investment were strongly concentrated in the hands of US and UK firms, and second that, because of the nature of the advantages and their differences in their cross-border production and transaction costs, these advantages were generally best exploited from a foreign location.

It is nevertheless true that most existing and potential foreign investors outside the US were facing balance of payments difficulties in the 1960s and early 1970s, while a war-ravaged Europe was still short of resources, especially capital and technology to revitalize her industries. Because of this,

home governments were reluctant to encourage outward investment, except where it was perceived to support domestic economic activities or was made to acquire consumer goods and services which could not be produced domestically. Chapters 5 and 14 have shown that very little recognition was given to the possible complementarity between domestic and foreign investment, although in their research into the effects of outward MNE activity from the UK, Reddaway *et al.* (1968) did discover some substantial technical feedback effects in a number of cases.

In spite of their lack of enthusiasm for outward investment, most governments maintained an open or a neutral stance towards it. By 1971, at least 15 countries offered some kind of investment insurance or guarantee scheme. In the same year, virtually all countries permitted foreign tax payments to be credited against domestic tax liabilities and/or deferred taxation on foreign income until it was repatriated. Yet, in the 1960s, all major investing countries were concerned about the possible negative effects of capital exports on their national economies. As Chapter 14 has shown, several of these (the UK, US, Japan, France and Sweden) used controls to try and remedy adverse balance of payments situations. By contrast, Germany and Japan tried to *increase* their foreign direct investment outflows to reduce their balance of payments surpluses (Bergsten *et al.*, 1978).

Only Sweden and Japan had any kind of comprehensive policy towards outbound investment. In 1974, the Swedish government passed a law which authorized the government to block an outflow of capital whenever it was perceived to conflict with the objectives of national economic policy. A key component of the law was that any application to export capital needed to be justified on balance of payments grounds. In addition, it had to include the views of labour unions. In practice, this law was generally ineffective as most Swedish MNEs were able to finance their foreign operations without transferring additional capital out of Sweden.

The Japanese case was (and still is) very different. From the mid-1960s, Japan has adopted a systemic approach to both inward and outward direct investment. At that time it set up a single agency to ensure that outbound MNE activity was consistent with national economic objectives. Initially, the emphasis was directed towards protecting the employment of Japanese workers, increasing the exports of manufactured goods and safeguarding supplies of energy and raw materials for her domestic industries. Subsequently, Japan encouraged the export of labour-intensive and low-productivity industries, such as textiles and clothing, especially to neighbouring developing countries in Asia. It did so both to reduce its foreign exchange reserves – thereby heading off the revaluation of the yen – and to release domestic resources which could be redeployed more productively in higher technology sectors.

Still later in the 1970s, Japanese MNEs began to set up offshore manufacturing subsidiaries in the electronics and other sectors to undertake the labour-intensive parts of producing medium to high technology products. Also in the 1970s, Japanese investors began to make inroads into the high income markets of the US and Europe, initially in response to the rising value of the yen and protectionist measures, but later as part of their globalization strategies and markets.

Unlike other developed countries, Japan has evolved a holistic and integrated strategy towards outward direct investment. Even today such a strategy is inseparable from its more general industrial, trade and technology policies, as well as from its policies towards inward direct investment. Although it is accepted that, in the case of some firms and for at least some period of time, Japanese investment may be *substitutable* for domestic investment, the policy is based on the essential *complementarity* between the two. For, first and foremost, Japanese outward direct investment is designed to promote the long-term competitiveness of the Japanese economy. In so far as it can capture global markets more effectively than by other means, it helps to provide the revenue to finance additional domestic innovatory activity, and to release indigenous resources for more productive uses. Investment in resource-based sectors – especially in developing countries – helps to guarantee the supplies (at the right quality and price) of raw materials and semi-processed goods for Japanese factories. Investment in labour-intensive manufacturing processes and/or products helps the investing company to maintain competitive prices in world markets. At the same time, Japan can claim that she is performing a useful 'tutorial' function to developing countries, by assisting them to more fully utilize and upgrade their own resources.

As far as the governments of other developed nations are concerned, although the criteria for evaluating the costs and benefits of the foreign activities of their MNEs have changed over the years, there is little evidence that they have yet integrated their actions into their broader macro-organizational strategies. However, there are signs that this could happen in the 1990s. The major reason for this is that the globalization of production and markets, particularly within the Triad, is forcing industrialized countries to reinterpret their strategies towards sustaining and advancing the competitiveness of their resources and capabilities. When the contribution of direct capital exports is viewed in this light, it is entirely possible that, far from adopting an adversarial policy, governments may seek to encourage certain types of outward investment, or at least reduce any structural impediments on the ability of firms to engage in such investment.

A review of recent macro-organizational policies pursued by Western governments reveals only a slight change in emphasis which can, in any case, be attributed to the internationalization of business. Rarely in the writings and speeches of politicians are policy statements specifically linked to the global activities of their firms. Since, in the public mind, these activities are still associated with the export of jobs or technology, this is perhaps understandable. Nevertheless, we believe it is misguided as, increasingly, outward and domestic investment are not in competition with each other. The one exception seems to be in the area of anti-trust policy where governments, particularly the US authorities, have taken a more relaxed attitude in the belief that both domestic and cross-border mergers and alliances may sometimes help firms capture the economies of scale or scope demanded by global competition.

As it becomes better understood that the macro-organizational strategies pursued by governments are an important factor affecting the competitiveness of the resources and capabilities over which they have jurisdiction and that outward direct investment has a particular and special contribution to make in this process, it may be that governments will come to adopt a more positive attitude towards their own MNEs.[33] At the very least, governments should not allow their own firms to be penalized by the more favoured strategies of their foreign counterparts. It is to be accepted that some of the policies are structurally distorting and are better removed altogether, either by negotiation at the conference table or by pursuing strategic trade and related policies. In the case of government policies which, by reducing market failure, help their countries to invest overseas, then the best reaction by other governments is to try to reduce the transaction costs facing their own firms.

20.5   CONCLUSIONS

As yet, few governments explicitly attempt to integrate their actions designed to affect the costs and benefits of MNE activity into their general economic policies. Nor, indeed, do they consider inward and outward investment alongside investment by unilateral domestic firms as complementary ways of advancing economic restructuring and growth.

This chapter has first outlined the main reactions of host governments to inward investment. It identified the reasons for cross-country differences in such policies and how they have evolved over the past 30 years. It suggested that, very gradually, as the contribution of the different kinds of inbound MNE activity has become better understood, and a more important feature on the landscape of most economies, that they have had to give equal attention to the appropriateness of their general policies, as well as those specifically addressed to MNEs. This has not only been made necessary by changes in the world economic scenario and the position of host governments in that scenario, but also, in some cases, by the increasing flexibility of MNEs in the siting of their value-added activities.

The chapter also argued that it is the balance between the competitive or O-specific advantages of MNEs (as perceived by the host countries) and the L advantages of countries (as perceived by the MNEs), together with the opportunity costs and negotiating strengths of the two parties, that determine the policy responses of host governments. This balance has changed over the past decade or so. Independently of world economic events, we have argued that it is necessary to take an evolutionary or dynamic approach to understand MNE–host government relationships. In particular, it is important to know how different kinds of outward and inward investment may affect the O-specific advantages of

the investing firms and the ESP configuration of the home and host countries. It is also critical to understand the ways in which national governments, either by design or accident, can affect inbound or outbound MNE activity and the way in which it is organized.

The role of governments in increasing or reducing market failure and their influence on the geographical concentration of related industries is also decisive as it affects both the L advantages of its location-bound resources and capabilities and the O-specific advantages of foreign MNEs. Finally, this chapter, like those before it, has also suggested that these various interactions need to be considered in the light of different developmental and/or economic restructuring strategies of governments, and in the context of some kind of asset-accumulation model.

Policies towards outbound and inbound direct investment have been generally formulated on the presumption that each is substitutable for domestic capital formation – either by MNEs or uninational firms. The growing convergence between the economic structures of the industrialized countries, the rising importance of the role of created assets in fashioning the competitiveness of firms and industries, and the increasing ease with which these assets can traverse national borders, has not only changed the nature and pattern of the global division of labour, but also the contribution of MNEs to that division of labour. Inward investment plays its part by providing new resources and capabilities, and by stimulating the better use of local resources and capabilities. Outward investment plays its part by tapping in to another nation's competitive advantages and by capturing new markets, both of which may help to sustain and upgrade domestic innovatory opportunities.

It is the synergy between international direct investment flows and the competitiveness of countries in the global economy which is beginning to force a reappraisal of the domestic macro-organizational policies of governments.

Finally, we believe that at the end of the day the main impact of MNE activity on governments – and particularly those in the Triad – will be to force them to adopt a systemic and strategically-led set of policies. The generic strategy must surely be to sustain, and, if possible, advance the competitiveness of its firms and location-bound resources in the global market place. But, in itself, this strategy can only be successful if all the components that, between them, determine economic prosperity are integrated and geared to a common objective. This means that fiscal, environmental, education, industrial trade and technology policies must all be strategy driven. And in each of these, directly or indirectly, governments must take account of the policies of their competitors, and how their efforts in affecting trade, migration and the activities of MNEs, they impinge upon the success of their own policies.

At the same time, we would echo a view expressed by Sylvia Ostry (1990) that action taken by national governments to assist their firms to compete in the global economy must not be a new form of protectionism. If this is the case, she warns, it could pose a serious threat to the very gains which the global market is intended to achieve. However, without multilateral guidelines or rules to deter such protectionism or mitigate its effects there is a real danger that the managed trade regimes of the inter-war years could be re-introduced – with even more damaging results – in the 1990s.[34]

Appendix
Changes in policies towards inbound direct investment by OECD countries in the 1980s

The changing attitudes and actions of OECD countries towards inbound MNE activity may be summarized under eight headings.

(1)   There has been a general liberalization of attitudes and policies towards inward direct investment and to the removal of restrictions and obstacles on most kinds of capital imports. Foremost among the liberalizing countries in the late 1980s have been France, Spain and Portugal; Greece is following a similar path in the early 1990s.

(2)   Many OECD countries have replaced fairly detailed and multi-faceted authorization procedures for inward investment by simple notification or verification devices. Authorization procedures are now usually confined to very large transactions and/or acquisitions. In most cases, only one authorizing ministry or agency is involved. The greatest progress towards liberalization has been made by Portugal, Spain and France.

(3)   Many sectorial restrictions have been lifted or greatly reduced. Sectors which used to be wholly denied to foreign investors have now been opened up. However, most EC countries still limit and/or regulate conditions

for non-EC foreign investment in the finance and insurance sectors (see 5 below), basic telecommunications services (Spain), broadcasting (Spain, the UK and France), publishing (France), nuclear power and oil-related activities (France), airlines (Spain, Italy, the UK, Ireland and Luxembourg), maritime transport – particularly the registration of ships and the access of foreign-owned vessels to cabotage – (most EC countries), fishing (Italy, Ireland, Denmark and France) and armaments manufacturers (Denmark, Spain, France and the Netherlands).

(4)   The reduction or elimination of all exchange controls on inward investment. Here the most radical reforms have occurred in France, Spain, Portugal and Greece. There is now a virtually free international capital market in the EC, although there are still some restrictions imposed on non-EC investment by France, Portugal and Greece.

(5)   Restrictions on the local financing of capital expenditure by non-residents have also been markedly reduced. Those that remain mainly relate to some general provisions on the access by non-residents to local capital markets, currently imposed by Italy, Portugal and Spain.

(6)   Provisions maintained by member countries on national security and public order grounds, however, remain extensive. Some have even been strengthened, especially in the strategic economic and 'cutting edge' technology sectors.

(7)   Rather less progress has been made on the liberalization of FDI in services. Reciprocity conditions, linking the recipient country's treatment of a foreign investor to that granted to the recipient country MNEs in the investor's country of origin, are still frequently imposed – particularly on US and Japanese MNEs. For example, in the banking sector, reciprocity conditions are being applied by Belgium, Germany and the UK; in the insurance sector, by Luxembourg and Portugal; and in other financial services, by Denmark and Portugal.

(8)   In spite of the liberalization of attitudes and policies towards inbound MNE activity, many countries, including those which otherwise adopt a most welcoming stance, still encourage, or even insist, that foreign investors should accept certain performance requirements. Often, adherence to these requirements is the price extracted by host governments for tax concessions and other incentives. To this extent – unwisely, in the views of some economists – EC countries have taken a leaf out of the books of developing countries by intervening in the normal market process. The two encouragements or requirements most widely imposed

– even by the most liberal minded governments, such as the UK – are, first, that over a certain period of time a given proportion of the value of a product sold by a foreign subsidiary in an EC country will actually be produced in the EC (the local content requirement); and second (and this is linked to the first), that an investing firm will, in due course, undertake at least some of its higher value added activities in its foreign subsidiary. Both these provisions are particularly directed to Japanese investors. The particular concern is lest Europe should simply become a low value added base servicing the higher value added activities of Japanese firms in their home country.

NOTES

1 This chapter should be read jointly with the policy-related sections of earlier chapters, especially Chapters 11 to 18.

2 That is, assuming that it has the will and the appropriate administrative competence and institutional machinery to do this!

3 Their expectations from particular foreign affiliates might vary depending upon the motives for the investment and the extent to which these affiliates are part of a globally-integrated network of activities.

4 But see, however, our analysis of taxation issues in Chapter 18. Vernon (1991) has also raised some possible tax-related conflicts that might arise between MNEs and the governments of the countries in which they operate.

5 For a rather similar analysis, but one which provides an excellent insight into four case studies of MNE–host country bargaining relations (*viz* IBM in Mexico, Toyota and Nissan in the US, SAS/Iberia in Argentina and Disney in France) see Grosse (1991). In particular, Grosse identifies the relative resources and stakes of the bargaining parties and the extent to which their interests are similar to each other as the key variable likely to determine the outcome of any bargaining relationship. For an earlier analysis of the comparative bargaining resources of host governments in Latin America, see Grosse and Aramburu (1990). On the basis of some field work in Venezuela, and the response to a mailshot by 55 of 165 large US industrial firms with investments in at least two of Latin America's largest countries, the authors found that firms with greater export activities, large scale operations, and more interests with the countries in question tended to enjoy superior bargaining outcomes than those who did not possess these attributes. Similarly, governments were likely to be in a more favourable

negotiating position in dealing with resource seeking MNEs, when the domestic market is large, and where there is strong competition between the prospective foreign investors (ibid., p. 233). For a recent application of resource dependency theory to the MNE–host government bargaining relationship, see Birkinshaw (1992). See also Behrman and Grosse (1990).

6 See pp. 566–8.

7 See Chapter 19 for some examples.

8 See Chapters 10, 14 and 18.

9 This, indeed, is a major motive for FDI in R&D marketing ventures, and also for the acquisition of foreign assets described in Chapter 3.

10 Which essentially concerns the application of the S to the E.

11 The following paragraphs draw substantially on Chapter 1 of Dunning (1988b).

12 During the years 1980 to 1985, almost two-thirds of the expropriation acts against foreign firms occurred in the period 1970 and 1976. In 1975 there was a peak of 83 expropriation acts in 28 countries.

13 See Chapter 21.

14 For further details, see Chapter 22.

15 Compare, for example, the international economic position of the US in the 1960s when it was the world's largest net outward direct investor with that of the US in the early 1990s when it is a substantial net inward direct investor.

16 For example, with few exceptions, the Indian Government will allow only a 40% participation by foreign owned firms in any particular sector.

17 For example, one survey (Brech and Sharp, 1984) estimated that in the 1980s the value of discretionary assistance given by the UK Government to seven Japanese companies setting up greenfield investments in the UK electronics industry totalled 27% to 29% of the total capital investment in the UK by these companies.

18 These, along with investment incentives and various corporate-related measures which affect trade are now referred to as TRIMS (Trade-related investment measures). For an analysis of the rationale of TRIMS and their effects on patterns of MNE behaviour, see UNCTC (1991c).

19 An example would be for the parent company to buy component parts for its affiliate(s) at discount prices, but not pass on the savings to the affiliate(s).

20 Thus, where TRIMS encourage the learning process of local firms in the cost efficient way, they may be acceptable; where, however, they protect inefficient indigenous producers, they may do more harm than good.

21 Described as O advantages in Chapter 5.

22 See also Chapter 6 of this monograph.

23 More specifically, evidence on the deterrent effect of taxation on FDI is mixed. Grubert and Mutti (1989), for example, calculated that if a host government were to halve its tax rate from 20% to 10% the stock of outward FDI would rise by 65%. Similarly, Shah and Slemrod (1991) found that US direct investment in Mexico showed 'a great deal of sensitivity to the Mexican regime'. Snoy (1985), in an examination of the location of US direct investment flows in Europe in the period 1966–69, concluded that any attempt to equalize corporate tax rates would bring about 'substantial changes' in the existing pattern. By contrast, some recent research by Wheeler and Mody (1983) suggests that in the 1980s differential tax rates had little effect on the location of outbound US investment.

24 For example, more than 40 states have some kind of office in Tokyo with the specific task of attracting Japanese investment to their states within the US.

25 Some of these are reviewed in Lim (1983), Guisinger (1985), and O'Sullivan (1985).

26 Hence, the strategic initiative talks between the US and Japan in 1989 and 1990, which were geared towards removing trade and investment barriers between the two countries.

27 Viz. the US, UK, Japan, France, Italy, Germany and Canada.

28 Especially in the field of information and biotechnology. For an appraisal of these developments and how they have affected MNE activity, see Van Tulden and Junne (1988).

29 As discussed in Chapter 5. For an assessment of the role of governments in shaping the competitive or comparative advantage of Nation States, see Lipsey and Dobson (1987).

30 According to Encarnation and Mason (1990), hostile

government rather than 'benign neglect' best explains the low level of foreign investment in Japan. Moreover, in spite of capital liberalization, the reluctance of large and powerful Japanese firms to do anything to open up the domestic market to foreign competition has stymied the attempts to foreign MNEs to gain a major foothold in most industrial sectors in Japan.

31 Some details are set out in UNCTC (1991e). The liberalization of measures towards inward direct investment include the relaxation of restrictions on access to sectors and industries (e.g. Nigeria, Guinea, Central African Republic), the relaxation of equity limitations (e.g. Nigeria and Ethiopia), the relaxation of regimes for repatriation of profits and capital (e.g. Ethiopia, Cote d'Ivoire, Nigeria, Guinea) and liberal incentive regimes (e.g. Guinea, Zaire, Zimbabwe).

32 See Chapter 2, Table 2.2.

33 Governments, like firms, behave as strategic oligopolists in the construction of their macro-organizational policies, which may affect the long-run competitiveness of their firms. Thus, if the Japanese Government should interfere with market forces to advance the competitiveness of (say) their auto industry which adversely affects that of the US auto industry, the US Government may wish to take 'strategic' action to counteract this action. It is, however, worth observing that the macro-organizational strategies of governments may enhance, as well as distort, the efficiency of the market mechanism. For a recent critical analysis of strategic trade policy, which is now spreading into the area of international direct investment policy, see Stegemann (1989). For a consideration of the interaction between national strategic policies, and regional or international regulatory (or consultative) organizations, see Chapter 21.

34 This point is taken up further in Chapter 21.

CHAPTER 21

GOVERNMENTS AND MNE ACTIVITY: THE SUPRA-NATIONAL OR MULTI-LATERAL RESPONSE

21.1 INTRODUCTION

The previous chapter considered some of the ways in which national governments might seek to influence, or respond to, MNE-related activity. However, there are reasons to suppose that, by itself, unilateral action may not always be fully effective or produce an optimal outcome for particular home or host countries. Each of these is linked to the perceived incapacity of individual governments to combat different kinds of structural or endemic market failure arising from, or associated with, the activities of MNEs. To overcome this incapacity, some kind of collaborative action by countries may be necessary. The rationale, form and appropriability of such action is the subject matter of this chapter.

There are three main reasons why national governments might require supra-national assistance in their dealings with MNEs. The first arises from the former's perceived weak bargaining positions *vis à vis* the latter as demonstrated by their incapacity to extract the desired share of any value added they create, or to effectively influence their patterns of behaviour. One way to redress the bargaining balance is for a group of countries to pursue collective and/or harmonized policies towards MNEs. Another may be to try to get agreement on some kind of multinational guidelines for the conduct of MNEs and their affiliates.

The second reason for multi-lateral action is where, because of market failure, the L-specific advantages of potential host countries are insufficient to attract the investments they need, or where structural market distortions in the home country

impede outward investment. Here cross-country efforts to reduce the disincentives to MNE activity may be justified.

Thirdly, the policies of national governments may be ineffective because they are counteracted by those of other countries. This is the case where the strategies of host (or home) governments towards FDI may conflict with the perceived best interests of the home (or host) country. For example, it is possible that a limitation on the remission of dividends imposed by a host country may conflict with the balance of payments interests of the investing country. The government of the country adversely affected can sometimes neutralize the other country's actions. However, only bilateral or multi-lateral cooperation can resolve the conflict. 'Beggar my neighbour' investment policies by governments towards MNEs may also be suboptimal in global welfare terms.

The following sections deal with these three issues – each of which needs to be reappraised in the light of the globalization of economic activity – in turn.

21.2 MULTINATIONAL ACTIONS TO ASSIST THE BARGAINING POWER OF HOST COUNTRIES

There are two reasons why countries might find themselves in a disadvantaged position in negotiating with MNEs. The first is that, as other chapters in this book have shown, host countries often compete with each other for the value-added activities both of foreign firms and of their own MNEs. Moreover, they often do so in highly imperfect market conditions. Indeed, they may sometimes exacerbate these conditions by their taxation or tariff policies. Only a collaborative effort to reduce these cross-border market distortions, or setting rules or guidelines of behaviour to avoid wasteful inter-country rivalry, can overcome these deficiencies. Thus, the European Commission has laid down certain limits on the amount and kind of fiscal incentives which may be offered by Member States to foreign investors.

Second, for reasons discussed in the previous chapter, some host countries may be at a disadvantage in bargaining with MNEs even where there is no competition for their resources and capabilities from other countries. In extreme cases, MNEs may be able not only to extract the entire economic rent arising from their activities, but also to use their leverage to engage in organizational and operational practices which, under other conditions, would be unacceptable. This lack of government bargaining power may be a result of ignorance, lack of experience or inappropriate policies. Alternatively, it may reflect the monopolistic control exerted by MNEs over the resources and capabilities they provide, or the markets which they serve.

In such cases, supra-national action may take four main forms. We shall briefly discuss each in turn.

(a) Collective action by countries

The first is for countries to group together to strengthen their bargaining position against MNEs and to formulate unified policies towards their activities. This, indeed, was one of the purposes of several of the regional integration schemes involving developing countries, as described in Chapter 17. These schemes not only lessen the possibility of MNEs playing the government of one country off against that of another, but also if a MNE tries to use its monopoly position in one country, it may find this adversely affects its profitability in another.

How far these common actions are successful depends on the extent to which a unified policy is likely to produce more beneficial results to the participants than 'going it alone'. This, in turn, rests on the form of the agreement between the member

countries and its distributional consequences *vis à vis* the terms and conditions which countries could have negotiated individually with the MNEs.[1] Moreover, it may be easier to obtain a collective agreement on some matters than others, and impossible to harmonize all at the same time.

For example, all countries in the EC have agreed to abide by the same local content standards for non-EC owned companies producing in the EC. There is also a common policy towards competition and restrictive practices, as well as some degree of harmonization about regional grants and incentives. However, there is little consensus on matters of corporate taxation. Nor is there much, for that matter, on exchange rate alignment, wages, hours of work, telecommunications policy, purchasing standards, government subsidization of R&D, social policy and a host of other factors no less significant in attracting inward investment.[2] Indeed, it may well be that, as and when one avenue of competition closes, another opens. The real question is whether the inter-country rivalry that exists is an expression of market-facilitating forces or an outcome of the distortion of such forces.

As Chapter 17 has indicated, history has shown that the experience of regional integration schemes in tilting the benefits of MNE investment towards particular countries is a mixed one. Often it would appear that the larger and more powerful members of an association have gained at the expense of the smaller members. As an example, in 1970 this led to a breakaway of the Andean group of countries from the Latin American Free Trade Area in which Brazil, Mexico and Argentina were perceived to be the main beneficiaries of MNE activity.

(b) Assisting national governments to re-evaluate their domestic policies

The second way to assist nations in their policies towards MNEs is by the education and training of government policy makers in not only economic management and administration, but also, more specifically, in the appropriate macro-economic and organizational policies to adopt towards, and in the light of, MNE activity. This latter task is one of the major tasks of the UN Centre on Transnational Corporations (UNCTC).[3] The UNCTC was set up in 1974 with the task of providing information about, and undertaking research on, MNEs (or transnational corporations, as the Centre prefers to call them), and of evaluating both the consequences of MNE activity and how host governments might maximize the net benefits arising from it.

Advice and guidance is provided in two main ways. The first is in the form of cross-country workshops on specific MNE-related issues (transfer pricing, the transfer of technology, negotiating hotel contracts, restrictive business practices, the economics of export processing zones, investment incentives, the managing of joint ventures, environmental standards and so on) in which experts and participants share knowledge and experience about the consequences of inward (or outward) direct investment and the policies adopted towards it. The second is by individual consultants, or teams of consultants, visiting a particular country to help the appropriate authorities identify and deal with specific matters of concern to the government of that country. Examples might be the preparation of foreign investment laws and regulations, the construction of a code of practice for technology transfer, the restructuring of taxation policy in the light of MNE activity, and administrative procedures in negotiating with inward investors.

Over the past 18 years, the Centre has arranged several hundred cross-country workshops or seminars and has sent advisory teams to a very large number of developing countries. A similar informational, educational and advisory function is provided by other branches of the UN (e.g. UNCTAD, UNIDO and ILO), the World Bank and a variety of development agencies and educational institutions. Multi-lateral action of this kind (provided the information is correct and the advice is sound!) can be of considerable help to host countries, in obtaining foreign resources and capabilities on satisfactory terms, in using these resources and capabilities wisely and, where appropriate, in refashioning their macro-economic and organizational policies. Parenthetically, it is worth observing that over the past two decades, the emphasis of the advisory work of the UNCTC (which, incidentally, tends to be initiated by countries rather than by the UNCTC itself) has shifted from being mainly concerned with ways and means of improving the bargaining position of host governments of developing countries *vis à vis* MNEs, to helping them devise

suitable economic strategies to maximize the benefits of *both* inbound and outbound FDI. A critical evaluation of the work of the UNCTC and the relationship between the UN and the international business community is contained in Dell (1990).

(c)   Codes and guidelines

The third way in which multi-lateral action can aid (or even replace) unilateral action is by the introduction of internationally acceptable codes of conduct or guidelines of behaviour. These codes or guidelines might be addressed either to MNEs or to the home and/or host governments. In both cases they are likely to be drawn up by the governments of individual countries (at least 48 developing countries have introduced foreign investment codes over the past decade), a regional (e.g. OECD, Andean Pact) or an international (UNCTC, UNCTAD) agency or commission. Guidelines directed specifically to MNEs have also been compiled by Chambers of Commerce, Trade Associations and individual MNEs. Neither codes nor guidelines normally have the force of law, but an acceptance of them does imply the willingness of both corporations and governments to abide by their provisions, except in the cases where they are perceived to operate against their own economic or political interests.

Codes may be general or specific. While the UNCTAD code addresses itself mainly to issues surrounding the transfer of technology, and the WHO code to health-related matters, the OECD guidelines are more comprehensive. They embrace, for example, such issues as ownership, transfer of technology, the disclosure of information, employment and training, labour standards, taxation, competition and the environment. The underlying principle of the guidelines is to inform MNEs about matters which are likely to be sensitive to host countries and to encourage them to behave in a way which is in keeping with the national well-being of the economies in which they operate. Though adherence to the OECD guidelines is not binding on the part of MNEs, the constituent member states have the right to publicize the names of flagrant or persistent offenders, and they have not hesitated to do so. In the first six years after the guidelines were published, at least 20 MNEs, such as Badger, Hertz, Black and Decker, Philips and Massey Ferguson, were all referred to the OECD as having broken the spirit or the letter of one or other of the guidelines. Most of the complaints were brought by trade unions concerning such matters as employee protection and trade union rights (Robinson, 1983).[4]

The OECD guidelines are also addressed to governments in their dealings with MNEs. In particular, they stress the need for governments to treat domestic and foreign firms in an equal and equitable manner, and to abide by their contractual obligations and international commitments. The guidelines also encourage the establishment of international machinery for the settlement of disputes.

The most ambitious code – and one which is having a long and protracted birth – is that being prepared by the UNCTC. A draft of its proposed contents (as of June 1992) is set out in an Appendix to this chapter. It is similar to, yet more far reaching than, the OECD guidelines. It is intended that at least its major provisions should become legally binding on the countries which are signatories to the code. Unlike the OECD guidelines, but rather like the Tripartite Agreement of the ILO, which it is intended to complement, the UNCTC code has been drafted with the particular interests of developing countries in mind. The reason why the code is taking so long to work out is because there are so many divergent views about both the costs and benefits of MNE activity and the precise wording of the provisions of the code. Indeed, in many respects, the rationale for such a code has largely disappeared. The international economy of the 1990s is a very different phenomenon from that of the 1970s when negotiations on the code first started. Not only have several countries adopted quite sophisticated laws, regulations and administrative procedures to ensure that inbound direct investment works to their best interests, but the perceived costs and benefits of such investment – not to mention national policies – have changed to such an extent that many governments now countenance certain patterns of MNE behaviour which, at one time, they would not have been prepared to tolerate. In other words, neither the expectations of host countries of FDI nor the internationalizing strategies of MNEs in the early 1990s are those of the 1960s and 1970s. Because of this, some of the underlying assumptions of the UNCTC code need to be rethought and some of its

contents redrafted to take account of the refashioning of international economic relations (UNCTC, 1990a).

In any event, allowing for the diverse economic and cultural characteristics of countries as well as their different needs and expectations of inward investment, it is questionable whether any general code of conduct for MNEs – much less for particular host countries – can be meaningfully implemented. Do not the provisions of codes have to be couched in such general terms that they become platitudinous and, because of this, extremely difficult to enforce? While there is some truth in this suggestion, it is worth observing that many MNEs and some countries have prepared their own guidelines for inward investors, and that there is a great deal of common ground between them.

Moreover, when interpreted as guidelines to normal practice, such codes can provide useful information, particularly to first-time foreign investors and small or medium-size MNEs. Even if the behaviour of most large established MNEs is entirely consistent with the proposed UNCTC code, it is possible that they (or, more correctly, their line managers) may be tempted to ignore some of its provisions whenever and wherever these are perceived to work against the best interests of the company (or that of a particular department). At the same time, the protracted negotiations over the code in which business representatives and governments have been involved, have yielded valuable (albeit often expensive!) insights into what each party expects from a foreign investment. As with any joint venture, success will critically depend on an identity (or near identity) of goals and ideologies as well as on the mutual forbearance and trust of the partners. The pity is that it is rarely the individuals who have been involved in the construction of the codes or guidelines who will be responsible for the negotiations concerning specific foreign investment projects.

(d)   A new international governance structure?

The fourth avenue of multi-lateral action is to devise an appropriate machinery of international governance to set the ground rules for the cross-border activities of MNEs and to monitor the responses of national authorities to these rules. This is exactly what GATT has done so successfully over the past four decades – at least until recently when trade and FDI issues have become inextricably linked with one another. However, the kinds of market failure – and especially the suboptimal policies of governments – that GATT was set up to eliminate or counteract are very different from those associated with international production. The imposition of TRIMS (trade-related investment measures) and TRIPS (trade-related intellectual property policies) by many countries is a case in point. To ensure a level playing field in the modern global economy, it follows that either existing international regimes will need to be modified – which is what the current round of negotiations is partly about – or new forms of governance structures should be set up. We shall return to this issue later in the chapter.

21.3   COLLECTIVE INVESTMENT SUPPORTING OR MARKET FACILITATING SCHEMES

The previous sections have identified some kinds of supra-national action which may be necessary to supplement – and in some cases, supplant – unilateral action towards, or in the light of, MNE activity.

In some instances, however, the problem facing national governments is not one of ensuring that MNE activity is supportive of their economic and social goals, but of getting the right kind of FDI in the first place. In what circumstances is it appropriate for some extra-national support to be provided for this purpose? The answer essentially depends on the reasons for a country's lack of drawing power, and, more particularly, the extent to which these arise from market imperfections and which may be overcome by some form of collaborative action.

Let us give two examples. In the case of the poorer developing countries, the main obstacles to attracting MNE activity are their inadequate domestic markets and/or supply capabilities. Of these latter, the lack of a suitably trained labour force and an inadequate transport and communications infrastructure are the most pressing constraints. In these instances, inter-government aid or multi-lateral loans from international agencies (e.g. the World Bank, European Development Bank, Asian Development Bank) are the most likely (and most useful) form of

multi-lateral support. In the past, MNEs have helped supply these resources (see Chapter 5). Even today, consortia of foreign investors or private banks act as a useful catalyst for development.

When the deficiencies just described are compounded by inappropriate administrative mechanisms and outdated institutions, it is even more difficult for individual countries to rid themselves of a vicious circle of economic inefficiency and political lethargy. A particularly good example of this kind of market failure is now being demonstrated in Central and Eastern Europe. The transition from a collectivist to a market-oriented economy is likely to involve costs which are far too great for commercial corporations, either singly or collectively, to bear. This is because the root problem is a systemic one. It is then entirely appropriate that the cost of setting up a new method of organizing the allocation of resources should be a supra-national or multi-lateral responsibility. In case one might be tempted to extend this reasoning to other parts of the world, let it be said immediately that the ratio between the social costs and benefits of removing or reducing systemic market failure varies considerably between countries and regions, as does the willingness of countries to embrace the disciplines and social consequences of a market system.

But suppose, as a second example, that MNE activity is being restricted by the presence of unacceptable non-commercial economic risks. Where these risks cannot be insured – and even some commercial risks (e.g. aircraft insurance) are so large they usually involve a consortia of insurance companies from several countries – multi-lateral investment insurance or trade credit guarantee schemes such as that offered by the World Bank or Multilateral Investment Guarantee Agencies (MIGA) might be an entirely legitimate instrument for reducing this disincentive to FDI. Similarly, some very large infrastructure capital projects are being wholly or partially funded by multi-lateral agencies, or a consortia of commercial or merchant banks. The Inter-American Development Bank is in the process of launching two schemes which are specifically designed to reduce obstacles to domestic and foreign investment, foster open investment and regimes, and provide grants and loan financing to Latin American countries. In Europe, a European Community Investment Partners (ECIP) programme is similarly offering financial support to enable participating developing countries to realize the potential of FDI in their development strategies. There are also a host of bilateral investment schemes or treaties which could be extended to facilitate FDI, particularly to the poorer developing countries.

Clearly, the extent and form of bilateral or multi-lateral action to counteract domestic or international market failure will depend upon the extent and composition of that failure, the costs and benefits of overcoming it, and the distribution of its costs and benefits among the countries affected by it. The setting up of a new futures market on the Singapore stock exchange is one thing; the introduction of a completely new social accounting system in Albania or the erstwhile Soviet Union is altogether another. Moreover, it is sometimes difficult to disentangle political and strategic from purely economic motives in giving supra-national advice and assistance on the organization of market oriented policies. Finally, a complete removal of market failure may only be possible if a country is prepared to surrender part of its national sovereignty, which it might not be prepared to do. Much depends on the tradeoffs involved. Even an industrialized country like the UK found that when it sought a loan from the IMF in 1976, this was only forthcoming on condition that certain changes were made to the macro-economic management of the British economy.

21.4   THE CASE OF EXTRA-TERRITORIALITY: HOW MIGHT HOME/HOST DIFFERENCES BE RECONCILED?

21.4.1   Introduction

We now turn to consider a group of problems which stem from the presence of a MNE or its affiliates in particular host countries, which cannot easily be resolved by negotiation between the MNE and the host country government. *Inter alia* these arise because the MNE is behaving in a way that is expected of it by its home government. If this is not perceived to be in the interests of the host government, only the acceptance by one government of the other's rights, or a bilateral agreement between the two governments, can resolve the issue.

Chapter 5 has described how much of the direct investment by European (especially British, French, Dutch and Belgian) MNEs in the 19th century was in their overseas colonies and was intended primarily to service the economic needs of the mother countries. UK-owned companies in India and much of Africa, French and Belgian companies in Africa, Dutch companies in South East Asia and Japanese companies in China served as arms of the economic policies of their mother countries. *De facto* (and, on occasions, *de jure*), they provided a transmission belt for the export of the laws, institutions, economic systems and political ideologies of the home countries to the countries in which they established outposts.

In his various writings Raymond Vernon has referred to the twin personality of the foreign affiliate of a MNE. On the one hand, he points out, it is subject to the laws of the country within which it operates; on the other, it has to abide by the decisions of its parent company, which is required to comply with the laws of the country in which it resides. Over the years, this dichotomy has led to considerable conflict between investing and recipient countries. This reached an extreme form in 1906 when American marines were despatched to guard US sugar plantations threatened with burning by the local population. A year later, when Honduras and Nicaragua were at war, the US Navy sent a war ship to protect American properties along the coast of Honduras. And in 1910, US forces landed at Bluefield in Nicaragua to protect the interests of US nationals and MNEs located on or around the Escondido River. These and other instances of this particular form of political extra-territoriality are cited by Wilkins (1970).

Nearly a century later, though extra-territoriality is less of an issue, it does lead to inter-government disputes from time to time. Let us give some examples of two kinds of extra-territoriality provisions. The first relates to the restriction of exports from the foreign affiliates of MNEs and the second to the cross-border extension of domestic anti-trust legislation. For a general examination of the US government's influence over the foreign operations of its own MNEs the reader is invited to consult Vernon (1985); the author concludes that between

1945 and the mid 1980s any such influence was exerted with 'a very light hand, almost to the point of invisibility' (p. 8).

21.4.2   Export embargos

A well publicized attempt by a home government seeking to restrict the exports of a foreign subsidiary of one of its MNEs was that made by the Reagan Administration in 1982. It concerned the export of compressors by the French subsidiary of the US Dresser Corporation to the Soviet Union where they were to be used in the construction of natural gas pipelines in Siberia. The US Government perceived such exports to be against its strategic interests and ordered the Dresser Corporation to cease trading with the Soviet Union. This action offended the French government,[5] which promptly ordered the US subsidiary to ignore the instructions of its parent company. After taking legal advice, the subsidiary decided to comply with French law and accepted the consequences of violating US policy. Earlier in 1974, the sale of locomotives by a Canadian subsidiary of another US MNE – Studebaker-Worthington – to Cuba took place despite US Treasury objections.

According to Keohane and Van Doorn Ooms (1975), the fact that the number of major inter-governmental conflicts arising from the extra-territorial application of US law by US MNEs has been so small is itself a vindication of US policy. The main vehicle of the extra-territorial provisions is the Trading with the Enemy Act, first enacted during the First World War. By the use of this Act, the US has, in the past, been able to dissuade its foreign subsidiaries from trading with China and Cuba. Certainly, it would seem that until the mid 1970s, the great majority of US companies complied with the sanctions voluntarily. The protests lodged by host governments were generally weak and did not confront the sovereignty issue directly.

One notable exception was an eyeball-to-eyeball altercation between the US and France in 1967. This concerned an agreement made by Fruehauf-France, a US subsidiary which was two-thirds owned by the American Freuhauf Company, to sell trailers to another French company – Berliet – for incorpora-tion into trucks which Berliet intended to sell to Communist China. The US Treasury Department directed the American parent to instruct its sub-sidiary to suspend the execution of the contract. This was done, but Berliet insisted on its contractual rights and threatened suit. The French directors of the subsidiary then acted independently. They sued the American directors and Fruehauf (US), alleging that substantial losses would be incurred if the US directive was implemented. The French court then appointed an administrator for Berliet so that it could meet its Chinese commitments. The French government also sent a warning to the US govern-ment that if it attempted to apply the Trading with the Enemy Act Regulations, it would 'cause a permanent threat to hand over the subsidiaries of American companies, in conflict with the sovereignty of the state in which the subsidiaries are located' Kobrin (1989). Faced with this situation, the US Treasury backed down and accepted defeat.

By the 1970s, the economic hegemony of the US had considerably waned and host governments were less inclined to acquiesce to the demands of American law and policy. In 1974, for example, when the US Treasury and State Department objected to the sales of auto products to Cuba by the Argentinean plants of the three major US auto producers, the host Government not only refused to discuss the matter but also threatened to impound the vehicles destined for Cuba, and, if necessary, to nationalize the subsidiaries. In the end, not only were the licences granted, but also Secretary Henry Kissinger acknowledged the inevitable conflict posed by US law. A year later, after yet another case involving the export of office furniture by the Canadian subsidiary of Litton Industries to Cuba, restrictions on the exports of subsidiaries located in countries which favoured trade with Cuba was lifted.

Kobrin (1989) has persuasively argued that although there may be many cases where the behaviour of the subsidiaries of an MNE may conflict with the interests of the home countries, the power of the latter to do anything about it largely depends on the strength of their economic, political and strategic (and sometimes military) capabilities, rela-tive not only to those of the host country, but also to the rest of the world. It also rests on the extent to which investing firms take an ethnocentric attitude to their foreign operations (see Chapter 8). Kobrin suggests that the decline in the economic and political hegemony of the US and the more geocentric approach to overseas production by the major US investors over the past two decades have encouraged host countries to resist any interference in their domestic affairs by the US government. Gilpin (1975, 1987) endorses this view, and argues that the falling US share of the world's stock of FDI (see Chapter 2) is itself a contributory factor to the inability or reluctance of the US authorities to enforce any extra-territorial policies or regulations.[6]

Over a longer time horizon, there is much to suggest that the erosion of Pax Britannica in the 19th and early 20th century coincided with a reduced involvement of the UK Government in the foreign affairs of its own MNEs. Various commentators, such as Bergsten *et al.* (1978), have argued that post World War II changes in the world economic scenario and the increasing degree of multinationality of many firms have combined to strengthen the resolve of host governments not to bow to pressures from home governments. More recently, the growing detente between Eastern Europe and the US as well as the increasing acceptance that to stay competitive in world markets, firms need both to export and to produce abroad, suggests that foreign subsidiaries are less likely to behave against the interests of home countries than once they were.

21.4.3 Extra-territoriality and anti-trust policy

We turn next to consider the attitude of foreign governments (particularly the US Government) towards the extra-territorial application of domestic anti-trust legislation. In the 1950s, such legislation was held responsible for destroying some existing US investments in the UK and inhibiting new investment (American Chamber of Commerce in London, 1955).

Gladwin and Walter (1980) identify three kinds of extra-territorial application of US anti-trust law.[7] The first is where there is a perceived intra-firm conspiracy to restrict competition between an American parent company and its foreign affiliate or, indeed, between its foreign affiliates. A case in point is the prosecution and subsequent conviction of the US Timken Roller Bearing in 1951 for its agreement not to compete with its English and French affiliates, and for its actions to prevent these subsidiaries from

competing in the Western Hemisphere. Second, a US court may order a US corporation to divest its interests in a foreign company should it believe that this reduces competition in the US market. For example, in 1950, US courts ordered Alcoa to dispose of its interests in the Canadian subsidiary Alcan, DuPont and, a year later, forced the divestment of DuPont in Canadian Industries as an Anglo-American venture. In both cases, this action was strongly resisted by the Canadian government.

Third, American companies may be forbidden to acquire companies in particular host countries. This application of anti-trust legislation has probably had the most far reaching consequences of all the extra-territorial measures imposed by the US. Its provisions have been used to block a potential, as well as an actual, erosion of competition. The classic case here was the ruling by US courts against the proposed acquisition by the Gillette Corporation of Braun AG in Germany in 1968, on the grounds that it would considerably reduce the contestability of the market for electric razors in the US.

The practice of extra-territorial anti-trust legislation is not limited to the US and does not only apply to the foreign subsidiaries of MNEs. Contracts concluded in cross-border collaborative agreements are subject to the same authority. However, over the past decade or so, there have been few cases of infringement of anti-trust legislation involving the three kinds of action brought to the US courts. This is notwithstanding the fact that the number of cross-border acquisitions, mergers and strategic alliances have mushroomed. Between 1987 and 1990, for example, the value of acquisitions of European firms by US corporations was greater than for the whole of the preceding fifteen years (Walter, 1992). In the US, too, several mergers and acquisitions have been allowed, which a decade earlier would certainly not have been permitted by the US courts.

All this suggests a changing attitude of governments to anti-trust legislation. This monograph has frequently stressed that to be competitive in a global marketplace, firms in R&D and information-intensive sectors either have to be very large to benefit from the economies of scale or scope, or need to conclude alliances with other companies (including their competitors) to lessen their resource commitments and gain access to new supply capabilities and/or markets. In many cases, however, this leads to more (domestic) industrial concentration.[8] The fact that this is not opposed by national authorities is explained partly by the generally increased exposure of domestic firms to foreign competition (particularly within free trade areas) and partly by the belief (which is not always correct) that size and global competitiveness go hand in hand, and that smaller firms need to merge or collaborate with each other to compete with their larger rivals. US attitudes have also been influenced by the more liberal treatment of the European Commission to industrial concentration and cartelization.

The other reason for the fewer prosecutions of firms for violation of extra-territorial anti-trust provisions by the US government has been the reduction in the power of the American authorities to enforce this legislation. There is a direct parallel with the emasculation of the Trading with the Enemy Act and similar legislation. Moreover, over the years, especially in the past decade, the US has had few important 'enemies'! Indeed, it is now encouraging trade with, and investment in, some of the very countries on which earlier it had placed export embargoes.

Other issues involving MNEs may also cause some friction between home and host nations. Many of them do not involve the issue of extra-territoriality as such, but arise because of the different laws, regulations and policies of countries, which MNEs can sometimes counteract or exploit, and in so doing, affect the cross-border distribution of costs and benefits. Perhaps the most obvious are taxation and transfer pricing. Earlier chapters have shown that host countries sometimes compete with each other in the investment incentives and tax breaks they offer to gain more inward direct investment. The nature of the competition for the benefits of MNE activity is rather different and less transparent – but each country would certainly like to gain as high a share of the taxable income as it can.

Suppose, for example, that corporation taxes in Country B are lower than in Country A. Chapter 18 has shown that *ceteris paribus* this would give an MNE from Country A which produces in Country B an incentive to switch taxable income from Country A to Country B by, for example, manipulating the prices on goods and services internally traded between these countries. Since it will lose tax revenue, Country A will regard TPM as against its interests. Country B, on the other hand, will stand to gain additional tax revenue. The outcome could be a conflict about the distribution of income between the two tax authorities, with the MNE being caught as 'pig in the middle'. This example, which is just one of many which could be given, serves to make a general point. *It is that, in many instances, the apparent conflict of interests between MNEs and Nation States conceal more fundamental conflicts of interest which exist between Nation States*. In the case just illustrated, although TPM may benefit the MNE, its real consequence is that it causes income to be redistributed between the citizens of Country A and those of Country B.

In a variety of other fields, the MNE may be a transferring agent, or even an arbitrager, of country-specific policy differences. Take, for example, some of the contemporary, environment-related policies identified in Chapter 19. If West Germany imposes costly health and safety regulations on its auto factories, this could, but not necessarily would, cause a relocation of production by both German and foreign-owned auto companies out of Germany to countries which set less stringent environmental standards. Similarly, differences in anti-pollution regulations between countries are likely to affect both the ownership and location of pollution-intensive value-added activities. Often host countries complain that foreign firms are exporting environmental practices, which are unacceptable to home countries, to their subsidiaries. At the same time, they would most probably object if the same home countries were to insist that their MNE affiliates should conform to their domestic environmental standards.

Similarly, conflicts between home and host countries might arise over the remission of dividends and the repatriation of capital between the foreign subsidiaries and their parent companies. Clearly, conflicts will arise whenever the assets of a foreign affiliate are expropriated by a host government without adequate compensation. To the US government, the action by Iran after the overthrow of the Shah of Persia in 1979 was no less an affront than was the interference of an American MNE – ITT – in the political affairs of Chile in 1973. However, the on-going issue of the right of a host country unilaterally to freeze the dividend remissions due to foreign investors because of its own internal economic difficulties, suggests a more subtle yet more difficult area of contention. It may not matter a great deal if the home country does not have its own balance of payments difficulties. But what if both the home and host countries are in similar financial straits? Then a straightforward conflict of interests arises, and one country might perceive that the other is extending its jurisdictional rights beyond its boundaries.

It is over such issues as these and those relating to securities legislation (Rubin, 1967), information disclosure and accounting procedures, the norms of business conduct (e.g. attitudes to bribery and corruption) and employment practices in racist regimes, that the MNE *qua* MNE may quite unwittingly introduce governments (particularly those of countries with very different cultures, ideologies and economic systems) to new areas of conflict. Most of these issues, however, have nothing to do with extra-territoriality *per se*.

Indeed, as quickly as one area of inter-governmental conflict disappears, another seems to arise. The response by MNEs to regional integration, as described in Chapter 17, has widespread ramifications for the political sovereignty of Nation States and the efficacy of unilateral policies. The growth of intra-industry trade and investment, and growing similarity of the economic structures of many advanced countries, is creating a new set of inter-country tensions. Moreover, as the trade and production of countries become increasingly linked by the operations of MNEs and cross-border alliances, these conflicts are likely to become more transparent. True to its schizophrenic nature, MNE activity can – at one and the same time – bring countries closer together and drive them further apart. Once again, much depends on the OLI configuration with which a MNE is faced and its strategic response to that configuration. We shall discuss some of the proposed solutions in the following section.

21.5 SETTING THE CONDITIONS FOR INTERNATIONAL INVESTMENT: THE ROLE OF INTERNATIONAL AGENCIES

21.5.1 Efforts directed to harmonizing action towards MNEs

In spite of the less confrontational stance between host countries and MNEs, between the host countries themselves, and between home and host countries, which has emerged over the past decade, MNEs may still be conduits or arbitragers of discord and fashioners of inter-government strategic competition for resources, capabilities and markets. For many years, inter-governmental organizations, such as GATT, have set the conditions under which trade in goods may be conducted freely and within the dictates of comparative advantage. Various rounds of the GATT have focused on the implications of how new technological and organizational developments affect such trade and the distribution of its benefits to the participating countries.

The adequacy of GATT to deal with trade which is not only increasingly undertaken by MNEs but frequently conducted within their own organizational boundaries has been questioned by many analysts in recent years, but to little avail. However, the whole question of international direct investment is now being considered by GATT for a different reason. Several countries, including the US and the UK, want to incorporate services into the provisions of GATT, which have so far been excluded. Because many services are not transportable over space, the only way in which foreign firms can supply them is through 'on the spot' production. Hence, the attitudes and policies of host countries towards inward investment in services *pari passu* also influence trade in services.

This is a controversial issue among GATT members and, indeed, for developing countries which are not signatories to the GATT, but are greatly affected by its decisions. There are two reasons for this. The first is that many services (e.g. transport, broadcasting, telecommunications and information-intensive services) are regarded as strategically sensitive. As a result, countries wish to maintain control over their production. The second reason is that some countries wish to be free to develop their own indigenous capacity in critical service sectors and feel they will have less freedom to do so if the sectors are dominated by foreign firms. Both issues are yet to be resolved.

More generally, in a world in which international commerce is being increasingly driven by MNE activity, there is a lot of sense in the idea that there should be some internationally acceptable framework for the governance of international production as there is for international trade. Indeed, the concept of a GATT for international investment – to be called GAII or GAIC (General Agreement on International Investment or International Corporations) – was put forward more than two decades ago by Kindleberger and Goldberg (1970). It was later reinterpreted by Wallace (1974), who proposed an International Investment Organization (IIO). In both cases it was believed that an international regulatory body, drawing on the principle of international law or internationally acceptable social controls, would help resolve some of the cross-border conflicts arising from MNE activity, particularly those to do with taxation and transfer pricing, capital repatriation, anti-trust legislation, balance of payments issues and security regulations.

However, though of intuitive appeal, a GATT for international production would be very difficult to put into practice. This is primarily because FDI, unlike trade, implies the actual presence in one country of a firm that is owned and controlled by nationals residing in another country. The implementation of rules or guidelines on the terms of trade of intermediate products between a MNE and its foreign affiliate is one thing. The construction of guidelines and regulations concerning the terms of foreign-owned production and the strategies of MNEs is quite another. While it may be comparatively easy to obtain broad agreement by firms and countries on matters like anti-dumping, import controls, export subsidies and accounting conventions, achieving consensus on the appropriate governance over trade-related investment measures (TRIMS) implemented by governments and MNEs in pursuance of their respective economies strategies, is likely to prove much more difficult. This is partly because many areas of MNE or government behaviour are not transparent or easily evaluated, and partly because many TRIMS may be facets of a more general set of economic measures over which neither companies nor countries would wish to surrender their sovereignty.

While a GATT type accord on FDI does not seem likely to transpire in the near future, there is some pressure by the leading industrial nations, in the current Uruguay round negotiations, to set guidelines for TRIMS. Since the strategic behaviour of both governments and MNEs is playing an increasing role in affecting the disposition of resources, and as advances in technology and new organization structures are facilitating this behaviour, the incorporation of some of the consequences of TRIMS into the ambience of GATT would be a useful step forward.

While the original idea of a GAII or GAIC was conceived by the leading capital exporting countries, a very different perspective on the need for some kind of international organization to influence the activities of MNEs was being voiced by some host – particularly developing – countries in the 1960s and 1970s. As transnational investment has become more balanced with the passing of years, this voice has grown louder, with the US (or at least some sections of the US community) now contributing to it. Basically, the proposition is that because of their ability to move assets around the world, MNEs may not only circumvent unpalatable national policies and controls, but may play one government off against another to advance their own objectives. At the same time, governments in the pursuance of their national goals may destructively compete with each other for inward investment. Such actions, so the protagonists argue, can only be properly resolved by inter-government cooperation or by supra-national regulation (Fudenberg and Maskin, 1986). However, one problem facing any such supervisory body would be to distinguish between those actions by MNEs which benefit world economic welfare by overcoming market inefficiencies and those which add to the power of large and wealthy countries to behave in a structurally distorting way.

All of the illustrations just cited are an outcome of the wider territorial boundaries of the MNE compared to those of governments, a fact which has long been acknowledged by international lawyers. In 1970, George Ball proposed a treaty that would establish a supra-national authority to administer a law governing the operations of international companies, but the idea was regarded as impractical at the time. Today, the gradual evolvement of a European Company Law does demonstrate that supra-national legislation is possible. A prerequisite for such legislation is a mutuality of interest and benefits for the countries concerned, and a general agreement on the distribution of the costs and benefits of MNE activity. Such conditions – and, on occasion, the lack of them – have fashioned the governance of the US for the past two centuries. It is now being accepted, in part at least, by an increasing number of countries comprising the EC. However, as and when countries converge in their ideologies, cultures, political frameworks and economic systems, the practicality of the Ball proposal will become rather more persuasive.

De facto, however, a reconciliation of the interests of countries has been substantially brought about by other means over the past 20 to 30 years. We have already described the evolution of a variety of codes of conduct as guidelines intended to set norms of behaviour of MNEs in each of its major dimensions, and also of the responsibility of government towards MNEs – particularly as regards national treatment. No less significant have been the changing attitudes of national governments towards MNEs, which cause them to review and reappraise the desirability for some kind of supra-national governance of MNE behaviour.

21.5.2 More general inter-country action, consequential upon MNE activity

In addition to supra-national agreements specifically directed towards MNEs, the growing significance of FDI in the global economy has prompted groups of countries and various international agencies to review some of their more general resolutions and initiatives. Foremost among these is the Charter of Rights and Duties of States, approved by the UN General Assembly in 1974. This Charter reasserts the sovereignty of Nation States – including their right to nationalize or expropriate the assets of foreign-owned companies. It decrees that nations are entitled to enjoy permanent and full control over their resources and wealth undertaken inside their national boundaries and overseas territories. While many of the provisions of the Charter are readily

acceptable by all countries, others (e.g. the rights of countries to organize export cartels, and to share fully and freely in technological advances emanating from outside their national boundaries) are not. Not surprisingly, the Charter has never had any legal force and some of its more controversial features have been quietly buried over the past 20 years.

Similarly, legislation, codes and guidelines relating to intellectual property rights and the transfer of technology have been modified and strengthened in the light of the operations of MNEs. In 1975, the International Confederation of Free Trade Unions (ICFTU) produced a code of conduct with respect to the labour-related activities of MNEs, as did the International Labour Organization (ILO) in 1976. International agreements on environmental protection, health and safety regulations, and accounting procedures, while not specifically addressed to MNEs, have nonetheless been modified in the light of the globalization of production and markets.

Chapter 17 has described a variety of schemes for regional economic integration. While none was primarily initiated to influence the behaviour of MNEs, the subsequent formulation of rules and guidelines by the regional authorities has most certainly taken serious account of their likely consequences on both inward and outward investment. Nowhere is this better demonstrated than in the case of the EC. Whereas the economic goals and actions of the European Commission have been generally consistent with those of MNEs[9] – indeed some European MNEs were the driving force behind the proposals to complete the internal market by 1992 (Franko, 1989) – the social policies have not been so well received. The whole question of European industrial democratization or co-determination, as, for example, contained in labour law and employee representation on boards of directors of German companies (e.g. the Vredling initiative),[10] have been bitterly opposed by MNEs, as have the rulings of the Commission in respect of anti-trust, tax evasion in transfer pricing and social security benefits.

In framing their regional policies and strategies, other integration schemes (e.g. LAFTA, CARICOM, ASEAN) have also been cognizant of the impact of their provisions on MNE activity in their areas. Almost certainly, the likely impact of rapid technological advances and the globalization of production for the competitiveness of individual Nation States has encouraged, rather than discouraged, collective action to promote more liberal markets and reduce both the domestic and cross-border transaction costs of firms producing within their regions.

However, in spite of supra-national schemes to promote the economic welfare of their participants, perhaps the main factors prompting the convergence or harmonization of domestic economic policies – including those specifically addressed to MNEs – are the dissemination of knowledge about the 'best practice' policies between countries and the internationalization of competitive pressures. Previous chapters have suggested that in the 1990s, countries, like firms, are increasingly behaving as strategic oligopolists. Moreover, although firms are the principle wealth creators in market economies, the role of governments in establishing the conditions for wealth creation is not only becoming increasingly significant, but is changing in character.

While competitive pressures and government action are helping to rid markets of many of their structural deficiencies, other forces making for the endemic failure of domestic and international markets are requiring governments to introduce new measures to ensure that their national champions are not disadvantaged *vis à vis* foreign competitors.

We have already cited the kind of supra-national action which may be necessary to reintroduce the market system in Central and Eastern European economies. The Canada–US Free Trade Agreement and the completion of the European internal market for 1992 are two regional collaborative efforts which are specifically intended both to lessen cross-border market distortions (at least, within the integrated region)[11] and to provide firms producing in these markets with the social, educational and communications infrastructure necessary for them to operate efficiently. *Such cooperative action is not governments replacing or distorting markets, but governments intervening to ensure markets can operate efficiently. It is not governments seeking to regulate MNEs, but governments seeking to upgrade and improve the organizational efficiency of their own resources and capabilities so that the competitive advantages of both foreign and domestic MNEs can be used in a way which will best advance their joint strategic interests.*

21.6   CONCLUSIONS: TOWARDS A NEW MULTI-LATERAL GOVERNANCE

The environment for collaborative action towards MNEs, or as a result of MNE activity, is very different in the early 1990s from that of two or more decades ago. At that time, multi-lateral actions were mainly directed at counteracting the perceived power of European and US MNEs, and intended structurally to distort the markets of the host countries in which they operated and to inhibit these countries from achieving their developmental goals. As a result of a lack of bargaining power and to avoid destructive competition for inward investment by competing host countries, it was suggested that some form of supra-national action was required. Sometimes this might be between host countries (e.g. to harmonize incentives offered to inward investors). Sometimes it might be between host and home countries (e.g. to reduce disputes on extra-territoriality or over dividend remissions). And sometimes a regional or international regulatory framework was thought to be the appropriate mechanism.

It is, however, worth noting that the emphasis of multi-lateral action was directed to strengthening national control procedures over MNEs which were perceived both to have too much economic power and to use that power in a socially detrimental way. The facts that these goals were not necessarily consistent with each other and that many of the government actions used to achieve these goals were structurally distorting in their own right, were largely overlooked in the discussion. Economic sovereignty was the God-given right of every country, whatever the means used to promote it! Resolutions in the UN and elsewhere (notably those directed to supporting the emergence of a New International Economic Order) proclaimed this message loud and clear.

Today, for many of the reasons already identified in this book, the situation is very different. Changes in the world economic scenario, in the character and structure of MNE activity, in the learning experiences of both countries and MNEs, and, most of all, the growing cross-border linkages of economic activity, have shifted attention away from bilateral relationships between MNEs and Nation States to the role that each may play in an international market system. This suggests that it is no longer sensible to take a compartmentalized approach to the way in which MNEs affect the goals of Nation States. Such interaction must be related to a systemic and holistic view of the organization of international resource allocation.[12] In this respect, there are signs that MNEs and host governments are viewing each other more positively and constructively than once they did. A caveat to this somewhat sanguine view is that the cooperation between firms and governments may not always be in the broader public interest. For example, firms may encourage governments to engage in strategic trade policies, which, far from reducing cross-border transaction costs and promoting healthy international competition, tend, by imposing artificial costs (e.g. non-tariff barriers) on their rivals, to shelter them from the winds of structural change (Rugman and Verbeke, 1990, 1991b). Moreover, without an overhaul of the institutional machinery of government and an upgrading in the competence of the executive bureaucrats, it is doubtful if even 'good' strategic trade policy could be efficiently administered.

More attention is now being focused on the relationship between the policies and actions of Nation States and the international system of which they are part. Multi-lateral action may still be necessary and may still be addressed to regulating MNE activity. However, today its main thrust is to ensure that the global economic order works so as to ensure that MNEs and other cross-border actors optimize their contribution to capabilities and competitiveness of Nation States. In the words of a UNCTC report (1990a), the question is no longer

> 'whether to regulate business but how to structure cooperative national approaches that facilitate rather than inhibit international transactions' (pp. 16–17);

and again, with particular reference to renewing discussions on the UN code of conduct,

> 'the major challenge is to structure a collective international approach to managing the systemic costs and benefits of a global economy driven by transnational business corporations' (p. 17).

The report then gives several illustrations of the kinds of problems now emerging in the international system, which are truly transnational in their impact and the manner in which they must be managed. To quote directly from the report:

> 'An obvious example is the protection of the environment which is not divisible territorially since pollution of the air or oceans can quickly spread beyond political boundaries requiring a cooperative international approach. The manufacture, transport, storage or disposal of hazardous wastes present other dangers that cannot be left solely to the discretion of national officials. Work and product health, safety and quality standards raise other common international issues, especially since products and services are rapidly and widely dispersed through an increasingly interdependent transnational network' (pp. 16–17).

The report goes on to conclude that:

> 'A supportive political framework is necessary for the continued growth of global stock markets and securities exchanges, linked data processing services and media transmission facilities. Similarly, the protection of international property rights, stability of component supply networks and the establishment of efficient and effective global market systems and franchising systems require compatible government approaches to regulatory goals and enforcement. These developments need coordinated definitions and regulatory processes which facilitate rather than impede business transactions.' (pp. 16–17)

In helping the international community to achieve these goals, MNEs may play a positive and constructive role, not only by influencing the geopolitical alignments between nations and regions, but also by providing many of the technological and organizational capabilities which may help overcome international market failure. Viewed in this light, an international facilitating framework which embraces the conduct and impact, as well as the government treatment, of MNEs could help to lessen friction and conflict between nations, while encouraging beneficial economic growth.

Only a decade ago scholars were forecasting an era of increasing supra-national controls on the behaviour of MNEs (Robinson, 1983). These have not, in general, materialized, mainly because of the shift in attitudes of both home and host countries towards their roles in the emerging global economy and how international direct investment may affect this role.

Yet, although governments are taking a more constructive view of MNE activity, certain systemic characteristics associated with the globalization of production and markets continue to give concern. Chief among these are the ease and speed with which MNEs are able to restructure their assets and relocate their production, and the cross-border oligopolistic strategies they pursue. Others relate to the perceived lack of social awareness or environmental sensitivity of some large international corporations.[13] Chapter 20 showed that these aspects of MNE activity require rigorous monitoring by governments, not so much with a view to regulating the conduct of MNEs, but rather to determine how governments, MNEs and the rest of the business community might work together to promote national and international economic welfare.

This chapter has argued that systemic market failure – particularly cross-border market failure – cannot always be fully counteracted, or compensated for, by national government actions because the uncertainties, externalities, and scale and scope of economies associated with the activities of hierarchies are no respecters of national boundaries. In such cases, depending on the costs and benefits involved to the participating countries, it may be appropriate for some kind of collaborative action to be taken between countries – be they host or home or both – towards MNEs. Such forms of alliances between countries might vary from very informal exchanges of information and views about MNE-related matters, to legally binding agreements and the abrogation of the sovereignty of Nation States in their acceptance of a common set of rules, regulations and policies towards, or as a consequence of, MNE activity. In between these extremes are a variety of 'soft' agreements (e.g. guidelines and codes); some are industry or country specific, while others are more general.

The main feature of the past two decades has been that the thrust of all these efforts has changed from regulating the behaviour of MNEs to conform with national or regional economic objectives to encouraging cross-border mechanisms that promote a positive interaction between national governments and MNEs. It is also being increasingly appreciated that this interface will be the most fruitful when

international structural distorting and endemic market failure is minimized. Only then can a systemic or mutually beneficial interface between the O advantages of MNEs and the L advantages of the countries in which they operate be achieved.[14]

At the same time, there can be no denying that inter-government relations, particularly among members of the Triad, have become more competitive as the structures of their economies have converged and as assets and intermediate products have become more internationally mobile. The result is that governments, like firms competing for the same resources and capabilities, have begun to behave as strategic oligopolists in a variety of policy-related areas, especially trade. But as in the corporate sector, competition among oligopolists can be destructive, unless the 'rules of the game' are clearly defined and the 'playing field' is reasonably level. This and the preceding chapter have argued that the existing international machinery for regulating cross-border commerce needs a complete overhaul to take account of the transnationalization of production and the activities of global companies. Unless this is brought about, there is a real possibility that the very real benefits which the global economy offers its participants will be severely eroded – if not lost altogether.

Appendix

United Nations Economic and Social Council: Proposed Text of the Draft Code of Conduct on Transnational Corporations

Contents

PREAMBLE

The General Assembly,

Recalling Economic and Social Council resolutions 1908 (LVII) of 2 August 1974 and 1913 (LVII) of 5 December 1974, establishing the Commission on Transnational Corporations and the United Nations Centre on Transnational Corporations with the mandate, as their highest priority of work, of concluding a Code of Conduct on Transnational Corporations,

Convinced that a universally accepted, comprehensive and effective Code of Conduct on Transnational Corporations is an essential element in the strengthening of international economic and social co-operation and, in particular, in achieving one of the main goals and objectives in that co-operation, namely, to maximize the contributions of transnational corporations to economic development and growth and to minimize the negative effects of the activities of these corporations,

Decides to adopt the following Code of Conduct on Transnational Corporations:

DEFINITIONS AND SCOPE OF APPLICATION

1. (a) This Code is universally applicable to enterprises, irrespective of their country of origin and their ownership, including private, public or mixed, comprising entities in two or more countries, regardless of the legal form and fields of activity of these entities, which operate under a system of decision-making, permitting coherent policies and a common strategy through one or more decision-making centres, in which the entities are so linked, by ownership or otherwise, that one or more of them may be able to exercise a significant influence over the activities of others and, in particular, to share knowledge, resources and responsibilities with the others. Such enterprises are referred to in this Code as transnational corporations.

(b) The term "entities" in the Code refers to both parent entities – that is, entities which are the main source of influence over others – and other entities, unless otherwise specified in the Code.

(c) The term "transnational corporation" in the Code refers to the enterprise as a whole or its various entities.

(d) The term "home country" means the country in which the parent entity is located. The term "host country" means a country other than the home country in which an entity other than the parent entity is located.

(e) The term "country in which a transnational corporation operates" refers to a home or host country in which an entity of a transnational corporation conducts operations.

2. For the application of this Code, it is irrelevant whether or not enterprises as described in paragraph 1 (a) above are referred to in any country as transnational corporations.

3. The Code is universally applicable in all States, regardless of their political and economic systems or their level of development.

4. The provisions of the Code addressed to transnational corporations reflect good practice for all enterprises. Subject to the provisions of paragraph 52, wherever the provisions of the Code are relevant to both, transnational corporations and domestic enterprises shall be subject to

the same expectations with regard to their conduct.

5. Subject to the relevant constitutions, charters or other fundamental laws of the regional groupings of States concerned, any reference in this Code to States, countries or Governments, also includes regional groupings of States, to the extent that the provisions of this Code relate to matters within these groupings' own competence, with respect to such competence.

6. In their interpretation and application the provisions of this Code are interrelated and each provision should be construed in the context of the other provisions.

ACTIVITIES OF TRANSNATIONAL CORPORATIONS

A. General

Respect for national sovereignty and observance of domestic laws, regulations and administrative practices

7. Transnational corporations shall respect the national sovereignty of the countries in which they operate and the right of each State to exercise its permanent sovereignty over its natural wealth and resources.

8. An entity of a transnational corporation is subject to the laws, regulations and established administrative practices of the country in which it operates.

9. Transnational corporations shall respect the right of each State to regulate and monitor accordingly the activities of their entities operating within its territory.

Adherence to economic goals and development objectives, policies and priorities

10. Transnational corporations should carry out their activities in conformity with the development policies, objectives and priorities set out by the Governments of the countries in which they operate and work seriously towards making a positive contribution to the achievement of such goals at the national and, as appropriate, the regional level, within the framework of regional integration programmes. Transnational corporations should co-operate with the Governments of the countries in which they operate with a view to contributing to the development process and should be responsive to requests for consultation in this respect, thereby establishing mutually beneficial relations with these countries.

11. Transnational corporations should carry out their operations in conformity with applicable intergovernmental co-operative arrangements concluded by the countries in which they operate.

Review and renegotiation of contracts and agreements

12. (a) Contracts or agreements between Governments and transnational corporations should be negotiated and implemented in good faith. In such contracts or agreements, especially long-term ones, review or renegotiation clauses should normally be included.

(b) In the absence of such clauses and where there has been a fundamental change of the circumstances on which the contract or agreement was based, transnational corporations, acting in good faith, should co-operate with Governments for the review or renegotiation of such contract or agreement.

Adherence to socio-cultural objectives and values

13. Transnational corporations should respect the social and cultural objectives, values and traditions of the countries in which they operate. While economic and technological development is normally accompanied by social change, transnational corporations should avoid practices, products or services which cause detrimental effects on cultural patterns and socio-cultural objectives as determined by Governments. For this purpose, transnational corporations should respond positively to requests for consultations from Governments concerned.

Respect for human rights and fundamental freedoms

14. Transnational corporations shall respect human rights and fundamental freedoms in the countries in which they operate. In their social and industrial relations, transnational corporations shall not discriminate on the basis of race, colour, sex, religion, language, social, national and ethnic origins or political or other opinion. Transnational corporations shall conform to government policies designed to extend equality of opportunity and treatment.

Non-collaboration by transnational corporations with the racist minority regime in South Africa

15. In accordance with the efforts of the international community towards the elimination of *apartheid* in South Africa,

(a) Transnational corporations shall refrain from operations and activities supporting and sustaining the racist minority regime of South Africa in maintaining the system of *apartheid*;

(b) Transnational corporations shall engage in appropriate activities within their competence with a view to eliminating racial discrimination and all other aspects of the system of *apartheid*;

(c) Transnational corporations shall comply strictly with obligations resulting from Security Council decisions and shall fully respect those resulting from all relevant United Nations resolutions.

Non-interference in internal affairs of host countries

16. Without prejudice to the participation of transnational corporations in activities that are permissible under the laws, regulations or established administrative practices of host countries, and without prejudice to paragraph 8 of the Code, transnational corporations shall not interfere in the internal affairs of host countries.

Non-interference in intergovernmental relations

17. Transnational corporations shall not interfere in intergovernmental relations provided that this provision shall not preclude such activities as are sanctioned within the framework of bilateral or multilateral co-operation.

18. Transnational corporations should not request Governments acting on their behalf to take the measures referred to in the second sentence of paragraph 65.

19. With respect to the exhaustion of local remedies, transnational corporations should not request Governments to act on their behalf in any manner inconsistent with paragraph 65.

Abstention from corrupt practices

20. (a) Transnational corporations shall refrain, in their transactions, from the offering, promising or giving of any payment, gift or other advantage to or for the benefit of a public official as consideration for performing or refraining from the performance of his duties in connection with those transactions.

(b) Transnational corporations shall maintain accurate records of any payments made by them to any public official or intermediary. They shall make available these records to the competent authorities of the countries in which they operate, upon request, for investigations and proceedings concerning those payments.

B. Economic, financial and social

Ownership and control

21. Transnational corporations should make every effort so to allocate their decision-making powers among their entities as to enable them to contribute to the economic and social development of the countries in which they operate.

22. To the extent permitted by national laws, policies and established administrative practices of the country in which it operates, each entity of a transnational corporation should co-operate with the other entities, in accordance with the actual distribution of responsibilities among them and consistent with paragraph 22, so as to enable each entity to meet effectively the requirements established by the laws, policies and regulations of the country in which it operates.

23. Transnational corporations should carry out their personnel policies in accordance with the national policies of each of the countries in which they operate which give priority to the employment and promotion of its nationals at all levels of management and direction of the affairs of each entity so as to enhance the effective participation of its nationals in the decision-making process.

24. Transnational corporations should contribute to the managerial and technical training of nationals of the countries in which they operate and facilitate their employment at all levels of management of the entities and enterprises as a whole.

Employment conditions and industrial relations

25. For the purposes of this Code, the principles set out in the Tripartite Declaration of Principles concerning Multinational Enterprises and Social Policy, adopted by the Governing Body of the International Labour Office, should apply in the field of employment, training, conditions of work and life and industrial relations.

Balance of payments and financing

26. Transnational corporations shall carry out their operations in conformity with laws and regulations and with full regard to the policy objectives set out by the countries in which they operate, particularly developing countries, relating to balance of payments, financial transactions and other issues dealt with in the subsequent paragraphs of this section. These obligations are without prejudice to multilaterally agreed trade rules and sound commercial practices.

27. Transnational corporations should respond positively to requests for consultation on their activities from the Governments of the countries in which they operate, with a view to contributing to the alleviation of pressing problems of balance of payments and finance of such countries.

28. Transnational corporations should, where appropriate, contribute to the promotion and diversification of exports in the countries in which they operate and to an increased utilization of goods, services and other resources which are available in these countries.

29. Transnational corporations should be responsive to requests by Governments of the countries in which they operate, particularly developing countries, concerning the phasing over a limited period of time of the repatriation of capital in case of disinvestment or remittances of accumulated profits, when the size and timing of such transfers

would cause serious balance-of-payments difficulties for such countries.

30. Transnational corporations should not, contrary to generally accepted financial practices prevailing in the countries in which they operate, engage in short-term financial operations or transfers or defer or advance foreign exchange payments, including intra-corporate payments, in a manner which would increase currency instability and thereby cause serious balance-of-payments difficulties for the countries concerned.

31. Transnational corporations should not impose restrictions on their entities, beyond generally accepted commercial practices prevailing in the countries in which they operate, regarding the transfer of goods, services and funds which would cause serious balance-of-payments difficulties for the countries in which they operate.

32. When having recourse to the money and capital markets of the countries in which they operate, transnational corporations should not, beyond generally accepted financial practices prevailing in such countries, engage in activities which would have a significant adverse impact on the working of local markets, particularly by restricting the availability of funds to other enterprises. When issuing shares with the objective of increasing local equity participation in an entity operating in such a country, or engaging in long-term borrowing in the local market, transnational corporations should consult with the Government of the country concerned upon its request on the effects of such transactions on the local money and capital markets.

Transfer pricing

33. In respect of their intra-corporate transactions, transnational corporations should not use pricing policies that are not based on relevant market prices, or, in the absence of such prices, the arm's length principle, which have the effect of adversely affecting the tax revenues, the foreign exchange resources or other aspects of the economy of the countries in which they operate.

Taxation

34. Transnational corporations shall not, contrary to the laws and regulations of the countries in which they operate, use their corporate structure and modes of operation, such as the use of intra-corporate pricing which is not based on the arm's length principle, or other means, to modify the tax base on which their entities are assessed.

Competition and restrictive business practices

35. For the purposes of this Code, the relevant provisions of the Set of Multilaterally Agreed Equitable Principles and Rules for the Control of Restrictive Business Practices

adopted by the General Assembly in its resolution 35/63 of 5 December 1980 apply in the field of restrictive business practices.

Transfer of technology

36. (a) Transnational corporations shall conform to the transfer of technology laws and regulations of the countries in which they operate. They shall co-operate with the competent authorities of those countries in assessing the impact of international transfers of technology in their economies and consult with them regarding the various technological options which might help those countries, particularly developing countries, to attain their economic and social development.

(b) Transnational corporations in their transfer of technology transactions should, in accordance with the criteria set forth in the Set of Multilaterally Agreed Equitable Principles and Rules for the Control of Restrictive Business Practices, avoid restrictive practices which adversely affect the international flow of technology, or otherwise hinder the economic and technological development of countries, particularly developing countries.

(c) Transnational corporations should contribute to the strengthening of the scientific and technological capacities of developing countries, in accordance with the science and technology established policies and priorities of those countries. Transnational corporations should undertake substantial research and development activities in developing countries and should make full use of local resources and personnel in this process.

Consumer protection

37. Transnational corporations shall carry out their operations, in particular production and marketing, in accordance with national laws, regulations, administrative practices and policies concerning consumer protection of the countries in which they operate. Transnational corporations shall also perform their activities with due regard to relevant international standards, so that they do not cause injury to the health or endanger the safety of consumers or bring about variations in the quality of products in each market which would have detrimental effects on consumers.

38. Transnational corporations shall, in respect of the products and services which they produce or market or propose to produce or market in any country, supply to the competent authorities of that country on request or on a regular basis, as specified by these authorities, all relevant information concerning:

Characteristics of these products or services which may be injurious to the health and safety of consumers including experimental uses and related aspects;

Prohibitions, restrictions, warnings and other public regulatory measures imposed in other countries on grounds of health and safety protection on these products or services.

39. Transnational corporations should disclose to the public in the countries in which they operate all appropriate information on the contents and, to the extent known, on possible hazardous effects of the products they produce or market in the countries concerned by means of proper labelling, informative and accurate advertising or other appropriate methods. Packaging of their products should be safe and the contents of the product should not be misrepresented.

40. Transnational corporations should be responsive to requests from Governments of the countries in which they operate and be prepared to co-operate with international organizations in their efforts to develop and promote national and international standards for the protection of the health and safety of consumers and to meet the basic needs of consumers.

Environmental protection

41. Transnational corporations shall carry out their activities in accordance with national laws, regulations, established administrative practices and policies relating to the preservation of the environment of the countries in which they operate and with due regard to relevant international standards. Transnational corporations should, in performing their activities, take steps to protect the environment and where damaged to rehabilitate it and should make efforts to develop and apply adequate technologies for this purpose.

42. Transnational corporations shall, in respect of the products, processes and services they have introduced or propose to introduce in any country, supply to the competent authorities of that country on request or on a regular basis, as specified by these authorities, all relevant information concerning:

Characteristics of these products, processes and other activities including experimental uses and related aspects which may harm the environment and the measures and costs necessary to avoid or at least to mitigate their harmful effects;

Prohibitions, restrictions, warnings and other public regulatory measures imposed in other countries on grounds of protection of the environment on these products, processes and services.

43. Transnational corporations should be responsive to requests from Governments of the countries in which they operate and be prepared where appropriate to co-operate with international organizations in their efforts to develop and promote national and international standards for the protection of the environment.

C. Disclosure of information

44. Transnational corporations should disclose to the public in the countries in which they operate, by appropriate means of communication, clear, full and comprehensible information on the structure, policies, activities and operations of the transnational corporation as a whole. The information should include financial as well as non-financial items and should be made available on a regular annual basis, normally within six months and in any case not later than 12 months from the end of the financial year of the corporation. In addition, during the financial year, transnational corporations should wherever appropriate make available a semi-annual summary of financial information.

The financial information to be disclosed annually should be provided where appropriate on a consolidated basis, together with suitable explanatory notes and should include, *inter alia*, the following:

(a) A balance sheet;

(b) An income statement, including operating results and sales;

(c) A statement of allocation of net profits or net income;

(d) A statement of the sources and uses of funds;

(e) Significant new long-term capital investment;

(f) Research and development expenditure.

The non-financial information referred to in the first subparagraph should include, *inter alia*:

(a) The structure of the transnational corporation, showing the name and location of the parent company, its main entities, its percentage ownership, direct and indirect, in these entities, including shareholdings between them;

(b) The main activity of its entities;

(c) Employment information including average number of employees;

(d) Accounting policies used in compiling and consolidating the information published;

(e) Policies applied in respect of transfer pricing.

The information provided for the transnational corporation as a whole should as far as practicable be broken down:

By geographical area or country, as appropriate, with regard to the activities of its main entities, sales, operating results, significant new investments and number of employees;

By major line of business as regards sales and significant new investment.

The method of breakdown as well as details of information provided should be determined by the nature, scale and interrelationships of the transnational corporation's operations, with due regard to their significance for the areas or countries concerned.

The extent, detail and frequency of the information provided should take into account the nature and size of the transnational corporation as a whole, the requirements of confidentiality and effects on the transnational corporation's competitive position as well as the cost involved in producing the information.

The information herein required should, as necessary, be in addition to information required by national laws, regulations and established administrative practices of the countries in which transnational corporations operate.

45. (a) Transnational corporations shall supply to the competent authorities in each of the countries in which they operate, upon request or on a regular basis as specified by those authorities, and in accordance with national legislation, all information required for legislative and administrative purposes relevant to the activities and policies of their entities in the country concerned.

(b) Transnational corporations shall, to the extent permitted by the provisions of the relevant national laws, regulations, established administrative practices and policies of the countries concerned, supply to competent authorities in the countries in which they operate information held in other countries needed to enable them to obtain a true and fair view of the operations of the transnational corporation concerned as a whole in so far as the information requested relates to the activities of the entities in the countries seeking such information.

(c) The provisions of paragraph 52 concerning confidentiality shall apply to information supplied under the provisions of this paragraph.

46. (a) With due regard to the relevant provisions of the ILO Tripartite Declaration of Principles concerning Multinational Enterprises and Social Policy and in accordance with national laws, regulations and practices in the field of labour relations, transnational corporations shall provide to trade unions or other representatives of employees in their entities in each of the countries in which they operate, by appropriate means of communication, the necessary information on the activities dealt with in this Code to enable them to obtain a true and fair view of the performance of the local entity and, where appropriate, the corporation as a whole. Such information shall include, where provided for by national law and practices, *inter alia*, prospects or plans for future development having major economic and social effects on the employees concerned.

(b) Procedures for consultation on matters of mutual concern should be worked out by mutual agreement between entities of transnational corporations and trade unions or other representatives of employees in accordance with national law and practice.

(c) Information made available pursuant to the provisions of this paragraph should be subject to appropriate safeguards for confidentiality so that no damage is caused to the parties concerned.

TREATMENT OF TRANSNATIONAL CORPORATIONS

A.   General provisions relating to the treatment of transnational corporations

47. In all matters relating to the Code, States shall fulfill, in good faith, their obligations under international law.

48. States have the right to regulate the entry and establishment of transnational corporations including determining the role that such corporations may play in economic and social development and prohibiting or limiting the extent of their presence in specific sectors.

49. Transnational corporations shall receive fair and equitable treatment in the countries in which they operate.

50. Subject to national requirements for maintaining public order and protecting national security and consistent with national constitutions and basic laws, and without prejudice to measures specified in legislation relating to the declared development objectives of the developing countries, entities of transnational corporations should be entitled to treatment no less favourable than that accorded to domestic enterprises in similar circumstances.

51. The importance of endeavouring to assure the clarity and stability of national policies, laws, regulations and established administrative practices is acknowledged. Laws and regulations affecting transnational corporations should be publicly and readily available. To the extent appropriate, relevant information regarding decisions of competent administrative bodies relating to transnational corporations should be disseminated.

52. Information furnished by transnational corporations to the authorities in each of the countries in which they operate containing confidential business information shall be accorded reasonable safeguards normally applicable in the area in which the information is provided, particularly to protect its confidentiality.

53. In order to achieve the purposes of paragraph 24 relating to managerial and technical training and employment of nationals of the countries in which transnational corporations operate, the transfer of those nationals between the entities of a transnational corporation should, subject to the laws and regulations of the countries concerned, be facilitated.

54. Transnational corporations are entitled to transfer all payments legally due. Such transfers are subject to the procedures laid down in the relevant legislation of host countries, such as foreign exchange laws, and to restrictions for a limited period of time emanating from exceptional balance of payments difficulties.

B.   Nationalization and compenstion

55. It is acknowledged that States have the right to nationalize or expropriate the assets of a transnational

corporation operating in their territories, and that adequate compensation is to be paid by the State concerned, in accordance with the applicable legal rules and principles.

C. Jurisdiction

56. An entity of a transnational corporation is subject to the jurisdiction of the country in which it operates.

D. Dispute settlement

57. Disputes between States and entities of transnational corporations, which are not amicably settled between the parties, shall be submitted to competent national courts or authorities. Where the parties so agree, or have agreed, such disputes shall be referred to other mutually acceptable or accepted dispute settlement procedures.

58. Where the exercise of jurisdiction over transnational corporations and their entities by more than one State may lead to conflicts of jurisdiction, States concerned should endeavour to avoid or minimize such conflicts, and the problems to which they give rise by following an approach of moderation and restraint, respecting and accommodating the interests of Other States.

INTERGOVERNMENTAL CO-OPERATION

59. It is acknowledged that intergovernmental co-operation is essential in accomplishing the objectives of the Code.

60. Intergovernmental co-operation should be established or strengthened at the international level and, where appropriate, at the bilateral, regional and interregional levels.

61. States should exchange information on the measures they have taken to give effect to the Code and on their experience with the Code.

62. States should consult on a bilateral or multilateral basis, as appropriate, on matters relating to the Code and its application and with respect to the development of international agreements and arrangements on issues related to the Code.

63. States should take into consideration the objectives of the Code as reflected in its provisions when negotiating bilateral or multilateral agreements concerning transnational corporations.

64. States should not use transnational corporations as instruments to intervene in the internal or external affairs of other States and should take appropriate action within their jurisdiction to prevent transnational corporations from engaging in activities referred to in paragraphs 16 and 17 of this Code.

65. Government action on behalf of a transnational corporation operating in another country shall be subject to the principle of exhaustion of local remedies provided in such a country and, when agreed among the Governments

concerned, to procedures for dealing with international legal claims. Such action should not in any event amount to the use of any type of coercive measures not consistent with the Charter of the United Nations and the Declaration on Principles of International Law concerning Friendly Relations and Co-operation among States in accordance with the Charter of the United Nations.

IMPLEMENTATION OF THE CODE OF CONDUCT

A. Action at the national level

66. In order to ensure and promote the implementation of the Code at the national level, States should, *inter alia*:

(a) Publicize and disseminate the Code;

(b) Follow the implementation of the Code within their territories;

(c) Report to the United Nations Commission on Transnational Corporations on the action taken at the national level to promote the Code and on the experience gained from its implementation;

(d) Take action to reflect their support for the Code and take into account the objectives of the Code as reflected in its provisions when introducing, implementing and reviewing laws, regulations and administrative practices on matters dealt with in the Code.

B. International institutional machinery

67. The United Nations Commission on Transnational Corporations shall assume the functions of the international institutional machinery for the implementation of the Code. In this capacity, the Commission shall be open to the participation of all States. Consistent with United Nations practices, it may establish the subsidiary bodies and specific procedures it deems necessary for the effective discharge of its functions. The United Nations Centre on Transnational Corporations shall act as the secretariat to the Commission.

68. The Commission shall act as the international body within the United Nations system for all matters related to the Code. It shall establish and maintain close contacts with other United Nations organizations and specialized agencies dealing with matters related to the Code and its implementation with a view to co-ordinating work related to the Code. When matters covered by international agreements or arrangements, specifically referred to in the Code, which have been worked out in other United Nations forums, arise, the Commission shall forward such matters to the competent bodies concerned with such agreements or arrangements.

69. The Commission shall have the following functions:

(a) To discuss at its annual sessions matters related to the Code. If agreed by the Governments engaged in consultations on specific issues related to the Code, the Commission shall facilitate such intergovernmental consultations to the extent possible. Representatives of trade unions, business, consumer and other relevant groups may express their views on matters related to the Code through the non-governmental organizations represented in the Commission.

(b) Periodically to assess the implementation of the Code, such assessments being based on reports submitted by Governments and, as appropriate, on documentation from United Nations organizations and specialized agencies performing work relevant to the Code and non-governmental organizations represented in the Commission. The first assessment shall take place not earlier than two years and not later than three years after the adoption of the Code. The second assessment shall take place two years after the first one. The Commission shall determine whether a periodicity of two years is to be maintained or modified for subsequent assessments. The format of assessments shall be determined by the Commission.

(c) To develop in the light of experience procedures for providing clarifications on provisions of the Code.

(d) To report annually to the General Assembly through the Economic and Social Council on its activities regarding the implementation of the Code.

(e) To facilitate intergovernmental arrangements or agreements on specific aspects relating to transnational corporations upon request of the Governments concerned. 70. The United Nations Centre on Transnational Corporations shall provide assistance relating to the implementation of the Code, *inter alia*, by collecting, analysing and disseminating information and conducting research and surveys, as required and specified by the Commission.

C. Review procedure

71. The Commission shall make recommendations to the General Assembly through the Economic and Social Council for the purpose of reviewing the provisions of the Code. The first review shall take place not later than six years after the adoption of the Code. The General Assembly shall establish, as appropriate, the modalities for reviewing the Code.

NOTES

1 Thus, one country may be prepared to sacrifice some economic rent to gain a larger amount of foreign investment. Harmonization may mean it gains a higher economic rent from each investment, but the total volume of investment falls.

2 Although, in December 1991, eleven of the twelve Member States of the EC (Britain was the exception) agreed to implement a social charter which *inter alia*

set down certain work standards, a minimum wage and industrial relations procedures.

3 Now the Division of Transnational Corporations and Management of the United Nations.

4 After 1979, most MNE–union and other disputes about implementation of the guidelines were settled at national level.

5 For a fascinating discussion of the different kinds of cross-border politico-market failures and the kind of international governance structures which might be set up to deal with them, see Eden and Hampson (1990).

6 For an expansion of Gilpin's views, see Gilpin (1987) and Chapter 12.

7 As set down, for example, in the Sherman Act of 1890 and the Clayton Act of 1914.

8 As measured by the percentage of the output of a domestic industry accounted for by the 'X' largest firms. Such a measure takes no account either of imports or of the foreign production of a domestically-based firm.

9 One exception is legislation designed to deregulate parallel import pricing, a practice which enables established MNEs in individual countries to charge different prices for the same goods. For a more detailed examination of the implications of this practice, see UNCTC (1980).

10 The Vredling initiative seeks to 'disinternalize' the control procedures of MNEs, at least in respect of EC labour matters, by insisting that each foreign subsidiary is treated as a separate legal entity and has to provide exactly the same kinds of information (e.g. with respect to products, investment plans and any plant closures) and abide by the same regulations (e.g. with respect to employee participation on company boards) as domestic firms (Robinson, 1983, pp. 61–3). For a more extended discussion of the Vredling proposal, see Blanpain (1983).

11 At the same time, it is possible that in their trading relationships with the rest of the world, a regional bloc may create new structural distortions.

12 Note, there is a parallel to considering the MNE as a system in organizing cross-border value-added activities and that of viewing the international economy as a global system of organizing the interaction of national economic markets.

13 In July 1991, the (UK) Church of England Synod voted to advise its members to boycott the purchase of Nescafe on the grounds that the company which made it – Nestlé – was behaving irresponsibly in its marketing of baby milk powder in the poorer countries of the Third World. Needless to say, Nestlé strongly denied this allegation.

14 The movement away from a confrontational to a cooperative MNE–Nation State stance is further discussed in Dunning (1991b).

PART 5

LOOKING FORWARD

This part consists of just one chapter, the purpose of which is to speculate a little about the future course and characteristics of MNE activity. The chapter suggests that such activity is likely to become more diversified in its origin and pluralistic in its organizational form in the 1990s, and that to understand its determinants and consequences, it will be necessary to take a more systemic approach to analysing its determinants and consequences.

While economists and organizational scholars are making some progress in analysing the competitive advantages of the large MNE in terms of its competence to orchestrate the activities of a network of intra- and inter-firm organizational relationships effectively, much less headway has been made on reviewing the complications of the global economy for the way in which governments organize for the overall management of the resources and capabilities under their jurisdiction. In particular, what does the dramatic growth of all forms of cross-border transnational relationships by MNEs mean for the workings of a domestic market economy? Do they aid or inhibit its efficiency? The volume concludes by asserting that it is the juxtaposition between the systemic organization of the cross-border assets by MNEs, as leading actors in the global market economy, and that of the location-bound assets of countries by governments to promote their competitive advantages in the global economy, that promises to be the kernel of fruitful research by international business scholars in the 1990s and beyond.

CHAPTER 22

THE FUTURE OF MNEs IN A GLOBAL ECONOMY

22.1 INTRODUCTION: THE FIVE STAGES IN THE EVOLUTION OF THE GLOBAL ECONOMY

For the most part, this book has adopted an evolutionary approach to explaining the value-added activities of MNEs and their interaction with the economies of which they are part. In doing so, we have used the eclectic paradigm of international production as our framework of analysis. This suggests that both the determinants of MNE activity and the response of policy makers to its economic and social consequences are functions of the dynamic interplay between the competitive or O-specific advantages of enterprises and the competitive or L-specific advantages of countries, as well as of the way in which this interplay is governed and organized.

In Chapter 3 we traced the growth of international production and its shifting industrial and geographical structure in terms of the strategic response of firms to a changing OLI configuration. That chapter as well as Chapters 7 and 8 used the eclectic paradigm to examine the organizational structures of MNEs, while Chapter 5 introduced the concept of the investment development path to explain the changing propensity of countries to attract inward direct investment or generate outward direct investment at different stages in their economic development.

In Part 3 of the monograph, we explored some of the more important economic consequences of MNE activity on the Nation States in which they operate. We argued that these, too, could be explained by reference to the interaction between the O advantages of firms and the L endowments of countries, and the relative attractions of exploiting the former across national boundaries through hierarchical, market or cooperative modes. We showed that such effects are likely to be country, sector and firm specific, and to vary according to both the stage of a country's development and the management and organizational strategies pursued by MNEs. Part 4 demonstrated that the OLI paradigm could also provide a useful framework for understanding the reactions and strategic policies pursued by home and host governments, and how these have changed over the past 20 years or more.

Considering both the growth of international production and the reactions of governments to the activities of MNEs, it is possible to trace five stages in the evolution of the global economy, each of which is distinguished by a different configuration of the competitive strengths and weaknesses of firms, and their strategic response to them, as well as that of the competitive strengths and weaknesses of Nation States, and the strategic response of governments to them. The following paragraphs briefly summarize the main features of these five stages.

22.1.1 Stage 1: Up to 1914

The *first* stage, which lasted from the mid 19th century to the First World War, was one in which the revolution in production and organizational methods and new forms of transport and energy heralded the emergence of the managed multi-plant firm, which occasionally extended beyond its national boundaries when it was commercially or strategically appropriate to do so. The O advantages of the embryonic MNEs lay mainly in the intangible assets they possessed, rather than in the perceived benefits of internalizing cross-border markets, while the L advantages of countries rested in the structure of their natural endowments, rather than in that of their created assets and capabilities. The organization of such activities was monocentric and, for the most part, MNEs acted as economic colonists, often aided and abetted by their mother countries. Host countries took little strategic action to affect inbound investment, either because they were powerless to do so, or because governments generally played a less important role than they do now in influencing market demand and the disposition of resources. Metropolitan countries were generally only interested in outbound direct investment in so far as it helped them to advance their colonial ambitions, although the initiation of strong anti-trust legislation by some home countries (e.g. the US) in the 1890s reduced the propensity of firms to engage in cross-border alliances.

22.1.2   Stage 2: The inter-war years

The *second* stage of the evolution of the global economy lasted from 1918 to the outbreak of the Second World War. It was characterized by the maturing of both US and European MNEs and a general move towards the integration of their affiliates into the economies in which they operated. The variables affecting the location of value-added activities underwent noticeable change as there was a general shift of host industrialized countries towards economic independence and protectionism – together with adoption of Keynesian economic policies. Much MNE activity in this period took the form of defensive market-seeking investment. Most MNEs consisted of a federation of loosely knit foreign affiliates, which were primarily geared towards providing the parent companies with access to foreign markets. Subsidiaries tended to be set up as truncated replicas of their parent companies.

As in Stage 1, few home or host countries had formulated specific policies towards MNE activity. A study of the literature of the period[1] reveals that, while policy makers paid some notice to the merits and demerits of *portfolio* capital movements, particularly under a managed currency system, they appeared little interested or concerned about the implications of either outward or inward direct.investment.

With the collapse of the international capital market in the 1930s and the growing role of FDI in some economies, notably Canada and Australia, scholars began to give more attention to the consequences of the activities of the branch plants of foreign (later to be called multinational) enterprises.[2] During this period, too, home countries generally took a more relaxed stance towards mergers and cartels, which led some firms to engage in cross-border alliances rather than FDI. However, as in Stage 1, the main gains of MNE activity arose from the economic rent derived from their proprietary rights rather than from those of multinationality *per se*. Natural factor endowments together with government-imposed import restrictions remained the main determinants of the location of economic activity. Structural distortions in cross-border markets counteracted the technological and organizational advances of the era and severely hampered international plant specialization and intra-firm trade.

22.1.3   Stage 3: 1945 to late 1960s

The *third* stage of the evolution of MNE activity was between 1945 and the late 1960s. These were the years in which the technological and economic hegemony of the US was at its zenith and the international agreements forged at Bretton Woods and GATT were having their most dramatic impact on trade liberalization. During these years, too, international direct investment, initially from the US and the UK but later from other Continental European countries and Japan, became an increasingly significant modality of international economic commerce. This reflected the growing importance of all kinds of proprietary rights as a form of competitive advantage of firms, as well as the strong pressures and incentives to exploit these rights from a foreign location.[3] *Inter alia* these latter pressures and incentives reflected the shortage of the currencies of the leading investing countries by the prospective importers; the rapidly rising demand for minerals, materials and foodstuffs by industrialized countries, especially those located in developing countries; and the incentives provided to attract import substituting investment, especially by Canada, Australia and some of the larger developing countries.

As the significance of foreign production and the number of MNE affiliates grew, the organizational philosophy of MNEs shifted from being mono- or ethnocentric to being polycentric, with many companies replacing their international divisions by cross-border functional/product or regional divisions. At the same time, in only a few of the larger high technology MNEs was there any real attempt to organize their subsidiaries as part of a closely controlled network of value-added activities or to exploit fully the risk-reducing or arbitrage advantages of producing in different economic or political environments. This was also a period in which Keynesian economic policies were in full vogue and governments were assuming a more important role in influencing national diamonds of competitive advantage (Porter, 1990). Towards the end of the period, the role of 'created' factor endowments (e.g. entrepreneurship, technology and human capital) was becoming a more important feature of the L attractions of countries, particularly among industrialized developed countries, between which the significance of intra-industry trade was also increasing.

22.1.4   Stage 4: From end 1960s to mid 1980s

The *fourth* stage, from the mid-1960s to the mid-1980s, was distinguished by a series of events which combined both to increase the propensity of MNEs to integrate and control many of their cross-border activities and to take a more geocentric stance towards these activities. The period was also marked by a movement towards regional integration in Europe and, to a lesser extent, in Asia and Latin America. This allowed MNEs in those regions to rationalize their value-added activities and recoup some of the advantages of product and plant specialization and intra-firm trade.

By the mid-1980s, most developing countries were relaxing some of their restrictive policies towards inbound investment that had been a characteristic of the early and mid 1970s. This mainly reflected a shift in their macro-economic policies from import substituting to export led or balanced growth, increasing unemployment and reduced rates of growth in these economies,[4] and/or the better understanding and expertise of governments in negotiating with MNEs. The period was also marked by a growth in alternative forms of international business involvement to that of the fully-owned foreign subsidiary, as well as a more pronounced heterogeneity of these forms across countries, industries and firms.

During these years, too, the international distribution of O advantages leading to MNE activity became more evenly balanced between the leading industrial economies – a fact most vividly demonstrated by the US becoming the world's largest inward, as well as the largest outward direct investor, by the mid 1980s.

22.1.5   Stage 5: Mid 1980s to date

The *fifth* and current state of evolution of the global economy is essentially distinguished from its predecessors by a series of dramatic changes in the world economic and political scenario; by a new generation of advances in information generation, processing and dissemination; and by the introduction of a range of generic technologies and organizational methods, which together are fundamentally altering the structure and organization of production and the transactional relationships between firms. At the same time, MNEs are becoming increasingly aware of the need to be responsive to the local supply conditions, institutional systems and markets of the countries in which they operate, and how these, in turn, may be used to strengthen their own O-specific resources and capabilities.

These factors and the response of MNEs to them are also affecting the configuration of the competitive advantages of nations. By the end of the 1980s, in most advanced industrial economies, not only were natural factor endowments assuming a less important locational role and engineered factor endowments a more important role, but also the actions of governments, through their willingness and ability to affect the quantity and quality of these endowments and their organization, were assuming a new significance.

These developments are causing a realignment of both the strategies of companies as they seek to remain innovatory and competitive in a global economy, and the macro-organizational strategies of countries as they seek to encourage domestic and foreign firms both to upgrade their indigenous resources and to use these resources more productively. The rise of MNEs from the Third World, the growth of cross-border strategic alliances, the increasing attention paid by governments to competitiveness as a goal in itself and the closer interaction between corporate and regional integration, are all illustrations of these developments.

In the early 1990s, although foreign direct investors of the earlier post-war period still exist, especially among emerging and smaller sized nations, the large international firm is evolving into a very different sort of institution. It is increasingly assuming the role of an orchestrator of production and transactions within a system of cross-border internal and external relationships, which may, or may not, involve equity investment, but which are intended to serve its global interests.

From being mainly a provider of capital, management and technology to its outlying affiliates, each operating more or less independently, and then a coordinator of the way in which resources are used within a closely knit family of affiliates, the decision-taking nexus of the MNE in the early 1990s has come to resemble the central nervous system of a much larger group of interdependent, but less formally governed activities aimed primarily at advancing the global competitive strategy and position of the core organization. This it does, first, by efficiently combining its O-specific resources with those it acquires from other firms or the market, second, by its technology, product and marketing strategies, and third, by the nature and form of alliances it concludes with other firms. The sixth largest industrial firm in the world in 1991 – IBM – has long been regarded as the leader in new forms of cross-border organization. Today, the company is no longer the manufacturer of a single integrated device, but rather the organizing centre of a community of interrelated goods and service companies. Similarly, ITT currently regards itself as a constellation of information-intensive companies, each supplying customized products to local or international markets. This is a far cry from 20 years ago when ITT was a leading producer of a whole variety of manufactured products.

In a renowned study, Bartlett and Ghoshal

(1989) have suggested that in the 1990s the competence of a firm to develop and manage a cross-border network of separate but interrelated value-added activities will be the key factor determining the success in the global competitive environment (p. 212). Such a competence, they argue, is three-pronged. First, it involves taking full advantage of the economies of scale and scope arising from global integration. Second, it involves a proper appreciation of differences in the supply capabilities and consumer needs in different countries. Third, it involves using the experience gained in global and national markets to strengthen the resource base of the firm as a whole. Such a balance between globalization, localization and learning experience will clearly vary according to the nature and range of products produced, where they are produced and firm-specific characteristics. It may also depend upon the channels of knowledge and expertise within the MNE and the way in which decisions are taken.

Not all, indeed, not even the majority of MNEs have reached this last stage of evolution and most never will. In this chapter, we shall be mainly concerned with the 500 or so largest MNEs which currently account for about four-fifths of the value of all foreign production. For these giant concerns, the stage is set for the emergence of a galaxy of technology-related and information-based networks of value-added activities, which will be far removed, in function and form, from their labour and resource-intensive predecessors.

A few such enterprises already exist and their sphere of influence is rapidly spreading. As Chapter 9 has demonstrated, one of the features of the past decade has been the dramatic escalation in the number of strategic and 'first-best' cooperative ventures concluded between large enterprises often domiciled in different countries. The express purpose of such alliances has been to reduce the transaction and production costs of activities at different stages of the value-adding chain, and/or to gain access to complementary resources and capabilities. Some of these strategic asset acquiring coalitions are very different in kind, purpose and scope to the joint ventures and non-equity arrangements of the earlier post-war period, which, more often than not, were made for defensive or second best reasons, e.g. in response to the exhortations of host governments.

There are several implications of the new style

MNEs for our theorizing about the determinants and effects of international production and of the response of governments to MNE-controlled activities. First, they cause us to reappraise our thinking about the nature, functions and boundaries of firms and markets, as well as the way each is organized. Second, they cast doubt on the usefulness of some of our existing classifications of economic activities and market forms. Third, they are profoundly affecting the pattern, ownership and location of international economic activity. Fourth, they require governments to rethink their domestic economic and macro-organizational strategies in the light of the much greater ease with which resources and capabilities can now move across national boundaries – and particularly within MNEs.

However, before speculating further into the future interaction between the competitive advantages of firms and Nation States, we wish to pay some attention to the main variables which are likely to bring these changes about. Most of these will be familiar to the reader by now as they have helped shape the core paradigm of this volume.

22.2 THE DETERMINANTS OF INTERNATIONAL PRODUCTION: A REPRISE

Throughout the last century, four main factors have been the driving force behind the emergence, growth and changing structure of international business activity. The first, and in the long run, the most important as it directly affects the other three, has been a series of major technological advances coupled with a continual upgrading in the quality of human capital. These events have not only made possible a new range of materials and products which our forefathers could scarcely have imagined but have also dramatically impacted on the way in which assets, goods, people and ideas are organized and moved over space. As a consequence of these advances, both the global structure of value-added activities and the modalities in which goods and services are exchanged across national borders have helped push back the industrial and territorial boundaries of firms, and have refashioned the competitive advantages of countries.

The second driving force has been the pace and structure of economic development. This may be measured in a variety of ways, but perhaps the most telling are the change in gross national product (GNP) per head and a variety of social welfare or human developments.[6] For example, over the period 1965–89, the annual average growth of world population was 1.9%, that of the world's GNP 1.6% and that of world merchandise trade (exports plus imports) 5.2% (World Bank, 1991). The most spectacular economic and social achievements have been recorded by Japan and several Asian developing countries. Nations such as South Korea, Taiwan, Thailand, Singapore, Malaysia and Hong Kong are the contemporary equivalents to the UK, Germany, France and the US of the 19th Century. Their progress has fundamentally affected the international allocation of economic activity and the composition of the world's largest firms.[7] Moreover, by their very distinctive business cultures, organizational patterns and government–industry relationships, Japan and the East Asian 'tigers' have helped fashion new cross-border hierarchical and cooperative business relationships.[8]

The third vehicle of change has been the attitude of governments towards the limits of their economic boundaries and the way in which their policies interact with international economic events. Though Nation States are no less schizophrenic than they used to be – in the sense that they want the benefits of economic interdependence without the costs – the general trend, again largely brought about by events beyond their control, has been towards, rather than away from, the globalization of production and trade. The current wave of intra-Triad protectionism in no way negates this proposition. Indeed, it is a perfectly understandable response of governments to some of the inevitable costs of restructuring occasioned, for example, by regional integration and the increasing Japanese presence in the US and Europe.

Both trade and MNE activity are absolutely and proportionally more important in the world economy than they have ever been.[9] Even countries which, historically, have pursued the most restrictionist policies towards FDI (e.g. India,[10] the People's Republic of China and some African countries) are now taking a more open stance (UN, 1992a). Also, the last major bastions of economic isolationism in

Central and Eastern Europe seem likely to become important actors on the international stage by the late 1990s. By one means or another, willingly or not, Nation States are becoming increasingly locked into each other's economic destinies. MNEs are both shaping and being shaped by government attitudes and world economic events. If anything, their role seems likely to become more influential in the future.

The *fourth* key factor affecting the growth and pattern of international (as well as domestic) business in recent years has been the way in which economic activity is organized.[11] This, in fact, is a consequence of the first three. Nonetheless, it reflects the increasing inappropriateness of traditional producing and transactional modes to cope with the demands of contemporary technology and consumer tastes. Historically, as Chapter 3 has shown, for much of the century after the industrial revolution the spot market remained the dominant form of organizing cross-border transactions, both among firms and between firms and people. During this period, the single-product enterprise continued to be the main vehicle of production. In the early 1990s, while the spot markets still account for the majority of transactions involving factor services and final goods, the transactions of intermediate products are being increasingly internalized within firms or jointly undertaken by two or more enterprises.

The stages of the evolution of MNE activity described earlier can be traced to a changing juxtaposition of these four forces, and how these, in turn, have impacted upon consumer tastes and aspirations, market structure, the ownership and management of firms, and the supply of money capital. The first movement abroad of firms in modern history coincided with a series of technological advances leading to the innovation and commercialization of new products and production methods, as well as of improved methods of transportation, communications and storage. These, in turn, fostered the search for new materials and energy sources to satisfy the demands of industrial products, and of new and better quality consumer goods to meet the rising real incomes of a growing population. However, because of uncertainties over the willingness or capability of supplying firms (which were mainly located in developing countries) to fulfil the terms of

their contracts, buying firms found it desirable to internalize these markets or invest in the production of the intermediate products themselves. Similarly, to ensure that the products would be effectively marketed, firms integrated forwards into foreign marketing and distribution networks. Later, as the roundaboutness of production increased and R&D became an important link in the value-added chain, manufacturing firms integrated forwards to lessen the risk of their proprietary technology being pirated, dissipated or inappropriately used.

The late 1960s saw a new generation of technological discoveries. However, this time the focus of interest was on process technology (notably automation and computerization) and telecommunications. These were also years of a widespread reduction in trade barriers – notably as initiated by successive GATT rounds, the EC and EFTA, and by preferential trade agreements, such as those agreed by the Lomé conventions. As described in Chapter 17, the developing countries also helped create free trade areas in Latin America, East Africa and the Caribbean, and, towards the end of the 1970s, in Asia. At the same time, both technological and organizational innovations were encouraging the specialization and common ownership of vertically and horizontally related activities. The idea of a world product mandate took shape; international sourcing in several industries became the norm; and there was a marked increase in the propensity of MNEs to integrate and centrally control their production, marketing and innovatory activities.

During these years, the world was becoming politically and economically less stable. The oil crisis, fluctuating currencies, uncertainties about the future supply of many commodities and the adversarial stance assumed by several governments towards inbound direct investment, all exacerbated cross-market failure. At the same time, the rapid growth of the economies of East Asia and the establishment of customs unions or free trade zones prompted a new international division of labour both between countries and within MNEs. In fact, as one group of foreign direct investors – mainly in the primary product sectors – was forced to divest, or partially divest, its overseas assets, another group – mainly in the high technology manufacturing and information-intensive service sectors – was rapidly investing in new 100% owned foreign affiliates.[12]

As we have seen, the main feature of this period was that the distinctive O-specific advantages of MNEs began to reside more in their ability to create, acquire and effectively organize the use of resources and competences across national boundaries, and less in the privileged possession of specific proprietary assets. However, effective control was generally thought to require full equity ownership. In sectors where such control was not deemed necessary, joint ventures or contractual agreements became the dominant form of foreign involvement.

22.3 CONTEMPORARY DEVELOPMENTS

22.3.1 Technological advances

The current phase in the evolution of MNE activity is marked by three new developments. The first is a series of major and, for the most part systemic, technological advances. These are not only having a widespread impact on the OLI configurations of MNEs and the diamonds of competitive advantage of the countries in which they operate (Porter, 1990), but are also bringing about major changes in the organization of economic activity. In the 1990s, inter-firm *cooperation* in the production and transaction of goods and services is becoming as much a feature of the macro-organizational system as are markets and hierarchies.

Contemporary innovatory advances are of two main kinds. First, there are those which are essentially directed towards aiding the efficiency of production. These include a number of core technologies which may be described as generic because they are multi- rather than uni-purpose in their application and affect a wide range of industrial activities. Examples include robotization, a range of biotechnological discoveries and the latest generation of microchip computer-related technologies.[13] Unlike their predecessors, these technologies are not only labour saving, but also economize on capital, raw materials and energy, and are more flexible in their use.

Another feature about the new technologies is that their efficient utilization frequently requires them to be fused with other technologies produced by a different group of firms. Optoelectronics, for example, is a marriage of electronics and optics and is yielding important commercial products such as optical fibre communication systems (Kodama, 1992). The latest generation of large commercial aircraft, for example, requires the combined skills of metallurgy, aeronautical engineering and aero-electronics. Current medical advances often need the technological resources of pharmacology, biotechnology, laser technology and genetic engineering for their successful commercialization. The design and construction of chemical plants involves innovatory inputs from chemical, engineering and materials sectors. New telecommunication devices embrace the latest advances in carbon materials, fibre optics, computer technology and electronic engineering. Modern industrial building techniques need to draw upon the combined expertise of engineering, materials and production technologies. In its venture to explore the sea-bed, Kenecott's mining consortium brings together a large number of technical disciplines and firms from many different industrial sectors (Contractor and Lorange, 1988). Since both the consumption and the production of most core technologies usually yield externalities of one kind or another, it follows that one or the other of the firms involved may be prompted to recoup these benefits by integrating the separate activities, particularly those which draw upon the same generic technology.

The second kind of innovatory advance is that which lowers the transaction costs of doing business. Contemporary advances in telematics and information technology are dramatically changing the feasibility and cost of data transmission and data-intensive services. Films, tapes, compact discs, written instructions and sources of information can be reproduced then transported over large distances at little cost. Consequently, not only is the need for the simultaneous presence of the buyer and seller of data drastically reduced, but also the timing of production and consumption need not be coincidental (UNCTC, 1988). A firm which is able efficiently to acquire, assemble, interpret and monitor information over a wide geographical area is thus afforded a major new O advantage. At the same time, a great deal of information cannot easily be bought or sold on the open market, as much of it is of value only to the firms that currently own it.

The successful production and implementation of both kinds of technology require not only substantial amounts of human and physical capital to exploit them effectively, but also regional or global markets to support their commercialization. They also demand the presence of a sophisticated educational, transport and telecommunications infrastructure, which governments can and do do much to influence (Porter, 1990; Dunning, 1991a). Consumers, too, can play their role by the kinds of demands they place on producers to upgrade and/or lower the costs of their products.

At the same time, the way in which firms acquire and utilize new resources and competences, and the value-added activities flowing from them, may necessitate alliances with other firms in different industrial sectors and/or countries. Chapter 9 has shown that such collaboration may be of two kinds: those which involve firms at the same stage of different value-added chains, and those which involve firms at different stages on the same value-added chain. In the first case, a number of specific collaborative arrangements with a large number of firms may yield the synergistic advantages sought. Though each of these relationships is perceived to advance the strategic objectives of the participating firms, they may be largely independent of each other. By contrast, in the second, the gains rest more on the opportunities for integrating and monitoring a network of transactional relationships between a cluster of industrial producers and consumers. Advances in data-transmitting facilities have affected the way in which firms organize both forms of alliances. For example, where technology which was previously idiosyncratic and tacit becomes standardized and codifiable, there is an increased incentive to externalize its use. On the other hand, the linking of various stages of production by robotic or computer technology might encourage more vertical integration between suppliers and users.

It seems likely that the kinds of technological advances just described will have a no less significant effect upon the location and ownership of economic activity than did earlier advances. Recent data on the international distribution of innovatory activity[14] suggests that while there has been some decentralization of R&D – particularly in resource-based sectors – the great bulk continues to be undertaken in the five leading industrial nations, *viz* the US, Japan, Germany, the UK and France. At the same time, it is clear that MNEs within the Triad are increasingly

seeking an innovatory presence in North America, Japan and Western Europe.[15] This is primarily taking place through joint ventures and A&Ms rather than through the upgrading of existing value-added activities by greenfield ventures.

Other research, notably that of Porter, has shown that in spite of a fairly similar structure of basic or *natural* resources among developed countries, that of *created* asset endowments[16] does differ. Hence, so will the capability of Nation States both to create and use human and physical capital. Countries also vary in their ability to supply or employ different types of technology. Some, including Japan, Germany and Singapore, are particularly adept in innovating technologies for use in the fabricating sectors. Others, like Belgium, the UK and Canada, appear to have a comparative advantage in process technology. Some do better in manufacturing goods that require mass production techniques; others are particularly competent at operating more flexible production systems or in supplying idiosyncratic products for specialized niche markets. Partly, at least, this may reflect their ability to supply the complementary assets (e.g. marketing skills) which technological innovation requires, as well as the presence of the necessary stimulus (provided, for example, by consumers, rival firms and tax incentives) for firms to be entrepreneurial and innovatory. Culture-specific attributes, the availability of different sorts of factor inputs, the character of inter- and intra-firm relationships, and attitudes towards risk and product innovations are no less important factors.

Indeed, studies of both countries and firms are increasingly suggesting that national and corporate culture and the institutional framework for technology creation and deployment – particularly the way in which firms combine their core assets with those acquired from other firms – are crucial competitive advantages in their own right (Bartlett and Ghoshal, 1989; Bartlett et al., 1990). Clearly, governments, directly or indirectly, can and do play an important role in affecting the amount and kind of innovatory activity. Indeed, the question at issue is less 'should governments intervene or not?' than 'how, or how much, should they intervene?'

In most countries which have recorded an active innovatory record in recent years, the direct involvement of governments has been much less than is generally supposed, apart from the funding of tertiary education and defence-related R&D. While some of the latter expenditure has generated results which have spilled over to the non-defence sector and, most certainly, has stimulated the supply of some kinds of trained manpower, it may also have crowded out other (in the long run, more worthy) forms of technological development.

Nevertheless, the main government impact on innovatory capacity has been indirect, through influencing in one way or another, the demand for and supply of capabilities for innovation-intensive products, and determining the innovatory ethos and institutional structure for upgrading human and physical capital. This includes the regulatory environment, macro-economic and organizational policy and micro-economic management, attitudes to financial markets and risk taking, and policies on corporate mergers, alliances and FDI and so on.

22.3.2   Economic development

For the past two decades, the global economy has been undergoing a major restructuring. As a consequence, the economic alignment of Nation States in the early 1990s is very different than that in the 1960s. According to observers like Kenichi Ohmae (1985, 1987), world economic events are becoming increasingly dominated by a Triad of three huge trading blocs – Western Europe, Japan and North America – which currently account for 75% of the world's output and trade and its companies for about 90% of all international production. Each of these blocs has its own geographical hinterland, in and between which there are usually close trading and investment relationships. These hinterlands probably account for another 10% to 12% of the world's output[17] (UNCTC, 1991a).

Although the contribution of the various sectors of economic activity to gross national product varies between the member countries of the Triad, the industrial structure of each has tended to converge over the past 30 years, during which time Japan has emerged as a major economic power and *Pax Americana* has passed the way of *Pax Britannica* 70 years earlier. Both technological advances and the actions of government have helped bring this situation about. Barring completely unforeseen events

or unusually inept macro-economic management, it seems likely that, for the foreseeable future, a triumvirate of economic powers will largely determine the course of economic events. According to some observers (Bergsten, 1990), this could lead to some instability in cross-border organizational systems as, in order to prevent any one of the Triad consultants from gaining complete economic hegemony, the other two might form some kind of strategic alliance.

It might also be supposed that at least some of the countries in the hinterland of the Triad countries will, themselves, become part of its core in the next decade. Taiwan and South Korea in Asia and Brazil and Mexico in Latin America are obvious candidates. As more economies become industrialized and better off, the role of intra-industry trade and investment, which has always been strongly income-elastic, is likely to increase, though the geographical composition of the leading MNEs is likely to change.

Within both developed and developing economies, the trend also seems to be towards an increasing role of both producer and consumer services in the value-added process. Even in the most advanced industrial countries, it is premature, if not misleading, to talk about deindustrialization, as much of the growth in producer services is directed to improving the long-term competitiveness of the manufacturing sector. Moreover, it is the case that the composition of output – be it of goods or services – in the emerging global economy is becoming increasingly determined by the disposition and productivity of man-made assets and capabilities rather than those of 'natural' resources. *Inter alia* this is shown by the quite dramatic fall in the percentage of raw materials and unskilled labour costs in the sales value of most products (Drucker, 1986).

Since the quintessence of the MNE is that it is a producer, organizer, user and disseminator of created assets and competences, it may be expected that these developments will favour its further growth. Much will depend, of course, on the extent to which the new information-based economy lowers or raises barriers to entry into particular markets and whether it generates its own cross-border economies of scale and scope.

Earlier chapters have identified the many ways in which MNEs may affect the development process. Chapter 4 introduced the concept of the investment development cycle or path and suggested that at different stages of a country's development, the OLI configuration affecting the propensity of its firms to engage in outward direct investment, or for it to be invested in by foreign firms, was both different and, to some extent at least, predictable. Combined with the technological accumulation model and the concepts of virtuous and vicious circles developed by Pavitt (1987) and Cantwell (1989c), we also demonstrated how both inward and outward investment, through its impact on the diamond of competitive advantage, might affect both the ability of a country's own firms to develop new competitive advantages in international markets and the efficiency of location-bound resources.

A priori, without knowledge of a country's resources and capabilities, market structure, presence of related industries, demand conditions and the form and extent of government involvement, it is difficult to make any precise predictions as to how MNE activity will interact with a country's economic development. However, as several chapters in Part 3 of this book sought to demonstrate, it can and does affect different countries very differently. At the same time, we have a much better idea than once we had about the situations in which FDI is likely to have beneficial consequences. Countries that pursue pro-market economic strategies, whose markets are large enough to promote domestic rivalry between firms, whose consumers demand sophisticated and high quality goods and services, whose regional and transport policies favour the development of industrial clusters and agglomerative economies, whose fiscal policies favour entrepreneurship and the upgrading of resources and capabilities, and who fully participate in international trade and commerce – these are the countries that are most likely to profit from inbound direct investment and whose own companies are likely to be the most competitive in international markets.

It is possible to identify and classify countries according to the extent to which they possess the above conditions and, indeed, according to whether inward investment is the most appropriate way for them to obtain the foreign resources needed for development. In theory, at least, it should also be possible to trace and compare the interaction between MNE activity and the economic development of countries over a period of time. However, to

the best of our knowledge there have been no systematic or comparative studies of this kind.[18] To what extent, for example, would the OLI configuration currently facing foreign firms investing in Japan and Japanese firms investing overseas have been different had Japan pursued a similar set of economic policies to those of West Germany in the post-Second World War period? How far is the distinctive diamond of competitive advantage offered by the Singaporean economy responsible for the beneficial impact of inward direct investment (Lecraw, 1985a)? What would the technological position of Mexican industry be today if it had concluded a free trade agreement with the US 30 years ago? Had India historically adopted its currently more liberal position towards both trade and FDI, would her economic development have been speedier and more in tune with her long-run comparative advantages than that which has actually occurred (Lall, 1985)?

The focus of this chapter, however, is directed more to the future. What is likely to be the future role of MNEs as an engine of economic development? To what extent are the competitive advantages of countries likely to change in such a way as to affect the level and structure of inward and outward direct investment?

An examination of the current patterns of development and of the policies pursued by different countries suggests that there remain tremendous opportunities for MNE activity, and that many of the technological and organizational advances previously documented are assisting both the pace of development and the opportunity to deploy foreign resources. This is especially noticeable in the Far East, where the next generation of Eastern 'tigers', *viz* Thailand, Indonesia and the Philippines, are not only recording impressive rates of growth, but are also fashioning macro-organizational policies to ensure that the contribution of inward investment is optimized.

A comparison between economic trends and the role of inward investment in these countries, as well as many of those in Latin America and almost all African sub-Saharan territories, reveals quite dramatic differences. Within the developing countries, the gap in income levels between the most and the least developed is widening. The conditions making for the success of East Asian NICs are conspicuously absent in most other developing countries. Part of the reason undoubtedly lies in the burden of foreign debt of the latter countries, but no less important is their failure to embrace appropriate economic management programmes and structural adjustments, and to accept the costs of interdependence as well as the benefits.

The rapidly changing situation in Central and Eastern Europe is demonstrating both the costs and the benefits of economic development, as well as the actual and potential roles of MNEs in that development (McMillan, 1991). In spite of much initial interest and a substantial initial influx of foreign capital, mainly in the form of joint ventures, the institutional, organizational and cultural problems of converting the various economies from collectivist to market-oriented systems are likely completely to dwarf any efforts of Western private enterprise to promote economic development for some years to come (Dunning, 1991d). In the opinion of McMillan (1991), one of the foremost analysts of FDI in Eastern Europe, until the educational, technological and institutional infrastructure is improved, there is unlikely to be a dramatic increase in foreign MNE participation in most Central and Eastern European economies. Except for East Germany, and possibly Czechoslovakia and Hungary, McMillan does not see this occurring until the second half of the 1990s.

22.3.3 New organizational forms[19]

The third development of the early 1990s relates to changes in the nature and scope of business enterprises, and especially the burgeoning of various forms of cross-border corporate alliances. At one time the boundaries of a firm were assumed to be constrained by its own entrepreneurial vision, technological capabilities, financial resources and organizational strengths (Penrose, 1958). Where firms diversified into new product lines or sought new markets, they usually did so in the belief that they could benefit from the economies of vertical or horizontal integration. Moreover, when considered at all, most inter-firm relationships were assumed to be combative, unstructured, short-term and to involve little or no control or influence by one party over the value-added activities of the other. Possible exceptions included some dealerships in durable consumer goods.

In the early 1990s, the situation is very different.

Even when firms are not vertically integrated by ownership, the importance attached to ensuring that upstream and/or downstream value-added activities are undertaken at the lowest production and transaction costs is increasingly demanding a more cooperative stance between suppliers and customers which, in some cases, amounts to quasi-integration. In some countries (e.g. the US and Germany) it is usual for the terms of the relationship to be formally codified in a legally binding contract. In others, notably in Japan and Korea, though no less binding, the ties may take the form of a moral commitment of the transacting parties based on forbearance, trust, reputation building and allegiance to group values (Buckley and Casson, 1988).

Horizontal relationships are even more heterogeneous. The acquisition, merger and joint equity venture are all well known, and cross-licensing agreements have been common since the turn of the century. What is new, and is the direct result of developments identified in previous paragraphs, is the phenomenal growth of non-equity strategic alliances between enterprises who, outside the alliances, may fiercely compete with each other. Chapter 9 has already examined the structure and *raison d'être* for these alliances; so far, there has been little substantive research on their economic consequences. However, to the student of international business – particularly one brought up in the neo-classical tradition – they offer new intellectual challenges. In what circumstances will firms choose to cooperate, rather than compete, with each other? Exactly where do collaborative ventures fit into the spot market/hierarchies continuum of transnational relationships? Are they more akin to other kinds of non-equity ventures or mergers, but limited in design and purpose, or do they require a complete reappraisal of the character of international business relationships?

The issue is further complicated because the terms of cooperative agreements vary so much. Costs and benefits may be direct or indirect. Viewed from the perspective of one or the other of the partners involved in an alliance, the direct costs include the capital invested in R&D facilities and human skills, the provision of physical and intangible assets, new training programmes, and marketing and distribution facilities. Indirect costs are those internal to the participating organizations but external to the cooperative agreement. These might include any negative spill-over effects on the firm's global competitive position (e.g. if its partner(s) to the alliance benefits more than it does). Direct benefits include jointly shared results of R&D, lower production costs, improved technological capacity, reduced risks, better market access, improved production techniques and/or productivity, spreading of administration overheads, new insights into managerial and organizational techniques, and a better appreciation of unfamiliar cultures and business methods. Indirect benefits include a relative strengthening in the firm's overall competitive position and additional economies of scope and/or integration.

There is every sign that the 1990s will lead to more pluralism in both domestic and transnational inter-firm relationships. Although, at the end of the day, firms are separate legal entities, it is likely that technological and organizational pressures – especially the rising costs of R&D and global marketing – will encourage more cross-border cooperative ventures. The main caveat surrounds the attitude of governments or regional authorities (e.g. the EC) to anything which smacks of a restraint on competition or an abuse of monopoly power.

At the same time, to achieve their objectives, firms normally have to operate in contestable markets. In the case of a single-product firm, the sources of competition (i.e. contestability) are easily identifiable and the impact of any horizontal or vertical alliance on its competitive position can be evaluated without too much difficulty. However, in the case of a multiple-product firm, its rivals consist of the universe of firms producing (or likely to produce) any of the products it supplies, or who compete (or are likely to compete) in any of the markets it serves. Moreover, no one competitor is likely to have exactly the same portfolio of value-added activities or markets as another.

Admittedly, most MNEs, apart from the conglomerates, can readily identify their main rivals, or potential rivals, together with their main strengths and weaknesses. However, as the boundaries of a firm's activities become increasingly difficult to draw – not withstanding the 'core competence' syndrome[20] (Prahalad and Hamel, 1990) – the architecture of contestable markets, as traditionally defined, will require redefining. Indeed, the main emphasis of

competition may switch from the kind of product portfolio a firm may offer its customers to its ability to manage and coordinate complementary inputs – especially those of diverse technologies and human capabilities – to produce a group of quite disparate products.

Elsewhere (Dunning, 1988a) we have described the headquarters of a modern MNE as a nerve centre and controller of a network of interrelated cross-border value-added activities.[21] Some of these activities the MNE will undertake itself; others it will undertake jointly with other firms. However, over each and all of these activities it will seek to exercise systemic control or influence. At the same time, the motivation for, and outcome of, any particular alliance formed is not only dyadic, as each relationship must take account of the effects it has on the network of relationships forged by the initiating firm.

Robertson (1948) once described firms as 'islands of conscious power in this ocean of unconscious cooperation, like lumps of butter coagulating in a pail of buttermilk'. However, the modern large firm, particularly the large MNE, is not an island set within an ocean of unconscious cooperation – except in so far that it is set apart from (i.e. can be identified as being different from) other firms (islands). Between the islands are a series of causeways which are linked to each other by mutual self-interest; these causeways help forge conscious, rather than unconscious, cooperation.

The Robertson analogy is deficient in another respect; it assumes that the size of firms (islands) is constant and independent of each other. Perhaps a more apt parallel might be drawn from molecular biology. Firms, like organisms, though separate entities, are inextricably linked with each other and, according to the nature and strength of the link, affect each other's form and structure. In addition, the way in which each organism is constructed and sustained will affect its characteristics and functions, as well as its ability to interact with, and impact on, other organisms. Finally, since organisms are constantly changing, as is their interaction with other living entities, they can only be fully understood by examining them within an evolutionary context.

Until recently, economists, unlike sociologists and organizational theorists, paid scant attention to the firm as a member of a clan decision-taking unit which perceives its own interests to be best served by maximizing the well-being of the clan to which it belongs. One notable exception was Richardson who, in 1972, put forward the concept of inter-company cooperation and affiliation 'as an alternative form of transactional relationship between firms'. He argued that coordination of economic activity by cooperation would be preferable to that by hierarchies whenever the transaction costs of organizing dissimilar activities are high; and it would be preferable to that of markets wherever the coordination requires not the matching of aggregate supply with aggregate demand but rather the plans of separate enterprises (Richardson, 1972).

To the extent that, like administrative fiat within a single firm, inter-firm cooperation is a market-replacing activity, at least some of the reasons for it should be found in the internalization literature. However, in so far as it involves more than one firm and there is a broad coincidence of objectives between the participants, the form of governance is group oriented. To distinguish between the two forms of governance, we might refer to inter-corporate cooperation as *collective internalization*. Such internalization might take the form of an equity joint venture or a non-equity agreement, although, strictly speaking, only the former is a *de jure* internalization.

Finally, returning to the eclectic paradigm, we foresee that the new style of MNEs of the 1990s will prosper when they are able:

(1) To create and sustain O-specific advantages which reflect both their individual hierarchical capacities and competences, and their success in combining these with those of other hierarchies in such a way that their overall and long-term competitive position is strengthened.

(2) To use a variety of modalities to exploit these advantages, which might arise from individual or collaborative production capabilities and/or transaction economies; these may vary along the market/hierarchies spectrum.

(3) To locate value-added activities, either individually or jointly with other firms, in a way that is consistent with the overall objectives of the company.

The additional dimension opened up by collective internalization essentially stems from the conflicts of interest that may arise about the way in which the collaboration should be organized. Such conflicts occur because of the differential impact which any decisions taken by the parties in respect of the alliance may have on their other activities. For example, take the question of where a jointly-owned R&D laboratory should be located. While it may be possible to identify the optimum location, where the laboratory is a standalone activity, in practice this is unlikely to be the case. The fact that a particular location may differently affect the strategic objectives of the two firms may give rise to conflict. Such conflicts may, and do, occur whenever the impact of market failure differently affects each partner in the sense that if the decisions were taken separately within the hierarchies they would have been different.

22.3.4   The role of government

The final development likely to determine the future course of MNE activity is the role of governments. We have already argued that national governments are increasingly having to accept the fact that the economic prosperity of their constituents is as much determined by what is happening in the world economy, as by what is happening within their boundaries; and that it is in the interests of the leading industrial nations, at least, to coordinate their macro-economic and organizational policies in a way that minimizes disturbances, instabilities and structural rigidities in the world economy. Yet, this collaborative stance is not inconsistent with the policies which governments might pursue to ensure that they can maintain and advance their own national competitive positions. The early 1990s are witnessing the emergence of globally-oriented economic policies among Nation States as well as among firms. The principle of comparative advantage, which was enunciated on the assumption that the resource endowments of nations complement, rather than compete, with each other, may require some reassessment in a world in which cross-border failure and the mobility of critical resources and capabilities are the norm rather than the exception; and where technology, human capital, market structures, organizational systems and country-specific cultural values, rather than natural factor endowments, determine the level and structure of a nation's competitive advantages (Lipsey, 1990).

Of the factors likely to influence the future interaction between governments and MNE activity in both developed and developing countries, there are three which we believe are worth stressing. The first concerns the role of governments in influencing the general economic climate; the second relates to the strategies of governments in promoting industrial competitiveness; and the third is the attitudes of national governments to global or regional integration.

(a) The economic milieu for international business

To suggest that the role of government in affecting the milieu for MNE activity is likely to increase in the next decade or more may seem to run counter to the current trend towards less government intervention and more liberalization of markets. Yet if one examines the factors currently voiced by MNEs in the siting of manufacturing and service activities in different countries, those which are most frequently cited are strongly influenced by government policy (Dunning, 1989; JETRO, 1990). As this volume has frequently emphasized, in most branches of manufacturing industry both natural resources and labour – particularly unskilled or semi-skilled labour – are accounting for a decreasing proportion of the value-added activity. Increasingly significant are the costs and availability of created capabilities and competences, the transport communications and information-facilitating infrastructure without which these assets could not be efficiently used and the role of governments as fashioners of economic ideologies and systems.

While all of these latter variables affect the revenue and *production* costs of firms, they have a much more profound influence on their intra- and inter-firm *transactional* costs and benefits. These transaction costs are in no way reduced by the liberalization of markets. This is because much of the kind of cross-border market failure which MNE activity internalizes is not a result of government-imposed distortions, but that which stems from the inability of the market system to optimize the creation and allocation of resources under conditions of uncertainty; and where the impact of the decisions

dictated by market forces affect individuals and institutions which are not party to the goods or services being exchanged.

(b) Governments as strategic oligopolists

At the same time, national governments are likely to adopt more proactive strategies to protect and advance the competitiveness of their resources and capabilities in the 1990s. Increasingly, too, governments are beginning to view their role as harvesters of at least part of the rent generated by *global* economic activity and as protectors of their own enterprises from unacceptable economic strategies pursued by other governments. In a very real sense, governments are assuming the role of strategic oligopolists, in a world economy dominated by the activities of large integrated MNEs. Sometimes, this role is played out at a micro-organizational level (e.g. in strategic tax, trade, technology and FDI policy[21]) and sometimes at a systemic or macro-organizational level. We believe that in the 1990s, political scientists, economists and business analysts will need to pay much more attention to the strategy-led organizational policies of national governments than they have done in the past.

As yet, the explicit acceptance by governments of this function and its implications for the wide range of economic and other policies is limited to a number of Asian countries. In the main, Western governments still confine their macro- and micro-economic organizational policies to offering investment grants, subsidies or fiscal incentives to selective firms, industries or regions; to providing information about foreign market opportunities; to financing or subsidizing some kinds of R&D and training programmes; and to participating in international forums (e.g. GATT and the US–Japan strategic initiative talks[22]) to ensure that the international playing field for trade and foreign investment is kept as level as possible. Sometimes, too, Western governments take direct retaliatory action against foreign firms that are perceived to operate against their national interests, for example, by means of anti-dumping legislation against exporters, or the imposition of performance requirements (e.g. TRIMS) on inward investors. Although these – and many other measures – may add up to an impressive package of interventionism, more often than not the strategies are piecemeal and uncoordinated, and are intended to achieve very specific goals other than that of advancing national competitiveness.

As Chapter 20 has already indicated, the most dramatic evidence of a systemic approach to competitiveness and international business is that practiced by the Japanese government. Throughout the last 30 years, the Japanese government, by a variety of means, has actively and consciously influenced the level, direction and location of economic activity. In so doing, it has not attempted to replace the market, but to work with the market to achieve a structure of innovatory and productive activity consistent with its perception of Japan's comparative dynamic advantage. In the early post-war period, *viz* up to the mid-1960s, government intervention was direct and all pervasive. Nowadays it is much more indirect and selective, but it is still underpinned by an integrated macro-organizational strategy, geared to a continuous upgrading of indigenous technological assets and human skills and to sustaining and enhancing the competitiveness of Japanese firms in global markets.

One well known Japanese economist has characterized post-war Japanese industrial and trade strategy as that of 'collaborative symbiosis' between government and industry (Ozawa, 1989). Ozawa contrasts this strategy with the fragmentary, adversarial and frequently changing economic policies of most Western nations which, he argues, have engendered much conflict and disharmony between the public and private sectors. This strategy has several familiar features. However, before summarizing them it is worth noting that the Japanese 'miracle' would not have come about, or come about so quickly, had Western industrial nations not been prepared to allow Japanese producers unrestricted access to their markets, natural resources, technology and educational facilities in the years following the Second World War.

According to Ozawa's research and that of Porter, which tells a similar story (Porter, 1990), the fundamental platform of post-war Japanese macro-organizational strategy has been the continual upgrading of its industrial structure through investment in educational and innovatory activities, and by promoting the appropriate entrepreneurial, work and savings ethos necessary to ensure the effective deployment of these assets. Inward and outward direct investment have been an integral part of that strategy rather than an adjunct to it.

For example, in the first stage of its post-war development, Japan concentrated on revitalizing its heavy metal and chemical industries. However, this made enormous demands on various primary products which Japan could not produce for itself. Hence, outbound investment by Japanese MNEs was directed towards guaranteeing a reliable and inexpensive supply of the necessary raw materials, minerals and energy. Later Japan moved to produce less resource-intensive and more knowledge-intensive goods. To do this, it needed Western technology and the latest management and marketing skills. However, rather than obtaining these assets via inward direct investment – as earlier Germany had done – Japan chose to acquire the necessary product and process technology by way of reverse engineering, licensing and other cooperative arrangements with Western firms, as well as by the training of Japanese scientists, engineers, educators, administrators and managers in the US and Europe.

As Japan restructured its industries, it did not completely surrender its involvement in sectors in which its comparative advantage was declining. That was not Japan's way. Instead, backed by low interest loans and tax breaks from the government, by strong technical and financial assistance from the Soga Shosha, the banks and by the Japan Overseas Development Corporation, and by one of the earliest overseas investment guarantee programmes, Japanese firms were urged to transfer their resource- and labour-intensive activities to developing countries. In so doing, they practised what Ozawa calls a 'hand my clothes down' strategy.

In the 1980s, the focus of Japanese investment shifted to Europe and the US. This again was deliberate strategy on the part of the Japanese MNEs, though it was spurred on by a bout of Western protectionism and a rising trade surplus with Japan's major competitors. The more comprehensive Japan's development strategy became, the more it was prepared to give a helping hand to its own firms and to developing countries to promote that strategy. It has also been prepared to use developing countries either as procurement bases for the labour-intensive manufacturing products, or as points of entry into European and US markets which wished to reduce their imports from Japan.

In the meantime, although Japan as begun to take a more liberal attitude towards inbound foreign investment and is now finding its neighbours less willing to sell its cutting edge technology without maintaining some control over it, it remains a substantial creditor on its international direct investment account. In March 1992, the value of Japan's outward direct investment stake was $352.4 billion, 15 times that of its inward investment stake of $22.8 billion.

(c)   Regional economic integration

Finally, on the role of governments in affecting the dynamics of international production, some mention should be given to the formation of regional customs unions and the conclusion of bilateral or multi-lateral trading agreements. This subject was dealt with at some length in Chapter 17. Here it is perhaps sufficient to underline the point that these supra- or inter-government initiatives may dramatically affect the pattern and organization of international business activity and have widespread effects on the competitive advantages of both firms and countries.

Let us reiterate just two examples which we gave in Chapter 17. The first example is the formation of the EC in 1958, which initially caused both a marked deflection of US direct investment away from the UK – which did not become a member until 1972 – and a rationalization in the structure of value-added activities of US-owned firms in the Community. In 1982, US affiliates in the EC exported one-quarter of their output to other parts of the EC, compared with less than 5% in 1957. More particularly, 70% of the exports in 1982 were intra-group, compared with less than 10% in 1957 (Dunning, 1991c). Later in the 1980s, the accession of Portugal and Spain to the EC resulted in a marked reorientation in government macro-organization strategy as well as a realignment of the structure in both countries (Herrera, 1992; Simoes, 1992). Spain, in particular, is proving especially attractive to Japanese investors.

The second example is the marked upsurge of all kinds of foreign direct investment in the EC in the past few years in anticipation of the completion of the internal market in 1992. Figures released in 1991 by the US Department of Commerce (Fahim-Nader, 1991) showed that the actual and anticipated capital expenditure by majority-owned US affiliates in the EC over the three years from 1989 to 1991 are likely to total $89.7 billion – 49.8% of the planned capital expenditures of all foreign affiliates. These figures compare with a figure invested in the same 12 countries of $42.5 billion between 1983 and 1985, which then represented 40% of worldwide capital expenditure of US affiliates.

The growth of Japanese investment in the EC is even more remarkable. In the three years from April 1988 to March 1991, Japanese firms invested more in the EC than over the whole of the previous 19 years. About three-quarters of that investment was in the services sectors.[23] Scholars wishing to study the impact of 1992 on the activities of MNEs would do well to take a dynamic and interactive perspective from the start and, particularly, to consider outward and inward direct investment as complementary determinants of the future competitiveness of the EC and of EC-based firms.

Notwithstanding the excitement generated by EC 1992, it is likely that the main thrust of inter-regional cooperation in the 1990s will occur in Asia and the Pacific, although any prospect of full economic union in that area must surely lie in the distant future. Already, there are signs of a South China Region emerging. Cross-border MNE activity, mainly financed by ethnic Chinese capital, is creating a new economic nexus between Taiwan, Hong Kong, Singapore and the coastal provinces of China (in particular, Guangdong and Fujian). In the later 1990s, it may well extend south into Indo-China. By mid 1990, the investment by Asian NICs in ASEAN and China considerably exceeded that of Japan and the other developed nations.[23]

At the same time, Japan itself is supporting a plan to enhance regional cooperation among Asian and Pacific countries within the auspices of APEC, the Asian-Pacific Economic Cooperation Conference. Finally, there are moves for closer economic ties between Australia and New Zealand.

The momentum for all these collaborative schemes as well as those in other parts of the world is being provided by the globalization of economic activity and the concentration of MNE activity in a number of regional blocs. In effect, countries are behaving like companies and are forming strategic alliances with their neighbours in order to protect or advance their national economic interests. In the

1990s, however, we envisage MNEs playing a more proactive role in influencing the form and contract of regional integration, simply because such integration is being driven by international market forces rather than by national or regional political imperatives.

22.4 CONCLUSIONS

Let us now draw together the threads of this chapter. A review of the dynamics of international production over the past two or more decades suggests a number of characteristics. The first is the movement towards the globalization of production and markets by the leading multinational companies and a more integrated governance of their operations, especially in the advanced industrial nations. At the same time, there is reason to suppose that the MNEs of the 1990s are adjusting their product and marketing profiles to take better account of specific factor endowments and location-specific consumer needs.

Second, we observe a variety of structural changes in both the geographical and industrial composition of MNE activity. Especially noticeable in the 1980s were the emergence of Japan as a major outward investor, the rise in inward investment in the US, the growth in two-way intra-industry investment and the increased role of A&Ms as a form of entry. In the 1990s, the opening up of Central and Eastern Europe, Europe 1992 and regional integration in the Americas, East Asia and the Pacific are likely both to broaden and intensify the role of MNEs and cross-border strategic alliances in the global economy.

All these events have led, or are likely to lead, to a changing interface between the strategically activist role of firms in response to a particular configuration of OLI variables and the strategic activist policies of national governments in response to their perception of their position in the world economy, and how the latter believe their own policies can – within the framework of a market system – facilitate the competitiveness of their firms and resources.

The changing political and economic scenario of the 1970s and 1980s has led to a considerable acceleration in the proactive strategies of firms and governments. Corporate strategies are now fashioning world economic events as much as they are being

fashioned by them. Governments have also become more active in shaping the dynamic restructuring of international production in several ways. At the same time, sharp differences between (Far) Eastern and Western government strategies towards competitiveness have begun to reveal themselves. In the West, policies have been mainly directed at disengaging the government from the market place, although in the international arena there has also been an increasing pressure for selective protectionism. By contrast, in East Asia the philosophy evolved has been one of symbiosis between governments and the private sector, so as to promote a systemic economic strategy geared to a continual upgrading of the productivity of domestic resources and of the competitive advantage of home country firms in international markets.

The developing interface between governments, MNEs and markets and the ways in which MNEs shape or are shaped by the interface are, perhaps, the two most critical questions likely to engage the attention of the international business scholar in the next decade or more. From the perspective of the early 1990s, it seems likely that largely unfettered markets will continue to determine the price and conditions of supply of unskilled labour, most primary commodities, many consumer goods and services and financial assets. But increasingly, one suspects, networks of firms – and often MNEs – will come to determine the pattern of transactions of intermediate products and property rights. This is partly because of the idiosyncratic character of many of these products, and partly because to optimize their value, their use needs to be coordinated under the same governance. Nevertheless, provided there is competition between firms and they are subject to the discipline of the market for the final products they produce, corporate networks may act as surrogates for markets and, indeed, help them to operate more efficiently.

At the same time, the role of national governments is also likely to change. All too frequently, the actions of governments have been seen as combative to those of both markets and firms. While frictions between MNEs and governments will undoubtedly continue in the 1990s (see Vernon (1987) for an elaboration of these), we foresee that, to overcome the kind of international market failure now emerging in the global economy (Eden and Hampson,

1990), governments will find that they need to work with, rather than against, firms. In particular, governments are now valuing the presence of MNEs because they realize that, to be competitive in global markets, they need to foster the unique technological and organizational assets of these firms, including those which arise from their multinationality *per se*.

Governments are also beginning to acknowledge that markets are not a free good. They have to be created and sustained and this takes both time and resources. Moreover, since, when markets operate well, they do so to the benefit of the community as well as of the participants in the markets, governments have a responsibility to see that these net social benefits of markets are maximized.[24] This role of government is as far removed from the *laissez faire* role recommended by the 19th Century liberal economists as it is from the interventionist role advised by socialist economists in the 1960s and 1970s. It is perhaps best described as a strategic activist market-facilitating role.

We would make one final point. Barring unforeseen disasters, and assuming that the leading nations of the world do not retreat into their protectionist shells, there is little doubt that the 1990s will see a continuation of the growth in world trade and that an increasing proportion of that trade will be MNE-related in some way or another. It also seems likely that cross-border direct investment flows will become increasingly similar to those of trade, particularly within the Triad, and that industries – including service industries – will become more rather than less internationally oriented.

One possible outcome of this scenario is that the nationality of a firm's ownership will become less relevant to the location of its wealth-creating activities and to its impact on national economic welfare. Even today, it can no longer be presumed that an American-owned or controlled firm will necessarily provide more economic benefits to the citizens of the US than the US subsidiary of a Japanese or German firm (Reich, 1990). Moreover, as and when the world takes on the characteristics of a global village, and as and when labour as well as capital and technology becomes mobile across national boundaries, then will the distinctions of the MNE, *qua* MNE, become less meaningful and, indeed, less relevant for national policy makers.

NOTES

1 Examples include Keynes (1924), Iversen (1935) and Royal Institute of International Affairs (1937).
2 See, for example, the writings of Southard (1931), Southard *et al.* (1936) and Lewis (1938).
3 Ownership advantages arising from the privileged possession of specific income-generating assets (see Chapter 5).
4 As explained in Chapter 13.
5 By macro-organizational strategies, we mean the actions pursued by governments to organize the creation and structural deployment of resources, capabilities and markets rather than their influence and control. By micro-organizational strategies, we mean actions taken by governments to affect a particular determinant of macro-organizational strategy (e.g. anti-trust policy, environmental control, R&D). The concept of macro- and micro-organizational strategy is further explored in Dunning (1993b).
6 For example, as regularly published by the World Bank in its *World Development Report*.
7 For a recent explanation of the growth of the East Asian economies in terms of the 'flying geese' paradigm, see Ozawa (1991c). For an examination of the changing composition of the world's largest firms in the 1980s see Franko (1989).
8 Particularly in respect of the role of government in shaping comparative advantage. See Lipsey and Dobson (1986) and Wade (1988).
9 For example, according to the US Department of Commerce, between 1985 and 1989, the sales of US foreign subsidiaries rose by 41.4% compared with an increase of 21.1% in their domestic sales. Between 1985 and 1989 the assets of Japanese firms abroad rose by 203.5% compared with a growth in Japanese exports of 56.7% and of Japanese GNP of 23.9%.
10 Since July 1991, India, for example, has allowed majority-owned FDI in selected industrial sectors.
11 The changing interaction between governments, firms and markets is discussed in some detail in Dunning (1991a, b).
12 As Chapter 2 has shown, between 1975 and 1988, the share of foreign direct assets owned by the leading industrialized nations directed to the primary sector fell from around 25% to 15%, while that directed to the service sector rose from around 30% to 45%.
13 For an excellent survey of the interaction between MNE activity and the technologies of the late 1980s, see Van Tulder and Junne (1988).
14 As, for example, summarized in Pearce (1989), Dunning (1992d).
15 One recent expression of which is the setting up of a new European technology centre by Sony in Wales.

See, for example, International Herald Tribune, 22 May, 1992.

16 Elsewhere referred to as transaction cost related endowments (Dunning, 1990).

17 Thus, for example, the US has a revealed advantage in supplying Latin American countries with capital, goods and services; Japan has an advantage in its dealings with South East Asia; while the UK's hinterland extends to much of the middle East and sub-Saharan (non-Francophile) Africa.

18 But see Dunning (1985) for a comparative analysis of the impact of MNE activity on the economic structure and international competitiveness of nine developed and three developing countries. Also in a cross-sectional study of 69 non-oil producing developing countries, Blomström, Lipsey and Zejan (1992) found there was a positive and significant relationship between FDI inflows averaged over the period 1965–85 and real GDP per capita for middle income countries. At the same time, the domestic investment variable was only marginally significant. Some work on this subject is also being undertaken by UNCTC (see UN, 1992a).

19 The following paragraphs draw heavily on some earlier writings of the author. See especially Dunning (1988b).

20 By which firms are seeking to group their value-added activities around (what they perceive to be) their core competitive competences. Prahalad and Hamel defined such competences as 'the collective learning in the organization, especially how to coordinate diverse production skills and integrate multiple streams of technology' (p. 82). The authors go on to argue that core competence is about harmonizing streams of technology and about the organization of wares and the delivery of value' (p. 83). Examples of core competences cited by Prahalad and Hamel include optics, images and microprocessor controls in the case of Canon (which has helped the company dominate markets as diverse as cameras, semiconductors, lithographic equipment and laser printers) and electronic controls, fluid power and electric power in the case of Vickers.

21 For the concept of strategic (direct) investment policy see UN (1992a). Paralleling strategic trade policy, strategic investment policy is concerned with maximizing the net rents to be earned through government intervention to facilitate the market for MNE activities, or to negate the structurally distorting effects of actions taken by foreign governments. Similarly, strategic tax policy takes into account the possible impact of any tax changes on the locational behaviour of MNEs and on the tax policies of other governments which are competing with them for resources and capabilities. Strategic science and technology policy considers *inter alia* the effect of disbarring foreign affiliates from joining government-sponsored R&D consortia, or the reactions of foreign governments which might include taking similar action. More generally, strategic macro-organizational policy is concerned with actions which national governments might take to capture the rents of international economic activity in a world in which there exists both systemic and structural market failure.

22 These talks took place mainly in 1989 and 1990. Their purpose was to iron out differences in the strategic economic initiatives – particularly with respect to trade, industrial and technology policy – undertaken by either the Japanese or US authorities which might be construed as anti-competitiive or structurally distorting to the other authority.

23 Since 1990, partly as a reaction to the explosive rate of growth in the previous three years, and partly as a result of the economic recession in Japan, the rate of new Japanese investment in services, and especially in banking and finance, has considerably slowed down.

24 The concept of the social market economy is one which, while acknowledging the virtues of the market system, recognizes the external (i.e. social) effects of any particular transaction or group of transactions, and also the failure of some markets to properly embrace either supply or demand uncertainties.

REFERENCES

Abdel-Malek T. (1985). *Canada's Direct Investment in Western Europe*. Technological Innovation Research Report. Ottawa: Government of Canada, Office of Industrial Innovation

Adler M. and Stevens G. V. G. (1974). The trade effect of direct investment. *Journal of Finance*, **29**, 655–76

Adler N. J. and Ghadar F. (1990). International strategy from the perspective of people and culture. In *Research in Global Strategic Management. International Business Research for the 21st century, Canadian New Research Agenda* (Rugman A. M., ed.). Greenwich, CN: JAI Press

Agarwal J. P. (1976). Factor proportions in foreign and domestic owned firms in Indian manufacturing. *Economic Journal*, **86**, 529–85

Agarwal J. P. (1980). Determinants of foreign direct investment: a survey. *Weltwirtschaftliches Archiv*, **116**, 739–73

Agarwal S. and Ramaswami S. N. (1992). Choice of foreign market entry mode, impact of ownership, location and internationalization factors. *Journal of International Business Studies*, **23**, 1–28

Aggarwal R. (1987). The strategic challenge of the evolving global economy. *Business Horizons*, **30**(4), 38–44

Aggarwal R. and Agmon T. (1990). The international success of developing country firms: role of government directed comparative advantage. *Management International Review*, **30**, 163–80

Agmon T. and Lessard D. R. (1977). Investor recognition of corporate international diversification. *Journal of Finance*, **32** (September), 1049–55

Agodo O. (1978). The determinants of US private manufacturing investments in Africa. *Journal of International Business Studies*, **9**(3), Winter, 95–107

Aharoni, Y. (1966). *The Foreign Investment Decision Process*. Boston: Harvard Graduate School of Business Administration, Division of Research

Aharoni Y. (1971). On the definition of multinational corporation. *Quarterly Review of Economics and Business*, **2**, November–December, 25–30

Ajami R. A. and Ricks D. A. (1981). Motives for the American firms investing in the United States. *Journal of International Business Studies*, **VII**, 25–46

Akhter S. H. and Lusch R. (1991). Environmental determinants of U.S. foreign direct investment in developed and developing countries: a structural analysis. *The International Trade Journal*, **V**, 329–60

Akoorie M. and Enderwick P. (1992). The international operations of New Zealand companies. *Asia Pacific Journal of Management*, **9**, 51–69

Al-Eryani M., Alam P. and Akhter S. (1990). Transfer pricing determinants of U.S. multinationals. *Journal of International Business Studies*, **21**, 409–24

Alchian A. and Demsetz H. (1972). Production, information costs and economic organisation. *American Economic Review*, **62**, December, 777–95

Aldrich H. (1979). *Organizations and Environments*. Englewood Cliffs, NJ: Prentice Hall

Alexander J. A. (1983). The determinants of research and development activity in domestic and foreign controlled industries. In *Multinationals and Technology Transfer* (Rugman A. M. ed.). New York: Praeger

Aliber R. Z. (1970). A theory of foreign direct investment. In *The International Corporation* (Kindleberger C. P., ed.). Cambridge, MA: MIT Press

Aliber R. Z. (1971). The multinational enterprise in a multiple currency world. In *The Multinational Enterprise* (Dunning, J. H., ed.). London: Allen and Unwin

Aliber R. (1983). A theory of foreign direct investment. In *The Multinational Corporation in the 1980s* (Kindleberger C. P. and Audretsch D. B., eds.). Cambridge, MA: MIT Press

Aliber R. Z. (1984). International Banking. *Journal of Money, Credit and Banking*, **16**, 661–76

Allen G. C. and Donnithorne A. G. (1954). *Western Enterprises in Far Eastern Economic Development: China and Japan*. London: Allen and Unwin

Almor-Ellemers T. and Hirsch S. (1991). *Patterns of Foreign Direct Investment: Israel, a Small Country Situated in between Trading Blocks*. Business and Economic Studies on European Integration WP 18–91. Copenhagen: Copenhagen Business School

Alworth J. S. (1988). *The Finance, Investment and Taxation Decisions of Multinationals*. Oxford: Basil Blackwell

American Chamber of Commerce (1955). *The American Anti-Trust Laws and American Business Abroad*. London: American Chamber of Commerce

American Iron and Steel Association (1887). News item in Bulletin, 19 January 1887

Amey (1964). Diversified manufacturing businesses. *Journal of Royal Statistical Society, (Series A)*, **127**, Part 1

Anastassopoulos J. P., Blanc P. and Dussauge P. (1987). *State Owned Multinationals*. Chichester and New York: John Wiley & Sons

Anderson E. and Coughlan A. T. (1987). International market entry and expansion via independent or integrated channels of distribution. *Journal of Marketing*, **51**, 71–82

Anderson E. and Gatignon H. (1986). Modes of foreign entry: transaction costs and propositions. *Journal of International Business Studies*, **17**, 1–26

Andrews, M. (1972). *American Investment in Irish Industry*. Senior Honours Thesis. Harvard: Harvard University

Archibugi D. and Pianta M. (1989). *The Technological Specialization of Advanced Countries*. Brussels: Commission of European Communities. Mimeo

Archer H. J. (1986). An eclectic approach to the historical study of UK multinational enterprises. PhD Thesis, University of Reading

Archer H. J. (1990). The role of the entrepreneur in the emergence and development of U.K. multinational enterprises. *Journal of European Economic History*, **19**, 293–309

Arpan J. (1972). *International Intracompany Pricing, Non-American Systems and Views*. New York: Praeger

Arrow K. (1970). Political and economic evaluation of social effects and externalities. In *The Analysis of Public Output* (Margolis, J., ed.). New York: National Bureau of Economic Research

Artisien P., Rojec M. and Svetlick M. (1991). Yugoslav foreign direct investment in less developed countries. In *Multinational Enterprises in Less Developed Countries* (Buckley P. and Clegg J., eds.). Basingstoke and London: Macmillan

Atyas I. and Dutz M. (1993). Financial distress and the response of TNCs. In *TNCs, Market Structure and Industrial Performance* (Newfarmer R. and Frischtak C., eds.). UN Library on Transnational Corporations. London and New York: Routledge

Audretsch D. B. (1989). *The Market and the State*. New York and London: Harvester Wheatsheaf

Awadzi W. K. (1987). *Determinants of Joint Venture Performance: A Study of International Joint Ventures in the United States*. Unpublished PhD Dissertation, Louisiana State University

Baden-Fuller C. W. F. and Stopford J. M. (1991). Globalisation Frustrated: The Case of White Goods. Bath and London: Mimeo. *Strategic Management Journal*, **12** 493–507

Bagchi A. K. B. (1972). *Private Investment in India 1900–1939*. Cambridge: Cambridge University Press

Bailey P. J. (1979). *Employment effects of multinational enterprises: A survey of relevant studies relating to the Federal Republic of Germany*. Working Paper #2, ILO Publications on Multinationals. Geneva: ILO Office

Bailey P. J. and Parisotto A. (1991). *Multinational Enterprises: What Role can they play in Employment Generation in Developing Countries*. Paper presented at International Conference on Migration, Rome, 13–15 March 1991

Bain J. S (1956). *Barriers to New Competition*. Cambridge, MA: Harvard University Press

Balassa B. (1965). Trade liberalisation and revealed comparative advantage. *Manchester School of Economic and Social Studies*, **33**, 99–123

Balassa B. (1977). Revealed comparative advantage revisited: an analysis of relative export shares of the industrial countries. *Manchester School of Economic and Social Studies*, **45**, 327–44

Balassa B. (1980). The process of industrial development and alternative development strategies. Princeton Department of Economics. *Essays in International Finance*, No. 141, December

Balasubramanyam V. N. (1984). Factor proportions and productive efficiency of foreign owned firms in the Indonesian manufacturing sector. *Bulletin of Indonesian Economic Studies*, **XX**, 70–94

Balasubramanyam V. N. (1989). Incentives and discentives for foreign direct investment in less developed countries. *Weltwirtschaftliches Archiv*, **120**, 720–35

Balasubramanyam V. N. (1991). Putting TRIMS to good use. *World Development*, **19**, 1215–24

Ball D. A. and McCullogh D. A. (1988). *International Business*. Plano, TX: Business Publications

Bandera V. N. and White J. T. (1968). US direct investments and domestic markets in Europe. *Economia Internazionale*, **21**, February, 117–33

Baran P. and Sweezy P. (1966). *Monopoly Capital: An Essay on the American Economic and Social Order*. Harmondsworth: Penguin

Baranson J. (1979). *Technology and the Multinationals*. Lexington, MA: Lexington Books

Barlow E. R. (1953). *Management of Foreign Manufacturing Subsidiaries*. Cambridge, MA: Harvard University Press

Barnet R. and Miller R. (1974). *Global Reach. The Power of the Multinational Corporations*. New York: Simon and Schuster

Barney J. (1991). Firm resources and sustained competitive advantage. *Journal of Management*, **17**, 99–120

Bartlett C. A. (1986). Building and managing the transnational: the new organizational challenge. In *Competition in Global Industries* (Porter, M. E., ed.). Harvard: Harvard Business School Press

Bartlett C. A. and Ghoshal S. (1987). Managing across borders: new strategic requirements. *Sloan Management Review*, **28**, Summer, 7–17 *and* Managing across borders: new organizational responses. *Sloan Management Review*, **28**, Fall, 43–53

Bartlett C. A. and Ghoshal S. (1988). Managing innovations in the transnational corporations. In *Research on Multinational Management* (Bartlett C. A., Doz Y. and Hedlund G., eds.). London: Addison-Wesley

Bartlett C. A. and Ghoshal S. (1989). *Managing Across Borders – The Transnational Solution*. Boston: Harvard Business School Press

Bartlett C. A., Doz Y. and Hedlund G., eds. (1990). *Managing the Global Firm*. London and New York: Routledge

Basi R. S. (1964). *Determinants of United States Private Direct Investments in Foreign Countries*. Kent, Ohio: Kent State University, Bureau of Economic Research Printed Series No.3

Batra R. N. and Ramachandran R. (1980). Multinational firms and the theory of international trade and investment. *American Economic Review*, **70**, 278–90

Beamish P. W. (1984). *Joint Venture Performance in Developing Countries*. London: University of Western Ontario. Unpublished Doctoral Dissertation

Beamish P. W. (1985). The characteristics of joint ventures in developed and developing countries. *Columbia Journal of World Business*, **20**, 13–20

Beamish P. W. (1988). *Multinational Joint Ventures in Developing Countries*. London: Routledge

Beamish P. W. and Banks J. C. (1987). Equity joint ventures and the theory of the multinational enterprise. *Journal of International Business Studies*, **18**, 1–15

Beamish P. W., Killing J. P., Lecraw D. J. and Crookell H. (1991). *International Management Text and Cases*. Homewood: Irwin

Beckerman W. (1956). Distance in pattern of intra-European trade. *Review of Economics and Statistics*, **28**

Behrman J. N. (1962). Foreign associates and their financing. In *United States Private and Government Investment Abroad* (Mikesell R. F., ed.). Eugene: Oregon University Press

Behrman J. N. (1969). *Some Patterns in the Rise of the Multinational Enterprise*. Chapel Hill: University of North Carolina, Graduate School of Business Administration

Behrman J. N. (1970). *National Interests and the Multinational Enterprise*. Englewood Cliffs, New Jersey: Prentice Hall

Behrman J. N. (1972). *The Role of International Companies in Latin America: Autos and Petrochemicals*. Lexington, MA: Lexington Books

Behrman J. N. (1974). *Decision Criteria for Foreign Direct Investment in Latin America*. New York: Council of the Americas

Behrman J. N. and Grosse R. (1990). *International Business and Governments*. Columbia, South Carolina: University of South Carolina Press

Bello J. A. and Iyanda O. (1979). *Appropriate Technology Choice and Employment by Two Multinational Enterprises in Nigeria*. ILO Working Paper No. 17. Geneva: ILO

Bemis S. F. (1943). *The Latin American Policy of the United States*. New York: Harcourt, Brace and Co.

Bennett P. D. and Green R. T. (1972). Political instability as a determinant of direct foreign investment in marketing. *Journal of Marketing Research*, **9**, 162–86

Benvignati A. (1985). An empirical investigation of international transfer pricing by U.S. manufacturing firms. In *Multinationals and Transfer Pricing* (Rugman A. M. and Eden L., eds.). London: Croom Helm

Berg S. and Friedman P. (1977). Joint ventures, competition and technological complementarities. *Southern Economic Journal*, **43**(3), 1330–7

Berg S. and Friedman P. (1980). Causes and effects of joint ventures activity. *Antitrust Bulletin*, **25**(1), 143–68

Berg S. and Friedman P. (1981). Impacts of domestic joint ventures on industrial rates of return. *Review of Economics and Statistics*, **63**, 293–8

Bergsten C. F. (1974). Coming investment wars. *Foreign Affairs*, **53**, 135–52

Bergsten C. F. (1990). The world economy after the cold war. *Foreign Affairs*, **69**, 96–112

Bergsten C. F. and Graham E. (1992). Global corporations and national governments. *International Trade Journal*, **1**, 15–44

Bergsten C. F., Horst T. and Moran T. H. (1978). *American Multinationals and American Interests*. Washington, DC: The Brookings Institution

Bernard J. and Weiner R. (1989). Multinational corporations, international transfer prices and taxes. Evidence from the U.S. petroleum industry. In *Taxation in the Global Economy* (Razin A. S. and Slemrod J., eds.), pp. 123–59. New York: National Bureau of Economic Research

Berthoff R. T. (1953). *British Immigrants in Industrial America 1790–1900*. Cambridge: Harvard University Press

Biersteker T. J. (1978). *Contending Perspectives on the Multinational Corporations: Distortion or Development*. Cambridge, MA: The MIT Press

Birch F. D. (1976). *Tropical Milestones in Malaya and Thailand*. University of Melbourne, MA Thesis

Birkinshaw J. M. (1992). The MNE–host government relationship: a resource dependency perspective. Baltimore Academy of International Business (North East USA region). *Proceedings and Ten Best Papers*

Blainey R. (1984). History of multinational factories in Australia. In *Overseas Business Factories, Proceedings of the Fuji Conference* (Okochi A. and Inoue T., eds.), pp. 183–214. Japan: University of Tokyo Press

Blair A. R. (1987). The relative distribution of the United States direct investment. The U.K./E.E.C. experience. *European Economic Review*, **31**, 1137–44

Blanpain R. (1983). *The OECD Guidelines for Multinational Enterprises and Labor Relations 1979–1982*. Deventer, Netherlands: Kluwer Law and Taxation Publishers.

Blomström M. (1986). Foreign investment and productive efficiency: the case of Mexico. *Journal of Industrial Economics*, **XXXV**, 97–112

Blomström M. (1989). *Foreign Investment and Spillovers: A Study of Technology Transfer to Mexico*. London: Routledge

Blomström M. (1990). *Transnational Corporations and Manufacturing Export from Developing Countries*. ST/CTC/101. New York: United Nations

Blomström M. (1991). *Host country benefits of foreign investment*. Working Paper No. 3615. New York: National Bureau of Economic Research

Blomström M. and Lipsey R. E. (1991). Firm size and foreign operations of multinationals. *Scandinavian Journal of Economics*, **93**, 101–7

Blomström M. and Zejan M. (1991). Why do multinational firms seek out joint ventures. *Journal of International Development*, **3**, 53–63

Blomström M., Lipsey R. E. and Kravis I. B. (1988). Multinational Firms and Manufactured Exports from Developing Countries. Working Paper No. 2493. Cambridge, MA: NBER

Blomström M., Lipsey R. E. and Kulchyck K. (1988). US and Swedish Direct Investment and Exports. In *Trade Policy Issues and Empirical Analysis* (Baldwin R. E., ed.), pp. 259–97. Chicago: University of Chicago Press

Blomström M., Lipsey R. E. and Zejan M. (1992). *A Cross Country Study of Growth in Developing Countries*. Paper prepared for conference on Historical Perspectives on the International Convergences of Productivity, New York University, April

Boddewyn J. J. (1988). Political aspects of MNE theory. *Journal of International Business Studies*, **19**, 344–63

Boddewyn J. J., Halbrich M. B. and Perry A. C. (1986). Service multinationals: conceptualization, measurement and theory. *Journal of International Business Studies*, **17**, 45–56

Borner S. *et al.* (1985). Global structural change and international competition among industrial firms: the case of Switzerland. *Kyklos*, **38**, 77–103

Bornschier V. (1980). Multinational corporations and economic growth: a cross-national test of the decapitalisation thesis. *Journal of Development Economics*, **7**, 191–210

Bossom R. and Varon B. (1977). *Mining Industry and the Developing Countries*. Oxford: Oxford University Press

Boyle S. E. (1968). Estimate of the number and size distribution of domestic joint subsidiaries. *Antitrust Law and Economics Review*, **1**, 81–92

Brandt W. K. and Giddy I. (1977). *Profitability and Concentration of Foreign and Domestic Firms in Brazil*. Paper presented at Academy of International Business Annual Meeting, Orlando, August

Branscomb L. M. (1987). National and corporate technology strategies in an interdependent world economy. In *Technology of Global Industry* (Guile B. L. and Brooks H., eds.), pp. 246–57. Washington: National Academy Press

Brash D. T. (1966). *American Investment in Australian Industry*. Canberra: Australian University Press

Brech M. and Sharp M. (1984). *Inward Investment: Policy Options for the United Kingdom*. London: Routledge and Kegan Paul

Britain's Invisible Earnings (1988). London: Committee for Invisible Exports

British Business (1989). Overseas earnings from royalties net 24 million pounds in 1987. *British Business*, 15 September 1989

British Monopolies Commission (1973). Report on the Supply of Chlordiazepoxide and Diazepan. London: HMSO

Brown L. T., Rugman A. M. and Verbeke A. Japanese joint ventures with Western multinationals: Synthesizing the economic and cultural explanation of future. *Asia Pacific Journal of Management*, **6**, 225–42

Brown M. and McKern B. (1987). *Aluminium, Copper and Steel in Developing Countries*. Paris: OECD

Brown R. (1990). Chinese business and banking in South-East Asia. In *Banks as Multinationals* (Jones G., ed.). London and New York: Routledge

Brown S. R. (1979). The transfer of technology to China in the nineteenth century: the role of foreign direct investment. *Journal of Economic History*, **38**, 181–97

Brown W. B. (1976). Islands of conscious power: MNCs in the theory of the firm. *MSU Business Topics*, Summer, 37–45

Buckley P. J. (1987). *The Theory of the Multinational Enterprise*. Uppsala: Acta Universitas Upsalienis, Almquist and Wiksell International

Buckley P. J. (1988). Organization forms and multinational companies. In *Internal Organization, Efficiency and Profit* (Thompson S. and Wright M., eds.). Oxford: Philip Allan Publishers

Buckley P. J. (1990). Problems and developments in the core theory of international business. *Journal of International Business Studies*, **XXI**, 657–66

Buckley P. J. (1991). Developments in international business theory in the 1990s. *Journal of Marketing Management*, **7**, 15–24

Buckley P. J., ed. (1993). *Cooperative Forms of the TNC Activity*. UNCTC Library on Transnational Corporations. London: Routledge

Buckley P. J. and Artisien P. (1987). The employment impact of direct investment in Greece, Portugal and Spain. ILO Multinational Enterprise Working Paper No. 44. Geneva: ILO

Buckley P. J. and Artisien P. F. R. (1988). Policy issues of intra-EC direct investment. In *Multinationals and the European Community* (Dunning J. H. and Robson P., eds.). Oxford: Basil Blackwell

Buckley P. J. and Casson M. (1976). *The Future of the Multinational Enterprise*. London: Macmillan

Buckley P. J. and Casson M. (1981). The optimal timing of a foreign direct investment. *Economic Journal*, **91**, 75–87

Buckley P. J. and Casson M. (1985). *The Economic Theory of the Multinational Enterprise*. London: Macmillan

Buckley P. J. and Casson M. (1988). A theory of cooperation in international business. In *Cooperative Strategies in International Business* (Contractor F. J. and Lorange P., eds.), pp. 31–53. Lexington: D.C. Heath & Co.

Buckley P. J. and Casson M. (1991). Multinational enterprises in less developed countries: cultural and economic interactions. In *Multinational Enterprises in Less Developed Countries* (Buckley P. J. and Clegg J., eds.). London: Macmillan

Buckley P. J. and Dunning J. H. (1976). The industrial structure of US direct investment in the U.K.. *Journal of International Business Studies*, **7**, Summer, 5–13

Buckley P. J. and Mathew A. M. (1979). The motivation for recent first time direct investments in Australia by UK firms. *Management International Review*, **19**, 57–70

Buckley P. J. and Pearce R. D. (1979). Overseas production and exporting by the world's largest enterprises: a study in sourcing policy. *Journal of International Business Studies*, **10**, 1–20

Buckley P. J., Sparkes J. R. and Hartley A. G. (1979). EEC programme of research and actions on the development of labour market. Study 78/1, Commission of the European Communities, Brussels, October

Buckley P. J., Dunning J. H. and Pearce R. D. (1984). An analysis of the growth and profitability of the world's largest firms 1972–1977. *Kyklos*, **37**, 3–26

Buckley P. J., Pass C. L. and Prescott K. (1990). Foreign market servicing by multinationals: an integrated treatment. *International Marketing Review*, **74**

Buckley P., Pass, C. L. and Prescott P. (1988). Measures of international competitiveness: a critical study. *Journal of Marketing Management*, 175–200

Bureau of Industry Economics (1983a). *Australian Direct Investment in New Zealand*. Information Bulletin 3. Canberra: Australian Government Publishing Service

Bureau of Industry Economics (1983b). *Australian Direct Investment in Asean Countries*. Canberra: Australian Government Publishing Service

Bureau of Industry Economics (1984). *Australian Direct Investment Abroad: Effects on the Australian Economy*. Research report 14. Canberra: Australian Government Publishing Service

Burgenmeier B. (1986). Determinants of Swiss investment abroad: an empirical study. In *Technology, Policies and Economics* (Keller C., Matejka H. and Sezenasi K., eds.). Geneva: Graduate Institute of International Studies

Burgenmeier, B. (1991). Swiss foreign direct investment. In *Multinationals and Europe 1992* (Burgenmeier B. and Mucchielli J. L., eds.). London and New York: Routledge

Burns J. (1980). Transfer pricing decisions in U.S. multinational corporations. *Journal of International Business Studies*, **11**, Fall, 162–79

Burstall M., Dunning J. H. and Lake A. (1981). *The Impact of Multinational Enterprises on National Scientific and Technological Capacity: The Pharmaceutical Industry*. Paris: OECD

Business International (1980). *Locating a West European Office*. Geneva: Business International SA

Business International (1989). *Gaining a Competitive Edge in the New Europe*. Geneva and New York: Business International

Business Monitor (various dates). Census of Overseas Assets (for 1981, 1984 and 1987). London: Business Statistics Office, HMSO

Business Statistics Office (1990). Census of Production for 1988. London: HMSO

Business Week (1990). The Stateless Corporation. 14 May, 98–105

Business Week (1992). Could anything be finah than to be in Carolina. *Business Week*, 1 June, 33–4

Bye M. (1958). Self-financed multiterritorial units and their time horizon. *International Economic Papers*, **8**, 147–78

Cable J. and Yasuki M. (1985). Internal organization, business groups and corporate performance: an empirical test of the multidivisional hypothesis in Japan. *International Journal of Industrial Organization*, **3**, 401–20

Cable V. and Persaud B. (1987). *Developing With Foreign Investment*. London: Croom Helm

Cainarca G. C., Colombo, M. G., Mariotti S. (1988). *Cooperative Agreements in the Information and Communication Industrial System*. Milan: Politechnico de Milano

Cainarca G. C., Colombo M. G. and Mariotti S. (1990). *Agreements between firms and the technological life cycle of industry*. Milan: Politechnico de Milano

Callis H. (1942). *Foreign capital in South East Asia*. New York: New IPR International Research Series. Mimeo

Calvet A. L. (1980). *Markets and Hierarchies: Towards a Theory of International Business*. Ph.D Thesis, Sloan School of Management, Cambridge, MA

Calvet A. L. (1981). A synthesis of foreign direct investment theories and theories of multinational firms. *Journal of International Business Studies*, **12**, 43–59

Cameron R. (1961). *France and the Economic Development of Europe 1800–1914*. Princeton, NJ: Princeton University Press

Campbell D. C. and McElrath R. G. (1990). *The Employment Effects of Multinational Enterprises in the United States and of American Multinationals Abroad*. ILO Multinational Enterprises Programme Working Paper No. 64. Geneva: ILO

Cantwell J. A. (1981). *Technological Advantage as a Determinant of the International Economic Activity of Firms*. University of Reading Discussion Papers In International Investment and Business Studies, No. 105, October

Cantwell J. A. (1987). The reorganisation of European industries after integration: selected evidence on the role of transnational enterprise activities. *Journal of Common Market Studies*, **36**, 127–52

Cantwell J. A. (1989a). The changing form of multinational enterprise expansion in the twentieth century. In *Historical Studies in International Corporate Business* (Teichova A., Levy-Leboyer M. and Nussbaum H., eds.). Cambridge: Cambridge University Press

Cantwell J. A. (1989b). *The Methodological Problems Raised by the Collection of Foreign Direct Investment Data*. University of Reading Discussion papers in International Investment and Business Studies, No. 147

Cantwell J. A. (1989c) *Technological Innovation and Multinational Corporations*. Oxford: Basil Blackwell

Cantwell J. A. (1990). *The technological competence theory of international production and its implications*. University of Reading Discussion Papers in International Investment and Business Studies, Series B, III, November

Cantwell J. A. (1991a). A survey of theories of international production. In *The Nature of the Transnational Firm* (Pitelis C. N. and Sugden R., eds.). London: Routledge

Cantwell J. A. (1991b). The international agglomeration of technological activity. In *Global Research Strategy and International Competitiveness* (Casson M. C., ed.), pp. 104–32. Oxford: Basil Blackwell

Cantwell J. A. (1992a). The effects of integration on the structure of multinational corporation activity in the EC. In *Multinationals in the New Europe and Global Trade* (Klein M. W. and Welfens P. J., eds.). Berlin and New York: Springer-Verlag

Cantwell J. A. (1992b). The evolution of European industrial technology in the interwar years. *University of Reading Discussion Papers in International Economics*, **4**(33)

Cantwell J. A., ed. (1993). *Transnational Corporations and Innovatory Activities*. United Nations Library on Transnational Corporations. London: Routledge

Cantwell J. A. and Dunning J. H. (1991). Multinationals, technology and the competitiveness of European industries. *Aussenwirtschaft*, **46**(1), 45–65

Cantwell J. A. and Hodson C. (1991). Global R & D and British competitiveness. In *Global Research Strategy and International Competitiveness* (Casson M. C., ed.), pp. 133–82. Oxford: Basil Blackwell

Cantwell J. A. and Randaccio F. S. (1990). Catching up amongst the world's largest multinationals. *Economic Notes*, **19**, 1–23

Cantwell J. A. and Tolentino P. (1990). *Technology Accumulation and Third World Multinationals*. University of Reading, Discussion Papers in International Investment and Business Studies, No. 139

Cantwell J. A., Corley T. A. B. and Dunning J. H. (1986). Some theoretical antecedents to the eclectic paradigm of international production. In *Multinationals, Theory and History* (Hertner P. and Jones G., eds.). Aldershot: Gower

Carlos A. M. and Nicholas S. (1988). Giants of an earlier capitalism: The chartered trading companies as modern multinationals. *Business History Review*, **62** 450–71

Casson M. C. (1979). *Alternatives to the Multinational Enterprise*. London: Macmillan

Casson M. C. (1982a). Transaction costs and the theory of the multinational enterprise. In *New Perspectives in International Business* (Rugman A. M., ed.). London: Croom Helm

Casson M. C. (1982b). The theory of foreign direct investment. In *International Capital Movements* (Black J. and Dunning J. H., eds.). London: Macmillan

Casson M. C. (1985). The theory of foreign direct investment. In *The Economic Theory of the Multinational Enterprise* (Buckley P. and Casson M. C., eds.). London: Macmillan

Casson M. C. (1986). General theories of the multinational enterprise: Their relevance to business history. In *Multinationals: Theory and History* (Hertner P. and Jones G., eds.). Aldershot, Hants: Gower

Casson M. C. and Associates (1986). *Multinationals and World Trade: Vertical Integration and the Division of Labour in World Industries (with associates)*. London, Boston and Sydney: Allen and Unwin

Casson M. C. (1987). *The Firm and the Market*. Oxford: Basil Blackwell

Casson M. C. (1990). *Enterprise and Competitiveness: A Systems View of International Business*. Oxford: Clarendon Press

Casson M. C., ed. (1991). *Global Research Strategy and International Competitiveness*. Cambridge, MA: Basil Blackwell

Casson M. C. (1992). Internalization theory and beyond. In *New Directions in International Business* (Buckley P. J., ed.). Aldershot, Hants: Edward Elgar

Casson M. C. and Pearce R. D. (1987). *The Welfare Effects of Foreign Enterprise: A diagrammatic Analysis*. University of Reading Discussion Papers in International Investment and Business Studies, **98**, October

Casson M. C. and Pearce R. D. (1988). Intra-firm trade and the developing countries. In *Economic Development and International Trade* (Greenaway D., ed.). Basingstoke and London: Macmillan

Casson M. C. and Pearce R. D. (1990). Intra-firm trade and developing countries. In *Economic Development and International Trade* (Greenaway D., ed.), pp. 132–56. London: Macmillan

Castleman B. I. (1987). Work place health standards and multinational corporations in developing countries. In *Multinational Corporations, Environ-*ment and the Third World* (Pearson C. S., ed.). Durham, NC: Duke University Press

Castleman B. I. and Purkavastha B. I. (1985). The Bhopal disaster as a case study in double standards. In *The Export of Hazard* (Ives J. H., ed.), pp. 213–23. Boston and London: Routledge and Kegan Paul

Caves R. E. (1971). Industrial corporations: the industrial economics of foreign invesstment. *Economica*, **38**, February, 1–27

Caves R. E. (1974a). Causes of direct investment: foreign firms' shares in Canadian and United Kingdom manufacturing industries. *Review of Economics and Statistics*, **56**, August, 272–93

Caves R. E. (1974b). Multinational firms, competition and productivity in host country markets. *Economica*, **41**, May, 176–93

Caves R. E. (1980). Industrial organization, corporate strategy and structure. *Journal of Economic Literature*, **XVIII**, 64–92

Caves R. E. (1981). Intra-industry trade and market structure in the industrial countries. *Oxford Economic Papers*, **33**(2), July, 203–23

Caves R. E. (1982). *Multinational Enterprise and Economic Analysis*. Cambridge: Cambridge University Press

Caves R. E. and Mehra S. (1986). Entry of foreign multinationals into US manufacturing industry. In *Competition in Global Industries* (Porter M. E., ed.). Boston: Harvard Business School Press

Caves R. E., Porter M. E. and Spence A. M. (1979). *Competition in the Open Economy*. Cambridge: Harvard University Press

Cecchini P., Catinat M. and Jacquemin A. (1988). *The European Challenge 1992. The Benefits of a Single Market*. Aldershot, Hants: Wildwood House

Chakravarthy B. S. and Perlmutter H. V. (1985). Strategic planning for a global business. *Columbia Journal of World Business*, **20**, 3–10

Chandler A. D. Jr (1962). *Strategy and Structure: The History of American Industrial Enterprise*. Cambridge, MA: MIT Press

Chandler A. D. Jr (1977a). Institutional integration: an approach to comparative studies of the history of large scale business and enterprise. In *Strategy and Structure of Big Business* (Nakagawa K., ed.). Tokyo

Chandler A. D. Jr (1977b). *The Visible Hand: The Managerial Revolution in American Business*. Cambridge, MA: Harvard University Press

Chandler A. D. Jr (1980). The growth of transnational industrial firms in the U.K. and U.S.: a comparative analysis. *Economic History Review*, **33**(3), August, 396–410

Chandler A. D. Jr (1990). *Scale and Scope: The Dynamics of Industrial Capitalism*. Cambridge, MA: Harvard University

Chandler A. D. Jr and Daems H. (1974). The rise of managerial capitalism and its impact on investment strategy in the western world and Japan. In *The Rise of Managerial Capitalism* (Daems H. and Van der Wee H., eds.). Louvain: Louvain University Press

Chandler A. D. Jr and Daems H. (1980). *Managerial Hierarchies*. Cambridge, MA: Harvard University Press

Chapman S. D. (1985). British based investment groups before 1914. *Economic History Review*, **38**, 230–5

Chen E. (1983a). *Multinational Corporations, Technology and Employment*. London: Macmillan

Chen E. (1983b). Multinationals from Hongkong. In *The New Multinationals: The Spread of Third World Enterprises* (Lall S. *et al.*). Chichester: John Wiley

Chen J., ed. (1993). *Transnational Corporations and Technology Transfer*. United Nations Library on Transnational Corporations. London: Routledge

Chenery H. (1979). *Structural Change and Development Policy*. Oxford: Oxford University Press

Chenery H., Robinson S. and Syrquin M. (1986). *Industrialization and Growth*. Oxford: Oxford University Press

Cheng J. L. C. and Ramaswamy K. (1989). Towards a systems typology of MNCs: Some conceptual and research implications. Washington: Proceedings of the Annual National Conference of the Academy of Management, pp. 106–10

Chesnais F. (1988). Technical cooperation agreements between firms. *STI Review*, **4**, December, OECD, Paris, 57–119

Chi T. and Roehl T. (1989). *Transaction costs, model choice on the optimum share structure of joint ventures*. Washington: Mimeo

Chiu H.-J. (1992). *International Acquisition Strategy*. PhD thesis, University of Washington, Seattle

Cho K. R. (1988). Determinants of intra-firm trade: A search for a theoretical framework. *International Trade Journal*, **III**, Winter, 167–86

Chou Y.-M. (1992). Is an East Asian bloc emerging? In *Proc. International Trade Association Annual Conference*, Laredo, 1992, pp. 923–33

Chudnovsky D., ed. (1993). *Transnational Corporations and Industrialization*. United Nations Library on Transnational Corporations. London: Routledge

Chung B. S. and Lee C. H. (1980). The choice of production techniques by foreign and local firms in Korea. *Economic Development and Cultural Change*, **29**(1), 135–40

Clark C., Wilson F. and Bradley J. (1969). Industrial location and economic potential in Western Europe. *Regional Studies*, **3**, 197–212

Clark D. P., Sawyer W. C. and Sprinkle R. L. (1989). Determinants of industry participation under offshore assembly provisions in the US tariff code. *Journal of World Trade*, **23**(5), October, 123–30

Clark V. S. (1929). *A History of Manufacturers in the U.S.*, 3 vols. Washington: Carnegie Institution

Clarke C. and Brennan K. (1988). Allied forces. *Management Today*, November, 128–32

Clegg J. (1987). *Multinational Enterprises and World Competition*. London: Macmillan

Clough S. B. (1968). *Economic History of Europe*. New York: Walker

Clough, S. B. and Cole C. W. (1946). *Economic History of Europe*. Boston: D.C. Heath

Coase R.H. (1937). The nature of the firm. *Economica*, **4**, November, 386–405

Coase R. H. (1960). The problem of social cost. *Journal of Law and Economics*, **3**, 1–10

Cohen B. I. (1975). *Multinational Firms and Asian Exports*. New Haven and London: Yale University Press

Cohen B.I. *et al.*, eds. (1979). *The Multinational Corporation: A Radical Approach* (Papers by S. Hymer). Cambridge: Cambridge University Press

Cohen R. B. (1977). *Strategy and Structure of Multinational Corporations*. Mimeo

Collis D. J. (1991). A resource based analysis of global competition: the case of the bearings industry. *Strategic Management Journal*, **12**, 49–68

Commission of the European Communities (1976). *Survey of Multinational Enterprises*. Brussels: European Commission

Conan A. R. (1960). *Capital Imports into Sterling Countries*. London: Macmillan

Connor J. M. (1977). *The Market Power of Multinationals, A Quantitative Analysis of U.S. Corporations in Brazil and Mexico*. New York: Praeger

Connor J. M. and Mueller W. F. (1977). *Market power and the Profitability of Multinational Corporations in Brazil and Mexico*. Report to the Senate Subcommittee on Multinational Corporations. Washington DC: Government Printing Office

Contractor F. J. (1980). The composition of licensing fees and arrangements as a function of economic development of technology recipient nations. *Journal of International Business Studies*, **11**, Winter, 47–62

Contractor F. J. (1981). *International Technology Licensing Compensation, Costs and Negotiation*. Lexington, MA: Lexington Books

Contractor F. J. (1984a). Licensing and foreign direct investment in U.S. corporate strategy. In *International Technology Transfer: Concepts, Measures and Comparisons* (Rosenberg N. and Frischtak C., eds.). New York: Praeger

Contractor F. J. (1984b). Choosing between foreign direct investment and licensing: theoretical considerations and empirical tests. *Journal of International Business Studies*, **15**, 167–88

Contractor F. J. (1986). International business: an alternative view. *International Marketing Review*, Spring, **21**, 74–85

Contractor F. J. (1990). Ownership patterns of US joint ventures abroad and the liberalization of foreign government regulation in the 1980s: evidence from the benchmark surveys. *Journal of International Business Studies*, **21**, 55–73

Contractor F. J. and Lorange P. (1988). *Cooperative Strategies in International Business*. Lexington, MA: D.C. Heath

Cooper C. and Whelan N. (1972). *Science, Technology and Industry in Ireland. A Diagnosis and Some Policy Problems*. Quoted in OECD *Review of National Science Policy: Ireland*. Paris: OECD 1974

Cooper C., Kaplinsky R., Bell R. and Satyarakuit W. (1975). Choice of techniques for can making in Kenya, Tanzania and Thailand. In *Technology and Employment in Industry* (Bhalla A. S., ed.). Geneva: ILO

Copithorne L. W. (1971). International corporate transfer prices and government policy. *Canadian Journal of Economics*, **4**, August, 324–41

Coram T. C. (1967). *The Role of British Capital in the Development of the United States*. MSc Thesis, University of Southampton

Corley T. A. B. (1992). *Multinationals Theory and Business History: A study in Method*. Reading: University of Reading Discussion Papers in International Investment and Business Studies, No. 150, April

Coughlin C. C., Terza J. V. and Arromdee V. (1991). State characteristics and the location of foreign direct investment within the United States. *Review of Economics and Statistics*, **73**, 675–81

Cowling K. (1986). The internationalisation of production and deindustrialisation. In *Technological Change, Industrial Restructuring and Regional Development* (Amin A. and Goddard J., eds.). London: Allen and Unwin

Cowling K. and Sugden R. (1987). *Transnational Monopoly Capitalism*. Brighton: Wheatsheaf

Culem C. (1988). The locational determinants of direct investment among industrialized countries. *European Economic Review*, **32**, 885–904

Cunningham W. (1902). Localisation of industry. *Economic Journal*, **12**, 501–6

Cushman D. O. (1985). Real exchange rate risk, expectations and the level of direct investment. *Review of Economics and Statistics*, May, 297–308

Cyert R. M. and March J. G. (1963). *A Behavioral Theory of the Firm*. New York: Prentice Hall

Daniel P. (1991). A world of services. *Geoforum*, **22**, 359–76

Daniels J. D. (1971). *Recent Foreign Direct Investment in the United States*. New York: Praeger

Daniels J. D. (1986). Approaches to European management by the large US multinational firm. *Management International Review*, **2**, 27–42

Daniels J. D. (1987). Bridging national and global marketing strategies through regional operations. *International Marketing Review*, **4**, 29–43

Daniels J. D. and Bracker J. (1989). Profit performance: do foreign operations make a difference? *Management International Review*, **29** 6–16

Daniels J. D. and Radebaugh L. H. (1989). *International Business*. Reading, MA: Addison-Wesley

D'Arge R. (1969). Notes on custom unions and foreign direct investment. *Economic Journal*, **79**, June, 324–33

D'Arge R. C. (1971a). Customs union and direct foreign investments: a correction and further thoughts. *Economic Journal*, **81**, June, 352–55 and 357–60

D'Arge R. (1971b). Reply. *Economic Journal*, **81**, 357–60

Davenport-Hines R. P. T. (1983). Vickers' Balkan conscience: Aspects of Anglo Romanian armaments, 1918–1939. *Business History*, **XXV**(3), 287–319

Davenport-Hines R. P. T. (1986). *Glaxo as a Multinational Before 1963*. London: London Business History Unit. Mimeo

Davenport-Hines R. P. T. and Jones G., eds. (1989). *British Business in Asia since 1860*. Cambridge: Cambridge University Press

Davidson W. H. (1980). The location of foreign direct investment activity: Country characteristics and experience effects. *Journal of International Business Studies*, **11**, 9–22

Davidson W. H. (1988). Ecostructures and International Competitiveness. In *International Strategic Management* (Negandhi A. and Savara A., eds.). Lexington, MA

Davidson W. H. and McFetridge D. G. (1984). International technology transactions and the theory of the firm. *Journal of Industrial Economics*, **32**, 253–64

Davidson W. H. and McFetridge D. G. (1985). Key characteristics in the choice of international technology transfer. *Journal of International Business Studies*, **16**, 5–21

Davies R. B. (1969). Peacefully working to conquer the world: the Singer manufacturing company in foreign markets 1854–89. *Business History Review*, **63**

Davies S. W. and Lyons B. R. (1991). *Characterising Relative Performance: The Productivity Advantages of Foreign Owned Firms in the U.K.* Norwich: University of East Anglia. Mimeo

Deane R. S. (1970). *Foreign Investment in New Zealand Manufacturing*. Wellington: Sweet and Maxwell

Dell S. (1990). *The United Nations and International Business*. Durham and London: Duke University Press

Denison E. (1967). *Why Growth Rates Differ?* Washington DC: The Brookings Institution

Deutsche Bundesbank (1988). *Patent and license transaction with foreign countries and other exchanges of technological knowhow through service transactions in 1986 and 1987*. Monthly Report of the Deutsche Bundesbank, May

Dicken P. (1992). *Global Shift*. New York and London: The Guilford Press

Diejomaoh V. P. (1987). The economic integration process in Africa: experience, problems and prospects. In *Structural Change, Economic Interdependence and World Development* (Dunning J. H. and Usui M., eds.). London and Basingstoke: Macmillan

Dokopolou E. (1987). Technology transfer to the EEC periphery: the case of Greece. In *Industrial Change in Advanced Economics* (Hamilton F. E. I., ed.). London: Croom Helm

Dow M. B. and Kumar P. (1990). *Multinational Enterprises and Employment: The Canadian Experience*. ILO working paper No. 61. Geneva: ILO

Doz Y. (1986). *Strategic Management in Multinational Companies*. Oxford: Pergamon

Doz Y. (1988). Value creation through technology creation. *Aussenwirtschaft*, **43**, 175–90

Doz Y. and Hamel G. (1993). *The Competitive Logics of Strategic Alliances*. New York: Free Press

Doz Y. and Prahalad C. K. (1981). Headquarters influence and strategic control in MNCs. *Sloan Management Review*, **23**(1), 15–29

Doz Y. and Prahalad C. K. (1984). Patterns of strategic control in multinational corporations. *Journal of International Business Studies*, **15**(2), 55–72

Doz Y. and Prahalad C. K. (1987). A process model of strategic redirection in large complex firms: the case of multinational corporations. In *The Management of Strategic Change* (Pettigrew A., ed.), pp. 63–83. Oxford: Basil Blackwell

Doz Y. and Prahalad C. K. (1991). Managing DMNCs: a search for a new paradigm. *Strategic Management Journal*, **12**, 145–64

Doz Y., Shuen A. and Hamel G. (1992). *From intent to outcome: a process framework for partnerships*. Academy of Management Review (forthcoming)

Drucker P. F. (1986). The changed world economy. *Foreign Affairs*, **64**, 768–91

Dubin M. (1975). *Foreign Acquisitions and the Spread of the Multinational Firm*. DBA Thesis, Graduate School of Business Administration, Harvard Business School

Duerksen J. and Leonard H. J. (1980). Environmental regulation and the location of industry: an international perspective. *Columbia Journal of World Business*, **15**, 52–68

Dunning J. H. (1958). *American Investment in British Manufacturing Industry*. London: George Allen and Unwin. Reprinted by Arno Press, New York 1976

Dunning J. H. (1966). Further thoughts on foreign investment. *Moorgate and Wall Street*, Autumn, 5–37

Dunning J. H. (1969). Foreign capital in Europe. In *Economic Integration in Europe* (Denton G. R., ed.), pp. 286–306. London: Weidenfeld and Nicholson

Dunning J. H. (1970). *Studies in International Investment*. London: Allen and Unwin

Dunning J. H. (1971). *The Multinational Enterprise*. London: Allen and Unwin

Dunning J. H. (1973). The determinants of international production. *Oxford Economic Papers*, **25**(3), November, 289–336

Dunning J. H. (1974). *Economic Analysis and the Multinational Enterprise*. London: Allen and Unwin

Dunning J. H. (1976). *US Industry In Britain*. London: Wilton House

Dunning J. H. (1977). *United Kingdom Transnational Manufacturing and Resource Based Industries and Trade Flows in Developing Countries*. Geneva: UNCTAD

Dunning J. H. (1980). Toward an eclectic theory of international production: some empirical tests. *Journal of International Business Studies*, **11**(1), Spring/Summer, 9–31

Dunning J. H. (1981a). A note on intra-industry foreign direct investment. *Banca Nazionale del Lavoro Quarterly Review*, **139**, 427–37

Dunning J. H. (1981b). *International Production and the Multinational Enterprise*. London: Allen and Unwin

Dunning J. H. (1984). Non equity forms of foreign economic involvement and the theory of international productions. In *International Business Strategies in the Asia-Pacific Region* (Moxon R. W., Roehl T. W. and Truitt J. F., eds.). Greenwich, CN: JAI Press

Dunning J. H. (1985). The United Kingdom. In *Multinational Enterprises, Economic Structure and International Competitiveness* (Dunning J. H., ed.). Chichester and New York: John Wiley and Sons

Dunning J. H. (1986a). *Japanese Participation in British Industry*. London: Croom Helm

Dunning J. H. (1986b). *Decision-making Structure in US and Japanese Manufacturing Affiliates in the UK: Some Similarities and Contrasts*. Working Paper No. 41. Geneva: ILO

Dunning J. H. (1986c). The investment cycle revisited. *Weltwirtschaftliches Archiv*, **122**, 667–77

Dunning J. H. (1987). The investment development cycle and third world multinationals. In *Multinationals of the South* (Khan K., ed.). London: Francis Pinter

Dunning J. H. (1988a). Explaining International Production. London: Unwin Hyman

Dunning J. H. (1988b). Multinationals, Technology and Competitiveness. London: Allen and Unwin

Dunning J. H. (1988c). *Multinationals, Technology and Competitiveness*. London: Allen and Unwin

Dunning J. H. (1989). *Transnational Corporations and the Growth of Services: Some Conceptual and Theoretical Issues*. UNCTC Current Studies Series A, No. 9. New York: UNCTC

Dunning J. H. (1990). *The Globalization of Firms and the Competitiveness of Nations*. The Crafoord Lecture, 1989. Lund: Lund University Press

Dunning J. H. (1991a). Governments – markets – firms: towards a new balance? *The CTC Reporter*, No. 31, 2–9

Dunning J. H. (1991b). Governments and multinational enterprises: from confrontation to cooperation. *Millenium Journal of International Studies*, **20**, 223–44

Dunning J. H. (1991c). Governments organization and international competitiveness. In *Corporate and Industrial Strategies for Europe* (Mattson L. G. and Stymne B., eds.). Amsterdam: Elsevier Science Publishers

Dunning J. H. (1991d). The prospects for foreign direct investment in Eastern Europe. *Development and International Cooperation*, **VII**, 21–46

Dunning J. H. (1991e). European integration and transnational investment: the record assessed. In *Europe and America 1992 US–EC Economic Relations in the Single European Market* (Yannopoulos G., ed.). Manchester: Manchester University Press

Dunning J. H. (1992a). The competitive advantages of nations and TNC activities: a review article. *Transnational Corporations*, **1**, 135–68

Dunning J. H. (1992b). International direct investment patterns in the 1990s. In *The Global Race for*

Foreign Direct Investment in the 1990s (Oxelheim L., ed.). Berlin and New York: Springer-Verlag

Dunning J. H. (1992c). The governance of Japanese and US manufacturing affiliates in the U.K.: Some country specific differences. In *Country Competitiveness: Technology and the Organising of Work* (Kogut B., ed.). Oxford: Oxford University Press

Dunning J. H., ed. (1992d). *The Theory of Transnational Corporations*. United Nations Library on Transnational Corporations. London: Routledge

Dunning J. H. (1992e). Multinational enterprises and the globalisation of innovatory capacity. In *Technology, Management and International Business: Internationalisation of R&D and Technology* (Grandstrand O., Hakanson L. and Sjolander S., eds.). Chichester: Wiley

Dunning J. H. (1993a). Japanese and US manufacturing investment in Europe. Some comparisons and contrasts. In *Japanese Direct Investment in a Unifying Europe* (Mason M., ed.). Oxford: Oxford University Press

Dunning J. H. (1993b). *Global Business: The Challenge of the 1990s*. London and New York: Routledge

Dunning J. H. and Archer H. J. (1987). The eclectic paradigm and the growth of U.K. multinational enterprise 1870–1983. *Business and Economic History*, Second Series, **16**, 1–28

Dunning J. H. and Cantwell J. C., eds. (1987). *The IRM Directory of Statistics of International Investment and Production Statistics*. Basingstoke: Macmillan

Dunning J. H. and Gilman M. (1977). Alternative policy and prescriptions and the multinational enterprise. In *The Multinational Enterprise in a Hostile World* (Curzon G. and Curzon Y., eds.), pp. 31–55. London: Macmillan

Dunning J. H. and Gugler P. (1992). *Technology Based Cross Border Alliances*. GSM Working Paper Number 92–03, Rutgers University, Newark, New Jersey

Dunning J. H. and McQueen M. (1981). *Transnational Corporations in International Tourism*. New York: UNCTC

Dunning J. H. and Morgan E. (1980). Employee compensation in U.S. multinationals and indigenous firms: an exploratory micro/macro analysis. *British Journal of Industrial Relations*, **27**, 179–201

Dunning J. H. and Norman G. (1979). *Factors influencing the location of offices of multinational enterprises*. London: Location of Offices Bureau

Dunning J. H. and Norman G. (1983). The theory of the multinational enterprise: an application to multinational office location. *Environment and Planning*, **15**, 675–92

Dunning J. H. and Norman G. (1987). The location choice of offices of international companies. *Environment and Planning*, A, **19**, 613–31

Dunning J. H. and Pearce R. D. (1981). *The World's Largest Industrial Enterprises 1962–1977*. Farnham: Gower Press

Dunning J. H. and Pearce R. (1985). *The World's Largest Industrial Enterprises, 1962–1983*. Farnborough: Gower

Dunning J. H. and Robson P., eds. (1988). *Multinationals and the European Community*. Oxford: Basil Blackwell

Dunning J. H. and Rugman A. M. (1985). The influence of Hymer's dissertation on theory of foreign direct investment. *American Economic Review*, **75**, May, 228–32

Dunning J. H. and Steuer M. (1969). The effects of US direct investment on British technology. *Moorgate and Wall Street*, Autumn

Dunning J. H. and Stilwell F. (1978). Theories of business between the distribution of surplus profits. *Kyklos*, **31**, 601–23

East-West Business Directory (1990/1 and 1991/2). Ottowa: Carelton University, East–West Centre

Eastman H. C. and Stybolt S. (1967). *The Tariff and Competition in Canada*. London: Macmillan

ECA/UNCTC (1984a). *Transnational Corporations in Non-food Industries in Africa*. Addis Adaba: Joint ECA/UNCTC Unit E/ECA/UNCTC 44

ECA/UNCTC (1984b). *Transnational Corporations in the Cotton Industry in Tanzania*. Addis Adaba: Joint ECA/UNCTC Unit E/ECA/UNCTC

Economist (1990). The Human Condition. *The Economist*, 26 May, 80–1

Economist (1991). Stalling Japan's car makers. *The Economist*, 3 August, 65

Economou P. (1990). Enterprises from Eastern Europe and the USSR. *CTC Reporter*, No. 30, 46–7

Eden L. (1988). Equity and neutrality in the multinational taxation of capital. *Osgoode Hall Law Journal*, **26**, 367–408

Eden L. (1991). Multinational responses to trade and

technology changes: implications for Canada. In *Foreign Investment Technology and Growth* (McFetridge D., ed.). Ottawa: Investment Canada

Eden L. and Hampson F. O. (1990). *Clubs are Trumps: Towards a Taxonomy of International Regimes.* Carleton University Working Paper 90–02. Ottawa: Centre for International Trade and Investment Policy Studies

Eden L. and Molot M. A. (1992). Fortress or Free Market NAFTA and its implications for the Pacific Rim. In *Economic Relations in the Pacific in the 1990s* (Leaver J. and Ravenhill J., eds.). London: Routledge

Eisner R. and Pieper P. J. (1990). The world's greatest debtor nation? *North American Review of Economics and Finance*, **1**, 9–32

Eitman D. and Stonehill A. (1989). *Multinational Business Finance.* Reading, MA: Addison-Wesley, Fifth Edition

Ellis F. (1981). Export valuation and intra-firm transfers in the banana export industry in Central America. In *Multinationals Beyond The Market* (Murray R., ed.). Brighton: Harvester

Encarnation D. J. (1992). *Rivals Beyond Trade.* Ithaca and London: Cornell University Press

Encarnation D. J. and Mason M. (1990). The political economy of capital liberalization in Japan. *International Organization*, **44**, 42–51

Encarnation D. J. and Wells L. T. (1985). Sovereignty en garde: Organizing to negotiate with foreign investors. *International Organization*, **39**, 47–58

Enderwick P. (1985). *Multinational Business and Labour.* London: Croom Helm

Enderwick P. (1988). *Multinational Service Firms.* London: Routledge

Enderwick P. (1989). Multinational corporate restructuring and international competitiveness. *California Management Review*, **32**, 44–58

Enderwick P., ed. (1993). *Transnational Corporations and Human Resources.* UN Library on Transnational Corporations. London: Routledge

English H. E. (1964). *Industrial Structure in Canada's Competitive Position.* Montreal: Private Planning Association of Canada

Epstein B. and Newfarmer S. (1982). Imperfect international markets and monopolistic prices to developing countries. *Cambridge Journal of Economics*, **6**(1), 33–52

Erden D. (1988). Impact of Multinational Corporations in host countries executive training programs. *Management International Review*, **28**, 39–47

Ergas H. (1987). Does technology policy matter? In *Technology and Global Industry* (Brooks H. and Guile B. R., eds.). Washington: National Academy Press

Ergas H. (1988). *The Importance of Technology Policy.* Paris: OECD, Mimeo

ESCAP/CTC (1984). *Transnational Corporations and Transfer Pricing: A Case Study of the Pharmaceutical Industry of Thailand.* Bangkok: ESCAP/CTC

ESCAP and CTC Joint Unit (1981). *Transnational Corporations and Primary Commodity Exports From Asia and the Pacific.* Publication Series B, No. 1. Bangkok: ESCAP/UNCTC

ESCAP/CTC Joint Unit (1984). *Transnational Exportations and Transfer Pricing: A Case Study of the Pharmaceutical Industry of Thailand.* Bangkok: ESCAP

ESCAP/UNCTC (1979). *Activities of Transnational Corporation in the Cocoa Industry of Ghana.* Addis Adaba: Joint ECA/UNCTC Unit Working Paper No. 5

ESCAP/UNCTC (1984). *Transnational Corporations and Primary Product Exports from Asia and the Pacific.* Bangkok Joint CTC/ESCAP Unit on Transnational Corporations

Ethier W. J. (1986). The Multinational Firm. *Quarterly Journal of Economics*, **101**, 806–33

European Commission (1976). *Survey of Multinational Enterprises.* Vol. 1. Brussels: The European Commission

EUROSTAT (1991). *Direct Investment of the European Community.* Brussels: The European Commission

Evans P. A. L. (1984). On the importance of a generalist conception of human resource management: A cross-national look. *Human Resource Management*, Winter, 347–63

Evans P. B. (1977). Direct investment and industrial concentration. *Journal of Development Studies*, **13**, 373–85

Evans P. B. (1979). *Dependent Development: The Alliance of Multinational, State and Local Capital in Brazil.* Princeton, NJ: Princeton University Press

Fagre N. and Wells L. T. Jr (1982). Bargaining power of multinationals in host governments. *Journal of International Business Studies*, **13**, 9–24

Fahim-Nader M. (1991). Capital expenditures by majority owned foreign affiliates of U.S. companies, revised estimates for 1991. *Survey of Current Business*, September, 32–8

Fairchild L. (1977). Performance and technology of United States and national firms in Mexico. *Journal of Development Studies*, **14**(1), 14–34

Fairchild L. and Sosin K. (1986). Evaluating differences in technological activity between transnational and domestic firms in Latin America. *Journal of Development Studies*, **22**(4), 697–708

Fajnzylber F. and Martinez T. (1976). *Las Empresas Transnacionales su Expansion a Nivel Mundial y su Proyeccion en la Industria Mexicana (version preliminai)*. Mexico City: Fondo de cultura economica

Fatouros A., ed. (1993). *Transnational Corporations and the International Regulatory Framework*. United Nations Library on Transnational Corporations. London: Routledge

Feierabend I. K. and Feierabend R. L. (1976). Aggressive behavior in politics: a cross national study. *Journal of Conflict Resolution*, Fall

Fishwick F. (1982). *Multinational Companies and Economic Concentration in Europe*. Aldershot: Gower Publishing Company

Flowers E. B. (1975). *Oligopolistic Reaction in European Direct Investment in the United States*. Georgia State University, Georgia. Unpublished Doctoral Thesis

Flowers E. B. (1976). Oligopolistic reaction in European and Canadian Direct Investment in the United States. *Journal of International Business Studies*, **7**, 43–55

Foreman-Peck J. (1982). The American challenge of the twenties. Multinationals and the European motor industry. *Journal of Economic History*, **XLII**, December, 865–82

Forsyth D. J. C. (1972). *US Investment in Scotland*. New York: Praeger

Forsyth D. J. C. and Solomon, R. (1977). Choice of technology and nationality of ownership in manufacturing in a developing country. *Oxford Economic Papers*, **29**, 258–82

Fortune (1990). The World's Biggest Industrial Corporations. *Fortune*, 30 July, 269–94

Frank I. (1980). *Foreign Enterprise in Developing Countries*. Baltimore: John Hopkins University Press

Frank R. H. and Freeman R. T. (1978). *Distributional Consequences of Direct Foreign Investment*. London: Academic Press

Franke R. H., Hofstede G. and Bond M. H. (1991). Cultural roots of economic performance: a research note. *Strategic Management Journal*, **12**, 165–73

Frankel S. H. (1938). *Capital Investment in Africa*. London: Oxford University Press

Franko L. (1976). *The European Multinationals*. New York: Harper

Franko L. (1977). European multinational enterprises in the integration process. In *The Multinational Enterprise in a Hostile World* (Curzon G. and Curzon V., eds.). Basingstoke: Macmillan

Franko L. (1989). Global corporate competition: Who's winning and who's losing and the R&D factor as one reason why. *Strategic Management Journal*, **10**, 449–74

Franko L. (1991). Global corporate competition II. Is the large American firm an endangered species? *Business Horizons*, Nov./Dec., **34**, 14–22

Frischtak C. (1992). From monopoly to rivalry: policies to realize the competitive potential of transnational corporations. *Transnational Corporations*, **2**, forthcoming

Frischtak C., Hadjimichael B. and Zachau U. (1989). *Competitor Policies for Developing Countries*. Policy and Research Series No. 7. Washington: World Bank, Industry and Energy Department

Frobel F., Heinricks J. and Kreye O. (1980). *The New International Division of Labour*. Cambridge: Cambridge University Press

Frost K. A. and Stein J. C. (1989). *Exchange rates and foreign direct investment: an imperfect capital market approach*. Working Paper Series No. 2914. New York: National Bureau of Economic Research

Fudenberg D. and Maskin E. (1986). The folk theorem in repeated games with discounting or with incomplete information. *Econometrica*, **54**, 533–54

Fujita M. (1990). FDI between Japan and the United States. *CTC Reporter*, No. 29, 31–42

Fusfeld D. (1958). Joint subsidiaries in the iron and

steel industry. *American Economic Review*, **48**, 578–87

Galbraith C. S. and Kay N. W. (1986). Towards a theory of multinational enterprise. *Journal of Economic Behaviour and Organization*, **19**, 3–19

Garies H. (1971). Structure and functional aspects of a multinational pharmaceutical organisation. *Lex et Scientia*, **8**

Gaspari K. (1983). The multinational corporation in the 1980s. In *The Multinational Corporation in the 1980s* (Kindleberger C. P. and Audretsch D., eds.). Cambridge: MIT Press

Gatignon H. and Anderson E. (1988). The multinational corporation's degree of control over foreign subsidiaries: an empirical test of a transaction cost explanation. *Journal of Law, Economics and Organization*, **42**, 305–36

Geringer J. M. (1991). Strategic determinants of partner selection criteria in international joint ventures. *Journal of International Business Studies*, **22**, 41–62

Geringer J. M., Beamish P. W. and Da Costa R. C. (1989). Diversification strategy and internationalization. Implications for MNE performance. *Strategic Management Journal*, **10** 109–19

Gershenberg I. (1976). *The performance of multinationals and other firms in economically less-developed countries: a comparative analysis of Ugandan data*. Nairobi: Institute of Development Studies, Discussion Paper 234. Mimeo

Gershenberg I. (1987). *Multinational Enterprises, Transfer of Managerial Knowhow, Technology Choice and Employment Effects: A Case Study of Kenya*. ILO Working Paper No. 28. Geneva: ILO

Gershenberg I. and Ryan T. C. I. (1978). Does ownership matter? An analysis of transnational and other firms: an East African case. *Journal of Developing Areas*, **13**, 3–10

Ghemawat P., Porter M. E. and Rawlinson R. (1986). Patterns of international coalition activity. In *Competition in Global Industries* (Porter M. E., ed.). Boston: Harvard Business School Press

Ghoshal S. (1987). Global strategy: an organizing framework. *Strategic Management Journal*, **8** 425–40

Ghoshal S. and Bartlett C. A. (1990). The multinational corporations as an interorganizational network. *Academy of Management Review*, **15**(4), 603–25

Ghoshal S. and Nohria N. (1990). Internal differentiation within multinational corporations. *Strategic Management Journal*, **10**(4), 323–38

Ghoshal S. and Westney D. E (1992). *Organisation Theory and the Multinational Corporation*. London: Macmillan

Giddy I. H. (1978). The demise of the product cycle model in international business theory. *Columbia Journal of World Business*, Spring, **13**, 90–7

Gilpin R. (1975). *US Power and the Multinational Corporation*. London: Macmillan

Gilpin R. (1987). Trade, investment and technology policy. In *Emerging Technologies: Consequences for Economic Growth, Structural Change and Employment* (Giersch H., ed.), pp. 381–409. Tubingen: JCB Mohr

Gilroy B. Y. (1989). Intra-firm trade. *Journal of Economic Survey*, **3**, 325–43

Gladwin T. N. (1987). Environment, development and the multinational enterprise. In *Multinational Corporations, Environment, and the Third World* (Pearson C. S., ed.). Durham: Duke University Press

Gladwin T. N. and Walter I. (1980). *Multinationals Under Fire: Lessons in the Management of Conflict*. New York: John Wiley

Glickman N. and Woodward D. (1989). *The New Competitors: How Foreign Investors Are Changing The U.S. Economy*. New York: Basic Books

Globerman S. (1973). Market structure and R & D in Canadian manufacturing. *Quarterly Review of Economics and Business*, **13**, 59–67

Globerman S. (1979a). Foreign direct investment and spillover efficiency benefits in Canadian manufacturing industries. *Canadian Journal of Economics*, **12**, February, 42–56

Globerman S. (1979b). *U.S. Ownership of Firms in Canada*. Montreal: C.D. Howe Research

Globerman S. (1985). Canada. In *Multinational Enterprises, Economic Structure and International Competitiveness* (Dunning J. H., ed.). Chichester and New York: John Wiley and Sons

Goldberg M. A. (1972). The determinants of US direct investment in the EEC: a comment. *American Economic Review*, **62**, September, 692–99

Gomes-Casseres B. (1988). Joint venture cycles: the evolution of ownership strategies of US MNEs 1945–1975. In *Cooperative Strategies in International Business* (Contractor F. J. and Lorange P., eds.). Lexington, MA: D. C. Heath

Gomes-Casseres B. (1989a). Joint ventures in the face of global competition. *Sloan Management Review*, **30**, 17–26

Gomes-Casseres B. (1989b). Ownership structures of foreign subsidiaries. *Journal of Economic Behavior and Organization*, **2**, 1–25

Gomes-Casseres B. (1990). Firm ownership preferences and host government restrictions. An integrated approach. *Journal of International Business Studies*, **21**(1), 1–22

Goncalves R. (1986). Technological spillovers and manpower training. *Journal of Economic Development*, **1**, 119–32

Goodnow J. D. and Hansz J. E. (1972). Environmental determinants of overseas market entry strategies. *Journal of International Business Studies*, **3**, Spring, 33–50

Gordon M. J. and Fowler D. J. (1983). Performance of the multinational drug industry in home and host countries: a Canadian case study. In *The Multinational Corporations in the 1980s* (Kindleberger C. P and Audretsch D. B., eds.), pp. 139–61. Cambridge, MA: MIT Press

Graham E. M. (1975). *Oligopolistic Imitation and European Direct Investment in the United States*. D.B.A. Dissertation, Harvard University, unpublished

Graham E. M. (1978). Transatlantic investment by multinational firms: a rivalistic phenomenon. *Journal of Post Keynesian Economics*, **1**, 82–99

Graham E. M. (1981). *The terms of transfer of technology to the developing nations: a survey of the major issues, North–South Technology Transfer, The Adjustment Ahead*. Paris: OECD

Graham E. M. (1991a). Foreign direct investment in the United States and US interests. *Science*, **254**, 740–45

Graham E. M. (1991b). *Japanese control of R&D activities in the United States. Is this cause for concern?* Paper presented at conference on Japan's Growing Technological Capacity: Implications for the US Economy, Washington DC, October 23–24

Graham E. M. and Krugman P. R. (1989). *Foreign Direct Investment in the United States*. Washington: Institute for International Economics (Revised edition, 1991)

Grant R. M. (1987). Multinationality and performance among British manufacturing companies. *Journal of International Business Studies*, **18**, 79–89

Grant R. M. (1991). *Contemporary Strategy Analysis: Concepts, Techniques, Applications*. Oxford: Basil Blackwell

Gray H. P. (1972). *The Economics of Business Investment Abroad*. London: Macmillan Press

Gray H. P. (1982). Towards a unified theory of international trade, international production and direct foreign investment. In *International Capital Movements* (Black J. and Dunning J. H., eds.), pp. 58–83. London: Macmillan

Gray H. P., ed. (1992). *Transnational Corporations and International Trade and Payments*. UN Library on Transnational Corporations. London: Routledge

Gray H. P., ed. (1993). *Transnational Corporations and Trade and Payments*. United Nations Library on Transnational Corporations. London: Routledge

Gray J. M. and Gray H. P. (1981). The multinational bank: a financial MNC? *Journal of Banking and Finance*, **5**, 33–63

Green R. T. and Cunningham W. H. (1975). The determinants of U.S. foreign investment: an empirical examination. *Management International Review*, **15**, 113–20

Greenhill C. and Herbolzheimer E. (1981). Control of transfer prices in international transactions: the restrictive business practices approach. In *Multinationals Beyond The Market. Intra-firm Trade and the Control of Transfer Pricing* (Murray R., ed.). New York: John Wiley

Griffin K. (1978). *International Inequality and National Poverty*. London: Macmillan

Grosse R. E. (1982). Regional offices in multinational firms. In *New Theories of the Multinational Enterprise* (Rugman A., ed.). London and Canberra: Croom Helm

Grosse R. (1983). The Andean foreign investment code's impact on multinational enterprises. *Journal of International Business Studies*, **14**, Winter, 95–106

Grosse R. (1985). An imperfect theory of the MNE. *Journal of International Business Studies*, **16**, Spring, 20–37

Grosse R. (1988). *Competitive Advantages and Multinational Enterprises. A Latin American Application*. University of Miami, International Business and Banking Discussion Paper, 88–10, November

Grosse R. (1991). *The Bargaining Relationship Between Global Companies and National Governments*. Miami: Center for International Business Research

Grosse R. and Aramburu D. (1990). A bargaining of government relations: the Latin American case. *International Trade Journal*, **VI**, 209–38

Grosse R. and Kujawa D. (1992). *International Business*. Boston, MA: Irwin

Grosse R. and Behrman J. (1992). Theory in International Business. *Transnational Corporations*, **1**, 93–116

Group of Thirty (1984). *Foreign Direct Investment 1973–1987*. New York: Group of Thirty

Grubaugh S. J. (1987). Determinants of direct foreign investment. *Review of Economics and Statistics*, **69**(1), February, 149–52

Grubel H. G. (1968). Internationally diversified portfolios, welfare gains and capital flow. *American Economic Review*, **58**, December, 1299–314

Grubel H. G. (1974). Taxation and the rate of return from some U.S. asset holdings abroad 1960–69. *Journal of Political Economy*, May/June, **82**, 469–88

Gruber W., Mehta D. and Vernon R. (1967). The R&D factor in international trade and international investment of United States industries. *Journal of Political Economy*, **75**, February, 20–37

Grubert H. and Mutti J. (1991). Taxes, tariffs and transfer pricing in multinational corporation decision taking. *Review of Economics and Statistics*, **73**, pp. 285–93

Gugler P. (1991). *Les alliances strategies transnationales*. Fribourg: Universitaires Fribourg Suisse

Gugler P. (1992). Building transnational alliances to create competitive advantage. *Long Rate Planning*, **25**, 90–9

Gugler P. and Dunning J. H. (1991). *Technology Based Cross Border Alliances*. GSM Working Paper #92–03, Rutgers University

Guisinger S. E. (1986). Host-country policies to attract and control foreign investment. In *Investing in Development: New Roles for Private Capital* (Moran T. H., ed.), pp. 157–72. New Brunswick: Transition Books

Guisinger S. E. and Associates (1985). *Investment Incentives and Performance Requirements*. New York: Praeger

Gupta V. K. (1983). A simultaneous determination of structure, conduct and performance in Canadian manufacturing. *Oxford Economic Papers*, **35**, 281–301

Haex F., Halsberghe E. and Van den Bulcke D. (1979). *Buitenlandse en Belgische Ondernemingen in de Nationale Industrie*. Ghent: Diepenbeek

Hagedoorn J. and Schakenraad J. (1990a). Strategic partnering and technological cooperation. In *Perspectives in Industrial Economics* (Dankbaar B., Groenewegen J. and Schenk H., eds.). Dordrecht: Kluwer

Hagedoorn J. and Schakenraad J. (1990b). Inter-firm partnerships and cooperative strategies in core technologies. In *Explorations in the Economics of Technical Change* (Freeman C. and Soete L., eds.). London: Pinter

Hagedoorn J. and Schakenraad J. (1991). The internationalization of the economy, global strategies and strategic technology alliances. *Nouvelles de la Science et des Technologies*, **9**, 29–41

Hakanson L. (1981). Organization and evolution of foreign R&D in Swedish multinationals. *Geografiska*, **63B**, 47–56

Hakanson L. (1990). International decentralisation of R&D – the organizational challenges. In *Managing the Global Firm* (Bartlett C. A., Doz Y. and Hedlund G., eds.). London and New York: Routledge

Hakanson L. and Nobel R. (1989). *Overseas Research and Development in Swedish Multinationals*. Stockholm: Mimeo

Hakanson L. and Zander U. (1986). *Managing International Research and Development*. Stockholm: Svergies Mekanforbund

Halbach A. J. (1989). *Multinational Enterprises and Subcontracting in the Third World: A Study of Inter-Industrial Linkages*. ILO Working Paper No. 58. Geneva: ILO

Hallwood C. P. (1990). *Transaction Costs and Trade between Multinational Corporations*. Boston: Unwin, Hyman

Hamel G. and Prahalad C. K. (1985). Do you really have a global strategy? *Harvard Business Review*, July/August

Haddad M. and Harrison A. (1993). Are there dynamic externalities from foreign direct investment? Evidence from Morocco. In *TNCs, Market Structure and Industrial Performance* (Newfarmer R. and Frischtak C., eds.). UN Library on

Transnational Corporations. London and New York: Routledge

Hannah L. (1976). *Management Strategy and Business Development*. London: Macmillan

Harrigan K. (1985). *Strategies for Joint Ventures*. Lexington, MA: D. C. Heath and Co.

Hartman D. G. (1977). The effects of taxing foreign investment income. *Journal of Public Economics*, **13**, 213–30

Hartman D. G. (1981). *Domestic Tax Policy and Foreign Investment Income*. Working Paper No. 784. New York: National Bureau of Economic Research

Harvard Business School (1989). Europe, Case Study No. 9–389–130. Cambridge, MA: Harvard Business School

Harvey C. and Taylor P. (1987). Mineral wealth and economic development: foreign direct investment in Spain 1851–1913. *Economic History Review*, **XL**, 185–207

Haude D. (1991). Domestic agribusiness in peripheral countries: a challenge to established international firms. Paper presented at workshop organized by the Third World Centre, University of Nijmegen on 'Internationalization of National Economies', 18–20 December

Haug P., Hood N. and Young S. (1983). R & D intensity in the affiliates of US owned electronic companies manufacturing in Scotland. *Regional Studies*, **17**, 383–92

Hauser H., ed. (1989). *Technology and Public Policy*. Grusch, Switzerland: Vorlag Rugger

Hawawini G. and Schill M. (1992). *The Japanese Presence in the European Financial Sector. Historical Perspective and Future Prospects*. Paper presented to conference on Japanese Direct Investment in a Unifying Europe, Fontainbleau, France, INSEAD, 26–27 June. Mimeo

Hawkins R. G. (1972). *Job Displacement and the Multinational Firm: A Methodological Review*. Occasional Paper, No. 3, June. Washington: Center for Multinational Studies

Hawkins R. G. (1976). *Jobs, Skills and US Multinationals*. Statement to sub committee of International Economic Policy, Committee on International Relations House of Representatives, 5 February, 1976

Hawkins R. G., ed. (1979). *The Economic Effects of Multinational Corporations*. Greenwich: JAI Press

Hawkins R. G. and Gladwin T. N. (1981). Conflicts in the international transfer and technology: A US home country view. In *Controlling International Technology Transfer* (Sagafi-Nejad T., Moxon R. W. and Perlmutter H. V., eds.), pp. 202–62. New York and Oxford: Pergamon

Hawkins R. G. and Jedel M. J. (1975). US jobs and foreign investment. In *International Labor and the Multinational Enterprise* (Kujawa D., ed.). New York: Praeger

Hawrylyshyn B. (1971). The internationalisation of firms. *Journal of World Trade Law*, **5**(1), Jan./Feb., 72–82

He X. and Guisinger S. (1992). Does tax neutrality principle matter? Fresh funds investment versus reinvested earnings. Baltimore: Academy of International Business (North-East Chapter) Annual Proceedings

Heaton H. (1936). *Economic History of Europe*. New York: Harper and Brothers

Hedlund G. (1986). The hypermodern MNC – hetararchy. *Human Resource Management*, **25**, Spring

Hedlund G., ed. (1993). *Transnational Corporations and Organizational Management*. United Nations Library on Transnational Corporations. London: Routledge

Hedlund G. and Kogut B. (1992). Managing the MNCs: the end of the missionary era. In *TNCs and Organizational Issues* (Hedlund G., ed.). UN Library on Transnational Corporations. London and New York: Routledge

Hedlund G. and Rolander B. (1990). Actions in heterarchies: new approaches to managing the MNC. In *Managing the Global Firm* (Bartlett C. A., Doz Y. and Hedlund G., eds.). London and New York: Routledge

Helfgott R. B. (1973). Multinational corporations and manpower utilization in developing nations. *Journal of Developing Areas*, **7**, 235–46

Helleiner G. K. (1975a). The role of multinational corporations in the less developed countries – trade in technology. *World Development*, **3**, 161–89

Helleiner G. K. (1975b). Transnational enterprises in the manufacturing sector of the less developed countries. *World Development*, **3**, 641–50

Helleiner G. K. (1981). *Intra-firm Trade and the Developing Countries*, London: Macmillan

Helleiner G. K. (1989). Transnational corporations, direct foreign investment and economic development. In *Handbook of Development Economics* (Chenery H. and Srinivasan T. N., eds.). Amsterdam: Elsevier

Helleiner G. K. and Lavergne R. (1979). Intra-firm trade and industrial exports to the United States. *Oxford Bulletin of Economics and Statistics*, **41**, 297–312

Helpman E. and Krugman P. R. (1985). *Market Structure and Foreign Trade*. Cambridge: MIT Press

Hennart J. F. (1982). *A Theory of Multinational Enterprise*. Ann Arbor, MI: University of Michigan Press

Hennart J. F. (1986a). What is internalization? *Weltwirtschaftliches Archiv*, **122**, 791–804

Hennart J. F. (1986b). Internalization in practice; early foreign direct investments in Malaysian tin mining. *Journal of International Business Studies*, **17**, 131–43

Hennart J. F. (1986c). The tin industry. In *Multinationals and World Trade*. (Casson M. C. *et al.*, eds.). London: Allen and Unwin

Hennart J. F. (1987). Transaction costs and the multinational enterprise: the case of tin. *Business and Economic History*, **16**, 147–59

Hennart J. F. (1988). A transaction costs theory of equity joint ventures. *Strategic Management Journal*, **9**, 361–74

Hennart J. F. (1989). Can the new forms of investment substitute for the old forms: a transaction costs perspective. *Journal of International Business Studies*, **XX**, 211–33

Hennart J. F. (1991). The transaction costs theory of joint ventures: an empirical study of Japanese subsidiaries in the United States. *Management Science*, **37**, 483–97

Herrera J. D. (1992). Cross direct investment and technological capability of Spanish domestic firms. In *Multinational Investment in Modern Europe. Strategic Interaction in the Integrated Community* (Cantwell J. C., ed.). Aldershot, Hants: Edward Elgar

Hertner P. (1986). German multinational enterprise before 1914: Some case studies. In *Multinationals: Theory and History*. (Hertner P. and Jones G., eds.). Aldershot: Gower Press

Hertner P. and Jones G. (1986). *Multinationals Theory and History*. Aldershot and Brookfield VT: Gower

Hiemenz U. (1987). Foreign direct investment and industrialization in ASEAN countries. *Weltwirtschaftliches Archiv*, **123**, 121–34

Hill C. and Kim W. C. (1988). Searching for a dynamic theory of the multinational enterprise: a transaction cost model. *Strategic Management Journal*, **9**, 93–104

Hill C. W., Hwang P. and Kim W. C. (1990). An eclectic theory of the choice of international entry mode. *Strategic Management Journal*, **11**, 117–28

Hill H. and Johns B. (1985). The role of direct foreign investment in developing East Asian countries. *Weltwirtschaftliches Archiv*, **121**, 355–81

Hill M. O. (1974). Correspondence analysis: a neglected multivariate method. *Applied Statistics*, **23**, 340–54

Himmel E. (1922). *Industrielle Kapitalanglagender Schweiz in Auslande*. Langensalza: Hermann Beyer

Hipple F. S. (1990). Multinational companies and international trade: the impact of intra-firm shipments on U.S. foreign trade 1977–82. *Journal of International Business Studies*, **21**, 495–504

Hirsch S. (1967). *The Location of Industry and International Competitiveness*. Oxford: Oxford University Press

Hirsch S. (1976). An international trade and investment theory of the firm. *Oxford Economic Papers*, **28**, 258–70

Hirsch S. and Meshulach A. (1991). *Towards a Unified Theory of Internationalization*. Paper presented for 17th EIBA annual conference, Copenhagen, December 15–17, 1991

Hirschey M. (1981). R&D intensity and multinational involvement. *Economic Letters*, **7**, 87–93

Hirschman A. O. (1969). *How to divest in Latin America and why*. Essays in International Finance, 76. Princeton: Princeton University

Hladik K. J. (1985). *International Joint Ventures: An Economic Analysis of U.S. Foreign Business Partnerships*. Lexington, MA: Lexington Books

Hladik K. J. (1988). R&D and international joint ventures. In *Cooperative Strategies in International Business* (Contractor F. J. and Lorange P., eds.). Lexington: D. C. Heath and Co.

Hladik K. J. and Linden L. H. (1989). Is an international joint venture in R&D for you? *Research Technology Management*, **32**, July/August, 11–13

Hobson C. K. (1914). *The Export of Capital*. London: Constable White

Hofstede G. (1980). *Cultures Consequence: International Differences in Work-related Values*. Beverly Hills, CA: Sage

Hollander A. (1984). Foreign location decision by US transnational firms: an empirical study. *Managerial and Decision Economics*, **5**(1), March, 7–18

Hood N. and Young S. (1980). *European Development Strategies of US owned manufacturing companies located in Scotland*. Edinburgh: HMSO

Hood N. and Young S. (1982a). US multinational R&D: corporate strategies and policy implications for the U.K. *Multinational Business*, No. 2, 10–23

Hood N. and Young S. (1982b). *Multinationals in Retreat: The Scottish Experience*. Edinburgh: Edinburgh University Press

Hood N. and Young S. (1983). *Multinational Investment Strategies in the British Isles: A Study of MNEs in the Assisted Areas and in the Republic of Ireland*. London: HMSO

Hood N. and Young S. (1988). In *Multinational Corporate Integration and Regional Economic Integration* (Dunning J. H. and Robson P., eds.). Oxford: Basil Blackwell

Horaguchi H. and Toyne B. (1990). Setting the record straight. Hymer internalization theory and transaction cost economies. *Journal of International Business Studies*, **22**, 445–60

Hornell E., Vahlne J. E. and Wiedersheim P. F. (1973). *Export och Utlandsetableringar*. Stockholm: Almquist and Wiksell

Horst T. (1971). The theory of the multinational firm: optimal behaviour under different tariff and tax rates. *Journal of Political Economy*, **79**(5), 1059–72

Horst T. (1972a). Firm and industry determinants of the decision to invest abroad: an empirical study. *Review of Economics and Statistics*, **54**, August, 258–66

Horst T. (1972b). The industrial composition of US exports and subsidiary sales to the Canadian market. *American Economic Review*, **62**, March, 37–45

Horst T. (1974). *American Exports and Foreign Direct Investments*. Harvard Institute of Economic Research Discussion Paper No. 362, May

Horstman I. and Markusen J. R. (1986). *Licensing v Direct Investment: A Model of Internalization by the Multinational Enterprise*. University of Western Ontario. Mimeo

Hou Chi-ning (1965). *Foreign Investment and the Economic Development of China*. Cambridge, MA: Harvard University Press

Houston T. and Dunning J. H. (1976). *U.K. Industry Abroad*. London: Financial Times Publications

Hout T., Porter M. E. and Rudden E. (1986). How global companies win out? *Harvard Business Review*, September/October, 98–108

Hudson R. L. (1991). In Europe, electronics industry sends protectionist message to ICL. *Wall Street Journal*, 27 March, p. 2

Hufbauer G. C. (1966). *Synthetic Materials and the Theory of International Trade*. London: Gerald Duckworth

Hufbauer G. C. (1970). The impact of national characteristics and technology on the commodity composition of trade in manufactured goods. In *The Technology Factor in International Trade* (Vernon R., ed.). New York: Columbia University Press

Hufbauer G. C. (1992). *U.S. Taxation of International Income: Blue for Reform*. Washington: Institute of International Economics

Hufbauer G. C. and Adler M. (1968). *US Manufacturing Investment and the Balance of Payments*. Tax Policy Research Study Number 1. Washington, DC: US Treasury Department

Hughes H. and You Poh Seng (1969). *Foreign Investment and the Industrialization of Singapore*. Canberra: Australia National University Press

Hultman C. W. and McGee R. (1988). Factors influencing foreign investment in the US 1970–1986. *International Review of Economics and Business*, **XXXV**, Numbers 10-11, October/November, 1061–67

Huntingdon W. F. M. (1916). The relation of the government to foreign investment. *Annals of the American Academy of Political and Social Science*, **68**, November

Huss T. (1991). Transfer of technology: the case of the Chile foundation. *CEPAL Review*, **43**, 97–115

Hymer S. H. (1960). *The International Operations of National Firms: A Study of Direct Investment*. PhD Thesis, MIT: Published by MIT Press. (Also published under same title in 1976)

Hymer S. H. (1968). La grande firme multinationale. *Revue Economique*, **14**(b), 949–73

Hymer S. H. (1970). The efficiency contradictions of multinational corporations. *American Economic Review*, **60**, 441–48

Hymer S. H. (1971). The multinational enterprise and the law of uneven development. In *Economics and the World Order* (Bhagwati J., ed.). New York: World Law Fund

Hyun J. T. and Whitmore K. (1989). *Japanese Direct Foreign Investment: Patterns and Implications for Developing Countries*. Working Paper, Industry Series No. 1. Washington: Industry and Energy Department

ILO (1972). *Employment, Incomes and Inequality*. Geneva: ILO

ILO (1977). *Tripartite Declaration of Principles Concerning Multinational Enterprises and Social Policy*. Geneva: ILO

ILO (1981). *Employment Effects of Multinational Enterprises in Industrialized Countries*. Geneva: ILO

ILO (1984). *Technology Choice and Employment Generation by Multinational Enterprises in Developing Countries*. Geneva: ILO

ILO (1989). *The ILO Tripartite Declaration of Principles Concerning Multinational Enterprises and Social Policy – Ten*. Geneva: ILO

ILO (1991). *Multinational Banks and Labour Practices*. Geneva: ILO

Imai K. (1985). *Network Organisation and Incremental Innovation in Japan*. Institute of Business Research, Hitosubashi Discussion Paper No. 122, July

IMF (1977). *Balance of Payments Manual* 4th edn. Washington: IMF

IMF (1990). Tax policy and reform for foreign direct investment in developing countries. In *Organization of Economic Cooperation and Development, Taxation and International Capital Flows, A Symposium of OECD and Non-OECD Countries*, pp. 163–235. Paris: OECD

IMF (1993). *Balance of Payments Manual*. Washington: IMF. 5th edn.

Inman B. R. and Burton D. F. (1990). Technology and competitiveness: the new frontier. *Foreign Affairs*, **69**, Spring, 116–34

Institute for Studies on International Development (1991). *Indian Imports and Exports: Some Insights*. New Delhi: Institute for Studies of International Development

Irish C. (1987). Transfer pricing abuses and less developed countries. *The University of Miami Law Review*, **18**, Fall, 83–136

Itaki M. (1991). A critical assessment of the eclectic theory of the multinational enterprise. *Journal of International Business Studies*, **22**, 445–60

Itaki M. and Waterson M. (1990). *Europeans Multinationals and 1992*. Reading: University of Reading Discussion Paper in International Investment and Business Studies, No. 141

Iversen C. (1935). *Aspects of International Capital Movements*. London and Copenhagen: Levin and Munksgaard

Iyanda O. and Bello J. A. (1979). *Employment Effects of Multinational Enterprises in Nigeria*. Working Paper No. 10. Geneva: ILO

Jacques L. (1985). *The changing personality of US–Japanese joint ventures: a value added chain mapping paradigm*. Mimeo

Jansson H. (1982). *Interfirm Linkages in a Developing Economy: The Case of Swedish Firms in India*. Studia Oeconomiae Negotiorum 14. Uppsala: Acta Universitatis Uppalienses

Jansson H. (1983). *Purchasing Strategies of Transnational Corporations in Importing Substituting Countries*. Working Paper 1983/3. Uppsala: Centre for International Business Studies

Japan (1991). Japanese R&D Facilities in the UK. *Japan*. No. 507, 19 Feb, p. 3

Japan Update (1990). Direct investment in Japan: New developments. *Japan Update*, Winter, 12–15

Jenkins R. O. (1979). Transnational Corporations and their impact on the Mexican economy. In *Industrialization and the State in Latin America* (Carriere, ed.). Amsterdam: CEDLA Incidentele Publicaties, 14

Jenkins R. O. (1984). *Transnational Corporations and Industrial Transformation in Latin America*. London: Macmillan

Jenkins R. O. (1986). *Comparing Foreign Subsidiaries and Local Firms in Less Developed Countries; Theoretical Issues and Empirical Evidence*. University of East Anglia. Mimeo

Jenkins R. O. (1987a). Changing patterns in the Latin American automobile industry. In *Transnational Corporations and the Latin American Automobile Industry*, Ch. 11, pp. 206–238. London: Macmillan

Jenkins R. O. (1987b). *Transnational Corporations and Uneven Development. The Internationalization of Capital and the Third World*. New York: Methuen

Jenks L. H. (1938). *Migration of British capital to 1875*. London and New York: Jonathan Cape

JETRO (1981). *Japanese Manufacturing Operations in the U.S.: A Follow Up Study*. New York: JETRO

JETRO (1983). *Japanese Manufacturing Companies in Europe*. London: JETRO

JETRO (1988). *Current Management Structure of Japanese Manufacturing Enterprises in Europe*. 4th Survey Report. Tokyo: JETRO

JETRO (1989). *Current Management Structure of Japanese Manufacturing Enterprises in Europe*. 5th Survey Report. Tokyo: JETRO

JETRO (1990). *Current Management Situation of Japanese Manufacturing Enterprise in Europe*, 6th Survey Report. Tokyo: JETRO

JETRO (1991). *Current Management Situation of Japanese Manufacturing Enterprises in Europe*, 7th Survey Report. Tokyo: JETRO

Jo S.-H. (1976). *The impact of multinational firms in employment and incomes: The case study of South Korea*. ILO Working Paper. Geneva: ILO

Jo S.-H. (1980). Direct foreign private investment. In *Macroeconomic and Industrial Development in Korea* (Chong Kee Park, ed.), pp. 129–82. Seoul: Korea Development Institute

Johanson J. and Mattson L. G. (1987a). Internationalization in industrial systems – network approach. In *Strategies in Global Competition* (Hood H. and Vahlne J. E., eds.). Chichester and New York: John Wiley

Johanson J. and Mattson L. G. (1987b). Interorganizational relations in industrial systems: a network approach compared with a transaction cost approach. *International Studies of Management and Organization*, 17, 34–48

Johanson J. and Vahlne J. E. (1977). The internationalisation process of the firm – a model of knowledge development and increasing market commitments. *Journal of International Business Studies*, 8, 23–32

Johnson H. (1968). *Comparative Cost and Commercial Policy Theory for a Developing World Economy*. Stockholm: Almquist and Wiksell

Johnson H. (1970). The efficiency and welfare implications of the international corporations. In *The International Corporation* (Kindleberger C. P., ed.). Cambridge MA: MIT Press

Jones G. (1984a). Multinational chocolate: Cadbury overseas 1918–39. *Business History*, **XXVI**, 59–76

Jones G. (1984b). The growth and performance of British multinational firms before 1939: the case of Dunlop. *Economic History Review*, **XXXVI**, 35–53

Jones G. (1986). *British Multinationals: Origins, Management and Performance*. Aldershot: Gower

Jones G. (1988). Foreign multinationals and British industry before 1945. *Economic History Review*, **XLI**, 429–53

Jones G., ed. (1990). *Banks as Multinationals*. London and New York: Routledge

Jones G. (1991). The British government and foreign multinationals before 1940. In *Governments, Industries and Marketing* (Chick M., ed.). London: Edward Elgar

Jones G. (1992a). *British Multinational Banking Strategies on Historical Perspective*. University of Reading Discussion Papers in International Investment and Business Studies, No. 162, February

Jones G., ed. (1992b). *Transnational Corporations: A Historical Perspective*. United Nations Library on Transnational Corporations. London: Routledge

Jones S. R. H. (1987). Technology, transaction costs and the transition to factory production in the British silk industry. *Journal of Economic History*, **XLVII**, 71–96

Jordan G. L. and Vahlne J. E. (1981). *Domestic Employment Effects of Direct Investment Abroad by Two Swedish Multinationals*. International Labour Office, Multinational Enterprises Working Paper 13. Geneva: ILO

Jovanovic M. N. (1992). *International Economic Integration*. London and New York: Routledge

Juhl P. (1979). On the sectoral patterns of West German manufacturing investment in less developed countries: the impact of firm size, factor intensities and protection. *Weltwirtschaftliches Archiv*, **115**(3)

Juhl P. (1985). The Federal Republic of Germany. In *Multinational Enterprises, Economic Structure and International Competitiveness* (Dunning J. H., ed.). Chichester and New York: John Wiley and Sons

Julius de A. (1990). *Global Companies and Public Policies*. New York: Council on Foreign Relations Press

Kalirajan K. P. (1991a). A simulation determination of market concentration and industry performance in West Malaysian manufacturing. *Journal of Quantitative Economics*

Kalirajan K. P. (1991b). Government intervention in Malaysian manufacturing industries: a suggested methodology of measurement. *Applied Economics*, **23**, 1093–101

Katrak H. (1983). Global profit maximization and export performance of foreign subsidiaries in India. *Oxford Bulletin of Economics and Statistics*, **45**, 205–22

Katseli L. (1922). *Foreign direct investment and trade interlinkages in the 1990s: Experience and prospects of developing countries*. Paper presented to United Nations Symposium on Globalization and Developing Countries, The Hague, 30 March

Kawabe N. (1989). Japanese firms in the United States before the second world war: the case of Mitsui and Mitsubishi. In *Historical Studies in International Corporate Business* (Teichova A. and Levy-Lebayer M., eds.). Cambridge: Cambridge University Press

Kawaguchi N. B. (1978). *The role of Japanese firms in the manufacturing exports of developing countries*. Unpublished manuscript. May. Washington, DC: World Bank

Kay N. (1988). The R & D functions, corporate strategy and structure. In *Technical Change and Economic Policy* (Dosi G., ed.). London and New York: Pinter Publishers

Kay N., Robe J. P. and Zagnote P. (1987). *An approach to the analysis of joint ventures*. Florence: European University Institute

Keesing D. B. (1966). *Labor skills and comparative advantage*. American Economic Review Papers and Proceedings 1965 annual meeting

Keesing D. B. (1978). *Developing Countries Exports of Textiles and Clothing: Perspectives and Policy Changes*. May. Washington DC: World Bank. Mimeo

Kennett D. (1989). *The Determinants of European Direct Investment in the United States 1961–1987.*

London: University College Discussion Papers in Economics, 89–15

Keohane R. O. and Van Doorn Ooms (1975). The multinational firm and international regulation. In *World Politics and International Economics* (Bergsten C. F. and Krause L. B., eds.). Washington DC: Brookings Institution

Keynes J. M. (1924). Foreign investment and the national advantage. *The Nation and Athenaeum*, **35**, August, 584–87

Khan K., ed. (1987). *Multinationals of the South*. London: Francis Pinter

Kidron M. (1965). *Foreign Investment in India*. London: Oxford University Press

Killick T. (1982). Employment in foreign-owned plants. *British Business*, 26 November

Killing J. P. (1982). How to make a global venture work. *Harvard Business Review*, **60**(3), 120–27

Killing J. P. (1983). *Strategies for Joint Venture Success*. New York: Praeger

Kim S. H. and Miller S. W. (1979). Constituents of international transfer pricing decision. *Columbia Journal of World Business*, **14**, Spring, 69–77

Kim W. C. (1989). Developing a global diversification measure. *Management Science*, **35**(3), 376–83

Kim W. S. and Lyn E. O. (1987). Foreign direct investment theories, entry barriers and reverse investments in U.S. manufacturing industries. *Journal of International Business Studies*, **18**, 53–66

Kim W. S. and Lyn E. O. (1990). Foreign direct investment theories and the performance of foreign multinationals operating in the U.S. *Journal of International Business Studies*, **21**, 41–54

Kimura Y. (1989). Firm specific strategic advantages and foreign direct investment behavior of firms: the case of Japanese semi-conductor firms. *Journal of International Business Studies*, **20**, 296–314

Kindleberger C. P. (1969). *American Business Abroad*. New Haven, CN: Yale University Press

Kindleberger C. P., ed. (1970). *The International Corporation*. Cambridge, MA: MIT Press

Kindleberger C. P. (1974). Size of firm and size of nation state. In *Economic Analysis and the Multinational Enterprise* (Dunning J. H., ed.). London: Allen and Unwin

Kindleberger C. P. and Audretsch D. B., eds. (1983). *The Multinational Corporation in the 1980's*. Cambridge: MIT Press

Kindleberger C. P. and Goldberg P. M. (1970).

Towards a GATT for investment: a proposal for the supervision of the international corporation. *Law and Policy in International Business*, **2**, 295–323

Kirchner W. (1981). Russian tariffs and foreign industries before 1914. The German entrepreneur's perspective. *Journal of Economic History*, **XLI**, 361–80

Kirim A. (1986). Transnational corporations and local capital comparative conduct and performance in the Turkish pharmaceutical industry. *World Development*, **14**, 503–21

Kirkpatrick C. and Yamin M. (1981). The determinants of export subsidiary formation by US transnationals in developing countries: an inter-industry analysis. *World Development*, **9**, 373–82

Klein L. R. (1988). Components of Competitiveness. *Science*, **241**, 15 July, 308–13

Klein M. W. and Rosengren E. S. (1990a). *Determinants of Foreign Direct Investment in the United States*. Worcester, MA and Boston: Mimeo

Klein M. W. and Rosengren E. S. (1990b). *Foreign direct investment outflow from the United States: an empirical assessment*. Worcester and Boston: Mimeo

Klein M. W. and Rosengren E. S. (1991). Foreign exchange intervention as a signal of monetary policy. *New England Economic Review*, May/June, 39–50

Kline J. M. (1989). *The States and International Affairs*. Report prepared for US Advisory Commission on Intergovernmental Relations. Mimeo

Knickerbocker F. T. (1973). *Oligopolistic Reaction and the Multinational Enterprise*. Cambridge, MA: Harvard University Press

Knickerbocker F. T. (1976). *Market structure and market power consequences of foreign direct investment by multinational companies*. Occasional Paper 8, Washington Center for Multinational Studies

Knodgen G. (1979). Environmental and industrial siting results of a survey of investment by West German industry in developing countries. *International Institute for Environment and Society*, May

Kobrin S. J. (1976), The environmental determinants of foreign direct investment: an expost empirical analysis. *Journal of International Business Studies*, **VI**, 29–42

Kobrin S. J. (1978). When does political instability result in increased investment risk? *Columbia Journal of World Business*, **13**, Fall, 113–23

Kobrin S. J. (1982). *Managing Political Risk Assessment*. Berkeley: University of California Press

Kobrin S. J. (1986). *Testing the obsolescing bargain hypothesis in the manufacturing sector or the ink takes an awfully long time to dry*. Paper given in the 1986 Annual Meeting of the American Political Science Association, Washington DC, 26 August

Kobrin S. J. (1988). Trends in ownership of US manufacturing subsidiaries in developing countries: an inter-industry analysis. In *Cooperative Strategies in International Business* (Contractor F. J. and Lorange P., eds.). Lexington, MA: Lexington Books

Kobrin S. J. (1989). Enforcing export embargoes through multinational corporations: Why it does not work anymore. *Business In The Contemporary World*, (I), Winter, 31–42

Kobrin S. J. (1991). An empirical analysis of the determinants of global integration. *Strategic Management Journal*, **12**, 17–31

Kodama F. (1992). Japan's unique capability to innovate: technology, fusion and its international implications. In *Japan's Growing Technological Capability: Implications for the U.S. Economy* (Arrison T. S., Bergsten C. F. and Harris M., eds.). Washington DC: National Academy Press

Kogut B. (1983). Foreign direct investment as a sequential process. In *The Multinational Corporation in the 1980s* (Kindleberger C. P. and Audretsch D. B., eds.). Cambridge, MA: MIT Press

Kogut B. (1985a). Designing global strategies: corporate and competitive value added chain. *Sloan Management Review*, **25**, 15–28

Kogut B. (1985b). Designing global strategies: profiting from operational flexibility. *Sloan Management Review*, **26**, Fall, 27–38

Kogut B. (1988a). A study of life cycles in joint ventures. In *Cooperative Strategies in International Business* (Contractor F. J. and Lorange P., eds.). Lexington, MA: Lexington Books

Kogut B. (1988b). Joint ventures: theoretical and empirical perspectives. *Strategic Management Journal*, 319–22

Kogut B. (1989a). A note on global strategies. *Strategic Management Journal*, **10**, 383–89

Kogut B. (1989b). The stability of joint ventures: reciprocity and competitive rivalry. *Journal of Industrial Economics*, **38**, 183–93

Kogut B. (1990). 'The permeability of borders and the speed of learning among countries'. Globalization of Firms and the Competitiveness of Nations. Crafoord Lectures, Lund: University of Lund

Kogut B. (1991). Joint ventures and the option to acquire. *Management Science*, **37**, 19–33

Kogut B. (1992a). National organizing principles of work and the erstwhile dominance of the American multinational corporation. *Industrial and Corporate Change*, **1**, 263–303

Kogut B., ed. (1992b). *Country Competitiveness: Technology and the Organizing of Work*. Oxford: Oxford University Press

Kogut B. and Chang S. J. (1991). Technological capabilities and Japanese direct investment in the United States. *Review of Economics and Statistics*, **LXXIII**, 401–13

Kogut B. and Parkinson D. (1992). The diffusion of American organizing principles to Europe. In *Country Competitiveness, Technology and the Organization of Work* (Kogut B., ed.). Oxford: Oxford University

Kogut B. and Singh A. (1988). The effect of national culture on the choice of entry mode. *Journal of International Business Studies*, **19**, 411–32

Kojima K. (1973). Reorganization of north–south trade: Japan's foreign economic policy for the 1970's. *Hitsubashi Journal of Economics*, **13**, February, 1–28

Kojima K. (1978). *Direct Foreign Investment: A Japanese Model of Multinational Business Operations*. London: Croom Helm

Kojima K. (1982). Macroeconomic versus international business approach to foreign direct investment. *Hitsubashi Journal of Economics*, **23**, 630–40

Kojima K. (1983). Japanese direct foreign investment in Asian developing countries. In *Japan's Economy in a Comparative Perspective* (Fodella G., ed.). Tenterden, Kent: Paul Norbury Publications

Kojima K. (1985). Japanese and American direct investment in Asia. A comparative analysis. *Hitsubashi Journal of Economics*, **26**(2)

Kojima K. (1990). *Japanese Direct Investment Abroad*. Mitaka, Tokyo: International Christian University, Social Science Research Institute Monograph Series 1

Kojima K. (1992). *Internalization vs Cooperation of MNC's Business*. Paper presented at fifth International Conference on Multinational Enterprise, Taipei, 4–6 May 1992

Kojima K. and Ozawa T. (1984). Micro and macro economic models of foreign direct investment: towards a synthesis. *Hitsubashi Journal of Economics*, **25**(2), 1–20

Kokko A. (1990). *Host Country Competition and Technology Transfer by US Multinationals*. Stockholm: Stockholm School of Economics. Mimeo

Kolde E. (1968). *International Business Enterprise*. London: Prentice Hall

Koo B.-Y. (1985). Korea. In *Multinational Enterprises, Economic Structure and International Competitiveness* (Dunning J. H., ed.). Chichester and New York: John Wiley and Sons

Koopman K. and Montias J. M. (1971). On the description and comparison of economic systems. In *Comparison of Economic Systems* (Eckstein A., ed.). California: University of California Press

Kopits G. F. (1976a). Taxation and the Multinational Flow; A Critical Survey. *IMF Staff Papers*, **23**, 624–73

Kopits G. F. (1976b). Intra-firm royalties crossing frontiers and transfer pricing behaviour. *Economic Journal*, **86**, December, 791–805

Kopits G. F. (1979). Multinational conglomerate diversification. *Economia Internazionale*, **32**, 99–111

Kopits G. F. (1980). Effects of tax changes on direct investment abroad. In *United States Taxation and Developing Countries* (Hallawell R., ed.). New York: Columbia University Press

Koshiro K. (1982). How overseas investments affects employment at home? *Japan Economic Research Center Bulletin*, No. 417, June (Reprinted in *Economic Eye*, June 1982, 34–36)

Kotabe M. (1990a). Hollowing out of US multinationals and their global competitiveness. An intrafirm perspective. *Journal of Business Research*, **19**, 1–15

Kotabe M. (1990b). The relationship between offshore sourcing and innovativeness of US multinational firms: an empirical investigation. *Journal of International Business Studies*, **21**, 623–39

Kotabe M. and Omura G. S. (1989). Sourcing

strategies of European and Japanese multinationals: a comparison. *Journal of International Business Studies*, **20**, 113–29

Krause L. B. (1966). *Economic Integration and the United States*. Washington: The Brookings Institution

Kravis I. B. and Lipsey R. E. (1982). The location of overseas production for exports by U.S. multinational firms. *Journal of International Economics*, **12**, 201–23

Kravis I. B. and Lipsey R. E. (1988). *The Effect of Multinational Firms' Foreign Operations on Their Domestic Employment*. Working Paper No. 2760. Cambridge: National Bureau of Economic Research

Krey O., Heinrichs J. and Frobel F. (1988). *Multinational Enterprises and Employment*. ILO Working Paper No. 55. Geneva: ILO

Krugman P., ed. (1986). *Strategic Trade Policy and the International Economics*. Cambridge: MIT Press

Kuhn T. (1960). *The Structure of Scientific Revolutions, Institutions, Institutional Change and Economic Performance*. Cambridge: Cambridge University Press

Kujawa D. (1980). *Employment Effects of Multinational Enterprises: The Case of the United States*. ILO Working Paper No. 12. Geneva: ILO

Kujawa D. (1988). *American Attitudes Towards Japanese Direct Investment*. University of Miami International Business and Banking Discussion Papers, 88–8, September

Kumar K. and Kim K. Y. (1984). The Korean Manufacturing Multinationals. *Journal of International Business Studies*, **15**, Spring/Summer, 45–62

Kumar K. and McLeod M., ed. (1981). *Multinationals from Developing Countries*. Lexington, MA: D.C. Heath

Kumar M. S. (1984a). Social cost-benefit analysis of an export oriented project with foreign collaboration in India. *Industry and Development*, No. 10, 9–46

Kumar M. S. (1984b). *Growth, Acquisition and Investment*. Cambridge: Cambridge University Press

Kumar N. (1987a). Foreign investment and export orientation: the case of India. In *Direct Foreign Investment and Export Promotion: Policies and Experiences in Asia* (Seiji Naya *et al.*, eds.),

pp. 357–82. Kuala Lumpur and Honolulu, Hawaii: SEACEN Research and Training Center and East West Resource Systems Institute

Kumar N. (1987b). Technology imports and local research and development in Indian manufacturing. *The Developing Economies*, **25**, 220–33

Kumar N. (1987c). Intangible assets, internalisation and foreign production: direct investments and licensing in Indian manufacturing. *Weltwirtschaftliches Archiv*, **123**, 325–45

Kumar N. (1990). *Multinational Enterprises in India*. London: Routledge

Kumar N. (1991). *Determinants of country choice in relocation of production. The case of US multinationals*. New Delhi: Mimeo

Kuwahara Y. (1989). *Decision Making Structures and Processes in Multinationals in Japan*. Working Paper No. 35. Geneva: ILO

Kuwahara Y., Harada T. and Mizuno Y. (1979). *Employment Effects of Foreign Direct Investments in ASEAN Countries*. Working Paper No. 3. Geneva: ILO

Lado A. A. and Kedia B. (1990). *Determinants of solo versus alliance strategic choice: an integrative framework*

Lahera E. (1988). Technical change and production restructuring. *CEPAL Review*, No. 36, 33–47

Lall S. (1973). Transfer-pricing by multinational manufacturing firms. *Oxford Bulletin of Economics and Statistics*, **35**(3), 173–93

Lall S. (1976). Financial and profit performance of MNCs in developing countries: some evidence from an Indian and Colombian sample. *World Development*, **4**, 713–24

Lall S. (1978). The pattern of intra firm exports by US multinationals. *Oxford Bulletin of Economics and Statistics*, **40**, August, 209–22

Lall S. (1979a). The international allocation of research activity by US multinationals. *Oxford Bulletin of Economics and Statistics*, **41**, November, 313–31

Lall S. (1979b). Multinationals and market structure in an open developing economy. The case of Malaysia. *Weltwirtschaftliches Archiv*, **114**(2), 325–50

Lall S. (1979c). Developing countries as exporters of technology: a preliminary analysis. In *International Development and Resource Transfer* (Giersch H., ed.). Tubingen: Mohr

Lall S. (1980a). Monopolistic advantages and foreign involvement by US manufacturing industry. *Oxford Economic Papers*, **32**, 102–22

Lall S. (1980b). Vertical interfirm linkages: an empirical study. *Oxford Bulletin of Economics and Statistics*, **42**, 203–6

Lall S. (1983). *The New Multinationals*. Chichester and New York: John Wiley

Lall S. (1985). India. In *Multinational Enterprises, Economic Structure and International Competitiveness* (Dunning J. H., ed.). Chichester and New York: John Wiley and Sons

Lall S. (1987). Multinationals and technology development in host LDCs. In *Structural Change, Economic Interdependence and World Development* Vol. 4. (Dunning J. H. and Usui M., eds.). London: Macmillan

Lall S., ed. (1992). *Transnational Corporations and Economic Development*. United Nations Library on Transnational Corporations. London: Routledge

Lall S. and Mohammad S. (1983). Multinationals in Indian big business: industrial characteristics of foreign investments in a heavily regulated economy. *Journal of Development Economics*, **13**, 143–57

Lall S. and Siddharthan N. S. (1982). The monopolistic advantages of multinationals: lessons from foreign investment in the US. *The Economic Journal*, **92**, September, 668–83

Lall S. and Streeten P. (1977). *Foreign Investment, Transnational and Developing Countries*. London and Basingstoke: Macmillan

Landi J. (1986). *The Sourcing Policies of MNEs: A Case Study of Nigeria*. University of Reading, PhD Thesis

Langdon S. W. (1975). Multinational corporations, taste transfer and underdevelopment: a case study from Kenya. *Review of African Political Economy*, No. 2, 12–35

Langdon S. W. (1978). The multinational corporation in the Kenya political economy. In *Readings on the Multinational Corporation in Kenya* (Kaplinsky R., ed.). Nairobi: Oxford University Press

Langdon S. W. (1981). *Multinational corporations in the political economy of Kenya*. London: Macmillan

Larimo J. (1990). *Foreign Direct Investment Performance*. Paper presented at annual meeting, EIBA, Madrid, December

Lawrence P. R. (1987). Competition: a renewed focus for industrial policy. In *The Competitive Challenge* (Teece D. J., ed.). Cambridge, MA: Ballinger

Lawrence P. R. and Lorsch J. W. (1967). *Organization and Environment*. Homewood, IL: Irwin

Lecraw D. J. (1977). Direct investment by firms from less developed countries. *Oxford Economic Papers*, **29**, Nov.

Lecraw D. J. (1979). Choice of technology in low wage countries: a new classical approach. *Quarterly Journal of Economics*, Nov.

Lecraw D. J. (1983). Peformance of transnational corporations in less developed countries. *Journal of International Business Studies*, **14**, Spring/Summer. 15–33

Lecraw D. J. (1984). Bargaining power, ownership and the profitability of transnational corporations. *Journal of International Business Studies*, **15**, 27–43

Lecraw D. J. (1985a). Hymer and public policy in LDCs. *American Economic Review Papers and Proceedings*, **75**(2), 239–44

Lecraw D. J. (1985b). Singapore. In *Multinational Enterprises, Economic Structure and International Competitiveness* (Dunning J. H., ed.). Chichester and New York: John Wiley and Sons

Lecraw D. J. (1985c). Some evidence on transfer pricing by TNCs. In *Multinationals, Transfer Pricing* (Rugman A. M. and Eden L., eds.). London: Croom Helm

Lecraw D. J. (1991). Transnational corporations in host developing countries; a preliminary report. In *Multinational Enterprises in Less Developed Countries* (Buckley P. J. and Clegg J., eds.). Basingstoke and London: Macmillan

Lecraw D. J. and Morrison A. J. (1991). Transnational Corporations–Host Country Relations: A Framework for Analysis. *South Carolina Essays in International Business*, No. 9

Lecraw D. J. and Morrison A. (1992). *Transnational Corporations and Business Strategy*. UN Library on Transnational Corporations. London: Routledge

Lee W.-Y. (1986). *Foreign Investment in Korea: A Survey*. Seoul: Mimeo

Leonard H. J. (1984). *Are environmental regulations driving US industry overseas? An issue report*. Washington DC: The Conservation Foundation

Lessard D. R. (1976). World, country and industry relations in equity returns: implications for risk reduction through international diversification. *Financial Analysts Journal*, **32**, 32–8

Lessard D. R. (1982). Multinational diversification and direct foreign investment. In *Multinational Business Finance* (Eiteman D. K. and Stonehill A., eds.). Reading, MA: Addison-Wesley

Lessard D. R. (1985). Transfer prices, taxes, and financial markets: implications of international financial transfers within the multinational corporations. In *International Financial Management, Theory and Applications* (Lessard D. R., ed.), pp. 426–47. New York: Wiley and Sons

Lessard D. R. and Shapiro A. (1973). Guidelines for global financing choices. *Midland Corporate Finance Journal*, Winter, 68–80

Levis M. (1979). Does political instability in developing countries affect foreign investment flow? An empirical examination. *Management International Review*, **19**, 59–68

Levy B. (1983). *The Industrial Economics of Entrepreneurship and Dependent Development*. PhD Thesis in Business Economics, Harvard University

Levy D. and Gomes-Casseres B. (1989). *Technology Collaboration in Europe, HBS Case 9-389-130*. Boston, MA: Harvard Business School

Levy H. and Sarnat M. (1970). International diversification of investment portfolios. *American Economic Review*, **60**, 668–75

Lewis C. (1938). *America's Stake in International Investment*. Washington, DC: Brookings Institution

Li J. T. and Guisinger S. (1991). Comparative business failures of foreign controlled firms in the United States. *Journal of International Business Studies*, **22**, 209–24

Li J. T. and Guisinger S. (1992). The globalization of service multinationals in the 'triad' nations: Japan, Europe and North America. *Journal of International Business Studies*, **23**, forthcoming

Lim D. (1977). Do foreign companies pay higher wages than their local counterparts in Malaysian manufacturing? *Journal of Development Economics*, **7**, 55–66

Lim D. (1983). Fiscal incentives and direct foreign investment in less developed countries. *Journal of Development Studies*, **19**, 207–12

Lim L. Y. C. and Pang E. F. (1977). *The Electronics Industry in Singapore: Structure Technology and Linkages*. Singapore: University of Singapore, Economic Research Press Monograph Series No. 7

Lim L. Y. C. and Pang E. F. (1982). Vertical linkages and multinational enterprises in developing countries. *World Development*, **10**, 585–95

Lim L. Y. C. and Pang E. F. (1991). *Foreign Direct Investment and Industrialization in Malaysia, Taiwan and Thailand*. Paris: Development Centre of the OECD

Lincoln J. (1992). Work Organization in Japan and the United States. In *Country Competitive Technology and the Organizing of Work* (Kogut B., ed.). Oxford: Oxford University Press

Link A. and Tassey G., eds. (1990). *Cooperative Research. A New Strategy for Competitiveness*. Norwell, MA: Kluwer Academic Publishers

Lipsey R. E. (1991). Foreign direct investment in the United States and US trade. *Annals of the American Academy of Political and Social Science*, No. 516, 76–90

Lipsey R. E. and Dobson N. (1986). *Shaping Comparative Advantage*. Ontario: Prentice Hall for C.D. Howe Institute

Lipsey R. E. and Weiss M. Y. (1981). Foreign production and exports in manufacturing industries. *Review of Economics and Statistics*, **63**, 488–94

Lipsey R. E. and Weiss M. Y. (1984). Foreign production and exports of individual firms. *Review of Economics and Statistics*, **66**, 304–8

Lipsey R. E., Kravis I. B. and Roldan R. R. (1982). Do multinational firms adapt factor proportions to prices? In *Trade and Employment in Developing Countries: Factor Supply and Substitution* (Krueger A. O., ed.). Chicago: University of Chicago Press

Lipsey R. G. (1991). *Economic Growth: Science and Technology and Institutional Change in the Global Economy*. CIAR Publication No. 4. Toronto: Canadian Institute for Advanced Research

Little I. .M. .D., Scitovsky T. and Scott M. (1970). *Industry and Trade in Some Developing Countries*. London: Oxford University Press

Little J. S. (1986). The effects of foreign direct investment on U.S. employment during recession and structural change. *New England Economic Review*, Nov./Dec., 40–8

Litvak E. and Rothman J. (1970). Towards the theory and practice of coordination between formal organizations. In *Organizations and Clients: Essays in the Sociology of Service* (Rosengren W. R., Lefton M. and Bidwell C. W., eds.). Columbus, Ohio: Merrill

Litvak I. A. and Maule C. J. (1977). Transnational corporations and vertical integration: the banana case. *Journal of World Trade Law*, 2(6), 537–49

Long F. (1981). *Restrictive Business Practices, Transnational Corporations and Development. A Survey*. The Hague: Martinus Nijhoff Publishing

Lundgren N. (1977). Comment (on a chapter by J. H. Dunning). In *The International Allocation of Economic Activity* (Ohlin B., Hesselborn P. O. and Wijkman P. M., eds.). London: Macmillan

Lundström R. (1986). Swedish multinational growth before 1930. In *Multinationals: Theory and History* (Hertner P. and Jones G., eds.). Aldershot: Gower Publishing Co.

Lunn J. L. (1980). Determinants of US direct investment in the EEC. *European Economic Review*, 13, January, 93–101

Lunn J. L. (1983). Determinants of US direct investment in the EEC, revisited again. *European Economic Review*, 21, May, 391–3

Luostarinen R. (1979). *Internationalization of the Firm*. Helsinki: Acta Acadamie Oeconomicae, Helsinki School of Economics

Luostarinen R. and Welch L. (1990). *International Business Operations*. Helsinki: Helsinki School of Economics

Lustig N. (1991). *Bordering on Partnership: The US–Mexico Agreement*. Mimeo

Macharzina K. (1991). Paradigm shift in international business research: from partist and eclectic approaches to the gains paradigm. *Management International Review*, 31, Special Issue, 23–43

MacManus J. C. (1972). The theory of the multinational firm. In *The Multinational Firm and the Nation State* (Paquet G., ed.). Toronto: Collier Macmillan

Maddala G. S. (1983). *Limited-Dependent and Qualitative Variables in Econometrics*. New York: Cambridge University Press

Magee S. P. (1977a). Information and the multinational corporation. An appropriability theory of foreign direct investment. In *The New International Economic Order* (Bhagwati J. N., ed.). Cambridge, MA: MIT Press

Magee S. P. (1977b). Multinational corporations, the industry technology cycle and development. *Journal of World Trade Law*, 2(4), 297–321

Magee S. P. (1979). Jobs and the multinational corporations: The home country perspective. In *The Economic Effects of Multinational Corporations* (Hawkins R. G., ed.). Greenwich: JAI Press

Mamalakis M. (1970). The American copper companies and the Chilean government, 1920–1967. In *Foreign Investment in the Petroleum and Mineral Industries: Case Studies of Investor–Host Country Relations* (Mikesell R. F., ed.). Baltimore: John Hopkins University Press

Manrique G. (n.d.). *An Industrial Organizational Approach to the Study of Multinational Corporations in Development*. Mimeo

Mansfield E. and Romeo A. (1984). Reverse transfer of technology from overseas subsidiaries to American firms. *IEEE Transactions on Engineering Management*, EM–31, August, 610–27

Markusen J. R. (1984). Multinationals, multi-plant economies and the gain from trade. *Journal of International Economics*, 16, 205–16

Martinez J. and Jarillo J. C. (1989). The evolution of research on coordination mechanisms in multinational corporations. *Journal of International Business Studies*, Fall, 20(3), 489–514

Marton K. (1986). *Multinationals, Technology and Industrialization*. Lexington, MA: D.C. Heath

Mason F. R. (1920). *American Silk Industry and the Tariff*. Cambridge, MA: American Economic Association

Mason M. (1987). Foreign direct investment and Japanese economic development 1899–1931. *Business and Economic History*, 16, 93–107

Mason M. (1992). *The Lost Link Rediscovered: The Origins and Evolution of Japanese Direct Investment in Europe*. Paper presented at a conference on Japanese Direct Investment in a Unifying Europe, Fontainbleau, France, 26–27 June

Mason R. H. (1973). Some observations on the choice of technology by multinational firms in developing countries. *Review of Economics and Statistics*, 55, 349–55

Mason R. H. (1980). A comment on Professor Kojima's Japanese type versus American type of technology transfer. *Hitosubashi Journal of Economics*, **20**, 42–52

Mataloni R. J. Jr (1990). US multinational companies: operations in 1988. *Survey of Current Business*, **70**, June, 31–44

McAleese D. (1985). American investment in Ireland. In *The Irish in America: Emigration Assimilation and Import* (Drudy P. J., ed.). Cambridge: Cambridge University Press

McAleese D. and Counahan M. (1979). 'Snitchers' or 'Snatchers'. Employment in Multinational Corporations during the Recession. *Oxford Bulletin of Economics and Statistics*, **41**, November, 345–58

McAleese D. and McDonald D. (1978). Employment growth and the development of linkages in foreign owned and domestic manufacturing enterprises. *Oxford Bulletin of Economics and Statistics*, **40**, 321–39

McConnell J. and Nantell J. (1985). Common stock returns and corporate combinations: The case of joint ventures. *Journal of Finance*, **40**, 519–36

McFetridge D. G. (1987). The timing, mode and terms of technology transfer: Some recent findings. In *Governments and International Technology Transfer* (Safarian A. E. and Bertin G., eds.). London: Croom Helm

McGee J. and Thomas H. (1986). Strategic groups: theory research and taxonomy. *Strategic Management Journal*, **7**, 141–60

McGuinness N. W. (1983). The influence of research and development on foreign sales performance. In *Multinationals and Technology Transfers: The Canadian Experience* (Rugman A. M., ed.). New York: Praegers Publishers

McKay J. P. (1970). *Pioneers for Profit: Foreign Entrepreneurship and Russian Industrialisation, 1885–1913*. Chicago, IL: University of Chicago Press

McKern B. (1976). *Multinational Enterprises and Natural Resources*. Sydney: McGraw-Hill

McKern B., ed. (1993). *Transnational Corporations and Natural Resources*. United Nations Library on Transnational Corporations. London: Routledge

McManus J. C. (1972). The theory of the multinational firm. In *The Multinational Firm and the Nation State* (Pacquet G., ed.). Toronto: Collier, MacMillan

McMillan C. (1987). *Multinationals from the Second World*. London: Macmillan Press

McMillan C. (1989). *The East West Business Directory 1989*. Ottawa: Carleton University/Duncan Publishing

McMillan C. (1991). *The East West Business Directory 1990/91*. Ottawa: Carleton University/Duncan Publishing

Meeks P. J. (1986). West–west technology transfer: the dilemma of cooperation and conflict. In *The Political Economy of International Technology Transfer* (McIntyre J. R and Papp D. S., eds.). New York and London: Quorum Books

Meller P. and Mizala A. (1982). US multinationals and Latin American manufacturing employment absorption. *World Development*, **10**(2), 115–26

Mellors J. (1973). *Corporate Taxation and the Location of Overseas Direct Investment*. Reading: University of Reading Discussion Papers in International Investment and Business Studies, Number 5, May

Meyer H. E. (1978). Those worrisome technology exports. *Fortune*, 22 May, 106–9

Miami News (1988), *Global outlook the real thing Coca-Cola Executives affair*. Miami News, 11 February

Michalet C.-A. and Chevallier T. (1985). France. In *Multinational Enterprises, Economic Structure and International Competitiveness* (Dunning J. H., ed.). Chichester and New York: John Wiley and Sons

Michel A. and Shaked I. (1986). Multinational corporations versus Domestic corporations financial performance and characteristics. *Journal of International Business Studies*, **16**, 89–106

Micossi S. and Viesti G. (1991). Japanese investments in manufacturing in Europe. In *European Integration: Trade and Industry* (Winters L. A. and Venables A., eds.). Cambridge: Cambridge University Press

Mikesell R. F., ed. (1970). *Foreign Investment in the Petroleum and Mineral Industries: Case Studies of Investor–Host Country Relations*. Baltimore: John Hopkins University Press

Millington A. L. and Bayliss B. T. (1991). Non-tariff barriers and U.K. Investment in the European Community. *Journal of International Business Studies*, **XXI**, 695–710

Miranti P. J. and Gray H. P. (1992). *Problems in Estimating a Nation's International Investment Position*. New Brunswick: Rutgers University, Mimeo

MITI (1989). *Dai-sankai Kaigai Jigyo Katsudo Kihan Dhosan Kaigai Toshi Tokei, Soran*. Tokyo, Keibun Shuppan, May

Moose J. (1968). *US Direct Investment Abroad in Manufacturing and Petroleum. A recursive model*. Unpublished Doctoral Thesis. Cambridge: Harvard Business School

Moran T., ed. (1993). *Governments and Transnational Corporations*. United Nations Library on Transnational Corporations. London: Routledge

Morgenstern R. D. and Muller R. E. (1976). Multinationals versus local corporations in LDCs: An econometric analysis of export performance. *Southern Economic Journal*, January, **42**(3), 399–406

Morley S. and Smith G. W. (1973). The effects of changes in the distribution of income on labour, foreign investment and growth in Brazil. In *Authoritarian Brazil* (Stepan A., ed.). New Haven: Yale University Press

Morley S. and Smith G. W. (1977a). The choice of technology: Multinational firms in Brazil. *Economic Development and Cultural Change*, **25**(2), 239–64

Morley S. and Smith G. W. (1977b). Limited search and the technology choices of multinational firms in Brazil. *Quarterly Journal of Economics*, **91**, 263–88

Morris O. and Hergert M. (1988). Trends in international collaborative agreements. *Columbia Journal of World Business*, Summer, **23**, 15–21

Morrison A. J., Ricks D. A. and Roth K. (1991). Globalization versus regionalization: Which way for the multinational? *Organizational Dynamics*, Winter, 17–29

Morse G. W. and Farmer M. C. (1986). Location and investment effects of a tax abatement program. *National Tax Journal*, **34**

Mowery D., ed. (1988). *International Collaborative Ventures in U.S. Manufacturing*. Cambridge: Ballinger

Mowery D. (1989). Collaborative ventures between US and foreign manufacturing firms. *Research Policy*, **18**, 19–32

Mowery D. (1990). *New developments in US Technology and Trade Policies. Declining Hegemon, Wounded Giant or Ambivalent Gulliver*. Working Paper No. 90–1. Berkeley, California: School of Business

Mowery D. (1991). *The Challenges of International to US Technology Policy*. Berkeley, California: School of Business CCC Working Paper No. 91–4

Mowery D. and Rosenberg N. (1989a). New developments in US technology policy: implications for competitiveness and international trade policy. *California Management Review*, **32**, 107–24

Mowery D. and Rosenberg N. (1989b). *Technology and the Pursuit of Economic Growth*. New York: Cambridge University Press

Moxon R. (1975). The motivation for investment in offshore plants: the case of the US electronics industry. *Journal of International Business Studies*, **6**(1), Spring, 51–65

Moxon R. (1979). The cost, conditions and adaptation of MNC technology in developing countries. In *The Economic Effects of Multinational Corporations* (Hawkins R. G., ed.). Greenwich, CN: JAI Press

Mullar-Sebastian A. (1983). The product life cycle theory: empirical evidence. *Journal of International Business Studies*, **14**, 95–106

Munro D. G. (1934). *United States and the Caribbean Area*. Boston: World Peace Foundation

Murphy N. R. V. (1989). The effects of taxes and rates of return on foreign direct investment in the United States. Some econometric comments. *National Tax Journal*, **XLII**, 205–7

Murphy K. M., Shleifer A. and Vishny R. W. (1989). Industrialization and the Big Push. *Journal of Political Economy*, **97**, October, 447–59

Murray R., ed. (1981). *Multinationals Beyond the Market*. Brighton, Sussex: Harvester

Musgrave P. B. (1969). *United States Taxation of Foreign Investment Income: Issues and Arguments*. Cambridge, MA: The Law School of Harvard University

Musgrave P. B. (1987). Taxes on capital income and corporations. In *Tax Coordination in the European Community* (Cnossen, S., ed.), pp. 197–225. Devenber: Kluwer Law and Taxation Publishers

Myrdal G. (1970). *The Challenge of World Poverty*. New York: Pantheon

Mytelka L. K. (1978). Licensing and Technology Dependence in the Andean Group. *World Development*, **6**, 447–59

Mytelka L. K. (1979). *Regional Development and the Global Economy*. New Haven, CN: Yale University Press

Mytelka L. K., ed. (1991). *Strategic Partnerships. States, Firms and International Competition*. London: Francis Pinter

Mytelka L. K. and Delapierre M. (1987). The alliance strategies of European firms and the role of ESPRIT. *Journal of Common Market Studies*, **26**, 231–55

Nader F. M. (1990). Capital expenditures by majority-owned foreign affiliates of US affiliates of US companies, revised estimates for 1991. *Survey of Current Business*, September, 32–8

Nakamoto M. (1992). Plugging into each other's strength. *Financial Times*, 27 March

National Academy of Sciences (1987). *Balancing the National Interest*. Washington DC: National Academy Press

National Science Foundation (1988). *The Science and Technology Resources of Japan: A Comparison with the United States*. Washington, DC: National Science Foundation, NSF Report 88–318

National Science Foundation (1989). *International Science and Technology Data Update*. Washington, DC: National Science Foundation

Natke P. (1985). A comparison of import pricing by foreign and domestic firms in Brazil. In *Multinationals and Transfer Pricing* (Rugman A. M. and Eden L., eds.). London: Croom Helm

Nau H. R. (1986). International technology transfer security and economic considerations under the Reagan administration. In *The Political Economy of International Technology Transfer* (McIntyre J. R. and Papp D. S., eds.). New York and London: Quorum Books

Negandhi A. (1983). External and internal functioning of American, German and Japanese multinational corporations' decision making and policy issues. In *Governments and Multinationals: The Policy of Control Versus Autonomy* (Goldberg W. H., ed.). Cambridge: Delgeschlager, Gunn and Hain

Negandhi A. and Baliga R. (1981). Internal functioning of American, German and Japanese multinational corporations. In *The Management of Headquarters Subsidiary Relationships in Multinational Corporations* (Otterbeck L., ed.), pp. 107–20. Aldershot: Gower

Negandhi A. and Welge M. (1984). *Beyond Theory Z: Global Rationalization Strategies of American, German and Japanese Multinational Companies*. Greenwich, CN: JAI Press Inc.

Nelson R. (1990). US technological leadership: where did it come from and where did it go. *Research Policy*, **19**, 117–32

Nelson R. R. (1991). *Why do Firms Differ and How Does it Matter?* Berkeley, CA: Consortium on Competitiveness and Cooperation Working Paper 91–7

Newfarmer R. S. (1979). Oligopolistic tactics to control markets and the growth of TNCs in Brazil's electrical industry. *Journal of Development Studies*, **15**, 108–40

Newfarmer R. S., ed. (1985). *Profits Progress and Poverty*. Notre Dame, Indiana: University of Notre Dame Press

Newfarmer R. S. and Frischtak C., eds. (1993). *Transnational Corporations, Market Structure and Industrial Performance*. United Nations Library on Transnational Corporations. London: Routledge

Newfarmer R. S. and Marsh L. (1981a). *Profitability of foreign and domestic firms*. North–South Economic Linkages. Washington, DC: U.S. Department of Labor

Newfarmer R. S. and Marsh L. C. (1981b). Foreign ownership, market structure and industrial performance: Brazil's electrical industry. *Journal of Development Economics*. **8**. 47–75

Newfarmer R. S. and Mueller W. F. (1975). *Multinational corporations in Brazil and Mexico: Structural sources of economic and non economic power*. Washington, DC: U.S. Senate Subcommittee on Multinational Corporations

Nicholas S. (1982). British multinational investment before 1939. *Journal of European Economic History*, **11**, 605–30

Nicholas S. (1983). Agency contracts, institutional modes, and the transition to foreign direct investment by British manufacturing multinationals before 1939. *Journal of Economic History*, **XLIII**, 675–86

Nicholas S. (1986). The theory of multinational enterprise as a transactional mode. In *Multinationals: Theory and History* (Hertner P. and Jones G., eds). Aldershot: Gower

Nicholas S. (1989). Location choice performance and the growth of British multinational firms. *Business History*, **31**, 122–41

Nigh D. (1985). The effect of political events on US

direct foreign investment: a pooled time-series cross sectional analysis. *Journal of International Business Studies*, **16**(1), Spring, 1–17

Nigh D. (1986). Political events and the foreign direct investment decision: an empirical examination. *Managerial and Decision Economics*, **7**(2), June, 99–106

Nigh D., Cho K. R. and Krishnan S. (1986). The role of location related factors in U.S. banking involvement abroad: an empirical examination. *Journal of International Business Studies*, **17**, 59–71

Nippon Electric Company (1984). *The First 80 Years*. Tokyo: NEC

Nordström R. (1991). *The Internationalization Process of the Firm Searching for New Patterns and Explanations*. Stockholm: Stockholm School of Business, IIB dissertation

North D. (1981). *Structure and Change in Economic History*. New York: Norton

North D. (1985). Transaction costs in history. *Journal of Economic History*, **42**, 566–76

O'Brien T. F. (1989). Rich beyond the dreams of avarice: the Guggenheims in Chile. *Business History Review*, **63**, 122–59

O'Farrell P. N. (1983). Ireland. In *Industrial Mobility and Migration in the European Community* (Klaassen L. H. and Molle W. T. M., eds.), pp. 301–51. Aldershot: Gower Publishing Co.

O'Farrell P. N. and Crouchley R. (1984). Industrial closures in Ireland 1973–81: Analysis and implications. *Regional Studies*, **17**, 411–27

O'Hearn D. (1990). TNCs intervening mechanisms and economic growth in Ireland: a longitudinal test and extension of the Bornschier model. *World Development*, **18**, 417–29

O'Suilleabhain M. (1982). *Employment Effects of Multinational Enterprises: The Case of the Republic of Ireland*. ILO Working Paper No. 22. Geneva: ILO

O'Sullivan P. (1985). Determinants and impact of foreign direct investment in host countries. *Management International Review*, **24**, 28–35

OECD (1979). *Transfer Pricing and Multinational Enterprises*. Report of the OECD Committee on Fiscal Affairs, Paris.

OECD (1981). *East-West Trade: Recent Development in Countertrade*. Paris: OECD

OECD (1983). *Aluminium Industry: Energy Aspects of Structural Change*. Paris: OECD

OECD (1985). *Structural Adjustment and Multinational Enterprises*. Paris: OECD

OECD (1989). *Investment Incentives and Disincentives Effects on International Direct Investment*. Paris: OECD

OECD (1991a). Global Firm Cooperation and Competition. Globalisation Developments and Industrial Policy Issues for the Nineties. Paris: OECD, Directorate for Science Technology and Industry Committee. (To be published in 1992 under the title *Technology and the Economy*. Paris: OECD)

OECD (1991b). *The Revised Benchmark Definition of Foreign Direct Investment*. Paris: OECD, July. Mimeo

OECD (1991c). *Measures Affecting Direct Investment in OECD Countries*. Paris: OECD

Ohmae K. (1985). *Triad Power*. New York: Free Press

Ohmae K. (1987). *Beyond National Borders*. Homewood: Dow Jones-Irwin

Ohmae K. (1990). *The Borderless World*. New York: Harper Business

Okada Y. (1991). *Cooperative Sectoral Governance Structure of Japanese Automobile Manufacturing in Asean Countries Framework for Analysis*. Niigata-Ken International University of Japan: Mimeo

Oliver N. and Wilkinson B. (1989). Japanese manufacturing techniques and personnel and industrial practice in Britain: evidence and implications. *British Journal of Industrial Relations*, **XXVII**, March, 73–92

Oman C. (1984). *New Forms of International Investment in Developing Countries*. Paris: Development Center of OECD

Oman C. (1989). *New Forms of Investment in Developing Countries: Mining, Petrochemicals, Automobiles, Textiles, Food*. Paris: Development Center of OECD

Orr D. (1975). The industrial composition of US exports and subsidiary sales to the Canadian market: Comment. *American Economic Review*, **65**, March, 230–4

Osenghale B. D. (1992). *Strategic reaction of US multinationals to abrupt changes in host government policies: an expost study*. Annual Meeting of Academy of International Business: Ten Best Papers Proceedings. Baltimore: Loyola College

Ostry S. (1990). *Governments and Corporations in a*

Shrinking World: Trade and Innovation Policies in the United States, Europe and Japan. New York: Council on Foreign Relations

Ostry S. (1992). The domestic domain: the new international policy area. *Transnational Corporations*, **1**, 7–26

Otterbeck L., ed. (1981). *The Management of Headquarter Subsidiary Relationships in Multinational Corporations*. London: Gower

Owen R. F. (1982). Inter-industry determinants of foreign direct investment. In *New Theories of Multinational Enterprise* (Rugman A., ed.). London: Croom Helm

Ozawa T. (1979). *Multinationalism: Japanese Style*. Princeton: Princeton University Press

Ozawa T. (1981). Technology transfer and control systems: the Japanese experience. In *Contracting International Technology Transfer* (Sagafi-Nejad T., Moxon R. W. and Perlmutter H. V., eds.), pp. 376–426. New York and Oxford: Pergamon

Ozawa T. (1985). Japan. In *Multinational Enterprises, Economic Structure and International Competitiveness* (Dunning J. H., ed.). Chichester and New York: John Wiley and Sons

Ozawa T. (1987a). Can the market alone manage structural upgrading? A challenge posed by economic interdependence. In *Structural Change, Economic Interdependence and World Development* Vol. 4 (Dunning J. H. and Usui M., eds.). London and Basingstoke: Macmillan

Ozawa T., ed. (1987b). *Role of General Trading Firms in Trade and Development*. Tokyo: Asian Productivity Association

Ozawa T. (1989). *Japan's Strategic Policy Towards Outward Direct Investment*. Fort Collins: Colorado State University, July. Mimeo

Ozawa T. (1990). Europe 1992 and Japanese multinationals: transplanting a subcontracting system in the expanded market. In *Multinationals and Europe 1992* (Burgenmeier B. and Mucchielli J. L., eds.). London: Routledge

Ozawa T. (1991a). Japan in a new phase of multinationalism and industrial upgrading: functional integration of trade, growth and foreign direct investment. *Journal of World Trade*, **25**, 43–60

Ozawa T. (1991b). Japanese multinationals and 1992. In *Multinationals and Europe 1992* (Burgenmeier B. and Mucchielli J. L., eds.). London and New York: Routledge

Ozawa T. (1991c). The dynamics of Pacific rim industrialization: How Mexico can join the flock of flying geese. In *Mexico's External Relations in the 1990's* (Roett R., ed.). Boulder and London: Lynne Rienner

Ozawa T. (1992). Foreign direct investment and economic development. *Transnational Corporations*, **1**, 27–54

Pack H. (1976). The substitution of labour for capital in Kenyan manufacturing. *Economic Journal*, **86**, 45–58

Pamuk S. (1981). 'A note on the portfolio-direct composition of private foreign investment in the Ottoman empire in 1914'. Ankara: University of Ankara. Mimeo

Panic M. and Joyce P. L. (1980). U.K. manufacturing industry; international integration and trade performance. *Bank of England Quarterly Bulletin*, March, **20**(1), 42–55

Papanastassiou M. and Pearce R. D. (1990). *Host country characteristics and the sourcing behaviour of UK manufacturing industry*. University of Reading, Department of Economics, Discussion Papers in International Investment and Business Studies, Series B, Vol II, No. 140

Papandreou V. A. (1980). *Multinational Enterprises, Market Industrial Structure and Trade Balance in Less Developed Countries: The Case of Greece*. PhD Thesis, University of Reading

Papke L. E. (1987). Subnational taxation and capital mobility: Estimates of tax-price elasticities. *National Tax Journal*, **40**, 191–203

Parry G. (1977). *Multinational Manufacturing Enterprises and Imperfect Competition*. Australia, Centre for Applied Economics Research, University of New South Wales Occasional Papers No. 1.

Parry T. G. (1974). Technology and the size of the multinational corporation subsidiary: evidence from the Australian manufacturing sector. *Journal of Industrial Economics*, **2**, 125–34

Parry T. G. (1979). Competition and monopoly in multinational corporation relations with host countries. *The Economic Effects of Multinational Corporations* (Hawkins R. G., ed.). Greenwich, CN: JAI Press

Parry T. G. (1980). *The Multinational Enterprise,*

International Investment and Host Country Imports. Greenwich, CN: JAI Press

Parry T. G. (1982). The multinational enterprise and two stage technology transfer to developing countries. In *Technology Transfer to Developing Countries* (Hawkins R. G., ed.). Greenwich, CN: JAI Press

Parry T. G. and Watson J. F. (1978). Technology flows and foreign investment in the Australian manufacturing sector. *Australian Economic Papers*, **2**, 125–34

Pate J. L. (1969). Joint venture activity, 1960–1968. Economic Review, Federal Research Bank of Cleveland, pp. 16–23

Patel P. and Pavitt K. (1991). Large firms in the production of the world's technology: an important case of non-globalization. *Journal of International Business Studies*, **22**, 1–21

Paterson D. G. (1976). *British Direct Investment in Canada: Estimates and Determinants*. Toronto: University of Toronto Press

Pavitt K. (1987). International patterns of technological accumulation. In *Strategies in Global Competition* (Hood N. and Vahlne J. E., eds.). London: Croom Helm

Pavitt K. (1988). Uses and abuses of patent statistics. In *Handbook of Quantitative Studies of Science and Technology* (Van Raan A., ed.). Amsterdam: Elsevier

Pearce R. D. (1987). *Host Countries and the R & D of Multinationals: Issues and Evidence*. University of Reading Discussion Papers in International Investment and Business Studies, Number 101

Pearce R. D. (1989). *The Internationalisation of Sales by leading enterprises: some firm, industry and country determinants*. University of Reading Discussion Papers in International Investment and Business Studies, Series B, No. 135

Pearce R. D. (1990a). *Overseas production and exporting performance: some further investigations*. University of Reading Discussion Papers in International Investment and Business Studies, No. 135

Pearce R. D. (1990b). *The Internationalization of Research and Development*. London: Macmillan

Pearce R. D. and Singh S. (1992). Internationalisation of R & D among the world's leading enterprises. In *Technology, Management and International Business: Internationalisation of R & D and Technology* (Grandstrand O., Sjolander S. and Hakanson L., eds.). Chichester: Wiley

Pearson C. S., ed. (1987). *Multinational Corporations, Environment and the Third World*. Durham, NC: Duke University Press

Pelkmans J. (1987). The community's vivid core: processes in industrial product markets. In *Structural Change, Economic Independence and World Development*. Vol. 4. Economic Interdependence (Dunning J. H. and Usui M., eds.). London and Basingstoke: Macmillan

Penrose E. T. (1956). Foreign investment and growth of the firm. *Economic Journal*, **60**, 220–35

Penrose E. T. (1958). *The Theory of the Growth of the Firm*. Oxford: Basil Blackwell

Penrose E. (1971). Monopoly and competition in the international petroleum industry. In Penrose E. *The Growth of Firms, Middle East Oil and Other Essays*. London: Frank Cass

Peredis T. (1991). *Strategic alliance for smaller firms*. Toronto: York University. Mimeo

Perlmutter H. (1969). The tortuous evolution of the multinational enterprise. *Columbia Journal of World Business*, **4**(1), 9–18

Peters L. S. (1991). *Technology Strategies of Japanese Subsidiaries and Joint Ventures in the United States*. Paper presented at International Trade and Finance Association, Marseille, 31 May–2 June 1991

Peters L. S. (1992). *Technology Management and the Research and Development Activities of Multinational Enterprises*. Troy, New York: Centre for Science and Technology Centre Working Paper, School of Management, Rensselare Polytechnic Institute

Petrochilas G. A. (1984). The determinants of foreign direct investment in the Greek economy. *British Review of Economic Issues*, **6**(4), Spring, 27–54

Petrochilas G. A. (1989). *Foreign Direct Investment and the Development Process*. Aldershot: Avebury

Pfeffer J. and Nowak P. (1976). Joint ventures and interorganizational interdependence. *Administrative Science Quarterly*, **21**(3), 398–418

Phillips A. (1969). The significance of Nigeria's income tax relief incentives. *The Nigerian Journal of Economic and Social Studies*, **11**, No. 2, July, 143–64

Pintz W. (1987). Environmental negotiations in the Tedi mine in Papua New Guinea. In *Multinational Corporations, Environment and the Third World*

(Pearson C. S., ed.). Durham: Duke University Press

Plasschaert S. (1985). Transfer pricing problems in developing countries. In *Multinational and Transfer Pricing* (Rugman A. M. and Eden L., eds.), pp. 247–66. London: Croom Helm

Plasschaert S. (1993). *Transnational Corporations: Transfer Pricing and Taxation*. UN Library on Transnational Corporations. London and New York: Routledge

Plummer A. (1934). *International Combines in Modern History*. London: Pitman

Porter M. E. (1979). The structure within industries and companies' performance. *Review of Economics and Statistics*, **LXI**, 214–27

Porter M. E. (1980). *Competitive Strategy*. New York: The Free Press

Porter M. E. (1985). *Competitive Advantage*. New York: The Free Press

Porter M. E., ed. (1986). *Competition in Global Industries*. Boston: Harvard Business School Press

Porter M. E. (1990). *The Competitive Advantage of Nations*. New York: The Free Press

Porter M. E. and Fuller M. B. (1986). Coalitions and global strategy. In *Competition in Global Industries* (Porter M. E., ed.). Boston: Harvard Business School Press

Posner M. V. (1961). International trade and technical papers. *Oxford Economic Papers*, **13**, October, 323–41

Possas M. L. (1979). Employment Effects of Multinational Enterprises in Brazil. ILO Working Paper No. 7 (MNE Programme). Geneva: ILO Office

Prahalad C. K. and Doz Y. (1987). *The Multinational Mission*. London and New York: The Free Press

Prahalad C. K. and Hamel G. (1990). The core competence of the corporation. *Harvard Business Review*, May/June, 79–91

Prakash O. (1985). *The Dutch East India Company and the Economy of Bengal 1630–1720*. Princeton, NJ: Princeton University Press

Prasartset S. (1990). Technological domination by transnational corporations in Thailand. In *Transnational Corporations and China's Open Door Policy* (Teng W. and Wang N. T., eds.). Lexington: D. C. Heath

Pugel T. A. (1978). *International Market Linkages and U.S. Manufacturing*. Cambridge: Ballinger

Pugel T. A. (1981). The determinants of foreign direct investment: an analysis of US manufacturing industries. *Managerial and Decision Economics*, **2**, 220–28

Pugel T. A. (1985). The United States. In *Multinational Enterprises, Economic Structure and International Competitiveness* (Dunning J. H., ed.). Chichester and New York: John Wiley and Sons

Pugel T. A. (1986). *The Industry Determinants of Foreign Direct Investment into the United States*. New York: Stern School of Business, New York University. Mimeo

Putterman L., ed. (1986). *The Economic Nature of the Firm. A Reader*. Cambridge: Cambridge University Press

Radetzki M. (1977). Where should developing countries' minerals be processed? The country view versus the multinational view. *World Development*, **5**, 325–34

Raghunathan S. P. and Chandran R. (1990). *Globality: Dimensions, Quantification and Measurement*. Temple University, Philadelphia. Mimeo

Rangachand U. K. (1981). Characteristics of research and development performing firms in Canadian manufacturing. *Research Policy*, **11**, 193–203

Ray M. (1990). *Standardizing Employment Growth Rates of Foreign Multinationals and Domestic Firms in Canada: From Shift Share to Multifactor Partitioning*. ILO Working Paper No. 62. Geneva: ILO

Read R. (1983). The growth and structure of multinationals in the banana trade. In *The Growth of International Business* (Casson M. C., ed.). London: Allen and Unwin

Read R. (1986). The banana industry. In *Multinationals and World Trade: Vertical Integration and the Division of Labour in World Industries* (Casson M. C., ed.). London: Allen and Unwin

Reddaway N. B., Potter S. T. and Taylor C. T. (1968). *The Effects of UK Direct Investment Overseas*. Cambridge, MA: Cambridge University Press

Reich R. B. (1987). The rise of technonationalism. *The Atlantic*, May, 63–9

Reich R. B. (1990). Who is us. *Harvard Business Review*, January/February, 53–64

Reich R. B. (1991). Who is them. *Harvard Business Review*, March/April, 77–88

Reich R. B. and Mankin E. D. (1986). Joint ventures with Japan give away our future. *Harvard Business Review*, April, 79–86

Renforth W. E. (1974). *A Comparative Study of Joint International Business Ventures with Family or Non-family Firm Partners: The Caribbean Community Experience*. Unpublished doctoral dissertation, Indiana University

Reuber G. L. (1973). Foreign Investment in Canada: A Review. In *Contemporary Economic Problems in Canada* (Auld D., ed.). Toronto: Holt, Rinehart and Winston

Reuber G. L. *et al.* (1973). *Private Foreign Investment in Development*. Oxford: Clarendon Press

Richardson G. B. (1972). The organisation of industry. *Economic Journal*, **82**, 883–96

Ricketts M. (1989). *The Economics of Business Enterprise: New Approaches to the Firm*. Brighton: Wheatsheaf Books

Ricotta E. (1987). *Accordi di Collaborazione: Strumenti Flessibili per Strategie Globali*. Unpublished Report, For-Start, Rome

Riedel J. (1975). The nature and determinants of export-oriented direct foreign investment in a developing country: a case study of Taiwan. *Weltwirtschaftliches Archiv*, **III**(3), 505–28

Rippy F. J. (1959). *British Investment in Latin America*. Hamden, CN: Archon Books

Robertson D. (1948). *The Control of Industry*. Cambridge: Cambridge University Press

Robinson H. J. (1961). *The Motivation and Flow of Private Foreign Investment*. Stanford, CA: Stanford Research Institute

Robinson J. (1983). *Multinationals and Political Control*. Aldershot: Gower

Robinson R. D. (1978). *International Business Management*. Hinsdale, IL: The Dryden Press

Robinson W. (1982). *Imperialism, Dependency, and Peripheral Industrialisation: The Case of Japan in Indonesia*. Paper presented at the Fourth National Conference, Asian Studies Association of Australia, Melbourne, May

Robock S. H. and Simmonds K. (1989). *International Business and Multinational Enterprises*. 4th edn. Boston, MA: Irwin Publishers

Robson P., ed. (1993). *Transnational Corporations and Economic Integration*. United Nations Library on Transnational Corporations. London: Routledge

Rolfe S. E. (1969). *The International Corporation*. New York and Paris: International Chamber of Commerce

Roman P. D. and Puett J. F. (1983). *International Business and Technological Innovation*. New York, Amsterdam and Oxford: North Holland

Root F. R. (1987). *Entry Strategies for International Markets*. Lexington, MA: Lexington Books

Root F. R. and Ahmed A. A. (1978). The influence of policy instruments on manufacturing direct foreign investment in developing countries. *Journal of International Business Studies*, **9**, Winter, 81–93

Root F. R. and Ahmed A. A. (1979). Empirical determinants of manufacturing direct foreign investment in developing countries. *Economic Development and Cultural Change*, **27**(4), July, 751–67

Ros J. (1987). *Eficienca Tenica. Un Anaeisis Estato y Sectorial*. Mexico City: ILET

Rosenberg N. (1976). *Perspectives on Technology*. Cambridge, MA: Cambridge University Press

Rosenberg N. (1981). The international transfer of industrial technology: past and present. In *OECD North/South Technology Transfer. The Adjustments Ahead*. Paris: OECD

Rosenberg N., ed. (1982). *International Technology Transfer*. Chichester: John Wiley

Rosenbluth G. (1970). The relation between foreign control and concentration in Canadian industry. *Canadian Journal of Economics*, **3**, February

Rosenthal G. and Cohen I. (1976). *Algunas Reflecciones en Torno al Marco Conceptual de la Integraccion Economica Centroamerica*. Mexico City: CEPAL

Rostow W. W. (1959). *The Stages of Economic Growth*. London: Macmillan

Roumeliotis P. (1977). La politique des prix d'importation et exportation des enterprises multinationales en Greece. *Revue Tiers Monde*, **18**, April/June, 353–65

Royal Institute of International Affairs (1937). *The Problem of International Investment*. London: Cass

Rubin S. and Wallace D., eds. (1993). *Transnational Corporations and National Law*. United Nations Library on Transnational Corporations. London: Routledge

Rugman A. M. (1975). Motives for foreign investment: the market imperfections and risk diversification hypothesis. *Journal of World Trade Law*, **9**, September–October, 567–73

Rugman A. M. (1979). *International Diversification and the Multinational Enterprise*. Lexington, MA: Lexington Books

Rugman A. M. (1980). Internalisation as a general theory of foreign direct investment, a reappraisal of the literature. *Weltwirtschaftliches Archiv*, **116**(2), 365–79

Rugman A. M., ed. (1981). *Inside The Multinationals: The Economics of Internal Markets*. London: Croom Helm

Rugman A. M., ed. (1982). *New Theories of the Multinational Enterprise*. London: Croom Helm

Rugman A. M. (1983). The comparative performance of U.S. and European multinational enterprises. *Management International Review*, **23**, 4–14

Rugman A. M. (1986a). Canadian research and development. *Managing International Risk*. Cambridge: Cambridge University Press

Rugman A. M. (1986b). New theories of the multinational enterprise: an assessment of internalisation theory. *Bulletin of Economic Research*, **38**, 101–18

Rugman A. M. (1986c). European multinationals: an international comparison of size and performance. In *European Approaches to International Management* (Macharzina K. and Staehle W. H., eds.). Berlin and New York: Walter de Gruyter

Rugman A. M. (1987). *Outward Bound Canadian Direct Investment in the United States*. Toronto and Washington: C. T. Howe Institute and National Planning Association

Rugman A. M. (1990). Strategic trade policy is not a good strategy. *Hitosubashi Journal of Commerce and Management*, **25**, December, 75–97

Rugman A. M. (1990b). *Multinationals and Canada –United States Free Trade*. Columbia: University of South Carolina Press

Rugman A. M. (1991). Diamond in the rough. *Business Quarterly*, **55**, 61–4

Rugman A. M. and Eden L., eds. (1985). *Multinationals and Transfer Pricing*. London: Croom Helm

Rugman A. M. and McIlveen J. (1985). *Megafirms: Strategies for Canada's Multinationals*. Toronto: Methuen

Rugman A. M. and Verbeke A. (1989). Strategic Management and Trade Policy. *Journal of International Economic Studies*, **3**, 139–52

Rugman A. M. and Verbeke A. (1990a). Multinational corporate strategy and the Canada–US free trade agreement. *Management International Review*, **3**, 253–66

Rugman A. M. and Verbeke A. (1990b). *Global Corporate Strategy and Trade Policy*. London and New York: Routledge

Rugman A. M. and Verbeke A. (1991). Trade barriers and corporate strategies in international companies: the Canadian experience. *Long Range Planning*, **24**, June, 66–72

Rugman A. M., Lecraw D. J. and Booth L. D. (1985). *International Business: Firm and Environment*. New York: McGraw-Hill

Rutenberg D. P. (1970). Organizational archetypes of a multinational company. *Management International Science*, **16**(6), February, 337–49

Rutenberg S. (1971). *Needed! a Constructive Foreign Trade Policy*. Washington DC: AFL-C10

Sabi M. (1988). An application of the theory of foreign direct investment. *Journal of International Business Studies*, **19**, 433–48

Safarian A. E. (1966). *Foreign Ownership of Canadian Industry*. Toronto: University of Toronto Press

Safarian A. E. (1969). *The Performance of Foreign Owned Firms in Canada*. Montreal and Washington: Private Association of Canada

Safarian A. E. (1983). *Governments and Multinationals: Policies in the Developed Countries*. Washington DC: British North-American Committee

Safarian A. E. (1985). *Foreign Direct Investment: A Survey of Canadian Research*. Montreal: Institute for Research on Public Policy

Safarian A. E. (1991). Firm and government strategies. In *Multinationals and Europe 1992* (Burgenmeier B. and Mucchelli J. L., eds.). London and New York: Routledge

Sagari S. B. (1990). US Direct Investment in the Banking Sector Abroad. Washington: The World Bank. Mimeo

Saki M. (1988). An application of the theory of foreign direct investment to multinational banking in LDCs. *Journal of International Business Studies*, **XIX**, 433–47

Saunders R. S. (1982). The determinants of inter-industry variation of foreign ownership in Canadian manufacturing. *Canadian Journal of Economics*, **15**(1), February, 77–84

Sauvant K. P. (1986a). *International Transaction in Services: The Politics of Transborder Flows*. Boulder, CO: Westview Press

Sauvant K. P. (1986b). *Trade and Foreign Direct Investment in Data Services*. Boulder, CO: Westview Press

Sauvant K. P. and Mallampally P., eds. (1993). *Transnational Corporations and Services*. United Nations Library on Transnational Corporations. London: Routledge

Scaperlanda A. (1967). The EEC and US foreign investment: some empirical evidence. *Economic Journal*, **77**, March, 22–6

Scaperlanda A. (1968). The EEC and US foreign direct investment: some evidence: a reply. *Economic Journal*, **78**, September, 720–23

Scaperlanda A. E. (1992). Direct investment controls and international equilibrium: the US experience. *Eastern Economic Journal*, **18**

Scaperlanda A. and Balough R. (1983). Determinants of US direct investment in the EEC revisited. *European Economic Review*, **21**, 381–90

Scaperlanda A. and Mauer L. J. (1969). The determinants of US direct investment in the EEC. *American Economic Review*, **59**, September, 558–68

Scaperlanda A. and Mauer L. J. (1973). The impact of controls on US direct foreign investment in the EEC. *Southern Economic Journal*, **39**, 419–23

Scherer F. M. (1971). *Industrial Market Structure and Economic Performance*. Chicago: Rand McNally

Schive C. (1978). *The impact of foreign direct investment on the economy of Taiwan*. Taipei: Research, Development and Evaluation Commission, ROC (in Chinese)

Schive C. and Hsueh K. T. (1985). *Taiwan's Investment in ASEAN Countries and its Competitiveness*. Taipei: R.O.C. National University

Schmitz A. (1970). The impact of trade blocs on foreign direct investment. *Economic Journal*, **80**, 724–31

Schmitz A. and Bieri J. (1972). EEC tariffs and US direct investment. *European Economic Review*, **3**, October, 259–70

Schneider F. and Frey B. S. (1985). Economic and political determinants of foreign direct investment. *World Development*, **13**(2), February, 161–75

Schollhammer H. (1974). *Locational Strategies of International Firms*. Studies in International Economics and Business, No. 1. Los Angeles: Center for International Business Pepperdine University

Schroter H. (1988). Risk and control in multinational enterprise: German businesses in Scandinavia, 1918–1939. *Business History Review*, **62**, 420–33

Scott B. R. and Lodge G. R., eds. (1985). *US Competitiveness in the World Economy*. Boston: Harvard Business School Press

Shah A. and Slemrod J. (1991). Does tax matter for foreign direct investment. *World Bank Economic Review*, **5**

Shan W. (1991). Environmental risks and joint venture sharing arrangements. *Journal of International Business Studies*, **22**, 555–78

Shan W. (1992). Environmental risks and joint venture sharing arrangements. *Journal of International Business Studies*, forthcoming

Shapiro D. M. (1983). The comparative profitability of Canadian and foreign controlled firms. *Managerial and Decision Economics*, **4**, 97–105

Shelp R. *et al.* (1984). *Service Industries and Economic Development*. New York: Praeger

Shepherd D., Sibertson A. and Strange R. (1985). *British Manufacturing Investment Overseas*. London and New York: Methuen

Shulman J. S. (1975). *Transfer Pricing in Multinational Business*. Boston: Soldiers Field Press

Sibunruang A. and Brimble P. (1988). *The Employment Effects of Manufacturing Multinational Enterprises in Thailand*. ILO Working Paper No. 54. Geneva: ILO

Siddharthan N. S. and Kumar N. (1990). The determinants of inter-industry variations in the proportions of intra-firm trade: the behaviour of US multinationals. *Weltwirtschaftliches Archiv*, **126**, 581–91

Siggel E. (1986). Protection, distortions and investment incentives in Zaire. *Journal of Development Economics*, **22**, 295–319

Simoes V. C. (1985). Portugal. In *Multinational Enterprises, Economic Structure and International Competitiveness* (Dunning J. H., ed.). Chichester and New York: John Wiley and Sons

Simoes V. C. (1992). European integration and the pattern of foreign direct investment inflow in Portugal. In *Multinational Investment in Modern Europe. Strategic Interactions in the Integrated Community* (Cantwell J., ed.). Aldershot, Hants and Brookfield, Vermont: Edward Elgar

Simon H. A. (1947). *Administrative Behavior*. New York: Macmillan (3rd edition, 1976)

Simon H. A. (1955). A behavioral model of rationale choice. *Quarterly Journal of Economics*, **69**, February

Simon H. A. (1959). Theories of decision-making in economics and behavioral science. *American Economic Review*, **49**, 253–83

Sleuwagen L. (1985). Monopolistic advantages and the international operation of firms: Disaggregated evidence from US based multinationals. *Journal of International Business Studies*, **16**, Fall, 125–33

Smith A. (1776). *An Inquiry Into the Nature and Causes of the Wealth of Nations*. London. Reprinted in 1976 by W. Strahan and T. Cadwell, Oxford: Clarendon Press

Snoy B. (1975). *Politiques Fiscales Nationales et Strategies des Societes Multinationales dans la C.E.E.* Universite Catholique de Louvaine, C.R.I.D.E.

Snoy B. (1985). *Taxes on Direct Investment Income in the EEC. A Legal and Economic Analysis*. New York: Praeger

Solomon R. G. and Ingham K. P. D. (1977). Discriminating between MNC subsidiaries and indigenous companies: a comparative analysis of the British mechanical engineering industry. *Oxford Bulletin of Economics and Statistics*, **39**, 127–38

Solvell D., Zander I. and Porter M. E. (1991). *Advantage Sweden*. Stockholm: Norstedts

Sourrouville J. V. (1976). *The impact of transnational enterprises on employment and income: the case of Argentina*. Geneva: ILO, World Employment Programme Working Paper Number 7. Mimeo

Southard F. A. Jr (1931). *American Industry in Europe*. Boston: Houghton Mifflin

Southard F. A. Jr, Marshall H. and Taylor K. W. (1936). *Canadian American Industry*. New Haven: Yale University Press

Spencer B. J. and Brander J. A. (1983). International R & D rivalry and industrial strategy. *Review of Economics and Studies*, **50**, 707–20

Stegemann K. (1989). Policy rivalry among nation states: what we can learn from models of strategic trade policy. *International Organisation*, **43**(1), 73–100

Stekler L. and Stevens G. V. G. (1991). *The Adequacy of US Direct Investment Data (Washington Federal Reserve System)*. Discussion papers in International Finance, No. 401. June

Stern R. M. (1975). Testing trade theories. In *International Trade and Finance* (Kenen P. B., ed.). London: Cambridge University Press

Steuer M. D. *et al.* (1973). *The Impact of Foreign Direct Investment on the United Kingdom*. London: HMSO

Stevens G. V. (1974). Determinants of investment. In *Economic Analysis and the Multinational Enterprise* (Dunning J. H., ed.). London: Allen and Unwin

Stiglitz J. E. (1987). Learning to learn, localized learning and psychological progress. In *Economic Policy and Technological Development* (Dasgupta P. and Stoneman P., eds.). Cambridge: Cambridge University Press

Stobaugh R. (1969). Where in the world to put that plant. *Harvard Business Review*. January–February, 132–4

Stobaugh R. B. *et al.* (1976). *Nine Investments abroad and their impact at home: Case studies on multinational enterprises and the US economy*. Boston: Harvard Business School Press

Stone I. (1977). British direct and portfolio investment in Latin America before 1941. *Journal of Economic History*, **XXXVII**, 690–722

Stonehill A. (1965). *Foreign Ownership in Norwegian Enterprises*. Oslo: Central Bureau of Statistics

Stonehill A. and Dullum K. B. (1990). Corporate wealth maximisation takeovers and the market for corporate control. *National Konomist Tidsskrift*, 79–96

Stonehill A. and Moffett M. H., eds. (1993). *Transnational Corporations and Financial Management*. United Nations Library on Transnational Corporations. London: Routledge

Stoneman P. (1989). *Overseas Financing for Industrial R & D in the U.K.* Paper delivered to British Association, Section F, September

Stopford J. M. (1974). The origins of British-based multinational manufacturing enterprises. *Business History Review*, **48**, 303–35

Stopford J. M. (1976). Changing perspectives on investment of British manufacturing multinationals. *Journal of International Business Studies*, **7**, Fall/Winter, 15–18

Stopford J. M. (1979). *Employment Effects of Multinational Enterprises in the United Kingdom*. ILO Working Paper No. 5. Geneva: ILO

Stopford J. M. (1982). *The World Directory of Multinational Enterprises*. Basingstoke: Macmillan

Stopford J. M. (1992). *The World Directory of Multinational Enterprises*. Basingstoke: Macmillan 2nd edition

Stopford J. M. and Strange S. (1991). *Rival States, Rival Firms*. Cambridge: Cambridge University Press

Stopford J. M. and Turner L. (1985). *Britain and the Multinationals*. Chichester: John Wiley

Stopford J. M. and Wells L. T. Jr (1972). *Managing the Multinational Enterprise. Organization of the Firm and Ownership of the Subsidaries*. New York: Basic Books

Stopford J. M., Dunning J. H. and Haberich K. O. (1980). *The World Directory of Multinational Enterprises*. Basingstoke: Macmillan

Stowsky J. (1987). *The Weakest Link: Semi Conductor Production Equipment, Linkages and International Trade*. Working Paper No. 27. Berkeley, CA: Berkeley Round Table in the International Economy

Streeten P. (1974). The theory of development policy. In *Economic Analysis and the Multinational Enterprise* (Dunning J. H., ed.). London: Allen and Unwin

Stubenitsky F. (1970). *American Direct Investment in Netherlands Industry*. Rotterdam: Rotterdam University Press

Stuckey J. A. (1983). *Vertical Integration and Joint Ventures in the Aluminium Industry*. Cambridge, MA: Harvard University Press

Subramaniam K. K. (1972). *Import of Capital and Technology*. New Delhi: People

Subramaniam K. K. and Pillai M. P. (1979). *Multinationals and Indian Exports*. New Delhi: Allied Publishers

Subunruang A. (1988). *The Employment Effects of Manufacturing Multinational Enterprises in Thailand*. ILO Multinational Enterprises Programme Working Paper No. 54. Geneva: ILO

Sugiyama S. (1988). *Japan's Industrialization in the World Economy, 1851–1899 Export Trade and Overseas Competition*. London: Athlone

Sullivan D. (1992a). *The Threshold of Internationalization: Replication, Extension and Reinterpretation*. Tulane: Tulane University. Mimeo

Sullivan D. (1992b). Measuring the degree of internationalization of a firm. *Journal of International Business Studies*, forthcoming

Sunkel O. (1972). Big business and dependica: a Latin America view. *Foreign Affairs*, **50**, 517–31

Survey of Current Business, (various dates). The International Direct Investment Position of the US. (Annual article – usually in August or September)

Svedberg P. (1978). The portfolio-direct composition of private foreign investment in 1914 revisited. *Economic Journal*, **88**, 763–77

Svedberg P. (1981). Colonial enforcement of foreign direct investment. *Manchester School of Economic and Social Studies*, **49**, March, 21–38

Svedberg P. (1982). Colonialism and foreign direct investment profitability. In *International Capital Movements* (Black J. and Dunning J. H., eds.). London: Macmillan

Swedenborg B. (1979). *The Multinational Operations of Swedish Firms: An Analysis of Determinants and Effects*. Stockholm: Industriens Utredningsinstitut

Swedenborg B. (1985). Sweden. In *Multinational Enterprises, Economic Structure and International Competitiveness* (Dunning J. H., ed.), Chichester and New York: John Wiley and Sons

Swedenborg B. (1990). *The EC and the locational choice of Swedish multinational companies*. Working Paper No. 284. Stockholm: Industrial Institute for Economic Social Research

Sweeney R. J. (1992). The competition for foreign direct investment. In *The Global Race for Foreign Direct Investment in the 1990s* (Oxelheim L., ed.). New York: Springer-Verlag

Swiss Association of Entrepreneurs (1982). *Research and Development in the Swiss Private Sector*. Quoted in Borner *et al.* 1985

Szekely G., ed. (1991). *Manufacturing Across Borders and Oceans*. San Diego: Center for US-Mexican Studies, University of California, San Diego

Taggart J. H. (1989). *Classification of Foreign R & D Strategies in the Pharmaceutical Industry*. Paper presented at 15th annual conference of EIBA, Helsinki, Finland, December

Taggart J. H. (1991). Determinants of the foreign R&D locational decision in the pharmaceutical industry. *R&D Management*, **21**, 229–40

Tallman S. B. (1988). Home country political risks and direct foreign investment in the United States. *Journal of International Business Studies*, **19**, 219–34

Tallman S. B. (1991). Strategic management models and resource based strategies among MNEs in a host market. *Strategic Management Journal*, **12**, 69–82

Tallman S. B. and Shankar O. (1990). *Economic and behavioral models of international cooperative ventures: a management synthesis*. Mimeo

Tanaki N. (1990). The Yokohama specie bank: a multinational in the Japanese interest 1879-1913. In *Banks as Multinationals* (Jones G., ed.). London and New York: Routledge

Tang R. Y. (1979). *Transfer Pricing Practices in the United States and Japan*. New York: Praeger

Tang R. Y. (1981). *Multinational Transfer Pricing: Canadian and British Perspectives*. London: Butterworth

Tang R. Y. (1992). Transfer Pricing in the 1990s. *Management Accountancy*, February 22–6

Teece D. J. (1976). *The Multinational Corporation and the Resource Cost of International Technology Transfer*. Cambridge, MA: Ballinger

Teece D. J. (1977). Technology transfer by multinational firms: The resource cost of transferring technological knowhow. *Economic Journal*, **87**, June, 242–61

Teece D. J. (1981a). The multinational enterprise: market failure and market power considerations. *Sloan Management Review*, **22**, 3–18

Teece D. J. (1981b). The market for know-how and efficient international transfer of technology. *Annals of American Academy of Political and Social Science*, **458**, 81–96

Teece D. J. (1984). Economic analysis and strategic management. *California Management Review*, **26**, Spring, 87–108

Teece D. J. (1986). Transaction cost economics and the multinational enterprise. *Journal of Economic Behaviour and Organization*, **I**, 21–45

Teece D. J. and Mowery D. C. (1992). The changing place of Japan in the global scientific and technological enterprise. In *Japan's Growing Technological Capability* (Arrison T. S., Bergsten C. F., Graham E. M. and Harris M. C., eds.). Washington DC: National Academy of Sciences

Teichova A. (1974). *An Economic Background to Munich*. Cambridge: Cambridge University Press

Telesio P. (1979). *Technology Licensing and Multinational Enterprise*. New York: Praeger

Terpstra V. and David K. (1991). *The Cultural Environment of International Business*, 3rd edn. Cincinnati: South Western Publishing Co.

Terpstra V. and Yu C. (1988). Determinants of foreign investment of US advertising agencies. *Journal of International Business Studies*, **19**, 33–46

Thorelli H. B. (1987). Networks: between markets and hierarchies. *Strategic Management Journal*, **7**, 37–51

Tignor R. (1987). British textile companies and the Egyptian economy. *Business and Economic History*, **16**, 53–68

Tolchin M. and Tolchin S. (1988). *Buying into America. How foreign money is changing the face of our nation*. New York: Times Books

Tolentino P. E. (1992). *Technology Innovation and Third World Multinationals*. London and New York: Routledge

Tomlinson B. R. (1989). British business in India. In *British Business in Asia since 1860* (Davenport-Hines R. P. T. and Jones G., eds.). Cambridge: Cambridge University Press

Tomlinson J. W. L. (1970). *The Joint Venture Process in International Business*. Cambridge: MIT Press

Tomlinson J. W. and Thompson M. (1977). *A Study of Canadian Joint Ventures in Mexico*. Working paper, University of British Columbia, Vancouver

Torrisi C. R. (1985). The determinants of direct foreign investment in a small LDC. *Journal of Economic Development*, July, 29–45

Transnationals (1992). China as outward investors. *Transnationals*, **4**, July, 1–6

Tsai P.-L. (1991). Determinants of foreign direct investment in Taiwan. *World Development*, **19**, 275–85

Tsetsekos G. P. and Gombola M. J. (1991). *Foreign and Domestic Divestments: Evidence on Valuation of Plant Closings*. Philadelphia: Drexel University. Mimeo

Tsurumi Yoshi (1976). *The Japanese are Coming: A Multinational Interaction of Firms and Policies*. Cambridge, MA: Ballinger

UN (1949). *International Capital Movements during the Interwar Period*. New York: UN

UN (1991). *Transnational Corporations and Issues Relating to the Environment*. Report of Secretary General presented at 17th session of Commission on Transnational Corporations, New York: E/C 10/ 1991/3

UN (1992a). *World Investment Report 1992. Transnational Corporations and Engines of Growth*. New York: Transnational Corporations and Management Division, Department of Economic and Social Development

UN (1992b). *World Investment Directory Volumes 1 and 2*. (Other volumes to follow.) New York: UN

UN (1992c). *Technology Transfer in Services in Latin America*. New York: UN. Forthcoming

UN (1992d). *From the Common Market to EC 92: Regional Economic Integration in the European Community and Transnational Corporations*. New York: UN

UN (1993). *World Investment Directory*. Volumes 3, 4 and 5. New York: UN

UNCTAD (1973). *Report of Expert Group on Restrictive Business Practices in Relation to Trade and Development of Developing Countries*. TD/B/C2/119. Geneva: UNCTAD

UNCTAD (1975). *The Role of the Patent System in the Transfer of Technology to Developing Countries*. TD/B/AC.11/19/Rev.1. New York: United Nations

UNCTAD (1978). Empirical evidence of dominant positions or market power through the use of transfer pricing mechanism. *Dominant Positions of Market Power of Transnational Corporations: Use of Transfer Pricing Mechanism*, Ch.4, pp. 20–7. Geneva: UNCTAD

UNCTAD (1981). *The Set of Multilaterally Agreed Principles and Rules for the Control of Restrictive Business Practices*. New York and Geneva: UNCTAD

UNCTAD (1983a). *Monitoring of technology transfer agreements by regulatory agencies: An overview of policies and issues*. Geneva: UNCTAD

UNCTAD (1983b). *The Role of Transnational Enterprises in Latin American Economic Integration Efforts: Who Integrates for Whom and For Whose Benefits*. TO/B/C/7/38, 1983. Geneva: UNCTAD

UNCTAD (1985). *Services and the Development Process*. UN/TD/1008/Rev 1. New York: UN Publications

UNCTC (1973). *Multinational Corporations in World Development*. United Nations Publications, Sales Number E73.II.A.11

UNCTC (1978). *Transnational Corporations and World Development: A Reexamination*. E/C 10/38. New York: UN

UNCTC (1980). *Transnational Reinsurance Operations*. New York: UNCTC

UNCTC (1981a). *Transnational Corporations in the Bauxite/Aluminium Industry*. ST/CTC/20. New York: UN

UNCTC (1981b). *Salient Features and Trends in Foreign Direct Investments*. Mimeo

UNCTC (1982). *Regional Integration Cum/Versus Corporation Integration*. New York: UNCTC

UNCTC (1983a). *National Legislation and Regulations Relating to Transnational Corporations*. ST/CTC/35. New York: UN

UNCTC (1983b). *Transnational Corporations and World Development: Third Survey*. E83, II, A 19. New York: UN

UNCTC (1985a). *Trends and Issues in Foreign Direct Investment and Related Flows*. E.85.II.A.15. New York: UN

UNCTC (1985b). *Environmental Aspects of the Activities of Transnational Corporations: A Survey*. New York: United Nations Centre on Transnational Corporations

UNCTC (1987). *Transnational Corporations and Non-fuel Primary Commodities in Developing Countries*. New York: UN

UNCTC (1988). *Transnational Corporations in World Development*, 4th Survey. New York: UN

UNCTC (1989). *Foreign Direct Investment and Transnational Corporations in Services*. Sales No. E 89 II A.1. New York: UN

UNCTC (1990a). *The New Code Environment*. New York: UN

UNCTC (1990b). *Non-conventional Transnational Corporations* E/C 10/1990/18. Report to the 16th session of Commission on Transnational Corporations

UNCTC (1990c). *Regional Integration and Transnational Corporations in the 1990s: Europe 1992,*

North America and Developing Countries. UNCTC Current Series A, No. 15. New York: UN

UNCTC (1990d). *New Approaches to Best Practice Manufacturing: The Role of Transnational Corporations and Implications for Developing Countries*. Current Series A No. 12. New York: United Nations

UNCTC (1990e). *The Role of Free Economic Zones in the USSR and Eastern Europe*. Current Series A No. 14. New York: UN

UNCTC (1991a). *World Investment Report, The Triad in Foreign Direct Investment*. New York: UN

UNCTC (1991b). *Transnational Corporations and Industrial Hazards Disclosure*. New York: UN

UNCTC (1991c). *The Impact of Trade Related Measures on Trade and Development*. New York: UN

UNCTC (1991d). *Transnational Corporations and Issues Relating to the Environment*. Report of the Secretary General, New York, Commission on Transnational Corporations, 17th Session, Stem 4, E/C/10/1991/3, March

UNCTC (1991e). *Government Policies and Foreign Direct Investment*. New York: UN

UNCTC (1992a). *Foreign Direct Investment and Technology Transfer in India*. New York: UN

UNCTC (1992b). *The Determinants of Foreign Direct Investment*. New York: UN

UNCTC (1992c). *Foreign Direct Investment and Industrial Restructuring in Mexico*. UNCTC Current Studies Series A No. 18. New York: UN

UNCTC (1992d). *Third World Foreign Direct Investment*. New York: UN

UNCTC (various dates). *National Legislation and Regulation Relating to Transnational Corporations*. Vols. 1–7, various dates 1978/1989. New York: UN

UNESCO (1987). *Statistical Year Book*. Paris: UNESCO

UNESCO (1990). *Statistical Year Book*. Paris: UNESCO

UNIDO (1980). *Export processing zones in developing countries*. UNIDO working papers on Structural Changes, No. 10, UNIDO/ICIS, 176, Vienna, August

US Department of Commerce (1981). *US Direct Investment Abroad 1977*. Washington, DC: Bureau of Economic Analysis International Investment Division.

US Department of Commerce (1985). *US Direct Investment Abroad, 1982 Benchmark Survey*. Washington, DC: US Government Printing Office

US Department of Commerce (1988). *Foreign Direct Investment in the U.S.* Washington, DC: US Department of Commerce

US Department of Commerce (1991). *US Direct Investment Abroad, 1989 Benchmark Survey*. Provisional Results. Washington: Bureau of Economic Analysis

US Department of Commerce (various dates). *Foreign Direct Investment in the US*. Washington, DC: US Department of Commerce

US Department of Commerce (various dates). *The International Investment Position of the US*. Annual article usually in August or September

US Tariff Commission (1970). *Economic Factors Affecting the Use of Items 807.00 and 806.30 of the Tariff Schedules of the United States*. Washington, DC: Government Printing Office

US Tariff Commission (1973). *Implications of Multinational Firms for World Trade and Investment and for US Trade and Labor*. Washington DC: US Government Printing Office

Vahlne J. E. and Nordström K. A. (1992). *Is the globe shrinking: Psychic distance and the establishment of Swedish sales subsidiaries during the last 100 years*. Stockholm. Mimeo

Vahlne J. E. and Wiedersheim P. F. (1973). Ekonomiskt avstand- Model och empirisk undersokning. In *Export och Utlandsetableringar* (Hornell E., Vahlne J. E. and Wiedersheim P. F., eds.). Stockholm: Almquist and Wiksell

Vaitsos C. V. (1974). *Intercountry Income Distribution and Transnational Enterprises*. Oxford: Clarendon Press

Vaitsos C. V. (1975). The process of commercialization of technology in the Andean pact. In *International Firms and Imperialism* (Radice H., ed.). London: Penguin

Van den Bulcke D. (1984). *European Headquarters of American Multinational Companies in Belgium and Brussels*. Brussels: ICHEC

Van den Bulcke D. (1985). Belgium. In *Multinational Enterprises, Economic Structure and International Competitiveness* (Dunning J. H., ed.). Chichester and New York: John Wiley

Van den Bulcke D. and Halsberghe E. (1979). Employment Effects of Multinational Enterprises: A Belgian Case Study. ILO Working Paper No. 1. Geneva: ILO

Van den Bulcke D. and Van Pachterbeke M. A. L. (1985). *European Headquarters of American Enterprises in Brussels and Belgium*. Brussels: ICHEC

Van der Wee H. and Goosens M. (1990). Belgium. In *International Banking, Foreign Investment and Industrial Finance 1870–1914* (Borykin V. I. and Cameron R., eds.). Oxford: Oxford University Press

Van Tulder R. and Junne G. (1988). *European Multinationals in Core Technologies*. Chichester: John Wiley

Vaupel J. W. and Curhan J. P. (1969). *The Making of a Multinational Enterprise*. Cambridge, MA: Harvard University Press

Vaupel J. W. and Curhan J. P. (1974). *The World's Largest Multinational Enterprises*. Cambridge, MA: Harvard University Press

Vendrell-Alda J. L. M. (1978). *Comparing Foreign Subsidiaries and Domestic Firms: A Research Methodology Applied to Efficiency in Argentine Industry*. New York: Garland

Vernon R. (1966). International investment and international trade in the product cycle. *Quarterly Journal of Economics*, **80**, 190–207

Vernon R. (1971a). The multinational enterprise: power vs. sovereignty. *Foreign Affairs*, **49**, July, 736–51

Vernon R. (1971b). *Sovereignty at Bay: The Multinational Spread of U.S. Enterprises*. New York: Basic Books

Vernon R. (1973). *Sovereignty at Bay*. Harmondsworth: Penguin

Vernon R. (1974). The location of economic activity. In *Economic Analysis and the Multinational Enterprise* (Dunning J. H., ed.). London: Allen and Unwin

Vernon R. (1977). *Storm Over the Multinationals: The Real Issues*. Cambridge, MA: Harvard University Press

Vernon R. (1979). The product cycle hypothesis in the new international environment. *Oxford Bulletin of Economics and Statistics*, **41**, 255–67

Vernon R. (1982). Technological effects on international trade: a look ahead. In *Emerging Technologies: Consequences for Economic Growth,*

Structural Change and Employment (Giersch H., ed.), pp. 145–66. Tubingen: JCB Mohr

Vernon R. (1983). Organizational and institutional responses to international risk. In *Managing International Risk* (Herring R. J., ed.). Cambridge, MA: Cambridge University Press

Vernon R. (1985). *Government Control Over Its Multinational Enterprises: The U.S. Case*. Cambridge, MA: Center for Business and Government, John F. Kennedy School of Government

Vernon R. (1986). The curious character of the international technology market. In *The Political Economy of International Technology Transfer* (McIntyre J. R. and Papp D. S., eds.). New York and London: Quorum Books

Vernon R. (1987a). Codes on transnationals: ingredients for an effective international regime. In *Structural Change, Economic Interdependence and World Development* (Dunning J. H. and Usui M., eds.). London: Macmillan

Vernon R. (1987b). Coping with technological change: US problems and prospects. In *Technology Global Industry* (Guile B. R. and Brooks H., eds.). Washington: National Academy Press

Vernon R. (1991). Sovereignty at Bay: Twenty Years After. *Millenium*, **20**, 191–96

Vernon R. and Wells L. (1981). *Manager in the International Economy*. Cambridge: Harvard University Press

Veuglers R. (1991). Locational determinants and ranking of host countries: an empirical assessment. *Kyklos*, **44**, 363–82

V.E.V. (1984). *Enquete Buitenlandse Vestigingen*. Antwerp

Von-Grebmer K. (1987). International transfer pricing in the pharmaceutical industry. *Interfax*, 4–5, 92–99

Vunez W. P. (1990). *Foreign Direct Investment and Industrial Development in Mexico*. Paris: Development Center of the OECD

Wade R. (1988). The role of government in overcoming market failure in Taiwan, Republic of Korea and Japan. In *Achieving Industrialization in East Asia* (Hughes H., ed.). Cambridge: Cambridge University Press

Wallis K. (1968). The EEC and US foreign investment: some empirical evidence re-examined. *Economic Journal*, **78**, September, 717–19

Walsh F. (1979). *Foreign Direct Investment and*

Regional Planning in the Irish Republic. Paper presented at the symposium of the Commission on Industrial Systems, Rotterdam

Walter I. (1992). Patterns of mergers and acquisitions, 1985–90. In *The Global Race for Foreign Direct Investment in the 1990s* (Oxelheim L., ed.). Berlin and New York: Springer-Verlag

Warr P. G. (1984). Korea's Masan free export zone: benefits and costs. *The Developing Economies*, **22**, 169–84

Warr P. G. (1987). Malaysia's industrial enclaves: benefits and costs. *The Developing Economies*, **25**, 30–55

Wavre P. A. (1988). Swiss investment in Italy from the 18th to 20th century. *Journal of European Economic History*, **XVII**, 85–102

Weekly J. K. and Aggarwal R. (1987). *International Business*. Chicago: The Dryden Press

Weintraub S. (1990). *Marriage of Convenience Relations between Mexico and the United States*. New York: Oxford University Press

Welch L. S. and Luostorinen R. (1988). Internationalization: evolution of a concept. *Journal of General Management*, **14**(2), 34–55

Wells L. T., ed. (1972). *The Product Life Cycle and International Trade*. Cambridge, MA: Harvard University Press

Wells L. T. (1973). Economic man and engineering man: choice of technology in a low wage country. *Public Policy*, **21**, 39–42

Wells L. T. (1983). *Third World Multinationals*. Cambridge, MA: MIT Press

Wells L. T. (1986). Investment incentives: an unnecessary debate. *CTC Reporter*, Autumn, 58–60

Wernerfelt B. (1984). A resource based theory of the firm. *Strategic Management Journal*, **5**, 171–80

Wertheimer H. W. (1971). The international firm and international aspects of policies on mergers. In *International Conference on Monopolies, Mergers and Restrictive Practices* (Heath J. B., ed.). London: HMSO

Westney E. (1992). Country patterns in R&D organizations: the United States and Japan. In *Country Competition: Technology and Organizing of Work* (Kogut B., ed.). Oxford: Oxford University Press

Westney E. and Ghoshal S., eds. (1992). *Organization Theory and the Multinational Corporation*. Basingstoke and London: Macmillan

Westphal L., Rhee Y. W. and Pursell G. (1979). Foreign influences on Korean industrial development. *Bulletin of the Oxford University Institute of Economics and Statistics*, **41**(4), 359–88

Wheeler D. and Mody A. (1991). International investment location decisions: the case of U.S. firms. *Journal of International Economics*, forthcoming

White L. J. (1978). The evidence on appropriate factor proportions for manufacturing in less developed countries: a survey. *Economic Development and Cultural Change*, **27**, 27–59

Wilkins M. (1970). *The Emergence of Multinational Enterprise: American Business Abroad from the Colonial Era to 1914*. Cambridge, MA: Harvard University Press

Wilkins M. (1974). *The Maturing of Multinational Enterprise: American Business Abroad from 1914 to 1970*. Cambridge, MA: Harvard University Press

Wilkins M. (1976). Multinational companies and the diffusion of technology to Africa: an historical perspective. In *Importing Technology into Africa* (Babatunde D., ed.). New York: Praeger

Wilkins M. (1977a). Modern European economic history and the multinationals. *Journal of European Economic History*, **6**, 575–95

Wilkins M. (1977b). Cross-currents: American investments in Europe, European investments in the United States. In *Business and Economic History* (Uselding P., ed.), **6**, 22–35

Wilkins M. (1978). The free standing company 1870–1914. *Economic History Review*, **41**, 259–82

Wilkins M. (1979). *Foreign Enterprise in Florida*. Gainesville: University of Florida Press

Wilkins M. (1986). Japanese multinational enterprise before 1914. *Business History Review*, **60**, 199–231

Wilkins M. (1988a). European and North American multinationals 1870–1914: comparison and contrasts. *Business History*, **30**, 8–45

Wilkins M. (1988b). The history of European multinationals 1870–1914: comparisons and contrasts. *Business History*, **30**, 8–45

Wilkins M. (1989). *Foreign Investment in the United States*. Cambridge, MA: Harvard University Press

Wilkins M. (1990a). Banks over borders: Some evidence from their pre-1914 history. In *Banks as Multinationals* (Jones G., ed.). London and New York: Routledge

Wilkins M. (1990b). Japanese multinationals in the United States: continuity and change 1879–1990. *Business History Review*, **64**, 585–629

Wilkins M., ed. (1991). *The Growth of Multinationals*. Aldershot: Edward Elgar

Williams J. H. (1929). The theory of international trade reconsidered. *Economic Journal*, **39**, 195–209

Williamson O. E. (1975). *Markets and Hierarchies: Analysis and Antitrust Implications*. New York: The Free Press

Williamson O. E. (1979). Transaction cost economics. The governance of contractual relations. *Journal of Law and Economics*, **22**, 223–61

Williamson O. E. (1980). Emergence of the visible hand: Implications for industrial organization. In *Managerial Hierarchies* (Chandler A. D. Jr and Daems H., eds.). Cambridge, MA: Harvard University Press

Williamson O. E. (1985). *The Economic Institutions of Capitalism*. New York: The Free Press

Williamson O. E. (1986). *Economic Organisation*. Brighton: Wheatsheaf Books

Williamson P. J. (1986). Multinational enterprise behavior and domestic industry adjustment under import threat. *Review of Economics and Statistics*, **LXVIII**, 359–68

Willmore L. N. (1976). Direct foreign investment in central American manufacturing. *World Development*, **4**, 499–517

Willmore L. N. (1986). The comparative performance of foreign and domestic firms in Brazil. *World Development*, **14**, 489–502

Willmore L. N. (1989). Determinants of industrial concentration – A Brazilian case study. *World Development*, **17**, 1601–18

Wilson C. (1974). The multinational in historical perspective. In *Strategy and Structure of Big Business* (Nakagawa K., ed.). Tokyo: Tokyo University Press

Wolf B. M. (1977). Industrial diversification and internationalisation: some empirical evidence. *Journal of Industrial Economics*, **26**, December, 177–91

World Bank (1989). *Foreign Direct Investment from the Newly Industrialised Countries*. Industry and Energy Department Working Paper Industry Series No. 22. Washington: The World Bank

World Bank (1991). *World Development Report*. Oxford: Oxford University Press

World Bank (various dates). *The World Development Report*. Oxford: Oxford University Press (an annual publication)

World Economic Forum and IMEDE (1989). World Competitive Report. 9th edn. Geneva: World Economic Forum

World Economic Forum and IMEDE (1990). *The World Competitiveness Report*. Geneva: The World Economic Forum and IMEDE

World Economic Forum and IMEDE (1991). *World Competitive Report*. 11th edn. Geneva: World Economic Forum

Wortmann M. (1990). Multinationals and the internationalization of R & D: New development in German companies. *Research Policy*, **19**, 175–83

Wright G. (1990). The origins of American industrial success, 1879–1940. *American Economic Review*, **80**, 651–68

Wyatt S. M. E., Bertin G. and Pavitt K. (1985). Patents and multinational corporations; results from questionnaires. *World Patent Information*, **7**, 196–212

Yamawaki H. (1991). *Location Decisions of Japanese Multinational Firms in European Manufacturing Industries*. Catholic University of Louvain. Mimeo

Yang H. C., James W. and Lane W. R. (1985). Stock market recognition of multinationality of a firm and international events. *Journal of Business Finance and Accounting*, **12**, Summer, 263–74

Yannopoulos G. N. (1990). Foreign direct investment and European integration: the evidence from the formative years of the European Community. *Journal of Common Market Studies*, **28**, March, 235–59

Yannopoulos G. N., ed. (1991). *Europe and America 1992: US–EC Economic Relations in the Single European Market*. Manchester: Manchester University Press

Yannopoulos G. N. (1992). Multinational corporations and the single European market. In *Multinational Investment in Modern Europe. Strategic Interaction in the Integrated Community* (Cantwell J. C., ed.). Aldershot, Hants and Brookfield Vermont: Edward Elgar

Yannopoulos G. N. and Dunning J. H. (1976). MNEs and regional development: an exploratory paper. *Regional Studies*, **10**, November, 389–401

Yasumuro K. (1992). *European Headquarters of Japanese MNCs: Heterarchial Approach for Global Business Organization*. Paper presented at 5th International Conference on Multinational Enterprise, Taipei, May 1992

Yeh R.-S., and Sagafi-Nejad T. (1987). Organizational characteristics of American and Japanese firms in Taiwan. Academy of Management Best Papers Proceedings (1987), 111–15

Yonekawa S. (1985). The formation of general trading companies: a comparative study. Japanese Yearbook on Business History, Number 5: 1988. Tokyo: Japan Business History Institute, 1989

Yong Y. S. (1988). Employment Effects of Multinational Entrepreneurs in Malaysia. ILO Multinational Enterprises Programme Working Paper No. 53. Geneva: ILO

Yoshihara H. (1985). Multinational growth of Japanese manufacturing enterprises in the postwar period. *Proc. Fuji International Conference on Business History*. Tokyo: University of Tokyo Press

Yoshino M. Y. (1976). *Japan's Multinational Enterprises*. Honolulu: Hawaii University Press

Young S., Hood N., and Hamill J. (1985). *Decision-making in Foreign Owned Multinational Subsidiaries in the U.K.* ILO Working Paper No. 35. Geneva: ILO

Young S., Hood N. and Hamill J. (1988). *Foreign Multinationals and the British Economy*. London: Routledge

Young S., McDermott M. and Dunlop S. (1990). Non E.C. multinationals and the single market challenge. In *Multinationals and Europe 1992* (Burgenmeier B. and Mucchielli J. L., eds.). London and New York: Routledge

Yu C. M. and Ito K. (1988). Oligopolistic reaction and foreign direct investment: the case of the U.S. tire and textile industry. *Journal of International Business Studies*, **19**, 449–60

Author Index

Singh, S.   167, 168, 243, 304, 305, 308, 311, 312, 330
Slemrod, J.   573
Sleuwagen, L.   155
Smith, A.   294
Snoy, B.   510, 526
Solomon, R. G.   297, 424
Solvell, D. *et al.*   341
Sosin, K.   405, 425
Sourrouille, J. V.   381
Southard, F. A. Jr   68, 94, 123, 137, 616
Spencer, B. J.   316
Stegemann, K.   322
Stein, J. C.   74, 157, 173
Stekler, L.   13
Stern, R. M.   94
Steuer, M. D. *et al.*   391, 400, 403, 433, 434
Stevens, G. V.   13, 90, 510
Stilwell, F.   55
Stobaugh, R.   364
Stone, I.   135
Stonehill, A.   127, 432, 433, 513
Stoneman, P.   305
Stopford, J. M.   8, 11, 52, 72, 100, 108, 111, 114, 122, 123, 142, 145, 209, 314, 347, 364, 391, 393
Stowsky, J.   458
Strange, S.   209
Streeten, P.   283, 391, 398, 399, 405, 413, 433
Stubenitsky, F.   433
Subramaniam, K. K.   405, 452
Sugden, R.   67, 500
Sugiyama, S.   116
Sunkel, O.   541
Svedberg, P.   63, 118, 135
Swedenborg, B.   71, 94, 149, 150, 151, 153, 164, 165, 199, 403, 413, 508
Sweezy, P.   67

T

Taggart, J. H.   311
Tallman, S. B.   95, 153, 190, 238, 257, 258, 259

Tang, R. Y.   518, 520, 521, 526
Taylor, C. T.   124
Taylor, K. W.   123
Taylor, P.   113, 134
Teece, D. J.   67, 70, 78, 187, 299, 312, 329, 332, 335, 347, 490
Teichova, A.   118
Telesio, P.   72, 347
Terpstra, V.   152, 153, 155, 535
Terza, J. V.   485, 561
Thomas, H.   426, 443
Thompson, M.   258
Tignor, R.   123
Tolchin, M. and Tolchin, S.160, 542
Tolentino, P. E.   87, 175, 269
Tomlinson, B. R.   101, 134, 240, 258
Torrisi, C. R.   172
Toyne, B.   94
Tsurumi, Y.   72
Turner, L.   123, 145, 347, 391, 393

U

UN   12, 39, 64, 118, 170, 174, 311, 380, 434, 439, 443, 451, 469, 484, 502, 503, 504, 603, 617
UNCTAD   406, 516, 522
UNCTC   8, 11, 14, 16, 36, 48, 53, 118, 171, 177, 192, 203, 247, 289, 298, 402, 404, 429, 434, 436, 443, 450, 454, 455, 457, 458, 461, 494, 497, 503, 536, 539, 541, 542, 543, 562, 572, 577, 587, 596, 607
UNESCO   300, 303

V

Vahlne, J. E.   156, 365
Vaitsos, C.   516, 517

Van Den Bulcke, D.   65, 304, 305, 365, 371, 387, 403, 436
Van Der Wee, H.   105
Van Doorn Ooms   580
Van Tulder, R.   490, 573, 616
Varon, B.   460
Vaupel, J. W.   53, 109, 120, 126, 127, 138, 177, 256
Verbeke, A.   154, 345, 444, 587
Vernon, R.   11, 12, 70, 71, 72, 73, 86, 106, 138, 146, 180, 199, 233, 309, 348, 400, 427, 444, 572, 579, 615
Veuglers, R.   164, 167, 181
VEV   164
Viesti, G.   152

W

Wade, R.   88, 616
Wallace, D.   584
Wallender, H.   342
Wallis, K.   486
Walsh, F.   486
Walter, I.   160, 432, 494, 581
Wavre, P. A.   98, 107, 134
Waterson, M.   492
Watson, J. F.   330
Weekly, J. K.   220, 233
Weidersheim P. F.   156
Weiner, R.   518
Weiss, M. Y.   199, 383, 397
Welge, M.   225
Wells, L. T.   11, 72, 146, 180, 199, 233, 244, 297
Wernerfelt, B.   95
Westney, E.   233
Westphal, L. *et al.*   404
Wheeler, D.   573
White, L. J.   170, 294, 486
Whitmore, K.   36, 142, 181
Wilkins, M.   98, 99, 100, 101, 102, 105, 106, 107, 108, 111, 112, 113, 114, 115, 116, 118, 124, 129, 134, 135, 139, 145, 146, 203, 313, 347, 541, 579
Wilkinson, B.   377

SUBJECT INDEX

A

A & Ms   120, 126, 135, 146,
   432–3, 491, 494, 562–3
   data banks   12
   in Europe   504
   policy   440
absorptive capacity   380
accounting conventions   10
activities
   advances in banking   115
   aggressive   56
   'alternative' position   282–3
   attribution   282
   banking   115, 124
   competitors   462
   costs and benefits   556
   'counterfactual' position
      282–3
   data   6
      deficiencies on quality   7
   defensive   56
   determinants   66–95
   developed countries
      recipients   22
   developing countries
      recipients   22
   early history   96
   early theories   68
   economic development   277–9
   economic organization   604
   general theories   68, 75–90
   impact   264–7
   innovative   310–11
   insurance   115
   inter-war years   119

manufacturing industry   28
mining   124
non-wealth creating   533–4
oil   124, 135
organization in 1945–1960
   126
partial theories   68
primary industry   28
quality and availability   6
relocation   371
resource-based   120
secondary processing   124
service on training   374
sources of data   8–9
spill-over effects   390
time series studies   170–4
trends since 1960   15
'why', 'where' and 'how'   67
administration costs   202
administrative authority   567
advantages   153
   comparative   378
   competitive   265
   diamond and competitive   420
   European firms   106, 122
   Japanese firms   106
   O-specific   269, 270
   US firms   106
advertising   160
   agencies   155
   expenditure advantages
      151–2
   sales ratios   436
affiliates
   foreign
      balance of payments   388–9

size   432–4
   trade   388–9
   number   46
after-sales service   459
agency failures   135
agreements
   agency   134
   buyer-seller cooperative
      246–9
   contractual   248
   franchise   247
   Japanese collaborative   255
   licensing   247
   production sharing   247
   R & D cooperative   251
agribusiness   454–5, 458, 469,
   472
alternative positions   336, 363,
   388, 399, 401, 531
anti-competitive behaviour   438
anti-trust
   law   581
   legislation   126
aptitudes and skills   358
ASEAN   498–9
   pricing practices   517
Asian industrializing countries
   17
assets
   accumulation   315
   created   288
   upgrading   315
auto industry   447–8, 458, 463,
   488
   India   450
   Nigeria   450